Heinrich C. Mayr Jiri Laza
Gerald Quirchmayr Pavel V

Database and Expert Systems Applications

12th International Conference, DEXA 2001
Munich, Germany, September 3-5, 2001
Proceedings

Springer

Series Editors

Gerhard Goos, Karlsruhe University, Germany
Juris Hartmanis, Cornell University, NY, USA
Jan van Leeuwen, Utrecht University, The Netherlands

Volume Editors

Heinrich C. Mayr
University of Klagenfurt, IFI -IWAS
Universitaetsstr. 65, 9020 Klagenfurt, Austria
E-mail: heinrich@ifit.uni-klu.ac.at

Jiri Lazansky
Czech Technical University, Faculty of Electrical Engineering
Technicka 2, 166 27 Prague 6, Czech Republic
E-mail: lazan@labe.felk.cvut.cz

Gerald Quirchmayr
University of South Australia, School of Computer and Information Science
Mawson Lakes Campus, Mawson Lakes, SA 5095
E-mail: Gerald.Quirchmayr@unisa.edu.au

Pavel Vogel
Technical University of Munich, Department of Information Systems
Orleanstr. 34, 81667 Munich, Germany
E-mail: vogel@in.tum.de

Cataloging-in-Publication Data applied for

Die Deutsche Bibliothek - CIP-Einheitsaufnahme
Database and expert systems applications : 12th international conference ; proceedings / DEXA 2001, Munich, Germany, September 3 - 5, 2001. Heinrich C. Mayr ... (ed.). - Berlin ; Heidelberg ; New York ; Barcelona ; Hong Kong ; London ; Milan ; Paris ; Tokyo : Springer, 2001
(Lecture notes in computer science ; Vol. 2113)
ISBN 3-540-42527-6
CR Subject Classification (1998): H.2, H.3, I.2.1, H.4, H.5, J.1

ISSN 0302-9743
ISBN 3-540-42527-6 Springer-Verlag Berlin Heidelberg New York

Springer-Verlag Berlin Heidelberg New York
a member of BertelsmannSpringer Science+Business Media GmbH

http://www.springer.de

Typesetting: Camera-ready by author, data conversion by PTP Berlin, Stefan Sossna
Printed on acid-free paper SPIN 10839825 06/3142 5 4 3 2 1 0

Lecture Notes in Computer Science 2113
Edited by G. Goos, J. Hartmanis and J. van Leeuwen

Springer
Berlin
Heidelberg
New York
Barcelona
Hong Kong
London
Milan
Paris
Tokyo

Preface

DEXA 2001, the 12th International Conference on Database and Expert Systems Applications was held on September 3–5, 2001, at the Technical University of Munich, Germany. The rapidly growing spectrum of database applications has led to the establishment of more specialized discussion platforms (DaWaK conference, EC-Web conference, and DEXA workshop), which were all held in parallel with the DEXA conference in Munich.

In your hands are the results of much effort, beginning with the preparation of the submitted papers. The papers then passed through the reviewing process, and the accepted papers were revised to final versions by their authors and arranged with the conference program. All this culminated in the conference itself. A total of 175 papers were submitted to this conference, and I would like to thank all the authors. They are the real base of the conference. The program committee and the supporting reviewers produced altogether 497 referee reports, on average of 2.84 reports per paper, and selected 93 papers for presentation.

Comparing the weight or more precisely the number of papers devoted to particular topics at several recent DEXA conferences, an increase can be recognized in the areas of XMS databases, active databases, and multi- and hypermedia efforts. The space devoted to the more classical topics such as information retrieval, distribution and Web aspects, and transaction, indexing and query aspects has remained more or less unchanged. Some decrease is visible for object orientation.

At this point we would like to say many thanks to all the institutions which actively supported this conference and made it possible. These are:

- The Technical University of Munich
- FAW
- DEXA Association
- Austrian Computer Society

A conference like DEXA would not be possible without the enthusiastic efforts of several people in the background. First we would like to thank the whole program committee for the thorough referee process. Many thanks also to Maria Schweikert (Technical University of Vienna) and Monika Neubauer and Gabriela Wagner (FAW, University of Linz).

July 2001

Jiri Lanzanski
Heinrich C. Mayr
Gerald Quirchmayr
Pavel Vogel

Program Committee

General Chairperson:
Heinrich C. Mayr, University of Klagenfurt, Austria

Conference Program Chairpersons:
Jiri Lazansky, Czech Technical University, Czech Republic
Gerald Quirchmayr, University of Vienna, Austria
Pavel Vogel, Technical University of Munich, Germany

Workshop Chairpersons:
A Min Tjoa, Technical University of Vienna, Austria
Roland R. Wagner, FAW, University of Linz, Austria

Publication Chairperson:
Vladimir Marik, Czech Technical University, Czech Republic

Program Committee Members:
Michel Adiba, IMAG - Laboratoire LSR, France
Hamideh Afsarmanesh, University of Amsterdam, The Netherlands
Jens Albrecht, Oracle GmbH, Germany
Ala Al-Zobaidie, University of Greenwich, UK
Bernd Amann, CNAM, France
Frederic Andres, NACSIS, Japan
Kurt Bauknecht, University of Zurich, Switzerland
Trevor Bench-Capon, University of Liverpool, United Kingdom
Alfs Berztiss, University of Pittsburgh, USA
Jon Bing, University of Oslo, Norway
Omran Bukhres, Purdue University, USA
Luis Camarinah-Matos, New University of Lisbon, Portugal
Antonio Cammelli, IDG-CNR, Italy
Wojciech Cellary, University of Economics at Poznan, Poland
Stavros Christodoulakis, Technical University of Crete, Greece
Panos Chrysanthis, Univ. of Pittsburgh & Carnegie Mellon Univ., USA
Paolo Ciaccia, University of Bologna, Italy
Christine Collet, LSR-IMAG, France
Carlo Combi, University of Udine, Italy
William Bruce Croft, University of Massachusetts, USA
John Debenham, University of Technology, Sydney, Australia
Misbah Deen, University of Keele, United Kingdom
Nina Edelweiss, University of Rio Grande do Sul, Brazil
Johann Eder, University of Klagenfurt, Austria
Thomas, Eiter , Technical University of Vienna, Austria
Gregor Engels, University of Paderborn, Germany
Peter Fankhauser, GMD-IPSI, Germany
Eduardo Fernandez, Florida Atlantic University, USA

Simon Field, IBM Research Division, Switzerland
Peter Funk, Mälardalen University, Sweden
Antonio L. Furtado, University of Rio de Janeiro, Brazil
Georges Gardarin, University of Versailles, France
Parke Godfrey, York University, Canada
Georg Gottlob, Technical University of Vienna, Austria
Paul Grefen, University of Twente, The Netherlands
Abdelkader Hameurlain, Université Paul Sabatier, France
Igor T. Hawryszkiewycz, University of Technology, Sydney, Australia
Mohamed Ibrahim, University of Greenwich, UK
Yahiko Kambayashi, Kyoto University, Japan
Magdi N. Kamel, Naval Postgraduate School, USA
Nabil Kamel, American University in Cairo, Egypt
Gerti Kappel, University of Linz, Austria
Kamalar Karlapalem, University of Science and Technology, Hong Kong
Randi Karlsen, University of Tromsö, Norway
Rudolf Keller, University of Montreal, Canada
Myoung Ho Kim, KAIST, Korea
Masaru Kitsuregawa, Tokyo University, Japan
Gary J. Koehler, University of Florida, USA
Donald Kossmann, Technical University of Munich, Germany
Jaques Kouloumdjian, INSA, France
Petr Kroha, Technical University Chemnitz-Zwickau, Germany
Josef Küng, University of Linz, Austria
Michel Leonard, University of Geneve, Switzerland
Tok Wang Ling, National University of Singapore, Singapore
Mengchi Liu, University of Regina, Canada
Fred Lochovsky, Hong Kong Univ. of Science and Technology, Hong Kong
Peri Loucopoulos, UMIST, United Kingdom
Sanjai Kumar Madria, University of Missouri-Rolla, USA
Akifumi Makinouchi, Kyushu University, Japan
Vladimir Marik, Czech Technical University, Czech Republic
Simone Marinai, University of Florence, Italy
Subhasish Mazumdar, New Mexico Tech, USA
Robert Meersman, Free University Brussels, Belgium
Elisabeth Metais, University of Versailles, France
Mukesh Mohania, Western Michigan University, USA
Sophie Monties, EPFL, Switzerland
Tadeusz Morzy, Poznan University of Technology, Poland
Günter Müller, University of Freiburg, Germany
Erich J. Neuhold, GMD-IPSI, Germany
Gultekin Ozsoyoglu, University Case Western Research, USA
Georgios Pangalos, University of Thessaloniki, Greece
Stott Parker, University of Los Angeles (UCLA), USA
Oscar Pastor, Technical University of Valencia, Spain
Marco Patella, University of Bologna, Italy
Barbara Pernici, Politecnico di Milano, Italy

Günter Pernul, University of Essen, Germany
Fausto Rabitti, CNUCE-CNR, Italy
Isidro Ramos, Technical University of Valencia, Spain
Haralad Reiterer, University of Konstanz, Germany
Norman Revell, Middlesex University, UK
Sally Rice, Unversity of South Australia, Australia
John Roddick, Flinders University of South Australia, Australia
Colette Rolland, University Paris I, Sorbonne, France
Elke Rundensteiner, Worcester Polytechnic Institute, USA
Domenico Sacca, University of Calabria, Italy
Marinette Savonnet, University of Bourgogne, France
Erich Schweighofer, University of Vienna, Austria
Timos Sellis, National Technical University of Athens, Greece
Michael H. Smith, University of California, USA
Giovanni Soda, University of Florence, Italy
Harald Sonnberger, EUROSTAT, Luxembourg
Günther Specht, Technical University of Ilmenau, Germany
Uma Srinivasan, CIRO, Australia
Bala Srinivasan, Monash University, Australia
Olga Stepankova, Czech Technical University, Czech Republic
Zbigniew Struzik, CWI, Amsterdam, The Netherlands
Makoto Takizawa, Tokyo Denki University, Japan
Katsumi Tanaka, Kobe University, Japan
Zahir Tari, University of Melbourne, Australia
Stephanie Teufel, University of Fribourg, Germany
Jukka Teuhola, University of Turku, Finland
Bernd Thalheim, Technical University of Cottbus, Germany
Jean Marc Thevenin, University of Toulouse, France
Helmut Thoma, IBM Global Services Basel, Switzerland
A Min Tjoa, Technical University of Vienna, Austria
Roland Traunmüller, University of Linz, Austria
Aphrodite Tsalgatidou, University of Athens, Greece
Susan Urban, Arizona State University, USA
Krishnamurthy Vidyasankar, Memorial University of Newfoundland, Canada
Roland R. Wagner, University of Linz, Austria
Michael Wing, Middlesex University, UK
Werner Winiwarter, Software Competence Center Hagenberg, Austria
Gian Piero Zarri, CNRS, France
Arkady Zaslavsky, Monash University, Australia

External Reviewers

Alessandro Vullo
Andrea Passerini
Elisabetta Grazzini
Matilde Celma
Pepe Carsí
Pedro Sánchez
J.H. Canós
Kalpdrum Passi
Pascal van Eck
Herman Balsters
Rashid Jayousi
Costas Vassilakis
Heiko Ludwig
Eleni Berki
Thomas Neligwa
Jan-Hendrik Hausmann
Jochen Küster
Marc Lohmann
Katharina Mehner
Stefan Sauer
Annika Wagner
Yon Dohn Chung
Jin Hyun Son
Sara Comai
Hartmut Liefke
Marcus Herzog
Barbara Catania
Brian Henderson Sellars
Franz Puntigam
Maurizio Vincini
Jochen Renz
Thomas Lukasiewicz
Xubo Zhang
Michel Klein
Fredj Dridi
Torsten Priebe
Torsten Schlichting
Ingo Frommholz
Surya Nepal
Guoren Wang
Pit Koon Teo
Wai Lup Low
Katsumi Takahashi
Miyuki Nakano
Yibin Su
Haiyun Zheng
Zdenek Kouba
Petr Miksovsky
Jiying Wang
Kaiyang Liu
Ralf Busse
Jute Pfleschutz
Peter Dawabi
Lionel Brunie
Elisabeth Kapsammer
Siegfried Reich
Simon Cuce
Jeffrey Tan
Maria Indrawan
Campbell Wilson
M Viswanthan
Jose-Luis Zechinelli
Nikos Karayannidis
Theodore Dalamagas
Panos Vassiliadis
Morad Benyoucef
Gianni Mainetto
Giuseppe Amato
Pasquale Pagano
Claudio Gennaro
Tuyet Tram Dang Ngoc
Edgard Benitz-Guerrero
Khalid Belhajjame
Claudia Roncancio
Tanguy Nedelec
Sapia Carsten
Wohner Wolfgang
Hahn Charlie
Fenk Robert
Bauer Michael
Reiner Bernd
Francesco Buccafurri,
Mario Cannataro,
Luigi Pontieri,
Domenico Ursino
Ioannis Mavridis

Table of Contents

Invited Talk

Advanced Databases I

Information Retrieval Aspects I

Digital Libraries

User Interfaces

Advanced Databases II

Information Retrieval Aspects II

Multimedia Databases

Workflow Aspects

Advanced Databases III

Information Retrieval Aspects III

Active Databases

Spatial Databases

Advanced Databases IV

Distributed Databases

Web Aspects I

Knowledge Aspects I

XML

Datawarehouses

Web Aspects II

Knowledge Aspects II

Hypermedia

Index Aspects

Object-Oriented Databases I

Transaction Aspects I

Query Aspects I

Object-Oriented Databases II

Transaction Aspects II

Query Aspects II

DEXA Position Paper

XML Databases: Modeling and Multidimensional Indexing

Rudolf Bayer
Institut für Informatik
TU-München

Abstract. The talk will discuss several relational models for XML-Databases and methods, how to map XML-Data to relational data. For each relational model there is a standard technique, how to rewrite XML-Queries in order to transform them into relational SQL-Queries.

The relational models and the queries will be considered in combination with classical and multidimensional (UB-tree) indexes and qualitative performance analyses will be presented depending on the relational models and the indexes used. Based on these analyses a recommendation will be given for mapping XML to the relational world.

H.C. Mayr et al. (Eds.): DEXA 2001, LNCS 2113, p.1, 2001.

Updatability in Federated Database Systems

Mong Li Lee, Sin Yeung Lee, and Tok Wang Ling

School of Computing, National University of Singapore
email{leeml, jlee, lingtw}@comp.nus.edu.sg

Abstract. It is important to support updates in federated database systems. However, not all updates on the federated schema are possible because some may violate certain constraints in the local databases which are involved in the federation. In this paper, we give a formal framework which characterizes the conditions under which a federated schema object type is updatable. We study the steps involved to systematically map an update request on an external view of a federated schema into the equivalent update(s) on the local databases. We also consider the situation where semantically equivalent object types may not model exactly the same set of objects in the real world. We ensure that the set constraints (EQUAL, SUBSET, DISJOINT) between the instance sets of equivalent object types are not violated after an update.

1 Introduction

A federated database system (FDBS) is a collection of cooperating but autonomous component database systems. [16] proposed a five-level schema architecture (Figure 1) which includes the *local schema* (conceptual schema of a local database system), the *component schema* (equivalent local schema modeled in a canonical or common data model), the *export schema* (subset of a conceptual schema), the *federated schema* (integration of multiple export schemas), and the *external schema* (a view of the federated schema). There are 3 important issues in a FDBS:

1. Translation from the local schema to component schema with semantic enrichment [3,11,13].
2. Integration of multiple export schemas into a federated schema [1,15,18,7].
3. Translation of retrieval and update requests specified in terms of external schema to requests on underlying database systems.

While the first two issues have been extensively studied by many researchers, the third issue, however, has not been deeply studied. Updates in FDBS are quite different from view updates in centralized databases. The former involves a federated schema which is an integration of multiple schemas, while the latter involves views of an underlying conceptual schema. To support updates in an FDBS, it is necessary to determine how to which local databases to propagate the update to. This entails us to consider how the various local schemas have been integrated into the federated schema.

Consider two SUPPLIER-PART databases with base tables SUPPLIER, PART and SUPPLY and export schemas ES1 and ES2 respectively. Suppose ES1

H.C. Mayr et al. (Eds.): DEXA 2001, LNCS 2113, pp. 2–11, 2001.

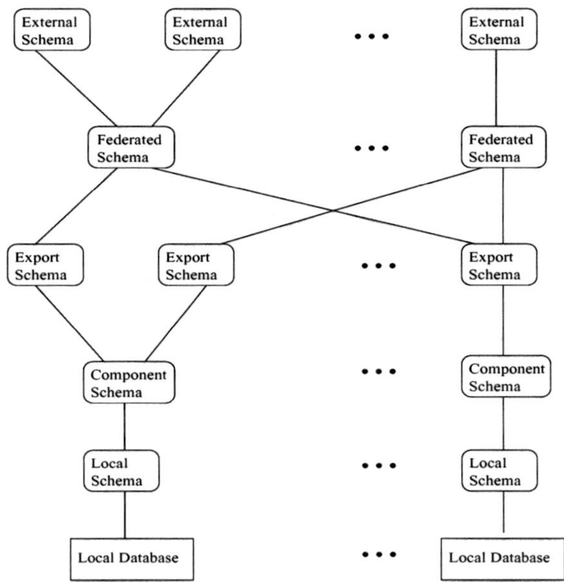

Fig. 1. The five level architecture

consists of entity types SUPPLIER, PART and relationship set SUPPLY, while ES2 has only entity type SUPPLIER with a multivalued attribute PARTNO. An integration of these two export schemas will give us a federated schema that is the same as ES1. Assuming that we have an external schema that is the same as the federated schema. Then a request to delete a relationship $supply(s1, p1, 10)$ from the external schema is translated to deleting the same relationship $supply(s1, p1, 10)$ from the federated schema. This federated schema deletion will be propagated to the export schemas in various ways. In ES1, it is translated to a deletion of $supply(s1, p1, 10)$ from relationship set SUPPLY. In ES2, the deletion will be translated to an update to the multivalued attribute PNO of SUPPLIER. The latter situation would not have occured in centralized databases. Furthermore, the set of objects in a local databases may need to obey certain set constraints. For example, the set of students in in the science department database should be a subset of the set of students in the university database. If an update is propagated to the science department database, then it must also be propagated to the university database.

The rest of the paper is organized as follows. Section 2 reviews the Entity-Relationship (ER) model and explains the update issue in a FDBS. Section 3 gives a framework for the integration of export schemas. Section 4.1 examines when and how an update to the federated schema can be propagated to the set of export schemas. Section 4.2 discusses how to maintain the consistency of the local databases after an update. We conclude the paper in Section 5.

2 Preliminaries

In this section, we will discuss the advantages of adopting the ER model as the CDM and examine what is involved in supporting updates in a FDBS.

2.1 The Entity-Relationship Approach

Many existing FDBS prototypes use the relational model as the CDM. However, the relational model does not possess the necessary semantics for defining all the integration mappings that might be desired. Updating views in relational model is inherently ambiguous [6]. The trend is to use semantic data models such as object-oriented (OO) data model [2,4] and the ER data model [18]. Unfortunately, the OO models suffer from several inadequacies such as the lack of a formal foundation, lack of a declarative query language, a navigational interface, conflicts in class hierarchy etc. The structural properties of the OO model can be derived from the ER approach [19]. Hence, although ER model does not have an equivalent concept of object methods yet, we will adopt the more established and well-defined ER model as the CDM in our FDBS. In this paper, we assume that the ER data model supports single-valued, multivalued and composite attributes, weak entity types (both EX-weak and ID-weak), recursive relationship sets, and special relationship sets such as ISA, UNION, INTERSECT etc [8].

2.2 The Update Issue

In the traditional problem of updating databases through views, a user specifies an an update U against a database view $V[DB]$. The view update mapper M map the update U on $V[DB]$ to another database update U_M on DB, which results in a new database $U_M(DB)$. The new view of the database is therefore $V[U_M(DB)]$. The mapping is *correct* if $V[U_M(DB)] = U(V[DB])$, that is, the view changes precisely in accordance with the user's request. On the other hand, an update on the external schema of a FDBS has to be translated to the equivalent updates on the local schemas. We identify five mappings that are required.

1. Map update request on external schema modeled using data models such as relational, network, or hierarchical models to corresponding update on external schema modeled using ER model.
2. Map update request on ER external schema to corresponding updates on ER federated schema.
3. Map updates on federated schema into updates on the ER export schemas which have been integrated to form the federated schema.
4. Map updates on export schemas into updates on their respective ER component schemas.
5. Map updates on the component schemas into updates on their corresponding local schema which may not be modeled using the ER model.

Algorithms for mappings (1) and (5) can be found in [9] and [14,5,13] respectively. Mappings (2) and (4) are similar to the translation of ER view updates. [10,12] give the theory and algorithms to handle these mappings. Mapping (3), which has not been investigated in the literature, involves the propagation of an update on the federated schema to updates on the various export schemas. The integration feature, which is non-existent in traditional view updates, makes this mapping unique and is the focus of the paper.

3 Integration of Schemas

It is important to know the original modeling constructs of a federated object type (entity type, relationship set, attribute), in the export schemas to determine the updatability of the federated object type. Structural conflicts occur when related real world concepts are modeled using different modeling constructs in the different schemas. [7] enumerates the possible original modeling structures of a federated schema object type:

1. A federated schema entity type is an entity type, or as an attribute of an entity type or a relationship set in the export schemas.
2. A federated schema relationship set is a relationship set, or a relationship between an attribute and its owner entity type in the export schemas.
3. A federated schema attribute is an attribute in the export schemas.

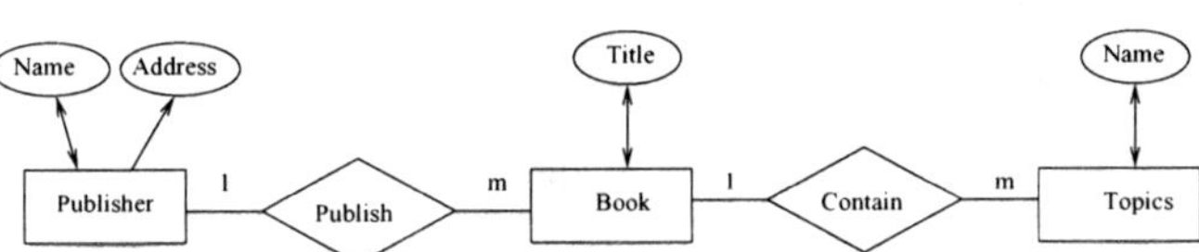

Fig. 2. Schema S1

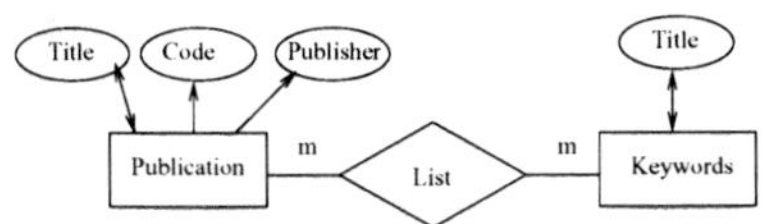

Fig. 3. Schema S2

Example 1. Consider schemas S1 and S2 in Figure 2 and 3. We have

1. S1.Topics = S2.Keywords
2. S1.Topics.Name = S2.Keywords.Title
3. S1.Publisher = S2.Publication.Publisher
4. S1.Book ISA S2.Publication

The structural conflict between S1.Publisher and S2.Publication.Publisher can be resolved by transforming the attribute S2.Publication.Publisher into an entity type Publisher (Figure 4). A new relationship set Print is created. We merge S1 and S2'. Since we have S1.Book ISA S2.Publication, an ISA relationship is created between Book and Publication. Any redundant relationship sets and entity types are removed. Figure 5 shows the integrated schema.

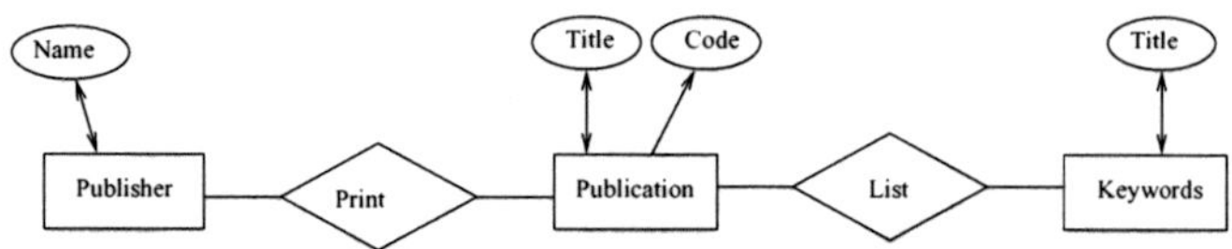

Fig. 4. Schema S2' - Attribute Publisher in S2 is transformed into an entity type

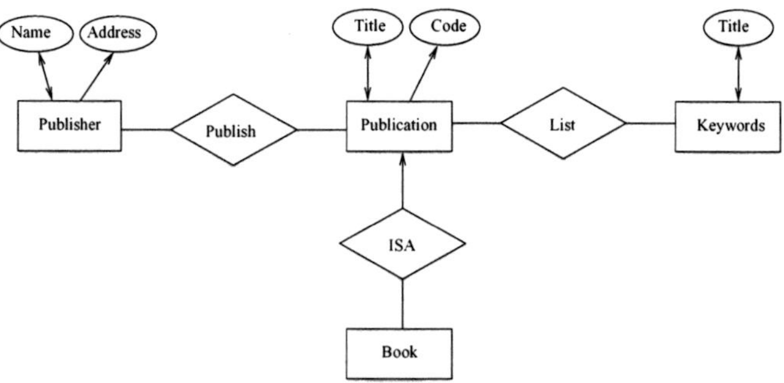

Fig. 5. Final schema S3 after integrating S1 and S2

We will now present the notations used to indicate how an integrated entity type/relationship set/attribute is obtained from the export schemas.

Definition 1. *Let E_F be an entity type in a federated schema. If E_F is obtained by integrating a set of objects I_k in export schemas S_k respectively, then we denote $E_F = Integrate < I_1, \cdots, I_n >$. Object I_k is of the form:*

1. $S_k.E_j$ if I_k is an entity type E_j in export schema S_k,

2. $S_k.E_j.A$ if I_k is an attribute A of an entity type E_j in schema S_k,

3. $S_k.R_j.A$ if I_k is an attribute A of relationship set R_j in schema S_k ◇.

Definition 2. *An integrated schema relationship set R_F is denoted as $Integrate < I_1, \cdots, I_n >$ if R_F is obtained by integrating a set of objects I_k where I_k is of the form:*

1. $S_k.R_j$ if I_k is a relationship set R_j in export schema S_k, or

2. $S_k.E_j\%A$ if I_k is the implicit relationship between an attribute A and its owner entity type E_j in export schema S_k ◇.

Definition 3. *An integrated schema attribute A_F which is obtained by integrating a set of objects I_k, is denoted by $A_F = Integrate < I_1, \cdots, I_n >$ where all the I_k are either of the form $S_k.E_j.A$ or of the form $S_k.R_j.A$. That is, the I_k are equivalent entity types (or relationship sets).* ◇.

For example, the integrated entity type Publisher can be represented as *Integrate* < S1.Publisher, S2.Publication.Publisher>. This indicates that Publisher is obtained from an entity type in the export schema S1 and an attribute Publisher in S2. The integrated relationship set Publish = *Integrate* <S1.Publish, S2.Publication%Publisher>. S2.Publication%Publisher denotes the implicit relationship between entity type Publication and its attribute Publisher. The integrated attribute Title = *Integrate* <S1.Topics.Name, S2.Keywords.Title>. Note that the entity types Topics and Keywords are equivalent. [11] shows that that an attribute of an entity type in one schema cannot be equivalent to an attribute of a relationship set in another schema because their semantics are inherently different.

4 Updatability of Federated Schemas

In this section, we will investigate the conditions under which an update on the federated schema is acceptable. There are two steps involved:
1. Decide the set of objects in the export schemas which a federated schema update can propagate to.
2. Decide if update propagation is consistent with the set constraints that exist among the objects in the local databases.

4.1 Propagating Updates

Definition 4. *A federated schema entity type (or a relationship set) S_F is* insertable *wrt an export schema S_E if we can insert some corresponding entities (or relationships) in S_E and the translation of the update is correct. The deletion of a federated schema entity type (or a relationship set) can be similarly defined. A federated schema attribute is* modifiable *wrt an export schema S_E if we can modify some corresponding attribute in S_E and the translation of the modification is correct* ◇.

Theorem 1 (Update propagation for federated schema entity type). *Let $E_F = Integrate < I_1, \cdots, I_n >$ be a federated schema entity type. If E_F is insertable and deletable, then an insertion or deletion on E_F will be propagated to some I_k where I_k is an entity type.*

Proof. Assume that any identifier or key conflicts have been resolved. If I_k is an entity type, then a request to insert an entity into E_F will be translated into requests to insert corresponding entities with key value and other attribute values of E_F into I_k. Similar argument can be applied to deletion. Hence, E_F is insertable and deletable wrt I_k. If I_k is an attribute, then any insertion or deletion on E_F will not be propagated to I_k since an attribute needs to be associated with an owner entity/relationship. Similarly, When we delete an entity from E_F, we cannot delete the corresponding key value from some attribute I_k because this would mean deleting some implicit relationship between the attribute and its owner entity type/relationship set ◇.

Example 2. Let Publisher=*Integrate* <S1.Publisher,S2.Publication.Publisher> where the concept publisher is modeled as an entity type Publisher in S1 and as an attribute Publisher of Publication in S2. The integrated entity type Publisher is both insertable and deletable as follows. An insertion of a new publisher into Publisher at the federated schema is propagated to S1 by inserting the new publisher into S1.Publisher. Note that the insertion will not be propagated to S2 because publisher is modeled as an attribute in S2 and needs to be associated with a publication.

The next theorem determines how the insertion or deletion of a federated relationship set is propagated to the export schemas. The modification of a relationship set can refer to the modification of attributes of the relationship set, or the modification of an association among the participating entities of the relationship set. The former is handled in Theorem 3 while the latter is equivalent to a deletion followed by an insertion.

Theorem 2 (Update propagation for federated schema relationship set). *Let R_F be a federated schema relationship set. $R_F = Integrate < I_1, \cdots, I_n >$ where I_k corresponds to a relationship set or an implicit relationship E%A between an entity type E and an attribute A in some export schema. Then R_F is always both insertable and deletable wrt to any I_k.*

Proof. *If I_k is a relationship set, then insertion is similar to the case of entity type. If I_k is an implicit relationship E%A, then I_k is a binary relationship set, and R_F must be a binary relationship set involving two entities E_1 and E_2. Without loss of generality, let E correspond to E_1 and attribute A correspond to the identifier of E_2. If A is a single-valued attribute, then we can insert into E%A by first retrieving the corresponding entity in E using the key value of E1. If the value of A is NULL, that is, this relationship instance does not yet exist in E_1 and E_2, then set the value of A to the identifier value of E_2. If A is a multivalued attribute, then update A by inserting the new value into A. Similarly, to delete E%A, set the value of A to NULL if A is a single-valued attribute, or remove the deleted value from A if A is a multivalued attribute* ◇.

Example 3. Consider the integrated relationship set Publish with participating entity types Publisher and Publication. If Publish is integrated from S1.Publish and S2.Publication%Publisher, then the integrated relationship set Publish is both insertable and deletable as follows. The insertion of a new relationship $(IEEE, Computer)$ into Publish is propagated to S1 by inserting $(IEEE, Computer)$ into S1.Publish. The insertion is also propagated into S2 by retrieving publication "Computer" from S2.Publication and inserting the value "IEEE" to multivalued attribute Publisher.

Theorem 3 (Modification of a federated schema attribute). *Let A_F be an attribute in the federated schema. $A_F = Integrate < I_1, \cdots, I_n >$ where each I_k is an attribute. The owners of the attributes $I_1, \cdots, I_k$ are all equivalent entity types $E_1, \cdots, E_n$ (or relationship sets $R_1, \cdots, R_n$). Then A_F is always modifiable wrt any I_k.*

Proof. *If a federated schema entity type E_F (or relationship set R_F) is the owner of attribute A_F whose value is to be modified, then we will use the key value of E_F (or R_F) to retrieve the corresponding entity in E_k (or relationship in R_k). If A_k is a single-valued attribute of E_k, then modify the value of A_k to new value. If A_k is a multivalued attribute of E_k, then remove the old value from the set attribute A_k and insert the new value into A_k. Hence, A_F is modifiable wrt any I_k* $\diamond$.

4.2 Maintaining Set Constraints

We have shown when an update from the federated schema can be propagated to the export schemas. However, an update can be propagated to an export schema does not imply that the update WILL be propagated. One of the further considerations is to maintain set constraints among various local databases. An update will be propagated only if no set constraint is violated. In this section, we consider the following three set constraints. Note that these constraints are not necessarily mutually exclusive. For instance, EQUAL is a special case of SUBSET.

1. EQUAL - Two entity types (or relationship sets) are EQUAL, if they model exactly the same set of objects (or relationships) in the real world.
2. SUBSET - An entity type E_1 (or a relationship set R_1) is a SUBSET of another entity type E_2 (or a relationship set R_2 respectively) if for any database instance, the set of objects in the real world modeled by E_1 (or R_1 respectively) is a subset of the set of objects in the real world modeled by E_2 (or R_2 respectively).
3. DISJOINT - Two entity types (or two relationship sets) obeys the DISJOINT constraint if for any database instance, the sets of objects in the real world modeled by both entity types (or both relationship sets) are disjoint.

Lemma 1 (Enforce set constraints for attribute modification). *Let $A = Integrate < A_1, \cdots, A_n >$, where A is a federated schema attribute of an object type (entity type or relationship set) and A_k is an attribute of an object type O_k in the export schemas. The execution of a modification request on the value of a federated schema attribute cannot violate the set relations between any two object types O_i and O_j* $\diamond$.

On the other hand, an insertion and deletion of entity type and relationship set can violate some set constraints. The following theorem describes the condition such that an insertion or a deletion will not violate any of the three given set constraints.

Theorem 4 (Enforce set constraints for entity type and relationship set insertion and deletion). *Let $O = Integrate < O_1, \cdots, O_n >$, where O is a federated schema object type, which can be either an entity type or a relationship set, and O_k are equivalent object types in the export schemas. Suppose the insertion of an object x into federated schema object O is propagated to some export* *schema* $O' \in \{O_1, \cdots, O_n\}$. *This insertion does not violate any set constraint if and only if all the following two conditions hold*

1. x *is also inserted into each of the* $O_k \in \{O_1, \cdots, O_n\}$ *if either* O' *EQUAL* O_k *or* O' *SUBSET* O_k *holds.*

2. x *is not inserted into any of the* $O_k \in \{O_1, \cdots, O_n\}$ *if* O' *DISJOINT* O_k *holds.*

Similarly, Suppose the deletion of an object x *from federated schema object* O *is propagated to some export schema* $O' \in \{O_1, \cdots, O_n\}$. *The deletion of an object* x *from* O' *does not violate any set constraint if and only if* x *is also deleted from all of the* $O_k \in \{O_1, \cdots, O_n\}$ *if either* O' *EQUAL* O_k *or* O_k *SUBSET* O' *holds* $\diamond$.

The above theorem only decides if a set of update propagations are correct. In general, there can be many different update propagations that does not violate any set constraint. The decision of which propagation to be finally chosen will be determined by the user or application.

Example 4. Suppose S1.Publisher is modeled as a weak entity type. In this case, we may assume that S1.Publisher EQUAL S2.Publication.Publisher. According to Theorem 1, an insertion to the integrated entity type Publisher can be propagated to S1 but not S2. According to Theorem 4, an insertion of S1 will violate some set constraint if S2 is not inserted at the same time. In this case, the insertion into the integrated schema entity type Publisher is not valid. However, when S1.Publisher is modeled as a normal entity type, we can only assume that S2.Publication.Publisher SUBSET S1.Publisher. An insertion into S1 without an insertion into S2 will not violate any set constraints. In this case, an insertion into the integrated schema entity type Publisher will be valid. Intuitively, this conclusion is sound as the publishers modeled by S2 are "published publishers". A new publisher without any publication can be inserted into S1 but not S2.

5 Conclusions

In this paper, we have examined the issue of supporting updates in an ER based FDBS. We discussed how an update against the external schema of a FDBS needs to be translated into equivalent updates on the local databases via the federated schema, export schemas, component schemas and local schemas. The crucial step involves mapping an update on the federated schema to equivalent export schemas updates. This step requires the determination of the updatability (insertable or deletable) of a federated schema entity type or relationship set. We examined when and how a federated schema update can be propagated to updates on various export schemas, and ensure that such an update does not violate any of set constraints.

References

1. Batini C. and Lenzerini M. A methodology for data schema integration in the ER model. In *IEEE Trans. on Software Engineering, Vol 10*, 1984.

2. Bertino E. Integration of heterogeneous data repositories by using object-oriented views. In *First Int. Workshop on Interoperability in Multidatabase Systems*, 1991.
3. Castellanous M. and Saltor F. Semantic enrichment of database schema: An object-oriented approach. *First Int. Workshop on Interoperability in Multidatabase*, 1991.
4. Drosten K., Kaul M. and Neuhold E. Viewsystem: Integrating heterogeneous information bases by object-oriented views. In *IEEE 6th Int. Conf. On Data Engineering*, 1990.
5. Johannesson P. and Kalman K. A method for translating relational schemas into conceptual schemas. In *Proc. of 8th Int. Conf. on ER Approach*, 1989.
6. Keller A.M. Algorithms for translating view updates to database updates for views involving selections, projections and joins. In *Proc. of ACM SIGACT-SIGMOD Symposium*, 1985.
7. Lee M.L. and Ling T.W. Resolving structural conflict in the integration of ER schemas. In *Proc. 14th Int. Conf. on ER Approach*, 1995. Australia.
8. Ling T.W. A normal form for ER diagrams. In *Proc. 4th Int. Conf. on ER Approach*, 1985.
9. Ling T.W. External schemas of ER based database management systems. In *Proc. 7th Int. Conf. on ER Approach*, 1988.
10. Ling T.W. and Lee M.L. A theory for ER view updates. In *Proc. 11th Int. Conf. on ER Approach*, 1992.
11. Ling T.W. and Lee M.L. Relational to ER schema translation using semantic and inclusion dependencies. In *Journal of Integrated Computer Aided Engineering, 2(2)*, 1995.
12. Ling T.W. and Lee M.L. View update in ER approach. In *Data and Knowledge Engineering, Vol 19*, 1996.
13. Markowitz M. and Markowsky J. Identifying extended ER object structures in relational schemas. In *IEEE Trans. on Software Engineering, 16(8)*, 1990.
14. Navathe S.B. and Awong A.M. Abstracting relational and hierarchic data with a semantic data model. In *Proc of 7th Int. Conf. on ER Approach*, 1987.
15. Navathe S., Larson J. and Elmasri R. A theory of attribute equivalence in schema integration. In *IEEE Trans. on Software Engineering, Vol 15*, 1989.
16. Sheth A.P. and Gala S.K. Federated database systems for managing distributed, heterogenous, and autonomous databases. In *ACM Computing Surveys, 22(3)*, 1990.
17. Spaccapietra S., Parent C., and Dupont Y. Model independent assertions for integration of heterogenous schemas. In *VLDB Journal, (1)*, 1992.
18. Spaccapietra S. and Parent C. View integration: A step forward in solving structural conflicts. In *IEEE Trans. on Knowledge and Data Engineering, 6(2)*, 1994.
19. Teo P.K. Ling T.W. and Yan L.L. Generating object-oriented views from an ER based conceptual schema. In *3rd Int. Symposium on Database Systems for Advanced Applications*, 1993.

Designing Semistructured Databases: A Conceptual Approach

Mong Li Lee[1], Sin Yeung Lee[1], Tok Wang Ling[1],
Gillian Dobbie[2], Leonid A. Kalinichenko[3]

[1] School of Computing, National University of Singapore, Singapore
{leeml, jlee, lingtw}@comp.nus.edu.sg
[2] Dept of Computer Science, University of Auckland, New Zealand
gill@cs.auckland.ac.nz
[3] Institute for Problems of Informatics, Russian Academy of Sciences, Russia
leonidk@synth.ipi.ac.ru

Abstract. Semistructured data has become prevalent with the growth of the Internet. The data is usually stored in a database system or in a specialized repository. Many information providers have presented their databases on the web as semistructured data, while others are developing repositories for new applications. Designing a "good" semistructured database is important to prevent data redundancy and updating anomalies. In this paper, we propose a conceptual approach to design semistructured databases. A conceptual layer based on the Entity-Relationship model is used to remove redundancies at the semantic level. An algorithm to map an ER diagram involving composite attributes weak entity types, recursive, n-ary and ISA relationship sets, and aggregations to a semistructured schema graph (S3-Graph) is also given.

1 Introduction

It is increasing important to design good semistructured databases. While many information providers have presented their databases on the web as semistructured data, others are developing repositories for new applications. Consider the building of an e-commerce application. This involves designing and maintaining repositories of data including product catalogs, customer and vendor information and business-to-business transactions. Currently application builders must define and create objects and relationships in the underlying databases, as the details of the schema are not expressed in the data. As with traditional databases, poorly designed databases contain redundant data, leading to undesirable anomalies. A design methodology that seamlessly maps from the objects and relations in the database, to the hierarchical elements and attributes in semistructured data is also required.

In this paper, we describe the research that forms the basis of a methodology to build applications with semistructured data. This comprises three steps:

1. model the underlying database using ER diagrams [1],
2. normalize the ER diagrams [4],
3. model the views on the data using S3-graphs [3].

H.C. Mayr et al. (Eds.): DEXA 2001, LNCS 2113, pp. 12–21, 2001.

Introducing a normalized layer has the following advantages. First, anomalies and redundancies can be removed at the semantic level. Second, customized XML views can be generated from the normalized model. Third, data can be stored in relational databases with controlled redundancy. The contribution of this paper is an algorithm that maps ER diagrams to semistructured schema graphs (S3-Graphs), forming a seamless mapping between how the stored data is modeled and the semistructured views of the data. Our study also reveals similarites between the S3-Graph and the hierarchical model and nested relations in that all have limitations in modeling situations with nonhierarchical relationships given their tree-like structures.

The rest of the paper is organized as follows. Section 2 reviews background concepts such as the S3-graph and the ER approach. Section 3 shows how the ER approach can be used to design a semistructured database and gives a comprehensive algorithm to translate an ER diagram into a normal form semistructured schema graph. Finally, we conclude in Section 4.

2 Preliminaries

Data modeling people have acknowledged the fact that if the database attributes are fixed in structure, the modeling power of the data model is greatly reduced. In this section, we review some of the concepts of a semistructured data graph and a semistructured schema graph (S3-Graph) defined in [3]. We also review the ER approach and discuss how it can be used to model semistructured data.

2.1 SemiStructured Graph

With the introduction of XML, semistructured data becomes widespread. XML has characteristics which are very similar to semistructured data: self-describing, deeply nested or even cyclic, and irregular. Graph-based complex object models such as Object Exchange Model (OEM) [7], Document Object Model (DOM) [2], Araneus Data Model (ADM) [6] and semistructured graph [3] provide a natural framework for describing semistructured XML repositories and their DTDs. Figure 1 shows a semistructured data graph. The data graph is basically a labeled graph in which vertices correspond to objects and edges represent the object-subobject relationship. Each edge has a label describing the precise nature of the relationship. Each object has an object identifier (oid) and a value. The value is either atomic or complex, that is, a set of object references denoted as a set of (label, oid) pairs.

Figure 2 shows the schema of the semistructured data graph in Figure 1. A *SemiStructured Schema Graph (S3-Graph)* is a directed graph where each node is either a *root node* or a *component node*. We differentiate nodes in a semistructured data graph from the S3-graph by using the & symbol instead of #. Node #1 is a root node representing the entity Student. Node #2 is both a component node as well as a leaf node. Node #3' is a component node which references the root node Course (Node #3). Each directed edge in the

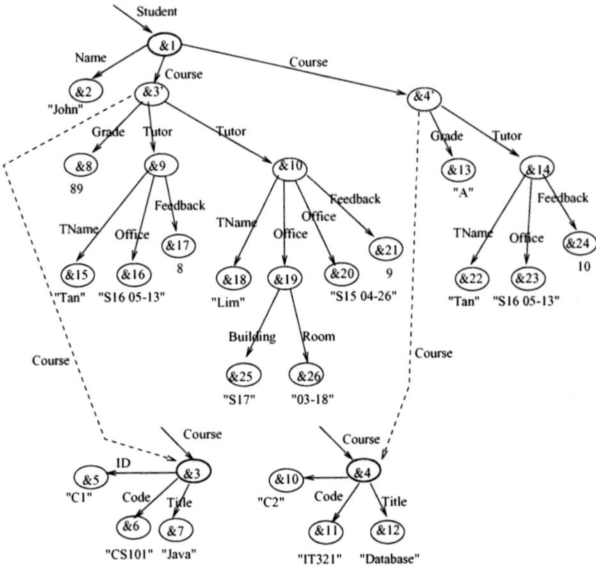

Fig. 1. A semistructured data graph.

S3-graph is associated with a *tag* indicating the relationship between the source and destination nodes. The tag may be suffixed with a "*" indicating multiple occurences. A node V_1 is connected to node V_2 by a *component edge* (a solid arrow line) with a tag T if V_2 is a component of V_1. If T is suffixed with a "*", the relationship is interpreted as "Entity type represented by V_1 has many T". Otherwise, it is interpreted as "Entity type represented by V_1 has at most one T". A node V_1 is connected to node V_2 via a *referencing edge* (a dashed arrow line) if V_1 references the entity represented by node V_2. A node V_1 is pointed by a *root edge* (a solid arrow line with no source node) tagged T if the entity type represented by V_1 is owned by the database.

The design of our example database is not a good one due to data redundancy. The two instances "$\ll$ &9 $\gg$" and "$\ll$ &14 $\gg$" in Figure 1 actually represent the same tutor "Tan" and his office "S16 05-13". If a tutor changes his office, then all occurences of this information must be changed to maintain consistency. [3] employs a decomposition method to restructure a S3-graph to remove anomalies. As in relational databases, the decomposition approach does not ensure a good solution.

2.2 The Entity-Relationship Approach

The ER model [1] incorporates the concepts of entity types, relationship sets and attributes which correspond to structures naturally occuring in information systems and database applications. An *entity type* is a collection of similar objects which have the same set of predefined common properties or attributes.

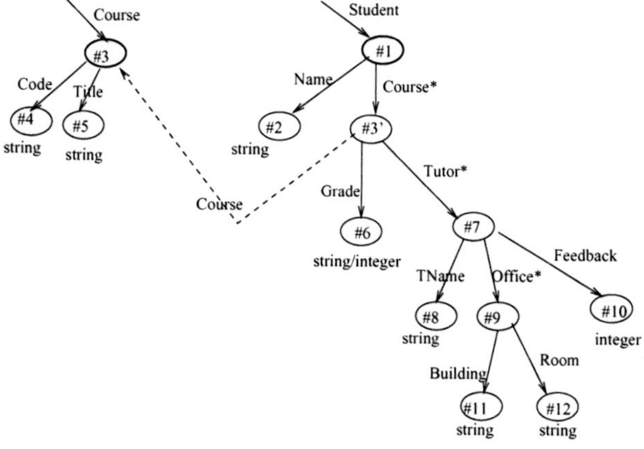

Fig. 2. Schema of the semistructured graph in Figure 1.

Attributes can be single-valued, multivalued or composite. A minimal set of attributes whose values uniquely identify an entity in an entity type is called a *key*. A *relationship* is an association among two or more entities. A *relationship set* is a collection of similar relationships with a set of predefined common attributes. If the existence of an entity in one entity type depends on the existence of a specific entity in another entity type, such a relationship set and entity type are called *existence dependent relationship set* and *weak entity type*. A relationship set which involves weak entity types is a weak relationship set. An entity type which is not weak is a regular entity type. If an entity in one entity type $E1$ is also in another entity type $E2$, we say that $E1$ ISA $E2$. The ER model also supports *recursive* relationships involving entities in the same entity type. Relationship sets can be viewed as a high level entity type known as *aggregation*.

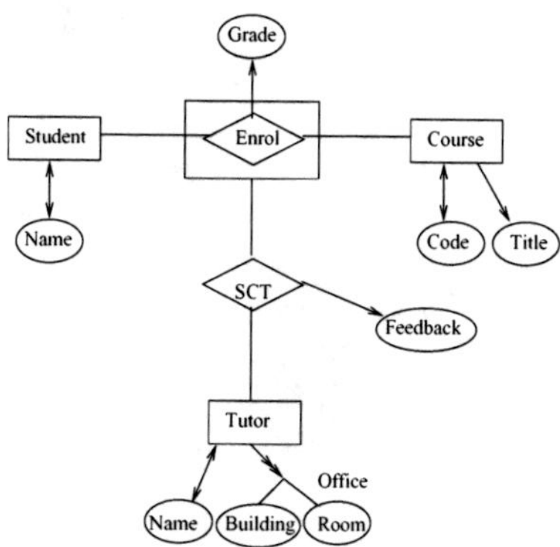

Fig. 3. Entity-Relationship diagram for Student-Course-Tutor example.

Figure 3 shows the ER diagram for the Student-Course-Tutor database. The relationship set Enrol captures the association that a student is enrolled in a course and has a single-valued attribute Grade. Since a student taking a course is taught by some tutors, we need to associate the relationship set Enrol with entity type Tutor. This association is captured in SCT where Enrol is viewed as an entity type participating in other relationship sets. The ER diagram is also in normal form.

3 ER to S3-Graph Translation

The task of designing a "good" semistructured database can be made easier if we have more semantics. For example, [4] proposes a normal form for the ER model and [5]uses the normal form ER to design normal form nested relations. This top-down approach has two advantages. First, normalizing an ER diagram removes ambiguities, anomalies and redundancies at the semantic level. Second, converting a normalized ER diagram into a set of nested relations results in a database schema with clean semantics, in a good normal form. An S3-graph is similar to the nested relations and hierarchical model in that they have a tree-like structure and allow repeating groups or multiple occurences of objects. All these models represent hierarchical organizations in a direct and natural way, but they are problematic when representing nonhierarchical relationships. Duplication of data is necessary when representing many-to-many relationships or relationships that involve more than two participating entity types. The problem of handling symmetric queries with data duplication also exists in semistructured data. Keys and foreign keys are used in nested relations while virtual pairing by logical parent pointers to represent many-to-many relationships are used in the hierarchical model to allow symmetric queries. In S3-graphs, we will show how referencing edges can be used to remove redundancies.

We will now describe the translation of an ER diagram to an S3-Graph. If the ER diagram is not in normal form, then the S3-Graph obtained may contain redundancy. However, if the ER diagram is in normal form, then the S3-Graph obtained will be in normal form (S3-NF). Anomalies in the semistructured database are removed and any redundancy due to many-to-many relationships and n-ary relationships are controlled.

Algorithm: Translation of an ER diagram to a S3-Graph.
Input: an ER diagram; Output: the equivalent S3-Graph
Step 1. Transform the ER diagram to a normal form ER diagram.
Step 2. Map regular entity types.
Step 3. Map weak entity types.
Step 4. Map relationship sets with no aggregations[1] .
Step 5. Map relationship sets with aggregations.
Step 6. Map ISA relationship sets.

[1] The participating entity types of a relationship set R may be aggregations or simply entity types.

Step 1. *Transform the ER diagram to a normal form ER diagram.*
Detailed steps with examples are described in [4].

Step 2. *Map regular entity types.*
Each regular entity type E becomes a root node N of an S3-Graph.

(a) Each single-valued and multivalued attribute A of E is mapped to a component node N_A connected to E by a component edge tagged A. If A is multivalued, then the tag is suffixed by an "*". N_A is also a leaf node labeled with the data type of A.

(b) Each composite attribute A of E is mapped to a component node N_A connected to E by a component edge tagged A. Each component attribute C of A is mapped to a component node N_C connected to N_A by a component edge with tag C.

Step 3. *Map weak entity types.*
Each weak entity type W becomes a component node N_W connected to the node N corresponding to its owner entity type E by a component edge tagged W suffixed by an "*". Attributes of W are mapped in the same way as the attributes of a regular entity type.

Step 4. *Map regular relationship sets with no aggregations.*

Case (1) *R is a binary relationship set.*
Let R be a binary relationship set with participating entity types E_A and E_B. E_A and E_B are mapped to root nodes N_A and N_B respectively. Depending on the application, there are several ways to map R:

(a) R is mapped to a component node N_R.
N_A is connected to N_R by a component edge tagged R_A and N_R connected to N_B by a referencing edge tagged R_B.

(b) R is mapped to a component node N_R.
N_B is connected to N_R by a component edge tagged R_B and N_R connected to N_A by a referencing edge tagged R_A.

(c) R is mapped to component nodes N_R and $N_{R'}$.
N_A is connected to N_R by a component edge tagged R_A and N_R connected to N_B by a referencing edge tagged R_B, while N_B is connected to $N_{R'}$ by a component edge tagged $R'_B$and $N_{R'}$ connected to N_A by a referencing edge tagged R'_A.

(d) R is mapped to a root node N_R.
N_R is connected to N_A and N_B by referencing edges tagged R_A and R_B respectively.

If R is a one-to-one relationship set, then all the tags of the component and referencing edges are not suffixed by an "*". If R is a many-to-many relationship set, then the tags are suffixed by an "*". If R is a one-to-many relationship set, then without loss of generality, let the cardinalities of E_A and E_B in R be 1 and m respectively. If we have N_A connected to N_R by a component edge, then the tag of the component edge is suffixed by an "*". Otherwise, if we have N_B connected to N_R by a component edge, then the tag is suffixed by an "*". Tags of component edges for $N_{R'}$ are similarly suffixed.

Attributes of R are mapped to component nodes in the same way as attributes of regular entity types. Figure 4 summarizes the mapping of binary relationship sets. Note that mappings (a) and (b) do not allow symmetric queries to be answered efficiently, while mapping (c) has controlled data redundancy. The relationship set R is "flattened" in mapping (d) to allow symmetric queries without duplication.
Note that if R is a recursive relationship set, then only one entity type, say E_A is involved in R with roles r1 and r2. The mapping for a recursive relationship set is similar to binary relationship sets except that the edges are tagged with the rolenames of E_A.

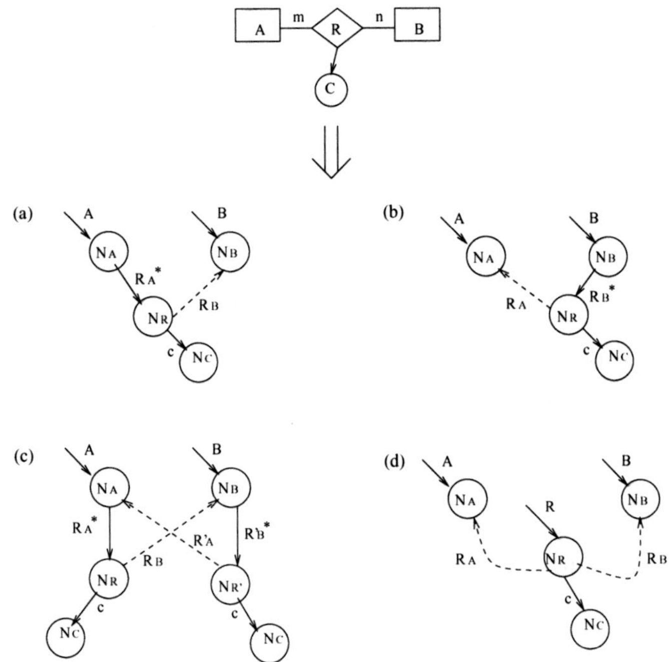

Fig. 4. Different ways to map a binary relationship set in an ER diagram to S3-graph

Case (2) *R is a n-ary relationship set where* $n > 2$.
Let the participating entity types of R be E_1, E_2, ..., E_m, where $m > 2$. E_1, E_2, ..., E_m are mapped to root nodes N_1, N_2, ..., N_m respectively. There are several ways to map R as shown in Figure 5.

(a) Map R to a component node N_R. Without loss of generality, connect N_1 to N_R by a component edge tagged R_{E1}. Then N_R has a referencing edge tagged $R_{E1}, R_{E2}, ..., R_{Em}$ to each of the root nodes N_2, N_3, ..., N_m respectively.

(b) First choose a path to link the participating entity types of R. Let $\prec V_1, V_2, V_3, \cdots, V_k \succ$ be the path, vertex V_1 corresponds to some participating entity type of R which is associated with some root node N_1, and vertex V_i, $2 \leq i \leq k$, corresponds to either a participating entity type of R or a combination of participating entity types of R. Next, create component nodes $N_{R2}, N_{R3}, ..., N_{Rk}$ that is associated with $V_2, V_3, ..., V_k$ respectively. Root node N_1 has a component edge tagged $R2_{E1}$ to node N_{R_2}, while each node N_{R_i}, where $2 \leq i \leq k-1$, has a component edge tagged $R_{i+1_{E1}}$ to $N_{R_{i+1}}$, and a referencing edge(s) tagged R_{Ei} to the root node(s) that is associated with the participating entity type(s) of R corresponding to V_i.

(c) "Flatten" the relationship set by mapping R to a root node N_R. N_R is connected to N_1, N_2, ..., N_m by referencing edges tagged $R_{E1}, R_{E2}, ..., R_{Em}$ respectively.

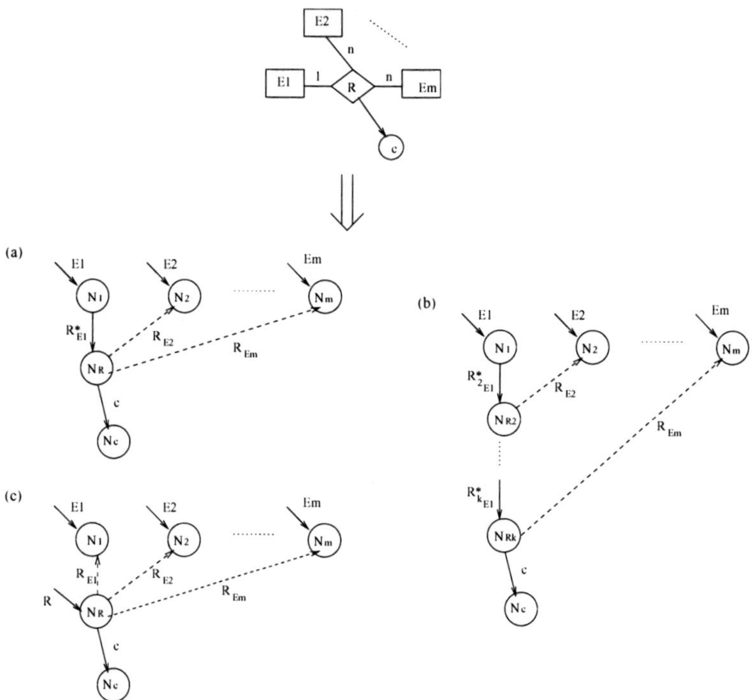

Fig. 5. Different ways to map a n-ary relationship set in an ER diagram to S3-graph

Step 5. *Map regular relationship sets with aggregations.*

Aggregations are a means of enforcing inclusion dependencies in a database. Let R be a regular relationship set and E_1, E_2, ..., E_m and E_{A_1}, E_{A_2}, ..., E_{A_n} be the participating entity types of R. Entity types E_1, E_2, ..., E_m have been mapped to root nodes N_1, N_2, ..., N_m respectively. Relationships in the aggregations E_{A_1}, E_{A_2}, ..., E_{A_n} have been mapped to nodes N_{A_1}, N_{A_2}, ...,

N_{A_n} respectively. Depending on the application, use the various alternatives in Step 4 to map R to a node N_R and link N_R to the nodes N_i and N_{A_j}, where $1 \leq i \leq m$, $1 \leq j \leq n$.

Step 6. *Map special relationship set ISA.*
Given A ISA B, map A and B to nodes N_A and N_B respectively and the ISA relationship set to a referencing edge tagged ISA connecting N_A to N_B.

Example. The ER diagram in Figure 3 can be translated to the semi-structured schema graph in Figure 6 as follows. The entity types Student, Course and Tutor become entity nodes #1, #3, #7 respectively. The attributes also become nodes and are connected to their owner entity type by component edges. We need to process the relationship Enrol before SCT because Enrol is involved in an aggregation. Enrol is mapped to an entity node #13 with component edges to entity nodes Course and Student. The attribute Grade is a component of the entity node #13. Next, we map the relationship set SCT to an entity node #15 which has component edges to entity nodes Enrol and Tutor. The attribute Feedback is a component of node #15. The S3-Graph obtained does not contain data redundancy. Note that the relationship sets Enrol and SCT have been flattened in the S3-Graph in Figure 6 because we want to answer symmetric queries with no redundant data. However, if an application only process queries which retrieve the courses taken by a student, and do not need to find students who take a given course, then Figure 7 shows an alternative way to map the ER diagram. Note that this schema cannot answer symmetric queries effectively.

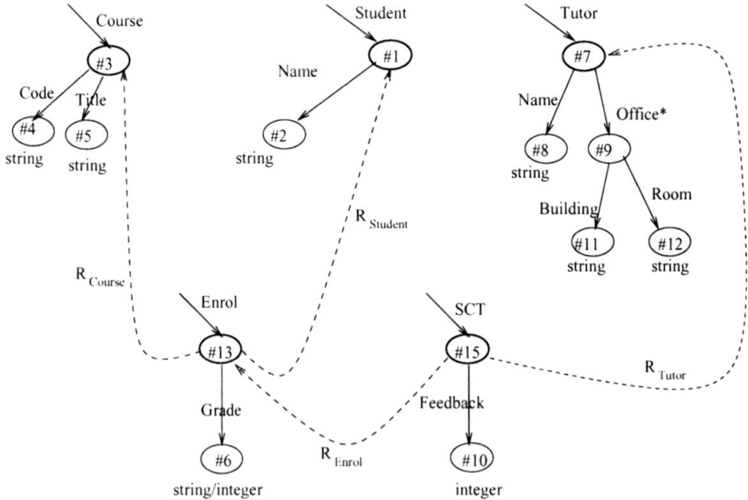

Fig. 6. An S3-Graph for the ER diagram in Figure 3

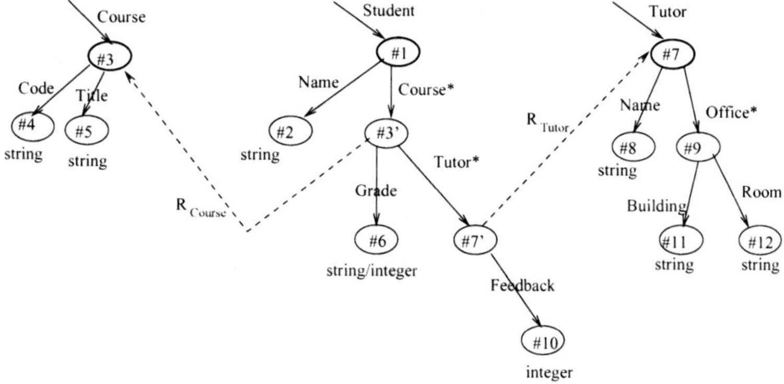

Fig. 7. An alternative S3-Graph for the ER diagram in Figure 3

4 Conclusion

To the best of our knowledge, this is the first paper that presents a conceptual approach for designing semistructured databases which can be associated with some schema. We envisage the growing importance of well designed semistructured databases with the development of new e-commerce applications that require the efficient design and maintenance of large amounts of data. The introduction of an ER-based conceptual layer allows us to remove anomalies and data redundancies at the semantic level. We have developed an algorithm to map an ER diagram involving weak entity types, recursive, n-ary and ISA relationship sets, and aggregations to a normal form S3-Graph. Using the mappings proposed, XML DTDs and customised XML views can be generated from the normal form ER diagrams. Relational tables can also be created from the normalized ER diagram to store the XML data with controlled or no redundancy.

References

1. P.P. Chen. The ER model: Toward a unified view of data. *ACM Transactions on Database Systems*, Vol 1, No 1, 1976.
2. Document Object Model(DOM). *http://www.w3.org/TR/REC-DOM-Level-1.*
3. S.Y. Lee, M.L. Lee, T.W. Ling, and L. Kalinichenko. Designing good semistructured databases. In *Proc. of 18th Int. Conference on ER Approach*, 1999.
4. T.W. Ling. A normal form for entity-relationship diagrams. In *Proc. of 4th Int. Conference on Entity-Relationship Approach*, pages 24–35, 1985.
5. T.W. Ling. A normal form for sets of not-necessarily normalized relations. In *Proc. of 22nd Hawaii Int. Conference on Systems Science*, pages 578–586, 1989.
6. G. Mecca, P. Merialdo and P. Atzeni. Araneus in the Era of XML. *IEEE Bulletin on Data Engineering*, 1999.
7. Y. Papakonstantinou, H. Garcia-Molina, and J. Widom. Object exchange across heterogeneous information sources. In *IEEE Int. Conference on Data Engineering*, 1995.

Meaningful Change Detection on the Web*

S. Flesca[2], F. Furfaro[2], and E. Masciari[1,2]

[1] ISI-CNR, 87036 Rende, Italy
{masciari}@si.deis.unical.it
[2] DEIS, Univ. della Calabria, 87036 Rende, Italy
{flesca,furfaro}@si.deis.unical.it

Abstract. In this paper we present a new technique for detecting changes on the Web. We propose a new method to measure the similarity of two documents, that can be efficiently used to discover changes in selected portions of the original document. The proposed technique has been implemented in the CDWeb system providing a change monitoring service on the Web. CDWeb differs from other previously proposed systems since it allows the detection of changes on portions of documents and specific changes expressed by means of complex conditions, i.e. users might want to know if the value of a given stock has increased by more than 10%. Several tests on stock exchange and auction web pages proved the effectiveness of the proposed approach.

1 Introduction

Due to increasing number of people that use the Web for shopping or on-line trading, services for searching information and identifying changes on the Web have received renewed attention from both industry and research community. Indeed, users of e-commerce or on-line trading sites frequently need to keep track of page changes, since they want to access pages only when their information has been updated. Several systems providing change monitoring services have been developed in the last few years[9,10,13,8]. Generally, these systems periodically check the status of the selected web pages, trying to identify how the page of interest has been changed. The lack of a fixed data structure makes the problem of detecting, efficiently and effectively, meaningful changes on the web a difficult and interesting problem. Most of the systems developed so far are not completely satisfactory since they are only able to check if a page has been modified. For instance, the system Netmind can only detect changes on a selected text region, a registered link or image, a keyword, or the timestamp of the page [9]. Consider, for instance, an auction on-line web page (e.g. eBay, Auckland, etc.), an user wants to be alerted only if a change occurs in one of the items he wants to buy, i.e. if the quotation of an article has been changed or if new items of the desired kind are available on the site.

Change detection systems should provide the possibility of specifying the changes the user is interested in: to select the region of the document of interest,

* Work partially supported by the Murst projects Data-X and D2I

H.C. Mayr et al. (Eds.): DEXA 2001, LNCS 2113, pp. 22–31, 2001.

the items inside the region whose changes have to be monitored, and conditions on the type of changes which must be detected. Systems detecting changes on HTML pages with fixed structure are not able to satisfy these kind of user needs since the page regions considered depend on the user's request. Current techniques for detecting document differences are computationally expensive and unable to focus on the portion of the page that is considered of interest to the user [3,2,15]. A technique able to detect changes with a reasonable degree of efficiency and accuracy is necessary. The general problem of finding a minimum cost edit script that transforms a document into its modified version is computationally expensive (NP-hard) [3,2]. However, in many application contexts, like the one considered in the above example, users are only interested in the changes made and not in the sequence of updates which produce the new document. For the on-line trading example, users are interested in the change on the quotation of a stock or in the insertion of a new stock, regardless of the changes in the whole structure or the intermediate changes.

In this paper we present a different approach that, instead of looking for the exact sequence of changes that permits the new document to be produced from the old version, pays attention to how much the changes have modified the document under observation. Our technique represents the document as a tree and permits the user to focus on specific portions of it, e.g. sub-trees. The paper also describes the architecture of a system, called CDWeb system, which allows users to monitor web pages, specifying the information and the type of changes they consider relevant. The main contributions of this paper are the definition of a new efficient technique that allows users to measure Web document differences in a quantitative way, the definition of a language to specify web update triggers and the implementation of a system for change detection on the web.

2 Web Changes Monitoring

In this section we define an efficient technique for the detection of *meaningful changes* in web documents. We are mainly interested in changes that add, delete or update information contained in specific portions of a Web page. To specify the information that has to be monitored, the user selects the region of the document of interest (a sub-tree of the document tree), the items inside the region (sub-trees of the previously selected sub-tree) whose changes have to be monitored, and conditions on the type of changes which must be detected. The system has to identify first the region of interest (i.e. the portion of the document that is most similar to the region selected in the old version) and to verify, for each item the associated conditions.

To retrieve the sub-tree of interest in the updated document it is necessary to define a similarity measure between document sub-trees and use it to compare all the possible sub-trees with the old one. The similarity measure of two trees is defined by considering the similarities of the sub-trees. It is worth noting that the use of the minimum cost edit script, transforming a given document into the new one [2], to detect changes is not feasible for this kind of application since it is computationally expensive. Our technique can be seen as the computation of an edit script characterized by a null cost for the "move" operation (and no glue and copy operations are considered). The null cost assumption is not a real limitation, since the type of applications considered are only interested in semantic changes (the position of the stock quote is not of interest). The similarity measure is defined by considering the complete weighted bipartite graph $((N_1, N_2), E)$ where N_1 and N_2 are, respectively, the nodes of the two sub-trees; the weight of each edge $(x, y) \in E$ is the similarity of the two nodes. The similarity of two trees is defined by considering the associations of nodes (edges of the bipartite graph) which give the maximum degree of similarity. The association constructed is then used to obtain quantitative information about changes.

Document Model. Several different data models have been proposed to represent Web documents. For instance, the WWW Consortium (W3C) has defined a kind of "generic" model, named *Document Object Model* (DOM), which defines a set of basic structures that enable applications to manipulate HTML and XML documents.

In this work we represent structured documents as unordered labeled trees, i.e. we do not consider the order of document elements but only the hierarchical information about them. Generally each node of the tree corresponds to a structuring HTML tag in the document.

The document model is defined in a formal way as follows. We assume the presence of an alphabet Σ of content strings, of a set of element types τ, that contains the possible structuring markup, and a set of attribute names A.

Definition 1. *(Document Tree) A* document tree *is a tuple* $T = \langle N, p, r, l, t, a \rangle$, *where* N *is the set of nodes of the tree,* p *is the parent function associating each node (except the root* r*) of the tree with its parent,* r *is the distinguished root of* T, l *is a labeling function from* $leaf(T)$ *to* Σ^+, t *is a typing function from* N *to* τ *and* a *is an attribute function from* N *to* $A \times \Sigma^*$.

Essentially a document tree is an unordered tree whose nodes (named also elements) are characterized by their markup type and the associated set of attribute-value pairs. Leaf nodes have associated the actual textual content of the document. Given a document tree T, whose root is r, and a node e_n of T, we denote with $T(e_n)$ the sub-tree of T rooted at e_n.

Furthermore we define two new functions characterizing an element w.r.t. the whole document tree, $type(e_n)$ and $w(e_n)$. If $r, e_2, \cdots e_n$ is the path from the root r to the element e_n, $type(e_n) = t(r)t(e_2)\cdots t(e_n)$, whereas $w(e_n) = \{s | s$ is a word[1] contained in $l(e) \wedge e \in leaf(T(e_n))\}$. We also define $a(e_n)$ as the set of attributes associated to e_n. Essentially $w(e_n)$ is a set of words contained in the various text strings associated to the leaves of the subtree rooted at e_n, and $type(n)$ is the concatenation of type label in the path starting from the root of the tree and ending in e_n, i.e. the *complete* type of the element.

[1] A word is a substring separated by blank to the other substring

Example 1. Consider the portion of an HTML document shown in the right side of Fig. 1.

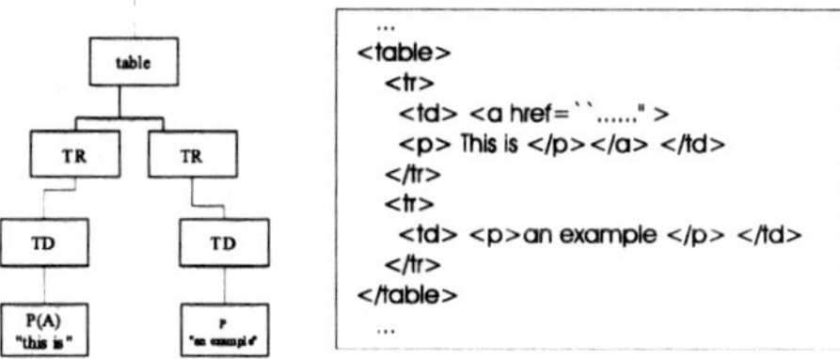

Fig. 1. A document tree

It corresponds to the HTML document tree shown in the left side of Fig. 1, where for each node are reported the corresponding HTML tag, and attributes (text is not shown for non leaf elements). The root element r of this sub-tree is characterized by $w(r)$= { This, is, an, example }, $type(r)$={table} and $a(r)$={ $\emptyset$ }, whereas for the node p relative to the first paragraph we have $w(p)$= { This, is }, $type(p)$={table.tr.td.p} and $a(p)$={ A }.

A tree similarity measure. To detect changes in the selected portion of a web page, we first have to retrieve this portion of the document in the new document version. Since in the new version of the web page text can be added or removed before and after the portion of the document we are interested in, we cannot rely on its old position in the document tree to perform this task, and consequently, we have to find the portion of the new document that is the most similar to the old one. One possibility to perform this task is to follow one of the approaches that compute minimum edit script between tree structures[3, 2]. However the use of these techniques is not suitable for our problem, since, in general, the problem of finding a minimum cost edit script is computationally expensive, and we cannot use heuristics to compute the similarity degree. We define a simple similarity measure between document trees. In the definition of this measure there are two main issues to be achieved: it should be possible to compute it efficiently, and it must be *normalized*, allowing the comparison of different pairs of trees and the selection of the most similar one.

To define the similarity between documents we first associate each element of the selected document to its current version in the new document, and then consider the similarity degree of the two documents w.r.t. this association. So, we first have to define a measure of similarity between single elements and then use it to define a similarity measure between whole trees. Given a document tree $T = \langle N, p, r, l, t, a \rangle$ and an element r' of N, the *characteristic* of r' ($\psi(r')$) is a triple $< type(r'), a(r'), w(r') >$.

The similarity measure of two elements is defined on the basis of the similarity between each component of the characteristics of the elements being considered. We define the following functions measuring similarity between the different components of element characteristics. Given two trees T_1 and T_2, and two nodes r_1 and r_2 we define:

$$intersect(w(r_1), w(r_2)) = \frac{|w(r_1) \cap w(r_2)|}{|w(r_1) \cup w(r_2)|}$$

$$attdist(a(r_1), a(r_2)) = \frac{\sum_{a_i \in \{a(r_1) \cap a(r_2)\}} Weight(a_i)}{\sum_{a_i \in \{a(r_1) \cup a(r_2)\}} Weight(a_i)}$$

$$typedist(type(r_1), type(r_2)) = \frac{\prod_{i=0}^{suf}(2^{max-i})}{\prod_{i=0}^{max}(2^i)}$$

The function $intersect(w(r_1), w(r_2))$ returns the percentage of words that appear in both $w(r_1)$ and $w(r_2)$. The function $attdist(a(r_1), a(r_2))$ is a measure of the relative weight of the attributes that have the same value in r_1 and r_2 w.r.t. all the attributes in r_1 and r_2. The attributes are weighted differently because some attributes are generally considered less relevant than other, for instance the attribute "href" is considered more relevant than formatting attributes, like "font". The definition of the function $typedist(type(r_1), type(r_2))$ take care of the difference between the complete types of element, suf represents the length of the common suffix between $type(r_1)$ and $type(r_2)$ and max denotes the maximum cardinality between $type(r_1)$ and $type(r_2)$. We can now to define similarity between two document tree elements.

Definition 2. *(Element Similarity) Given two document trees T_1 and T_2 and two elements r_1 and r_2 of characteristics $\langle type(r_1), a(r_1), w(r_1)\rangle$ and $\langle type(r_2), a(r_2), w(r_2)\rangle$, the similarity of r_1 and r_2 ($CS(r_1, r_2)$) is defined as:*

$$CS(T_1', T_2') = -1 + 2 \times (\alpha * typedist(type(r_1), type(r_2)) + \beta * attdist(a(r_1), a(r_2)) + \gamma * intersect(w(r_1), w(r_2))) \text{ where } \alpha + \beta + \gamma = 1.$$

The value of α,β,γ are given by the user on the basis of the type of changes you want to detect (see section 5.1). Clearly the similarity coefficient takes values from the interval [-1,1], where -1 corresponds to the maximum difference and 1 to the maximum similarity. A element that is deleted (resp. inserted) has assumed to have similarity 0 with elements of the new (resp. old) document.

Detecting document changes. Once we have defined element similarity, we can complete the definition of our technique. To compare two document sub-trees, we consider the complete weighted bipartite graph $((N_1, N_2), E)$ where N_1 and N_2 are, respectively, the nodes of the two sub-trees; the weight of each edge $(x, y) \in E$ is $CS(x, y)$. We use this weighted graph to establish association between elements belonging to the old and new version of the document. Obviously not all the possible associations can be considered valid since node association must correspond to an effective document transformation. Also we do not want to consider all the possible transformations, since it is not probable that complex transformations correspond to rewriting of some information already present in the document, at least for the type of applications we are considering.

Document mappings. All the possible changes that can occur in a document must correspond to a change in the association between the nodes in the document tree of the original pages and the nodes in the document tree of the newest pages. As stated above, not all the associations can be considered valid. For example if we do not want to deal with paragraph splitting or joining then only one to one associations are valid. Also we do not consider *glue* or *copy* operations [3,2] since they seems to be not relevant in this contest.

In general we are interested in associations that correspond to some type of *editing* of the document that add, change or delete some meaningful information in the document, for instance the text of a paragraph or the destination of a hypertext link. Before defining valid *edit mapping* we introduce some notation. Given two document trees $T = \langle N, p, o, r, l, t \rangle$ and $T' = \langle N', p', o', r', l', t' \rangle$. A *Tree Mapping* from T to T' is a relation $M \subseteq N \times N'$, such that $\langle r, r' \rangle \in M$. Given two document trees T and T', a tree mapping M from T to T' and a node x in N, we denote with $M_{x,.}$ the set of nodes of N' associated with x in M; analogously, given a node y in N' we denote with $M_{.,y}$ the set of nodes of N associated with y in M.

Definition 3. *(Edit Mapping) Given two document trees* $T = \langle N, p, o, r, l, t \rangle$ *and* $T' = \langle N', p', o', r', l', t' \rangle$. *An* edit mapping M *from* T *to* T' *is a tree mapping such that* $\forall x \in N$ *if* $|M_{x,.}| > 1$ *then* $|M_{.,y}| = 1$ *for each* y *in* $M_{x,.}$.

Intuitively if $|M_{x,.}| > 1$ the original node has been split while if $|M_{.,y}| > 1$ many nodes in the original tree have been merged. A mapping between two trees T and T' is said to be *Simple* if it associates each node in T with at most one node in N' and each node in T' with at most one node in N. Given two document trees T and T' and a tree mapping M we denote with $ext(M)$ the set of mappings M' from T to T' such that $M \subseteq M'$. The number of valid edit mapping may be very large due to the completeness of the graph, but we can strongly reduce the number of edges to be considered for the mapping. This can be done by considering the edges that have a weight greater than a predefined threshold.

A cost model for mapping. Once we have defined the valid association between document trees we have to define the cost of these associations, that is: if we consider the nodes in the new subtree as the new version of the associated nodes in the original sub-tree, how similar can we consider the new document sub-tree to the old one? To define document similarity we need to define node similarity.

Definition 4. *Given two document trees* T_1, T_2 *and two sub-trees* T_1', T_2' *and an edit mapping* M *from* T_1' *to* T_2', *the similarity of* $x \in N_1$ *w.r.t.* M *is defined as:*

$$Sim_M(x) = \left\{ \begin{matrix} avg_{<x,y>\in M} CS(x,y) \text{ if } |\{<x,y>\in M\}| > 0. \\ 0 \text{ otherwise.} \end{matrix} \right\}$$

Thus, given a bipartite graph $\langle (N_1, N_2), E \rangle$, Definition 4 computes the similarity of a node x in N_1 by considering the average of the similarities of the pairs of elements $\langle x, y\rangle$ for each y related to x by the edit mapping. Using the previous definition we can now define the concept of similarity among document sub-trees.

Definition 5. *Given two document trees T_1, T_2, two subtrees T_1' of T_1 ,T_2' of T_2 and an edit mapping M from T_1' to T_2', the similarity of T_1', T_2' w.r.t. M is defined as follows:*

$$Sim_M(T_1', T_2') = \frac{\sum_{x \in N_1 \cup N_2} Sim_M(x)}{|N_1'| + |N_2'|}.$$

Finally, we define document sub-tree similarity considering the similarity obtained by the edit mapping that maximizes the similarity between two sub-trees.

Definition 6. *(Tree Similarity) Given two document trees T_1, T_2, two subtrees T_1' of T_1 ,T_2' of T_2, and letting $\mathcal{M}$ be the set of possible mappings from T_1' to T_2'. The similarity coefficient of T_1', T_2' ($Sim(T_1', T_2')$) is defined as:*

$$Sim(T_1', T_2') = \max_{M \in \mathcal{M}} Sim_M(T_1', T_2')$$

Searching for the most similar subtree. Once we have defined similarity between document sub-trees we can approach the problem of detecting document changes. Here we consider only simple changes, i.e. changes that are detectable using a simple mapping; these changes are insertion, deletion, or textual modification. Note that some types of move operations are also detectable; in particular changes that move an element e from the sub-tree rooted in the parent of e to another sub-tree that is not contained in $T(e)$ and does not contain $T(e)$.

Before presenting the technique used to detect changes we introduce the concept of *similarity graph*, that will be used in the algorithm searching for the most similar sub-trees. Given two document trees $T_1 = \langle N_1, p_1, r_1, l_1, t_1, a_1\rangle$ and $T_2 = \langle N_2, p_2, r_2, l_2, t_2, a_2\rangle$, the *similarity graph* associated to T_1, T_2 (denoted $WG(T_1, T_2)$) is a weighted bipartite graph $\langle (N_1, N_2), E\rangle$ where E is the set of weighted edges defined as follows: $E = \{\langle x, y, CS(x, y)\rangle \mid \forall x \in N_1, y \in N_2\}$

Furthermore given a similarity graph $WG(T_1, T_2) = \langle N,\ E\rangle$, we define the projection of a similarity graph on a set of nodes $N' \subseteq N$ as $\pi_{N'} WG(T_1, T_2) = \langle N',\ \{\ \langle x, y, c\rangle | \langle x, y, c\rangle \in E \wedge (x \in N' \vee y \in N')\}\rangle$, i.e. the sub graph representing the piece of the document to be monitored. To define the algorithm that for a given sub-tree finds the most similar sub-tree in the new document, we refer to the Maximum Matching problem. Indeed, given two document sub-trees $T_1 = \langle N_1, p_1, r_1, l_1, t_1, a_1\rangle$ and $T_2 = \langle N_2, p_2, r_2, l_2, t_2, a_2\rangle$, the following lemma assures that we can use the Hungarian algorithm to compute a simple edit mapping between two sub-trees. .

Proposition 1. *Given two document trees T_1, T_2 and two subtrees T_1', T_2', and a simple edit mapping M between T_1' and T_2', then $Sim_M(T_1', T_2') = Sim(T_1', T_2')$ if M is a maximum weight matching on $WG(T_1', T_2')$.*

3 Web Update Queries

To better exploit the change detection technique defined in the previous section, we need to provide the possibility of specifying general conditions on data being observed. A trigger will be executed only if the associated condition is verified.

In this section we introduce a language to specify this type of triggers, named *Web update queries* (web trigger). A web update query allows the user to select some specific portions of the document, that will be monitored (we refer to these portions as *target-zones*). These are the portions of the document where the information which is considered relevant is contained. Inside this zone you can specify a set of sub-zones, named targets. When specifying the trigger condition, the user can ask for verification if the information in a target has been modified. Usually, each target is a leaf of an HTML Tree that is considered relevant by the user. Web update queries are expressed using the syntax sketched below:

```
< WebTrigger >          ::= CREATE Webtrigger < name >
                            ON < zone-list >
                            CHECK < target-list >
                            NOTIFY BY < notify >
                            WHEN < target-condition >
                            [BETWEEN < date > AND < date >]
                            [EVERY < polling-interval >]
< zone-list >           ::= < target-zone >< zone-name > INSIDE URL |
                            < target-zone >< zone-name > INSIDE URL ,
                            < zone-list >
< notify >              ::= < email address > | < alert >
< target-list >         ::= < target >< zone-name > . < target-name >
                            < target-list >| ε
< target >              ::= NEW-ITEM | < HTML SubTree >
< target-zone >         ::= < HTML SubTree >
< target-condition >    ::= < target-name > DELETED |
                            < target-name > CHANGED(< min threshold >)
                            < target-name > CONTAINS < string > |
                            < target-name > CONTAINS ATTRIBUTE
                            '['< attname >, < string > ']' |
                            < target-name > OF TYPE < typename >
< polling-interval >    ::= < number-of-minutes >
```

where < *HTML SubTree* > represents a subtree of the document representation discussed in the above section. Note that web update queries should be specified using a visual interface, since it is the best way to specify the < *HTML SubTree* > involved in the trigger definition. The non terminal symbol < *target-condition* > in the trigger syntax table represents simple boolean conditions that can be used in the *when* clause. In particular when specifying conditions in the *when* clause it is possible to access both the old and new target values using the *NEW* and *OLD* properties of target items, as shown in the example below. Furthermore you can cast target item type from the predefined *string* type to *number* and *date* type. Using the *CREATE WebTrigger* command a user can create a web trigger on the CDWeb personal server, that handles change detection on his behalf. The server maintains a local copy of the target zones to be monitored and a list of the target predicates that can fire user notification.

Example 2. Consider the web page shown in Fig. 2 that contain information about stock prices on *NASDAQ* and suppose that a user would like to be notified if the quotation for "Cisco System" stock has a percentage variation of 5%. The user can run CDWeb and once the item relative to "Cisco System" has been selected (you can do this by simply selecting the table entry indexed by "CSCO") a Web Trigger can be set as shown in Fig. 2:

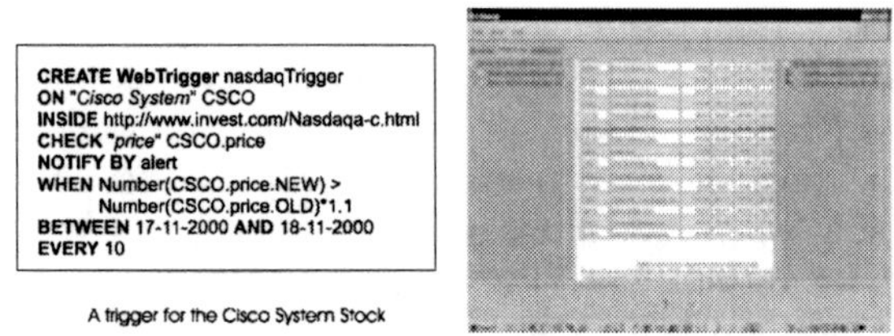

Fig. 2. The Nasdaq example.

where "*Cisco System*" and "*price*" are respectively an HTML subtree and leaf element of it that the user can choose using the CDWeb browser by simply double click on the table row for Cisco system quotation and then click on the price column. If the condition specified in the WHEN clause is verified, the user is notified by an alert.

4 System Architecture

In this section we describe the evaluation process of web update queries in the *CDWEB* system that allows users to specify and execute web update queries using a visual interface. Change detection results are shown when triggers are raised. The system is implemented in java, and HTML documents are manipu-

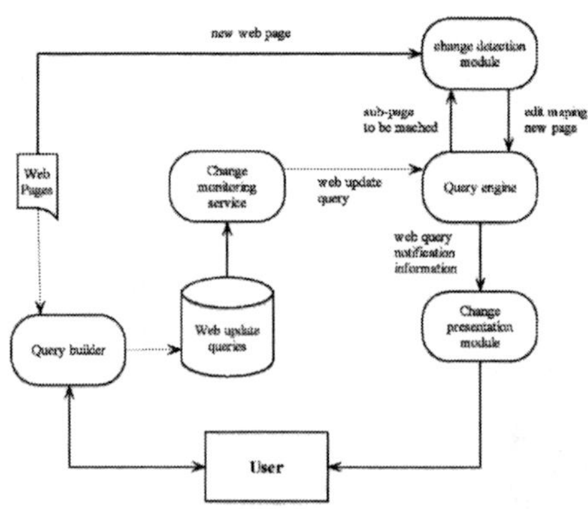

Fig. 3. System Architecture

lated by means of performed using the swing document libraries, that are based on a document model very similar to the model here used. The architecture of the system is reported in Fig. 3 and consists of five main modules: are the *change monitoring service*, the *query engine*, the *change detection module*, the *query builder* and the *change presentation module.* The system is composed of two main applications, a visual query editor, that handles query specification, and an active query engine, that evaluates web update queries. The system maintains an object store where the objects describing the currently active web update queries are serialized. Each query object maintains information about the list of target zones(document sub-trees) referred to in the query, and for each target zone the list of targets contained inside that zone.

References

1. S. Chawathe, A. Rajaraman, H. Garcia-Molina, and J. Widom Change detection in hierarchically structured information. In *Proc. of the ACM SIGMOD Int. Conf. on Management of Data*, pages 493-504, Montreal, Quebec, June 1996.
2. S. Chawathe, H. Garcia-Molina Meaningful change detection in structured data. In *Proc. of the ACM SIGMOD Int. Conf. on Management of Data*, pages 26-37, Tuscon, Arizona, May 1997.
3. S. Chawathe, S. Abiteboul, J. Widom Representing and querying changes in semistructured data. In *Proc. of the Int. Conf. on Data Engeneering*, pages 4-13, Orlando, Florida, February 1998
4. F. Douglis, T. Ball, Y. Chen, E. Koutsofios WebGuide: Querying and Navigating Changes in Web Repositories. In *WWW5 / Computer Networks*, 28(7-11), pages 1335-1344, 1996.
5. Fred Douglis, Thomas Ball: Tracking and Viewing Changes on the Web. In *Proc. of USENIX Annual Technical Conference*, pages 165-176, 1996.
6. F. Douglis, T. Ball, Y. Chen, and E. Koutsofios. The AT&T Internet Difference Engine: Tracking and Viewing Changes on the Web. In *World Wide Web*, 1(1), pages 27-44, Baltzer Science Publishers, 1998.
7. L. Liu, C. Pu, W. Tang, J. Biggs, D. Buttler, W. Han, P. Benninghoff, and Fenghua. CQ: A personalized update monitoring toolkit. In *Proc. of the ACM SIGMOD Int. Conf. on Management of Data*, 1998
8. L. Liu, C. Pu, W. Tang WebCQ - Detecting and delivering information changes on the web. In *Proc. of CIKM'00*, Washington, DC USA, 2000.
9. NetMind. http://www.netmind.com
10. TracerLock. http://www.peacefire.org/tracerlock
11. Wuu Yang. Identifying Syntactic differences Between Two Programs. In *Software - Practice and Experience (SPE)*, 21(7), pp. 739-755, 1991.
12. J. T. Wang, K. Zhang and G. Chirn. Algorithms for Approximate Graph Matching. In *Information Sciences* 82(1-2), pp. 45-74, 1995.
13. Webwhacker. http://www.webwhacker.com
14. J. Widom and J. Ullman. C^3: Changes, consistency, and configurations in heterogeneous distributed information systems. *Unpublished, available at http://www-db.stanford.edu/c3/synopsis.html*,1995
15. K. Zhang, J. T. Wang and D. Shasha. On the Editing Distance between Undirected Acyclic Graphs and Related Problems. In *Proc. of Combinatorial Pattern Matching*, pp. 395-407, 1995.

Definition and Application of Metaclasses

Mohamed Dahchour

University of Louvain, IAG School of Management, 1 Place des Doyens, 1348 Louvain-la-Neuve, Belgium,
dahchour@qant.ucl.ac.be

Abstract. Metaclasses are classes whose instances are themselves classes. Metaclasses are generally used to define and query information relevant to the class level. The paper first analyzes the more general term *meta* and gives some examples of its use in various application domains. Then, it focuses on the description of metaclasses. To help better understand metaclasses, the paper suggests a set of criteria accounting for the variety of metaclass definitions existing in the literature. The paper finally presents the usage of metaclasses and discusses some questions raised about them.

1 Introduction

Common object models (and languages and database systems based on them) model real-world applications as a collection of objects and classes. Objects model real-world entities while classes represent sets of similar objects. A class describes structural (attributes) and behavioral (methods) properties of their instances. The attribute values represent the object's status. This status is accessed or modified by sending messages to the objects to invoke the corresponding methods. In such models, there are only two abstraction levels: *class level* composed of classes that may be organized into hierarchies along inheritance (i.e., isA) mechanism, and *instance level* composed of individual objects that are instances of the classes in the class level.

However, beyond the need for manipulating individual objects, there is also the need to deal with classes themselves regardless of their instances. For example, it should be possible to query a class about its name, list of its attributes and methods, list of its ancestors and descendents, etc. To be able to do this, some object models (e.g., Smalltalk [11], ConceptBase [16], CLOS [18]) allow to treat classes themselves as objects that are instances of the so-called *metaclasses*. With metaclasses, the user is able to express the structure and behavior of classes, in such a way that messages can be sent to classes in the same way that messages are sent to individual objects in usual object models. Systems supporting metaclasses allow to organize data into an architecture of several abstraction levels. Each level describes and controls the lower one.

Existing work (e.g., [11,16,18,19,26,10,21]) only deal with particular definitions of metaclasses related to specific systems. This work deals with metaclasses in general. More precisely, the objectives of the paper are:

H.C. Mayr et al. (Eds.): DEXA 2001, LNCS 2113, pp. 32–41, 2001.

- clarify the concept of metaclasses often confused with ordinary classes;
- define a set of criteria characterizing a large variety of metaclass definitions;
- present some uses of metaclasses;
- discuss some problems about metaclasses raised in the literature.

The rest of the paper is organized as follows. Section 2 analyzes the more general term *meta* and gives some examples of its use beyond the object orientation. Section 3 defines the concept of metaclasses. Section 4 presents a set of criteria accounting for the variety of metaclass definitions found in the literature. Section 5 describes the mechanism of method invocation related to metaclasses. Section 6 presents the usage of metaclasses and Section 7 analyzes some of their drawbacks. Section 8 summarizes and concludes the paper.

2 Meta Concepts

The word *meta* comes from Greek. According to [29], meta means "occurring later than or in succession to; situated behind or beyond; more highly organized; change and transformation; more comprehensive". Meta is usually used as a prefix of another word. In the scientific vocabulary, meta expresses the idea of change (e.g., metamorphosis, metabolism) while in the philosophical vocabulary, meta expresses an idea of a higher level of generality and abstractness (e.g., metaphysics, metalanguage). In the computing field *meta* has the latter sense and it is explicitly defined as being a "prefix meaning one level of description higher. If X is some concept then meta-X is data about, or processes operating on, X" [15]. Here are some examples of use of meta in computing:

- *Metaheuristic.* It is an heuristic about heuristics. In game theory and expert systems, metaheuristics are used to give advice about when, how, and why to combine or favor one heuristic over another.
- *Metarule.* It is a rule that describes how ordinary rules should be used or modified. More generally, it is a rule about rules. The following is an example of metarule:

  "If the rule base contains two rules R_1 and R_2 such that:
  $R_1 \equiv A \wedge B \Rightarrow C$
  $R_2 \equiv A \wedge \text{not } B \Rightarrow C$
  then the expression B is not necessary in the two rules; we can replace the two rules by R_3 such that $R_3 \equiv A \Rightarrow C$"

  Metarules can be used during problem solving to select an appropriate rule when conflicts occur within a set of applicable rules.
  Meta-heuristics and meta-rules are known in knowledge-based systems under a more generic term, *metaknowledge.*
- *Metaknowledge.* It is the knowledge that a system has about how it reasons, operates, or uses domain knowledge. An example of metaknowledge is shown below.

  "If more than one rule applies to the situation at hand, then use rules supplied by experts before rules supplied by novices"

- *Metalanguage.* It is a language which describes syntax and semantics of a given language. For instance, in a metalanguage for C++, the (meta)instruction ⟨variable⟩ "=" ⟨expression⟩ ";" describes assignment statement in C++, of which "x=3;" is an instance.
- *Metadata.* In databases, metadata means data about data and refer to things such as a data dictionary, a repository, or other descriptions of the contents and structure of a data source [22].
- *Metamodel.* It is a model representing a model. Metamodels aim at clarifying the semantics of the modeling constructs used in a modeling language. For instance a metamodel for OML relationships is proposed in [14]. Figure 1 shows a metamodel for the well-known ER model.

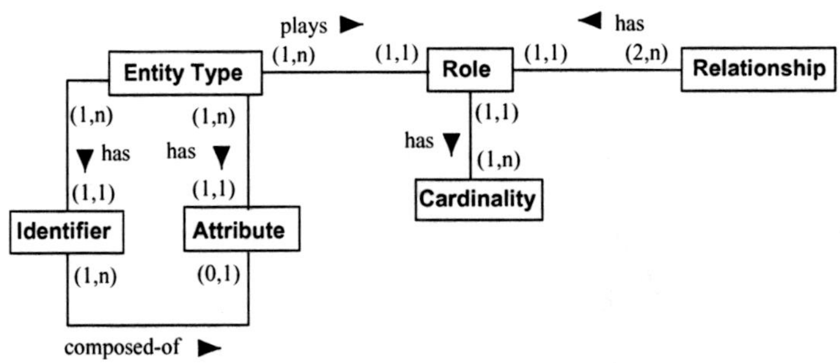

Fig. 1. Metamodel of the ER model.

The basic concepts of the ER model are the following: *entity types*, *relationships* associating entity types, *roles* played by participating entity types, *attributes* characterizing entity types or relationships themselves, *identification* structures identifying in a unique manner the entity types, and *cardinalities* related to the roles. Each of these concept appears as a *metatype* in the metamodel shown in Figure 1.

3 The Metaclass Concept

In a system with metaclasses, a class can also be seen as an object. *Two-faceted constructs* make that double role explicit. Each two-faceted construct is a composite structure comprising an object, called the *object facet*, and an associated class, called the *class facet*. To underline their double role, we draw a two-faceted construct as an object box adjacent to a class box. Like classes, class facets are drawn as rectangular boxes while objects (and object facets) appear as rectangular boxes with rounded corners as in Figure 2.

MC is a metaclass with attribute A and method M1(..). Object I_MC is an instance of MC, with a0 as value for attribute A. I_MC is the object facet of a two-faceted construct with C as class facet. A is an *instance attribute* of MC

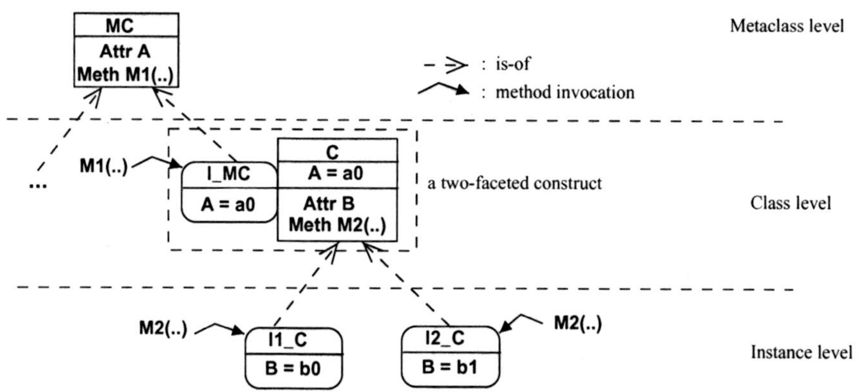

Fig. 2. Class/metaclass correspondence.

(i.e., it receives a value for each instance of MC) and a *class attribute* of C (i.e., its value is the same for all instances of C). For instances I1_C and I2_C of C, attribute A is either inapplicable (e.g., an aggregate value on all instances) or constant, i.e., an instance attribute with the same value for all instances. In addition to the class attribute A, C defines attribute B and method M2(..). The figure shows that methods like M1(..) can be invoked on instances of MC (e.g., I_MC), while methods like M2(..) can be invoked on instances of C (e.g., I1_C and I2_C).

Note that the two-faceted construct above is useful only to illustrate the double facet of a class that is also an object of a metaclass. Otherwise, in practice, both the object facet I_MC and its associated class facet C (see Figure 2) are the same thing, say, I_MC_C defined as shown in Figure 3.

```
Metaclass MC    Class I_MC_C instanceOf MC
  Attributes      Values
    A:AType         A=a0

  Methods         Attributes
    M1(..)          B:BType
End
                  Methods
                    M2(..)
                End
```

Fig. 3. Definition of class I_MC_C as an instance of metaclassMC.

Systems with metaclasses comprise at least three levels: token (uninstantiable object), class, and metaclass, as shown in Figure 4. Additional levels, like Metaclass in Figure 4, can be provided as root for the common structure and behavior of all metaclasses. The number of levels of such hierarchies varies from one system to another.

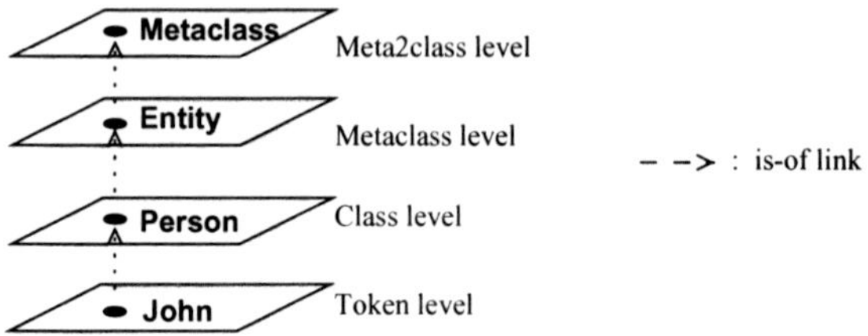

Fig. 4. Levels of systems with a metaclass concept.

4 Various Metaclass Definitions

Substantial differences appear in the literature about the concept of metaclass. We suggest the following criteria to account for the variety of definitions.

- **Explicitness:** the ability for programmers to explicitly declare a metaclass like they do for ordinary classes. Explicit metaclasses are supported by several *semantic models* (e.g., TAXIS [23], SHM [2]), *object models and systems* (e.g., VODAK [19], ADAM [26], OSCAR [10], ConceptBase [16]), *knowledge representation languages* (e.g., LOOPS [1], KEE [9], PROTEUS [28], SHOOD [25], Telos [24]), and *programming languages* (e.g., CLASSTALK [21], CLOS [18]). On the contrary, Smalltalk [11] and Gemstone [3], for example, only support implicit system-managed metaclasses. Of course, explicit metaclasses are more flexible [21]. They can, for example, be specialized into other metaclasses in the same way that ordinary classes can.
- **Uniformity:** the ability to treat an instance of a metaclass like an instance of an application class. More generally, for a system supporting instantiation trees of arbitrary depth, uniformity means that an object at level i ($i \geq 2$), instance of a (meta)class at level i+1, can be viewed and treated like an object at level i-1, instance of a (meta)class at level i. Thus, for example, in Figure 4, to create the Entity metaclass, message new is sent to Metaclass; to create the Person class, the message new is sent to the Entity metaclass; and, again, to create the terminal object John, message new is sent to the Person class. While most metaclass systems support uniformity, Smalltalk-80 and Loops, for example, do not.
- **Depth** of instantiation: the number of levels for the hierarchy of classes and metaclasses. While, for example, Smalltalk has a limited depth in its hierarchy of metaclasses, VODAK and CLOS allow for an arbitrary depth.
- **Circularity:** the ability to use metaclasses in a system for a uniform description of the system itself. To ensure finiteness of the depth of instantiation tree, some metaclass concepts have to be instances of themselves. CLOS and ConceptBase, for example, offer that ability. Smalltalk does not.
- **Shareability:** the ability for more than one class to share the same user-defined metaclass. Most systems supporting explicit metaclasses provide shareability.

- **Applicability:** whether metaclasses can describe classes only (the general case) or other concepts also. For example, TAXIS extends the use of metaclasses to procedures and exceptions, while ConceptBase uses attribute metaclasses to represent the common properties of a collection of attributes.
- **Expressiveness**: the expressive power made available by metaclasses. In most systems, metaclasses represent the structure and behavior of their instances only as shown in Figure 2. In some systems like VODAK [19], metaclasses are able to describe both their direct instances (that are classes) and instances of those classes. The metaformulas of Telos and ConceptBase can also specify the behavior of the instances of a metaclass and of the instances of its instances.
- **Multiple classification**: the ability for an object (resp., class) to be an instance of several classes (resp., metaclasses) not related, directly or indirectly, by the generalization link. At our knowledge, only Telos and ConceptBase support this facility.

Note that this list of characteristics has been identified by carefully analyzing a large set of systems supporting metaclasses. We cannot, however, claim their exhaustiveness. The list remains open to other characteristics that could be identified by exploring other systems. Note also that these criteria are very useful in that they much help designers to select the more suitable system (with metaclasses) to define their specific needs.

5 Method Invocation

In systems with metaclasses, messages can be sent to classes in the same way that messages are sent to individual objects in usual object models. To avoid ambiguity, we show below how messages are invoked at each level of abstraction and how objects are created. Henceforth, the term object will denote tokens, classes, or metaclasses. Two rules specify the method-invocation mechanism[1].

Rule 1. When message Msg is sent to object o, method Meth which responds to Msg must be available (directly or indirectly by inheritance) in the class of o.

Rule 2. An object o is created by sending a message, say new(), to the class of o. Consequently, according to *Rule 1*, new() must be available in the class of o's class.

The following messages illustrate the two rules above. They manipulate objects of Figure 4.

- John→increaseSalary($1000). In this message, increaseSalary is sent to object John to increase the value of salary by $1000. Method increaseSalary is assumed to be available in the class of John, i.e., Person.

[1] These rules assume that the target object system represents object behavior with *methods*. Systems like ConceptBase that represent object behavior using constraints and deductive rules are not concerned with message-passing rules.

- John := Person→new(). In this message, new is sent to object Person in order to create object John as an instance of Person. According to *Rule 1*, method new must be available in the class of Person, i.e., Entity.

Most object systems provide for built-in primitives and appropriate syntax to define classes (e.g., Person), their attributes (e.g., salary), and methods (e.g., increaseSalary). However, to illustrate how metaclasses affect classes, just as classes affect tokens, we show in the following how messages can be sent to the Entity metaclass to build classes and their features.

- Person := Entity→new(). In this message, Person is created as an instance of Entity. Once again, this assumes that method new is available in Entity's class, i.e., Metaclass.
- Entity→addAttributes(Person, { [attrName:name, attrDomain: String]; [attrName:salary, attrDomain: Real]}). This message adds attributes name and salary to the newly created object Person. Similarly, a message can be sent to object Entity to add a new method to object Person.

6 Usage of Metaclasses

Various reasons warrant a metaclass mechanism in a model or a system. Typically, metaclasses extend the system kernel, blurring the boundary between users and implementors. Explicit metaclasses can specify knowledge to:

- Represent group information, that concerns a set of objects as a whole. For example, the average age of employees is naturally attached to an EmployeeClass metalevel.
- Represent class properties unrelated to the semantics of instances, like the fact that a class is concrete or abstract[2], has a single or multiple instances, has a single superclass or multiple superclasses.
- Customize the creation and the initialization of new instances of a class. The message new which is sent to a class to create new instances can incorporate additional arguments to initialize the instance variables of the newly created instance. Furthermore, each class can have its own overloaded new method for creating and initializing instances.
- Enhance the extensibility and the flexibility of models, and thus allow easy customization. For example, the semantics of generic relationships can be defined once and for all in a structure of metaclasses that provides for defining and querying the relationships at the class level, creating and deleting instances of participating classes, and so on (see e.g., [13,19,5,7,20,6]).
- Extend the basic object model to support new categories of objects (e.g., remote objects or persistent objects) and new needs such as the authorization mechanism. This kind of extension requires the ability to modify some basic

[2] Here, an abstract class, in the usual sense of object models, is an incompletely defined class without direct instances, whose complete definition is deferred to subclasses.

behavioral aspects of the system (object creation, message passing), and has often been faced by allowing these aspects to be manipulated in a metaclass level.

- Define an existing formalism or a development method within a system supporting metaclasses. This definition roughly consists in representing the modeling constructs involved in that formalism or method (i.e., its ontology) with a set of metaclasses of the target system. For example, Fusion [4], an object development method, was partially integrated in ConceptBase [12] using metaclasses.
- Integrate heterogeneous modeling languages within the same sound formalism. For example, a framework combining several formalisms for the requirement engineering of discrete manufacturing systems was defined along the lines of ConceptBase in [27]. The combined formalisms are: CIMOSA (for the purpose of eliciting requirements), i* (for the purpose of enterprise modeling), and the Albert II language (for the purpose of modeling system requirements).

7 Problems with Metaclasses

Some authors (e.g., [17]) have pointed out some problems with metaclasses. These problems have been analyzed in part in [8]. We summarize the main issues.

- *Metaclasses make the system more difficult to understand.* We agree with [8] that, once programmers are familiar with metaclasses, having a single mechanism for both data and metadata helps them progress from object design to object *system* design.
- *By themselves, metaclasses do not provide mechanisms to handle all the run-time consequences of extending the data model.* This is true for most systems. However, some systems like ADAM [8] and ConceptBase introduce the notion of active rules to enforce some constraints in order to keep the database in a consistent state.
- *Metaclasses do not facilitate low-level extensions.* For most systems this is true since metaclasses describe the model or class level, above the structures that specify storage management, concurrency, and access control. Thus, in such systems, metaclasses do not let applications define policies at all levels. However, this is not a general rule. In fact, systems such as ConceptBase and VODAK provide for a mechanism of metaclass that allows to describe both the class and instance level in a coordinated manner.
- *With metaclasses, programmers must cope with three levels of objects: instances, classes, and metaclasses.* We agree that it can be difficult at the beginning to play with the three levels.

After presenting these problems, the authors conclude that the metaclass approach is not satisfactory. We agree with [8] that this conclusion may be be valid when talking about programming languages, but we believe that explicit metaclasses are a powerful mechanism for enhancing database extensibility, uniformity, and accessibility by addressing these issues at the class level (see e.g., [6]).

8 Conclusion

Metaclasses define the structure and behavior of class objects, just as classes define the structure and behavior of instance objects. In systems with metaclasses, a class can also be seen as an object. We used the two-faceted constructs to make that double role explicit. Substantial differences appear in the literature about the concept of metaclass. We suggested a set of criteria to account for the variety of definitions, namely, uniformity, depth of instantiation, circularity, shareability, applicability, and expressiveness. We then presented the method-invocation mechanism between objects at various levels of abstraction. We also presented some uses of metaclasses and analyzed some of their drawbacks pointed out in the literature.

References

1. D.G. Bobrow and M.J. Stefik. *The LOOPS Manual.* Xerox Corp., 1983.
2. M.L. Brodie and D. Ridjanovic. On the design and specification of database transactions. In M. L. Brodie, J. Mylopoulos, and J. W. Schmidt, editors, *On Conceptual Modelling.* Springer-Verlag, 1984.
3. P. Butterworth, A. Ottis, and J. Stein. The Gemstone Database Management System. *Communications of the ACM*, 34(10):64–77, 1991.
4. D. Coleman, P. Arnold, S. Bodoff, C. Dollin, H. Gilchrist, F. Hayes, and P. Jeremaes. *Object-Oriented Development: The Fusion Method.* Prentice Hall, 1994.
5. M. Dahchour. Formalizing materialization using a metaclass approach. In B. Pernici and C. Thanos, editors, *Proc. of the 10th Int. Conf. on Advanced Information Systems Engineering, CAiSE'98*, LNCS 1413, pages 401–421, Pisa, Italy, June 1998. Springer-Verlag.
6. M. Dahchour. *Integrating Generic Relationships into Object Models Using Metaclasses.* PhD thesis, Département d'ingénierie informatique, Université catholique de Louvain, Belgium, March 2001.
7. M. Dahchour, A. Pirotte, and E. Zimányi. Materialization and its metaclass implementation. To be published in IEEE Transactions on Knowledge and Data Engineering.
8. O. Díaz and N.W. Paton. Extending ODBMSs using metaclasses. *IEEE Software*, pages 40–47, May 1994.
9. R. Fikes and J. Kehler. The role of frame-based representation in reasoning. *Communications of the ACM*, 28(9), September 1985.
10. J. Göers and A. Heuer. Definition and application of metaclasses in an object-oriented database model. In *Proc. of the 9th Int. Conf. on Data Engineering, ICDE'93*, pages 373–380, Vienna, Austria, 1993. IEEE Computer Society.
11. A. Goldberg and D. Robson. *Smalltalk-80: The Language and its Implementation.* Addison-Wesley, 1983.

12. E.V. Hahn. Metamodeling in ConceptBase - demonstrated on FUSION. Master's thesis, Faculty of CS, Section IV, Technical University of München, Germany, October 1996.
13. M. Halper, J. Geller, and Y. Perl. An OODB part-whole model: Semantics, notation, and implementation. *Data & Knowledge Engineering*, 27(1):59–95, May 1998.
14. B. Henderson-Sellers, D.G. Firesmith, and I.M. Graham. OML metamodel: Relationships and state modeling. *Journal of Object-Oriented Programming*, 10(1):47–51, March 1997.
15. D. Howe. *The Free On-line Dictionary of Computing*. 1999.
16. M. Jarke, R. Gallersdörfer, M.A. Jeusfeld, and M. Staudt. ConceptBase : A deductive object base for meta data management. *Journal of Intelligent Information Systems*, 4(2):167–192, 1995.
17. S.N. Khoshafian and R. Abnous, editors. *Object Orientation: Concepts, Languages, Databases, User Interfaces*. John Wiley & Sons, New York, 1990.
18. G. Kiczales, J. des Rivières, and D. Bobrow. *The Art of the Metaobject Protocol*. MIT Press, 1991.
19. W. Klas and M. Schrefl. *Metaclasses and their application*. LNCS 943. Springer-Verlag, 1995.
20. M. Kolp. *A Metaobject Protocol for Integrating Full-Fledged Relationships into Reflective Systems*. PhD thesis, INFODOC, Université Libre de Bruxelles, Belgium, October 1999.
21. T. Ledoux and P. Cointe. Explicit metaclasses as a tool for improving the design of class libraries. In *Proc. of the Int. Symp. on Object Technologies for Advanced Software, ISOTAS'96*, LNCS 1049, pages 38–55, Kanazawa, Japan, 1996. Springer-Verlag.
22. L. Mark and N. Roussopoulos. Metadata management. *IEEE Computer*, 19(12):26–36, December 1986.
23. J. Mylopoulos, P. Bernstein, and H. Wong. A language facility for designing interactive, database-intensive applications. *ACM Trans. on Database Systems*, 5(2), 1980.
24. J. Mylopoulos, A. Borgida, M. Jarke, and M. Koubarakis. Telos: Representing knowledge about informations systems. *ACM Trans. on Office Information Systems*, 8(4):325–362, 1990.
25. G.T. Nguyen and D. Rieu. SHOOD: A desing object model. In *Proc. of the 2nd Int. Conf. on Artificial Intelligence in Design*, Pittsburgh, USA, 1992.
26. N. Paton and O. Diaz. Metaclasses in object oriented databases. In R.A. Meersman, W. Kent, and S. Khosla, editors, *Proc. of the 4th IFIP Conf. on Object-Oriented Databases: Analysis, design and construction, DS-4*, pages 331–347, Windermere, UK, 1991. North-Holland.
27. M. Petit and E. Dubois. Defining an ontology for the formal requirements engineering of manufacturing systems. In K. Kosanke and J.G. Nell, editors, *Proc. of the Int. Conf. on Enterprise Integration an Modeling Technology, ICEIMT'97*, Torino, Italy, 1997. Springer-Verlag.
28. D.M. Russinof. Proteus: A frame-based nonmonotonic inference system. In W. Kim and F.H. Lochovsky, editors, *Object-Oriented Concepts, Databases and Applications*, pages 127–150. ACM Press, 1989.
29. M. Webster. *The WWWebster Dictionary*. 2000.

XSearch: A Neural Network Based Tool for Components Search in a Distributed Object Environment

Aluízio Haendchen Filho[1], Hércules A. do Prado[2], Paulo Martins Engel[2], and Arndt von Staa[1]

[1]PUC – Pontifícia Universidade Católica do Rio de Janeiro, Departamento de Informática, Rua Marquês de São Vicente 225, CEP 22453-900, Rio de Janeiro, RJ, Brasil
{aluizio, arndt}@inf.puc-rio.br
[2]Universidade Federal do Rio Grande do Sul, Instituto de Informática, Av. Bento Gonçalves, 9500, CEP 91501-970, Porto Alegre, RS, Brasil
{prado, engel}@inf.ufrgs.br

Abstract. The large-scale adoption of three-tier partitioned architectures and the support provided by the distributed object technology has brought a great flexibility to the information systems development process. In addition, the development of applications based on these alternatives has led to an increasing amount of components. This boom in the components amount was remarkably influenced by the Internet arising, that incorporated a number of new components, as HTML pages, java scripts, servlets, applets, and others. In this context, to recover the most suitable component to accomplish the requirements of a particular application is crucial to an effective reuse and the consequent reduction in time, effort and cost. We describe, in this article, a neural network based solution to implement a components intelligent recovering mechanism. By applying this process, a developer will be able to stress the reuse, while avoiding the morbid proliferation of nearly similar components.

1 Introduction

The large-scale adoption of architectures partitioned in interface, logical, and data tiers, levered up by the Internet, has brought an unprecedented flexibility to the development of information systems. However, the development of applications based on these alternatives has led to a considerable increment of the number of components. One important challenge of this scenery is posed by the question: in a repository with an enormous amount of alternatives, how to recover the most suitable component to accomplish the requirements of a particular application?

In this article, we describe a solution based on an artificial neural network, the associative Hopfield Model (HM) [2] [5], to locate and recover components for business applications. The HM is particularly interesting to record sparse signals, as is the case of software component descriptors. Moreover, in the application phase, the model allows to recover similes based in the description of the desired component requirements. A tool, called *XSearch* was implemented that validates this approach. We also present a small example that illustrates the applicability of the tool.

H.C. Mayr et al. (Eds.): DEXA 2001, LNCS 2113, pp. 42–51, 2001.

After discussing the context of the work in the next chapter, we give the details of our approach in Chapter 3. Chapter 4 describes the tool functions, presenting different kinds of resources that are used to build the neural network. Chapter 5 illustrates how the tool works by means of an example. Some techniques related to component recovery issues are described in Chapter 6.

2 Context

This paper uses results from Software Engineering (SE) and Artificial Intelligence (AI), aiming to support the information systems development process. To clarify the proposed approach context, we describe the applied distributed object architecture (DOA), the multi-tier model, and the technology applied to create the DOA. The knowledge of these characteristics simplify to understanding the components that compose a typical distributed object environment and the deployment descriptors that are mapped to the neural network. To avoid confusion when referring to parts of the architecture and the topology of the HM, we reserved the word „tier" to be used when describing the software engineering context and „layer" to be used in the HM.

In this paper we use the platform J2EE, from Sun Microsystems, particularly, the component model EJB (Enterprise Java Beans). EJB was designed to cope with the issues related to the management of business distributed objects in a three-tier architecture [7]. The J2EE Platform provides an application model distributed in tiers; it means that many parts of an application can run in different devices. On the other hand, it also enables different client types, to access transparently information from an object server in any platform. Figure 1 shows the components and services involved in a typical J2EE multi-tier environment.

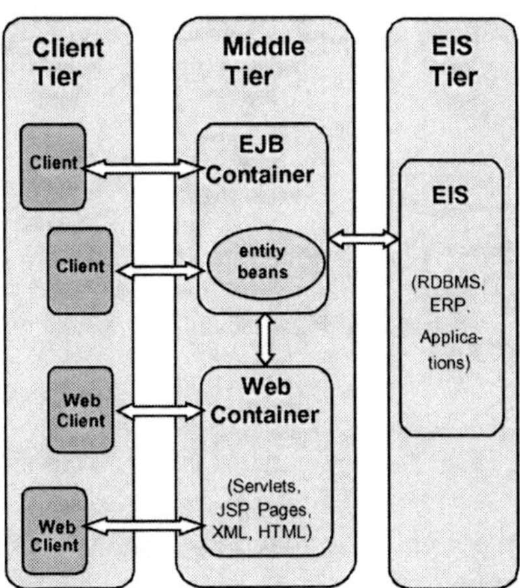

Fig. 1. The multi-tier model applied in a J2EE environment

The *client tier* supports a variety of client types, inside or outside the corporation firewall. The *middle tier* supports client services through *web containers* and EJB components that provide the business logic functions. *Web containers* provide support to client requisitions processing, performing time processing answers, such as invoking JSP methods, or *servelets*, and returning the results to the client [7]. EIS (Enterprise Information Systems) tier includes the RDBMS applied to the data persistency. Behind the central concept of a component based development model we find the notion of *containers*. *Containers* are standard processing environments that provide specific services to components [7].

A serv*er-side* component model defines an architecture to develop distributed objects. These models are used in the middle tier and manage the processing, assuring the availability of information to local or remote clients. The object server comprises the business object set, which is in this tier. Server-side component models are based in interface specifications. Since a component adheres to the specifications, it can be used by the CTM (*Component Transaction Monitor*). The relationship between a server-side component and the CTM is like a CD-ROM and a CD player: the component (CD-ROM) must be adequate to the player specification [7].

3 Proposed Approach

Considering the context previously described, the approach consists of the application of a HM to retain information about components and recover the most similar one with respect to a particular set of requirements. Figure 2 represents an overview of the whole process whose steps are described next.

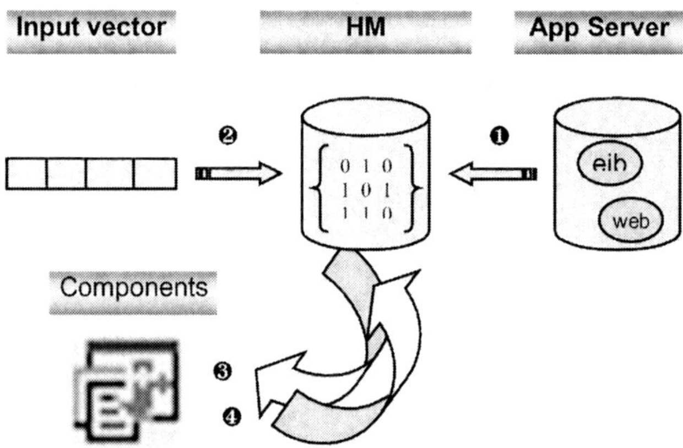

Fig. 2. Representation process overview.

(1) The tool scans the application server and creates a HM, representing all components in the environment;
(2) The developer presents the specifications of the desired component to the interface. These specifications are mapped to the input layer of the HM;
(3) The tool recovers the most similar component;
(4) New components are incrementally incorporated to the HM.

In this chapter, we describe: (a) the component descriptors, provided by J2EE platform, used to build the HM; (b) the HM topology; and (c) how the descriptors are codified in the HM.

3.1 The Deployment Descriptors

The deployment descriptors works very similarly to a property file, in which attributes, functions, and behavior of a bean are described in a standard fashion. In our approach, the component descriptors are used to relate requirements of a desired component to the components already existing in an environment. Starting at these descriptors, the tool locates the component or framework most suitable to be reused or customized. Figure 3 shows an example of directory structures in that appear many components that belong to a specific package (*Product*) of an application (*Application*).

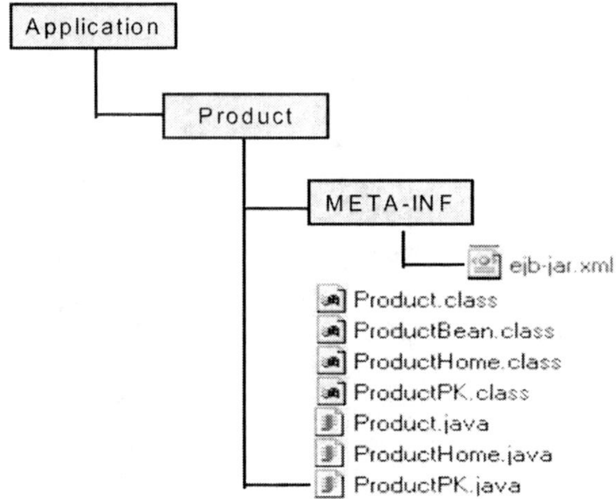

Fig. 3. The Product beans files.

When a bean class and its interfaces are defined, a deployment descriptor is created and populated with data about the bean. Usually, IDEs (Integrated Development Environments) are provided by the tools that work with EJB, through property sheets similar to those presented by Visual Basic, Delphi and others. After the description of these properties, by the developer, the component descriptor can be packaged in a JAR (Java Archive) type file. A JAR file contains one or more enterprise beans, including a class bean, remote interfaces, home interfaces, and primary keys (only for the *EntityBean* types), for each bean [8]. The component descriptor of a bean must be saved as a *ejb.jar.xml* file and must be located in the same directory where are the other components (interfaces and primary key) of the bean. Normally, in applications, we create directory structures that match with the structures from the application packages.

Notice that the components belonging to the package Product form a set of files that includes the classes *Product.class*, *ProductHome.class*, *ProductBean.class* and

ProductPK.class, beyond the files *.java* (Product.java, ProductHome.java, *Product PK.java*). When a JAR file containing a *JavaBean* (or a set of *JavaBeans*) is loaded in an IDE, the IDE examine the file in order to determine which classes represent beans. Every development environments know how to find the JAR file in the META-INF directory.

3.2 The Hopfield Model

The adoption of a discrete HM is justified by three main arguments: (1) we are assuming a stable set of components that are going to be stored in the model; (2) the components descriptors are typically represented by, or can be converted to, a binary form; and (3) the descriptors vector is quite sparse, since different components share very few descriptors. Our HM (see Figure 4) has two layers: the input one, where the binary descriptors are mapped, and the representation layer, where the traces of the vectors are represented.

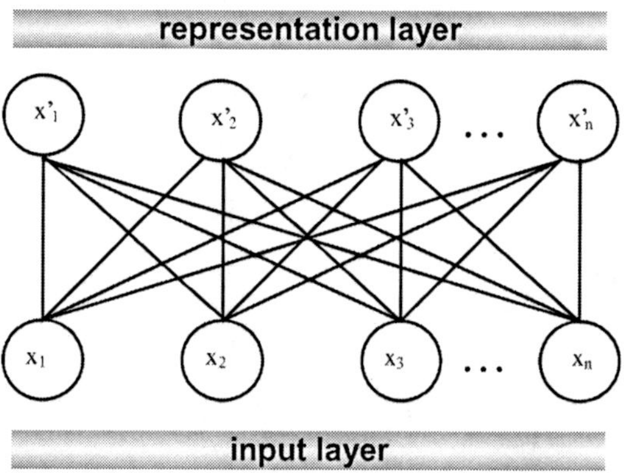

Fig. 4. The auto-associative architecture of HM.

The HM can be seen as a non-linear auto-associative memory that always converges to one of the stored patterns, as a response to a presentation of an incomplete or noisy version of that pattern. The stable points in the network phase space are the fundamental memories or prototype states of the model. A partial pattern presented to the network can be represented as an initial point in the phase space. Since this point is near the stable point, representing the item to be recovered, the system must evolve in time to converge to this memorized state. The discrete version of HM uses the formal McCulloch-Pitts neuron that can take one from 2 states (+1 or –1). The network works in two phases: storage and recovering. Let us suppose that we want to store a set of *p* *N*-dimensional binary vectors, denoted by:

$$\{\xi_\mu \mid \mu = 1,2,\ldots,p\}$$

These are the p vectors corresponding to the fundamental memories. $\xi_{\mu,i}$ represents o i-th element from the fundamental memory ξ_μ. By the external product-storing rule, that is a generalization of the Hebb rule, the synaptic weight of neuron i to neuron j is defined by:

$$w_{ji} = \frac{1}{N} \sum_{\mu=1}^{p} \xi_{\mu,j} \xi_{\mu,i} \quad \text{with} \quad w_{ii} = 0$$

Defining **w** the N by N matrix of synaptic weights, in which w_{ji} is its ji-th element, we can write:

$$\mathbf{w} = \frac{1}{N} \sum_{\mu=1}^{p} \xi_\mu \xi_\mu^T - \frac{p}{N}\mathbf{I}$$

$\xi_\mu \xi_\mu^T$ represents the external product of the vector ξ_μ with itself, and **I** denote the identity matrix. During the recovering phase, a ***N***-dimensional binary vector of proof ($\pm$)**x** is imposed to the network. A proof vector is typically a noisy or incomplete version of a fundamental memory. By this way a prototype is recovered that represent the most probable reuse candidate component.

3.3 Coding Components in the Network

Taking into account the context of distributed objects and the adopted platform, we are going to consider initially three kinds of basic components: (1) components of the *bean entity* type, (2) components of the *bean section* type and (3) components of the *web* type. For each one of the basic components it is built a different input vector and, as a consequence, a different HM, making the search and recovery process faster and more efficient. By this way, different kinds of networks can be generated, being each one more adequate for a particular objective. Filtering processes, running when interacting with the user, allow one to establish networks for different component classes. The input vector stores the description of the searched component and is defined by the developer. Figure 5 shows a particular example of an input vector layout for an *entity bean* component type.

<table>
<tr><th colspan="6">Interface</th><th colspan="8">State</th><th colspan="7">Behavior</th></tr>
<tr><td colspan="3">Client</td><td colspan="3">Dbms</td><td colspan="3">Integer</td><td colspan="3">Char</td><td colspan="2">...</td><td colspan="4">CTM Trans</td><td colspan="3">Methods</td></tr>
<tr><td>C1</td><td>C2</td><td>...</td><td>D1</td><td>D2</td><td>...</td><td>I1</td><td>I2</td><td>...</td><td>C1</td><td>C2</td><td>...</td><td>...</td><td>...</td><td>T1</td><td>T2</td><td>...</td><td>T7</td><td>M1</td><td>M2</td><td>...</td></tr>
</table>

Fig. 5. Input vector data groups to the *GenericNetwork*.

Three different data groups compose the vector of one *GenericNetwork*: Interface, State, and Behavior. Each group is briefly described next. The fields in this vector are Boolean, receiving value 1 when the property holds, and -1 otherwise. These data groups are defined when configuring the HM. Each cell is coded as the contents of the JAR files are analyzed and according to the following guidelines:

C1, C2, ... represents the different characteristics of a client that interacts with the entity bean, like: the existence or not of the local and remote interfaces, if the client is from a EJB type, and others;

D1, D2, ... holds the DBMS names in the environment, obtained during the interaction with the user when generating the network;

I2, I2, ... represents, each one, a quantity of „int" type attributes occurring in the component. For example, if a component has 2 attributes of „int" type, the cell I2 receives 1 and the remaining I1, I3, ... receive –1. The same rule applies to the other data type (char, Str, Ima, and so on).

CTM can have at maximum 7 cells, as described further in the Behavior topic.

4 The *XSearch* Functions

XSearch is totally configurable, assuring a high flexibility to simulate alternative HMs, varying the descriptors. By simulating different HMs, the developer can look for a better tradeoff between search performance and precision. Among the advantages of using a neural network, a Hopfield Model in this case, the most important are the simplification of the process and the reduction of processing time. Comparing our approach to an exhaustive search in a relational database, we can see that the operations in the latter alternative overcome those in the neural network. Following we list the key operations for each alternative:

Tasks in a relational model

(a) Traverse all the component base to each element in the input vector: n = table size; m = input vector size; Cost = n x m
(b) Compare for each interaction;
(c) Sort the selected components by similarity.
(d) Get the address and recover the component.

Task in our approach

(a) Make the product of the input vector by the neural network.

After recovering a vector describing a component candidate for reuse, it is necessary to locate this component in its specific repository. Indexing the component in a binary tree with each descriptor as a node and having its address as leaf solves this problem.

The example presented in Section 3.3 has shown a composition of a generic network *GenericNetwork*), more adequate to recover components that possess a great amount of methods combined with many attributes, interfaces, and other characteristics. Almost all the time, we need to recover a component from a less general set of specifications. For example, recover a session bean that possesses only two or three methods. In this case, a specific network to locate components can be faster and more efficient than a *GenericNetwork*. To cope with this question, considering a component of EJB type, the following *QuickNets* can be generated: (a) *StateNet*: deals with only the State group of the component; (b) *BehaviorNet*: considers only the Behavior group; (c) *ClientNet*: help in finding the components located outside the application server; and (d) *PKNets*: network that allows recover components that access databases.

To avoid the pattern mixing, due to successive extensions, the HM comprises only the original components (from which extensions can be generated). From this original component, a list of its extensions is created. When a component is recovered, a sequential search on its extension list is performed to try an extension that is more similar than the component. To find the most similar extension, the Hamming distance [2] is applied.

Dictionaries play important roles in the system. When generating the network, after configuring the environment with the wizard, a process scans the application server to identify and classify components, attributes, and methods. Moreover, the dictionaries simplify the search, when recovering components by name or all components that apply a specific method or contain a specific attribute.

5 Example

In this chapter we present a small example illustrating how a component is recovered according to a list of requirements stated by the developer: (a) component type: entity bean; (b) client type: ejb1.1; (c) DBMS vendor: ORACLE; (d) attributes: two integer type fields, two String fields, one Date type, and two double type fields and (e) Methods: the component must include a set of methods like *ejbCreate*, *ejbStore*, *ejbRemove*.

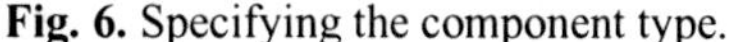

Fig. 6. Specifying the component type.

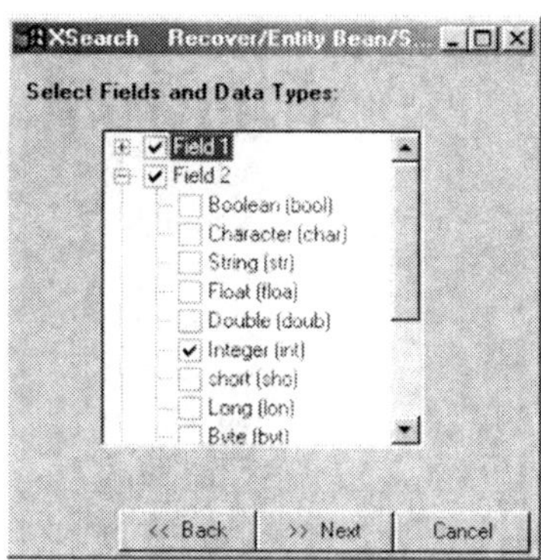

Fig. 7. Requirements for the state part.

One start window, not shown, enables the HM configuration, and includes the specification of limits for the three data groups (interface, state, and behavior). One limit, for example, is the number of fields in the state data group. Another configuration item is the folder to be scanned when building the HM.

Figure 6 shows the window that enables the user to specify the component type. The other operation recovers a component of the type selected in this window. It must be clear that, when choosing the component type (entity, session, or web), automatically the specific HM that holds the component characteristics is also chosen.

The window in Figure 7 allows the user to specify the component requirements. An example of state requirement specification is shown. Suppose we have a component base and a required component as described in Table 1. In this case, the HM will recover the component C_2. Note that, for the sake of simplicity, we adopted a general specification of behavior as transactional or non-transactional. The level of specification depends on the user preferences when configuring the tool. For space limitation it was not included in Table 1 examples of methods.

Table 1. Components base and components state

Description	*Components base*						*Req. Cmp.*
	C_1	C_2	C_3	C_4	C_5	C_6	
Client	ejb1.0	ejb1.1	java	ejb1.1	ejb1.0	ejb1.0	ejb1.1
DBMS	INF	ORA	SYB	INF	ORA	ORA	ORA
#int	2	2	1	2	2	4	2
#char	1	-	-	1	-	2	1
#Str	-	1	-	-	1	-	1
#Ima	1	1	1	-	-	1	1
#doub	1	2	-	-	-	-	2
#date	1	1	-	-	1	1	1
...	...	...	...	...	...	...	...

ORA: Oracle; SYB: Sybase; INF: Informix; Ima: Image; bool: boolean; doub: double.

6 Related Works

Recovering components for reuse has been approached in several recent publications. Some of them cope with this question by creating standard libraries for reuse. Michail [1] shows how to discover standard libraries in existing applications using Data Mining techniques. He applies „generalized association rules" based in inheritance hierarchies to discover potential reusable components. By browsing generalized association rules, a developer can discover patterns in library usage in which take into account inheritance relationships.

Küng [10], for example, applies the associative memory model *Neunet* in data mining, where the basic idea is to develop simple neural units and connections between the nodes. This is made by applying one binary representation to hold a connection between two units or not. The network shows a behavior similar to our approach. Another version – *Fuzzy Neunet* [11] - processes the signals which are normally between –1 and +1 [10].

Cohen [3] considers the recovery problem as an instance of a learning approach, focussing the behavior. Recently, library reengineering has been assessed, analyzing their use in many existing applications [6]. Constructing lattices do this provides insights into the usage of the class hierarchy in a specific context. Such a lattice can be used to reengineer the library class hierarchy to better reflect standard usage [1] [6].

7 Conclusions

An important advantage of our proposal is that, by adopting the HM, it is possible to simplify and to locate and recover faster components to be reuse. Also, tool supports the network maintenance, since the model allows one to perform an online update on the network as new components are inserted in to the repository. Moreover, the tool can be reconfigured to include new descriptors in the HM, requiring the HM to be rebuilt.

To generate and maintain a neural network in a highly dynamic environment requires many tasks, like monitoring the environment; keeping the neural network updated when including, modifying, or excluding components; and presenting the search results. To perform these laborious tasks a multi-agent system has been implemented.

The increasing complexity in the modern computational environment has required more refined tools and resources that simplify and increase the efficiency of the development process. This is true even when considering the traditional CASE tools [9]. The application of Artificial Intelligence techniques can contribute significantly to provide many of these resources, as we have shown in this paper.

References

1. Michail, A.: Data Mining Library Reuse Patterns using Generalized Association Rules. In Proceedings of 22nd International Conference On Software Engineering, Limerick, Ireland, 2000. IEEE Computer Society Press.
2. Freeman, J. A.: Neural Networks - Algorithms, Applications, and Programming Techniques, Addison-Wesley Publishing, Menlo Park CA, 1992.
3. Cohen, W. W. et al.: Inductive specification recovery: Understanding. Software by learning from example behaviors. Automated Software Engineering, 2(2): 107-129, 1995.
4. Fayad, M. E. et al.: Application Frameworks: Object-Oriented Foundations of Frameworks Design. New York: John Wiley & Sons, 1999.
5. Haykin, S.: Neural networks: a comprehensive foundation, Prentice Hall, Inc., Englewood Cliffs, New Jersey, 1999.
6. Snelting, G. et al.: Reengineering class hierarchies using concept analysis. In Proceedings of 6th IEEE International Conference On Automated Software Engineering, pages, 1998.
7. Kassen, N.: Designing Enterprise Applications with the Java2 Platform, Enterprise Edition, Addison-Wesley, Boston, 2000.
8. Monson-Haefel, R.: Enterprise Java Beans, O'Reilly & Associates, Inc., California, 1999.
9. Wang, Y. et al.: A Worldwide Survey of Base Process Activities Towards Software Engineering Process Excellence. In Proceedings of 20th International Conference On Software Engineering, Kyoto, Japan, 1998. IEEE Computer Society Press.
10. Küng, J.: Knowledge Discovery with the Associative Memory Modell Neunet. In Proceedings of 10th International Conference DEXA'99, Florence, Italy, 1999. Springer-Verlag, Berlin.
11. Andlinger, P. Fuzzy Neunet. Dissertation, Universität Linz, 1992.

Information Retrieval by Possibilistic Reasoning

Churn-Jung Liau[1] and Y.Y. Yao[2]

[1] Institute of Information Science
Academia Sinica, Taipei, Taiwan
liaucj@iis.sinica.edu.tw
[2] Department of Computer Science
University of Regina
Regina, Saskatchewan, Canada S4S 0A2
yyao@cs.uregina.ca

Abstract. In this paper, we apply possibilistic reasoning to information retrieval for documents endowed with similarity relations. On the one hand, it is used together with Boolean models for accommodating possibilistic uncertainty. The logical uncertainty principle is then interpreted in the possibilistic framework. On the other hand, possibilistic reasoning is integrated into description logic and applied to some information retrieval problems, such as query relaxation, query restriction, and exemplar-based retrieval.

Keywords: Possibilistic logic, Boolean models, Description logic, Similarity-based reasoning.

1 Introduction

In the last two decades, we have witnessed the significant progress in the information retrieval(IR) research. To meet the challenge of information explosion, many novel models and methods have been proposed. Among them, the logical approach is aimed at laying down a rigorous formal foundation for the IR methods and leads to a deeper understanding of the nature of the IR process. Since the pioneering work of Van Rijsbergen[20], several logical approaches to IR have been proposed. These approaches usually rely on some philosophical logics or knowledge representation formalisms, such as modal logic[14], relevance logic[13], many-valued logic[16], description logic[12,13], and default logic[5]. This list is by no means exhaustive and further references and surveys can be found in [8, 9].

In the logical approaches, it is common to give the documents and queries some logical representation and the retrieval work is reduced to establishing some implication between documents and queries. However, it is also well-known that classical logical implication is not adequate for the purpose after Van Rijsbergen introduced the *logical uncertainty principle* (LUP). To cope with the problem, many logical models for IR are thus extended with some uncertainty management formalisms, such as probability[19], fuzzy logic[15], or Dempster-Shafer

H.C. Mayr et al. (Eds.): DEXA 2001, LNCS 2113, pp. 52–61, 2001.

theory[6,7]. Though these extensions cover almost all the mainstream theories of uncertainty reasoning, the management of possibilistic uncertainty has received less attention. Possibilistic uncertainty is due to the fuzziness of information. In particular, in [17], it is shown that possibilistic uncertainty arises naturally from the degrees of similarity. Since the matching between documents and queries has been recognized as a kind of similarity in traditional models of IR (such as the vector models), the logical models should also have the capability of dealing with possibilistic uncertainty.

Possibility theory[21] is the main theory for the management of possibilistic uncertainty. Some logical systems based on possibility theory have been developed and extensively studied in artificial intelligence literature[3,10]. In these logics, two measures are attached to the logical formulas for denoting their possibility and necessity. These measures are shown to be closely related to modal logic operators, so their evaluations rely on a set of possible worlds and a similarity relation between them. In IR terms, this means that the uncertainty of a Boolean query matching with a document will depend on the similarity between documents. In fact, the inferential IR approach based on fuzzy modal logic in [15] can be seen as an application of the possibility measures. However, the full utilization of possibilistic reasoning power remains to be explored. Also, though it is well-known that possibility theory can be seen as a special case of Dempster-Shafer theory, the former can provide some simplicity over the latter in the representation of similarity relation.

In this paper, it would be shown that possibilistic reasoning can enhance the uncertainty management capability of similarity-based IR models. On the one hand, possibility theory will be used in combination with Boolean models to accommodate possibilistic uncertainty. Then it is shown that LUP can be interpreted in the possibilistic framework. On the other hand, due to the modal flavor of possibility and necessity measures, it is easy to integrate possibilistic reasoning into description logic, so we will propose a possibilistic description logic model for IR. This logic will be a possibilistic extension of $\mathcal{ALC}$[18].

In the rest of the paper, we will first review some notions of possibility theory and description logic. Then we present the possibilistic extensions of Boolean and description logic IR models in two respective sections. Finally, we conclude the paper with some remarks.

2 Preliminaries

2.1 Possibility Theory and Possibilistic Logic

Possibility theory is developed by Zadeh from fuzzy set theory[21]. Given a universe U, a *possibility distribution* on U is a function $\pi : U \rightarrow [0,1]$. In general, the normalized condition is required, i.e., $\sup_{u \in U} \pi(u) = 1$ must hold. Thus, π is a characteristic function of a fuzzy subset of U. Two measures on U can be derived from π. They are called possibility and necessity measures and denoted by Π and N respectively. Formally, $\Pi, N : 2^U \to [0,1]$ are defined as

$$\Pi(X) = \sup_{u \in X} \pi(u),$$

$$N(X) = 1 - \Pi(\overline{X}),$$

where $\overline{X}$ is the complement of X with respect to U.

In the IR application, the possibility distributions are in general induced from a similarity relation. Given a universe U, a similarity relation $R : U \times U \to [0,1]$ is a fuzzy relation on U satisfying that for all $u, v \in U$,

(i) reflexivity(also called separation in [4]): $R(u,v) = 1$ iff $u = v$, and
(ii) symmetry: $R(u,v) = R(v,u)$.

A binary operation $\otimes : [0,1]^2 \to [0,1]$ is a t-norm if it is associative, commutative, and increasing in both places, and satisfying $1 \otimes a = a$ and $0 \otimes a = 0$ for all $a \in [0,1]$. Some well-known t-norms include Gödel t-norm $a \otimes b = \min(a,b)$, product t-norm $a \otimes b = a \cdot b$, and Łukasiewicz t-norm $a \otimes b = \max(0, a+b-1)$. A similarity relation is called a $\otimes$-similarity if it in addition satisfies the $\otimes$-transitivity:

$$R(u,v) \otimes R(v,w) \leq R(u,w)$$

for all $u, v, w \in U$. For each $u \in U$, the fuzzy relation R can induce a possibility distribution π_u such that $\pi_u(v) = R(u,v)$ for all $v \in U$. The necessity and possibility measures corresponding to π_u are denoted by N_u and Π_u respectively.

2.2 Description Logics

In this subsection, we introduce a description logic, called $\mathcal{ALC}$[18]. The alphabets of $\mathcal{ALC}$ consists of three disjoint sets, the elements of which are called concept names, role names, and individual names respectively. The roles terms of $\mathcal{ALC}$ are just role names and denoted by R (sometimes with subscripts) and the concept terms are formed according to the following rules.

$$C ::= A \mid \top \mid \bot \mid C \sqcap D \mid C \sqcup D \mid \neg C \mid \forall R : C \mid \exists R : C$$

where A is metavariable for concept names, R for role terms and C and D for concept terms. The wffs of $\mathcal{ALC}$ consists of terminological and assertional formulas. Their formation rules are as follows.

1. If C and D are concept terms, then $C = D$ is a terminological formula.
2. If C is a concept term, R is a role term, and a, b are individual names, then $R(a,b)$ and $C(a)$ are assertional formulas.

The terminological formula $C \sqcap \neg D = \bot$ is abbreviated as $C \sqsubseteq D$.

The Tarskian semantics for $\mathcal{ALC}$ are given by assigning sets to concept names and binary relations to roles names. Formally, an interpretation for $\mathcal{ALC}$ is a pair $I = (U, \llbracket \cdot \rrbracket)$, where U is a set of universe and $\llbracket \cdot \rrbracket$ is an interpretation function which assigns each concept name a subset of U, each role name a subset of $U \times U$, and each individual name an element of U. The domain of $\llbracket \cdot \rrbracket$ can be extended to all concept terms by induction

1. $\|\top\| = U$ and $\|\bot\| = \emptyset$.
2. $\|\neg C\| = U \backslash \|C\|$, $\|C \sqcap D\| = \|C\| \cap \|D\|$, and $\|C \sqcup D\| = \|C\| \cup \|D\|$.
3. $\|\forall R : C\| = \{x \mid \forall y((x,y) \in \|R\| \Rightarrow y \in \|C\|)\}$
4. $\|\exists R : C\| = \{x \mid \exists y((x,y) \in \|R\| \wedge y \in \|C\|)\}$

An interpretation $I = \langle U, \|\cdot\|\rangle$ satisfies a wff

$$C = D \Leftrightarrow \|C\| = \|D\|,$$

$$R(a,b) \Leftrightarrow (\|a\|, \|b\|) \in \|R\|,$$

$$C(a) \Leftrightarrow \|a\| \in \|C\|.$$

If I satisfies a wff φ, it will be written as $I \models \varphi$. A set of wffs Σ is said to be satisfied by I, written as $I \models \Sigma$, if I satisfies each wff of Σ and Σ is satisfiable if it is satisfied by some I. A wff φ is an $\mathcal{ALC}$-consequence of Σ, denoted by $\Sigma \models_{\mathcal{ALC}} \varphi$ or simply $\Sigma \models \varphi$, iff for all interpretations I, $I \models \Sigma$ implies $I \models \varphi$, and φ is $\mathcal{ALC}$-valid if it is the $\mathcal{ALC}$-consequence of $\emptyset$.

3 Possibilistic Reasoning in Boolean Models

An IR model in general consists of three components (D, Q, F), where D is a collection of documents, Q is the query language(i.e. the set of possible queries), and $F : D \times Q \to O$ is a retrieval ranking function with values in a total ordered set O. What makes differences between the models is the representation of documents and queries and the definition of retrieval ranking function. The models considered in this section will have a logical representation for the documents and queries and the retrieval ranking function will be determined by the possibilistic reasoning mechanism.

3.1 Boolean Models with Complete Information

In Boolean models, we have a propositional query language. The set of index terms $\mathcal{A}$ is taken as the set of propositional symbols and the wffs of the query language Q are formed from the index terms by Boolean connectives $\neg$, $\wedge$, and $\vee$. An interpretation is just a two-valued truth assignment $d : \mathcal{A} \to \{0, 1\}$ and the assignment can be extended to the whole set Q as usual. Let Ω be the set of all interpretations. In the Boolean models with complete information, a document is just an interpretation, so D is a subset of Ω. In this model, a document d is matched with a query φ if $d(\varphi) = 1$, so the retrieval ranking function is completely determined by the satisfaction relation between interpretations and wffs. This retrieval ranking function is two-valued, so it in fact returns an yes/no answer instead of a ranked list.

What possibilistic logic can help is to improve the ranking capability of the above retrieval ranking function. To use possibilistic reasoning, we assume that there exists a similarity relation on the set D. The similarity relation can be imposed extraneously or generated automatically. One approach to the automatic generation of similarity relation is by using the Dalal's distance[2,11]. Let $\mathcal{A}$ be a finite set and d_1 and d_2 be two documents, then the Dalal's distance between d_1 and d_2 is the proportion of $\mathcal{A}$ in which d_1 and d_2 do not agree, i.e.

$$\delta(d_1, d_2) = \frac{|\{p \in \mathcal{A} : d_1(p) \neq d_2(p)\}|}{|\mathcal{A}|}$$

Thus, a similarity relation R on D can be defined by

$$R(d_1, d_2) = 1 - \delta(d_1, d_2) = \frac{|\{p \in \mathcal{A} : d_1(p) = d_2(p)\}|}{|\mathcal{A}|}$$

Note that the similarity so defined is a Łukasiewicz t-norm similarity.

As mentioned above, given a similarity relation R on D, we can induce a possibility distribution π_d for each $d \in D$. The possibility distribution induces necessity and possibility measures on the set of interpretations. Since each query can be identified with its corresponding models, the necessity and possibility measures can be naturally extended to the set of queries. Thus we can further define a ordering $\succ_\varphi$ between documents according to the query φ:

$$\begin{aligned} d_1 \succ_\varphi d_2 \Leftrightarrow\ & \Pi_{d_1}(\varphi) > \Pi_{d_2}(\varphi) \\ & \text{or } \Pi_{d_1}(\varphi) = \Pi_{d_2}(\varphi) \text{ and } N_{d_1}(\varphi) > N_{d_2}(\varphi) \end{aligned}$$

In other words, the ranking function is defined as $F : D \times Q \to [0,1]^2$, where $[0,1]^2$ is ordered by the lexicographical ordering $>_{lex}$ and for $d \in D$ and $\varphi \in Q$, $F(d,\varphi) = (\Pi_d(\varphi), N_d(\varphi))$. Then $d_1 \succ_\varphi d_2$ iff $F(d_1,\varphi) >_{lex} F(d_2,\varphi)$.

Because of the reflexivity of similarity relation, each possibility distribution π_d is normalized, so according to possibilistic logic, we have

$$N_d(\varphi) > 0 \Rightarrow \Pi_d(\varphi) = 1.$$

Thus the ordering $d_1 \succ_\varphi d_2$ can be divided into two cases:

1. $1 > \Pi_{d_1}(\varphi) > \Pi_{d_2}(\varphi)$: thus $N_{d_1}(\varphi) = N_{d_2}(\varphi) = 0$, this means that neither d_1 nor d_2 satisfies φ, then they are ordered according to their nearness to φ since $\Pi_d(\varphi)$ corresponds to the minimal distance (or maximal similarity) from d to the documents satisfying φ. This can be seen as an interpretation of LUP in the possibilistic framework and in fact the same principle has been used in [11] in the case of Dalal's distance. However, we can further distinguish the documents satisfying φ by their distances to $\neg\varphi$, that is
2. $N_{d_1}(\varphi) > N_{d_2}(\varphi) > 0$: thus $\Pi_{d_1}(\varphi) = \Pi_{d_2}(\varphi) = 1$, this means that both d_1 and d_2 have zero distance to φ since they satisfy φ by the reflexivity of similarity relation. However, $N_d(\varphi) = 1 - \Pi_d(\neg\varphi)$ measures their distance to $\neg\varphi$. The larger the $N_d(\varphi)$, the further d is from $\neg\varphi$. From the viewpoint of information need, this means that the documents close to both φ and $\neg\varphi$ may be ambiguous and should be considered less matching the need. The use of necessity measure will improve the precision but reduce the recall, so it is particularly useful in meeting the challenge of information explosion.

In summary, a Boolean model with complete information is a tuple

$$(\mathcal{A}_{bc}, Q_{bc}, \Omega_{bc}, D_{bc}, R_{bc}, F_{bc})$$

where $\mathcal{A}_{bc}$ is the set of index terms, Q_{bc} the propositional language formed from $\mathcal{A}_{bc}$, $\Omega_{bc} = 2^{\mathcal{A}_{bc}}$ the set of interpretations for Q_{bc}, $D_{bc} \subseteq \Omega_{bc}$ a set of documents, R_{bc} a similarity relation on Ω_{bc}, and F_{bc} the ranking function defined above. Note that the domain of R_{bc} is extended to the whole Ω_{bc} for handling queries not satisfied by any documents. For a query φ satisfiable in classical logic, if there are not any documents meeting its requirement, then $\Pi_d(\varphi) = N_d(\varphi) = 0$ when R_{bc} is a similarity relation on D_{bc}. However, by extending the domain of R_{bc}, we can order the documents in D_{bc} according to their distances to the interpretations satisfying φ but not in D_{bc}. Since Q_{bc} and Ω_{bc} are completely determined by $\mathcal{A}_{bc}$, the model can sometimes be abbreviated as $(\mathcal{A}_{bc}, D_{bc}, R_{bc}, F_{bc})$.

3.2 Boolean Models with Incomplete Information

In Boolean model with incomplete information, only partial description instead of complete information is given for each document, so the model is a tuple $(\mathcal{A}_{bi}, Q_{bi}, \Omega_{bi}, D_{bi}, R_{bi}, F_{bi})$, where $\mathcal{A}_{bi}, Q_{bi}$, Ω_{bi}, and R_{bi} are as above, however D_{bi} is now a subset of Q_{bi} since each document is described by a sentence in the propositional language. As for the ranking function F_{bi}, we have several choices at our disposal.

1. Consider each possible interpretation ω of the document description. Let $\psi_d \in Q_{bi}$ be a description for document d and φ a query, then $F_{bi} : D_{bi} \times Q_{bi} \to [0,1]^2$ can be defined in two ways.
   a) Optimistic way:
   $$F_{bi}^{\exists}(d, \varphi) = \max_{>_{lex}} \{F_{bc}(\omega, \varphi) : \omega(\psi_d) = 1\}$$
   b) Pessimistic way:
   $$F_{bi}^{\forall}(d, \varphi) = \min_{>_{lex}} \{F_{bc}(\omega, \varphi) : \omega(\psi_d) = 1\}$$
2. According to the LUP, "a measure of the uncertainty of $\psi_d \to \varphi$ relative to a data set is determined by the minimal extent to which we have to add information to the data set, to establish the truth of $\psi_d \to \varphi$", however, what remain unspecified in the principle are the information measure and the implication $\to$. In the possibilistic framework, the information measure is given by the pair of possibility and necessity measures induced from the similarity relation. Let us first consider the material implication $\psi_d \supset \varphi =_{def} \neg\psi_d \vee \varphi$. Let $\triangle$ denote $\forall$ or $\exists$, then we have also two definitions of ranking function based on optimistic or pessimistic way of looking at the document.
   $$F_{bi}^{\triangle\supset}(d, \varphi) = F_{bi}^{\triangle}(d, \psi_d \supset \varphi)$$

3. In [10], it is shown that the possibility theory can provide a natural semantics for conditional implication based on the Ramsey test. Essentially, given an interpretation ω, we can define an ordering $>_\omega$ on the set Ω_{bi} in the way that $u >_\omega v$ iff $\pi_\omega(u) > \pi_\omega(v)$. An ω-maximal model of a wff φ is an interpretation u satisfying φ and for all v satisfying φ, $v \not>_\omega u$. Thus we can define $\omega(\psi_d \rightarrow \varphi) = 1$ iff all ω-maximal models of ψ_d satisfy φ. In this way, each interpretation in Ω_{bi} can also assign truth values to the wffs of conditional logic, so the possibility and necessity measures can also be extended to the conditional wffs. This results in our definition of a new form of ranking function:

$$F_{bi}^{\triangle\rightarrow}(d, \varphi) = F_{bi}^{\triangle}(d, \psi_d \rightarrow \varphi).$$

4 Possibilistic Description Logic

In the IR applications of DL's, it is shown that the instance checking problem is especially relevant[12,13,19]. In those applications, a set of DL wffs is called a document base and the IR problem is to determine whether an individual i is an instance of a concept term C. Here a document base contains all descriptions of documents and thesaurus knowledge and an individual represents a document, whereas a concept term is just a query, so the problem just amounts to checking whether a document meets the information need expressed by the query. What makes DL-based approach advantageous is its capability to represent background knowledge (in particular, thesaurus knowledge) in the document base. However, classical DL's also lack the necessary uncertainty management mechanisms, so a probabilistic extension of DL's has been provided in [19].

Though probabilistic DL is definitely a must in dealing with the uncertainty problem of DL-based IR, it does not utilize the similarity between individuals. Obviously, the uncertainty due to randomness and that due to fuzziness are two orthogonal forms of properties and need separate formalisms for handling them. In the last section, we have seen that possibilistic reasoning is an appropriate tool for handling similarity-based reasoning in classical IR. In this section, we will try to propose a possibilistic extension of $\mathcal{ALC}$ and show that it is appropriate for DL-based IR. The logic is called $\mathcal{PALC}$.

To represent the individuals and concepts uniformly, we will use the basic hybrid language proposed in [1]. Let A, i, R be metavariables respectively for concept names, individual names, and role names and C and D be for concept terms, then the formation rules of concept terms are as follows:

$$\begin{aligned} C ::= {} & \top \mid \bot \mid A \mid i \mid \neg C \mid C \sqcap D \mid C \sqcup D \mid \forall R : C \\ & \mid \exists R : C \mid [\alpha]C \mid [\alpha]^+ C \mid \langle\alpha\rangle C \mid \langle\alpha\rangle^+ C \end{aligned}$$

where $\alpha \in [0, 1]$. Note that an individual name is also a concept term. The intended meaning is to treat it as a singleton set. Thus we will not need assertional formulas any more. The wffs of $\mathcal{PALC}$ are just terminological ones of the form $C = D$ for concept terms C, D. The definition of $C \sqsubseteq D$ is as in $\mathcal{ALC}$. For convenience, we will write $i : C$ or $C(i)$ for $i \sqsubseteq C$ and $(i,j) : R$ or $R(i,j)$ for $i \sqsubseteq \exists R : j$. The new modalities $[\alpha], [\alpha]^+, \langle\alpha\rangle$, and $\langle\alpha\rangle^+$ are for quantifying the necessity and possibility measures induced from a similarity relation. For example, an individual is in $\langle\alpha\rangle C$ iff it is similar to some element of C at least to the degree α. These modalities are also called numeral modalities.

For the formal semantics, a $\mathcal{PALC}$ interpretation is a triple $I = (U, \| \cdot \|, E)$, where E is a similarity relation on U and $(U, \| \cdot \|)$ is an $\mathcal{ALC}$ interpretation except $\| \cdot \|$ now assigns to each individual name a singleton subset instead of an element of U. Let $E_\alpha = \{(u,v) : E(u,v) \geq \alpha\}$ and $E_\alpha^+ = \{(u,v) : E(u,v) > \alpha\}$ denote the α-cut and strict α-cut of E respectively, then the following rules are added to the interpretation of concept terms:

5. $\|[\alpha]C\| = \{x \mid \forall y((x,y) \in E_\alpha \Rightarrow y \in \|C\|)\}$
6. $\|[\alpha]^+C\| = \{x \mid \forall y((x,y) \in E_\alpha^+ \Rightarrow y \in \|C\|)\}$
7. $\|\langle\alpha\rangle C\| = \{x \mid \exists y((x,y) \in E_\alpha \wedge y \in \|C\|)\}$
8. $\|\langle\alpha\rangle^+C\| = \{x \mid \exists y((x,y) \in E_\alpha^+ \wedge y \in \|C\|)\}$

The definitions of satisfaction, validity, etc. are all the same as those for $\mathcal{ALC}$, so the IR problem under the $\mathcal{PALC}$ framework is still the instance checking problem.

For the application of $\mathcal{PALC}$ to IR problems. Let us consider some examples.

Example 1 (Query relaxation) Let Σ be a document base in $\mathcal{PALC}$ and C be a concept term in which the numeral modalities do not occur, then for the query C, our problem is to find document i such that $\Sigma \models C(i)$. However, sometimes, if C is too restrictive, then it may not provide enough recall to meet the user's need. In this case, we may try to relax the query by using the concept term $\langle\alpha\rangle C$ for some $\alpha < 1$.

For example, in using an on-line hotel reservation system, the user may input a query C as follows:

$$\texttt{near–train–station} \sqcap \neg\texttt{expensive} \sqcap \texttt{pet–allowed} \sqcap \exists\texttt{has–room–type}.(\texttt{single} \sqcap \texttt{non–smoking})$$

and the system consequently find a hotel satisfying the requirement. However, unfortunately, upon checking the availability during the specified period the user wants, no rooms are available. In this case, the user may relax the query to $\langle 0.8\rangle C$ for finding a hotel nearly satisfying his requirement.

Example 2 (Query restriction) On the other hand, sometimes the query term is too loose so that there are too much recall. In this case, we may further require that $[\alpha]C$ must be satisfied for some $\alpha > 0$. Note that $[\alpha]C$ requires the documents must not have similarity to elements in $\neg C$ with degree exceeding α. Thus, the desired documents must be not only in C but also far enough from $\neg C$.

Example 3 (Exemplar-based retrieval) In some cases, in particular, for the retrieval of multimedia information, we may be given an exemplar or standard document and try to find documents very similar to the exemplar but satisfying some additional properties. In this case, we can write the query term as $\langle\alpha\rangle i \sqcap C$, where i is the name for the exemplar and C denotes the additional properties. According to the semantics, $j : \langle\alpha\rangle i$ will be satisfied by an interpretation $I = (U, \llbracket \cdot \rrbracket, E)$ iff $E(a_j, a_i) \geq \alpha$ where a_i and a_j be the elements of $\llbracket j \rrbracket$ and $\llbracket i \rrbracket$ respectively. Thus, a document j will meet the query if it can satisfy the properties denoted by C and is similar to the exemplar to some degree α.

The last example also suggests that we may have to specify the aspect on which the similarity is derived. For example, we may require the documents which are similar to the exemplar on the style or on the color. To model the situation, we should have more than one similarity relations and corresponding numeral modalities. However, this can be achieved by a straightforward generalization of $\mathcal{PALC}$. For example, let T denote a set of aspects, we can add to our language different modalities $[\alpha]_t$, etc. for all $t \in T$.

5 Concluding Remarks

We have presented some applications of possibilistic reasoning to IR problems. On the one hand, it can be used in combination with Boolean IR models to improve the precision and provide a finer ranking of the retrieval results. On the other hand, it can be easily integrated into the DL-based approach to help some IR tasks, such as query relaxation, query restriction and exemplar-based retrieval, etc. The scope of the applications is that the document collection must be endowed with some similarity relations. However, in most cases, the similarity relation can be automatically generated from the document representation, though it can also be given extraneously by some experts. The automatic generation of similarity relation may be time-consuming in the large collection of documents. It need $O(n^2)$ time if the computation of similarity degree between any two documents needs constant time. Fortunately, the generation process can be executed in advance when the collection is constructed, so it can be completed in a preprocessing phase.

References

1. P. Blackburn. "Representation, reasoning, and relational structures: a hybrid logic manifesto". *Logic Journal of IGPL*, 8(3):339–365, 2000.
2. M. Dalal. "Investigations into a theory of knowledge base revision: Preliminary report". In *Proceedings of the 7th National Conference on Artificial Intelligence*, pages 475–479. AAAI Press, 1988.
3. D. Dubois, J. Lang, and H. Prade. "Possibilistic logic". In D.M. Gabbay, C.J. Hogger, and J.A. Robinson, editors, *Handbook of Logic in Artificial Intelligence and Logic Programming, Vol 3 : Nonmonotonic Reasoning and Uncertain Reasoning*, pages 439–513. Clarendon Press - Oxford, 1994.

4. F. Esteva, P. Garcia, L. Godo, and R. Rodriguez. "A modal account of similarity-based reasoning". *International Journal of Approximate Reasoning*, pages 235–260, 1997.
5. A. Hunter. "Using default logic in information retrieval". In C. Froidevaux and J. Kohlas, editors, *Symbolic and Quantitative Approaches to Reasoning and Uncertainty : European Conference ECSQARU'95*, LNAI 946, pages 235–242. Springer-Verlag, 1995.
6. M. Lalmas. "Dempster-Shafer's theory of evidence applied to structured documents: modelling uncertainty". In *Proceedings of the 20th Annual International ACM SIGIR Conference in Research and Development of Information Retrieval*, pages 110–118. ACM Press, 1997.
7. M. Lalmas. "Information retrieval and Dempster-Shafer's theory of evidence". In A. Hunter and S. Parsons, editors, *Applications of Uncertainty Formalisms*, LNAI 1455, pages 157–176. Springer-Verlag, 1998.
8. M. Lalmas. "Logical models in information retrieval: introduction and overview". *Information Processing and Management*, 34(1):19–33, 1998.
9. M. Lalmas and P. Bruza. "The use of logic in information retrieval modeling". *Knowledge Engineering Review*, 13(3):263–295, 1998.
10. C.J. Liau and I.P. Lin. "Possibilistic Reasoning—A Mini-survey and Uniform Semantics". *Artificial Intelligence*, 88:163–193, 1996.
11. D.E. Losada and A. Barreiro. "Using a belief revision operator for document ranking in extended boolean models". In *Proceedings of the 22nd Annual International ACM SIGIR Conference in Research and Development of Information Retrieval*, pages 66–73. ACM Press, 1999.
12. C. Meghini, F. Sebastiani, U. Straccia, and C. Thanos. "A model of information retrieval based on a terminological logic". In *Proceedings of the 16th Annual International ACM SIGIR Conference in Research and Development of Information Retrieval*, pages 298–307. ACM Press, 1993.
13. C. Meghini and U. Straccia. "A relevance terminological logic for information retrieval". In *Proceedings of the 19th Annual International ACM SIGIR Conference in Research and Development of Information Retrieval*, pages 197–205. ACM Press, 1996.
14. J.Y. Nie. "An information retrieval based on modal logic". *Information Processing and Management*, 25(5):477–491, 1989.
15. J.Y. Nie. "Using fuzzy modal logic for inferential information retrieval". *Informatica*, 20:299–318, 1996.
16. T. Rölleke and N. Fuhr. "Retrieval of complex objects using a four-valued logic". In *Proceedings of the 19th Annual International ACM SIGIR Conference in Research and Development of Information Retrieval*, pages 206–214. ACM Press, 1996.
17. E. Ruspini. "On the semantics of fuzzy logic". *Int. J. of Approximate Reasoning*, 5:45–88, 1991.
18. M. Schmidt-Schauß and G. Smolka. "Attributive concept descriptions with complements". *Artificial Intelligence*, 48(1):1–26, 1991.
19. F. Sebastiani. "A probabilistic terminological logic for modelling of information retrieval". In W.B. Croft and C.J. van Rijsbergen, editors, *Proceedings of the 17th Annual International ACM SIGIR Conference in Research and Development of Information Retrieval*, pages 122–130. ACM Press, 1994.
20. C.J. van Rijsbergen. "A non-classical logic for information retrieval". *The Computer Journal*, 29:481–485, 1986.
21. L.A. Zadeh. "Fuzzy sets as a basis for a theory of possibility". *Fuzzy Sets and Systems*, 1(1):3–28, 1978.

Extracting Temporal References to Assign Document Event-Time Periods*

D. Llidó[1], R. Berlanga[1], and M.J. Aramburu[2]

[1]Departament of Languages and Computer Systems
[2]Departament of Engineering and Science of Computers
Universitat Jaume I, E-12071, Castellón (Spain)
{dllido, berlanga, aramburu}@uji.es

Abstract. This paper presents a new approach for the automatic assignment of document event-time periods. This approach consists of extracting temporal information from document texts, and translating it into temporal expressions of a formal time model. From these expressions, we are able to approximately calculate the event-time periods of documents. The obtained event-time periods can be useful for both retrieving documents and finding relationships between them, and their inclusion in Information Retrieval Systems can produce significant improvements in their retrieval effectiveness.

1 Introduction

Many documents tell us about events and topics that are associated to well-known time periods. For example, newspaper articles, medical reports and legal texts, are documents that contain many temporal references for both placing the occurrences and relating them with other events. Clearly, using this temporal information can be helpful in retrieving documents as well as in discovering new relationships between document contents (e.g. [1] [2] and [3]).

Current Information Retrieval Systems can only deal with the publication date of documents, which can be used in queries as a further search field. As an alternative approach, in a new object-oriented document model, named TOODOR [4], is presented. In this model two time dimensions are considered: the publication date, and the event-time period of documents. Furthermore, by means of its query language, called TDRL [5], it is possible to retrieve documents by specifying conditions on their contents, structure and time attributes.

However, TOODOR assumes that the event-time period of a document is manually assigned by specialists, which is an important limitation. By one hand, this task is subjective as it depends on the reader's particular interpretation of the document texts. On the other hand, in applications where the flow of documents is too high, the manual assignment of event-time periods is impracticable. Consequently, it is

* This work has been funded by the Bancaixa project with contract number PI.1B2000-14 and the CICYT project with contract number TIC2000-1568-C03-02.

H.C. Mayr et al. (Eds.): DEXA 2001, LNCS 2113, pp. 62–71, 2001.

necessary to define an automatic method for extracting event-time periods from document contents.

In this paper we present an approach to extracting temporal information from document contents, and its application to automatically assigning event-time periods to documents. Moreover, with this work we demonstrate the importance of these attributes in the retrieval of documents.

The paper is organized as follows. Section 2 describes the semantic models on which the extraction system relies. Section 3 presents our approach to extracting temporal references from texts. Section 4 describes how event-time periods can be calculated with the extracted dates. Finally, Section 5 presents some conclusions.

2 Semantic Models

This section describes the semantic models on which the proposed information extraction method relies, these are: a representation model for documents, and a time model for representing the temporal information extracted from texts.

2.1 Documents and Their Time Dimensions

This work adopts the document model of TOODOR [4]. Under this model, complex documents are represented by means of object aggregation hierarchies. The main novelty of this model is that document objects have associated two time attributes, namely: the publication time and the event time. The former indicates when the document has been published, whereas the latter expresses the temporal coverage of the topics of the document.

The publication time plays an important role in the extraction of temporal expressions, because several temporal sentences, such as "today" and "tomorrow", take it as point of reference.

The event-time period of a document must express the temporal coverage of the relevant events and topics reported by its contents. Since the relevance of a topic depends on the interpretation of the document contents, event-time periods are inherently indeterminate. As a general rule, we assume that the location of these periods will coincide approximately with the temporal references appearing in the document, where a temporal reference is either a date or a period mentioned in the document texts. In this way, event-time periods could be either extracted automatically from the texts, or manually assigned by users.

2.2 Time Model

Temporal sentences in natural language usually involves the use of the calendar granularities. In concrete, we can express time instants, intervals, and spans at several granularity levels. In this section we provide a time model that takes into consideration the time entities appearing in temporal sentences.

2.2.1 Granularities

The proposed time model relies on the granularity system of Figure 1. From now on, we will denote each granularity of this system by a letter: day (*d*), week (*w*), month (*m*), quarter (*q*), semester (*s*), year (*y*), decade (*x*) and century (*c*). As shown in Figure 1, these granularities can be arranged according to the finer-than relationship, which is denoted with $\prec$ [6]. Note that unlike other time models of the literature, in written text it is usual to relate granularities that do not satisfy this relationship (e.g. "the first week of the year"). In Figure 1 they are represented with dashed lines.

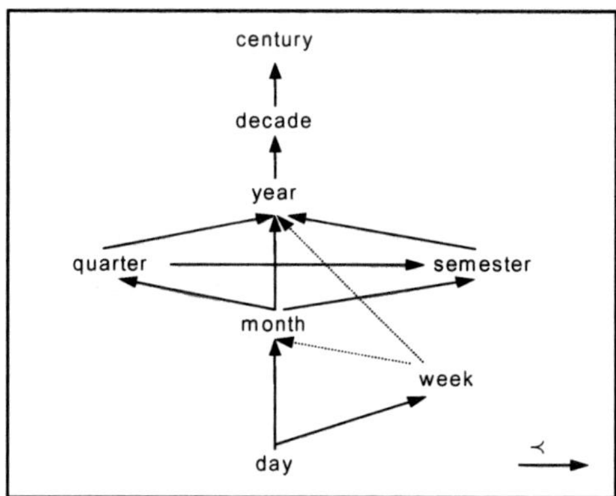

Fig. 1. Granularity System

In our model, two types of granularity domains are distinguished, namely: relative and absolute domains. A relative domain for a granularity *g* is defined in terms of another coarser granularity *g'* ($g \prec g'$), which is denoted with *dom*(*g, g'*). For instance, the domain of days relative to weeks is defined as *dom*(*d, w*)={1,...,7}. Relative domains are always represented as finite subsets of the natural numbers. Thus, we will denote with *first*(*g, g'*) and *last*(*g, g'*), the first and last elements of the domain *dom*(*g, g'*) respectively.

An absolute domain for a granularity *g*, denoted with *dom*(*g*), is always mapped onto integer numbers (e.g. centuries and years). Time models from the literature associate absolute domains to granularities (called *ticks*), defining over them the necessary mapping functions to express the finer-than relationship [6].

2.2.2 Time Entities

In this section, we define the time entities of our time model in terms of the granularity system described above.

A *time point* is expressed as the following alternate sequence of granularities and natural numbers $T = g_1\ n_1\ g_2\ n_2 ...\ g_k\ n_k$. In this expression, if g_i is a relative granularity then n_i must belong to the domain $dom(g_i, g_{i-1})$ with $1 < i \leq k$, otherwise $n_i \in dom(g_i)$. Consequently, the sequence of granularities must be ordered by the finer-than relationship, i.e. $g_{i+1} \prec g_i$ with $1 \leq i \leq k$. From now on, the finest granularity of a time point *T* is denoted with *gran*(*T*).

A *time interval* is an anchored span of time that can be expressed with two time points having the same sequence of granularities:

$$I = [T_1, T_2], \text{ where } T_1 = g_1\ n_1 \ldots g_k\ n_k\ , T_2 = g_1\ n'_1 \ldots g_k\ n'_k \text{ y } n_i \leq n'_i \text{ for all } 1 \leq i \leq k$$

We will use the functions *start*(I) and *end*(I) to denote the starting and end points of the interval I respectively. Besides, the finest granularity of I, denoted with *gran*(I), is defined as the finest granularity of its time points.

Finally, a *span of time* is defined as an unanchored and directed interval of time. This is expressed as $S = \pm\, n_1\ g_1 \ldots\ n_k\ g_k$, where the sign (±) indicates the direction of the span (+ towards the future, - towards the past), n_i ($1 \leq i \leq k$) are natural numbers, and the granularities g_i with $1 \leq i < k$ are ordered (i.e. $g_{i+1} \prec g_i$).

2.2.3 Operators

This section describes the main operators that are used during the resolution of temporal sentences from the text. Firstly, we define the refinement of the a point $T = n_1 g_1 \ldots n_k\ g_k$ to a finer granularity g as follows:

$$refine(T, g) = [T_1, T_2]$$
$$\text{where } T_1 = g_1\ n_1 \ldots g_k\ n_k\ g\ first(g, g_k), \text{ and } T_2 = g_1\ n_1 \ldots g_k\ n_k\ g\ last(g, g_k)$$

Note that this operation can only be applied to granularities with relative domains. Similarly, we define the refinement of a time interval I to a finer granularity g ($g \prec gran(I)$) as follows:

$$refine(I, g) = [start(refine(start(i), g)), end(refine(end(i), g))]$$

The abstraction is the inverse operation to the refinement. Applying it, any time entity can be abstracted to a coarser granularity. We will denote this operation with the function *abstract*(T, g), where g is a granularity that must be contained in T. This operation is performed by truncating the sequence of granularities up to the granularity g. For example, *abstract*(`y2000m3d1`, y) = `y2000`.

Finally, the shift of a time point $T = g_1\ n_1 \ldots g_k\ n_k$ by a time span $S = n\ g$ is defined as follows:

$$shift(T, S) = g_1\ n'_1 \ldots g_i\ n'_i\ g_{i+1}\ n_{i+1} \ldots g_k\ n_k$$

where $g_i = g$, and $n'_1 \ldots n'_i$ are the new quantities associated to the granularities resulting from $n + n_i$ and propagating its overflow to the coarser granularities. These are some examples:

shift(`y1999m3`, `+10m`) = `y2000m1`
shift(`y2001`, `-2y`) = `y1999`
shift(`y1998m2w2`, `-3w`) = `y1998m1w4`

3 Temporal Information Extraction

To calculate the event-time period of a document we apply a sequence of two modules. The first module, named date extraction module, first searches for temporal expressions in the document text, then extracts dates, and finally inserts XML tags with the extracted dates. Figure 2 shows an example of a tagged document. In our approach we use the tag TIMEX defined in [7], to which we have added the attribute VALUE to store the extracted dates. Figure 3 presents the different stages of the date extraction module.

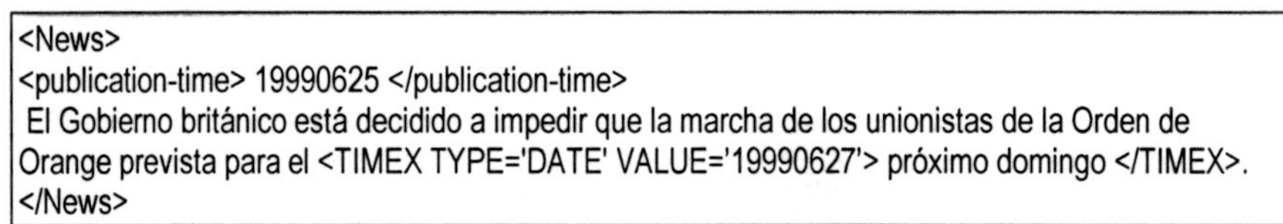
<News>
<publication-time> 19990625 </publication-time>
El Gobierno británico está decidido a impedir que la marcha de los unionistas de la Orden de Orange prevista para el <TIMEX TYPE='DATE' VALUE='19990627'> próximo domingo </TIMEX>.
</News>

Fig. 2. Example of XML tagged document.

Regarding to the second module, named event-time extraction module, it processes all the TIMEX tags of the document to approximately obtain its event-time period. This section is focused on describing how the first module works, whereas Section 4 describes the second module.

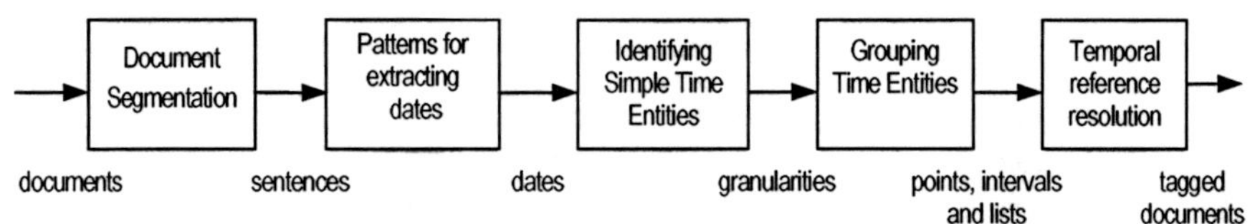

Fig. 3. Stages of the Date Extraction Process.

In the date extraction module, the main problem to solve is similar to that of any natural language processing system, that is the ambiguity. This appears in several contexts:

- *Syntactic ambiguity*. We need to know which words belong to the same temporal expression. After testing several syntactic analysers, we have concluded that they are not able to identify whole phrase like "In May of this year".
- *Word sense disambiguation*. We need to fix indefinite phrases like "in the last years", vague adverbial words like "now", "recently", and references to events like "since the beginning of these negotiations".
- *Semantic ambiguity*. We need to distinguish between temporal expressions that identify either spans, intervals or dates.

The approach we propose in this work consists of applying a shallow semantic-syntactic parser to extract temporal information. Similarly to Information Extraction systems [8], we begin with a lexical analysis that looks-up words related to temporal expressions into a dictionary (time granularities, day of weeks, months, holidays, etc.), and name recognition of standard date expressions. This is followed by a partial syntactic analysis of the sentences that contain these words, in order to search for more words that probably belong to the same temporal expression. Afterwards, the selected words are coded with their semantic meaning in terms of the formal time model. Finally, these codes are properly combined to obtain dates, intervals and time spans. Next section illustrates the grammatical elements necessary for all this process, and the following stages are described afterwards.

3.1 Grammatical Elements

By analysing the range of temporal expressions in natural language, we have classified the words belonging to these expressions in three categories that give us the semantic information necessary to assign the corresponding date. These are:

- *Granularities*, which are words that identify calendar granularities (e.g. "day", "month", "years", "semester", etc.)
- *Time head nouns*, which are words closely related with the calendar granularities. Specifically, these words represent the proper granularities and its synonyms (e.g. "journey"), the granularities values (e.g. "July", "Monday") as well as relevant dates and periods like "Hallowing night", "Christmas", "autumn", etc.
- *Quantifiers*, which are the cardinal, ordinal and indefinite adjectives, as well as the roman numbers (e.g. "first", "second", "two", etc.)
- *Modifiers*, which are words that grammatically can take part in a temporal expression. In this group we can find words for expressing intervals or periods like "during" and "between", words for indicating the temporal direction of spans like "past" and "next", and words for specifying a position within a time interval like "beginning" and "end".

All these elements are always translated into codes representing their temporal meaning in the formal time model of Section 2.2. We use the notation $e \Rightarrow c$ to denote the translation of a temporal expression e into its corresponding representation c in the formal model. This translation is performed as follows:

- *Time head nouns* are always encoded as time entities. For example, since Monday is the first day of the week, we encoded it as "Monday" ⇒ "wd1". Other head nouns can be encoded as time intervals, for instance "autumn" ⇒ "[m9d21, m12d26]".
- *Quantifiers* are all encoded as natural numbers. Additionally, ordinal and cardinal numbers must be distinguished in order to identify the time entity they are referring to. For instance, "first day" is encoded as "d1" (time point), whereas "two days" is encoded as "2d" (span). The order of a quantifier with respect to a granularity changes its meaning. For instance we must distinguish between "day two" ⇒ "d2" (time point) and "two days" ⇒ "2d" (span).
- *Modifiers* are used to express the direction of time spans, namely: towards the past '–', towards the future '+', and at present time '0'. For instance, "last Monday" is

encoded as "–wd1", and "next three days" as "+3d". Besides, modifiers can also refer to both other time entities, denoted with the prefix r, and events, denoted with the prefix R. For example, consider the following translations "that day" ⇒ "rd" and "two days before the agreement" ⇒ "R–2d the agreement".

3.2 Date Extraction Module

The basic structural unit in our document model is the paragraph. However in the extraction date module, as in most Information Extraction systems, it is necessary to split them into smaller units to extract complex temporal expressions. For this purpose, we make use of the usual separators of sentences (e.g. '!', ';',. '?', '-', ':', etc.) Since some of these symbols are also used for other purposes such as numeric expressions, we need to define and apply a set of patterns to correctly split sentences.

3.2.1 Extraction of Dates

During this stage, regular expressions are applied in order to extract basic temporal expressions for dates. These are common date formats (e.g. \d{2,4}\/\d{1,2}\/\d{1,2}) and relative temporal expressions referred to the publication date (e.g. "today", "this morning", "weekend", etc.). These regular expressions have been obtained by analysing the most frequent temporal sentences.

3.2.2 Identifying Simple Temporal Expressions

In this stage all the sentences having temporal head nouns are analysed to extract simple time entities. Sometimes these head nouns appear in usual temporal expressions like "every Monday", "each weekend", "each morning", which do not denote any time entity of our model. To avoid misunderstandings on interpreting such expressions and improve the efficiency of the extraction process, a list of patterns for rejecting them has been defined. Once checked that a temporal expression does not match any of these patterns, the algorithm proceeds to search for modifiers and quantifiers in the head's adjacent words. As a result, the identified head and its modifiers/quantifiers are translated into a single time entity.

3.2.3 Grouping Simple Time Expressions

Once the simple time entities from a sentence are extracted, we have to analyse them in order to detect if they are the components of a more complex time entity. Thus, this phase we must determine whether they constitute a single date (e.g. "May last year" ⇒ "y0m5–1y"), a time interval (e.g. "from May to July" ⇒ "from m5 to m7" ⇒ "[m5, m7]"), a list of dates (e.g. "On Wednesday and Friday" ⇒ "on wd4 and wd6" ⇒ "{wd4, wd6}"), or two different expressions (e.g. "I won yesterday and you today").

Starting from a set of temporal expressions, we have defined a list of regular expressions for grouping simple time entities. For instance, the pattern 'from \entity to \entity' is used to identify a time interval. In this way, when a sentence contains several encoded time entities, the algorithm tries to apply these patterns to identify complex time entities.

3.2.4 Resolution of Temporal References

Most of the identified time entities can be finally translated into concrete dates, which will be used by the event-time generator. More specifically, only those time entities that contain the granularities either of year or century are translated into dates. In this process we take into account the relationships and operations specified between time entities as well as the time references of the document. To perform these tasks, the system makes use of regular expressions as follows:

- If the sentence matches the pattern '\granularity[0-9]+', the date (or interval date) is extracted by applying the refine operation on the temporal expression. *Example*: "y1999" ⇒ refine(y1999, d) = [y1999m1d1, y1999m12d31]
- If the sentence matches the pattern '(+|-)?\granularity0\D', the date is extracted by applying the denoted shift operation to the publication date. If the shift sign is omitted, the system tries to determine it by using the tense of the verb within the same sentence. *Example*: "The meeting will be on Monday" ⇒ "The meeting will be on +w0d1"
- If the sentence matches the pattern 'r(+|-)\granularity\d+', the date is extracted by applying the denoted shift operation to the most recent cited date.
- If the sentence matches the pattern 'r(+|-)\d+\granularity', we proceed as before.

The rest of cases are not currently analysed to extract concrete dates. However, their study can be of interest in order to extract further knowledge about events and their relationships. For instance, temporal expressions containing references to events, for examples "R+2d the agreement", can be very useful to identify named events and their occurrences. However, this analysis will be carried out in future works.

4 Generating Event-Time Periods

In this section we describe the module in charge of analysing the extracted dates of each document, and of constructing the event-time period that covers its relevant topics. As in Information Retrieval models, we assume that the relevance of each extracted date is given by its frequency of appearance in the document (i.e. the TF factor). Thus, the most relevant date is considered as the reference time point of the whole document. If all dates have a similar relevance, the publication date is taken as the reference point. This approach differs from others in the literature, where the publication date is always taken as the reference time point.

The algorithm for constructing the event-time period of a document groups all the consecutive dates that are located around the reference time point, and whose relevance is greater than a given threshold.

Currently, both the date extraction module and the event-time generator have been implemented in the Python language. To perform the dictionary look-ups when solving temporal references, the date extraction module uses the TACAT system [9], which is implemented in Perl.

4.1 Preliminary Results

To evaluate the performance of the date extraction module we have analysed four newspapers containing 1,634 time expressions. The overall *precision* (valid extracted dates / total extracted dates) of the evaluated set was 96.2 percent, while the overall *recall* (valid extracted dates / valid dates in the set) was 95.2 percent. Regarding the execution times, each news is tagged in 0.1 seconds. These results, obtained on a dual Pentium III-600 MHz, are very satisfactory for our applications.

To study the properties of the generated event-time periods, we have applied the extraction modules to 4,274 news. Then we have classified them into the following four classes:

1. *Class A*: news whose event-time periods contain the publication date and are smaller than three days.
2. *Class B*: news whose event-time periods do not contain the publication date and are smaller than three days.
3. *Class C*: news whose event-time periods are between four and fourteen days.
4. *Class D*: news whose event-time periods are greater than fourteen days.

Table 1. Classification of documents according to their event-time period.

Class A	*Class B*	*Class C*	*Class D*
21%	53%	9%	11%

The obtained results are given in Table 1. It is worth pointing out that near 6% of the articles have no event-time assigned. These cases are due to the lack of dates in the document contents. Moreover, around 42% of the articles contain dates located at least 14 days before or after the publication date. These dates are references to other past or future events, probably described in other newspaper articles. The extraction of these dates can be very useful to automatically link documents through their time references.

5 Related Work

The extraction of temporal information from texts is a recent research field within the Information Retrieval area. In [7] it has been shown that near 25% of the tagged tokens in documents are time entities, whereas near 31% of the tags corresponds to person names. The relevance of temporal information is also demonstrated in [2], where the impact of time attributes on Information Retrieval systems is analyzed. Extracting temporal information is also important in the topic detection and tracking tasks. However, the proposed methods in the literature (e.g. [1]) use the publication date as the event time. The work presented in [2] tries to calculate event-time periods by grouping similar news located in consecutive publication dates. This approach can produce errors because an event is published one or more days after its occurrence.

There are other works in the literature dedicated to automatically extract dates from dialogues [11] and news [12]. The main limitation of these approaches is that only absolute temporal expressions [7] are analyzed to extract dates. In [12], some simple relative expressions can also be analyzed by applying the tense of verbs to disambiguate them.

6 Conclusions

In this paper a new method for extracting temporal references from texts has been presented. With this method event-time periods can be calculated for documents, which can be used in turn for retrieving documents and discovering temporal relationships. The proposed method is based on the shallow parsing of natural language sentences containing time entities. These are translated into a formal time model where calculations can be performed to obtain concrete dates. Future work is focused on the automatic recognition of events by using the extracted dates and the chunks of texts where they appear. Another interesting task consists of solving the temporal expressions that refers to other events.

References

1. J. Allan, R. Papka and V. Lavrenko. "On-Line New Event Detection and Tracking". 21st ACM SIGIR Conference, pp. 37-45, 1998.
2. R. Swan and J. Allan. "Extracting Significant Time Varying Features from Text," CIKM Conference, pp. 38-45, 1999.
3. R. Berlanga, M. J. Aramburu and F. Barber. "Discovering Temporal Relationships in Database of Newspapers". In *Tasks and Methods in Applied Artificial Intelligence*, LNAI 1416, Springer Verlag, 1998.
4. M. J.Aramburu and R. Berlanga. "Retrieval of Information from Temporal Document Databases". ECOOP Workshop on Object-Oriented Databases, Lisboa, 1999.
5. M. J. Aramburu and R. Berlanga. "A Retrieval Language for Historical Documents". 9th DEXA Conference, LNCS 1460, pp. 216-225, Springer Verlag, 1998.
6. C. Bettini et al. "A glossary of time granularity concepts". In *Temporal Databases: Research and Practice*, LNCS 1399, Springer-Verlag, 1998.
7. "The task definitions, Named Entity Recognition Task Definition" Version 1.4, http://www.itl.nist.gov/iad/894.01/tests/ie-er/er_99/doc/ne99_taskdef_v1_4.ps
8. R. Grishman. "Information Extraction: Tehniques and Challenges. International Summer School" SCIE-97. Edited by Maria Teresa Pazienza, Springer-Verlag, pp 10-27, 1997.
9. Castellón, M. Civit and J. Atserias. "Syntactic Parsing of Unrestricted Spanish Text". International Conference on Language Resources and Evaluation, Granada (Spain), 1998.
10. J. Wiebe et al. "An empirical approach to temporal reference resolution.". Second Conference On Empirical Methods in Natural Language Processing, Providence, 1997.
11. M. Stede, S. Haas, U. Küssner. "Understanding and tracking temporal descriptions in dialogue". 4th Conference on Natural Language Processing, Frankfurt, 1998.
12. D.B. Koen and W. Bender, "Time frames: Temporal augmentation of the news," IBM Systems Journal Vol. 39 (3/4), pp. 597-616, 2000.

Techniques and Tools for the Temporal Analysis of Retrieved Information

Rafael Berlanga[1], Juan Pérez, María José Aramburu[2], and Dolores Llidó[1]

[1] Department of Languages and Computer Systems
[2] Department of Engineering and Science of Computers
Universitat Jaume I, Castellón, Spain
{berlanga,aramburu, dllido}@nuvol.uji.es

Abstract. In this paper we present a set of visual interfaces to query newspapers databases with conditions on their contents, structure and temporal properties. Query results are presented in various interfaces designed to facilitate the reformulation of query conditions and the analysis of the temporal distribution of news. The group of techniques and tools here described has shown useful for the temporal analysis of information from documents in a way that current systems do not support.

1 Introduction

In many professional fields, an important part of the work consists of searching, organising and analysing documents information. Nowadays, by means of the World Wide Web and other computer-based systems, professionals have available huge amounts of searchable digital documents. Analysing information is a research task, mainly driven by the initial expectations of the researcher, and that must start by organising properly the original documents. By these reasons, to improve the results of research activities, current document retrieval systems need to be completed with new tools for organising information. Furthermore, these tools should apply new techniques for the visualisation of retrieved information.

In many areas, it is particularly interesting the analysis of how and when the topics of the documents have taken place. In these cases, researchers look for the antecedents of current happenings, in order to obtain information about their relationships with previous events. Similarly, the task of elaborating stories and chronicles includes the discovery of the time periods that are associated to the occurrences of past events.

Current information and documents retrieval systems do not provide users with the proper tools and interfaces for carrying out these tasks. A possible reason for this resides in that current models of documents representation and retrieval are not prepared for the processing of query results in a similar way to traditional databases. In this paper, we present a set of visual interfaces to analyse the temporal distribution of the information that has been retrieved from a large repository of documents. The practical usefulness of the proposed interfaces has been proven over a large digital library of newspapers [1].

H.C. Mayr et al. (Eds.): DEXA 2001, LNCS 2113, pp. 72–81, 2001.

The rest of the paper is organised as follows. Firstly, the underlying documents database and visual interfaces are briefly described. Sections 4 and 5 explain the techniques applied to analyse the evolution of topics and to evaluate temporal patterns. Section 6 explains how to calculate the relevance of retrieved documents, and section 7 how to implement all these techniques. Conclusions are in section 8.

2 Storage and Retrieval System

The techniques and tools presented in this paper have been developed over a document storage and retrieval system that contains a large amount of digital newspapers. This repository has been implemented by means of the Oracle database management system, with the Context tool for text management, and by following the approach presented in [5]. The data and query models adopted for this system were also presented in previous papers, being denoted TOODOR (Temporal Object-Oriented Document Organisation and Retrieval) [2] and TDRL (Temporal Document Retrieval Language) [3], respectively.

In the TOODOR data model, each document has assigned a time period denoted event time, which expresses the temporal coverage of the relevant events and topics reported by its contents. This temporal attribute is very useful when retrieving information from the documents stored in the repository. Firstly, it allows retrieving with better precision the documents relevant to user queries. Secondly, it can be applied to the evaluation of temporal relationships between document contents, as for example, cause-effect relationships and topic co-occurrence. Finally, it serves to analyse the evolution of the topics described in the documents of the repository. To perform these operations, TDRL provides a complete set of temporal predicates and operators, and a syntax based on OQL. Logically, to be executed by Oracle, TDRL sentences must be previously translated into equivalent SQL queries.

3 Interfaces for Information Retrieval

For users not trained to handle database query languages, the specification of sentences in TDRL can be very difficult, especially when applying its predicates to define temporal relationships between documents. Something similar happens when analysing query answers, because for extracting conclusions from query results, presenting them as tabular raw data combining attributes, text and temporal information is of little help. Instead of this, it is preferable to specify queries in some graphical and intuitive interface, easy to use for non-specialised users, and that can be adapted to many different kinds of query conditions, that is, without loosing the expressiveness of TDRL. Similarly, the graphical presentation of processed query results would improve the capacity of analysis of the users, at the same time that would facilitate the reformulation of queries until satisfactory results were obtained.

Thus, the main objective of this work is to provide a set of interactive user interfaces to analyse the temporal evolution of the contents of a documents repository in an intuitive and useful way.

3.1 Description of the Interfaces

The interface for the definition of query variables is the initial one and it is presented in Figure 1. It allows for the specification of conditions on the structure and contents of the documents in the repository, representing each variable a set of documents that satisfy a group of conditions. In this component, it is also possible to define a temporal window for each variable, so that the documents are restricted to those published during those dates.

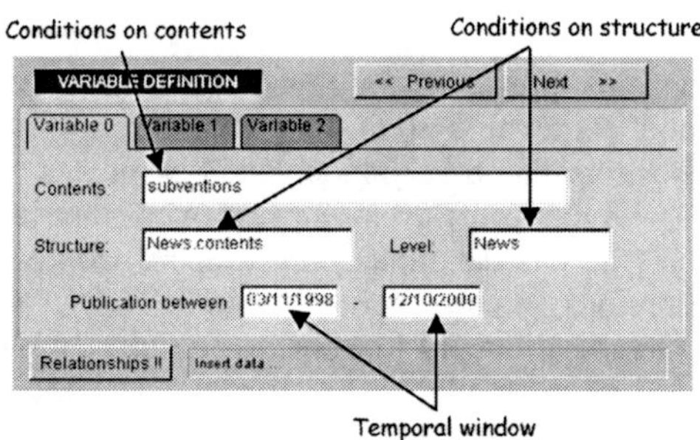

Fig. 1. Interface for the specification of initial query conditions

After specifying the variables of the query, the interface of Figure 2 can be used for defining the temporal relationships that will constitute the temporal pattern to analyse. The set of temporal relationships available is equivalent to the set of temporal predicates of TDRL, being also possible to specify the temporal granularity at which they should be evaluated. In this interface, each query variable is represented by an icon that has associated the number of documents satisfying the corresponding initial conditions. From the variables of the query, the user will be able to choose one of them as the objective of the query, that is, the set of documents to retrieve. This and the rest of parameters of the query can be modified at any moment, so that it is possible to adjust it depending on the intermediate results, or to analyse these results from different perspectives. Each time that these parameters are redefined, the number of documents associated to each variable varies dynamically.

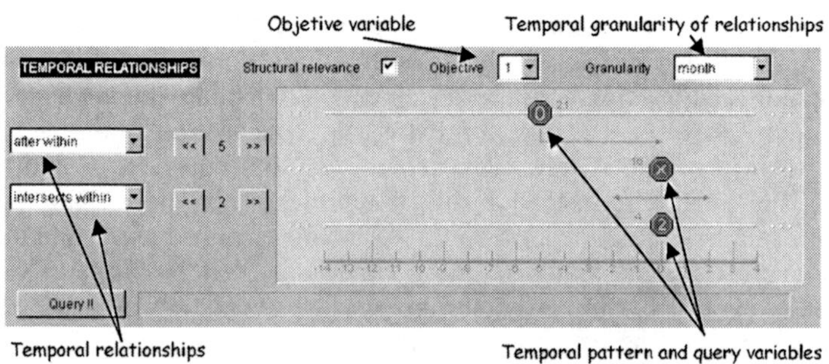

Fig. 2. Interface for the specification of temporal patterns

Finally, in the interface of Figure 3, users can see the list of documents that instantiate the objective variable ordered by relevance. At selecting one of them, its text is visualised together with a histogram of the words that occur more frequently in it. In this interface, users can find out and select some topics to feed back the initial query, and refine the results.

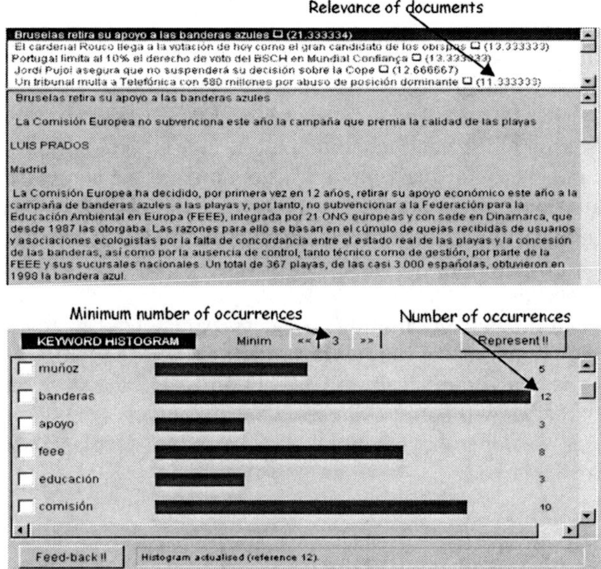

Fig. 3. Visualisation of the texts and histogram of keywords

To visualise the query results in a format that facilitates the temporal analysis of information, users can apply the components in Figure 4, denoted respectively temporal histogram and chronicles. The first component shows a bar chart expressing the relevance of the required information in each span of time of the query temporal window. This relevance is calculated as a combination of the frequency and relevance of the documents found in that period. The second component represents the periods of time during which different occurrences of the event described in the query are happening. Each one of these time periods is calculated by grouping the consecutive event times of the documents in the answer, and therefore, this interface expresses the temporal distribution and frequency of events. Like before, the user can adjust the parameters of these interfaces as needed, and visualise the contents of the documents associated to a chart bar by clicking on it.

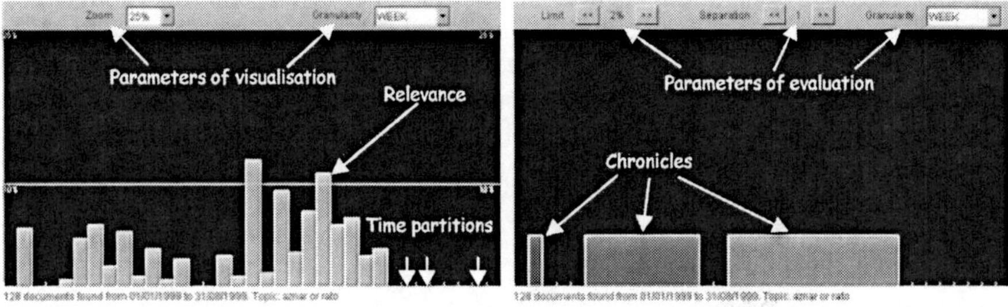

Fig. 4. Query results presented as temporal histograms and chronicles

3.2 Implementation Requirements

The implementation of the interfaces previously described presents several requirements with respect to the processing and refinement of query results. They can be enumerated as follows:

1. The evaluation of the initial query conditions and the temporal pattern is a costly task that needs some preprocessing in order to optimise its execution. By this reason, it is necessary to design some algorithms of optimisation to decide the order of execution of the query conditions.
2. To generate the charts for the temporal histogram and the chronicles, it is required to design algorithms to group query results based on documents event-time periods and query granularity. Furthermore, these algorithms should calculate the relevance of each group, considering in each case several parameters as topic relevance or structural properties.
3. Users can perform the redefinition of query parameters at any time, including changes in the granularity of queries or in their retrieval conditions. Therefore, it is necessary to design some scheme of execution to refine query answers in some efficient way that is, without re-evaluating the query completely.

In the following sections the solutions that we have developed to satisfy these requirements are explained.

4 Analysis of Topic Evolution

In this section, the processing of query results for visualising the temporal evolution of document topics is described. This process applies temporal aggregation functions to group documents by their event times, and in this way, to draw the two presentations of Figure 4. The time model of TDRL [3] provides us with two mechanisms for performing these grouping operations:

1. Regular time partitions based on several time granularities (i.e.: weeks, months, etc.). These are similar to those defined by the Group-By clause of TSQL2 [7].
2. Irregular time partitions defined by documents with intersecting event times. These were denoted Chronicles in [3] and can be applied to analyse the periods of occurrence of the topics described by documents.

4.1 Elaboration of Histograms

After evaluating a query, each regular time partition defined by the chosen granularity level has associated a possibly empty set of documents whose event-time periods fall into the partition. The degrees of relevance of these documents can be combined to calculate the relevance of the whole partition. More specifically, for a retrieval condition IRE, each retrieved document *d* has associated an index of relevance denoted *rel*(*d,* IRE). In our model, this index is evaluated by the normal TF-IDF factor [4], and the degree of structural relevance defined in Section 6.

Given a finite and regular time line partition $\{P_i\}_{i=1...k}$, each time interval P_i will have associated the following functions:

$docs(P_i, \text{IRE}) = \{d \mid event\text{-}time(d) \cap P_i \neq \emptyset \wedge rel(d, \text{IRE})>0\}$

$$sum(P_i, \text{IRE}) = \sum_{\forall d \in docs(P_i, \text{IRE})} rel(d, \text{IRE})$$
$$avg(P_i, \text{IRE}) = sum(P_i, \text{IRE}) \, / \, |docs(P_i)|$$

From these functions, we define the relevance of each partition as:

$$rel(P_i, \text{IRE}) = \alpha \cdot sum(P_i, \text{IRE}) + (1-\alpha) \cdot (sum(P_i,\text{IRE}) \cdot avg(P_i,\text{IRE}) \, / \, |docs(P_i, \text{IRE})|)$$

In other words, the relevance of each time partition is defined as the pondered sum of the relevance of the documents in the partition, and a factor that considers the ratio between the sum of relevances, their average, and the number of documents in the partition. The α constant is experimentally calculated, in our experiments a value of 0.3 produces good results.

The presentation of the function $rel(P_i, \text{IRE})$ (left hand of Figure 4) as a histogram shows the relevance of each time partition with respect to the IRE retrieval condition. This is useful to analyse the distribution of the relevant documents along time.

4.2 Elaboration of Chronicles

For the construction of chronicles, we start from a regular time line partition defined by choosing a granularity level. These partitions are applied to group the documents whose event-time periods intersect, and that have a minimum level of relevance with respect to the query. Each of these groups of documents corresponds to a chronicle and the algorithm that calculates them is presented in Figure 5. The algorithm takes two input parameters: the maximum number of empty time partitions that will be allowed between the documents of a chronicle (separation), and the minimum index of relevance (limit) that must have a partition to be considered as non-empty.

The purpose of the limit parameter is to remove the documents that are not relevant for the query, whereas the separation parameter indicates the degree of tolerance to apply when building the chronicles. In this way, when the limit is increased, the information is more filtered, and when the separation is increased, the information is less fragmented. The right chart of Figure 4 shows the chronicles evaluated from the document distribution represented at the left.

```
Def chronicle_generator(partitions {Pi}i=1..k, limit, separation):
  is_chronicle=false; gaps=0
  for each i (1≤i ≤k):
          if rel(Pi, IRE)<limit and is_chronicle:
                  if gaps>separation:
                          is_chronicle=false
                          create chronicle with the interval from ini to end
                  else: gaps=gaps+1
          elif rel(Pi,IRE)≥limit:
                  if not is_chronicle: gaps=0; ini=i; end=i
                  elif docs(Pi,IRE) ∩ docs(Pi+1,IRE) ≠ Ø: end=i
                  else: gaps=gaps+1
  return the generated chronicles
end chronicle_generator
```

Fig. 5. Algorithm for the elaboration of chronicles

5 Evaluation of Temporal Patterns

In TDRL, a temporal pattern consists of a set of temporal relationships between the event-time periods of the documents in the query (see Figure 2). Here it is an example of TDRL sentence with a temporal pattern defined:

```
select a from #.Finantial.#.Article as a, Column as b, Article as c
where  contains(a, 'agricultural subsidies', 0.7) and contains(b, 'EEC meeting', 0.8)
and    contains(c, 'agricultural agreement', 0.8)
and    after-within(10 day, a.et, b.et) and intersects-within(3 day, b.et, c.et)
```

In a TDRL query, there are a set of query variables $v_1,\ldots,v_n$, with some unary conditions over them $c_1,\ldots,c_n$, and a possibly empty set of temporal relationships between them, R_{ij} with $1\leq i \leq n$, $1 \leq j \leq n$ and $i\neq j$. One of these variables is the objective of the query and denotes the set of documents to retrieve. Initially, a possible strategy of query evaluation could apply join operations over the query variables in the following way:

$$(\mathrm{SEL}_{c1}(v_1) \times_{R1,2} \mathrm{SEL}_{c2}(v_2) \times_{R2,3} \mathrm{SEL}_{c3}(v_3) \times_{R3,4} \mathrm{SEL}_{c4}(v_4) \ldots)$$

However, given that temporal relationships are not very restrictive, the number of tuples that results from the join operations is too large for an efficient execution. By this reason, a new scheme of optimisation must be designed to execute queries.

After considering several alternatives, the best results were obtained with the application of semi-join operators by executing a chain of nested EXISTS as shown in Figure 6. As the order of nesting of the semi-joins modifies the total time of execution, it is important to elaborate a good strategy. In a query, each variable has associated a different group of unary conditions that produces a domain for the variable with a given cardinality. Our strategy consists of nesting more deeply those variables with a larger domain, evaluating the variables with smaller cardinalities in last term. In this way, the total time of execution is reduced.

```
SELECT v1 FROM repository v1 WHERE c1 AND
      EXISTS ( SELECT v2 FROM repository v2 WHERE c2 AND r1,2 AND
            EXISTS (SELECT v4 FROM repository v4 WHERE c4 AND
                  EXISTS ( SELECT v3 FROM repository v3 WHERE c3 AND r3,4 AND r2,3 )
))
```

Fig. 6. Example of nesting of EXISTS clauses

Figure 7 summarises the proposed algorithm of optimisation for queries with a temporal pattern. In it, the objective variable is denoted by v_{obj}, and the cardinality of the domain of a variable v_i by n_i. The *Order*(v_i) operator returns the order of nesting assigned to the variable v_i. Logically, the position of the objective variable is always the first. The *Conjunction* operator returns the *and* of the query conditions. Finally, by means of *Cond*[*o*], all the conditions over the variable with order *o* are represented.

For variables with similar domains, the behavior of this algorithm may be unsatisfactory, given that the only criteria considered by Step 2 is the cardinality of the variables domains. The final algorithm introduces an additional parameter to take into account the temporal relationships defined between variables.

Step 1: Calculate the number of elements of the domain of each non-objective variable:
$\forall v_i \mid v_i \neq v_{obj}$ calcule n_i in paralell
Step 2: Sort the variables and construct the operator *Order*:
Order(v_{obj}) $\leftarrow$ 0;
Order($v_i \neq v_{obj}$) $\leftarrow$ increasing order of the variable v_i in terms of its n_i.
Step 3: Construct the sets of conditions corresponding to each nesting level:
Step 3.1: Inicialise the sets of retrieval conditions associated to each variable:
$\forall v_i$, *Cond*[o] $\leftarrow \{c_i\}$; with o = *Order*(v_i)
Step 3.2: Iterative construction of the sets of conditions:
For each variable v_i so that $v_i \neq v_{obj}$, and with o = *Order*(v_i), taken in reverse order of Step 2:
Step 3.2.1: $\forall v_j \mid$ *Order*(v_j) $< o \wedge \exists r_{i,j}$, *Cond*[o] $\leftarrow$ *Cond*[o] $\cup \{r_{i,j}\}$;
Step 3.2.2: *Cond*[o-1] $\leftarrow$ *Cond*[o-1] $\cup$
{EXISTS SELECT v_i FROM *repository* v_i WHERE *Conjunction*(*Cond*[o])};
Step 4: Construct the final SQL sentence:
SQL-sentence $\leftarrow$ SELECT v_{obj} FROM *repository* v_{obj} WHERE *Conjunction*(*Cond*[0]);

Fig. 7. Algorithm of optimisation of queries with temporal patterns

6 Relevance of Retrieved Documents

In many applications with documents, the logical position of the retrieved elements must be considered to calculate their relevance for the query. For example, with newspapers, the topics that appear in the title, or in the first paragraphs, are more relevant than those that appear in any other part of the news. This section describes how the structural relevance of documents has been included in our query model, and how it can be combined with the relevance based in the frequency of terms (TF-IDF) to calculate a final relevance for each document.

In our implementation of TDRL, each document element has associated a code, denoted *Scode* [5], that indicates its location in the database logical schema. More specifically, this code is a sequence of codified pairs (*elem*, *order*), that describes the schema path followed to insert the element. As it was explained in [5], it is possible to define a function of relevance for these codes as follows:

$$relevance\_struc: \{Scode\} \rightarrow [0, 100]$$

In our current approach, this function has been defined in this way:

$$relevance\_struc(Scode) = \Sigma_{(elem,\, order) \in Scode}\, weight(elem)/(order + 1)$$

The function *weight* returns a degree of relevance for each element of the database logical schema. Those elements considered more relevant in the context of an application (titles, keywords, etc.) will have assigned a higher degree of relevance. Each pair (*elem*, *order*) of a *Scode* will have a degree of relevance that depends on the type of the *elem* component. In the case of multi-valued elements, this relevance degree is modified depending on the order of the element. In this way, it is possible to assign a higher importance to the first paragraphs of the document, as required by many applications.

Finally, to combine the structural relevance with the TF-IDF factor, the next formula is applied:

$$relevance(doc) = (\, 2 \cdot relevance\_struc(doc.SCode) + TF\text{-}IDF_{doc}\,) \,/\, 3$$

This formula has been obtained by experimentation in the newspapers field, and as it can be seen, the structural relevance has higher importance than the frequencies based factor. In other application areas, this ratio may vary.

7 Implementation

To implement the application presented in this paper, we have designed a three-tier architecture with the different components organised as Figure 8 shows. The upper layer contains the components that visualise the interfaces described in Section 3. The components that translate queries into SQL sentences are in the intermediate layer, together with the components to process query answers and generate the results that are visualised in the upper layer. This layer is also in charge of storing intermediate query results, and in this way to accelerate the re-execution of queries when their parameters are modified. Finally, in the lower layer is the Oracle data base server. The application interfaces used to connect the three layers are also represented in this figure.

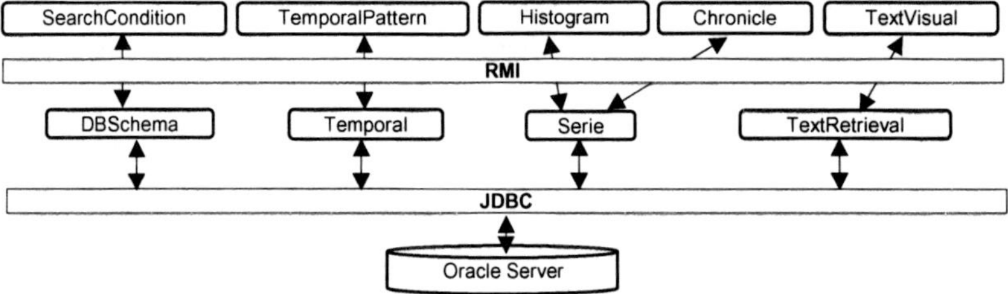

Fig. 8. Proposed multi-tier architecture

The main property of this architecture is that each of the three layers can be developed over independent and heterogeneous platforms. In this way, the database server and client processes can be executed apart from those of the intermediate layer, which are much more costly in time and space. Other interesting property of this architecture is that it offers independence with respect to the location and evolution of the database server. From the point of view of the client components, any changes in the server will be transparent and properly managed by the intermediate layer.

8 Conclusions

In this paper we have presented a set of techniques and tools developed to help in the analysis of the temporal distribution of the happenings described by documents. In our solution we assume that each document has assigned an event-time attribute indicating the time of occurrence of the described happenings. At the moment we are also working on the development of techniques for extracting these attributes from documents texts automatically [6].

As a related work, in [8] the TimeMines system is presented, which starting from a repository of time tagged news, generates timelines indicating the most important topics, how much coverage they receive, and their time spans. The purpose of timelines is similar to our chronicle generators, but they apply statistical methods and text mining techniques to extract knowledge about time-dependent stories.

Our results are being applied to large repositories of newspapers, where users want to discover the relationships between the occurrences of pre-established happenings, or to build the sequence of occurrences that has led to a given event, or simply to write the story of some topic. The interfaces presented have been implemented in Java and can be executed from a web navigator over our newspapers database. A demo is available at http://www3.uji.es/~berlanga/Demos/demo.zip.

Acknowledgments. This work has been funded by the Bancaixa project with contract number PI.1B2000-14, and the CYCIT project with contract number TIC2000-1568-C03-02.

References

1. Aramburu, M. and Berlanga, R.: An Approach to a Digital Library of Newspapers: *Information Processing & Management*, Pergamon Press, Vol. 33(5), pp. 645-661, 1997.
2. Aramburu, M. and Berlanga, R.: Metadata for a Digital Library of Historical Documents: *Proceedings of the 8th International Conference on Database and Expert Systems Applications*. Springer Verlag, LNCS 1308, pp 409-418, 1997.
3. Aramburu, M. and Berlanga, R.: A Retrieval Language for Historical Documents: *Proceedings of the 9th International Conference on Database and Expert Systems Applications*. Springer Verlag, LNCS 1460, pp. 216-225, 1998.
4. Baeza-Yates, R.: Modern information retrieval: Addison-Wesley Longman, 1999.
5. Berlanga, R., Aramburu, M. and Garcia, S.: Efficient Retrieval of Structured Documents from Object-Relational Databases: *Proceedings of the 10th International Conference on Database and Expert Systems Applications*, Springer Verlag, LNCS 1677, pp. 426-435, 1999.
6. Llidó, D., Berlanga, R. and Aramburu, M.: Extracting Temporal References to Assign Document Event-Time Periods: *Proceedings of the 12th International Conference on Database and Expert Systems Applications*, Springer Verlag, 2001.
7. Snodgrass, R.: The TSQL2 Temporal Query Language: Kluwer Academic Press, 1995.
8. Swan, R. and Jensen, D. : Automatic generation of overview timelines: *Proceedings of the 23rd Annual International ACM SIGIR Conference on Research and Development in Information Retrieval*, ACM, pp. 49-56, 2000.

Page Classification for Meta-data Extraction from Digital Collections

Francesca Cesarini, Marco Lastri, Simone Marinai, and Giovanni Soda

Dipartimento di Sistemi e Informatica - Università di Firenze
Via S.Marta, 3 - 50139 Firenze - Italy Tel: +39 055 4796361.
{cesarini, lastri, simone, giovanni}@mcculloch.ing.unifi.it
http://mcculloch.ing.unifi.it/~docproc

Abstract. Automatic extraction of meta-data from collections of scanned documents (books and journals) is a useful task in order to increase the accessibility of these digital collections. In order to improve the extraction of meta-data, the classification of the page layout into a set of pre-defined classes can be helpful. In this paper we describe a method for classifying document images on the basis of their physical layout, that is described by means of a hierarchical representation: the Modified X-Y tree. The Modified X-Y tree describes a document by means of a recursive segmentation by alternating horizontal and vertical cuts along either spaces or lines. Each internal node of the tree represents a separator (a space or a line), whereas leaves represent regions in the page or separating lines. The Modified X-Y tree is built starting from a symbolic description of the document, instead of dealing directly with the image. The tree is afterwards encoded into a fixed-size representation that takes into account occurrences of tree-patterns in the tree representing the page. Lastly, this feature vector is fed to an artificial neural network that is trained to classify document images. The system is applied to the classification of documents belonging to Digital Libraries, examples of classes taken into account for a journal are "title page", "index", "regular page". Some tests of the system are made on a data-set of more than 600 pages belonging to a journal of the 19th Century.

1 Introduction

Meta-data are "data about data" and generally provide high level information about a set of data. In the field of Digital Libraries, appropriate meta-data allow users to effectively access digital material. When dealing with scanned books and journals three main categories of meta-data can be taken into account: administrative (e.g. the ISBN code of a publication), descriptive (e.g. the number of pages of a book), and structural (e.g. the title of a chapter). Whereas administrative and descriptive meta-data are frequently already available in electronic standard formats, or can be easily extracted from library cards, structural meta-data can be computed from a digital book only after an accurate analysis of the content of the book. In order to automatically extract structural meta-data from a scanned book, document image analysis techniques can be taken into

H.C. Mayr et al. (Eds.): DEXA 2001, LNCS 2113, pp. 82–91, 2001.

account. An useful task for the automatic extraction of structural meta-data is page classification, that is appropriate for both extracting page-level meta-data and narrowing the set of pages where to look for some meta-data. Page-level meta-data have a one-to-one correspondence of the meta-data with a physical page. Significant examples are the table of contents page, and pages containing pictures. Page classification can be helpful also for locating meta-data which appear only in some pages, for instance identifying the title page can help to retrieve the title of a book.

Page classification has been addressed with different objectives and methods. Most work concerned form classification methods that are aimed at selecting an appropriate reading method for each form to be processed [1,2]. Other approaches address the problem of grouping together similar documents in business environments, for instance separating business letters from technical papers [3]. In the last few years the classification of pages in journals and books received more attention [4,5]. An important aspect of page classification are the features that are extracted from the page and used as input to the classifier. *Sub-symbolic* features, like the density of black pixels in a region, are computed directly from the image. *Symbolic* features, for instance the number of horizontal lines, are extracted from a segmentation of the image. *Structural* features (e.g. relationships between objects in the page) can be computed from a hierarchical description of the document. *Textual* features, for instance presence of some keywords, are obtained from the text in the image recognized by an OCR (Optical Character Recognition) program.

In this paper we describe a page classification system aimed at splitting pages (belonging to journals or monographs in Digital Libraries) on the basis of the type of page; the input is a structural representation of the page layout. Examples of classes taken into account are *advertisement*, *first page*, and *index*. The structural representation is based on the Modified X-Y tree, a hierarchical description of page layout. The page is classified by using artificial neural networks (multilayer perceptron trained with Back-propagation) working on an appropriate encoding of the Modified X-Y tree corresponding to the page. This page classifier is under development in the domain of the METAe European project[1]. METAe is focused on the semi-automatic extraction of structural meta-data from scanned documents of historical books and journals, in order to make the digital conversion of printed material more reliable in terms of digital preservation. Key components of the project are layout analysis, page classification and specialized OCR for automatic meta-data extraction.

The paper is organized as follows, in Section 2 we describe the structural representation of documents, in Section 3 we analyze the proposed classification method. Experimental results are reported in Section 4, while conclusions are drawn in Section 5.

---

[1] METAe: the Metadata engine. http://meta-e.uibk.ac.at

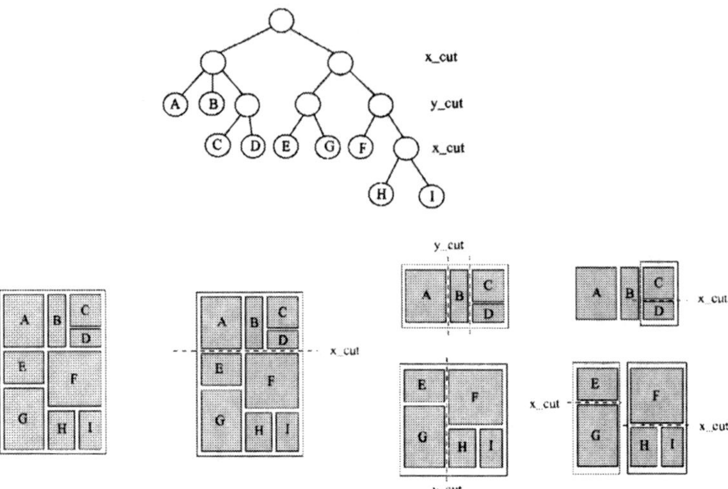

Fig. 1. Example of X-Y tree decomposition. In the upper-left part of the image we show the original page. The three images in the lower part describe the position of cuts at different levels of segmentation.

2 Document Layout Representation

The structure of the page is represented with a hierarchical representation (the Modified X-Y tree, MXY tree in the following) that is an extension of the classical X-Y tree representation. In this section, we first review the X-Y tree decomposition algorithm, and afterwards describe the MXY tree extension that is designed in order to deal with documents containing lines. Finally the building of the MXY tree starting from a symbolic description of the page is analyzed.

2.1 The Modified X-Y Tree

The Modified X-Y tree [6] is an extension of the X-Y tree designed in order to deal with documents containing lines in their layout. The X-Y tree [7] is a top-down data-driven method for page layout analysis. The basic assumption behind the X-Y tree segmentation is the property that elements of the page (columns, paragraphs, figures) are generally laid out in rectangular blocks. Furthermore, the blocks can usually be grouped in such a way that blocks that are adjacent to one another within a group have one dimension in common. The method consists in using thresholded projection profiles in order to split the document into successively smaller rectangular blocks [8]. A projection profile is the histogram of the number of black pixels along parallel lines through the document (see Figure 3 for an example). Depending on the direction of parallel lines the profile can be horizontal or vertical. To reduce the effects of noise, frequently a thresholded projection profile is considered. The blocks are split by alternately making horizontal and vertical "cuts" along white spaces which are found by using the thresholded projection profile. The splitting process is stopped when

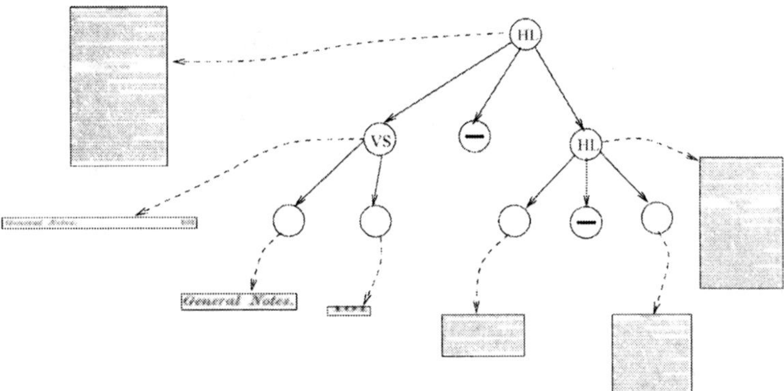

Fig. 2. The MXY tree of a page. Dotted lines point out to images of regions described in the corresponding nodes. VL (HL) denote Vertical (Horizontal) cutting Line; VS (HS) denote Vertical (Horizontal) cutting Space. Nodes with a line indicate leaves corresponding to line separators.

a cutting space (either horizontal or vertical) cannot be found or when the area of the current region is smaller than a pre-defined threshold. The result of such segmentation can be represented in a X-Y tree, where the root is for the whole page, the leaves are for blocks of the page, whereas each level alternately represents the results of horizontal (x_cut) or vertical (y_cut) segmentation. Figure 1 contains an example of a page segmented into blocks and the corresponding X-Y tree representation.

Two improvements to this approach have been proposed in literature. The *lossless optimization* proposed in [9] is based on the consideration that it is sufficient to perform the projections only up to the threshold T_p. In [10], projections profiles are obtained by using bounding boxes of connected components instead of single pixels in order to reduce the computational cost for calculating the projection profile. This method is tightly related to the symbolic extraction of MXY tree that we propose in Section 2.2.

When dealing with documents containing lines, the X-Y tree algorithm can give rise to uneven segmentations for the presence of regions delimited by lines. The MXY tree extends the basic X-Y tree approach by taking into account splitting of regions into sub-parts by means of cuts along horizontal and vertical lines, in addition to the classical cuts along white spaces. Each node of an MXY tree is associated either to a region of the page or to a horizontal or vertical line. In particular, internal nodes can have four labels (corresponding to two cutting directions, and two cutting ways), and leaves can have 4 labels. Figure 2 shows an example of a page with the corresponding MXY-tree.

2.2 Symbolic Building of Modified X-Y Tree

When using the X-Y tree (and also the MXY tree) for document segmentation, the purpose is to extract the blocks composing the page, and the algorithm is applied directly to the document image. To this purpose, appropriate algorithms

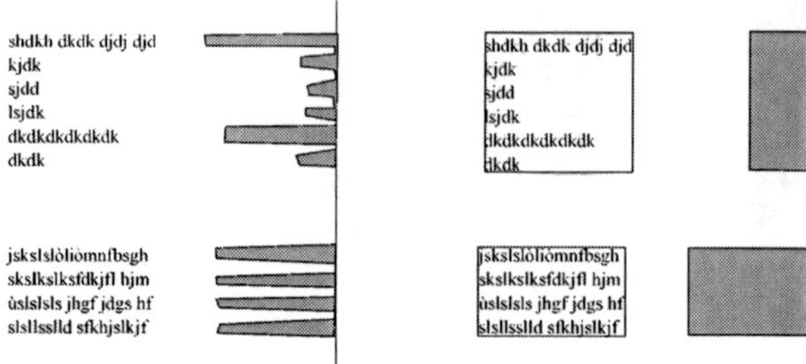

Fig. 3. Two approaches for computing the projection profile of textual regions. Left: the classic method which computes the profile directly from the image. Right: the profile is computed taking into account an uniform contribution for each block.

must be considered for the extraction and analysis of the projection profile, and for the location of separating lines (Section 2.1). However, the MXY tree data structure can be taken into account also for hierarchically representing the layout of the page, and this representation is helpful for understanding the meaning of items in the page, and also for page classification. In order to build an MXY representation of a document already split into its constituents blocks (e.g. provided by a commercial OCR), we developed an algorithm for the symbolic extraction of the MXY tree of a segmented document. Another advantage of the use of this algorithm is the possibility of integrating the algorithm with other approaches (e.g. bottom-up methods) that are less sensitive to the skew of the page, but which provide less structured representations of the page.

The input to the algorithm is a list of rectangular regions (corresponding to the objects in the page), and the list of horizontal and vertical lines. Since the input format is quite simple, various segmentation algorithms can be easily adapted in order to deal with this algorithm. The page classifier that we describe in this paper (Section 3), was integrated with a commercial OCR that is able to locate regions corresponding to text, and regions corresponding to images. Since horizontal and vertical lines are not provided by the OCR package, we look for them in zones of the image not covered by regions found by the OCR. Moreover, in order to locate segmentation points corresponding to horizontal and vertical white spaces, we compute an approximate projection profile (Figure 3). This profile is computed by considering an uniform contribution from each region extracted by the OCR both in the horizontal and in vertical direction. The amount of contribution to the profile depends on the average number of black pixels in each region, and this value can be either computed directly from the image or estimated on the basis of the number of characters in the region. A side effect of this approach is that noise in the image (not included in segmented regions) does not affect the MXY tree building. This approach is similar to the use of connected components for computing profiles [10] described in Section 2.1. The main difference is that in our approach we use whole regions instead of connected components, and the contribution to the projection profile is related to the density of the region.

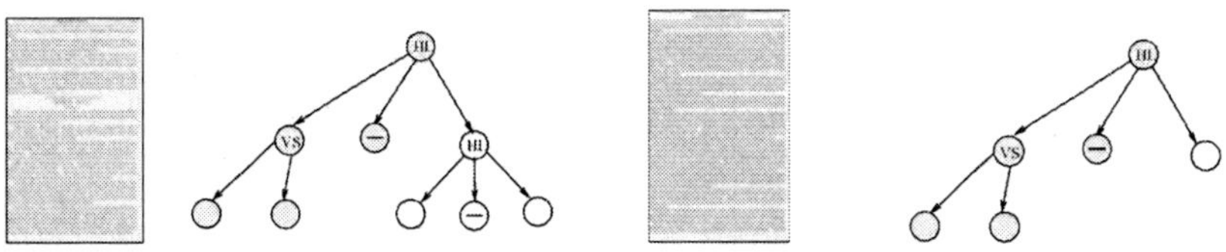

Fig. 4. A common subtree between the MXY trees of two pages of the same class.

3 Page Classification

Page classification is performed with a sequence of operations that is aimed at encoding the hierarchical structure of the page into a fixed-size feature vector. MXY trees are coded into a fixed-size representation that takes into account the occurrences of some specific tree-patterns in the tree corresponding to each document image. Lastly, this feature vector is fed to an MLP that is trained to classify document images according to the labels assigned to training data. Most classifiers (e.g. decision trees and neural networks) require a fixed-size feature vector as input. Some approaches have been considered for the mapping of a graph-based representation into a fixed-size vector. One approach (e.g. [11]) is based on the assignment of some pre-defined slots of the vector to each node and edge of the graph. This approach is appropriate when the maximum size of the graph is bounded, and when a robust ordering algorithm of nodes and edges is available. Another method is based on generalized N-grams [12], and the tree structure of logical documents is represented by probabilities of local tree node patterns similar to mono-dimensional N-grams, which are generalized in order to deal with trees. The generalization is obtained by considering "vertical" N-grams (describing ancestor and child relations) in addition to the more usual "horizontal" N-grams (corresponding to sibling relations).

In this paper, we use an encoding method that is used for the classification of trees describing the page layout. The basic idea that is behind this coding is the observation that similar layout structures often have similar sub-trees in the corresponding MXY representation (Figure 4). In real cases, because of noise and content variability, we cannot expect to find exactly the same sub-tree in all the trees of a given class. For instance, a block of text can be sometimes split into two or more sub-parts for other documents. Due to this size variability of the common sub-trees, we describe each tree by counting the occurrences of some tree-patterns composed by three nodes. This approach is somehow similar to generalized N-grams [12]. The main difference with respect to generalized N-grams is that the tree-patterns considered are composed by three nodes connected one to the other by a path in the tree. On the contrary, generalized N-grams include also patterns made by three siblings without taking into account their parent. Trees composed by three nodes can have two basic structures: one composed by a root and two children (referred to as balanced tree-pattern), and one composed by a root, a child, and a child of the second node. Four labels can be assigned to each internal node: HS, VS (for cuts along spaces), HL, VL (for cuts along lines). Each leaf can have four labels: hl (Horizontal line), vl (vertical line), T

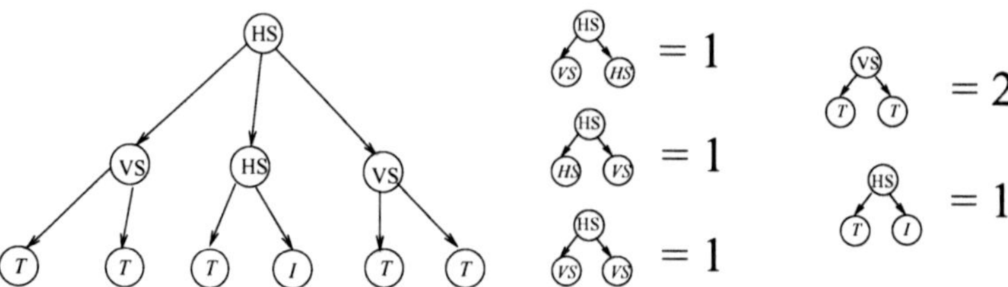

Fig. 5. A simple MXY tree; in the right part of the figure we show the balanced tree patterns in the tree, with the corresponding occurrences. Non adjacent nodes are considered in the pattern having HS as root and VS as leaves.

(text region), and I (image). Leaves of tree-patterns can correspond either to a leaf of the MXY tree or to an internal node, consequently internal nodes of a tree pattern can have four values, whereas leaves can have eight values. Taking into account all the combinations of labels, 512 possible tree patterns can be defined. A special care is required by the balanced tree-patterns. Since siblings in the MXY tree can be ordered according to their horizontal or vertical position (depending on the cutting direction described in their parent), the relative position between contiguous blocks is preserved in this description. However, due to noise (or simply variable layouts of the documents), one sub-tree can differ from the reference one only for a node that is inserted between two representative siblings. In order to overcome this problem, when computing the tree-patterns appearing in a MXY tree, we look also for non-adjacent children (Figure 5), and this is another difference with respect to generalized N-grams.

The encoding just described takes into account only discrete attributes in the nodes of the tree. To consider also some information about the size of regions considered in the tree nodes, we added four values in the feature vector, that take into account the size of textual blocks belonging to the same tree-pattern. Textual blocks are labeled as "small" or "big" depending on the ratio of their area with respect to the area of the page. Blocks with area lower than a fixed threshold are labeled as "small", whereas larger blocks are labeled as "big". Therefore each tree-pattern containing textual leaves can belong to one of four classes according to the possible combinations of size labels of the leaves. The four features bringing size information are obtained by computing the relative distribution of each of the four combinations in the MXY tree. The addition of these features provides increased classification performance as discussed in the following section.

After extracting the vectorial representation of the MXY tree corresponding to a document, various algorithms can be taken into account for the actual classification. In this paper we addressed the problem with a classical MLP-based classifier (trained with the Backpropagation algorithm), which takes the normalized feature vector as input, whereas outputs describe, with an one-hot coding, the membership of each pattern. One problem with such an approach (that is common to other classification methods) is the large size of the feature vector, since many combinations of node labels can be considered. From a prac-

Fig. 6. Examples of the classes considered in our experiments. From left to right: advertisement, first page, index, receipts, regular.

tical point of view, we can easily find out that few tree-patterns can be found in actual documents of a given data set, as we will analyze in the next section.

4 Experimental Results

We made a set of experiments in order to evaluate the improvements in classification that can be achieved by considering the information about the relative size of textual blocks, and by using non-adjacent leaves when computing occurrences of balanced tree-patterns. Moreover, we analyzed the results that can be achieved using few patterns in the training set. The experiments are made with a data-set of pages belonging to a historical journal: the *American Missionary*, that is available in the on-line Digital Library *Making of America*[2]. We considered five classes having different layout, and appearing in each issue of the journal. Samples of the 5 classes are shown in Figure 6. Some classes have a very stable layout (e.g. the first page and the index), whereas other classes have a more variable layout (e.g. the advertisement class) and give rise to most errors.

For each experiment the documents are split into two classes: one is used for training, and the other is considered for testing purposes. The training set was furtherly divided into three sub-sets in order to perform a three-folder cross validation that allowed us to find the optimal number of epochs required for MLP training. A simple feature selection step was performed by removing from the feature vectors all the items that never appear in the training set. In this way we used a feature vector containing only 177 elements, instead of the 512 possible combinations of labels assigned to nodes. The classification results obtained with an MLP having 177 inputs, 20 hidden nodes, and 5 outputs are summarized in Table 1. A pattern is rejected when the difference between the highest MLP output and the next one is lower than 0.2 (the outputs are in the range [0,1]).

As described in Section 3, in order to take into account the size of textual blocks, we added to the basic features four block size features. First, we selected the most appropriate threshold (that discriminates among "small" and "big"

[2] Document images can be downloaded from the web site of the collection: *http://cdl.library.cornell.edu/moa/*.

Table 1. Confusion table of the test set, when using the basic features.

	Output class					
True class	adv	first page	index	receipts	regular	Reject
adv	37	0	1	6	5	2
first page	0	56	0	0	0	3
index	0	0	53	0	0	0
receipts	0	0	0	57	1	1
regular	0	1	0	2	79	0

Table 2. Confusion table of the test set, when adding the textual block size features considering a threshold of 28 %.

	Output class					
True class	adv	first page	index	receipts	regular	Reject
adv	36	0	0	6	4	5
first page	0	58	1	0	0	0
index	0	0	52	0	0	1
receipts	1	0	0	56	1	1
regular	0	0	0	1	79	3

blocks), by evaluating the performances with different values of this threshold. From this experiment we selected a threshold value of 28 % as an optimal one (the corresponding confusion table is reported in Table 2). Comparing Table 2 with Table 1 we can see that a lower error rate is achieved when introducing the information about the block area.

Another experiment was performed in order to evaluate the gain that can be achieved when considering tree-patterns generated from non-adjacent siblings. In this experiment we generated feature vectors considering only adjacent siblings. Also in this case the threshold for size selection of blocks was 28 %, and we obtained an error rate of 6.8 % that is higher than the 4.7 % achieved when considering non-adjacent siblings. The last experiment concerns an empirical analysis of the requirements of the proposed method in terms of number of training samples (Table 3). From this experiment we can see that also with few training patterns, the performance are not excessively deteriorated.

5 Conclusions

We propose a method for the classification of document images belonging to Digital Libraries, that can be useful for the automatic extraction of structural meta-data. The method is based on a vectorial encoding of the MXY tree representing the document image. Each item in the feature vector describes the occurrences of some tree-patterns in the tree corresponding to the document. After an extensive test on a data-base of more than 600 pages we can conclude that an encoding taking into account non-contiguous siblings (and that uses information on the relative size of textual siblings) is appropriate; moreover with this approach we are able to obtain reasonable performances also when dealing

Table 3. Classification error versus number of training samples. Each value corresponds to the average of 10 tests obtained by randomly selecting the corresponding number of training samples. The test set is fixed and is composed by 300 samples different from those taken into account for training.

Error (%)	17.4	10.9	9.2	9.5	7.1	6.5	5.7	5.4	5.3	4.7
Number of training samples	30	60	90	120	150	180	210	240	270	300

with few training samples. Future work is related to the use of other feature selection approaches, and on tests on other kinds of documents. Moreover, other classifiers will be taken into account in place of the MLP-based classifier considered in this paper. We would like to thank Oya Y. Rieger from Cornell University for her help in collecting data taken into account for our experiments.

References

1. S. L. Taylor, R. Fritzson, and J. Pastor, "Extraction of data from preprinted forms," *Machine Vision and Applications*, vol. 5, no. 5, pp. 211–222, 1992.
2. Y. Ishitani, "Flexible and robust model matching based on association graph for form image understanding," *Pattern Analysis and Applications*, vol. 3, no. 2, pp. 104–119, 2000.
3. A. Dengel and F. Dubiel, "Clustering and classification of document strcture -a machine learning approach," in *Proceedings of the Third International Conference on Document Analysis and Recognition*, pp. 587–591, 1995.
4. J. Hu, R. Kashi, and G. Wilfong, "Document image layout comparison and classification," in *Proceedings of the Fifth International Conference on Document Analysis and Recognition*, pp. 285–288, 1999.
5. C. Shin and D. Doermann, "Classification of document page images based on visual similarity of layout structures," in *SPIE 2000*, pp. 182–190, 2000.
6. F. Cesarini, M. Gori, S. Marinai, and G. Soda, "Structured document segmentation and representation by the modified X-Y tree," in *Proceedings of the Fifth International Conference on Document Analysis and Recognition*, pp. 563–566, 1999.
7. G. Nagy and S. Seth, "Hierarchical representation of optically scanned documents," in *Proceedings of the International Conference on Pattern Recognition*, pp. 347–349, 1984.
8. G. Nagy and M. Viswanathan, "Dual representation of segmented technical documents," in *Proceedings of the First International Conference on Document Analysis and Recognition*, pp. 141–151, 1991.
9. T. M. Ha and H. Bunke, "Model-based analysis and understanding of check forms," *International Journal of Pattern Recognition and Artificial Intelligence*, vol. 8, no. 5, pp. 1053–1081, 1994.
10. J. Ha, R. Haralick, and I. Phillips, "Recursive X-Y cut using bounding boxes of connected components," in *Proceedings of the Third International Conference on Document Analysis and Recognition*, pp. 952–955, 1995.
11. A. Amin, H. Alsadoun, and S. Fischer, "Hand-printed arabic character recognition system using an artificial network," *Pattern Recognition*, vol. 29, no. 4, pp. 663–675, 1996.
12. R. Brugger, A. Zramdini, and R. Ingold, "Modeling documents for structure recognition using generalized N-grams," in *Proceedings of the Fourth International Conference on Document Analysis and Recognition*, pp. 56–60, 1997.

A New Conceptual Graph Formalism Adapted for Multilingual Information Retrieval Purposes

Catherine Roussey, Sylvie Calabretto, and Jean-Marie Pinon

LISI, INSA of Lyon, 20 Avenue A. Einstein 69621 VILLEURBANNE Cedex, FRANCE
{croussey,cala,pinon}@lisi.insa-lyon.fr

Abstract. In this paper, a graph formalism is proposed to describe the semantics of document in a multilingual context. This formalism is an extension of the Sowa formalism of conceptual graphs [8] in which two new concepts are added: *vocabulary* and *term*. Based on recent works, we propose a new comparison operator between graphs taking the specific needs of information retrieval into account. This operator is the core of the comparison function used in our multilingual documentary system, called SyDoM. SyDoM manages XML documents for virtual libraries. An English collection of articles has been used to evaluate SyDoM. This first evaluation gives better results than traditional Boolean documentary system.

Keywords. Digital libraries, information retrieval, knowledge engineering, information modeling, conceptual graph, multilingual information retrieval system

1 Introduction

The emergence of web applications has deeply transformed the access to information. Particularly document exchanges between countries are facilitated. Consequently, document collections contain documents written in various languages. Thanks to this technical revolution, libraries became digital libraries able to manage multilingual collections of documents and Information Retrieval (IR) systems retrieve documents written in different languages.

To take the multilingual aspect of such collections into account, it is necessary to improve the representation of documents. In multilingual context, terms are no more sufficient to express the document contents. It is thus necessary to work on elements more significant than terms, namely "concepts".

Moreover, according to recent works [2], semantics of indices have to be enhanced. A solution is to transform the usual list of keywords into a more complex indexing structure, in which relations link concepts. That is the reason why, the Sowa formalism of **Conceptual Graph** (CG) [4] is chosen to express the document contents. Nevertheless, one of the drawbacks of IR system based on CG is the time consuming effort to carry on a retrieval process. Moreover, the CG matching function produce lot of

H.C. Mayr et al. (Eds.): DEXA 2001, LNCS 2113, pp. 92–101, 2001.

silence[1] that decrease the recall rate. In this article, an adaptation of the CG formalism is proposed in order to improve the retrieval effectiveness of our system.

First of all, the principles of the CG formalism, used in IR system, are presented. Afterwards, we propose the semantic graph formalism and its corresponding matching function. Finally, the validation of our proposition is presented.

2 Conceptual Graph Formalism

A conceptual graph [4] is a graph composed of concept nodes, relation nodes and edges that link concept and relation nodes. A concept node is labeled by a *type* and possibly a *marker*. *Type* corresponds to a semantic class and *marker* is a particular instance of a semantic class. In the same way, a relation node is only labeled by a *type*. A specialization relation, noted $\leq$ classifies concept types and relation types in a hierarchy. Specialization relations are useful to compare graphs by the Sowa projection operator. This operator defines a specialization relation between graphs. As shown in Figure 1, there is a projection of a graph *H* onto a graph *G* if there exists in *G* a "*copy*" of the graph *H* where all nodes are specialization of *H* nodes.

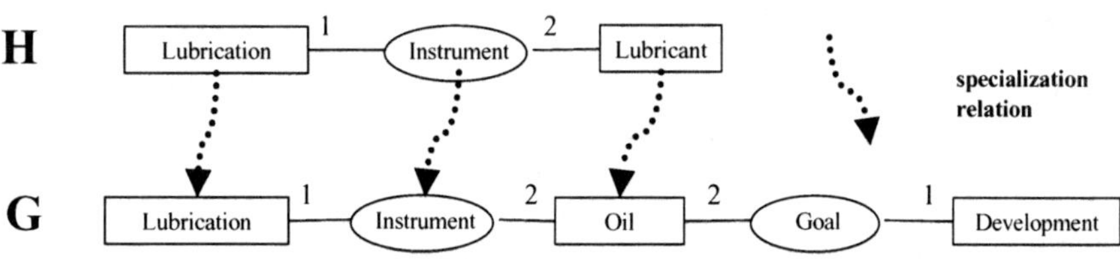

Fig. 1. A projection example.

the matching function of IR system is based one the projection operator. For example, the previous graph *H* represents a query and the graph *G* corresponds to the document index. If there is a projection of *H* onto *G* the document is considered relevant for the query.

3 State of the Art

Several IR systems, based on CG formalism, have been developed:

1. Ounis and all [2] have developed the RELIEF system. Even if in graph theory a projection cannot be performed in polynomial time, one of the contributions of this work is to propose a fast matching function, based on inverted file and acceleration tables.
2. Genest [1] has noted that the projection operator is not adapted to IR purpose. First, matching functions based on projection give Boolean results. Secondly, document is not relevant for a query, if its index graph contains only one node, which is a

[1] Relevant documents not retrieved (forgotten) by the IR system..

generalization of the query node or if graph structures are different. In order to take such problems into account, Genest defines some transformations on conceptual graph. Moreover a mechanism is proposed to order sequences of transformations. As a consequence, the matching function based on projection becomes a ranking function and orders relevant documents for a query.

Our proposition considers improvements of the Ounis and Genest methods, by proposing a graph matching function optimized for the information retrieval needs. First a graph formalism is presented allowing the document description in a multilingual context.

4 Semantic Graph Model

We have simplified the CG formalism to get it closer to a documentary language. So, concepts are limited to generic concepts because descriptors represent main notions and not individual object. Moreover, the comparison between graphs should not be based on graph structure.

4.1 Semantic Thesaurus

We proposed an extension of the Sowa formalism in which two kinds of knowledge are identified in a semantic thesaurus:

1. Domain knowledge organizes domain entity in two hierarchies of types. Types defined a pivot language used to represent document and query graphs
2. Lexical knowledge associates terms, belonging to a vocabulary, to types. Terms are used to present semantic graphs in the user's native language.

4.1.1 Domain Conceptualization or Support

A support S is a 2-tuple $S = (T_C, T_R)$ such as:

- T_C is a set of concept types partially ordered by the specialization relation, noted $\leq$, and it has a greatest element, noted T.
- T_R *is a* set of binary relation types[2] partially ordered by $\leq$ and it has a greatest element, noted T_2.

4.1.2 Semantic Thesaurus

A semantic thesaurus, noted M, (composed of P languages) is a 3-tuple $M = (S, V, \lambda)$ such as :

- S is a support (cf. § 4.1.1).
- V is a set of vocabularies, split into set of terms belonging to the same language (a vocabulary). $V = V_{L1} \cup V_{L2} \cup \ldots \cup V_{Lj} \cup \ldots \cup V_{LP}$ such as V_{Lj} is a set of terms belonging to the language Lj.

[2] In general, a type of relation can have any arity, but in this paper, relations are considered to be only binary relations like case relations or thematic roles associated with verbs [5].

– $\lambda = \{ \lambda^{VL1}_{\ldots,} \lambda^{VLj}_{\ldots,} \lambda^{VLP} \}$ is a set of P mapping such as $\lambda^{VLj} : T_C \cup T_R \rightarrow V_{Lj}$ is a mapping λ^{VLj} *(t)* which associates a term of the language $Lj \in V_{Lj}$ with a type $t \in T_C \cup T_{R}$.

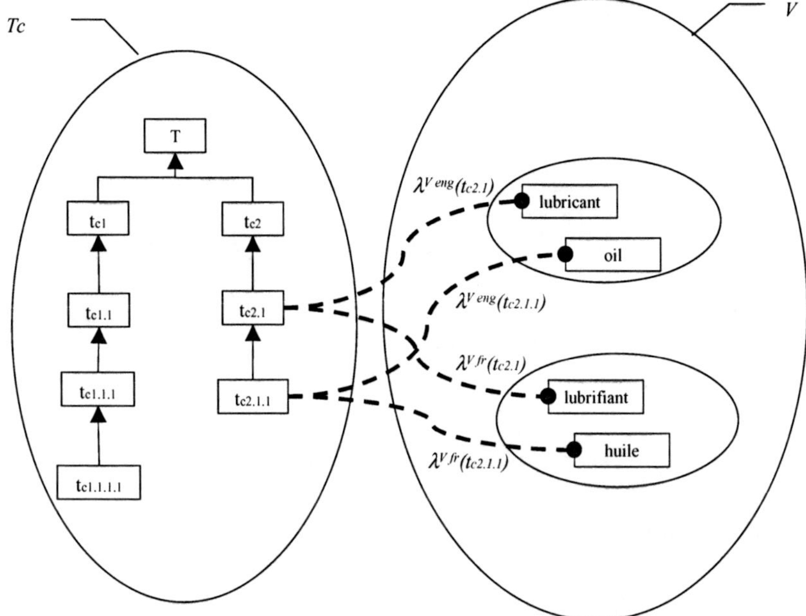

Fig. 2. An example of semantic thesaurus.

Figure 2 presents an example of mapping λ, in which V is composed of two vocabularies: an English vocabulary, noted V_{eng} , and a French vocabulary, noted V_{fr}. Each concept type is linked to a term of each vocabulary. For example, the concept type $t_{c2.1}$ is linked to the English term λ^{Veng} $(t_{c2.1})$*="lubricant"* and it is also linked to a French term λ^{Vfr} $(t_{c2.1})$*="lubrifiant"*.

From this semantic thesaurus defining domain knowledge and lexical knowledge, our formalism, called **semantic graph**, is defined. A semantic graph is a set of concept nodes connected to each other by relations. Comparing to Conceptual Graph, the notion of **arch** is defined as a couple of concept nodes labeled by a relation type.

4.2 Semantic Graph

A semantic graph is a 4-tuple $Gs = (C, A, \mu, \nu)$ related to a semantic thesaurus M, such that :

– C is a set of concept nodes[3] contained in *Gs*.
– $A \subset C \times C$ is a set of arches contained in *Gs*.

[3] In this article, "concept node" and "concept" are equivalent expressions.

- $\mu: C \rightarrow T_C, A \rightarrow T_R$. μ is a mapping, which associated for each concept node, $c \in C$, a label $\mu(c) \in T_C$, $\mu(c)$ is also called the ***type*** of c. μ associated for each arch, $a \in A$, a label $\mu(a) \in T_R$. $\mu(a)$ is also called the ***type*** of a.
- ν is a set of mapping $\nu = \{\nu^{VL1}, \ldots, \nu^{VLj}, \ldots, \nu^{VLP}\}$ such that the mapping $\nu^{VLj}: C \cup A \rightarrow V_{Lj}$ associates an arch, $a \in A$ or a concept node, $c \in C$, with a term of the language Lj. $\nu(a)^{VLj} \in V_{Lj}$ is called the ***term*** of a for the language Lj. $\nu(c)^{VLj} \in V_{Lj}$ is called the ***term*** of c for the language Lj.

Thanks to previous definitions, there exist different representations for the same semantic graph depending of the label used.

1. The first representation of semantic graph labels each graph component with its type. So for a concept node c, its label is $\mu(c)$.
2. The second kind of semantic graph representation labels each graph component with a term chose in a vocabulary defined in the semantic thesaurus. So for a concept node c, its label is $\nu(c) = \lambda(\mu(c))$. Indeed, there exist several representations of the same semantic graph depending of the chosen vocabulary.

Now, the pseudo-projection operator comparing semantic graph is presented.

4.2.1 Pseudo-Projection Operator

The pseudo projection operator is an extension of the projection operator of Sowa conceptual graph. A pseudo projection defines morphism between graphs with less constraints than the Sowa original operator does. The pseudo projection of a graph H in a graph G means that, H is "comparable" to G. The formalization of the pseudo-projection operator is as follows:

Pseudo projection operator: A pseudo projection from a semantic graph $H = (C_H, A_H, \mu_H, \nu_H)$ to a semantic graph $G = (C_G, A_G, \mu_G, \nu_G)$ is a mapping Π: $A_H \rightarrow A_G$, $C_H \rightarrow C_G$ which associates an arch of H with an arch of G and a concept node of H with a set of concept nodes of G. Π has the following properties:

1. Arches are preserved but concept nodes cannot be preserved.
2. Types can be restricted or increased.

Remark: A concept node can have several images by Π. As a consequence, the pseudo-projection operator makes no differences between a graph containing several concept nodes typed by t_c, for example, and another graph containing a unique concept node typed by t_c. That is the reason why, a semantic graph is considered to contain a unique concept node by type. That is defined as the *normal form* of a graph.

4.3 Similarity Functions

The result of the pseudo-projection operator between graphs is Boolean: pseudo-projection exists or does not exist. Often, a matching function of IR system orders the result documents. Thus, a similarity function between graphs is defined. To this end, various similarity functions are presented. Each similarity function returns a normalized float value ranging between 0 and 1. First, thanks to the specialization relation, a similarity function between types will be defined.

4.3.1 Similarity Function between Types

The similarity function, noted *sim,* between types is an asymmetrical function. *sim* is defined as follows:

- If two types are not comparable then the similarity function returns 0.
- If two types are identical then the similarity function returns 1.
- If a type $t_{2.1}$ specializes another type t_2 directly, i.e. there is not intermediate type between $t_{2.1}$ and t_2 in the type hierarchy, then the similarity function returns a constant value lower than 1. For example, $sim(t_{C2.1}, t_{C2}) = V_G$ and $sim(t_{C2}, t_{C2.1}) = V_S$ V_S and V_G are fixed arbitrary.
- If a type $t_{2.1.1}$ specializes another type t_2 not directly, i.e. there is an intermediate type $t_{2.1}$ between $t_{2.1.1}$ and t_2 in the type hierarchy then the similarity function between $t_{2.1.1}$ and t_2 is the product of the similarity functions between $(t_{2.1.1}, t_{2.1})$ and $(t_{2.1}, t_2)$. For example, $sim(t_{C2.1.1}, t_{C2}) = sim(t_{C2.1.1}, t_{C2.1}) \times sim(t_{C2.1}, t_{C2})$

4.3.2 Similarity Function between Arches

The similarity function between two arches, noted Sim_A computes the average of the similarity type between each arch component.
For example, a_H is an arch such as $a_H = (c_H, c'_H)$ and $\mu(a_H) = t_{rH}$ and a_G is an arch such as $a_G = (c_G, c'_G)$ and $\mu(a_G) = t_{rG}$.

$$Sim_A \ (a_H, \ a_G) = \frac{sim(t_{rH}, \ t_{rG}) + \ sim(\mu(c_H), \ \mu(c_G)) + sim(\mu(c'_H), \ \mu(c'_G))}{3} \quad (1)$$

4.3.3 Similarity Function between Graphs

The similarity function, noted sim_G, between a graph $H = (C_H, A_H, \mu_H, \nu_H)$ and a graph $G = (C_G, A_G, \mu_G, \nu_G)$ is the average of the similarity function between each arch and concept node of H and their images in G by Π. Because a concept node can have several images by Π, we take the maximum of the similarity function between a concept and their images.

$$\text{simG} \ (H,G) = \frac{\sum_{a \in A_H} sim_A(a, \ \Pi(a)) + \sum_{c \in C_H} Max(sim(\mu_H(c), \ \mu_G(\Pi(c))))}{|C_H| + |A_H|} \quad (2)$$

5 Algorithms

After introducing our semantic graph formalism, we shall concentrate on the implementation of the matching function between graphs. Search algorithms evaluate all the pseudo-projections from the query graph to the index graphs stored in the database.

During indexing, all the possible query subgraphs comparable with each index graph are memorized. Finding documents relevant for a query graph consists of identifying the subgraphs of the current query corresponding to possible query subgraphs, stored beforehand in the database.

The semantic graphs are composed of arches and concept nodes. Thus the document content are represented by two different indices: a list of arches and a list of concepts, from which the normal form of semantic graph can be rebuilt.

Following the works of Ounis [2], our algorithms are based on the association of inverted files and acceleration tables. The inverted file groups in the same entry all the documents indexed by an indexing entity. The acceleration tables store, for each indexing entity, the list of the comparable entities as well as the result of the similarity function between the comparable entity and the indexing entity. The acceleration tables pre-compute all possible generalizations or specializations of the indexing entities. The construction of the inverted file and the acceleration table is done off-line, as part of the indexing procedure.

There is a search algorithm for each kind of indexing entities. Because these two algorithms are similar, only the search algorithm for arches is presented.

```
GraphReq is a query graph composed of nbArc arches,
noted ArcReq, and of nbConcept concept nodes
ListDocResult is a list of documents weighted by the
value of the similarity function between the query
graph GraphReq and the index graph of document.

For each arch ArcReq of GraphReq do
   ListArcIndex ←FindArcComparable(ArcReq)
   For each(ArcIndex, WeightArc) of ListArcIndex do
     ListDoc ← FindListDoc(ArcIndex)
     For each Doc of ListDoc do
       If ListDocArc.Belong(Doc) Then
         Weight ←ListDocArc.FindWeight(Doc)
         NewWeight ← max(Weight, WeightArc)
         ListDocArc.ReplaceWeight(Doc, NewWeight)
       Else
         ListDocArc.Add(Doc, WeightArc)
       Endif
     Endfor
   Endfor
   For each (Doc, WeightArc) of ListDocArc do
     If ListDocResult.Belong(Doc) Then
       Weight ← ListDocResult.FindWeight(Doc)
```

```
        NewWeight ← Weight + (WeightArc / (nbArc +
nbConcept))
        ListDocResult.ReplaceWeight(Doc, NewWeight)
      Else
        ListDocResult.Add(Doc, WeightArc)
   Endfor
Endfor
```

FindArcComparable(**ArcReq**) returns a list of arches (**ArcIndex**) comparable to **ArcReq**, weighted by the value of the similarity function between **ArcReq** and **ArcIndex**, noted **WeightArc**.

Usually, the cost of a projection operator between graphs is prohibitive, because in graph theory, it is equivalent to find a morphism between indefinite structures. To overcome this problem, the graph structure is limited, that is to say a semantic graph is supposed to contain a unique concept node .

6 Experiment

An information retrieval module based on semantic graph has been developed. This module is a component of the documentary system called SyDoM (Multilingual Documentary System) [3]. The system is implemented in JAVA on top of a relational database system. SyDoM is composed of three modules:

1. The semantic thesaurus module manages the documentary language (addition of new vocabulary or new domain entity).
2. The indexing module indexes and annotates XML documents with semantic graph using a set of metadata associated to the semantic thesaurus.
3. The retrieval module performs multilingual retrieval. The users choose their query component in the semantic thesaurus presented in their native language. As example, Figure 3 presents a French query graph dealing with combustion model.

The library Doc'INSA associated to the National Institute of Applied Science of Lyon gives us a test base of English articles. These articles deal with mechanics and they are called *pre-print of the Society of Automotive Engineers (SAE)*. During manual indexing, only titles are taken in account. For our first experiments, approximately fifty articles were indexed manually and ten queries were performed.

Our system was compared to the Boolean system used at Doc'INSA. Indices of Doc'INSA system were generated automatically from those of SyDoM, to avoid variability. Figure 4 presents this evaluation. The average precision were computed for ten recall intervals. We can notice that relation treatments and hierarchy inference improve significantly the quality of the answer even for manual indexing.

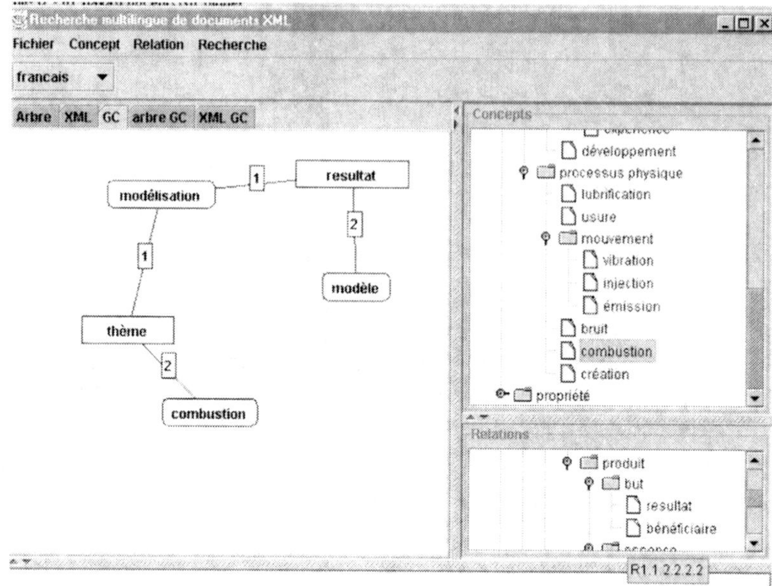

Fig. 3. SyDoM interface is composed of a graph editor and a browser of semantic thesaurus (concept and relation hierarchies). To build their queries, users select graph component in the hierarchies. The graph can be presented in different language by changing the language vocabulary thanks to the top left button.

7 Conclusion

In this paper, a solution was proposed to the challenge of using complex knowledge representation formalism for information retrieval purpose. Moreover, a graph formalism is presented to describe the semantics of document contents in a multilingual

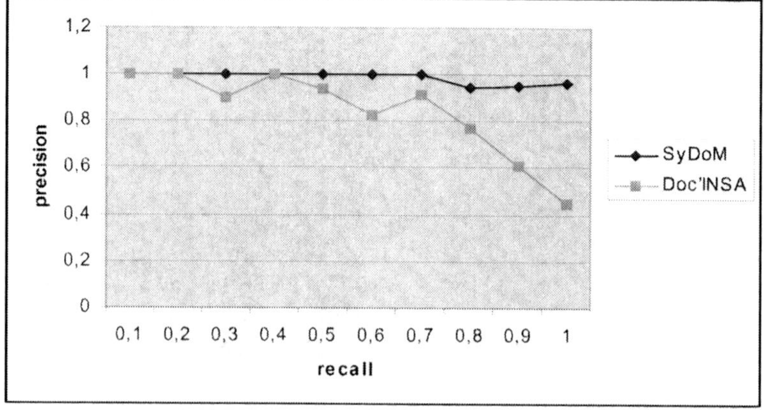

Fig. 4. Evaluation of SyDoM (threshold = 0.6) and Doc'INSA system.

context. This formalism is an extension of the Sowa formalism of Conceptual Graphs. Starting from recent works, a new comparison operator between graphs is proposed not based on graph structure comparison. This choice enables us to decrease the complexity of the search algorithm. Our proposition is validated by the prototype SyDoM dedicated to digital libraries. SyDoM has been evaluated by querying in French, an English collection of articles. At this stage, SyDoM gives better results than traditional documentary system. The next step would be to compare our system with RELIEF [2] or Genest One [1]. Such experiments would test if our proposition -comparing to the extension of CG proposed by Genest- could have similar results with less computational time.

References

1. D. Genest. Extension du modèle des graphes conceptuels pour la recherche d'information. PhD Thesis, Montpellier University, Montpellier, France (2000).
2. I. Ounis, M. Pasça. RELIEF: Combining Expressiveness and Rapidity into a Single System. Proceedings of 18th SIGIR Conference, Melbourne, Australia, (1998), 266-274.
3. C. Roussey, S. Calabretto, J. M. Pinon Un modèle d'indexation pour une collection multilingue de documents. Proceedings of the 3rd CIDE Conference, Lyon, France, (2000) 153-169.
4. J. Sowa. Conceptual Structures: Information Processing in Mind and Machine. The System Programming Series, Addison Wesley publishing Company, (1984).
5. J. Sowa. Knowledge Representation: Logical, Philosophical, and Computational Foundations. Brooks Cole Publishing Co., Pacific Grove, CA., (2000).

Flexible Comparison of Conceptual Graphs*

M. Montes-y-Gómez [1], A. Gelbukh [1], A. López-López [2], and R. Baeza-Yates [3]

[1] Center for Computing Research (CIC), National Polytechnic Institute (IPN), 07738, Mexico.
mmontesg@susu.inaoep.mx, gelbukh@cic.ipn.mx
[2] Instituto Nacional de Astrofísica, Optica y Electrónica (INAOE), Mexico.
allopez@inaoep.mx
[3] Departamento de Ciencias de la Computación, Universidad de Chile, Chile.
rbaeza@dcc.uchile.cl

Abstract. Conceptual graphs allow for powerful and computationally affordable representation of the semantic contents of natural language texts. We propose a method of comparison (approximate matching) of conceptual graphs. The method takes into account synonymy and subtype/supertype relationships between the concepts and relations used in the conceptual graphs, thus allowing for greater flexibility of approximate matching. The method also allows the user to choose the desirable aspect of similarity in the cases when the two graphs can be generalized in different ways. The algorithm and examples of its application are presented. The results are potentially useful in a range of tasks requiring approximate semantic or another structural matching – among them, information retrieval and text mining.

1 Introduction

In many application areas of text processing – e.g., in information retrieval and text mining – simple and shallow representations of the texts are commonly used. On one hand, such representations are easily extracted from the texts and easily analyzed, but on the other hand, they restrict the precision and the diversity of the results.

Recently, in all text-oriented applications there is a tendency to use richer representations than just keywords, i.e., representations with more types of textual elements. Under this circumstance, it is necessary to have the appropriate methods for the comparison of two texts in any of these new representations.

In this paper, we consider the representation of the texts by conceptual graphs [9,10] and focus on the design of a method for comparison of two conceptual graphs. This is a continuation of the research reported in [15].

Most methods for comparison of conceptual graphs come from information retrieval research. Some of them are restricted to the problem of determining if a graph, say, the query graph, is completely contained in the other one, say, the document graph [2,4]; in this case neither description nor measure of their similarity is obtained. Some other, more general methods, do measure the similarity between two conceptual graphs, but they typically describe this similarity as the set of all their common elements allowing duplicated information [3,6,7]. Yet other methods are focused on question answering [12]; these methods allow a flexible matching of the graphs, but they do not compute any similarity measure.

* Work done under partial support of CONACyT, CGEPI-IPN, and SNI, Mexico.

H.C. Mayr et al. (Eds.): DEXA 2001, LNCS 2113, pp. 102–111, 2001.

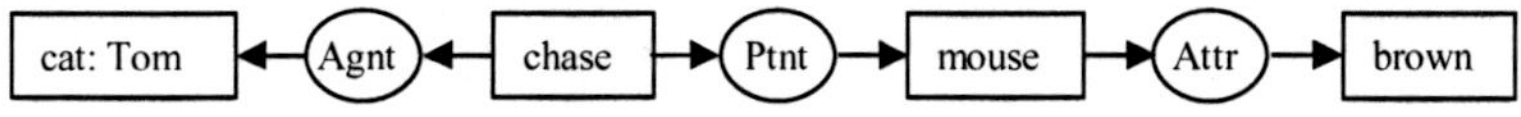

Fig. 1. A simple conceptual graph

The method we propose is general but flexible. First, it allows measuring the similarity between two conceptual graphs as well as constructing a precise description of this similarity. In other words, this method describes the similarity between two conceptual graphs both quantitatively and qualitatively. Second, it uses domain knowledge – a thesaurus and a set of *is-a* hierarchies – all along the comparison process, which allows considering non-exact similarities. Third, it allows visualizing the similarities between two conceptual graphs from different points of view and selecting the most interesting one according to the user's interests.

The paper is organized as follows. The main notions concerning conceptual graphs are introduced in section 2. Our method for comparison of two conceptual graphs is described in section 3, matching of conceptual graphs being discussed in subsection 3.1 and the similarity measure in subsection 3.2. An illustrative example is shown in section 4, and finally, some conclusions are discussed in the section 5.

2 Conceptual Graphs

This section introduces well-known notions and facts about conceptual graphs.

A conceptual graph is a finite oriented connected bipartite graph [9,10]. The two different kinds of nodes of this bipartite graph are concepts and relations.

Concepts represent entities, actions, and attributes. Concept nodes have two attributes: type and referent. Type indicates the class of the element represented by the concept. Referent indicates the specific instance of the class referred to by the node. Referents may be generic or individual.

Relations show the inter-relationships among the concept nodes. Relation nodes also have two attributes: valence and type. Valence indicates the number of the neighbor concepts of the relation, while the type expresses the semantic role of each one.

Figure 1 shows a simple conceptual graph. This graph represents the phrase "*Tom is chasing a brown mouse*". It has three concepts and three relations. The concept [cat: Tom] is an individual concept of the type *cat* (a specific cat Tom), while the concepts [chase] and [mouse] are generic concepts. All relations in this graph are binary. For instance, the relation (attr) for *attribute* indicates that the mouse has brown color. The other two relations stand for *agent* and *patient* of the action [chase].

Building and manipulating conceptual graphs is mainly based on six canonical rules [9]. Two of these rules are the generalization rules: unrestrict and detach.

Unrestrict rule generalizes a conceptual graph by unrestricting one of it concepts either by type or referent. Unrestriction by type replaces the type label of the concept with some its supertype; unrestriction by referent substitutes individual referents by generic ones.

Detach rule splits a concept node into two different nodes having the same attributes (type and referent) and distributes the relations of the original node between the two resulting nodes. Often this operation leads to separating the graph into two unconnected parts.

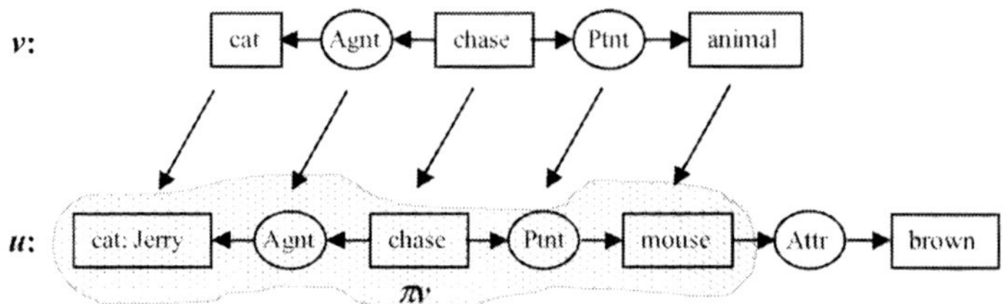

Fig. 2. Projection mapping π: $v \rightarrow u$ (the highlighted area is the projection of v in u).

A conceptual graph v derivable from the graph u by applying a sequence of generalization rules is called a generalization of the graph u; this is denoted as $u \leq v$. In this case there exists a mapping π: $v \rightarrow u$ with the following properties (πv is a subgraph of u called a projection of v in u; see Figure 2):[1]

- For each concept c in v, πc is a concept in πv such that $type(\pi c) \leq type(c)$. If c is an individual concept, then $referent(\pi c) = referent(c)$.
- For each relation node r in v, πr is a relation node in πv such that $type(\pi r) = type(r)$. If the i-th arc of r is linked to a concept c in v then the i-th arc of πr must be linked to πc in πv.

The mapping π is not necessarily one-to-one, i.e., two different concepts or relations can have the same projections ($x_1 \neq x_2$ and $\pi x_1 = \pi x_2$, such situation results from application of detach rule). In addition, it is not necessarily unique, i.e., a conceptual graph v can have two different projections π and π' in u, $\pi' v \neq \pi v$.

If u_1, u_2, and v are conceptual graphs such that $u_1 \leq v$ and $u_2 \leq v$, then v is called a common generalization of u_1 and u_2. A conceptual graph v is called a maximal common generalization of u_1 and u_2 if and only if there is no other common generalization v' of u_1 and u_2 (i.e., $u_1 \leq v'$ and $u_2 \leq v'$) such that $v' \leq v$.

3 Comparison of Conceptual Graphs

The procedure we propose for the comparison of two conceptual graphs is summarized in Figure 3. It consists of two main stages. First, the two conceptual graphs are matched and their common elements are identified. Second, their similarity measure is computed as a relative size of their common elements. This measure is a value between 0 and 1, 0 indicating no similarity between the two graphs and 1 indicating that the two conceptual graphs are equal or semantically equivalent.

The two stages use domain knowledge and consider the user interests. Basically, the domain knowledge is described as a thesaurus and as a set of user-oriented *is-a* hierarchies. The thesaurus allows considering the similarity between semantically related concepts, not necessarily equal, while the *is-a* hierarchies allow determining similarities at different levels of generalization.

---

[1] Here, the functions $type(c)$ and $referent(c)$ return the type and referent of the concept c, respectively; the function $type(r)$ returns the type of the relation r. By $type(a) \leq type(b)$ we denote the fact that $type(b)$ is a supertype of $type(a)$.

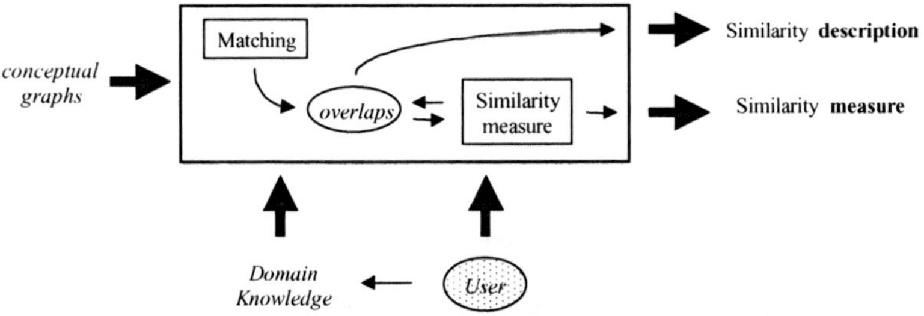

Fig. 3. Comparison of conceptual graphs

3.1 Matching Conceptual Graphs

Matching of two conceptual graphs allows finding all their common elements, i.e., all their common generalizations. Since the projection is not necessarily one-to-one and unique, some of these common generalizations may express redundant (duplicated) information. In order to construct a precise description of the similarity of the two conceptual graphs (e.g. G_1 and G_2), it is necessary to identify the sets of compatible common generalizations. We call such sets *overlaps* and define them as follows.

Definition 1. A set of common generalizations $O = \{g_1, g_2, \ldots, g_n\}$ is called *compatible* if and only if there exist projection maps[2] $\{\pi_1, \pi_2, \ldots, \pi_n\}$ such that the corresponding projections in G_1 and G_2 do not intersect, i.e.:

$$\bigcap_{i=1}^{n} \pi_{G_1} g_i = \bigcap_{i=1}^{n} \pi_{G_2} g_i = \varnothing$$

Definition 2. A set of common generalizations $O = \{g_1, g_2, \ldots, g_n\}$ is called *maximal* if and only if there does not exist any common generalization g of G_1 and G_2 such that either of the conditions holds:

1. $O' = \{g_1, g_2, \ldots, g_n, g\}$ is compatible,
2. $\exists i : g \leq g_i$, $g \neq g_i$, and $O' = \{g_1, \ldots, g_{i-1}, g, g_{i+1}, \ldots, g_n\}$ is compatible.

(i.e., O cannot be expanded and no element of O can be specialized while preserving the compatibility of O.) .

Definition 3. A set $O = \{g_1, g_2, \ldots, g_n\}$ of common generalizations of two conceptual graphs G_1 and G_2 is called overlap if and only if it is compatible and maximal.

Obviously, each overlap expresses completely and precisely the similarity between two conceptual graphs. Therefore, the different overlaps may indicate different and independent ways of visualizing and interpreting their similarity.

Let us consider the algorithm to find the overlaps. Given two conceptual graphs G_1 and G_2, the goal is to find all their overlaps. Our algorithm works in two stages.

At the first stage, all similarities (correspondences) between the conceptual graphs are found, i.e., a kind of the product graph is constructed [6]. The product graph P expresses the Cartesian product of the nodes and relations of the conceptual graphs,

---

[2] Recall that projection map and thus the projection for a given pair v, u is not unique.

but only considers those pairs with non-empty common generalizations. The algorithm is as follows:

For each concept c_i of G_1
  For each concept c_j of G_2
    $P \leftarrow$ the common generalization of c_i and c_j.
For each relation r_i of G_1
  For each relation r_i of G_2
    $P \leftarrow$ the common generalization of r_i and r_j.

At the second stage, all maximal sets of compatible elements are detected, i.e., all overlaps are constructed. The algorithm we use in this stage is an adaptation of a well-known algorithm for the detection of all frequent item sets in a large database [1].

Initially, we consider that each concept of the product graph is a possible overlap. At each subsequent step, we start with the overlaps found in the previous step. We use these overlaps as the seed set for generating new large overlaps. At the end of the step, the overlaps of the previous step that were used to construct the new overlaps are deleted because they are not maximal overlaps and the new overlaps are the seed for the next step. This process continues until no new large enough overlaps are found. Finally, the relations of the product graph are inserted into the corresponding overlaps. This algorithm is as follows:

$Overlaps_1 = \{$all the concepts of $P\}$
For ($k = 2$; $Overlaps_{k-1} = \varnothing$; $k{+}{+}$)
    $Overlaps_k \leftarrow$ overlap_gen ($Overlaps_{k-1}$)
    $Overlaps_{k-1} \leftarrow Overlaps_{k-1} - \{$elements covered by $Overlaps_k\}$
$MaxOverlaps = \bigcup_k Overlaps_k$
For each relation r of P
  For each overlap O_i of $MaxOverlaps$
    If the neighbor concepts of r are in the overlap O_i
      $O \leftarrow r$

The *overlap_gen* function takes as argument $Overlaps_{k-1}$, the set of all large (k-1) overlaps and returns $Overlaps_k$, the set of all large k-overlaps. Each k-overlap is constructed by joining two compatible (k-1) overlaps. This function is defined as follows:

$$Overlaps'_k = \{X \cup X' \mid X, X' \in Overlaps_{k-1}, |X \cap X'| = k-2\}$$
$$Overlaps_k = \{X \in Overlaps'_k \mid X \text{ contains } k \text{ members of } Overlaps_{k-1}\}$$

with the exception of the case $k = 2$ where

$$Overlaps_2 = \{X \cup X' \mid X, X' \in Overlaps_1, X \text{ and } X' \text{ are compatibles concepts}\}.$$

In the next section we give an illustration of matching of two simple conceptual graphs; see Figure 4.

It is well-known [5,6] that matching conceptual graphs is an NP-complete problem. Thus our algorithm has exponential complexity by the number of common nodes of the two graphs. This does not imply, however, any serious limitations for its practical application for our purposes, since the graphs we compare represent the results of a shallow parsing of a single sentence and thus are commonly small and have few nodes in common. Since our algorithm is an adaptation of the algorithm called

APRIORI [1] that was reported to be very fast, ours is also fast (which was confirmed in our experiments); in general, algorithms of exponential complexity are used quite frequently in data mining. For a discussion of why exponential complexity does not necessarily present any practical problems, see also [14].

3.2 Similarity Measure

Given two conceptual graphs G_1 and G_2 and one of their overlaps, O, we define their similarity s as a combination of two values: their conceptual similarity s_c and their relational similarity s_r.

The conceptual similarity s_c depends on the common concepts of G_1 and G_2. It indicates how similar the entities, actions, and attributes mentioned in both conceptual graphs are. We calculate it using an expression analogous to the well-known Dice coefficient [8]:[3]

$$s_c = 2\left(\sum_{c\in\bigcup O}\left(weight(c)\times\beta\left(\pi_{G_1}c,\pi_{G_2}c\right)\right)\right)\Big/\left(\sum_{c\in G_1}weight(c)+\sum_{c\in G_2}weight(c)\right)$$

Here $\bigcup O$ is the union of all graphs in O, i.e., the set of all their nodes and arcs; the function *weight* (c) gives the relative importance of the concept c, and the function $\beta(\pi_{G_1}c, \pi_{G_2}c)$ expresses the level of generalization of the common concept $c \in \bigcup O$ relative to the original concepts $\pi_{G_1}c$ and $\pi_{G_2}c$. The function *weight*(c) is different for nodes of different types; currently we simply distinguish entities, actions, and attributes:

$$weight(c) = \begin{cases} w_E & \text{if } c \text{ represents an entity} \\ w_V & \text{if } c \text{ represents an action} \\ w_A & \text{if } c \text{ represents an attribute} \end{cases}$$

where w_E, w_V, and w_A are positive constants that express the relative importance of the entities, actions, and attributes respectively. Their values are user-specified. In the future, a less arbitrary mechanism for assigning weights can be developed.

The function $\beta(\pi_{G_1}c, \pi_{G_2}c)$ can be interpreted as a measure of the semantic similarity between the concepts $\pi_{G_1}c$ and $\pi_{G_2}c$. Currently we calculate it as follows:[4]

$$\beta\left(\pi_{G_1}c,\pi_{G_2}c\right) = \begin{cases} 1 & \text{if } type\left(\pi_{G_1}c\right)=type\left(\pi_{G_2}c\right) \text{ and } referent\left(\pi_{G_1}c\right)=referent\left(\pi_{G_2}c\right) \\ depth\,/\left(depth+1\right) & \text{if } type\left(\pi_{G_1}c\right)=type\left(\pi_{G_2}c\right) \text{ and } referent\left(\pi_{G_1}c\right)\neq referent\left(\pi_{G_2}c\right) \\ 2d_c\,/\left(d_{\pi_{G_1}c}+d_{\pi_{G_2}c}\right) & \text{if } type\left(\pi_{G_1}c\right)\neq type\left(\pi_{G_2}c\right) \end{cases}$$

---

[3] Because of its simplicity and normalization properties, we take the Dice coefficient as the basis for the similarity measure we proposed.

[4] In this definition, the condition *type*($\pi_{G_1}c$) = type($\pi_{G_2}c$) is also satisfied when *type*($\pi_{G_1}c$) and *type*($\pi_{G_2}c$) are synonyms, which is defined by the thesaurus.

In the first condition, the concepts $\pi_{G_1} c$ and $\pi_{G_2} c$ are the same and thus $\beta(\pi_{G_1} c, \pi_{G_2} c) = 1$.

In the second condition, the concepts $\pi_{G_1} c$ and $\pi_{G_2} c$ refer to different individuals of the same type, i.e., different instances of the same class. In this case, $\beta(\pi_{G_1} c, \pi_{G_2} c) = depth / (depth + 1)$, where *depth* indicates the number of levels of the *is-a* hierarchy. Using this value, the similarity between two concepts having the same type but different referents is always greater that the similarity between any two concepts with different types.

In the third condition, the concepts $\pi_{G_1} c$ and $\pi_{G_2} c$ have different types, i.e., refer to elements of different classes. In this case, we define $\beta(\pi_{G_1} c, \pi_{G_2} c)$ as the semantic similarity between *type*($\pi_{G_1} c$) and *type*($\pi_{G_2} c$) in the *is-a* hierarchy. We calculate it using a similar expression to one proposed in [11]. In this third option of our formula, d_i indicates the distance – number of nodes – from the type i to the root of the hierarchy.

The relational similarity s_r expresses how similar the relations among the common concepts in the conceptual graphs G_1 and G_2 are. In other words, the relational similarity indicates how similar the neighbors of the overlap in both original graphs are (see more details in [13]). We define the immediate neighbor of the overlap O in a conceptual graph G_i, $N_O(G_i)$, as the set of all the relations connected to the common concepts in the graph G_i:

$$N_O(G_i) = \bigcup_{c \in O} N_{G_i}(\pi_{G_i} c), \text{ where } N_G(c) = \{r \mid r \text{ is connected to } c \text{ in } G\}.$$

With this, we calculate the relational similarity s_r using the following expression – also analogous to the Dice coefficient:

$$s_r = 2\left(\sum_{r \in O} weight_O(r)\right) \Bigg/ \left(\sum_{r \in N_O(G_2)} weight_{G_1}(r) + \sum_{r \in N_O(G_2)} weight_{G_2}(r)\right)$$

Here $weight_G(r)$ indicates the relative importance of the conceptual relation r in the conceptual graph G.[5] This value is calculated by the neighbor of the relation r. This kind of assignment guarantees the homogeneity between the concept and the relation weights. Hence, we compute $weight_G(r)$ as:

$$weight_G(r) = \sum_{c \in N_G(r)} weight(c) \Big/ |N_G(r)|, \quad \text{where } N_G(r) = \{c \mid c \text{ is connected to } r \text{ in } G\}.$$

Now that we have defined the two components of the similarity measure, s_c and s_r, we combine them into a cumulative measure s. First, the combination should be roughly multiplicative, for the cumulative measure to be proportional to each of the two components. This would give the formula $s = s_c \times s_r$. However, we note that the relational similarity has a secondary importance, because its existence depends on the existence of some common concept nodes and because even if no common relations

---

[5] This function also holds for overlaps because an overlap is also a set of conceptual graphs (see the definition 3.1).

exist between the common concepts of the two graphs, there exists some level of similarity between them. Thus, while the cumulative similarity measure is proportional to s_c, it still should not be zero when $s_r = 0$. So we smooth the effect of s_r using the expression:

$$s = s_c \times (a + b \times s_r)$$

With this definition, if no relational similarity exists between the two graphs (s_r = 0) then the general similarity only depends on the value of the conceptual similarity. In this situation, the general similarity is a fraction of the conceptual similarity, where the coefficient a indicates the value of this fraction.

The coefficients a and b reflect user-specified balance ($0 < a, b < 1, a + b = 1$). The coefficient a indicates the importance of the part of the similarity exclusively dependent on the common concepts and the coefficient b expresses the importance of the part of the similarity related with the connection of these common concepts. The user's choice of a (and thus b) allows adjusting the similarity measure to the different applications and user interests. For instance, when $a > b$, the conceptual similarities are emphasized, while when $b > a$, stresses structural similarities.

4 An Illustrative Example

Our method for comparison of two conceptual graphs is very flexible. On one hand, it describes qualitatively and quantitatively the similarity between the two graphs. On the other hand, it considers the user interests all along the comparison process.

To illustrate this flexibility, we compare here two simple conceptual graphs. The first one represents the phrase "Gore criticizes Bush" and the second one the phrase "Bush criticizes Gore".[6] The figure 4 shows the matching of these two graphs. Notice that their similarity can be described in two different ways, i.e., by two different and independent overlaps. The overlap O_1 indicates that in both graphs "a candidate criticizes another candidate", while the overlap O_2 indicates that both graphs talk about Bush, Gore, and an action of criticizing.

The selection of the best overlap, i.e., the most appropriate description of the similarity, depends on the application and the user interests. These two parameters are modeled by the similarity measure. Table 1 shows the results for the comparison of these two conceptual graphs. Each result corresponds to a different way of evaluating and visualizing the similarity of these graphs. For instance, the first case emphasizes the structural similarity, the second one the conceptual similarity, and the third one focuses on the entities. In each case, the best overlap and the longer similarity measure are highlighted.

5 Conclusions

In order to start using more complete representations of texts than just keywords in the various applications of text processing, one of the main prerequisites is to have an appropriate method for the comparison of such new representations.

[6] Bush and Gore were candidates at U.S. president elections in 2001.

We considered representation of the texts by conceptual graphs and proposed a method for comparison of any pair of conceptual graphs. This method works in two main stages: matching conceptual graphs and measuring their similarity. Matching is mainly based on the generalization rules of conceptual graph theory. Similarity measure is based on the idea of the Dice coefficient but it also incorporates some new characteristics derived from the conceptual graph structure, for instance, the combination of two complementary sources of similarity: conceptual and relational similarity.

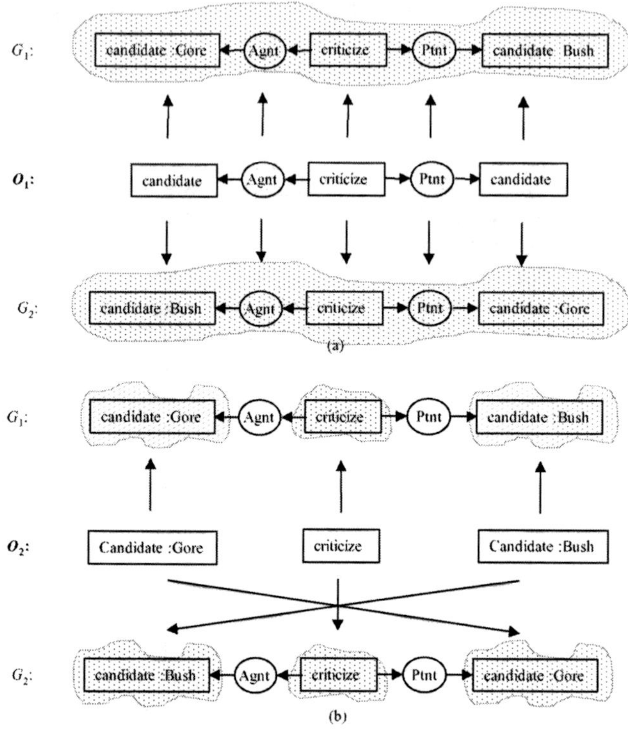

Fig. 4. Flexible matching of two conceptual graphs

Our method has two interesting characteristics. First, it uses domain knowledge, and second, it allows a direct influence of the user.

The domain knowledge is expressed in the form of a thesaurus and a set of small (shallow) *is-a* hierarchies, both customized by a specific user. The thesaurus allows considering the similarity between semantically related concepts, not necessarily equal, while the *is-a* hierarchies allow determining the similarities at different levels of generalization.

The flexibility of the method comes from the user-defined parameters. These allow

Table 1. The flexibility of the similarity measure

Conditions	Overlap	s_c	s_r	s
$a = 0.1$, $\mathbf{b = 0.9}$ $w_E = w_V = w_A = 1$	[candidate]←(agt)←[criticize]→(pnt)→[candidate]	0.86	1	0.86
	[candidate:Bush] [criticize] [candidate:Gore]	1.00	0	0.10
$\mathbf{a = 0.9}$, $b = 0.1$ $w_E = w_V = w_A = 1$	[candidate]←(agt)←[criticize]→(pnt)→[candidate]	0.86	1	0.86
	[candidate:Bush] [criticize] [candidate:Gore]	1.00	0	0.90
$a = 0.5$, $b = 0.5$ $\mathbf{w_E = 2}$ $w_V = w_A = 1$	[candidate]←(agt)←[criticize]→(pnt)→[candidate]	0.84	1	0.84
	[candidate:Bush] [criticize] [candidate:Gore]	1.00	0	0.50

analyzing the similarity of the two conceptual graphs from different points of view and also selecting the best interpretation in accordance with the user interests.

Because of this flexibility, our method can be used in different application areas of text processing, for instance, in information retrieval, textual case-based reasoning, and text mining. Currently, we are designing a method for the conceptual clustering of conceptual graphs based on these ideas and an information retrieval system where the non-topical information is represented by conceptual graphs.

References

1. Agrawal, Rakesh, and Ramakrishnan Srikant (1994), "Fast Algorithms for Mining Association Rules", Proc. 20th VLDB Conference, Santiago de Chile, 1994.
2. Ellis and Lehmann (1994), "Exploiting the Induced Order on Type-Labeled Graphs for fast Knowledge Retrieval", Lecture Notes in Artificial Intelligence 835, Springer-Verlag 1994.
3. Genest D., and M. Chein (1997). "An Experiment in Document Retrieval Using Conceptual Graphs". Conceptual structures: Fulfilling Peirce's Dream. Lecture Notes in artificial Intelligence 1257, August 1997.
4. Huibers, Ounis and Chevallet (1996), "Conceptual Graph Aboutness", Lecture Notes in Artificial Intelligence, Springer, 1996.
5. Marie, Marie (1995), "On generalization / specialization for conceptual graphs", Journal of Experimental and Theoretical Artificial Intelligence, volume 7, pages 325-344, 1995.
6. Myaeng, Sung H., and Aurelio López-López (1992), "Conceptual Graph Matching: a Flexible Algorithm and Experiments", Journal of Experimental and Theoretical Artificial Intelligence, Vol. 4, 1992.
7. Myaeng, Sung H. (1992). "Using Conceptual graphs for Information Retrieval: A Framework for Adequate Representation and Flexible Inferencing", Proc. of Symposium on Document Analysis and Information Retrieval, Las Vegas, 1992.
8. Rasmussen, Edie (1992). "Clustering Algorithms". Information Retrieval: Data Structures & Algorithms. William B. Frakes and Ricardo Baeza-Yates (Eds.), Prentice Hall, 1992.
9. Sowa, John F. (1984). "Conceptual Structures: Information Processing in Mind and Machine". Ed. Addison-Wesley, 1984.
10. Sowa, John F. (1999). "Knowledge Representation: Logical, Philosophical and Computational Foundations". 1st edition, Thomson Learning, 1999.
11. Wu and Palmer (1994), "Verb Semantics and Lexical Selection", Proc. of the 32nd Annual Meeting of the Associations for Computational Linguistics, 1994.
12. Yang, Choi and Oh (1992), "CGMA: A Novel Conceptual Graph Matching Algorithm", Proc. of the 7th Conceptual Graphs Workshop, Las Cruces, NM, 1992.
13. Manuel Montes-y-Gómez, Alexander Gelbukh, Aurelio López-López (2000). *Comparison of Conceptual Graphs*. O. Cairo, L.E. Sucar, F.J. Cantu (eds.) MICAI 2000: Advances in Artificial Intelligence. Lecture Notes in Artificial Intelligence N 1793, Springer-Verlag, pp. 548-556, 2000.
14. A. F. Gelbukh. "Review of R. Hausser's 'Foundations of Computational Linguistics: Man-Machine Communication in Natural Language'." *Computational Linguistics*, 26 (3), 2000.
15. Manuel Montes-y-Gómez, Aurelio López-López, and Alexander Gelbukh. *Information Retrieval with Conceptual Graph Matching*. Proc. DEXA-2000, 11th International Conference on Database and Expert Systems Applications, Greenwich, England, September 4-8, 2000. Lecture Notes in Computer Science N 1873, Springer-Verlag, pp. 312–321.

Personalizing Digital Libraries for Learners

Su-Shing Chen, Othoniel Rodriguez, Chee-Yoong Choo, Yi Shang, and Hongchi Shi

University of Missouri-Columbia
Columbia, MO 65211
schen@risc1.ecn.missouri.edu

Abstract. User-centered digital libraries for education are developed. Instead of static contents on the web searched and retrieved in a traditional sense, we investigate personalized, dynamic information seeking in the learning environment of digital libraries. Learning objects and user profiles are important components of the digital library system. In their existing metadata standards, personalizing agents are designed and developed for realizing peer-to-peer educational and learning technologies on the Internet.

1 Introduction

Education is an interactive process between learners and teachers in a peer-to-peer fashion. Digital libraries have great potential for education [2]. But if personalization is not supported on these large-scale systems, their functions will not be fully utilized. Personalization in web-based education has taken place in research of adaptive and intelligent technologies (e.g., [1]). However current web-based personalization research does not have the large scale and the integrative nature of digital libraries. Our contribution is to integrate personalization technology into digital libraries. This paper reports such a recent effort – NBDL (National Biology Digital Library) – supported by the NSF for biological education [5]. The NBDL project is a core integration system of the NSF NSDL (National SMETE Digital Library) Program [10]. The NBDL consortium consists of the University of Missouri, University of Illinois, NCSA, and Missouri Botanical Garden. The main collection is the Tropicos collection of more than 1 million botanical specimens. The federated search engine, Emerge, can access seamlessly networked biological databases, including Medline, Pubmed, Entrez genetic databases, Library of Congress, and Tropicos. The NSF NSDL Program is a large-scale program consisting of many collection and service projects covering science, mathematics, engineering and technology education.

Personalization is essential to user-centered digital libraries. This specific situation provides us with learning-object and learner standards already established [5-8], thus theories and technologies (e.g., [2]) can be developed, tested, and validated more explicitly. In addition to the main search engine and primary collections, we are developing a user-centered digital library LOVE (Learning Object Virtual Exchange), which collects non-traditional learning-objects, such as tutorials, lecture notes, software, examinations, projects, and field trips. Our innovation of personalization manifests in three dimensions of LOVE: (1) managing learning-related history, goals,

H.C. Mayr et al. (Eds.): DEXA 2001, LNCS 2113, pp. 112–121, 2001.

and accomplishments of learners and learner-groups, (2) engaging a learner in a learning experience pedagogically, and (3) discovering learning opportunities for learners in the LOVE collection and the NBDL digital library. The goal of the NSF NSDL Program is to enhance education through cumulating modern technologies, but is not to replace completely teachers by web-based learning systems. Thus LOVE is an intelligent environment supporting peer-to-peer learning. It exploits technologies, such as multiagent systems (e.g., [12]), but also human involvement of teachers, (K-12) parents, reviewers, editors, and students, all as users.

2 LOVE: Design Objectives

LOVE is intended for the community of teachers, (K-12, university, and life-long) learners, authors, editors, and reviewers. It complements the primary collections of NBDL. Our main design objectives of LOVE as a digital library are adaptivity, interactivity and openness. Adaptivity is needed to select and customize the learning resources to the learners and to the context in which the learning is taking place. These two aspects exhibit a wide range of variability for digital libraries. Such systems can not make a priori assumptions about the characteristics of the learner, such as educational background, cognitive style, etc., nor about the context and purpose for the learning process. Instead it must be able to adapt dynamically based on explicit knowledge about these aspects that need to be maintained independently of the more generic learning content knowledge.

In the following, we describe the overall NBDL architecture of which LOVE is a subsystem:

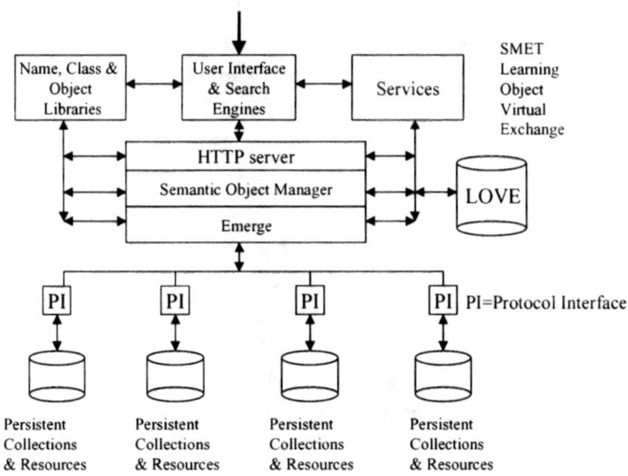

Fig. 1. NBDL Architecture

In the LOVE collection, we will provide learning objects in standardized forms so that intelligent agents can index user profiles and learning objects and match them directly. In the persistent collections of legacy data (e.g., the Library of Congress and National Library of Medicine), we will not be able to directly match the two parties. Instead we would develop data mining techniques in the "Semantic Object Manager" and "Emerge" (search engine) for matching them. The LOVE architecture consists of the collection managed by a community (e.g., a school district) and several networked services, which implement various educational technologies as multiagents described in later sections.

3 Learning Objects: Metadata Standards

The IEEE Learning Technology Standards Committee (IEEE-LTSC P1484) has undertaken the initiative of drafting a set of standards among which they define a data model for Learning Object Metadata (LOM) [6], [9]. This standard has received the endorsement of other consortiums dealing with educational standards such as ARIADNE, IMS (Instructional Management Systems) Consortium, and SCORM (Shareable Courseware Object Reference Model) for the ADL-Net (Advanced Distributed Learning Network) within the DOD.

Several of these standards are being endorsed by the IMS Consortium, who in addition is developing the Content Packaging Information Model, which describes a self-standing package of learning resources [7]. The IMS Content Packaging Information Model describes data structures that are used to provide interoperability of Internet-based content with content creation tools, learning management systems, and run time environments. The objective of the IMS Content Packaging Information Model is to define a standardized set of structures that can be used to exchange content. These structures provide the basis for standardized data bindings that allow software developers and implementers to create instructional materials that interoperate across authoring tools, learning management systems and run time environments that have been developed independently by various software developers.

The IEEE Learning Technology Standards Committee (IEEE-LTSC P1484) has undertaken the initiative of drafting a set of standards among which they define a data model for Learning Object Metadata (LOM) [6], [9]. This standard has received the endorsement of other consortiums dealing with educational standards such as ARIADNE, IMS (Instructional Management Systems) Consortium, and SCORM (Shareable Courseware Object Reference Model) for the ADL-Net (Advanced Distributed Learning Network) within the DOD.

Several of these standards are being endorsed by the IMS Consortium, who in addition is developing the Content Packaging Information Model, which describes a self-standing package of learning resources [7]. The IMS Content Packaging Information Model describes data structures that are used to provide interoperability of Internet-based content with content creation tools, learning management systems, and run time environments. The objective of the IMS Content Packaging Information Model is to define a standardized set of structures that can be used to exchange content. These structures provide the basis for standardized data bindings that allow software developers and implementers to create instructional materials that interoperate across authoring tools, learning management systems and run time environments that have been developed independently by various software developers.

The IEEE-LTSC LOM model is an abstract model, however, the IMS Consortium has provided one possible binding specification using pure XML and XML-Schema standards. The XML Schema introduces an unambiguous specification of low-level

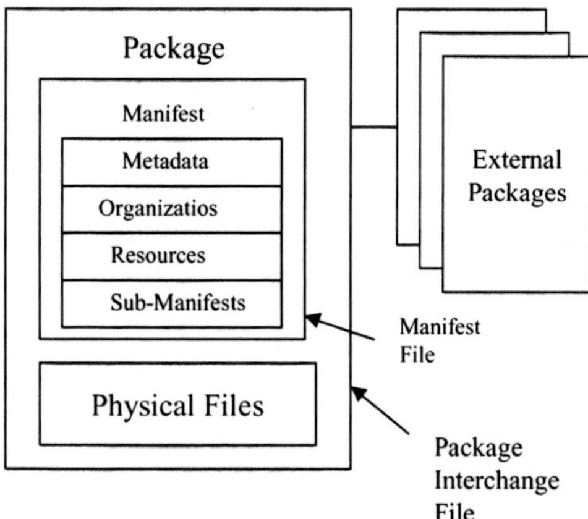

Fig. 2. IMS Content Packaging Conceptual Model [7]

and intermediate level data types and structures that assure a higher level of interoperability between XML documents. We will adopt this model to develop our LOVE collection. The current LOM model includes the following nine metadata elements, some of which can occur multiple times:

1. General: title, cat/entry, language, description, keyword, coverage, aggregation level.
2. Lifecycle: version, status, contributor.
3. MetaMetaData: identifier, catalog/entry, contributor, metadata scheme, language.
4. Technical: format, size (bytes), location, requirements (installation, platforms), duration.
5. Pedagogical: interactivty type, learning resource type, interactivity level, semantic density, intended end user role, learning context, age range, typical learning time, description on how to be used.
6. Rights: cost, copyright, description of condition of use.
7. Relation: kind, resource (target).
8. Annotation: person, date, description, comment.
9. Classification: taxon, taxon-path.

From this set, the Relation and Classification elements and sub-elements are specifically relevant from the perspective of supporting LOVE design objectives: adaptivity, interactivity, and openness. The Relation element provides a best practice set of controlled vocabulary for kind-of-relations pairings with the target LO or resource with which the current LO holds this kind-of-relation. Their use for navigation between LO's, in a kind of semantic networks, is very important. Note that these relations do not have to link to other LO's necessarily, so relations with other resources that may provide associated active-content is a possibility here. The Classification element provides the principal mechanism for extending the LOM model by allowing it to reference a Taxonomy and describe associated taxon-path sub-elements corresponding to the LO. Thus Classification provides for multiple alternative descriptions of the LO within the context and meaning of several Taxonomies.

In our LOVE collection, LO's will represent small capsules of knowledge in a form suitable for didactic presentation and assimilation by learners. We believe that the LO metadata standardization will introduce a large degree of interoperability and re-use, promoting the widespread investment in, and adoption of, educational technology. Each learning object by being highly atomic and complete in capturing a concept or "learning chunk" provides the opportunity for the configuration of a large number of course variations. The resulting fine-grained course customization is expected to lead to "just-in time", "just-enough", "just-for-you", training and performance support courseware. This implies the traversal of a subject matter domain in a highly flexible way and learner-specific way. However this flexibility must comply with inter-LO dependencies and restrictions, which in turn will require new goal-driven more intelligent navigation facilities.

4 User Profiles: Learner Model Standards

Tracking learners' patterns and preferences for adapting the digital library system to their needs is perhaps the most important aspect of user-centered digital libraries. In addition to LOM, the IMS is also defining a standard model for learners called the IMS LIP (Learner Information Packaging) Model [8]. IMS LIP is based on a data model that describes those characteristics of a learner needed for the general purposes of:

- Recording and managing learning-related history, goals, and accomplishments.
- Engaging a learner in a learning experience.
- Discovering learning opportunities for learners.

Since some IMS LIP elements are narrowly specific to formal classroom learning context, and not relevant to digital libraries, we will not use them. In user profiling of our LOVE collection, we will tentatively use the following metadata, subject to NSDL community decisions:

Identification
Affiliation
Privacy
Security
Relationship
Accessibility (e.g., disability)
Goal
Competency
Performance
Portfolio
Interest
Preference
Activity

The LOVE community is composed of learners, but also creators, reviewers, catalogers, librarians, and editors. Its user profiles are manifold. For examples,

1. Learners: finding resources, managing resources once retrieved, sharing resources with others, talking to other community members;
2. Teachers: tutoring, advising, managing resources;

3. Parents: advising, coordinating with other parents and teachers;
4. Creators: contributing resources;
5. Reviewers: gaining access for quality assurance and review, rating resources, finding rated resources;
6. Editors: adding resource descriptions;
7. Catalogers: ingesting content into digital libraries; and
8. Librarians: analyzing collection.

The relationships between learners, reviewers, editors, parents, catalogers, and librarians of LOVE are hierarchical with different authorities. Learners are basic users without any authority, while reviewers and editors will have authority over content materials of LO's. Catalogers and librarians will have the final authority to manage the LOVE collection. At present, we have not decided the role of parents, because it will be a matter of each school district. At least, parents will have a supporting role to enhance K-12 students. Either proactive or on-demand, personalization services are derived by matching metadata patterns of both learning objects and learner/user models. Learners would have at least the following needs:

1. accessibility (e.g., styles, disabilities, cognitive level, language),
2. personal profile on creators/vendors available to judge resource quality,
3. dynamic "portfolio" of their own ratings and assessment,
4. dynamic "portfolio" shared in a limited way with other LOVE members.

Getting profile information for learners/users will be iterative over time. Generally we can expect users to provide profile information only in incremental times. Moreover profile information touches upon privacy issues. We are in the process of building user profiling for NBDL, which will be extended later to the whole NSDL Program.

5 Theories: Multiagent Systems

Personalization of digital libraries for education rests its theories on multiagent systems (e.g., [11], [12]). These theories are general multiagent theories specialized to education. Under our LOVE design-objectives, personalization means system adaptivity, interactivity and openness. Multiagents are required to manipulate and represent many user profiles, learning objects, and learning experiences. Multiagents are intelligent software that incorporates many Artificial Intelligence (AI) and Distributed AI research results, but also exhibit emergent intelligent behavior resulting from the combined interaction among several agents and their shared environment. In our perspective, key properties of multiagents are autonomous, proactive, interactive, adaptive, scalable, and decentralized. These properties support personalization in several ways. Our contribution is to develop practical and scalable multiagents as operations on metadata describing user profiles, learning objects, and learning experiences.

In the following, we define multiagents in the LOVE environment. Autonomous agents can incorporate a set of goals that steer their planning, behavior and reactions as they carry out their assigned tasks. Autonomous agents can continuously support the interaction with users. Proactive agents take the initiative in guiding users based on high level learning goals and low level tasks selections. Interactive agents possess complex behavior and can incorporate meaningful responses to users by closely tracking their inputs and reactions. Interactivity means the agents or significant portions of them execute on the local desktop thus avoiding network links latencies and bandwidth limitations. Adaptive agents are capable of exhibiting a wide range of adaptivity, by properly modeling users and their contexts in user profiles, and understanding learning objects interdependencies. Scalable agents are able to tackle problems whose computational complexity is usually not scalable when using standard monolithic algorithm approaches. This is achieved through off-loading some of the potential agent-to-agent interaction complexity to interaction within a shared environment of standardized formats, styles, and protocols. Decentralized agents can interact directly with the user without tight coupling with central services, thus reducing the performance requirements on the network and improving the scalability.

In the LOVE environment, agents are inherently modular services and able to communicate using a certain inter-agent language in XML asynchronously. Thus our multiagent architecture is highly flexible allowing the re-use and creative re-combination of different agents and the independent development and deployment of new agents with improved functionality, performance and embodying new ideas on digital libraries. Multiagents permit experimentation and incremental improvement of the system. They make also possible inter-disciplinary work and cooperation among different NSDL teams, allowing highly focused development of specialized agents that can be tested and deployed to real-world learning environments without having to obsolete and start from scratch every time. The re-usability of learning objects coupled with the modularity of agents, provide for steady and continuous improvement both in the quality of content and the quality of delivery of digital libraries.

Although we can conceive of several partitioning alternatives for a minimum set of functions required within the LOVE learning environment, an intuitively appealing break-up is one, which follows the traditional human roles in current educational settings. This role re-distribution among agents might not be necessarily the best one but has the advantage to help the architectural specification of the LOVE learning environment by exploiting existing metaphors that enhance comprehension of the NSDL architecture. Actual experience with the NSDL Program may suggest a more optimized approach to role partitioning and re-distribution.

The following is a sample of the kinds of personalizing agents that we will develop. The learner-agent is a proxy for the learner on interactions with other parts of the system. Its responsibilities include learner enrollment into a particular course, presentation of pre-selected material to the learner, capturing learner responses, forwarding these to a teacher-agent, also forwarding learner input during learner-driven navigation. The teacher-agent is responsible for performing the role of an intelligent tutor choosing optimal navigation of the course learning units and the interactive tasks required from the learner. The recommender-agent provides content adaptation and navigation support for learner-driven navigation. A major responsibility of this agent is updating the learner model, including keeping track of learner cumulative performance portfolio. The course-agent is customized based on the content of a course. It is responsible for the unwrapping of course content packages. The timely retrieval of all learning resources identified by a course manifest, including active content and any additional delivery mechanisms. The register-agent manages the learner enrollments into courses, and may enforce some desired curricular sequencing among courses, and other high level policies dealing with long-term learning and development goals. This agent is responsible for the security and privacy of learner public and private information, its storage and retrieval.

6 Learning Technologies and Implementation Issues

The two major predecessor learner technologies impacting education are intelligent tutoring systems (ITS) and adaptive hypermedia systems (AHS) (e.g., Brusilovsky [1]). The goal of ITS is the use of knowledge about the domain and learner profiles to support personalized learning. There are at least four core functions: curriculum sequencing, intelligent analysis of student's solutions, interactive problem solving support, example-based problem solving support. We will adopt these ideas to the LOVE environment. Curriculum sequencing is to provide the learner with the most suitable individually planned sequence of knowledge units to learn and sequence of learning tasks (examples, questions, problems, etc.). Sequencing is further divided into active sequencing dealing with a learning goal and passive sequencing dealing with remedial knowledge. Active sequencing can involve fixed system-level selection of goals and adjustable learner selections of a subset of the goals. Most systems provide high level sequencing of knowledge in concepts, lessons, and topics, and low level sequencing of task in problems, examples, and examinations within a high level goal. Not all systems adopt intelligent sequencing at both the high and low level. The learner knowledge is used to drive active sequencing as a function of the "gap" between the goals and the knowledge. Sequencing can also be driven by learner preferences with regards to lesson media. The sequencing can be generated statically before the learner begins interacting with the system or dynamically while the learning process is taking place.

Curriculum sequencing has become a favorite technology on web-based learning due to its relatively easy implementation. Historically most ITS had focused on problem solving support technologies with sequencing being left as the responsibility of a human tutor. Problem solving support technologies are intelligent analysis of learner's solutions, interactive problem solving and example-based problem solving support. Intelligent analysis of learner's solutions uses the learner final answers to perform knowledge diagnosis, provide error feedback and update learner model. Interactive problem solving support continually tracks learner problem solving process, identifies difficulties and can provide error indication for each individual step, hint at alternative solutions, or provide wizard-like step by step help. These interactive tutors can not only help the learner every step of the way but also update the learner model. Example-based problem solving support is shifted from identifying errors or step by step support, to suggesting previously solved examples that are relevant to the problem at hand.

Adaptive hypermedia systems (AHS) will be another important feature of LOVE. Adaptive presentation is to adapt the content of a hypermedia page to the learner's goal, knowledge and other information stored in the learner model. In this technology, pages are not static, but are adapted to learner goals, knowledge level, etc. Some systems perform low-level conditional text techniques, while others can generate adaptable summaries, or preface to pages. The latter can take the form of adaptively inserted warnings about learner readiness to learn a given page. Adaptive navigation support is to support the learner in hyperspace orientation and navigation by changing the appearance of visible links. The technique can be seen as a generalization of curriculum sequencing but within the hypermedia context, and offering more options for direct/indirect guidance. Direct guidance guides learners to next "best" link. Contrary to curriculum sequencing where pages are built on demand and only system can guide learners to page, here the page must pre-exist. Direct guidance usually provides one-level sequencing versus two-level sequencing available in traditional curriculum sequencing. Adaptive link annotation modifies the link colors, associates icons with links, and provides other differentiation cues that help learner selection. Adaptive link hiding makes the links selectively invisible when the learner is not ready to learn that material. Adaptive link sorting sorts links in terms of the next best choice for navigation. Adaptive collaboration support forms different matching groups for collaboration, like identifying a collaboration group adequate to a learner characteristics or finding a qualified learner-tutor among the other learners. Finally, intelligent class monitoring looks for miss-matching user profiles or outlying learners.

The theory of multiagents provides the foundation of learner-agent, teacher-agent, and course-agent, and learning technologies supply the didactic model of the LOVE environment. However practical implementation issues involve a framework of browsers, applets, servlets, and distributed services in the LOVE environment. In the browser, the active portion is at the client in the form of an applet. It takes advantage of the browser facilities to present material and interact with the learner. Although allowing the applet to be a relatively thin client, the reliance on the browser imposes and inherits all the browser limitations, constraining the ultimate flexibility. For example, a heavyweight browser must always remain in the background, and if the browser window is closed the applet is also terminated. In addition interaction between the applet and the network is severely constrained. The distributed service framework implements decentralized agents. A portion of the functionality is implemented as a service and other parts as a remote service-object that accesses the service. The client-side is the service-object that knows how to communicate with the parent service probably using a proprietary protocol. The client-side service-object is downloaded from a look-up service that makes publicly available the parent service through a discovery protocol. For example, this is the scheme implemented by JINI [4]. One of the advantages of this approach is the centralization of the learner model at the parent service site. A potential disadvantage is the centralized nature of the parent service.

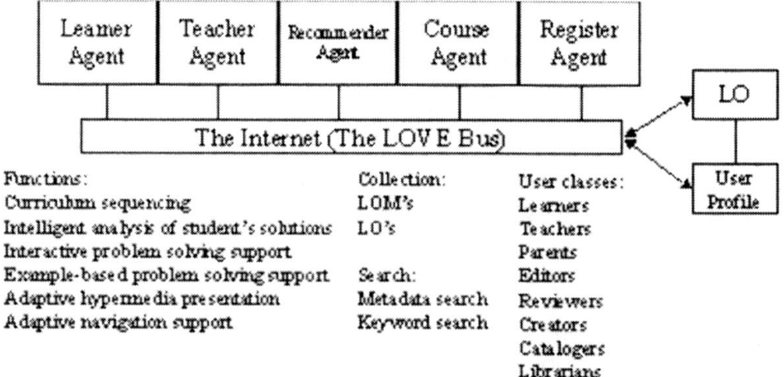

Fig. 3. The LOVE Architecture

References

[1] Brusilovsky, P., Adaptive and Intelligent Technologies for Web-based Education, In: C. Rollinger and C. Peylo, (eds.) Künstliche Intelligenz, Special Issue on Intelligent Systems and Teleteaching, 1999, 4, 19-25.

[2] Chen, S. Digital Libraries: The Life Cycle of Information, Better Earth Publisher, 1998, http://www.amazon.com.

[3] Deitel, H.M., Deitel, P.J., Nieto, T.R., Internet and World Wide Web: How to Program, Prentice-Hall.

[4] Edwards, W. Core JINI, Sun Microsystems Press, 1999.

[5] Futrelle, J., Chen, S., and Chang, K., NBDL: A CIS framework for NSDL, The First ACM-IEEE Joint Conference on Digital Libraries, Roanoke VA, June 24-28, 2001.

[6] IMS Learning Resource Metadata Information Model, http://www.imsproject.org/metadata/.

[7] IMS Content Packaging Information Model, http://www.imsproject.org/content/packaging/.

[8] IMS Learner Information Packaging Model, http://www.imsproject.org/profiles/lipinfo01.html

[9] LOM: Base Scheme - v3.5 (1999-07-15), http://ltsc.ieee.org/doc/wg12/scheme.html.

[10] SMETE.ORG, http://www.smete.org/nsdl/.

[11] Shang, Y. and Shi, H. IDEAL: An integrated distributed environment for asynchronous learning, Distributed Communities on the Web, LNCS, No. 1830, Kropf et al (ed.), pp. 182-191.

[12] Weiss, G. (Editor), Multiagent Systems: A Modern Approach to Distributed Artificial Intelligence, The MIT Press, 1999.

Interface for WordNet Enrichment with Classification Systems

Andrés Montoyo[1], Manuel Palomar[1] and German Rigau[2]

[1]Department of Software and Computing Systems, University of Alicante, Alicante, Spain
{montoyo, mpalomar}@dlsi.ua.es
[2]Departament de Llenguatges i Sistemes Informàtics, Universitat Politécnica de Catalunya
08028 Barcelona, Spain
g.rigau@lsi.upc.es

Abstract. This paper presents an interface that incorporate a method to enrich semantically WordNet 1.6. with categories or classes from other classification systems. In order to build the WordNet enriched it is necessary the creation of a interface to label WordNet with categories from different available classification systems. We describe features of the design and implementation of the interface to obtain extensions and enhancements on the WordNet lexical database, with the goal of providing the NLP community with additional knowledge. The experimental results, when the method is applied to IPTC Subject Reference System, show that this may be an accurate and effective method to enrich the WordNet taxonomy. The interface has been implemented using programming language C++ and providing a visual framework.

1 Introduction and Motivation

Lexical resources are an essential component of language enabled systems. They are one of the main ways of representing the knowledge which applications use in Natural Language Processing (NLP) system, such as Information Retrieval (IR), Information Extraction (IE), Machine Translation (MT), Natural Language Interface or Text Summarization.

Byrd in [3], proposes the integration of several structured lexical knowledge resources derived from monolingual and bilingual Machine Read Dictionaries (MRD) and Thesaurus. The work reported in [20] used a mapping process between two thesaurus and two sides of a bilingual dictionary. Knight in [7], provides a definition match and hierarchical match algorithms for linking WordNet [9] synsets and LDOCE [16] definitions. Knight and Luk in [8], describe the algorithms for merging complementary structured lexical resources from WordNet, LDOCE and a Spanish/English bilingual dictionary. A semiautomatic environment for linking DGILE [2] and LDOCE taxonomies using a bilingual dictionary are described in [1]. A semiautomatic method for associating Japanese entries to an English ontology using a Japanese/English bilingual dictionary is described in [14]. An automatic method to enrich semantically the monolingual Spanish dictionary DGILE, using a Spanish/English bilingual dictionary and WordNet is described in [17]. Several methods

H.C. Mayr et al. (Eds.): DEXA 2001, LNCS 2113, pp. 122–130, 2001.

for linking Spanish and French words from bilingual dictionaries to WordNet synsets are described in [18]. A mechanism for linking LDOCE and DGILE taxonomies using a Spanish/English bilingual dictionary and the notion of Conceptual Distance between concepts are described in [19]. The work reported in [4] used LDOCE and Roget's Thesaurus to label LDOCE. A robust approach for linking already existing lexical/semantic hierarchies, in particular WordNet 1.5 onto WordNet 1.6, is described in [5].

This paper presents an interface that incorporate a method to enrich semantically WordNet 1.6. with categories or classes from other classification systems. In order to build the WordNet enriched it is necessary the creation of a interface to label WordNet with categories from different available classification systems.

The organisation of this paper is as follows: After this introduction, in Section 2 we describe the technique used (Word Sense Disambiguation (WSD) using Specification Marks Method) and its application. In Section 3, we briefly describe the method for labelling the noun taxonomy of the WordNet. In section 4, we describe the user interface which allows the enrichment of WordNet. In Section 5, some experiments related to the proposal method are presented, and finally, conclusions and an outline of further lines of research are shown.

2 Specification Marks Method

WSD with Specification Marks is a method for the automatic resolution of lexical ambiguity of groups of words, whose different possible senses are related. The method requires the knowledge of how many of the words are grouped around a specification mark, which is similar to a semantic class in the WordNet taxonomy. The word-sense in the sub-hierarchy that contains the greatest number of words for the corresponding specification mark will be chosen for the sense-disambiguating of a noun in a given group of words. Detailed explanation of the method can be found in [12], while its application to NLP tasks are addressed in [15].

2.1 Algorithm Description

The algorithm with Specification Marks consists basically of the automatic sense disambiguating of nouns that appear within the context of a sentence and whose different possible senses are related. Its context is the group of words that co-occur with it in the sentence and their relationship to the noun to be disambiguated. The disambiguation is resolved with the use of the WordNet lexical knowledge base (1.6).

The input for the WSD algorithm will be the group of words $w=\{w_1, w_2, ..., w_n\}$. Each word w_i is sought in WordNet, each one has an associated set $s_i=\{s_{i1}, s_{i2}, ..., s_{in}\}$ of possible senses. Furthermore, each sense has a set of concepts in the IS-A taxonomy (hypernym/hyponym relations). First, the concept that is common to all the senses of all the words that form the context is sought. We call this concept the Initial Specification Mark (ISM), and if it does not immediately resolve the ambiguity of the word, we descend from one level to another through WordNet's hierarchy, assigning new Specification Marks. The number of concepts that contain the subhierarchy will then be counted for each Specification Mark. The sense that corresponds to the Specification Mark with highest number of words will then be chosen as the sense disambiguation of the noun in question, within its given context.

2.2 Heuristics

At this point, we should like to point out that after having evaluated the method, we subsequently discovered that it could be improved, providing even better results in disambiguation. The results obtained in [13] demonstrate that when the method is applied with the heuristics, the percentages of correct resolutions increases. We therefore define the following heuristics:

Heuristic of Hypernym: This heuristic solves the ambiguity of those words that are not directly related in WordNet (i.e. plant and leaf). But the word that is forming the context is in some composed synset of a hypernym relationship for some sense of the word to be disambiguated (i.e. leaf#1 → plant organ).

Heuristic of Definition: With this heuristic, the word sense is obtained using the definition (gloss used in WordNet system) of the words to be disambiguated (i.e. sister, person, musician).

Heuristic of Common Specification Mark: With this heuristic, the problem of fine-grainedness is resolved (i.e. year, month). To disambiguate the word, the first Specification Mark that is common to the resulting senses of the above heuristic is checked. As this is the most informative of the senses, it is chosen. By means of this heuristic it tries to resolve the problem of the fine grainedness of WordNet. Since in most of the cases, the senses of the words to be disambiguated differ very little in nuances, and as the context is a rather general one it is not possible to arrive at the most accurate sense.

Heuristic of Gloss Hypernym: This heuristic resolves the ambiguity of those words that are neither directly related in WordNet nor are in some composed synset of a hypernym relationship for some senses of the word to be disambiguated. To solve this problem we use the gloss of each synset of a hypernym relationship.

Heuristic of Hyponym: This heuristic resolves the ambiguity of those words that are not directly related in WordNet (i.e. sign and fire). But the word that is forming the context is in some composed synset of a hyponym relationship for some sense of the word to be disambiguated (i.e. sign#3→ Visual signal → watch fire).

Heuristic of Gloss Hyponym: This heuristic resolves the ambiguity of those words that are neither directly related in WordNet nor are in some composed synset of a hyponym relationship for some sense of the word to be disambiguated. To resolve this problem we use the gloss of each synset of a hyponym relationship.

3 WordNet Enrichment

The classification systems provide a means of arranging information so that it can be easily located within a library, World Wide Web, newspapers, etc. On the other hand, WordNet presents word senses that are too fine-grained for NLP tasks. We define a way to deal with this problem, describing an automatic method to enrich semantically WordNet 1.6. with categories or classes from the classification systems using the Specification Marks Method. Categories, such as Agriculture, Health, etc, provide a natural way to establish semantic relations among word senses. These groups of nouns are the input for the WSD module. This module will consult the WordNet knowledge base for all words that appear in the semantic category, returning all of their possible senses. The disambiguation algorithm will then be applied and a new file will be returned, in which the words have the correct sense as assigned by WordNet. After a new file has been obtained, it will be the input for the rules module. This module will apply a set of rules for finding out the super-concept in WordNet. This super-concept in WordNet is labelled with its corresponding category of the classification system. Detailed explanation of the method can be found in [11].

4 Interface

In order to build the enriched WordNet it is necessary the creation of a interface to label WordNet with categories from different available classification systems. This interface is made up of a set of computer programs that do all the work leading ultimately to a labelled lexical knowledge base of WordNet.

This section describes features of the design and implementation of the interface to obtain extensions and enhancements on the WordNet lexical database, with the goal of providing the NLP community with additional knowledge.

The design of the interface is composed of four processes: (i) selecting the classify-cation systems and their categories, (ii) resolving the lexical ambiguity of each word, (iii) finding out the super-concept and (iiii) organization and format of the WordNet database. These processes are illustrate in the figure 1.

In order to validate our study, we implemented the interface using programming language C++. It is shown in figure 2, with necessary given explanations below. And due to the physical distance between the different members of the group of investigation who use the interface, this has been developed to work through the local area network (LAN). The user interface offers the operations followed:

Select the classification system. A classification systems selection window contains option buttons. The user clicks on the appropriate button to select the desired classification system. We have considered the classification systems such as IPTC, Dewey classification, Library of Congress Classification and Roget´s.

Open category. The user clicks on this command button to select a category of the selected classification system in the previous step. The group of words that belong to the selected category appear in the left text window of the interface, named Input Category.

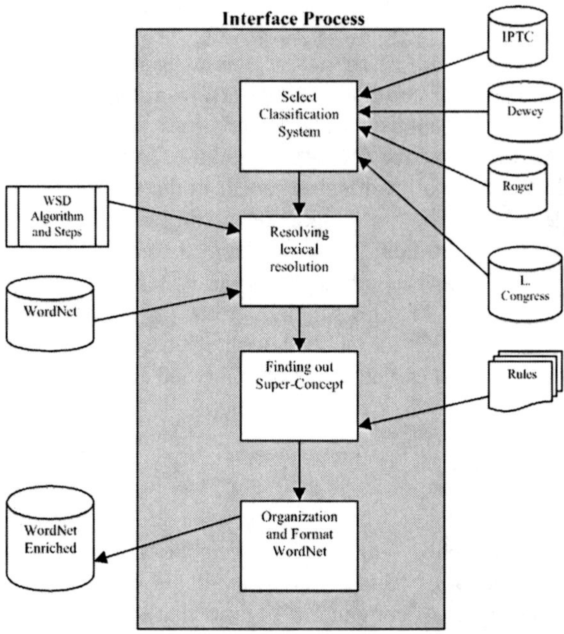

Figure 1: Interface Process

Run Interface. The processes, resolving the lexical ambiguity and finding out the super-concept, were implemented in a unique function. The command button Run Interface allows one to run this function, and the output information that belongs to the group of words of the selected category appear in the right text window of the interface, named Output Labelled Synsets. This output information is made up of WordNet Sense Word and Super-Concept obtained for each word belonging to the category. For example:

WordNet Sense Word	Super-Concept
{10129713} disease#1	{10120678} <IPTC.Health> ill Health

Save Category. If this command button is clicked, the information above is organizated, formatted and storaged in the WordNet lexical database for each super-concept, their full hyponyms and meronyms.

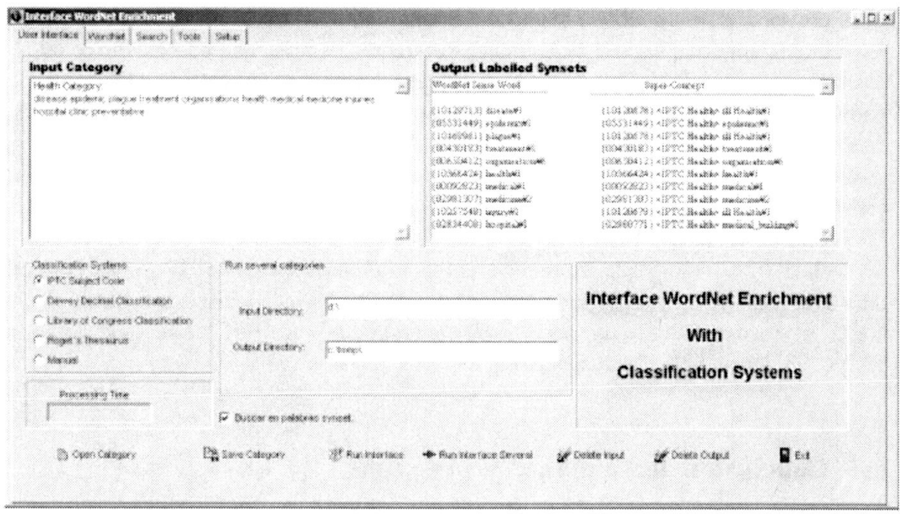

Figure 2: User Interface

5 Experiments And Results

In this section we will describe a set of experiments and the results obtained. The goal of the experiments is to assess the effectiveness of the proposed method to enrich semantically WordNet 1.6. with categories from the classification systems. A brief description of the resources used is included in this section to introduce the reader in the test environment.

The first goal was to assess the effectiveness of the disambiguation of the Specification Marks method. It was carried out on random sentences taken from the Semantic Concordance Corpus (Semcor [10]) and Microsoft Encarta Encyclopaedia Deluxe (Encarta), and the IPTC Subject Reference System (classification system). The method tested on IPTC Subject Reference System but this method can also be applied to other classification systems such as Library of Congress Classification(LC), Roget's Thesaurus or Dewey Decimal Classification (DDC).

These classification systems are divided in categories or classes, which are in turn subdivided into groups of words that are strongly related. In this work we intend to enrich WordNet 1.6. with synsets that have been annotated with one or more categories of the previous classification systems.

In the first approach we wanted to verify that, the Specification Mark Method can obtain successful results, and therefore this method can be applied successfully on any corpus. The percentages of correct resolutions achieved with these two corpora were Semcor 67,4% and Encarta 65,9% respectively. We should like to make a clear distinction, however, it does not require any sort of training, no hand-coding of lexical entries, or the hand-tagging of texts.

In the second approach we tested the Specification Mark Method on word clusters related by categories over IPTC Subject Reference System. The percentage of correct resolution was 96.1%. This successful percentage was because the method uses the knowledge of how many of the words in the context are grouped around a semantic class in the WordNet taxonomy.

Once it has been shown that the WSD Specification Marks Method works well with classification systems, we tested the method of combining the semantic categories of IPTC and WordNet.

Each IPTC category was computed as the amount of synsets of WordNet correctly labelled, synsets incorrectly labelled and words unlabelled (synsets are not in WordNet). After, we evaluate the precision[1], coverage and recall of the method obtaining 95,7%, 93,7% and 89,8%, respectively.

6 Conclusion and Further Work

This paper applies the WSD Specification Marks Method to assign a category of a classification system to a WordNet synset as to full hyponyms and meronyms. We enrich the WordNet taxonomy with categories of the classification system.

The experimental results, when the method is applied to IPTC Subject Reference System, indicate that this may be an accurate and effective method to enrich the WordNet taxonomy.

The WSD Specification Marks Method works successfully with classification systems, that is, categories subdivided into groups of words that are strongly related. Although, this method has been tested on IPTC Subject Reference Systems, but can also be applied to other systems that group words about a single category. These systems are Library of Congress Classification(LC), Roget's Thesaurus or Dewey Decimal Classification(DDC).

A relevant consequence of the application of the Method to enrich WordNet is the reduction of the word polysemy (i.e., the number of categories for a word is generally lower than the number of senses for the word). That is, category labels (i.e., Health, Sports, etc), provide a way to establish semantic relations among word senses, grouping then into clusters. Therefore, this Method intends to resolve the problem of the fined-grainedness of WordNet´s sense distinctions [6].
The researchers are therefore capable of constructing variants of WSD, because for each word in a text a category label has to be chosen instead of a sense label.

---

[1] Precision is given by the ratio between correctly synsets labelled and total number of answered (correct and incorrect) synsets labelled. Coverage is given by the ratio between total number of answered synsets labelled and total number of words. Recall is given by the ratio between correctly labelled synsets and total number of words

Acknowledgements

This research has been partially funded by the UE Commission (NAMIC IST-1999-12302) and the Spanish Research Department (TIC2000-0335-C03-02 and TIC2000-0664-C02-02).

References

1. Ageno A., Castellón I., Ribas F., Rigau G., Rodríguez H., and Samiotou A. 1994. TGE: Tlink Generation Environment. *In proceedings of the 15th International Conference On Computational Linguistic (COLING'94)*. Kyoto, (Japan).
2. Alvar M. 1987. Diccionario General Ilustrado de la Lengua Española VOX. *Bibliograf S.A.*. Barcelona, (Spain).
3. Byrd R. 1989. Discovering Relationship among Word Senses. *In proceedings of the 5th Annual Conference of the UW Centre for the New OED*, pages 67-79. Oxford, (England).
4. Chen J. and Chang J. 1998. Topical Clustering of MRD Senses Based on Information Retrieval Techniques. *Computational Linguistic* **24**(1): 61-95.
5. Daudé J., Padró L. And Rigau G. 2000. Mapping WordNets Using Structural Information. *In Proceedings 38th Annual Meeting of the Association for Computational Linguistics(ACL00)*. Hong Kong. (Japan).
6. Ide N. and Véronis J. 1998. Introduction to the Special Issue on Word Sense Disambiguation: The State of the Art. *Computational Linguistics* **24** (1): 1-40.
7. Knight K. 1993. Building a Large Ontology for Machine Translation. *In proceedings of the ARPA Workshop on Human Language Technology*, pages 185-190. Princenton.
8. Knight K. and Luk S. 1994. Building a Large-Scale Knowledge Base for Machine Translation. *In proceedings of the American Association for Artificial Inteligence.*
9. Miller G. A., Beckwith R., Fellbaum C., Gross D., and Miller K. J. 1990. WordNet: An on-line lexical database. *International Journal of Lexicography* **3**(4): 235-244.
10. Miller G., Leacock C., Randee T. and Bunker R. 1993. A Semantic Concordance. *Proc. 3rd DARPA Workshop on Human Language Tecnology*, pages 303-308, Plainsboro, (New Jersey).
11. Montoyo A., Palomar, M. and Rigau, G. (2001) WordNet Enrichment with Classification Systems. WordNet and Other Lexical Resources: Applications, Extensions and Customisations Workshop. (NAACL-01) The Second Meeting of the North American Chapter of the Association for Computational Linguistics. Carnegie Mellon University. Pittsburgh, PA, USA.
12. Montoyo, A. and Palomar M. 2000. Word Sense Disambiguation with Specification Marks in Unrestricted Texts. *In Proceedings 11th International Workshop on Database and Expert Systems Applications (DEXA 2000)*, pages 103-108. Greenwich, (London).
13. Montoyo, A. and Palomar, M. 2001. Specification Marks for Word Sense Disambiguation: New Development. *2nd International conference on Intelligent Text Processing and Computational Linguistics (CICLing-2001)*. México D.F. (México).
14. Okumura A. and Hovy E. 1994. Building japanese-english dictionary based on ontology for machine translation. *In proceedings of ARPA Workshop on Human Language Technology*, pages 236-241.
15. Palomar M., Saiz-Noeda M., Muñoz, R., Suárez, A., Martínez-Barco, P., and Montoyo, A. 2000. PHORA: NLP System for Spanish. *In Proceedings 2nd International conference on*

Intelligent Text Processing and Computational Linguistics (CICLing-2001). México D.F. (México).

16. Procter P. 1987. Longman Dictionary of common English. *Longman Group*. England.
17. Rigau G. 1994. An Experiment on Automatic Semantic Tagging of Dictionary Senses. *In International Workshop the Future of the Dictionary*. Grenoble, (France).
18. Rigau G. and Agirre E.1995. Disambiguating bilingual nominal entries against WordNet. *Seventh European Summer School in Logic, Language and Information (ESSLLI'95)*. Barcelona, (Spain).
19. Rigau G., Rodriguez H., and Turmo J. 1995. Automatically extracting Translation Links using a wide coverage semantic taxonomy. *In proceedings fifteenth International Conference AI'95, Language Engineering'95*. Montpellier, (France).
20. Risk O. 1989. Sense Disambiguation of Word Translations in Bilingual Dictionaries: Trying to Solve The Mapping Problem Automatically. *RC 14666, IBM T.J. Watson Research Center*. Yorktown Heights, (United State of America).

An Architecture for Database Marketing Systems

Sean W.M. Siqueira[1], Diva de S. e Silva[1], Elvira M[a] A. Uchôa[1], M[a] Helena L.B. Braz[2], and Rubens N. Melo[1]

[1] PUC-Rio, Rua Marquês de São Vicente, 255, Gávea, 22453-900, Rio de Janeiro, Brazil, {sean, diva, elvira, rubens}@inf.puc-rio.br
[2] DECivil/ICIST, Av. Rovisco Pais, Lisboa, Portugal
mhb@civil.ist.utl.pt

Abstract. Database Marketing (DBM) refers to the use of database technology for supporting marketing activities. In this paper, an architecture for DBM systems is proposed. This architecture was implemented using HEROS - a Heterogeneous Database Management System as integration middleware. Also, a DBM metamodel is presented in order to improve the development of DBM systems. This metamodel arises from the main characteristics of marketing activities and basic concepts of Data Warehouse technology. A systematic method for using the proposed DBM architecture is presented through an example that shows the architecture's functionality.

1 Introduction

Database Marketing (DBM) refers to the use of database technology for supporting marketing activities ([8], [9]). Therefore, DBM is a marketing process driven by information and managed by database technology. It allows marketing professionals to develop and to implement better marketing programs and strategies.

In some corporations, DBM systems work only as a system for inserting and updating data, just like a production system. In others, they are used only as a tool for data analysis. In addition, there are corporations that use DBM systems for both operational and analytical purposes. Once analytical processing has been researched in Data Warehouse (DW) [31], DBM systems could use concepts of DW technology to guide to a solution for specific problems of the marketing area.

This paper presents an architecture for DBM systems considering operational and analytical aspects. Also, a DBM metamodel is proposed based on the main characteristics of marketing activities and DW concepts, allowing better understanding of the application area. This metamodel guides the development of DBM systems, contributing to improve their efficacy and efficiency. An implementation of the proposed architecture using a Heterogeneous Database Management System (HDBMS) as integration middleware and an application example is also described.

The remainder of this paper is organized as follows: In section 2, the most relevant concepts to the understanding of the architecture are introduced. Section 3 presents the proposed architecture for DBM systems, compares HDBMS to other data access/integration solutions and describes an implementation of this architecture using

H.C. Mayr et al. (Eds.): DEXA 2001, LNCS 2113, pp. 131–144, 2001.

HEROS HDBMS as integration middleware. In section 4, the conceived DBM metamodel is described. In section 5, a systematic method for using the architecture is detailed through an example that shows the architecture's functionality. Finally, in Section 6, related works and some final remarks are presented.

2 Fundamentals

In this paper, DBM denotes the use of database technology for supporting marketing activities while marketing database (MktDB) refers to the database system. There are many different concepts in the specialized literature for DBM. PricewaterHouse& Coopers [4] proposed three different levels of DBM in order to better organize these concepts:

- *Direct Marketing* – Companies manage customer lists and conduct basic promotion performance analyses.
- *Customer Relationship Marketing* – Companies apply a more sophisticated, tailored approach and technological tools to manage their relationship with customers.
- *Customer-centric Relationship Management* – Customer information drives business decisions for the entire enterprise, thus allowing the retailer to directly dialogue with individual customers and ensure loyal relationships.

Besides these levels, some usual functions/processes of marketing such as householding, prospecting, campaign planning/management, merchandise planning and cross selling are mentioned in ([4], [6]). These functions/processes should also be supported by DBM systems.

An architecture for DBM systems should satisfy operational and analytical requirements. Usually, analytical systems need the integration of data from several sources, internal and/or external to the corporation, in a MktDB ([9], [15]). This MktDB is used by marketing tools/systems for data analysis and also for planning and execution of marketing strategies.

Some tools like *Xantel Connex* ([33]), *MarketForce* ([7]) and *The Archer Retail Database Marketing Software* ([27]) consider only operational DBM requirements; thus they do not provide analytical aspects. Other tools, such as *ProfitVision* [16], *Decisionhouse* ([25]), *SAP FOCUS* ([13]), *Pivotal Software* ([24]) and *ERM Central* ([5]) consider only analytical DBM requirements. Finally, there are some tools, like *IBM marketing and sales application* ([23]), that consider both operational and analytical DBM requirements. They have a MktDB that considers the analytical aspect and they allow operational applications to use their own databases that are optimized for operational tasks.

Analytical processing in support of management's decision has been researched in DW context. According to William H. Inmon [31], a DW is subject oriented, integrated, non-volatile collection of data that is time-variant and used in support of management's decisions.

Generally, a DW is modeled using the dimensional model [26] that is an intuitive technique to represent business models that allows high-performance access. Business models are domain dependent and refer to the area of the system. Usually, the dimensional model is implemented in a schema similar to a star. This resulting schema is called *star schema*. In this schema, there is a central data structure called „fact structure“ that stores business measures (facts). Business measures are indicators of some action/activity of business.

3 Proposed Database Marketing Architecture

Based on the characteristics of operational and analytical DBM systems, an architecture for DBM systems is proposed and the use of a HDBMS as integration midlleware is highlighted. This architecture is implemented using HEROS – a HDBMS.

3.1 Specification of the Proposed DBM Architecture

The work described in this paper presents a four-layer architecture (Fig. 1) for DBM systems.

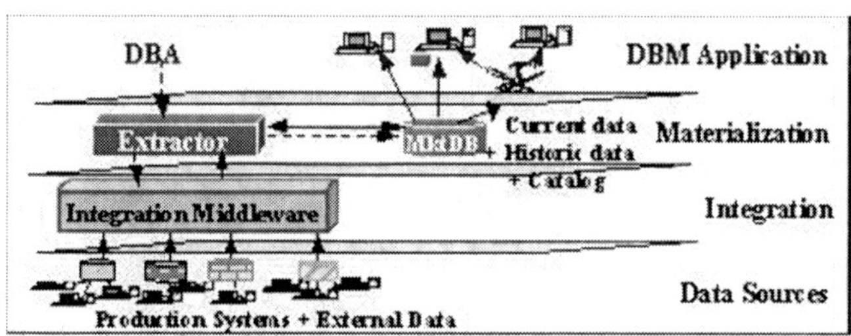

Fig. 1. Proposed DBM Architecture

In the proposed architecture, the *Data Sources* layer refers to data from production systems of the company and from external sources. External data sources refer to data outside the corporation, such as data obtained from market research or data from other corporations. They are important to complement the information of the company. Data sources can be centralized or distributed, homogeneous or heterogeneous, and comprise relevant data to marketing activities.

The *Integration* layer is responsible for providing an integrated view from several component data sources, eliminating inconsistency and heterogeneity, besides consolidating and aggregating data whenever it is necessary. In this layer, all the processes for identifying duplications, standardizing names and data types, comparing data, removing strange and excessive data, identifying synonymous and homonymous, and treating any other kind of heterogeneity/inconsistency are executed.

The *Materialization* layer refers to the materialization of integrated data in a new database. This layer is responsible for giving persistence to data resulting from integration process. It allows better performance in the execution of marketing queries, because a query submitted to a persistent MktDB (where integrated data were previously stored) executes faster than doing the whole integration processes „on the fly". The execution of integration processes increases network traffic and processing time in local systems that must also execute local applications.

The materialization layer is composed by a MktDB and an extractor:

- MktDB corresponds to the database system responsible for storing the integrated data, guaranteeing their persistence and security, as well as allowing the *DBM Application* layer to access them. This MktDB stores current data (resulting from new data loads), historic data (resulting from preview loads that remain stored in the database) and a catalog for supporting the translation of the output of the integration middleware to the MktDB format.
- The extractor is responsible for activating integration processes, translating the output of the integration middleware to the MktDB format and, finally, loading the MktDB. It generates a persistent view of the integrated data.

In the proposed architecture, the MktDB is used to data analysis. This database system is based on the multidimensional modeling that presents better performance in query-only environments. Operational applications can extract data from this MktDB to their own database where data are stored in a model that is more adequate to operational aspects.

The *DBM Application* layer embodies tools for marketing activities. These tools or systems access data from the MktDB and allow the execution of marketing functions/processes. Therefore, through this layer, it is possible to visualize, analyze and manipulate data from the MktDB.

Generally, this layer is composed by OLAP tools, statistical and data mining tools and/or marketing-specific applications:

- OLAP tools present a multidimensional view of data, allowing sophisticated analyses through easy navigation and visualization of a large volume of data ([1]).
- Tools for statistical analysis and data mining[1] are used for clients/products segmentation and valuation or for discovering patterns and information, allowing personalized services ([17], [18]).
- Finally, marketing-specific applications like campaign management, merchandise planning, media selection and scheduling, retention analysis and inventory management can also be performed in this layer.

3.1.1 Integration Middleware

Indifferently to which requirements are considered in DBM systems, it is necessary to have integrated access to data from several sources. There are many different ways to provide this kind of access.

In database community, HDBMS are one of the solutions for integrating heterogeneous and distributed data. A HDBMS ([28], [3]) is a layer of software for controlling and coordinating heterogeneous, autonomous and pre-existing data sources, interconnected by communication networks. By heterogeneity, it is meant not only technological differences (hardware and software), but also differences in data models, database systems and semantics.

The analysis about the level of integration that exists among the component systems allows heterogeneous database systems (HDBS) to be classified into tightly

---

[1] Data mining refers to extraction of hidden information from large databases. Data mining tools predict trends and future behavior.

coupled or loosely coupled HDBS [3]. In loosely coupled HDBS, the end-user must know in which sources are located data that he/she wants to access and their paths. The HDBMS just supply mechanisms to facilitate this access. In tightly coupled HDBS, the end-user has an integrated and homogeneous view of data. It gives the illusion that there is only one system.

The use of a tightly coupled HDBMS as integration middleware was considered appropriated to DBM systems according to the following reasons:

Commercial products vs. HDBMS

Some DBM tools consider an existing database or use only their own database as data source, e.g.: *Xantel Connex* and *MarketForce*. Other tools, such as *ProfitVision* and *DIALOG++*, presume the existence of a DW that would be responsible for data integration processes.

Other tools use proprietary solutions exploring ODBC drivers to access/integrate data, e.g.: The Archer™ Retail Database Marketing Software, Decisionhouse, SAP FOCUS, Pivotal Software, ERM Central and IBM marketing and sales application.

Commercial products generally behave as „black" boxes. The integration procedures are hidden from the users that are responsible for the DBM definition. This fact obstructs the user's perception about extraction and cleansing processes, creating the possibility of errors in the resulting data. Moreover, these commercial products don't consider the semantic heterogeneity. It must be treated through other programs/procedures, in some phase before the use of these products.

The use of tightly coupled HDBMS to integrate heterogeneous data presupposes that the database administrator that is responsible for the DBM definition knows local data schemas and translation processes. Once this knowledge is recognized by the HDBMS, it will treat the heterogeneity and will carry out data integration processes. In order to include a new data source, the local user (DBA) needs only to define the characteristics of this source in the HDBMS. This approach contributes to a more organized and transparent process. Tightly coupled HDBMS support the development of a DBM without the need of external programs.

Mediators and Wrappers vs. HDBMS

Although it was found no tool or research work using mediators [14] and wrappers [20] in DBM systems, they are frequently used for data access/integration. Wrappers and mediators are software programs, which are developed to assist a specific class of problem. They usually work as „black" boxes and do not allow accessing their logic. Therefore, they are less flexible than a HDBMS as an integration middleware that is responsible for data extraction, transformation and integration. The use of a HDBMS implies in representing data schemas and their mappings that facilitates data understanding and project changes.

3.2 Implementation of the DBM Architecture

Once the use of tightly coupled HDBMS as integration middleware was considered appropriate, it was decided to use HEROS – HEteRogeneous Object System – in the proposed architecture. HEROS is a tightly coupled HDBMS at development in the Computer Science Department of PUC-Rio (Catholic University of Rio de Janeiro). It allows the integration of a set of HDBS in a federation. These HDBS are cooperative but autonomous, and queries and updates can be executed with transparency in relation to data location, access paths and any heterogeneity or redundancy [10].

Therefore HEROS HDBMS is responsible for all the processes for data integration and consolidation. The use of HEROS HDBMS allows any kind of system, even non-conventional ones, to be easily integrated. There is only the need for specializing some classes in HEROS' data model [11].

The extractor, which is responsible for activating HEROS, triggering data integration, decoding HEROS' output and loading the MktDB was implemented using C++ for its core and Visual Basic for the front end. The database management system (DBMS) used for the MktDB was Oracle 8.0.

4 Proposed Database Marketing Metamodel

In the development of DBM systems, it is very important to understand marketing processes and activities. A DBM metamodel could incorporate marketing semantic in order to guide the project and therefore to provide higher quality to DBM systems. However, during this research, no DBM metamodel was found in the literature, so it was decided to propose a DBM metamodel based on fundamental concepts related to marketing activities.

4.1 Characteristics of Marketing Activities

A marketing activity implies in answering four important questions [30]:

- *Who* should I target?
- *What* should I target them with?
- *When* should I do it?
- *How* should I bring the offer to market?

Once marketing activities refer to exchange of products/services, it is possible to generalize the considerations above:

- An exchange involves a deal with two (or more) partners. Then, „*Who*" represents the corporation's partner in a marketing activity.
- In this exchange relationship, the corporation must offer some product or service. „*What*" refers to the product or service that the corporation is offering.
- A marketing activity occurs on a specific moment in time. Then, „*When*" is a temporal aspect in the MktDB, and represents the moment of the exchange.
- Finally, characteristics of the marketing activity are represented by „*How*". However, it is possible to detail it in two aspects:
    - *Which* promotion channel should I use? – representing the communication channel used to present the promotion.
    - *How* promotion should be done? – representing the promotional strategy, discount policies, etc.

Analyzing the three DBM levels (section 2) and functions/processes supported by DBM systems, two new important questions, not found in the literature, were introduced:

- *Where* should I offer it? – representing a spatial aspect in the MktDB. It is related to the physical and/or geographic space where the marketing activity occurs.
- *Why* should I do it? – representing the purpose of the marketing activity.

4.2 Metamodel

To express these fundamental questions in DBM systems, a metamodel was proposed. This DBM metamodel explores concepts and characteristics of marketing activities and uses some concepts of multidimensional modeling (facts and dimensions structures) that are used in DW area. It increases the semantics and brings the analytical perspective to the DBM systems.

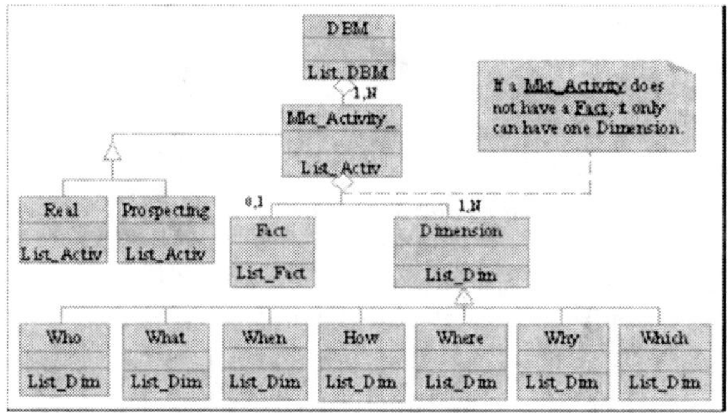

Fig. 2. DBM Metamodel

Fig. 2 represents the DBM metamodel, using the UML notation [22]. As DBM refers to the use of database technology to support marketing activities, a DBM system may be represented as a set of marketing activities (Mkt_Activity) such as sales or promotions. If the company executes these activities, they are considered Real (representing internal data or complementary data if it comes from an external source). If these activities refer to benchmarking or monitoring of other company's activities, Prospecting represents them.

Each marketing activity has at least one „perspective of the data" (Dimension). This perspective provides information for comparative analysis. Exploring the concepts and characteristics of marketing activities, the questions *Who*, *What*, *When*, *Where*, *How*, *Why* and *Which* are the different perspectives of data about marketing activities and represent the Dimensions. Finally, if there is more than one dimension, they are related to a specific subject that is responsible for combining them. This specific subject is represented by Fact. More detail can be found at [29].

If this metamodel is instantiated in a HDBMS, integration processes have more DBM semantic and become less liable to errors, reducing the possibility of failure of the DBM project.

5 Systematic Method for Using the Proposed Architecture

The development and use of a DBM system based on the proposed architecture should be guided by a systematic method that embraces three stages: the construction/development of the DBM system, the load of the resulting MktDB and the use of the MktDB by marketing applications.

In order to evaluate the architecture it was considered an example, detailed in [29]. In this paper, a simplified version of this example is used to present the proposed systematic method. All aspects related to the example are printed in Italics.

The example refers to a virtual bookstore – Book House – that wants to know its customers and their characteristics in detail. Through this knowledge, Book House intends to increase sales using a list of prospects (potential customers), which is obtained from a specialized company (Editora Abril, a Brazilian publishing house). It is considered a customer of „Book House" everyone who has bought any product (book) from the company.

The development of a DBM system – using the proposed architecture – follows seven steps [29]:

1. Identification of the DBM level:

According to meetings with enterprise managers, level one of DBM - direct marketing - is the most suitable level to Book House. It is desired to generate a simple list of promotional prospectus to potential customers, starting data selection/segmentation from characteristics of the best current customers.

2. Identification of necessary marketing functions/processes:

Among the marketing functions/processes that need to be supported by the Book House's MktDB, prospecting and campaign management are the two most important. Prospecting refers to getting a list of people that have not yet bought at „Book House". Campaign management is responsible for coordinating prospectus-mailing activities to prospects and verifying possible answers (purchases and contacts).

3. Business interviews and data gathering for identifying and understanding data sources:

After analysis of several data systems of the enterprise and other data sources that are necessary to the desired marketing activities, two data sources were considered in the development of Book House's MktDB. One data source refers to real data that comes from the enterprise and the other refers to prospecting data.

The first data source is related to Book House's sales system. This data source, which is identified in Book House's DBM system as Sales Component, uses Oracle DBMS. The other data source, called Ext_Customer Component, corresponds to prospecting about potential customers bought from Editora Abril. This component uses Postgres DBMS. Fig 3 shows the component's local schemas, with some simplifications.

4. Integrate data using the Integration Middleware:

In HEROS HDBMS, data integration is executed through the definition of a set of schemas. The schema architecture used by HEROS HDBMS is shown in Fig 4. In this architecture, each data source has a local schema, represented in its own data model. This local schema is translated to HEROS' object oriented data model, resulting in an export schema. All export schemas must be integrated, resulting in a global schema, with no heterogeneity. Finally, end user's views can be created from this global schema, generating external schemas. A HEROS' federation consists of an integrated set of autonomous component systems.

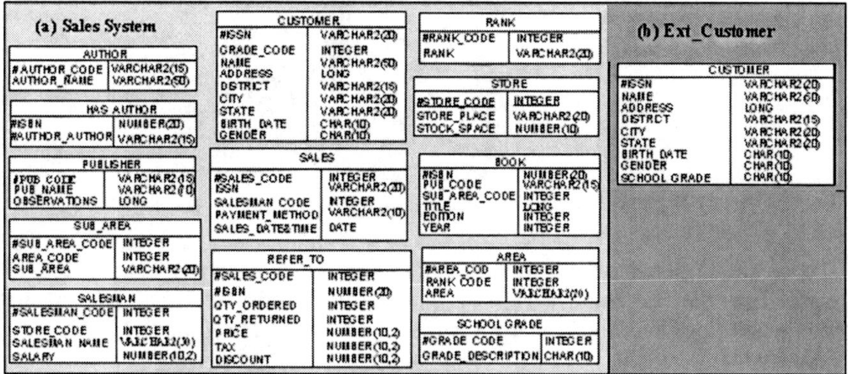

Fig. 3. Local Schemas of (a) *Sales System* and (b) *Ext_Customer*

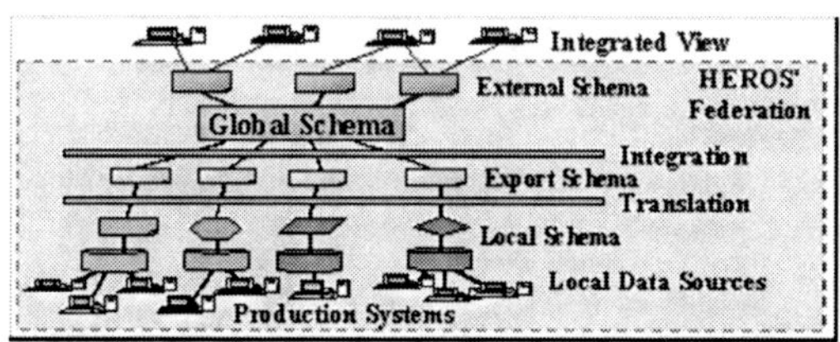

Fig. 4. Schema Architecture used by HEROS

As the implementation of the proposed architecture for DBM system involves the use of HEROS HDBMS as integration middleware, it is necessary to follow the steps for the creation of a HEROS' federation [12]:

a) To define a new HEROS' federation and to explain data semantic of each local system into HEROS' data dictionary:

   The BookHouse DBM federation was defined in HEROS and the data semantic of each local system was explained.

b) To create an export schema for each local schema (at present, this is necessary because HEROS' active rules mechanism has not yet been developed. This mechanism would create the export schemas automatically).

   For the creation of export schemas, it is necessary to represent the local schemas (Sales Systems and Ext_Customer) in HEROS' data model. Another component system – HEROS – must be defined in the federation in order to be used as a working area in the integration process. Therefore, in addition to classes representing local schemas (Customer, Book, Time, Sale and E_Customer), another class – Work_Area – is defined. Fig 5 presents the classes of the export schemas concerning the example. Each method in the classes of the export schema must call local procedures that will be executed in the component systems. Such local procedures are mainly responsible for executing data extraction from the component system. The detailed procedures and execution paths for this example can be found at [29].

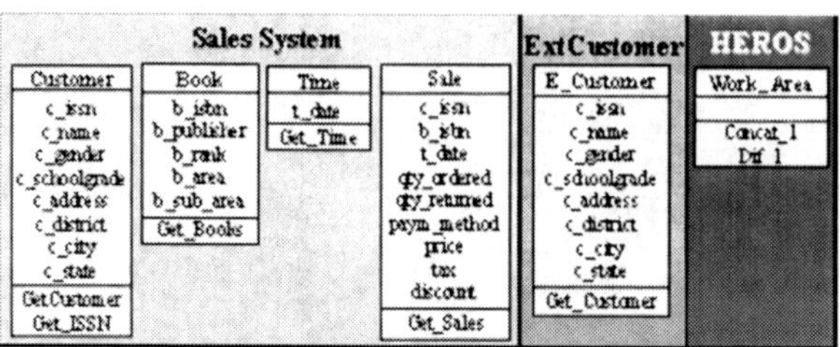

Fig. 5. Export Schemas of the Component Systems

c) To create a global schema. For creating this global schema, it is necessary to specialize the metamodel classes, integrating export schemas and to define command trees in order to achieve data semantic integration and consolidation.

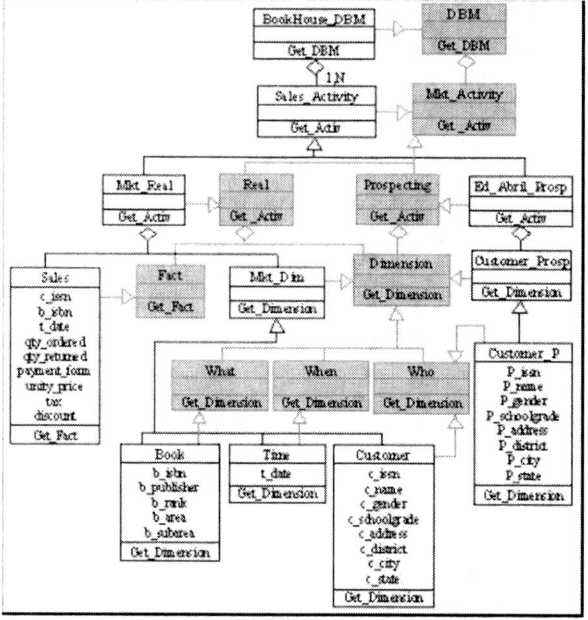

Fig. 6. Global Schema of „Book_House" Federation

The DBM metamodel was instantiated into HEROS' global schema and then specialized according to the semantic of the example. Fig 6 shows the global schema for BookHouse DBM, representing the metamodel through gray boxes and the specialization for the example through white boxes.

One Real Marketing Activity – Mkt_Real – and one Prospect Marketing Activity – Ed_Abril_Prosp composes the BookHouse DBM. The Real Marketing Activity is composed by a Fact – Sales – and by three Marketing Dimensions: Book (the „what" aspect), Time (the „when" aspect) and Customer (the „who" aspect). The Prospecting Marketing Activity is composed by only one Marketing Dimension: Customer_P that represents the „who" aspect.

A query relative to a global class may be decomposed into sub-queries for other classes in the global schema and afterwards into sub-queries for classes in the export schemas through the execution trees related to the global procedures. The execution trees for the example are detailed in [29] and they are responsible for treating the semantic heterogeneity and data consolidation.

5. Creation of tables for storing integrated data in the MktDB:

In the example, MktDB is a relational DBMS because almost all DBM tools access this type of DBMS. Tables Sale, Customer, Book, Time and Customer_Prosp were created in Oracle DBMS.

6. Creation of a mapping catalog between the output of the integration middleware and MktDB's tables:

This catalog corresponds to the mapping between HEROS' output and attributes of the MktDB's tables. Therefore, it enables the extractor to load the MktDB. *Table 1 represents the catalog for the example.*

Table 1. Catalog of Mappings between HEROS' output and MktDB persistent tables

Corp Unit	DBM	HEROS' Output Position	Table Name	Table Attribute
Book house	BookHouse DBM	1	Sales	c_issn
		2		b_isbn
		3		t_date
		4		qty_ordered
		5		qty_returned
		6		paym_method
		7		unit_price
		8		tax
		9		discount
		10	Customer	c_issn
		11		c_name
		12		c_gender
		13		c_schoolgrade
		14		c_address
		15		c_district
		16		c_city
		17		c_state
		18	Book	b_isbn
		19		b_publisher
		20		b_rank
		21		b_area
		22		b_subarea
		23	Time	t_date
		24	Customer_Prosp	p_issn
		25		p_name
		26		p_gender
		27		p_schoolgrade
		28		p_address
		29		p_district
		30		p_city
		31		p_state

7. Definition and configuration of DBM tools:

For the example, some tools for campaign management such as Lodgistics (from DataLodgic), NCR Target Marketing & Campaign Management solution (from NCR) and Trail Blazer (from Aspen Software Corp.) were analyzed. However, it was decided to develop a specific application (BSA – BookHouse Sales Analysis) to access/analyze data from the resulting database in order to improve performance analysis and enable strategic actions. One of the screens of BSA is shown in Figure 7.

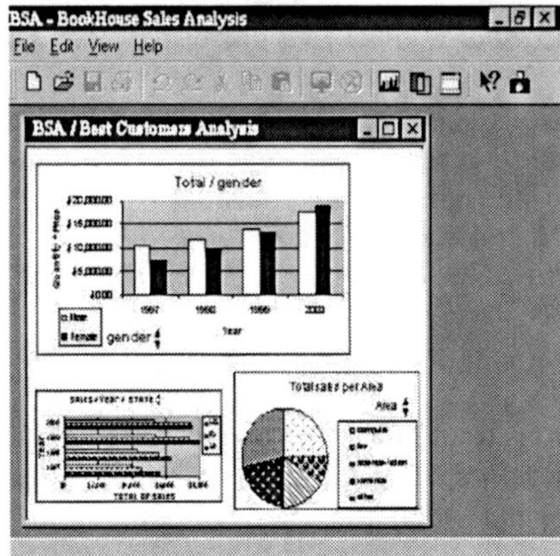

Fig. 7. Print Screen of module Best Customers Analysis from BSA

After the development of the DBM system, the MktDB is loaded through the activation of the extractor by the DBA and it is used through marketing tools.

6 Conclusions

This paper presented an architecture for DBM systems, focusing data integration processes in the creation of a MktDB and considering some concepts of DW technology. There was found no similar work in the literature. The survey conducted during the development of the work presented in this paper showed that there are some works on DBM systems, but they focus different characteristics. On the business field, the main works consider aspects related to customer loyalty and selection of customers ([32], [21]). On data mining area, some techniques have been proposed to allow knowledge discovery on customer data ([2]). Also, DW systems have been used to store data for data analysis in DBM systems. However, no work treating data integration for DBM systems, considering operational and analytical aspects was found.

The proposed architecture is adequate to all levels of DBM (Direct Marketing, Customer Relationship Marketing and Customer-centric Relationship Management) because it considers analytical and operational aspects of marketing activities. It considers a MktDB that uses multidimensional modeling – facts and dimensions structures – and allows operational marketing applications to use the resulting MktDB as a data source.

HEROS HDBMS was used as integration middleware, providing the necessary transparency about data models, localization and other details to end-users.

The proposed DBM metamodel makes possible a business-oriented view because it was based on marketing concepts and characteristics. It guides the definition of the necessary data and therefore the MktDB becomes semantically richer and more reliable.

The systematic mechanism for using the architecture conducts the development of DBM systems, allowing faster and more reliable DBM projects.

The main contributions of the work presented in this paper are:

- the proposal of an architecture for DBM systems;
- the definition of a DBM metamodel;
- and the use of HEROS HDBMS as integration middleware in an implementation of the proposed architecture.

As future work, it is suggested the development of a tool and a systematic mechanism for automatic refresh of the MktDB. A monitor responsible for detecting changes in data sources and, automatically, triggering a new load of the MktDB could perform this refresh. It should also be able to perform scheduled loads of the MktDB.

Other interesting aspect is the research/development of tools in order to automate some marketing functions/processes using the semantic offered by the resulting MktDB. Then, it would be possible, for instance, after a load of the MktDB, to automatically trigger a new marketing campaign to prospects according to automatic analysis of the profile of the best customers. Therefore, some marketing activities could be performed automatically.

References

[1] A. Berson & S. J. Smith: *Data Warehousing, Data Mining & OLAP*, McGraw-Hill Companies, Inc., 1997

[2] A. Berson & S. Smith & K. Thearling: *Building Data Mining Applications for CRM* ; McGraw Hill, 2000.

[3] A. P. Sheth & J. A. Larson, „Federated Database Systems for Managing Distributed, Heterogeneous, and Autonomous Databases" in *ACM Computing Surveys*, Vol. 22, N. 3, September 1990

[4] Coopers & Lybrand Consulting (CLC), „Database Marketing Standards for the Retail Industry", Retail Target Marketing System Inc., 1996

[5] Customer Analytics to Integrate MyEureka! Within its Enterprise Relationship Management Suite – http://www.informationadvantage.com/pr/ca.asp

[6] D. M. Raab, „Database Marketing", DM Review, January 1998

[7] D. M. Raab, „MarketFirst Software", DM News, May 1998 – http://raabassociates.com/a805mark.htm

[8] D. Shepard, *Database Marketing*, Makron, 1993

[9] D. Shepard, *The New Direct Marketing: How to Implement a Profit-Driven Database Marketing Strategy*, 3rd edition, McGraw-Hill, 1998

[10] E. M. A Uchôa & S. Lifschitz & R. N. Melo, „HEROS: A Heterogeneous Object-Oriented Database System", *DEXA Conference and Workshop Programme*, Vienna, Austria, 1998

[11] E. M. A. Uchôa & R. N. Melo, „HEROS^{fw}: a Framework for Heterogeneous Database Systems Integration", *DEXA Conference and Workshop Programme*, Florence, Italy, 1999

[12] E. M. A. Uchôa: *HEROS – A Heterogeneous Database System: Integrating Schemas*. Computer Science Department – Pontifícia Universidade Católica do Rio de Janeiro (PUC-Rio). M.Sc. Thesis, 1994 (in Portuguese)

[13] Focus Group Approach – Facilitator Manual – http://p2001.health.org/VOL05/FOCUSGRP.SAP.HTM

[14] G. Wiederhold, "Mediators in the Architecture of Future Information Systems"; *IEEE Computer*, March 1992

[15] J. F. Naughton, „Database Marketing Applications, Relational Databases and Data Warehousing", http://www.rtms.com/papers/dbmarket.htm, Janeiro 1999

[16] J. McMillan, „Hyperion and HNC Software Sign Reseller Agreement to Deliver Profitability Analysis Solutions to the Financial Industry“, http://psweb1.hyperion.com/hyweb/imrsnews.nsf/newsdate/87C87DF6955AE94385 2568C500547C24
[17] K. Thearling, „From Data Mining to Database Marketing“, http://www3.shore.net/~kht/text/wp9502/wp9502.htm
[18] K. Thearling, „Understanding Data Mining: It's All in the Interaction“, DS, December 1997
[20] M. T. Roth & P. Schwarz, „Don't Scrap it, Wrap it! A Wrapper Architecture for Legacy Data Sources“, Proceedings of the 23 VLDB Conference, Athens, Greece, 1997
[21] N. Narayandas, „Measuring and Managing the Consequences of Customer Loyalty: An Empirical Investigation“, http://www.hbs.edu/dor/abstracts/9798/98-003.html
[22] OMG Unified Modeling Language Specification, version 1.3, June 1999 http://www.rational.com/media/uml/post.pdf
[23] P. Gwynne, „Digging for Data“, http://www.research.ibm.com/resources/magazine/1996/issue_2/datamine296.html
[24] Pivotal eRelationship™ – Our award-winning customer relationship management (CRM) solution enables universal collaboration“, http://www.pivotal.com/solutions/eRelationship.htm
[25] Quadstone, „Decisionhouse ™“, http://www.quadstone.com/systems/decision/index.html
[26] R. Kimball: *The Data Warehouse Toolkit*, John Wiley & Sons, Inc., 1996
[27] RTMS/Customer Insight“, http://www.rtms.com/papers/lybrand.html
[28] S. Ram: *Guest Editor's Introduction: Heterogeneous Distributed Database Systems*. In: IEEE Computer, Vol.24, N.12, December 1991.
[29] S. W. M. Siqueira: *An Architecture for Database Marketing Systems using HEROS – a HDBMS*. Computer Science Department – Pontifícia Universidade Católica do Rio de Janeiro (PUC-Rio). M.Sc. Thesis, 1999 (in Portuguese)
[30] T. Suther, „Customer Relationship Management: Why Data Warehouse Planners Should Care About Speed and Intelligence in Marketing“, DM Review, January 1999
[31] W. H. Inmon: *Building the Data Warehouse*, John Wiley & Sons, Inc., 1996
[32] W. Hoyer, „Quality, Satisfaction and Loyalty in Convenience Stores — Monitoring the Customer Relationship“, University of Texas at Austin - Center for Customer Insight, http://hoyer.crmproject.com/
[33] Xantel Connex version 2.4, http://www.ask-inet.com/html/news_relase3.htm

NChiql: The Chinese Natural Language Interface to Databases

Xiaofeng Meng and Shan Wang

Information School, Renmin University of China
Beijing 100872, China
xfmeng@public.bta.net.cn, swang@mail.ruc.edu.cn

Abstract: Numerous natural language interface to databases (NLIDBs) developed in the mid-eighties demonstrated impressive characteristic in certain application areas, but NLIDBs did not gained the expected rapid and wide commercial acceptance. We argue that there are two good reasons explain why: limited portability and poor usability. This paper describes the design and implementation of NChiql, a Chinese natural language interface to databases. In order to bright the essence of these problems, we provide an abstract model (AM) in NChiql. We try to give a solution for these problems based on the model in our system. In this paper, we depict a novel method based on database semantics (SCM) to handle the Chinese natural language query, which greatly promotes the system's usability. The experiments show that NChiql has good usability and high correctness.

1 Introduction

A natural language interface to database (NLIDB or NLI) is a system that allows the user to access information stored in a database by typing requests expressed in some natural language (e.g. Chinese, English). Since the early 1960s, much of the research on NLIDB has been motivated by its potential use for communicating with DBMS. Prototype NLIDBs appeared in the late sixties and early seventies. The best-known NLIDBs of that period is LUNAR, a natural language interface to a database containing chemical analyses of moon rocks. By the late seventies several more NLIDB had appeared. Although some of the numerous NLIDBs developed in the mid-eighties demonstrated impressive characteristic in certain application areas, NLIDBs did not gained the expected rapid and wide commercial acceptance [5]. Two good reasons explain why:

First, it is the *portability problem*. Existing systems can only cope with questions referring to a particular knowledge domain (e.g. questions about university, questions about company sales). So when we want to transfer a existing NLIDB to different knowledge-domains, it is very expansive or impossible.

Second, the *usability problem*. Existing NLIDBs are brittle and users are often frustrated in using them. That's caused by the coverage mismatch, i.e. users can not distinguish between the limitations in the system's conceptual coverage and the system's linguistic coverage.

H.C. Mayr et al. (Eds.): DEXA 2001, LNCS 2113, pp. 145–154, 2001.

In order to bright the essence of these problems, we provide an abstract model (AM) in NChiql. We try to give a solution for these problems based on the model in our system.

The remainder of this paper is organized as follows: In Section 2, an abstract model in NChiql is presented. Section 3 explain the natural language query processing in NChiql. The experiment results are provided in Section 4. Section 5 concludes the paper.

2 Abstract Model in Nchiql

Generally, there are three level models involved in a NLIDB, which are user's linguistic model, domain conceptual model and data model. The Figure 1 shows that the domain conceptual model is usually fixed for a specific domain, but the corresponding data models in computers may be various. Similarly, users can employ different linguistic models to express the same concepts. For example, "what are sale on the second floor" and "what we can buy on the second floor", or "what is his salary" and "how much does he earn every month".

The task of NLIDBs is to map the user's linguistic model to machine's data model. However, the distance between them is very far. Data models do not contain any semantic information. On the other hand, linguistic models are flexible and varied. Most systems have to introduce an intermediate representation - conceptual models. Linguistic models are first mapped to unambiguous conceptual models and then to definite data models from the conceptual models. All of these are illustrated in Figure 1, which is called abstract model.

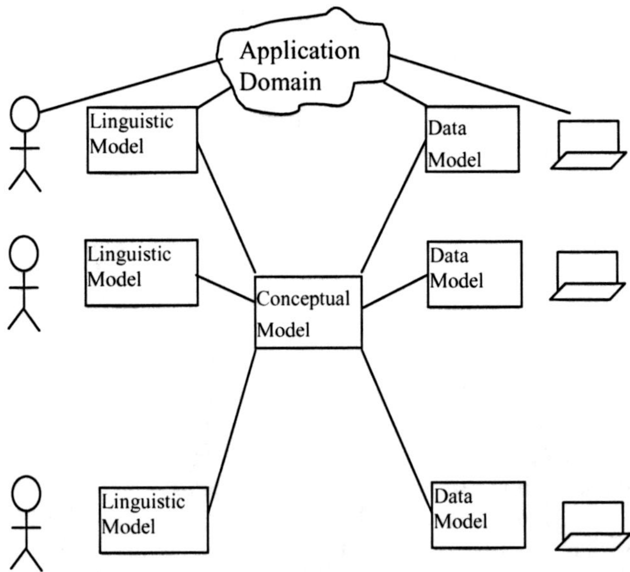

Fig. 1. The Abstract Model in Nchiql

The introduction of conceptual models can bridge the gap of linguistic models and data models to some extent. Most NLIs choose logical forms as the conceptual models. Although E-R models are also available to express conceptual model, they are developed for database design and cannot express complete semantics. They have to be extend to cover linguistic models in NLIs. Based on the idea, we provide a Semantic Conceptual Model (SCM) to serve as the conceptual models in NChiql,. SCM can describe not only the semantics of words, but also combination relationship among different words that involve in linguistic models. So it's more powerful than the E-R model in term of semantics expression.

Each application domain has different vocabulary and domain knowledge. So when a NLIDB is portable from one domain to another, the three models will be changed based on application domain. Linguistic model and data model can be obtained by domain experts and database designers respectively. The difficulty is how to generate conceptual model from domain, namely how to build the bridge. We think that's the essence for the problems mentioned above. So in order to solve the problem of portability, it must enable the system to generate conceptual model automatically or semi-automatically.

Based on the relationship among the three models, we give an extracting method in NChiql that can build the SCM automatically [8]. The performance is 15-20 minutes in an evaluation of transporting NChiql to a new domain.

Besides the three models in AM, there are two mappings existing among them, that's Linguistic model to conceptual model mapping, and Conceptual to Data mapping. Actually, the Processing of a natural language query in NLIDBs is the processing of the two mapping. The first mapping is the sentence analysis processing, and the second is the translation to database query.

3 Chinese Natural Language Query Processing Based on SCM in Nchiql

The goal of language processing in NLIDB is to translate natural language to database query. So it's not necessary to understand the deep structure of sentences, as long as we can reach the translation goal. On the other hand, different from common language, natural query language has its own features: First, it mainly includes three kinds of sentences: the imperative, the question and the elliptical in term of language structure. Second, the database concept model limits the semantic content of the natural query statements, that's to say, the query statements only involve the words that have direct relationship with database model (E-R Model). Based on the consideration, we depict a novel language processing method based on the database semantic, namely SCM. It includes the following steps:

1. Based on the Chinese query language features, a word segmentation algorithm is designed to handle the delimiting problem;
2. Based on the semantic word segmentation, a revised dependency grammar is depicted to parse the language structures;
3. Based on the semantic dependency tree, the outcome of second step, we give a set of heuristic rules for translation to database query, e.g.SQL.

3.1 Word Segmentation Based on SCM in NChiql

The initial step of any language analysis task is to tokenize the input statement into separated words with certain meaning. For many writing systems, using white space as a delimiter for words yields reasonable results. However, for Chinese and other systems where white space is not used to delimit words, such trivial schemes will not work. Therefore, how to segment the words in a Chinese natural language becomes an important issue.

Most of literatures [2,3,5] on Chinese segmentation are rooted in the natural language processing (NLP). However, NLIDB, as one of the typical application domain of NLP, has its own processing features. It is very possible to apply the achievement in NLP to NLIDB, but it may not be the best way.

The goal of language processing in NLIDB is to translate natural language to database query. So it's not necessary to understand the deep structure of sentences, as long as we can reach the translation goal. Generally, the conventional segmentation methods mark the word with Part of Speech (POS) such as noun, verb, adjunct, and pronoun etc. These methods can not reflect the database semantic associated with the words. However, in NLIDB we do not care which class a word belongs to, but care what semantic it represents in database. According to this design principle, we give a novel word segment method based on the database semantic. The advantage of the word-segmenter is simple and efficient. The performance was 99% above precision to our real test queries [9].

Definition 1. The *database description* of a given word in a specific application domain (DOM) is defined as D(ω:DOM)=*(o,[t,c])*, where ω represents the given word; *o* represents the corresponding database object (entity, relation, attribute) of ω; *t* represents the data type(data type, length, precision) of a database object; *c* represents the verb case of a database object.

3.2 Sentence Analysis in NChiql

The next step of language analysis is sentence analysis. Many researches have shown[10] that Chinese languages are suitable to be represented by Dependency Grammar(DG). We argue that Chinese natural language queries are especially suitable to be parsed by DG. Under the scope of database, the dependency relationship is very simple and clear.

In SCM, there are three kinds of the association among the database objects:

1) modifying /modified association;
2) relationship association; and
3) part-of association.

In the query language, every words which have specific database semantic will associate with other words as the above relationship. The query goals and query conditions can be clustered based on the associations. Based on the idea, we put forward a dependency analysis method ground on database semantics.

We know that DG parsing can be represented as dependency trees. Basically, the nodes in the dependency tree are three attributes tuple as below:

(<dependant-no>,<governor-no>, <dependant-relation>)

a dependency tree is the collection of the nodes.

In NChiql, we extend the above tree. First the node is extended to four attributes tuple: (<dependant-no>,<governor-no>,<dependant-relation> , D)
where D is the database semantic description as defined in Definition 1. It will be useful to the query translation to SQL. We design special values for <dependant-relation> based on the database requirements. We have the following dependent relations :

- value based relation
- relationship based relation
- VP based relation
- aggregation based relation
- quantifier based relation
- compare based relation
- conjunction based relation

The tree consisting of the above extended nodes is called the database semantic dependency tree, or for short, semantic dependency tree(SDT).

3.3 Translation to Database Query Based on Set-Block in NChiql

SDT is a hierarchical tree structure. As mentioned in the above section, STD has combined database semantics in sentence analysis. Therefore, the SDT has both the sentence structure and semantic information used in the translation to database query (i.e.SQL).

The nodes in SDT can be classified to the following types:

Attribute value node (AVD): it's related to some like "Attribute = value" expression, i.e. a selection predicate.

Entity node (ED): it's related to a database object such as table name.

Relationship node (RD): it's related to a join condition.

Operation node (OD): it's related to some operators like AND/OR, GREAT/LESS, SOME/ALL, etc..

AVDs give the restrictive condition. But restrictive objects should be given by EDs. So a semantic block in database translation should consists of several nodes that have internal dependent relationship among each other. ED plus at least one AVD can be a semantic block. Also, a OD plus ED or semantic unit can serve as a semantic unit.

Definition 2. A *semantic block* can be defined as a subtree rooted Rs in SDT:

1) Rs should be a ED; or

2) Rs should be a OD with database object sub-nodes;

3) sub node of Rs should be AVD, RD, or semantic block.

It's a recursive definition that reflects the nest feature in semantic blocks.

Clearly, the semantic block is a recursive definition that reflects the nested block nature in database queries. Essentially, s semantic block is a set in database evaluation. So we can call it as set block too. In database scope, set block can be defined as below.

Definition 3. Let SetBlock = (Obj , Cond , T) , where:

Obj = $\{o \mid o \in R \vee o \in U\}$, U denoted all attributes , R denoted all relations;

Cond = cond1$\wedge$cond2…$\vee$condi$\vee$condi+1…$\wedge$condn;

Condi = A_{i1} Op V 或A_{i1} Op A_{i2} , or {SQL where conditions}, $1 \le i \le n$, $A_{i1}, A_{i2} \in U$, V denoted values , Op $\in$ { $>,<,\le,\ge\ne,=$};

T= {t | t = the relation that A_{ij} belongs to , $1 \le i \le n$, $1 \le j \le 2$}

It can be found that semantic block can acts as the basic unit in the translation from a natural language query to a database query (SQL). Semantic blocks enable us to adopt a "divide-and-conquer" strategy for translation. This method consists of two steps. In the first step, the SDT is transformed to a tree with nested blocks, where each block is a subtree (based on Definition 2). In the second step, blocks that correspond to subqueries (based on Definition 3) are evaluated in an inside-out manner. When a block is evaluated, the root of the corresponding subtree is reduced; that is, the block corresponding to the root of subtree are returned as an intermediate result, a possible SQL subquery. After every blocks are evaluated, we can obtain a series subqueries. So it's an important stage to integrate the subqueries to a final SQL statement.

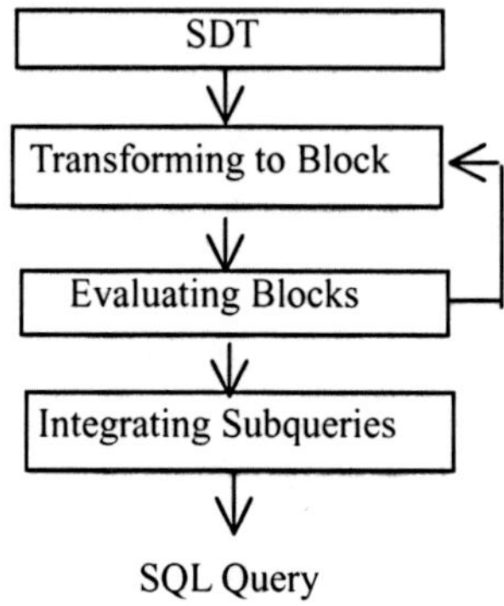

Fig. 2. Translation process Flow

Based on the above discussion, the translation process flow is shown in Figure 2.

3.4 Run-Time System Structure and Implementation

Figure 3 illustrates the run-time system structure and functional components of Nchinql. The part included in the box is the language processing function, the outside is the user interface function. NChiql have good ability of leaning and guidance. We explain the processing flow in Figure 3 as below:

⊙ Users face the Guidance function, which can help users to lean the system scope and typical query statements;

(1) Users input their natural language query statement by voice or writing devices;

(2) Natural language query is passed to Language Analyzer through Interface Agent;

(3)(4)(5)(6) Language Analyzer read Semantic Dictionary to process word segmentation and sentence analysis. When it meets the words that can not be identified, Language Analyzer returns the words to Interface Agent which call the Learning module to handle the new words with the interaction of users. The result will be sent to Language Analyzer to process further;

(7) The result of Language Analyzer is SDT, which can be used as middle language for translation and paraphrasing;

(8)(9) To be confirmed the result of Language Analyzer by users, middle language is generated to natural language by paraphrasing module. If the analysis result does not meet the user's requirement, system will stop the processing and return to user interface to revise the paraphrasing result;

(10)(11) If the result is right, middle language is translated to SQL;

(12)(13) The Executing module call DBMS to handle the SQL, and the query results are handover to Response Analysis to help user understanding the results.

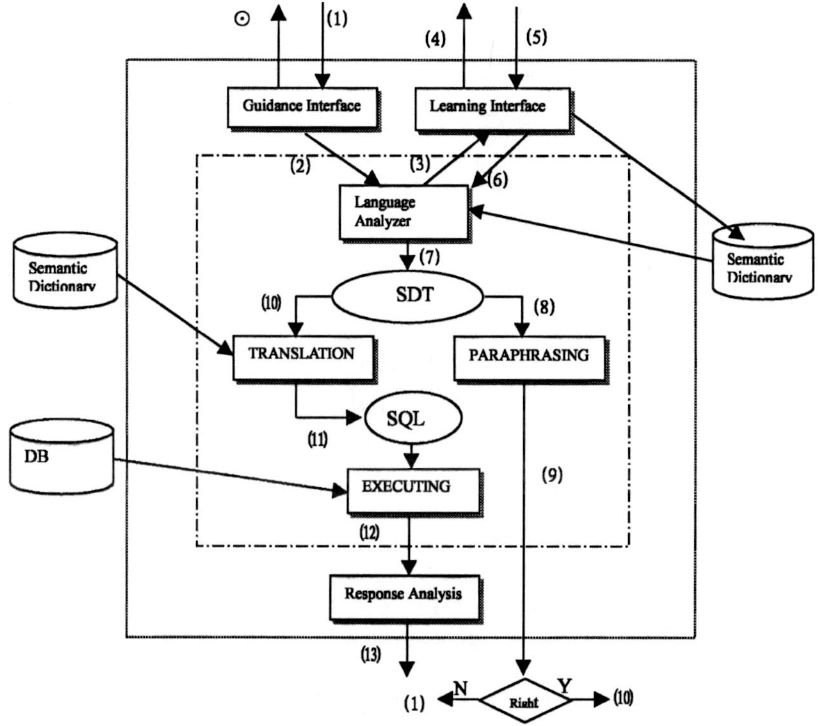

Fig. 3. Run-time structure in NChiql

4 System Evaluation

4.1 Test Data Collection and Analysis

To conduct the evaluation, an investigation has been designed for two purposes: (1) collecting the test data for the evaluation; (2) analyzing the data to find out the sentence distribution.

There were 44 subjects under study in this experiment with very diverse backgrounds. In fact, the educational backgrounds of these subjects varied drastically including master program students, undergraduates as well as persons with only secondary school level education. Their ages varied between 14 and 23. Two methods are used for the investigation:

– Passive investigation: Each subject should answer our questionnaire by natural language query. The questionnaire consists of 30 problems shown with pictures. Additional help were available, but did not inflect their language usage. Each question can be expressed with several different queries.

– Active investigation: Each subject give any questions under the specific domain.

We collected 1126 query sentences through the passive investigation and 124 query sentences through active investigation. There are four kind of sentence involved in answers, including imperative query, question query, elliptical query, and multi-sentence query. Table 1 and 2 describe the percentage of each kind of query.

Table 1. Natural language query percentage (passive investigation)

	imperative	question	elliptical	multi-sentence	others	error	total
No. of sentences	620	289	35	94	18	70	1126
percentage %	55.1	25.7	3.1	8.3	1.6	6.2	100

Table 2. Natural Language query percentage (active investigation)

	imperative	question	elliptical	multi-sentence	others	error	total
No. of sentences	48	48	2	7	5	14	124
percentage %	38.7	38.7	1.7	5.6	1.6	11.3	100

From the table 1 and table 2, we can see that imperative query and question query are the dominant usage in natural language query (with the percentage of 80.8 and 77.4% respectively)。 It should note here, all the subjects are not knowledgeable in database and SQL. So their query usage does not be inflected by database query (e.g. SQL).

Based on the investigation, we select the imperative query and question query as the test objects(See Table 3).

Table 3. Testing Queries

	imperative	question	total
Number of test sentences	130	31	162

4.2 Usability Test

In the language processing, system will interact with users for some ambiguity or unknown words in order to obtain the right answer. The number of interaction with users in NChiql is the main factor in term of usability. The test result is shown in Table 5.

Table 4. Usability Test

	No of interaction									
	0	1	2	3	4	5	6	7	8	9
No of Testing queries	46	44	46	12	5	2	2	1	1	3

From the Table 4, we can see that almost 148 sentences (of 162 sentences, 91.36%) need the interaction with users no more than three times, and only 8.64% sentences need over three times interaction. This result shows that Nchiql has the good usability. That proves that Nchiql has good ability of leaning and disambiguating.

4.3 Correctness Test

For a query, There are two results: one is the answer required by users (called UR), the other is the system output (called SR). It's a correct result when SR is equal to UR. Unfortunately, SR is not always equal to UR. Basically, there are following relationship between SR and UR:

- Equality(EQ): combining with the interaction, EQ can be evaluated as the following cases:
  - EQ(<3): System can output a correct result with no more than three interactions;
  - EQ(>3): System can output a correct result with more than three interactions.
- Part Equality (PEQ) : SR partly matches UR. There are two cases too:
  - PEQ1: System can output a SR, but its contents are less or more than UR. For example, users want to find student's name and age, but the system outputs a small result(just including name or age attribute) or a big result (including more attributes besides name and age).
  - PEQ2: System can output a SR, SR is related to US. For example, users want to find student's name, but system gives the student's address.
- Not Equality(NEQ) : System can output a SR, but it's not related to UR semantically.

Table 5 shows the correctness test result.

Table 5. Correctness Test (1)

	EQ	PEQ	NEQ
No of sentences	139	22	1
percent%	85.8	13.58	0.62

Table 5. Correctness Test (2)

	EQ<3	EQ>3
No of sentences	123	16
percent%	88.49	11.51

There are 85.8% sentences can be processed correctly. Among them, there are 88.49% sentences can be handled correctly with no more than three interactions. So we can conclude that NChiql has good usability and high correctness.

5 Conclusion

Now there are two main problems hinder NLIDBs to gain the rapid and wide commercial acceptance: portability and usability. In order to bright the essence of these problems, we provide an abstract model (AM) in NChiql. In this paper we depict a novel language processing method based on the database semantic, namely

SCM. The experiment results show that NChiql has good usability and high correctness.

In the future , we will explore how to utilize the techniques in NChiql to query Web by natural language.

Acknowledgements. This work is sponsored by the Natural Science Foundation of China (NSFC) under grant number 69633020. We would like to thank Shuang Liu and Mingzhe Gu of Renmin University of China for their great help and valuable advice in the evaluation and the detailed implementation of NChiql.

References

[1] Hendrix G.G., Natural Language Interface, *American Journal of Computational Linguistics*, 1982, 8(2):56-61.

[2] Wu X., Ichikawa T., Cercone N., Knowledge-base Assisted Database Retrieval Systems, World Scientific, 1996.

[3] Hendrix G G and Lewis W. H., Transportable Natural Language Interface to Database, *American Journal of Computational Linguistic*, Vol.7,1981.

[4] Grosz B.,et al., Team: An Experiment in the Design of Transportable Natural-Language Interfaces, *Artificial Intelligence* , 1987, 12: 173-243.

[5] Cha S K., et al., Kaleidoscope Data Model for An English-like Query Language, *Proc. of the 17th International Conference on VLDB,* September 3-6, 1991, Spain: 351-361.

[6] Androutsopoulos L., et al, Natural Language Interfaces to Database - An Introduction, URL: http://xxx.lanl.gov/abs/cmp-lg. Also in *Journal of Natural Language Engineering*, Combridge University press, 1995, 1(1): 29-81.

[7] Epstein S S, Transportable Natural Language Processing Through Simplicity - the PRE System, ACM Transaction on Office Information Systems, 1985, 3(2): 107-120.

[8] Meng X F, Zhou Yong, Wang Shan, Domain Knowledge Extracting in a Chinese Natural Language Interface to Database: NChiql, In Proc of PAKDD'99, Beijing: Spinger-Verlag , 1999: 179-183.

[9] Meng X F, Liu S, Wang S, Word Segmentation based on Database Semantic in NChiql,, Journal of Computer Science and Technology, 1998, 5(4):329-344.

[10] Zhang X X, et al., Encyclopedia of Computer Science and Technology, Tsinghua Press, 1999:1008-1011

Pattern-Based Guidelines for Coordination Engineering

Patrick Etcheverry, Philippe Lopistéguy, and Pantxika Dagorret

Laboratoire d'Informatique U.P.P.A
IUT de Bayonne – Pays Basque
Château Neuf – 64100 Bayonne – France
{Patrick.Etcheverry, Philippe.Lopisteguy, Pantxika.Dagorret}@iutbayonne.univ-pau.fr

Abstract. This paper focuses on coordination engineering. We state that coordination engineering can be approached through a double point of view. On the one hand, coordination problems are recurrent and on the other hand, tested forms of coordination exist. We define a typology of coordination problems that can be solved by the enforcement of well known coordination forms. We highlight a correlation between our approach and the context-problem-solution formulation of patterns. We present a catalogue of coordination patterns that makes an inventory of a set of coordination problems, and a set of solutions that describe how these problems can be solved. After describing an example of coordination pattern, we finally present guidelines that use the catalogue in a framework of process coordination engineering.

1 Two Key Components for a Coordination Problem Solving

This paper focuses on the problem of coordination specification, which is a recurrent problem in numerous domains. Indeed, it appears in each process (human or software) composed by a great number of activities that have to be performed by different actors (or processors).

Coordination difficulties exist within every society composed by entities which are able to act in an autonomous way and have to reach a common goal. The problem we point out is the difficulty to describe and, therefore, to solve coordination problems within a complex process. This paper aims to present an approach to describe coordination problems and elaborate solutions to solve them. This approach is based on the analysis of coordination problem [4], [13], [15], [5] from which we point out two fundamental and recurrent issues: on the one hand, the need to identify several coordination principles and, on the other hand, the need to identify situations where such principles can be applied.

Consequently, we consider that any intent to control coordination must attempt to solve the two previously outlined problems: identification of coordination situations, and identification of coordination forms that manage these situations. Our proposal is strongly based on this fundamental statement. Indeed, the two previous points will be

H.C. Mayr et al. (Eds.): DEXA 2001, LNCS 2113, pp. 155–164, 2001.

considered as two structural axes for solutions modelling as well as they will give rise to methodological steps in the construction of solutions to coordination problems.

Firstly, our contribution is presented as a catalogue of coordination patterns that makes an inventory of a set of situations, where coordination problems occur, and a set of solutions that describe how these problems can be solved. Secondly, we propose a four steps approach that helps designers to specify the coordination forms that have to be adopted by the activities of the modelled process. For each step, we list inputs, deliverables, the corresponding pattern clauses on which it relies and the models/languages needed to perform it. We also indicate adapted methodologies to carry out the step and precise existing computer-based tools that are able to support these methodologies.

2 Situations of Coordination

2.1 Situation Vocabulary = Vocabulary of the Domain

We aim to elaborate guidelines that help to carry out coordination within human or software processes. Consequently, specification of situations and coordination forms has to be performed in terms of elements that belong to the considered processes, that means in terms of the considered domains. Despite the specificity of each process, it is possible to define a common vocabulary allowing a generic description of any process.

We consider that a *process* is basically composed of a set of *activities* that combine and use *resources*. An activity corresponds to an action of the process. It can be elementary, or composed of other activities. A resource is an entity belonging to the activities environment and needed for activities progress. We define three types of resources: actors (human being or software, and more generally, any component of the organisation able to process an activity), devices and documents. Moreover, activities and resources have interactions, like resource utilisation (by an activity) and temporal constraints (between activities). This point has been developed in [7] and presented as a complete model of process.

2.2 Typology of Coordination Situations

Our typology of coordination situations relies on [13] which studies the recurrent and interdisciplinary characteristics of coordination problems. Coordination is defined as "the management of dependencies between activities", where the main types of dependencies are: production-expenditure of resources, resource sharing, simultaneity constraints and tasks - sub-tasks relationships.

Subsequently, we define a coordination situation as a situation where one of these four dependencies can be identified between activities of a given process.

For each coordination situation, we describe, on the one hand, the characteristics of this situation and on the other hand, the coordination problems related to it.

Production - Expenditure of Resources

Characterisation: This situation arises when an activity produces a resource which is used by another activity. The production - expenditure relation is not limited to material flows, it also extends to informational flows.

Example: In manufacturing processes, a typical example occurs when the result produced at one stage of the assembly line is used as input for the following stage.

Associated coordination problems: We distinguish three families of problems related to the production - expenditure of resources:
- Prerequisite problems: these problems happen when the following constraint cannot be satisfied: a P activity producer of an R resource must be finished before a C activity consumer of R begins. This rule implies two sub-constraints: P activity exists and P must produce R before R expenditure begins.
- Transfer problems: these problems are related to resource "transportation", from production activity until expenditure activity (wrong data communication channel, wrong resource deposit place, etc).
- Usability problems: these problems happen when the produced resource cannot be expended because of its format and/or its properties (access rights, etc).

Sharing Resources

Characterisation: This situation arises when activities must share a limited resource. It is necessary to have a resource allocator which manages the resource demands formulated by the activities. Resource allocation is probably one of the most largely studied coordination mechanisms: for example, economy, organisation theory and data processing are major domains interested by this issue.

Examples: sharing a storage space, sharing a person's working time, etc.

Associated coordination problem: It is related to concomitant accesses to the shared resource.

Simultaneity Constraints

Characterisation: This situation arises when activities must satisfy one or more temporal constraints among the following ones [11]: "A activity *before* B activity", "A activity *starts* B activity", "A activity *overlaps* B activity", "A activity *during* B activity", etc.

Example: Planning a rendezvous is a typical situation which supposes simultaneity constraints satisfaction ("A activity *starts* B activity", which means that activities A and B must start at the same time).

Associated coordination problems: They deal with difficulties to respect the control of temporal constraints.

Tasks and Subtasks Relationships

Characterisation: This situation happens when the goal to reach is divided into sub-goals and the associated activities are distributed to several actors.

Example: Retrieval information activity on Internet, where different search engines are in charge of exploring different sites.

Associated coordination problems: Three kinds of coordination problems emerge. The first problem consists in determining the goal to reach. The second problem consists in splitting the task into sub-tasks. The last problem consists in allocating the sub-tasks to the actors.

3 Coordination Forms

A coordination form defines a mechanism that expresses coordination principles. The study of various works [15], [8], [3] and [5] points out that all detailed coordination forms are enclosed in coordination forms described in [15]. Thus, we rely upon this nomenclature for identifying coordination forms. Any coordination is expressed according to three basic mechanisms: mutual adjustment, supervision, and standardisation (which is declined in four particular under-forms).

3.1 Supervision

Characterisation: It is the coordination form where a supervisor gives instructions and controls the execution of a set of tasks.

Example: In computer systems, the supervision mechanism is used in systems based on a master - slave architecture. In Management domain, supervision is based on hierarchical levels: leaders supervise managers which themselves supervise operators.

3.2 Standardisation

Characterisation: It is the coordination form where activities have to respect norms. These norms can focus on: behavior to carry out, results to reach, qualifications to have or standards to respect.

Example: TCP/IP protocol specifies a behaviour that has to be adopted by communicating machines.

3.3 Mutual Adjustment

Characterisation: This mechanism carries out the activities coordination by informal communication. It is a particularly suitable mechanism for complex situations where numerous activities interact.

Example: An organisation in charge of sending a man on the moon for the first time is compelled to use this coordination mechanism. This project requires a very elaborated labour division between thousands of specialists. The project success largely depends on the specialists capability to adjust one with each other [15].

4 Coordination Patterns Catalogue

Our analysis of current research works about coordination leads us to state that the presented coordination situations can be managed by the introduced coordination forms.

4.1 Patterns as a Combination of Situations and Coordination Forms

The catalogue of coordination patterns we propose relies on the former statement. Indeed, for [10], a pattern is "a solution to a problem in a given context". The *context* refers to all recurrent situations in which the pattern is applied. The *problem* expresses a set of forces (goals and constraints) which take place in the context. The *solution* refers to a model that can be applied to solve these forces. Thus, by analysing coordination issue according to the context-problem-solution point of view, we identify situations (*contexts*) where coordination forms must be employed to construct solutions (*solutions*) to coordination problems (*problems*). To take up [14] point of view, we consider the set of coordination patterns as a catalogue of solution schemas that can be applied in order to specify and solve coordination problems.

Each pattern results from the connection of one coordination situation and one coordination form introduced in the former section. Then, the pattern catalogue is composed of the combination of coordination situations and coordination forms. It is presented in the bellowing table. For example, mapping a supervision mechanism with the task allocation problem leads to specify a pattern, marked (*) in the catalogue, which focuses on task allocation solutions thanks to supervision techniques.

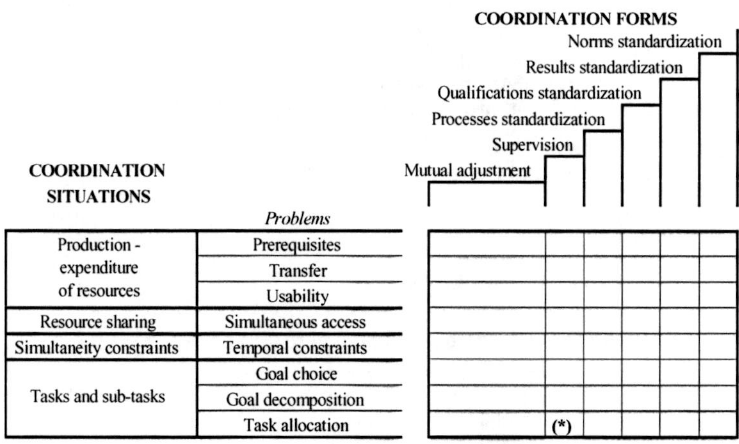

Fig. 1. Patterns catalogue structure

4.2 An Example of Pattern

We describe patterns according to a framework derived from those presented in [1] and [9]. The coordination pattern presented results from mapping the task allocation problem and the supervision mechanism. We present an informal description of each clause.

Name	*Task allocation by supervision*
Examples	- In MIMD multiprocessors architectures, process distribution to multiple processors deals with task allocation problems. When allocation is carried out in a centralised way, the "task allocation by supervision" pattern is applicable. - This pattern is applicable to the multi-agent planning mode called "centralised planning for multiple agents" [8].
Context	This pattern can be used each time the problem deals with distributing tasks between several actors (human, hardware or software). The context elements are a set of tasks and a set of actors.
Consider-ed Problem	The pattern deals with the problem of tasks allocation between several actors. The difficulty consists in determining who does what. The problem is how to establish links between tasks to achieve and potential actors.
How to build the solution	To solve the problem, it is necessary to have a strategy based on the supervision mechanisms. The strategy has to establish links between tasks and actors. The strategy is distributed between the supervisor and the potential actors, and is controlled by the supervisor. The supervisor: - knows the tasks to be carried out - knows the potential actors able to perform tasks - has an algorithm of tasks allocation - is informed of the acceptance or not of the tasks assignments Each actor is provided with communication and behaviour capabilities: - reception of instructions - sending of notifications to received instructions - instruction interpreter and task performance capabilities
Solution	The supervisor decides the links to establish. It is informed by the actors of their tasks acceptance. Actors can be required to carry out tasks and notify the supervisor concerning their acceptance or refusal.

Strengths and compro-mises	This solution with centralised structure facilitates control and allows dynamic adaptation of the supervisor's strategy. This pattern is recommended in strongly dynamic environments where re-planning is an essential activity. The weakness of the pattern is the weakness of centralised systems. If the supervisor undergoes a fault, coordination will not be correctly ensured. In a costly communication environment, this pattern is not efficient because its success strongly depends on the exchanges between the supervisor and actors.
Associat-ed patterns	Each pattern related to task allocation brings a different solution. Thus, in order to remedy defaults of this pattern (see Strengths and compromises), it is recommended to use the "task allocation by standardisation" pattern (processes standardisation, results standardisation) which needs few communication.

5 Using the Catalogue to Solve Coordination Problems

We present an approach that uses the catalogue in a process modelling context [12]. We propose a four steps approach that helps designers to specify the coordination forms that have to be adopted by the components of the modelled process. For each step, we list inputs, deliverables, the models/languages and the corresponding pattern clauses on which it relies. We also indicate adapted methodologies to carry out the step and precise existing computer-based tools that are able to support the step.

5.1 Describing Activities According to a Process Approach

Objectives: The aim of this step consists in describing the various activities that must be carried out in order to achieve the process goal. It does not focus on how activities are carried out but on how activities are connected to achieve the final goal.

Input data: It is made up of informal knowledge about the process to be modelled. Knowledge is parcelled and held by different actors of the process.

Deliverables: A schema of the process describing its components in terms of: actors, activities, resources, roles, and relations between them.

Models, languages: Deliverables are described thanks to a process model defined in [2] with a semi-formal modelling language (Unified Modelling Language [17]).

Methodology: Methods belonging to requirements engineering and knowledge acquisition domains are well adapted to carry out this step.

Tools for Information Technology based support: A collective process editor has been developed in order to support the achievement of this step [6]. It allows the proper actors of the process to participate simultaneously at the process description.

5.2 Identifying Situations That Generate Coordination Problems

Objectives: The goal of this step consists in analysing the described process and identifying the situations in which problems need coordination solutions.

Input data: The process schema produced by the previous step.

Deliverables: A set of situations and associated problems extracted from the process schema.

Models, languages: Deliverables of this step are situations described thanks to the process model used in the previous step.

Methodology: Situations are identified by analysing the existing dependencies between components (activities, resources, ...) and comparing them to the situations typology defined in the patterns catalogue.

Tools for Information Technology based support: Pattern recognition systems are of interest in this step. They identify and suggest situations in the process schema that can match with situations of the catalogue.

5.3 Choosing a Coordination Form for Each Coordination Problem

Objectives: The aim of this step consists in associating a coordination form to each identified coordination situation.

Input data: A set of situations and associated problems extracted from the process schema and identified in the previous step.

Deliverables: A set of pairs: coordination situation extracted from the process schema ; associated coordination form, which define the coordination canvas of the process. There is one pair [coordination situation ; coordination form] for each extracted situation, and it defines the way the named situation will be managed.

Models, languages: no specific language to describe a set of pairs.

Methodology: The assignment of a catalogue's coordination form to a coordination situation is carried out thanks to the comparison between characteristics and constraints of the situation's environment (organisation: distributed / centralised / hierarchical, communication: quality / rapidity ...) with advantages and drawbacks of the coordination forms (local / global knowledge and decision, communication usage ...). These correlation aspects are treated in the *Strengths and compromises* clause and the *Associated patterns* clause of the pattern. The choice of forms can also be guided by the analysis of previously acquired experience.

Tools for Information Technology based support: Case based reasoning systems are of interest in this step.

5.4 Carrying out Coordination

Objectives: The aim of this step consists in producing a solution for each extracted coordination situation by the enforcement of the corresponding coordination form.

Inputs: A set of pairs [coordination situation ; coordination form] defined in the previous step.

Deliverables: A set of solutions derived from the pairs [coordination situation ; coordination form]. Each solution assigns procedures (directives, rules) to the situation components and brings, when necessary, new elements needed to implement the solution (queues, stacks …).

Models, languages: The procedures assigned by the solution are specified in terms of mechanisms (directives, rules) belonging to the form.

Methodology: *How to build* and *Solution* pattern clauses describe how to carry out this step. The objective consists in using the specific mechanisms of the form to express the procedures to be applied by the components. Adapted methodologies for carrying out this step concern engineering of procedures production and engineering of procedures implementation into situation components. For example, business process reengineering in management domain.

Tools for Information Technology based support: The tools facilitate the implementation of the procedures within situation components. For instance, multi-agent systems are suitable to implement procedures derived from negotiation forms.

6 Conclusion

The whole approach is based on the strong distinction between two axes: situations and forms of coordination. According to these two axes, coordination description is an original way to present coordination problems. Specification of solutions by the means of patterns constitutes a framework that allows answering to fundamental questions of [16] "… why, when, where and how is coordination carried up …". Indeed, each pattern describes a solution (how to) in order to solve a coordination problem (why) that arises in a situation (when / where) [9]. The proposal of a pattern catalogue structured according to these two main axes allows a large enumeration of solutions and any extension of each axes leads to the extension of the whole catalogue. Our presented approach also relies upon the two axes. Consequently, it suggests the designer a prior specification of problematic situations. The analysis of their environment facilitates then an adapted choice of the form to be adopted. Moreover, the organisation of both catalogue and approach according to the two axes ensures a usefulness help of the described patterns in the approach.

References

1. C. Alexander, S. Ishikawa, M. Silverstein, M. Jacobson, I. Fiskdahl-King, S. Angel: A Pattern Language. Oxford University Press, New York, (1977)
2. C. Bareigts, P. Etcheverry, P. Dagorret, P. Lopistéguy: Models of process specification for Organisational Learning. UK Conference on Communications and Knowledge Management, Swansea, Wales, UK, (2000)
3. B. Chaib-draa, S. Lizotte: Coordination in unfamiliar situations. Third French-speaking days, IAD & SMA, Chambery-St Baldoph, (1995)

4. K. Crowston, C.S. Osborn: A coordination theory approach to process description and redesign. Technical report number 204, Cambridge, MA, MIT, Centre for Coordination Science, (1998)
5. K.S. Decker: Environment Centred Analysis and Design of Coordination Mechanisms. Department of Computer Science, University of Massachusetts, UMass CMPSCI Technical Report, (1995)
6. P. Etcheverry, P. Dagorret, G. Bernadet, N. Salémi, A. Coste: A cooperative editor for process design. Bayonne, (1999)
7. P. Etcheverry, P. Dagorret, P. Lopistéguy: Know-how capitalization, a process approach. Interdisciplinary Research Center, Bayonne, (1999)
8. J. Ferber: Multi-Agent Systems - Towards a collective intelligence. InterEditions – ISBN: 2-7296-0665-3, (1997)
9. E. Gamma, R. Helm, R. Johnson, J. Vlissides: Design Patterns - Elements of Reusable Object-Oriented Software. Addison-Wesley publishing company - ISBN: 0-201-63361-2, (1995)
10. D. Lea: Patterns Discussion http://g.oswego.edu/dl/pd-FAQ/pd-FAQ.html, (1997)
11. T.D.C. Little, A. Ghafoor: Interval-Based Conceptual Models for Time-Dependent Multimedia Data. In IEEE Trans. on Knowledge and Data Engineering (Special Issue: Multimedia Information Systems), Vol. 5, N°4, pp 551-563, (1993)
12. P. Lorino: The value development by processes. in French Review of Management, (1995)
13. T.W. Malone and K. Crowston: The Interdisciplinary Study of Coordination. ACM Computing Surveys, 26 (1), pp 87-119, (1993)
14. M. Mattsson: Object-Oriented Frameworks. A survey of methodological issues. Licentiate Thesis, Lund University, Department of Computer Science, (1996)
15. H. Mintzberg: Management. Travel Toward Organizations Centre. Organizations Editions, Paris, (1990)
16. H. S. Nwana, L. C. Lee and N. R. Jennings: Coordination in Software Agent Systems. The British Telecom Technical Journal, 14 (4) 79-88, (1996)
17. J. Rumbaugh, G. Booch, I. Jacobson: The Unified Modeling Language Reference Manual. Addison-Wesley, (1998)

Information Management for Material Science Applications in a Virtual Laboratory

A. Frenkel[1], H. Afsarmanesh[1], G. Eijkel[2], and L.O. Hertzberger[1]

[1] University of Amsterdam, Computer Science Department
Kruislaan 403, 1098 SJ, Amsterdam, The Netherlands
{annef, hamideh, bob}@science.uva.nl

[2] Institute for Atomic and Molecular Physics (AMOLF)
Kruislaan 407, 1098 SJ, Amsterdam, The Netherlands
eijkel@amolf.nl

Abstract. The goal of Virtual Laboratory project (VL), being developed at the University of Amsterdam, is to provide an open and flexible infrastructure to support scientists in their collaboration towards the achievement of a joint experiment. The advanced features of VL provide an ideal environment for experiment-based applications, such as the Material Analysis of Complex Surfaces (MACS) experiments, to benefit from different developed interfaces to the hardware and software required by the scientists. To properly support the information management in this collaborative environment, a set of innovative and specific mechanisms and functionalities for efficient storage, handling, integration, and retrieval of the MACS-related data, as well as data analysis tools on the experiment results, are being developed. This paper focuses on the information management in the MACS application case and describes its implementation using the Matisse ODBMS system.

1 Introduction

The aim of the Virtual Laboratory (VL) project[1] is to provide an open and flexible framework that support the collaboration between groups of scientists, engineers and scientific organizations that decide to share their knowledge, skills and resources (e.g. data, software, hardware, complex devices, etc.) towards the achievement of a joint experiment [1], [2], [11]. The advanced features of VL provide an ideal environment for experiment-based applications to benefit from different developed interfaces to the hardware and software required by the scientists.

One of the experiment-based application cases proposed for the VL, is focused on the Material Analysis of Complex Surfaces (MACS) experiments. These experiments involve large and complex physics related devices, such as the Fourier Transformed Infra-Red imaging spectrometer (FTIR) and the nuclear microprobe (μBeam). This

[1] This research is supported by the ICES/KIS organization.

H.C. Mayr et al. (Eds.): DEXA 2001, LNCS 2113, pp. 165–174, 2001.

application case benefits from VL since it is possible to operate these devices remotely in a multiple-user collaboration way and also from the possibility to combine results from different experiments, creating in this way new research opportunities.

In order to support the information management involved in this collaborative environment, a set of innovative and specific mechanisms and functionalities for efficient storage, handling, integration, and retrieval of the MACS related data, through the VL, are being developed. These mechanisms and functionalities enable scientists to search through the large amount of stored data in order to identify patterns and similarities. Therefore, the database model is carefully designed to enable an efficient way to store and access the data produced in such scientific environments.

The focus of this paper is on describing these information management mechanisms and functionalities specific for the MACS case that are being implemented using the Matisse ODBMS. This paper is organized as follows. Section 2 describes the Virtual Laboratory environment and its reference architecture. In Section 3, the specific domain, i.e. the MACS experiment case is covered. Section 4 presents the development approach and the functional details that support the information management system developed for the MACS application using the Matisse ODBMS system. Section 5 addresses the main conclusions of this paper and some of the future work that is planned in the context of this research project.

2 The Virtual Laboratory Environment

The Virtual Laboratory environment provides a framework for groups of scientists, engineers and scientific organizations that interact and cooperate with each other towards the achievement of a common experiment. Such an experimental environment enables researchers, at different locations, to work in an interactive way, as in any laboratory, i.e. the scientists are able to create and conduct the experiments in the same natural and efficient way as if they were in their laboratory.

One of the most important characteristics of the experimental domains is the manipulation of large data sets produced by the experiment devices, as described in [1]. To be able to handle the resulting experiment data sets, three main requirements are supported within the VL architecture:

- Proper management of large data sets: i.e. storage, handling, integration, and retrieval of large data sets. For example, in such a scientific environment, the size of data sets can range from a few megabytes (e.g. DNA micro-array experiments data sets) to tens of gigabytes (e.g. FTIR imaging micro-spectrometer data sets).
- Information sharing and exchange for collaboration activities: scientists are able to share both the devices used to perform the experiments and the data sets generated by those experiments. They must be able also to look at these data sets and compare them to the ones from previous experiments or other public databases, in order to find similarities and patterns.
- Distributed resource management: must be properly considered in order to meet the high performance and massive computation and storage requirements.

The Virtual Laboratory architecture, shown in Fig. 1, has incorporated these and other functional requirements through the design of different system components. In particular, the VL architecture consists of three main architecture components:

1. The *Application Environment* contains the scientific application domains considered in the VL (e.g. MACS application case, DNA Micro-array application case, and others), including certain specific domain functionalities.
2. The *VL Middleware* enables the VL users to access low level distributed computing resources. The VL middleware provides: the *VL user interface* that enables the scientists to define and execute the experiments; the *Abstract Machine* (AM) that is the intermediate layer between the Grid infrastructure and the VL users, as described in [2]; and three main functional components: the *VIMCO* component provides the functionalities to store and retrieve both the large data sets and the data analysis results, the advance functionalities for intelligent information integration and the facilities for information sharing based in a federated approach [1]. The *ComCol* component provides the appropriate mechanisms for the data and process handling based on the Grid technology. The *ViSE* component offers a generic Virtual Simulation and Exploration environment where 3D visualization techniques are offered to analyze large data sets. The functionality provided by each one of these components is integrated through the *VL integration architecture.*
3. The *Distributed Computing Environment* provides the network platform that enables efficient usage of the computing and communication resources. At present, a Gigabit Ethernet connection is being used. In the near future, it will be extended to a Wide-Area environment using a GigaPort network based on the Surfnet5 backbone, which will result in a speed of 80 gigabits per second and a client connection capacity of 20 Gigabits per second [6]. The Grid infrastructure provides the platform to manage data, resources, and processes in distributed collaborative environments, such as the VL scientific applications. The Globus toolkit offers a set of tools to manage the resources in Data-Grid systems [5], [2], [7], [15].

The functionalities provided by the VIMCO layer and the specific domain tools developed in the VL Interface layer specifically for the Material Science applications are described in details in the following sections.

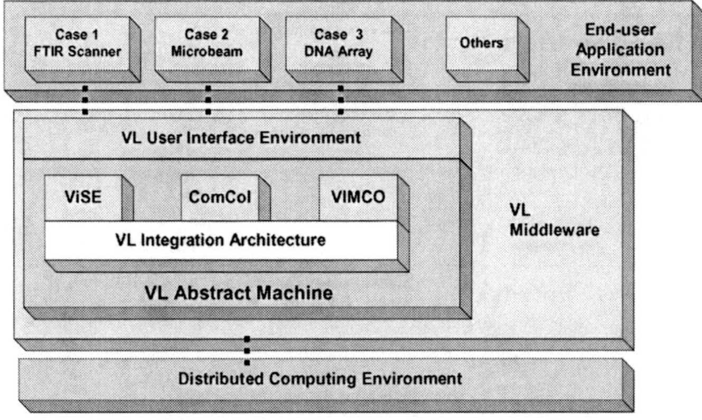

Fig. 1. Virtual Laboratory reference architecture

3 Material Science Application in VL

The goal of the Material Science application is to the study materials and their properties and understanding what happens on surfaces when materials interact. In this section, the Material Analysis of Complex Surface experiment, a specific case of the Material Science application, is described.

3.1 Material Analysis of Complex Surface Experiment

The Material Analysis of Complex Surface (MACS) experiments try to identify and determine the elements that compose complex surfaces, regardless of the nature of the sample. Some application areas that benefit from this kind of experiments (some of which are currently implemented or considered) includes: art conservation and restoration (e.g. analysis of binding media and organic pigments in old master paintings), bio-medical science (e.g. identification of arteriosclerotic deposits in mice), medical research (e.g. studies of trace elements in brain tissues), and others.

The MACS experiment itself can be divided into three phases as shown in Fig. 2, as the preprocessing, the experimentation process, and the analysis of results. The preprocessing phase is where references to related research and images of the object are collected and analyzed. After this, the sample that will be used during the experiment process is extracted from the object. This process includes several extraction protocols and procedures to be followed. Then usually the sample needs to be treated, for example with reagents and solutions, in order to fulfill the requirements of the device used in the material analysis process for the experimentation phase.

The material analysis process is performed with a set of specialized and complex

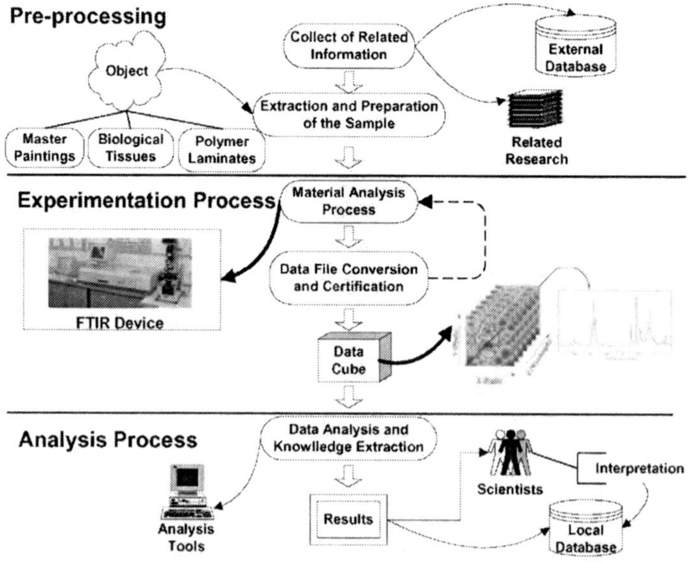

Fig. 2. Material Analysis of Complex Surfaces Experiment

hardware equipments. At present, the FTIR and the µBeam devices are available. The FTIR facility is a non-dispersive infrared imaging spectrometer coupled to an infrared microscope used to examine the infrared radiation absorbed by complex surfaces, as described in [8] and [4]. The µBeam device provides a highly focused beam of ions, with a spatial resolution in the sub-micrometer range, that can be used to identify trace elements on a surface with a sensitivity of 10^{-15} grams as described also in [8].

After the full scan process finishes, the outcome of the experiment is a set of data files, containing the experiment results and the device parameters. This data set consists of a stack of images, known as *hyper-spectral data cube*. Afterwards, these data files are converted into a format that can be used in the analysis phase. Also a quality control process is carried out to certify that the generated data complies with some standards, otherwise the data is discarded and the material analysis process is redone.

The large amount of data produced by these devices makes the analysis phase longer and more effort consuming than the experiment phase itself. For example, the size of one single data cube can range from 16 to 100 Mbytes and considering that every day up to 20 data cubes can be generated, it is understandable that individual scientists cannot do this analysis. Therefore, a set of analysis tools needs to be integrated into the application to facilitate the work of the scientists, e.g. correlation analysis, multivariate data analysis (PCA, pLS) and others.

4 The MACS Information Management System

The main goal of this system is to design and develop an open and flexible environment to facilitate the experimentation process for physicists involved in MACS-related experiments. This application case is being developed at the CO-IM group [14] at the University of Amsterdam in collaboration with the physics institutes AMOLF and NIKHEF.

The first phase to build the MACS system focuses on the specific mechanisms and functionalities that need to be developed for the information management of the data produced by the FTIR and the µBeam devices. Thus, first the identification of the information management requirements including the study of the structures of the input and output data and the study of the operations on the data of the application domain was done. The next step was the development of the MACS database that included: the design of the database, the development of database prototype, the design and development of tools to load the database, the population of the database with the FTIR and/or µBeam data, and the design and development of the user and query interfaces. The second phase will focus on the development of data analysis and knowledge extraction tools that will be used to process, analyze and present the results in such a way that valuable knowledge can be extracted from the large amount of data generated by these complex devices, i.e. information about experimental resources, experimental parameters and conditions, and raw or processed results.

4.1 MACS Process-Data Model

After studying and analyzing the way in which the MACS experiments are performed, (including data, objects, and processes), a process-data flow model was designed. For this design, the Virtual Laboratory Experiment Environment Data (VL-EED) model was used as a reference model [10]. The VL-EED model is a generic database model for experimentation environments. This model is the result of the careful study of several applications, within the context of the VL project. Therefore, it was possible to determine the generic characteristics of scientific experiments and design a generic schema to store experimental information. The VL-EED model is a template that facilitates the creation of new experiment-based schemas, preventing in this way the duplication of modeling effort, i.e. the database managers do not have to create a new "schema" for each new experimental application. It also enables a more efficient way to share and access the data from different experiment-based application tools, e.g. data analysis tools, browser and query tools.

The VL-EED model (shown in Fig. 3) can be viewed as a hierarchy with the class *Project* as the root. Under each project a number of *experiments* can be performed. Each experiment consists of *experiments elements* that can be either *processes* or *data elements*. The experiments and the experiment elements can have *comments*. The processes are actions that can be described by *protocols* (i.e. standard procedures) and can have *properties*. The processes may be carried out with the use of *hardware* or *software* tools with their *parameters* and whose *vendor* is an *organization*. In addition, a *person* that belongs to an *organization* (both with an *address)* performs the experiments and processes. The relationships between experiments and experiment elements

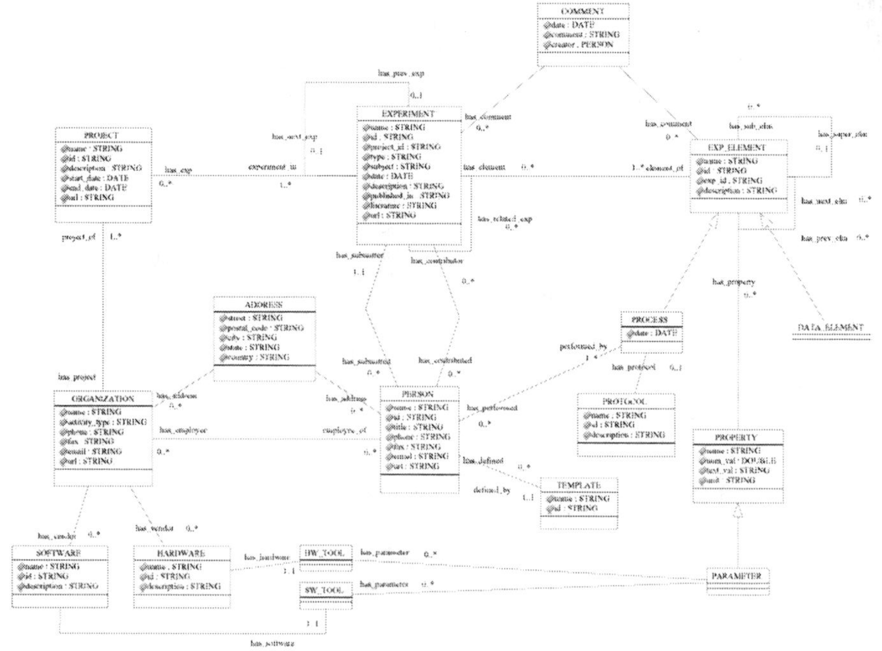

Fig. 3. Virtual Laboratory Experiment Environment Data model

are represented by the recursive-relations *has_prev_elm* and *has_next_elm*. The goal of this representation is to enable a flexible and random process-data flow.

The MACS process-data flow model (shown in Fig. 4) covers the information specific for the material science experiments. Due to the fact that the VL-EED model is flexible and extendible, it was easy to develop the domain specific data model on top of it. Following the VL-EED definition, the MACS experiments consist of experiment elements that can be extended to *data elements* and/or *processes*. The data elements can be subdivided into *active elements* and *passive elements* considering their participation during the different experimental phases. Thus, the passive elements are just used during the experiment process while the active elements are generated and/or modified by one or more experimental processes. In the figure, for instance, the set of *Passive data elements* is represented by gray rectangles (e.g. Object, Physics Devices, Analysis Tool, etc.). And the *Active data elements*, represented by lined rectangles (e.g. Sample, Data Cube, etc. The *Processes* elements are represented by ovals (e.g. Sample Extraction, Material Analysis, Data Cube Analysis, etc.).

4.2 MACS Information Management System Development

The MACS database system was developed using the Matisse object-oriented database management system, which provides a set of database management tools for proper handling of large and complex data from database applications. Some of the advantages of considering Matisse ODBMS for this application include its flexible and dynamic data model, its support to manage many multimedia data types, and the high level of scalability and reliability that it provides, as mentioned in [12].

In order to create the description of the MACS schema in Matisse, the data definition language MATISSE ODL was used. The MACS ODL file provides the description of the persistent data for both of the VL-EED and the MACS schema as a set of object classes, including the attributes and relationships. Once, the MACS ODL file is ready, the next step is to interpret it using the MATISSE *mt_odl* utility, which creates

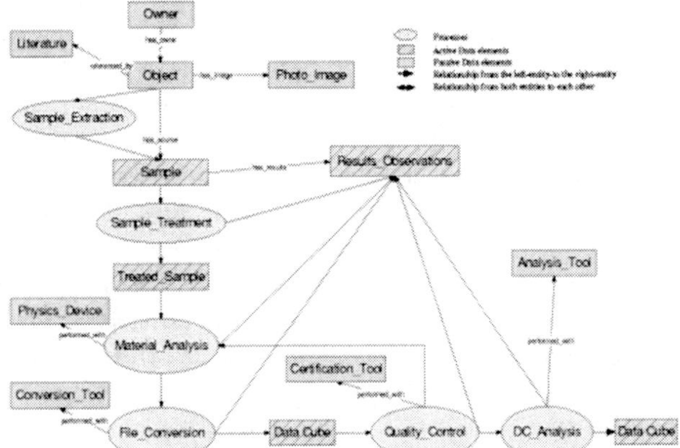

Fig. 4. MACS Process Data Flow

the actual MACS schema in the database. Thus the MACS database schema is stored in the database and can be manipulated like the other objects through the use of APIs.

Once the database is set up, the transference of the data from some existing external sources can be done with the loader tool specially developed for this purpose. Thus, the MACS Database Loader is responsible for providing the proper means for uploading data into the MACS database. Therefore, instead of creating one object at a time it is possible to load many objects at once. The format of the source data file of is based on the Object Interchange Format (OIF) file. This format is a specification language proposed in the ODMG standard to dump/load databases objects to/from files, as described in [13]. The MACS Database Loader (presented in Fig. 4) was implemented using Java, in order for the application to be portable between platforms, and also to offer the possibility of using the program as an applet, allowing it to also run remotely from a web browser. For the integration with the MACS database, the Matisse Java API was used [9].

The Matisse Java API, developed at the University of Amsterdam, is a set of library functions that provides a high-level and object-oriented Java access to the Matisse ODBMS. It provides a set of generic data management functions that encapsulate Matisse C API commands. In this way, the applications that are developed do not have to deal with Matisse specificities, and may just provide the necessary information through the access functions. These functions do not necessarily imply a one-to-one mapping in relation to Matisse commands; they can encapsulate a sequence of Matisse commands. The functions contained in this library include: the *DB Access* functions (e.g. to connect and perform the transactions on Matisse DB), the *Data access* functions (e.g. to select, update and delete the data in the Matisse DB), and the *Meta-data Access* functions (e.g. to perform operations on the database schema).

4.3 The MACS Information Management System in the Virtual Laboratory

Considering as a scenario case, the experiment for the analysis of highly oxidised diterpenoid acids of Old Master paintings described in detail in [3], a typical experiment developed within the VL environment would consist of the following steps:

1. Through the VL user interface environment (of the VL middleware), the user logs in to the system, and through a VL web-based interface he/she is able to access the VL resources that include physical devices, software and data elements.
2. Using further features of the VL Abstract Machine, the experiment is defined by selecting a number of experiment elements, i.e. processes and data elements and connecting them in order to create a process-data flow. The definition of the experiments is performed using a drag-and-drop interface, which may also provide an intelligent assistant (i.e. VL-AM Assistant) to help the user, during the design of the VL experiment, as described in [2]. It is also possible to load a previous experiment, i.e. an experiment that was performed earlier, or even a pre-defined experiment (i.e. a experiment template).
3. Every application provides a set of user-friendly tools, either specific domain tools or generic tools, to look at the data sets stored in VIMCO. Through the MACS user

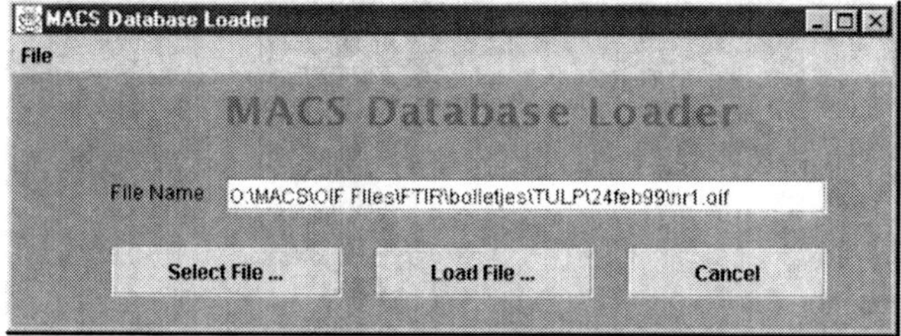

Fig. 4. MACS Database Loader user interface

interface facilities, the user can access, at any time, the data collected from the ex periments. In this case, the MACS interface allows the user to perform queries on the MACS database, to apply some analysis processes in order to extract valuable information and to provide the facilities to access visualization tools.

4. When the setup of the experiment is finished, the experiment is submitted to the system. At this moment, the VL Abstract Machine Run Time System (VL-AM RTS), uses the tools provided by the Globus toolkit for the Data-Grid management to send the different parts of the experiment, throughout the distributed environment (within the computational grid), according to the computational requirements and the availability of the resources needed.
5. During the execution of the experiment, through the VL user interface environment of the VL middleware, the user is able to supervise their experiments using monitoring tools. Also, it is possible for the user to change the experiment parameters at any moment, in order to adjust the experiment process.

5 Conclusions and Future Work

In the VL environment, an important requirement is the appropriate management of the large amount of data produced by the large and complex devices used in the scientific experiments. The information management system developed for the Material Science application in the VL project and its implementation using Matisse ODBMS supports the efficient storage, handling, integration, and retrieval of such data sets. The MACS component, integrated in the VL environment, provides a comprehensive and friendly environment to scientists of the Material Science application.

The user-friendly interfaces that allow the VL users to access the data stored in the Matisse database are now under development. Such query/search component will enable the VL user to search through the data and look for similarities or patterns. A query component that includes sophisticated search commands is being considered and will result in a more powerful tool. For instance, these query tools can be used to extract slices from the data cubes and together with specialized tools perform some calculations (e.g. chemometrics, correlation analysis methods) on these data slices. Additionally, some data mining and knowledge extraction technology should be offered to analyze the large data sets, to process either the raw data generated by different devices from different applications or the processed experiment-results. This technology is presently being considered to process, analyze and present the results in such a way that some valuable knowledge can be extracted from the large amount of data. The stored data that will be used may include information about experimental resources, experimental parameters and conditions, and raw or processed results. The easy retrieval and manipulation of the large data sets together with sophisticated data analysis and knowledge extraction tools give the scientists new research possibilities.

References

[1] Afsarmanesh, H., Benabdelkader, A., Kaletas, E.C., et al. *Towards a Mulit-layer Architecture for Scientific Virtual Laboratories.* In *8th International Conference on High Performance Computing and Networking - EuropeHPCN 2000.* 2000. Amsterdam, The Netherlands: Springer.

[2] Belloum, A., Hendrikse, Z.W., Groep, D.L., et al. *The VL Abstract Machine: a Data and Process Handling System on the Grid.* In *High Performance Computing and Networking Europe, HPCN 2001.* 2001. Amsterdam, The Netherlands.

[3] Berg, K.J.v.d., Boon, J.J., Pastorova, I., et al., *Mass spectrometric methodology for the analysis of highly oxidized diterpenoid acids in Old Master paintings.* Journal of Mass Spectrometry, 2000. **35**(4): p. 512-533.

[4] Eijkel, G.B., Afsarmanesh, H., Groep, D., et al. *Mass Spectrometry in the Amsterdam Virtual Laboratory: development of a high-performance platform for meta-data analysis.* In *13th Sanibel Conference on Mass Spectrometry: informatics and mass spectrometry.* 2001. Sanibel Island, Florida, USA.

[5] Foster, I., Kesselman, C., and Tuecke, S., *The Anatomy of the Grid: enabling scalable virtual organizations, www.globus.org/research/papers/anatomy.pdf.* 2000.

[6] Gigaport, *Gigaport Homepage (www.gigaport.nl).* 2001.

[7] Global Grid Forum, *http://www.gridforum.org/.* 2001.

[8] Groep, D., Brand, J.v.d., Bulten, H.J., et al., *Analysis of Complex Surfaces in the Virtual Laboratory.* 2000, Amsterdam, The Netherlands.

[9] Kaletas, E.C., *A Java Based Object-Oriented API for the Matisse OODBMS.* 2001, University of Amsterdam: Amsterdam.

[10] Kaletas, E.C. and Afsarmanesh, H., *Virtual Laboratory Experiment Environment Data model.* 2001, University of Amsterdam: Amsterdam.

[11] Massey, K.D., Kerschberg, L., and Michaels, G. *VANILLA: A Dynamic Data Schema for A Generic Scientific Database.* In *9th International Conference on Scientific and Statistical Database Management (SSDBM '97).* 1997. Olympia, WA, USA: Institute of Electrical and Electronics Engineers (IEEE).

[12] Matisse, *Matisse Tutorial.* 1998.

[13] ODMG, *The Object Data Standard: ODMG 3.0.* Series in Data Management Systems, ed. Gray, J., et al. 2000: Morgan Kaufmann Publishers, Inc.

[14] The CO-IM Group, UvA, *http://carol.wins.uva.nl/~netpeer/.*

[15] The Globus Project, *http://www.globus.org/.* 2001.

TREAT: A Reverse Engineering Method and Tool for Environmental Databases

Mohamed Ibrahim, Alexander M. Fedorec, and Keith Rennolls

The University of Greenwich, London, UK
{M.T.Ibrahim, A.M.Fedorec, K.Rennolls} @Greenwich.ac.uk

Abstract. This paper focuses on some issues relating to data modelling, quality and management in a specific domain: forests. Many forest domain specialists e.g., botanists, zoologists, economists and others collect vast volumes of data about the forest fauna and flora, climate, soil, etc. The favourite tools for managing this data are spreadsheets and/or using popular DBMS packages such as Access or FoxPro. The use of these tools introduces two major problems: loss of semantics and poor data structure. These problems and associated issues are examined in this the paper.

To address these problems, we propose a method for database reverse engineering from spreadsheet tables to a conceptual model and suggest a design of a prototype tool (TREAT). We also explain the motivation for and the methodology and approach that we adopted. The interactive process used to identify the constituents of the spreadsheet tables and data semantics are explained. Semi-automated analysis of the associations between the data items in terms of the domain knowledge, constraints and functional dependencies between the data items are also described. The output from the tool may be selected as either an Entity-Relationship or Object or Object-Relational model.

Keywords. Data management, reverse engineering, data modelling.

1. Introduction

There are many vast, valuable, and expensive tropical forest inventories kept by many countries in the tropics, and controlled by many different organizations [27, 28]. In some cases the aims of the inventory can be tightly specified which is likely to be the case if the aims are restricted to the management of the timber resources. However, such limited aims are the exception rather than the rule. For example, even if the considerations of the inventory are only those of timber management, the question of *sustainable* forest management for timber production must be faced. It is accepted [27, 28, 29], information requirements for a sustainable forest management plan go well beyond those required for the management of a single crop to final clear. For example, issues such as site degradation and continuing interaction between local communities and the forest edges, for economic reasons, are quite important and must be considered in the overall scheme of things.

However, there are other important aims in forest management that have become to be recently recognized. To give an example, there are the monitoring and

H.C. Mayr et al. (Eds.): DEXA 2001, LNCS 2113, pp. 175-185, 2001.

conservation of biodiversity, and also the management of medicinal and pharmaceutical resources in forests. In such areas, even the yardsticks of measurement are not well developed, since the inherent structure of tropical rain forests, and its relationship to biodiversity and medicinal plant communities are not well understood and are the subject of continuing ecological and environmental research.

This paper is organized as follows. In section 2, we offer some observations based on practical field experiences of the authors. This is then followed by discussion of some issues of data modelling in section 3. In section 4, we discuss some practical experience in model extraction and share with the reader some of the problems we faced in this respect. Sections 5 and 6 deal with our proposed method for reverse-engineering and a prototype tool which we dubbed our 'TREAT'. In section 7, we discuss our conclusions and suggest further work.

2. Observations on Data Management Practice

Date describes a database as "nothing more than a computer-based record keeping system: that is a system whose overall purpose is to record and maintain information" [1]. In current database theory it is convenient when considering design and structure to assume that there is just one database containing the totality of all stored data in the system. It can be shown that subsequent physical partitioning and distribution of data for practical implementation and performance reasons does not invalidate this assumption [2]. Thus databases are considered '*integrated*', that is, a unification of several otherwise distinct data files with any redundancy among those files partially or wholly eliminated. For example, a forestry database may contain both species records, giving name, genus, family, etc, and study plot records listing trees with their heights, diameters and so on. There is clearly no need to include the genus of each tree in the study plot records as this can always be discovered from the species records.

As well as being an integrated repository for stored data, databases are also '*shared*'. Sharing is a consequence of integration and implies that different users may access individual data items for different purposes. Any given user will normally be concerned with only a subset of the total database and different user's subsets may overlap in many different ways. Thus a given database will be perceived by different users in a variety of different ways and two users sharing the same subset of the database may have views of that subset which differ considerably at a detailed level. For example the same forest data set may be employed in resources assessment for production, dynamics monitoring for conservation or environmental impact assessment for protection.

An integrated and shared repository of information implies a central responsibility for the data and database management. Although long accepted in areas of commerce and business where data is recognised as a valuable asset, this is in stark contrast to the situation that prevails in many areas of forestry research where each application has its own private files and local copies of data.

Indeed studies by Boehm have shown that a requirement incorporated into an unstructured system by someone who was not the original author typically takes 40 times the development effort of incorporating the requirement when the system was initially implemented [5]. Data that had been collected and generated at enormous cost was therefore lost or beyond practical use to other research.

3. Issues in Data Modelling

The work in this paper stems from practical recent experiences with the Indonesian Forest Sector. The overall aim of this European Commission funded project is to strengthen the Ministry of Forestry's capacity for forest planning and management at a provincial level. Botanical, zoological and soil surveys have been conducted and this with socio-economic, climatic, geological, topographic and other data is being incorporated into a comprehensive and user-friendly Integrated Forest Resource Information System (IFRIS) to complement the National Forest Inventory [8, 16].

Our prime concern was to recover the data model of this wealth of data using an information systems perspective and hence forward engineer the required information systems based on sound foundations. Whilst there are many kinds of information system, our initial interest was restricted to two main systems: Operational Transaction Processing (TP) and Decision Support Systems (DSS) aspects of the IFRIS data.

TP systems are concerned with standard day-to-day operations such as entering, modifying and reporting on 'operational' data and are characterized by the traditional ACID concepts of atomicity, consistency, isolation and durability [9]. The collation and management of field study data would typically be within the remit of TP. DSS, on the other hand, supports the strategic exploration of 'informational' data by a 'knowledge worker'. This sort of information processing often takes the form of 'What if?' queries as exemplified by a researcher's explorations into biodiversity metrics or those of a senior manager concerned with ecological or environmental impact analysis.

Management Information Systems (MIS) would clearly be essential in the longer term to bodies responsible for on-going forest management or conservation or, for example, those seeking ISO14000 certification [10], and therefore an important aspect of IFRIS. With restricted time and limited access to potential end-users, little progress could be made in the required analysis.

The standard approach to building TP, MIS and DSS information systems is to bridge the semantic gap from problem domain to the solution space via a set of models that may be transformed and refined at each step [11]. Whilst different authors use different terms, the standard models are conceptual, logical, and physical. Quality is assured by applying verification and validation to each refinement. The first of these steps maps semantics from the real-world problem to a conceptual model that embodies an abstract representation of the user mini real world.

There are many design solutions to any system and the actual result will be dependent on the paradigm employed in the modeling and the target technology. Irrespective of the adopted paradigm, the models will normally coincide with the deliverables of the standard analysis, design and implementation phases of the classical software engineering lifecycle [12].

Each of the information models may be viewed in terms of the data and processes on that information and consist of three main components:

1. Structure: including objects, properties and association between objects,
2. Operations to manipulate the structure,
3. Domain knowledge and Constraints to ensure validity of:
   - the (static) database states, and
   - the operations and transition between states.

Although ER modelling has been successfully employed for the data modelling of pictorial or spatial and temporal entities [15], OO has clear advantages in the analysis and design of a system presentation layer that employs event driven interaction with multimedia objects such as a GIS based user interface. However, as our concern with Indonesian Forest sector was with data management and the storage layer of TP and DSS systems targeted at relational DBMS systems, it was felt that structured data analysis based on ER models was adequate given the limited local skills available.

4. Practical Model Extraction Experience

An example of the data modeling, undertaken in Indonesia, is the analysis of botanical data held in spreadsheets [16]. Spreadsheets are popular and flexible data manipulation tools however they have no data dictionary or other explicit mechanism to act as a repository for meta-data and no input or state transition validation facilities. The implicit metadata is limited to data-type information of cell values and range relationships for embedded formulae provided by the audit facilities of the spreadsheet system.

The botanical data consists of sets of Microsoft Excel workbooks, each of which represents a study area and contains two related worksheets of tree and plot data. An example of the plot data is presented figure 1.

The second worksheet is the related plot data. The size of this data set depends on the number of transects in the study area and the number of plots within the transects. Typically there are a few tens of records.

An example of tree data is given in figure 2. Again the sheet has been transposed and restricted to three records to fit the printed page. In this table it can be seen that, without domain specific knowledge of transects, plots and subplots or an understanding of the representation of sample data as arrays of percentages, interpretation may be extremely difficult. It can thus be seen that discovering what the data means is hard and time-consuming without 'proper' documentation. The actual process of producing a data model from the spreadsheet data required many iterations of file-gazing, reading available documents and reports and interaction with domain experts - for completeness an example data model manually produced from this botanical data is given in figure 3. It was therefore of interest to explore how much of this effort could be automated.

Pengisi	Jonar Purba	Jonar Purba	Jonar Purba
Tempat	Pemunyian	Pemunyian	Pemunyian
Tinggi	300	315	325
Azimuth	200	130	200
Habitat	1	3	5
Tanggal	21-Jun-96	22-Jun-96	22-Jun-96
T	1	1	1
P	1	2	3
Ukuran plot	50	100	50
No. Pohon	1	36	105
Miring	0505050505xxxxxxxxxx	05050515151010151515	0505050505xxxxxxxx
Dominan	xxxxxxxxxxxxxxxxxxxx	xxxxxxxxxxxxxxxxxxxx	xxxxxxxxxxxxxxxxxx
Tajuk Utama	xxxxxx38xxxxxxxxxxxx	xx743841xxxxxx887487	64xx425661xxxxxxxx
Strata ke2	7869596471xxxxxxxxxx	81628782768689646871	9178746954xxxxxxxx
Strata ke3	6746314827xxxxxxxxxx	46345241546748414258	7154584140xxxxxxxx
pohon kecil	2614112015xxxxxxxxxx	24192128273118192326	3928291815xxxxxxxx
Tanlunak	xxxxxxxxxxxxxxxxxxxx	xxxxxxxxxx0204xxxxxx	xxxxxxxxxxxxxxxxxx
palm	xxxxxx0202xxxxxxxxxx	010304xxxx02xxxxxxxx	xxxx0201xxxxxxxxxx
pandan	xxxxxxxxxxxxxxxxxxxx	xxxxxxxxxxxxxxxxxxxx	02xx03xxxxxxxxxxxx
Pakis	xxxxxxxxxxxxxxxxxxxx	xxxxxxxxxxxxxxxxxxxx	xxxxxxxxxxxxxxxxxx
rotan_m	0503020403xxxxxxxxxx	03040608060402060709	0804060503xxxxxxxx
rotan_r	0203040101xxxxxxxxxx	01020203050201020403	0301040301xxxxxxxx
liana_L5	xx02030502xxxxxxxxxx	01010102xx01xxxx0102	xxxx03xxxxxxxxxxxx
liana_K5	0812080605xxxxxxxxxx	05040306050312080508	0504080703xxxxxxxx
bambu	xxxxxxxxxx	xxxxxxxxxx	xxxxxxxxxx
Epifit	11232xxxxx	x211xxx11x	xx11xxxxxx
Belukar tua	xxxxxxxxxxxxxxxxxxxx	xxxxxxxxxxxxxxxxxxxx	xxxxxxxxxxxxxxxxxx
Belukar tua	xxxxxxxxxxxxxxxxxxxx	xxxxxxxxxxxxxxxxxxxx	xxxxxxxxxxxxxxxxxx

Fig. 1. Example Plot Worksheet Data

5. The Design of a Reverse-Engineering Tool

Much work has been done within the software engineering community on automated 'reverse-engineering' of process models from code and re-engineering the systems [17]. Unfortunately reverse engineering of data models is not as well explored. Chikofsky and Cross define reverse engineering as the "Process of analysing a system to identify components and their inter-relationships in order to create representations in another form, usually at a higher level of abstraction" [18].

Re-Engineering is defined as the "process of re-implementing a design recovered by means of reverse engineering, possibly in a different environment". The relationship between the concepts is shown in figure 4. The term 'reverse engineering' comes from the practice of analysing existing hardware (created by a competitor or even an enemy) to understand its design. As the goal is to create an alternative representation, usually at a higher level of abstraction, it is also known as 'design recovery'.

Re-engineering employs reverse engineering to recover a design followed by forward engineering to re-implement the system in a changed form. Re-engineering does not necessarily involve changing the system's external appearance or functionality. One of the benefits of database reverse engineering identified by

Premerlani [19] is the identification of errors in original data design – he reports that 50% of the database systems he studied had major errors.

Idno	11101	11101	11101	11101
TreeNo.	1	2	3	4
x	9.9	6.2	5.4	6.1
y	0.7	2.8	4.8	7.5
d	16.2	12.6	13.7	13.9
Ht	9	6	10	9
Hb	6	4	8	5.5
Ba	0.020614662	0.012470598	0.01474305	0.015176646
Vol	0.061843986	0.024941196	0.049143498	0.045529937
Ht/D	55.55555556	47.61904762	72.99270073	64.74820144
T	1	1	1	1
P	1	1	1	1
SubP	1	1	1	1
Lf	1	1	1	1
coll	-.	RIZ.	HAS	RIZ.
N_Herb	-	124	531	125
Fam	MORA	DIPT	RUBI	DIPT
Genus	Artocarpus	Shorea	Neonauclea	Shorea
Species	elasticus	assamica	calycina	ovalis
Gen_Spe	Art_ela	Sho_ass	Neo_cal	Sho_ova
freq.	2	2	2	20
Sp_rank	24	24	24	6
Author	-	-	-	-
Cnt of Gen_Spe	Gen_Spe	*** ***	Act_gla	Act_glo
	Total	328	1	2
Gen_Spe	*** ***	Act_gla	Act_glo	Ade_mic
Total	328	1	2	3
Rank	0	25	24	23
		26	26	26
N_Herb	2	2	2	2
coll	RIZ.	RIZ.	RIZ.	RIZ.
***	***	***	***	***

Fig. 2. Tree data - (sample only)

As incomplete information is the norm and undocumented metadata is held in the head of the author a fully automated tool for reverse engineering the forest botanical data is infeasible. The goals were therefore to:

1. Automate as much as is possible
2. Ensure quality by verification of transforms
3. Assist the analyst/domain expert where the process cannot be automated by:
   (i) pruning of the search space, and
   (ii) presentation of relevant information.

The desired output would be a sound data model with an explicit representation of the entities, relationships and a stable structure that could support the diverse information needs of TP, MIS and DSS.

The resultant tool is called TREAT – which, in the best software engineering tradition is an acronym for 'Trial Reverse Engineering Automated Tool'. It was developed using Microsoft Visual Basic Version 5 for Excel 97 and presents a set of interactive steps which briefly are as follows.

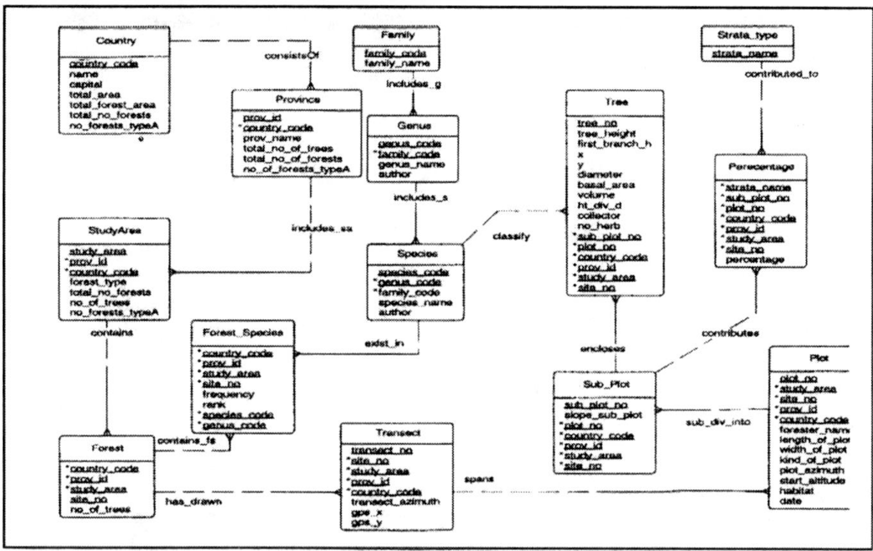

Fig. 3. ER Model - Forest Botanical data

The first step is to set up and initialize a symbol table of spreadsheet objects and data dictionary to be populated with the identified entities, relationships and attributes. The symbol table lists each workbook and the worksheets within the workbooks, the ranges, data types and names of the ranges of each dataset. This is achieved by iteratively prompting the user to select ranges of headings and of data.

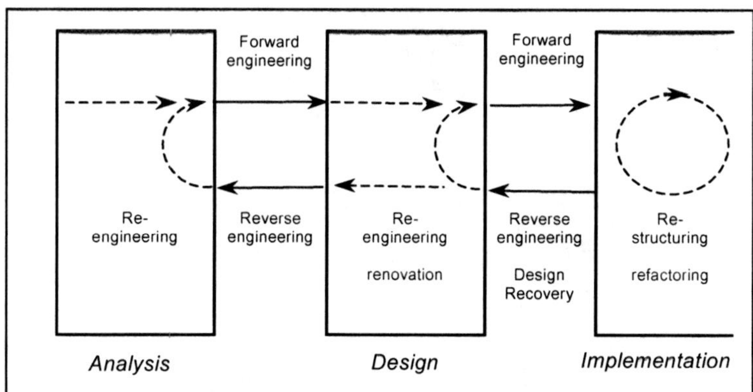

Fig. 4. Concepts in Reengineering

The data dictionary is initialized with a dummy 'super-entity' from which further entities will hang. Drawing on the information in the symbol table each workbook is represented as a tentative entity as are each of the worksheets within the workbooks. As each new entity is formed it is allocated a temporary unique name of the form TE*nnn*, (the user is given the opportunity to change this to something more meaningful at a later stage).

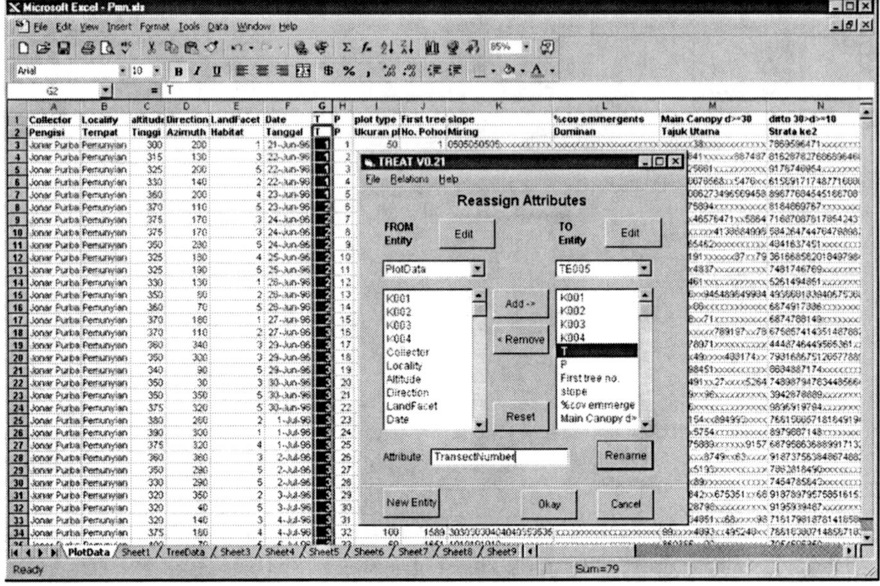

Fig. 5. Example of TREAT – First Pass Amendment of Entity-Attribute List

The symbol table is then processed. Each column entry is made an attribute of the enclosing sheet entity and the column reference, name and data type is entered into the data dictionary. As each row is a record each cell is an instance value and could later be forward engineered into a new database.

Having initialized the symbol table and data dictionary we perform an automatic attribute analysis. This consists of pairing and comparing the data values in each of the datasets allocated to the same entity and logging the nature of the relation between them. A set of predicates are used, largely derived from Semmen's [23] and Fraser's [24] respective formal specifications of ER models, to indicate which columns should

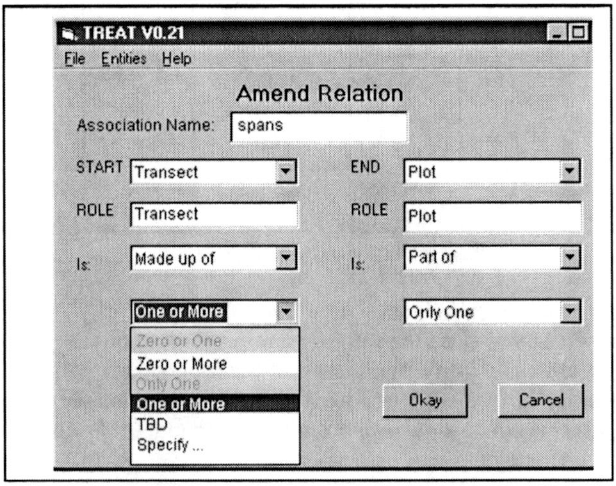

Fig. 6. TREAT Modification of Relations

be factored out into new entities and what is the cardinality of the relation between the existing entity and the new one. The mapping relations of prime interest are the functions; in particular bijections, which indicate potential attributes of the same entity, and the forward and reverse injections that suggest attributes of entities with a one-to-many cardinality. As a sequence of injective functions is transitive these are also used to indicate indirect dependencies between entities. The relation log (which is actually part of the symbol table) is also used to provide proof obligations on further transforms, restrict and validate the manual changes to the model and provide verification constraints on the final data model and future database modifications.

After the automatic attribute analysis has generated a new set of candidate entities and nominally assigned attributes and relations to them they must be reviewed manually. Following [25], examples of two of these dialogue boxes are given in figures 5 and 6. On completion of a step control progresses to the next step or iteration. In practice there is much iteration, backtracking and re-ordering of steps and so facilities are provided through pull-down menus and command buttons for the user to navigate to any of the key steps.

6. Notes on 'Our' TREAT

Numerous problems and exceptions were found in formulating our predicate set which could not be resolved from just the information content of the source data. Some of these problems were due to the syntactic style of the original data (for example the formulation of strata data as uniquely identified attributes rather than a repeating group of homogeneous attributes, and the use of repeating groups within the strata variables). It may be feasible (but probably not cost-effective) to include algorithms to search for and handle many of these problems. However the majority of real problems were due to loss of semantics. These problems required considerable domain knowledge to resolve and it is clear from this that the reverse engineering process could never be fully automated.

The tool therefore 'suggests' data refinements and the process still requires substantial domain expertise to clarify the semantics of the entities, attributes and relations between them. Because the process is primarily an iterative factoring and decomposition of existing objects, the data model produced is fundamentally hierarchical. Whilst techniques have been suggested by Blaha and Premerlani for transforming hierarchical and network data structures to fully relational or object-relational models [26] the process still demands considerable data modeling and systems analysis expertise and cannot be automated.

7. Conclusion & Further Work

In this paper we have stressed the importance of data modeling and data management for forestry data sets and outlined some important information systems concepts for data analysis. We have presented examples of botanical data and discussed some of the problems associated with the data being held in spreadsheets or poorly structured personal databases. In particular we have noted the loss of semantic data, lack of metadata and formal documentation and therefore the difficulty in integrating and sharing that data in operational and informational information systems.

Finally, the design and implementation of a proof of principle prototype for a tool (TREAT) to facilitate the reverse engineering of data models from these data sets is described. Whilst limited in functionality, the tool has been found to help structure the systems analyst/domain expert knowledge elicitation process and could potentially reduce the substantial time and effort currently required for data analysis of existing forestry data sets. Work is planned for enhancing the functionality of TREAT further and examining the possibility of implementation a fully automated version.

References

1. Date, C.J., An Introduction to Database Systems, Addison-Wesley, 1995
2. Umar, A., Object-Oriented Client/Server Internet Environments, Prentice-Hall, 1997
3. Korth, H.F., Silberschatz, A., Database Research Faces the Information Explosion, *Communications of the ACM,* **40**(2), Feb 1997, pp. 139-142
4. DeLisi,C., Computation and the Human Genome Project: An Historical Perspective, in G.I. Bell and T.G.Marr (eds.) *Computers and DNA*, Addison-Wesley, 1988, pp. 13-20
5. Boehm, B., Software Engineering Economics, Prentice-Hall, 1981
6. Fisher, G., Experimental Materials Databases, in M.J.Bishop (ed.), *Guide to Human Genome Computing*, Academic Press, 1994, pp. 39-58
7. Burks, C., The Flow of Nucleotide Sequence Data into Data Banks., in G.I. Bell and T.G.Marr (eds.) *Computers and DNA*, Addison-Wesley, 1988, pp. 35-46
8. Legg, C.A., Integrated Forest Resource Information System, Brochure prepared for FIMP, Jakarta, 1998
9. Hennessey, P., Ibrahim, M.T., Fedorec, A.M., Formal Specification, Object Oriented Design and Implementation of an Ephemeral Logger for Database Systems, in R.Wagner and H. Thoma (Eds.), *Database and Expert Systems Applications (DEXA '96)*, Springer-Verlag, 1996, pp.333-355
10. ISO14000, International Standard ISO 14000 – Introduction, http://www.quality.co.uk/iso14000.htm, 1998
11. Furtado,A.L., Neuhold, E.J., Formal Techniques for Database Design, Springer-Verlag, 1986
12. Dawson,C.W., Dawson,R.J., *Towards more flexible management of software systems development using meta-models*, Software Engineering Journal, May 1995, pp.79-88
13. Chen, P. The Entity-Relationship Model: Towards a Unified View of Data, *ACM Trans. Database Systems*, **1**(1), 1976, pp. 9-36
14. Rumbaugh,J., Blaha, M., Premeralni, W., Eddy, F., Lorensen, W., Object-Oriented Modeling and Design, Prentice-Hall, 1991
15. Pizano, A., Klinger, A., Cardenas, A., Specification of Spatial Integrity Constraints in Pictorial Database, *IEEE Computer*, **22**(12), Dec 1989, pp.59-71
16. Ibrahim, M.T., FIMP (Forest Inventory Management Project) Database Management Report, 1998, in preparation
17. Sneed, H., Planning the Reengineering of Legacy Systems, *IEEE Software* Jan 1995
18. Chikofsky,E., Cross II,J., Reverse Engineering and Design Recovery: A Taxonomy, *IEEE Software*, **7**(1), Jan 1990, pp.13-19
19. Premerlani, W., Blaha, M., An Approach for Reverse Engineering of Relational Databases, *Communications of the ACM*, **37**(5), May 1994, pp.42-49
20. Holtzblatt, L.J., *et.al*, Design Recovery for Distributed Systems, *IEEE Trans Software Engineering*, **23**(7), July 1997, pp.461-472

21. Markosian, L., *et al,* Using an Enabling Technology to Reengineer Legacy Systems, *Communications of the ACM,* **37**(5), May 1994, pp. 58-71
22. Aiken.P., Muntz, A., Richards, R., DoD Legacy Systems, Reverse Engineering Data Requirements, *Communications of the ACM*, **37**(5), May 1994, pp. 26-41
23. Semmens, L., Allen, P., Using Yourdon and Z: an Approach to Formal Specification, J.E.Nicholls (Ed.) *Proc Z User Workshop, Oxford 1990*, Springer-Verlag, 1991, pp. 228-253
24. Fraser, M.D., Informal and Formal Requirements Specification Languages: Bridging the Gap, *IEEE Trans Software Engineering*, **17**(5), May 1991, pp. 454-466
25. Sockut, G.H., Malhotra, A Full-Screen Facility for Defining Relational and Entity-Relationship Database Schemas, *IEEE Software*, **5**(6), Nov 1988, pp.68-78
26. Blaha, M., Premerlani, W., Object Oriented Modeling and Design for Database Applications, Prentice-Hall, 1998
27. Laumonier, Y., B.King,C.Legg, K.Rennolls (eds.), Data Management and Modelling using Remote Sensing and GIS for Temporal Forest Land Inventory, Proceedings of An Interantional Conference on, EU, 1999.
28. EC/IUFRO, FIRS (Forest Information from Remote Sensing), Proceedings of Conference on Remote Sensing and Forest Monitoring, Rogow, Poland 1-3June 1999; EC 2000.

A Very Efficient Order Preserving Scalable Distributed Data Structure

Adriano Di Pasquale[1] and Enrico Nardelli[1,2]

[1] Dipartimento di Matematica Pura ed Applicata, Univ. of L'Aquila, Via Vetoio, Coppito, I-67010 L'Aquila, Italia. {dipasqua,nardelli}@univaq.it
[2] Istituto di Analisi dei Sistemi ed Informatica, Consiglio Nazionale delle Ricerche, Viale Manzoni 30, I-00185 Roma, Italia.

Abstract. SDDSs (Scalable Distributed Data Structures) are access methods specifically designed to satisfy the high performance requirements of a distributed computing environment made up by a collection of computers connected through a high speed network. In this paper we present and discuss performances of ADST, a new order preserving SDDS with a worst-case constant cost for exact-search queries, a worst-case logarithmic cost for update queries, and an optimal worst-case cost for range search queries of $O(k)$ messages, where k is the number of servers covering the query range. Moreover, our structure has an amortized almost constant cost for any single-key query. Finally, our scheme can be easily generalized to manage k-dimensional points, while maintaining the same costs of the 1-dimensional case.
We report experimental comparisons between ADST and its direct competitors (i.e., LH*, DRT, and RP*) where it is shown that ADST behaves clearly better. Furthermore we show how our basic technique can be combined with recent proposals for ensuring high-availability to an SDDS. Therefore our solution is very attractive for network servers requiring both a fast response time and a high reliability.

Keywords: Scalable distributed data structure, message passing environment, multi-dimensional search.

1 Introduction

The paradigm of SDDS (*Scalable Distributed Data Structures*) [9] is used to develop access methods in the technological framework known as *network computing*: a fast network interconnecting many powerful and low-priced workstations, creating a pool of perhaps terabytes of RAM and even more of disk space.

The main goal of an access method based on the SDDS paradigm is the management of very large amount of data implementing efficiently standard operations (i.e. inserts, deletions, exact searches, range searches, etc.) and aiming at *scalability*, i.e. the capacity of the structure to keep the same level of performances while the number of managed objects changes.

The main measure of performance for a given operation in the SDDS paradigm is the number of point-to-point messages exchanged by the sites of

H.C. Mayr et al. (Eds.): DEXA 2001, LNCS 2113, pp. 186–199, 2001.

the network to perform the operation. Neither the length of the path followed in the network by a message nor its size are relevant in the SDDS context. Note that, some variants of SDDS admit the use of multicast to perform range query.

There are several SDDS proposals in the literature: defining structures based on hashing techniques [3,9,12,16,17], on order preserving techniques [1,2,4,7,8, 10], or for multi-dimensional data management techniques [11,14], and many others.

LH* [9] is the first SDDS that achieves worst-case constant cost for exact searches and insertions, namely 4 messages. It is based on the popular linear hashing technique. However, like other hashing schemes, while it achieves good performance for single-key operations, range searches are not performed efficiently. The same is true for any operation executed by means of a scan involving all the servers in the network.

On the contrary, order preserving structures (e.g., RP* [10] and DRT* [5]) achieve good performances for range searches and a reasonably low (i.e. logarithmic), but not constant, worst-case cost for single key operations.

Here we present and discuss experimental results for ADST, the first order preserving SDDS proposal achieving single-key performances comparable with the LH*, while continuing to provide the good worst-case complexity for range searches typical of order preserving access methods (e.g., RP* and DRT*). For a more detailed presentation of the data structure see [6].

The technique used in our access method can be applied to the distributed k-d tree [14], an SDDS for managing k-dimensional data, with similar results.

2 Distributed Search Trees

In this section we review the main concepts relative to distributed search trees, in order to prepare the way for the presentation of our proposal and to allow its better comparison with previous solutions.

Each server manages a unique *bucket* of keys. The bucket has a fixed capacity b. We define a server "to be in overflow" or "to go in overflow" when it manages b keys and one more key is assigned to it. When a server s goes in overflow it starts the *split* operation. This operation basically consists of transfer half of its keys to a new fresh server s_{new}. Consequently the interval of keys I managed is partitioned in I_1 and I_2. After the split, s reduces its interval I to I_1. When s_{new} receives the keys, it initializes its interval to I_2. This is the first interval managed by s_{new} and we refer to such an interval as the *basic interval* of a server.

From a conceptual point of view, the splits of servers build up a virtual distributed tree, where each leaf is associated to a server, and a split creates a new leaf, associated to the new fresh server, and a new internal node.

Please note that the lower end of the interval managed by a server never changes. A split operation is performed by locking the involved servers. Its cost is a constant number of messages, typically 4 messages. We recall that since in the SDDS paradigm the length of a message is not accounted in the complexity, then it is assumed that all keys are sent to the new server using one message.

After a split, s manages $\frac{b}{2}$ keys and s_{new} $\frac{b}{2}+1$ keys. It is easy to prove that for a sequence of m intermixed insertions and exact searches we may have at most $\lfloor \frac{m}{A} \rfloor$ splits, where $A = \frac{b}{2}$.

The splits of a server is a local operation. Clients and the other servers are not, in general, informed about the split. As a consequence, clients and servers can make an *address error*, that is they send the request to a wrong server.

Therefore, clients and servers have a local indexing structure, called *local tree.* Whenever a client or a server performs a request and makes an *address error*, it receives information to correct its local tree. This prevents a client or a server to commit the same address error twice.

From a logical point of view the local tree is an incomplete collection of associations $\langle server,\ interval\,of\,keys\rangle$: for example, an association $\langle s, I(s)\rangle$ identifies a server s and the managed interval of keys $I(s)$. A local tree can be seen as a tree describing the partition of the domain of keys produced by the splits of servers. A local tree can be wrong, in the sense that in the reality a server s is managing an interval smaller than what the client currently knows, due to a *split* performed by s and yet unknown to the client.

Note that for each request of a key k received by a server s, k is within the *basic interval* I of s, that is the interval s managed before its first division. This is due to the fact that if a client has information on s, then certainly s manages an interval $I' \subseteq I$, due to the way overflow is managed through *splits.* In our proposal, like other SDDS proposals, we do not consider deletions, hence intervals always shrinks. Therefore if s is chosen as the server to which to send the request of a key k, it means that $k \in I' \Rightarrow k \in I$.

Given the local tree $lt(s)$ associated to server s, we denote as $I(lt(s))$ the interval of $lt(s)$, defined as $I(lt(s)) = [m, M)$, where m is the minimum of lower ends of intervals in the associations stored in $lt(s)$, and M is the maximum of upper ends of intervals in the associations stored in $lt(s)$.

From now on we define a server s *pertinent* for a key k if $k \in I(s)$, and *logically pertinent* if $k \in I(lt(s))$.

3 ADST

We now introduce our proposal for a distributed search tree, that can be seen as a variant of the systematic correction technique presented in [2].

Let us consider a split of a server s with a new server s'. Given the leaf f associated to s, a split conceptually creates a new leaf f' and a new internal node v, father of the two leaves. This virtual node is associated to s or to s'. Which one is chosen is not important: we assume to associate it always with the new server, in this case s'. s stores s' in the list l of servers associated to nodes in the path from the leaf associated to itself and the root. s' initializes its corresponding list l' with a copy of the s' one (s' included).

Moreover if this was the first split of s, then s identifies s' as its *basic server* and stores it in a specific field. Please note that the interval $I(v)$ now corresponds to the *basic interval* of s.

After the split s sends a correction message containing the information about the split to s' and to the other servers in l. Each server receiving the message corrects its local tree. Each list l of a server s corresponds to the path from the leaf associated with s to the root.

This technique ensures that a server s_v associated to a node v knows the exact partition of the interval $I(v)$ of v and the exact associations of elements of the partition and servers managing them. In other words the local tree of s_v contains all the associations $\langle s', I(s') \rangle$ identifying the partition of $I(v)$. Please note that in this case $I(v)$ corresponds to $I(lt(s_v))$.

This allows s_v to forward a request for a key belonging to $I(v)$ (i.e. a request for which s_v is logically pertinent) directly to the right server, without following the tree structure. In this distributed tree, rotations are not applied, then the association between a server and its basic server never changes.

Suppose a server s receives a requests for a key k. If it is pertinent for the requests ($k \in I(s)$) then it performs the request and answers to the client. Otherwise if it is logically pertinent for the requests ($k \in I(lt(s))$) then it finds in its local tree $lt(s)$ the pertinent server and forwards it the requests. Otherwise it forwards the requests to its basic server s'. We recall that $I(lt(s'))$ corresponds to the basic interval of s, then, as stated before, if the request for k is arrived to s, k has to belong to this interval. Then s' is certainly logically pertinent.

Therefore a request can be managed with at most 2 address errors and 4 messages.

The main idea of our proposal is to keep the path between any leaf and the root short, in order to reduce the cost of correction messages after a split. To obtain this we aggregate internal nodes of the distributed search tree obtained with the above described techniques in compound nodes, and apply the above technique to the tree made up by compound nodes. For this reason we call our structure ADST (Aggregation in Distributed Search Tree).

Please note that the aggregation only happens at a logical level, in the sense that no additional structure has to be introduced.

Each server s in ADST is conceptually associated to a leaf f. Then, as a leaf, s stores the list l of servers managing compound nodes in the path from f and the (compound) root of the ADST. If s has already split at least one time, then it stores also its *basic server* s'. In this case s' is a server that manages a compound node and such that $I(lt(s'))$ contains the *basic interval* of s.

Any server records in a field called *adjacent* the server managing the adjacent interval on its right. Moreover, if s manages also a compound node $va(s)$, then it also maintains a local tree, in addition to the other information (see figure 1).

The way to create compound nodes in the structure is called *aggregation policy.* We require that an aggregation policy creates compound nodes so that the height of the tree made up by the compound nodes is logarithmic in the number of servers of the ADST. In such a way the cost of correcting the local trees after a split is logarithmic as well.

One can design several aggregation policies, satisfying the previous requirement. The one we use is the following.

(AP): To each compound node va a bound on the number of internal nodes $l(va)$ is associated. The bound of the root compound node ra is $l(ra) = 1$. If the compound node va' father of va has bound $l(va')$, then $l(va) = 2l(va') + 1$.

In figure 2 an example of ADST is presented.

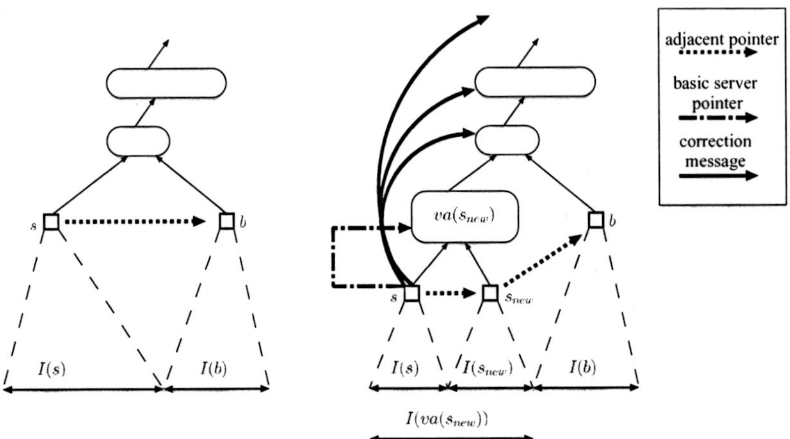

Fig. 1. Before (left) and after (right) the split of server s with s_{new} as new server. Intervals are modified accordingly. Correction messages are sent to server managing compound nodes stored in the list $s.l$ and *adjacent* pointers are modified. Since the aggregation policy decided to create a new compound node and s_{new} has to manage it, then s_{new} is added to the list $s.l$ of servers between the leaf s and the compound root nodes, s_{new} sets $s_{new}.l = s.l$. If this is the first split of s, then s sets s_{new} as its *basic server*.

We now show how a client c looks for a key in ADST: c looks for the pertinent server for k in its local tree, finds the server s, and sends it the request. If s is pertinent, it performs the request and sends the result to c.

Suppose s is not pertinent. If s does not manage a compound node, then it forwards the request to its *basic server* s'. We recall that $I(lt(s'))$ includes the basic interval of s, then, as stated before, if the request for k is arrived to s, k has to belong to this interval. Therefore s' is certainly logically pertinent: it looks for the pertinent server for k in its local tree and finds the server s''. Then s' forwards the request to s'', which performs the request and answers to c. In this case c receives the local tree of s' in the answer, so to update its local tree (see figure 3).

Suppose now that s manages a compound node. The way in which compound nodes are created ensures that $I(lt(s))$ includes the basic interval of s itself. Then s has to be logically pertinent, hence it finds in $lt(s)$ the pertinent server and sends it the request. In this case c receives the local tree of s in the answer.

For an insertion, the protocol for exact search is performed in order to find the pertinent server s for k. Then s inserts k in its bucket. If this insertion causes

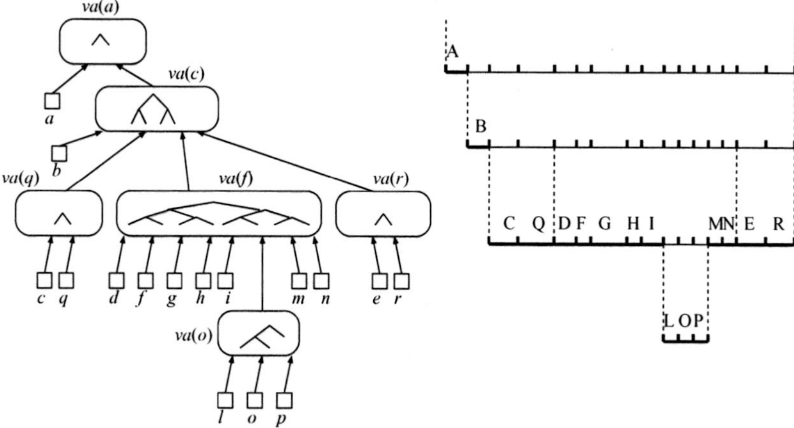

Fig. 2. An example of ADST with policy AP. Lower-case letters denote servers and associated leaves, upper-case letters denote intervals of data domain. The sequence of splits producing the structure is $a \to b \to c \to d \to e$, then $d \to f \to g \to h \to i \to l \to m \to n$, then $l \to o \to p$, then $c \to q$ and finally $e \to r$, meaning with $x \to y$ that the split of x creates the server y.

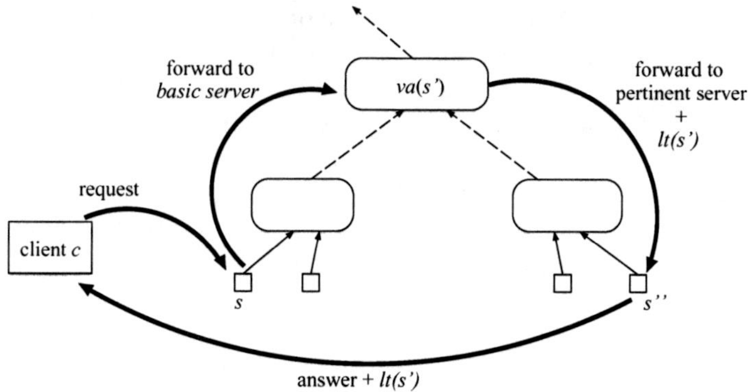

Fig. 3. Worst-case of the access protocol

s to go in overflow then a split is performed. After the split, correction messages are sent to the servers in the list l of s.

Previous SDDSs, e.g LH*, RP*, DRT*, etc., do not explicitly consider deletions. Hence, in order to compare ADST and previous SDDSs performances, we shall not analyze behavior of ADST under deletions.

To perform a range search the protocol for exact search is performed in order to find the server s pertinent for the leftmost value of the range. If the range is not completely covered by s, then s sends the request to server s' stored in its field *adjacent*. s' does the same. Following the adjacent pointers all the servers covering the range are reached and answer to the client. The operation stops whenever the server pertinent for the rightmost value of the range is reached (see figure 4).

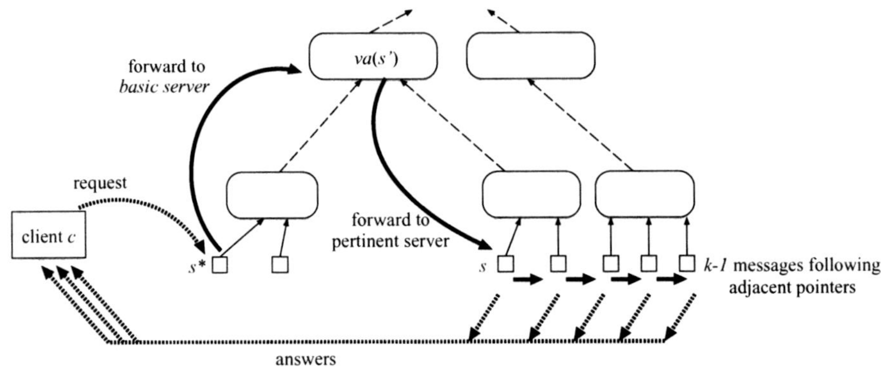

Fig. 4. Worst-case of the range search. s is the server pertinent for the leftmost value of the range.

In the following we give the main results of ADST. Detailed descriptions can be found in the extended version of the paper [6].

An exact search and an insertion that does not cause a split have in an ADST a worst-case cost of 4 messages. A split and the following corrections of local trees have in an ADST a worst-case cost of $\log n + 5$.

A range search has in an ADST a worst-case cost of $k+1$ messages, where k is the number of servers covering the range of query, without accounting for the single request message and the k response messages.

Moreover, under realistic assumptions, a sequence of intermixed exact searches and insertions on ADST has an amortized cost of $O(1)$ messages. The basic assumption is that $\frac{\log n}{b} < 1$. For real values of b, e.g. hundreds, thousands or more, the assumption is valid for SDDSs made by up to billions of servers.

ADST has a good load factor, under any key distribution, like all the other order preserving structures, that is 0.5 in worst case and about 0.7 ($= \ln 2$) as expected value.

Another important performance parameter for an SDDS is the convergence of new client's index. This is the number of requests that a new client starting with an initial index has to perform in order to have an index reflecting the exact structure of the distributed file: this means that the client does not make address errors until new splits occur in the structure. The faster is the convergence, the lower is the number of address errors made by clients.

In ADST a new client is initialized with a local tree containing the server associated to the compound root node, or the unique server, in the case ADST is made up just by one server. Due to the correction technique used after a split, this server knows the exact partition of data domain among servers. Then it is easy to show that a new client obtains a completely up-to-date local tree after just one request.

Also in this case ADST notably improves previous results. In particular we recall that, for an n-servers SDDS, the convergence of a new client's index requires in the worst-case:

- n messages in any structure of DRT family.
- $O\left(\frac{n}{0.7f}\right)$ messages in RP*s, where f is the fanout of servers in the kernel.
- $O(\log n)$ messages in LH*.

4 Experimental Comparison

In this section we discuss results of experimental comparisons between ADST performances and RP*, DRT* and LH* ones with respect to sequences of intermixed exact-searches and insertions. The outcome is that ADST behaves clearly better than all its competitors.

As discussed previously ADST presents worst-case constant costs for exact searches, worst-case logarithmic costs for insertions whenever a split occurs, and amortized constant costs for sequences of intermixed exact-searches and insertions. On the other hand, LH* is the best SDDS for single key requests, since it has worst-case constant costs for both exact searches and insertions, and constant costs in the amortized case as well.

The objective of our experimental comparison is to show which is the difference between ADST and its direct competitors. We have not considered in our experimental comparison the case of deletions since this case is not explicitly analyzed in LH*, RP* and DRT*.

In our experiments we perform a simulation of SDDS using the CSIM package [15], which is the standard approach in the SDDS literature for this kind of performance evaluation. We analyze structures with a capacity of buckets fixed at $b = 100$ records, that is a small, but reasonable, value for b. Later we describe the behavior of the structures with respect to different values of b. We consider two situations: a first one with 50 clients manipulating the structures and a second one with 500 clients. Finally, we consider three random sequences of intermixed insertions and exact searches: one with 25% of insertions, one with 50% of insertions and one with 75%.

We have considered a more realistic situation of fast working clients, in the sense that it is possible that a new request arrives to a server before it has terminated with updating operations. This happens more frequently when considering 500 clients with respect to the case of 50 clients.

The protocol of operations is the usual one. In case of exact searches an answer message arrives to the client which issued the request, with the information to correct the client index. In case of insertions, the answer message is not sent back. This motivates the slightly higher cost for the structures in case of low percentage of inserts, even if more exact searches means more possibility to correct an index of a client.

Note that, although all costs in LH* are constant, while ADST has a logarithmic split cost, in practice ADST behaves clearly better with respect to LH* in this environment, as shown in figure 5, 6, 7, 8, 9 and 10. This is fundamentally motivated by the better capacity of ADST to update client indexes with respect to LH*, and then to allow clients to commit a lower number of address errors. This difference of capability is shown by the fact that while LH* slightly increases its access cost passing from 50 to 500 clients, for ADST the trend is opposite: with 500 clients access cost is slightly decreased with respect to 50.

The logarithmic cost of splits for ADST become apparent for lower values of b, where the weight of term $\frac{\log n}{b}$ increases its relative weight. However lower values for b, e.g. 10, are not realistic for an SDDS involving a large number of servers. On the contrary the situation shown in figures is even more favourable to ADST for larger values of b, like for example 1000 or more (in this case the term $\frac{\log n}{b}$ decreases its relative weight). This also happens for larger number of clients querying the structure, due to the relevant role played by the correction of client indexes.

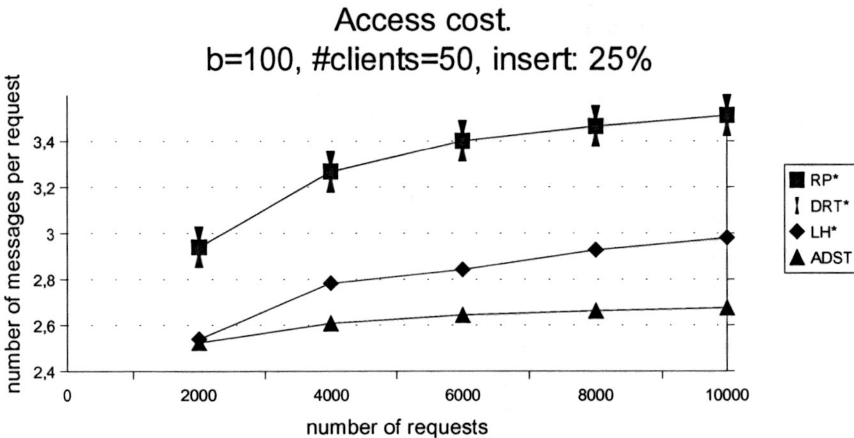

Fig. 5. Access cost for a bucket capacity $b = 100$ and for a number of clients $c = 50$ and a sequence of requests of intermixed exact searches and inserts, with 25% of inserts.

Other possible experiments could have involved the load factor of the structures, but there we fundamentally achieve the results of other order preserving SDDSs. For a series of experimental comparisons see [7].

For range searches, ADST is clearly better than LH*, where a range search can require to visit all the servers of the structure, even for small ranges. This is a direct consequence of the fact that ADST preserves the order of data.

For other order preserving proposals (e.g. RP*s, BDST), the worst-case range search cost is $O(k + \log n)$ messages, when using exclusively the point-to-point protocol, without accounting for the request message and the k response mes-

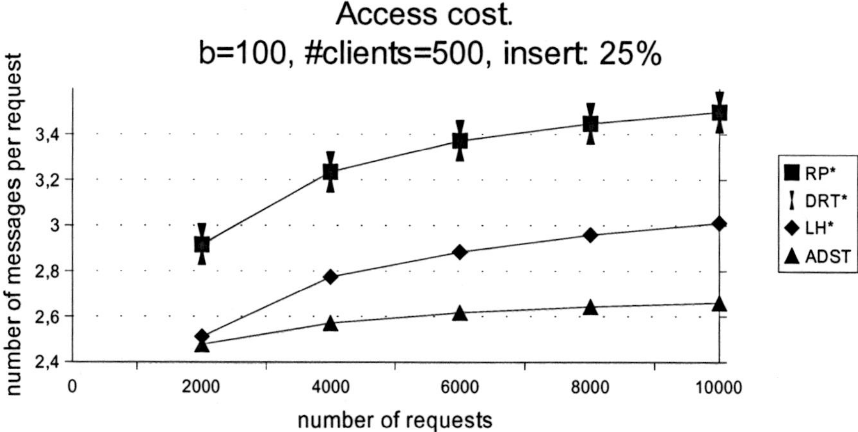

Fig. 6. Access cost for a bucket capacity $b = 100$ and for a number of clients $c = 500$ and a sequence of requests of intermixed exact searches and inserts, with 25% of inserts.

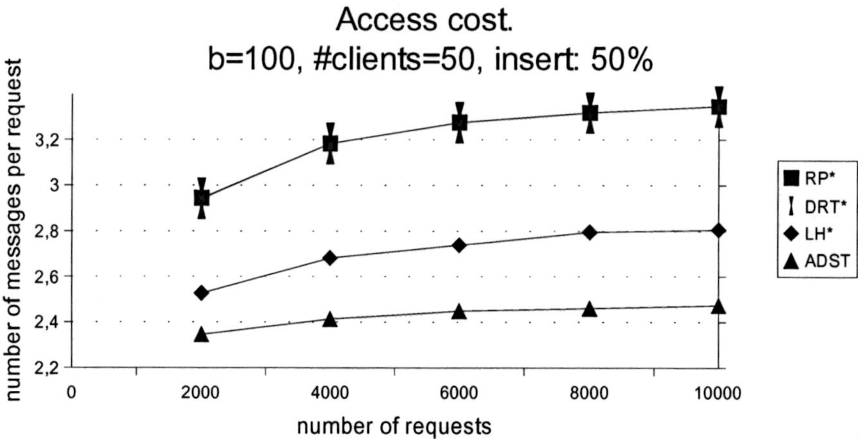

Fig. 7. Access cost for a bucket capacity $b = 100$ and for a number of clients $c = 50$ and a sequence of requests of intermixed exact searches and inserts, with 50% of inserts.

sages. The logarithmic term is due to the possibility that the request arrives to a wrong server and then has to go up in the tree to find the server associated to the node covering the entire range of the query. The base of the logarithm is a fixed number (it is equal to 2 for BDST and to the fanout of servers in the kernel for RP*s), while n is assumed unbounded.

Hence, in the case of use of point-to-point protocol, our algorithm clearly improves the cost for range search with respect to other order preserving proposals

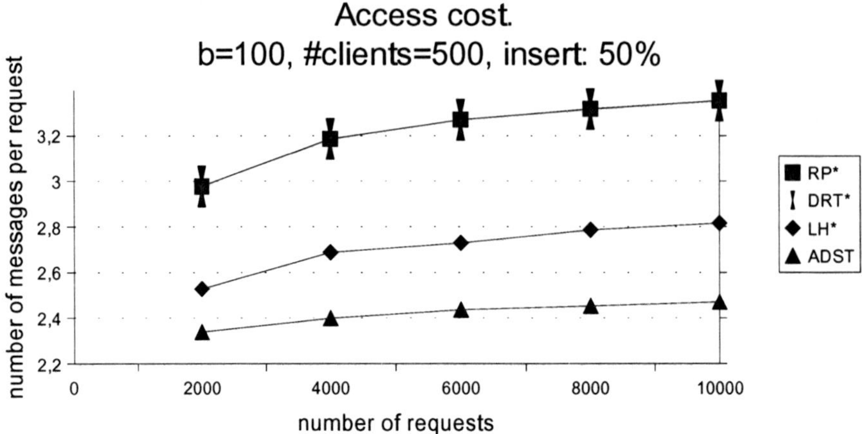

Fig. 8. Access cost for a bucket capacity $b = 100$ and for a number of clients $c = 500$ and a sequence of requests of intermixed exact searches and inserts, with 50% of inserts.

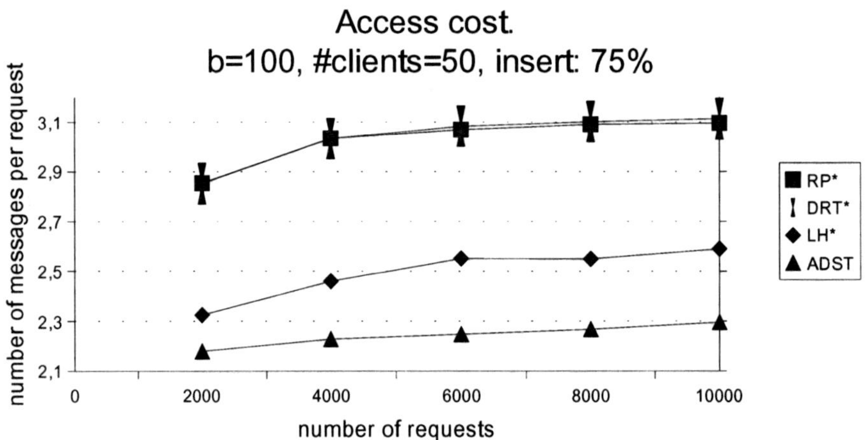

Fig. 9. Access cost for a bucket capacity $b = 100$ and for a number of clients $c = 50$ and a sequence of requests of intermixed exact searches and inserts, with 75% of inserts.

and reaches the optimality. Whenever multicast is used, all proposals have the same cost since in this case the nature of access method does not affect the cost.

5 Extensions

The basic ADST technique can be extended to:

- manage k-dimensional data. This is obtained considering the distributed k-d tree with index at client and server sites [14];
- manage deletions.

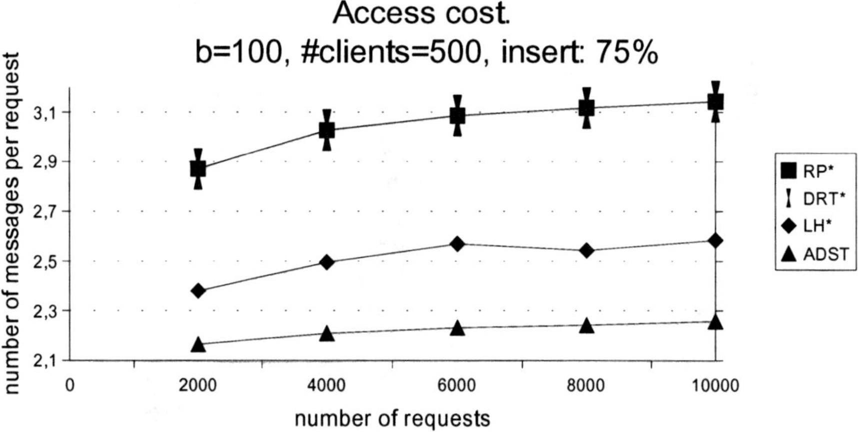

Fig. 10. Access cost for a bucket capacity $b = 100$ and for a number of clients $c = 500$ and a sequence of requests of intermixed exact searches and inserts, with 75% of inserts.

The detailed presentation of the extensions would exceed the limit of the paper and can be found in extended version of this paper [6]. In the following we just consider the fault tolerance extension of ADST.

5.1 High Availability

In this section we want to focus on the fact that our scheme is not restrictive with respect to techniques for fault tolerance in SDDSs, and we can consider ADST as an access method completely orthogonal to such techniques.

In particular we focus on the techniques for high availability using *Reed Solomon codes* and in general based on *record grouping* [13] and on the very interesting scalable availability provided by this scheme. One of the important aspect of this work is that with full availability of buckets, the normal access method can be used, while recovery algorithms have to be applied whenever a client cannot access a record in normal mode. In such a case we say an operation enters in *degraded* mode.

A more detailed description of record grouping and of techniques based on Reed Solomon codes would exceed the limits of this paper, hence we give only a brief sketch in the following.

In [13] LH* is used as access method in normal mode. The operations in *degraded* mode are handled by the coordinator. From the managed state of file, it locates the bucket to recover, and then proceeds with the recovery using the parity bucket. But for the search of the bucket to recover, the access method does not influence the correctness of the recovery algorithm, based on parity buckets. Moreover the coordinator is, in some sense, considered always available.

As already stated in [13], the same technique may be applied to other SDDS than LH*. For example we consider ADST. Buckets can be grouped and the parity bucket can be added in the same way as in [13]. We just have to associate a rank to a record in a bucket. This can be the position of the record at the moment of insertions.

ADST technique is used in normal mode. Whenever an operation enters in *degraded* mode, it is handled by the coordinator. We assume that the coordinator is the server s managing the compound root node (or a server with a copy of the local tree of s that behaves like the coordinator in LH*. This is not important here). From the request entered in degraded mode, the coordinator finds the server and then the bucket pertinent for the request. Then s can proceed with the recovery, following algorithms of [13].

The cost of operations in degraded mode are just increased with the cost of the recovery. In this case we want to emphasize that ADST, extended for achieving high availability, still keeps better worst-case and amortized case performances than the extensions of other proposals, e.g. RP*s or DRT, to a high availability schema.

6 Conclusions

We presented an evaluation of performances of ADST (Aggregation in Distributed Search Tree). This is the first order preserving SDDS, obtaining a constant single-key query cost, like LH*, and at the same time an optimal cost for range queries, like RP* and DRT*. More precisely our structure features: (i) a cost of 4 messages for exact-search queries in the worst-case, (ii) a logarithmic cost for insert queries producing a split in the worst-case, (iii) an optimal cost for range searches, that is a range search can be answered with $O(k)$ messages, where k is the number of servers covering the query range, (iv) an amortized almost constant cost for any single-key query.

The experimental analysis compares ADST and its direct competitors, namely LH*, RP* and DRT*. The outcome is that ADST has better performances than LH* (hence better than RP* and DRT*) in the average case for single-key requests. Moreover ADST is clearly better with respect to other order preserving SDDSs, like RP* and DRT*, for range searches (hence better than LH*).

ADST can be easily extended to manage deletions and to manage k-dimensional data. Moreover, we have shown that ADST is an orthogonal technique with respect to techniques used to guarantee fault tolerance, in particular to the one in [13], that provides a high availability SDDS.

Hence our proposal is very attractive for distributed applications requiring high performances for single key and range queries, high availability and possibly the management of multi-dimensional data.

References

1. P. Bozanis, Y. Manolopoulos: DSL: Accomodating Skip Lists in the SDDS Model, *Workshop on Distributed Data and Structures (WDAS 2000)*, L'Aquila, June 2000.
2. Y. Breitbart, R. Vingralek: Addressing and Balancing Issues in Distributed B^+-Trees, *1st Workshop on Distributed Data and Structures (WDAS'98)*, 1998.
3. R.Devine: Design and implementation of DDH: a distributed dynamic hashing algorithm, *4th Int. Conf. on Foundations of Data Organization and Algorithms (FODO)*, Chicago, 1993.
4. A.Di Pasquale, E. Nardelli: Fully Dynamic Balanced and Distributed Search Trees with Logarithmic Costs, *Workshop on Distributed Data and Structures (WDAS'99)*, Princeton, NJ, Carleton Scientific, May 1999.
5. A.Di Pasquale, E. Nardelli: Distributed searching of k-dimensional data with almost constant costs, *ADBIS 2000*, Prague, Lecture Notes in Computer Science, Vol. 1884, pp. 239-250, Springer-Verlag, September 2000.
6. A.Di Pasquale, E. Nardelli: ADST: Aggregation in Distributed Search Trees, Technical Report 1/2001, *University of L'Aquila*, February 2001, submitted for publication.
7. B. Kröll, P. Widmayer: Distributing a search tree among a growing number of processor, in *ACM SIGMOD Int. Conf. on Management of Data*, pp 265-276 Minneapolis, MN, 1994.
8. B. Kröll, P. Widmayer. Balanced distributed search trees do not exists, in *4th Int. Workshop on Algorithms and Data Structures(WADS'95)*, Kingston, Canada, (S. Akl et al., Eds.), Lecture Notes in Computer Science, Vol. 955, pp. 50-61, Springer-Verlag, Berlin/New York, August 1995.
9. W. Litwin, M.A. Neimat, D.A. Schneider: LH* - Linear hashing for distributed files, *ACM SIGMOD Int. Conf. on Management of Data*, Washington, D. C., 1993.
10. W. Litwin, M.A. Neimat, D.A. Schneider: RP* - A family of order-preserving scalable distributed data structure, in *20th Conf. on Very Large Data Bases*, Santiago, Chile, 1994.
11. W. Litwin, M.A. Neimat, D.A. Schneider: k-RP^*_s - A High Performance Multi-Attribute Scalable Distributed Data Structure, in *4th International Conference on Parallel and Distributed Information System*, December 1996.
12. W. Litwin, M.A. Neimat, D.A. Schneider: LH* - A Scalable Distributed Data Structure, *ACM Trans. on Database Systems*, 21(4), 1996.
13. W. Litwin, T.J.E. Schwarz, S.J.: LH^*_{RS}: a High-availability Scalable Distributed Data Structure using Reed Solomon Codes, *ACM SIGMOD Int. Conf. on Management of Data*, 1999.
14. E. Nardelli, F.Barillari, M. Pepe: Distributed Searching of Multi-Dimensional Data: a Performance Evaluation Study, *Journal of Parallel and Distributed Computation (JPDC)*, 49, 1998.
15. H. Schwetman: Csim reference manual. Tech. report ACT-ST-252-87, Rev. 14, MCC, March 1990
16. R.Vingralek, Y.Breitbart, G.Weikum: Distributed file organization with scalable cost/performance, *ACM SIGMOD Int. Conf. on Management of Data*, Minneapolis, MN, 1994.
17. R.Vingralek, Y.Breitbart, G.Weikum: SNOWBALL: Scalable Storage on Networks of Workstations with Balanced Load, *Distr. and Par. Databases*, 6, 2, 1998.

Business, Culture, Politics, and Sports – How to Find Your Way through a Bulk of News?

On Content-Based Hierarchical Structuring and Organization of Large Document Archives

Michael Dittenbach[1], Andreas Rauber[2], and Dieter Merkl[2]

[1] E-Commerce Competence Center – EC3,
Siebensterngasse 21/3, A–1070 Wien, Austria
[2] Institut für Softwaretechnik, Technische Universität Wien,
Favoritenstraße 9–11/188, A–1040 Wien, Austria
www.ifs.tuwien.ac.at/{~mbach, ~andi, ~dieter}

Abstract. With the increasing amount of information available in electronic document collections, methods for organizing these collections to allow topic-oriented browsing and orientation gain increasing importance. The *SOMLib* digital library system provides such an organization based on the *Self-Organizing Map*, a popular neural network model by producing a map of the document space. However, hierarchical relations between documents are hidden in the display. Moreover, with increasing size of document archives the required maps grow larger, thus leading to problems for the user in finding proper orientation within the map. In this case, a hierarchically structured representation of the document space would be highly preferable.
In this paper, we present the *Growing Hierarchical Self-Organizing Map*, a dynamically growing neural network model, providing a content-based hierarchical decomposition and organization of document spaces. This architecture evolves into a hierarchical structure according to the requisites of the input data during an unsupervised training process. A recent enhancement of the training process further ensures proper orientation of the various topical partitions. This facilitates intuitive navigation between neighboring topical branches. The benefits of this approach are shown by organizing a real-world document collection according to semantic similarities.

1 Introduction

With the increasing amount of textual information stored in digital libraries, means to organize and structure this information have gained importance. Specifically an organization by content, allowing topic-oriented browsing of text collections, provides a highly intuitive approach to exploring document collections. As one of the most successfull methods applied in this field we find the *Self-Organizing Map* (*SOM*) [5], a popular unsupervised neural network model, which is frequently being used to provide a map-based representation of document

H.C. Mayr et al. (Eds.): DEXA 2001, LNCS 2113, pp. 200–210, 2001.

archives [7,2,10,6]. In such a representation, documents on similar topics are located next to each other. The obvious benefit for the user is that navigation in the document archive is similar to the well-known task of navigating in a geographical map. With the *SOMLib* digital library [9] we developed a system using the *SOM* as its core module to provide content-based access to document archives. This allows the user to obtain an overview of the topics covered in a collection, and their importance with respect to the amount of information present in each topical section.

While these characteristics made the *SOM* a prominent tool for organizing document collections, most of the research work aims at providing one single map representation for the complete document archive. As a consequence, hierarchical relations between documents are lost in the display. Moreover, it is only natural that with increasing size of the document archive the maps for representing the archive grow larger, thus leading to problems for the user in finding proper orientation within the map. We believe that the representation of hierarchical document relations is vital for the usefulness of map-based document archive visualization approaches.

In this paper we argue in favor of establishing such a hierarchical organization of the document space based on a novel neural network architecture, the *Growing Hierarchical Self-Organizing Map* (*GHSOM*) [3]. The distinctive feature of this model is its problem dependent architecture which develops during the unsupervised training process. Starting from a rather small high-level *SOM*, which provides a coarse overview of the various topics present in a document collection, subsequent layers are added where necessary to display a finer subdivision of topics. Each map in turn grows in size until it represents its topic to a sufficient degree of granularity. Since usually not all topics are present equally strong in a collection, this leads to an unbalanced hierarchy, assigning more "map-space" to topics that are more prominent in a given collection. This allows the user to approach and intuitively browse a document collection in a way similar to conventional libraries.

The hierarchical structuring imposed on the data represents a rather strong separation of clusters mapped onto different branches. While this is a highly desireable characteristic helping in understanding the topical cluster structure in large data sets, it may lead to misinterpretations when long-streched clusters are mapped and expanded on two neighboring, yet different units of the *SOM*. This can be alleviated by ensuring proper orientation of the maps in the various branches of the hierarchy, allowing navigation between branches. We present the the benefits of such a hierarchical organization of digital libraries, as well as the stability of the process using a set of experiments based on a collection of newspaper articles from the daily Austrian newspaper *Der Standard*. Specifically, we compare two different representations of the topical hierarchy of this archive resulting from different parameter settings.

The remainder of this paper is organized as follows. In Section 2 we provide a brief review of related architectures followed by a description of the principles of the *SOM* and *GHSOM* training in Section 3. Subsequently, we provide a detailed discussion of our experimental results in Section 4 as well as some conclusions in Section 5.

2 Related Work

A number of extensions and modifications have been proposed over the years in order to enhance the applicability of *SOMs* to data mining, specifically inter- and intra-cluster similarity identification. The *Hierarchical Feature Map*(*HFM*) [8] addresses the problem of hierarchical data representation by modifying the *SOM* architecture. Instead of training a flat *SOM*, a balanced hierarchical structure of *SOMs* is trained. Data mapped onto one single unit is represented at a further level of detail in the lower-level map assigned to this unit. However, this model merely represents the data in a hierarchical way, rather than really reflecting the hierarchical structure of the data. This is due to the fact that the architecture of the network has to be defined in advance, i.e. the number of layers and the size of the maps at each layer is fixed prior to network training. This leads to the definition of a balanced tree which is used to represent the data. What we want, however, is a network architecture definition based on the actual data presented to the network.

The shortcoming of having to define the size of the *SOM* in advance has been addressed in several models, such as the *Incremental Grid Growing (IGG)* [1] or *Growing Grid*(*GG*) [4] models. The former allows the adding of new units at the boundary of the map, while connections within the map may be removed according to some threshold settings, possibly resulting in several separated, irregular map structures. The latter model, on the other hand, adds rows and columns of units during the training process, starting with an initial 2×2 *SOM*. This way the rectangular layout of the *SOM* grid is preserved.

3 Content-Based Organization of Text Archives

3.1 Feature Extraction

In order to allow content-based classification of documents we need to obtain a representation of their content. One of the most common representations uses word frequency counts based on full text indexing. A list of all words present in a document collection is created to span the feature space within which the documents are represented. While hand-crafted stop word lists allow for specific exclusion of frequently used words, statistical measures may be used to serve the same purpose in a more automatic way. For our experiments we thus remove all words that appear either in too many documents within a collection (e.g. say in more than 50% of all documents) or in too few (say, less than 5 documents) as these words do not contribute to content representation. The words are further weighted according to the standard $tf \times idf$, i.e. term frequency times inverse document frequency, weighting scheme [11]. This weighting scheme assigns high values to words that are considered important for content representation. The resulting feature vectors may further be used for *SOM* training.

3.2 Self-Organizing Map

The *Self-Organizing Map* is an unsupervised neural network providing a mapping from a high-dimensional input space to a usually two-dimensional output space while preserving topological relations as faithfully as possible. The *SOM* consists of a set of i units arranged in a two-dimensional grid, with a weight vector $m_i \in \Re^n$ attached to each unit. Elements from the high dimensional input space, referred to as input vectors $x \in \Re^n$, are presented to the *SOM* and the activation of each unit for the presented input vector is calculated using an activation function. Commonly, the Euclidean distance between the weight vector of the unit and the input vector serves as the activation function. In the next step the weight vector of the unit showing the highest activation (i.e. the smallest Euclidean distance) is selected as the 'winner' and is modified as to more closely resemble the presented input vector. Pragmatically speaking, the weight vector of the winner is moved towards the presented input signal by a certain fraction of the Euclidean distance as indicated by a time-decreasing learning rate α. Thus, this unit's activation will be even higher the next time the same input signal is presented. Furthermore, the weight vectors of units in the neighborhood of the winner as described by a time-decreasing neighborhood function ϵ are modified accordingly, yet to a less strong amount as compared to the winner. This learning procedure finally leads to a topologically ordered mapping of the presented input signals. Similar input data is mapped onto neighboring regions on the map.

3.3 Growing Hierarchical Self-Organizing Map

The key idea of the *GHSOM* is to use a hierarchical structure of multiple layers where each layer consists of a number of independent *SOMs*. One *SOM* is used at the first layer of the hierarchy. For every unit in this map a *SOM* might be added to the next layer of the hierarchy. This principle is repeated with the third and any further layers of the *GHSOM*.

Since one of the shortcomings of *SOM* usage is its fixed network architecture we rather use an incrementally growing version of the *SOM*. This relieves us from the burden of predefining the network's size, which is rather determined during the unsupervised training process. We start with a layer 0, which consists of only one single unit. The weight vector of this unit is initialized as the average of all input data. The training process then basically starts with a small map of 2×2 units in layer 1, which is self-organized according to the standard *SOM* training algorithm.

This training process is repeated for a fixed number λ of training iterations. Ever after λ training iterations the unit with the largest deviation between its weight vector and the input vectors represented by this very unit is selected as the error unit. In between the error unit and its most dissimilar neighbor in terms of the input space either a new row or a new column of units is inserted. The weight vectors of these new units are initialized as the average of their neighbors.

An obvious criterion to guide the training process is the quantization error q_i, calculated as the sum of the distances between the weight vector of a unit i

and the input vectors mapped onto this unit. It is used to evaluate the mapping quality of a *SOM* based on the mean quantization error (*MQE*) of all units in the map. A map grows until its *MQE* is reduced to a certain fraction τ_1 of the q_i of the unit i in the preceding layer of the hierarchy. Thus, the map now represents the data mapped onto the higher layer unit i in more detail.

As outlined above the initial architecture of the *GHSOM* consists of one *SOM*. This architecture is expanded by another layer in case of dissimilar input data being mapped on a particular unit. These units are identified by a rather high quantization error q_i which is above a threshold τ_2. This threshold basically indicates the desired granularity level of data representation as a fraction of the initial quantization error at layer 0. In such a case, a new map will be added to the hierarchy and the input data mapped on the respective higher layer unit are self-organized in this new map, which again grows until its *MQE* is reduced to a fraction τ_1 of the respective higher layer unit's quantization error q_i.

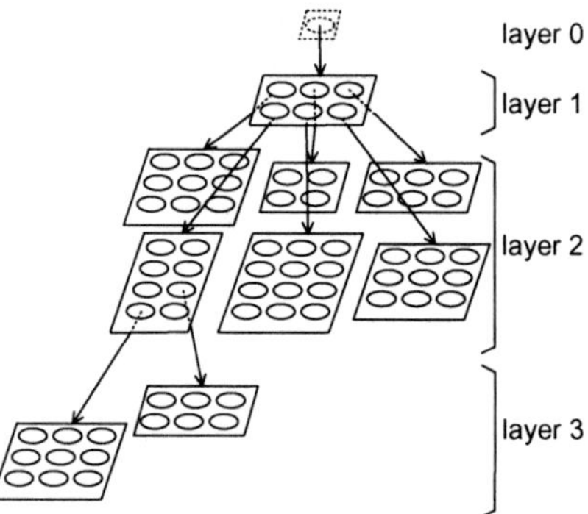

Fig. 1. *GHSOM* reflecting the hierarchical structure of the input data.

A graphical representation of a *GHSOM* is given in Figure 1. The map in layer 1 consists of 3×2 units and provides a rough organization of the main clusters in the input data. The six independent maps in the second layer offer a more detailed view on the data. Two units from one of the second layer maps have further been expanded into third-layer maps to provide sufficiently granular data representation.

Depending on the desired fraction τ_1 of *MQE* reduction we may end up with either a very deep hierarchy with small maps, a flat structure with large maps, or – in the most extreme case – only one large map, which is similar to the *Growing Grid*. The growth of the hierarchy is terminated when no further units are available for expansion. It should be noted that the training process does not necessarily lead to a balanced hierarchy in terms of all branches having the same depth. This is one of the main advantages of the *GHSOM*, because the structure of the hierarchy adapts itself according to the requirements of the input space.

Therefore, areas in the input space that require more units for appropriate data representation create deeper branches than others.

The growth process of the *GHSOM* is mainly guided by the two parameters τ_1 and τ_2, which merit further consideration.

- τ_2: Parameter τ_2 controls the minimum granularity of data representation, i.e. no unit may represent data at a coarser granularity. If the data mapped onto one single unit still has a larger variation a new map will be added originating from this unit, representing this unit's data in more detail at a subsequent layer.
  This absolute granularity of data representation is specified as a fraction of the inherent dissimilarity of the data collection as such, which is expressed in the *mean quantization error* of the single unit in layer 0 representing all data points.
  If we decide after the termination of the training process, that a yet more detailed representation would be desirable, it is possible to resume the training process from the respective lower level maps, continuing to both grow them horizontally as well as to add new lower level maps until a stricter quality criterion is satisfied. This parameter thus represents a global termination and quality criterion for the *GHSOM*.
- τ_1: This parameter controls the actual growth process of the *GHSOM*. Basically, hierarchical data can be represented in different ways, favoring either (a) lower hierarchies with rather detailed refinements presented at each subsequent layer, or (b) deeper hierarchies, which provide a stricter separation of the various sub-clusters by assigning separate maps.
  In the first case we will prefer larger maps in each layer, which explain larger portions of the data in their flat representation, allowing less hierarchical structuring. In the second case, however, we will prefer rather small maps, each of which describes only a small portion of the characteristics of the data, and rather emphasize the detection and representation of hierarchical structure.
  Thus, the smaller the parameter τ_1, the larger will be the degree to which the data has to be explained at one single map. This results in larger maps as the map's mean quantization error (*MQE*) will be lower the more units are available for representing the data. If τ_1 is set to a rather high value, the *MQE* does not need to fall too far below the *mqe* of the upper layer's unit it is based upon. Thus, a smaller map will satisfy the stopping criterion for the horizontal growth process, requiring the more detailed representation of the data to be performed in subsequent layers.

In a nutshell we can say, that, the smaller the parameter value τ_1, the more shallow the hierarchy, and that, the lower the setting of parameter τ_2, the larger the number of units in the resulting *GHSOM* network will be.

In order to provide a global orientation of the individual maps in the various layers of the hierarchy, their orientation must conform to the orientation of the data distribution on their parents' maps. This can be achieved by creating a coherent initialization of the units of a newly created map, i.e. by adding a fraction of the weight vectors in the neighborhood of the parent unit. This initial orientation of the map is preserved during the training process. By providing a global orientation of all maps in the hierarchy, potentially negative effects of splitting a large cluster into two neighboring branches can be alleviated, as it is possible to navigate across map boundaries to neighboring maps.

4 Two Hierarchies of Newspaper Articles

For the experiments presented hereafter we use a collection of 11,627 articles from the Austrian daily newspaper *Der Standard* covering the second quarter of 1999. To be used for map training, a vector-space representation of the single documents is created by full-text indexing. Instead of defining language or content specific stop word lists, we rather discard terms that appear in more than 813 (7%) or in less than 65 articles (0.56%). We end up with a vector dimensionality of 3,799 unique terms. The 11,627 articles thus are represented by automatically extracted 3,799-dimensional feature vectors of word histograms weighted by a $tf \times idf$ weighting scheme and normalized to unit length.

4.1 Deep Hierarchy

Training the *GHSOM* with parameters $\tau_1 = 0.07$ and $\tau_2 = 0.0035$ results in a rather deep hierarchical structure of up to 13 layers.[1] The layer 1 map depicted in Figure 2(a) grows to a size of 4×4 units, all of which are expanded at subsequent layers. Among the well separated main topical branches we find *Sports*, *Culture*, *Radio-* and *TV programs*, the Political Situation on the Balkan, *Internal Affairs*, *Business*, or *Weather Reports*, to name but a few. These topics are clearly identifiable by the automatically extracted keywords using the *LabelSOM* technique [10], such as *weather*, *sun*, *reach*, *degrees* for the section on *Weather Reports*[2]. The branch of articles covering the political situation on the Balkan is located in the upper left corner of the top-layer map labeled with *Balkan*, *Slobodan Milosevic*, *Serbs*, *Albanians*, *UNO*, *Refugees*, and others.

We find the branch on *Internal Affairs* in the lower right corner of this map listing the three largest political parties of Austria as well as two key politicians as labels. This unit has been expanded to form a 4×4 map in the second layer as shown in Figure 2(b). The upper left area of this map is dominated by articles related to the *Freedom Party*, whereas, for example, articles focusing on the *Social Democrats* are located in the lower left corner. Other dominant clusters on this map are *Neutrality*, or the elections to the *European Parliament*, with one unit carrying specifically the five political parties as well as the term *Election* as labels. Two units of this second layer map are further expanded in a third

[1] The maps are available for interactive exploration at `http://www.ifs.tuwien.ac.at/~andi/somlib/experiments_standard`

[2] We provide English translations for the original German labels.

layer, such as, for example, the unit in the lower right corner representing articles related to the coalition of the *People's Party* and the *Social Democrats.* These articles are represented in more detail by a 3 × 4 map in the third layer.

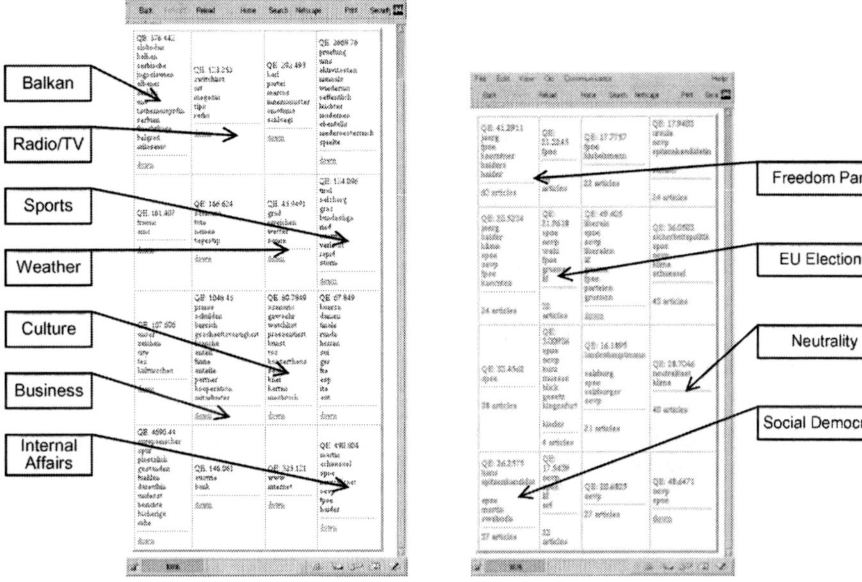

(a) Top layer map: 4×4 units; Main topics

(b) Second layer map: 4×4 units; Internal Affairs

Fig. 2. Top and second level map.

4.2 Shallow Hierarchy

To show the effects of different parameter settings we trained a second *GHSOM* with τ_1 set to half of the previous value ($\tau_1 = 0.035$), while τ_2, i.e. the absolute granularity of data representation, remained unchanged. This leads to a more shallow hierarchical structure of only up to 7 layers, with the layer 1 map growing to a size of 7 × 4 units. Again, we find the most dominant branches to be, for example, *Sports*, located in the upper right corner of the map, *Internal Affairs* in the lower right corner, *Internet*-related articles on the left hand side of the map, to name but a few. However, due to the large size of the resulting first layer map, a fine-grained representation of the data is already provided at this layer. This results in some larger clusters to be represented by two neighboring units already at the first layer, rather than being split up in a lower layer of the hierarchy. For example, we find the cluster on *Internal Affairs* to be represented by two neighboring units. One of these, on position (6/4), covers solely articles related to the *Freedom Party* and its political leader *Jörg Haider*, representing one of the most dominant political topics in Austria for some time now, resulting in an accordingly large number of news articles covering this topic. The neighboring unit to the right, i.e. located in the lower right corner on position (7/4), covers other *Internal Affairs*, with one of the main topics being the elections to the *European Parliament*. Figure 3 shows these two second-layer maps.

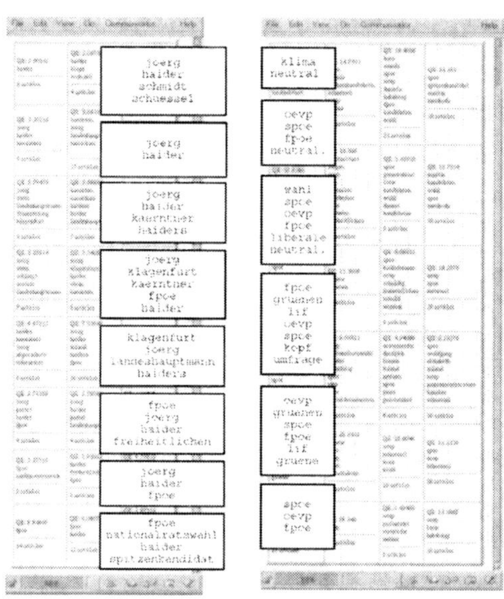

Fig. 3. Two neighboring second-layer maps on Internal Affairs

However, we also find, articles related to the *Freedom Party* on this second branch covering the more general *Internal Affairs*, reporting on their role and campaigns for the elections to the *European Parliament*. As might be expected these are closely related to the other articles on the *Freedom Party*, which are located in the neighboring branch to the left. Obviously, we would like them to be presented on the left hand side of this map, so as to allow the transition from one map to the next, with a continuous orientation of topics. Due to the initialization of the added maps during the training process, this continuous orientation is preserved, as can easily be seen from the automatically extracted labels provided in Figure 3. Continuing from the second layer map of unit (6/4) to the right we reach the according second layer map of unit (7/4), where we first find articles focusing on the *Freedom Party*, before moving on to the *Social Democrats*, the *People's Party*, the *Green Party* and the *Liberal Party*.

We thus find the global orientation to be well preserved in this map. Even though the cluster of *Internal Affairs* is split into two dominant sub-clusters in the more shallow map, the articles are organized correctly on the two separate maps in the second layer of the map. This allows the user to continue his exploration across map boundaries. For this purpose, the labels of the upper layers neighboring unit may serve as a general guideline as to which topic is covered by the neighboring map. In the deeper hierarchy, these two sub-clusters are represented within one single branch in the second layer of the map, covering the upper and the lower area of the map, respectively.

5 Conclusions

Automatic topical organization is crucial for providing intuitive means of exploring unknown document collections. While the *SOM* has proven capable of handling the complexities of content-based document organization, its applicability is limited, firstly, by the size of the resulting map, as well as secondly, by the fact that hierarchical relations between documents are lost within the map display.

In this paper we have argued in favour of a hierarchical representation of document archives. Such an organization provides a more intuitive means for exploring and understanding large information spaces. The *Growing Hierarchical Self-Organizing Map* (*GHSOM*) has shown to provide this kind of representation by adapting both its hierarchical structure as well as the sizes of each individual map to represent data at desired levels of granularity. It fits its architecture according to the requirements of the input space, reliefing the user from having to define a static organization prior to the training process.

Multiple experiments have shown both its capabilities of hierarchically orginzing document collection according to their topics, as well as the benefits of providing a better overview of, especially, larger collections, where single map-based representations tend to become unacceptably large. Furthermore, by preserving a global orientation of the individual maps, navigation between neighboring maps is facilitated. The presented model thus allows the user to intuitively explore an unknown document collection by browsing through the topical sections.

References

1. J. Blackmore and R. Miikkulainen. Incremental grid growing: Encoding high-dimensional structure into a two-dimensional feature map. In *Proceedings of the IEEE International Conference on Neural Networks (ICNN'93)*, volume 1, pages 450–455, San Francisco, CA, USA, 1993. `http://ieeexplore.ieee.org/`.
2. H. Chen, C. Schuffels, and R. Orwig. Internet categorization and search: A self-organizing approach. *Journal of Visual Communication and Image Representation*, 7(1):88–102, 1996. `http://ai.BPA.arizona.edu/papers/`.
3. M. Dittenbach, D. Merkl, and A. Rauber. The growing hierarchical self-organizing map. In *Proceedings of the International Joint Conference on Neural Networks (IJCNN 2000)*, volume VI, pages 15 – 19, Como, Italy, 2000. IEEE Computer Society. `http://www.ifs.tuwien.ac.at/ifs/research/publications.html`.

4. B. Fritzke. Growing Grid – A self-organizing network with constant neighborhood range and adaption strength. *Neural Processing Letters*, 2(5):1 – 5, 1995. `http://pikas.inf.tu-dresden.de/~fritzke`.
5. T. Kohonen. *Self-organizing maps.* Springer-Verlag, Berlin, 1995.
6. T. Kohonen, S. Kaski, K. Lagus, J. Salojärvi, J. Honkela, V. Paatero, and A. Saarela. Self-organization of a massive document collection. *IEEE Transactions on Neural Networks*, 11(3):574–585, May 2000. `http://ieeexplore.ieee.org/`.
7. X. Lin. A self-organizing semantic map for information retrieval. In *Proceedings of the 14. Annual International ACM SIGIR Conference on Research and Development in Information Retrieval (SIGIR91)*, pages 262–269, Chicago, IL, October 13 - 16 1991. ACM. `http://www.acm.org/dl`.
8. R. Miikkulainen. Script recognition with hierarchical feature maps. *Connection Science*, 2:83 – 101, 1990.
9. A. Rauber and D. Merkl. The SOMLib Digital Library System. In *Proceedings of the 3. European Conference on Research and Advanced Technology for Digital Libraries (ECDL99)*, LNCS 1696, pages 323–342, Paris, France, 1999. Springer. `http://www.ifs.tuwien.ac.at/ifs/research/publications.html`.
10. A. Rauber and D. Merkl. Using self-organizing maps to organize document collections and to characterize subject matters: How to make a map tell the news of the world. In *Proceedings of the 10. International Conference on Database and Expert Systems Applications (DEXA99)*, LNCS 1677, pages 302–311, Florence, Italy, 1999. Springer. `http://www.ifs.tuwien.ac.at/ifs/research/publications.html`.
11. G. Salton. *Automatic Text Processing: The Transformation, Analysis, and Retrieval of Information by Computer.* Addison-Wesley, Reading, MA, 1989.

Feature Selection Using Association Word Mining for Classification

Su-Jeong Ko and Jung-Hyun Lee

Department of Computer Science & Engineering
Inha University, Inchon, Korea
{sujung@nlsun.inha.ac.kr},{jhlee@inha.ac.kr}

Abstract. In this paper, we propose effective feature selection method using association word mining. Documents are represented as association-word-vectors that include a few words instead of single words. The focus in this paper is the association rule in reduction of a high dimensional feature space. The accuracy and recall of document classification depend on the number of words for composing association words, confidence, and support at Apriori algorithm. We show how confidence, support, and the number of words for composing association words at Apriori algorithm are selected efficiently. We have used Naive Bayes classifier on text data using proposed feature-vector document representation. By experiment for categorizing documents, we have proved that feature selection method of association word mining is more efficient than information gain and document frequency.

1 Introduction

A growing number of statistical classification methods and machine learning techniques have been applied to text classification in recent years, including multivariate regression models[17], nearest neighbor classification[8], Bayes probabilistic approaches[6], decision trees, neural networks[15], symbolic rule learning[11] and inductive learning algorithms[3]. A major characteristic or difficulty of text classification problems is the high dimensionality of the feature space. This is prohibitively high for many learning algorithms. It is highly desirable to reduce the naïve space without sacrificing classification accuracy.

There are a little feature selection methods in statistical learning of text classification, including term selection based on document frequency, information gain, mutual information, and term strength[9,10,18]. Information gain method is most effective but too expensive. Document frequency can be reliably used instead of information gain but is not a principled criterion for selecting predictive feature. Term strength is compared favorably with the other methods with up to 50% vocabulary reduction but is not competitive at higher vocabulary reduction levels. In contrast, mutual information has relatively poor performance due to its bias towards favoring rare terms [18].

In this paper, we propose effective feature selection method using association word mining for classification. The focus in this paper is the association rule in reduction of a high dimensional feature space using Apriori algorithm[16]. The accuracy and recall

H.C. Mayr et al. (Eds.): DEXA 2001, LNCS 2113, pp. 211–220, 2001.

of document classification depend on the number of words for composing association words, confidence, and support at Apriori algorithm. We show how confidence, support, and the number of words for composing association words at Apriori algorithm are selected efficiently.

In order to evaluate the performance of feature selection using association word mining designed in this paper, we compare feature selection methods with information gain and document frequency. In this case, we use Naïve Bayes classifier on text data using proposed feature-vector document representation[7].

2 Feature Selection Methods

Scoring of individual features can be performed by using some of the methods used in machine learning for feature selection during the learning process[18].

2.1 Document Frequency(DF)

Document frequency is the number of documents in which a term occurs. We computed the document frequency for each unique term in the training corpus and removed from the feature space those terms whose document frequency was less than some predetermined threshold.

2.2 Information Gain(IG)

Information gain is frequently employed as a term goodness criterion in the field of machine learning. It measures the number of bits of information obtained for category prediction by knowing the presence or absence of a term in a document. Let $\{c_i\}_{i=1}^{m}$ denote the set of categories in the target space. The information gain of term t is defined to be:

$$G(t) = \sum_{i=1}^{m} \Pr(c_i)\log\Pr(c_i) + \Pr(t)\sum_{i=1}^{m} \Pr(c_i \mid t)\log\Pr(c_i \mid t) + \Pr(\bar{t})\sum_{i=1}^{m} \Pr(c_i \mid \bar{t})\log\Pr(c_i \mid \bar{t})$$

2.3 Mutual Information(MI)

If one considers the two-way contingency table of a term t and a category c, where A is the number of times t and c co-occur, B is the number of time the t occurs without c, C is number of times c occurs without t, and N is the total number of documents, then the mutual information criterion between t and c is defined to be:

$$I(t,c) \approx \log \frac{A x N}{(A+C) x (A+B)}$$

2.4 Term Strength(TS)

Term strength is originally proposed and evaluated for vocabulary reduction in text retrieval. Let x and y be a arbitrary pair of distinct but related documents, and t be a term, then the strength of the term is defined to be:

$$s(t) = Pr(t \in y \mid t \in x)$$

3 Feature Selection Using Association Word Mining

3.1 Feature Selection for Document Representation

We adopt the commonly used 'bag-of-words'[12] document representation scheme, in which we ignore the structure of a document and the order of words in the document[5]. 'bag-of-words' is composed of nouns pruned stop-list from results after morphological analysis[13,14]. In this paper, we represent 'bag-of-words' as 'bag-of-association words'. The feature vectors represent the association words observed in the documents. The association word-list in the training set consists of all the distinct words that appear in the training samples after removing the stop-words.

The AW (association word)_list is defined to be : AW=$\{(w_{11}\&w_{12}\ldots\&w_{1(r-1)}\Rightarrow w_{1r}), (w_{21}\&w_{22}\ldots\&w_{2(r-1)}\Rightarrow w_{2r}),\ldots,(w_{k1}\&w_{k2}\ldots\&w_{k(r-1)}\Rightarrow w_{kr}),\ldots,(w_{p1}\&w_{p2}\ldots\&w_{p(r-1)}\Rightarrow w_{pr})\}$. Here, each of $\{ w_{k1}, w_{k2},\ldots,w_{k(r-1)}, w_{kr} \}$ in $(w_{k1}\&w_{k2}\ldots\&w_{k(r-1)}\Rightarrow w_{kr})$ represents a word for composing association word. "p" in AW represents the number of association words in a document. "r" in AW represents the number of words in an association word. "&" in pairs of words means that pairs of words have a high degree of semantic relatedness. "$w_{k1}\&w_{k2}\ldots\&w_{k(r-1)}$" is antecedent of association word $(w_{k1}\&w_{k2}\ldots\&w_{k(r-1)}\Rightarrow w_{kr})$ and "w_{kr}" is consequent of association word $(w_{k1}\&w_{k2}\ldots\&w_{k(r-1)}\Rightarrow w_{kr})$.

3.2 Confidence and Support at Apriori Algorithm

Apriori algorithm [1,2] extracts association rule between words through data mining [15]. Mining association rule between words consists of two stages. In the first stage, composition having transaction support in excess of min_support is found to constitute frequent word item. In the second stage, frequent word item is used to create association rule from database. As for all frequent word item(L), find subset instead of all empty set of frequent word item. As for each subset(A), if ratio of support(L) against support(A) is not less than min_confidence, rule of A=>(L-A) type is displayed. Support of this rule is support(L).

In order to constitute association word, confidence and support should be decided. Equation (1) to decide confidence can be obtained as follows. Equation (1) is the result of dividing the number of transaction that includes all items of W1 and W2 with the number of transaction that includes item of W1.

$$Confidence(W1\text{->}W2)=Pr(W2|W1) \quad (1)$$

Fig. 1 indicates accuracy and recall of extracted association word in times of diversifying confidence of one hundred web documents. One hundred web documents are those collected in game class from one of eight classes into which web document related to computer is classified for this experiment. Criteria of recall and accuracy of mining result has been evaluated through use of words thesaurus of WordNet[19]. For the evaluation, synonym, hyponyms and hypernyms of words related to game has been extracted from WordNet. And we extract to make 300 association words. If mining association words are not included in these 300 association words, it is regarded as error. Accuracy represents ratio of association word regarded as error against mining association word. Recall is ratio of inclusion of mining association word into association words made for evaluation.

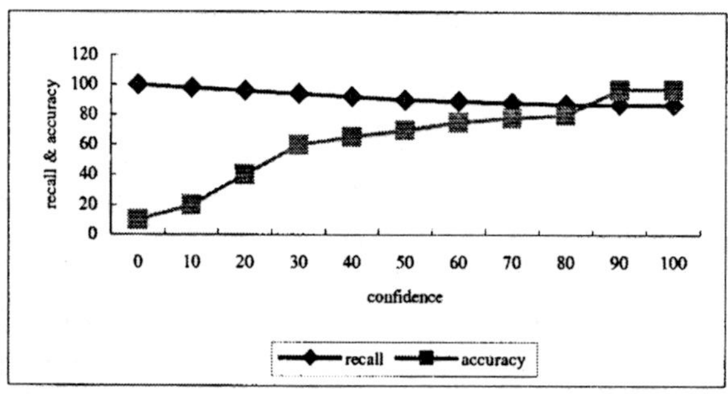

Fig. 1. The accuracy and recall of extracted association word in times of diversifying confidence of one hundred web documents

Fig. 1 shows that the bigger confidence the more accurate association words become but the lower recall becomes. However recall is almost consistent and accuracy recorded high at not less than 85 of confidence. Accordingly, in order to extract the most proper association word, confidence should be fixed at not less than 85. Equation (2) to decide support represents frequency of each association word among all word sets. Equation (2) is result of dividing the number of transaction that includes all items of W1 and W2 with the number of all transactions within database.

$$Support(W1\text{->} W2)=Pr(W1 \cup W2) \quad (2)$$

If support is large, frequency can be low but important association word can be omitted, and less important association word with high frequency such as (basics & method & use & designation => execution) is extracted. Fig. 2 represents change in accuracy and recall according to change in support of one hundred web documents. Criteria of evaluating accuracy and recall are the same as confidence.

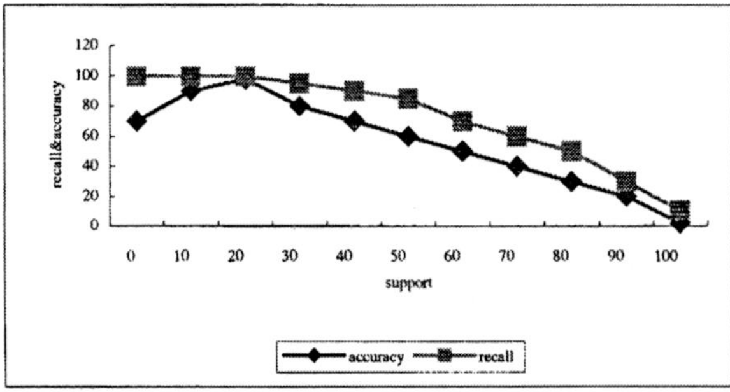

Fig. 2. The change in accuracy and recall according to change in support of one hundred web documents

Curve of accuracy and recall is identical at support of 22 and at this point, the most proper association word is extracted. However, if support is not less than 22, both accuracy and recall become lower. Accordingly, in order to extract the most trustworthy association word, support of not more than 22 should be designated.

3.3 Generating Feature

Our document representation includes not only 2 association words but also up to 5 association words occurring in document. At confidence 90 and support 20 in Apriori algorithm, we can capture some characteristic word combinations, in which the number of words increases. The process of generating feature is performed in n database retrieval, where n-association words are generated in the last pass. For illustration we show in Fig. 3(a) the accumulated number of features during the process of generating feature on 1000 web documents gathered by HTTP down loader. Let AW denote association word in generating feature. In Fig. 3(a), we can see that the number of feature generated using 2-AW is larger than the others(149890 for 2-AW vs. 13932 for 3-AW vs. 3802 for 4-AW vs. 98 for 5-AW).

Fig. 3(b) shows the result of classification using new features generated. In order to evaluate the performance of classification using each AW(2-AW, 3-AW, 4-AW, 5-AW), we use Naïve Bayes classifier on 500 web documents. We have gathered 500 web documents in game class at yahoo retrieval engine by HTTP down loader. In case that Naïve Bayes classifier using AW classifies documents into the other classes except game class, it is incorrect classification. The accuracy of classification is rate of documents correctly classified for 500 documents. In Fig. 3(b), time(sec) is the response time for document classification. As the graph shows, 2-AW has a very bad speedup performance. On the other hand, the accuracy of classification using 2-AW is higher than using 4-AW but is lower than using 3-AW. The classification using 3-AW has much more accuracy than the others. In addition, 3-AW has a good speedup comparatively. 4-AW has a very good speedup performance. On the other hand, the accuracy of classification using 4-AW is much lower than the others. Therefore, it is relevant to use 3-association words format at feature selection for document classification.

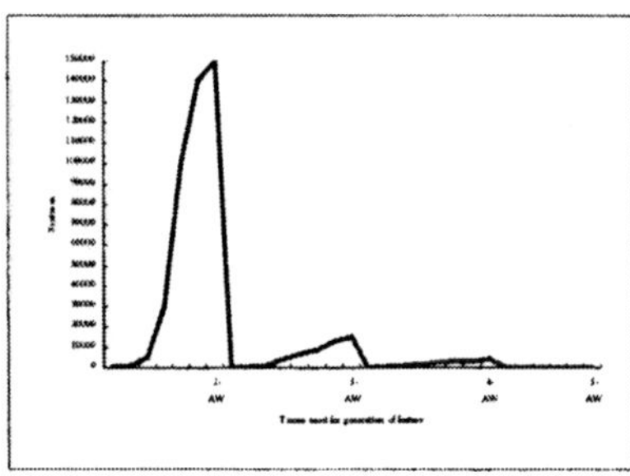

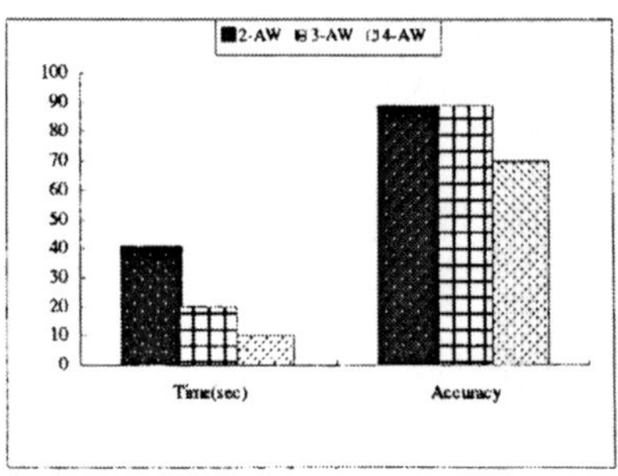

(a) Generating feature (b) Result of classification

Fig. 3. The accumulated number of features during the process of generating feature on 1000 web documents and the result of classification

4 Document Classification by Naïve Bayes

This chapter illustrates how Naïve Bayes classifier using association word mining classify web documents.

4.1 Naïve Bayes Classifier

In order to classify document, we use Naïve Bayes classifier[8]. Naïve Bayes classifier classifies document through learning stage and classifying stage. In order to learn, we must choose Equation (3) for estimating the probability of association words. In particular, we shall assume that the probability of encountering a specific association word AW_k is independent of the specific association word position being considered.

$$P(AW_k | v_j) = \frac{n_k + 1}{n + |AWKB|} \tag{3}$$

Here, n is the total number of association word positions in all training examples whose target value is v_j. n_k is the number of times association word AW_k is found among n association word positions. $|AWKB|$ is the total number of distinct association words found within the training data. In second stage, new web document can be categorized by Equation (4).

$$v_{NB} = \operatorname*{argmax}_{v_j \in AWKB} P(v_j) \prod_{i \in positions} P(AW_i | v_j) \tag{4}$$

4.2 Feature Selection and Document Classification

In order to classify document, we first represent document as 3-association words feature using Apriori algorithm. Apriori algorithm can mine association words at confidence 90 and support 20 and 3-association rule. In order to experiment, web documents on field of computer are classified into 8 classes. A basis of classification follows a statistics that the established information retrieval engines- yahoo, altavista and so on - classify words on field of computer. In Table 1, we show an example of 3-association words using Apriori algorithm.

Table 1. An example of 3-association words format for feature selection

Class	Antecedent	Consequent	Average confidence	Average support
Game	game&composition sports&participation	choice play	91.30%	20.1039%
Graphic	method¢er manufature&use	evaluation process	90.10%	21.4286%
News& media	news&offer inforamtion&flash	guide radio	99.9%	20.2838%
Semiconductor	system&business activity&technique	computer system	96.20%	20.3839%
Security	world&netizen person&maniplation	hacker communication	96.30%	21.7583%
Internet	content&site management&shopping	web electronic	94.90%	19.3838%
Publication	input&edit output&color&kind	publication print	95.30%	18.2129%
Hardware	board&printer slot&Pentium	machine computer	96.20%	21.2532%

Table 2 shows examples of how Naïve Bayes classifier classifies web document(D) using Equation (3) and Equation (4). Apriori algorithm extracts association words, which represent the web document(D). Association words that represent web document(D) are {*game&participation=>event, domain&network=>host, laser&inkjet=>printer, game&technique =>development, composition&choice=> play*}. In Table 2, Naïve Bayes classifier in Equation (4) assigns class1 to web document(D).

Table 2. Documents classification by Naïve Bayes classifier

Association word	Class 1	Class 2	Class 3	Class 4	Class 5	Class 6	Class 7	Class 8
game&participation=>event	1(0.100386)							
Domain&network=>host						1(0.00635)		
laser&inkjet=>printer								1(0.0321)
game&technique=>development	1(0.100386)							
composition&choice=> play	1(0.086614)							
class	<u>0.1724</u>					0.0013		0.00642

5 Evaluation

In order to evaluate the performance of feature selection using association word mining(AW), we compare feature selection methods with IG and DF. We experiment on Naïve Bayes document classification with 1000 web documents gathered by HTTP down loader.

It is important to evaluate accuracy and recall in conjunction. In order to quantify this with single measure, we use F-measure in Equation (5), which is a weighted combination of accuracy and recall[4].

$$F\_measure = \frac{(\beta^2 + 1)PR}{\beta^2 P + R} \qquad P = \frac{a}{a+b} 100\% \qquad R = \frac{a}{a+c} 100\% \tag{5}$$

P and R in Equation (5) represent the accuracy and recall. "a" is the number of documents, which appear in both classes. "b" is the number of documents, which appear in class categorized by first method but not in class categorized by second method. "c" is the number of documents, which appear in class categorized by second method but not in class categorized by first method. The larger F-measure is, the better performance of classification is. Here, β represents the relative weight of recall for accuracy. For β=1.0, the weight of accuracy and recall is same. The larger β is than 1.0, the larger relative weight of recall for accuracy is. In this experiment, we show the results of F-measure for β=1.0 and changing β from 0.5 to 1.4.

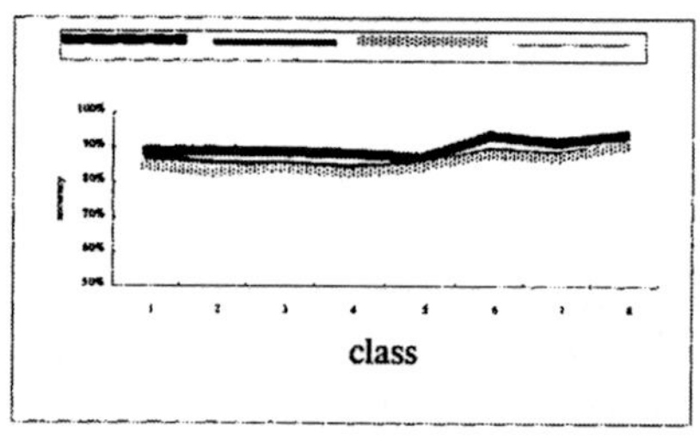

(a) Accuracy of classification

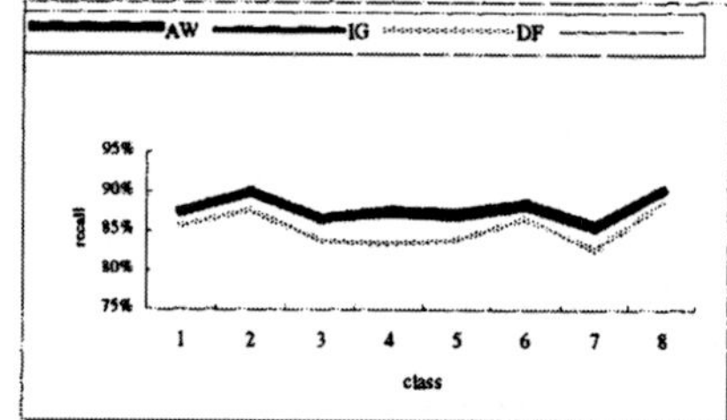

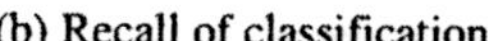
(b) Recall of classification

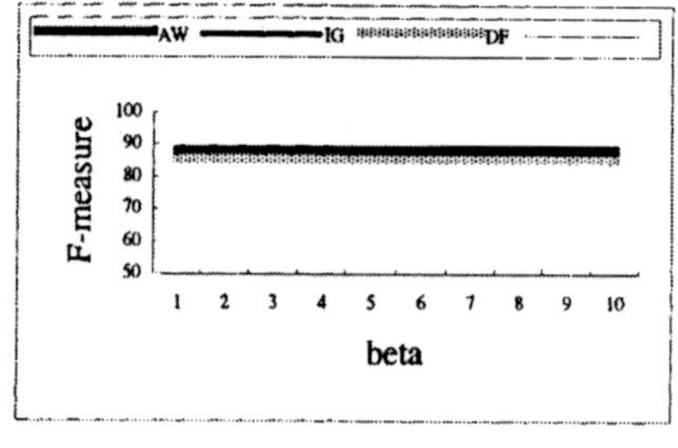

(c) F-measure at varying β

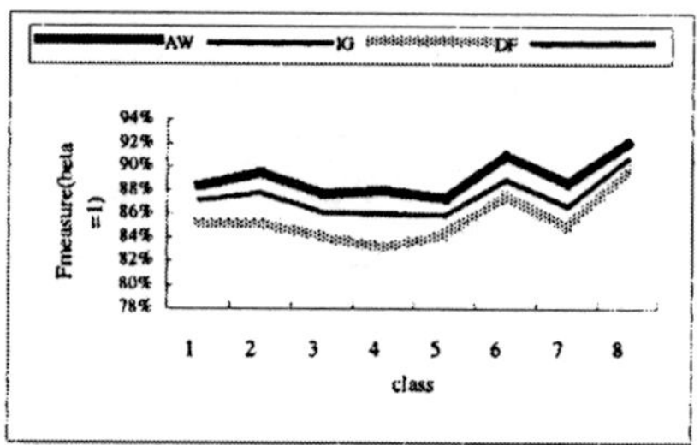

(d) F-measure of classification

Fig. 4. Performance of the AW method compared to IG method and DF method

Fig. 4 summarizes the performance of three methods. In Fig. 4(a), we can see that AW is much more accuracy than the other methods(average 90.17 for AW vs. 87.33 for IG vs. 85.72 for DF). In Fig. 4(b), we can see that both AW, as well as IG, have a significant advantage in recall(average 87.92 for AW vs. 87.47 for IG) but DF is low in recall(average 85.33 for DF). In addition, AW has an advantage than IG substantially. In Fig. 4(c), at varying with change for with β from 0.5 to 1.4, we can see that all methods have similar performance in accuracy and recall. In Fig. 4(d), we can see that AW has higher performance than the other methods(average 89.02 for AW vs. 87.39 for IG vs. 85.50 for DF).

These results are encouraging and provide empirical evidence that the use of AW can lead to improved performance on document classification.

6 Conclusion

In this paper, we have proposed feature-vector document representation that includes association words instead of just single words. We believe that the contributions of this paper are twofold. First, we have shown that feature of association rule is able to extract at confidence 90 and support 20 significantly. Second, we have shown that when association words are composed of 3-words, performance of document classification is most efficient.

We have used Naïve Bayes classifier on text data using proposed feature-vector document representation. In order to evaluate the performance of feature selection using association word mining designed in this paper, we compared feature selection methods with information gain and document frequency. By experiment for classifying documents, we have proved that feature selection method of association word mining is much more efficient than information gain and document frequency. In the future, the availability of association rule for feature space reduction may significantly ease the application of more powerful and computationally intensive learning methods, such as neural networks, to very large text classification problems that are otherwise intractable.

References

1. R. Agrawal and R. Srikant, "Fast Algorithms for Mining Association Rules," Proceedings of the 20th VLDB Conference, Santiago, Chile, 1994.
2. R. Agrawal and T. Imielinski and A. Swami, "Mining association rules between sets of items in large databases," In Proceedings of the 1993 ACM SIGMOD Conference, Washington DC, USA, 1993.
3. W. W. Cohen and Y. Singer, "Context sensitive learning methods for text categorization," Proceedings of the 19th Annual International ACM SIGIR Conference on Research and Development in Information Retrieval, pp. 307-315, 1996.
4. V. Hatzivassiloglou and K. McKeown, "Towards the automatic identification of adjectival scales: Clustering adjectives according to meaning," Proceedings of the 31st Annual Meeting of the ACL, pp. 172-182, 1993.
5. D. D. Lewis, *Representation and Learning in Information Retrieval*, PhD thesis(Technical Report pp. 91-93, Computer Science Dept., Univ. of Massachussetts at Amherst, 1992.

6. D. D. Lewis and M. Ringuette, "Comparison of two Learning algorithms for text categorization," Proceedings of the Third Annual Symposium on Document Analysis and Information Retrieval, 1994.
7. Y. H. Li and A. K. Jain, "Classification of Text Documents," Computer Journal, Vol. 41, No. 8, pp. 537-546, 1998.
8. T. Michael, *Maching Learning*, McGraw-Hill, pp. 154-200, 1997.
9. D. Mladenic, "Feature subset selection in text-learning," Proceedings of the 10th European Conference on Machine Learning, pp. 95-100, 1998.
10. D, Mladenic and M. Grobelnik, "Feature selection for classification based on text hierarchy," Proceedings of the Workshop on Learning from Text and the Web, 1998.
11. I. Moulinier and G. Raskinis and J. Ganascia, "Text categorization: a symbolic approach," Proceedings of Fifth Annual Symposium on Document Analysis and Information Retrieval, 1996.
12. M. Pazzani, D. Billsus, *Learning and Revising User Profiles: The Identification of Interesting Web Sites*, Machine Learning 27, Kluwer Academic Publishers, pp. 313-331, 1997.
13. V. Rijsbergen and C. Joost, *Information Retrieval*, Butterworths, London-second edition, 1979.
14. G. Salton and M. J. McGill, *Introduction to Modern Information Retrieval*, McGraw-Hill, 1983.
15. E. Wiener and J. O. Pederson and A. S. Weigend, "A neural network approach to topic spotting," Proceedings of the Fourth Annual Symposium on Document Analysis and Information Retrieval, 1995.
16. P. C. Wong and P. Whitney and J. Thomas, "Visualizing Association Rules for Text Mining," Proceedings of the 1999 IEEE Symposium on Information Visualization, pp. 120-123, 1999.
17. Y. Yang and C. G. Chute, "An example-based mapping method for text categorization and retrieval," ACM Transaction on Information Systems, pp. 253-277, 1994.
18. Y. Yang and J. O. Pedersen, "A Comparative Study on Feature Selection in Text Categorization," Proceedings of the Fourteenth International Conference on Machine Learning, pp. 412-420, 1997.
19. Cognitive Science Laboratory, Princeton University, "WordNet - a Lexical Database for English," http://www.cogsci.princeton.edu/~wn/.

Efficient Feature Mining in Music Objects

Jia-Ling Koh and William D.C. Yu

Department of Information and Computer Education
National Taiwan Normal University
Taipei, Taiwan 106, R.O.C.
jlkoh@ice.ntnu.edu.tw

Abstract. This paper proposes novel strategies for efficiently extracting repeating patterns and frequent note sequences in music objects. Based on bit stream representation, the bit index sequences are designed for representing the whole note sequence of a music object with little space requirement. Besides, the proposed algorithm counts the repeating frequency of a pattern efficiently to rapidly extracting repeating patterns in a music object. Moreover, with the assist of appearing bit sequences, another algorithm is proposed for verifying the frequent note sequences in a set of music objects efficiently. Experimental results demonstrate that the performance of the proposed approach is more efficient than the related works.

1 Introduction

Data mining has received increasing attention in the area of database, with the conventional alphanumeric data having been extensively studied [4]. However, the mining of multimedia data has received lesser attention. Some interesting patterns or rules in multimedia data can be mined to reveal the hidden useful information. In the melody of a music object, many sequences of notes, called repeating patterns, may appear more than once in the object. For example, "sol-sol-sol-mi" is a well-known melody that repeatedly appears in Beethoven's Fifth Symphony. The repeating pattern, an efficient representation for content-based music retrieval, can represent the important characteristics of a music object. Moreover, the sequence of notes that frequently appear in a set of music objects, an interesting pattern called a frequent note sequence, can be used for music data analysis and classification.

Hsu [5] proposed an effective means of finding repeating patterns of music objects based on a data structure called *correlative matrix*. The correlative matrix was used to record the lengths and appearing positions of note patterns that are the intermediate results during the extracting process. However, as the lengths of music objects increase, the memory requirement increases rapidly. The authors of [5] proposed a new approach in 1999 for discovering repeating patterns of music objects [8]. In this approach, the longer repeating pattern was discovered by using string-join operations to repeatedly combine shorter repeating patterns. Therefore, the storage space and execution time is reduced. However, the approach is inefficient when there exist many

H.C. Mayr et al. (Eds.): DEXA 2001, LNCS 2113, pp. 221–231, 2001.

repeating patterns whose length are extremely close to the length of the longest repeating patterns.

Mining frequent note sequences that differ from mining frequent item sets must consider the order of data items. Agrawal [2] extended the Apriori approach [1] to mine the sequential orders that frequently appear among the item sets in customer transactions. Bettini [3] adopted the finite automata approach to extract the frequent sequential patterns. However, the lengths and the ending of the repeating patterns and frequent note sequences in music objects can not be predicted, such that the terminating state of the finite automata can not be defined. Wang [9] designed suffix tree structure for representing the data set. Although capable of confirming the appearance of a certain data sequence efficiently by tracing the path of the suffix tree, that approach requires much storage space.

In light of above developments, this paper presents an efficient approach for extracting all maximum repeating patterns in a music object. Based on bit stream representation, the *bit index sequences* are designed for representing the whole note sequence of a music object with little space requirement. In addition, the repeating frequency of a candidate pattern can be counted by performing bit operations on bit index sequences so that repeating patterns can be verified efficiently. Moreover, an extended approach for mining frequent note sequences in a set of music objects is provided. Also based on bit stream representation, the *appearing bit sequences* are designed for representing the music objects in which a note sequence appears. With the aid of appearing bit sequences and bit index sequences, the number of music objects in which a note sequence appears can be counted by performing bit operations. Therefore, the frequent note sequences can be extracted efficiently.

The rest of this paper is organized as follows. Section 2 introduces the basic definitions of the problem domain. Section 3 describes the proposed data structure and algorithm for extracting repeating patterns. By extending the idea proposed in Section 3, Section 4 introduces the algorithm for extracting frequent note sequences in a set of music objects. Next, Section 5 summarizes the experimental results that demonstrate the efficiency of the proposed algorithm. Finally, we conclude with a summary and directions for future work in Section 6.

2 Repeating Patterns and Frequent Note Sequences

A repeating pattern is a consecutive sequence of notes appearing more than once in a music object and a frequent note sequence is the one appearing among a set of music objects frequently. As important features in music objects, these two kinds of patterns can be used for content-based retrieval and analysis of music data.

[*Def. 2.1*] Let X denote a note sequence consisting of $P_1P_2...P_n$, where n denotes a positive integer and each P_i (i=1, ..., n) denotes a note. The length of X is denoted by length(X), whose value is n.

[*Def. 2.2*] Let X denote a note sequence consisting of $P_1P_2...P_n$ and X' denote another note sequence consisting of $Q_1Q_2...Q_m$, where m and n are positive integers and each P_i (i=1, ..., n) and Q_j (j=1, ..., m) denotes a note, respectively. X' is called a *sub-pattern* of X if

(1) $m \leq n$,

(2) and $\exists$ positive integer i, $i \leq n$, such that $P_i P_{i+1} \ldots P_{i+m-1} = Q_1 Q_2 \ldots Q_m$.

[*Def. 2.3*] Let X denote a note sequence consisting of $P_1 P_2 \ldots P_n$, where n denotes a positive integer and each P_i (i=1, ..., n) denotes a note. The set containing all the sub-patterns of X is $\{X' | X' = P_i \ldots P_j$, where i, j $\in$ positive integers, $i \geq 1$, $j \leq n$, and $i \leq j\}$, which is denoted by SUBP(X).

[*Def. 2.4*] A note sequence X is a *repeating pattern* in music object M, if X satisfies

(1) $X \in$ SUBP(the entire note sequence of M), and

(2) $Freq_M(X) \geq$ *min-freq*.

$Freq_M(X)$ denotes the repeating frequency of X in M. Besides, *min-freq* denotes a constant value, which can be specified by users. Hereinafter, *min-freq* is set to be 2.

[*Def. 2.5*] The note sequence X is a *maximum repeating pattern* in M if X is a repeating pattern in M, and there does not exist another repeating pattern X' in M such that X is a sub-pattern of X' and $Freq_M(X)$ is equal to $Freq_M(X')$.

[Example 2.1]

Table 1. Music example for example 2.1

Music ID	Music Melody
M1	DoMiMiMiSoSo
M2	SoMiMiFaReRe
M3	SoSoSoMiFaFaFaRe
M4	SoDoDoReSoDoDo

Consider the music objects as shown in Table 1. In music object M1, $Freq_{M1}$("Mi") = 3, $Freq_{M1}$("So") = 2, and $Freq_{M1}$("MiMi") = 2. Because the repeating frequencies of these three patterns are larger than or equal to *min-freq*, "So", "Mi", and "MiMi" are repeating patterns in M1. In addition, these three patterns are also maximum repeating patterns in M1. In music object M4, $Freq_{M4}$ ("So") = 2, $Freq_{M4}$ ("Do") = 4, $Freq_{M4}$ ("SoDo") = 2, $Freq_{M4}$ ("DoDo") = 2, and $Freq_{M4}$ ("SoDoDo") = 2. These five patterns are repeating patterns in music object M4. However, only "Do" and "SoDoDo" are maximum repeating patterns.

[*Def. 2.6*] Let MS denote a set of music objects. The note sequence Y is a *frequent note sequence* in MS, if $Sup_{MS}(Y) \geq$ *min-sup*,

where $Sup_{MS}(Y) = \sum_{M \in MS} Contains_M(Y)$,

$Contains_M(Y) = 1$, if $Freq_M(Y) \geq 1$

$Contains_M(Y) = 0$, otherwise.

In the definition, *min-sup* denotes a constant value, which is used to require that a frequent note sequence must appear in at least *min-sup* music objects in MS. Besides, the notation $Sup_{MS}(Y)$ is named the *support* of Y in MS.

[*Def. 2.7*] The note sequence Y is a *maximum frequent note sequence* in MS if Y is a frequent note sequence in MS, and there does not exist another frequent note sequence Y' in MS such that Y is a sub-pattern of Y'.

[*Def. 2.8*] Let P and Q denote a note in music object M, respectively. Q is named an adjacent note of P if note sequence PQ appears in M. We also say Q is *adjacent to* P. Moreover, PQ is an *adjacent note pair* in M.

3 Repeating Patterns Mining

3.1 Bit Index Table

The bit index table is designed based on bit stream representation. A *bit index sequence* is constructed for each note in the note sequence of a music object. The length of the bit index sequence equals the length of the note sequence. Assume that the least significant bit is numbered as bit 1 and the numbering increases to the most significant bit. If the *i*th note in the note sequence is note N, bit *i* in the bit index sequence of N is set to be 1; otherwise, the bit is set to be 0. That is, the bits in the bit index sequence of note N represent the appearing locations of N in the music object. Consider the note sequence "DoDoDoMiMi" as an example. The bit index sequence of "Do", denoted by BIS_{Do}, is 00111. Then, the entire note sequence of a music object is represented by a bit index table that consists of bit index sequences for various notes in the music object. Consider the music object with note sequence "SoSoSoMFaFaFa Re". The length of the sequence is 8, which contains four various notes. Table 2 presents the corresponding bit index table.

Table 2. Example of bit index table

Note	Bit index sequence
Re	10000000
Mi	00001000
Fa	01110000
So	00000111

For each note P, the number of bits with value 1 in its bit index sequence implies the repeating frequency $Freq_M(P)$. Suppose a note sequence consists of two notes P and Q. The repeating frequency of the note sequence PQ also can be counted efficiently by performing bit operations on bit index sequences as described in the following. Initially, the bit index table provides the corresponding bit index sequences of note P and Q, BIS_P and BIS_Q. The left shift operation on BIS_P is performed. An **and** operation on the previous result and BIS_Q is then performed to get the bit index sequence of PQ. The bits with value 1 in the sequence correspond to the positions in music object M where PQ appears. In addition, the number of bits with value 1 represents $Freq_M(PQ)$. Similarly, this strategy can be applied to verify whether a note sequence ST, consisting of a note sequence S with length(S) ≥ 1 and a note T, is a repeating pattern. Hereinafter, Frequent_Count(M, P) represents the function for counting the repeating frequency of note sequence P in music object M.

[Example 3.1]

Given the bit index table of music object M as shown in Table 2, where the represented note sequence is "SoSoSoMiFaFaFaRe". The process for evaluating whether the note sequences "SoSo" and "SoSoMi" are repeating patterns is as follows.

<1> Frequent_Count(M, SoSo)

1) Obtain the bit index sequence of the second note "So", BIS_{So} = 00000111.
2) Perform the left shift operation on BIS_{So}, which is 00000111. The resultant sequence is then assigned to temporal variable t, t =shl(BIS_{So}, 1) =00001110.
3) Perform $r = t \wedge BIS_{So}$, and the resultant bit sequence is 00000110.
4) Count the number of 1s in the bit sequence r and get $Freq_M$(SoSo) = 2. This implies that "SoSo" appears in M two times and, thus, is a repeating pattern in M.

<2> Frequent_Count(M, SoSoMi)

1) Obtain BIS_{Mi} = 00001000.
2) BIS_{SoSo} , 00000110, is obtained from the previous step. Perform the left shift operation and assign it to variable t. t = 00001100.
3) Perform $r = t \wedge BIS_{Mi}$, and, in doing so, bit sequence 00001000 is obtained.
4) The number of 1s in the bit sequence r is 1. This indicates that $Freq_M$(SoSoMi) = 1 and, thus, "SoSoMi" is not a repeating pattern in M.

3.2 Algorithm for Mining Repeating Patterns

This subsection presents an algorithm, named MRP algorithm, for mining repeating patterns by applying the bit index table. Redundancy may occur among the repeating patterns and, therefore, only the maximum repeating patterns are extracted. The algorithm consists of two phases: mining repeating patterns and extracting maximum repeating patterns.

The mining phase applies the depth first search approach. First, the candidate pattern consists of a single note. If the pattern is a repeating pattern, the algorithm constructs a new candidate pattern by adding an adjacent note to the old one and verifies the repeating frequency. If the new candidate is a repeating pattern, the process will continue recursively. Otherwise, the process returns to the old candidate pattern before adding a note and attempts to add another note to the sequence.

Consider the music object with note sequence "ABCABC". The candidate pattern with length 1, "A", is initially chosen and its repeating frequency is then counted. Since the repeating frequency of "A" equals 2, "A" is a repeating pattern. Next, an adjacent note of "A" is added, and the candidate pattern "AB" is constructed as well. After verifying that "AB" satisfies the definition of a repeating pattern, the candidate "ABC" is then constructed. Although "ABC" is verified to be a repeating pattern, a repeating pattern with length 4 can not be obtained by adding any note to "ABC". Thus, the recursive process is terminated and the status returns to the sequence "AB" and then back to the sequence "A". When the process returns the status back to the sequence "A", no other adjacent notes of "A" can be added. Next, another candidate pattern with length 1, "B", is chosen and the above process repeats. After that, the repeating patterns "B" and "BC" are found. In addition, the final candidate pattern with length 1, "C", is also a repeating pattern.

Among the extracted repeating patterns, not all repeating patterns are maximum repeating patterns. Therefore, the second phase is required to investigate the sub-pattern relationship and repeating frequencies for every pair of repeating patterns to remove the non-maximum repeating patterns. In order to reduce processing cost of the second phase, the following property is applied in the mining phase for removing a part of non-maximum repeating patterns.

If repeating pattern T is constructed from repeating pattern S by adding a note, S is a sub-pattern of T. Therefore, we can make sure that S is not a maximum repeating pattern if S and T have the same repeating frequency and S can be removed in the mining phase. In the example illustrated above, the repeating frequency of sequence "AB" is 2, and so is sequence "ABC". Therefore, "AB" is not a maximum repeating pattern. Similarly, "A" is not a maximum repeating pattern. Therefore, only sequences "ABC","BC", and "C" remain in the result because they are possibly maximum repeating pattern and require the processing of second phase. This strategy can filter out many non-maximum repeating patterns, such that it is more efficient when extracting the maximum repeating patterns during the second phase.

Among the possible maximum repeating patterns remained in set RP, no two repeating patterns exist that have the same repeating frequency and one is the prefix of the other. These patterns are stored in a table as shown in Table 3. In addition to the note sequence of the repeating pattern, the other three columns are used to store the length, repeating frequency, and the final starting position where the pattern appears in the music object. Applying the table allows us to extract the maximum repeating patterns without performing string matching.

The function MMRP() is used to extract the maximum repeating patterns. The pseudo codes for function MMRP() are shown below. The first two predicates in the "if clause" are used to verify whether if note sequence T is a sub-pattern of sequence S. If T is a sub-pattern of S and has the same repeating frequency with S, T is not a maximum repeating pattern and is removed from the results.

```
Function MMRP()
{for each note sequence S in RP
      for each note sequence T in RP and T ≠ S
         i := the final starting position where S appears
         j := the final starting position where T appears
         if((i <
  j)and(length(S)+i≥length(T)+j)and(Freq_M(S)=Freq_M(T))
            RP = RP - {T}
      end for }
```

Table 3. Example of maximum repeating patterns

Repeating pattern	Length	Repeating frequency	Final starting position
ABC	3	2	4
BC	2	2	5
C	1	2	6

Consider the note sequence "ABCABC". Table 3 displays the possible maximum repeating patterns extracted in the mining phase. Both the final starting positions of "BC" and "C" are larger than the one of "ABC". These patterns have the same result by adding the final starting positions and the lengths of the patterns. Moreover, their repeating frequencies are all the same. Therefore, only "ABC" is a maximum repeating pattern among these patterns.

4 Frequent Note Sequences Mining

This section describes a novel algorithm for mining frequent note sequences in a set of music objects. The note combination structure is designed for storing the adjacent note pairs appearing in a set of music objects. Applying the structure allows us to produce the candidate frequent note sequences efficiently in the mining process.

4.1 Note Combination Structure

The note combination structure is a two-dimensional array named *NC table*. Notably, the index values of the array correspond to the distinct notes. The data stored in array NC[M][N] is a bit stream representing the music objects in which the note sequence MN appears and is named the *appearing bit sequence* of MN. The length of the sequence equals the number of music objects. If MN appears in the *i*th music object, bit *i* in the appearing bit sequence is set to be 1; otherwise, the bit is set to be 0. In the following, $Appear_S$ denotes the appearing bit sequence of a note sequence S.

Table 4. Example of NC table

	Do	Re	Mi	Fa
Do	000	011	100	000
Re	000	000	011	000
Mi	000	000	000	111
Fa	110	000	000	000

[Example 4.1] Consider the note sequences of three music objects: "DoReMiFa", "ReMiFaDoRe", and "MiFaDoMi". All the adjacent note pairs appearing in the first music object are "DoRe", "ReMi", and "MiFa". Because "DoRe" appears in music object 1, the first bit of the appearing bit sequence in NC[Do][Re] is set to be 1. Table 4 presents the NC table for these three music objects.

The bit sequence stored in NC[Do][Re], which is 011, represents that the note sequence "DoRe" appears in music object 1 and 2. Similarly, $Appear_{MiFa}$ is stored in NC[Mi][Fa]. The sequence "111" implies that "MiFa" appears in all the music objects.

For a single note P, the appearing bit sequence of P, denoted as $Appear_P$, represents the music objects in which note P appears. This sequence can be obtained via performing **or** operations on the sequences stored in the row and column indexed by P. Then the number of bits with value 1 in $Appear_P$ represents the support of P.

For a note sequence consisting of two notes, P and Q, $Appear_{PQ}$ is obtained from the NC table directly. Therefore, the support of PQ also can be counted efficiently according to the number of 1s in $Appear_{PQ}$.

Suppose a note sequence S with length n ($n \geq 2$) is a frequent note sequence. And a new candidate note sequence is constructed by adding a note Q to S. In order to reduce the processing cost of frequent note sequence verification, information in the NC table is used to filter out the non-frequent note sequences as early as possible. Suppose the last note in S is P. The note sequence SQ remains as a candidate if both the following two requirements are satisfied.

1. The number of bits with value 1 in $Appear_{PQ}$, stored in NC[P][Q], is larger than or equal to *min_sup*.
2. Perform $Appear_S \wedge Appear_{PQ}$. The number of 1s in the resultant sequence is larger than or equal to *min_sup*.

The result of $Appear_S \wedge Appear_{PQ}$ is an approximation of $Appear_{SQ}$, which represents the music objects in which both S and RQ appear. If the number of bits with value 1 in this sequence is larger than or equal to *min-sup*, both S and RQ are frequent note sequences. However, further verification is required by invoking function Frequent_Count() to verify if SQ is actually a note sequence in the corresponding music objects specified by the bits with value 1.

4.2 Algorithm for Mining Frequent Note Sequences

This subsection presents MFNS algorithm designed for mining frequent note sequences, which mainly consists of the following three steps.

[Step 1] Bit index tables and NC table construction.

The note sequences of the given music objects are scanned sequentially. The bit index table for each music object and the NC table for the given music objects are then constructed.

[Step 2] Frequent note sequences extraction.

Similar to the mining phase in MRP algorithm, this step also applies the depth first search approach to extract the frequent note sequences. Initially, the candidate note sequence consists of a single note. The information in the NC table and bit index tables is used to verify if a candidate is a frequent note sequence and construct a new candidate sequence recursively.

[Step 3] Maximum frequent note sequences extraction.

This step extracts maximum frequent note sequences. For any two frequent note sequences P and P', if P is the sub-pattern of P', P is not a maximum frequent note sequence and removed from the result.

[Example 4.2] Table 4 displays the NC table of a set of music objects, and *min-sup* is set to be 2. Frequent note sequence mining according to step 2 of the algorithm is performed as follows.

<1> Select note "Do" as the first note of candidate note sequences.

After performing $Appear_{DoRe} \vee Appear_{DoMi} \vee \ldots \vee Appear_{FaDo}$, the outcome is "111". The sequence represents that "Do" appears in all the music objects and is a frequent note sequence. Then note "Re" is chosen to added adjacent to "Do".

$Appear_{DoRe}$="011" implies that "DoRe" appears in two music objects and is a frequent note sequence. Next, note "Mi" is chosen to construct candidate sequence "DoReMi". The outcome is "011" after performing $Appear_{DoRe}$ ("011") ∧ $Appear_{ReMi}$ ("011"). This occurrence implies that "DoRe" and "ReMi" appear in the first and second music objects. It is necessary to verify whether if "DoReMi" exists in the first and second music objects.

Closely examining the bit index sequences of "DoReMi" in the first and second music objects reveals that "DoReMi" only appears in the first music. Therefore, "DoReMi" is not a frequent note sequence. Next, no other notes can be added to the frequent note sequences "DoRe" and "Do", individually, to construct new candidates. Therefore, the mining process for the frequent note sequences begins with "Do" terminates. "Do" and "DoRe" are the extracted frequent note sequences.

<2> Select note "Re" as the first note of candidate note sequences.

Applying the same mining process allows us to extract the frequent note sequences "Re", "ReMi", and "ReMiFa" sequentially. Next, the note "Do" is chosen to construct a candidate pattern "ReMiFaDo". However, after performing the **and** operation on $Appear_{ReMiFa}$ ("011") and $Appear_{FaDo}$("110"), there is only one bit with value 1 in the resultant sequence, implying that only the second music object contains "ReMiFa" and "FaDo" at the same time. Therefore, "ReMiFaDo" is obviously not a frequent note sequence. The frequent note sequences beginning with "Re" are "Re", "ReMi", and "ReMiFa".

Similarly, notes "Mi" and "Fa" are chosen as the first note of candidate note sequences individually, and the above process repeats. Finally, the extracted frequent note sequences beginning with "Mi" are "Mi", "MiFa", and "MiFaDo". The frequent note sequences beginning with "Fa" are "Fa" and "FaDo".

For a frequent note sequence K, K is not a maximum frequent note sequence if K is a prefix of another frequent note sequence. Such sequences are not stored in MaxFNS when mining frequent note sequences. Therefore, step 3 can be performed more efficiently via only considering the frequent note sequences in MaxFNS. Among the extracted frequent note sequences, only "DoRe", "ReMiFa", "MiFaDo" and "FaDo" are stored in MaxFNS, which are possible maximum frequent note sequences. After step 3 is performed, only the maximum frequent note sequences "DoRe", "ReMiFa", and "MiFaDo" remain.

5 Performance Study

The efficiency of the proposed MRP algorithm is evaluated by comparing it with two related approaches: the correlative matrix approach [5] and the string join method [8].

The algorithms are implemented and performed on a personal computer. The data sets used in the experiments include synthetic music objects and real music objects. Herein, the *object size* of a music object is defined as the length of the note sequence and the *note count* represents the number of various notes appearing in the music object. In addition, the total repeating frequency of repeating patterns in a music object is the *RP repeating frequency* and the number of maximum repeating patterns is named *RP count.* Due to page limit, the parameter setting of synthetic music objects for each experiment refers to [7].

According to the results of the experiments shown in Fig.1, the execution time of MRP algorithm is less than 0.2 seconds for the real music objects and less than 0.01 seconds for the synthetic music objects. The proposed algorithm is more efficient than the other two approaches. Moreover, the memory requirement of MRP algorithm is less than the other ones, thus confirming that the algorithm proposed herein is highly appropriate for mining maximum repeating patterns.

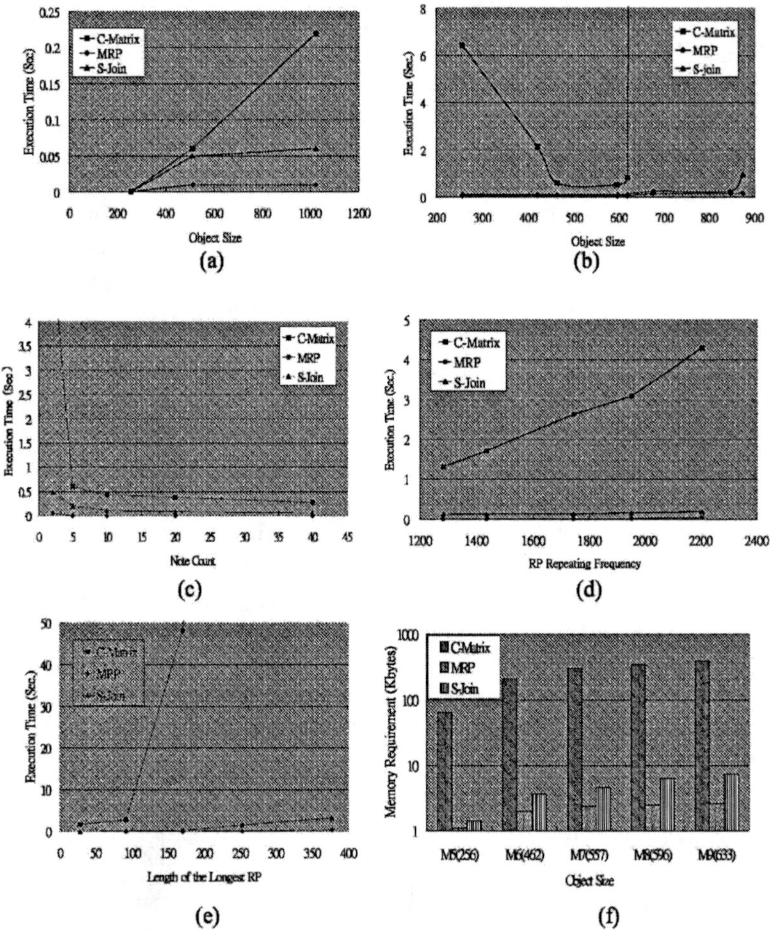

Fig. 1. (a) illustrates the execution time versus the object size of synthetic music objects. (b) shows the results of eight real music objects. (c) indicates that the execution time is inversely proportional to the note count. (d) reveals that the RP repeating frequency more significantly influence the execution time of correlative matrix approach than the MRP algorithm and the string join method do. (e) reveals that all the execution times of the three algorithms increase with an increasing length of the longest repeating pattern. (f) shows that the size of memory requirement for MRP algorithm is the least among the three algorithms.

6 Conclusion

This paper presents a novel means of mining the maximum repeating patterns in the melody of a music object. With the design of bit index sequence representation, the repeating frequency of a candidate pattern can be counted efficiently. In addition, the proposed approach is extended to extract frequent note sequences in a set of music objects. With the aid of appearing bit sequence representation and note combination structure, MFNS algorithm is proposed for generating candidate sequences and verifying the frequent note sequences efficiently.

Experimental results indicate that both execution time and memory requirement of the proposed MRP algorithm are less than the other two related works for mining maximum repeating patterns. Moreover, our approach is extended to mine the frequent note sequences in a set of music objects, which has seldom been mentioned previously.

From the extracted repeating patterns, a future work should address issues on music data clustering and classification. Furthermore, the music association rules should be analyzed for frequent note sequences to develop the intelligent agent so that similar music objects can be automatically retrieved. Finally, a future application will extend the proposed techniques to DNA and protein sequence mining.

References

1. R. Agrawal and R. Srikant, "Fast Algorithms for Mining Association Rules in Large Databases," in *Proc. 20th International Conference on Very Large Data Bases,* 1994.
2. R. Agrawal and R. Srikant, "Mining Sequential Patterns," in *Proc. the IEEE International Conference on Data Engineering (ICDE),* Taipei, Taiwan, 1995.
3. C. Bettini, S. Wang, S. Jajodia, and J.-L. Lin, "Discovering Frequent Event Patterns with Multiple Granularities in Time Sequences," *IEEE Trans. on Knowledge and Data Eng.*, vol. 10, no. 2, 1998.
4. M.S. Chen, J. Han and P.S. Yu, "Data Mining: an Overview from a Database Perspective," *IEEE Trans. Knowledge and Data Eng.*, Vol. 8, No. 6, Dec.1996.
5. J.-L. Hsu, C.-C. Liu, and A.L.P Chen, "Efficient Repeating Pattern Finding in Music Databases," in *Proc. the 1998 ACM 7th International Conference on Information and Knowledge Management (CIKM'98),* 1998.
6. Roberto J. and Bayardo Jr., "Efficiently Mining Long Patterns from Databases," in *Proc. ACM SIGMOD International Conference on Management of Data,* 1998.
7. J.-L. Koh and W.D.C. Yu, "Efficient Repeating and Frequent Sequential Patterns Mining in Music Databases," Technique report in Department of information and computer education, National Taiwan Normal University.
8. C.-C. Liu, J.-L. Hsu and A.L.P. Chen, "Efficient Theme and Non-Trivial Repeating Pattern Discovering in Music Databases," in *Proc. IEEE International Conference on Data Engineering,* 1999.
9. K. Wang, "Discovering Patterns from Large and Dynamic Sequential Data," *Journal of Intelligent Information Systems (JIIS)*, Vol. 9, No. 1, 1997.

An Information-Driven Framework for Image Mining

Ji Zhang, Wynne Hsu, and Mong Li Lee
School of Computing, National University of Singapore
{zhangji, whsu, leeml}@comp.nus.edu.sg

Abstract. Image mining systems that can automatically extract semantically meaningful information (knowledge) from image data are increasingly in demand. The fundamental challenge in image mining is to determine how low-level, pixel representation contained in a raw image or image sequence can be processed to identify high-level spatial objects and relationships. To meet this challenge, we propose an efficient information-driven framework for image mining. We distinguish four levels of information: the Pixel Level, the Object Level, the Semantic Concept Level, and the Pattern and Knowledge Level. High-dimensional indexing schemes and retrieval techniques are also included in the framework to support the flow of information among the levels. We believe this framework represents the first step towards capturing the different levels of information present in image data and addressing the issues and challenges of discovering useful patterns/knowledge from each level.

1 Introduction

An extremely large number of image data such as satellite images, medical images, and digital photographs are generated every day. These images, if analyzed, can reveal useful information to the human user. Unfortunately, there is a lack of effective tools for searching and finding useful patterns from these images. Image mining systems that can automatically extract semantically meaningful information (knowledge) from image data are increasingly in demand. Image mining deals with the extraction of implicit knowledge, image data relationship, or other patterns not explicitly stored in the images and between image and other alphanumeric data. It is more than just an extension of data mining to image domain. It is an interdisciplinary endeavor that draws upon expertise in computer vision, image processing, image retrieval, data mining, machine learning, database, and artificial intelligence [6]. Despite the development of many applications and algorithms in the individual research fields, research in image mining is still in its infancy. The fundamental challenge in image mining is to determine how low-level, pixel representation contained in a raw image or image sequence can be processed to identify high-level spatial objects and relationships.

In this paper, we propose an information-driven framework for image mining. We distinguish four levels of information: (1) the Pixel Level comprises the raw image information such as image pixels and the primitive image features such as color, texture, and shape; (2) the Object Level deals with object or region information based on the primitive features in the Pixel Level; (3) the Semantic Concept Level takes into consideration domain knowledge to generate high-level semantic concepts from the identified objects and regions; (4) the Pattern and Knowledge Level incorporates

H.C. Mayr et al. (Eds.): DEXA 2001, LNCS 2113, pp. 232–242, 2001.

domain related alphanumeric data and the semantic concepts obtained from the image data to discover underlying domain patterns and knowledge. High-dimensional indexing schemes and retrieval techniques are also included in the framework to support the flow of information among the levels. This framework represents the first step towards capturing the different levels of information present in image data and addressing the question of what are the issues and work that has been done in discovering useful patterns/knowledge from each level.

The rest of this paper is organized as follows: Section 2 presents an overview of the proposed information-driven image mining architecture. Section 3 describes each of the information level. Section 4 discusses how each of the information level can be organized and indexed. Section 5 gives the related work and we conclude in Section 6.

2 Information-Driven Image Mining Framework

The image database containing raw image data cannot be directly used for mining purposes. Raw image data need to be processed to generate the information that is usable for high-level mining modules. An image mining system is often complicated because it employs various approaches and techniques ranging from image retrieval and indexing schemes to data mining and pattern recognition. Such a system typically encompasses the following functions: image storage, image processing, feature extraction, image indexing and retrieval, patterns and knowledge discovery. A number of researchers have described their image mining framework from the functional perspective [6, 25, 37]. While such functional-based framework is easy to understand, it fails to emphasize the different levels of information representation necessary for image data before meaningful mining can take place.

Figure 1 shows our proposed information-driven framework for image mining. There are four levels of information, starting from the lowest Pixel Level, the Object Level, the Semantic Concept Level, and finally to the highest Pattern and Knowledge Level. Inputs from domain scientists are needed to help identify domain specific objects and semantic concepts. At the Pixel Level, we are dealing with information relating to the primitive features such as color, texture, and shape. At the Object Level, simple clustering algorithms and domain experts help to segment the images into some meaningful regions/objects. At the Semantic Concept Lever, the objects/regions identified earlier are placed in the context of the scenes depicted. High-level reasoning and knowledge discovery techniques are used to discover interesting patterns. Finally, at the Pattern and Knowledge Level, the domain-specific alphanumeric data are integrated with the semantic relationships discovered from the images and further mining are performed to discovered useful correlations between the alphanumeric data and those found in the images. Such correlations discovered are particularly useful in the medical domain.

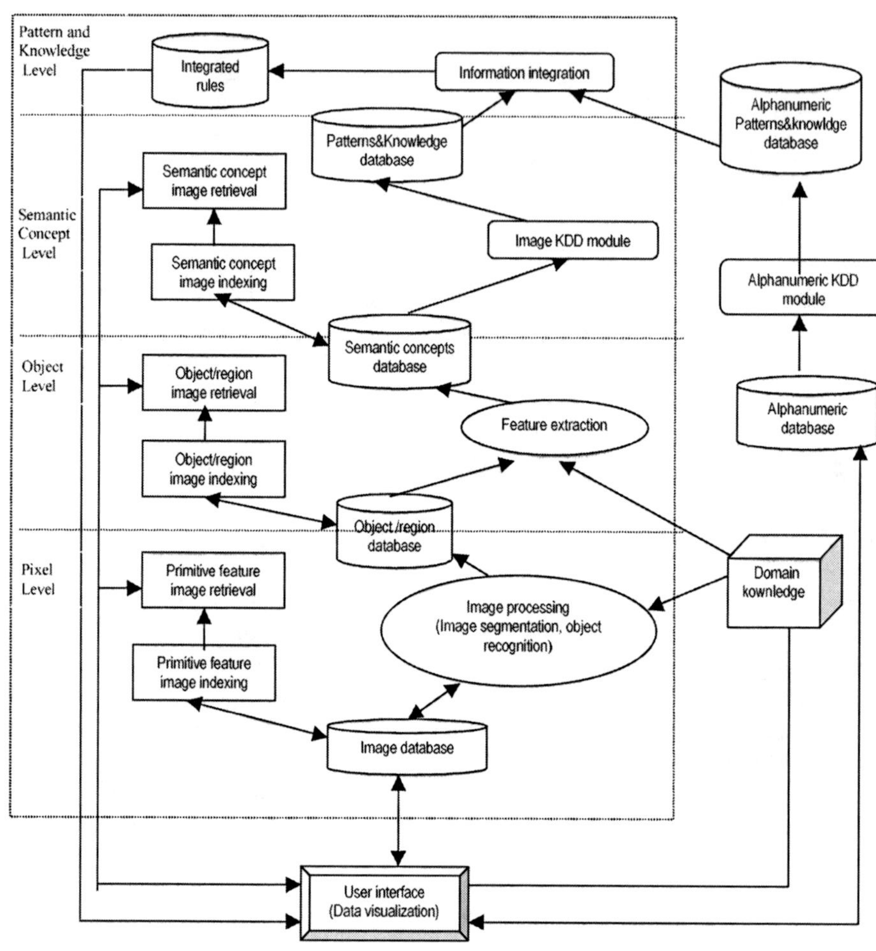

Fig. 1

3 The Four Information Levels

In this section, we will describe the four information levels in our proposed framework. We will also discuss the issues and challenges faced in extracting the required image features and useful patterns and knowledge from each information level.

3.1 Pixel Level

The Pixel Level is the lowest layer in an image mining system. It consists of raw image information such as image pixels and primitive image features such as color, texture, and edge information.

Color is the most widely used visual feature. Color is typically represented by its RGB values (three 0 to 255 numbers indicating red, green, and blue). The distribution of color is a global property that does not require knowledge of how an image is composed of component objects. Color histogram is a structure used to store the proportion of pixels of each color within an image. It is invariant to under translation and rotation about the view axis and change only slowly under change of view angle, change in scale, and occlusion [32]. Subsequent improvements include the use of cumulative color histogram [31], and spatial histogram intersection [30].

Texture is the visual pattern formed by a sizable layout of color or intensity homogeneity. It contains important information about the structural arrangement of surfaces and their relationship to the surrounding environment [27]. Common representations of texture information include: the co-occurrence matrix representation [12], the coarseness, contrast, directionality, regularity, roughness measures [33], the use of Gabor filter [22] and fractals [17]. [22] develop a texture thesaurus to automatically derive codewords that represent important classes of texture within the collection.

Edge information is an important visual cue to the detection and recognition of objects in an image. This information is obtained by looking for sharp contrasts in nearby pixels. Edges can be grouped to form regions.

Content-based image retrieval focus on the information found at the Pixel Level. Researchers try to identify a small subset of primitive features that can uniquely distinguish images of one class from another class. These primitive image features have their limitation. In particular, they do not have the concept of objects/regions as perceived by a human user. This implies that the Pixel Level is unable to answer simple queries such as "retrieve the images with a girl and her dog" and "retrieve the images containing blue stars arranged in a ring".

3.2 Object Level

The focus of the Object level is to identify domain-specific features such as objects and homogeneous regions in the images. While a human being can perform object recognition effortlessly and instantaneously, it has proven to be very difficult to implement the same task on machine. The object recognition problem can be referred to as a supervised labeling problem based on models of known objects. Given a target image containing one or more interesting objects and a set of labels corresponding to a set of models known to the system, what object recognition does is to assign correct labels to regions, or a set of regions, in the image. Models of known objects are usually provided by human input a priori. An object recognition module consists of four components: model database, feature detector, hypothesizer and hypothesis verifier [15]. The model database contains all the models known to the system. The models contain important features that describe the objects. The detected image primitive features in the Pixel Level are used to help the hypothesizer to assign likelihood to the objects in the image. The verifier uses the models to verify the hypothesis and refine the object likelihood. The system finally selects the object with the highest likelihood as the correct object.

To improve the accuracy of object recognition, image segmentation is performed on partially recognized image objects rather than randomly segmenting the image. The techniques include: "characteristic maps" to locate a particular known object in images [16], machine learning techniques to generate recognizers automatically [6], and use a set of examples already labeled by the domain expert to find common objects in images [10]. Once the objects within an image can be accurately identified, the Object Level is able to deal with queries such as "Retrieve images of round table" and "Retrieve images of birds flying in the blue sky". However, it is unable to answer queries such as "Retrieve all images concerning Graduation ceremony" or "Retrieve all images that depicts a sorrowful mood."

3.3 Semantic Concept Level

While objects are the fundamental building blocks in an image, there is "semantic gap between the Object level and Semantic Concept level. Abstract concepts such as happy, sad, and the scene information are not captured at the Object level. Such information requires domain knowledge as well as state-of-the-art pattern discovery techniques to uncover useful patterns that are able to describe the scenes or the abstract concepts. Common pattern discovery techniques include: image classification, image clustering, and association rule mining.

(a) Image Classification

Image classification aims to find a description that best describe the images in one class and distinguish these images from all the other classes. It is a supervised technique where a set of labeled or pre-classified images is given and the problem is to label a new set of images. This is usually called the classifier. There are two types of classifiers, the parametric classifier and non-parametric classifier. [7] employ classifiers to label the pixels in a Landset multispectral scanner image. [37] develop a MM-Classifier to classify multimedia data based on given class labels. [36] proposed IBCOW (Image-based Classification of Objectionable

Websites) to classify websites into objectionable and benign websites based on image content .

(b) Image Clustering

Image clustering groups a given set of unlabeled images into meaningful clusters according to the image content without a priori knowledge [14]. Typical clustering techniques include hierarchical clustering algorithms, partitioning algorithms, nearest neighbor clustering, and fuzzy clustering. Once the images have been clustered, a domain expert is needed to examine the images of each cluster to label the abstract concepts denoted by the cluster.

(c) Association Rule Mining

Association rule mining aims to find items/objects that occur together frequently. In the context of images, association rule mining is able to discover that when several specific objects occur together, there is a high likelihood of certain event/scene is being described in the images. An association rule mining algorithm works in two steps. The first step finds all large itemsets that meet the minimum support constraint. The second step generates rules from all the large itemsets that satisfy the minimum confidence constraint. [25] present an algorithm that uses association rule mining to discover meaningful correlations among the blobs/regions that exists in a set of images. [37] develop an MM-Associator that uses 3-dimensional visualization to explicitly display the associations in the Multimedia Miner prototype.

With the Semantic Concept Level, queries involving high-level reasoning about the meaning and purpose of the objects and scene depicted can be answered. Thus, we will able to answer queries such as: “Retrieve the images of a football match” and “Retrieve the images depicting happiness”. It would be tempting to stop at this level. However, careful analysis reveals that there is still one vital piece of missing information – that of the domain knowledge external to images. Queries like: “Retrieve all medical images with high chances of blindness within one month”, requires linking the medical images with the medical knowledge of chance of blindness within one month. Neither the Pixel level, the Object level, nor the Semantic Concept level is able to support such queries.

3.4 Pattern and Knowledge Level

To support all the information needs within the image mining framework, we need the fourth and final level: the Pattern and Knowledge Level. At this level, we are concerned with not just the information derivable from images, but also all the domain-related alphanumeric data. The key issue here is the integration of knowledge discovered from the image databases and the alphanumeric databases. A comprehensive image mining system would not only mine useful patterns from large collections of images but also integrate the results with alphanumeric data to mine for further patterns. For example, it is useful to combine heart perfusion images and the associated clinical data to discover rules in high dimensional medical records that may suggest early diagnosis of heart disease.

IRIS, an Integrated Retinal Information System, is designed to integrate both patient data and their corresponding retinal images to discover interesting patterns and trends on diabetic retinopathy [13]. BRAin-Image Database is another image mining system developed to discover associations between structures and functions of human brain [23]. The brain modalities were studied by the image mining process and the brain functions (deficits/disorders) are obtainable from the patients' relational records. Two kinds of information are used together to perform the functional brain mapping.
By ensuring a proper flow of information from low level pixel representations to high level semantic concepts representation, we can be assured that the information needed at the fourth level is derivable and that the integration of image data with alphanumeric data will be smooth. Our proposed image mining framework emphasizes the need to focus on the flow of information to ensure that all levels of information needs have been addressed and none is neglected.

4 Indexing of Image Information

While focusing on the information needs at various levels, it is also important to provide support for the retrieval of image data with a fast and efficient indexing scheme. Indexing techniques used range from standard methods such as signature file access method and inverted file access method, to multi-dimensional methods such as K-D-B tree [26], R-tree [11], R*-tree [3] and R+-tree [29], to high-dimensional indexes such as SR-tree [18], TV-tree [20], X-tree [4] and iMinMax [24].

Searching the nearest neighbor is an important problem in high-dimensional indexing. Given a set of n points and a query point Q in a d-dimensional space, we need to find a point in the set such that its distance from Q is less than, or equal to, the distance of Q from any other points in the set [19]. Existing search algorithms can be divided into the following categories: exhaustive search, hashing and indexing, static space partitioning, dynamic space partitioning, and randomized algorithms. When the image database to be searched is large and the feature vectors of images are of high dimension (typically in the order of 10^2), search complexity is high. Reducing the dimensions may be necessary to prevent performance degradation. This can be accomplished using two well-known methods: the Singular Value Decomposition (SVD) update algorithm and clustering [28]. The latter realizes dimension reduction by grouping similar feature dimensions together.

Current image systems retrieve images based on similarity. Euclidean measures may not effectively simulate human perception of a certain visual content. Other similarity measures such as histogram intersection, cosine, correlation, etc., need to be utilized.

One promising approach is to first perform dimension reduction and then use appropriate multi-dimensional indexing techniques that support Non-Euclidean similarity measures [27]. [11] develop an image retrieval system on Oracle platform using multi-level filters indexing. The filters operate on an approximation of the high-dimension data that represents the images, and reduces the search space so that the computationally expensive comparison is necessary for only a small subset of the data. [12] develop a new compressed image indexing technique by using compressed image features as multiple keys to retrieve images.

Other proposed indexing schemes focus on specific image features. [21] present an efficient color indexing scheme for similarity-based retrieval which has a search time that increases logarithmically with the database size. [34] propose a multi-level R-tree index, called the nested R-trees for retrieving shapes efficiently and effectively. With the proliferation of image retrieval mechanisms, a performance evaluation of color-spatial retrieval techniques was given in [35] which serves as guidelines to select a suitable technique and design a new technique.

5 Related Work

Several image mining systems have been developed for different applications. The MultiMediaMiner [37] mines high-level multimedia information and knowledge from large multimedia database. [8] describes an intelligent satellite mining system that comprises of two modules: a data acquisition, preprocessing and archiving system which is responsible for the extraction of image information, storage of raw images, and retrieval of image, and an image mining system, which enables the users to explore image meaning and detect relevant events. The Diamond Eye [6] is an image mining system that enables scientists to locate and catalog objects of interest in large image collections. These systems incorporate novel image mining algorithms, as well as computational and database resources that allow users to browse, annotate, and search through images and analyze the resulting object catalogs. The architectures in these existing image mining systems are mainly based on module functionality. In contrast, we provide a different perspective to image mining with our four level information image mining framework. [6, 25] primarily concentrate on the Pixel and Object level while [37] focus on the Semantic Concepts level with some support from the Pixel and Object levels.

It is clear that by proposing a framework based on the information flow, we are able to focus on the critical areas to ensure all the levels can work together seamlessly. In addition, with this framework, it highlights to us that we are still very far from being able to fully discover useful domain information from images. More research is needed at the Semantic Concept level and the Knowledge and Pattern level.

6 Conclusion

The rapid growth of image data in a variety of medium has necessitated a way of making good use of the rich content in the images. Image mining is currently a bourgeoning yet active research focus in computer science. We have proposed a four-level information-driven framework for image mining systems. High-dimensional indexing schemes and retrieval techniques are also included in the framework to support the flow of information among the levels. We tested the applicability of our framework by applying it to some practical image mining applications. The proposal of this framework is our effort to provide developers and designer of image mining systems a standard framework for image mining with an explicit information hierarchy. We believe this framework represents the first step towards capturing the different levels of information present in image data and addressing the question of what are the issues and challenges of discovering useful patterns/knowledge from each level.

References

1. Annamalai, M and Chopra, R.: Indexing images in Oracles8i. ACM SIGMOD, (2000)
2. Babu, G P and Mehtre, B M.: Color indexing for efficient image retrieval. Multimedia Tools and applications, (1995)
3. Beckmann, N, Kriegel, H P, Schneider, R and Malik, J.: The R*-tree: An efficient and robust access method for points and rectangles. ACM SIGMOD, (1990)
4. Berchtold, S, Keim, D A and Kriegel, H P.: The X-tree: An index structure for high dimensional data. 22nd Int. Conference on Very Large Databases, (1996)
5. Bertino, E, Ooi, B C, Sacks-Davis, R, Tan, K L, Zobel, J, Shilovsky, B and Catania, B.: Indexing Techniques for Advanced Database Systems. Kluwer Academic Publisher (1997)
6. Burl, M C et al.: Mining for image content. In Systems, Cybernetics, and Informatics / Information Systems: Analysis and Synthesis, (1999)
7. Cromp, R F and Campbell, W J.: Data mining of multi-dimensional remotely sensed images. International Conference on Information and Knowledge Management (CIKM), (1993)
8. Datcu, M and Seidel, K.: Image information mining: exploration of image content in large archives. IEEE Conference on Aerospace, Vol.3 (2000)
9. Eakins, J P and Graham, M E.: Content-based image retrieval: a report to the JISC technology applications program. (http://www.unn.ac.uk/iidr/research/cbir/report.html), (1999)
10. Gibson, S et al.: Intelligent mining in image databases, with applications to satellite imaging and to web search, Data Mining and Computational Intelligence, Springer-Verlag, Berlin, (2001)
11. Guttman, A.: R-trees: A dynamic index structure for spatial searching. ACM SIGMOD. (1984)
12. Haralick, R M and Shanmugam, K.: Texture features for image classification. IEEE Transactions on Systems, Man, and Cybernetics, Vol 3 (6) (1973)
13. Hsu, W, Lee, M L and Goh, K G.: Image Mining in IRIS: Integrated Retinal Information System, ACM SIGMOD. (2000)

14. Jain, A K, Murty, M N and Flynn, P J.: Data clustering: a review. ACM computing survey, Vol.31, No.3. (1999)
15. Jain, R, Kasturi, R and Schunck, B G.: Machine Version. MIT Press. (1995)
16. Jeremy S. and Bonet, D.: Image preprocessing for rapid selection in "Pay attention mode". MIT Press. (2000)
17. Kaplan, L M et al.: Fast texture database retrieval using extended fractal features. Proc SPIE in Storage and Retrieval for Image and Video Databases VI (Sethi, I K and Jain, R C, eds). (1998)
18. Katayama, N and Satoh, S.: The SR-tree: An index structure for high-dimensional nearest neighbour queries. ACM SIGMOD. (1997)
19. Knuth, D E.: Sorting and searching, the Art of Computer Programming, Vol.3. Reading, Mass. Addison-Wesley (1973)
20. Lin, K, Jagadish, H V and Faloutsos, C.: The TV-tree: An index structure for high-dimensional data. The VLDB Journal, 3 (4). (1994)
21. Ma, W Y and Manjunath, B S.: A texture thesaurus for browsing large aerial photographs, Journal of the American Society for Information Science 49(7) (1998)
22. Manjunath, B S and Ma, W Y.: Texture features for browsing and retrieval of large image data, IEEE Transactions on Pattern Analysis and Machine Intelligence, 18, (1996)
23. Megalooikonomou, V, Davataikos, C and Herskovits, E H.: Mining lesion-deficit associations in a brain image database. ACM SIGKDD. (1999)
24. Ooi, B C, Tan, K L. Yu,S and Bressan. S.: Indexing the Edges - A Simple and Yet Efficient Approach to High-Dimensional Indexing, 19th ACM SIGMOD-SIGACT-SIGART Symposium on Principles of Database Systems (2000).
25. Ordonez, C and Omiecinski, E.: Image mining: a new approach for data mining. IEEE. (1999)
26. Robinson, J T.: The K-D-B tree: A search structure for large multidimensional dynamic indexes. ACM SIGMOD. (1981)
27. Rui, Y, Huang, S T et al.: Image retrieval: Past, present and future. Int. Symposium on Multimedia Information Processing. (1997)
28. Salton, J and McGill, M J.: Introduction to Modern Information Retrieval. McGraw-Hill Book Company. (1983)
29. Sellis, T, Roussopoulous, N and Faloutsos.: C. R^{+}-tree: A dynamic index for multi-dimensional objects. 16th Int. Conference on Very Large Databases. (1987)
30. Stricker, M and Dimai, A.: Color indexing with weak spatial constraints. Proc SPIE in Storage and Retrieval for Image and Video Databases IV. (1996)
31. Stricker, M and Orengo, M.: Similarity of color images. Proc SPIE in Storage and Retrieval for Image and Video Databases III. (1995)
32. Swain, M J and Ballard, D H.: Color indexing. International Journal of Computer Vision **7**(1). (1991)
33. Tamura, H et al.: Textural features corresponding to visual perception. IEEE Transactions on Systems, Man and Cybernetics 8(6). (1978)
34. Tan, K L, Ooi, B C and Thiang, L F.: Retrieving Similar Shapes Effectively and Efficiently. Multimedia Tools and Applications, Kluwer Academic Publishers, accepted for publication, 2001
35. Tan, K L, Ooi, B C and Yee, C Y.: An Evaluation of Color-Spatial Retrieval Techniques for Large Image Databases, Multimedia Tools and Applications, Vol. 14(1), Kluwer Academic Publishers. (2001)

36. Wang, J Z, Li, J et al.: System for Classifying Objectionable Websites, Proceedings of the 5th International Workshop on Interactive Distributed Multimedia Systems and Telecommunication Services (IDMS'98), Springer-Verlag LNCS 1483, (1998)
37. Zaiane, O R and Han, J W.: Mining MultiMedia Data. CASCON: the IBM Centre for Advanced Studies Conference (http://www.cas.ibm.ca/cascon/), (1998)

A Rule-Based Scheme to Make Personal Digests from Video Program Meta Data

Takako Hashimoto[1,2], Yukari Shirota[3], Atsushi Iizawa[1,2], and Hiroyuki Kitagawa[4]

[1] Information Broadcasting Laboratories, Inc., Tokyo, Japan
{takako, izw }@ibl.co.jp
[2] Software Research Center, Ricoh Company Ltd., Tokyo, Japan
{takako, izw }@src.ricoh.co.jp
[3] Faculty of Economics, Gakushuin University, Tokyo, Japan
yukari.shirota@gakushuin.ac.jp
[4] Institute of Information Sciences and Electronics, University of Tsukuba, Japan
kitagawa@is.tsukuba.ac.jp

Abstract. Content providers have recently started adding a variety of meta data to various video programs; these data provide primitive descriptors of the video contents. Personal digest viewing that uses the meta data is a new application in the digital broadcasting era. To build personal digests, semantic program structures must be constructed and significant scenes must be identified. Digests are currently made manually at content provider sites. This is time-consuming and increases the cost. This paper proposes a way to solve these problems with a rule-based personal digest-making scheme (PDMS) that can automatically and dynamically make personal digests from the meta data. In PDMS, depending on properties of the video program contents and viewer preferences, high-level semantic program structures can be constructed from the added primitive meta data and significant scenes can be extracted. The paper illustrates a formal PDMS model. It also presents detailed evaluation results of PDMS using the contents of a professional baseball game TV program.

1 Introduction

The digitization of the video contents has experienced rapid growth with the recent advance of digital media technology such as digital broadcasting and DVD (digital video discs). In digital media environments, various video meta data can be attached to the video program contents.

Personal digest viewing is an application that uses such meta data. These meta data can be used to make personal digests automatically and dynamically, and to present them on such viewer terminals as TVs and personal computer monitors. To build personal digests of video programs, higher-level semantic program structures must be constructed from the primitive meta data, and significant scenes need to be extracted. Appropriate semantic structures and scene extraction strategies, however, depend heavily on program content properties. Beyond that, in making personal digests, viewer preferences should be reflected in the significant scene extraction. We therefore need a scheme that is adaptable to target program contents and viewer preferences. To achieve this scheme, this paper presents a personal digest-making scheme (called PDMS) based on rule descriptions using video program meta data. In PDMS, higher-level semantic scenes are extracted using rules designating occurrence patterns

H.C. Mayr et al. (Eds.): DEXA 2001, LNCS 2113, pp. 243–253, 2001.

of meta data primitives. Other rules are used to calculate scene significance. Scenes with high significance scores are selected to compose digests. Viewer preferences can be reflected in calculating significance. Processes involved in the digest making can be tuned flexibly depending on properties of the program contents and viewer preferences.

Section 2 of this paper describes related work and our approach. Section 3 explains our personal digest-making scheme. Section 4 describes our prototype digest viewing system based on PDMS, which is applied to the TV program content of a professional baseball game. Section 5 summarizes important points and briefly describes future work.

2 Related Work and Our Approach

This section describes work related to our personal digest-making scheme. Generally speaking, methods for making video digests are divided into two groups. The first is based on image and speech recognition technology, and the second is based on meta data, which are added by content providers. Various researchers have been looking into the first group [1, 2, 3, 4, 5, 6, 7]. An advantage of the first group is that the technology makes it possible to automatically construct index structures to build digests without a lot of manual labor. Technical reliability, however, is not high and the recognition process is expensive. The second group, on the other hand, features high reliability. Despite the cost of providing meta data, we consider this approach more practical for use in digital broadcasting services because of its reliability and efficiency. Moreover, many content providers are starting to supply primitive meta data in addition to video contents. For these reasons, our approach follows the second group.

There are some researches based on meta data [8, 9, 10, 11, 12]. Zettsu et al., for example, proposed a method of finding scenes as logical units by combining image features and attached primitive meta data [10]. Ushiama and Watanabe proposed a scheme of extracting scenes using regular expressions on primitive meta data [11]. Their work concentrates on process to extract semantic structures such as scenes from primitive meta data. It does not present schemes for processes to evaluate scene significance and to select important scenes to compose digests. Kamahara et al. proposed a digest making method using scenario templates to express the synopsis of the digest video [5, 12]. This method is useful in building typical digests focused on the story of the video program. This method, however, has two problems: The first is that it is difficult to prepare all scenario templates that are assumed as digests. The second is that it is hard to build digests in the middle of a video program. In our scheme, scene significance is calculated more dynamically, and viewer preferences are also taken into account.

3 Personal Digest-Making Scheme

3.1 Inputs to PDMS

There are three kinds of data given to PDMS: *video data*, *primitive descriptors*, and *viewer preferences*. The video data and primitive descriptors should be produced by content providers. At home, viewers input their preferences through user interfaces.

Video Data: This data is a video stream, which is expressed as a sequence of frames $f_1..f_n$. Each frame has a frame identifier (*fid*) and *time code* to specify the starting point in the video program. A sub-sequence of frames in the following explanation is referred to as a *frame sequence*.

Primitive Descriptor: *Primitive descriptors* are video program meta data. Each primitive descriptor is expressed as the following tuple: *(pid, type, ffid, lfid, {attr*$_1$*, ..., attr*$_n$*})*. *Pid* is the primitive descriptor's identifier. *Type* is a type of the description. For example, when the video content is a baseball game, it includes *beginning_of_game*, *beginning_of_inning*, *hit*, *out*, *additional_run*, and so on. *Type* values are decided and registered in advance at the content providers. Each primitive descriptor has the first and last frame identifiers: *ffid* and *lfid*. Items *{ attr*$_1$*, ..., attr*$_n$ *}* are attributes of the descriptor. They are decided according to the *type* value. Fig. 1 shows an example of primitive descriptors. Each line corresponds to one primitive descriptor.

```
1, beginning_of_game, 100,,Giants, Carp, Tokyo Dome, Oct. .., 0-0, start
2, beginning_of_inning, 130,,1 ,Carp, 0-0,, top
3, at_bat, 2800,, Nomura, Kuwata,,,,0-0, ,
4, pitch, 2950,,Nomura, Kuwata, straight, ,0-0-0,,,,
5, hit, 3130,, right,liner
6, at_bat,4250,,Tomashino, Kuwata, Nomura, ,,0-0,,
7, pitch,5135,,Tomashino, Kuwata, straight, ,0-0-0, Nomura,,,
8, hit,5340,,left, liner
9, additional_run, 6150,,1, Nomura, 1,, 1-0,,
10, beginning_of_inning, 8680,, Kanamoto,Kuwata,Nomura,,,2-0,,
:
52 ,out, 23440,,strikeout, ,Ogata
```

Fig. 1. Primitive Descriptor Example

Viewer Preference: A *viewer preference* is expressed as follows: *(uid, prefid, name, category, weight)*. *Uid* is the viewer's identifier and *prefid* is the identifier of the viewer preference. *Name* is the preference item name and *category* designates the category of the preference item. *Weight* expresses the degree of the viewer's preference (0<= *weight* <=1). Preference examples are indicated as follows:

(1, 1, "Giants", "Team Name", 0.8) // the fan of team Giants
(1, 2, "Brown", "Player Name", 1) // the fan of player Brown

Here, viewer 1 registers two viewer preferences.

3.2 Data Generated in PDMS

This section describes data generated in PDMS: *scenes*, *annotations*, *status parameters* and *preference parameters*.

Scene: A *scene* is a frame sequence corresponding to a semantic unit. A scene is expressed as follows: *(sid, type, ffid, lfid)*. *Sid* is the scene's identifier. *Type* expresses the scene's type. *Ffid* and *lfid* express the first and last frame identifiers. For baseball programs, an *inning* type scene is defined as a frame sequence starting from a primitive descriptor *beginning_of_inning* and ending just before the next occurrence of *beginning_of_inning*. A *batting* type scene (the frame sequence from a primitive descriptor *at_bat* to just before the next *at_bat)* is also defined. In the *batting* type scene, when a primitive descriptor *hit* and a primitive descriptor *additional_run* appear in this order, the frame sequence from the *hit* to the *additional_run* becomes an *RBI(run batted in)_hit* type scene (see Fig. 2).

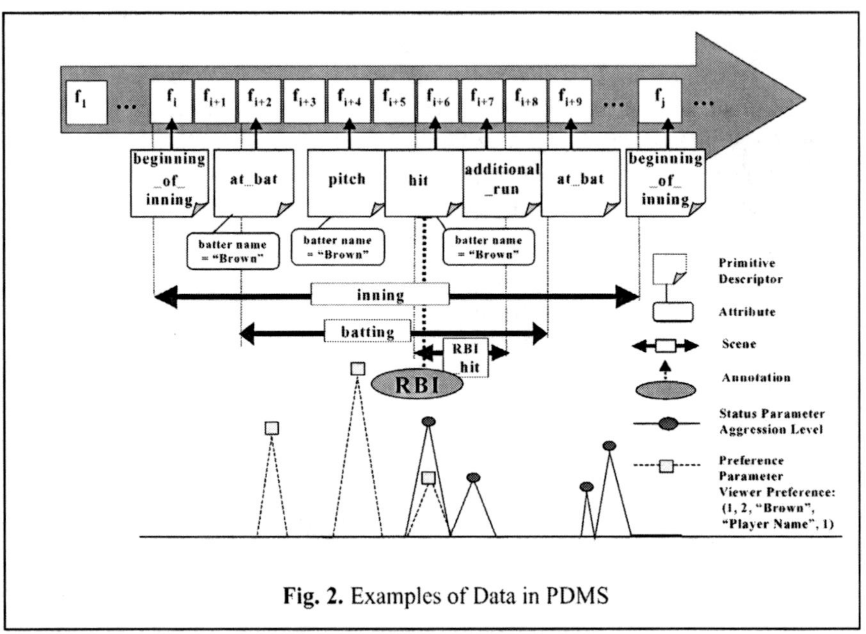

Fig. 2. Examples of Data in PDMS

Annotation: An *annotation* is a text data item used to add semantic information to a primitive descriptor. For baseball programs, when an *RBI_hit* type scene is extracted, an annotation *RBI* is added to the primitive descriptor *hit* (Fig. 2). We can also think of such annotations as *come_from_behind* and *the_first_run*.

Status Parameter: A *status parameter* expresses the significance of each frame of the video. For baseball programs, there is the *Aggression Level* status parameter. The value of *Aggression Level* increases when aggressive primitive descriptors such as *hit* and *additional_run*, or aggressive annotations such as *RBI*, appear (Fig. 2). *Aggression Level* expresses the aggressive importance. We can also use *Pitching Level* to express the pitcher's condition, *Excitement Level* to express an exciting situation, and various others for baseball programs. Users can specify which parameter to use.

Preference Parameter: A *preference parameter* expresses the degree of a viewer's preference. Each viewer has one preference parameter. When a primitive descriptor related to the viewer's preference appears, the value of the preference parameter increases. For example, suppose the viewer's preference *(1, 2, "Brown", "Player Name", 1)* is given. If a primitive descriptor related to the player *"Brown"* occurs such as *at_bat, pitch,* and *hit* in which the batter's name is *"Brown,"* the value of his or her preference parameter increases (see Fig. 2).

3.3 Rules for Making Digests

This section explains the rules for generating scenes and annotations, and for changing values of status parameters and preference parameters.

Scene Extraction Rule: Scenes and annotations are derived by *scene extraction rules.* Fig. 3 shows two examples of scene extraction rules. In the first rule, an *inning* type scene is extracted. In the second rule, an *RBI_hit* type scene is extracted, and an annotation *RBI* is also generated and added to the primitive descriptor *hit.*

Status Parameter Calculation Rule: Fig.3 also shows a *status parameter calculation rule* example. An occurrence of the primitive descriptor *hit* and the generation of the annotation *RBI* invoke the execution of this rule. Then, the value of the status parameter is calculated. In Fig.3, the value of *Aggression Level* is increased by 2points.

Preference Parameter Calculation Rule: A *preference parameter calculation rule* is invoked by an occurrence of a primitive descriptor related to the viewer's preference. Fig. 3 shows an example of a preference calculation rule. The viewer's identifier, preference item name, category name, and weight is referred to by $X, $Name, $Category, and $Weight. In this rule, when a primitive descriptor *at_bat* in which the batter's name matches the viewer's favorite player appears, the value of the preference parameter is increased by "(4* $Weight)."

```
<scene extraction rule> // extract an "inning" type scene
   <trigger> <start> beginning_of_inning </>
      <regexp> beginning_of_inning (.)*  beginning_of_inning </> </> <type> inning
</> </>
<scene extraction rule> // extract an "RBI_hit" type scene
  <trigger> <start> at_bat </> <end> at_bat </>  <regexp> \( hit \)  additional_run (.)
</> </>
      <type> RBI_hit </> <annotation> <name> RBI </> <refer> \1 </> </>
<status parameter calculation rule >
   <rule> <trigger description> hit </> <calculation> <name> Aggression Level </>
      <op> + </> <value> 2</> </> </>
   <rule> <trigger annotation> RBI </> <calculation> <name> Aggression Level </>
      <op> + </> <value> 2</> </> </> </>
<preference parameter calculation rule >
  <rule> <trigger description>
        t_bat[$Category == "Player Name" && batter_name == $Name] </>
     <calculation> <name> Preference Level ($X) </> <op> +</>
        <value> (4* $Weight) </> </> </>
  <rule> <trigger description>
        pitch[$Category == "Player Name" && batter_name == $Name] </>
     <calculation> <name> Preference Level ($X) </> <op> +</>
        <value> (5* $Weight) </> </> </>
  <rule> <trigger description>
        hit[$Category == "Player Name" && batter_name == $Name] </>
      <calculation> <name> Preference Level ($X) </> <op> + </>
        <value> (2* $Weight)
</> </> </> </>
```

Fig. 3. PDMS Rule Examples

3.4 Digest Making Process in PDMS

In the following, we explain the digest making process in PDMS, which consists of two steps (See Fig. 4).

Step 1: Scene/annotation extraction and parameter calculation
First, the system analyzes the input meta data. Then, scenes are extracted and annotations are generated, both based on scene extraction rules. The status/preference parameters are also calculated based on the corresponding rules.

Step 2: Selection of significant scenes
To select significant scenes, user inputs three kinds of data:
(1) *Total Digest Time*: the total time of the digest;
(2) *Scene Unit*: the unit of each extracted scene or granularity; and
(3) *Parameters to select*: a set of status and preference parameters selected by the viewer among the given parameters.

Depending on these inputs, significant scenes that are judged change. As Fig. 4 shows, extracted scenes depend on the *Selected Parameters* where scenes S_i and S_k are extracted if *Aggression Level* is selected; scenes S_i and S_j are extracted if *Aggression Level* and *Preference Level* are selected.

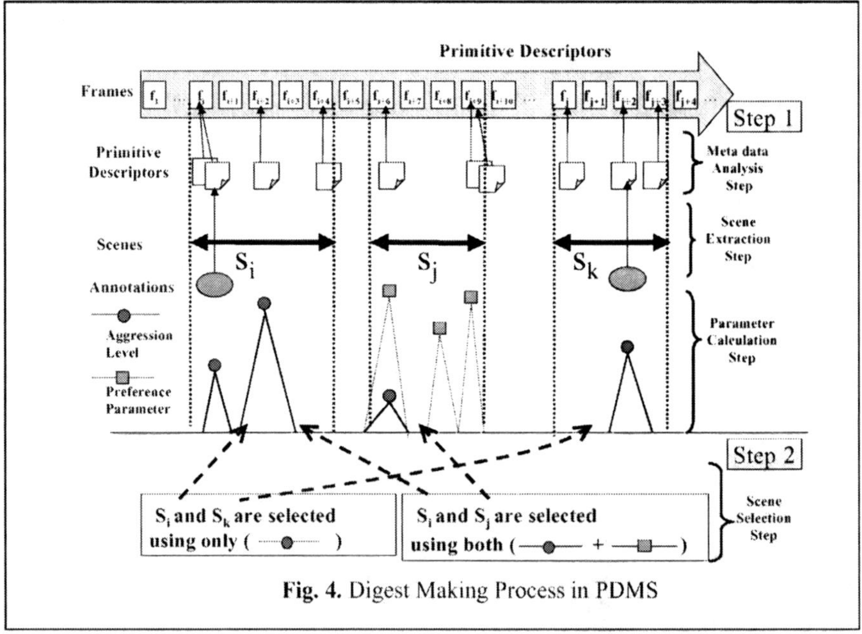

Fig. 4. Digest Making Process in PDMS

4 Prototype System

4.1 System Architecture

As Fig. 5 shows, the system consists of three modules and two kinds of databases: a *meta data analysis module*, a *scene extraction module*, a *parameter calculation module*, *rule databases*, and a *semantic structure database*.

First, the meta data analysis module receives the broadcast data and continually monitors for an occurrence of a primitive descriptor (See (1) in Fig. 5). After parsing and checking data consistency, the module notifies the other modules of the primitive descriptor occurrence, issuing a *primitive descriptor occurrence event.*

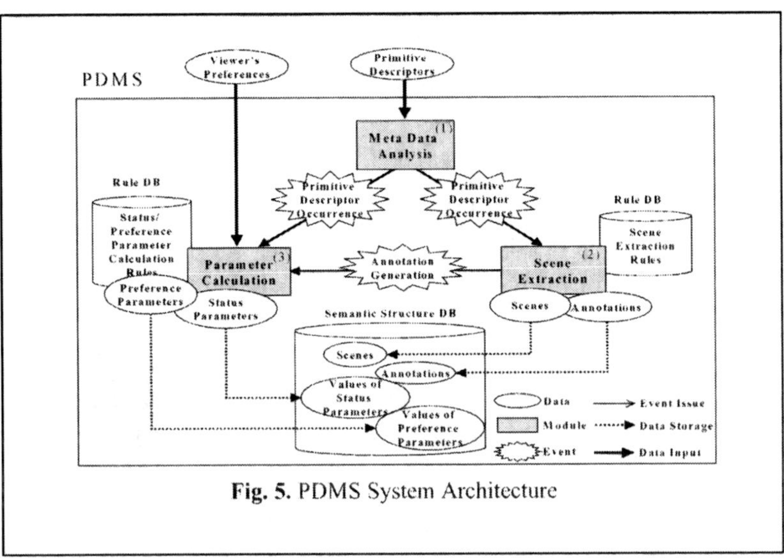

Fig. 5. PDMS System Architecture

The scene extraction module tries to find a primitive descriptor occurrence pattern corresponding to a scene or an annotation from a sequence of incoming primitive descriptors (See (2) in Fig. 5). The extracted scenes and the generated annotations are stored in the semantic structure database. If an annotation is generated, the scenes extraction module notifies the parameter calculation module by issuing an *annotation generation event*. The parameter calculation module then starts to calculate the parameter values (See (3) in Fig. 5). Parameter values are also calculated from a sequence of incoming primitive descriptors.

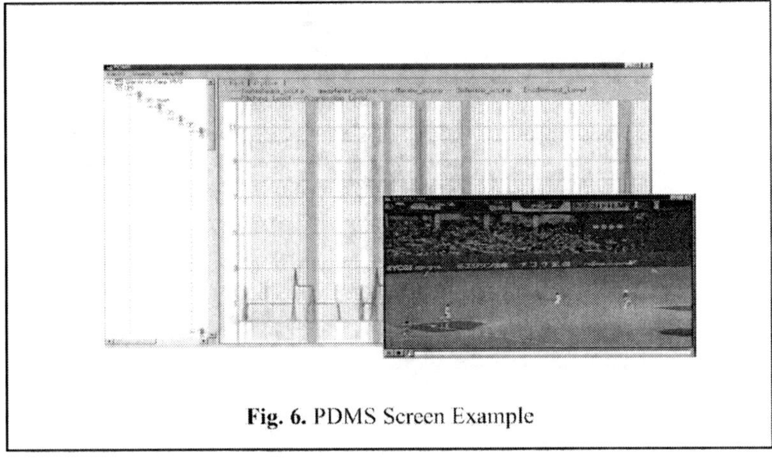

Fig. 6. PDMS Screen Example

Fig. 6 shows values of status parameters internally calculated of which horizontal axis shows time (For a home user interface, the internal calculation results are not presented.). The extracted scene is highlighted as a bar. Clicking the bar, you can see the extracted scene on the screen, as shown in Fig. 6.

4.2 Evaluation of PDMS Effectiveness

This section evaluates effectiveness of our PDMS using actual professional baseball content broadcast by the Nippon Television Network Corporation. This sample content is a game between the Giants and the Carp held in the Tokyo Dome. The scores are as follows:

	1	2	3	4	5	6	7	8	9	
Carp	1	0	0	0	0	3	0	0	0	4
Giants	3	3	0	0	0	0	0	1	x	7

To evaluate effectiveness, we made two types of digests, depending on viewer preferences. The first type is called a generic digest that does not take into account of each viewer's preferences; the digest is middle-of-the-road. The second type is called a preference digest, which is skewed by viewer's preferences.

To authenticate PDMS, we use a baseball game database provided by Nippon Television Network Corporation, the content provider [13]. Sports correspondents write the game digest articles presented on the database, ensuring high reliability. If a scene selected by PDMS is included in the database digest, we can say the scene is appropriate for a generic digest.

Generic Digest

Table 1 lists the selected scenes as a generic digest by our system under the following conditions:

· *Total Digest Time: 3min.*
· *Scene Unit: throwing scene*
· *Selected Parameters: {Aggression Level, Excitement Level, Pitching Level}*

Our system extracted each scene in maximum 30-second segments. As Table 1 shows, every scene extracted by our system was appropriate. The correctness is 100%. The DB article also extracted six scenes.

Table 1. Extracted Scenes as for a Generic Digest

Inning	Team	Selected Scene	Result
Top of 1st	Carp	Batter Etoh got a sacrifice hit.	OK
Bottom of 1st	Giants	Batter Takahashi hit an RBI.	OK
		Batter Kawai hit an RBI.	OK
Bottom of 2nd	Giants	Batter Matsui hit a home run.	OK
Top of 6th	Carp	Batter Etoh hit a homerun.	OK
Bottom of 8th	Giants	Batter Motoki got a sacrifice hit.	OK

Preference Digests

To evaluate preference digests, we use preference data of two viewers: A and B. Viewer A preferences are *(1, 1, "Nishi", "Player Name", 0.5)* and Viewer B preferences are *(2, 1, "Nishi", "Player Name", 1)*. The preference data show that Viewer A is an ordinary fan of batter *Nishi*, with a weight of 0.5. Viewer B is an enthusiastic fan of batter *Nishi*, with a weight of 1. The preference digests are made under the following conditions:

· *Total Digest Time: 3min*
· *Scene Unit*: *throwing scene*
· *Selected Paramteres: {Aggression Level, Excitement Level, Pitching Level}*

Table 2 lists the two viewers' resultant data. Both digests are skewed by batter *Nishi*'s scenes. Batter *Nishi*'s scenes occupy the following:

Viewer A: 2 (scenes) / 6 (scenes) = 33.3% when w=0.5
Viewer B: 4 (scenes) / 6 (scenes) = 66.6% when w=1.0.

The number of preference scenes increases according to the preference weights.

Evaluation results show that scenes extracted by our system are appropriate for a generic digest and that the number of preference scenes can be controlled by the preference weight.

Table 2. Extracted Scenes for Preference Digests

Viewer	Inning	Team	Selected Scene
(A)	Top of 1st	Carp	Batter Etoh got a sacrifice hit.
	Bottom of 1st	Giants	***Batter Nishi walked to 1st base.***
			Batter Takahashi hit an RBI.
	Bottom of 2nd	Giants	***Batter Nishi struck out.***
			Batter Matsui hit a home run.
	Top of 6th	Carp	Batter Etoh hit a home run.
(B)	Bottom of 1st	Giants	***Batter Nishi walked to 1st base.***
			Batter Takahashi hit an RBI.
	Bottom of 2nd	Giants	***Batter Nishi struck out.***
			Batter Matsui hit a home run.
	Bottom of 4th	Giants	***Batter Nishi grounded out to third.***
	Bottom of 7th	Giants	***Batter Nishi fled out.***

5 Conclusions and Future Work

This paper described a personal digest-making scheme that can be adapted to various programs and viewer preferences. We proposed a rule-based scheme called PDMS to make personal digests from video program meta data. PDMS extracts higher-level semantic structures and calculates scene significance based on rules. Viewer preferences can be reflected in the significance calculation. Therefore, using PDMS, viewers can make personal digests flexibly and dynamically on their TVs or personal computers. We applied our prototype system based on PDMS to build digests of a TV program content for a professional baseball game and evaluated its effectiveness. We verified that our prototype could extract important scenes selected manually by the content provider and flexibly make personal digests according to the weight of viewer preferences.

Acknowledgements. The authors would like to thank Nippon Television Network Corporation for providing the baseball program contents. We are also indebted to Ms. Hiroko Mano at Ricoh Company Ltd., Takeshi Kimura at NHK (Japan Broadcasting Corporation) Science & Technical Research Laboratories and Mr. Hideo Noguchi and Mr. Kenjiro Kai at Information Broadcasting Laboratories, Inc. for their detailed comments on an earlier draft of this paper.

References

1. Y. Nakamura and T. Kanade: Semantic Analysis for Video Contents Extraction - Spotting by Association in News Video, *Proc. of ACM Multimedia*, Nov. 1997, pp. 393-401.
2. M. A. Smith and T. Kanade: Video Skimming and Characterization through the Combination of Image and Language Understanding, *Proc. of the 1998 Intl. Workshop on Content-Based Access of Image and Video Database (CAIVD '98),* IEEE Computer Society, 1998, pp. 61-70.
3. A. G. Hauptmann and D. Lee: Topic Labeling of Broadcast News Stories in the Informedia Digital Video Library, *Proc. of the 3rd ACM International Conference on Digital Libraries*, ACM Press, June 23-26, 1998, Pittsburgh, PA, USA, pp. 287-288.
4. A. G. Hauptmann and M. J. Witbrock: Story Segmentation and Detection of Commercials in Broadcast News Video, *Proc. of the IEEE Forum on Research and Technology Advances in Digital Libraries*, IEEE ADL '98, IEEE Computer Society, April 22-24, 1998, Santa Barbara, California, USA, pp. 168-179.
5. J. Kamahara, T. Kaneda, M. Ikezawa, S. Shimojo, S. Nishio, and H. Miyahara: Scenario Language for automatic News Recomposition on The News-on Demand, *Technical Report of IEICE DE95-50*, Vol. 95, No. 287, pp.1-8, 1995 (in Japanese).
6. M. Nishida and Y. Ariki: Speaker Indexing for News Articles, Debates and Drama in Broadcasted TV Programs, *Proc. of the IEEE International Conference on Multimedia Computing and Systems (ICMCS) Volume II*, 1999, pp. 466-471.
7. Y. Ariki and K. Matsuura: Automatic Classification of TV News Articles Based on Telop Character Recognition, *Proc. of the IEEE International Conference on Multimedia Computing and Systems (ICMCS) Volume II*, 1999, pp. 148-152.
8. Y. Shirota, T. Hashimoto, A. Nadamoto, T. Hattori, A. Iizawa, K. Tanaka, and K. Sumiya: A TV Programming Generation System Using Digest Scenes and a Scripting Markup Language, *Proc. of HICSS34 34th Hawaii International Conference on System Science and CD-ROM of full papers*, Jan. 3-6, 2001, Hawaii, USA.
9. Takako Hashimoto, Yukari Shirota, Atsushi Iizawa, and Hideko S. Kunii: Personalized Digests of Sports Programs Using Intuitive Retrieval and Semantic Analysis, Alberto H. F. Laender, Stephen W. Liddle, and Veda C. Storey (Eds.): *Conceptual Modeling - ER 2000, Proc. of 19th International Conference on Conceptual Modeling*, Salt Lake City, Utah, USA, October 9-12, 2000, *Lecture Notes in Computer Science*, Vol. 1920, Springer, 2000, pp. 584-585.
10. K. Zettsu, K. Uehara, and K. Tanaka: Semantic Structures for Video Data Indexing, Shojiro Nishio, and Fumio Kishino (Eds.): *Advanced Multimedia Content Processing, First International Conference, AMCP '98*, Osaka, Japan, November, 9-11, 1998, *Lecture Notes in Computer Science*, Vol. 1554, Springer, 1999, pp. 356-369.

11. T. Ushiama and T. Watanabe: A Framework for Using Transitional Roles of Entities for Scene Retrievals Based on Event-Activity Model, *Information Processing Society of Japan Transactions on Database*, Vol. 40, No. SIG 3(TOD 1), Feb. 1999, pp. 114-123 (in Japanese).
12. J. Kamahara, Y. Nomura, K. Ueda, K. Kandori, S. Shimojo, and H. Miyahara: A TV News Recommendation System with Automatic Recomposition, Shojiro Nishio, and Fumio Kishino (Eds.): *Advanced Multimedia Content Processing, Proc. of First International Conference, AMCP '98*, Osaka, Japan, November, 9-11, 1998, *Lecture Notes in Computer Science*, Vol. 1554, Springer, 1999, pp. 221-235.
13. Nippon Television Network Corporation. http://www.ntv.co.jp

Casting Mobile Agents to Workflow Systems: On Performance and Scalability Issues

Jeong-Joon Yoo[1], Young-Ho Suh[2], Dong-Ik Lee[1], Seung-Woog Jung[3], Choul-Soo Jang[3], and Joong-Bae Kim[3]

[1]Department of Info. and Comm., Kwang-Ju Institute of Science and Technology
1 Oryong-Dong Buk-Gu Kwangju, Korea (Republic of)
[2]Internet Service Department, Electronics and Telecommunications Research Institute
[3]EC Department, Electronics and Telecommunications Research Institute
161 Kajong-Dong Yusong-Gu, Taejon, Korea (Republic of)
{jjyoo, dilee}@kjist.ac.kr
{yhsuh, swjung, jangcs, jjkim}@etri.re.kr

Abstract. In this paper we describe two important design issues of mobile agents-based workflow systems; in architecture and workflow execution levels. Solutions for better performance and scalability of workflow systems are proposed. We suggest 3-layer architecture and agent delegation model in architecture and workflow execution levels of workflow systems respectively. Mobile agents effectively distribute workloads of a naming/location server and a workflow engine to others based on the proposed methods. In consequence, the performance and the scalability of workflow systems are improved. This effectiveness is shown through comparison with client server-based and another mobile agent-based workflow systems with stochastic Petri-nets simulation. Simulation results show that our approach not only outperforms others in massive workflow environment but also comes up with the scalability of previous mobile agent-based workflow systems.

1 Introduction

A workflow management system, in short a WFMS, is a system that defines, creates and manages the execution of workflows through one or more workflow engines which interpret the process definition, interact with workflow participants and, if required, invoke the use of IT tools and applications [1]. Due to the inherent characteristics of the client-server paradigm, only workflow engines of most existing WFMS such as FlowMark [2], Action Workflow [3] and FloWare [4] have to interpret the process definition, interact with workflow participants. As the number of workflow process increases, these overhead given to workflow engines degrades the system performance significantly. Though distributed version of client-server based WFMSs [5] are introduced to break up this centralized overhead, the inherent characteristics of the client-server paradigm place similar limitation in scalability of WFMSs. To overcome this limitation mobile agent-based WFMSs have been considered [6].

A mobile agent is a software program that can migrate over a heterogeneous network autonomously and acts on behalf of a user or another entity [7]. In this paper, autonomy of a mobile agent in the contexts of WFMS implies that an agent can

H.C. Mayr et al. (Eds.): DEXA 2001, LNCS 2113, pp. 254–263, 2001.

manage by itself. More specifically, if a set of tasks is assigned to an agent, the agent can perform all the tasks without any interaction with workflow engines. With the autonomy and the mobility features remote interactions can be reduced; as a result, performance and scalability is improved. DartFlow is the first WFMS based on mobile agents for highly flexible and scalable WFMSs [6]. Since the mobile agent carries the workflow definition by itself, it can decide the next tasks to perform without help of workflow engines. However, DartFlow also has problems in the scalability and performance as; (i) the existence of centralized location/naming server which may become bottle-neck. (ii) too big agent code size, that introduces much communication overhead (referred to as an *agent migration overhead* in this paper).

In this paper, we tackle on the performance and the scalability of mobile agent-based WFMSs by considering the above (i) and (ii). We suggest '3-layer architecture' and 'agent delegation model' as solutions for the issue (i) and (ii) respectively. We show the effectiveness of proposed solutions through stochastic Petri-nets and compare with previous WFMSs. Through this paper, throughput is considered as a measure of performance. Furthermore throughput = 1/response time, where response time is duration from creation of a workflow instance to the completion. Scalability is sensitivity to throughput with respect to the number of workflow instances.

The rest of this paper is organized as follows; In Section 2, we describe design issues and approaches for better performance and scalability of WFMS based on mobile agents. In Section 3, we compare the performance and the scalability of agent delegation models through stochastic Petri-nets simulation. One of agent delegation models with 3-layer architecture is again compared with previous WFMSs. Finally, Section 4 is the conclusion with future work.

2 Design Issues and Approaches for Increasing Performance and Scalability

In this section we explain design issues and suggest some approaches for better performance and scalability. We try to solve two problem of mobile agent-based workflow system described before as; (i) the existence of centralized location/naming server which may become a bottle-neck point. (ii) too big agent code size, that introduces much communication overhead (referred to as an *agent migration overhead* in this paper). We suggest three-layer architecture for (i) and agent delegation models for (ii).

2.1 System Architectural Level: 3-Layer Architecture

To enjoy the advantages of mobile agents we must provide an efficient location management for mobile agents, so that agents can communicate with others for the purpose of dynamic reconfiguration etc. In order to provide location-independent name resolution scheme, location/naming server is required to map a symbolic name to the current location of the agent. However, a centralized location/naming server may be potential performance bottle-neck in mobile agent systems - this may be unacceptable in such a system that a huge number of agents are executed in parallel.

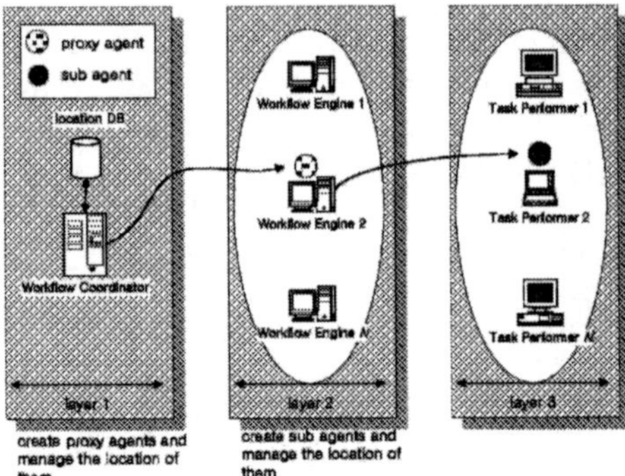

Fig. 1. 3-layer architecture of a WFMS

Thus to exert potential advantages of the mobile agent paradigm, particularly in terms of performance and scalability, an efficient mechanism of location management for mobile agents must be provided in the mobile agent system level.

Fig. 1 shows the 3-layer architecture of a WFMS which is suggested as a solution for the described problem. In this figure, instead that a mobile agent (referred to in the text as a *proxy agent*) migrates over task performers in layer 3 to execute the delegated workflow instance, the proxy agent creates several agents with help of a workflow engine in layer 2 and delegates a sub-workflow process to each sub-agent. We refer to a mobile agent being responsible for part of workflow process as a *sub-agent*. The role of sub-agents is defined and used later in agent delegation model. In the conventional mobile agent systems, the location of not only proxy agents but also sub-agents is managed by a centralized location/naming server. On the other hand, the location of sub-agents is managed by the corresponding proxy agent in our systems. In this 3-layer architecture the location management is gracefully distributed in a hierarchical way. Trivially, any centralized location/naming server that can be a bottle-neck is not required.

2.2 Agent Execution Level: Agent Delegation Model

Agent migration overhead is a source of performance degradation. On the other hand, a process migration distributes workloads of a host to others. Considering them, a certain 'workflow process decomposition policy' must be provided to reduce agent migration overhead and to increase the load distribution. It is beyond scope of the paper to find the optimum solution for agent delegation model. The agent delegation model is a kind of workflow process decomposition policy. Here we propose some non-trivial division methods and claim that these strategies are necessary. Assuming that there are two trivial division methods as follows (a and b), we can define some non-trivial division methods.

a. minimum model (referred to as *min*)
   Each task consisting a workflow process is assigned to a mobile agent as shown in Fig. 2(a). When a mobile agent completes its own task, it does not return back home but reports the results to the corresponding workflow engine. Then the

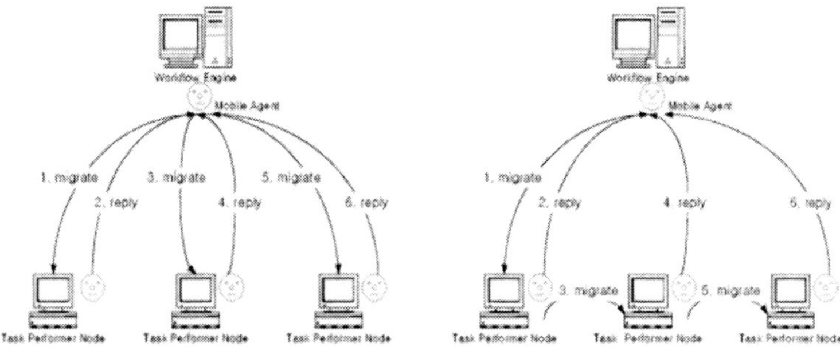

Fig. 2. Trivial Agent Delegation Models: (a) *min* (b) *max*

workflow engine updates local database, executes scheduler to decide the next task and assign it to another mobile agent. If the number of workflow processes increases, the number of mobile agents generated is increased. Thus the workflow engine becomes a bottle-neck and hence the scalability is decreased.

b. maximum model (referred to as *max*)
   All tasks consisting a workflow process are assigned to a mobile agent as shown Fig. 2(b). A mobile agent itself migrates to the task performers, performs tasks, and determines the next tasks. A mobile agent residing in task performers can take loads off workflow engines.

The *max* is in favor of scalability, while the *min* is in favor of performance (It is shown later in Section 3). In this paper, we adopt these two trivial agent delegation models as references. We try to enhance performance by proposing a comparatively good delegation model that is a hybrid model of *min* and *max* as follows;

c. Non-trivial agent delegation model: *min*-based *max* model
   Algorithm for *min*-based *max* model is shown in Fig. 3. ELEMENT is an object data type for *task*s, *join*s, *split*s, or *termination*s. TASKS_QUEUE is a queue for tasks. As an example, consider a workflow process shown in Fig. 4(a), ignore dotted boxes in this phase.

```
Initialization: Find every AND-split path that is not included in any other AND-split paths and
                define each branch of the AND-split paths as a PARALLEL BRANCH.
                For the remaining parts define each unit task as a sub-process.
perform the following procedure for every PARALLEL BRANCHs

ELEMENT Decomposition(PARALLEL BRANCH) {
TASK_QUEUE q;
ELEMENT currentElement;
  set currentElement as the first element of PARALLEL BRANCH;
  do {
    switch (currentElement.type) {
        case TASK: add currentElement into q;
                   currentElement = currentElement.next; // next element
                   break;
        case SPLIT: define a set of tasks in q as a sub-process and delete tasks from q;
                   for (int i=0;i<# of branches; i++)
                     currentElement = Decomposition(branch);
                     // branch is assumed to be a PARALLEL BRANCH
                   currentElement = currentElement.next;
                   break;
        case JOIN: define a set of tasks in q as a sub-process;
                   return currentElement; // local q will be automatically deleted
        case TERMINATION: define a set of tasks in q as a sub-process;
                   return currentElement;
    } // end of switch
  } while (currentElement.type != TERMINATION);
} // end of algorithm
```

Fig. 3. Algorithm for *min*-based *max* model

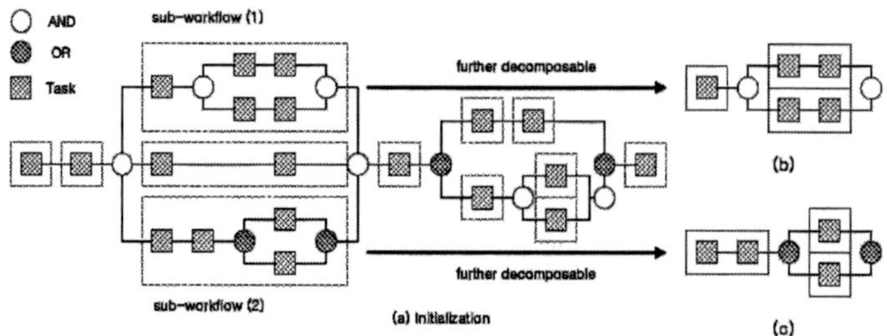

Fig. 4. An example of the proposed delegation model: (a) initialization, (b) after a sub-agent completes one task, another two sub agents assigned two tasks for each parallel routing are generated, (c) after a sub-agent completes two tasks for sequential routing, another sub-agents assigned one task for each parallel routing is generated

In the initialization phase, the process is decomposed into a set of sub-processes enclosed by dotted boxes. Two sub-workflow processes (1) and (2) are further decomposed into solid boxes in Fig. 4(b) and (c) respectively by the *Decomposition* procedure in Fig. 3.

This model is compared with other alternatives, such as *min*, *max*, and the maximum-based minimum model, which adopts the *max* as the basic model and partially includes the *min* in AND-splits of a workflow process (applying *Decomposition* procedure without *Initialization* in Fig. 3).

3 Experimental Comparisons

In this section, we evaluate the performance and the scalability of our design strategy – the mobile agent-based workflow system adopting the 3-layer architecture and the delegation model. Our system is compared with the previous workflow systems such that client server-based and another mobile agent-based workflow systems. In our simulation, the performance corresponds to absolute elapsed time needed to complete a fixed number of workflow instances, while the scalability is considered as an oblique of the performance graphs. We use *UltraSAN* simulation tool [8] for stochastic Petri-nets simulation.

3.1 Simulation Models

In this sub-section, we show stochastic Petri-nets model and its parameters of our simulation models.

Agent delegation models

Simulation models for the *min* and *max* are shown in Fig. 5(a) and (b). Simulation models for the *min*-based *max* and *max*-based *min* models are the combination of (a) and (b) as described before. As an example, in Fig. 4(c), there are one mobile agent having two tasks for sequential routing and two mobile agents having single task for each parallel routing. A Petri-net model of hybrid delegation model for this case is shown in Fig. 5(c). All of models in Fig. 5 consist of a 'workflow engine', 'task performer', and 'channel'. Important simulation parameters for *min*, *max*, *min*-based

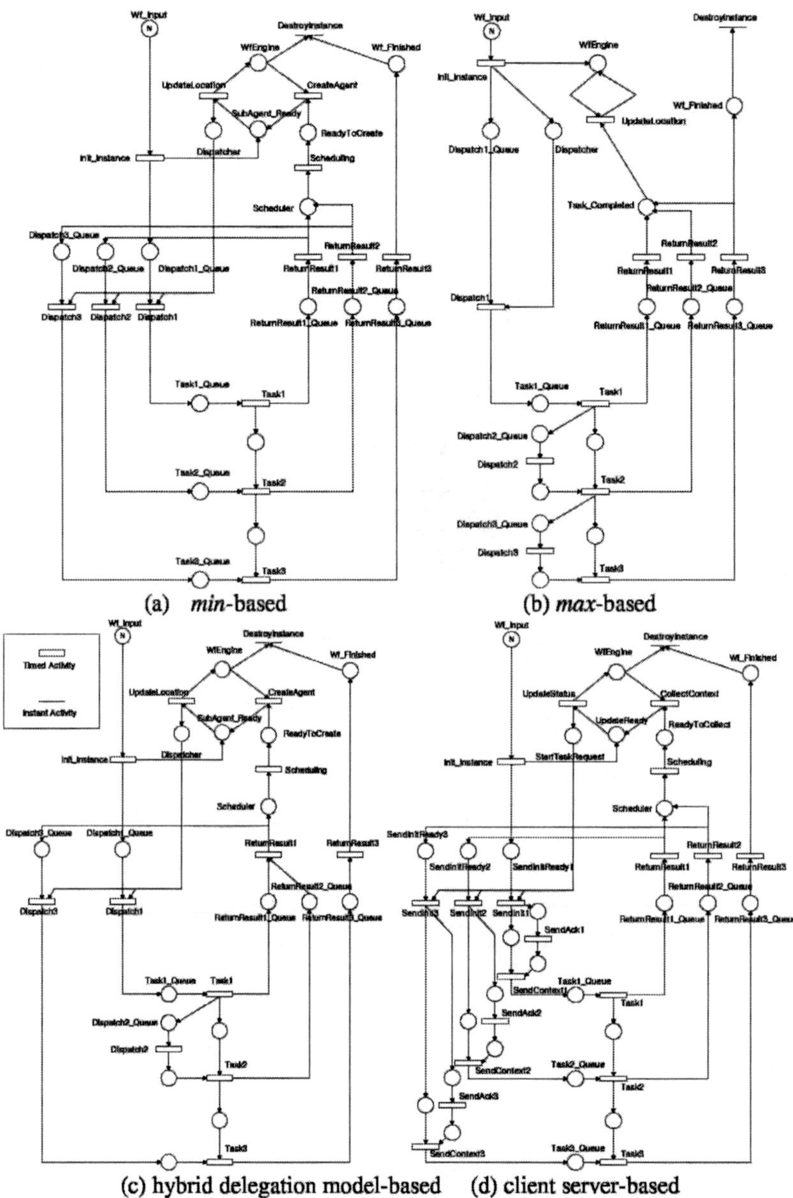

Fig. 5. Petri net models for agent delegation model-based workflow system

max and *max*-based *min* agent delegation models are shown in Table 1. All transitions are changed by the load dependent rate function as shown in Table 2. As well, the agent transmission rates are also changed depending on the agent size as shown in Table 3. Agent migration rates are determined by the literature of [9] together with an assumption of 'A transmission time of code and/or data is proportional to the size of them'. Scheduling rates are observed in Hanuri/TFlow [10].

Table 1. Parameters for agent delegation models

Minimum model			
Transition name	Rate	Type	Semantics
CreateAgent	19.2	Exponential	Load dependent
InitInstance	1.0	Exponential	Load dependent
Scheduling	1.1	Exponential	Load dependent
ReturnResult	15.4	Exponential	Load dependent
Dispatch	0.769	Exponential	Load dependent
Task	19.2	Exponential	Load dependent
Maximum model			
Transition name	Rate	Type	Semantics
InitInstance	1.0	Exponential	Load dependent
UpdateLocation	7.69	Exponential	Load dependent
ReturnResult	15.4	Exponential	Load dependent
Dispatch	0.046	Exponential	Load dependent
Task	19.2	Exponential	Load dependent
Minimum-based maximum model, Maximum-based minimum model			
Transition name	Rate	Type	Semantics
InitInstance	1.0	Exponential	Load dependent
Scheduling	1.1	Exponential	Load dependent
UpdateLocation	7.69	Exponential	Load dependent
ReturnResult	15.4	Exponential	Load dependent
Dispatch	Refer to Table 3	Exponential	Load dependent
Task	19.2	Exponential	Load dependent

Table 2. Parameters for load dependent rate

$\mu = \lambda(1-x/(B+1))^{\alpha}$	Value	Meaning
λ	Rate in Table 1	Constant rate for a single server semantic
B	100	Buffer size
x	-	Number of customers
α	0.7	Controller for rate change

Table 3. '*Dispatch*' rate for *min-based max* and *max-based min*

The number of task assigned to sub-agents	Sub-agent size (*Kbytes*)	Migration rate (*Dispatch*)
1	20	0.769
2	30	0.485
3	40	0.385
4	50	0.297
5	60	0.256
6	70	0.214
32	330	0.046

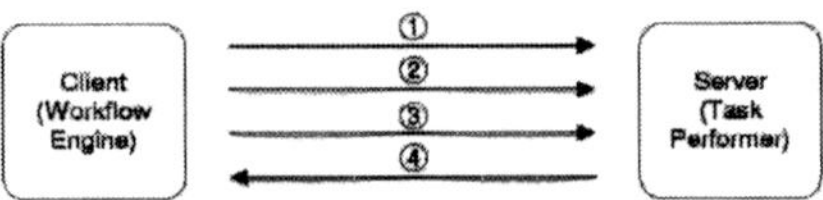

① ask task performer to create a context
② send context information to task performer
③ ask task performer to execute a task
④ return results

Fig 6. Remote interactions for a task execution in client server-based WFMS

Table 4. Parameters for the client server-based workflow system

Transition	Rate	Type	Semantics
SendInit	154	Exponential	Load dependent
SendContext	1.54	Exponential	Load dependent
ReturnResult	15.4	Exponential	Load dependent
Ack	154	Exponential	Load dependent

A client server model

To compare the performance and the scalability of our systems with client server-based workflow system we define remote interactions between a client and a server as shown in Fig. 6. In the first step of Fig. 6, a workflow engine asks a task performer to create a context, and the task performer makes a space for a context and returns an acknowledgement message, about 100*Bytes*. After receiving the acknowledgement message, the workflow engine sends the context information of the control data and relevant data, about 10*Kbytes*, to the task performer in the second step. In the third step, the workflow engine asks the task performer to execute the task with the information of the context. Then the task performer can begin the task. After completing the task, the task performer returns the results, about 1*Kbyte*. The parameter values for a client server-based workflow system are summarized in Table 4. The simulation model is shown in Fig. 5(d).

3.2 Evaluations and Analysis

From now on, we evaluate the performance and the scalability of agent delegation models with various parameters such as the number of branches of a workflow process, the number of tasks consisting the branch (referred to as *task length*), and the number of workflow processes to reflect diverse workflow system environments. One of agent delegation models is chosen to compare the performance and the scalability of client server-based workflow systems.

Relation between workflow structure and simulation time

Fig. 7 shows the relation between the number of branch in a workflow process and the simulation time. In this simulation we fix up the number of process as 100 and 1000. In case that the number of workflow process is 100 (referred to in the text as *small-scale* workflow system), *min* outperforms all other models. But in case that the number of workflow process is 1000 (referred to in the text as *large-scale* workflow systems), *min*-based *max* model outperforms all others. These results say that *min* is more sensitive to the number of workflow process than the other models. The bottleneck in a centralized workflow engine caused more sensitiveness of *min* to the number of workflow process. This result is true of the case that the task length is increased as shown in Fig. 8.

Relation between the number of workflow process and simulation time

In this simulation we evaluate the performance and the scalability of agent delegation model on the diverse number of workflow process. We adopt the workflow structure shown in [11] as a target. As shown in Fig. 9 *min* outperforms all other agent delegation models in case of small-scale workflow systems. But min-based max outperforms all others in case of large-scale workflow systems. It also comes up with the scalability of *max*.

Comparison with other workflow systems

In this simulation min-based max model with 3-layer architecture, client server-based workflow systems, and another mobile agent-based workflow systems are evaluated. As shown in Fig. 10, a workflow system applying 3-layer architecture and an agent delegation model not only outperforms client server-based and DartFlow workflow systems in case of massive workflow environments such as telecommunication and manufacturing enterprises but also preserves the scalability of DartFlow. Therefore,

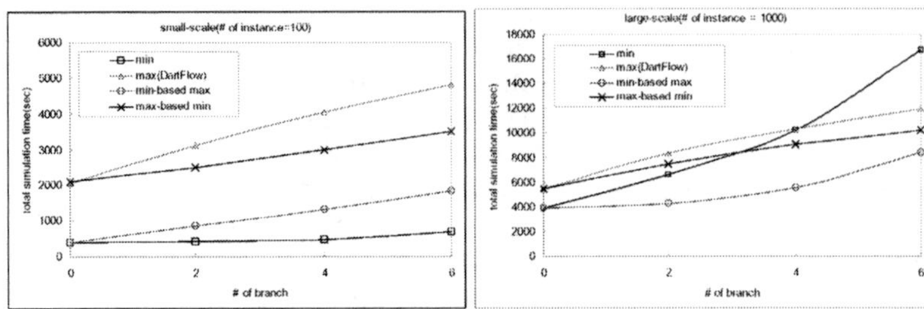

(a) the number of workflow process=100 (b) the number of workflow process=1000

Fig. 7. The relation between the number of branch and the simulation time

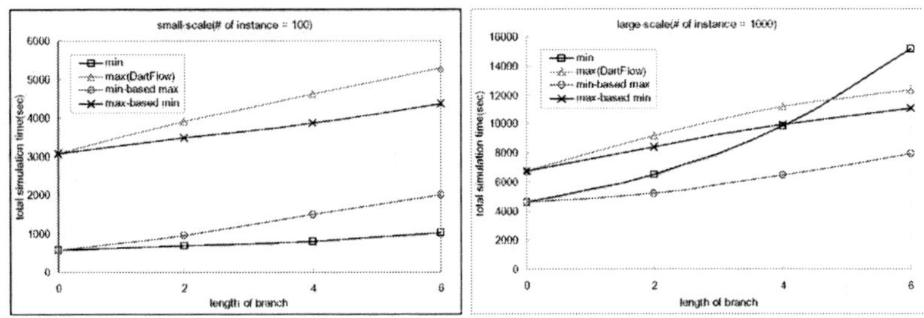

(a) the number of workflow process=100 (b) the number of workflow process=1000

Fig. 8. The relation between the length of branch and the simulation time

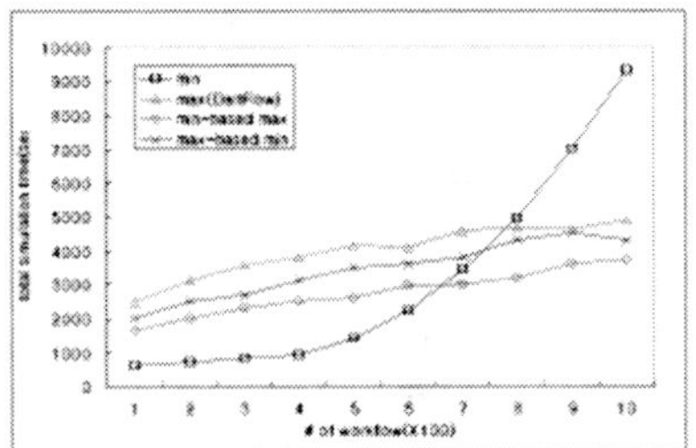

Fig. 9. The relation between the number of process and the simulation time

we conclude that the 3-layer architecture and agent delegation models address a good solution for increasing the performance and the scalability of workflow systems.

4 Conclusions

In this paper, we explained design issues of mobile agent-based workflow systems. In our proposed system, mobility of agents is mainly used to transport parts of a workflow implementation towards decentralized processing elements. Autonomy of agents is used to reduce the remote interactions between workflow engines and task performers. Because the workflow structure is frequently changed, uploading the parts of workflow implementation toward decentralized processing elements in advance is not an efficient method. By hierarchical distribution of control in architecture level as well as workflow execution level, potential advantages of a mobile agent in workflow systems are realized in terms of performance and scalability. We showed the effectiveness of proposed strategy with an *UltraSAN* simulation tool. As the stochastic Petri-nets simulation results has shown, the proposed model outperforms the client server-based and the *max*-based workflow systems in case of massive workflow environments as well as comes up with the scalability of *max*-based workflow systems. Although the code size for error handling is not considered, we will consider it in our future work.

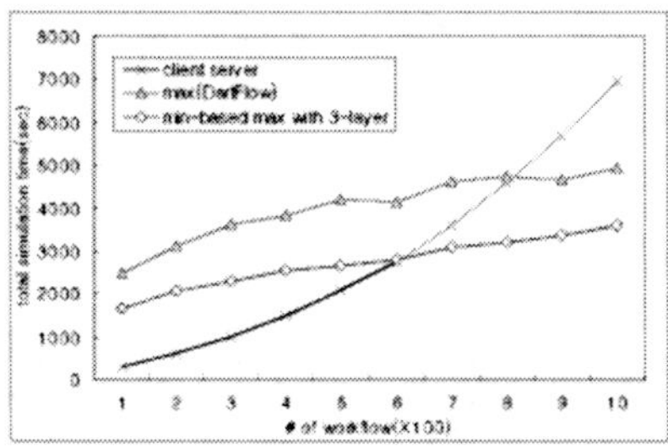

Fig. 10. Comparisons of the performance and the scalability of workflow systems

Acknowledgments. This work was partially supported by Korea Science and Engineering Foundation (KOSEF) under contract 98-0102-11-01-3.

References

1. WfMC, "Workflow Management Coalition Terminology and Glossary: WfMC Specification," 1999.
2. Frank Leymann, and Dieter Roller, "Business Process Management with FlowMark," *Spring Compcon, Digest of Papers, pp. 230-234*, 1994.
3. Action Workflow website: "http://www.actiontech.com/"
4. FloWare website: "http://www.plx.com/"
5. G. Alonso, C. Mohan et al., "Exotica/FMQM: A Persistent Message-Based Architecture for Distributed Workflow Management," *In IFIP WG8.1 Working Conference on Information System Development for Decentralized Organizations, pp. 1-18*, 1995.
6. Ting Cai, Peter A. Gloor, and Saurab Nog, "DartFlow: A Workflow Management System on the Web using Transportable Agents," *DartMouth College, Technical Report PCS-TR96-283*, 1996.
7. Colin G. Harrison, David M. Chess, and Aaron Kershenbaum, "Mobile Agents: Are they a good idea?," *Research Report, IBM Research Division, T.J.Watson Research Center*, 1995.
8. D. D. Deavours, W. D. Obal II, M. A. Qureshi, W. H. Sanders, and A. P. A. van Moorsel., "UltraSAN Version 3 Overview," *In Proceedings of International Workshop on Petri Nets and Performance Models*, 1995.
9. Manfred Dalmeijer, Eric Rietjens, Dieter Hammer, Ad Aerts, and Michiel Soede, "A Reliable Mobile Agents Architecture," *In Proceedings of the Int. Symposium on Object-Oriented Real-Time Distributed Computing*, 1998.
10. Kwang-Hoon Kim, Su-Ki Paik, Dong-Su Han, Young-Chul Lew, and Moon-Ja Kim, "An Instance-Active Transactional Workflow Architecture for Hanuri/TFlow," *In proceedings of International Symposium on Database, Web and Cooperative Systems*, 1999.
11. Qinzheng Kong, and Graham Chen, "Transactional Workflow for Telecommunication Service Management," *In Proceedings of International Symposium on Network Operations and Management*, 1996.

Anticipation to Enhance Flexibility of Workflow Execution

Daniela Grigori, François Charoy, and Claude Godart

LORIA - INRIA Lorraine, Campus Scientifique
BP 239, 54506 Vandoeuvre les Nancy – France
{dgrigori, charoy, godart}@loria.fr

Abstract. This paper introduces an evolution to classical workflow that allows more flexible execution of processes while retaining its simplicity. On the one hand it allows to describe processes in the same way that they are in design and engineering manuals. On the other hand it allows to control these processes in a way that is close to the way they are actually enacted. This evolution is based on the concept of anticipation, i.e. the weakening of strict sequential execution of activity sequences in workflows by allowing intermediate results to be used as preliminary input into succeeding activities. The architecture and implementation of a workflow execution engine prototype allowing anticipation is described.

1 Introduction

Current workflow models and systems are mainly concerned with the automation of administrative and production business processes. These processes coordinate well-defined activities that execute in isolation, i.e. synchronize only at their *start* and *terminate* states. If current workflow models and current workflow systems apply efficiently for this class of applications, they show their limits when one wants to model the subtlety of cooperative interactions as they occur in interactive or creative processes, typically co-design and co-engineering processes. Several research directions are investigated to provide environments that are more adaptable to user habits. These directions are described in section 2. They propose most of the time complex evolutions to the basic workflow model. Our approach consists in adding flexibility to workflow execution with minimal changes of the workflow model. We try to reach this goal by relaxing the way the model is interpreted; users can take some initiative regarding the way they start the assigned activities, leaving the burden of consistency management to the execution engine.

In this paper we introduce the idea of *anticipation* as a way to support more flexible execution of workflows. The principle is to allow an activity to start its execution even if all "ideal" conditions for its execution are not fulfilled. Anticipation is very common in creative applications: reading a draft, starting to code without complete design, illustrate this idea. Anticipation allows to add flexibility to workflow execution in a way that can not be modeled in advance. It can also be used to accelerate process execution as it increases parallelism in activity execution.

H.C. Mayr et al. (Eds.): DEXA 2001, LNCS 2113, pp. 264–273, 2001.

The paper is organized as follows. In the next section, we motivate our approach. In section 3 we describe our view of anticipation in workflows and the constraints related to it in order to ensure consistent execution of a process. Section 4 is dedicated to the implementation of a workflow engine allowing anticipation. Finally, section 5 concludes.

2 Related Work

In the literature we can find several works addressing the problem of workflow flexibility. The first approach considers *the process as a resource for action* [16]. Basically, it means that the process is a guide for users upon which they can build their own plan. It is not a definitive constraint that has to be enforced. Thus, users keep the initiative to execute their activities. They are not constrained by the predefined order of activities but are inspired by it and encouraged to follow it.

Authors of [14] propose to enhance the workflow model with goal activities and regions in order to allow its use as a resource for action. A goal node represents a part of the procedure with an unstructured work specification; its description contains goals, intent or guidelines. Authors of [1] argues that a plan as a resource for action must support users awareness, helping them to situate in the context of the process, either to execute it or to escape to it in order to solve a breakdown.

The second approach uses the process as a constraint for the flow of work, but it is admitted that it may change during its lifetime. The process can be dynamically adapted during its execution. ADEPTflex [15], Chautauqua [5], WASA [17] and WIDE [3] provide explicit primitives to dynamically change running workflow instances. These primitives allow to add/delete tasks and to change control and data flow within a running workflow instance. Constraints are imposed on the modifications in order to guarantee the syntactic correctness of the resulting process instance.

The third approach consists in evolving the process model itself to allow for more flexible execution. In this case, flexibility has to be modelled and is anticipated during the process modelling step. This is one of the branches that are followed by the COO project [7] and by other similar work [6]. In Mobile [10], the authors define several perspectives (functional, behavioral, informational, organizational, operational) for a workflow model, the definitions of perspectives being independent of one another. Descriptive modeling is defined as the possibility to omit irrelevant aspects in the definition of a perspective. In [11], [7], [12] other examples of descriptive modeling are presented as techniques for compact modeling. The authors propose simple modeling constructs that better represent real and complex work patterns to be used, instead of a composition of elementary constructs.

The first two approaches consider flexibility at the level of the process execution itself. In one case, the model is a guide to reach a goal; in the other case, the model is a path to reach a goal that may change during its course. In the third approach, it is the model that evolves to provide the requested flexibility.

In this paper we consider a fourth way which is not based on the way the process model is used or instantiated, neither on the way it can be evolved or modelled, but which adds flexibility in the workflow management system execution engine itself. This has the advantage of retaining the simplicity of the classical model and may also be adapted to other approaches. It is a first step toward a simple model that could support a more flexible execution suited to engineering processes.

3 Flexibility of the Execution Model

In this part we describe the evolution of the workflow execution engine to support flexible execution and data flow, and how we tackle the consistency problems that arise.

The workflow model that we use is very simple. It provides the basics to support control and data flow modeling. We provide here a minimal description allowing the explanation of the evolution we propose on the workflow engine. Our workflow model is based on process graphs. A process is represented as a directed graph, whose nodes are activities. An activity having more than one incoming edge is a join activity; it has an associated join condition. For an *or-join* activity the associated join condition is the disjunction of conditions associated to incoming edges. For an *and-join* activity the associated join condition is the conjunction of conditions associated to incoming edges. An activity having more than one outgoing edge is a fork activity.

Activities have input data elements and produce output data elements. The circulation of data between activities is represented by edges between output elements of an activity and input data element of another activity. The consumer must be a direct or transitive successor of the producer activity.

In summary, a process model is represented by a directed graph whose nodes are activities and whose edges represent control flow and data flow constraints.

3.1 Anticipation

Traditional workflow management systems impose an end-start dependency between activities [4]. This means that an activity can be started only after the preceding ones have completed. However, in cooperative processes that do not use coordination support, activities overlap and start their work with intermediate[1] results (in opposition to final results[2]) of preceding activities, even if all conditions for their execution are not completely fulfilled.

Anticipation is the mean we propose to support this natural way to execute activities while retaining the advantage of explicit coordination. Anticipation allows an activity to start its execution earlier regarding the control flow defined in the process model. When preceding activities are completed and all activation conditions are met, an anticipating activity enters the normal executing state, i.e. it continues its execution as if it never anticipated. At this time, final values of its input parameters are available. Having already been started, the activity is able to finish its execution earlier. The anticipation allows a more flexible execution, preserving, at the same time, the termination order of activities.

---

[1] Intermediate result: result produced by an activity during its execution, before its end.

[2] Final result: result produced by an activity when it completes.

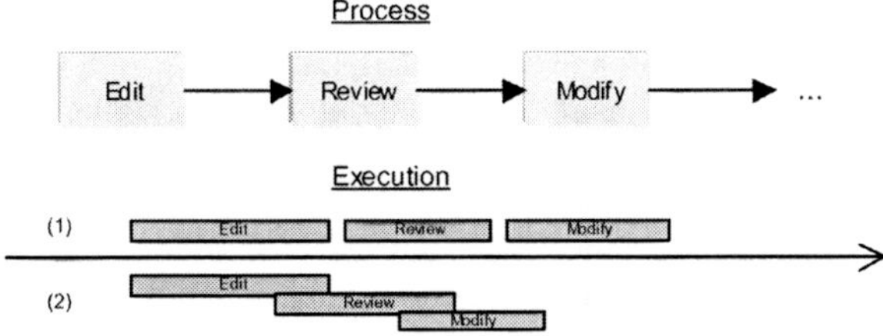

Fig. 1. Execution without (1) and with (2) anticipation

Example of Fig. 1 is an execution with anticipation (2). The *Edit* activity provides an intermediate draft of the edited document to *Review*. In this case *Review* and *Modify* activities can be started earlier. The whole process can thus be terminated earlier.

The possibility to anticipate requires some modifications of the workflow execution model. Our approach is to extend the traditional model (we start from the model defined in [13]) to take into account anticipation. Two new activity states are added: *ready to anticipate* and *anticipating* state. The *ready to anticipate* state indicates that the activity can start to anticipate. When an agent having the adequate role chooses it from its *to do list*, the activity enters the *anticipating state.* Fig. 2 depicts a state transition diagram including the new added states. Note that before to complete, even if an activity has started to anticipate, it must pass through executing state.

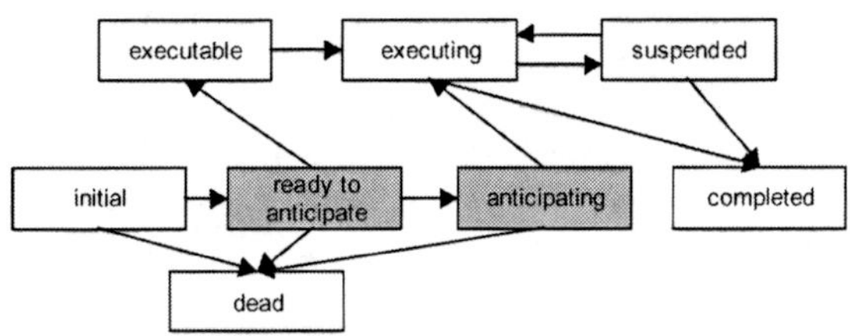

Fig. 2. State transition diagram for activities

When a process is started, all activities are in *initial* state, except the start activities (activities with no incoming edges), that are in *executable* state.

Transition from *initial* to *ready to anticipate* state. Concerning the moment when an activity in initial state can start to anticipate, several strategies can be considered:

1. *Free anticipation* – an activity in *initial* state may anticipate at any moment (*ready to anticipate* state merged with *initial* state). Control flow dependencies defined in the process model are interpreted at execution time as end-end dependencies; i.e. an activity can finish its execution only when the preceding one has. In our example, it would mean that *Modify* could start at any time. Free anticipation should be reserved to very special cases.
2. *Control flow dictated anticipation* – an activity may anticipate when its direct predecessor has started to work, i.e. is in *anticipating* or *executing* state. For an *or-join* activity, at least one of its predecessors must be in the *anticipating* or *executing* state. For an *and-join* activity, all the preceding activities must have been

started. In this case, the traditional start-end dependency between activities is relaxed, being replaced with a start-start dependency. In our example, that means that *Modify* can start as soon as *Review* has started.

3. *Control flow and data flow dictated anticipation* – an activity can anticipate when its predecessors are in *anticipating*, *executing* or *completed* state and for all its mandatory inputs, there are values available. In this case, the *Modify* activity could start only with a draft document and some early versions of the comments.

These three strategies have an impact on the general flexibility of the process execution. While the first one is very open but can lead to a lot of inconsistencies, the last one is more rigid and remove most of the interest of anticipation. In the remainder of the paper, we will consider that the implemented policy is the second one.

Transition from *ready to anticipate* to *anticipating*. As soon as an activity becomes *ready to anticipate,* it is scheduled, i.e. it is assigned to all agents who actually qualify under its associated staff query. It is important to note that users know the state of activity and can decide to anticipate. When one of these agents starts to anticipate, the activity passes in *anticipating* state and disappears from the *to do list* of the other agents.

Transition from *anticipating* to *executing*. An activity in *anticipating* state passes to *executing* state when it is in a situation where it would be allowed to start its execution if it was not anticipating.

Transition from *ready to anticipate* to *executable*. An activity in *ready to anticipate* state passes to *executable* state in the same conditions as traditionally an activity passes from *initial* to *executable*.

Transition from *anticipating* to *dead*. An activity in *anticipating* state passes to *dead* state if it is situated in a path that is not followed in the current workflow instance. Such a transition has the same motivations as for a traditional workflow activity to go from the *initial* state to the *dead* state. An anticipating activity makes the hypothesis that it will be executed. This is not sure. However, we think that, due to the nature of the applications we consider, this situation will not occur frequently: the objective of anticipation is to make the right decision at the right time thanks to rapid feedback.

We can see from this description that modifications of the workflow execution engine to provide anticipation are not very important. In order to gain all the benefits of anticipation of activity execution, it is necessary to allow also early circulation of data between activities, i.e. publication of early or intermediate results in the output container of executing activities.

3.2 Data Flow Supporting Intermediate Results

As we consider mainly interactive activities, user can decide to provide output data before their end and possibly with several successive versions. New activity operations are introduced, *Write* and *Read*. These operations can be used by users (or even special tools) to manage publication of data during activity execution. *Write* operation updates an output element and makes it available to succeeding activities.

Consider that activity A invokes the operation *Write(aout1)* to publish its output data *aout1*. Suppose that in data flow definition, two edges exist that have *aout1* as origin: an edge (aout1, bin1) between A and B activity and another one, (aout1, cin1) between A and C activity. If B or C is in anticipating state, it must be notified about the existence of new data (pull mode) or notified of arrival of data in their input container (push mode).

Read operation is used by anticipating activities in pull mode to update an input data with the new version published by the preceding activity. For unstructured data, a mechanism must be provided to synchronize with new versions (merge for instance). For text files, this is a common feature supported by version management systems.

Activities are no more isolated in black box transactions. They can provide results that can be used by succeeding activities. If the succeeding activities are interactive activities, the users in charge can consider taking this new value into account. They may also choose to wait for a more stable value supposed to arrive at a later time. Breaking activity isolation is necessary in order to benefit from the ability to anticipate but it may also cause some problems of inconsistency. These problems and the way to address them will be described in the section 3.4.

Besides supporting early start, anticipation can be used to provide rapid feedback to preceding activities. A communication channel can be created backward of the defined flow of activities. As anticipation allows successive activities to execute partly in parallel, it is natural to imagine that people may have some direct feedback (e.g. comments) to provide to user of preceding activities. In the example of Fig. 1, the *Review* activity can provide early comments while the *Edit* activity is still running.

3.3 Anticipation to Increase Parallelism between a Process and Its Subprocess

In a traditional workflow, an activity is a black box that produces output data at the end of its execution. In our approach, an activity may fill an output parameter in its output container as soon as it is produced. These partial results become available to succeeding activities. They can enter anticipating state and initiate actions based on these results. For instance, let consider the activity of sending a letter to a customer; the letter can be prepared in anticipating state with available data and really sent out in executing state. In this way, the process execution is accelerated.

Anticipation is especially useful when the activity is a sub-process. The output container of the activity is the output container of the process implementing it. Similar to an activity, a process can gradually fill data produced by its activities in its output container. These data become available for subsequent activities; otherwise they would have to wait the end of the sub-process. Anticipation allows increasing the parallelism between the main process and the sub-process implementing the activity.

To illustrate this, we can use the example of [9] depicted in Fig. 3; it represents a typical process to handle the delivery of products by a retail company. The G*et item* activity takes care of the stock control; it can be implemented as a sub-process which verifies if the item is available and otherwise orders it; finally an invoice is produced. The output data of the sub-process are the warehouse where the product is available and the delivery date. As soon as the product is in stock or the date when it will be received from manufacturer is known, the acknowledgement to the customer can be prepared. Similarly, the *Prepare Shipment* is initiated as soon as it is known from which warehouse the product will be delivered and at what date it will be available.

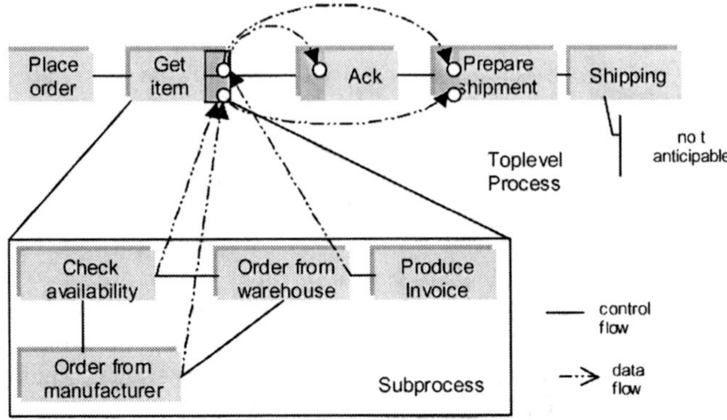

Fig. 3. Inter-process data communication

For this kind of process, control and data flow dictated anticipation can be applied efficiently. However, the *Shipping* activity can not be anticipated. This is a typical activity that can be executed only when all the preceding activities are terminated.

3.4 Synchronization and Recovery

Publishing intermediate results is important to take advantage of anticipation. However, an activity that has published results during its execution may fail or die, after it has published a result. The problem is *how to compensate* the visibility of such results (it can be related to *dirty read* in traditional concurrency theory). In order to assure this, the following rules are applied:

1. An activity that has read an intermediate result must read the corresponding final result if necessary (it is different from the intermediate result). An activity can enter completed state only from executing state. When an anticipating activity enters executing state, previous activities have been completed and their final results available.
2. An activity cannot produce intermediate results if it is not currently "certain" that it will enter the normal executing state. Independently of the anticipation strategy, we adopt a conservative approach concerning the moment when an anticipating activity may publish data requiring the preceding activity to be in executing state. Of course, this is an optimistic approach: nothing ensures that the preceding activities will not be canceled.
3. In case where an executing activity is canceled, anticipating activities that published data may need to be compensated. As only direct successors could publish data, the influence of canceling an activity is limited. After the state change, the status of anticipating activities is recomputed. They may go to dead state; the work done in anticipating state is lost. Otherwise, they remain anticipating. New updated values will be provided by the execution of their preceding activities. They will have to resynchronize with the next valid input.

As we can see, anticipation does not have an important impact on the general problem of workflow recovery, as long as activities do not have side effects. The work done in anticipating state may be lost but this is the price of flexibility. In case of activities having side effects outside of the scope of the workflow system, we are still obliged to introduce a special case described in the next section.

3.5 Suitability and Applicability of Anticipation

Anticipation is not suitable in any situation and not applicable for any activity type. For instance, it cannot be applied for an automatic activity having effects that cannot be compensated. However, it can be applied for automatic activities that are of retry type (flexible transactions). For example, an activity that searches available flight tickets in a database, can be automatically restarted at each modification of its inputs if the execution speed of the process is more important for the application than the overload created in the external database. A similar example is an activity that compiles a program at each modification of one of its modules.

During the definition phase of the process, it may not be possible to know in advance when anticipation will occur but it is possible to know which activities must not anticipate. These activities will be marked as such and will follow a more classical execution model.

In this part we have described how a simple modification of the classical model can enhance the flexibility of workflow execution in different ways. Now we are going to present how it is integrated in a larger framework to support cooperative workflow execution.

4 Implementation

We are currently implementing a workflow execution engine allowing anticipation. It is part of the MOTU prototype whose goal is to provide a framework to support cooperative work of virtual teams. The prototype is written in Java[3].

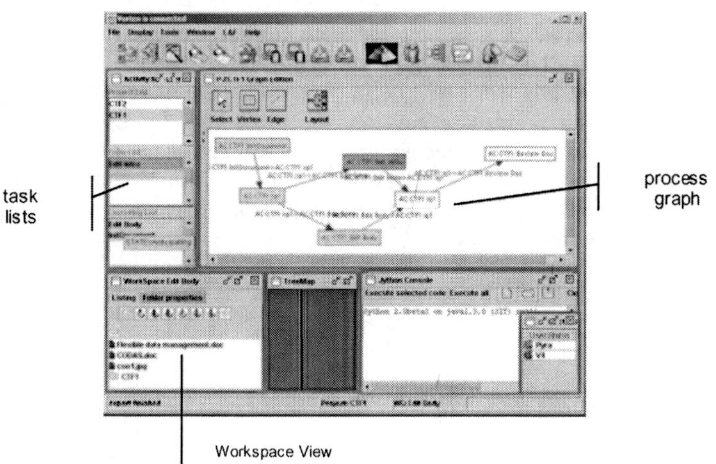

Fig. 4. Motu Client

[3] motu.sourceforge.net

The basis for the implementation is a non-linear version management server that provides the functionalities for public and private workspace management. This system has been extended with a basic workflow execution engine that provides dynamic process instantiation and implements anticipation. It also supports a cooperative transaction manager that allows exchanges of data between concurrently executing activities.

Anticipation is implemented as part of the Workflow execution engine. Activities that are not anticipatable can be specified. To each activity is associated a Coo Transaction[8]. This Coo transaction provides support for optimistic concurrency control between activities. A Coo Transaction[2] has a private base (a workspace) that contains a copy of all the objects accessed (read and updated) by activities; it also serves as communication channel between successive activities.

5 Conclusion

In this paper, we have presented a simple yet powerful way to modify workflow systems classical behavior to provide more flexible execution of processes. Compared to other approaches that try to provide flexibility in workflow models, the one we propose is simpler to understand for end users. This simplicity is essential in cooperative processes allowing graphical representation, helping their participants to situate in the context of the process and facilitating manual interventions for dynamical modifications. We showed that extending existing systems with anticipation is simple since it requires just updating the state transition management of the execution engine and some adaptation to the way data are transmitted between activities. Anticipation also provides substantial benefits regarding activities execution, especially for interactive activities: parallelism of execution between successive activities, possibility of early feedback between successive activities, potential acceleration of the overall execution.

Of course, there is also the risk of doing some extra work but as we mainly target interactive activities, we believe that users are able to evaluate the opportunity to use anticipation and what they may gain from it.

The next step of this work will be to consolidate the integration of the workflow model with cooperative transactions and to provide a set of operators to allow dynamic modification of the process during its execution. We believe that flexible execution, cooperative data exchange and dynamic process definition provide a cooperative environment allowing richer interactions between users and preserving coordination control on the process.

References

1. Agostini, A. and G. De Michelis, *Modeling the Document Flow within a Cooperative Process as a Resource for Action*, . 1996, University of Milano.
2. Canals, G., *et al.*, *COO Approach to Support Cooperation in Software Developments.* IEE Proceedings Software Engineering, 1998. **145**(2-3): p. 79-84.
3. Casati, F., *et al. Workflow Evolution.* in *15th Int. Conf. On Conceptual Modeling (ER'96).* 1996.

4. Workflow Management Coalition, *The Workflow Reference Model*, . 1995.
5. Ellis, C. and C. Maltzahn. *Chautaqua Workflow System*. in *30th Hawaii Int Conf. On System Sciences, Information System Track,*. 1997.
6. Georgakopoulos, D. *Collaboration Process Management for Advanced Applications*. in *International Process Technology Workshop*. 1999.
7. Godart, C., O. Perrin, and H. Skaf. *coo: a Workflow Operator to Improve Cooperation Modeling in Virtual Processes*. in *9th Int. Workshop on Research Issues in Data Engineering Information technology for Virtual Entreprises (RIDEVE'99)*. 1999.
8. Grigori, D., F. Charoy, and C. Godart. *Flexible Data Management and Execution to Support Cooperative Workflow: the COO approach*. in *The Third International Symposium on Cooperative Database Systems for Advanced Applications (CODAS'01)*. 2001. Beijing, China.
9. Hagen, C. and G. Alonso. *Beyond the Black Box: Event-based Inter-Process Communication in Process Support Systems*. in *9th International Conference on Distributed Computing Systems (ICDCS 99)*. 1999. Austin, Texas, USA.
10. Jablonski, S. *Mobile: A Modular Workflow Model and Architecture*. in *4th international Working Conference on Dynamic Modeling and Information Systems*. 1994. Noordwijkerhout, NL.
11. Jablonski, S. and C. Bussler, *Workflow management - Modeling Concepts, Architecture and implementation*. 1996: International Thomson Computer Press.
12. Joeris, G. *Defining Flexible Workflow Execution Behaviors*. in *Enterprise-wide and Cross-enterprise Workflow Management - Concepts, Systems, Applications', GI Workshop Proceedings - Informatik'99, Ulmer Informatik Berichte Nr. 99-07, University of Ulm*. 1999.
13. Leymann, F. and D. Roller, *Production Workflow*. 1999: Prentice Hall.
14. Nutt, G.J. *The Evolution Toward Flexible Workflow Systems*. in *Distributed Systems Engineering*. 1996.
15. Reichert, M. and P. Dadam, *ADEPTflex - Supporting dynamic Changes of Workflows Without Losing Control. Journal of Intelligent Information Systems*, 1998. **10**.
16. Suchmann, L.A., *Plans and Situated Action. The Problem of Human-Machine Communication*, in *Cambridge University Press*. 1987.
17. Weske, M. *Flexible Modeling and Execution of Workflow Activities*. in *31st Hawaii International Conference on System Sciences, Software Technology Track (Vol VII)*. 1996.

Coordinating Interorganizational Workflows Based on Process-Views

Minxin Shen and Duen-Ren Liu

Institute of Information Management, National Chiao Tung University, Taiwan

{shen, dliu}@iim.nctu.edu.tw

Abstract. In multi-enterprise cooperation, an enterprise must monitor the progress of private processes as well as those of the partners to streamline interorganizational workflows. In this work, a process-view model, which extends beyond the conventional activity-based process model, is applied to design workflows across multiple enterprises. A process-view is an abstraction of an implemented process. An enterprise can design various process-views for different partners according to diverse commercial relationships, and establish an integrated process that is comprised of private processes as well as the process-views that these partners provide. Participatory enterprises can obtain appropriate progress information from their own integrated processes, allowing them to collaborate more effectively. Furthermore, interorganizational workflows are coordinated through virtual states of process-views. This work develops a regulated approach to map the states between private processes and process-views. The proposed approach enhances prevalent activity-based process models to be adapted in open and collaborative environments.

1 Introduction

During cross-enterprise collaboration, each participatory enterprise needs to conceal its private processes to preserve autonomy. However, successful collaboration among multiple enterprises requires information sharing. Therefore, modelers should provide various external interfaces of a private process that not only conceals sensitive information but also reveals that which is essential to cooperation. Outside partners can monitor and control the progress of a private process through these external interfaces. To automate interorganizational workflows, modelers must also incorporate the process information as provided via partners' external interfaces into internal processes. Furthermore, an ideal process model should describe internal processes and external interfaces uniformly to increase comprehensibility.

Our previous study [9] proposed a process-view model that enhances the capability of process abstraction in conventional activity-based process models [4]. A process-view, i.e., a virtual process, is abstracted from an actual process. According to distinct organizational role's requirements, a process modeler can design various process-views, hence providing the appropriate process information to each participant. However, the preliminary process-view model does not consider managing workflows within interorganizational collaboration. Therefore, this work extends the process-view model to endeavor these issues.

H.C. Mayr et al. (Eds.): DEXA 2001, LNCS 2113, pp. 274–283, 2001.

A process-view abstracts critical commercial secrets and is an external interface of an internal process. An enterprise can design process-views, which are unique to each partner. Process-views of participatory enterprises comprise a collaboration workflow. Furthermore, the *virtual states* of a process-view present progress status of an internal process. An enterprise can monitor and control the progress of partners through the virtual states of their process-views. The proposed approach provides a modeling tool to describe interorganizational workflows as well as an interoperation mechanism to coordinate autonomous, heterogeneous and distributed workflow management systems (WfMSs).

The remainder of this paper is organized as follows. Section 2 presents the process-view model and its applications within inter-enterprise cooperation. Section 3 summarizes the procedure of defining an ordering-preserved process-view presented in [9]. Next, Section 4 presents the coordination of interorganizational workflows through the virtual states of process-views and then Section 5 discusses some properties of process-view based approach and related work. Conclusions are finally made in Section 6.

2 Process-View Based Coordination Model

A process that may have multiple process-views is referred to herein as a *base process*. A process-view is an abstracted process derived from a base process to provide abstracted process information. Based on the process-view definition tool, a modeler can define various process-views to achieve different levels of information concealment.

Definition 1 (Base process). A base process *BP* is a 2-tuple ⟨*BA*, *BD*⟩, where

1. *BD* is a set of dependencies. A dependency *dep*(*x*, *y*, *C*) indicates that *x* is completed and *C* is true is one precondition of whether activity *y* can start.
2. *BA* is a set of activities. An activity is a 4-tuple ⟨*AID*, *SPLIT_flag*, *JOIN_flag*, *SC*⟩, where (a) *AID* is a unique activity identifier within a process. (b) *SPLIT_flag*/*JOIN_flag* may be "NULL", "AND", or "XOR". NULL indicates this activity has only one outgoing/incoming dependency (Sequence). AND/XOR indicates the AND/XOR JOIN/SPLIT ordering structures defined by WfMC [15]. (c) *SC* is the *starting condition* of this activity. If *JOIN_flag* is NULL, *SC* equals the condition associated with its incoming dependency. If *JOIN_flag* is AND/XOR, *SC* equals Boolean AND/XOR combination of all incoming dependencies' conditions.
3. $\forall x, y \in BA$, (a) if $\exists dep(x, y, C)$, then *x* and *y* are adjacent; (b) the *path* from *x* to *y* is denoted by $x \rightarrow y$. (c) *x* is said to have a higher *order* than *y* if $\exists x \rightarrow y$, i.e., *x* proceeds before *y*, and their *ordering relation* is denoted by $x > y$ or $y < x$. If $\nexists\, x \rightarrow y$ and $y \rightarrow x$, i.e., *x* and *y* proceed independently, their ordering relation is denoted by $x \infty y$.

2.1 Virtual Process: A Process-View

A process-view is generated from either base processes or other process-views and is considered a *virtual process*. A process-view is defined as follows:

Definition 2 (Process-view). A process-view is a 2-tuple ⟨*VA*, *VD*⟩, where (1) *VA* is a set of virtual activities. (2) *VD* is a set of virtual dependencies. (3) Analogous to base process, $\forall va_i, va_j \in VA$, the *path* from va_i to va_j is denoted by $va_i \rightarrow va_j$; the *ordering relation* between va_i and va_j may be ">", "<", or "∞".

A virtual activity is an abstraction of a set of base activities and corresponding base dependencies. A virtual dependency is used to connect two virtual activities in a process-view. Figure 1 illustrates how the components of our model are related. Section 3 demonstrates how to abstract virtual activities and dependencies from a base process. Notably, within an interorganizational environment, a participant's role represents an external partner.

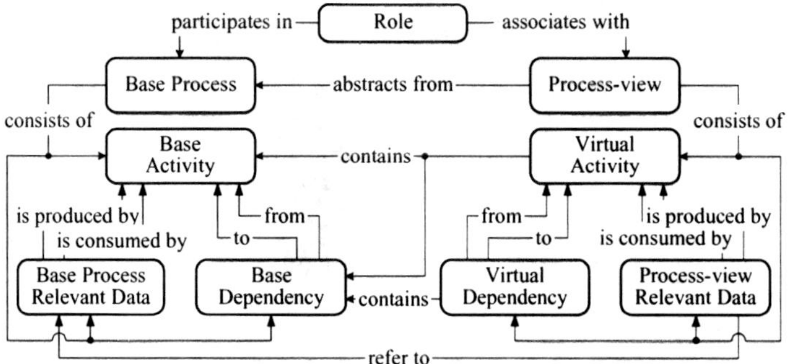

Fig. 1. Process-view model

2.2 Process-View Based Coordination

Figure 2 illustrates the cooperation scenario and system components, in which three systems cooperate through process-views. To enhance the interoperability through open techniques, process-views' interactions (solid bi-arrow lines) are implemented based on industrial standards, such as CORBA and XML. However, each enterprise determines its proprietary implementation of the communication autonomously (blank bi-arrow lines) among base processes, process-views and integrated processes.

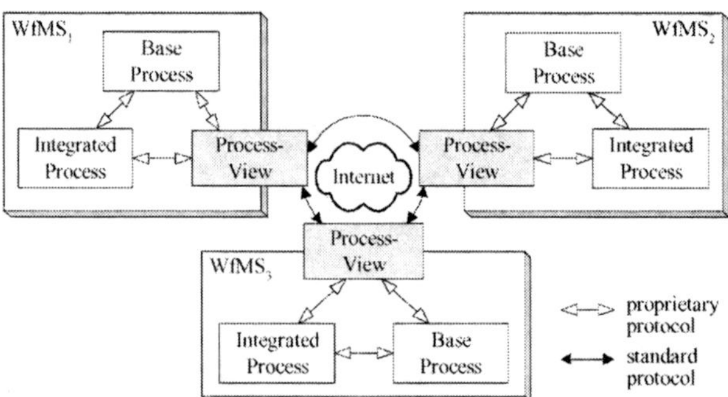

Fig. 2. System architecture and interaction scenario

A process-view is an external view (or interface) of the private base process and is derived through the procedure described in Section 3. An *integrated process* is a specific view of the interorganizational workflow that is based on a participatory enterprise's perspective, which consolidates private processes and partners' process-views. Notably, the integrated process is also a virtual process. Each of its virtual activity/dependency is either a base one of a private base process or a virtual one of partners' process-views.

As a base activity/process, a virtual activity/process is associated with a set of states to present its run-time status. A virtual state is employed to abstract the execution states of base activities/processes contained by a virtual activity/process. To monitor and control the progress of a private process through the virtual states of its public process-view, two rules are proposed in Section 4 to map the states between a base and a virtual process. Therefore, an enterprise can coordinate with its partners through virtual states of process-views.

2.3 Three Phase Modeling

Collaboration modeling is a complex negotiation procedure. Process design is divided into three phases: *base process phase*, *process-view phase* and *integration phase*. Figure 3 illustrates the three phases for the cooperation between enterprise *A* and *B*.

- Base process phase is the traditional build phase. A process modeler specifies the activities and their orderings in a business process, which is based on a top-down decomposition procedure that many activity-based process models support.
- Next, designing a process-view is a bottom-up aggregation procedure. A process modeler can define various process-views for the partners according to diverse cooperation relationships.
- Finally, a process modeler forms an integrated process, or a personalized view of an interorganizational workflow through consolidating private base process and partners' process-views.

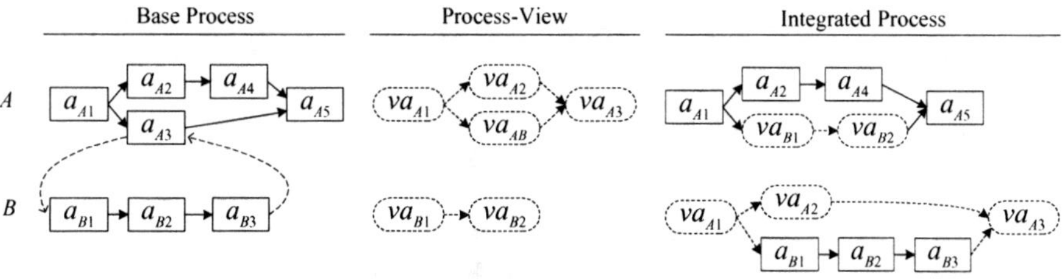

Fig. 3. Three phases of designing interorganizational workflows

3 Ordering-Preserved Process-View

Enterprises cooperate through process-views. According to the different properties of a base process, various approaches can be developed to derive a process-view. A novel ordering-preserved approach to derive a process-view from a base process has been presented in [9] and is summarized in this section. The ordering-preserved

approach ensures that the original execution order in a base process is preserved. A *legal* virtual activity in an ordering-preserved process-view must follow three rules:
Rule 1 (Membership). A virtual activity's member may be a base activity or a previously defined virtual activity.
Rule 2 (Atomicity). A virtual activity, an atomic unit of processing, is completed if and only if each activity contained by it either has been completed or is never executed. A virtual activity is started if and only if one activity contained by it is started. In addition, if an ordering relation, $\Re$ (i.e., >, < or ∞), between two virtual activities is found in a process-view, then an implied ordering relation $\Re$ exists between these virtual activities' respective members.
Rule 3 (Ordering preservation). The implied ordering relations between two virtual activities' respective members must conform to the ordering relations in the base process.

Based on the above rules, virtual activities and dependencies in an ordering-preserved process-view are formally defined as follows:
Definition 3 (Virtual Activity). For a base process $BP = \langle BA, BD\rangle$, a virtual activity *va* is a 6-tuple $\langle VAID, A, D, SPLIT\_flag, JOIN\_flag, SC\rangle$, where

1. *VAID* is a unique virtual activity identifier within a process-view.
2. *A* is a nonempty set, and its members follow three rules:

   Its members may be base activities that are members of *BA* or other previously defined virtual activities that are derived from *BP*.

   The fact that *va* is completed implies that each member of *A* is either completed or never executed during run time; the fact that *va* is started implies that one member of *A* is started.

   $\forall x \in BA$, $x \notin A$, the ordering relations between x and all members (base activities) of *A* are identical in *BP*, i.e., $\forall y, z \in BA$, $y, z \in A$, if $x \Re y$ exists in *BP*, then $x \Re z$ also exists in *BP*.
3. *D* is a nonempty set, and its members are dependencies whose succeeding activity and preceding activity are contained by *A*.
4. *SPLIT_flag*/*JOIN_flag* may be "NULL" or "MIX". NULL suggests that *va* has only one outgoing/incoming virtual dependency (Sequence) while MIX indicates that *va* has more than one outgoing/incoming virtual dependency.
5. *SC* is the *starting condition* of *va*.

The *SPLIT_ flag* and *JOIN_ flag* cannot simply be described as AND or XOR since *va* is an abstraction of a set of base activities that may associate with different ordering structures. Therefore, MIX is used to abstract the complicated ordering structures. A WfMS evaluates *SC* to determine whether *va* can be started. The abbreviated notation $va = \langle A, D\rangle$ is used for brevity.
Definition 4 (Virtual Dependency). For two virtual activities $va_i = \langle A_i, D_i\rangle$ and $va_j = \langle A_j, D_j\rangle$ that are derived from a base process $BP = \langle BA, BD\rangle$, a virtual dependency from va_i to va_j is $vdep(va_i, va_j, VC_{ij}) = \{ dep(a_x, a_y, C_{xy}) \mid dep(a_x, a_y, C_{xy}) \in BD, a_x \in A_i, a_y \in A_j \}$, where the virtual condition VC_{ij} is a Boolean combination of C_{xy}.

The procedure of defining an ordering-preserved process-view is summarized as follows: A process modeler must initially select essential activities. The process-view definition tool then generates a legal minimum virtual activity that encapsulates these essential activities automatically. The above two steps are repeated until the modeler determines all required virtual activities. The definition tool then generates all virtual dependencies between these virtual activities as well as ordering fields (*JOIN/SPLIT_flag*) and starting condition (*SC*) of each virtual activity automatically. [9] presents the algorithm that implements the process-view definition tool.

4 Coordinating Inter-enterprise Processes through Virtual States

In this section, the mechanism that coordinates inter-enterprise processes through activity/process states is described. During run time, cooperative partners monitor and control the progress of inter-enterprise processes through the execution states (virtual states) of virtual activities/processes. First, the states and operations of base activity/process are described. Then, the state mapping rules to coordinate base processes, process-views and integrated processes during run-time are proposed.

4.1 Generic States and Operations

The state of a process or activity instance represents the execution status of the instance at a specific point. A state transition diagram depicts the possible run-time behavior of a process/activity instance. Currently, both WMF and Wf-XML support the generic states as shown in Figure 4, in which WfExecutionObject is a generation of a process or activity instance [11]. Furthermore, the hierarchical structure of states imposes superstate/substate relationships between them.

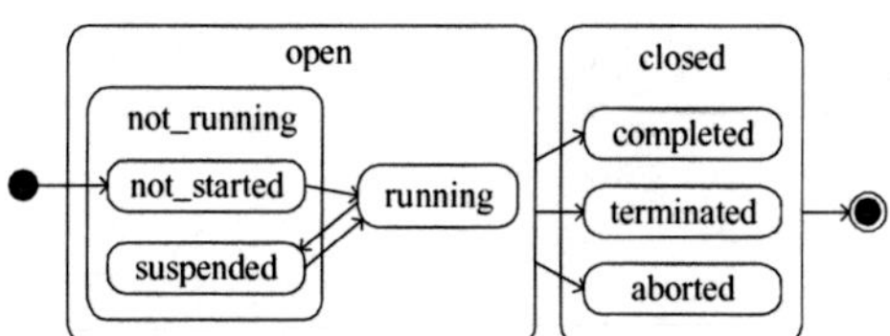

Fig. 4. States of a WfExecutionObject [11]

After a WfExecutionObject is initiated, it is in *open* state, however, upon completion, it enters *closed* state. The *open* state has two substates: *running* indicates that the object is executing, and *not_running* suggests that the object is quiescent since it is either temporarily paused (in *suspended* state) or recently initialized and prepared to start (in *not_started* state). The state *completed* indicates that the object has been completed correctly. Otherwise, the object stops abnormally, i.e., in *terminated* or *aborted* state.

The operations, e.g., *suspend*, *terminate*, and *change_state*, that are used to control a WfExecutionObject change the state of a WfExecutionObject as well as its associated WfExecutionObjects. The operation *get_current_state*, as defined in WMF, returns the current state of a WfExecutionObject instance. In the following section, state function f_s is employed to substitute this operation for brevity.

4.2 State Mapping

Both base and virtual activities/processes support the same set of the previously mentioned generic states and operations. In this section, consistent mapping of the execution states between virtual processes/activities and its member processes/ activities is discussed. Two cooperation scenarios can trigger state mapping. First, virtual activities/processes must respond to the state change that occurred in base activities/processes, i.e., the mapping occurs from base activities/processes to virtual activities/processes. Second, base activities/processes must react to the request to change the state as triggered by virtual activities/processes, i.e., the mapping occurs from virtual activities/processes to base activities/processes.

State Mapping between a Base Process and a Process-View

The virtual state of a process-view simply equals the state of its base process. For example, a process-view is in the *suspended* state if its base process is also in the same state. However, state mapping between virtual activities and its member activities must follow atomicity rule (Rule 2) as follows.

Active state. Atomicity rule states that a virtual activity is *active*, i.e., in *open* state, if at least one member activity is active. *Active degree* (or grade) of active states is introduced to extend the atomicity rule for state mapping. Active states are ranked as follows: *running* > *suspended* > *not_started*. Since an activity has been executed for a while prior to suspension, but never runs before the *not_started* state, the *suspended* state is more active than the *not_started* state. The atomicity rule is extended as follows: if two or more member activities of a virtual activity *va* are active and states of member activities compose a state set Q, then the (virtual) state of *va* equals the most active state in Q.

Inactive state. Atomicity rule also states that a virtual activity is *inactive*, i.e., in *closed* state, if all members are either inactive or never initialized. According to the definition of the *closed* state and its substates in [11, 14], an execution object, WfExecutionObject, is stopped in *completed* state if all execution objects contained within it are *completed*. Second, an execution object is stopped in *terminated* state if all execution objects contained within it are either *completed* or *terminated*, and at least one is *terminated*. Finally, an execution object is stopped in *aborted* state if at least one execution object contained within it is *aborted*. Therefore, based on these definitions, the state of an inactive virtual activity can be determined.

In sum, a virtual activity responds to the state change of member activities according to the following rule. Notably, $f_s(a)$/ $f_s(va)$ denotes the state/virtual state of a member activity *a*/ virtual activity *va*.

Rule 4 (State Abstraction). Given a virtual activity $va = \langle A , D\rangle$. If $\exists a \in A$, $f_s(a)$ = *open* or its substate, then let the state set $Q = \{f_s(a), \forall a \in A\}$, $f_s(va)$ equals the most active state in Q. If $\forall a \in A$, $f_s(a)$ = *closed* or its substate, and $\exists a \in A$, $f_s(a)$ = *aborted*, then $f_s(va)$ = *aborted*. If $\forall a \in A$, $f_s(a)$ = either *terminated* or *completed*, and $\exists a \in A$, $f_s(a)$ = *terminated*, then $f_s(va)$ = *terminated*. If $\forall a \in A$, $f_s(a)$ = *completed*, then $f_s(va)$ = *completed*.

Figure 5 depicts the state transitions of a virtual activity that are triggered by the state transitions of its member activities.

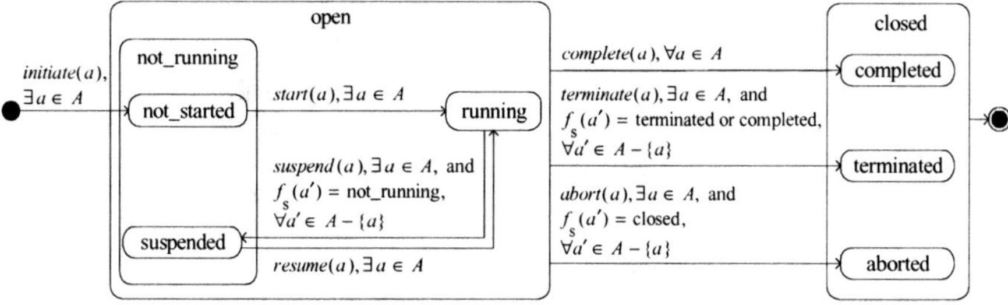

Fig. 5. State transitions of a virtual activity $va = \langle A, D \rangle$

When invoking an operation of a virtual process/activity object, the object propagates the operation to underlying base process/activity object. A process-view affects the entire base process, while a virtual activity only affects its member activities. For example, invoking *create_ process* operation on a process-view definition initiates a process-view and its corresponding base process. However, applying *suspend* operation on a virtual activity only suspends its member activity(s). If an external event or API call alters the state of a virtual activity/process, then the influence of state transition in base activities/processes depends on the following rule:

Rule 5 (State Propagation). For a virtual activity $va = \langle A, D \rangle$, when requesting va to be in state s, $\forall a \in A$, if a transition from state $f_s(a)$ to state s is valid, then the state of a transfers from $f_s(a)$ to s; otherwise, $f_s(a)$ is not changed. Next, according to Rule 4, the state of va can be derived. If $f_s(va) \neq s$, then an *InvalidState* exception [11] throws and member activities rollback to their original states. If $f_s(va) = s$, then the state transitions of member activities are committed. For a process-view PV, when requesting PV to be in state s, if its base process BP can transfer to s, then the state transitions of PV and BP are committed; otherwise, an *InvalidState* exception are returned to the request and PV and BP rollback to their original states.

State Mapping between an Integrated Process and Its Underlying Processes

Since each virtual activity in an integrated process only maps to an activity in the private process or a partner's process-view, state mapping at the activity level is direct. If virtual activity a's underlying activity can transfer to state s when requesting that a to be in state s, then the transition is committed; otherwise, the transition fails. Similarly, if the activities within an integrated process IP can transfer to state s when requesting IP to be in state s, then the request is committed; otherwise, the transition fails.

5 Discussion

Several investigations defined and implemented *interaction points* among cooperating enterprises. Casati and Discenza [2] introduced event nodes in a process to define the tasks that exchange information with partners. Lindert and Deiters [8] discussed the data that should be described in interaction points from various aspects. Van der Aalst [13] applied a message sequence chart to identify interactions among enterprises. In these approaches, the external interface is the set of interaction points. Above investigations ensure that only interaction points are public and the structure of internal processes remains private.

A widely used modeling method uses an activity as an external interface to abstract a whole process enacted by another enterprise. The notion is based on service information hiding [1], i.e., a consumer does not need to know the internal process structure of a provider. Therefore, the activity can be viewed as a business service that an external partner enacts. This approach resembles the traditional nested sub-process pattern in which a child sub-process implements an activity within a parent process. Various investigations are based on the paradigm of *service activity* such as [5, 10, 12]. Via service activity states, a consumer can monitor service progress. Most approaches only support Workflow Management Coalition (WfMC) specified activity states [15] to comply with interoperation standards such as Wf-XML [14] and Workflow Management Facility (WMF) [11]. To reveal a more semantic status of the service provider's process, CMI [5] enables modelers to define application-specific states that extend from standard activity ones.

This work focuses mainly on supporting collaborative workflow modeling and interoperation. Conventional approaches are restricted by original granularity of process definitions that is not intended for outside partners. Therefore, determining which parts of private processes should be revealed to partners is extremely difficult. Process-view model enables a modeler to generate various levels of abstraction (granularity) of a private process flexibly and systematically. A process-view can be considered a compromised solution between privacy and publicity.

Meanwhile, in parallel with the publication of our work, Chiu et al. proposed a workflow view that provides partial visibility of a process to support interorganizational workflow in an e-commerce environment [3]. A workflow view contains selected partial activities of a process. In contrast, a process-view is derived from bottom-up aggregation of activities to provide various levels of aggregated abstraction of a process. Interorganizational workflows are coordinated through virtual states of process-views. The generic states/operations that was defined in standards were adopted to use the existing standards as a backbone to integrate heterogeneous and distributed systems in multi-enterprise cooperation. This work has developed a regulated approach to manage the states mapping between base processes/activities and virtual processes/activities. Although only generic states and operations are discussed herein, the adopted hierarchical structure of states facilitates further extension regarding specific application domains, e.g., the CMI approach [5].

WISE [7] proposed a framework to compose a virtual business process through the process interfaces of several enterprises. In addition, CrossFlow [6] proposed a framework, which is based on service contract, to manage WfMS cooperation between service providers and consumers. These projects focus on providing broking architectures to exchange business processes as business services. Our contribution is a systematic approach from which external interfaces can be derived. The process-view model can be extended to support the trading architectures that WISE and CrossFlow proposed.

6 Conclusion

A process-view model to conduct interorganizational workflow management was presented herein. Notably, a process-view is an abstracted process that can be viewed as an external interface of a private process. The proposed approach not only preserves the privacy of an internal process structure, but also achieves progress monitoring and control. Moreover, enterprises interact through the virtual states of process-views that conform to interoperation standards. Therefore, distributed, heterogeneous and autonomous WfMSs can be integrated in an open environment. The proposed approach alleviates the shortcomings of inter-enterprise workflow collaboration.

Acknowledgements. The work was supported in part by National Science Council of the Republic of China under the grant NSC 89-2416-H-009-041.

References

1. A. P. Barros and A. H. M. ter Hofstede, "Towards the Construction of Workflow - Suitable Conceptual Modelling Techniques", *Information Systems Journal*, 8(4), pp. 313-337, 1998.
2. F. Casati and A. Discenza, "Modeling and Managing Interactions among Business Processes", *Journal of Systems Integration*, 10(2), pp. 145-168, 2001.
3. D. K. W. Chiu, K. Karlapalem, and Q. Li, "Views for Inter-Organization Workflow in an E-Commerce Environment", *Proceedings of the 9th IFIP Working Conference on Database Semantics (DS-9)*, Hong Kong, China, April 24-28, 2001.
4. D. Georgakopoulos, M. Hornick, and A. Sheth, "An Overview of Workflow Management - from Process Modeling to Workflow Automation Infrastructure", *Distributed and Parallel Databases*, 3(2), pp. 119-153, 1995.
5. D. Georgakopoulos, H. Schuster, A. Cichocki, and D. Baker, "Managing Process and Service Fusion in Virtual Enterprises", *Information Systems*, 24(6), pp. 429-456, 1999.
6. P. Grefen, K. Aberer, Y. Hoffner, and H. Ludwig, "CrossFlow: Cross-Organizational Workflow Management in Dynamic Virtual Enterprises", *Computer Systems Science & Engineering*, 15(5), pp. 277-290, 2000.
7. A. Lazcano, G. Alonso, H. Schuldt, and C. Schuler, "The WISE Approach to Electronic Commerce", *Computer Systems Science & Engineering*, 15(5), pp. 345-357, 2000.
8. F. Lindert and W. Deiters, "Modeling Inter-Organizational Processes with Process Model Fragments", *Proceedings of GI workshop Informatik'99*, Paderborn, Germany, Oct. 6, 1999.
9. D.-R. Liu and M. Shen, "Modeling Workflows with a Process-View Approach", *Proceedings of the 7th International Conference on Database Systems for Advanced Applications (DASFAA'01)*, pp. 260-267, Hong Kong, China, April 18-22, 2001.
10. M. z. Muehlen and F. Klien, "AFRICA: Workflow Interoperability Based on XML-Messages", *Proceedings of CAiSE'00 workshop on Infrastructures for Dynamic Business-to-Business Service Outsourcing (IDSO'00)*, Stockholm, Sweden, June5, 2000.
11. Object Management Group, "Workflow Management Facility", Document number formal/00-05-02, April 2000.
12. K. Schulz and Z. Milosevic, "Architecting Cross-Organizational B2B Interactions", *Proceedings of the 4th International Enterprise Distributed Object Computing Conference (EDOC 2000)*, pp. 92-101, Los Alamitos, CA, USA, 2000.
13. W. M. P. van der Aalst, "Process-Oriented Architectures for Electronic Commerce and Interorganizational Workflow", *Information Systems*, 24(8), pp. 639-671, 1999.
14. Workflow Management Coalition, "Interoperability Wf-XML Binding", Technical report WfMC TC-1023, May 1, 2000.
15. Workflow Management Coalition, "The Workflow Reference Model", Technical report WfMC TC-1003, Jan. 19, 1995.

Strategies for Semantic Caching*

Luo Li[1], Birgitta König-Ries[2], Niki Pissinou[2⇧], and Kia Makki[2]

[1] Center for Advanced Computer Studies, U. of Louisiana at Lafayette
luoli@cacs.louisiana.edu

[2] Telecommunications and Information Technology Institute, Florida International University
niki|kia@eng.fiu.edu

Abstract. One major problem with the use of mediator-based architectures is long query response times. An approach to shortening response times is to cache data at the mediator site. Recently, there has been growing interest in semantic query caching which may generally outperform the page and tuple caching approaches. In this paper, we present two semantic-region caching strategies with different storage granularities for mediators accessing relational databases. In contrast to most existing approaches, we do not only cache the projection result of queries but also the condition attributes, resulting in a higher cache hit rate. Additionally, we introduce the Profit-based Replacement algorithm with Aging Counter (PRAG), which incorporates the semantic notion of locality into the system.

1 Introduction

Mediators are software components that homogenize and integrate information stemming from different data sources [Wied92]. Mediator-based architectures are used successfully in applications where transparent access to heterogeneous information sources is needed. Whenever a user query is sent to a mediator, this query is expanded into one to the underlying information sources and results are gathered from these sources. A major disadvantage stemming from this kind of "view-like behavior" is that query response times tend to be very long. For many applications this is not acceptable. For example, consider a mobile and wireless system that has the typical characteristics of frequent disconnections and expensive connections charged by connection time [PMK2000]. In such a system long response times can result in the user being disconnected by the time the result arrives and in high costs associated with querying.

A first step in making mediator architectures more usable in application areas that require short response times is to make query results instantly available. Caching them in the mediator can do this. Then, when a query arrives, before contacting the underlying information source, the mediator checks if all or part of the required

* This work was supported in part by the National Science Foundation (NSF) under grants CCR9986080, CCR9988336, NSF EPSCOR for the MONISA project, DUI9751414

⇧ On leave from: Center for Advanced Computer Studies, University of Louisiana at Lafayette

H.C. Mayr et al. (Eds.): DEXA 2001, LNCS 2113, pp. 284–298, 2001.

information is in its cache. This materialization has two key advantages: First, partial results are available even if a mediator becomes disconnected from its source. Second, the response times and thus costs and the likelihood of disconnections are reduced. While these advantages are of particular importance in mobile and wireless applications, more traditional systems can also profit from the above approach.

Several caching strategies are available for mediator architectures. Besides traditional tuple and page caching, there has been growing interest in semantic query caching, where the cache is organized in semantic regions containing semantically related query results. Due to the semantic locality (i.e., subsequent queries often are related conceptually to previous queries), semantic caching generally outperforms the page and tuple caching approaches [CFZ94].

Different classes of mediators cater to different information needs. In this paper, we are looking at mediators answering queries on information sources with hot-spots, i.e., small areas of the database that are queried frequently. Semantic caching works particularly well for this class of mediators. Hot-spots are common in a wide variety of applications: A library's database may get many queries on bestsellers; an online travel system may have lots of queries about certain places; a movie database may have mainly queries on movies with top ratings. Currently, we are restricting our investigation to non-join queries in read-only applications such as the ones mentioned above. Although this leaves out a number of interesting applications, we believe the remaining to be of considerable importance warranting sophisticated support.

In order to achieve a high utilization of data, in our work we do not only cache the projection results of a query, but also the condition attributes. Additionally, we introduce a Profit-based Replacement algorithm with Aging Counter (PRAG). The remainder of this paper is organized as follows: Section 2 introduces the basic ideas of semantic-region caching and provides our approaches. Two strategies with different storage granularities are studied, and the profit-based replacement algorithm PRAG is introduced. Section 3 provides our experimental results; Section 4 gives an overview of related work. Section 5 summarizes the paper and presents an outlook on future work.

2 Materializing Hot-Spots Using Semantic Caching

In this section, we show how semantic caching can be applied in order to reduce mediator response times for mediators accessing relational databases with a hot-spot pattern. We summarize the semantic caching method described in [DFJ+96], and describe in detail our solutions to the open questions posed in [DFJ+96].

2.1 Preliminaries

[DFJ+96] proposes a semantic model for client-side caching and replacement in a client-server database system. Semantic caching uses semantic descriptions to describe the cached data instead of a list of physical pages, which is used in page caching, or tuple identifiers, which are used in tuple caching. The cache is organized as a collection of semantic regions. Each region groups tuples sharing the same semantic description, a query statement corresponding to the cached data. By using these descriptions, the client can determine what data is available in the cache.

When a query is asked, it is split into a remainder query and a probe query. The probe query is used to retrieve data from the cache, while the remainder query is sent to the database to retrieve data that is not available in the cache. In order to keep the cache organization optimal, semantic regions will be split and merged dynamically based on the queries posed. Thus, semantic descriptions may change over time. The semantic region is also the unit of replacement in case the cache becomes full. Sophisticated value functions incorporating semantic notions of locality can be used for this task. Additionally, for this purpose, information about the reference history is maintained for each region. [DFJ+96] presents the basic ideas of semantic caching, but it does not provide any implementation details. In the following, we provide these implementation details.

2.2 Our Implementation

In order to implement semantic caching, two problems need to be addressed: The first one is the development of a caching strategy, namely the decision of what data to store in the cache. The second one is the development of a replacement algorithm. This algorithm is used to decide which entries to replace in the cache if the cache does not have enough empty space to add a new region. In the following subsections, we look at both problems.

2.2.1 Caching Strategies

In this section, we describe two caching strategies for mediators that support queries to databases containing hot-spots. The existence of hot-spots implies that the same data items will be accessed frequently, therefore, it makes sense to store these data items in the mediator.

We assume that this approach is used for queries that access a single table. If there is no specific declaration, q_i(i=1,2,3…) is used to denote a general query:

```
SELECT qi_project_attributes
FROM R
WHERE qi_condition(qi_condition_attributes)
```

where q_i is the query name; *q_i_project_attributes* indicates q_i's selection list; *q_i_condition_attributes* indicates the attributes used in q_i's WHERE clause; *q_i_condition(q_i_condition_attributes)* indicates the predicate of q_i, i.e. its WHERE clause; *R* is the relation name.

The general idea is to materialize and store region(s) whenever a query is posed. For each region, two data structures are maintained: one is the "real" data (i.e., the tuples retrieved from the database), the other is the meta-data entry for the region. This contains cache location, semantic description, size, and reference information. When a query is submitted to the mediator, it is first compared with the semantic description of regions that we have cached. Then, the query is split into a remainder query, which will be sent to the server, and a probe query, which will be executed in the local cache. Once query execution is completed, regions in the cachet are reorganized if necessary and the reference history is updated. We have developed two different strategies for building and storing regions. While the first one reduces storage usage, the second one aims at optimizing performance.

Implementation Method 1: Optimizing Storage Usage

Suppose there is no cached data in the mediator at the beginning and query q_i on relation *R* arrives, what data should we retrieve from the database and materialize? In [DFJ+96], complete tuples of the underlying relation are stored. Most other approaches (e.g., [RD2000], [LC98], [GG99]) materialize only part of each tuple. The straightforward method is to materialize exactly the query result. In this case, the semantic description $d(r_i)$ of region r_i is query q_i. However, this is not satisfying, since we want to take advantage of the region(s) to answer future queries. If we create region r_i this way, the region can be used only for a query identical to query q_i. However, if the incoming query q_j is not identical to q_i, region r_i can not be used for answering q_j, even if the region contains the result or part of the result of q_j. Consider as an example the following queries q_i and q_j on the relation *Movie(title, year, length, type, studioName)*. q_i has been materialized as region r_i[1].

```
qi: SELECT title, type
    FROM movie
    WHERE year > 1995
```

$d(r_i)$: : <q_i>

```
qj: SELECT title, type
    FROM movie
    WHERE year > 1997
```

Obviously, the result of q_j is contained in r_i. However, the only columns that we stored for q_i are its projection attributes, that is, TITLE and TYPE. We lose information about the condition attribute, the column YEAR. When query q_j comes, we cannot use region r_i to answer it.

To solve this problem, when generating a region for a query, we do not only store the projection attributes, but also the condition attributes in the semantic region. For example, the semantic description of q_i's region is:

```
d(ri):SELECT             qi_project_attributes             ∪
qi_condition_attributes ∪ ROWID
  FROM R
  WHERE qi_condition(qi_condition_attributes)
```

Note that we store an extra column, ROWID, in the region, which will be used for region splitting and merging. This is an artificial primary key for a tuple in the scope of the whole database.

---

[1] We use <*q*> as an abbreviation for query *q*.

For simplicity, in what follows, we use "q_i_*all_attributes*" to denote "q_i_*project_attributes*$\cup q_i$_*condition_attributes*", and "q_i_*condition()*" to denote "q_i_*condition*(q_i_*condition_attributes*)".

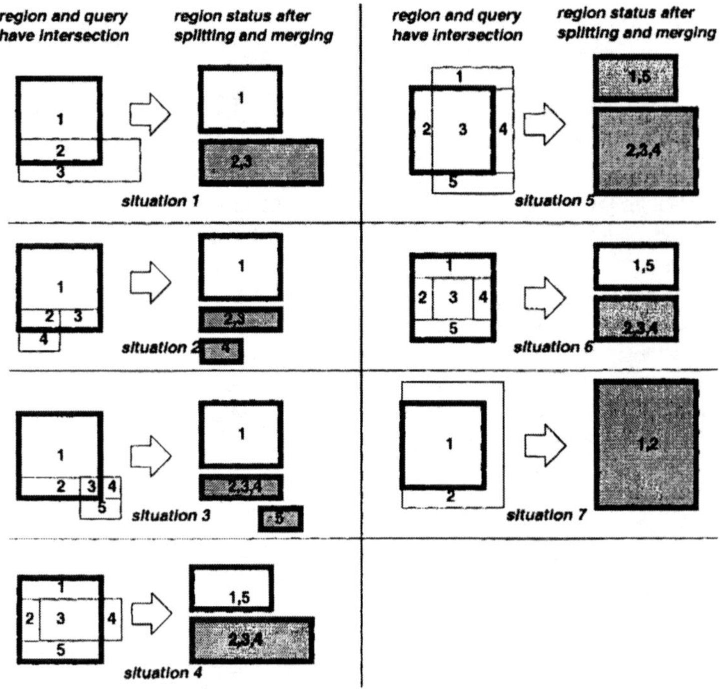

Fig. 1. Region Splitting and Merging

As described above, when a query is submitted to the mediator, we compare its semantic description with that of all the cached regions. Then we can decide how they intersect and generate the probe query and remainder query and retrieve the necessary data from the remote database. Finally, in order to maintain a well-organized cache, if the query results and an existing region overlap, the regions need to be split and merged.

In Figure 1, we show all seven possible situations of overlap between a region and a new query[2]. For each situation in the figure, the left side indicates how the query intersects with a cached region; the right side indicates how the region is split and merged. The boxes in Figure 1 represent relations with rows (the horizontal) representing tuples and columns (the vertical) representing attributes: the ones with bold lines represent cached regions, the ones with thin lines represent query results. We also add some dashed lines to mark the fragments of a region. These fragments are numbered from 1 to 5. The shadowed boxes indicate the region whose reference information is updated after splitting and merging operations. The exact way for

[2] It is also possible that a query overlaps with more than one region. Extending the approaches to deal with this case is straightforward.

splitting and merging the regions, as well as how the query execution is performed, depends on the type of overlap.

Consider as an example Situation 1. Suppose the semantic description for region r_i is q_i and the semantic description for the new query is q_j. From the figure, we can see that q_i and q_j meet the following condition:

(q_i_all_attributes) $\subseteq$ *(q_j_all_attributes)*

However, it is not necessary that the following condition be satisfied:

q_j_condition_attributes $\subseteq$ *(q_i_all_attributes)*

If it is met, however, we can execute the probe query pq_j and the remainder queries rq_{j1} and rq_{j2} shown in Figure 2 in parallel, which will shorten the response time.

Probe query for q_j:

```
Pqj:
        SELECT *
        FROM ri
        WHERE qj_condition()
```

Remainder queries for q_j, (*R* is the corresponding table in the database)

```
Rqj1:
    SELECT(qj_all_attributes-qi_all_attributes, ROWID
    FROM R
    WHERE qi_condition() ∩ qj_condition()

Rqj2:
    SELECT qj_all_attributes, ROWID
    FROM R
  WHERE ¬qi_condition() ∩ qj_condition()
```

Fig. 2. Example Probe and Remainder Queries

After we get all the necessary data from the database, we split and merge the region as necessary using the relational operations INSERT and DELETE. We will also update the semantic description and reference history for the changed regions. The original semantic description of r_i was:

```
SELECT qi_all_attributes, ROWID
FROM R
WHERE qi_condition()
```

The updated semantic description of r_i is:

```
SELECT qi_all_attributes, ROWID
FROM R
WHERE qi_condition()∩¬qj_condition()
```

The semantic description of the newly created region is the query q_j.

Let us now consider the second variant of Situation 1, in which the condition q_j*_condition_attributes* ⊆ (q_i*_all _attributes)* is not met. In this case, we cannot execute the probe query until we receive the result of the remainder query from the remote database. Once we do, we execute similar operations of splitting and merging.

After performing the splitting and merging operations, the reference information of each new region should be updated. For the regions that contain (part of) the result of the new query, we update the reference information; these regions are shown in Figure 1 by shadowed boxes. For the regions that do not contain any result of the new query, we keep the reference information unchanged. The reference information is maintained for region replacement, which will be analyzed in detail in Section 2.2.

Implementation Method 2: Optimizing Performance

The method described above minimizes storage usage. The drawback of this approach is that for each relation, a number of differently structured regions may exist, which makes region splitting and merging complicated. We have thus developed a second strategy that achieves uniform regions by storing complete tuples in the semantic region. While this clearly increases storage usage, the advantage is an improved performance due to easier region splitting and merging.

For example, suppose that the mediator receives a query q_i on relation *R*. If this is the first time that the mediator receives a query on relation *R*, the mediator will initialize the region space for it. If, however, there has been such a table in the cache already, the mediator will add the tuples to it directly. After we add the tuples to the cache table, we will create/update the meta-data entry for this region. The region is only a conceptual unit in this strategy: all regions from the same relation are stored together in a single cache table. The only way to distinguish them is to reference their semantic descriptions. For this strategy, we only record the condition of a query as its semantic description. We do not have to record the projection information.

When a new query is submitted to the mediator, it is divided into probe query(s) and remainder query(s) as with the first strategy. However, for this strategy (as opposed to the previous one) the splitting and merging operation is simple, as we maintain only one cache table for all the regions that come from the same relation. Suppose that a new query q_j is asked. To generate the probe query and the remainder query, we will analyze the region whose semantic description is q_i.

The probe query (or its condition) should be: q_i*_condition()* ∩ q_j*_condition()*, or just q_i*_condition()* which will be applied to region of q_i. The remainder query should be: ¬q_i*_condition()* ∩ q_j*_condition()*.

After we get the tuples from the database, we insert them into the corresponding cache table. We add a new meta-data entry for q_j whose semantic description is the same as q_j; and we update the semantic description for region q_i to q_i*_condition()* ∩ ¬q_j*_condition()*.

Note that if the condition q_i*_condition_attributes* ⊆ q_j*_condition_attributes* is met, we may possibly determine that the region can answer the query completely. In this case, we do not have to send a query to the database. We just have to update the semantic descriptions as explained above.

2.3 Replacement Issues

Up to now, we have dealt with adding entries to the cache. When the cache size is exceeded, a replacement policy needs to be used to determine which entries to remove. [DFJ+96] suggests that "a semantic description of cached data enables the use of sophisticated value functions that incorporate semantic notions of locality". However, [DFJ+96] does not give a detailed general solution to this issue[3]. [SSV96] provides a cache replacement algorithm called LNC-RA (Least Normalized Cost Replacement / Admission) based on a profit model. The algorithm uses the following statistics for each retrieved set RS_i corresponding to a query q_i:

$$profit(RS_i) = \frac{\lambda_i \cdot C_i}{S_i}$$

where

- λ_i: average rate of reference to query q_i.
- S_i: size of the set retrieved by query q_i.
- C_i: cost of execution of query q_i.

If a new query (or data set) RS_i is submitted the result size of which is bigger than the empty space available in the cache, LNC-RA will scan the cache to find all cached data sets whose profit is less than that of the current query. If the total size of all such data sets is greater than that of the new query, region replacement will happen.

There are several problems with the LNC-RA algorithm. In [SSV96], λ_i is defined as: $\lambda_i = K/(t - t_K)$. K is the size of sliding window; t is current time and t_K is the time of the K-th reference. However, for a newly retrieved region, we cannot calculate the value of λ, because the denominator "t - t_l" is equal to zero. Another problem of LNC-RA, is that LNC-RA tends to evict newly retrieved data sets first. This is because it first considers all retrieved sets having just one reference in their profit order, then the ones with two references, etc. Since newly retrieved data sets always have fewer reference times (which means smaller value of λ and profit), this strategy will lead to "thresh" in cache: new data sets are admitted then evicted fast.

In order to prevent this phenomenon, we should gather enough reference information for a new region before it is evicted. We have therefore developed a Profit-base Replacement algorithm with Aging Counter (PRAG). For each region or retrieved set RS_i, the profit of it is still equal to $(\lambda_i \bullet C_i) / S_i$ [SSV96]. However, we introduce an "aging counter" strategy to solve the problems mentioned above. For each region, we assign an "aging counter". The principles of the aging counter are as follows: Each time a region is admitted, its aging counter is set to an initial value[4]. A region cannot be evicted unless its aging counter is equal to zero. When there is not enough space in the cache, we test each region in the cache and decrease its aging counter by one. When a region is referenced, its aging counter will be reset to the initial value.

---

[3] However, [DFJ+96] talks about a Manhattan Distance function. This approach particularly suits mobile navigation applications where geographic proximity is a suitable means to express semantic closeness.

[4] See Section 3 for a discussion on how to determine this initial value.

```
CreateRegion(r)
  Calculate r.profit;
  r.agingCounter = PredefinedAgingTimes;
UpdateRegion(r)
  Recalculate r.profit;
  r.agingCounter = PredefinedAgingTimes; //Reset
ReplaceRegion(r)
  freeSpace=0;
  V=Ø;
  for( each region ri in cache){
     if( ri.agingCounter <= 0){
        V= V ∪ {ri};
        freeSpace=freeSpace + sizeof(ri);
     }else
     ri.agingCounter = ri.agingCounter - 1;
  }
  if ( freeSpace > = sizeof(r) ){
     evict n regions in V with least profit such
                                           that
```

$$\sum_{j=1}^{n} sizeof(r_j) >= sizeof(r);$$

```
     admit r in cache;
   }
```

Fig. 3. PRAG algorithm

The aging counter has two functions. The first function is the "aging function." If a region has not been referenced recently, its aging counter will decrease gradually. When it decreases to zero, the region is ready to be replaced. The second function is that the aging counter allows a new region to stay in the cache for a period of time during which the new region can get the necessary reference information. This overcomes the thresh problem. The "zero denominator" problem is solved also, since we do not use any value that could be zero as denominator. The algorithm is shown in Figure 3.

3 Simulation Results

We have performed extensive experiments to compare the performance of the PRAG replacement algorithm with other commonly used algorithms. In particular, we examine the performance of three algorithms, i.e. LRU (Least Recently Used), MRU (Most Recently Used) and PRAG, on different types of queries. The performance is in inverse proportion to the response time. We use the performance of the LRU algorithm as the measurement unit, that is, we always consider its performance as 1. The measurement of MRU and PRAG is represented by the ratio of their performance to that of LRU. We use three types of query sets with different patterns:

1) "very hot" query set in which 99% of queries are within 1% of all the tuples;
2) "hot" query set in which 90% of queries are within 10% of all the tuples;
3) random query set in which the queries are random.

For each type of query set, we test a size of 1000, 2000, 3000, 4000, and 5000 queries respectively. We use a simulation environment to simulate the database, the mediator and the network. The parameters for the simulation environment are:

- the size of the database is 2MB;
- the number of relations is 10;
- the total number of tuples is about 16000;
- for each attribute, the values are distributed evenly within its domain;
- the transmission speed of the network is 40KBPS
- the transmission delay of the network is 0.4s;
- the transmission speed of the disk is 40MBPS;
- the transmission delay of the disk is 1ms;
- the size of each cache block is 128 bytes.

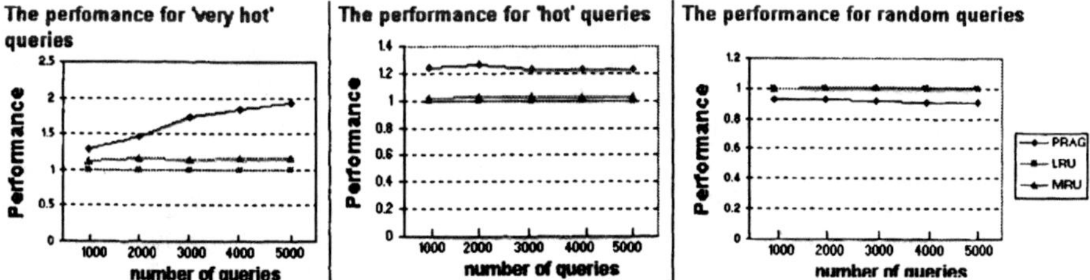

Fig. 4. Performance comparison for different types of the query set

In Figure 4, the X-axis denotes the size of the query set and the Y-axis denotes the performance. We use a cache with a size of 192KB to perform this test. The LRU and MRU algorithm show almost the same performance for each type of the query sets; however, the PRAG algorithm shows a different behavior. In Figure 4a, the PRAG algorithm has a much better performance for the "very hot" query set than LRU and MRU. What is more, the larger the query set is, the better the performance of PRAG is compared with that of LRU and MRU. This is due to the property of the "very hot" query set, i.e., 99% of queries are within 1% of all tuples. After a certain amount of queries to warm up the cache, the PRAG algorithm is able to fill the cache with as many hot regions as possible. Non-hot regions, thus, are not likely to be admitted. So, the more referenced the cache is, the higher the benefit gained using PRAG.

For the "hot" query set, which is shown in Figure 4b, we can find that the performance of PRAG is better than LRU and MRU while keeping a stable ratio. This is because there are about 10% random queries whose data scopes would be the whole information source and which cannot be effectively cached. However, because the PRAG algorithm has a better ability to recognize hot regions, its performance stays 25% higher than that of LRU and MRU.

The result in Figure 4c indicates that the performance of the PRAG algorithm will be a little worse than that of LRU and MRU for random query sets. This is because the PRAG algorithm always tries to keep the region having larger profit value in cache. However, for the random case, no query will be more likely to be referenced again soon than other queries. In that case, PRAG may try to keep a region with high profit value (which it recognized as hot region) for a longer time than necessary. LRU and MRU degrade to a FIFO algorithm, which seems to be the best solution for random query sets.

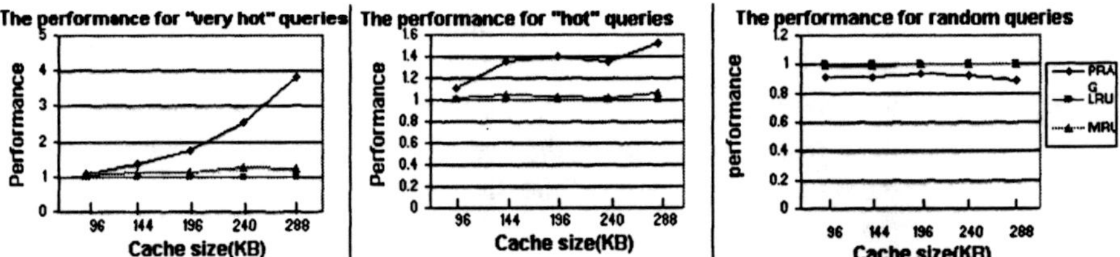

Fig. 5. Performance comparison for different cache sizes

Our next experiment examines the performance of the three algorithms on different cache sizes. In Figure 5, the X-axis denotes the size of the cache and the Y-axis denotes the performance. The size of query set is fixed at 3000 queries. Again, the LRU and MRU algorithm show almost the same performance for each type of the query sets. In Figure 5a, the PRAG algorithm has a much better performance for the "very hot" query set than LRU and MRU and the ratio are getting higher when the cache size increases. The advantage will be more remarkable if the cache size is near or greater than the total size of all hot regions. In that case, the PRAG algorithm will keep almost all hot regions in the cache and is able to answer almost all queries directly without contacting the information source any more. In fact, the performance will be improved for both LRU and MRU; however, the rate of improvement is not as large as for PRAG.

For the "hot" query set (Figure 5b), the ratio of performance for PRAG algorithm increases with the cache size's increasing. When the cache size is large enough, the ratio of performance for PRAG algorithm keeps stable later on.

The explanations for Figure 5c are similar to that of Figure 4c. The ratio of performance for PRAG is insensitive to the cache size.

Another interesting problem is how the initial value of the aging counter affects the performance of the PRAG algorithm. The experimental result is shown in Figure 6. First, we examine the curve corresponding to the "hot" query set. When the initial aging-times is equal to zero, the algorithm degrades to the pure profit algorithm without aging counter. In such a case, a hot region may be evicted at any time. Thus, there is no guarantee that a hot region will stay in the cache for a period of time to gather reference information. With the initial aging-times increasing, the PRAG algorithm is getting smarter and its performance is improved. This is due to the PRAG algorithm obtaining more reference information for regions by which it is able to distinguish hot regions from non-hot regions. However, the aging counter has both positive and negative effect for the PRAG algorithm. On the one hand, it allow hot regions to get enough reference information; on the other hand, the non-hot regions will keep staying in cache before their aging counters decrease to zero, which will affect the performance. If the aging counter is larger than necessary, the negative effect will counteract the positive effect. We can see that the performance curve for "hot" query decreases after the initial aging-times reaches a certain value.

Then, we examine the curve corresponding to "very hot" query set in Figure 6. The performance of PRAG algorithm is improved when the initial aging-times increases from zero. The explanations are similar to the case above. However, the performance is not affected so much as the initial aging-times continues to increase. This is due to the property of the "very hot" query set in which 99% of queries are hot ones. Thus, most regions in the cache are hot regions. Even if the initial aging-times is very large, the few non-hot regions will not take much effect.

We also find that the performance of PRAG is improved for random query set when the initial value of the aging counter increases. This can be explained as follows: if the initial value of the aging counter is zero, the replacement policy will be based on profit only. Regions with larger profit value are prone to stay in cache, getting more chance to be reference again, obtaining larger profit value and keeping staying in the cache. Thus, the "valid" cache size decreases and the utilization of cache space is low. When the initial value of the aging counter is too small, the situation is similar. With increasing initial value of the aging counter, regions with small profit value get a chance to stay in the cache and regions with large profit value may be replaced if their aging counters decrease to zero. The replacement policy approaches FIFO when the initial value of aging counter is large enough.

Now, we analyze the problem how to find an appropriate initial aging-times for the PRAG algorithm. Our solution is based on the assumption that if a region is referenced more than twice during its aging time, it can be considered a hot region. In other words, the appropriate value for aging times should be the average number of queries between two subsequent references to a certain hot region. The value of the average number can be estimated as:

$$AgingTimes = \frac{HotRegionNumbers}{HotQuery\%}$$

where

$$\begin{aligned}
&HotRegionNumbers \\
&= TotalRegionNumbers \times HotRegion\% \\
&= \frac{DatabaseSize}{AverageRegionSize} \times HotRegion\% \\
&= \frac{DatabaseSize}{CacheSize \,/\, AverageNumberOfRegionsInCache} \times HotRegion\%
\end{aligned}$$

Our experimental results, depicted in Figure 6, support this formula. For a database size of 2 MB, a cache size of 192 KB and 3000 queries, as used in our experiments, the formula suggests an initial aging counter of 47.11 for the hot query set, the experiments show best performance at 45, for the very hot query set the numbers are 14.55 and 15, respectively.

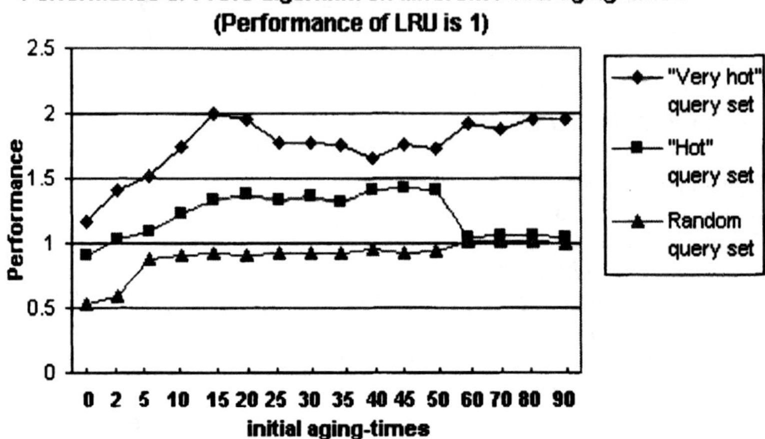

Fig. 6. Performance of PRAG on different initial aging-times

4 Related Work

There are several techniques that use semantic information about the query and cache to improve the efficiency of query evaluation or shorten the response time. [DFJ+96] proposes a semantic model for client-side caching and replacement in a client-server database system. As described in Section 2, it provides some key semantic caching solutions. [DFJ+96] however does not describe any implementation strategies or a general replacement algorithm. In view of this, this paper extends the semantic caching model provided by [DFJ+96] and proposes a PRAG algorithm for replacement issues.

[GG97] and [GG99] extend the SQC (semantic query caching) paradigm by broadening the domain of applications of SQC into heterogeneous database environments and by presenting a logic framework for SQC. Within that framework they consider the various possibilities to answer a query. Possible (overlap) relations between cache and query are studied in [GG99]. However, in contrast to our caching strategy that caches both the projection attributes and condition attributes, its caching strategy only caches the projection attributes, which leads to the ability of utilizing the cache to answering queries being weak.

[GG96] and [GGM96] address the issue of semantic query optimization for bottom-up query evaluation strategies. They focus on the optimization technique of join elimination, and propose a framework that allows for semantic optimization over queries that employ views. We do not consider query optimization in this paper; however, the technology can always be employed to archive efficient query evaluation, which would further decrease the query response time. [KB94] proposes a client side data-caching scheme for relational databases. It focuses on the issue of "cache currency" which deals with the effect of update at the central database on the multiple client caches. The result can also be applied to our semantic caching model when considered in a distributed environment.

[RD2000] studies the issue of semantic caching in a background of mobile computing, it extends the existing research in three ways: formal definitions associated with semantic caching are presented, query processing strategies are investigated, and the performance of the semantic cache model is examined through a detailed simulation study, which shows its effectiveness in mobile computing. Similar to [GG99], its does not consider the strategy of caching both the projection and condition attributes either.

[LC98] and [LC99] provide a semantic caching scheme suitable for web database environments with web sources that have very limited querying. Possible match types and detailed algorithms for comparing the input query with stored semantic views are studied in [LC98]; a seamlessly integrated query translation and capability mapping between the wrappers and web sources in semantic caching is described in [LC99]. It should be further studied whether our semantic caching scheme can be applied to web sources because web sources "have typically weaker querying capabilities than conventional database"[LC99]. However, the replacement algorithm PRAG is a general one and can be applied to the web data sources.

5 Summary and Future Work

Materialization of mediator results is a promising first step in adapting mediator architectures for mobile and wireless applications. In this paper, we present materialization strategies for mediators used to query databases whose query profile shows some hot-spots. For such environments, [DFJ+96] proposes a semantic-region caching. We have extended this work. The main advantages of our approach are optimized methods to define semantic regions in a relational DBMS environment and a profit-based algorithm PRAG for region replacement. Our analysis shows that our caching strategies optimize storage space requirements and performance respectively. Experimental results show that the PRAG algorithm outperforms other popular replacement algorithms in environments with hot or very hot query sets.

Currently, we are implementing both strategies to support our analytical conclusions on performance gains using extensive benchmark results. Also, we are working on strategies to support mediators with join-queries.

References

[CFZ94] Michael J. Carey, Michael J. Franklin, Markos Zaharioudakis: *Fine-grained sharing in page server database system*. In Proc. of ACM-SIGMOD 1994 International Conference on Management of Data, Minneapolis, Minnesota, pages 359-370, May 1994.

[DFJ+96] Shaul Dar, Michael J. Franklin, Björn Thór Jónsson, Divesh Srivastava, Michael Tan: *Semantic Data Caching and Replacement*. In Proc. of: Intl. Conf. on Very Large Databases (VLDB), Bombay, India, pages 330-341, September 1996.

[GG96] Parke Godfrey, Jarek Gryz: *A Framework for Intensional Query Optimization*. In Proc of: Workshop on Deductive Database and Logic Programming, held in conjunction with the Joint International Conference and Symposium on Logic Programming, Bonn, Germany, pages 57-68, September 1996.

[GG97] Parke Godfrey, Jarek Gryz: *Semantic Query Caching for Heterogeneous Databases.* In Proc. of : 9th Intl. Symposium on Methodologies for Intelligent Systems (ISMIS), Zakopane, Poland, June 1996.

[GG99] Parke Godfrey, Jarek Gryz: *Answering Queries by Semantic Caches.* In Proc. of: 10th Intl. Conf. on Database and Expert Systems Applications (DEXA), Florence, Italy, pages 485-498, 1999.

[GGM96] Parke Godfrey, Jarek Gryz, Jack Minker: *Semantic Query Optimization for Bottom-Up Evaluation.* In Proc. of: 9th Intl. Symposium on Methodologies for Intelligent Systems (ISMIS), Zakopane, Poland, pages 561 –571, June 1996.

[KB94] M. Keller, Julie Basu: *A Predicate-based Caching Scheme for Client-Server Database Architectures.* In Proc. of: IEEE Conf. on Parallel and Distributed Information Systems, Austin, Texas, pages 229-238, September 1994.

[LC98] Dongwon Lee, Wesley W. Chu: *Conjunctive Point Predicate-based Semantic Caching for Wrappers in Web Databases.* In Proc of: ACM Intl. Workshop on Web Information and Data Management (WIDM'98), Washington DC, USA, November 1998.

[LC99] Dongwon Lee, Wesley W. Chu: *Semantic Caching via Query Matching for Web Sources.* In Proc. of ACM Conf. on Information and Knowledge Management (CIKM) , Kansas City, MO, pages 77-85, 1999.

[PMK2000] Niki Pissinou, Kia Makki and Birgitta König-Ries: *A Middleware Based Architecture to Support Mobile Users in Heterogeneous Environments.* In: Proc. of: Intl. Workshop on Research Issues in Data Engineering (RIDE), San Diego, CA, 2000.

[RD2000] Qun Ren, Margaret H. Dunham: *Semantic Caching in Mobile Computing.* Preliminary version (submitted). Available at: http://www.seas.smu.edu/~mhd/pubs/00/tkde.ps

[SSV96] Peter Scheuermann, Junho Shim, Radek Vingralek. *WATCHMAN: A Data Warehouse Intelligent Cache Manager.* In Proc. of: Intl. Conf. on Very Large Databases (VLDB), Bombay, India, September 1996.

[Wied92] Gio Wiederhold. *Mediators in the Architecture of Future Information Systems.* IEEE Computer 25(3): 38-49 (1992)

Information Flow Control among Objects in Role-Based Access Control Model

Keiji Izaki, Katsuya Tanaka, and Makoto Takizawa

Dept. of Computers and Systems Engineering
Tokyo Denki University
Email {izaki, katsu, taki}@takilab.k.dendai.ac.jp

Abstract. Various kinds of applications have to be secure in an object-based model. The secure system is required to not only protect objects from illegally manipulated but also prevent illegal information flow among objects. In this paper, we discuss how to resolve illegal information flow among objects in a role-based model. We define safe roles where no illegal information flow occurs. In addition, we discuss how to safely perform transactions with unsafe roles. We discuss an algorithm to check if illegal information flow occurs each time a method is performed.

1 Introduction

Various kinds of object-based systems like object-oriented database systems, JAVA [10] and CORBA [13] are widely used for applications. Object-based systems are composed of multiple objects cooperating to achieve some objectives by passing messages. An object is an encapsulation of data and methods for manipulating the data. Methods are invoked on objects in a nested manner. The object-based system are required to not only protect objects from illegally manipulated but also prevent illegal information flow among objects in the system.

In the access control model [11], an access rule $\langle s, o, t \rangle$ means that a subject s is allowed to manipulate an object o in an access type t. Only access requests which satisfy the access rules are accepted to be performed. However, the *confinement* problem [12] is implied, i.e. illegal information flow occurs among subjects and objects. In the *mandatory lattice-based* model [1,3,16], objects and subjects are classified into security classes. Legal information flow is defined in terms of the *can-flow* relation [3] between classes. Access rules are specified so that only the legal information flow occurs. For example, if a subject s reads an object o, information in o flows to s. Hence, the subject s can read the object o only if a *can-flow* relation from o to s is specified. In the role-based model [6,17,19], a *role* is defined to be a collection of access rights, i.e. pairs of access types and objects, to denote a job function in the enterprise. Subjects are granted roles which show their jobs. In an object-based system, the methods are invoked on objects in a nested manner. The purpose-oriented model [18,20] discusses which methods can invoke another method in the object-based system. In the paper [15], a *message filter* is used to block read and write requests if illegal information flow occurs. The authors [9] discuss what information flow to *possibly*

H.C. Mayr et al. (Eds.): DEXA 2001, LNCS 2113, pp. 299–308, 2001.

occur among objects if subjects issue methods by the authority of the roles in case every method invocation is not nested. Since methods are invoked in the nested manner in the object-based systems, we have to discuss information flow to occur among objects. We define a *safe* role where no illegal information flow occurs by performing any transaction with the role. In addition, we discuss an algorithm to check for each method issued by a transaction if illegal information flow occurs by performing the method. By using the algorithm, some methods issued by a transaction can be performed even if the transaction is in a session with an unsafe role. Data flowing from an object o_1 to o_2 can belong to o_2 some time after the data flows. We discuss how to manage timed information flow.

In section 2, we classify methods from information flow point of view. In section 3, we discuss information flow to occur in a nested invocation. In section 4, we discuss how to resolve illegal information flow.

2 Object-Based Systems

An object-based system is composed of objects which are encapsulations of data and methods. A transaction invokes a method by sending a request message to an object. The method is performed on the object and then the response is sent back to the transaction. During the computation of the method, other methods might be invoked. Thus, methods are invoked in a nested manner.

Each subject plays a *role* in an organization. In the role-based model [6,17,19], a *role* is modeled to be a set of *access rights*. An access right $\langle o, t\rangle$ means that t can be performed on the object o. A subject s is granted a role which shows its job function in an enterprise. This means that the subject s can perform a method t on an object o if $\langle o, t\rangle \in r$. If a subject s is in a *session* with r, s can issue methods in r. Each subject can be in a session with at most one role.

Each method t on an object o is characterized by the following parameters:

1. *Input type* $= I$ if the method t has input data in the parameter, else N.
2. *Manipulation type* $= M$ if the object o is changed by t, else N.
3. *Derivation type* $= D$ if data is derived from o by t, else N.
4. *Output type* $= O$ if data is returned to the invoker of t, else N.

Each method t of an object o is characterized by a *method type* $mtype(t)$ $= \alpha_1\alpha_2\alpha_3\alpha_4$, where input $\alpha_1 \in \{I, N\}$, manipulation $\alpha_2 \in \{M, N\}$, derivation $\alpha_3 \in \{D, N\}$, and output $\alpha_4 \in \{O, N\}$. For example, a method class "$IMNN$" shows a method which carries data in the parameters to an object and changes the state of the object. Here, N is omitted in the method type. For example, "IM" shows $IMNN$. Especially, "N" shows a type $NNNN$. Let MC be a set $\{IMDO, IDO, IMO, IO, IMD, ID, IM, I, MDO, DO, MO, O, MD, D, M, N\}$ of sixteen possible method types. A *counter* object c supports methods *display*(*dsp*), *increment*(*inc*), and *decrement*(*dec*). $mtype(dsp) = DO$ and $mtype(inc) = mtype(dec) = IMD$. A notation "$\beta_1, ..., \beta_k \in mtype(t)$" ($k \leq 4$) shows $mtype(t) = \alpha_1\alpha_2\alpha_3\alpha_4$ and $\beta_i \in \{\alpha_1, \alpha_2, \alpha_3, \alpha_4\}$ ($i \leq k$). For example, $I \in mtype(inc)$ and $ID \in mtype(dec)$. In the object-based systems, objects are created and dropped. $IM \in mtype(created)$ and $N \in mtype(drop)$. The method type $mtype(t)$ is specified for each method t by the owner of the object.

We assume that each subject does not have any persistent storage. That is, the subject does not keep in record data obtained from objects. The subject issues one or more than one method to objects. A sequence of methods issued by the subject is referred to as a *transaction*, which is a unit of work. Each *transaction* T can be in a session with only one role r. A transaction has a temporary memory. Data which the transaction derives from objects may be stored in the temporary memory. On completion of the transaction, the memory is released. Any transaction does not share data with the other transactions. In this paper, objects show persistent objects.

Suppose T with a role r invokes a method t_1 on an object o_1 since $\langle o_1, t_1 \rangle \in r$. Suppose t_1 invokes another method t_2 on an object o_2. Here, we assume $\langle o_2, t_2 \rangle \in r$. That is, $\langle o, t \rangle \in r$ for every method t invoked on an object o in T.

3 Nested Invocation

3.1 Invocation Tree

Suppose a transaction T invokes a method t_1 on an object o_1 and a method t_2 on an object o_2. Then, t_1 invokes a method t_3 on an object o_3. The invocations of methods are represented in a tree form named *invocation tree* as shown in Figure 1. Each node $\langle o, t \rangle$ shows a method t invoked on an object o in the transaction T. A dotted directed edge from a parent to a child shows that the parent invokes the child. A notation "$\langle o_1, t_1 \rangle \vdash_T \langle o_2, t_2 \rangle$" means that a method t_1 on an object o_1 invokes t_2 on o_2 in the transaction T. A node $\langle \_, T \rangle$ shows a root of invocation tree of T. Here, $mtype(T)$ is N according to the assumption.

If a method serially invokes multiple methods, the left-to-right order of nodes shows an invocation sequence of methods, i.e. tree is ordered. Suppose $\langle o_1, t_1 \rangle \vdash_T \langle o_2, t_2 \rangle$ and $\langle o_1, t_1 \rangle \vdash_T \langle o_3, t_3 \rangle$ in an invocation tree of a transaction T. If t_1 invokes t_2 before t_3, $\langle o_2, t_2 \rangle$ *precedes* $\langle o_3, t_3 \rangle$ ($\langle o_2, t_2 \rangle \prec_T \langle o_3, t_3 \rangle$). In addition, $\langle o_4, t_4 \rangle \prec_T \langle o_3, t_3 \rangle$ if $\langle o_2, t_2 \rangle \vdash_T \langle o_4, t_4 \rangle$. $\langle o_2, t_2 \rangle \prec_T \langle o_4, t_4 \rangle$ if $\langle o_3, t_3 \rangle \vdash_T \langle o_4, t_4 \rangle$. The relation "$\prec_T$" is transitive. T invokes t_1 before t_2 as shown in Figure 1. Here, $\langle o_1, t_1 \rangle \prec_T \langle o_2, t_2 \rangle$ and $\langle o_3, t_3 \rangle \prec_T \langle o_2, t_2 \rangle$.

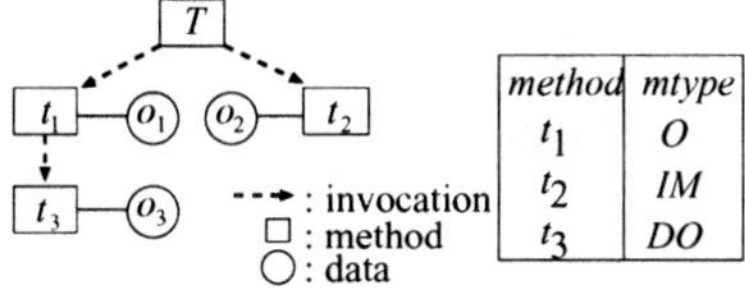

method	mtype
t_1	O
t_2	IM
t_3	DO

Fig. 1. Invocation tree.

3.2 Information Flow

Suppose $mtype(t_3) = DO$, $mtype(t_2) = IM$, and $mtype(t_1) = O$ in Figure 1. In a transaction T, data is derived from an object o_3 through the method t_3. The data is forwarded to t_1 as the response of t_3. The data is brought to t_2 as the input parameter. and is stored into o_2 through t_2. Thus, the information in o_3 is brought to o_2. A straight arc indicates the information flow in Figure 2. This example shows that information flow among objects may occur in a nested invocation.

[Definition] Suppose a pair of methods t_1 and t_2 on objects o_1 and o_2, respectively, are invoked in a transaction T.

1. Information *passes down* from $\langle o_1, t_1\rangle$ to $\langle o_2, t_2\rangle$ in T ($\langle o_1, t_1\rangle \overset{T}{\rightharpoondown} \langle o_2, t_2\rangle$) iff t_1 invokes t_2 ($\langle o_1, t_1\rangle \vdash_T \langle o_2, t_2\rangle$) and $I \in mtype(t_2)$, or $\langle o_1, t_1\rangle \overset{T}{\rightharpoondown} \langle o_3, t_3\rangle \overset{T}{\rightharpoondown} \langle o_2, t_2\rangle$ for some $\langle o_3, t_3\rangle$ in T.
2. Information *passes up* from $\langle o_1, t_1\rangle$ to $\langle o_2, t_2\rangle$ in T ($\langle o_1, t_1\rangle \overset{T}{\rightharpoonup} \langle o_2, t_2\rangle$) iff $\langle o_2, t_2\rangle \vdash_T \langle o_1, t_1\rangle$ and $O \in mtype(t_2)$, or $\langle o_1, t_1\rangle \overset{T}{\rightharpoonup} \langle o_3, t_3\rangle \overset{T}{\rightharpoonup} \langle o_2, t_2\rangle$ for some $\langle o_3, t_3\rangle$ in T. □

[Definition] Information *passes* from $\langle o_1, t_1\rangle$ to $\langle o_2, t_2\rangle$ in an ordered transaction T ($\langle o_1, t_1\rangle \underset{O}{\overset{T}{\rightarrow}} \langle o_2, t_2\rangle$) iff $\langle o_1, t_1\rangle \overset{T}{\rightharpoondown} \langle o_2, t_2\rangle$, $\langle o_1, t_1\rangle \overset{T}{\rightharpoonup} \langle o_2, t_2\rangle$, $\langle o_1, t_1\rangle \overset{T}{\rightharpoondown} \langle o_3, t_3\rangle \overset{T}{\rightharpoonup} \langle o_2, t_2\rangle$ and $\langle o_1, t_1\rangle \prec_T \langle o_2, t_2\rangle$, or $\langle o_1, t_1\rangle \underset{O}{\overset{T}{\rightarrow}} \langle o_3, t_3\rangle \underset{O}{\overset{T}{\rightarrow}} \langle o_2, t_2\rangle$ for some $\langle o_3, t_3\rangle$ in T. □

[Definition] Information *passes* from $\langle o_1, t_1\rangle$ to $\langle o_2, t_2\rangle$ in an unordered transaction T ($\langle o_1, t_1\rangle \underset{U}{\overset{T}{\rightarrow}} \langle o_2, t_2\rangle$) iff $\langle o_1, t_1\rangle \overset{T}{\rightharpoondown} \langle o_2, t_2\rangle$, $\langle o_1, t_1\rangle \overset{T}{\rightharpoonup} \langle o_2, t_2\rangle$, or $\langle o_1, t_1\rangle \underset{U}{\overset{T}{\rightarrow}} \langle o_3, t_3\rangle \underset{U}{\overset{T}{\rightarrow}} \langle o_2, t_2\rangle$ for some $\langle o_3, t_3\rangle$ in T. □

Suppose t_1 is invoked before t_2, i.e. $\langle o_1, t_1\rangle \prec_T \langle o_2, t_2\rangle$ in Figure 2. $\langle o_3, t_3\rangle \overset{T}{\rightharpoonup} \langle o_1, t_1\rangle \overset{T}{\rightharpoonup} \langle \_, T\rangle \overset{T}{\rightharpoondown} \langle o_2, t_2\rangle$. $\langle o_1, t_1\rangle \underset{O}{\overset{T}{\not\rightarrow}} \langle o_2, t_2\rangle$ if $\langle o_2, t_2\rangle \prec_T \langle o_1, t_1\rangle$. However, $\langle o_1, t_1\rangle \underset{U}{\overset{T}{\rightarrow}} \langle o_2, t_2\rangle$. A relation "$\overset{T}{\rightarrow}$" shows "$\underset{O}{\overset{T}{\rightarrow}}$" or "$\underset{U}{\overset{T}{\rightarrow}}$". A notation "$o_1 \overset{T}{\rightarrow} o_2$" shows "$\langle o_1, t_1\rangle \overset{T}{\rightarrow} \langle o_2, t_2\rangle$" for some methods t_1 and t_2. Here, $T \overset{T}{\rightarrow} o$ and $o \overset{T}{\rightarrow} T$ indicate $\langle \_, T\rangle \overset{T}{\rightarrow} \langle o, t\rangle$ and $\langle o, t\rangle \overset{T}{\rightarrow} \langle \_, T\rangle$, respectively. According to the definitions, $o_1 \underset{U}{\overset{T}{\rightarrow}} o_2$ if $o_1 \underset{O}{\overset{T}{\rightarrow}} o_2$.

[Definition] $\langle o_1, t_1\rangle$ *flows into* $\langle o_2, t_2\rangle$ in a transaction T ($\langle o_1, t_1\rangle \overset{T}{\Rightarrow} \langle o_2, t_2\rangle$) iff $\langle o_1, t_1\rangle \overset{T}{\rightarrow} \langle o_2, t_2\rangle$, $D \in mtype(t_1)$, and $M \in mtype(t_2)$. □

In Figure 2, $\langle o_3, t_3\rangle \overset{T}{\Rightarrow} \langle o_2, t_2\rangle$ where $\langle o_3, t_3\rangle$ is a *source* and $\langle o_2, t_2\rangle$ is a *sink*. Here, data in o_3 flows into o_2. "$\langle o_1, t_1\rangle \overset{T}{\Rightarrow} \langle o_2, t_2\rangle$" can be abbreviated as $o_1 \overset{T}{\Rightarrow} o_2$. $T \overset{T}{\Rightarrow} o$ if $T \overset{T}{\rightarrow} o$ and o is a sink. $o \overset{T}{\Rightarrow} T$ if $o \overset{T}{\rightarrow} T$ and o is a source. $o_1 \overset{r}{\Rightarrow} o_2$ for a role r iff $o_1 \overset{T}{\Rightarrow} o_2$ for some transaction T with r.

[Definition] Information in o_i *flows into* o_j ($o_i \Rightarrow o_j$) iff $o_i \overset{r}{\Rightarrow} o_j$ for some role r and $o_i \Rightarrow o_k \Rightarrow o_j$ for some object o_k. □

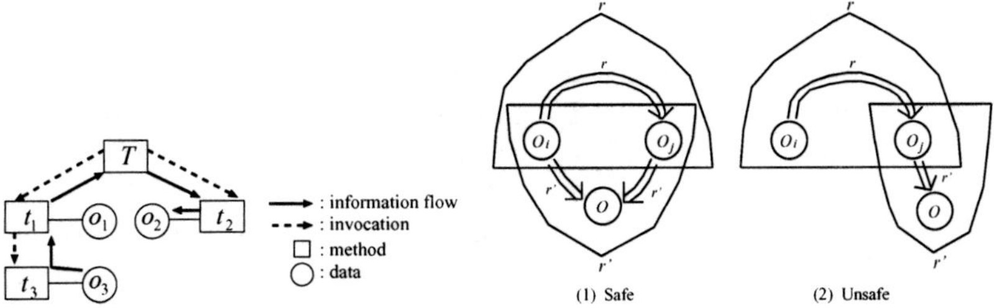

Fig. 2. Information flow.

Fig. 3. Safeness.

$o_i \Rightarrow o_j$ is *primitive* for a role r if $o_i \Rightarrow o_j$. $o_i \Rightarrow o_j$ is *transitive* for a role r iff $o_i \stackrel{r}{\Rightarrow} o_j$ is not primitive for r, i.e. $o_i \Rightarrow o_k \stackrel{r}{\Rightarrow} o_j$ but $o_i \stackrel{r}{\not\Rightarrow} o_j$ for some o_k. If $o_i \Rightarrow o_j$ is transitive for r, a transaction T with r may get data in o_i through o_j even if T is not allowed to get data from o_i.

[Definition] "$o_i \Rightarrow o_j$" is *illegal* iff $o_i \Rightarrow o_j$ is transitive for some role r. □

[Definition] A role r *threatens* another role r_1 iff for some objects o_i, o_j, and o, $o_i \stackrel{r_1}{\Rightarrow} o_j \stackrel{r}{\Rightarrow} o$ and $o_i \Rightarrow o$ is transitive for r. □

Suppose information in o_i might flow into an object o_j ($o_i \stackrel{r_1}{\Rightarrow} o_j$) by performing a transaction T_1 with a role r_1. Even if a transaction T_2 is not granted a role to derive data from o_i, T_2 can get data in o_i from o_j if T_2 is granted a role r to derive data from o_j. Thus, if there is another role r threatening a role r_1, illegal information flow might occur if some transaction with r is performed.

[Definition] "$o_i \stackrel{r}{\Rightarrow} o_j$" is *safe* for a role r iff r is not threatened by any role. □

Figure 3 shows a system including a pair of roles r and r' where $o_i \stackrel{r}{\Rightarrow} o_j$. For another role r', $o_i \stackrel{r'}{\Rightarrow} o$ and $o_j \stackrel{r'}{\Rightarrow} o$ in Figure 3 (1). Since r' does not threaten r, $o_i \stackrel{r}{\Rightarrow} o_j$ is safe. In Figure 3 (2), $o_j \stackrel{r'}{\Rightarrow} o$ but $o_i \stackrel{r'}{\not\Rightarrow} o$. However, T is not allowed to derive data from o_i. Hence, r' threatens r and $o_i \stackrel{r}{\Rightarrow} o_j$ is not safe. $o_i \Rightarrow o$ is illegal. This is a *confinement* problem on roles. It is noted that o may show a transaction. For example, the transaction T manipulates o_j through a *DO* method t. Here, $o_i \stackrel{r'}{\Rightarrow} T$.

[Definition] A role r is *safe* iff r neither threatens any role nor is threatened by any role. □

A transaction is *safe* iff the transaction is in a session with a *safe* role. An *unsafe* transaction is in a session with an *unsafe* role.

[Theorem] If every transaction is safe, no illegal information flow occurs. □

That is, no illegal information flow occurs if every role is safe. The paper [9] discusses an algorithm to check whether or not illegal information flow possibly occurs if the method is performed.

3.3 Invocation Models

Suppose a transaction T is in a session with a role r. It is not easy to make clear what transactions exist for each role and how each transaction invokes methods. Hence, we first discuss a basic (B) model where there is one transaction T_r which is in a session with a role r and invokes all the methods in r, i.e. $\langle\_, T_r\rangle \vdash_r \langle o, t\rangle$ for every $\langle o, t\rangle$ in the role r. An invocation tree of T_r is an unordered, two-level tree. Here, $\langle\_, T_r\rangle \xrightarrow{r} \langle o, t\rangle$ if $\langle o, t\rangle \in r$ and $I \in mtype(t)$ according to the definition of $\rightarrow$. $\langle o, t\rangle \xrightarrow{r} \langle\_, T\rangle$ if $\langle o, t\rangle \in r$ and $o \in mtype(t)$. $\xrightarrow{r}$ is transitive. $\langle o, t\rangle \stackrel{r}{\Rightarrow} \langle\_, T\rangle$ iff $\langle o, t\rangle \xrightarrow{r} \langle\_, T_r\rangle$ and $D \in mtype(t)$. $\langle\_, T_r\rangle \stackrel{r}{\Rightarrow} \langle o, t\rangle$ iff $\langle\_, T_r\rangle \xrightarrow{r} \langle o, t\rangle$ and $M \in mtype(t)$. $\langle o_1, t_1\rangle \stackrel{r}{\Rightarrow} \langle o_2, t_2\rangle$ iff $\langle o_1, t_1\rangle \xrightarrow{r} \langle\_, T_r\rangle$ and $\langle\_, T_r\rangle \xrightarrow{r} \langle o_2, t_2\rangle$. Here, $r \stackrel{r}{\Rightarrow} o$ and $o \stackrel{r}{\Rightarrow} r$ show "$\langle\_, T_r\rangle \stackrel{r}{\Rightarrow} \langle o, t\rangle$" and "$\langle o, t\rangle \stackrel{r}{\Rightarrow} \langle\_, T_r\rangle$" for some method t, respectively. "$\underset{B}{\stackrel{r}{\Rightarrow}}$" shows "$\stackrel{r}{\Rightarrow}$" in the B model.

Next, suppose a collection of transactions are *a priori* defined. $Tr(r)$ is a set of transactions which are in sessions with r. Let $N(T)$ be a set $\{\langle o, t\rangle \mid t$ is invoked on o in a transaction $T\}$ and $Al(r)$ be $\{\langle o, t\rangle \mid \langle o, t\rangle \in N(T)$ for every transaction T in $Tr(r)\}$ ($\subseteq r$). Suppose two transactions T_1 and T_2 are in sessions with a role r. T_1 invokes a method t_1 on an object o_1. T_2 invokes a method t_2 on an object o_2 and then t_2 invokes a method t_3 on an object o_3 and t_4 on o_4. Here, $Tr(r) = \{T_1, T_2\}$. $N(T_1) = \{\langle o_1, t_1\rangle\}$, and $N(T_2) = \{\langle o_2, t_2\rangle, \langle o_3, t_3\rangle, \langle o_4, t_4\rangle\}$. $Al(r) = N(T_1) \cup N(T_2)$. There are two cases: invocation sequence of methods is *a priori* fixed or not, i.e. invocation tree of each transaction is ordered(O) or unordered(U). In the basic (B) model, T_r invokes t_1 and t_2. Since $o_1 \stackrel{r}{\Rightarrow} T_r \stackrel{r}{\Rightarrow} o_2 \stackrel{r}{\Rightarrow} o_3$, $o_1 \stackrel{r}{\Rightarrow} o_3$, i.e. information in o_1 possibly flows to o_2. In the unordered (U) and ordered (O) models, there is no information flow between o_1 and o_3, because o_1 and o_3 are manipulated by T_1 and T_2, respectively. If the transactions are not ordered, $o_4 \stackrel{r}{\Rightarrow} o_3$ as shown in Figure 4. On the other hand, if the transactions are ordered, o_4 is manipulated before o_3. Hence, $o_4 \stackrel{r}{\not\Rightarrow} o_3$. $o_i \underset{O}{\stackrel{r}{\Rightarrow}} o_j$ if $o_i \underset{U}{\stackrel{r}{\Rightarrow}} o_j$. $o_i \underset{U}{\stackrel{r}{\Rightarrow}} o_j$ if $o_i \underset{B}{\stackrel{r}{\Rightarrow}} o_j$.

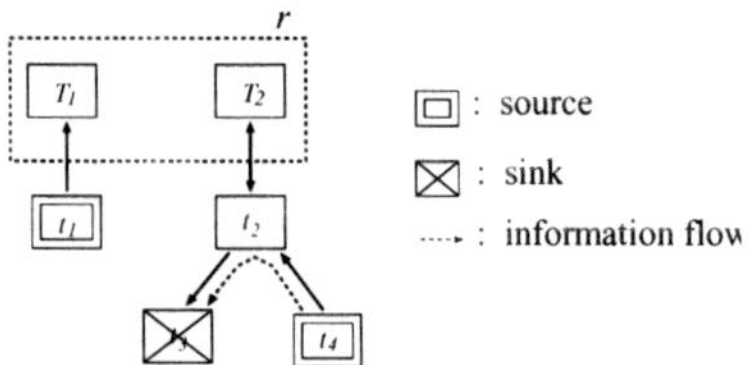

Fig. 4. Invocation trees.

4 Resolution of Illegal Information Flow

4.1 Flow Graph

Every safe transaction is allowed to be performed because no illegal information flow occurs. As discussed in Figure 4, $o_1 \stackrel{r}{\Rightarrow} o_3$ does not hold in the U and O models even if $o_1 \stackrel{r}{\Rightarrow} o_3$ in the B model. $o_1 \stackrel{r}{\Rightarrow} o_3$ in the U model but $o_1 \stackrel{r}{\Rightarrow} o_3$ does not hold in the O model. This means it depends on an invocation sequence of methods whether or not illegal information flow occurs. The paper [9] discusses how to decide if a role is safe and an algorithm for each method issued by an unsafe transaction to check whether or not illegal information flow *possibly* occurs if the method is performed. However, it is not easy, possibly impossible to decide whether or not each role is safe if roles include large number of objects and roles are dynamically created and dropped. In this paper, we discuss an algorithm to check whether or not illegal information flow *necessarily* occurs if each method issued by every transaction is performed. A system maintains a following directed *flow graph* G.

[Flow graph]

1. Each node in G shows an object in the system. Here, each transaction is also an object. If an object is created, a node for the object is added in G. Initially, G includes no edge.
2. A directed edge $o_1 \rightarrow_\tau o_2$ is created if $o_i \stackrel{T}{\Rightarrow} o_j$ by performing a transaction T of a role r at time τ. If $o_1 \rightarrow_{\tau_1} o_2$ already exists in G, $o_1 \rightarrow_{\tau_1} o_2$ is changed to $o_1 \rightarrow_\tau o_2$ if $\tau_1 < \tau$.
3. For each object o_3 such that $o_3 \rightarrow_{\tau_1} o_1 \rightarrow_\tau o_2$ in G,
   3.1 $o_3 \rightarrow_\tau o_2$ no edge from o_3 to o_2 in G and $\tau_2 < \tau$. go to Step 2.
   3.2 $o_3 \rightarrow_{\tau_2} o_2$ if $o_3 \rightarrow_{\tau_3} o_2$ is already in G and $\tau_2 > \tau_3$. □

Figure 5 shows a flow graph G including four objects o_1, o_2, o_3, and o_4. First, suppose $o_1 \rightarrow_4 o_2$ and $o_2 \rightarrow_3 o_4$ hold in G. Then, information flow $o_2 \stackrel{r_1}{\Rightarrow} o_3$ occurs by performing a transaction at time 6. Here, a directed edge $o_2 \rightarrow_6 o_3$ is created in G. Since $o_1 \rightarrow_4 o_2 \rightarrow_6 o_3$, information flowing to o_2 from o_1 at time 4 might flow to o_3 by the transaction. Hence, $o_1 \rightarrow_6 o_3$ since $4 < 6$ [Figure 5 (2)]. Then, $o_3 \stackrel{r_2}{\Rightarrow} o_4$ at time 8. $o_3 \rightarrow_8 o_4$. Since $o_1 \rightarrow_4 o_2 \rightarrow_6 o_3 \rightarrow_8 o_4$, an edge $o_1 \rightarrow_8 o_4$ is also created and another edge $o_2 \rightarrow_8 o_4$ is tried to be created. However, "$o_2 \rightarrow_3 o_4$" in G. Since $3 < 8$, the time 3 of the edge "$o_2 \rightarrow_3 o_4$" is replaced with 8 [Figure 5 (3)]. In Figure 5 (3), information in the objects o_1, o_2, and o_3 flow into o_4. Let $In(o)$ be a set $\{o_1 \mid o_1 \rightarrow_\tau o \text{ in } G\}$ of objects whose information has flown into an object o. For example, $In(o_4) = \{o_1, o_2, o_3\}$ in Figure 5.

Suppose a method t is issued to an object o in a transaction T with a role r. Methods invoked in T are logged in an ordered invocation tree form in a log L_T. From the invocation tree in L_T, every information flow relation "$o_i \stackrel{T}{\Rightarrow} o_j$" is obtained. If the following condition is satisfied, t can be invoked in o.

[Condition for a method t] [Figure 6] $DO \in mtype(t_2)$ and $\langle o_2, t_2 \rangle \in r$,

1. for every "$o_1 \rightarrow_\tau o$" in L_T if $IM \in mtype(t)$,
2. for every "$o_2 \rightarrow_\tau o$" in G if $DO \in mtype(t)$. □

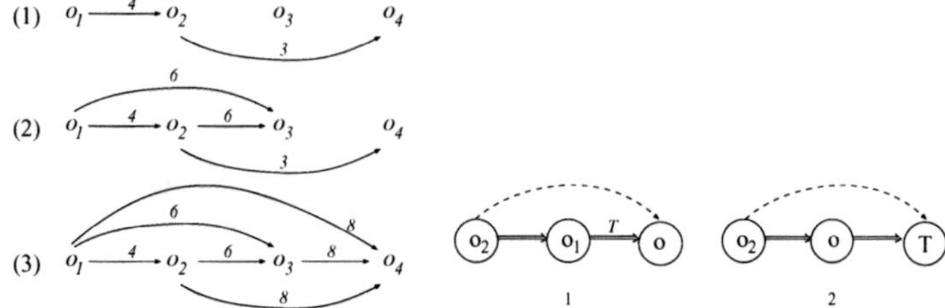

Fig. 5. Flow graph G.

Fig. 6. Condition.

In the condition 1, data in some object o_2 might have been brought into o_1 ($o_2 \stackrel{T}{\Rightarrow} o_1$) before the transaction T manipulates the object o. In the condition 2, T issues t to derived data from o.

4.2 Timed Information Flow

Suppose some data in an object o_i illegally flows to another object o_j by performing a transaction T with a role r at time τ ($o_i \rightarrow_\tau o_j$ in G). Security level of data is changing time by time. After it takes some time δ, the data brought from o_i is considered to belong to o_j. An edge "$o_i \rightarrow_\tau o_j$" is *aged* if $\tau + \delta < \sigma$ where σ shows the current time. Every aged edge is removed from the graph G for σ. In Figure 5, suppose $\delta = 10$. If σ gets 14, an edge timed 4 is aged now and removed. Figure 7 shows the flow graph G obtained here. Suppose some transaction T with a role r_1 issues a request t_3 on an object o_3 which $DO \in mtype(t_3)$ in Figure 5(3) but data in o_1 is not allowed to be derived. In Figure 5(3), T is rejected according to the conditions. However, the *DO* method t_3 can be performed in Figure 7 because of no illegal information flow from o_1 to T.

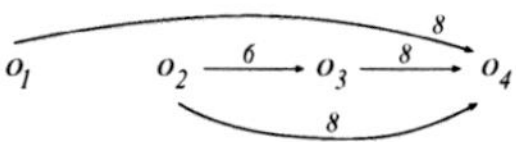

Fig. 7. Flow graph.

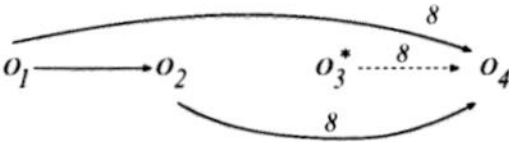

Fig. 8. Flow graph.

Suppose an object o_3 is dropped in a flow graph G of Figure 5(3). Since "$o_3 \stackrel{4}{\rightarrow} o_4$" exists in G, some data in o_3 might have been copied in o_4. Hence, only transaction which is granted to manipulate o_3 is allowed to manipulate o_4 even after o_3 is dropped.

[Drop of an object] An object o is dropped.

1. A node o is marked.
2. Every incoming edge in $In(o)$ is removed from G.
3. Every outgoing edge in $Out(o)$ is marked. □

Figure 8 shows a flow graph G obtained by dropping the object o_3 a through the algorithm from Figure 5(3). The node o_3 is marked $*$. A dotted edge from o_3 to o_4 shows a marked edge. All incoming edges to o_3, i.e. "$o_1 \rightarrow_6 o_3$" and "$o_2 \rightarrow_6 o_3$" are removed from G. Here, suppose some transaction T issues a DO method t_4 on o_4. t_4 is rejected if T is not allowed to derived data from o_3 even if o_3 is dropped already. Because there is still data of o_3 in o_4. Each marked edge is removed after it takes δ time units. If a marked node o does not have any outgoing edge, i.e. $Out(o) = \phi$, o is removed from G.

[Remove of aged edge]

1. For any edge "$o_i \rightarrow_\tau o_j$" in G, the edge is removed if $\tau + \delta \leq \sigma$.
2. Every marked node o_i is removed if $Out(o_i) = \phi$. □

5 Concluding Remarks

This paper discussed an access control model for the object-based system with role concepts. We discussed how to control information flow in a system where methods are invoked in a nested manner. We first defined a safe role where no illegal information flow possibly occurs in types of invocation models; basic (B), unordered (U), and ordered (O) models. We presented the algorithm to check if each method could be performed, i.e. no illegal information flow occurs after the method is performed. By using the algorithm, some methods issued by an unsafe transaction can be performed depending on in what order a transaction performs the methods. We also discussed a case that security level is *time-variant*. Information flowing to another object can be considered to belong to the object after some time.

References

1. Bell, D. E. and LaPadula, L. J., "Secure Computer Systems: Mathematical Foundations and Model," *Mitre Corp. Report,* No. M74–244, *Bedford, Mass.,* 1975.
2. Castano, S., Fugini, M., Matella, G., and Samarati, P., "Database Security," Addison-Wesley, 1995.
3. Denning, D. E., "A Lattice Model of Secure Information Flow," *Communications of the ACM,* Vol. 19, No. 5, 1976, pp. 236–243.
4. Fausto, R., Elisa, B., Won, K., and Darrell, W., "A Model of Authorization for Next-Generation Database Systems," *ACM Trans on Database Systems,* Vol. 16, No. 1, 1991, pp. 88–131.
5. Ferrai, E., Samarati, P., Bertino, E., and Jajodia, S., "Providing Flexibility in Information Flow Control for Object-Oriented Systems," *Proc. of 1997 IEEE Symp. on Security and Privacy,* 1997, pp. 130–140.
6. Ferraiolo, D. and Kuhn, R., "Role-Based Access Controls," *Proc. of 15th NIST-NCSC Nat'l Computer Security Conf.,* 1992, pp. 554–563.
7. Harrison, M. A., Ruzzo, W. L., and Ullman, J. D., "Protection in Operating Systems," *Comm. of the ACM,* Vol. 19, No. 8, 1976, pp. 461–471.
8. Izaki, K., Tanaka, K., and Takizawa, M., "Authorization Model in Object-Oriented Systems," *Proc. of IFIP Database Security,* 2000.

9. Izaki, K., Tanaka, K., and Takizawa, M., "Information Flow Control in Role-Based Model for Distributed Objects," *Proc. of IEEE Int'l Conf. on Parallel and Distributed Systems*, 2001.
10. Gosling, J. and McGilton, H., "The Java Language Environment," Sun Microsystems, Inc, 1996.
11. Lampson, B. W., "Protection," *Proc. of 5th Princeton Symp. on Information Sciences and Systems,* 1971, pp. 437–443. (also in *ACM Operating Systems Review,* Vol. 8, No. 1, 1974, pp. 18–24.)
12. Lampson, B. W., "A Note on the Confinement Problem," *Comm. of the ACM,* Vol. 16, No. 10, 1973, pp. 613–615.
13. Object Management Group Inc., " The Common Object Request Broker : Architecture and Specification," Rev. 2.1, 1997.
14. Oracle Corporation,"Oracle8*i* Concepts", Vol. 1, Release 8.1.5, 1999.
15. Samarati, P., Bertino, E., Ciampichetti, A., and Jajodia, S., "Information Flow Control in Object-Oriented Systems," *IEEE Trans. on Knowledge and Data Engineering* Vol. 9, No. 4, 1997, pp. 524–538.
16. Sandhu, R. S., "Lattice-Based Access Control Models," *IEEE Computer,* Vol. 26, No. 11, 1993, pp. 9–19.
17. Sandhu, R. S., Coyne, E. J., Feinstein, H. L., and Youman, C. E., "Role-Based Access Control Models," *IEEE Computer,* Vol. 29, No. 2, 1996, pp. 38–47.
18. Tachikawa, T., Yasuda, M., and Takizawa, M., "A Purpose-oriented Access Control Model in Object-based Systems," *Trans. of IPSJ,* Vol. 38, No. 11, 1997, pp. 2362–2369.
19. Tari, Z. and Chan, S. W., "A Role-Based Access Control for Intranet Security," *IEEE Internet Computing,* Vol. 1, No. 5, 1997, pp. 24–34.
20. Yasuda, M., Higaki, H., and Takizawa, M., "A Purpose-Oriented Access Control Model for Information Flow Management," *Proc. of 14th IFIP Int'l Information Security Conf. (SEC'98)*, 1998, pp. 230–239.

Object Space Partitioning in a DL-Like Database and Knowledge Base Management System

Mathieu Roger, Ana Simonet, and Michel Simonet

TIMC-IMAG Faculté de Médecine de Grenoble
38706 La Tronche Cedex – France
Mathieu.Roger@imag.fr, {Ana,Michel}.Simonet@imag.fr

Abstract. The p-type data model was designed first to answer database needs. Some of its features were and still are quite unusual for a DBMS and, by some aspects, make it nearer Description Logic (DL) systems than classical DBMS. Views play a central role in the model. They are defined in a hierarchical manner, with constraints on role (attribute) types as in DLs, and instance classification (view recognition) is a basic mechanism in p-type implementation by the Osiris system.
In this paper we recall the main characteristics of p-types and their semantics as a DL system. We insist on the modelling of unknown values, whose treatment leads to a three-value instance classification system. We develop database specific aspects and particularly the partitioning of the object space and its use for the management of data.

1 Introduction

The P-type data model was defined in the early eighties [Sales 84] with in mind the objective of making the end-user central to the system. This was achieved by giving views a first-class status. In the database world, views are synonym to shortcuts for SQL queries. They are neither persistent nor updatable, thus rendering them unable to satisfy the ANSI-SPARC requirements [ANSI/X3], where views constitute the external level of the three-level hierarchy and should constitute the only user interface with the database. To be more explicit, no database user except the DBA should deal with the relational tables. Even the database programmer should use only views. Everyone knows this is impossible with current database implementations, where the database cannot be updated through views, except in very simple cases. The interest in views has been increased by the recent development of Data Warehouses, where views have become an essential constituent. Much work is being done in the Data Warehouse community to optimise query evaluation by making the views persistent. However, views are still considered logically as queries and practically as secondary tables that have to be built and maintained parallel to the main table, the fact table. Because huge volumes of data are ordinary, physical space management becomes a central problem. Disk space has to be shared between views and indexes [Bellatreche 00]. It is somewhat paradoxical that views, which were intended to achieve logical independence and were placed at the higher conceptual level in the three-level architecture, have been lowered to the physical level, together with files and indexes.

H.C. Mayr et al. (Eds.): DEXA 2001, LNCS 2113, pp. 309–318, 2001.

The similarity between views and concepts in Description Logics (DLs) has been pointed out early. Both "define" subsets of objects of a more general concept (a table is a relational representation of a concept). Work has been done on using views – considered as defined concepts[1] – to optimise query evaluation [Beneventano et al., 93]. Through this kind of work, database research can benefit from the theoretical work that is being done in the field of DLs. Most of this work concerns the complexity of concept classification depending on the kind of properties the system allows to define the concepts.
However, there are important differences between DL systems and DBMS. DLs deal with conceptual aspects, not the physical ones related to object management. DLs do not deal with the management of large quantities of objects, which is the purpose of databases. They do not even consider object evolution. They deal only with a given state of the world, concerning a small amount of static, non-evolving objects. On the other hand, databases do not consider – even today – instance classification, i.e., determination of the current views of an object.
The Osiris system, which implements the p-type data model, can be considered at the crossing of both currents: databases and DLs. From databases, it retains the importance of sharing large amounts of data between different categories of users; hence the central place of views and their role that is not limited to that of "named queries". With DLs it shares the importance given to concept management. The specific aspects of Osiris with respect to both paradigms concern mainly a category of constraints used to define the views, namely Domain Constraints, and particularly their use for object management and query optimisation.
In this paper we make a presentation of the p-type data model in the DL style, which enables us to situate its language in the DL classification. This has given us confidence in the possibilities of implementing certain features in a feasible manner. The DL paradigm has also proved useful to express many specific aspects of the model, such as the partitioning of the object space, and even generalise it. Therefore this experience has been fruitful.
In this introduction we have outlined some essential characteristics of the p-type data model. In the following, we present a DL model of p-types. We first recall the main results of a previous study [DEXA00]. We show how the explicit treatment of unknown values leads to a three-value instance classification model where views can be Valid, Invalid or Potential for a given object. We then present the principle of a partitioning of the object space that is based on constraints on predefined domains and extended to constraints on views. We show how this partitioning can be used for the management of data in a database perspective: persistent views and object indexing. We present the current solution in the Osiris system and the problems posed by the generalization of constraints from predefined to user-defined domains.

---

[1] "Defined" concepts are defined by necessary and sufficient conditions. They are opposed to "primitive" concepts, which are defined only by necessary conditions. Therefore, it is mandatory to explicitly assign an object to a primitive concept and then let the system classify it into the defined concepts whose properties it satisfies. For example, an object p1 being assigned to the primitive concept PERSON will be classified into the defined concepts ADULT, MINOR, MALE, etc., according to its properties.

2 Previous Results: p-types Syntax and Semantics

In this section we recall the main results about the formal definition of the syntax and semantics of the concept language of p-types in a DL-like manner. This work was presented in [DEXA 00]. The modeling has been improved since, but its principle and its results remain mostly the same.
We do not consider the external form of p-types, i.e., the syntax used in the Osiris system. We consider a concept language whose semantics is that of p-types, which presents some characteristics that make it a database-oriented model. Description Logics deal with concept definition and classification. In defining P-types a designer is not interested only in the ontological aspects of the system, i.e., the concepts that are taken into consideration, but in their use in a database context. This leads to a decision to transform some concepts into classes of objects and others into views. A class must be understood in the programming sense: an object belongs to a unique class and does not change its class during its lifetime. Views are subsets of objects of a given class. Contrary to the common database perspective, P-type views are not shortcuts for queries. They are defined by logical properties on the attributes of the class and therefore behave as *defined concepts* in a DL. Similarly, classes behave as *primitive concepts*. This means that an object must be explicitly assigned to a class and then is automatically classified into its views. This is what happens in Osiris. Any object is created in a given class and automatically classified into the views of this class.

Table 1. Syntax and semantics for **type concept language** constructs, R ranges over roles, A over types and C,D over type concepts.

Construct Name	Syntax	Semantics
Attribute Typing	$\forall$R.A	$\{ x \in \Delta^I \mid \forall y \in \Delta^I: (x,y) \in Relation^I \Rightarrow y \in A^I\}$
Mono valued Attribute	(= 1 R)	$\{x \in \Delta^I \mid \#\{y \in \Delta^I: (x,y) \in Relation\} = 1 \}$
Intersection	C $\cap$ D	$C^I \cap D^I$

In this section we give a definition of the concept language syntax for OSIRIS. On an operational point of view, this language is used to specify databases schemes.
Let us consider:

- a set of types ***T*** (ranged over by A,B,T) containing predefined types INT, REAL, CHAR, STRING, namely Predefined,
- a set of views ***V*** (ranged over by U,V) containing predefined views $\{]v_1,v_2[, [v_1,v_2[,]v_1,v_2] , [v_1,v_2], \{a_1,\ldots,a_n\} \mid v_1$ and v_2 are both elements of one of the types INT, CHAR or REAL and a_i are all elements of one of the types INT,REAL, CHAR or STRING$\}$ namely PredefinedViews
- a set of roles ***R*** (ranged over by R).

Table 2. Syntax and Semantics for **types concept language** constructs, R ranges over roles, U,V over view concepts.

Construct Name	Syntax	Semantics
Intersection	$U \cap V$	$V^I \cap U^I$
Negation	$\neg U$	$\{x \in \Delta^I \mid x \notin U^I\}$
	Undefined(R)	$\{x \in \Delta^I \mid x \in \text{Undefined}\}$
	$\forall R.V$	$\{x \in \Delta^I \mid \forall y \in \Delta^I: (x,y) \in Rel^I \Rightarrow y \in V^I\}$
	$\forall R. \neg V$	$\{x \in \Delta^I \mid \forall y \in \Delta^I: (x,y) \in Rel^I \Rightarrow y \notin V^I\}$
	$\exists R.V$	$\{x \in \Delta^I \mid \exists y \in \Delta^I (x,y) \in Rel^I \text{ and } y \in V^I\}$
Elementary Constraints	$\exists R. \neg V$	$\{x \in \Delta^I \mid \exists y \in \Delta^I (x,y) \in Rel^I \text{ and } y \notin V^I\}$

We define two separate languages that are mostly sub languages of the ALC language family [Domini et al., 96]. One of these languages is called **type concept language** (namely **TL**), and is used to declare the types of the application considered as primitive concepts. The other one is called **view concept language** (namely **VL**), and is used to declare views (i.e., subsets of types) considered as defined concepts. This distinction is a central point of the Osiris system, and it has also been used in [Buchheit et al., 98]. The purpose of such a distinction is to emphasize the fact that types are inherently primitive concepts and views are defined concepts. A **type scheme** is a set S of axioms of the type:

1. $A \subseteq C$, where $A \in$ *T-Predefined* and $C \in$ TL
2. $A \subseteq \neg B$, where $A \in$ ***T*** and $B \in$ ***T***
3. $R \subseteq A \times B$, where $R \in$ ***R***, $A \in$ ***T****-Predefined* and $B \in$ ***T***
4. $V = A \cap U$, where $V \in$ ***V***, $A \in$ ***T*** and $U \in$ VL

Such that:

- ***Uniqueness of a type definition:*** for all $A \in$ ***T****-Predefined*, there is one axiom $A \subseteq C$ in S. Such types are called *p-types*.
- ***A role belongs to a single type and all roles are defined:*** for all R there is exactly one axiom $R \subseteq A \times B$ and $A \subseteq C$ such as C uses R.
- ***Types are disjoint:*** for all A,B in ***T***, there is an axiom $A \subseteq \neg B$.
- ***Uniqueness of a view definition:*** for all $V \in$ ***V*** there is exactly one axiom $V = U$.
- ***Views form a hierarchy:*** considering the binary relation of view inclusion "V uses U in its definition, $V = U \cap \ldots$", the directed graph formed by views as node and this relation is acyclic and every connex compound has a unique root called *minimal view*.
- ***A view is a subset of a unique type:*** for each view V there is exactly one type A such as minimal_view(V) = $A \cap \ldots$.

An **interpretation** I = (ΔI,.I) of a given type scheme S is given by a set Δ^I and an interpretation function $^{.I}$ such that initial concepts and roles are interpreted in the following way:

- A^I is a subset of Δ^I for all A in ***T***
- V^I is a subset of Δ^I for all V in ***V***
- R^I is a triplet <Relation, Undefined, Unknown> with Relation $\subseteq \Delta^I \times \Delta^I$, Undefined $\subseteq \Delta^I$, Unknown $\subseteq \Delta^I$ and $\{x \in \Delta^I \mid \exists\, y \in \Delta^I \text{ and } (x,y) \in \text{Relation}\} \subseteq \Delta^I$ - (Undefined $\cup$ Unknown)

Concept constructs are interpreted according to table 1 and 2.

Example. We give an example of type scheme:

- PERSON $\subseteq$ ∀partners. PERSON $\cap$ ∀ age. INT $\cap$ (= 1 age) $\cap$ ∀follow. COURSE $\cap$ ∀teach. COURSE $\cap$ ∀ namePERSON. STRING $\cap$ (= 1 namePERSON)
- COURSE $\subseteq$ ∀teacher. PERSON $\cap$ (= 1 teacher) $\cap$ ∀ nameCOURSE. STRING$\cap$ (= 1 nameCOURSE)

- VIEWPERSON = PERSON $\cap$ ¬Undefined(age) $\cap$ ¬Undefined(partner) $\cap$ ¬Undefined(namePERSON) $\cap$ ∀ age. [0, 100]
- STUDENT = VIEWPERSON $\cap$ ¬Undefined (follow) $\cap$ ∀ age. [0, 50[
- TEACHER = VIEWPERSON $\cap$ ¬Undefined (teach) $\cap$ ∀ age. [18, 70[
- TEACHINGASSISTANT = STUDENT $\cap$ TEACHER
- MAJOR = VIEWPERSON $\cap$ ∀ age. [18, 100[
- VIEWCOURSE = COURSE$\cap$¬Undefined(teacher)$\cap$¬Undefined(nameCOURSE)

Remark. The undefined set in a role interpretation represents the objects for which the role has no meaningful value. It is the case for the function 1/x: it is undefined for x=0. As in Description Logics we assume that names, i.e., the elements from Δ^I, are unique (unique name assumption), in the context of our database system these names are oids.

Definition. Given I and J two interpretations of a scheme S, we say that J is **a more specific interpretation** than I (noted as J $\subseteq$ I) iff:

- $\Delta^I \subseteq \Delta^J$
- For all A in ***T***, $A^I \subseteq A^J$.
- For all V in ***V***, $V^I \subseteq V^J$.
- For all R in ***R***, R^I = <Relation_1 , Undefined_1, Unknown_1>, R^J = <Relation_2 , Undefined_2, Unknown_2>, $\text{Relation}_1 \subseteq \text{Relation}_2$, $\text{Undefined}_1 \subseteq \text{Undefined}_2$ and $\text{Unknown}_2 \subseteq \text{Unknown}_1$.

In other words, J a more specific interpretation than I contains less unknown information and possibly more objects than I.

Definition. An interpretation I is said **finite** if Δ^I is finite.

Definition. An interpretation I is said to be **complete** if for every R $\in$ ***R***, such as R^I = <Relation, Undefined, Unknown>, we have Unknown = $\varnothing$.

Remark. Intuitively, a interpretation is complete if all the values for all the objects are known.

Definition 8. Given a scheme S, we say that a finite interpretation I may **satisfy an axiom**. More precisely:

1. I **satisfies** $A \subseteq C$ iff $A^I \subseteq C^I$
2. I **satisfies** $A \subseteq \neg B$ iff $A^I \cap B^I = \emptyset$
3. I **satisfies** $R \subseteq A \times B$ iff Relation $\subseteq A^I \times B^I$, Undefined $\subseteq A^I$ and Unknown $\subseteq A^I$, where R^I = < Relation, Undefined, Unknown>
4. I **satisfies** $V = A \cap U$ iff $V^I = A^I \cap U^I$

Definition. We say that a finite interpretation **satisfies** a type scheme S (or that I is a valid interpretation of S) iff:
1. I satisfies every axiom of S
2. For each p-type A, with minimal view V, we have $A^I = V^I$.
3. There exists a complete interpretation J such that J satisfies S and $J \subseteq I$.

Remark. This Definition needs a few explanations. First, we only consider finite interpretations because they best match our intuition: we do not believe that it is the purpose of computers to deal with infinity. Constraint 1 is classical and means that an interpretation for a concept follows its definition. Constraint 2 means that minimal views are primitive concepts. Constraint 3 deals with the unknown values. It means that in a valid interpretation, if a value is unknown, then it will be possible to put some actual value in the future.

Definition. We say that a view V_1 **subsumes** a view V_2, iff $V_2^I \subseteq V_1^I$ for all valid complete interpretation I.

Remark. As in Description Logics, deduction does not deal with unknown values. The unknown values only appear when building the extension of a specific database, which is during the "using phase" of a database. Before inserting any object in the database, that is building a specific interpretation, the only thing one can do is to deduce facts that are true for every interpretation.

3 Application to Databases

The goal of this section is to show how the object space of a p-type can be partitioned in order to store the objects of an interpretation, i.e., the actual set of objects of the database. This partition may also be used for computing the subsumption relationship, as in [Calvanese 96] where *compound concepts* form a semantic driven partitioning analogous to the equivalence classes introduced in this section. We give the intuition of the partitioning, starting with the partition of an attribute when it is defined over a predefined type (which is the case in the current implementation of the Osiris system). Then we extend this partitioning to the case where attribute types are views.

Definition. Given a role R from a p-type A, let us call constraints(R) the set of all elementary constraints involving R; a **stable sub-domain for R** is either a subset of constraints(R) or the stable sub-domain sds-undefined$_R$. The interpretations of a stable sub-domains s are repectively $s^I = A^I \cap C_i^I - \cup C_j^I$, where$C_i \in s$ and $C_j \notin s$; and sds-undefined$_R^I$ = Undefined, where R^I = <Relation, Undefined, Unknown>.

Definition. A stable sub-domain s is said to be **consistent** iff for some valid interpretation I we have $s^I \neq \emptyset$.

Example. Consistent stable sub-domains for the PERSON p-type and age role in example are:

Sds11={ ∀age.[0,50], ∀age.[0,70], ∀age.[0,100]} :
those whose age is between 0 and 50 (included)

Sds12={ ∀age.[0,70], ∀age. [0,100]} :
those whose age is between 50 (excluded) and 70 (included)

Sds13={ ∀age.[0,100]} :
those whose age is between 70 (excluded) and 100 (included)

Sds14={ } : those whose age is not between 0 (included) and 100 (included)

Property. Given an interpretation I and a role R, the R's stable sub-domains' interpretations form a partition for A^I.

Proof. Let $o \in A^I$. For a constraint C from constraint(R), either o belongs to C^I, or o belongs to $\neg C^I$. As this is true for each constraint, we have the result.

Definition. Given a p-type A whose roles are $R_1, \ldots, R_n$, an **eq-class** for A is $(s_1, \ldots, s_n)$ where each s_i is a stable sub-domain for R_i with interpretation $(s_1, \ldots, s_n)^I = \cap s_i^I$.

Remark. One can see an eq-class as a hyper-square, as in figure 1.

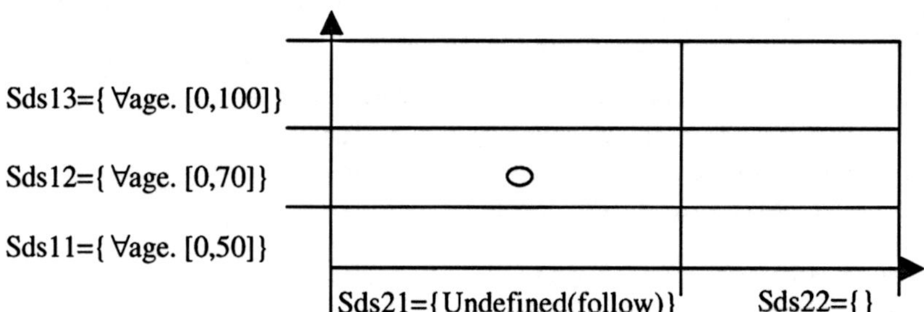

Fig. 1. Example of graphical representation of eq-classes. Graphical representation for a virtual space of a p-type; only consistent stable sub-domains are represented. The circle symbolizes an object with values *follow=Undefined and age=60.*

Property. Given an interpretation I, the interpretations of Eq-classes are the equivalence classes for the relationship between objects: o1 ≈ o2 iff for each constraint C, either both o1 and o2 belong to C^I, or both o1 and o2 belong to $\neg C^I$.

The following properties and definitions deal with the storage of a specific interpretation. So we assume that we have a valid interpretation I and we concentrate on a single p-type A.

Property. Given an object o from I such that, for each $R \in \boldsymbol{R}$, with R^I = <Relation, Undefined, Unknown>, we have $o \notin$ Unknown (i.e. **o is completely known**), then there exists a unique eq-class eq, called EquivalentClass(o,I) such as $o \in eq^I$.

Definition. Given a valid interpretation I, and an object o, we define **Possible**(o,I) as the set of eq-classes associated with o in every more specific interpretation of I.

Property. If o is completely known, then Possible(o,I) = {EquivalentClass(o,I)}.

The idea would be to index each object with the Possible(o,I) set. In fact, as we do not need so much information, we will use instead an approximation of Possible(o,I).

Definition. Given a p-type A with role R, a **general stable sub-domain** is either a stable sub-domain or the general stable sub-domain sds-unknown_R with interpretation $\text{sds-unknown}_R^I = A^I$.

Definition. Given a p-type A whose roles are R_1, ..., R_n, a **general eq-class** is $(s_1, \ldots, s_n)$ where each s_i is a general stable sub-domain for R_i with interpretation $(s_1, \ldots, s_n)^I = \cap s_i^I$.

Definition. Given an object o, we define **GeneralEquivalentClass(o,I)** = $(s_1, \ldots, s_n)$ where s_i is either the stable sub-domain such that $o \in s_i^I$ if o is not unknown for R_i, or sds-unknown_R.

Property. Given an object o and a J valid complete more specific interpretation than I, then we have:

$$\cup_{eq \in \text{Possible}(o,I)} eq^J \subseteq \text{GeneralEquivalentClass}(o,I)^J.$$

Proof. Suppose o is completely known, then Possible(o,I) = {EquivalentClass(o,I)} and GeneralEquivalentClass(o,I) = EquivalentClass(o,I).
Now suppose than o is not completely known.
Let us reorder the roles from A, such as R1, ..., Rk are the roles for which o is known and Rk+1, ..., Rn the roles for which o is unknown. Then let sds1, ..., sdsk the stables sub-domains for o according to each Ri for I in 1..k. We have:

$$\text{eq in Possible}(o,I) \Rightarrow eq = (\text{sds1}, \ldots, \text{sdsk}, \ldots).$$

We also have

$$\text{GeneralEquivalentClass}(o,I)=(\text{sds1},\ldots,\text{sdsk},\text{sds-Unknown}_{Rk+1},\ldots,\text{sds-Unknown}_{Rn}).$$

As for each Ri, I in k+1 .. n, we have $\text{sdsi}^J \subseteq \text{sds-Unknown}_{Ri}^J$, we have :

$$eq^J \subseteq \text{GeneralEquivalentClass}(o,I)^J.$$

Definition. Given a view V of p-type A and a general eq-class eq, we define **Validity(eq,V)**, the validity of eq with regards to V, as :

- **True** if $eq^I \subseteq V^I$ for every valid interpretation I.
- **False** if $eq^I \cap V^I = \varnothing$ for every valid interpretation I.
- **Possible** if $eq^I \cap V^I \neq \varnothing$ and $eq^I \cap \neg V^I \neq \varnothing$ for every valid interpretation I.

Definition. Given a general eq-class eq of p-type A with views V1, ...,Vn, we call **ValidityVector(eq)** the set of couples (Vi, Validity(eq,Vi)).

Solution. We can associate with each general eq-class its validity vector and the set of objects that belong to the interpretation of the general eq-class. This is the way we implement object indexation as shown in figure 2.

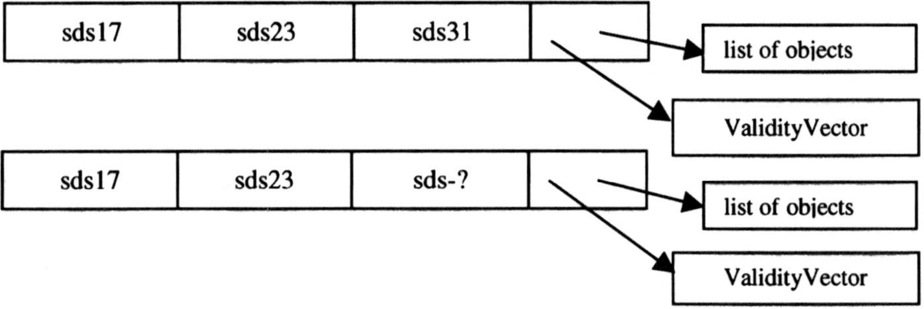

Fig. 2. Example of general eq-classes for object indexation. Two general eq-classes, with their associated object list and validity vector. The second eq-class has a general stable sub-domain unknown (quoted here as sds-?).

4 Conclusion and Future Work

This paper continues the work initiated in [Roger et al. 00]. In particular we present a way of partitioning data according to the semantics. The notion of eq-classes provides semantic-driven partitioning and even if the number of eq-classes is exponential according to the size of the type scheme, only populated eq-classes need to be represented. Thus the number of eq-classes never exceeds the number of objects. This is the central idea of the p-type model as it has proven to be valuable for object indexation and logical deduction as stated in [Calvanese 96]. This convergence between databases and knowledge bases through semantic-driven partitioning allows us to consider the possibility of reusing previous results about concept classification. Future work will consist in extending the expressiveness of the language by reusing previous work on description logics, for example cardinality constraints [Calvanese 96]. We will also study the influence of concepts on a level "above" p-types, which reduces the gap between the p-type data model and that of description logics. An example of such a concept would be "old things" that would gather objects from different p-types according to the role *age*.

References

[ANSI/X3]: ANSI/ X3/ SPARC Study group on database management systems. Interim report, ACM SiGMOD Bulletin 7, N2, 1975.

[Bellatreche,00]: L. Bellatreche, *Utilisation des Vues Matérialisées, des Index et de la Fragmentation dans la Conception d'un Entrepôt de Données*, Thèse d'Université, Université Blaise Pascal, Clermont-Ferrand, France, Dec. 2000.

[Beneventano et al., 93]: Beneventano, Bergamaschi, Lodi, Sartori, *Using subsumption in semantic query optimisation*, IJCAI Workshop on object based representation systems, Août 1993.

[Bucheit et al., 98]: Buchheit, Domini, Nutt, Schaerf, *A refined architecture for terminological systems: terminology = schema + views*, Artificial Intelligence, Vol 99, 1998.

[Calvanese 96]: Diego Calvanese, *Finite Model Reasoning in Description Logics*, in Proceedings of Knowledge Representation 1996.

[Domini et al., 96]: Domini, Lenzerini, Nardi, Schaerf, *Reasoning in description logics*, Principles of Knowledge Representation, pp. 191-236, CSLI Publications, 1996.

[Sales 84]: A. Sales, *Types abstraits et bases de données*, Thèse, Université scientifique et médicale de Grenoble,1984.

[Simonet et al., 94]: A. Simonet, M. Simonet, *Objects with Views and Constraints : from Databases to Knowledge Bases*, Object-Oriented Information Systems OOIS'94 - London, Springer Verlag, pp 182-197, Dec. 1994.

[Simonet, 88]: A. Simonet, *Les P-TYPES: un modèle pour la définition de bases de connaissances centrées-objets cohérentes*, R.R. 751-I laboratoire Artemis, Grenoble, Novembre 1988.

[Simonet et al., 98]: A. Simonet, M. Simonet, C. G. Bassolet, X. Delannoy, R. Hamadi, *Static Classification Schemes for an Object System*, In: FLAIRS-98, 11th Int. FLorida Artificial Intelligence Research Society Conference, AAAI Press, pp 254-258, May 1998.

[Roger, 99]: M. Roger, *Requêtes dans un SGBD-BC de type objet avec vues*, Rapport de Dea, UFR IMA, Grenoble, 1999.

[Roger et al., 00]: M. Roger, A. Simonet and M Simonet, *A Description Logics-like Model for a Knowledge and Data Management System*, in DEXA 2000.

A Genome Databases Framework

Luiz Fernando Bessa Seibel and Sérgio Lifschitz

Departamento de Informática
Pontificia Universidade Católica do Rio de Janeiro (PUC-Rio)
Rio de Janeiro - Brasil
{seibel,sergio}@inf.puc-rio.br

Abstract. There are many Molecular Biology Databases, also known as Genome Databases, and there is a need for integrating all this data sources and related applications. This work proposes the use of an object-oriented framework for genome data access and manipulations. The framework approach is an interesting solution due to the flexibility, reusability and extensibility requirements of this application domain. We give a formal definition of our Genome Databases Framework using UML class diagrams, that explore the structural part of the architecture. A brief discussion on the Framework functionalities is also presented.

1 Introduction

Many molecular biology projects are currently active [19]. In spite of all the benefits one may expect from them, it has become a challenging problem to deal with large volumes of DNA and protein sequences, besides other related data (such as annotations) (e.g., [2,9,23,10]). DNA and protein sequences are text strings and this is one of the reasons why molecular biologist started keeping them in text files. With new technologies available, the sequencing process and genetic code production has increased in such a way that the total volume of data became large enough, motivating the use of DBMSs.

Database technology is already present in this research area but to a little extent, i.e., even if some projects include DBMS-like software to store all the data, most does not use DBMS's functionalities [2,19]. Moreover, most users still work with flat text-based files downloaded from public repositories and data manipulation is done through programs like BLAST search (e.g., [5]). There exists many Molecular Biology Databases, also known as Genome Databases, such as the GenBank Sequence Database [13], the Annotated Protein Sequence Database (Swiss-Prot) [27] and A C. elegans Database [1]. It is important to note that many so-called databases are not always complete database systems but, rather, file systems with own storage, manipulation and access methods.

We are interested here in a basic, though very important, problem that is related to the definition of a suitable structure for representing and integrating this kind of genome data. It is a well-known problem for genome and molecular biology data users that the information widely spread in different sites are not easy to deal with in a single and uniform way. Each research group that is

H.C. Mayr et al. (Eds.): DEXA 2001, LNCS 2113, pp. 319–329, 2001.

currently generating or processing these data usually work in a independent manner, using different data models to represent and manipulate mostly the same information. There are object-oriented systems (e.g., AceDB [1]), relational (e.g., Swiss-Prot [27]) and semi-structured text-based files (e.g., GenBank [13]).

The usual approach to handle this problem is to use a specific integrated model and system that should capture all the needed data for a particular application (e.g., [8]). Since it is a research area that is often changing, with new structural information being incorporated together with new application requirements, it is very difficult to decide upon which data model should be considered in this context. Thus, every existing approach based on a chosen model may not be well adapted to all users and application needs.

In this work we propose the use of an object-oriented framework [11] approach to deal with these Genome data integration problem. A framework is an incomplete software system, which contains many basic pre-defined components (frozen spots) and others that must be instantiated (hot spots) for the implementation of the desired and particular functionality. There are multiple object-oriented framework classifications. Our framework belongs to a class called "specific to the application domain". Indeed, molecular biology (genome) research area.

We claim that, using a framework and the software systems instantiations it may generate, we have a better solution to most of the questions that arise in this domain. Our proposed framework, briefly introduced in [20], will be discussed and formalized here, with UML class diagrams that explore its structural part. Due to space limitations, we will only give an idea of the framework's dynamic part. This is further explained in [26].

We first motivate our work in the next section, listing a sample of the existing genome data sources and tools, together with some of the most important approaches in the literature. Then, in Section 3, we give an overview of our framework, presenting its basic architecture, a discussion on its functionalities and an instantiation of the biological model. This is followed by the details of the framework modules, shown in Section 4. We conclude in Section 5 with contributions, future and ongoing work.

2 Motivation and Related Work

There are many interesting problems for the database research community, besides simply providing a way to store and give reliable and efficient access to large volumes of data. Among them, we can mention the works on appropriate user interfaces and the interaction between different data collections [4,28]. Some other issues involve the definition of an appropriate ontology [3,15], as well as buffer management [18] and indexes [14].

Molecular genome projects, through sequencing, have produced very large collections of DNA data of multiple organisms. An important problem in this research area is how to deal with gene and other genome sites in order to identify their functions. It is important to enable comparisons between different species' genome data that may be similar and, probably, have the same function.

Many research groups have developed tools to provide integration, structuring, comparison and presentation of genome sequences and related information. In [17,9,21] the authors identify the most important integration strategies:

- (*hyperlink navigation for joining information*) The idea here is to allow users to jump through registers of different data sources, either through existing links among them (e.g., Entrez [19]) or navigation systems that create the links among different data sources (e.g., SRS [19]). Thus, in a first movement, the user accesses a data source register and, in what follows, the user asks for a link to another data source where the desired information is; or
- (*multidatabases*) Another strategy includes those that use integration tools that implement queries to the different pre-existing data sources. These queries may be formulated through special languages (e.g., [7] and CPL/Kleisli [19]) that allow representing complex data types, with an access driver implemented for each data source to be accessed; or
- (*data warehouses*) An alternative strategy consists of using a mediator that is responsible for determining the data sources that participate in the query, creating an access plan, translating concepts and syntax, assigning the queries to the distributed environment and integrating the results [17]. We deal here with implementation of a data instance that collects the biological information available in several sources.

When genome and molecular biology information structuring are taken into account, other research groups propose and discuss data models that are suitable to represent them. We can cite the OPM semantic-based object-oriented model [8], the DDBJ DNA Database presented in [24] and, more recently, the data warehouse-like approach proposed in [25]. Usually genome projects develop own system interfaces that differ in the way they show their data and results from data manipulation. For example, AceDB [1] offer a powerful graphical interface that enables the user to visualize the chromosome map in details.

We have chosen here an approach that is based on an object-oriented framework. The basic idea for choosing a framework is that we needed a tool for integrating genome information that is spread in a distributed environment (mostly available in the web). Furthermore, this information changes because new biological information and descriptions emerge often. All data is used by distinct and, at the same time, similar applications. Thus, properties like flexibility, extensibility and software reusability are required.

The biology data model, once initially defined, need to incrementally aggregate new information from the different existing data sources. Through an object-oriented framework, it becomes possible to generate interfaces and database instances, executing the most important genome applications in a uniform and integrated way. Our approach integrates the information through the instantiation of particular scientific data warehouses, which respond to high performance requests of the related applications.

3 Framework General Description

Our Genome Databases Framework provides basically six functionalities:

1. Schemas capture of existing and different data sources;
2. Matching of the architecture objects to those objects in the captured schema;
3. Capture of data belonging to the data sources;
4. Definition of new ad-hoc schemas;
5. Data generation in a format required by a molecular biology application;
6. Execution of algorithms instantiated as methods of the biology classes.

The first one assumes that there exists a converter (wrapper) for the data sources being considered. When the second functionality is not directly obtained, a new biology object is created and associations must be created. This matching may establish relationships such as "is synonym of". The ability of capturing the data is the third functionality mentioned and is needed once the associated schema has been already captured. For this, there is another type of converter. Listed next, in fourth place, is a common demand for new specific applications schemas, together with a new associated data set. As there are multiple stored data formats, one may need to convert them to a particular format, mandatory for the execution of a given application (e.g., FASTA file format for BLAST programs). This is what the fifth functionality is related to and, finally, the framework must be able to execute all the involved methods.

Besides the above mentioned functionalities, we have chosen XML Schema to define the data sources schemas and XML for storing data [29]. This is due to (i) the intrinsic characteristic of the information in the biology data sources; (ii) the known advantages of semi-structured data models in this context [16]; and (iii) to the eventual adoption of XML by many commercial CASE tools.

Framework Architecture

The framework being proposed is divided in four modules: Administrator, Captor, Driver and Converter. Their relationship and an overview of the framework architecture is depicted in Figure 1.

The hot spots of our framework are the *Biology Model and Algorithms*, the *Wrappers* associated to biology data sources and the *Application Drivers*. When instantiated, they implement a particular functionality, defining an application over the molecular biology application domain.

The Administrator module performs the interface with the users to provide management of the biological data model: schemas and/or data capturing requests or the execution of algorithms instantiated in the framework. Therefore, this module contains a biology class model that is committed with the existent data sources, as well as with the methods that are associated to these classes.

The Captor module is responsible for the data and schemas repository. The Converter provides access to the biology data sources, translating schemas to XML Schema and data to XML. Finally, the Drivers module implements the interface generation between biology applications and the framework.

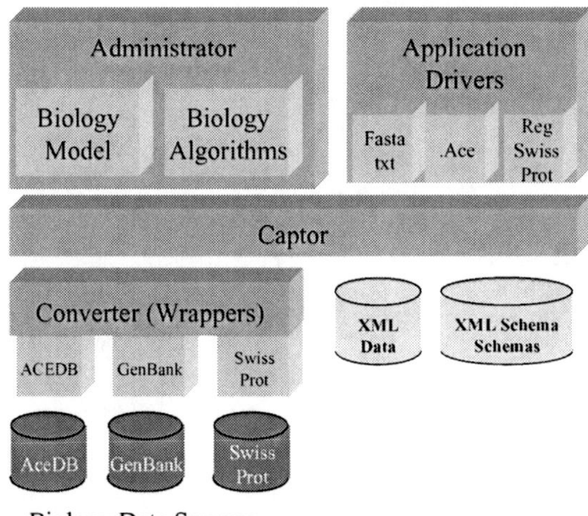

Fig. 1. The Framework Architecture

Overview of Framework Dynamics

When a user asks for a schema (or data) from a given data source to the Administrator, this module sends the request to the Captor, which in turn sends it to the corresponding biology data wrapper. These schemas/data capturing may only be done if the correspondent wrapper have been previously developed in the framework. The wrapper implements the mapping of the data sources schema to XML Schema and data to XML. The schemas and the data obtained are stored in their respective repositories.

The user may also ask the Administrator module for generating a file for a given biology application. Much like as described before, such a request can only be done if the associated driver have been previously instantiated in the architecture. The Administrator module triggers the driver in order to execute its task. Then, the driver requests data to the Captor, which manipulates the data repository. There are multiple biology applications that ask for a given file name and its localization in order to proceed with the execution.

The architecture also allows the execution of a biology algorithm instantiated in the architecture, which may work on the available data stored in the repository. The construction of interfaces between the framework and the existent biology applications can also be done through the Application Driver, i.e., data may be requested in specific formats for a class of applications.

An Example of Biology Model

We present here an instantiation of the *Biology Model* to give an idea of the objects involved in the biology application domain, as well as the algorithms associated to each one of these objects.

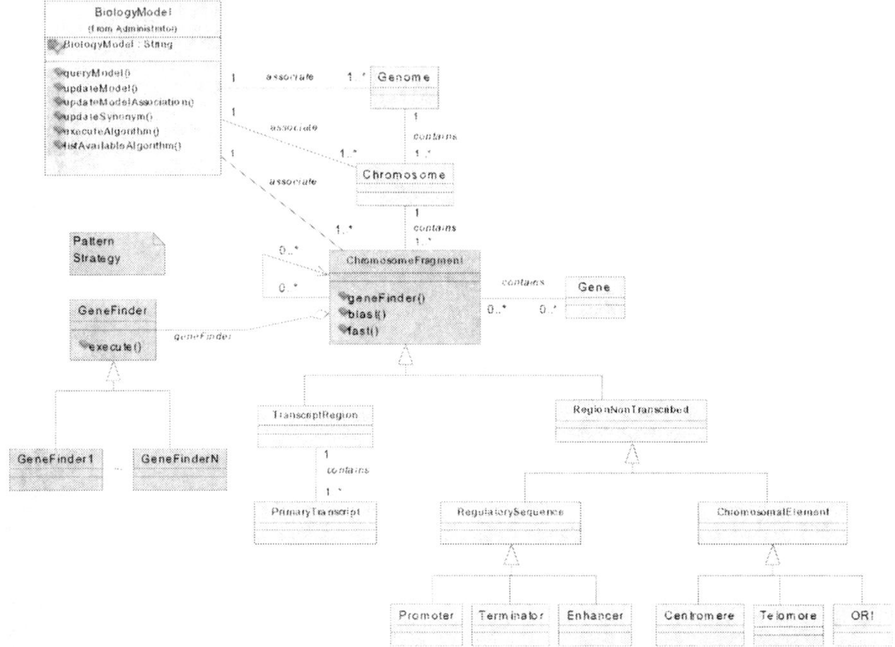

Fig. 2. Example of Genome Class diagram

The model presents only a small part of the application domain objects, specifically the pieces of information related to the genome. Other facts refer, for example, to the proteome, transcriptome and metabolone. The biology model - a framework hot spot in our case - can be extended so that all information currently available at the biology data sources are considered.

In the model depicted in Figure 2, one may observe that chromosomes form the genome and that each is considered a set of *Chromosome Fragments*, which consist of DNA sequences. A Chromosome Fragment can be either a Transcript Region or a Non-Transcript Region. The latter can be a Regulatory Sequence or a Chromosomal Element, and so forth. The algorithms that may be executed over the objects in the chromosome fragments class are, for example, GeneFinder-type methods, like Blast and Fast [22]. These type of algorithms are those that run discovery (mining) processes of DNA regions in the fragments for which genes formation is possible.

4 Framework Modules

We present here the architecture of each module Each module has a class that represents its interface with the other modules. We use the Facade pattern [12] in their implementation. The framework is described and formally specified using the Unified Modeling Language (UML) [6]. Although a complete formal definition of our framework would contain both structural and functional specification (through class and sequence diagrams), as explained before only the static part will be presented. We will focus on module's classes and related functionalities. The attributes and methods will not be detailed but are quite immediate.

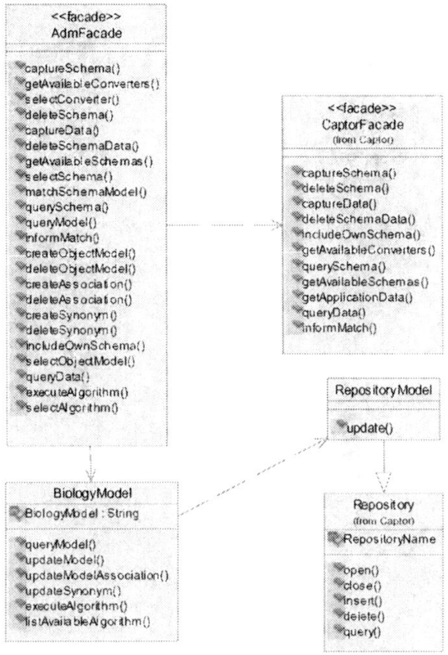

Fig. 3. Classes Diagram of the Administrator Module

Administrator Module

The 3 classes in this module are: *AdmFacade*, *BiologyModel* and *RepositoryModel*. The class *AdmFacade* is the path to all framework functionalities. The users interact with this class in order to capture schemas or data from a given data source or to obtain the matching between a biology schema, defined in the architecture, and the schema that was captured from a data source. When there is no direct matching, new objects can be added to (or suppressed from) the model. Also, object associations can be done (or undone) and objects can be recognized as synonyms of other objects. An user can create a new schema and a data instantiation that are appropriate to a given application. One can, via the Administrator module, generate data for external applications, query schemas and data repositories or even run biology programs.

The class *BiologyModel* manipulates the biology model, allowing its expansion. Classes that are part of the Administration module may be extended or modified by programmers. They are, indeed, hot spots of the proposed framework. The *Strategy* pattern [12] is used to permit the creation of algorithms families associated to the biology model's classes. This way the programmers can implement variations of the available algorithms. Finally, the class *RepositoryModel* provides object persistency as well as their retrieval from the Repository.

Captor Module

The class *CaptorFacade* provides (i) the capture and storage of biology data sources' schemas/data; (ii) management of own specific schemas, defined from the objects of the biology model available in the framework; (iii) exclusion of own or captured schemas/data; and (iv) query execution over the repository class.

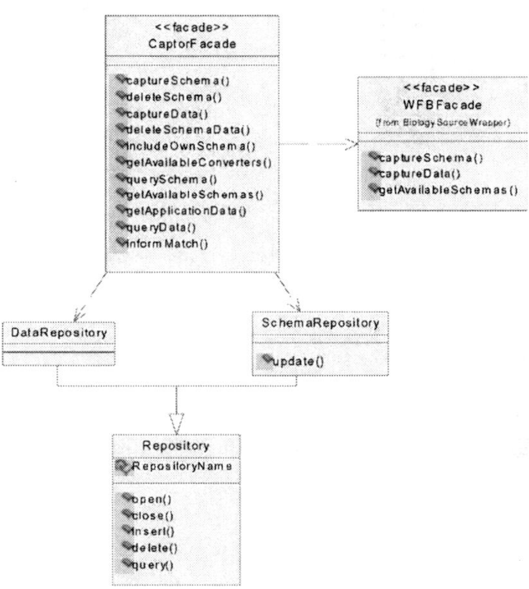

Fig. 4. Classes Diagram of the Captor Module

The second class, called *Repository*, provides persistency of schemas and data, besides enabling data retrieval. It is worth to remember that the schemas are stored in XML Schema and all data in XML. So, there is a need for access and manipulation languages, such as XQuery [30], to deal with the Repository.

WrapperBiologySources Module

This module is composed by classes *WFBFacade* and *DataSourceWrapper*.

The *WFBFacade* is an interface class between the framework modules and the biology data wrappers. There will be various converters in the architecture, one for each data source. Therefore, the relationship between the WFBFacade and the Wrappers is of the type one-to-many.

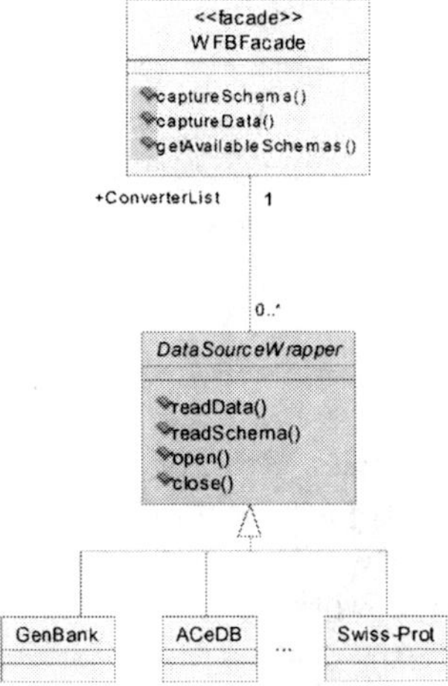

Fig. 5. Classes Diagram of the WrapperBiologySources Module

The *DataSourceWrapper* represents the implementation of each wrapper. A wrapper will contain two distinct functionalities. On one hand, it has the ability to capture the biology data source schema and, on the other hand, the capture of the source's data itself. The DataSourceWrapper class is a hot spot of the architecture.

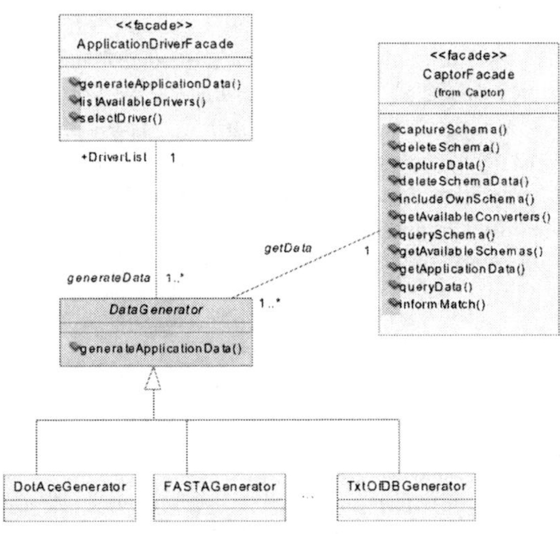

Fig. 6. Class Diagram of the DriverBiologyApplication Module

DriverBiologyApplication Module

The following classes compose the *DriverBiologyApplication module*: the *ApplicationDriverFacade* is an interface class between the modules of the framework and the drivers that generate data for the biology applications. There will exist multiple application drivers in the architecture, one for each application program to be used. Thus, the relationship between the ApplicationDriverFacade and the drivers is "one-to-many" type. The *DataGenerator* represents the implementation of each driver. The driver is also a framework hot spot.

For instance, a driver can generate data in a text format, according to the syntax used in GenBank or Swiss- Prot, or even in FASTA format to be used in the execution of algorithms that work on them. Moreover, a driver may be the implementation of an interface with a system available in the Web. It can send the available data in the framework repositories to a system that will execute and manipulate them. The driver can also be a data service, allowing an application to be connected to the framework, receiving the data stored there.

5 Final Comments

We proposed and detailed a genome database framework that integrates molecular biology data sources and allows the execution of programs and queries in a uniform way. This is quite different from previous approaches, that lie on particular data models and structures, only appropriate to specific contexts.

The main contribution is based on the idea that our framework works much like data warehouses do but provide in addition flexibility and reusability. The users of such a tool may access a heterogeneous environment of information sources and can deal with schema evolution based on a meta-model, i.e., independent of each distinct data model used. New schemas can be built via framework instantiation, with the help of an ontology and a biology data model.

We are currently working on the framework implementation and we hope to have a prototype available soon, with all functionalities, although still with restricted access to data sources. We are also interested in the definition and representation of a specific ontology for the molecular biology and genome area, which will be used in the existing data sources. Moreover, we plan to explore further the schema evolution characteristics of the framework.

References

1. AceDB: http://genome.cornell.edu/acedoc/index.html
2. M. Ashburner and N. Goodman, "Informatics, Genome and Genetics Databases", Current Opinion in Genetics & Development 7, 1997, pp 750–756.
3. P. Baker, C.A. Goble, S. Bechhofer, N.W. Patton, R. Stevens and A. Brass, "An Ontology for Bioinformatics Applications", Bioinformatics 15(6), 1999, pp 510–520.
4. M.I. Bellgard, H.L. Hiew, A. Hunter, M. Wiebrands, "ORBIT: an integrated environment for user-customized bioinformatics tools", Bioinformatics 15(10), 1999, pp 847–851.

5. Blast: http://ww.ncbi.nlm.nih.gov/BLAST/
6. G. Booch, J. Rumbaugh and I. Jacobson, "The Unified Modeling Language User guide", Addison-Wesley Longman, 1999.
7. P. Buneman, S.B. Davidson, K. Hart, G.C. Overton and L. Wong, "A Data Transformation System for Biological Data Sources", VLDB Conference, 1995, pp 158–169.
8. I.A. Chen and V.M. Markowitz, "An Overview of the Object Protocol Model and the OPM Data Management Tools", Information Systems 20(5), 1995, pp 393–418.
9. S.B. Davidson, C. Overton and P. Buneman, "Challenges in Integrating Biological Data Sources", Journal of Computational Biology 2(4), 1995, pp 557–572.
10. R.F. Doolittle (editor), "Methods in Enzymology", Academic Press, 1990.
11. M.E. Fayad, D.C. Schmidt and R.E. Johnson, "Building Application Frameworks", Addison-Wesley, 1999.
12. E. Gamma, R. Helm, R. Johnson and J. Vlissides, "Design Patterns: Elements of reusable object-oriented software", Addison-Wesley Longman, 1995.
13. GenBank: http://www.ncbi.nlm.nih.gov/Genbank/index.html
14. E. Hunt, M.P. Atkinson and R.W. Irving, "A Database Index to Large Biological Sequences", to appear in VLDB Conference, 2001.
15. Gene Ontology: http://www.geneontology.org/
16. V. Guerrinia and D. Jackson, "Bioinformatics and XML", On Line Journal of Bioinformatics, 1(1), 2000, pp 1–13.
17. P. Karp, "A Strategy for Database Interoperation", Journal of Computational Biology 2(4), 1995, pp 573–586.
18. M. Lemos, "Memory Management for Sequence Comparison", MSc Thesis (in Portuguese), Departamento de Informática, PUC-Rio, August 2000.
19. S. Letovsky (editor), "Bioinformatics: Databases and Systems", Kluwer, 1999.
20. S. Lifschitz, L.F.B. Seibel and E.M.A. Uchôa, "A Framework for Molecular Biology Data Integration", Procs. Workshop on Information Integration on the Web (WIIW), 2001, pp 27-34.
21. V.M. Markowitz and O. Ritter, "Characterizing Heterogeneous Molecular Biology Database Systems", Journal of Computational Biology, 2(4), 1995, pp 547–556.
22. J. Meidanis and J.C. Setúbal, "Introduction to Computational Molecular Biology", PWS Publishing Company, 1997.
23. F. Moussouni, N.W. Paton, A. Hayes, S. Oliver, C.A. Goble and A. Brass, "Database Challenges for Genome Information in the Post Sequencing Phase", Procs 10th Database and Expert Systems Applications (DEXA), 1999, pp 540–549.
24. T. Okayama, T. Tamura, T. Gojobori, Y. Tateno, K. Ikeo, S. Miyasaki, K. Fukami-Kobayashi and H. Sugawara, "Formal Design and Implementation of an Improved DDBJ DNA Database with a New Schema and Object-oriented Library", Bioinformatics 14, 1998, pp 472–478.
25. N.W. Patton, S.A. Khan, A. Hayes, F. Moussoni, A. Brass, K. Eilbeck, C.A. Goble, S.J. Hubbard, S. G. Oliver, "Conceptual modeling of genomic information", Bioinformatics 16(6), 2000, pp 548– 557.
26. L.F.B. Seibel and S. Lifschitz, "A Genome Databases Framework", Technical Report (MCC) PUC-Rio, Departamento de Informática, 2001.
27. Swiss-Prot: http://www.ebi.ac.uk/swissprot
28. Tambis Project: http://img.cs.man.ac.uk/tambis/
29. XML: http://www.w3.org/XML/
30. Xquery: http://www.w3.org/TandS/QL/QL98/pp/xquery.html

Lock Downgrading: An Approach to Increase Inter-transaction Parallelism in Advanced Database Applications[1]

Angelo Brayner
University of Fortaleza - UNIFOR, Dept. of Computer Science
60811-341 Fortaleza - Brazil
brayner@unifor.br

Abstract. In this paper, we propose a concurrency control protocol, denoted *Cooperative Locking*, which extends the two-phase locking protocol by introducing the notion of downgrading of locks proposed in [9]. The basic idea of the proposed protocol is to provide the following functionality: after using an object in a transaction, the user can downgrade a lock on an object to a less restrictive mode before the transaction ends its execution. The prime goal of our proposal is to provide a high degree of inter-transaction parallelism while ensuring serializability of schedules.

1 Introduction

The classical model for concurrency control in DBMSs adopts *serializability* as the correctness criterion for the execution of concurrent transactions. In existing DBMS, serializability is ensured by the two-phase locking (2PL) protocol [7]. The 2PL protocol implements a locking mechanism which requires that a transaction obtains a lock on a database object before accessing it. A transaction may only obtain a lock if no other transaction holds an incompatible lock (e.g., a lock for a read operation is incompatible with a write lock) on the same object. When a transaction obtains a lock, it is retained until the transaction ends its execution (by a commit or an abort operation).

However, in recent years, database concepts have been applied to areas such as computer-aided design and software engineering (CAD and CASE), geographic information systems (GIS) and workflow management systems (WFMS). These advanced database applications consist of long-living transactions and present a cooperative environment. Waiting for locks may cause unacceptable delays for concurrent transactions belonging to this class of database applications. Accordingly, the 2PL protocol is not adequate for controlling concurrency in such applications.

In this work, we propose an extension to the 2PL protocol by introducing the notion of lock mode downgrading presented in [9] (this notion appears also in [10] as *lock release conversion*, but it is not used as a primitive in the locking mechanism). Härder and Rothermel propose that *a transaction holding a lock in mode M can downgrade it to a less restrictive mode.* This notion is used by the authors to implement controlled downward inheritance of locks to provide more intra-transaction parallelism in the processing of nested transactions.

[1]Research supported by the University of Fortaleza - UNIFOR.

H.C. Mayr et al. (Eds.): DEXA 2001, LNCS 2113, pp. 330–339, 2001.

In our proposal, we use lock downgrading as a primitive in the locking protocol in order to obtain more inter-transaction parallelism. Such a feature can optimize the processing of long-living transactions. With the notion of lock downgrading, the user may relax the blocking property of locks on database objects. Lock downgrading ensures more cooperation among transactions accessing the same set of database objects. For that reason, we denote our proposal Cooperative Locking (CL, for short).

This paper is organized as follows. In the next section, we briefly outline some concepts of the conventional transaction model which are used in this paper. Section 3 motivates and discusses the Cooperative Locking protocol. In Section 4, we compare the results of our proposal with other works. Section 5 concludes the paper.

2 The Model

A database is a collection of disjoint objects. The values of these objects may be read and modified by transactions. A transaction is modeled as a finite sequence of *read* and *write* operations on database objects, where $r_i(x)$ ($w_i(x)$) represents a read (write) operation executed by a transaction T_i on object x. To each transaction, an identifier, denoted *TRID*, is associated which uniquely identifies it.

A schedule models an interleaved execution of transactions. Two operations of different transactions conflict iff they access the same database object and at least one of them is a write operation. With $p <_S q$, we indicate that the operation p is executed in the schedule S before q. The Serialization Graph for a schedule S over $\mathcal{T}= \{T_1, T_2, \cdots, T_n\}$ is a directed graph $SG(S) = (N, E)$ where each node in N corresponds to a transaction in $\mathcal{T}$, and E contains edges of the form $T_i \longrightarrow T_j$ if and only if $T_i, T_j \in N$ and two operations p in T_i and q in T_j are in conflict, with $p <_S q$. We say that a transaction T_j indirectly conflicts with T_i, if there is an edge $T_i \longrightarrow T_j$ in E^+, where $SG^+(S) = (N, E^+)$ is the transitive closure of the serialization graph SG of the schedule S, and $T_i, T_j \in \mathcal{T}$. A schedules S is said to be conflict serializable, i.e. $S \in$ CSR, iff $SG(S)$ is acyclic [4]. A schedule S is correct if it is either serial or conflict serializable.

3 The CL Protocol

3.1 The Protocol

Upgrading of locks is the only lock conversion supported by 2PL. Cooperative Locking extends 2PL by introducing a mechanism which enables two different types of lock conversion on a database object O:

- Upgrading of locks: A transaction holding a lock type L on O can upgrade it to a *more* restrictive type L', if no other transaction holds a conflicting lock with L' on O;
- Downgrading of locks: A transaction holding a lock type L on O can downgrade it to a *less* restrictive type L'.

Cooperative locking supports three lock types: *Nil*, *read lock* (rl) and *write lock* (wl). The lock type Nil denotes the absence of locks. The other lock types have been discussed exhaustively. Figure 1 shows the compatibility table among lock types. The columns represent lock types which a transaction T_i holds on a database object. The rows represent locks which are requested by another transaction T_j on the same object. An entry "+" in the table denotes that the lock types are compatible. On the other hand, an entry "−" denotes that the lock types are not compatible.

	Nil	rl_i	wl_i
rl_j	+	+	-
wl_j	+	-	-

Figure 1: Compatibility table for locks in a *CL* protocol.

A *CL* scheduler[2] manages locks according to the following rules:

(R1) A transaction may *acquire* a lock of type read on an object O, if no other transaction holds a write lock on O.

(R2) A transaction may *acquire* a lock of type write on an object O or *upgrade* a lock it holds to write lock, if no other transaction holds a read or write lock on O.

(R3) A transaction holding a write lock may *downgrade* it to read lock or *Nil*.

(R4) A transaction holding a read lock may *downgrade* it to *Nil*.

(R5) Once a transaction has downgraded a lock, it may not upgrade the lock.

(R6) Once a transaction has released a lock, it may not acquire any new locks (2-phase rule).

The process of lock downgrading can make an object used by a transaction T visible to other transactions. The object may become visible for read or for update operations. For instance, if a transaction T downgrades a write lock on an object O to a read lock, other transactions can read O but not update it. Notwithstanding, if T downgrades the write lock to *Nil*, other transactions can read and update O.

The user should explicitly request a lock downgrading. To represent such a transaction request, we will use the notation $dg(O, L)$, where O denotes the object whose lock should be downgraded to type L according to rules (R3) and (R4).

It is easy to see that, differently from lock upgrading, the action of downgrading a lock does not provoke deadlocks. On the other hand, lock downgrading may sometimes present undesirable side-effects. To illustrate such a side-effect, consider that a *CL* scheduler has already scheduled the following operations: $S = w_1(x)dg_1(x, rl)r_2(x)w_2(y)c_2$. Assume that the commit operation c_2 has been successfully processed and, after that, the scheduler receives $w_1(y)$ and schedules it. A nonserializable schedule is produced ($SG(S)$ contains a cycle). In order to avoid such undesirable side-effects, the *CL* protocol must perform special control on transactions which have executed at least one lock downgrading. Before describing how this control is carried out, we have to define data structures which are needed for it.

Definition 1. The CL protocol should maintain the following data structures:

1. $rl\_set(O)$: This structure represents a set containing TRIDs of all transactions which are currently holding a read lock on the object O.

[2] A scheduler which implements a Cooperative Locking protocol.

2. $wl\_set(O)$: Set of TRIDs from transactions currently holding a write lock on O.
3. dg_set: Set whose elements are TRIDs of all active (not committed) transactions which have downgraded at least one lock. After a transaction has committed or aborted, it is removed from the set dg_set;
4. $TCG(T)$: For each transaction T in dg_set, a directed graph, called *transaction conflict graph* for T ($TCG(T)$) is constructed as follows:
   (a) The nodes represent transactions which *directly* or *indirectly* conflict with T, where the conflicting operations occur *after* T *has downgraded a lock*;
   (b) The edges represent the conflicts among the transactions represented in $TCG(T)$. Hence, the $TCG(T)$ contains edges of the form T → T' if and only if an operation p in T conflicts with an operation q belonging to T' and $p < q$;
   (c) The $TCG(T)$ must be acyclic;
   (d) After T has ended its execution, the $TCG(T)$ can be deleted. ◇

Example 1. Consider the schedule S over set $\mathcal{T} = \{T_1, T_2, T_3, T_4\}$ of transactions, where: $S = w_1(x)c_1r_2(x)w_2(y)dg_2(y, rl)r_3(y)w_3(z)c_3r_4(z)c_4w_2(v)$
The following graph represents the transaction conflict graph for T_2:
$TCG(T_2)$: $T_2 \longrightarrow T_3 \longrightarrow T_4$
The conflict between T_1 and T_2 occurs before T_2 has downgraded wl on y to rl. For that reason, T_1 is not represented in $TCG(T_2)$. On the other hand, T_3 conflicts with T_2 after the latter has downgraded a lock. By item 4.a of Definition 1, T_3 should be represented in the graph. Transaction T_4 represents a node in $TCG(T_2)$ because T_4 *indirectly conflicts* with T_2. ◇

Theorem 1. Let CL be the set of all schedules produced by a *Cooperative Locking* protocol. Then CL ⊂ CSR.
Proof. Let S be a schedule over a set $\mathcal{T}$ of transactions produced by a CL protocol, that is, S ∈CL.
Case 1. No transaction has requested lock downgrading in S. Suppose, by way of contradiction, that S is not conflict serializable, that is S ∉CSR. Hence, the serialization graph of S is cyclic. Without loss of generality, consider that the cycle in $SG(S)$ has the following form: $T_i \to T_j \to \cdots \to T_i$. It follows from this that, for some operations $p_i(x), q_i(y)$, the transaction T_i may obtain a lock on y after having released a lock on x, a contradiction to the 2-phase rule. Thus, CL ⊆ CSR. Consider the following schedule: $S' = r_1(x)w_2(x)w_1(z)$. Clearly, S' ∈ CSR\CL, because, according to the CL protocol (rule R2), transaction T_2 must wait for the end of T_1 in order to execute the operation $w_2(x)$. Thus, CL ⊂ CSR, as was to be proved.
Case 2. At least one transaction in S downgrades a lock. By way of contradiction, suppose that S ∉ CSR. Hence, the serialization graph of S contains at least one cycle. Without loss of generality, consider that $SG(S)$ has the following cycle: $T_i \to T_j \to \cdots \to T_i$. The edge $T_i \to T_j$ is the result of two conflicting operations

$p_i(x)$ in T_i and $q_j(x)$ in T_j, where $p_i(x) <_S q_j(x)$. Now consider that the transaction T_i has downgraded a lock on object x on which the transaction T_j executes operation q_j. By Definition 1, a transaction conflict graph for T_i ($TCG(T_i)$) should be constructed for which $T_i \rightarrow T_j \rightarrow \cdots \rightarrow T_i$ is a subgraph, a contradiction, because, by item 4.c of Definition 1, $TCG(T_i)$ must be acyclic. Thus, CL $\subseteq$ CSR. The schedule $S' = w_1(z)r_1(x)dg_1(x, Nill)w_2(x)r_2(z)w_1(y)$. Clearly, $S' \in$ CSR$\backslash$CL, because T_2 may not acquire a read lock on z while T_1 holds a write lock on z, consequently, T_2 may not execute $r_2(z)$ before T_1 ends. Therefore, CL $\subset$ CSR, as was to be proved. ◇

Theorem 1 shows that a scheduler implementing cooperative locking enforces serializability. It is important to note that in the absence of lock downgrading, a *CL* scheduler behaves like a 2PL scheduler. This is shown in case 1 of the proof for Theorem 1. This property represents an important result of our proposal, since it assures that a cooperative locking mechanism may be implemented on the top of any 2PL scheduler.

3.2 Implementation Aspects

Using the structures described in Definition 1, a *CL* scheduler performs the operations shown in Figure 2. These two procedures can be summarized as follows. When a transaction T_i requires a lock L for a given object O, the scheduler verifies whether there is a conflicting lock associated to O on behalf of another transaction T_j ($i \neq j$). If any T_j holds a conflicting lock on O, the scheduler should delay the processing of setting L until T_j releases its lock on O. In fact, the delay function ($delay(rl_i(O))$ or $delay(wl_i(O))$) blocks transaction T_i until T_j releases the lock. If there is no conflicting lock, the scheduler must verify whether transaction T_i has downgraded any lock. Hence, if T_i is not an element of *dg_set*, the lock can be set. Otherwise, it must be checked whether the execution of the corresponding operation to the required lock introduces a cycle in $TCG(T_i)$. This is performed by the function *check*(TCG(TRID)). If no cycle is produced, the required lock may be granted. Otherwise, the required lock should be rejected and the transaction aborted.

```
Read_Lock(TRID,O)
/* read locking protocol */
if wl_set(O) = ∅
  if TRID ∉ dg_set
    rl_set(O)←rl_set(O) ∪ {TRID};
  else
    check(TCG(TRID))
    if exists_cycle
      reject(rl(O))
    else
      rl_set(O)←rl_set(O) ∪ {TRID};
else
  delay(rl(O));
```

```
Write_Lock(TRID,O)
/* write locking protocol */
if wl_set(O)=∅ and rl_set(O)=∅
  if TRID ∉ dg_set
    wl_set(O)←wl_set(O) ∪ {TRID};
  else
    check(TCG(TRID))
    if exists_cycle
      reject(wl(O))
    else
      wl_set(O)←wl_set(O) ∪ {TRID};
else
  delay(wl(O));
```

Figure 2: Procedures to set read/write locks.

Figure 3 shows the procedure executed by a *CL* scheduler when it receives a lock downgrading request. The parameter L_{old} denotes the lock on object O which is to be downgraded to L_{new}. Only *rl* or *Nil* are valid values for L_{new} . Here it is important to underline the difference between downgrading a lock to *Nil* and releasing a lock. When a transaction T downgrades a lock to *Nil*, the scheduler should monitor the execution of T more closely in order to ensure that serializability will not be jeopardized. For that reason, T should be inserted in *dg_set* and the graph $TCG(T)$ should be constructed and maintained by the scheduler. By releasing a lock, a transaction can not induce inconsistencies in the execution of concurrent executions (this is ensured by the two-phase rule). Thus, no additional control is necessary.

Evidently, aborting transactions introduces several difficulties for the processing of long-living transactions. However, we propose mechanisms which can minimize the drawbacks of transaction aborts. It is also important to note that other proposals extending 2PL, such as *Altruistic Locking* [2, 11] and *Locks with Constrained Sharing* [1], also suffer from the problem of having to abort transactions.

3.3 Reducing the Negative Effects of Transaction Aborts

As mentioned before, a *CL* scheduler is sometimes forced to abort transactions. In this section, we present two strategies which can reduce the frequency of aborts.

The basic function of a concurrency control mechanism is to synchronize conflicting operations. There are two kinds of conflicts: *read-write* (*write-read*) conflicts and *write-write* conflicts. Sometimes, it may be meaningful to decompose the synchronization realized by a concurrency control mechanism in two subfunctions: *(i)* synchronization of conflicting read-write (write-read) operations, denoted *rw-synchronization* and *(ii)* synchronization of conflicting write-write operations, denoted *ww-synchronization*. In order to illustrate this fact, consider that a *CL* scheduler has already scheduled the following operations:

$S = rl_1(x)r_1(x)dg_1(x, Nil)wl_2(x)w_2(x)wl_2(z)w_2(z)c_2$

Now, suppose that, after c_2 has already been scheduled and performed, the scheduler receives the operation $w_1(z)$. For that reason, a $wl_1(z)$ is requested. By the *CL* protocol, $wl_1(z)$ can not be granted, the operation $w_1(z)$ should be rejected, and the transaction T_1 aborted. However, suppose that the scheduler has granted the write lock on O, but has not executed the operation $w_1(z)$ (i.e. the scheduler ignores $w_1(z)$). This yields the same value for the object z as executing the actions of rejecting $w_1(z)$ and aborting T_1. Therefore, from the *ww*-synchronization perspective, the actions of rejecting $w_1(z)$ and aborting T_1 were unnecessary.

We can summarize the observation described above as follows. Let T_j be a transaction which has executed a *write operation* on O before the *CL* scheduler receives $wl_i(O)$ (write lock request of T_i on O). If $wl_i(O)$ can be granted (because T_j has already committed or downgraded the write lock to *Nil*) and the operation $w_i(O)$ introduces a cycle in $TCG(T_i)$, then the scheduler only has to grant the write lock and ignore the operation $w_i(O)$ without aborting T_i. This is the sufficient condition to produce a result similar to the one produced by a correctly synchronized execution of the two conflicting write operations. To illustrate this fact, consider the following schedule:

$S = rl_1(x)r_1(x)dg_1(x, Nil)wl_2(x)w_2(x)wl_1(z)w_1(z)c_1wl_2(z)w_2(z)c_2.$

If a *CL* scheduler has already scheduled the operations of S and then receives $wl_1(z)$, T_1 should be aborted, because a cycle would be produced in $TCG(T_i)$, if $w_1(z)$ were executed. However, the scheduler can "correct" S on-the-fly without aborting T_1. It only needs to grant the write lock for T_1 and ignore operation $w_1(z)$. If this rule is applied, the execution of S produces the same database state as does the execution of the following schedule S', which is a correct one:

$S' = rl_1(x)r_1(x)dg_1(x, Nil)wl_2(x)w_2(x)wl_1(z)w_1(z)c_1wl_2(z)w_2(z)c_2.$

This *ww*-synchronization rule is called *Thomas' Write Rule* (TWR) [4] in the literature. To minimize the negative effects of aborting transactions, we introduce the TWR concept in the CL protocol. The key idea is to verify the applicability of the TWR whenever the scheduler receives a lock request for a *write* operation and this operation produces a cycle in the TCG of the transaction requiring the lock. For that reason, we have to extend the write locking protocol of Figure 2. The extended protocol is shown in Figure 4.

```
dg_Lock(TRID,O,L_old,L_new)
dg_set←dg_set ∪ {TRID};
if L_new=rl
  wl_set(O)←wl_set(O) \ {TRID};
  Read_Lock(TRID,O);
else
  if L_old=rl
    rl_set(O)←rl_set(O) \ {TRID};
  else
    wl_set(O)←wl_set(O) \ {TRID};
```

Figure 3. Downgrading of locks.

```
Write_Lock(TRID,O)
/* write locking protocol using TWR */
if wl_set(O)=∅ and rl_set(O)=∅
  if TRID ∉ dg_set
    wl_set(O)←wl_set(O) ∪ {TRID};
  else
    check(TCG(TRID))
    if exists_cycle
      if apply_twr
        wl_set(O)←wl_set(O) ∪ {TRID};
/* the lock is setted, but the write
operation is not executed */
      else
        reject(wl(O))
    else
      wl_set(O)←wl_set(O) ∪ {TRID};
else
  delay(wl(O));
```

Figure 4. Granting write locks applying TWR.

The basic function of *apply_twr* in the protocol of Figure 4 is to verify whether or not the TWR is applicable. This can be done by identifying the form of the cycle in the function *check*(TCG(TRID)), where TRID represents the transaction requesting the lock.

Another approach to reduce the side-effects of aborting transactions is to avoid cascading aborts in the CL protocol by introducing the following constraint: *A transaction may only downgrade read locks.* This constraint guarantees that a *write lock* may not be downgraded to a *read lock* or *Nil.* Write locks may only be released at transaction commit. This solution is useful for applications whose (long-living) transactions basically consist of many read-only operations and few write operations. However, it is restrictive for long-living transactions with many write operations.

The approach described above solves the cascading abort problem. However, it introduces other problems and restrictions. In fact, avoiding cascading aborts for long-living transactions is too expensive and perhaps impracticable. For that reason, several proposals introduce the notion of compensating transactions, instead of avoiding cascading aborts, as for example in [5, 8].

4 Related Work

As already mentioned, *Altruistic Locking* [2, 11] and *Locks with Constrained Sharing* [1] are also proposals based on the release of locks before a transaction ends.

The Altruistic Locking (*AL*) protocol extends 2PL by introducing the *donate* operation. A donate operation encapsulates the information that an object will not be used by a transaction. Hence, a donate operation converts a write or read lock to *Nil*. However, it does not have the same semantic as releasing a lock. If a transaction donates an object, it still holds a lock on the object. Locks are released according to the two-phase rule of the 2PL protocol. In order to guarantee serializability, the following condition, denoted *altruistic locking rule* [11], must be ensured by the AL protocol: if a transaction T_j accesses an object donated by a transaction T_i, each operation $op_j(O)$ in T_j can only be executed if the object O has been donated by T_i or after the first unlock operation in T_i. Observe that the transaction T_j may wait for the end of T_i to execute an operation $op_j(O)$, although there is no lock on the object O and transaction T_i will never execute any operation on O. Hence, the altruistic rule is too restrictive.

The CL protocol relaxes the altruistic locking rule. For that reason, we can say that the CL protocol provides a higher degree of inter-transaction parallelism than AL. In [6] we show that $\text{ALT} \subset \text{CL}$.

Although the AL protocol has been proposed to increase concurrency when long transactions are processed, it may cause that short transactions wait for the end of long transactions. To overcome such a restriction, some extensions are proposed in [11]. These extensions are based on the pre-declaration of the access set of transactions. However, because of the interactive nature of transactions in some advanced database applications (e.g., transactions in design activities), the access patterns of such transactions are not predictable.

In the AL protocol, a donate operation downgrades read or write locks to *Nil*. On the other hand, the CL protocol provides a controlled downgrading of locks. The user can specify, for example, if a write lock should be downgraded to read lock or to *Nil*. Thus, the user can decide if an updated object can be seen by other transactions for read-only operation or for update.

The *Locks with Constrained Sharing* (LCS) protocol introduces the notion of *ordered shared* locks. The basic idea here is that two transactions may hold conflicting locks on the same object, if the following condition is ensured: the order in which the conflicting locks are acquired must be the same to execute the corresponding operations. For example, if $rl_1(x) < wl_2(x)$, then $r_1(x) < w_2(x)$. The lock $wl_2(x)$ is said to be *on hold* and it remains on hold until transaction T_1

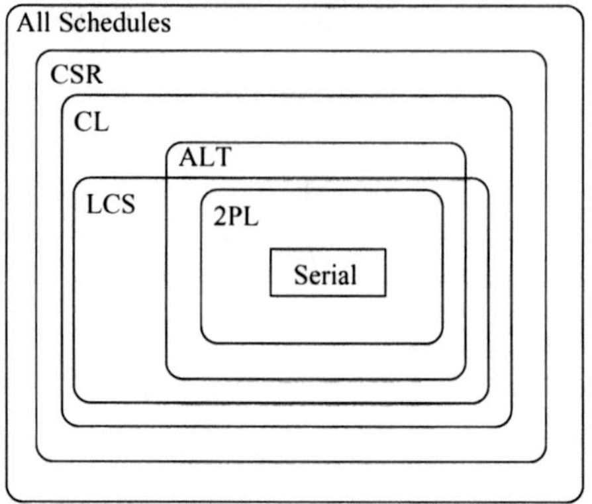

Figure 3: Relationship among different classes of schedules.

executes an unlock operation on x. In addition to the 2PL rules , this protocol ensures serializability through the following constraint: a transaction may not release any of its lock, if it has locks on hold. This constraint, however, can be too restrictive. To illustrate this fact, consider that a LCS scheduler has already scheduled the following operations:

$S = wl_1(x)w_1(x)rl_2(x)r_2(x)$, where $T_1 = w_1(x)r_1(v)\dots w_1(z)c_1$; $T_2 = r_2(x)c_2$

Consider that, after operation $r_2(x)$ is processed, the scheduler receives the operation c_2. According to the LCS protocol, the execution of c_2 must be delayed until T_1 releases its locks on x. As in *Altruistic Locking*, we have here the situation in which short transactions may wait for the end of long transactions. In [6] we show that LCS $\subset$ CL.

In Figure 3, we present a Venn diagram depicting the relationships among classes of schedules produced by the protocols discussed in this paper.

One may argue that, in our proposal, the rate of aborts increases. However, this problem also exists in *LCS* and *AL* protocols.

In a concurrency control mechanism using the *LCS* protocol, transactions should be aborted under the same conditions as in a *CL* protocol, more precisely, when non-serializable (incorrect) schedules are produced. For example, the following schedule may be produced by a *LCS* scheduler: $S = w_1(x)r_2(x)w_2(y)r_1(y)$. In [1], such phenomenon is called *deadly-embrace situation* and the authors propose that one of the involved transactions should be aborted.

The *AL* protocol increases the rate of aborts, since the frequency of deadlocks is increased. To show this fact, consider the following transactions:

$T_1 = w_1(x)donate_1(x)w_1(z)c_1$; $T_2 = r_2(x)r_2(y)c_2$; $T_3 = r_3(z)w_3(x)c_3$

Now, suppose that an *AL* scheduler has already scheduled the following operations: $S = r_3(z)w_1(x)donate_1(x)r_2(x)$. If, after scheduling $r_2(x)$, the scheduler receives $r_2(y)$, this operation should be delayed until T_1 ends (*altruistic locking rule*). Thus, transaction T_2 should wait for the end of T_1. On the other hand, T_1 can only end if T_3 ends, since T_3 holds a lock on z and T_1 is waiting for a lock on z in order to execute $w_1(z)$. In turn, transaction T_3 should wait for the end of T_2, because T_2 holds a lock on x and T_3 can not execute $w_3(x)$. Therefore, transactions T_1, T_2 and T_3 are involved in a deadlock. One of them has to be aborted, possibly causing cascaded aborts. For example, if T_1 is chosen to be aborted, T_2 should also be aborted. Note that a similar deadlock situation is also produced if the scheduler receives $w_1(z)$ or $w_3(x)$ after scheduling $r_2(x)$. If the CL protocol were used to synchronize the transactions in such a scenario, no deadlock situation had been induced.

5 Conclusions

In this paper, we have proposed an extension to the two-phase locking protocol which provides a higher degree of parallelism among transactions. We have shown that, although the Cooperative Locking protocol is more permissive than the 2PL, it ensures serializability of schedules. Moreover, we have also shown that Cooperative Locking provides more concurrency among transactions than other proposals extending the 2PL protocol, such as Altruistic Locking and Locks with Constrained Sharing.

Of course, our proposal does not completely solve all problems existing in the processing long-living transactions. However, it can provide a *higher degree of inter-transaction parallelism* as compared to 2PL, Altruistic Locking and Locks with Constrained Sharing.

References

[1] Agrawal, D. and Abbadi, A. E. Locks with Constrained Sharing. In *Proceedings of the 9th ACM Symposium on PODS*, pages 85–93, New York, 1990.

[2] Alonso, R., Garcia-Molina, H., Salem, K. Concurrency control and recovery for global procedures in federated database systems. *A quartely bulletin of the Computer Society of the IEEE technical comittee on Data Engineering*, 10(3), 1987.

[3] Berenson, H., Bernstein, P., Gray, J., Melton, J., O'Neil, E. and O'Neil, P. A Critique of ANSI SQL Isolation Levels. In *Proceedings of 1995 ACM SIGMOD Conference*, pages 1–10, June 1995.

[4] Bernstein, P. A., Hadzilacos, V. and Goodman, N. *Concurrency Control and Recovery in Database Systems.* Addison-Wesley, 1987.

[5] Biliris, A., Dar, S., Gehani, N., Jagadisch, H. V. and Ramamritham, K. ASSET: A System for Supporting Extended Transactions. In *Proceedings of the 1994 ACM SIGMOD Conference*, pages 44–54, May 1994.

[6] Brayner, A. *Transaction Management in Multidatabase Systems.* Shaker-Verlag, 1999.

[7] Eswaran, K.P., Gray, J.N., Lorie, R.A. and Traiger, I.L. The Notions of Consistency and Predicate Locks in a Database System. *Communications of the ACM*, 19(11):624–633, November 1976.

[8] Garcia-Molina, H. and Salem, K. . SAGAS. In *Proceedings of the ACM SIGMOD Conference*, pages 249–259, 1987.

[9] Härder, T. and Rothermel, K. Concurrency Control Issues in Nested Transactions. *VLDB Journal*, 2(1):39–74, 1993.

[10] Korth, H. F. Locking Primitives in a Database System. *Journal of the ACM*, 30(1):55–79, 1983.

[11] Salem, K., Garcia-Molina, H. and Shands, J. Altruistic Locking. *ACM Transactions on Database Systems*, 19(1):117–165, March 1994.

The SH-tree: A Super Hybrid Index Structure for Multidimensional Data

Tran Khanh Dang, Josef Küng, and Roland Wagner

Institute for Applied Knowledge Processing (FAW)
University of Linz, Austria
{khanh, jkueng, rwagner}@faw.uni-linz.ac.at

Abstract. Nowadays feature vector based similarity search is increasingly emerging in database systems. Consequently, many multidimensional data index techniques have been widely introduced to database researcher community. These index techniques are categorized into two main classes: SP (space partitioning)/KD-tree-based and DP (data partitioning)/R-tree-based. Recently, a hybrid index structure has been proposed. It combines both SP/KD-tree-based and DP/R-tree-based techniques to form a new, more efficient index structure. However, weaknesses are still existing in techniques above. In this paper, we introduce a novel and flexible index structure for multidimensional data, the SH-tree (Super Hybrid tree). Theoretical analyses show that the SH-tree is a good combination of both techniques with respect to both presentation and search algorithms. It overcomes the shortcomings and makes use of their positive aspects to facilitate efficient similarity searches.

Keywords. Similarity search, multidimensional index, bounding sphere (BS), minimum bounding rectangle (MBR), super hybrid tree (SH-tree).

1 Introduction

Feature based similarity search has a long development process which is still in progress now. Its application range includes multimedia databases [33], time-series databases [32], CAD/CAM systems [34], medical image databases [27], etc. In these large databases, feature spaces have been usually indexed using multidimensional data structures.

Since Morton introduced the space-filling curves in 1966 up to now, many index structures have been developed. A survey schema that summarizes the history of multidimensional access methods from 1966 to 1996 has been presented in [1]. This summary and two recent publications [2, 19] show that multidimensional index techniques can be divided into two main classes: Index structures based on space partitioning (SP-based) or KD-tree-based such as kDB-tree [6], hB-tree [7], LSD-tree and LSDh-tree [8, 9], Grid File [10], BANG file [11], GNAT tree [29], mvp-tree [35], SKD-tree [28], etc. Index structures based on data partitioning (DP-based or R-tree-based) consist of R-trees and its improved variants [12, 13, 14], X-tree [15], SS-tree [5], TV-tree [3], SR-tree [4], M-tree [20], etc. The remains, which can not be categorized into the above schema, are called dimensionality reduction index techniques [19] like Pyramid technique [16, 17], UB-tree [18], space-filling curves

H.C. Mayr et al. (Eds.): DEXA 2001, LNCS 2113, pp. 340–349, 2001.

(see [1] for a survey). Recently, the Hybrid tree[1] [2, 19], a hybrid technique has been proposed. It is formed by combining both SP and DP based techniques. For detailed explanations of classification, see [1, 2, 19].

This paper is organized as follows: Section 2 discusses motivations, which lead us to introduce the SH-tree. Section 3 is devoted to discuss structure and advanced aspects of the SH-tree. Section 4 presents update operations, query algorithms with the SH-tree. Section 5 gives conclusions and future work.

2 Motivations

The SR-tree [4] has shown superiorities over the R*-tree and the SS-tree by dividing feature space into both small volume regions (using bounding rectangles–BRs) and short diameter regions (using bounding spheres–BSs). Nevertheless, the SR-tree must incur the fan-out problem: only one third of the SS-tree and two third of the R*-tree [4]. The low fan-out causes the SR-tree based searches to read more nodes and to reduce the query performance. This problem does not occur in the KD-tree based index techniques: the fan-out is constant for arbitrary dimension numbers.

Recently, the Hybrid tree [2, 19] has been introduced. It makes use of positive characteristics of both SP-based and DP-based index techniques. It depends on the KD-tree based layout for internal nodes and employs bounding regions (BRs) as hints to prune while traversing the tree. To overcome the access problem of unnecessary data pages, the Hybrid tree also applies a dead space eliminating technique by coding actual data regions (CADR) [9]. Although the CADR technique partly softens the unnecessary disk access problem, it is still not a high efficient solution to solve the entire problem. It strongly depends on the number of bits used to code the actual data region and, in some cases, this technique does not benefit regardless of how many bits are used to code space. Figure 1a and 1b show examples like that in 2-dimensional space. Here the whole region is coded irrespective of how many bits are used. Figure 1c shows an example where the benefit from coding the actual data region is not interesting, especially for range queries. This is due to the high remaining dead space ratio in the coded data region. Besides, when new objects locate outside the bounds of feature space already indexed by the Hybrid tree, the encoded live space (ELS) [19] must be recomputed from scratch.

Furthermore, the SP/KD-tree based index techniques in common recursively partition space into two subspaces using a single dimension until the data object number in each subspace can be stored in a single data page as the Hybrid tree, the LSDh-tree, etc. This partitioning way leads cluster of data to be quickly destroyed because the objects stored in the same page are "far away" in the real space. This problem could significantly influence the search performance; increase the number of disk accesses per range query [1]. It is contrary to the DP/R-tree based index techniques as the SS-tree, the SR-tree, etc. They try to keep near objects in the feature space into each data page.

To alleviate these problems and take inherent advantages of the SR-tree (the R-tree based techniques as a whole), together with introducing novel worth attentions we

---

[1] Internal nodes presentation idea is similar to one introduced by Ooi et al in 1987 for the Spatial KD-tree [28].

will present the SH-tree in the successive section. In the SH-tree, the fan-out problem will be overcome by employing the KD-tree presentation for partitions of internal nodes. The data cluster problem as mentioned above, however, is softened by still keeping the SR-tree-like structure for presentation of balanced and leaf nodes of the SH-tree (c.f. section 3.1). Section 3 will detail these ideas.

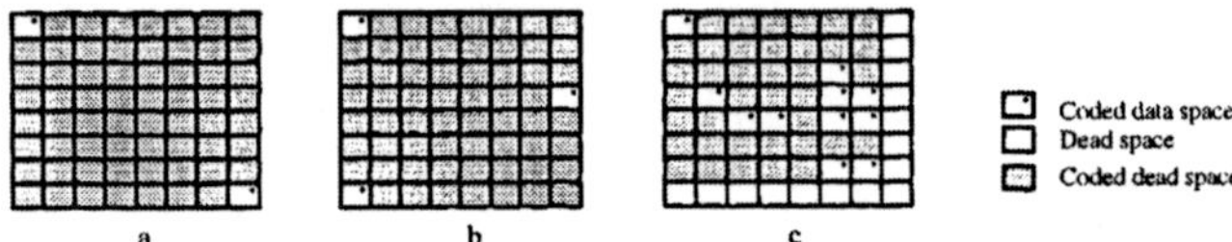

Fig. 1. Some problems with coding actual data region

3 The SH-tree

This section is dedicated to introduce the SH-tree. We are going to discuss how to split multidimensional space into subspaces and introduce a very special hybrid structure of the SH-tree.

3.1 Partitioning Multidimensional Space in the SH-tree

Because the SH-tree is planned to apply not only for point data objects, but also for extended data objects we choose no overlap-free space partitioning. This approach easily controls objects that cross a selected split position and solve the storage utilization problem. The former had been described in the SKD-tree [28] and the latter has happened to the kDB-tree, which shows uninterestingly slow performance even in 4-dimensional feature vector spaces [21].

There are three node kinds in the SH-tree: Internal, balanced and leaf nodes. Each internal node i has structure <d, lo, up, other_info>, where d is split dimension, *lo* represents the left (lower) boundary of the right (higher) partition, *up* represents the right (higher) boundary of the left (lower) partition and *other_info* consists of additional information as the data object number of its left, right child. While up=lo means no overlap between partitions, up>lo indicates that partitions overlap. This structure is similar to ones introduced in the SKD-tree [28] and the Hybrid tree [2]. The supplemental information also gives hints to develop a cost model for the nearest neighbor search in high-dimensional spaces, query selectivity estimation, etc. Moreover, let BR_i denote bounding rectangle of internal node i. The BR of its left child is defined as $BR_i \cap (d \leq up)$. Note that $\cap$ denotes geometric intersection. Similarity, the BR of its right child is defined as $BR_i \cap (d \geq lo)$. This allows us to apply algorithms used in the DP/R-tree based techniques to the SH-tree.

Balanced nodes are just above leaf nodes and they are not hierarchical (figure 2). Each of them has a similar structure to that of an internal node of the SR-tree This is a specific characteristic of the SH-trees. It conserves the data cluster, in part, and makes the height of the SH-tree smaller as well as employing the SR-tree's superior aspects. Moreover, it also shows that the SH-trees are not simple in binary shape as in the KD-tree based techniques. They are also multi-way trees as R-tree based index techniques:

BN: <B_1, B_2, …B_n> (minBN_E ≤ n ≤ maxBN_E)

B_i: <BS, MBR, num, child_pointer>

A balanced node consists of entries B_1, B_2, … B_n *(minBN_E ≤ n ≤ maxBN_E)* where *minBN_E* and *maxBN_E* are the minimum and maximum number of entries in the node. Each entry B_i keeps information of a leaf node including four components: a bounding sphere *BS*, a minimum bounding rectangle *MBR*, the object number of leaf node *num* and a pointer to it *pointer*. Furthermore, computing MBS (minimum BS) of a given objects set is not feasible in a high-dimensional space, since the time complexity is exponential in the dimension number [25]. Therefore, the SH-tree preliminarily uses MBRs and only BSs. See [4] for the calculation formula of BS.

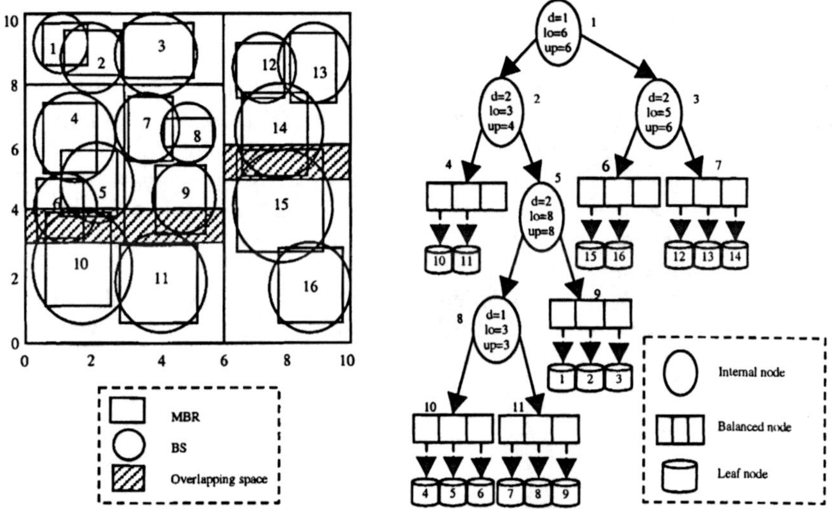

Fig. 2. A possible partition of a data space and corresponding mapping to the SH-tree

Each leaf node of the SH-tree has the same structure as that of the SS-tree (because the SR-tree [4] is just designed for point objects but the SH-tree is also planned for both points and extended objects):

LN: <L_1, L_2, …L_m> (minO_E ≤ m ≤ maxO_E)

Li: <obj, info>

A leaf node consists of entries L_1, L_2, … L_n *(minO_E ≤ n ≤ maxO_E)* where *minO_E* and *maxO_E* are minimum and maximum number of entries in a leaf. Each entry *Li* consists of a data object *obj* and information in the structure *info* as a feature vector, the radius bounds the object's extent in the feature space, object's MBR, etc. If objects in database are complex, then *obj* is its identifier instead of a real data object. In addition, in case that the SH-tree is only applied for point data objects, each *Li* is similar to that of the SR-tree: *Li: <obj, feature_info>*. In this case, the other information of the objects is no longer needed. For example, the parameter *radius* is always equal to zero and MBR is the point itself.

Figure 2 shows a possible partition of a feature space and its corresponding mapping to the SH-tree. Assume we have a 2-dimensional feature space D with a size of (0,0,10,10). With (d, lo, up)=(1,6,6), the BRs of left and right children of the internal node 1 are $BR_2=D\cap(d\leq 6)=(0,0,6,10)$ and $BR_3=D\cap(d\geq 6)=(6,0,10,10)$, individually. For the internal node 2, (d, lo, up)=(2,3,4), $BR_4=BR_2\cap(d\leq 4)=(0,0,6,4)$, $BR_5=BR_2\cap(d\geq 3)=(0,3,6,10)$ and so on. The BRs information is not stored in the SH-tree, but it is computed when necessary.

Furthermore, the storage utilization of the SH-tree must ensure that each balanced node is filled with at least *minBN_E* entries and each data page contains at least *minO_E* objects. Therefore, each subspace according to a balanced node holds N data objects and N satisfies the following condition:

$$\text{minO\_E} \times \text{minBN\_E} \leq N \leq \text{maxO\_E} \times \text{maxBN\_E} \qquad \textbf{(1)}$$

3.2 The Extended Balanced SH-tree

For almost index techniques based on the KD-tree, the tree structure is not balanced (e.g., the LSD/LSDh-tree, the SKD-tree). It means that there are leaf nodes that are farther away from the root than all others are. The experiments of [29] have shown that a good balance is not crucial for the performance of the index structure. In this section, we introduce a new conception for the balance problem in the SH-tree: *extended balance*. The motivation is to retain acceptable performance of the index structure and reduce maintenance cost for its exact balance.

Suppose that *p, b, b_min, b_max* denotes leaf node number, balanced node number, minimum and maximum number of balanced nodes in the SH-tree, respectively. The following inequality holds:

$$\text{b\_min} = \left\lceil \frac{p}{\max BN\_E} \right\rceil \leq \text{b} \leq \left\lceil \frac{p}{\min BN\_E} \right\rceil = \text{b\_max} \qquad \textbf{(2)}$$

The SH-tree's height *h* satisfies the following inequality:

$$1 + \lceil \log_2 \text{b\_min} \rceil \leq \text{h} \leq \lceil \log_2 \text{b\_max} \rceil + 1 \qquad \textbf{(3)}$$

Inequality (3) is used to evaluate whether the SH-tree is "balanced" or not. The meaning of balance here is loose. It does not mean that path length of every leaf node from the root is equal. We call this extended balance in the SH-tree. If the height *hl* of each leaf node in the SH-tree satisfies (3), i.e. $1+\lceil \log_2 \text{b\_min} \rceil \leq \text{hl} \leq \lceil \log_2 \text{b\_max} \rceil+1$, then the SH-tree is called an *extended balanced tree (EBT)*, and otherwise it is not a balanced tree. The extended balance conception generalizes the conventional balance conception: if inequality (3) becomes $1+\lceil \log_2 \text{b\_min} \rceil=\text{h}=\lceil \log_2 \text{b\_max} \rceil+1$, then an EBT becomes a *conventional balanced tree (CBT)*.

If *minBN_E*=2 and *maxBN_E*=3, the SH-tree in figure 3 is not a CBT or an EBT; it is not a balanced tree. The inequality (3) can be also extended as follows:

$$1 + \lceil \log_2 \text{b\_min} \rceil - x \leq \text{h} \leq \lceil \log_2 \text{b\_max} \rceil + 1 + x \qquad \textbf{(4)}$$

or a more general form:

$$1 + \lceil \log_2 \text{b\_min} \rceil - x \leq \text{h} \leq \lceil \log_2 \text{b\_max} \rceil + 1 + y \qquad \textbf{(5)}$$

In (4), (5) x and y are acceptable "errors". These parameters give more flexibility to the SH-tree but they must be carefully selected to prevent from creating a too much unbalanced tree. The SH-tree does not satisfy (3) but (4) or (5) will be called *loosely extended balanced tree (LEBT)*. For example, concerning the SH-tree in figure 3 then (3) becomes $4 \le h \le 4$ (here b_min=$\lceil 16/3 \rceil$=6 and b_max=8). If the SH-tree satisfies this condition, it really becomes a CBT (also EBT). We can readjust this condition with x=1 and get the new condition concerning (4): $3 \le h \le 5$. With respect to the new condition, the above SH-tree can be considered a LEBT. The parameter x (and y) in (4) (and (5)) depends on many attributes, say *p*, *minBN_E*, *maxBN_E* and so on. If x is suitably chosen, the maintenance cost of the SH-tree is substantially decreased but does not affect the querying performance.

In general, if the SH-tree fails to satisfy (4), it needs to be reformed. The reformation can entirely reorganize the SH-tree (also called dynamic bulk loading) or suitably change splitting algorithm. Henrich has presented a hybrid split strategy for KD-tree based access structures [22]. It depends on weighted average of the split positions calculated using two split strategies, data dependence and distribution dependence. Notice that the dynamic reformation operation usually incurs substantial costs including both I/O accesses and CPU time. An efficient algorithm for the SH-tree reformation is still an open problem.

3.3 Splitting Nodes in the SH-tree

In the context of dynamic databases, which means that the SH-tree is incrementally created and in that process, the data objects can be added or deleted, we present leaf nodes splitting and balanced nodes splitting in the SH-tree.

Leaf nodes splitting. The boundary of a leaf node in the SH-tree is the geometric intersection between its MBR and BS, but BS is isotropic thus it is not suitable for choosing the split dimension. Therefore, the choice of the split dimension depends on its MBR. This problem is solved in the same way as that of the Hybrid tree including overlap free splitting. The selected split dimension must minimize the disk access number. Without loss of generality, assume that the space is d-dimensional and extent of MBR along the ith dimension is e_i, i= [1,d]. Let range query Q be a bounding box with each dimension of length r. Prove as done in [4] to get result: the split dimension is k if $\frac{r}{e_k + r}$ is the minimum. Therefore, split dimension k is chosen such that its extent in MBR is the maximum, i.e. e_k=max(e_i), i=[1,d]. The next step is to select the split position. First, we check if it is possible to split in the middle without violating the utilization constraint. If it is impossible, we distribute data items equally into two nodes. This way also solves the special case as shown in the hB-tree [7]. Figure 3 shows this case as an example in two-dimensional space.

Balanced nodes splitting. Because the balanced node has the similar structure to internal nodes of the SR-tree and the R*-tree, the internal nodes splitting algorithm of the R*-tree [24] can be applied to split overfull balanced nodes of the SH-tree. With the SH-tree, however, if the sibling of an overfull balanced node is also a balanced node and still not full, then an entry of the overfull balanced node can be shifted to the

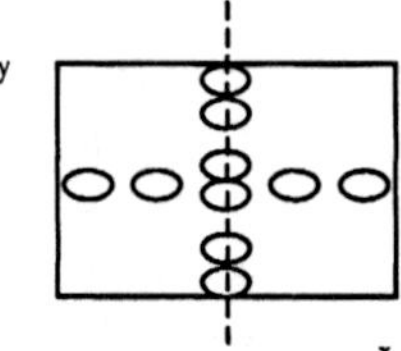

Fig. 3. Assume the split dimension *x* is chosen and the minimum data object number of each partition is three. There is no suitable split position if we apply the way of the Hybrid tree as described in [2]. In this case and other similar cases, the SH-tree distributes data items equally into two nodes.

sibling to avoid a split. This method also increases the storage utilization [36, 9]. Thus, the modified splitting algorithm for the balanced nodes can be concisely described: First, try to avoid a node splitting as just discussed. If it fails, the split algorithm similar to that of the R*-tree is employed. Notice that, in the SH-tree, the balanced node split does not cause propagated splits upwards or downwards, which is called cascading splits [7] and happened to the kDB-tree [6].

4 The SH-tree Operations

4.1 Insertion

Let NDO be a new data object to insert into the SH-tree. First, the SH-tree must be traversed from the root to locate leaf node *w*, which NDO will belong to. The best candidate is the node whose MBR is closest to NDO[2]. Ties are broken based on the nodes' data object number. If there is an empty entry in this leaf, NDO is inserted. Conversely, the leaf is an overflow leaf node, then one object of this leaf can be redistributed to the sibling, which is still not full, to make space for NDO. This idea is the same as that of [36] but does not recursively go upward like that, the siblings here are locally located in the balanced node. In fact, the predefined constant *l* of the algorithm in [36] is similar to the current entry number (CEN) of the balanced node (minBN_E ≤ CEN ≤ maxBN_E). The parameter CEN for the SH-tree's corresponding redistribution algorithm is different from each balanced node; this is a difference from the one presented in [36]. If a split is still compulsory, it can only propagate upwards at most one level. Figure 4 illustrates the split propagation in the SH-tree. In that, assume leaf node P_1 is selected to insert a NDO and P_1's entry number is *maxO_E* already. Moreover, suppose that the redistribution is also failed. Consequently, P_1 is split into P_1' and P_1". Nevertheless, because *maxBN_E*=2 (*minBN_E*=1) in this example, the balanced node B_1 is later split into B_1' and B_1". At last, a new internal node N is created. The split process is stopped and has no more propagation to upper level (root node R in this example).

[2] The distance metric used here is MINDIST, described in [26]

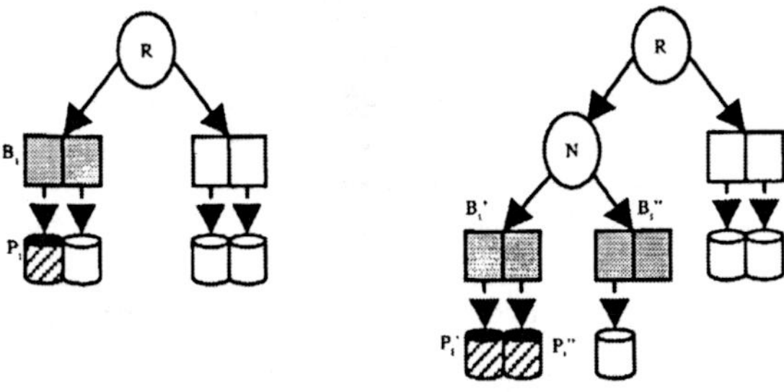

Fig. 4. Split in the SH-tree

4.2 Deletion

After determining which leaf node contains the object and removing the object, the leaf may become under-full (it means that the object number kept in this leaf is less than *minO_E*). There are some solutions to solve this problem as discussed in [23]. An under-full leaf node can be merged with whichever sibling has least enlargement or its objects can be scattered among sibling nodes. Both of them can cause the node splitting, especially the latter can lead into a propagated splitting, say the balanced nodes splitting. The R-tree [23] employed re-insertion policy instead of two ones above. The SR-tree, the SS-tree, the R*-tree and the Hybrid-tree also employ this policy. We propose a new algorithm to solve the under-full leaf problem called *eliminate-pull-reinsert*. The algorithm is similar to eliminate-and-reinsert policy as well. However, because reinsertion can cause the splits of leaf and balanced nodes, thus after deleting the object, if the leaf node is under-full, we apply a "pull" strategy to get one object from the sibling so that this sibling still ensures utilization constraints. This also depends on the idea in section 4.1 but in a contrary direction. While the under-full leaf here "pulls" one object from the sibling, the overflow one, in section 4.1, "shifts" one object to the sibling. If the pull policy still does not solve the problem, the objects of the under-full leaf node are reinserted. Note that, the pull policy can also propagate to only the siblings located in the same balanced node.

4.3 Search

The search operations of the SH-tree are similar to the SR-tree for the balanced nodes, leaf nodes and similar to the R-tree for the internal nodes. Because of the space limitation, we do not present them here. The detail discussion is referred to [31].

5 Conclusions and Future Work

In this paper, we introduced the SH-tree for indexing multidimensional data. The SH-tree is a flexible multidimensional index structure to support similarity searches in information systems. It is a well-combined structure of both the SR-tree and the KD-tree based techniques. The SH-tree carries positive aspects of both the KD-tree and the R-tree families. While the fan-out problem of the SR-tree is overcome by employing the KD-tree like representation for partitions of internal nodes, the SH-tree still take advantages of the SR-tree by using the balanced nodes, which are the same as internal nodes of the SR-tree. Moreover, the tree operations in the SH-tree are similar to the R-tree family but there are many modifications to adapt them to the new structure. We also introduced a new concept for the SH-tree, the extended balanced tree (EBT). It implies that the SH-trees are not necessary to be exactly balanced, but the querying performance is still not deteriorated and the maintenance cost for the tree balance is reduced.

As a part of the future work, we intend to compare the SH-tree to the SR-tree, the LSDh-tree and some other prominent multidimensional index structures as X-tree, SS-tree, M-tree, etc. We also plan to deploy the SH-tree for indexing features in similarity search systems [30].

References

1. V. Gaede, O. Günther. Multidimensional Access Methods. ACM Computing Surveys, Vol. 30, No. 2, June 1998.
2. K. Chakrabarti, S. Mehrotra. The Hybrid Tree: An Index Structure for High Dimensional Feature Spaces. Proc. of 15th International Conference on Data Engineering 1999. IEEE Computer Society.
3. King-Ip Lin, H.V. Jagadish, C. Faloutsos. The TV-Tree: An Index Structure for High-Dimensional Data. VLDB Journal, Vol. 3, No. 1, January 1994.
4. N. Katayama, S. Satoh. The SR-Tree: An Index Structure for High Dimensional Nearest Neighbor Queries. Proc. of the ACM SIGMOD International Conference on Management of Data, 1997.
5. D.A. White, R. Jain. Similarity Indexing with the SS-Tree. Proc. of the 20th International Conference on Data Engineering, 1996. IEEE Computer Society.
6. J.T. Robinson. The k-D-B-Tree: A Search Structure for Large Multidimensional Dynamic Indexes. Proc. of ACM SIGMOD International Conference on Management of Data, 1981.
7. D.B. Lomet, B. Salzberg. The hB-Tree: A Multiattribute Indexing Method with Good Guaranteed Performance. ACM Trans. on Database Systems, Vol. 15, No. 4, Dec. 1990.
8. A. Henrich, H.W. Six, P. Widmayer. The LSD Tree: Spatial Access to Multidimensional Point and Nonpoint Objects. Proc. of 15th VLDB, August 1989.
9. A. Henrich. The LSD/sup h/-tree: An Access Structure for Feature Vectors. Proc. of 14th International Conference on Data Engineering, 1998. IEEE Computer Society.
10. J. Nievergelt, H. Hinterberger, K.C. Sevcik. The Grid File: An Adaptable, Symmetric Multikey File Structure. ACM Trans. on Database Systems Vol. 9, No. 1, March 1984.
11. M. Freeston. The BANG file: A new kind of grid file. Proc. of the ACM SIGMOD Annual Conference on Management of Data, 1987.
12. A. Guttman. R-Trees: A Dynamic Index Structure for Spatial Searching. Proc. of ACM SIGMOD Conference, 1984.
13. T.K. Sellis, N. Roussopoulos, C. Faloutsos. The R+-Tree: A Dynamic Index for Multi-Dimensional Objects. Proc. of 13th VLDB, September 1987.
14. N. Beckmann, H.P. Kriegel, R. Schneider, B. Seeger. The R*-Tree: An Efficient and Robust Access Method for Points and Rectangles. SIGMOD Conference 1990.
15. S. Berchtold, D.A. Keim, H.P. Kriegel. The X-tree: An Index Structure for High-Dimensional Data. Proc. of 22nd VLDB, September 1996.

16. S. Berchtold, C. Böhm, H.P. Kriegel. The Pyramid Technique: Towards Breaking the Curse of Dimensionality. Proc. of ACM SIGMOD International Conference on Management of Data, June 1998.
17. J. Küng, J. Palkoska. An Incremental Hypercube Approach for Finding Best Matches for Vague Queries. Proc. of the 10th International Workshop on Database and Expert Systems Applications, DEXA 99. IEEE Computer Society.
18. R. Bayer. The Universal B-Tree for Multidimensional Indexing. Technical Report TUM-I9637, November 1996. (http://mistral.informatik.tu-muenchen.de/results/publications/)
19. K. Chakrabarti, S. Mehrotra. High Dimensional Feature Indexing Using Hybrid Tree. Technical Report, Department of Computer Science, University of Illinois at Urbana Champaign. (http://www-db.ics.uci.edu/pages/publications/1998/TR-MARS-98-14.ps)
20. P. Ciaccia, M. Patella, P. Zezula. M-tree: An Efficient Access Method for Similarity Search in Metric Spaces. Proc. of VLDB 1997.
21. D. Greene. An implementation and performance analysis of spatial data access methods. Proc. of 5th International Conference on Data Engineering 1989. IEEE Computer Society.
22. A. Henrich. A hybrid split strategy for k-d-tree based access structures. Proc. of the fourth ACM workshop on Advances on Advances in geographic information systems, 1997.
23. A. Guttman. R-Trees: A Dynamic Index Structure for Spatial Searching. SIGMOD, Proc. of Annual Meeting, June 1984.
24. N. Beckmann, H.P. Kriegel, R. Schneider, B. Seeger. The R*-tree: an efficient and robust access method for points and rectangles. Proc. of ACM SIGMOD International Conference on Management of Data, 1990.
25. R. Kurniawati, J.S. Jin, J.A. Shepherd. The SS+ -tree: An Improved Index Structure for Similarity Searches in a High-Dimensional Feature Space. SPIE Storage and Retrieval for Image and Video Databases V, San Jose, CA, 1997.
26. N. Roussopoulos, S. Kelley, F. Vincent. Nearest neighbor queries. Proc. of ACM SIGMOD International Conference on Management of Data, 1995.
27. F. Korn, N. Sidiropoulos, C. Faloutsos, E. Siegel, Z. Protopapas. Fast Nearest Neighbor Search in Medical Image Databases. Proc. of VLDB 1996.
28. B.C. Ooi, K.J. McDonell, R. Sacks-Davis. Spatial kd-Tree: A Data Structure for Geographic Databases. Proc. of COMPSAC 87, Tokyo, Japan.
29. S. Brin. Near Neighbor Search in Large Metric Spaces. Proc. VLDB 1995.
30. FAW Institute, Johannes Kepler University Linz. VASIS – Vague Searches in Information Systems. (http://www.faw.at/cgi-pub/e_showprojekt.pl?projektnr=10)
31. D.T. Khanh, J. Küng, R. Wagner. The SH-tree: A Super Hybrid Index Structure for Multidimensional Data. Technical Report, VASIS Project. (http://www.faw.uni-linz.ac.at)
32. C. Faloutsos, M. Ranganathan, Y. Manolopoulos. Fast subsequence matching in time-series databases. ACM SIGMOD International Conference on Management of Data, 1994.
33. Thomas Seidl, Hans-Peter Kriegel: "Efficient User-Adaptable Similarity Search in Large Multimedia Databases". VLDB 1997.
34. S. Berchtold, H.P. Kriegel. S3: Similarity Search in CAD Database Systems. Proc. of ACM SIGMOD International Conference on Management of Data, 1997.
35. T. Bozkaya, M. Ozsoyoglu. Indexing Large Metric Spaces for Similarity Search Queries. ACM Transactions on Database Systems. Vol. 24, No. 3, September 1999.
36. A. Henrich. Improving the performance of multi-dimensional access structures based on k-d-trees. Proc. of the 12nd International Conference on Data Engineering, 1996.

Concept-based visual information management with large lexical corpus

Youngchoon Park, PanKoo Kim[1], Forouzan Golshani, Sethuraman Panchanathan

Department of Computer Science and Engineering
Arizona State University
Tempe, AZ 85287-5406
{ycpark, golshani, panch}@asu.edu

[1]Collage of Computer Engineering
Chosun University
KwangJu Korea
{pkkim}@chosun.mina.ac.kr

Abstract.

Most users want to find visual information based on the semantics of visual contents such as a name of person, semantic relations, an action happening in a scene, ...etc. However, techniques for content-based image or video retrieval are not mature enough to recognize visual semantic completely, whereas retrieval based on color, size, texture and shape are within the state of the art. Therefore, smart ways to manage textual annotations in visual information retrieval are necessary. In this paper, a framework for integration of textual and visual content searching mechanism is presented. The proposed framework includes ontology-based semantic query processing through efficient semantic similarity measurement. A new conceptual similarity distance measure between two conceptual entities in a large taxonomy structure is proposed and its efficiency is demonstrated. With the proposed method, an information retrieval system can benefit such as (1) reduction of the number of trial-and-errors to find correct keywords, (2) Improvement of precision rates by eliminating the semantic heterogeneity in description, and (3) Improvement of recall rates through precise modeling of concepts and their relations.

1. Introduction

Regardless of media type, users tend to find media objects based on their perceptual understanding of the media content [16]. Such perceptual understanding can be a semantic recognition of a localized visual object in an image, an emotional perception of a certain sound clip, an abstracted summary of a news video clip or a particular semantic event captured from a movie clip. These facts have been explored in our human factors study in visual information retrieval. To enable conceptual level querying, the semantics of media content should be captured and represented in computable form. Semantic refers to the both "meaning" and "description purpose" of a media object in this paper. However, current content-based media

---

[1] Corresponding author, This work was supported by grant No. 2001-1-30300-002-3 from the Basic Research Program of the Korea Science & Engineering Foundation.

H.C. Mayr et al. (Eds.): DEXA 2001, LNCS 2113, pp. 350–359, 2001.

retrieval techniques are not mature enough to answer semantic related queries [12]. This is due to the difficulties in extraction of semantic information from low-level media data.

The most frequently employed semantic annotation mechanism is to use keywords or to use simple natural language sentences with advanced text retrieval techniques [2] [12] [18]. However, our recent human factors study reported in [15] shows that keyword-based visual content annotation and retrieval requires a sophisticated handling of keywords since, two people may use the same term with probability < 0.28 to describe or retrieve information. This term mismatch has created difficulties in information retrieval.

A promising solution for providing smart retrievals (semantic/knowledge level retrievals) of media object based on the content is to use *concept-based indexing and retrieval* [16]. Concept-based indexing and retrieval of media content attempts to explore beyond the standard keyword, and audio-visual feature based indexing approaches, which use simple counting of the words or media features from the given user query. Concept-based indexing technique uses knowledge of conceptual interrelationships [7][6] among concepts to find correspondences /semantic relations between the concepts in user query and that occur in media contents. Fig. 1 depicts a scenario of concept based indexing and retrieval. In this scenario, users may access all types of media content from a unified conceptual view. The emphasis of concept-based indexing is not so much in what is indexed, but rather in how the index is presented. With conceptual index, now users are allowed to access various media data by using single retrieval view (conceptual view).

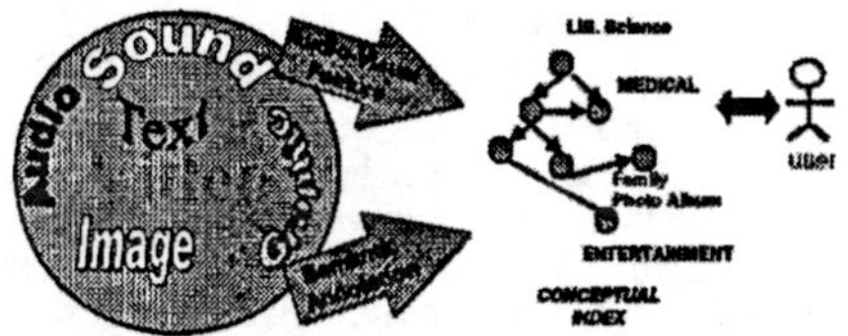

Fig. 1. Concept based media indexing and retrieval

In this research, WordNet™ being used as a general ontology to provide concept-based visual information indexing and retrieval. To support the concept-based similarity search combining with visual information retrieval, we propose a method for computerized conceptual similarity calculation in conceptual ontology space. The proposed similarity model will consider edges, depth, as well as existence of common ancestors. The forth factor tells that mutual information that shared by two concept also be a part of similarity calculation in our approach.

The main points of this paper as follows:

- A framework for semantic integrated information indexing and retrieval.
- A method for qualitative (not quantitative) measurement of semantic distance between two conceptual entities in a linguistic ontology hierarchy is proposed and its efficiency is evaluated.

2. Related Works

Our previous work presented in [8][17] introduces a semantic integrated visual information retrieval that allows users to post concepts and visual properties (i.e., sketch, color, etc.) as search criteria at the same time. Then system individually processes each search option and integrates them as results. Similar query processing can be found in [13] that proposes a terminology server architecture that manages semantic relations among words. The terminology sever returns semantically similar terms for a semantic query processing. Both approaches utilizes lexical thesaurus as a minimization mechanism for heterogeneity in keyword annotations and utilize term rewriting mechanism. In terminology server [13], terms are maintained with corresponding a semantic type and a relation, (i.e, "apple" *is-a* fruit). [8] uses WordNet™ [4] as a term management system that returns a set of terms considered to be similar (or related) to the given user search options and corresponding WordNet™ scene relations. With a set of words, query reformulation is performed to process semantic query processing which still performs pattern matching based query operation. However, query rewriting has a drawback in practical implementation. Since some of abstract concepts such as "plant" or "product name" may have hundreds of semantic entities, a number of logical relations in WHERE clause possibly degenerates the performance of query processing. In addition, browsing and navigation of database requires additional operations such as tracking of semantic hierarchy.

One solution to tackle the above problem is to employee a similarity-based indexing and a semantic distance [16] [14] [18] among terms in semantic query processing. In this approach, triangular inequality may improve the overall performance of search. The problem of semantic distance computation on corpus statistics and lexical taxonomy has been studies during the last decade. However, only two distinct approaches have been reported in literatures. The first approach is edge-based approach and the second is information content-based approach.

Sussna [12] defines a similarity distance between two conceptual entities as a weighted path length A weight between two conceptual entities is defined as follows:

$$w(C_i, C_j) = \frac{w(C_i \xrightarrow{R} C_j) + w(C_j \xrightarrow{R'} C_i)}{2d} \tag{1}$$

where, $w(C_x \xrightarrow{R} C_y) = \max_R - \frac{\max_R - \min_R}{n_R(C_x)}$. In equation (1), $\xrightarrow{R}$, d, $\max_R$, $\min_R$ and $n_R(C_x)$ represent a relation type R, the maximum weight for relation type R, the minimum weight for relation type R and the number of relations of type R leaving a conceptual entity C_x. This approach considers three distinct criteria in similarity measurement. $w(C_x \xrightarrow{R} C_y)$ measures the density of connections and connection type (i.e., ISA and IS-A-PART-OF cannot have the same connection strength). Depth of concept, d is involved in computation. The distance, d shrinks as one descends the hierarchy, since differentiation is based on finer and finer details. Finally the similarity distance between two concepts is defined as the minimum path length.

Information content-based approach [16] uses entropy measure that is computed on the basis of child node population. Even though, this method is derived from solid theory, it does not use the conceptual structure provided by ontology. Moreover, its similarity measure is too coarse.

The similarity distance two conceptual entities are defined on the basis information content. Information content of a conceptual entity, $H(C)$ is measured by using the number of words that subsumed by C. Resnik proposed the following similarity measure.

$$D(C_i, C_j) = \max_{C_k \in Se(C_i, C_j)} [-\log p(C_k)], \; p(C_k) = \frac{frequency(C_k)}{N} \tag{2}$$

where, N is the total number of words observed, and $Se(c_i, c_j)$ is the set of concepts that subsume both c_i and c_j.

Information content-based approach does not require detailed understanding of taxonomy and consider semantic dissimilarity that is not independent from link types. In contrast, edge based-approach is more natural and closer to the human perceptual measurement on concept discrimination. Depth, link type and link density are typically used as features in this model. However, it often fails to make a correct measurement because of non-uniform distribution of links and depths.

3. Proposed Similarity measurement between concepts

Concept is a unique mental experience and keyword is a symbolic expression of those mental experiences. The problem of polysemy (same symbolic representation but represents different meanings) is caused by the mapping procedure from a keyword to a corresponding concept. Since multiple concepts may share the same symbolic expressions, this problem can be removed by adding type information indicating the class of concept.

Let us consider a simple taxonomy structure illustrated in Fig. 2. The first observation can be illustrated with concepts, A, B and C. Let *Sim*(B,A) and *Sim*(B,C) are similarity distances

between a concept B to A and B to C respectively. Institutively, *Sim*(B,C) should be closer than *Sim*(B,A), since B and C share more parents than B and A. Let us consider, *Sim*(B,C) and *Sim*(B, D). In this case, it is not obvious to see which one is closer unless we know additional information such as a link type. Suppose, the type of link 12, and 13 are ISA. The type of link 14 is PART-OF. Then we may say that B and C are more similar than *Sim*(B,D). Let us look at others, *Sim*(E,G) and *Sim*(E,B). Both have the same type link. Based on the depth level consideration, (as depth level increase, classification is based on finer and finer criteria) E and B are more similar, in general. However, we don't know the quantity of similarity. With examples, we may have rough idea of similarity computation with conceptual hierarchy. First, let us design a similarity metric to calculates two adjacent nodes (one of them is a parent).
Given two adjacent conceptual entities C_i^l and C_j^{l-1} connected through a link $L_{i\rightarrow j}^T$, where T indicates a type of link. Without considering the number of shared parents, a semantic distance of two adjacent concepts; $Sim_{ADJ}(C_i^l, C_j^{l-1})$ is defined as follows.

$$Sim_{ADJ}(C_i^l, C_j^{l-1}) = w(L_{i\rightarrow j}^T)\cdot [H(C_i^l) - H(C_j^{l-1})]\cdot f(d), \quad (3)$$

where, $w(L_{i\rightarrow j}^T)$ indicates the weight function that decides the weight value based on the link type $t_{i\rightarrow j}$, $H(C_i)$ indicates the information content, entropy of C_i. $H(C_i)$ is defined as follows:

$$H(C_i) = -\log(P(C_i)) \quad (4)$$

Therefore, a link strength between two concepts, one of them is a parent and the other is a child is justified as weighted information content difference between adjacent concepts. $f(d)$ is a function that returns a depth factor. A link strength between two adjacent nodes is defined are (1) a link type, (2) amount of shared information, and (3) their topological location in a conceptual space. Probability $P(C_i)$ can be easily calculated by using the following equation.

$$P(C_i) = F(C_i)/N_{total} \quad (5)$$

where, $F(C_i)$ returns a number of words subsumed by the concept, C_j^{l-1}, and N_{tota} is the total number of words in a taxonomy . So far, we have designed a function that calculates the connection strength between two concepts.

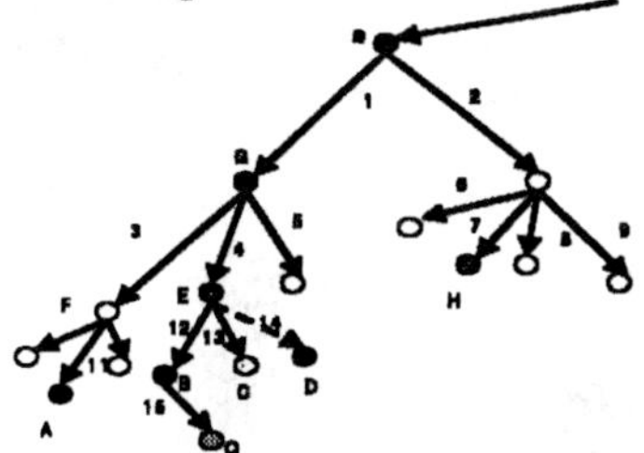

Fig.2. A simple taxonomy structure

The next desideratum for the similarity computation is an amount of information shared by common parents with depth consideration. Let us consider two similarities, Sim(A,Q) and Sim(A,H). As you see, A and Q share @ and G, while, A and H share only @. With edge-based computation, Sim(A,H) and Sim(A,Q) have the same number of edges that is 5. Based on the conceptual organization structure, Sim(A,Q) should be smaller than Sim(A,H). Because A and Q share more common concepts in parent levels than A and H.
Three concepts A, H and Q are in the same conceptual cluster with respect to the classification conditions applied to the node @. However, with respect to the conditions applied to the node G, A and Q are in the same conceptual space, but H is not. An information theocratic analysis may be applied to understand this circumstance. Randomness of concepts in conceptual structure subsumed by the node @ is larger than that of the node G. In other words, semantic dissimilarity distribution made up from all concept pairs, subsumed by G is less scattered than that of @. Because concepts subsumed by G has been classified with finer-grained decision

conditions. With this evidence, we may say that semantic closeness between two concepts should be affected by the depth and the number of parent nodes. Then the next step is to develop a function to measure the amount of shared information by parents. Shared information content SI between two conceptual entities, C_i and C_j is defined as follows:

$$SI(C_i, C_j) = \max[-\log(P(C_p))] \tag{6}$$

where, C_p is a parent node of the both C_i and C_j, and its depth is the maximum compared to other shared parents of C_i and C_j. Entropy of the root/empty concept is 0 since probability is 1. Since we assumed that a conceptual structure is a hierarchical structure, as depth increase, probability decrease (entropy will increase).

Now, we will expand the above equation to handle the case where more than one edges are in the shortest path between two concepts. Suppose we have the shortest path P, from two concepts C_i and C_j. , $P = \{(t_0, C_0, C_1), (t_1, C_1, C_2), \ldots, (t_{n-1}, C_{n-1}, C_n)\}$.

Then, similarity distance measure between C_i and C_j is as follows:

$$Sim_{edge}(C_i, C_j) = \sum_{k=0}^{n} w(t_k) \cdot Sim_{ADJ}(C_k, C_{k+1}) \tag{7}$$

The above similarity measurement is only considering the link types and number of edges. What is missing in this formulation is a slot for shared concepts (As the number of shared concept increases, more similar). To incorporate this into our similarity measurement, we propose the following equation.

$$Sim(C_i, C_j) = \frac{\sum_{k=0}^{n} w(t_k) \cdot Sim_{ADJ}(C_k, C_{k+1})}{wF} \tag{8}$$

The above equation tells that the entire similarity is proportional to the shared information. As SI increase, wF increases (the total similarity is a proportional to the amount of shared concepts). One example of wF is $e^{SI(C_i, C_j)}$. A simplest form of $w(t)$ is step function. If an edge type is ISA then $w(t)$ returns 1 and otherwise returns a certain number that is less than 1.

With a well-defined weighting function, the similarity metric may return negative value when two concepts are antonyms each other. For instance, two concept, man and woman are in the relation of "antonym" that is directly visible lexical ontology such as WordNet. In other words, they are linked through single edge. However, they share concepts, "entity", "life from", "person". Such shared information makes them as similar concepts in similarity computation. However, antonym relation eventually prevents this situation.

A similarity distance, $Sim(C_i, C_j)$ of two conceptual entities C_i and C_j is a symmetric.

$$Sim(C_i, C_j) = Sim(C_j, C_i) \tag{9}$$

A content similarity between two visual objects VO_i and VO_j, $S^C(VO_i, VO_j)$ is defined as follows:

$$S^C(VO_i, VO_j) = \alpha \times S^s(VO_i, VO_j) + \beta \times S^v(VO_i, VO_j) \tag{10}$$

where, α and β are weight coefficients for conceptual similarity and visual similarity. By adjusting those two values, users can express which attributes are more important in similarity search. S^V is a visual similarity measurement between two visual objects. For instance, histogram similarity [11] or shape similarity [16] belongs to S^V.

4. Semantic Query Processing

Our semantic description of a media is based on the conceptual graph formulation (CGF) with strong restrictions in concept type and relation type assignment. CGF is a knowledge representation mechanism in which knowledge is modeled and expressed with concepts and relations. A conceptual graph is a bipartite graph where nodes of one class represent concepts, nodes of the other class represent relations between concepts, and the partially ordered labels represents types and referents [19]. Semantics of CGF is interpreted with first order logic. One of the reasons to choose CGF as our semantic annotation mechanism is that it provides a unified way to describe, store and retrieve the contents (can be used in both description and query). In addition, its graphical representation of semantic content is a semi-formal concept description language that strikes a balance between human comprehension and the possibility of computational support. In addition to the standard CG notation, we have add following rules:

Rule 1. Concept type restriction. A concept type is defined as a full path with semantic relations from an empty (root) concept to a target concept in an ontology.
Rule 2. Relation type restriction. A relation type is defined as a full path with semantic relations from an empty (root) relation type to a target relation type in an ontology.
Rule 3. A referent of a conceptual relation must be predefined in the lexical ontology and it must be a noun.
Rule 4. A referent of a concept must have a concept type.
Rule 5. No general marker "*" in CG is allowed in description.

The purpose of the third restriction is to make mapping from natural language to logical expression more systematic. In conceptual graph based content representation, it is required to invent a relation name for clarifying semantic meaning. In fact, we have noticed that annotators often invent their own relation names such as author-of, teacher-of, friend-of in conceptual-graph based knowledge representation. Since those words are fully understood by a binary relation. Based on the relational interpretation mechanism presented in [9] [19] and default relation called "has" in CG, an semantic interpretation of a simple relation on two concepts r(c1,c2) is "c1 and c2 has a relation r".

The above restrictions ensure that all concept types appeared in a description have corresponding conceptual categories defined in ontologies, and relations must be handled by a lexical ontology. In a CG, a concept is represented as a rectangle and a circle represents relation between concepts. A concept has a concept type and a referent, which is an instance of the concept type. A relation has a relation type and a referent that is an instance of the relation type. Concept types and relation types are managed in a concept hierarchy. Therefore, they provide partial ordering relations.

Fig. 3 illustrates a graphical representation of the concept, "Red Mustang", and its semantic disambiguation process by adding concept type information.

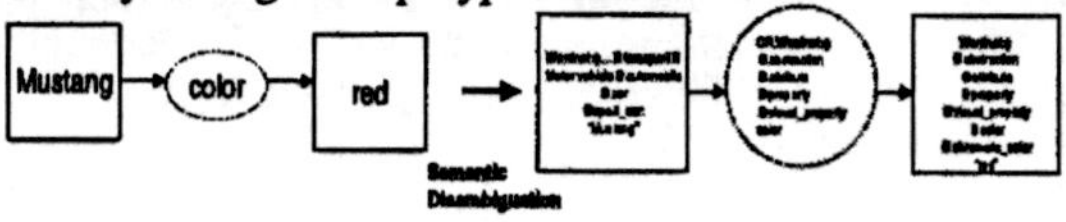

Fig.3. Semantic disambiguation process of a concept "Red Mustang"

4.1 Conceptual Browsing and Presentation of the content

For the purpose of semantic retrieval, we need a query language and query processor. Unlike SQL, or other query languages (most of them are designed for data retrieval), our query language requires more expressiveness power. Some examples of queries that can be handled are as follows:

1) Find media objects that contain an "automobile".
2) Find media objects that contain "US President Clinton is wearing a blue suit"
3) Find media objects that contain "A man is holding a ball"

To present queries, a user may use a visual query tool equipped with concept graph drawing and ontology browser. The first query is translated into

```
SELECT CONCEPT
FROM CONCEPT_TBL
WHERE CONCEPT LIKE "automobile";
```

The statement, WHERE CONCEPT LIKE '*automobile*'; is SQL compliant and it means that a user want to find concept descriptions that contains a string, "automobile". Most text retrieval engines provide at this level search. More sophisticated search systems rewrite the query for concept level retrieval by adding similar terms such as "car", "sedan", etc. When a database system did not find any matched results against the given query, query relaxation is required based on the user's search view. If a user really means to find a media object with exact match then, no further query processing is necessary. However, if a user want to find media objects that contain a concept of "automobile", then semantic query processing has to be take in placed. This will be the most frequently occurring situation in content-based retrievals. Then the given term "automobile" becomes a concept. A query processor will look up ontology and find a set of possible conceptual interpretations of "automobile". For instance, in WordNet there is only one conceptual interpretation that is "4-wheeled motor vehicle". Then query processor generates a concept type string that contains conceptual inheritance information (from empty concept to the target concept, "automobile"). The next step is a replacement of the string "automobile" to a wildcard "*" and add the concept type string to the current query. The resulting query is as follows:

```
SELECT CONCEPT
FROM CONCEPT_TBL
WHERE CONCEPT LIKE "CE.Wordnet:ϕ@entity@object@artifact@instrumentation@transport@Motor vehicle@automobile";
```

The above query is semantically equivalent to "Find media objects that contain a "4-wheeled motor vehicle". Then we may have a number of media objects annotated with "car", "sport car", "mustang", etc.

The second query example contains several concepts and relations such as "US President", "Clinton", "wear", "blue", "suit", "hold" "basketball", etc. This example requires more complex query processing and need user's feedback or weighting scheme in retrieval. Suppose we have the following semantic annotations in our database. They are "General Clinton is wearing blue suit and holding a baseball", D1, "US President, Clinton is wearing a blue suit and holding a basketball", D2 and "Vice President, Al Gore i wearing a red polo shirt and holding a basketball", D3. Graphical representations and index entries of the query and D2 are shown in Figure 4.

CR.Wornet:ϕ...Title(CE.Wornet:ϕ...#Clinton, CE.Wornet:ϕ...#US President) ∧
CR.Wornet:ϕ...Holding(CE.Wornet:ϕ...#Clinton, CE.Wornet:ϕ...#Basketball) ∧
CR.Wornet:ϕ...Wearing(CE.Wornet:ϕ...#Clinton, CE.Wornet:ϕ...#Suit) ∧
CR.Wornet:ϕ...Visual_property(CE.Wornet:ϕ...#Suit, CE.Wornet:ϕ...#Blue);

(a)

CR.Wornet:ϕ...Title(CE.Wornet:ϕ...#Clinton, CE.Wornet:ϕ...#US President) ∧ CR.Wornet:ϕ...Holding(CE.Wornet:ϕ...#Clinton, CE.Wornet:ϕ...#Basketball);

(b)

Fig. 4. **(a) Simplified CG representation of the "US President Clinton is wearing a blue suit and holding a basketball", (b) Simplified CG representation of query, "US President is wearing a blue suit" Shaded partial graph in (a) is corresponding to (b)**

To retrieve media objects, a query process will formulate a query, Q that is equivalent to Figure 4(b). The query is as follows:

```
SELECT CONCEPT
FROM CONCEPT_TBL
WHERE  CONCEPT LIKE ';*CR.Wornet:ϕ...Title(CE.Wornet:ϕ...#Clinton, CE.Wornet:ϕ...#US President)*;' AND
 CONCEPT LIKE ';*CR.Wornet:ϕ...Holding(CE.Wornet:ϕ...#Clinton, CE.Wornet:ϕ...#Basketball)*;';
```

The above query looks index entries in database and find a set of descriptions that contains both CR.Wornet:ϕ…Title(CE.Wornet:ϕ…#Clinton, CE.Wornet:ϕ…#US President) and CR.Wornet:ϕ…Holding(CE.Wornet:ϕ…#Clinton, CE.Wornet:ϕ… #Basketball). Still, we are using standard SQL for querying. Since, this particular implementation only uses string matching operations provided by SQL, it is simple and easy to incorporate to any RDBMS. Suppose a user find media objects with the third example " A man is holding a ball". A semantically equivalent query is shown below.

```
SELECT CONCEPT
FROM CONCEPT_TBL
WHERE  CONCEPT LIKE ';*CR.Wornet:ϕ...Holding(CE.Wornet:ϕ...@man*,CE.Wornet:ϕ...@ball*)*;';
```

The above query will retrieve all media objects that contain at lease two conceptual elements whose types are "man" and "ball" and one semantic relation whose type is "holding".

So far, we have demonstrated how we can index and retrieve semantic descriptions with traditional RDBMS. More advanced database systems such as deductive database systems can be used to manage document management. Proposed method allows approximate matching along specialization and generalization and on relations. Suppose, user want to generalize a relation, "holding" then the resulting query is as follows:

```
SELECT CONCEPT
FROM CONCEPT_TBL
WHERE  CONCEPT LIKE ';*CR.Wornet:φ...Possesion*(CE.Wornet:φ...@man*,CE.Wornet:φ...@ball*)*;';
```

Similarity matching on concepts and relations is possible. Given three conceptual descriptions, "US President Bill Clinton has a rose", C1 and "A man holds a flower", C2, and US President Bill Clinton has a daughter", C3. Within these examples, most human will agree that C1 is more similar to C2 than C3. Given two concept-relation based semantic annotations denoted by $SC_i = R_i(CA_1,CA_2,\ldots,CA_n)$ and $SC_j=R_j(CB_1,CB_2,\ldots,CB_n)$, the similarity measurement of two semantic annotations can be calculated with the following form based on concept and relation based similarity retrieval.

$$Sim(SC_i,SC_j) = aSim(R_i,R_j) + \mathbf{W}^T\sum_{k=1}^{n} Sim(CA_k,CB_k) \quad (11)$$

where, $\mathbf{W}^T$ is a weighting matrix whose size is $1 \times k$, and a is a weighting factor for relation similarity.

5. Experimental Results

In the experiment, we constructed a sample image database containing nearly 22,300 randomly selected images. These images were mostly color pictures with non-uniform background. Each image has two or three concepts.

The search options selected for these experiments were:

1. Retrieval based on LSI (Latent Semantic Indexing, we use singular value decomposition).
2. Retrieval based on information content.
3. Retrieval based on term re-writing
4. Retrieval based on the proposed method.

Our previous work on feature extraction technique called spatial distribution model of color [8] that is as a visual feature in the experiment is a good indicator of color contents of images and is the basis of an effective method for image indexing. Let us look at few examples. The first query is a simple search for images that look like the image that contains the picture of sunset (query image is the top-left image in Fig. 5). The search option is spatial color distribution with concept, and the results of the retrieval are presented in Fig.5(a) and Fig.5(b) shows the retrieval of visual content only. As you notice, there are four erroneous retrievals appeared in the Fig.5(b) (marked with circles).

(a) (b)

Fig.5. Retrieval of sunset scenes (a)with/ (b)without concept, Erroneous retrievals are marked as circle

To evaluate the retrieval performance of the proposed method, we use the two traditional metrics, namely, precision and recall. They are good indicators for correctness of matches and the relevance of retrieved images. Recall measures the ability of the systems to retrieve all images that are relevant, whereas precision measures the ability of the system in retrieving only images that are relevant. In this experiments, 22,312 images were considered as a test set. We ran 10 different test queries against this image set with three distinct annotated text retrieval methods. To verify the correctness of retrieval, we manually investigated the retrieval-answers. The host system for the tests was a Pentium III machine with a 500 MHz processor and 512 MB of memory. In most cases, the response time is less than a second.

The graph shown in Fig.6 that is an average of 10 different queries. Queries contain the both visual and concept options such as "sunset", "folk-dance", "mustang", "nimbus", "motor-cycle",...,etc.). The results clearly indicate that both precision and recall rates of the proposed method are superior to other methods. Because, the existing term-frequency based text retrieval techniques such as LSI require a number of information from query (for instance, co-occurrence matrix of query document) that are not applicable in both annotated concept retrieval. Such lacking of available statistical information produces the poor results.

There is a significant precision dropping in recall ranges from 0.3 to 0.4. This is due to the fact that WordNet has not adequate semantic clusters at the top level ontology.

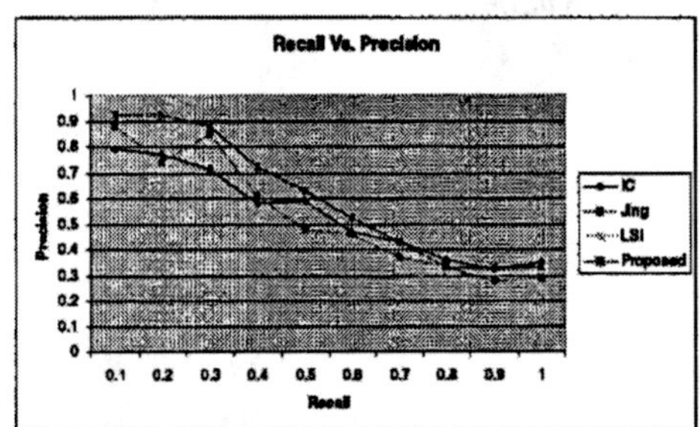

Fig. 6. Result of averaged 10 trials

In summary, techniques for content-based image or video retrieval are not mature enough to recognize visual semantic completely. Retrieval based on color, size, texture and shape are within the state of the art. Therefore, it is necessary to use captions or text annotations to photos or videos in content access of visual data.

6. Conclusion

In this paper, efficient concept encoding, indexing and similarity based retrieval mechanism are presented and its performance aspects are proven though turning test and semantic integrated visual information retrieval over large data set. The proposed similarity matching technique is generic enough to use in various application areas including natural language processing, information retrieval, etc.

Even though, lexical ontologies such as WordNet are proven to be useful tools in content-based indexing and retrieval, their taxonomy structures are not naturally followed by human perceptual classification of things. We have already started to develop an ontology specifically for information classification and retrieval on the basis of general top ontologies and WordNet vocabularies.

A new media object management technique called relation-based indexing and retrieval is introduced and its detailed implementation method is presented. Explicit representation of concepts and their relations transforms the problem of concept-based retrieval as full-text retrieval. We have shown, simple string matching operations can handle semantic query processing. Such string matching-based retrieval of concepts and relations can be seen as a semantic type filtering. It can be integrated into semantic similarity matching technique proposed in this research as a pre-filtering method.

Reference

1. Gianni Amati and Iadh Onis, Conceptual Graphs and First Order Logic, The Computer Journal, Volume 43, Number 1, 2000
2. S., Deerwester, et al., "Indexing by Latent Semantic Indexing," *Journal of the American Society for Information Science*, 41(6), 1990.
3. Gerard Robert Ellis, Managing Complex Objects, Ph.D, Thesis, Department of Computer Science, University of Queensland, 1995
4. Christiane Fellbaum (ed.), *WordNet: An Electronic Lexical Database*, MIT Press, 1998
5. D. Fensel, J. Angele, and R. Studer, The Knowledge Acquisition And Representation Language KARL, IEEE Transactions on Knowledge and Data Engineering, 10(4):527-550, 1998.
6. D. Fensel, J. Angele, S. Decker, M. Erdmann, H.-P. Schnurr, S. Staab, R. Studer, and A. Witt: On2broker: Semantic-Based Access to Information Sources at the WWW. In Proceedings of the World Conference on the WWW and Internet (WebNet 99), Honolulu, Hawaii, USA, October 25-30, 1999.
7. D. Fensel, M. Crubezy, F. van Harmelen, and M. I. Horrocks: OIL & UPML: A Unifying Framework for the Knowledge Web. In Proc. of the Workshop on Applications of Ontologies and Problem-solving Methods, ECAI'00, Berlin, Germany August 20-25, 2000.
8. Forouzan Golshani and Youngchoon Park, "ImageRoadMap: A New Content-Based Image Retrieval System", Lecture Notes in Computer Science (LNCS) 1308, Springer-Verlag, pp. 225-239, 1997.
9. N. Guarino, "Concepts, Attributes and Arbitrary Relations: Some Linguistic and Ontological Criteria for Structuring Knowledge Base:, Data and Knowledge Engineering. Vol.8, No2, 1992, Pp. 249-261
10. Nicola Garino et.al., "OntoSeek:Content-based Access to the Web", *IEEE Intelligent Systems*, Vol. 14, No. 3, May/June 1999
11. F. Idris and S. Panchanathan, "Review of Image and Video Indexing Techniques", *Journal of Visual Communication and Image Representation*-Special Issue on Indexing, Storage and Retrieval of Images and Video, June 1997.
12. Jay J. Jiang David W. Conrath "Semantic Similarity Based on Corpus Statistics and Lexical Taxonomy", Proc. of International Conference Research on Computational Linguistics (ROCLING X), 1997, Taiwan
13. W.-S. Li, K.S. Candan, K. Hirata, and Y. Hara, "A Hybrid Approach to Multimedia Database Systems through Integration of Semantics and Media-based Search, LNCS -, Springer-Verlag, Vol. 1274, P. 182-197, August, 1997.
14. Sussna, M., 1993, "Word Sense Disambiguation for Free-text Indexing Using a Massive Semantic Network", Proceedings of the Second International Conference on Information and Knowledge Management, CIKM'93, 67-74
15. ISO/IEC JTC 1/SC 29/WG 11/N3815, MPEG-7 Multimedia Description Schemes XM (Version 6.0), January 2001, Pisa, IT
16. Resnik, P., 1995, "Using Information Content to Evaluate Semantic Similarity in a Taxonomy", Proceedings of the 14th International Joint Conference on Artificial Intelligence, Vol. 1,448-453, Montreal, August 1995
17. Y.C. Park, F. Golshani, S. Panchanathan, "Conceptualization and Ontology: Tools for Efficient Storage and Retrieval of Semantic Visual Information", *Internet Multimedia Management Systems Conference*, Boston, MA, November 2000.
18. C.J. van Rijsbergen. A non-classical logic for information retrieval. *The Computer Journal*, 29(6): 481-485, 1986.
19. John F. Sowa, Knowledge Representation: Logical, Philosophical, and Computational Foundations, PWS Publishing Co., Pacific Grove, CA, 1999

Pyramidal Digest: An E cient Model for Abstracting Text Databases

Wesley T. Chuang and D. Stott Parker

Computer Science Department, UCLA, Los Angeles, CA 90095, USA
{yelsew, stott}@cs.ucla.edu

Abstract. We present a novel model of automated composite text digest, the Pyramidal Digest. The model integrates traditional text summarization and text classi cation in that the digest not only serves as a summary" but is also able to classify text segments of any given size, and answer queries relative to a context.

Pyramidal" refers to the fact that the digest is created in at least three dimensions: scope, granularity, and scale. The Pyramidal Digest is de ned recursively as a structure of extracted and abstracted features that are obtained gradually — from speci c to general, and from large to small text segment size — through a combination of shallow parsing and machine learning algorithms. There are three noticeable threads of learning taking place: learning of characteristic relations, rhetorical relations, and lexical relations.

Our model provides a principle for e ciently digesting large quantities of text: progressive learning can digest text by abstracting its signi cant features. This approach scales, with complexity bounded by O n log n , where n is the size of the text. It o ers a standard and systematic way of collecting as many semantic features as possible that are reachable by shallow parsing. It enables readers to query beyond keyword matches.

1 Introduction

When facing enormous volumes of text information, the fact that syntactic analysis does not scale has encouraged nding an alternative way for determining large-scale meaning without syntax: to consider shallow parsing and to gauge understanding" on the basis of query relevance and learning accuracy. With this in mind, in this paper we shift the syntax-then-semantics mentality to a semantics-then-syntax one. Our bias is that microscopic" syntactic categories should play only a minimal role in determining the meaning of lengthy documents, given that we wish to retrieve exact information as well as understand" the text at any level. These goals together require the system to retrieve keywords as well as retrieve an abstract context."

Putting syntactic structure temporarily aside, however, does not immediately protect us from the complexity of semantics. Viewing text documents as long segments formed by consecutive words, we can assign meanings to any subsegment. A word has many possible meanings and it can relate to other words. A

H.C. Mayr et al. (Eds.): DEXA 2001, LNCS 2113, pp. 360–369, 2001.

segment of words, too, can be abstracted with meanings and can be related to other segments. Based on the goals of retrieving keywords as well as context, we are in need of a model that digests the original text e ciently and accurately by analyzing these semantic relations, and by extracting as many features as possible. Because the relations are too numerous, the best way to accomplish this is with a machine learning approach. The advantage of a learning approach is that we can make good tradeo s between e ciency and accuracy. Learning is possible even with minimal data, and results can be improved with experience.

We regard whatever is learned as a *digest* or *abstract.* This introduces a new kind of summarization, both from the point of view of its function and of its representation.

In the past, text summarization has focused on natural language generation, or on extracting sentences from the text. By contrast, our approach to text digesting permits summarization to be integrated with *text classi cation*, in which the goal is to determine the topic or category of a text document as well as meaning of a text segment of any size. Our notion of digest has several novelties. For one, our digest takes into account the visual e ect of a structure. There is no doubt that pictures can reduce cognitive load, and so can structures. A second novelty is that our digest can take a new *composite* or *vectorized* form. Speci cally, we represent digests with a combination of text segments of different lengths. A third novelty is that we push summarization one step further, so that abstractions of the combined text segments form the digest.

```
- BOOK NAME:‘‘Handbook of Internal Medicine’’
  - DEPTH1
    - NAME:‘‘Emergencies’’
      • extractplus
      • abstract
      - DEPTH2
        - NAME:‘‘Cardiovascular’’
          • extractplus
          • abstract
          • segments
           NAME
        • NAME:‘‘Shock’’
         DEPTH2
       NAME
    - NAME:‘‘SyptomsSigns’’
      - extractplus
        - terms  pain chest headach hurt sever ...   terms
        • sentences
         extract
      - abstract  protection body_part ache protection ...   abstract
      - DEPTH2
        • NAME:‘‘AbdominalPain’’
        - NAME:‘‘ChestPain’’
          - extractplus
            - terms  chest pain correl diagnosi littl ...   terms
            • sentences
             extractplus
          - abstract  body_part ache ...   abstract
          - segments
            - rhetoricals
              - reason
                • satellite
                • nucleus
                 reason
              • example
               rhetoricals
            • contents
             segments
           NAME
        • NAME:‘‘HeadFacePain’’
         DEPTH2
       NAME
    • NAME:‘‘Infectious’’
     DEPTH1
   BOOK
```

Fig. 1. An example digest in XML.

Example 1. In Figure 1, we illustrate one level from a multilevel of an example digest in XML after processing a small portion of a book see 9 . A digest has a nested format and contains various sizes of segments. It is a composite summary of the original text. In later sections, we will explain how this digest is obtained. We can see that the sample digest above has a hierarchical or nested nature. Every **Name** tag represents a concept." The concept has both an **extractplus** and **abstract** . **extractplus** contains extracted words to digest a scope. The reason for the plus" is that this extract also includes additional synonyms; it is not extracted purely from the original text. **abstract** , on the other hand, contains words that abstract the scope portion of the book covered by this digest. Under **segments** , it contains sentence segments that are considered to be important for example, with rhetorical signi cance such as **reason** , **example** , etc. from the original text.

The novel way to extract and abstract text features across several dimensions scale, granularity, and scope makes the resulting digest not only become a *composite* summary, but also become some kind of a contextual *index*," which is di erent from traditional inverted index, or B-tree index. This contextual index is very convenient for context retrieval.

2 Related Work

A concept hierarchy or taxonomy is usually used in order to determine or classify the topic of documents, or of larger text granularities exceeding that of documents 1 . We show a way to extend the classi cation capability down to sentence segment and word granularity.

At the sentence granularity, previous work mostly considered extracted sentences to be text summaries 11, 5 . Structural aspect of the text was exploited in 3 . Other summarization systems have been concerned with generating a coherent summary 8, 12 . 10 made use of machine learning algorithms to determine the sentences to be extracted. 3 combined the structural aspect into learning and extracted sentence segments as a summary. Our work though integrate the summary into so-called *digest* to serve as a summary" as well as an index."

Research into lexical relations in WordNet 6 has drawn interests into word sense identi cation or word sense disambiguation 13 . Hirst et al. use *lexical chains* — chain of words — to represent context 7 . Their work di er from ours is that we only consider word senses for su ciently representative words, which are merged into the digest. In addition, context is very important for producing a summary or retrieving information as shown in 14 . With our digest, context can be e ciently captured and represented by segments of various sizes connected at some strength along several dimensions.

3 A Pyramidal Digesting Model

3.1 Relationships of Text at Di erent Granularities

Viewing text documents as long segments and their subsegments, we obtain a hierarchy of text segment sizes. To digest text from this hierarchy, we can then re ect the whole spectrum of segment sizes. Every segment of text is potentially the basis for part of the summary, and it may participate in many complicated semantic relations. Because of this, we have strived to employ methods that can manage large texts well — methods that can scale. Surface shallow" parsing thus becomes a reasonable choice. But we also need a method that can extract su cient semantics from the text surface."

De nition 1. *Consider a document* $\boldsymbol{C}$ *where multiple documents can be lumped into one vector as a vector* $w_1, w_2, \ldots w_n$ *, where* w_i *is either a word or a discourse marker e.g. punctuation, or cue words such as because", but", .., etc .*

De nition 2. *A text segment* $\boldsymbol{S}$ *is any sequence of consecutive words in* $\boldsymbol{C}$*. That is,* $\boldsymbol{S} = C\ i{:}j$ *, where* $i\ \ j$ *and* $0\ \ \ i,j\ \ \ |\boldsymbol{C}|$*.*

De nition 3. *A semantic relation* $\boldsymbol{R}$ *is a binary relation on text segments, i.e.,* $R\ \boldsymbol{S}_i,\ \boldsymbol{S}_j$ *, where* $\boldsymbol{S}_i$*,* $\boldsymbol{S}_j$ *are text segments.*

The number of relations can grow exponentially. In the interest of simplicity, we present only a few relations.

Above paragraph granularity: We focus on text segments of a size comparable to descriptions of basic concepts" in the hierarchy 2 . Intuitively, the meaning of any two chapters can be described by how they di er from each other with respect to certain relations. Such *characteristic relations*, if mapped into a concise form, not only indicate their characteristic di erences, but also serve as a summary of connections among text segments, which we call *blocks*, at this granularity.

At sentence-segment granularity: We concentrate on segments that are enclosed by discourse markers 3 . There are an enormous number of possible semantic relations. Fortunately, in practice it is su cient to analyze only those segments that are separated by discourse markers e.g. punctuation, or cue words such as because", but", .., etc. . There are words in the sentence that signal so-called rhetorical relations" between sentence segments; 3 gives a detailed account.

At word granularity: We work on the words' semantic relations for a small number of representative words. Whether in a given document or in a dictionary, there are many relations between words, such as synonymic and hypernymic relations 6 . Two synonyms in a summary can be grouped into one; several words that depict one idea can be elevated" into an abstraction, perhaps represented by another word.

3.2 Pyramidal Digest

De nition 4. *A Digest* D_i *at level* i*, consisting a collection of text segments, is induced from the previous level* D_{i-1} *of text segments.* $D_i = D_{i-1} - \sum_{j=1}^{|D|}\ \boldsymbol{S}_j\ \ f + \sum_{j=1}^{|D|}\ \ h\ \boldsymbol{S}_j\ - \boldsymbol{S}_j\ \ \ g$*, where* $h:\ \boldsymbol{S}\ \ \ \ g \rightarrow \boldsymbol{S}$ *is an abstraction function.* f, g *are machine learning functions with their de nitions to follow.* $-, +$ *are di erence and insertion operators, respectively and is multiplication.*

From the de nition, a digest is made by taking out text segments from the original document. Two operators are involved in shaping the digest, as de ned in the following.

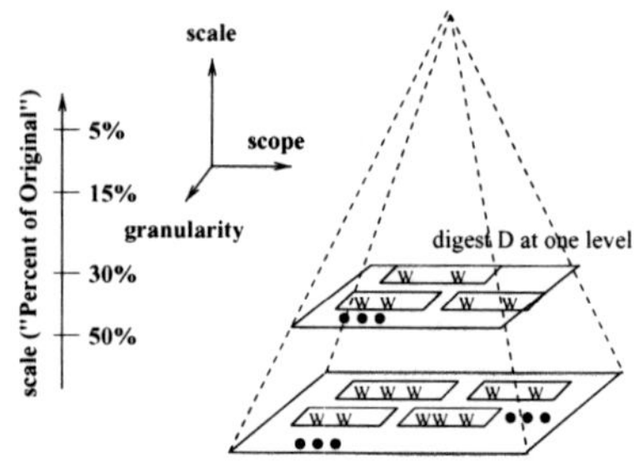

Fig. 2. A Pyramidal multilevel digest.

De nition 5. *Word occupation is a machine learning function f: S* S_1 S_2 *...* S_{n-1} R_1 R_2 *...* $R_m \rightarrow \{0, 1\}$ *that determines whether a segment S can occupy its original position or be eliminated in the next level of digest. Here n, m are the number of text segments, and number of semantic relations considered, respectively.*

De nition 6. *Word replacement is a machine learning function g:* S^n $R^m \rightarrow \{0, 1\}$ *that determines whether a segment can be replaced with another segment containing abstract words.*

De nition 7. *A Multilevel Digest is an instance of M= D, f, g, , which is a hierarchical structure, where is a partial order de ned over D.*

Documents, before being digested, are represented as the digest at the base level. To get a digest at a level above, we permit a machine learning algorithm to learn which text segments should be taken out by word occupation and which segments should be replaced with word replacement . Since the two operators only reduce the number of words, it can be proved that digests obey a partial order.

3.3 A Learning Model Unifying Classi cation and Summarization

One of the great principles of summarization, essentially *Occam's razor*, is that the simplest description is preferred. This is implicit in our machine learning approach, in which simpler and more abstract digests are produced level after level. At every granularity of summarization, it is classi cation that governs the learning process. At a high granularity, we classify big text segments, nding their characteristic di erences. At the granularity of sentence segments, we observe their rhetorical di erences, and classify them into essential and non-essential sentence segments.

$word_1$	$word_2$	$word_3$	...	$word_{k-1}$	$word_k$	...	Concept
pain	common	symptom	...	management	trigger	...	1
correlation	severity	chest	...	pain	cause	...	2
pain	somatic	skin	...	tissue	neuropath	...	1
abdominal	mucosal	muscle	...	in ammation	hollow	...	3
substernal	pressure	meals	...	emotion	arousal	...	2
chronic	pain	distraught	...	migraine	headache	...	1
:	:	:	...	:	:	...	:

Table 1. Classify block-size segments into target concepts.

At the granularity of word segments, we look into their sense di erences, and classify them into synonyms and hypernyms that are compatible with the context.

Segment ID	title words	term freq	...	antithesis	cause	...	Important
1	1	2.3	...	1.5	0	...	Y
2	0	0.5	...	0	-3.5	...	N
3	2	5.7	...	0	0.5	...	N
4	2	7.2	...	-3.5	0	...	Y
5	0	1.1	...	0	0.33	...	N
6	0	3.5	...	2.5	0	...	N
:	:	:	...	:	:	...	:

Table 2. Classify sentence segments into targets.

As shown in Tables 1- 3, targets may be binary- or multiple-valued depending on how many target classes there are. During learning, target values are known because they are labeled either implicitly or by a human. Then classi - cation, and essentially classi cation, is used to predict what the target class is.

Example 2. Speci cally, in Table 1 a block segment containing certain words can be classi ed into a target concept. In Table 2, rhetorical as well as other features of a sentence segment can be classi ed into either the important or unimportant class. In Table 3, judging from its neighboring words, a word's sense can be classi ed in a way that agrees with the context. These classi cation processes can be very e cient with complexities bounded by O n log n time, as explained in 2,4 .

$word$	$neighbor_1$	$neighbor_2$	...	$neighbor_{k-1}$	$neighbor_k$	...	Sense
chest	pulmonary	embolism	...	aortic	dissection	...	1
headache	migraine	acute	...	ergotamines	aspirin	...	2
pain	sensory	stimuli	...	viscera	nerve	...	1
symptom	pain	common	...	cause	factor	...	1
immune	infectious	disease	...	tool	medicine	...	1
tension	onset	bilateral	...	tight	band	...	3
:	:	:	...	:	:	...	:

Table 3. Classify words into target senses.

4 Learning to Create a Digest

We now explain how learning takes place at various granularities of the text body, and how summaries created for each granularity are combined.

Example 3. Examine the following text segments. We break it into three di erent granularities — document paragraph here , sentence-segment, and word, as shown in Figure 3. Then, the encoded relations are subjected to classi cation or learning as mentioned in Tables 1- 3.

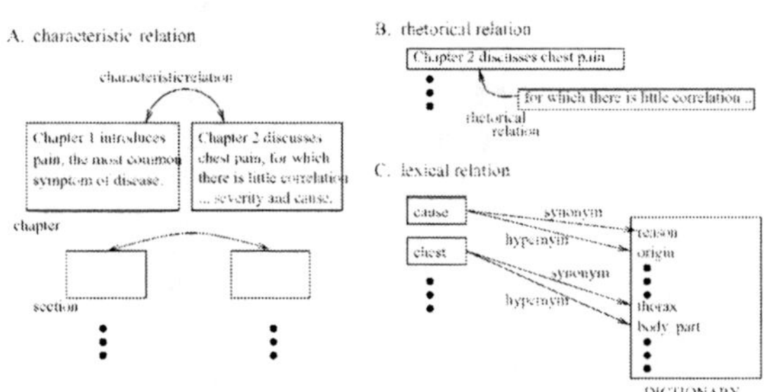

Fig. 3. Relations for machine learning to learn.

''Chapter 1 introduces pain, the most common symptom of disease, whereas Chapter 2 discusses chest pain, for which there is little correlation between severity and cause.''

These three threads, which learn relations at di erent granularities, create a digest for one *level* in the pyramid." There is another dimension which is seen as the vertical scale" dimension in Figure 2. This can be described as admitting fewer and fewer concepts into the target summary, so that a digest will be formed gradually, from speci c to general.

4.1 Scale Digest in All Levels

A popular Microsoft product, AutoSummarizer, provides the capability of producing a summary of length that is any given percentage of the original. If we stack these summaries, from higher percentage to lower, they, too, form a pyramid" as shown in Figure 2. This pyramid, however, is di erent from ours. Microsoft summaries consist of sentences extracted from the original, while ours contain segments of di erent sizes, and are both extracted and abstracted — i.e. they include words not in the original text. Nevertheless, we can compare our digest to Microsoft summaries by viewing only our sentence segment summaries inside the digest. Sentence segments are clauses; they are about the same size as sentences. In 3 , comparison has been made for one scale; we will use the same data as in 3 , but make more comparisons in the next section for di erent scales.

4.2 Supervised versus Unsupervised Learning

To create summaries of di erent scales for our pyramidal digest, we divide it into supervised and unsupervised methods. The pseudocode in Figure 4 illustrates how either supervised learning or unsupervised learning is applied to create the pyramidal digest that encompasses di erent granularities and di erent scales of summaries.

Supervised learning requires humans to manually label data, and is considered by many people to be too expensive. But there are ways to improve it. For example, labeled data can be obtained by feeding initial data to some heuristic function or existing search engines.

4.3 A Comparison with MS Word AutoSummarizer

In the following, we take only a portion i.e. sentence segments from several levels i.e. scale at 50 , 30 , 15 , and 5 of our pyramidal digest, both with supervised and unsupervised learning, and compare the results with summaries produced by the Microsoft AutoSummarizer.

```
for scale = 50 downto 5
  if unsupervised
    Construct naturally nested concept structure
    Remember text segments in each concept".
  else
    Manually create concept hierarchy.
    Manually label text segments into each concept
  end
  Compute TFIDF feature vectors for each concept.
  Apply 2 's accuracy feedback algorithm.
  for every concept
    Obtain subset features by this scale.
    Find rhetorical relations of sentence segments.
    if unsupervised
      Apply 3 's heuristic function by this scale.
    else
      Manually label segments of this scale.
      Apply C4.5 or Naive Bayesian or DistAl 3 .
    end
    Add segments to the digest.
    for top k = scale |TFIDF| rep. words.
      if unsupervised
        Perform classi cation phase of Accuracy
          Feedback algorithm at word granularity
      else
        Manually label word senses.
        Accuracy feedback at word granularity.
      end
      Add the -nyms to the digest feature vector.
    end
  end
end
```

Fig. 4. Learning to create the pyramidal digest.

For every scale, Microsoft Word summary performs the worst in every category — average accuracy, precision, and recall. Note that Microsoft summary is only compared to a portion of our pyramidal digest. In Figure 5 a , we averaged the overall precision and recall, and plotted it for methods in di erent scales. It can be seen that all methods drop as the scale approaches zero. There was a unusual spike for unsupervised learning near the lower end of the scale. This is because very few segments are in the denominator of the precision and recall equation; it often gets either 100 or 0 .

Figure 5 b shows the average test accuracy for di erent methods in di erent scales. Microsoft receives the lowest. As scale approaches zero, somewhat against our intuition, accuracy increases. This is because accuracy not only counts those that are correctly retrieved but also those that are correctly not retrieved.

5 Contextual Retrieval

A bene t of this pyramidal digest is that it better re ects context. Digests along the scope" dimension draw attention to segments from di erent positions in the sequence, and these di erent positions correspond to di erent contexts. Digests along the granularity" dimension highlight connections between context and

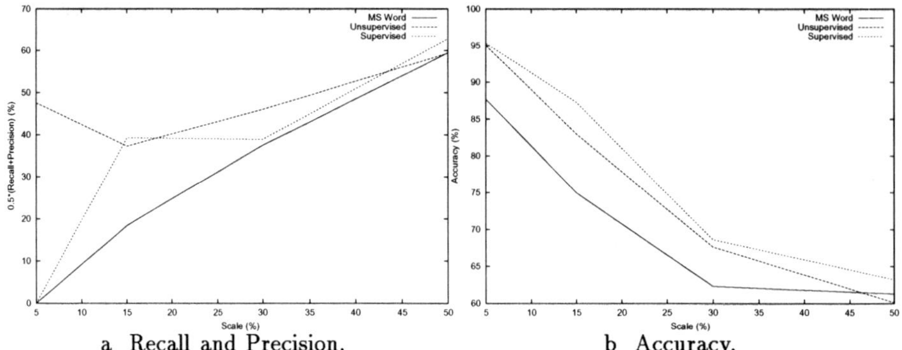

a Recall and Precision. b Accuracy.

Fig. 5. Evaluation in di erent scales.

text segments of di erent size. Last, digests along the scale” dimension capture di erences in user perceptions of context. This coincides with the assumption that di erent users want di erent sizes of summary. Our model produces a digest by focusing only on nearby context and never wastes time in considering far-reaching relationships.

After learning, the multilevel digest consists of text segments connected to others by some strength measure. This enables a given query string to be matched against the context, part of which is abstract information.

5.1 Abstract Information

Such abstract information is obtained in two ways. One abstract information is hypernym, which is inferred by following the WordNet's lexical hierarchy 6 after we learn the correct sense at the word granularity. The other abstract information is learned in supervised learning when we permit abstract terms in model summary. Contextual retrieval exploits this abstract information so that queries are carried out beyond keyword matches.

6 Summary and Discussion

When evaluated according to the criteria in section 4.3, we can see that our digest produced strictly better results than the Microsoft summary. The sentence segments portion of the digest performs better than Microsoft's summary in the categories of recall, precision and learning accuracy. But sentence segments are not the only information in our digest. The digest also contains extracted, abstracted, synonymized etc. segments of various scope in the original.

The experiments also indicate several tradeo s. First, there is a tradeo between supervised and unsupervised learning. Depending on how much humans can be involved in the process, the digest can be improved. Even when humans are not present, learning can still proceed without sacri cing much in performance. The second tradeo we have learned from the experiment is between retrieval relevance and scale from Figure 5 . It may be that we prefer shorter and more abstract digests, but it becomes more and more di cult to obtain such a digest when the scale is reduced. Third, from an information retrieval point of view, a higher level digest will retrieve more abstract information, but at the same time, more irrelevant information.

Nevertheless, the digest, or composite summaries, capture much information in a concise form. They basically index all important" parts of the original text, and can be used as an index for contextual retrieval as described in section 5. In addition, the pyramidal digest has many interesting potential applications such as XML summarizers, search engines, and e-Book etc.

References

1. Soumen Chakrabarti, Byron Dom, Rakesh Agrawal, and Prabhakar Raghavan. Using taxonomy, discriminants, and signatures for navigating in text databases. In *Proceedings of the 23rd VLDB Conference*, 1997.
2. Wesley Chuang, Asok Tiyyagura, Jihoon Yang, and Giovanni Giu rida. A fast algorithm for hierarchical text classi cation. In *Proceedings of the DaWak Conference*, 2000.
3. Wesley Chuang and Jihoon Yang. Extracting sentence segments for text summarization: A machine learning approach. In *Proceedings of the 23rd SIGIR Conference*, 2000.
4. Richard O. Duda, Peter E. Hart, and David G. Stork. *Pattern Classi cation*. John Wiley & Sons, 2000.
5. H.P. Edmundson. New methods in automatic extracting. *Journal of the ACM*, 16 2 :264 285, 1969.
6. Christiane Fellbaum, editor. *WordNet: An Electronic Lexical Database*. The MIT Press, 1998.
7. Graeme Hirst and David St-Onge. *WordNet: An Electronic Lexical Database*, chapter Lexical Chains as Representation of Context for the Detection and Correction Malapropisms, pages 305 332. The MIT Press, 1997.
8. Eduard Hovy and Chin-Yew Lin. *Advances in Automatic Text Summarization*, chapter Automated Text Summarization in SUMMARIST. MIT Press, 1999.
9. Kurt Isselbacher, Eugene Braunwald, Jean Wilson, Joseph Martin, Anthony Fauci, and Dennis Kasper, editors. *Harrison's Principles of Internal Medicine*. McGraw-Hill, 13rd edition, 1994.
10. Julian Kupiec, Jan O. Pedersen, and Francine Chen. Proceedings of the 18th acm sigir conference. In *A Trainable Document Summarizer*, pages 68 73, 1995.
11. H.P. Luhn. The automatic creation of literature abstracts. *IBM Journal of Research and Development*, 2 2 :159 165, 1958.
12. Dragomir R. Radev and Kathleen McKeown. Generating natural language summaries from multiple on-line sources. *Computational Linguistics*, 24 3 :469 500, 1998.
13. Mark Sanderson. Word sense disambiguation and information retrieval. In *Proceedings of the SIGIR Conference*, pages 142 151, 1994.
14. Ayse P. Saygin and Tuba Yavuz. Query processing in context-oriented retrieval of information. In *Joint Conference on Intelligent Systems*, 1998.

A Novel Full-Text Indexing Model for Chinese Text Retrieval[1]

Shuigeng Zhou, Yunfa Hu* and Jiangtao Hu*

State Key Lab of Software Engineering
Wuhan University, Wuhan, 430072, China
zhousg@whu.edu.cn

*Department of Computer Science
Fudan University, Shanghai, 200433, China
jthu@fudan.edu.cn

Abstract. Text retrieval systems require an index to allow fast access to documents at the cost of some storage overhead. This paper proposes a novel full-text indexing model for Chinese text retrieval based on the concept of adjacency matrix of directed graph. Using this indexing model, retrieval systems need to keep only indexing data, rather than indexing data and original text data as the traditional retrieval systems do, thus system space cost as a whole can be reduced drastically while retrieval efficiency is maintained satisfactory. Experiments over five real-world Chinese text collections are carried out to demonstrate the effectiveness and efficiency of this model.

1 Introduction

With the rapid growth of electronic Chinese documents published in Mainland China, Taiwan, Singapore, etc., there is an increasing need for Chinese text retrieval systems that support fast access to large amount of text documents. Full text retrieval systems are a popular way of providing support for on-line text access. From the end-user point of view, full text searching of on-line documents is appealing because a valid query is just any word or sentence of the document. Generally, full-text retrieval systems have an index to allow efficient retrieval of documents. Many text-indexing methods have been developed and used, such as inverted lists [1], signature files [2], PAT trees [3] and PAT arrays [4].

Although word-based indexing is widely used in English [1], it is not easily applied to Chinese. This is because written Chinese text has no delimiters to mark word boundaries. The first step toward word-based indexing of Chinese text is to break a sequence of characters into words, which is called word segmentation. Word segmentation is known to be a difficult task because accurate segmentation of written Chinese text may require deep analysis of the sentences [5]. On the other hand, character-based indexing methods don't depend on word segmentation, thus is suitable for Chinese text. Recently, there is an increasing research on character-based indexing for text retrieval of Chinese and other Oriental languages [6-7]. However, character-based full-text indexing costs too much storage space because each

[1] This work was supported by China Postdoctoral Science Foundation and the Natural Science Foundation of China (No. 60003016).

H.C. Mayr et al. (Eds.): DEXA 2001, LNCS 2113, pp. 370–379, 2001.

character in text database is indexed and its positional information is stored to support exact searching. So it is unfavorable for some application areas where storage resources are very limited, e.g., CD-based text retrieval systems.

This paper presents a novel full-text indexing model for Chinese text retrieval. By treating a text database as a directed graph and extending the concept of adjacency matrix of directed graph, we propose the adjacency-matrix based full-text indexing model. By using this model, retrieval system's space cost as a whole can be cut down drastically while retrieval efficiency is maintained satisfactory. The only precondition for the proposed model is that sufficient main memory is available to support an in-memory adjacency matrix. Given this precondition, the model described can support efficiently searching of string in large text databases.

In Section 2, we describe the novel full-text indexing model. In Section 3 we introduce the implementation techniques. We present the experimental results in Section 4 and conclude the paper in Section 5.

2 The Model

We begin with a *Chinese character set* Σ: a finite set of Chinese characters, letters, digits, punctuation marks and other symbols that may occur in Chinese text documents. A *text string* or simply *string* over Σ is a finite sequence of characters from Σ. The *length* of a string is its length as a sequence. We denote the length of a string w by $|w|$. Alternatively a string w can be considered as a function $w:\{1,\ldots,|w|\}\rightarrow\Sigma$; the value of $w(j)$, where $1\leq j\leq|w|$, is the character in the jth position of w. To distinguish identical characters at different positions in a string, we refer to them as different occurrences of the character. That is, the character $l\in\Sigma$ occurs in the jth position of the string w if $w(j)=l$.

Definition 1. Given a string w over Σ, let $V\subseteq\Sigma$ be the set of unique characters in w, there exists a *directed graph* $TDG=<V_g, E_g>$ where V_g is a set of vertices and $V_g=V$, i.e., each character in V corresponds to a vertex in V_g; E_g is a set of directed edges, each of which corresponds to a bigram appearing in w and its direction points from the first character to the second one. Because a character may occur at different positions in a string, the directed graph of a string is usually a *directed cyclic graph*.

Example 1. Consider a Chinese text string w_1: "家事国事天下事事事关心", its directed graph is illustrated in Fig. 1 where V_g = {"家", "国", "天", "下", "事", "关", "心"}, E_g={"家事", "事国", "国事", "事天", "天下", "下事", "事事", "事关", "关心"}.

Definition 2. A *simple string*, or simply *s-string*, is a string in which at most one character can occur twice. Equivalently, an *s-string* is a string whose directed graph contains at most one cycle.

Lemma 1. All bigrams in an s-string are unique.

Proof. By contradiction, if two or more similar bigrams exist in an s-string, then the s-string's directed graph must contain at least two cycles, which indicates it cannot be an s-string.

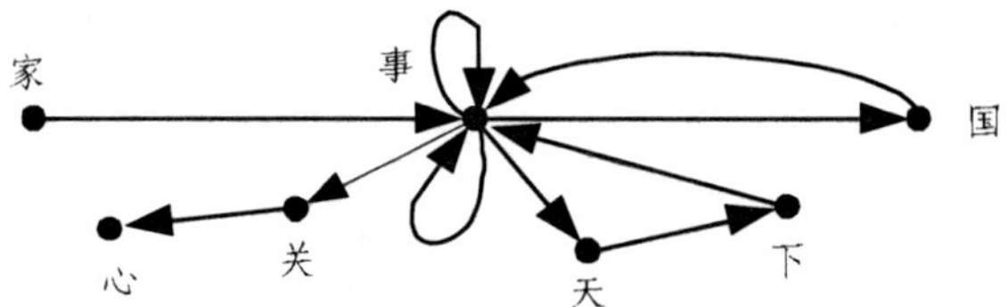

Fig. 1 The directed graph of string w_1

In what follows, we give an algorithm to segment an arbitrary string into a sequence of s-strings.

Algorithm 1. Segment an arbitrary string w into a sequence of s-strings

1) Set k=1;
2) Scan string w from its first character $w(1)$ to its last character $w(|w|)$
3) if there are two characters $w(i)$, $w(j)$ such that $w(j)= w(i)$ $(1\leq j<i\leq |w|)$ goto 5);
4) else goto 9);
5) $s_k= w(1)\, w(2)\ldots w(\mathrm{i})$;
6) if $i<|w|$ then do
7) $k=k+1$; $w= w(\mathrm{i})\, w(\mathrm{i}+1)\ldots w(|w|)$; goto 2);
8) else goto 10)
9) $s_k= w$;
10) The result is $(s_1,s_2,\ldots,s_k)$ where $s_i(|s_i|)=s_{i+1}(1)(1\leq i<k)$.

Definition 3. The *label* of an s-string is a natural number uniquely identifying the s-string. We specify that all s-strings of a string obtained by applying algorithm 1 are labeled in successive and incremental order. That is, the first s-string is labeled with l and the second with l+1, etc. The special and default case is that l=1.

Example 2 Applying algorithm 1 to w_1 in example 1, we get the following five s-strings: s_1= "家事国事", s_2= "事天下事", s_3= "事事", s_4= "事事", s_5= "事关心".

Lemma 2. If a string is segmented by algorithm 1, each bigram in the string is uniquely identified by a set of labels of the s-strings where the bigram occurs.
Proof. Each s-string is uniquely identified by its label (Definition 3); each bigram in an s-string is unique (Lemma 1); considering a bigram may occur in multiple s-strings, thus each bigram in a string can be uniquely identified by a set of labels of the s-strings where the bigram occurs.

Definition 4. The *weighted directed graph* of a string is established according to the following steps:

1) Segment the string using algorithm 1 and label the s-strings according to definition 3;

2) Construct the directed graph of the string according to definition 1.
3) Associate each edge in the directed graph with the label of the s-string where the edge's corresponding bigram locates.
4) Compact directed edges sharing a similar bigram to one directed edge and unite their corresponding labels to a set of labels as the compacted edge's weight.

Formally, denote $WDG=<V_w, E_w, L_w>$ the *weighted directed graph* of string w, V_w is the set of vertices and E_w is the set of directed edges as defined in definition 1, L_w is the set of labels associated with directed edges in E_w. Let $L_w(l^i, l^j)$ be the set of labels associated with directed edge $l^i l^j$, we have

$$L_w = \{L_w(l^i, l^j) \mid \forall l^i l^j : l^i l^j \in E_w \text{ and } l^i \in V_w \text{ and } l^j \in V_w\}.$$

Definition 5. The adjacency matrix of a string is formally defined as follows:

$$A = [a_{ij}],\ a_{ij} = L_w(l^i, l^j).$$

Example 3. Given a Chinese text string w_2: "我们的国家，我们的人民，你们的国家，你们的人民，他们的国家，他们的人民。". Segment w_2 into a sequence of s-strings and label them by the default fashion: s_1="我们的国家，我", s_2="我们的人民，你们", s_3="们的国家，你们", s_4="们的人民，他们", s_5="们的国家，他们", s_6="们的人民。". Eleven unique characters in w_2 constitute the vertices set V_w ={"我", "你", "他", "们", "的", "人", "民", "国", "家", "，", "。"}. Fourteen unique bigrams constitute the directed edges set E_w ={"我们", "们的", "的国", "国家", "家，", "，我", "的人", "人民", "民，", "，你", "你们", "，他", "他们", "民。"}. Fig.2 shows the weighted directed graph of string w_2.

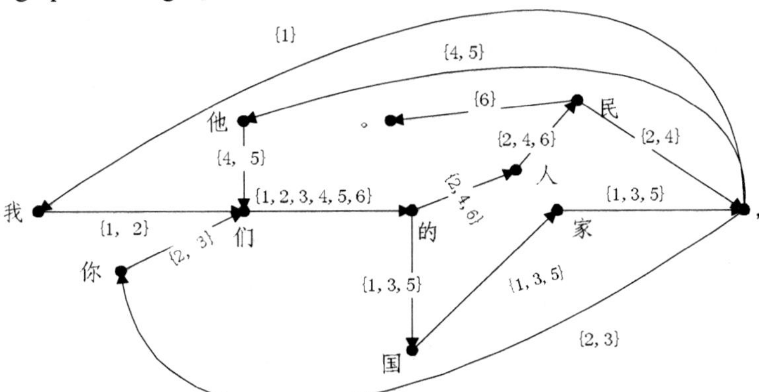

Fig. 2 Weighted directed graph of string w_2

Here, we use only 6 labels to represent 14 bigrams in w_2. However, if the character-based inverted lists were used, we would have to use 36 positions to identify 11 characters in w_2. We assume l^1= "我", l^2= "你" and so on, the corresponding adjacency matrix of Fig. 2 is a 11×11 matrix as shown in Fig. 3, in which: a_{14}= L_w ("我", "们")={1, 2}, d_{24}= L_w ("你", "们")={2, 3}, a_{34}= L_w ("他", "们")={4, 5}, a_{45}= L_w ("们" , "的")={1, 2, 3, 4, 5, 6}, a_{56}= L_w ("的" , "人")={2, 4,

6}, $a_{58}= L_w$ ("的", "国")={1, 3, 5}, $a_{67}= L_w$ ("人", "民")={2, 4, 6}, $a_{7\,10}= L_w$ ("民", "，")={2, 4}, $a_{7\,11}= L_w$ ("民", "。")={6}, $a_{89}= L_w$ ("国", "家")={1, 3, 5}, $a_{9\,10}= L_w$ ("家", "，")={1, 3, 5}, $a_{10\,1}= L_w$ ("，", "我")={1}, $a_{10\,2}= L_w$ ("，", "你")={2, 3}, $a_{10\,3}= L_w$ ("，", "他")={4, 5}; the other elements are empty.

$$A = \left| \begin{array}{ccccccccccc}
\Phi & \Phi & \Phi & a_{14} & \Phi & \Phi & \Phi & \Phi & \Phi & \Phi & \Phi \\
\Phi & \Phi & \Phi & a_{24} & \Phi & \Phi & \Phi & \Phi & \Phi & \Phi & \Phi \\
\Phi & \Phi & \Phi & a_{34} & \Phi & \Phi & \Phi & \Phi & \Phi & \Phi & \Phi \\
\Phi & \Phi & \Phi & \Phi & a_{45} & \Phi & \Phi & \Phi & \Phi & \Phi & \Phi \\
\Phi & \Phi & \Phi & \Phi & \Phi & a_{56} & \Phi & a_{58} & \Phi & \Phi & \Phi \\
\Phi & \Phi & \Phi & \Phi & \Phi & \Phi & a_{67} & \Phi & \Phi & \Phi & \Phi \\
\Phi & \Phi & \Phi & \Phi & \Phi & \Phi & \Phi & \Phi & \Phi & a_{7\,10} & a_{7\,11} \\
\Phi & \Phi & \Phi & \Phi & \Phi & \Phi & \Phi & \Phi & a_{89} & \Phi & \Phi \\
\Phi & \Phi & \Phi & \Phi & \Phi & \Phi & \Phi & \Phi & \Phi & a_{9\,10} & \Phi \\
a_{10\,1} & a_{10\,2} & a_{10\,3} & \Phi & \Phi & \Phi & \Phi & \Phi & \Phi & \Phi & \Phi \\
\Phi & \Phi & \Phi & \Phi & \Phi & \Phi & \Phi & \Phi & \Phi & \Phi & \Phi
\end{array} \right|$$

Fig. 3 Adjacency matrix of string w_2

Lemma 3. For a string w and its adjacency matrix A,
1) if bigram c_1c_2 occurs in w, then $a(c_1, c_2)\neq\Phi$;
2) if trigram $c_1c_2c_3$ occurs in w, then $(a(c_1, c_2)\cap a(c_2, c_3))\cup(\{a(c_1, c_2)+1\}\cap a(c_2, c_3))\neq\Phi$. Here, $\{a(c_1, c_2)+1\}$ represents a new set formed by adding 1 to each element in $a(c_1, c_2)$.
Proof. 1) if bigram c_1c_2 occurs in w, it must locate in some s-string(s), thus $a(c_1, c_2)\neq\Phi$; 2) if trigram $c_1c_2c_3$ occurs in w, then two cases exist: a) c_1c_2 and c_2c_3 locate in the same s-string, that is $a(c_1, c_2)\cap a(c_2, c_3) \neq\Phi$; b) c_1c_2 and c_2c_3 locate in two adjacent s-strings respectively. Considering the labels of two adjacent s-strings differ from each other by 1(definition 3), so $\{a(c_1, c_2)+1\}\cap a(c_2, c_3) \neq\Phi$. Combining these two cases, we have $(a(c_1, c_2)\cap a(c_2, c_3))\cup(\{a(c_1, c_2)+1\}\cap a(c_2, c_3))\neq\Phi$.

Definition 6. A *text database* is a collection of text documents, each of which is a string over Σ. Neglecting the boundary between any two adjacent documents, a text database can be seen as a long string, whose length is the sum of the lengths of all documents in the text database.

While constructing adjacency matrix of a text database, we request all documents in the text database are segmented separately. However, all s-strings are labeled globally. That is: 1) no s-string spans two or more adjacent documents; 2) for any two adjacent documents d_i and d_{i+1}, d_{i+1}'s first s-string is labeled just following the label of d_i's last s-string.

Definition 7. The *document index table* (*DIT*) of a text database is organized as a triple:

$$DIT = \{(l_1, c_1, c_2)\}.$$

Each document in the text database has a record in *DIT*. A record has three fields: l_1 is the label of the first s-string in a document; c_1 and c_2 are the first two characters of the document. Given two adjacent documents d_i and d_{i+1}'s first label: l_i, l_{i+1}, $[l_i, l_{i+1}-1]$ constitutes the label range of d_i's s-strings.

Definition 8. The *adjacency matrix based full-text indexing model* of a text database consists of two parts: the adjacency matrix and the document index table.

Unlike current indexing techniques, the proposed indexing model has the following unique characteristics: 1) Using bigrams as indexed terms and organizing all bigrams into an adjacency matrix corresponding to the text database's weighted directed graph. 2) After the indexing model is established, original text documents are not saved in the retrieval system, which results in a drastic reduction of system storage cost as a whole. While processing query, original text documents are reconstructed by using exclusively the indexing matrix and *DIT*. 3) Labels of s-strings rather than positions of indexed term are used for identifying different occurrences of indexed term, which provides an opportunity of cutting down indexing space overhead because the total number of s-strings in a text database is much smaller than the text database's length.

Using the proposed indexing model, an arbitrary string searching can be processes by applying lemma 3 iteratively. Generally, a query is processed with the following three steps: 1) Based on the adjacency matrix, retrieve the labels or label sequences of s-strings that the query string may locate in or span over. A query-processing algorithm is responsible for this sub-task. 2) According to *DIT*, find the desired document index records and corresponding label ranges. 3) Using the adjacency matrix and results from step 2), a text-reconstructing algorithm is used to reconstruct the text contents of all desired documents.

3 Implementation Techniques

The indexing adjacency matrix is usually a large, sparse matrix. Statistics for five test collections show that more than 97% of matrix elements are empty. In the process of index building, the adjacency matrix is dynamically expanding. We adopt a three-level in-memory structure for the indexing adjacency matrix as illustrated in Fig. 4. Notice that each matrix element corresponds to a bigram. The first level is a hash indexed by the first character of a bigram. Its maximum size is the number of all unique characters appearing in text database. Each element of the first-level hash consists of three components: the indexed character (*ch1*), number of the indexed character's successive characters (*number_of_ch2*) and a pointer to one instance of the second level. An instance of the second level is a hash indexed by the second character of the bigram, each of whose elements also includes three components: the indexed character (*ch2*), number of the labels (*number_of_labels*) associated with bigram (*ch1*, *ch2*) and a pointer to one instance of the third level. One instance of the third level is a hash indexed by the label of s-strings where a certain bigram locates.

While processing queries or reconstructing text documents, the indexing matrix is stable. We adopt a static in-memory structure for the indexing matrix then, which is quite similar to that in Fig.4, except 1) size-fixed arrays are used to replace the first-level hash and the second-level hashes in Fig.4; and 2) the third-level structure in Fig.4 is not used due to memory limitation. Label data is loaded to memory from disk whenever requested.

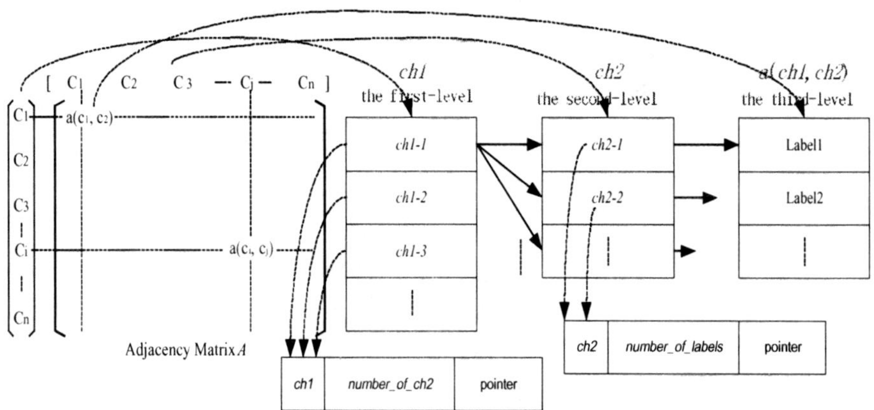

Fig. 4 In-memory structure of adjacency matrix (Used for matrix building)

On disk, indexing data is stored separately in two files. One file is used to store the labels of s-strings, i.e., data in the third level hashes. We refer to these data as label data; another is used to save structure information of the adjacent matrix, which corresponds to the data stored in both the first level hash and the second level hashes. We call these two files *label file* and *matrix file* respectively. In the label file, label data associated with each bigram is stored sequentially and successively. The matrix file has a structure as in Fig. 5. Here, *ch1* is the first character of a bigram, which specified the row where the bigram locates in the matrix; and *ch2* is the second of character of the bigram that determines which column the bigram is placed in the matrix. *ch2_number* indicates the number of successive characters of *ch1*. *label_numbe*r indicates the occurrences count of bigram (*ch1*, *ch2*) in text database, and *fp_seek* specifies the starting address where label data of bigram (*ch1*, *ch2*) is stored in the label file. *label_numbe*r and *fp_seek* use user defined data types because the ranges of their values are related to text database size. Using user defined data types can save storage space.

```
Struct {
  UNICHAR                     ch1;
  Usigned int                 ch2_number;
  Struct {
    UNCHAR                          ch2;
    LABEL_NUMBER_TYPE               label_number;
    FILE_ADDRESS                    fp_seek;
  } Column [ch2_number];
} ROW[Size_Of_Character_Set].
```

Fig. 5 Structure of the matrix file

A third file, the *document index file*, is used to store records in the document index table. These three files mentioned above are created when the indexing matrix is established. While processing queries or reconstructing text documents, data of the matrix file and the document index file is loaded into memory for improving retrieval efficiency. For the text collection of 182.2Mb in Table 1, the memory requirement is about 15Mb, which is available for current PCs.

The process of adjacency matrix building is simultaneously the process of text database building, which produces three resulting files: the matrix file, the label file and the document index file. As a new document arrives it is parsed and its bigrams are inserted into the in-memory adjacency matrix. At some point data in the adjacency matrix must be written to disk to release memory. We write only the label data, which is stored in the third-level hashes, to temporary files. Generally, a temporary file corresponds to a bigram. Notice the occurrences of different bigrams in text database are quite uneven. In the process of matrix building, some matrix elements (corresponding to frequently occurring bigrams) will expand rapidly with the arrival of new documents while others (corresponding to infrequently appearing bigrams) will expand slowly or not at all. In addition, new documents will contain previously unseen bigrams. To amortize disk writing cost, when data writing is requested, we move only the label data of bigrams that have accumulated more than L_s labels (L_s is a pre-specified threshold) since the last writing, so that label data of infrequent bigrams may be written only one time (the final time) during the process of matrix building. When all documents have been processed, label data in temporary files as well as these still in memory is merged into the final label file.

4 The Experiments

Five Chinese text collections of different sizes are used for experiments, which are listed in Table 1. All experiments are carried out on a PC with 2 CPUs of PII350 and 512M RAM.

Table 1 Test Collections

Test collection	TC-1	TC-2	TC-3	TC-4	TC-5
Size (Mb)	14.9	39.0	97.6	182.2	500.4

We first test space cost. Expansion ration is used to measure space cost of different indexing methods. We define expansion ration as $(s_{txt}+s_{ind})/s_{txt}$. Here, s_{txt} and s_{ind} are the sizes of text data and indexing data respectively. Fig. 6 shows the test results of expansion ration for four different indexing methods over fiver text collections. The four indexing methods are PAT array, bigram-based inverted lists, character-based inverted lists and the proposed new indexing model. We can see that our indexing method has the lowest expansion ration. When indexing TC-5, our method consumes about 750Mb less storage space than other methods do. We then test matrix building efficiency. Fig. 7 illustrates the results of matrix building speed for five text collections. Obviously, as the size of text collection grows, the frequency of disk writing also increases, which leads to processing efficiency going down. Following that, we test the efficiency of text reconstructing. Test results are demonstrated in Fig. 8. Basically, larger text collection has lower reconstructing efficiency. However, even for the largest test collection TC-4, its reconstructing speed surpasses 12kb/s, i.e., about 6000 characters/s, which is absolutely fast enough to meet the requirements of text reading and browsing of most ordinary people.

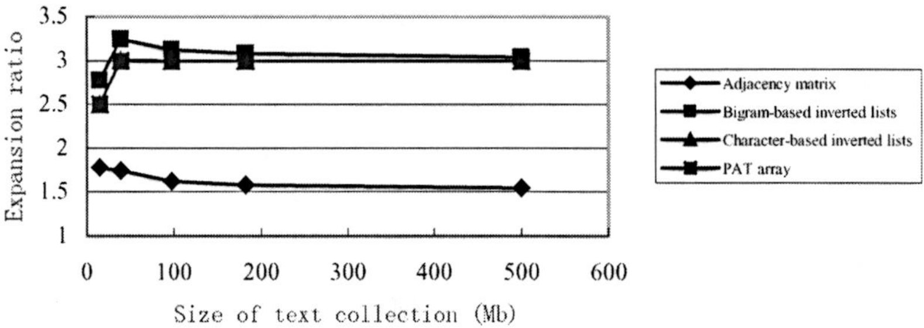

Fig. 6 Expansion ration comparisons among different indexing methods

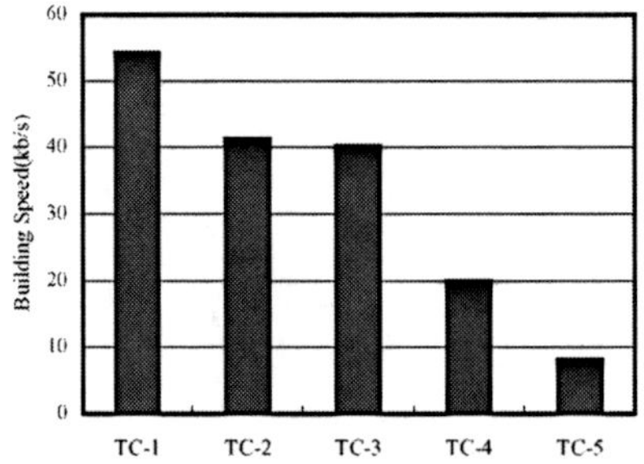

Fig.7 Matrix building speeds for text collections of different sizes

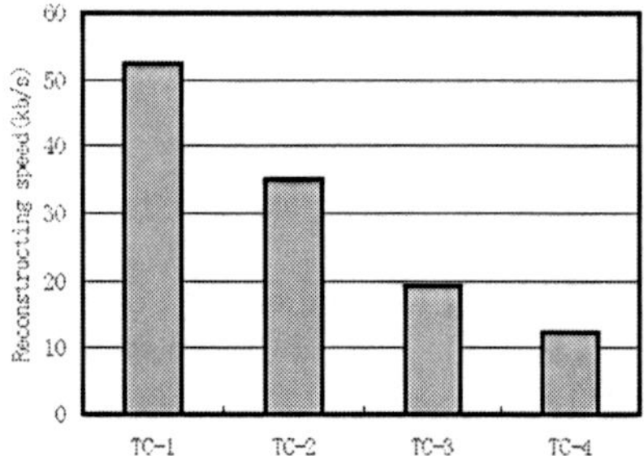

Fig.8 The impact of text collection size on text reconstructing speed

Finally, we examine the efficiency of query processing by using five kinds of query length: 2-character, 5-character, 10-character, 15-character and 20-character. To make experimental results more reasonable and reliable, a program is used to generate queries automatically and randomly. For each query length, 3000 queries generated randomly are processed to measure query efficiency. Results shown in Fig. 9 are average results over 3000 different queries of the same length. As the size of text collection becomes larger, the average amount of label data associated with each bigram increases. Consequently, more label data need to be read and processed while evaluating a query of a given length. Generally, query not longer than 10 characters can be processed within about 1 sec.

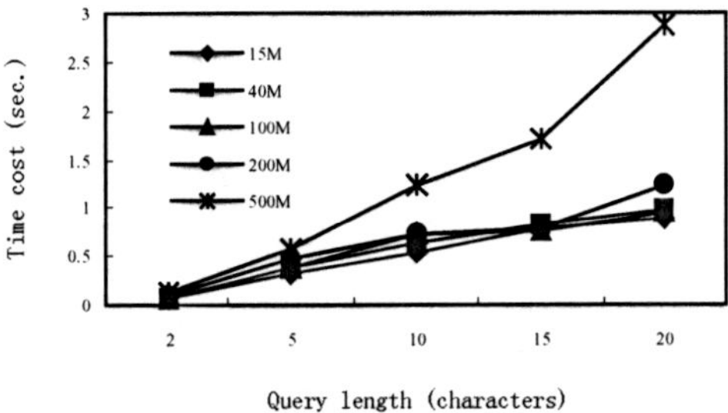

Fig. 9 The impact of query length on time cost of query processing

5 Conclusions

By treating text database as directed graph and extending the concept of adjacency matrix of directed graph, we propose the adjacency-matrix based full-text indexing model in this paper. The innovative ideas of this paper are 1) Organizing bigrams into an adjacency matrix, which makes it possible to reconstruct text contents by using exclusively indexing data; 2) using the labels of s-strings of text database to identify different occurrences of bigrams leads to further reduced indexing space overhead. Experimental results show that the proposed indexing model is effective and efficient. The new model can also be used for text retrieval of other Oriental languages such as Japanese and Korean.

References

[1] R. Baesa-Yates and B. Ribeiro-Neto. Modern Information Retrieval. Addison Wesley, Reading, Mass., 1999.

[2] C. Faltousos and S. Christodoulakis. Signature files: an access method for documents and its analytical performance evaluation. *ACM Trans. On Office Information Systems*, 2(4): 267-88, 1984.

[3] D. R. Morrison. PATRICIA- practical algorithm to retrieve information coded in alphanumeric. *Journal of the ACM*, 15(4): 514-534, 1968.

[4] G. Navarro. An optimal index for PAT arrays. In: *Proceedings of the Third South American Workshop on String Processing*, pp. 214-227, 1996.

[5] Z. Wu and G. Tseng. Chinese text segmentation for text retrieval: Achievements and Problems. Journal of the American Society for Information Science. 44:532-542, October 1993.

[6] Y. Ogawa & M. Iwasaki. A new character-based indexing method using frequency data for Japanese documents. In: *Proc. 18th ACM SIGIR Conf.*, pp. 121-128, 1995.

[7] K. L. Kwol. Comparing representations in Chinese information retrieval. In: *Proc. Of 20th ACM SIGIR Conf.*, pp.34-41, 1997.

Page Access Sequencing in Join Processing with Limited Buffer Space

Chen Qun, Andrew Lim and Oon Wee Chong

Department of Computer Science
National University of Singapore
Lower Kent Ridge Road, Singapore 119260
Email: {chenqun,alim,oonwc}@comp.nus.edu.sg

Abstract. When performing the join operation in relational databases, one problem involves finding the optimal page access sequence such that the number of page re-accesses is minimized, given a fixed buffer size. This paper presents a new heuristic for this problem (known as OPAS2) that generally outperforms existing heuristics.

Keywords: Join Processing, Query Processing, Heuristic Design

1 Introduction

The join operation is one of the most expensive and frequently executed operations in database systems. The main cost of join operations involves the fetching of data pages from secondary storage devices to the main memory buffer. Several approaches to this problem have previously been tried [2, 4, 7].

One strategy to minimise memory usage is to first scan the indices of the relevant relations to obtain a set of data page pairs (x, y), where page x contains some tuple which is joined with some tuple in page y. This information can then be used to find an efficient *page access sequence* to minimise the amount of memory required. This is an extension of the sort-merge join and the simple TID algorithm [1, 4].

There are two related problems when it comes to finding an optimal page access sequence for this strategy :

1. Given that there are no page reaccesses, what page access sequence will require the minimum number of buffer pages?
2. Given a fixed buffer size, what page access sequence will require the minimum number of page reaccesses?

The above problems are referred to as OPAS1 and OPAS2 respectively, for *optimal page access sequence* problems [6]. Both problems are believed to be NP-Complete. All previous works have concentrated on finding a good solution to OPAS1, and then adapting it to OPAS2 by including a page replacement

H.C. Mayr et al. (Eds.): DEXA 2001, LNCS 2113, pp. 380–389, 2001.

strategy when the maximum buffer size is reached. In this study, we present a new heuristic for OPAS2 that is not based on an OPAS1 strategy.

In Section 2, we define the symbols and terminology used in this report, along with the graph models used. Section 3 gives a brief description of existing heuristics. The new heuristic is presented in Section 4, with the experimental results analyzed in Section 5. Finally, in Section 6, we conclude our findings.

2 Terminology and Notation

2.1 Problem Definition

We can represent the page-pair information of a join by an undirected join graph $G = (V, E)$, where the set of vertices V represents the pages in the join, and the set of edges $E \subseteq V \times V$ represents the set of page-pairs which contains tuples to be joined with each other. As pages are fetched into the buffer, the join graph is updated as follows : An edge (x, y) is removed from the graph if the pages x and y have been fetched and joined. A vertex x is removed from the graph if the degree of x becomes zero. Such a page is said to be *released.*

A page access sequence (PAS) specifies the order of fetching the pages of the join graph into the buffer. For the OPAS2 problem, its definition is as follows:

Definition 1. *Let $G = (V, E)$ be a join graph. A* **page access sequence** $S =< p_1, p_2, \cdots, p_{|v|} >$ *is a sequence of pages from V where p_i denotes the ith page fetched into the buffer.*

This definition differs from an OPAS1 page access sequence in that the sequence of pages need not be distinct.

Definition 2. *For any page p, its* **resident degree** *is the number of distinct pages in the buffer that it is adjacent to. Its* **non-resident degree** *is the number of distinct pages not in the buffer that it is adjacent to. All pages are adjacent to itself.*

Definition 3. *Let $S =< p_1, p_2, \cdots, p_{|V|} >$ be a page access sequence for a join graph $G = (V, E)$ in a system with buffer size B. S is an* **optimal page access sequence** *iff $(|S| - |V|) \leq (|S'| - |V|)$ for all page access sequences S'.*

For any PAS, the total number of page re-accesses is the difference between the length of the PAS and the total number of pages to be read. An optimal page access sequence is thus one that minimizes this value.

Definition 4. *Let $S =< p_1, p_2, \cdots, p_{|v|} >$ be a page access sequence. $S' = < p_i, p_{i+1}, \cdots, p_{i+k} >, 1 \leq i \leq (|V| - k)$ is a* **segment of page access sequence S** *iff S' is a nonempty subsequence of S such that*

1. *No page is released by the entry of p_j for $i \leq j < i + k$,*
2. *One or more pages are released by the entry of p_{i+k}, and*
3. *One or more pages are released by the entry of p_{i-1} if $i > 1$.*

Thus, each PAS can be uniquely expressed as a sequence of m segments. We call a segment of length N that releases K pages an **N-Release-K segment**.

2.2 Types of Graphs

There are some types of graphs that are commonly used to model the conditions that arise in database systems. For our study, we make use of the following two types of graphs:

Bipartite Graph If G is a bipartite graph such that V = $V_1 \cup V_2$ and $V_1 \cap V_2 = \emptyset$, and *degree n%*, then Prob[$(v_i, v_j) \in$ E] =

1. $\frac{n}{100}$ if $v_i \in V_1$ and $v_j \in V_2$,
2. 0 otherwise.

A bipartite graph is partitioned into 2 sets of vertices, where the vertices within a set cannot be connected to each other. The bipartite graph models bi-relational joins, and is one of the most important join graphs in database systems.

Geometric Graph If G is a geometric graph with v vertices and the expected degree of each vertex $E(\theta) = k$, then G is generated as follows :

1. Compute d = $\sqrt{\frac{k}{v\pi}}$.
2. Generate v points randomly in a unit square, i.e. assign a pair of coordinates (x_k, y_k), $x_k, y_k \in [0, 1]$ to each vertex v_k.
3. Add (v_i, v_j) into E iff the distance between v_i and $v_j < d$, i.e. if $\sqrt{(x_i - x_j)^2 + (y_i - y_j)^2} < d$.

Thus in a geometric graph, there is only an edge if 2 points are "close enough", and therefore the points tend to form clusters. It is our opinion that a geometric graph is a good approximation of multi-relation joins, where each cluster approximates a relation.

3 Existing Heuristics

All existing heuristics for OPAS2 have so far been OPAS1 heuristics coupled with a page replacement strategy. In this section, we give a brief description of these heuristics.

Omiecinski's Heuristic (OH) [5] finds at each step the smallest number of fetches which would remove one page from the memory. The victim page when the buffer is full is the page with the smallest non-resident degree that is not adjacent to the page being brought into the buffer.

Chan and Ooi's Heuristic (COH) [6] does not restrict itself to removing pages from the buffer. At each step, it looks for the smallest number of pages to be read in order to release any page, or the *smallest minimal segment*, and puts it into the buffer in order of descending resident degree. When the buffer is full, the page replaced is the one with the smallest non-resident degree. COH generally outperforms OH for the OPAS1 problem, but performs worse for the OPAS2 problem when the buffer size is lower than a certain threshold.

In essense, the COH heuristic searches for the smallest N-Release-1 segments during each iteration. **Lim, Kwan & Oon's Heuristic (LKOH)** [3] extends COH by searching for N-Release-($K \geq 1$) page segments, such that $N - K$ is minimized while maximizing N. It has the added parameter L to limit the value of K in the search. LKOH outperforms COH significantly for geometric graphs, but the improvement is slight in the case of bipartite graphs.

4 The New Heuristic (CLOH)

In the OPAS2 problem, our performance metric is the number of page re-accesses. Therefore, it does not matter if there are few or no pages released early in the PAS, as long as the number of page re-accesses are ultimately minimized. A strategy that thus suggests itself is to create as many lightly-connected pages as possible within the memory buffer early in the algorithm. This is the basis of the new heuristic (CLOH).

CLOH brings the page with the highest resident degree into the buffer in each iteration. Ties are broken by selecting the page with the lowest non-resident degree. We also define a **release level** L, such that if there exists a page whose non-resident degree is L or less, we will bring in the segment that releases that page. The optimal value of L is determined quantitatively.

The page replacement strategy is slightly different depending on whether the threshold L has been reached. In the first case, when the smallest non-resident degree of all resident pages is greater than L, the victim page is the page with the largest non-resident degree that is not connected to the page being brought in. In the second case, when we are bringing in the smallest segment, the victim page has the additional condition of not being the page that is to be released at the end of the segment.

OPAS2-CLOH(G,L)

1. Choose a page p_i in the join graph G such that the degree of p_i is minimal. Bring p_i into the buffer.
2. if (the smallest non-resident degree of pages in the buffer is greater than L), then
   (a) Choose a page p_j such that of all the non-resident pages with the largest resident degree, p_j has the smallest non-resident degree.
   (b) if (the buffer is full) then remove from the buffer a page with the largest non-resident degree that is not connected to p_j.
   (c) Bring p_j into the buffer.
   (d) Delete all edges (p_i, p_j) from G where p_i and p_j are contained in the buffer. If the degree of a page becomes zero, then remove the page from the buffer (the page is released), and delete the vertex from G.
3. else
   (a) Choose a set of pages PAGES(G) to bring into buffer using the following strategy:

   i. Find a page p_j such that p_j has the minimal non-resident degree.
   ii. Select all pages outside the buffer which are connected with p_j. These pages make up PAGES(G).
 (b) for (every page p_k in PAGES(G))
   i. if (the buffer is full) then remove from the buffer a page with the largest non-resident degree that is not connected to p_k, and is not p_j.
   ii. Bring p_k into the buffer.
   iii. Delete all edges (p_i, p_k) from G where p_i and p_j are contained in the buffer. If the degree of a page becomes zero, then remove the page from the buffer (the page is released), and delete the vertex from G.
4. If G is empty, quit; else goto Step 1.

5 Testing and Evaluation

5.1 Bipartite Graph Results

For bipartite graphs, we randomly generated 20 instances with 500 vertices (250 vertices per partition) for each edge ratio of 5%, 10% and 15%. We then ran the OH, COH, LKOH and CLOH algorithms on these graphs, using a range of buffer sizes. For the LKOH heuristic, we used the L-value of 3 which gave the best results in the original work [3]. In the case of the new heuristic, we tested the effects of setting the release level L to various values. Our results show that in general, the best results are achieved with L set to between 2 and 4.

Table 1 gives the results for graphs with edge ratio 10%. The *Improvement* column gives the absolute difference between the best result obtained by CLOH using L at 2, 3, 4 and 5, and the best result obtained by the OH, COH and LKOH(3).

The results for graphs with edge ratio 5% and 15% are similar. The improvement patterns for all three cases (shown in figures 1, 2 and 3) are also similar. We note that CLOH outperforms all existing heuristics except for a narrow range of buffer sizes. Furthermore, the absolute improvement increases markedly as edge ratio increases, since denser graphs will have more heavily-connected vertices.

5.2 Geometric Graph Results

We randomly generated 20 geometric graphs of 500 vertices each for expected degrees of 25, 50 and 75. We ran the COH, OH, LKOH and CLOH algorithms on these graphs for a range of buffer sizes. Once again, the new heuristic outperforms all existing heuristics in general.

Table 2 gives the results for the set of geometric graphs with an expected degree of 75. For LKOH, we first ran the algorithm with the recommended L-value of 3. In the course of our experiments, we found that there were cases when an L-value of 5 gave a better result, and these figures are also included in the table. For CLOH, we ran the tests with release values of 2, 3 and 4,

Buffer Size	COH	OH	LKOH(3)	CLOH(2)	CLOH(3)	CLOH(4)	CLOH(5)	Improvement
10	4642	4610	4563	3366	3431	3503	3575	1197
20	3259	3202	3275	2901	2884	2946	3016	318
30	2597	2532	2533	2522	2469	2472	2536	63
40	2138	2055	2081	2140	2124	2039	2102	16
50	1801	1742	1870	1863	1843	1808	1751	-9
60	1629	1524	1580	1647	1581	1556	1503	21
70	1525	1318	1539	1456	1373	1324	1332	-6
80	1401	1248	1444	1327	1219	1224	1179	69
90	1367	1117	1419	1173	1141	1096	1071	46
100	1297	1080	1260	1052	1009	1023	1037	71
110	1210	1014	1271	992	944	958	931	83
120	1168	995	1118	930	911	924	923	84
130	1104	932	1067	888	857	842	901	90
140	1039	921	1113	816	838	872	910	105
150	1040	1088	973	807	827	860	829	166
160	1021	1076	987	724	727	721	724	266
170	891	1043	980	692	697	695	685	206
180	926	1026	901	670	678	683	668	233
190	916	1080	915	661	655	674	650	265
200	884	1047	859	650	642	638	634	225
210	853	978	763	621	624	626	615	148
220	742	815	797	608	607	603	603	139
230	631	667	638	606	598	509	592	122

Table 1. Comparison results for bipartite graphs with 250+250 vertices and edge ratio=10

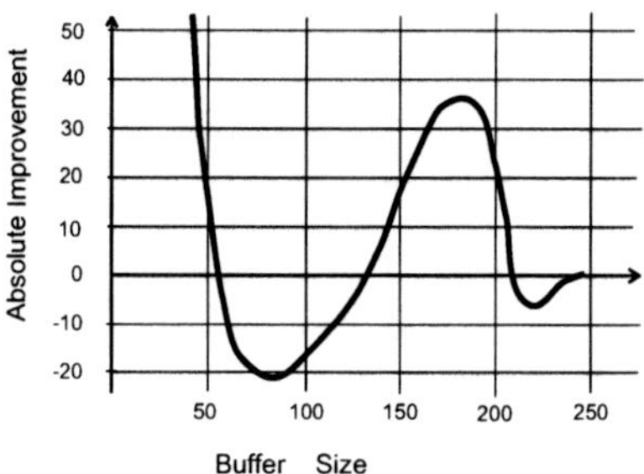

Fig. 1. Improvement of CLOH for BipartiteGraphs with 500 vertices and edge ratio=5%

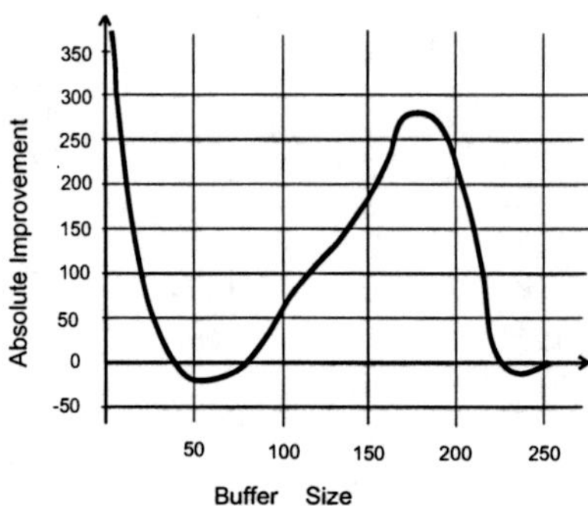

Fig. 2. Improvement of CLOH for BipartiteGraphs with 500 vertices and edge ratio=10%

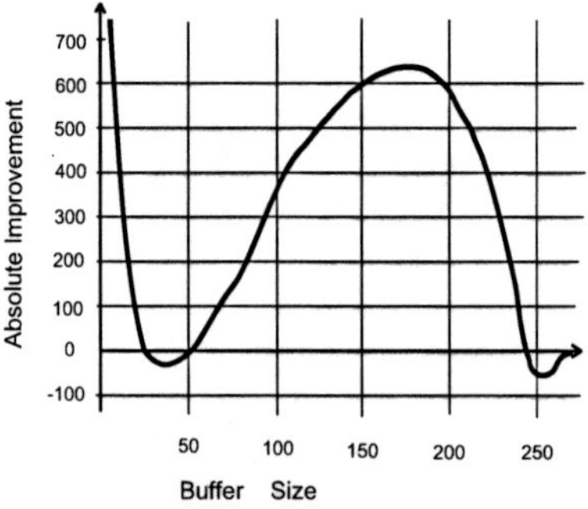

Fig. 3. Improvement of CLOH for BipartiteGraphs with 500 vertices and edge ratio=15%

which were found to give the best results. The *Improvement* column gives the absolute difference between the best values attained by COH, OH, LKOH(3) and LKOH(5), and that of CLOH for the three release values.

Buffer Size	COH	OH	LKOH(3)	LKOH(5)	CLOH(2)	CLOH(3)	CLOH(4)	Improvement
10	2395	2088	2482	2482	2035	2063	2035	53
15	1990	1454	1845	1851	1448	1410	1428	44
20	1534	1139	1494	1494	1139	1133	1074	65
25	1269	1113	1158	1158	949	984	901	212
30	1164	890	1054	1054	956	910	856	34
35	862	894	884	884	856	788	830	74
40	784	761	793	758	850	729	735	29
45	731	710	792	792	715	660	696	50
50	805	700	725	709	652	663	647	53
55	666	679	749	749	634	664	615	51
60	704	675	601	597	612	691	599	-2
65	631	607	598	585	607	609	604	-19
70	629	593	590	596	558	557	595	33
75	574	564	570	573	550	549	598	15
80	533	550	570	568	544	528	539	5
85	536	530	530	528	534	532	524	4
90	530	515	519	517	530	525	518	-3

Table 2. Comparison results for geometric graphs with 500 vertices and 75 expected degree

Experiments with graphs of expected degree 25 and 50 produced similar results. Figures 4, 5 and 6 give the improvement patterns for all three test sets. These figures show that CLOH gives better results over almost the entire range of buffer sizes.

5.3 Evaluation of the New Heuristic

Our experiments show that the CLOH heuristic outperforms all existing OPAS2 heuristics for both the bipartite and geometric graph models. Through quantitative analysis, we have ascertained that the best release level L for the CLOH algorithm is between 2 and 4, irrespective of buffer size and graph density. This bodes well for practical implementation of this heuristic.

6 Conclusion

In this paper, we proposed a new OPAS2 heuristic CLOH that differs from all previous heuristics in that it is not derived from simply giving an OPAS1 heuristic a page replacement strategy. In contrast, CLOH takes advantage of

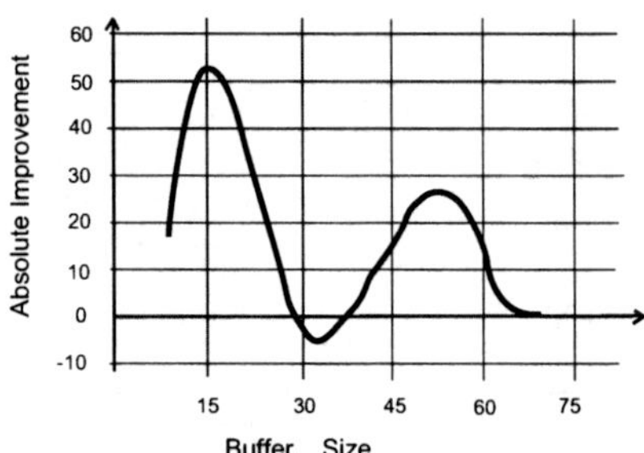

Fig. 4. Improvement of CLOH for GeometricGraphs with 500 vertices and Expected Degree=25

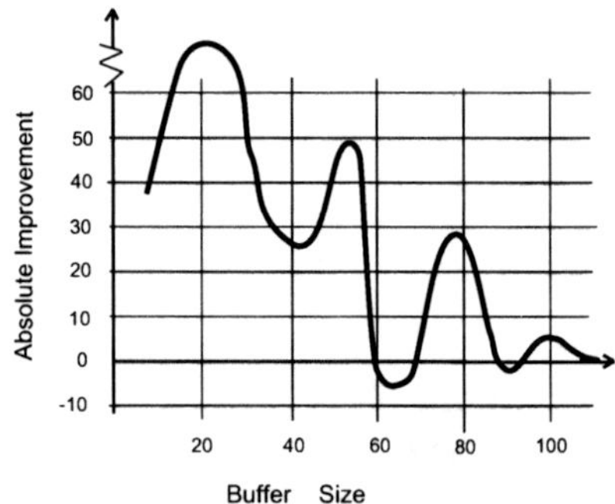

Fig. 5. Improvement of CLOH for GeometricGraphs with 500 vertices and Expected Degree=50

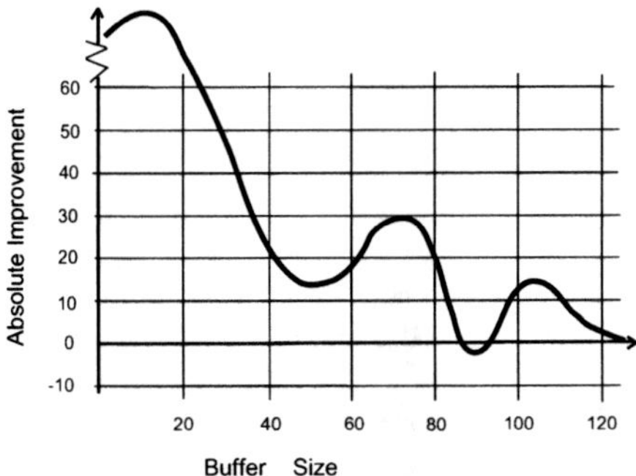

Fig. 6. OPAS2 Improvement of CLOH for Geometric Graphs with 500 vertices and Expected Degree=75

the fact that the performance metric for OPAS2 is page re-accesses, and makes use of the buffer space to create a situation of several lightly-connected pages in the memory. This is achieved by reading in the pages with the largest resident degree. Segments are released when their length is less than a release level L, which experiments have shown to be optimal at a value of 2 to 4.

References

1. M. W. Blasgen and K. P. Eswaran, *Storage and access in relational databases*, IBM Systems Journal, 16 (1977), pp. 363–377.
2. B. C. Desai, *Performance of a composite attribute and join index*, IEEE Trans. on Software Eng., 15 (1989), pp. 142–152.
3. A. Lim, J. Kwan, and W. C. Oon, *Page access sequencing for join processing*, in International Conference on Information and Knowledge Management, 1999, pp. 276–283.
4. P. Mishra and M. H. Eich, *Join processing in relational databases*, ACM Computing Surveys, 24 (1992), pp. 64–113.
5. E. R. Omiecinski, *Heuristics for join processing using nonclustered indexes*, IEEE Trans. Knowledge and Data Eng., 15 (1989), pp. 19–25.
6. B. C. Ooi and C. Y. Chan, *Efficient scheduling of page access in index-based join processing*, IEEE Trans. Knowledge and Data Eng., 9 (1997), pp. 1005–1011.
7. P. Valduriez, *Join indices*, ACM Trans. on Database Systems, 12 (1987), pp. 218–246.

Dynamic Constraints Derivation and Maintenance in the Teradata RDBMS

Ahmad Ghazal and Ramesh Bhashyam

NCR Corporation, Teradata Division
100 N. Sepulveda Blvd.
El Segundo, CA, 90245
{ahmad.ghazal,ramesh.bhashyam}@ncr.com

Abstract. We define a new algorithm that allows the Teradata query optimizer to automatically derive and maintain constraints between date type columns across tables that are related by referential integrity constraints. We provide a novel, quantitative measure of the usefulness of such rules. We show how the Teradata query optimizer utilizes these constraints in producing more optimal plans especially for databases that have tables that are value ordered by date. We also discuss our design for maintaining these constraints in the presence of inserts, deletes, and updates to the relevant tables. Finally, we give performance numbers for seven TPC-H queries from our prototype implementation based on the Teradata Database engine.

1 Introduction

Query optimization is important in relational systems that deal with complex queries on large volumes of data. Unlike previous generation navigational databases, a query on a relational database specifies what data is to be retrieved from the database but not how to retrieve it. Optimizing a relational query is not that important in transaction-oriented databases where only a few rows are accessed either because the query is well specified by virtue of the application or because it accesses the database using a highly selective index. In decision support and data mining applications, where the space of possible solutions is large and the penalty for selecting a bad query plan is high, optimizing a query to reduce overall resource utilization is important since it provides orders of magnitude overall performance improvement.

There has been lot of work on query optimization in relational and deductive databases [1,2,9,15,16]. Chaudhuri, et al in [8] has a good overview of query optimization in relational databases. One important optimization technique is to rewrite the user-specified query to be more performant.[1] The query is transformed into a logically equivalent query that performs better, i.e., costs less to execute [2,6]. There are basically two techniques for query transformation – Syntactic and

[1] Physical techniques and algorithms to improve execution are both outside the scope of this paper.

H.C. Mayr et al. (Eds.): DEXA 2001, LNCS 2113, pp. 390–399, 2001.

Semantic. Syntactic or algebraic transformations use the properties of the query operators and their mapping to rewrite the query. Some forms of magic set transformation [10,11], most forms of predicate push down, and transitive closure are techniques that fall under this category. Semantic query transformations use declarative structural constraints and semantics of application specific knowledge, declared as part of the database, to rewrite the query [1,2,4,18,20]. Semantic query transformation based rewrites are called Semantic Query Optimization or SQO [1].

The basic intent of a query rewrite is to reduce the number of rows processed. King in [2] mentions five transformations. We clarify these in the following and build upon them:

1. Predicate Introduction. A new predicate is inferred from domain knowledge and integrity constraints that are specified as part of the data model. The introduction of the predicate may reduce the number of rows that are read from the relation. For example, a range constraint may be introduced based on check constraint specified on a column.
2. Predicate MoveAround. Selection predicates may be pushed as far down in the execution tree as possible or moved sideways [11,17], or moved up when the predicates are expensive. [11] gives an example of a view that is restricted based on application specific information.
3. Operator MoveAround. A join operation may be commuted with an aggregation operation such that the aggregation may be pushed down across the join operation [12].
4. Join Elimination. A join may be deemed unnecessary and hence eliminated [1,5,14]. For example some portion of joins between relations that have a Primary Key – Foreign Key relationship (referred to in this paper as PK-FK relationship) can be eliminated especially if no attributes are projected from that relation. There are also other forms of partial or full join elimination based on materialized views.
5. Join Introduction. If a join with another table will help to reduce the rows processed from the original table then an extra join with the large table may be justified [2].
6. Others. The literature [2,7] also discusses other transformations such as index introduction and empty-set detection.

Notice that most of what is mentioned in the literature and almost all of what little is commercially implemented relate to transformations based on structural constraints and domain knowledge. As a point of interest, note that although the process of transformation is separate from the process of selecting the optimal plan they can be combined, as in Teradata, based on the cost of each transformation.

The researches in [2,7] are some of the earliest works in semantic query optimization. Structural constraint based semantic optimizations use functional dependencies, key dependencies, value constraints, and referential constraints that are defined on the relations [7,9]. Hammer and Zdonik [15] also discuss the use of application domain knowledge to perform query transformations. [13] shows semantic query transformations using dependency constraints, domain constraints, and constraints between two tables that have a join condition between them. [1,13] extends the classical notion of both integrity constraints and their application. [7] also discusses query optimization using two other types of constraints called implication integrity constraints and subset integrity constraints. These constraints are defined on chunks of data across relations. They define subset integrity constraints as a superset-subset relationship between the domains of two different attributes of two different relations and an implication integrity constraint as valid ranges of values that an attribute can have when some other attributes are restricted in the same or different relation.

There is not much work in the literature on dynamically derived constraints across multiple relations that are based on actual data stored in those relations. We explore this concept in this paper. Instead of using domain data [7, 13], we use actual data in relations and automatically derive and maintain constraints across two different relations. We then show how these can be used to optimize queries using the TPC-H query suite [3] as an example.

SQO could be very costly and may even cost more than the query execution time [19]. Shejar, et al in [19] presented a model for the trade-off between the cost and benefit of applying SQO. The problem of rule derivation we are considering in this paper, a sub-problem of SQO, is also a difficult one. The main difficulties we see are:

- What kind of rules should the optimizer find?
- Should the derivation process be completely automated?
- How can the optimizer decide if a rule is useful or not?

In this paper we show how we managed in the Teradata database engine to answer the above questions from our experience with real customer situations. We limit our analysis to the time dimension, specifically, we limit our analysis to: (1) relations that have a PK-FK structural relationship and (2) date attributes in those relations. Time is a key analytic dimension. Both customer relationship management (CRM) and strategic decision support applications limit their search space using time. They also attempt to co-relate transactions and behavior activities using time as a key dimension. For example, CRM queries are interested in understanding a customer's propensity for a product in a specific time frame. Similarly, the TPC-H workload often specifies time in its queries [3]. Also, we intend to make the DBMS automatically find these rules and we formally define a metric of how useful an SQO rule is. The following example illustrates the type of SQO problems we solved.

Example 1.

In the TPC-H benchmark LINEITEM and ORDERS are two tables. The ORDERS table gives details about each order. The LINEITEM table gives information about each item in the order; an order may have up to 7 items. O_ORDERDATE is an attribute of the ORDERS table and it represents the date the order was made. L_SHIPDATE is an attribute of the LINEITEM table and it denotes the date that line item was shipped. The LINEITEM and ORDERS tables have a PK-FK referential integrity structural constraint based on O_ORDERKEY=L_ORDERKEY. O_ORDERKEY is the primary key of ORDERS and L_ORDERKEY is a foreign key for LINEITEM. Line items of an order are shipped within 122 days of the order date. This fact can be written using the following rule:

(L_ORDERKEY=O_ORDERKEY)→[2]
(O_ORDERDATE+1≤L_SHIPDATE) and (L_SHIPDATE≤O_ORDERDATE+122)

The following query example (Q3 in TPC-H) illustrates the usefulness of such semantic rules.

```
SELECT
      L_ORDERKEY,
      SUM (L_EXTENDEDPRICE*(1-L_DISCOUNT) (NAMED
      REVENUE), O_ORDERDATE, O_SHIPPRIORITY
FROM CUSTOMER, ORDERS, LINEITEM
WHERE
            C_MKTSEGMENT  = 'BUILDING'
      AND   C_CUSTKEY     = O_CUSTKEY
      AND   L_ORDERKEY    = O_ORDERKEY
      AND   O_ORDERDATE   < '1995-03-15'
      AND   L_SHIPDATE    > '1995-03-15'
GROUP BY L_ORDERKEY, O_ORDERDATE, O_SHIPPRIORITY
ORDER BY REVENUE DESC, O_ORDERDATE;
```

The query has the condition (L_ORDERKEY = O_ORDERKEY) and using the rule (L_ORDERKEY=O_ORDERKEY) → (O_ORDERDATE +122 ≥ L_SHIPDATE and L_SHIPDATE ≥ O_ORDERDATE+1), the optimizer will add (ORDERDATE+122 ≥ L_SHIPDATE and L_SHIPDATE ≥ O_ORDERDATE+1) to the where clause of the query. In another phase of the optimizer, the transitive closure of the where-clause conditions are computed and the following range conditions on L_SHIDATE and O_ORDERDATE, that are specific to this query, are found:

L_SHIPDATE < '1995-07-15' and O_ORDERDATE > '1994-11-13'. Together with O_ORDERDATE<'1995-03-15' AND L_SHIPDATE>'1995-03-15', each of O_ORDERDATE and L_SHIPDATE has a range of approximately four months.

The new date constraints above could be very useful in one or both of the following situations:

- They could provide a fast access path to the corresponding table, for example, if ORDERS or one its secondary indexes are value ordered by O_ORDERDATE. Then in Example 1, only 4 months of data need to be accessed for ORDERS.
- The new constraints could reduce the size of an intermediate result. Note that this is applicable even if the derived constraints do not provide an access path to the table. For example, assume that ORDERS and CUSTOMER tables are

[2] → means implies.

hash distributed on O_ORDERKEY and C_CUSTKEY, respectively.[3] Also, assume that in the final execution plan of the query in example 1, ORDERS is re-hashed (re-distributed in Teradata terminology) on O_CUSTKEY to join with CUSTOMER. In this case, the new constraint O_ORDERDATE>'1994-11-13' could be applied prior to the re-hashing step which significantly reduces the amount of data that will re-hashed, sorted and stored on disk.

In this paper we discuss the automatic derivation of these date constraint rules. We refer to these derived date constraints rules as DDCR and the right hand side of a DDCR as DDC for the rest of this paper. We also discuss the maintenance of a DDCR in the presence of updates to the base relations. Finally, we discuss the performance gains that accrue from applying these constraints on some TPC-H queries by using the Parallel Teradata execution engine.

2 Rule Derivations and Usage

In this section we describe how Teradata finds a DDCR between columns of PK-FK tables. As mentioned before, for performance and practical aspects, the optimizer tries to discover such relationships under specific scenarios.

We studied some customer workloads and found that, frequently, date columns from PK-FK are semantically related by some range constraints. So our focus was to find such relationships between date columns from two tables that are PK-FK related.

A DDCR can be typically represented by (PK=FK) -> ($Date_2$ + C_1≤ $Date_1$ ≤ $Date_2$+C_2) where C_1, C_2 are constants and $Date_1$, $Date_2$ are date columns in the FK and PK tables, respectively.

The optimizer can initiate the DDCR derivation process when the user issues a collect statistics statement on a date column, $Date_1$, of a table that is either a PK or an FK table and the related table also has a date column $Date_2$. The basic idea of the algorithm is to find the values of C_1 and C_2 above. The high level algorithm is given below.

```
Procedure FindConstraint(T1.Date1,T2.Date2)

{Assume that T1 and T2 are PK-FK tables where Date1 and
Date2 are date columns in the FK and PK tables, res-
pectively. We also assume, without loss of gen-erality,
that both Date1 and Date2 are not nullable.}

begin
```

[3] Teradata is an MPP shared nothing architecture and tables are partitioned according to the hash value of a predefined primary index of that table.

1. Perform an inner join between T_1 and T2 using PK=FK as a join condition. The optimizer will choose the optimal join method, which is irrelevant to this algorithm. Note that we do not need to write the join results to spool since we will derive the relationship (constraint) between the two dates on the fly.

2. We create an initial constraint, which has an empty range. We call it a running constraint (RC).

3. For every row in the join result, assume that D_1, D_2 are the values of $Date_1$ and $Date_2$, respectively. From this join row we can deduce $Date_2 + (D_1 - D_2) \leq Date_1 \leq Date_2 + (D_1 - D_2)$. Merge RC with this new range. If RC is empty then set both C_1 and C_2 to $D_1 - D_2$, otherwise set $C_1 = minimum(C_1, D_1 - D_2)$ and $C_2 = maximum(C_2, D_1 - D_2)$.

4. The Result is a DDCR using the last value of RC and it is $(PK=FK) \rightarrow (Date_1 \leq Date_2 + C_2$ and $Date_1 \geq Date_2 + C_1)$

end.

The resulting DDCR of the previous algorithm will be stored as table level constraints for each table.

The above algorithm always yields a relationship between $Date_1$ and $Date_2$. However, the relationship may or may not be useful. For example, (L_ORDERKEY = O_ORDERKEY) → (L_SHIPDATE ≤ O_ORDERDATE+2557) is a useless rule for deriving a range constraint on either L_SHIPDATE or O_ORDERDATE for TPC-H since both of L_SHIPDATE and O_ORDERDATE have the same range of values and both are within 7 years (2557 days). Such rules will not benefit query optimization and will be just overhead.

We formally measured the "usefulness" of a DDCR using the following analysis. Assuming uniform distribution of $Date_1$ and $Date_2$, a DDCR is most useful when C_2-C_1 is minimized. Since both C_1 and C_2 are computed from D_1-D_2 in FindConstraint, the range of values for both is from $(D_1^{MIN} - D_2^{MAX})$ to $(D_1^{MAX} - D_2^{MIN})$ call them Low and High, respectively. The usefulness of a DDCR is measured as $(C_2 - C_1)/Size$, where Size is the interval size for the values of C_2-C_1, which is equal to (High-Low+1). The value of the usefulness function is between 0 and 1 and smaller values means more useful.

If we take the TPC-H workload as an example and the result of FindConstraint to be (L_ORDERKEY=O_ORDERKEY)→(O_ORDERDATE+122≥L_SHIPDATE and L_SHIPDATE≥O_ORDERDATE+1) then C_1=1, C_2=122,Low=-2557, High=2557 and the usefulness of this rule is 0.024. As a heuristic, the optimizer saves and maintains a DDCR only if the usefulness value is less than or equal to 0.5. Note that the usefulness function can be extended for non-uniform distribution of one or both of the date columns using collected statistics on these columns. This subject is outside the scope of this paper and we assume that the usefulness function for uniform distribution is a good approximation for the non-uniform case.

One problem with FindConstraint is that the DDC is a single interval, which may not be very useful in some cases. For example, if all line items in the TPC-H case were shipped within 122 days of the order date with the exception of one line item that was shipped after 500 days of its order. In this case, the final RC in the algorithm will be (O_ORDERDATE+500 ≥ L_SHIPDATE and L_SHIPDATE ≥ O_ORDERDATE+1). It is more useful if the algorithm finds a set of non-overlapping ranges like (O_ORDERDATE+122 ≥ L_SHIPDATE and L_SHIPDATE ≥ O_ORDERDATE+1) or (O_ORDERDATE+500 ≥ L_SHIPDATE and L_SHIPDATE ≥ O_ORDERDATE+500). If you apply this non-overlapping constraint to a query that has a range constraint on O_ORDERDATE, the optimizer can define the range of values for L_SHIPDATE as the union of two small non-overlapping ranges.

In our prototype, FindConstraint was modified to handle a union of non-overlapping ranges by maintaining a list of at most k running non-overlapping constraints,[4] RC_1, RC_2, … RC_k. If at any time there are k+1 non-overlapping RC's then the algorithm will pick two of them and merge them. The choice of which two to merge is done based on the nearest pair of intervals.

Also, the usefulness function is modified to handle a set of RC's rather than just one. First, the usefulness function is applied to each interval using the logic as described before. Then the usefulnesse of all the intervals are summed up to give the overall usefulness.

The optimizer uses a DDCR, like in Example 1, when the left-hand side of the rule exists in the query. To insure correctness, the optimizer adds the DDC to the largest conjunction that contains the left-hand side. The following example illustrates that.

Example 2.

Consider the DDCR: (L_ORDERKEY=O_ORDERKEY) → (O_ORDERDATE+122 ≥ L_SHIPDATE and L_SHIPDATE ≥ O_ORDERDATE+1) and the query condition (L_ORDERKEY=O_ORDERKEY and L_SHIPDATE > '1999-05-01' and L_QTY > 100) OR (L_ORDERKEY <> O_ORDERKEY and L_QTY < 200). In this case the optimizer rewrites the query condition to be (L_OR-

[4] The value of k depends on how the optimizer handles OR cases. It is set to 10 in our prototype.

DERKEY=O_ORDERKEY and L_SHIPDATE > '1999-05-01' and L_QTY > 100 and O_ORDERDATE+122 ≥ L_SHIPDATE and L_SHIPDATE ≥ O_ORDERDATE+1) OR (L_ORDERKEY <> O_ORDERKEY and L_QTY < 200).

2.1 Redundancy Detection and Removal

The DDC of a DDCR by itself does not provide any benefit to optimizing a query and therefore it is redundant. The reason is that the DDC, which is date range between two date columns, does not provide a fast access path to either relations and does not reduce the size of an intermediate result. It is useful for a query if it helps transitive closure to derive single column date ranges. Based on that, the optimizer uses the following rule to add the DDC of a DDCR:

- When the left-hand side of a DDCR is present in some conjunction in the query condition, we add the DDC only if at least one of the date columns is also referenced in that conjunction. The date column must be referenced in a condition of the form "Date **op** Constant", where **op** $\in \{<,=,>,\geq,\leq,\neq\}$.[5]

If you apply this rule to Example 2, the addition of (O_ORDERDATE+122 ≥ L_SHIPDATE and L_SHIPDATE ≥ O_ORDERDATE+1) happens because L_SHIPDATE is referenced in another condition in the same conjunction of (L_ORDERKEY=O_ORDERKEY).

After the query execution plan is found, the optimizer simply removes all DDC's since they are not useful by themselves.

2.2 Rule Maintenance

In this section, we show a high level approach to maintain DDCR in the presence of inserts, deletes and updates to either the PK or the FK table. Overall, this maintenance is performed within the PK-FK system enforcement. The general approach is the following:

1. If the operation is an insert to the PK table, do nothing. This is because new rows in the PK table do not have any matches in the FK table.
2. If the operation is an insert to the FK table, produce a join[6] of the new rows with the PK table. Apply algorithm FindConstraint to the join result, merge with the existing DDCR and replace the existing DDCR with the new one.
3. If the operation is a delete to either of the tables, choose between taking-no-action and redoing DDCR after some number of deletes. There are multiple options depending on the specific workload. Taking no action would merely reduce the "usefulness" of the DDCR. If the deletes were not frequent, re-computing the

---

[5] **op** is restricted to the same comparisons that our transitive closure implementation has.

[6] This join will be very fast, especially in the Teradata RDBMS, with the Row Hash Match Scan join algorithm.

entire DDCR periodically may suffice. In DSS and CRM applications, deletes are not as frequent as inserts.

4. If the operation is an update to a column that is not a PK,[7] FK, or the relevant date columns for the DDCR, in either of the tables, then there is no action to be taken. If it is otherwise, do the same approach as a delete followed by an insert.

3 Experimental Results

We have tested our prototype on the TPC-H benchmark with 10GB workload. LINEITEM is hash partitioned on L_ORDERDEY and value ordered by L_SHIPDATE and ORDERS is hash partitioned on O_ORDERKEY and value ordered by O_ORDERDATE.[8] With the new rules, 7 queries out of the 22 queries ran faster and the other 15 queries were not affected. The table below shows the execution time before and after the semantic query optimization is applied. It also, displays the percentage of time reduction this optimization provided.

TPC-H Query	Query Time without the new rules	Query Time with the new rules	Savings
Q3	523	55	89%
Q4	369	41	89%
Q5	804	217	73%
Q7	510	348	32%
Q8	827	365	56%
Q10	390	176	55%
Q12	175	133	24%

4 Conclusions and Future Work

We introduced a new algorithm that automatically derives integrity constraint rules across two PK-FK relations. These rules are dynamic and dependent on the actual data stored in the database. We invented a new function that assesses the value of these new rules before incorporating them in the database. We show the applicability of these constraints in semantic query optimization using TPC-H as an example.

We also give algorithms to automatically maintain these constraints in the presence of inserts, deletes, and updates to the tables used in the constraint. We show the performance results of our prototype with the Teradata RDBMS on TPC-H queries.

---

[7] In the Teradata RDBMS, updates to PK columns are discouraged but not prohibited.

[8] Currently, the Teradata RDBMS does not support value ordering for base tables and value ordering for LINEITEM and ORDERS were simulated using single table join indexes.

We expect to focus our future work on various structural and dynamic integrity-constraint based semantic query optimization. Specifically, we believe transitive closure and constraint move around can be specialized for time.

References

1. U. Chakravarty, J J.Grant and J Minker. Logic Based approach to semantic query optimization. ACM TODS, 15(2):162-207, June 1990.
2. J. J. King. Quist: A system for semantic query optimization in relational databases. Proc. 7th VLDB, pages 510-517, September 1981.
3. Transaction Processing Performance Council, 777 No. First Street, Suite 600, San Jose, CA 95112-6311, TPC-H Benchmark™, 1.2.1
4. H. Pirahesh, J. M. Hellerstein, and W. Hasan. Extensible/rule based query rewrite optimization in Starbust. In Proc. Sigmod, pages 39-48, 1992.
5. Qi Cheng, Jack Gryz, Fred Koo, et al. Implementation of two semantic query optimization techniques in DB2 Universal Database. Proc. 25th VLDB, pages , September 1999.
6. M. Siegel, E. Scorie and S. Salveter. A method for automatic rule derivation to support semantic query optimization. ACM TODS, 17(4):563-600, December 1992.
7. Sreekumar T Shenoy and Z Meral Ozsolyoglu. A System for Semantic Query Optimization. Proceedings of the ACM SIGMOD Annual Conference on Management of data 1987, 181-195.
8. Surajit Chaudhuri, An overview of query optimization in relational systems. Proceedings of the 17th ACM SIGACT-SIGMOD-SIGART symposium on Principles of database systems, 1998, 34-43.
9. M. Jarke, J. Koch, Query Optimization in Database Systems. ACM Computing Surveys 16 (1984), 111-152
10. I.S. Mumick, S.J. Finkestein, H. Pirahesh, R. Ramakrishnan. Magic Conditions. ACM Transactions Database Systems Mar 1996, 107-155
11. I.S. Mumick, S.J. Finkestein, H. Pirahesh, R. Ramakrishnan. Magic Is Relevant. ACM SIGMOD International Conference on Management of data May 23-26, 1990 247-258
12. Yan W. P., Larson P. A., "Performing Group-By before Join", International Conference on Data Engineering, Feb. 1993, Houston.
13. G.D. Xu. Search Control in Semantic Query Optimization. Tech. Rep, Dept of Computer Science, Univ. of Mass, Amherst, 1983
14. J. Gryz, L. Liu, and X. Qian. Semantic query optimization in DB2: Initial results. Technical Report CS-1999-01, Department of Computer Science, York University, Toronto, Canada, 1999.
15. M. T. Hammer and S. B. Zdonik. Knowledge based query processing. Proc. 6th VLDB, pages 137-147, October 1980.
16. M. Jarke, J. Clifford, and Y. Vassiliou. An optimizing PROLOG front end to a relational query system. SIGMOD, pages 296-306, 1984.
17. A. Y. Levy, I. Mumick, and Y. Sagiv. Query optimization by predicate move-around. In Proc. Of VLDB, pages 96-108, 1994.
18. H. Pirahesh, T. Y. Leung, and W Hassan. A rule engine for query transformation in Starburst and IBM DB2 C/S DBMS. ICDE, pages: 391-400, 1997.
19. S. Shekar, J. Srivistava and S. Dutta, A formal model of trade-off between optimization and execution costs in semantic query optimization. Proc. 14th VLDB, pages : 457-467, Los Angeles, 1988.
20. S. T. Shenoy and Z.M. Ozsoyoglu. Design and implementation of a semantic query optimizer. IEEE transactions on Knowledge and data Engineering, Sep 1989 1(3) 344-361

Improving Termination Analysis of Active Rules with Composite Events

Alain Couchot

Université Paris Val de Marne, Créteil, France
alaincouchot@minitel.net

Abstract. This article presents an algorithm for static analysis of termination of active rules with composite events. We refine the concept of triggering graph, including in the graph not only rules, but also events (primitive events and composite events). Our termination algorithm improves the previous termination algorithms, thanks to the notions of composite path and maximal order *M* path preceding a rule, replacing the classical notion of cycle. Both composite events and overall conditions of rules paths can be taken into account for rules termination analysis. So, much more termination situations can be detected by our algorithm, especially when active rules defined with conjunction events or sequence events are used.

1 Introduction

This paper deals with the termination problem of active rules. Active rules (or Event-Condition-Action rules[7]) are intended to facilitate the work of design and programming databases. But writing a set of rules actually remains a tricky work, often devolved upon specialists. Indeed, a set of rules is not a structured entity : the global behavior of a set of rules can be hard to predict and to control [1]. In particular, research works have brought to the fore the termination problem of the rules (the execution of the rules can be infinite in some situations), or the confluence problem (the same rules do not necessarily give the same results, depending on the execution order of the rules).

In section 2, we expose the related work ; in section 3, we present a motivating example ; in section 4, we introduce the events/rules graphs, the composite paths and the maximal order *M* path preceding a rule ; in section 5, we propose a function for the evaluation of the truth value of the condition of a rule (due to a simple path and due to the maximal order *M* path preceding the rule) ; in section 6, we expose our algorithm for termination analysis ; section 7 concludes.

2 Related Work

The termination of the active rules is an undecidable problem, except when languages of rules with very limited possibilities are used [2]. The previous works on the static analysis of the active rules propose criteria supplying sufficient conditions allowing to

H.C. Mayr et al. (Eds.): DEXA 2001, LNCS 2113, pp. 400–409, 2001.

guarantee termination. The majority of works on the termination of the active rules exploit the concept of *triggering graph*.

[5] introduced, for the first time, the notion of *triggering graph*. This notion is clarified by [1] : a such graph is built by means of a syntactic analysis of rules ; the nodes of the graph are rules. Two rules *r1* and *r2* are connected by a directed edge from *r1* towards *r2* if the action of *r1* contains an triggering event of *r2*. The presence of cycles in a such graph means a risk of non-termination of the set of rules. The absence of cycles in the triggering graph guarantees the termination of the set of rules. However, the possible deactivation of the condition of the rule is not taken into account by this analysis. A finer analysis is led by [3, 4, 8, 9, 12], taking the possible deactivation of the condition of a rule into account. Generalized connection formulas are introduced by [8], in order to test if the overall condition of a path can be satisfied. [10] proposes a technique to remove a path instead of removing a node, [11] proposes a technique to unroll a cycle. [13] refines the triggering graphs, using partial and total edges, to take into account the influence of composite events.

Our work is based on the following observation : the algorithm proposed by [13], which deals with conjunction events, takes into account neither the path removing technique [10], nor the cycle unrolling technique [11]. A new technique must be designed, in order to take into account for termination analysis both the composite events and the overall conditions of active rules paths. Thanks to this new technique, termination cases can be discovered, which would not be discovered by a simple combination of the algorithms [13] and [3, 8, 9, 10, 11, 12].

3 Motivating Example

We present in this section an example, which motivates our proposition. We consider a banking application. The class *Account* has the following three methods :

rate_increase (*X*) : this method increases the loan rate of the account by *X* per cent.
overdraft_increase (*X*) : this method increases the allowed bank overdraft of the account by *X*.
capacity_increase (*X*) : this method increases the loan capacity of the account by *X*.

The context of the conjunction events is cumulative [6]. The coupling modes of the active rules are immediate. The active rules are instance oriented. The active rules are the following :

Rule R_1 : When the rate and the allowed overdraft of an account have been increased, increase the loan capacity of the account by 2000.

Event : A_1→rate_increase(X_1) *AND* A_1→overdraft_increase(Y_1)
Condition : -
Action : A_1→capacity_increase(2000)

Rule R_2 : When the rate or the loan capacity of an account have been increased, if the account is a stocks account, increase the allowed overdraft of the account by 200.

Event : A_2→rate_increase(X_2) *OR* A_2→capacity_increase(Y_2)
Condition : A_2.type = stocks_account
Action : A_2→overdraft_increase(200)

Rule R_3 : When the loan capacity of an account A has been increased, if the account A is a standard account, increase by 1.5 the rate of all the accounts of the same customer than the account A, which are stocks accounts.
Event : A_3→capacity_increase(X_3)
Condition : (A_3.type = standard_account) *AND* (B.customer = A_3.customer) *AND* (B.type = stocks_account)
Action : B→rate_increase(1.5)

Let us try to analyze termination of this rules set using the Refined Triggering Graph method [8, 12] improved with [13] ([13] deals with composite events). We build a modified triggering graph with partial edges and total edges (figure 1).

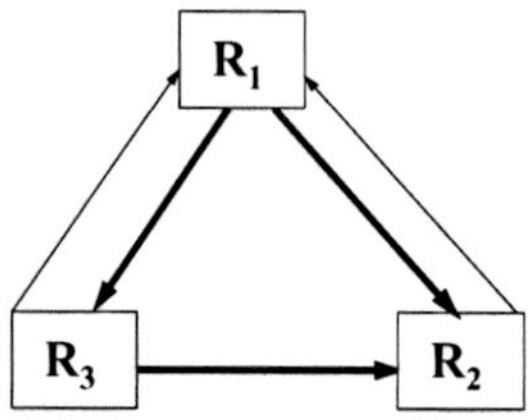

Fig. 1. Modified Triggering Graph with Partial and Total Edges. (the edges in thin lines are partial edges, and the edges in thick lines are total edges).

The cycles of the modified triggering graph are : (R_1, R_3, R_2, R_1), (R_1, R_3, R_1), (R_1, R_2, R_1). We have to detect false cycles. The cycle (R_1, R_3, R_2, R_1) is a false cycle (the path (R_2, R_1, R_3) is not activable, since the generalized connection formula along this path : (A_2.type = stocks_account) *AND* ($A_2 = A_1$) *AND*($A_1 = A_3$) *AND* (A_3.type = standard_account) can not be satisfied, and no rule action can modify an atom of this formula [8, 12]). The cycle (R_1, R_3, R_1) can trigger itself [13], and the cycle (R_1, R_2, R_1) can trigger itself [13]: these two cycles are not false cycles. Just one cycle can be detected as a false cycle. Therefore, the termination cannot be guaranteed by [8, 12], even improved by [13].

Let us analyze the behavior of this rules set more in detail.

Let us consider a rules process P. Each occurrence of R_1 during P requires an occurrence of R_3 and an occurrence of R_2 (due to the conjunction event of R_1), thus requires an occurrence of the path (R_3 ; R_1) and an occurrence of the path (R_2 ; R_1). Each occurrence of R_3 during P requires an occurrence of R_1, thus, requires an occurrence of the path (R_1 ; R_3). Thus, each occurrence of R_3 requires an occurrence of the path (R_3 ; R_1 ; R_3) and an occurrence of the path (R_2 ; R_1 ; R_3). But the path (R_2 ; R_1 ; R_3) is not activable. Thus, R_1 cannot appear an infinite number of times during a rules process. R_1 can be removed from the triggering graph. So, this rules set always terminates.

No previous algorithm and no combination of previous algorithms is able to detect termination of this rules set. This is due to the following fact : termination of this rules set can be guaranteed if we take into account at the same time the composite conjunction event of the rule R_1 and the fact that the path (R_2 ; R_1 ; R_3) is not activable. No previous algorithm deals at the same time with the composite conjunction events and the deactivation of a path. [13], which deals with composite conjunction events, do not deal with deactivation of conditions, and [10, 11], which deals with the deactivation of an overall condition of a path, do not deal with composite conjunction events.

4 Events/Rules Graphs

In this section, we propose a refinement of the triggering graphs proposed in the past : the triggering graphs we propose contain not only rules, but also events (primitive events and composite events). We develop then the notions of composite paths and maximal order *M* path preceding a rule.

4.1 Considered Active Rules

The active rules that we consider in this article follow the paradigm Event-Condition-Action. The database model is a relational model or an object oriented model. We do not make any assumption about the execution model of the rules (execution in depth, in width, or other model).

Each rule definition contains an unique event. A composite event is specified binding two events (primitive or composite) by means of one of the three binary operators : *AND*, *OR*, *SEQ*. *AND* is the conjunction operator, *OR* is the disjunction operator, and *SEQ* is the sequence operator.

We assume that the semantics of the conjunction events and the sequence events is defined by one of the three semantics defined by Snoop [6] : *recent context* (each occurrence of the composite event is computed with the most recent occurrence of each component event), *chronicle context* (each occurrence of the composite event is computed with the oldest occurrence of each component event), *cumulative context* (each occurrence of the composite event is computed with all the occurrences of each component event).

From the point of view of the termination analysis, it is important to note, for these three semantics, the following property : let us consider two (primitive or composite) events E_1 and E_2. If E_1 or E_2 can just occur a finite number of times during any rules process, the conjunction event (E_1 *AND* E_2) and the sequence event (E_1 *SEQ* E_2) can just occur a finite number of times during any rules process.

4.2 Graphical Representation of the Composite Events

We graphically represent a composite event by means of a tree. The leaves of the tree are the primitive events, which make up the composite event. The final node of the tree is the represented composite event. Each intermediate node is a composite event. A conjunction/disjunction/sequence event E has two incoming edges : the event E is the conjunction/disjunction/sequence of the origin nodes of the incoming edges. The tree is built by a syntactic analysis of the composite event.

4.3 Definition

An *events/rules graph* is an oriented graph, where the nodes are events and rules. Composite events are depicted using the tree representation showed above. There is an edge from a composite event E towards a rule R iff E is the composite event defined as the triggering event of the rule R. There is an edge from the rule R towards the event E iff E is a primitive event and R can raise E.

Example. For the active rules of the motivation example (section 3), the events/rules graph is shown figure 2. There are three primitive events : E_1 is raised by a call of the method rate_increase, E_2 is raised by a call of the method overdraft_increase, E_3 is raised by a call of the method capacity_increase.

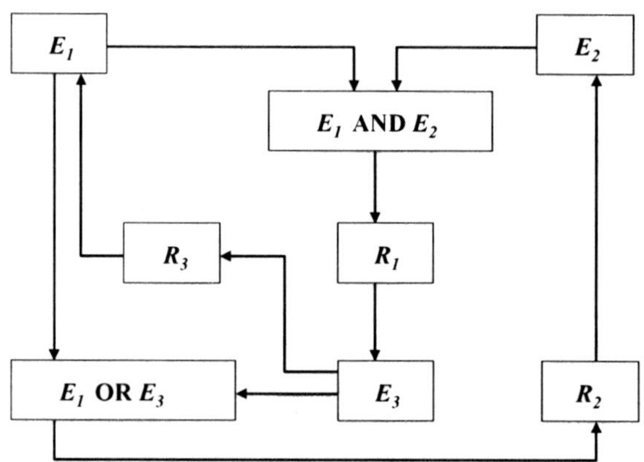

Fig. 2. Events/Rules Graph.

4.4 Composite Paths

We propose here the notion of *composite path*. This notion will be used for the evaluation of the truth value of the condition of a rule.

Simple Path. Let n be such that $n > 1$. Let N_1, N_2, ... N_i, ... N_n be n nodes (not necessarily all distinct) of an events/rules graph such that there is an edge from N_{i+1} to N_i. The tuple (N_1, N_2, ... N_n) make up a *simple path*. We adopt the following notation : $N_1 \leftarrow N_2 \leftarrow ... \leftarrow N_i \leftarrow ... \leftarrow N_n$. ($N_1$ is the last node of the path, N_n is the first node of the path).

Composite Path. A simple path is a particular case of *composite path*. Let $N_1 \leftarrow N_2 \leftarrow ... \leftarrow N_n$ be a simple path ($n > 1$). Let C_j ($1 \leq j \leq k$) be k composite paths such that the last node of C_j is N_n and such that the last edge of C_{j1} is different from the last edge of C_{j2}, (for $1 \leq j1 \leq k$, $1 \leq j2 \leq k$ and $j1 \neq j2$). Then, the tuple of paths $((N_1 \leftarrow N_2 \leftarrow ... \leftarrow N_n), C_1, ..., C_k)$ make up a *composite path*.

If N_n is a conjunction event or a sequence event, we denote this composite path in the following way : $((N_1 \leftarrow N_2 \leftarrow ... \leftarrow N_n) \leftarrow C_1)$ *AND* $((N_1 \leftarrow N_2 \leftarrow ... \leftarrow N_n) \leftarrow C_2)$ *AND* ... $((N_1 \leftarrow N_2 \leftarrow ... \leftarrow N_n) \leftarrow C_k)$.

If N_n is neither a conjunction event nor a sequence event, we denote this composite path in the following way : $((N_1 \leftarrow N_2 \leftarrow ... \leftarrow N_n) \leftarrow C_1)$ *OR* $((N_1 \leftarrow N_2 \leftarrow ... \leftarrow N_n) \leftarrow C_2)$ *OR* ... $((N_1 \leftarrow N_2 \leftarrow ... \leftarrow N_n) \leftarrow C_k)$.

Example. See figure 2. $(E_3 \leftarrow R_1 \leftarrow (E_1$ *AND* $E_2) \leftarrow E_1 \leftarrow R_3)$ *AND* $(E_3 \leftarrow R_1 \leftarrow (E_1$ *AND* $E_2) \leftarrow E_2 \leftarrow R_2)$ is a composite path, whose last node is E_3.

4.5 Maximal Order *M* Path Preceding a Rule

Let G be an events/rules graph. We replace the classical notion of cycle (used in the previous termination algorithms for the analysis of the triggering graphs) by the notion of *maximal order M path preceding a rule*. This is the composite path which contains all the simple paths preceding a rule. The number M corresponds to a limit on the length of the considered simple paths, and is fixed by the designer.

Let R_0 be a rule. The maximal order M path preceding R_0: *Max_Path*(R_3; 1 ;G) is built performing a depth search in the opposite direction of the edges. The computation is the following :

```
Path0 = ( R0 )
Max_Path(R ; M ; G) = Path_Building_Function ( Path0 )
Path_Building_Function (incoming variable : Pathin,
outgoing variable : Pathout )
    Let N be the first node of Pathin
    Let N1, N2, ... Np be the nodes of G
    such that there is an edge from Ni to N
    FOR each node Ni (1 ≤ i ≤ p)
      IF Ni appears less than M times in Pathin
          Pathi = Path_Building_Function (Pathin ← Ni )
      ENDIF
    ENDFOR
    IF N is a conjunction event or a sequence event
      Pathout = ( Path1 AND Path2 ... AND Pathp )
    ELSE
      Pathout = ( Path1 OR Path2 ... OR Pathp )
    ENDIF
```

Example. See figure 2. $Max\_Path(R_3; 1; G) = (R_3 \leftarrow E_3 \leftarrow R_1 \leftarrow (E_1\ AND\ E_2) \leftarrow E_1)$ $AND\ ((R_3 \leftarrow E_3 \leftarrow R_1 \leftarrow (E_1\ AND\ E_2) \leftarrow E_2 \leftarrow R_2 \leftarrow (E_1\ OR\ E_3))$
$OR\ (R_3 \leftarrow E_3 \leftarrow R_1 \leftarrow (E_1\ AND\ E_2) \leftarrow E_2 \leftarrow R_2 \leftarrow (E_1\ OR\ E_3) \leftarrow E_1))$

5 Evaluation of the Truth Value of the Condition of a Rule

We first introduce the notion of stabilization field of a rule. The usefulness of the notion of stabilization field is to represent in a uniform way the possible causes of deactivation of a condition of a rule due to a simple path. The truth value of the condition of the rule *R* due to a simple path will be stored by means of a function *TV*. The various stored truth values of the condition of the rule *R* will then be manipulated, thanks to the properties of the function *TV*, in order to deduce the truth value of the condition of *R* due to the maximal order *M* path preceding *R*.

5.1 Stabilization Field of a Rule

Definition. Let *Path* be a simple path of the events/rules graph such that the last node of *Path* is the rule *Last_Rule*. Let R_1, R_2, ..., R_n be *n* rules of the events/rules graph.

We say that the pair $(Path, \{R_1, R_2, \ldots, R_n\})$ is a *stabilization field* of *Last_Rule* iff we have the following property :
For each rules process *P* such that there is no occurrence of the rules R_1, R_2, ..., R_n during *P*, there is only a finite number of occurrences of *Path* during *P*.

Path is a *stabilizer* of *Last_Rule* ; $\{R_1, R_2, \ldots R_n\}$ is a *destabilizing set* associated to the stabilizer *Path*.

Previous termination algorithms [3, 4, 8, 9, 12] can be used to determine stabilization fields of a rule. For example, a simple path is a stabilizer of the last rule of the path, if there is a generalized connection formula along this simple path which cannot be satisfied [8, 10, 12] ; an associated destabilizing set contains all the rules whose action can modify the attributes contained in the atoms of the connection formula. Thanks to this notion, it is possible to represent in a uniform way the possible cases of deactivation of a condition of a rule listed by the previous termination algorithms [3, 4, 8, 9, 12].

5.2 Truth Value of the Condition of a Rule Due to a Simple Path

Let $Graph_1$ be the initial events/rules graph, or a subgraph of the initial graph ; let $Path_1$ be a simple path of $Graph_1$; let $Rule_1$ be the last rule of $Path_1$.

We evaluate the truth value of the condition of the rule $Rule_1$ due to the simple path $Path_1$ for the graph $Graph_1$ using a function *TV*, which associates a boolean value to the triple ($Rule_1$; $Path_1$; $Graph_1$).

The meaning of the function *TV* is the following :
If $TV\ (Rule_1 ; Path_1 ; Graph_1)$ is *FALSE*, this means that we are sure that, for each rules process *P*, composed of rules of $Graph_1$, there is only a finite number of occurrences of $Path_1$.

If TV ($Rule_1$; $Path_1$; $Graph_1$) is $TRUE$, this means that we are not sure of the truth value of the condition of $Rule_1$ due to $Path_1$ for $Graph_1$.

The function TV is determined using the two following formulas :

An unknown value TV ($Rule_1$; $Path_1$; $Graph_1$) is supposed equal to $TRUE$. **(1)**

We set down : $TV(Rule_1 ; Path_1 ; Graph_1) = FALSE$ **(2)**
if we can determine a stabilization field of $Rule_1$ ($Simple\_Path$, $\{R_1, R_2, ..., R_n\}$) such that $Simple\_Path = Path_1$; and no rule R_i ($1 \leq i \leq n$) is in $Graph_1$.

5.3 Truth Value of the Condition of a Rule Due to the Maximal Order *M* Path

We extend the previous function TV, in order to evaluate the truth value of the condition of a rule $Rule_1$ due to the maximal order M path preceding the rule $Rule_1$. For this, we apply the following formulas to $Max\_Path(Rule_1 ;M ;Graph_1)$:
($Graph_1$ is the initial events/rules graph, or a subgraph of the initial events/rules graph ; $Path_1$ and $Path_2$ are composite paths of $Graph_1$ such that $Path_1$ and $Path_2$ have the same last rule : $Rule_1$).

$TV(Rule_1; Path_1 \ OR \ Path_2; Graph_1) = TV(Rule_1; Path_1; Graph_1)$
$\quad OR \ TV(Rule_1; Path_2 ; Graph_1)$ **(3)**

$TV(Rule_1 ; Path_1 \ AND \ Path_2 ; Graph_1) =$
$\quad TV(Rule_1 ; Path_1 ; Graph_1) \ AND \ TV(Rule_1 ; Path_2 ; Graph_1)$ **(4)**

6 Termination Algorithm

The termination algorithm is composed of two main parts. The first part removes rules which are just triggered a finite number of times during any rules process, and events which are just raised a finite number of times during any rules process. The second part removes rules R whose condition is deactivated by the maximal order M path preceding R.

We sketch below our termination algorithm :

```
G = Initial Events/Rules Graph
WHILE nodes of G are removed
    WHILE nodes of G are removed
      Part One : Forward Deletion of Rules
      Remove from G the nodes without incoming edge
      Remove from G the conjunction events and the sequence events E
      such that an incoming edge of E has been removed
    ENDWHILE
    WHILE (all the rules of G have not been tested) AND
      (the condition of a rule has not been detected as deactivated)
      Part Two : Detection of the deactivation of the condition of a rule
      Choose a rule R
      Compute Max_Path(R ; M ; G)
```

```
        Evaluate TV (R ; Max_Path(R ; M ; G) ; G)
        IF TV (R ; Max_Path(R ; M ; G) ; G) = FALSE
            Remove R from G
        ENDIF
    ENDWHILE
ENDWHILE
```

Termination of the Rules Set. If the final graph is empty, termination of the rules set is guaranteed. If, after application of the termination algorithm, there are still rules in the final graph, these rules risk being triggered infinitely. The designer has then to examine, and possibly, to modify these rules.

Example. We analyze termination of the rules set of our motivation example (section 3). Let G be the initial events/rules graph of this rules set (figure 2). The Part One of the algorithm provides no result. Let us apply the Part Two of the algorithm. Let us then choose the rule R_3. The maximal order 1 path preceding R_3 is:

$$Max\_Path(R_3 ; 1 ; G) = (R_3 \leftarrow E_3 \leftarrow R_1 \leftarrow (E_1\ AND\ E_2) \leftarrow E_1)$$
$$AND\ ((R_3 \leftarrow E_3 \leftarrow R_1 \leftarrow (E_1\ AND\ E_2) \leftarrow E_2 \leftarrow R_2 \leftarrow (E_1\ OR\ E_3))$$
$$OR\ (R_3 \leftarrow E_3 \leftarrow R_1 \leftarrow (E_1\ AND\ E_2) \leftarrow E_2 \leftarrow R_2 \leftarrow (E_1\ OR\ E_3) \leftarrow E_1))$$

The pair $((R_3 \leftarrow E_3 \leftarrow R_1 \leftarrow (E_1\ AND\ E_2) \leftarrow E_2 \leftarrow R_2), \varnothing)$ is a stabilization field of R_3. We can establish this result using the Refined Triggering Graph method [8, 12]. (The generalized connection formula (A_3.type = standard_account) AND ($A_3 = A_1$) AND ($A_1 = A_2$) AND (A_2.type = stocks_account) can not be satisfied, and the attribute type can not be updated by any rule action.)

We can deduce :

$$TV(R_3 ; Max\_Path(R_3 ; 1 ; G) ; G) = TRUE\ AND\ (FALSE\ OR\ FALSE) = FALSE$$

R_3 can be removed. By forward deletion (Part One of the algorithm), the other nodes of the graph can be removed. Termination of this rules set is guaranteed by our algorithm. Note that no previous algorithm is able to detect the termination of this rules set.

7 Conclusion

We have presented an improvement of termination analysis of active rules with composite events. Our termination algorithm detects all the termination cases detected by the previous algorithms [3, 8, 9, 10, 11, 12, 13]. Much more termination situations are detected by our algorithm, especially when active rules with composite events are defined.

In the future, we plan to determine sufficient conditions to guarantee the termination of the union of several rules sets, designed by several designers, even if no designer knows all the rules : this can be useful for a modular design, when several active rules sets are designed by distinct designers.

References

1. A. Aiken, J. Widom, J.M. Hellerstein. Behavior of Database Production Rules: Termination, Confluence and Observable Determinism. In *Proc. Int'l Conf. on Management of Data (SIGMOD)*, San Diego, California, 1992.
2. J. Bailey, G. Dong, K. Ramamohanarao. Decidability and Undecidability Results for the Termination Problem of Active Database Rules. In *Proc. ACM Symposium on Principles of Database Systems (PODS)*, Seattle, Washington, 1998.
3. E. Baralis, S. Ceri, S. Paraboschi. Improved Rule Analysis by Means of Triggering and Activation Graphs. In *Proc. Int'l Workshop Rules in Database Systems (RIDS)*, Athens, Greece, 1995.
4. E. Baralis, J. Widom. An Algebraic Approach to Rule Analysis in Expert Database Systems. In *Proc. Int'l Conf. on Very Large Data Bases (VLDB)*, Santiago, Chile, 1994.
5. S. Ceri, J. Widom. Deriving Production Rules for Constraint Maintenance. In *Proc. Int'l Conf. on Very Large Data Bases (VLDB)*, Brisbane, Queensland, Australia, 1990.
6. S. Chakravarthy, D. Mishra. Snoop : An Expressive Event Specification Language for Active Databases. In *Data and Knowledge Engineering*, 14 , 1994.
7. U. Dayal, A.P. Buchmann, D.R. Mc Carthy. Rules are Objects too : a Knowledge Model for an Active Object Oriented Database System. In *Proc. Int'l Workshop on Object-Oriented Database Systems*, Bad Münster am Stein-Ebernburg, FRG, 1988.
8. A.P. Karadimce, S.D. Urban. Refined Triggering Graphs : a Logic-Based Approach to Termination Analysis in an Active Object-Oriented Database. In *Proc. Int'l Conf. on Data Engineering (ICDE)*, New-Orleans, Louisiana, 1996.
9. S.Y. Lee, T.W. Ling. Refined Termination Decision in Active Databases. In *Proc. Int'l Conf. on Database and Expert Systems Applications (DEXA)*, Toulouse, France, 1997
10. S.Y. Lee, T.W. Ling. A Path Removing Technique for Detecting Trigger Termination. In *Proc. Int'l Conf. on Extending Database Technology (EDBT)*, Valencia, Spain, 1998.
11. S.Y. Lee, T.W. Ling. Unrolling Cycle to Decide Trigger Termination. In *Proc. Int'l Conf. on Very Large Data Bases (VLDB)*, Edinburgh, Scotland, 1999.
12. M.K. Tschudi, S.D. Urban, S.W. Dietrich, A.P. Karadimce. An Implementation and Evaluation of the Refined Triggering Graph Method for Active Rule Termination Analysis. In *Proc. Int'l Workshop on Rules in Database Systems*, Skoevde, Sweden, 1997.
13. A. Vaduva, S. Gatziu, K.R. Dittrich. Investigating Termination in Active Database Systems with Expressive Rule Languages. In *Proc. Int'l Workshop on Rules in Database Systems*, Skoevde, Sweden, 1997.

TriGS Debugger – A Tool for Debugging Active Database Behavior[1]

G. Kappel, G. Kramler, W. Retschitzegger

Institute of Applied Computer Science, Department of Information Systems (IFS)
University of Linz, A-4040 Linz, AUSTRIA
email: {gerti, gerhard, werner}@ifs.uni-linz.ac.at

Abstract. Active database systems represent a powerful means to respond automatically to events that are taking place inside or outside the database. However, one of the main stumbling blocks for their widespread use is the lack of proper tools for the verification of active database behavior. This paper copes with this need by presenting TriGS Debugger, a tool which supports mechanisms for predicting, understanding and manipulating active database behavior. First, TriGS Debugger provides an integrated view of both active and passive behavior by visualizing their interdependencies, thus facilitating pre-execution analysis. Second, post-execution analysis is supported by tracing and graphically representing active behavior including composite events and rules which are executed in parallel. Third, TriGS Debugger allows to interactively examine and manipulate the active behavior at run-time.

1 Introduction

Active database systems have been developed since several years. Basic active facilities in terms of Event/Condition/Action rules (ECA rules) have already found their way into commercial database systems [1]. Although active facilities are suitable for a wide range of different tasks, they are not straightforward to use when developing active database applications [21]. The main reasons are as follows. First, the very special nature of active behavior, which is controlled dynamically by events rather than statically by a flow of control, the latter being the case for traditional applications based on passive database behavior. Second, while each single rule is easy to understand, complexity arises from the interdependencies among rules and between active and passive behavior. Finally, the inherent complexity of active behavior is increased by concepts such as composite events, cascaded rule execution, and parallel rule execution. The actual behavior of a set of rules responsible for a certain active behavior is very hard to understand without proper tool support. The special characteristics of active behavior, however, prevent the straightforward employment of traditional debuggers realized for application development based on

[1] The financial support by SIEMENS PSE Austria under grant No. 038CE-G-Z360-158680 is gratefully acknowledged.

H.C. Mayr et al. (Eds.): DEXA 2001, LNCS 2113, pp. 410–421, 2001.

passive database behavior. Therefore, specific approaches for the verification of active behavior have been investigated.

First of all, there are approaches supporting *static rule analysis* to determine certain qualities of a set of rules, like termination, confluence, and observable determinism [2], [3], [4], [18], [19], [24]. A major drawback of these approaches is that expressive rule languages which are not formally defined are hard to analyze, leading to imprecise results. Furthermore, on one hand it is not always obvious what action should be taken when a potential source of nontermination or nonconfluence is detected and on the other hand, the fact that a set of rules exhibits terminating and confluent behavior does not necessarily imply that it is correct. Due to these drawbacks, static rule analysis has no major influence on the development of active applications [21]. Most existing systems take a complementary approach in that they record the active behavior at run-time, and visualize rule behavior afterwards [5], [6], [7], [8], [9], [10], [23]. Besides mere recording and viewing, some systems let the rule developer control the active behavior by means of breakpoints and step-by-step execution, enabling the inspection of database states at any time during rule execution. However, existing systems often do not cope with the interdependencies between passive behavior and active behavior. They still lack proper debugging support for important aspects of rule behavior, like the composite event detection process [6], and parallel executed rules, which are not considered at all. Finally, the information overload induced by complex trace data is often not handled properly.

TriGS Debugger copes with these drawbacks and the special nature of active database behavior in three different ways. First, pre-execution analysis is allowed on the basis of an integrated view of active behavior and passive behavior. Second, post-execution analysis is supported by a graphical representation of active behavior which includes the detection of composite events and rules which are executed in parallel. Special emphasize is drawn on the complexity of the resulting trace data by allowing for filtering and pattern mining. Third, TriGS Debugger allows to interactively examine and manipulate the active behavior at run-time. In particular, mechanisms are provided to set breakpoints, to replay single events or event sequences, to (de)activate selected events and rules, and to modify rule properties and the rule code itself.

The remainder of this paper is organized as follows. The next section provides a concise overview of the active object-oriented database system TriGS as a prerequisite for understanding the work on the TriGS Debugger. In Section 3, the functionality of TriGS Debugger is presented from a rule developer's point of view. The paper concludes with some lessons learned from user experiences and points to future research.

2 Overview of TriGS

TriGS Debugger is realized on top of *TriGS (Triggersystem for GemStone)* [15] representing an active extension of the object-oriented database system GemStone [11]. The two main components of TriGS are *TriGS Engine* comprising the basic concepts employed in TriGS for specifying and executing active behavior and *TriGS Developer*, an environment supporting the graphical development of active database applications [22]. In the following, TriGS Engine is described as far as necessary for understanding the forthcoming sections.

Like most active systems, TriGS is designed according to the ECA paradigm. Rules and their components are implemented as *first-class objects* allowing both the definition and modification of rules during run-time. The structure of ECA rules in TriGS is defined by the following template in Backus-Naur Form:

```
<rule_definition> ::=
  DEFINE RULE <rule_name> AS
  ON <EselC>                    // Condition event selector
    IF <bool_expr> THEN         // Condition part
  [[WAIT UNTIL] ON <EselA>]       // Action event selector
    EXECUTE [INSTEAD] <action> // Action part
    [WITH PRIORITY <number>]
  [TRANSACTION MODES (C:{serial|parallel},
                       A:{serial|parallel})]
  END RULE <rule_name>.
```

The event part of a rule is represented by a *condition event selector* ($Esel_C$) and an optional *action event selector* ($Esel_A$) determining the events (e.g., a machine breakdown) which are able to trigger the rule's condition and action, respectively. Triggering a rule's condition (i.e., an event corresponding to the $Esel_C$ is signaled) implies that the condition has to be evaluated. If the condition evaluates to true, and an event corresponding to the $Esel_A$ is also signaled, the rule's action is executed. If the $Esel_A$ is not specified, the action is executed immediately after the condition has been evaluated to true. By default, the transaction signaling the condition triggering event is not blocked while the triggered rule is waiting for the action triggering event to occur. Blocking can be specified by the keyword `WAIT UNTIL`.

In TriGS, any message sent to an object may signal a *pre- and/or post-message event*. In addition, TriGS supports *time events*, *explicit events*, and *composite events*. Composite events consist of *component events* which may be primitive or composite and which are combined by different *event operators* such as conjunction, sequence and disjunction. The event starting the detection of a composite event is called *initiating event*, the event terminating the detection is called *terminating event*. TriGS allows to detect composite events whose component events are either signaled within a single transaction or within different transactions. It is even possible that component events span different database sessions each comprising one or more transactions [13]. For each event, a *guard*, i.e., a predicate over the event's parameters, may be specified, which further restricts the events able to trigger a condition or action, respectively. The condition part of a rule is specified by a Boolean expression, possibly based on the result of a database query (e.g., are there some scheduled jobs on the damaged machine?). The action part is specified again in terms of messages (e.g., display all jobs scheduled on the damaged machine and reschedule them on another machine). Considering rules incorporating message events, the keyword `INSTEAD` allows to specify that the action should be executed instead of the method corresponding to the message triggering condition evaluation. The execution order of multiple triggered rules, i.e., conditions and actions of different rules which are triggered at the same time, is controlled by means of *priorities*.

The *transaction mode* is specified separately for conditions and actions respectively. It defines, in which transaction *rule processing* comprising *rule scheduling* and *rule execution* takes place. Rule scheduling includes the detection of composite events and the determination of triggered conditions and actions. Rule execution refers to condition evaluation and action execution. In case of a *serial mode*, rule processing is done as part of the database session's transaction which has signaled the triggering event. In case of a *parallel mode* rule processing is done within transactions of separate database sessions. Rules incorporating composite events whose component events are signaled by different database sessions can have a parallel transaction mode only. This is also the case for rules which are triggered by events being signaled outside of a database session, e.g., time events. Rule scheduling is done within a dedicated database session running in a separate thread of control called *Parallel Rule Scheduler.* Rule execution is made efficient by means of several *Parallel Rule Processors* each running within a separate thread [14]. The number of these threads is dynamically controlled and depends on the utilization of the corresponding rule processors.

3 Functionality of TriGS Debugger

This section is dedicated to an in-depth description of the functionality of TriGS Debugger. TriGS Debugger as part of the TriGS Developer is operational, a more detailed description can be found in [16].

3.1 Providing an Integrated View on Active and Passive Schema

During pre-execution analysis, i.e., schema analysis, of an active system like TriGS it is not sufficient to exclusively focus on the active schema, because of the interdependencies between the active schema and the passive schema. For instance, rules may be triggered by method calls in case of message events. However, since these schemas are developed using different tools, namely GemStone (GS) Class Browser and TriGS Designer, respectively, it is difficult to keep track of the interdependencies between passive schema and active schema.

In order to provide an *integrated view* on the database schema TriGS Debugger supports a *Structure Browser* (cf. Fig. 1). The Structure Browser shows the passive object-oriented schema on the left side of the window by means of a *class hierarchy tree* comprising classes, methods, and class inheritance (cf. ①-③ in Fig. 1). This is complemented by a visualization of the active schema on the right side of the window, which comprises *rules* and their *event selectors*, no matter being primitive or composite (cf. ④-⑥). The interdependencies between passive schema and active schema are depicted by edges between methods and corresponding message event selectors.

In order to reduce information overload, guards, conditions, and actions of a rule are not explicitly shown within the Structure Browser. Rather, their existence is indicated by means of small black boxes only (cf. ⑦ and ⑧). Finally, the Structure Browser provides a *filtering mechanism* to cope with the fact that, when many classes and rules are visualized at once the display becomes cluttered. For example, it is possible to filter the methods and classes related to a particular rule and its event selectors. The filter result may be visualized in a context preserving way by means of highlighting using different colors (cf. ⑨).

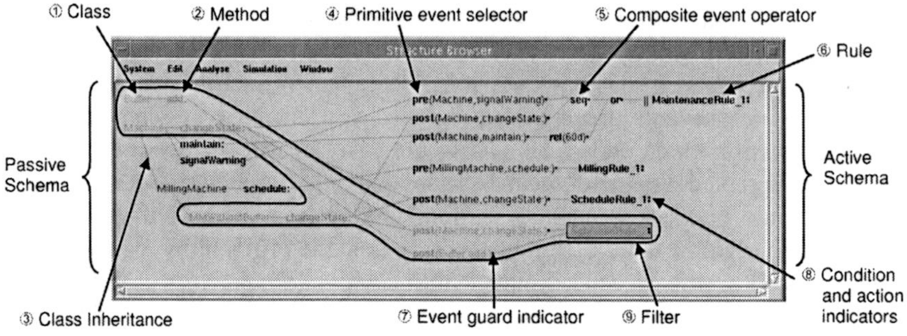

Fig. 1. Structure Browser

3.2 Visualizing Trace Data

Post-execution analysis, i.e., verification of the actual active behavior, requires tracing of events and rule executions, and visualization of traced data. For this, TriGS Debugger provides a *History Browser* (cf. Fig. 2), which may be opened at any time during or after the run of an active application to get a graphical snapshot of its behavior until that point in time. The visualization has been designed to highlight the relationships among events, like parallelism, event composition, or causal dependencies. In particular, the History Browser contains the following information:

- **Temporal Context.** Since active behavior occurs over time, a *timeline* (cf. ① in Fig. 2) organizes trace information in a *temporal context*, from top to bottom.
- **Event Detection.** Event detection of both primitive and composite events is visualized as *event graph*. This event graph is different from the event selector tree as depicted by the Structure Browser in that it represents events not at type level but rather at instance level. Since each event may be component of multiple composite events, a directed acyclic graph is formed.
- **Rule Execution.** The visualization of rule execution (cf. ④, ⑤) is decomposed into condition evaluation and action execution, because these two phases of rule execution may be triggered at different points in time by different events. Visualization of a condition evaluation comprises the begin of evaluation (cf. `evaluating` in Fig. 2) together with the name of the rule, possibly cascaded rule executions, and the end of evaluation indicated by the result of evaluation, i.e., true, false, an object, or nil. Action execution is visualized accordingly. The symbol "||" preceeding the begin of evaluation/execution denotes that the condition/action was performed by a Parallel Rule Processor outside the session which signaled the triggering event.

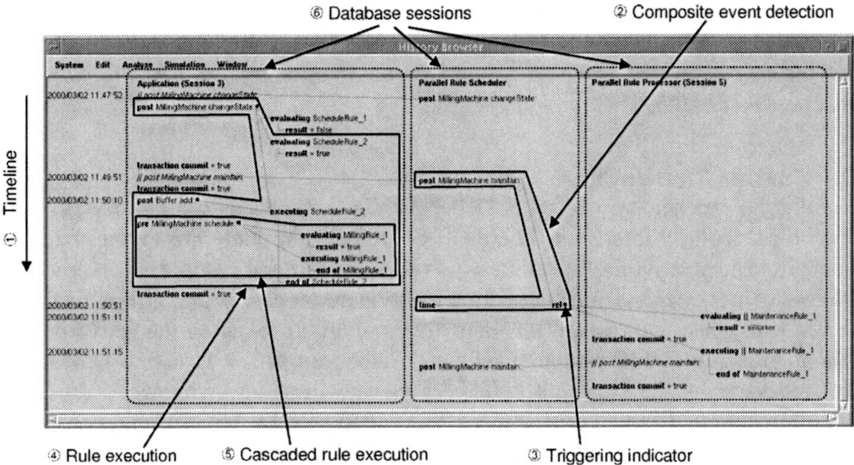

Fig. 2. History Browser

- **Database Sessions.** Database sessions during which events have been signaled or rules have been processed appear in the History Browser as parallel vertical tracks (cf. ⑥). According to the separation of serial rule processing and parallel rule processing in TriGS as discussed in Section 2, all trace data concerning a serial rule is shown within the track of the database session where the triggering event was signaled. This can be either an *Application Session* or a *Parallel Rule Processor Session*. Since events triggering parallel rules are processed within a dedicated database session, there is a special track labeled `Parallel Rule Scheduler` displayed right to the Application Session where all trace data of event detection for parallel rules is shown. As discussed in Section 2, parallel rules are executed by parallel rule processors in separate database sessions. The tracks of Parallel Rule Processor sessions are displayed right to the Parallel Rule Scheduler track.
- **Transactions.** Transaction boundaries within database sessions are represented by primitive events corresponding to commit/abort operations. Since committing a transaction may fail due to serialization conflicts, success or failure of a commit operation is indicated as well (cf. `transaction commit = true` in Fig. 2).

Further details are available by means of the integrated GS Inspector allowing the inspection and modification of trace data and related database objects, like condition results and action results as well as event parameters. However, one has to be aware that the Inspector shows the current state of an object, which may have changed since the time when, e.g., the object was used to evaluate the condition of a rule.

3.3 Customizing and Analyzing Trace Data

In case of a huge amount of events and rule executions a rule developer in looking for whether and why something has or has not happened will be overwhelmed by the sheer amount of information preserved in the trace data. Especially composite events, which may have to be traced over a long period of time and originating from various different sessions contribute to the complexity of visualization. To reduce the information overload, TriGS Debugger provides two complementary mechanisms allowing to customize the visualization of trace data, namely a *filtering mechanism* and a *pattern analyzer*.

3.3.1 Filtering Mechanism

The filtering mechanism of TriGS Debugger allows to focus the History Browser's view on particularly interesting details of the trace data, while preserving their order of occurrence by providing several *context independent* and *context dependent* filters. Whereas context dependent filters allow to navigate on causes and effects of selected parts of trace data, context independent filters allow to focus on the active behavior without selecting any particular trace data. Analogous to the Structure Browser, the filter results may be visualized either exclusively in a new window, or by simply highlighting them. Context independent filters supported by TriGS Debugger are:

- **Session.** With the session filter, it is possible to show/hide every track of the History Browser.
- **Time.** The time filter allows to focus on particular time intervals, specified either by begin and end time, or relative to the trace end, e.g. "the last 10 minutes".
- **Names of Event Selectors and Rules.** The view on a certain trace can be restricted to events conforming to certain event selectors, and/or having triggered evaluations and executions of certain rules.

The initial focus set by context independent filters can be modified step-by-step in an interactive manner by means of the following context dependent filters:

- **Cause.** The cause filter applied to a condition evaluation or an action execution shows the triggering event. Applying the cause filter to a primitive event results in either the rule execution during which it has been signaled, or the Application Session which signaled the event.
- **Direct/Indirect Effects.** The effect filter allows to focus either on direct effects only or on both direct and indirect effects of events and rule executions. Concerning a *primitive event*, the direct effects are the composite events terminated by that event, and the conditions/actions triggered, whereas the indirect effects are in addition all initiated composite events and all conditions/actions triggered by that initiated composite events. Concerning a *rule execution*, the direct effects are the primitive and composite events detected during execution as well as the first level of cascaded rule executions. The indirect effects of a rule execution include all levels of cascaded rule executions, as well as the events detected during these cascaded executions.
- **Time.** In order to focus on the temporal context of an event or of a rule execution, the time filter may be applied resulting in all events and rule executions within some time interval before and after the selected event/rule execution.

Fig. 3 is based on the same trace data as shown in Fig. 2, with filters being applied, thus making the trace data more readable. In particular, a context independent filter has been applied showing only the events signaled from Application Session 3 (cf. ①), and, based on the result of the first filter, a context dependent filter has been used to highlight the direct and indirect effects of the selected event (cf. ②).

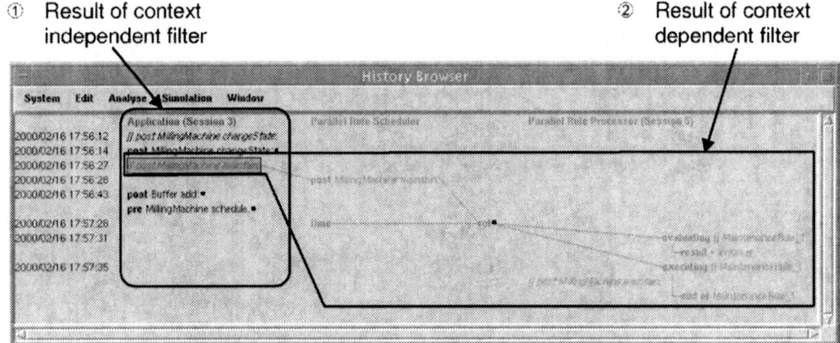

Fig. 3. Filtering Trace Data Within the History Browser

3.3.2 Pattern Analyzer

Besides filtering mechanisms, TriGS Debugger provides a *Pattern Analyzer*. In contrast to the History Browser, which shows each detected event and each executed rule in order of their occurrence, the Pattern Analyzer mines patterns of recurring active behavior and shows these patterns once, in an aggregated fashion. With this, a compact view on trace data is provided. Causal dependencies between rules and their components are visualized at one place, without having to browse through the whole history of trace data.

In order to mine patterns, the trace is analyzed step by step and similar trace data is aggregated into *equivalence classes*, whereby not only the equivalence of events and rule executions themselves is considered, but also the equivalence of relationships among them in terms of causal dependencies. Therefore, the *equivalence relation* is defined recursively, as follows:

- Two *primitive events* are considered equivalent if (1) they conform to the same primitive event selector, and (2) their causes, i.e., either the rule executions or the applications having signaled them, are in the same equivalence class.
- Equivalence of (partially detected) *composite events* is defined by the equivalence of their composition trees consisting of primitive component events (leafs) and event operators (nodes). Two such trees are equivalent if the root nodes are equivalent. Two nodes are in turn equivalent if (1) the event operator is the same, and (2) the child nodes/leafs are in the same equivalence class.
- Two *condition evaluations* are equivalent if (1) they belong to the same rule, and (2) the triggering events are in the same equivalence class.
- Two *action executions* are equivalent if (1) they belong to the same rule, and (2) the corresponding condition evaluations are in the same equivalence class, and (3) the action triggering events – if defined – are in the same equivalence class.

Patterns of behavior are visualized as a *directed acyclic graph*, with root nodes on the left representing equivalence classes of active behavior with outside cause, e.g., equivalence classes of primitive events raised by an application, and child nodes denoting equivalence classes of resulting active behavior. Note that this abstract view on rule behavior is similar to so-called *triggering graphs* as used in static rule analysis [2]. Unlike static rule analysis, which can be done before run-time, trace data patterns are not available until the application has been started. However, since trace data patterns represent the real active behavior of an application they have the advantage that *quantitative information* can be provided for each element of a pattern in terms of number of occurrences and execution time, comprising minimum, maximum and average values. *Qualitative information* in terms of, e.g., rule cycles is not automatically provided yet but rather subject to future work (cf. Section 4).

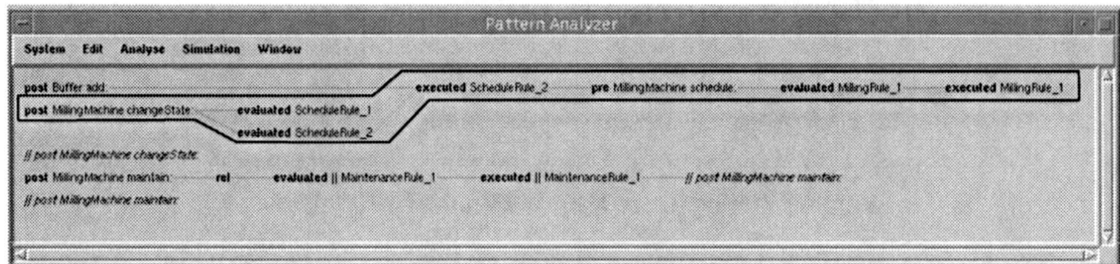

Fig. 4. Pattern Analyzer

Fig. 4 shows the Pattern Analyzer's view of the trace data as shown in Fig. 2. One can see at one place, e.g., all the direct and indirect consequences of the event `post(MillingMachine,changeState)`. Another insight is that `MillingRule_1` has been processed completely within the execution of `ScheduleRule_2`.

3.4 Interactive Rule Debugging

Besides the visualization and analyzing capabilities, TriGS Debugger allows to interactively control, examine and manipulate the active behavior by means of breakpoints, a replay and simulation mechanism and again by taking advantage of the other components of TriGS Developer and the standard GS tools.

First of all, TriGS Debugger allows to set breakpoints from within the History Browser and the Structure Browser. Breakpoints may be defined on all rule components namely *events*, *guards*, *conditions*, and *actions*. Whenever during rule processing TriGS Engine encounters a breakpoint, processing is stopped and a GemStone signal is thrown. On the front end, the GS Debugger has been extended to catch this signal and open a special breakpoint window. Depending on the rule component the breakpoint has been set on, different functionality is offered. In case the breakpoint has been set on a condition, one may choose to (1) proceed with condition evaluation, (2) continue under control of the GS Debugger in order to step through the condition's code, (3) skip the evaluation of the condition by setting the condition to either true or false, or (4) terminate the evaluation. Concerning breakpoints on events, one can in addition ignore the raised event, or continue until the next event is signaled. It has to be emphasized that since the standard GS Debugger can be incorporated from within the breakpoint window, one can control and examine the passive behavior of the application and its active behavior simultaneously.

TriGS Debugger offers similar interactive features for modifying the active behavior at run-time as the GS Debugger. Exploring the interpretative nature of GS, it is possible to modify rule code at run-time, even during a breakpoint halt. It is further possible to temporarily enable or disable certain events, guards, or rules and to modify rule priority settings.

The History Browser also supports a simple kind of event simulation [5], by allowing to replay events meaning that they are raised again. Either a single event or an arbitrary sequence of events can be selected from the event history in order to be replayed. By means of the GS Inspector, it is possible to modify event parameters before replaying, thus enabling the testing of guards and conditions. This way, an application scenario can be simulated, allowing to test a rule set without the need to run the application.

4 Lessons Learned and Future Work

TriGS Debugger has been already employed in a project aiming at the development of a schema generator that translates a conceptual schema modeled in terms of AOBD (Active Object/Behavior Diagrams), [17] into an executable TriGS schema [20]. The active behavior generated thereby is highly complex and therefore difficult to understand, since it makes extensive use of both composite events and parallel rules. This section discusses the lessons learned in the course of this project and points to future work.

Conflicts between parallel rules are hard to locate. The complexity of active behavior is not founded in single rules but in the interaction among rules [21]. With parallel executing rules, this interaction is multiplied by the possibility of concurrent access to database resources, which in turn may lead to serialization conflicts and abort of the corresponding transactions. It has been shown that parallel rules were involved in the most non-trivial bugs which had to be found and removed during development of the schema generator. Therefore we believe that debugging tools for parallel executing rules are even more important than for serial ones. Although TriGS Debugger facilitates debugging of parallel rules in that parallel database sessions, transactions, rules executed within a transaction, and success or failure of transactions are visualized, the reason of a conflict is not explained by the current prototype. In this sense it would be desireable to show the conflicting transactions/rules and the objects involved by a debugger. Furthermore, techniques for debugging parallel programs should be adopted. For instance, the *trace driven event replay* technique as already supported by TriGS Debugger could be used for semi-automatic detection of *race conditions* [12].

A history of database states would ease debugging. Trace data gathered by TriGS Debugger represents the history of event detections and rule executions, but it does not include the history of related database objects. This leads to the problem that one can inspect the current state of an object only. However the object may have changed since the time when it has been used, e.g., to evaluate the condition of a rule. Breakpoints are a cumbersome means to solve this problem, since they force a rule developer to interactively handle each break during an application test. Instead, it would be beneficial if a rule debugger could access a snapshot of the database state as it was at the time when a guard or condition was evaluated or an action was executed.

Active behavior requires active visualization. In order to support a rule developer in observing active behavior, a debugging tool should notify the developer automatically of any new rules which have been triggered or events which have been signaled. This could be achieved by updating the view(s) on trace data any time when considerable trace data has been added, or within certain time intervals. In the current prototype, the views of History Browser and History Analyzer have to be updated explicitly in order to check for new events/rule executions.

Trace analysis is a promising research topic. We consider analysis of trace data a promising alternative to static rule analysis. Especially in an environment like TriGS, which is based on the untyped language GS Smalltalk, static analysis is very restricted. Instead, we will focus on deriving qualitative information on active behavior from trace data. For instance, we plan to enhance the Pattern Analyzer to provide information on rule execution cycles. In general, TriGS Debugger should detect (patterns of) active behavior which is violating certain properties like termination or determinism, and this should be highlighted/visualized in both the History Browser's and Pattern Analyzer's view. Another possible application of trace data analysis would be to save trace data of different application tests (of different application versions) and compare them afterwards. Comparison might be in terms of execution order or encountered behavior patterns.

TriGS Debugger is not only specific to TriGS. TriGS Debugger has been designed specifically for TriGS, without having its application to other active database systems in mind. As such, the implementation of features like interactive rule debugging relies heavily on specific properties of the underlying TriGS/GS system. Nevertheless, the basic ideas of TriGS Debugger, like providing an integrated view on active and passive behavior, the visualization and filtering of trace data, and pattern analysis of trace data, can be applied to debuggers for active (object-oriented) database systems different from TriGS as well.

References

1. ACT-NET Consortium: The Active Database Management System Manifesto: A Rulebase of ADBMS Features. SIGMOD Record Vol. 25, 1996, pp. 40-49
2. Aiken, A., Widom, J., Hellerstein, J.: Behavior of database production rules: Termination, confluence, and observable determinism. SIGMOD Record, Vol. 21, 1992, pp. 59-68
3. Bailey, J., Dong, G., Ramamohanarao, K.: Decidability and Undecidability Results for the termination problem of active database rules. Proc. of the 17th ACM SIGMOD-SIGACT-SIGART Symposium on Principles of Database Systems, Seattle, 1998, pp. 264-273
4. Baralis, E.: Rule Analysis. Norman W. Paton (Ed.): Active Rules in Database Systems. Springer, New York, 1999, pp. 51-67
5. Behrends, H.: Simulation-based Debugging of Active Databases. In Proceedings of the 4th International Workshop on Research Issues in Data Engineering (RIDE) - Active Database Systems, Houston, Texas, IEEE Computer Society Press, 1994, pp. 172-180
6. Berndtsson, M., Mellin, J., Högberg, U.: Visualization of the Composite Event Detection Process. In Paton, N. W. and Griffiths, T. (eds.): International Workshop on User Interfaces to Data Intensive Systems (UIDIS'99). IEEE Computer Society, 1999, pp. 118-127

7. Chakravarthy, S., Tamizuddin, Z., Zhou, J.: A Visualization and Explanation Tool for Debugging ECA Rules in Active Databases. In Sellis, T. (ed.): Proc. of the 2nd Int. Workshop on Rules in Database Systems. Springer LNCS Vol. 985, 1995, pp. 197-212
8. Coupaye, T., Roncancio, C.L., Bruley, C., Larramona, J.: 3D Visualization Of Rule Processing In Active Databases. Proc. of the workshop on New paradigms in information visualization and manipulation, 1998, pp. 39-42
9. Diaz, O., Jaime, A., Paton, N.: DEAR: a DEbugger for Active Rules in an object-oriented context. In Proceedings of the 1st International Workshop on Rules in Database Systems, Workshops in Computing, Springer, 1993, pp. 180-193
10. Fors, T.: Visualization of Rule Behavior in Active Databases. In Proceedings of the IFIP 2.6 3rd Working Conference on Visual Database Systems (VDB-3), 1995, pp. 215-231
11. GemStone Systems Inc.: http://www.gemstone.com/products/s/, 2001
12. Grabner, S., Kranzlmüller, D., Volkert, J.: Debugging parallel programs using ATEMPT. Proceedings of HPCN Europe 95 Conference, Milano, Italy, May, 1995
13. Kappel, G., Rausch-Schott, S., Retschitzegger, W., Sakkinen, M.: A Transaction Model For Handling Composite Events. Proc. of the Int. Workshop of the Moscow ACM SIGMOD Chapter on Advances in Databases and Information Systems (ADBIS), MePhI, Moscow, September, 1996, pp. 116-125
14. Kappel, G., Rausch-Schott, S., Retschitzegger, W.: A Tour on the TriGS Active Database System - Architecture and Implementation. J. Carroll et al (eds.): Proc. of the 1998 ACM Symposium on Applied Computing (SAC). Atlanta, USA, March, 1998, pp. 211-219
15. Kappel, G., Retschitzegger, W.: The TriGS Active Object-Oriented Database System - An Overview. ACM SIGMOD Record, Vol. 27, No. 3, September, 1998, pp. 36-41
16. Kappel, G., Kramler, G., Retschitzegger, W.: TriGS Debugger – A Tool for Debugging Active Database Behavior. Technical Report 09/00, Dept. of Information Systems, University of Linz, Austria, March, 2000
17. Lang, P., Obermair, W., Kraus, W., Thalhammer, T.: A Graphical Editor for the Conceptual Design of Business Rules. Proc. of the 14th Int. Conference on Data Engineering (ICDE), Orlando, Florida, IEEE Computer Society Press, February, 1998, pp. 599-609
18. Lee, S.Y., Ling, T.W.: Unrolling cycle to decide trigger termination. In Proceedings of the 25th International Conference on Very Large Data Bases, 1999, pp. 483-493
19. Montesi, D., Bagnato, M., Dallera, C.: Termination Analysis in Active Databases. Proceedings of the 1999 International Database Engineering and Applications Symposium (IDEAS'99), Montreal, Canada, August, 1999
20. Obermair, W., Retschitzegger, W., Hirnschall, A., Kramler, G., Mosnik, G.: The AOODB Workbench: An Environment for the Design of Active Object-Oriented Databases. Software Demonstration at the Int. Conference on Extending Database Technology (EDBT 2000), Konstanz, Germany, March, 2000
21. Paton, N.W., Diaz, O.: Active Database Systems. ACM Computing Surveys Vol. 31, 1999, pp. 63-103
22. W. Retschitzegger: TriGS Developer - A Development Environment for Active Object-Oriented Databases. Proceedings of the 4th World Multiconference on Systemics, Cybernetics and Informatics (SCI'2000) and the 6th International Conference on Information Systems Analysis and Synthesis (ISAS'2000), Orlando, USA, July 23-26, 2000
23. Thomas, I.S. and Jones, A.C.: The GOAD Active Database Event/Rule Tracer. Proc. of the 7th Int. Conference on Database and Expert Systems Applications, Springer LNCS Vol. 1134, 1996, pp. 436-445
24. Vaduva, A., Gatziu, S., Dittrich, K.R.: Investigating Termination in Active Database Systems with Expressive Rule Languages. In Proceedings of the 3rd International Workshop on Rules In Database Systems, Skovde, Sweden, 1997, pp. 149-164

Tab-Trees: A CASE Tool for the Design of Extended Tabular Systems*

Antoni Ligęza, Igor Wojnicki, and Grzegorz J. Nalepa

Institute of Automatics, University of Technology AGH
al. Mickiewicza 30, 30-059 Kraków, Poland
ali@ia.agh.edu.pl, {wojnicki,gjn}@agh.edu.pl

Abstract. *Tabular Systems* constitute a particular form of rule-based systems. They follow the pattern of Relational Databases and Attributive Decision Tables. In *Extended Tabular Systems* non-atomic values of attributes are allowed. In order to assure safe, reliable and efficient performance of such systems, analysis and verification of selected qualitative properties such as completeness, consistency and determinism should be carried out. However, verification of them after the design of a system is both costly and late. In this paper another solution is proposed. A graphical CASE-like tool supporting the design of Extended Tabular Systems and providing verification possibilities is presented. The tool uses a new rule specification paradigm: the so-called *tab-trees*, covering the advantages of Attributive Decision Tables and Decision Trees. In the system the verification stage is moved into the design process. The background theory and the idea of tab-trees are outlined and presentation of a practical tool, the Osiris System, is carried out.

1 Introduction

Rule based systems constitute a powerful programming paradigm. They can be used in Active Databases, Deductive Databases, Expert Systems, Decision Support Systems and intelligent information processing. A particular form of such systems are Tabular Systems which try to stay close to Relational Databases (RDB) scheme and preserve their advantages. A tabular system can specify facts or rules; in the latter case some of the attributes refer to preconditions, while the rest refer to hypothesis or decision. Such systems can be embedded within the RDB structure, but if so all the values of attributes must be atomic ones. In an Extended Tabular System non-atomic values are allowed; they include subsets of the domain of an attribute, intervals (for ordered domains), and – in general – values of some lattice structure. A tabular system can consist of one or more tables, organised in a form of modular system [11].

In order to assure safe, reliable and efficient performance, analysis and verification of selected qualitative properties should be carried out [1,2,3,14,15,16]. In this paper we follow the line concerning control and decision support systems [5,

* Research supported from a KBN Project No.: 8 T11C 019 17.

H.C. Mayr et al. (Eds.): DEXA 2001, LNCS 2113, pp. 422–431, 2001.

12], where logical details were developed in [8,9,11]. Properties of interest include features such as, completeness, consistency and determinism. However, verification of them after the design of a rule-based system is both costly and late. In this paper another solution is proposed. A graphical CASE-like tool supporting the design of rule-based systems and providing verification possibilities is presented. The tool uses a new rule specification paradigm: the so-called *tab-trees* (also tabular-trees or tree-tables), covering the advantages of attributive decision tables and decision trees. The tool is aimed at synthesis of a single level, forward chaining rule-based systems in tabular form; the verification stage is moved into the design process. The background theory and the idea of the tab-trees are discussed and presentation of a practical tool, the Osiris System, is carried out. Osiris was implemented as a graphical CASE tool for design of Kheops-like rule-based systems under Unix environment.

The basic idea of the paper is to include the *verification* stage into the *design* process, as well as to support the design with flexible graphical environment of the CAD/CASE type. We follow the line proposed first in [7,8], where the so-called ψ-trees were proposed as a tool for support of logical design of complete and deterministic, non-redundant rule-based systems. We also use the ideas of tabular systems [9,11], which provide an approach following the attributive decision tables; the advantage of them is the easily readable, relational database-like format, which can be used both for data and knowledge specification.

As a result, a fully graphical environment supporting the design and including partially verification has been developed. A prototype system named *Osiris* cooperating with graphical user interface *gKheops* for the *Kheops* systems is presented. The tool is a generic one; the format of the rules to be generated can be adjusted for other systems as well.

2 Kheops

Kheops [5] is an advanced rule-based real time system. Its working idea is quite straightforward: it constitutes a reactive, forward interpreter. However, it is relatively fast (response time can be below 15 milliseconds) and oriented toward time-critical, on-line applications. Its distinctive features include compilation of the rule-base to the form of a specific decision tree which allows for checking some formal properties (e.g. completeness) and allows for evaluation of response time, dealing with time representation and temporal inference, and incorporation of specialized forms of rules, including universal quantification and C-expression. A more detailed description of Kheops can be found in [5].

The Kheops system was applied as one of the principal components in the TIGER project [12]. This was a large, real-domain application in knowledge-based monitoring, supervision, and diagnosis. The system operates on-line 24 hours a day and is applied for continuous monitoring, situation assessment and diagnosis of gas turbines. Its distinctive features include application of heterogenous tools, i.e. Kheops, IxTeT, and CA-EN, systems, i.e. it is a multi-strategy, multi-component system. Details about the TIGER system can be found in the literature quoted in [12].

3 Qualitative Properties Verification

3.1 Subsumption of Rules

Consider the most general case of subsumption; some particular definitions are considered in [1,9,11]. A rule subsumes another rule if the following conditions hold:

- the precondition part of the first rule is *weaker* (more general) than the precondition of the subsumed rule,
- the conclusion part of the first rule is *stronger* (more specific) than the conclusion of the subsumed rule.

Let the rules r and r', satisfy the following assumption: $\phi' \models \phi$ and $h \models h'$. The subsumed rule r' can be eliminated according to the following scheme:

$$\frac{\begin{array}{l} r : \phi \longrightarrow h \\ r' : \phi' \longrightarrow h' \end{array}}{r : \phi \longrightarrow h}$$

For intuition, a subsumed rule can be eliminated because it produces weaker results and requires stronger conditions to be satisfied; thus any of such results can be produced with the subsuming rule. Using tabular notation we have:

rule	A_1	A_2	...	A_j	...	A_n	H
r	t_1	t_2	...	t_j	...	t_n	h
r'	t'_1	t'_2	...	t'_j	...	t'_n	h'

rule	A_1	A_2	...	A_j	...	A_n	H
r	t_1	t_2	...	t_j	...	t_n	h

The condition for subsumption in case of the above tabular format takes the form $t'_j \subseteq t_j$, for $j = 1, 2, \ldots, n$ and $h' \subseteq h$ (most often, in practice $h' = h$ are atomic values). In the current version of *Osiris* subsumption is automatically eliminated due to the tabular partitioning of the attribute values to non-overlapping subdomains.

3.2 Determinism

A set of rules is *deterministic* iff no two different rules can succeed for the same state. A set of rules which is not deterministic is also referred to as *ambivalent*. The idea of having a deterministic system consists in a priori elimination of "overlapping" rules, i.e. ones which operate on a common situation.

From purely logical point of view the system is deterministic iff the conjunction of the precondition formulae $\phi \wedge \phi'$ is unsatisfiable. Calculation of $\phi \wedge \phi'$

is straightforward: for any attribute A_j there is an atom of the form $A_j = t_j$ in ϕ and $A_j = t'_j$ in ϕ', $i = 1, 2, \ldots, n$. Now, one has to find the intersection of t and t' – if at least one of them is empty (e.g. two different values; more generally $t_j \cap t'_j = \emptyset$), then the rules are disjoint. In the current version of *Osiris* determinism can be assured (if desired) thanks to non-overlapping partitioning of attribute domains. Normally, the check for determinism is to be performed for any pair of rules.

3.3 Completeness of Rule-Based Systems

For intuition, a RBS is considered to be *complete* if there exists at least one rule succeeding for any possible input situation [1,9]. In the following subsection logical (total) completeness is considered for a set of rules as below:

$$\begin{array}{lll} r_1 : & \phi_1 & \longrightarrow h_1 \\ r_2 : & \phi_2 & \longrightarrow h_2 \\ \vdots & \vdots & \vdots \ \vdots \\ r_m : & \phi_m & \longrightarrow h_m \end{array}$$

The approach proposed here comes from purely logical analysis based on the *dual resolution* method [6]; its algebraic forms are discussed in [9,11].

Consider the joint disjunctive formula of rule precondition of the form $\Phi = \phi_1 \vee \phi_2 \vee \ldots \phi_m$. The condition of logical completeness for the above system is $\models \Phi$, which simply means that Φ is a tautology. In the proposed approach, instead of logical proof [6], an algebraic method based on partitions of the domain attributes is used [9,11]; in effect, no exhaustive enumeration of detailed input states is necessary. In the current version of *Osiris* the check for completeness is performed automatically, when desired, during the design stage.

4 Graphical Design Concept

There is no general rule for knowledge representation and extraction. There are several approaches which have advantages and disadvantages depending on the purpose they are created for. That means there is a need for a brand new approach which would be able to give clear and efficient way to represent logical structures. The approach proposed below uses the so-called *tab-trees* or *tree-tables* for knowledge representation and it is analysed below along with some other representation methods.

4.1 Production Rules and Logic

This method relies on the *if-then-else* construct. It is well known form procedural programming languages. It could be described as:

$$IF\ condition\ THEN\ action1\ ELSE\ action2$$

It reads: if *condition* is true then perform *action*1 else perform *action*2. Often the *ELSE* part is absent or it is global, for all rules.

4.2 Decision Tables

Decision tables are an engineering way of representing production rules. Conditions are formed into a table which also holds appropriate actions. Classical decision tables use binary logic extended with "not important" mark to express states of conditions and actions to be performed.

The main advantage of decision tables is their simple, intuitive interpretation. One of the main disadvantages is that classical tables are limited to binary logic. In some cases the use of values of attributes is more convenient. A slightly extended table are OAV tables (OAT). OAV stands for Object-Attribute-Value (OAT – Object-Attribute-value-Table) and such a table is presented below.

Table 1. Object-Attribute-Value table.

attrib_1	attrib_2	...	action_1	action_2	...
v_11	v_12	...	w_11	w_12	...
v_21	v_22	...	w_21	w_22	...
⋮	⋮	⋱	⋮	⋮	⋱

The rows specify under what attribute values certain actions must be executed. Both `v_ij` and `w_kl` may take different values, not only *true*, *false* and *not important*.

4.3 Decision Trees

Tree-like representations are readable, easy to use and understand. The root of the tree is an entry node, under any node there are some branching links. The selection of a link is carried out with respect to a conditional statement assigned to the node. Evaluation of this condition determines the selection of the link. The tree is traversed top-down, and at the leaves final decisions are defined.

An example of a decision tree is given in Fig 1. Circles represent actions, rectangles hold attributes and parallelograms express relations and values.

Decision trees could be more sophisticated. The presented decision tree (Fig 1) is a binary tree; every node has only two links which express two different values of a certain attribute. There are also decision trees called ψ-trees [7,8]; in such trees a single node may have more then two links which makes the decision process more realistic, and allows to compare attributes with many different values in a single node. The structure of such trees is modular and hierarchical.

4.4 A New Approach: The Tab-Trees

The main idea is to build a hierarchy of OATs [7,8]. This hierarchy is based on the ψ-tree structure. Each row of a OAV table is right connected to the other OAV table. Such a connection implies logical AND relation in between.

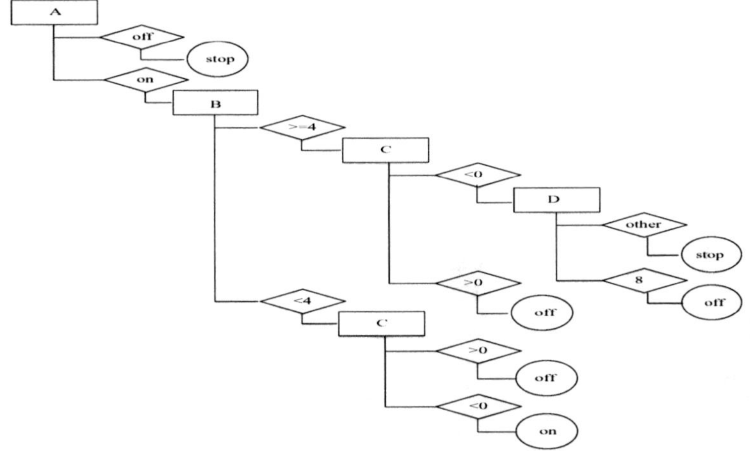

Fig. 1. An example of a decision tree.

OAV tables used in tree-table representation are divided into two kinds: attribute tables and action tables. Attribute tables are the attribute part of a classical OAT, Action tables are the action part. There is one logical limitation. While attribute tables may have as many rows as needed (a number of columns depends on the number of attributes), action tables may have only one row, it means that the specified action, or set of actions if there is more then one column, may have only one value set, which preserves the consistency.

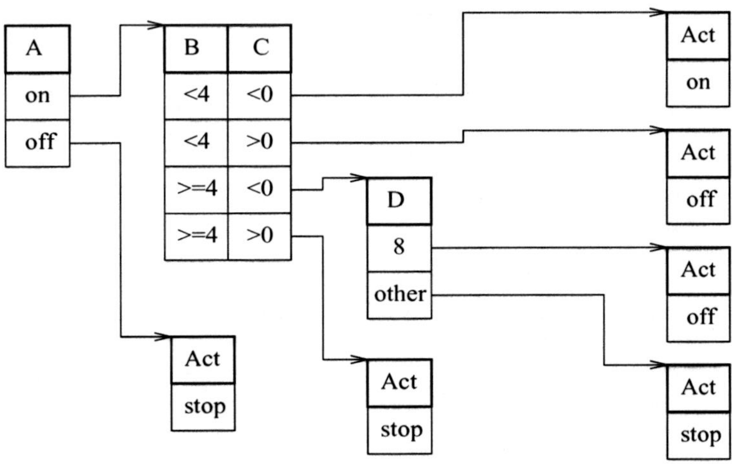

Fig. 2. An example of a tab-tree knowledge representation.

An example of a tab-tree representation is given in Fig 2. Note, that a tab-tree representation is similar to Relational Database (RDB) data representation scheme.

The main features of the tab-tree knowledge representation are:

- simplicity and transparency; intuitive way of representation,
- hierarchical, tree-like knowledge representation,
- highly efficient way of visualisation with high data density,
- power of the decision table representation,
- analogies to the RDB data representation scheme,
- flexibility with respect to knowledge manipulation.

5 The Osiris System

The Kheops [5] system has text oriented user interface. It is suitable for advanced users but not for beginners. The gKheops system solves problems with navigation through Kheops modes and allows to integrate editor with Kheops run-time environment. However, the user has still to know the sophisticated Kheops syntax. The main goal was to create such an environment that allows rapid development of Kheops rules using a graphical user interface and cooperates with gKheops. The name had been chosen to be *Osiris*[1]. *Osiris* should be designed to be as universal as possible to meet requirements not only for *Kheops*, but for almost all rule based expert systems without any major modifications.

The main features of the system include:

- graphical rule editor based on logic; it allows creating, modifying and storing rule structures,
- the editor uses a new tab-tree representation as a visualisation and development method of logical structures,
- rule-checking subsystem, completeness checking, which provides verification possibility in the development stage,
- mouse driven graphical user interface, easy to understand and use, following the RDB paradigm,
- automatic code generation for the Kheops system,
- integration with the gKheops to run the developed code,
- ability to expand or modify the system easily (e.g. to add code generation for other expert systems),
- high flexibility; the tabular components can be split and joint vertically if necessary.

Osiris is a multi-module system designed for UNIX environments (tested under Debian GNU/Linux, Sun Solaris 2.5). It consists of: a graphical environment for computer aided development of rules, a code generator for Kheops system, a validator, which provides on-line completeness checking and a run-time environment for created rules. The architecture of the Osiris is shown in Fig. 3

[1] It corresponds to an ancient Egyptian God whom Cheops (Kheops) could have owned his strength. The *Osiris* system was developed as a M.Sc. Thesis at Institute of Automatics AGH in Cracow, Poland.

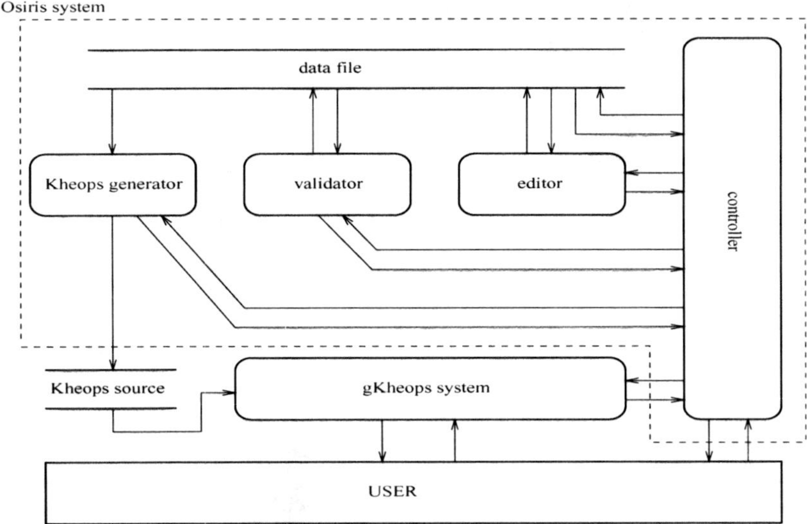

Fig. 3. The architecture of the Osiris

For visualisation and development the tree-table representation is chosen (see Section 4.4). Note that modules for code generation, verification, and a run-time environment (Generator, Validator, gKheops respectively) are separate applications. The Generator and the Validator use the compiler technology to process an Osiris datafile which describes the logical structures being developed. They produce a source code for Kheops and provide incompleteness checking, respectively. All modules are controlled by a single graphical user interface.

Osiris uses its own datafile for storing the logical structures. As a storing method an XML document is chosen. The datafile has well-defined grammar which allows to create a generator for almost any expert system and implement even sophisticated inconsistency checking algorithms.

What is also most important, Osiris provides a way to check the logical structures being developed against a possible incompleteness (the Validator) which moves the verification process to the development stage.

As a run-time environment a graphical user interface for Kheops, which is called gKheops is chosen. A sample session with the Osiris is shown in Fig 4.

6 The gKheops System

The gKheops system is a graphical user interface to Kheops expert system. Its main functions are launching and controlling Kheops, and aiding at creating and testing an expert system in Kheops environment. gKheops has a text editor for Kheops files and a syntax checker module. The interface is easy to use, intuitive and self documenting. It runs a process independent from Kheops itself. It uses Unix concurrent processes and inter process communication mechanisms that allow real-time communication with Kheops.

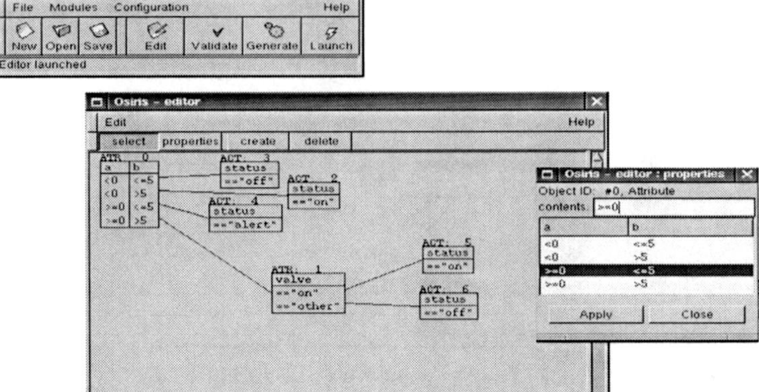

Fig. 4. A sample screen from a session with the Osiris system.

The gKheops system has been implemented in ANSI C and runs in the GNU/Linux and Unix environments. The interface is based on an advanced graphical toolkit called Gtk+. The Gtk+ library is available on any Unix-like platform in the X Window environment. The design of gKheops interface was made with Glade, which is a GUI builder for the Gtk+. The whole gKheops project was created entirely using *free software*. The syntax checker module consists of a Kheops language parser and scanner. The module was implemented using GNU Bison, a LALR(1) context-free parser generator, and Flex, which is a scanner generator. These tools are compatible with popular Yacc and Lex tools.

The gKheops system simplifies the development of expert systems in the Kheops environment by providing a coherent graphical interface to Kheops itself. It speeds up the process of launching and controlling Kheops, and is very useful in the process of debugging and testing an expert system.

7 Concluding Remarks

In this paper the first ideas for graphical, interactive, CASE-like environment for design of rule-based systems are proposed. The main aim of the system is to provide an intuitive, user-friendly environment, which covers both design and partial verification of qualitative properties. At the current, prototype implementation, the system provides the possibility of completeness checking, while features such as consistency, determinism and subsumption are achieved thanks to the structural specification of the design.

The system includes a new, the so-called tab-tree knowledge representation. It seems to be convenient, intuitive and readable, especially for people familiar with relational databases and decision trees. It should be mentioned that, only few tools support the design of the knowledge base in a similar way, e.g. or [18] (which uses mostly specific decision trees) or [19] (but mostly through knowledge-management tool).

References

1. Andert, E. P.: Integrated knowledge-based system design and validation for solving problems in uncertain environments. *Int. J. of Man-Machine Studies*, **36**, 1992, 357–373.
2. Coenen, F.: Verification and validation in expert and database systems: The expert systems perspective. A Keynote presentation in [17], 1998, 16–21.
3. Coenen, F.: Rulebase checking using a spatial representation. In [13], 1998, 166–175.
4. Coenen, F., B. Eaglestone and M. Ridley: Validation, verification and integrity in knowledge and data base systems: future directions. In [15], 1999, 297–311.
5. Gouyon, Jean-Paul: Kheops Users's Guide, *Report of Laboratoire d'Automatique et d'Analyse des Systemes*, No.: 92503, 1994, Toulouse.
6. Ligęza, A.: A note on backward dual resolution and its application to proving completeness of rule-based systems. Proceedings of the 13th Int. Joint Conference on Artificial Intelligence (IJCAI). Chambery, France **1**, 1993, 132–137.
7. Ligęza, A.: Towards design of complete rule-based control systems, *IFAC/IMACS International Workshop on Artificial Intelligence in Real-Time Control*, IFAC, Bled, Slovenia, 1995, 189-194.
8. Ligęza, A.: Logical support for design of rule-based systems. Reliability and quality issues, *ECAI-96 Workshop on Validation, Verification and Refinement of Knowledge-based Systems*, ECAI'96, Budapest, 1996, 28–34.
9. Ligęza, A.: Towards logical analysis of tabular rule-based systems. In [17], 1998, 30–35.
10. Ligęza, A.: Intelligent data and knowledge analysis and verification; towards a taxonomy of specific problems. In [15], 1999, 313–325.
11. Ligęza, A.: Towards logical analysis of tabular rule-based systems. *International Journal of Intelligent Systems*, **16**, 2001, 333–360.
12. Milne, R., C. Nicol, L. Travé-Massuyèz and J. Quevedo, TIGER: Knowledge based gas turbine condition monitoring, *Applications and Innovations in Expert Systems III*, SGES Publications, 1995, III, Cambridge, Oxford, 23–43.
13. Quirchmayr, G., Schweighofer, E. and T.J.M. Bench-Capon (Eds.): Database and Expert Systems Applications. Proceedings of the 9th Int. Conf., DEXA'98, Vienna, Springer-Verlag Lecture Notes in Computer Sciences. Berlin, **1460**, 1998.
14. Preece, A. D.: A new approach to detecting missing knowledge in expert system rule bases. Int. J. Man-Machine Studies. **38**, 1993, 661–668.
15. Vermesan, A. and F. Coenen (Eds.): Validation and Verification of Knowledge Based Systems – Theory, Tools and Practice. Kluwer Academic Publishers, Boston, 1999.
16. Vermesan, A. *et al.*: Verification and validation in support for software certification methods. In [15], 1999, 277–295.
17. Wagner, R. R. (ed.): Database and Expert Systems Applications. Proceedings of the Ninth International Workshop, Vienna; IEEE Computer Society, Los Alamitos, CA., 1998.
18. Attar Software, *XpertRule 3.0* http://www.attar.com/pages/info_xr.htm.
19. AITECH Katowice, *Sphinx 2.3*, http://www.aitech.gliwice.pl/.

A Framework for Databasing 3D Synthetic Environment Data

Roy Ladner[1], Mahdi Abdelguerfi[2], Ruth Wilson[1], John Breckenridge[1], Frank McCreedy[1], and Kevin B. Shaw[1]

[1]Naval Research Laboratory, Stennis Space Center, MS
{rladner, ruth.wilson, jbreck, mccreedy, shaw} @ nrlssc.navy.mil

[2]University of New Orleans, Computer Science Department, New Orleans, LA
mahdi @ cs.uno.edu

Abstract. Since 1994 the Digital Mapping, Charting and Geodesy Analysis Program at the Naval Research Laboratory has been developing an object-oriented spatial and temporal database, the Geographic Information Database (GIDB™). Recently, we have expanded our research in the spatial database area to include three-dimensional synthetic environment (3D SE) data. This work has focused on investigating an extension to the National Imagery and Mapping Agency's (NIMA's) current Vector Product Format (VPF) known as VPF+. This paper overviews the GIDB and describes the data structures of VPF+ and a prototyped 3D synthetic environment using VPF+. The latter was designed as a 3D Geographic Information System (3D-GIS) that would assist the U.S. Marine Corps with mission preparation and also provide onsite awareness in urban areas.

1 Introduction

The Digital Mapping, Charting and Geodesy Analysis Program (DMAP) at the Naval Research Laboratory has been actively involved in the development of a digital mapping database through its Geospatial Information Database (GIDB™). The GIDB is an object-oriented, CORBA compliant spatial database capable of storing multiple data types from multiple sources [GIDB]. The data is accessible both locally and remotely over the web through a Java Applet.

Recently we have expanded our work in the spatial database area to include three-dimensional synthetic environment (3D SE) data. Our synthetic environment work has focused on investigating an extension to the National Imagery and Mapping Agency's (NIMA's) current Vector Product Format (VPF) known as VPF+. VPF+ adds a new level of topology called Level 4 Full 3D Topology (Level 4). The topologic information encompasses the adjacencies involved in 3D manifold and non-manifold objects, and is described using a new, extended Winged-Edge data structure called *3D Non-Manifold Winged-Edge Topology*. This new level of topology is in

H.C. Mayr et al. (Eds.): DEXA 2001, LNCS 2113, pp. 432–441, 2001.

tended to facilitate the use of VPF in the 3D SE generation process by supporting a wide range of three-dimensional features expected to be encountered in a three-dimensional synthetic environment.

We have prototyped VPF+ in a 3D Geographic Information System (3D-GIS) that would assist the U.S. Marine Corps with mission preparation and also provide onsite awareness in urban areas. These operations require practice in physically entering and searching both entire towns and individual buildings. Our prototype, therefore, supplements the more traditional 2D digital-mapping output with a 3D interactive synthetic environment in which users may walk or fly across terrain, practice entry of buildings through doors and windows, and gain experience navigating the interiors of buildings.

2 DMAP's Spatial Database Experience

DMAP began investigating spatial database issues in 1994 with the development of the GIDB. The GIDB includes an object-oriented model, an object-oriented database management system (OODBMS) and various Spatial Analysis Tools. While the model provides the design of classes and hierarchies, the OODBMS provides an effective means of control and management of objects on disk such as locking, transaction control, etc. Spatial analysis tools include spatial query interaction, multimedia support and map symbology support. Users can query the database by area-of-interest, time-of-interest, distance and attribute. Interfaces are implemented to afford compatibility Arc/Info and Oracle 8i, among others.

Not only has the object-oriented approach been beneficial in dealing with complex spatial data, but it has also allowed us to easily integrate a variety of raster and vector data. Some of the raster data includes Compressed ARC Digitized Raster Graphics (CADRG), Controlled Image Base (CIB), jpeg and video. Vector data includes VPF, Shape, sensor data and Digital Terrain Elevation Data (DTED). The VPF data includes such NIMA products as Digital Nautical Chart (DNC), Vector Map (VMAP), Urban Vector Map (UVMAP), Digital Topographic Data Mission Specific Data Sets (DTOP MSDS), and Tactical Oceanographic Data (TOD).

Figure 1 gives an example of how the user may use this data over the web through the applet. The area-of-interest shown in the figure is for a portion of the U.S. Marine Corps Millennium Dragon Exercise that took place in September 2000 in the Gulf of Mexico. Using the applet interface to the GIDB the user was able to access the area of interest, bring in CIB imagery and overlay it with various vector data from DNC, MSDS and survey data from the Naval Oceanographic Office. The user was then able to zoom in and replace the CIB with CADRG imagery, and then zoom in further to see more of the detail of the MSDS data around the harbor in Gulfport, Mississippi.

In addition to spatial query features, the GIDB is capable of temporal query, such as wave height over a given time span for spatial objects (for instance, an ocean sensor), to provide statistics (min, max, mean, standard deviation) of this data and to provide data plots.

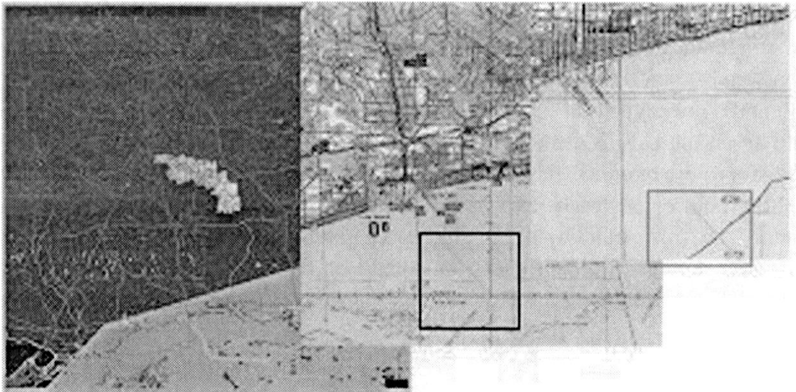

Fig. 1. Screen shots from Millennium Dragon exercise area. From left to right: (**1a**) CIB background with VMAP, DTOP MSDS, sensor data and DNC added. (**1b**) CADRG Data added, area-of-interest zoomed in. (**1c**) Additional zoom with CADRG and sensor data.

3 Motivations for the Current Work

NIMA is the primary provider of synthetic environment data to the Department of Defense and to the private sector. VPF and DTED are the formats used by NIMA to disseminate a significant amount of that data. Despite the widespread use of VPF, its shortcomings have been documented in the synthetic environment database generation systems used by a variety of government and private groups, involving different proprietary end-product formats, and across varying user needs [Trott 96]. These shortcomings involve VPF's arrangement of features into disjointed, thematic layers, its lack of attribute and geometric data appropriate to the reconstruction many 3D objects and its often lack of correlation with DTED data. Disjointed thematic feature data, in particular, requires considerable preprocessing and data integration to be usable in a 3D synthetic environment. These shortcomings add much time and money to the process of constructing synthetic environments from VPF data.

Non-manifold objects are those in which one of the following conditions exist: (1) exactly two faces are not incident at a single edge, (2) objects or faces are incident only through sharing a single vertex, or (3) a dangling edge exists [Gursoz 90, Lienhardt 91, and O'Rourke 95]. A dangling edge is one in which the edge is not adjacent to any face. Examples are given in Figure 2 where non-manifold conditions are noted by the bold edges. Non-manifold objects are commonplace in the real world, and they should be found in a synthetic environment (SE).

VPF uses winged-edge topology to provide line network, face topology and seamless coverages across tile boundaries [VPF 96]. However, it lacks the constructs necessary to maintain the adjacency relations in non-manifold objects. While an edge is adjacent to exactly two faces in VPF Level 3 topology, an edge may be adjacent to 0, 1, 2, 3 or more faces in a SE when a non-manifold condition is present. Though the winged-edge topology used by VPF relates each edge to exactly two faces (left and right, corresponding to two adjacent faces), the concept of a "left" and "right" face may be lacking in 3D non-manifold objects where multiple faces may be incident to the edge.

VPF also relates each connected node to exactly one of the edges to which each such node is connected. This allows for retrieval of all edges and faces to which the node is connected using the winged-edge algorithm. However, in a SE a connected node may connect two different 3D objects, two different faces or a dangling edge. Relating the connected node to only one edge in these circumstances will not be adequate for retrieval of all spatial primitives.

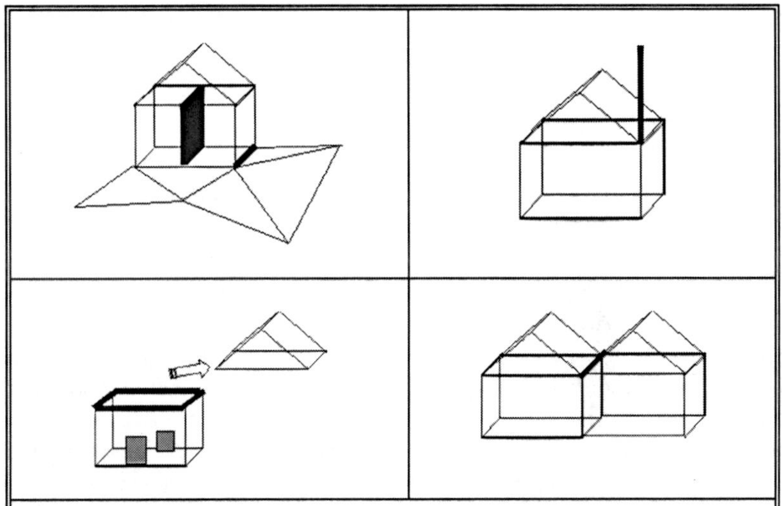

Fig. 2. Clockwise from top left: **(2a)** Multiple Faces Incident at a Single Edge. **(2b)** Dangling Edge and Building Joined Only By a Common Point. **(2c)** Two Buildings Sharing a Face With a Non-Manifold Condition at the bold Edge. **(2d)** Partial Building Creates Non-Manifold Condition.

There are a number of data structures that are capable of maintaining the adjacency relationships found in manifold and non-manifold objects. Notable are the Radial Edge [Weiler 86], the Tri-Cyclic Cusp [Gursoz 90] and the ACIS Geometric Modeler [Spatial 96]. The Radial Edge Structure is an edge based data structure that addresses topological ambiguities found with two non-manifold situations - the non-manifold edge and the non-manifold vertex. The Tri-Cyclic Cusp Structure is a vertex based data structure. This data structure addresses the topological relationships that the Radial Edge Structure addresses, and, in addition, is specifically intended to resolve ambiguities inherent in certain non-manifold representations that may not be easily eliminated by the Radial Edge structure as when two objects are joined only at a common point. The ACIS Geometric Modeler is a component-based package consisting of a kernel and various application based software components.

While these may provide a theoretical basis for a logical extension of the VPF standard, they could not be directly implemented. Our primary area of concern is modeling synthetic environments. These other data structures address a different application area, solid modeling, making them often inconsistent with Winged-Edge topology concepts found in the VPF standard.

There are also a number of major developers of synthetic environment database systems such as Loral Advanced Distributed Simulation, Inc., Lockheed Martin Information Systems (LMIS), Multigen, Inc., Evans & Sutherland (E&S) and Lockheed Martin Tactical Defense Systems (LMTDS). Their products include database formats such as the S1000, OpenFlight, TARGET, and specific image generator formats. Their emphasis, however, is on visual representation, not three-dimensional topological relationships.

4 The VPF+ Data Structure

Since VPF has widespread use and there are numerous VPF databases, the data structures described in this section are defined as a superset of VPF, known as VPF+, in order to facilitate the use of VPF in the 3D SE generation process. This superset introduces a new level of topology called Level 4 Full 3D Topology (Level 4) to accomplish 3D modeling. A boundary representation (*B-rep*) method is employed. B-rep models 3D objects by describing them in terms of their bounding entities and by topologically orienting them in a manner that enables the distinction between the object's interior and exterior.

The topologic adjacencies of three-dimensional manifold and non-manifold objects in the SE are described using a new, extended Winged-Edge data structure, referred to as *"Non-Manifold 3D Winged-Edge Topology"*. Geometric information includes both three-dimensional coordinates and Face and Edge orientation. Although this discussion is restricted to planar geometry, curved surfaces can also be modeled through the inclusion of parametric equations for Faces and Edges as associated attribute information.

Level 4 is a full 3D topology that is capable of representing comprehensive, integrated 3D synthetic environments. Such an environment can include the terrain surface, objects generally associated with the terrain surface such as buildings and roads, and it can include objects that are not attached to the terrain but are rather suspended above the terrain surface or below a water body's surface.

There are five main VPF+ primitives found in Level 4 topology: (1) *Entity node* – used to represent isolated features; (2) *Connected node* – used as endpoints to define edges; (3) *Edge* – an arc used to represent linear features or borders of faces; (4) *Face* – a two-dimensional primitive used to represent a facet of a three-dimensional object such as the wall of a building; and (5) *Eface* – a primitive that describes a use of a face by an edge. Unlike the topology of traditional VPF, the Level 4 topology of VPF+ does not require a fixed number of faces to be incident to an edge. The *Eface* is a new primitive that is introduced to resolve some of the ensuing ambiguities. Efaces describe a use of a Face by an Edge and allow maintenance of the adjacency relationships between an Edge and zero, one, two or more Faces incident to an Edge. This is achieved in VPF+ by linking each edge to all faces connected along the edge through a circular linked list of efaces. Each eface identifies the face it is associated with, the next eface in the list and the "next" edge about the face in relation to the edge common to the three faces. Efaces are also radially ordered in the linked list in a clockwise direction about the edge in order to make traversal from one face to the radially closest adjacent face a simple list operation.

In addition to the eface structure, VPF+ introduces several extensions to VPF consistent with non-manifold topology and 3D modeling. One extension is the Node-Edge relationship. While VPF relates each Connected Node to exactly one Edge, VPF+ allows for non-manifold Nodes. This requires that a Node point to one Edge in each object connected solely through the Node and to each dangling Edge (an edge that is adjacent to no face). This relationship allows for the retrieval of all Edges and all Faces in each object and the retrieval of all dangling Edges connected to the Node.

Significant to 3D modeling, VPF+ defines Two-Sided Faces. Faces are defined in VPF as purely planar regions. In VPF+ Faces may be one sided or two sided. A two sided Face, for example, might be used to represent the wall of a building with one side used for the outside of the building and the other side for the inside of the building. Feature attribute information would be used to render the two different surface textures and color. A one sided Face might then be used to represent the terrain surface.

Additionally, orientation of the interior and exterior of 3D objects is organized in relation to the normal vector of Faces forming the surface boundary of closed objects. This allows for easy distinction between an object's interior and exterior.

For more detail on VPF+ topologic structures the interested reader is referred to [Abdelguerfi 98].

Traditional VPF defines five categories of cartographic features: Point, Line, Area, Complex and Text. Point, Line and Area features are classified as Simple Features, composed of only one type of primitive. Each Simple Feature is of differing dimensionality: zero, one and two for Point, Line and Area Features respectively. Unlike Simple Features, Complex Features can be of mixed dimensionality, and are obtained by combining Features of similar or differing dimension.

For Level 4 topology, VPF+ adds a new Simple Feature class of dimension three. The newly introduced feature, referred to as *3D Object Feature*, is composed solely of Face primitives. This new feature class is aimed at capturing a wide range of 3D objects. Although 3D Objects are restricted to primitives of one dimension, 3D Objects of mixed dimensionality can be modeled through Complex Features using Simple Features of similar or mixed dimensionality as building blocks.

Software performance can be improved by identifying characteristics of real 3D objects that will allow storage of optional, unambiguous topological information that may otherwise require considerable processing time to derive. Clearly, portions of numerous 3D objects form closed volumes that divide 3D space into interior, exterior and surface regions. Optional topological information in these cases includes the classification of Faces as either inside of, outside of or part of the boundary of the 3D Object and the orientation of the interior and exterior of the object.

Though Area Features may geometrically exist in 3D space, they are topologically two dimensional, and are intended to model surface area. As with 3D Object Features, Area Features are Simple Features, and objects being modeled at this level are restricted to be composed only of Faces connected along incident Edges or at non-manifold Connected Nodes. Each face may be single sided or double sided, but an Area Feature will generally make use of only a single side of a double sided Face.

Tiling is the method used in VPF to break up large geographic data into spatial units small enough to fit the limitations of a particular hardware platform and media. Primitives that cross tile boundaries are split in VPF, and topology is maintained through *cross-tile topology*. The cross-tile constructs of VPF are extended in Level 4 in accordance with the organizational scheme of Non-Manifold 3D Winged-Edge topology. Tile boundaries in VPF+, however, consist of planar divisions.

5 The Prototyped Synthetic Environment

The synthetic environment prototype consists of the Military Operations in Urban Terrain site at Camp LeJeune, North Carolina. The MOUT site is a small city built by the Marine Corps for urban combat training. The MOUT site consists of approximately 30 buildings constructed in a variety of shapes and sizes to resemble what might be expected in an actual urban area. Since the area is supposed to resemble a combat environment, some are constructed to exhibit various degrees of damage. There is also a transportation network and the usual urban features associated with this type of setting such as trees, park benches, planters, flag poles, etc. Data for the site is readily available, which allowed for construction of a detailed 3D SE that closely matched its real world counterpart. MOUT buildings that exhibit damage, for example, are reproduced in the prototyped SE to show the same elements of damage.

The prototype provides a 3D synthetic environment alongside a more traditional 2D digital map. The map view offers general orientation and feature identification, while the 3D SE complements this with an immersive experience of the three-dimensional environment [Ladner 2000]. The combination should prove beneficial to a variety of uses.

A commercial-off-the-shelf OODBMS was used for the prototype database. Java2 and the Java3D API were used for interface into the database. The Java3D API provided reasonable performance for 3D interaction and easy implementation.

5.1 The User Interface

The user interface for the prototype consists of windows for displaying 2D digital maps and 3D synthetic environments. Each window is placed in a separate frame to allow for independent re-sizing according to the user's needs. On start-up, the user is given a map of the world, which allows selection of a user-defined area of interest (AOI) by dragging the mouse across and down the map.

Selection of an AOI causes the database to be queried. A digital map is drawn with all database features (Figure 3(a)). The user then has several options including zoom, pan, render features in 3D and identify objects. Rendering objects in 3D was left to a user decision rather than a default occurrence for performance reasons. Although the user can render all features in 3D, the user is given the choice of zooming and panning the map as a means of selecting features for 3D display. Only those features within the AOI are rendered in 3D, avoiding the unnecessary use of resources to extract unwanted feature geometry from the database.

Figures 3(b) - 5 show the 3D SE of the MOUT facility from various positions. The interface allows the user to move through the SE and into and out of buildings by use of the arrow keys. Movement can be by walking on or flying above the terrain. Drop-down menus allow the user to change speed, background texture and lighting conditions. Altering lighting conditions allows the viewer, for example, to obtain both day and night views of the 3D SE.

A feature is also provided that allows the user to track his position in the 3D SE. When activated, this feature places an icon on the map corresponding to the user's position in the 3D SE. As the user moves through the SE, the position of the icon is updated. The icon is oriented to correspond to the user's orientation in the SE.

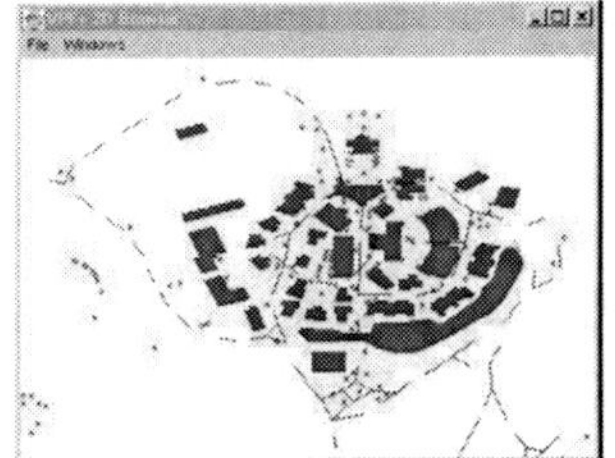

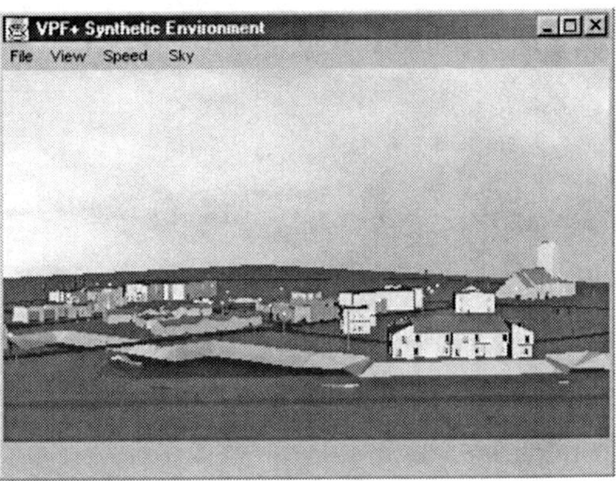

Fig. 3. From Left: (**3a**) 2D Map of the MOUT Facility. (**3b**) 3D View of the MOUT Facility from the Southwest.

6 Observations

This paper has described VPF+, a VPF-consistent data structure capable of supporting topologically consistent three-dimensional feature coverage. VPF Winged-Edge topology is insufficient to support the many topological adjacency relationships found in the 3D SE. The Non-Manifold 3D Winged-Edge Topology will support these relationships in a wide range of objects likely to be modeled in a 3D SE and provides a framework for the 3D synthetic environment generation process. VPF+ should be useful for commercial as well as the more traditional modeling and simulation applications, especially for developers who want to extend their geographic information system capability to add 3D topology.

Detailed data in the form of highly accurate representations of the interior and exterior of buildings was used in the prototype. Some SE applications do not require building interiors. For these, building exteriors with accompanying topology suffices. VPF+ topology will support these implementations as well. Continuing research into improved methods of automating the extraction of detailed 3D object geometry from satellite, aerial and panoramic imagery should be beneficial for providing detailed data over large areas, at least for building exteriors. On smaller areas, digitizers can be used to re-construct building interiors from building plans or CAD data can be imported. Where building plans are not available or where more rapid development is required, further work can concentrate on developing tools to project the interior layout of buildings based on photo-imagery, the building use and a basic material composition description, i.e. steel, brick, frame. This type of description should be easily obtainable.

Acknowledgments. The National Imagery and Mapping Agency and the U.S. Marine Corps Warfighting Lab sponsored this work.

Fig. 4. Street View of the MOUT Facility Looking North.

Fig. 5. View of the M OUT Facility from the West.

References

[Abdelguerfi 98] Mahdi Abdelguerfi, Roy Ladner, Kevin B. Shaw, Miyi Chung, Ruth Wilson, *VPF+: A Vector Product Format Extension Suitable for Three-Dimensional Modeling and Simulation,* tech. report NRL/FR/7441-98-9683, Naval Research Laboratory, Stennis Space Center, Miss., 1998.

[GIDB] Digital Mapping, Charting, and Geodesy Analysis Program Web site provides additional information about the Naval Research Laboratory's Geographic Information Database, http://dmap.nrlssc.navy.mil/dmap (current 16 May 2001).

[Gursoz 90] E. Levent Gursoz, Y. Choi, F. B. Prinz, "Vertex-based Representation of Non-Manifold Boundaries" in *Geometric Modeling for Product Engineering*, M.J. Wozny, J.U. Turner and K. Preiss (Editors), Elsevier Science Publishers, 1990, pp. 107-131.

[Ladner 2000] Roy Ladner, Mahdi Abdelguerfi, Kevin Shaw, *3D Mapping of an Interactive Synthetic Environment*, Computer, Vol. 33, No. 3, March 2000, pp. 35-39.

[Lienhardt 91] Pascal Lienhardt, *Topological models for boundary representation: a comparison with n-dimensional generalized maps*, Computer Aided Design, Vol. 23, No. 1, January 1991, pp. 59-82.

[O'Rourke 95] Joseph O'Rourke, *Computational Geometry in C*, Cambridge University Press, 1995, pp. 114-115.

[Spatial 96] Spatial Technology, Inc., *Format Manual*, 2425 55th Street, Building A, Boulder, CO 80301, 1996.

[Trott 96] Kevin Trott, *Analysis of Digital Topographic Data Issues in Support of Synthetic Environment Terrain Data Base Generation*, TEC-0091, U.S. Army Corps of Engineers, Topographic Engineering Center, November 1996.

[VPF 96] Department of Defense, *Interface Standard for Vector Product Forma*, MIL-STD 2407, 28 June 1996.

[Weiler 86] K.J. Weiler, *Topological Structures for Geometric Modeling*, PhD thesis, Rensselaer Polytechnic Institute, Troy, NY 1986.

GOLAP – Geographical Online Analytical Processing

Petr Mikšovský and Zdeněk Kouba

The Gerstner Laboratory for Intelligent Decision Making and Control
Faculty of Electrical Engineering
Czech Technical University
Technická 2, 166 27 Prague 6, Czech Republic
Phone: +420-2-24357666, Fax: +420-2-24357224,
{miksovsp, kouba}@labe.felk.cvut.cz

Abstract. Current geographical information systems (GIS) handle large amounts of geographical data stored usually in relational databases. Database vendors developed special database plug-ins in order to make retrieval of geographical data more efficient. Basically, they implement spatial indexing techniques aimed at speeding-up spatial query processing. This approach is suitable for those spatial queries, which select objects in certain user-defined area. Similarly as on-line transaction processing (OLTP) systems evolved into on-line analytical processing (OLAP) systems for supporting more complicated analytical tasks, similar evolution can be expected in the context of geographical information analytical processing. This paper describes the GOLAP system consisting of a commercial OLAP system enriched with a spatial index. Experiments comparing efficiency of original OLAP and the extended one are presented.

1. Introduction

OLAP systems are used mainly in such applications where it is possible to estimate the set of possible user's queries ahead. In such a case it is possible to calculate selected data aggregates in advance. The data warehouse then uses above-mentioned pre-calculated data aggregates instead of calculating everything from scratch.

Geographical Information Systems (GIS) do processing of spatial queries. As the evaluation of spatial queries is very expensive from the computational point of view, making use of pre-calculated spatial data aggregates would be appreciated. The approach of integrating the GIS with a data warehouse was presented on DEXA 2000 [3]. That work was restricted to situations, when the definition of geographical areas is stable like in case of administrative areas for example. In that case it is possible to pre-calculate data aggregates corresponding to those areas and store them in a data warehouse. Respective spatial queries asked to the GIS in the future are then translated to OLAP queries. It can be expected that in practical cases the response to an OLAP query will be much faster than the response to a corresponding spatial

H.C. Mayr et al. (Eds.): DEXA 2001, LNCS 2113, pp. 442–449, 2001.

query. However, let us imagine that we need to determine the average income of people living, for example, in the area with a diameter of 5 km around a city. It is an expensive task not only because of the huge number of arithmetic calculations, but also because of the complicated selection of appropriate objects (houses), which need to be taken into account. In the case of similar ad-hoc spatial queries such an approach does not help that much.

This paper describes a new approach, which is based on the idea of building-up the hierarchical structure of the geographical dimension of a data warehouse according to a spatial index having been constructed for a given population of GIS objects in a map. A prototype of a GOLAP (Geographical On-Line Analytical Processing) system implementing this idea has been developed. The efficiency of such a solution has been explored in a series of experiments.

2. GOLAP Components

The GOLAP system represents natural embedding of a spatial index into a commercial OLAP system. The prototype implementation makes use of the Microsoft SQL Server's Analytical Services. However, it is not restricted on this single OLAP system. Both the idea and the developed software creating spatial indices can be easily adapted to any other data warehouse platform. The following paragraphs describe briefly both the OLAP and the spatial index components, which are exploited by the system.

2.1 OLAP - Online Analytical Processing

Data warehouses are aimed at providing very fast responses to user queries. Usually, the OLAP layer of the data warehouse architecture [4] generates these queries. The data model of a data warehouse is designed to support fast evaluation of very complicated multi-dimensional queries. Considering define the following toy example for explaining the basic concepts of data warehouse modelling.

Let us consider an imaginary grocery chain consisting of nine supermarkets located in three districts in Bohemia. The districts are *Eastern Bohemia*, *Central Bohemia,* and *Western Bohemia*. Let the data warehouse store the data on turnover of particular supermarkets.

The data warehouse structure is represented by a cube, dimensions (axes) of which are *time*, *assortment*, and *location*. Every elementary cell of the cube contains a real number identifying the turnover achieved by the corresponding supermarket (position along the *location* axis) in the respective time slot (position along the *time* axis), and particular assortment item (position along the *assortment* axis). This number is called *fact*, *measure,* or *metric*. Let us choose the term *fact* to avoid ambiguity.

Data in an OLAP system are usually read-only for all users in order to minimise the overhead of a multiple access control. The content is updated in batches in predefined time periods by an ETL (Extraction, Transformation and Load) process. This is the only way how to modify the data stored in a data warehouse. The ETL process extracts data from data sources, transforms it to a multidimensional structure and preferably creates suitable pre-calculated aggregations.

2.2 Spatial Indexing

Generally, spatial data queries are very complex and their evaluation is time consuming. There are some supporting mechanisms, typically based on indexing techniques, which can speed-up spatial query evaluation. There are at least two spatial indexing techniques used frequently in commercial systems: *quad-trees* (e.g. Oracle8 Spatial Cartridge) and R-*trees* (e.g. Informix Spatial DataBlade). The GOLAP system currently makes use of R-trees, therefore a brief description of this technique follows.

R-tree [1] and its derivatives are spatial data structures devoted to indexing of more general objects than single points. In principle, an *R-tree* is a simple modification of a *B-tree*, where the leaf records contain pointers to data objects representing spatial objects. The important feature is that an *R-tree* node is implemented as a page in an external memory.

The indexing of spatial objects itself is given by a pair $< I, Id >$ (so called index records), where *I* is the minimal bounding hyper-cube (MBH) of the particular spatial object. Every MBH has basically the form of a tuple $(I_0, I_1, \ldots, I_n)$, where I_i is an interval $[a_i, b_i]$ describing lower and upper bounds along the dimension *i*.

The non-leaf nodes contain records (*I*, *pointer*). The *pointer* refers to such a sub-tree, which contains the nodes corresponding to all MBHs covered by the MBH *I*.

The *R-tree* is given an order (m, m_1), where *m* is the minimal number of edges leaving a node, whereas m_1 is the maximal one. It means that MBHs are constructed in such a way, that the number of edges leading from the corresponding node is at least m_1 but *m* as maximum. The MBHs may be overlapping. Figure 1 shows construction of an *R-tree* of the order *(2,3)*.

If the number of spatial objects is *E*, the depth of an *m*-ary *R-tree* is $\lceil \log_m E \rceil - 1$ in the worst case.

The *R-tree* is a dynamic data structure based on page splitting (in case of INSERT) and/or on page merging (in case of DELETE). In contrast to *B-trees* the search in an *R-tree* does not follow a single path, as the MBHs may be overlapping. It means that there may be several possibilities how to go on from a given node when searching an object.

There are many heuristics used for *R-tree* optimising. Basically, there is a tendency to separate MBHs as much as possible.

In principal the INSERT operation is very important for maintaining the *R-tree* to sustain its efficiency. The basic strategy of the algorithm implementing the INSERT operation is to find such a leaf in the tree, for which inserting an index record will invoke a minimum of nodes on the path from the leaf to the root requiring an update. The *R-tree* efficiency is very sensitive on the node splitting method.

The splitting procedure solves the problem how to partition an unordered set of index records. The idea is to minimise the probability, that both nodes will need to be investigated during a search. Therefore the volume of each MBH corresponding to the two nodes after splitting should be minimal. The complexity of the algorithm providing us with globally optimal solution is exponential. In practice, sub-optimal algorithms with linear or quadratic complexity [2] are used.

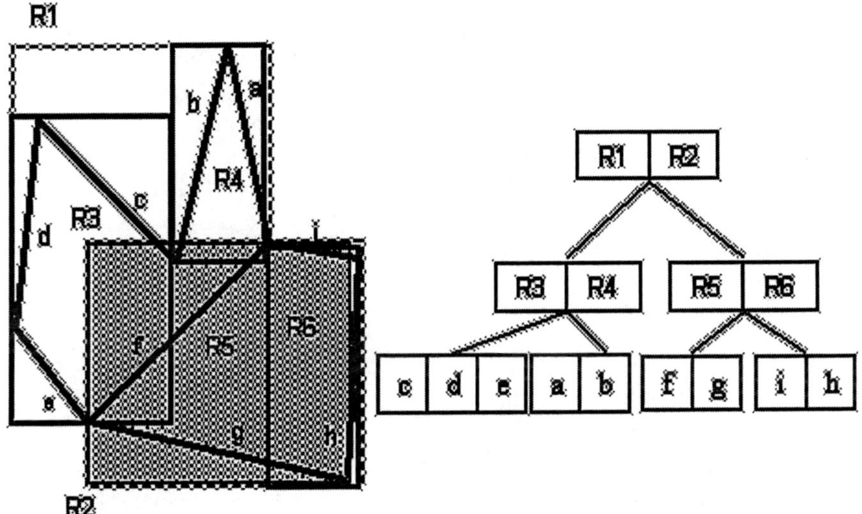

Fig. 1. Construction of an R-tree

3. GOLAP Architecture

The GOLAP system in fact consists of two parts: a *spatial index builder* and a *query evaluator*. The first of them (the *spatial index builder*) is responsible for building an R-tree for the given set of geographical objects. The index is a tree. Its leafs correspond to individual geographical objects, whereas the non-leaf nodes correspond to the respective MBHs. Only the ETL process uses the *spatial index builder* during the data warehouse creation/update. It creates an R-tree, which is then used as a template for definition of the geographical dimension of the data warehouse.

The second part (the *query evaluator*) is the user interface enabling the user to select an ad-hoc area to be analysed. The *query evaluator* selects a set of MBRs and single objects covering the explored area. Then it assembles the corresponding OLAP query and sends it to the OLAP engine.

4. Experimental Results

Currently, first series of experiments have been carried out. Basically, the results of these experiments confirmed our expectations concerning the comparison of a conventional OLAP and the GOLAP performance. The experiments were carried out on 2xPIII 866MHz, 256MB RAM workstation running MS Windows 2000 and MS SQL Server 2000 with Analytical Services.

Two random geographical data sets were generated. Both of them consisted of 100000 GIS objects distributed in a grid 10000x10000 points. One of them was based on a uniform geographical distribution, the other on a 2-dimensional normal (Gaussian) one. It simulates a more realistic distribution of objects in a geographical information system. The procedure generating the second data set started by a random selection of 100 centres ("cities"). Then 1000 GIS objects with a 2-dimensional normal distribution were generated around each of them.

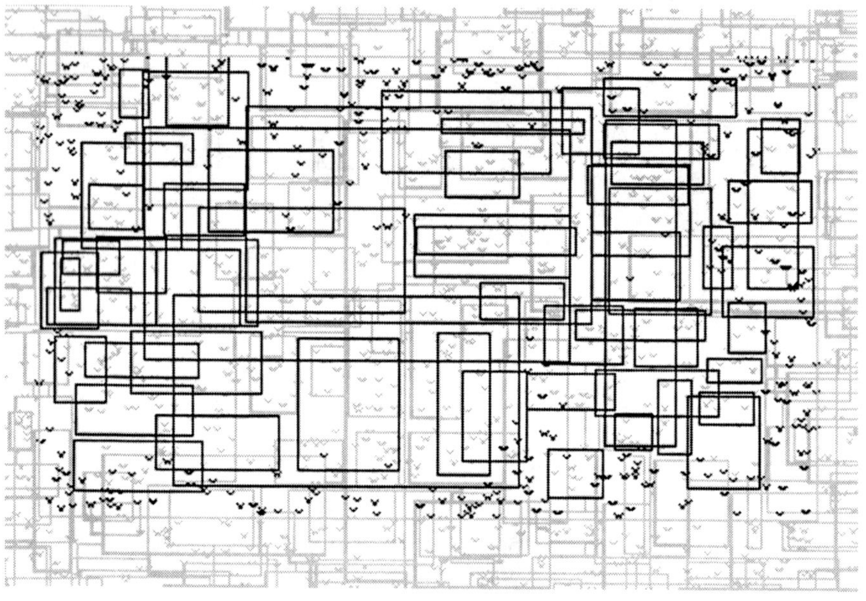

Fig. 2. Data set No. 1 - uniform distribution of GIS objects

The multidimensional schema used for experiments was simple. It included only one fact table and the geographical dimension. The fact table contained a single fact expressing the count of GIS objects in the respective area. The geographical dimension was constructed using the spatial index. An aggregation level is introduced to the geographical dimension for every level of nodes in the *R-tree*. Thus, a pre-calculated data aggregate can be stored in the data warehouse for each node (i.e. MBH) of the *R-tree*.

The spatial analysis capabilities of a conventional OLAP system are restricted to a simple filtering expressed in terms of SQL-based multidimensional queries (i.e.

Microsoft MDX in our case). On the other hand, the GOLAP is capable to analyse areas having a shape of a generic polygon. As the authors wanted to prove that the GOLAP is really useful, they choose a pessimistic strategy. It means that the experimental analysis was carried out on rectangular areas rather than on generic polygons. The reason is not the effort to reduce the expensive evaluation of polygons when using the spatial index, but defining fair conditions for comparing the response times of both systems. Even if this strategy degraded the capabilities of the GOLAP system and increased the "chance" of the conventional OLAP, the results are encouraging.

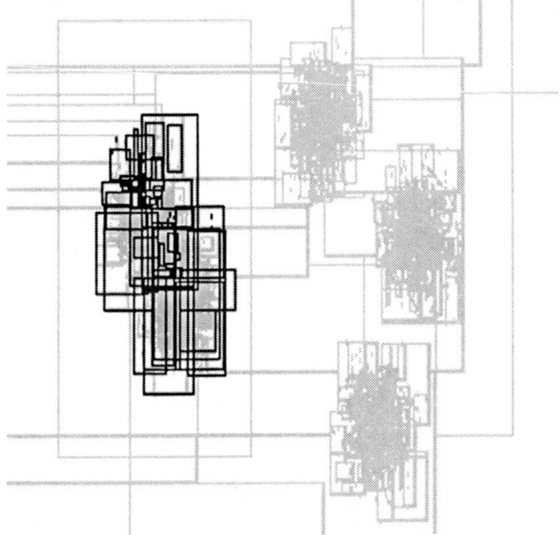

Fig. 3. Data set No. 2 - Gaussian distribution of GIS objects

For each data set areas of two sizes were analysed. The smaller one was a square of 1000 x 1000 points representing 1% of the whole grid. The bigger one was a square of 5000 x 5000 points representing 25% of the whole grid. For every data set and every size of the explored area 20 runs were carried out. The explored area was located in various positions (around the centres of clusters in case of the Gaussian distribution) in particular runs. The mean values over all 20 runs of both the response time and the number of GIS objects in the explored area are introduced in the Table 1.

Figure 2 and Figure 3 show results provided by the *query evaluator* module. Black rectangles represent those MBHs of the spatial index, which are fully contained in the explored area. The black points represent those GIS objects, which are contained in the explored area, but the MBHs covering them are not fully contained in it. These black rectangles and points correspond to data aggregates evaluated by the OLAP component of the GOLAP system.

In the case of direct evaluation by the conventional OLAP, all GIS objects (i.e. all the black and grey points in the figures) have to be evaluated. The ratio of the number of black rectangles and points to the number of all points determines the efficiency of the GOLAP.

Table 1. Experimental results

Area size [points]	Dataset	Objects	GOLAP		OLAP	Acceleration [%]
			R-tree objects	Avg. response time [s]	Avg. response time [s]	
1000x1000	unif.	1223	427	3.50	13.78	**393.7**
	gauss	1998	60	0.51	13.11	**2570.6**
5000x5000	unif	24852	2416	33.67	14.23	42.3
	gauss	21705	647	8.49	15.43	**181.7**

5. Conclusion

The paper describes a geographical extension of a conventional OLAP system capable to evaluate facts for ad-hoc defined areas. Without such an extension is the conventional OLAP applicable only for on-line analysis of pre-defined areas.

The solution is based on embedding a spatial index into multi-dimensional structure and exploiting such an index for evaluating complex spatial analytical queries. The prototype implementation called GOLAP has been developed. First series of experiments demonstrated that the proposed solution is useful. According to their results the GOLAP is 2 to 25 times faster than a conventional OLAP.

The GOLAP efficiency depends on the number of objects in the explored area, whereas the response time of the conventional OLAP system is roughly independent on it. The explanation is straightforward. The conventional OLAP system determines the target data aggregate corresponding to the explored area by accessing every single GIS object and testing if it belongs to the area. On the other hand the GOLAP calculates the result using the set of necessary data aggregates identified by the spatial index. Then it accesses the data warehouse only to retrieve those data aggregates without any filtering overheads.

It is obvious from the Table 1 that there exist situations when the conventional OLAP is faster than GOLAP (see 42% acceleration for the explored area of 25% of the whole map). The experiments support a conjecture that GOLAP's efficiency corresponds to the ratio *S/T*, where *S* is the number of GIS object in the explored area and *T* is the total number of them. Next research will be focused on more detailed analysis of this dependence. It will be aimed at finding the critical value of that ratio, when the conventional OLAP behaves better than GOLAP. We assume that the size of the explored area does not exceed 10% of the whole map in practical geographical analysis. As the critical value of the above-mentioned ratio seems to be far above the values used in practical analytical queries, we believe that GOLAP will be very efficient in praxis.

Another topic of next research is further optimising the OLAP queries generated by the spatial index. This optimisation will help to move the critical value even higher.

Acknowledgement. The work related to this paper has been carried out with support of the INCO-COPERNICUS No. 977091 research project *GOAL – Geographical Information On-line Analysis.* The authors want to express thanks to their colleagues from the *Gerstner Laboratory for Intelligent Decision Making and Control* for creating a friendly environment and to Jaroslav Pokorný for his excellent tutorial on spatial indexing techniques [5].

References

[1] Guttman, A.: *R-trees: a dynamic index structure for spatial indexing,* Proc. of SIGMOD Int. Conf. on Management of Data, 1984, pp. 47-54

[2] Gavrila, D.M.: *R-tree Index Optimization*, CAR-TR-718, Comp. Vision Laboratory Center for Automation Research, University of Maryland, 1994

[3] Kouba Z., Matoušek K., Mikšovský P.: *On Data Warehouse and GIS Integration,* In: Proceedings of the 11. International Conference on Database and Expert Systems Applications (DEXA 2000), Ibrahim, M. and Küng, J. and Revell, N. (Eds.), Lecture Notes in Computer Science (LNCS 1873), Springer, Germany

[4] Kurz A.: *Data Warehousing – Enabling Technology*, (in German), MITP-Verlag GmBH, Bonn, 1999, ISBN 3-8266-4045-4

[5] Pokorný J.:*Prostorové datové struktury a jejich použití k indexaci prostorových objektů (Spatial Data Structures and their Application for Spatial Object Indexing*), in Czech, GIS Ostrava 2000, Technical University Ostrava, Ostrava, Czech Republic, 2000, pp.146 –160

Declustering Spatial Objects by Clustering for Parallel Disks

Hak-Cheol Kim and Ki-Joune Li

Dept of Computer Science, Pusan National University, Korea
hckim@quantos.cs.pusan.ac.kr, lik@hyowon.pusan.ac.kr

Abstract. In this paper, we propose an efficient declustering algorithm which is adaptable in different data distribution. Previous declustering algorithms have a potential drawback by assuming data distribution is uniform. However, our method shows a good declustering performance for spatial data regardless of data distribution by taking it into consideration. First, we apply a spatial clustering algorithm to find the distribution in the underlying data and then allocate a disk page to each unit of cluster. Second, we analyize the effect of outliers on the performance of declustering algorithm and propose to handle them separately. Experimental results show that these approaches outperform traditional declustering algorithms based on tiling and mapping function such as DM, FX, HCAM and Golden Ratio Sequence.

1 Introduction

Spatial database systems, such as geographic information systems, CAD systems, etc., store and handle a massive amount of data. As a result, frequent disk accesses become a bottleneck of the overall performance of system. We can solve this problem by partitioning data onto multiple parallel disks and accessing them in parallel. This problem is referred to as declustering. For parallel disk accesses, we divide the entire data set into groups by the unit of disk page and assign a disk number so that partitioned groups should be accessed at the same time by a query.

Up to now, several declustering methods have been proposed. Most of them partition a data space into several disjoint tiles and match them with a disk number using mapping function[1,2,4,14,16]. They focussed only on an efficient mapping function from a partitioned tile to a disk number on the assumption that data is uniformly distributed. Therefore their methods, though give a good performance for uniform data, show a drop in efficiency for skewed data.

To be effective for a skewed data, a declustering algorithm must be reflected of the distribution in the underlying data. We can apply two approaches, parametric and nonparametric methods, to discover distribution. By the parametric method, we assume a parametric model such as normal distribution, gamma distribution, etc. However, we cannot adopt this approach because most of the real data distributions do not agree with these distribution models. Another approach, non-parametric methods, makes no assumption about distribution.

H.C. Mayr et al. (Eds.): DEXA 2001, LNCS 2113, pp. 450–459, 2001.

Several methods such as kernal estimation, histogram, wavelet and clustering methods belong to this category. Among these methods, we apply a spatial clustering method called SMTin[6] to detect data distribution.

By applying a spatial clustering method, our method is more flexible with the distribution than tiled partitioning methods and results in a high storage utilization and a low disk access rate. In addition to this contribution, we analyze the effect of outliers on the performance of declustering algorithm and propose a simple and efficient method to control them.

This paper is organized as follows. In section 2, we present related works and their problems and propose a new declustering algorithm in section 3. In section 4, we show the effects of outliers on the performance of declusteirng algorithm and our solutions. We show experimental results in section 5 and conclude this paper in section 6.

2 Background and Motivation

Since the performance of a spatial database system is more affected by the I/O cost than CPU cost, a great deal of efforts have been done to partition data onto multiple parallel disks and access those objects qualifying query condition simultaneously. Traditionaly this problem is called as declustering, which consists of the following two steps.

- step 1: grouping data set by the unit of disk page size
- step 2: distributing each group of data onto multiple disks

When we distribute objects onto multiple parallel disks, the response time of query q is determined as follows.

Definition 1. *Let M be the number of disks, then the number of disk accesses to process query q is*

$$DA_q = \max_{i=1}^{M}(DA_q(i)),\ \textit{where } DA_q(i) \textit{ is the number of i-th disk accesses}$$

Based on definition 1, Moon and Saltz defined the condition of the strict optimality of declustering algorithm[13].

Definition 2. Strictly Optimal Declustering
Let M be the number of disks, $DA_q(i)$ is the number of i-th disk accesses for a query q, then declustering method is strictly optimal if

$$\forall q,\ DA_q = \lceil \tfrac{N_q}{M} \rceil, where\ \ N_q = \textstyle\sum_{i=1}^{M} DA_q(i)$$

Previously proposed declustering methods tile a data space and assign disk number to each tile based on a certain mapping function. Disk Modulo(DM)[1], Field-wise Xor(FX)[2] and Hilbert Curve Allocation Method(HCAM)[4] use this scheme. Among these methods, Hilbert Curve Allocation Method proposed by C. Faloutsos and P. Bhagwat has been known to outperforms others[4]. Moon and Saltz proved that the scalability of DM and FX is limited to some degree. They proved that the scalability of DM is bounded by the query side and the scalability of FX is at best 25 percents by doubling the number of disks. For more details, see [13].

Recently, Bhatia and Sinha proposed a new declustering algorithm based on Golden Ratio Sequences[16]. Their analytical model and experimental results show that GRS outperforms not only traditional tile-based declustering methods such as DM, FX, HCAM, but also cyclic allocation method[14], which is a generalization of DM.

Most of these declustering methods are known to be not strictly optimal without some assumptions[1,2,4,8,14,16] and try only to find an optimal way in allocating each tile onto parallel disks on the assumption that data is uniformly distributed. However, they ignore the effects of a good grouping method on increasing the storage utilization for step 1. It is obvious that the maximum number of page accesses per disk grows as the total number of disk page occupied by objects increases. As a result, we might access more disk pages without a good grouping method.

In addition to this drawback, they did not consider outliers having an effect on the performance of declustering algorithm. We will explain its effects more closely in section 4.

3 Declustering Skewed Dataset

In section 2, we showed that previously proposed declustering algorithms have potential weakness by assuming uniform data distribution. we will show it in detail and propose a new declustering algorithm in this section.

3.1 Skewed Data and Declustering

First, we will describe how the performance of a tiling algorithm can be affected by data distribution. When the number of objects in a certain densed tile exceeds the disk page capacity, all the tiles must be split though they contain small number of objects that can fit into one disk page. This results in a low storage utilization and a poor performance in comparison with uniform data even if the same mapping function is used. We investigate this problem in the rest of this subsection in detail. Table 1 shows notations and their meanings to be used from now on.

Lemma 1. *When we apply the same tiling scheme, the number of total disk pages occupied by skewed data is more than that of uniform data.*

Proof. Let n_i be the number of objects in the *i-th* tile occupied by skewed data. Then $\sum_{i=1}^{T_s} n_i = N$. Since the distribution of data is skewed, $\min_{i=1}^{T_s}(n_i) < \max_{i=1}^{T_s}(n_i) = Bf_{max}$ and $\mathrm{avg}_{i=1}^{T_s}(n_i) = N/T_s < Bf_{max}$. For uniform data, the number of objects in a tile is N/T_u and if the storage utilization is maximum, the number of objects in a tile is Bf_{max}. It means that $N/T_u = Bf_{max}$. Therefore $N/T_s < N/T_u$ that is $T_s > T_u$. ■

Table 1. Notations and their meanings

Notation	Meaning
N	number of spatial objects in 2-D space
T_u, T_s	total number of tiles(disk pages) occupied by uniform data and skew data respectively
Bf_{max}	maximum disk blocking factor
d_u, d_s	density of uniform data and skewed data respectively
a_u, a_s	area of one tile for uniform data and skewed data respectively

Lemma 2. *For a given query q, Let $T_u(q)$ and $T_s(q)$ be the number of disk page accesses to process query q for uniform data and skewed data respectively. Then,*

$$T_u(q) < T_s(q)$$

Proof. We normalize the data space as $[0, 1]^2$. For completely uniform data, the number of disk pages T_u and the area of a tile are given as follows.

$$T_u = \frac{N}{Bf_{max}} \tag{1}$$

$$a_u = \frac{1}{T_u} = \frac{Bf_{max}}{N} \tag{2}$$

Since there are Bf_{max} objects in a tile, we obtain the following equation

$$d_u \cdot a_u = Bf_{max}, \qquad a_u = \frac{Bf_{max}}{d_u} \tag{3}$$

For skewed data, the number of objects contained in a tile is variable. We get the following equation for skewed data.

$$\max(d_s) \cdot a_s = Bf_{max}, \qquad a_s = \frac{Bf_{max}}{\max(d_s)} \tag{4}$$

It is evident that $d_u < \max(d_s)$, since $\max(d_s)$ is the maximum density of skewed data. Therefore we derive the following inequality from equation 3, 4.

$$a_s < a_u \tag{5}$$

For a query q whose area is A(q), the number of tiles contained by q for the uniform data, $T_u(q)$ and skewed data $T_s(q)$ are given as

$$T_u(q) = \frac{A(q)}{a_u}, \qquad T_s(q) = \frac{A(q)}{a_s} \tag{6}$$

From equation 5 and 6, we know that the number of tiles for the skewed data qualifying the same query condition is larger than that of uniform data, since $a_s < a_u$. ∎

From lemma 1 and 2, we come to a conclusion that tiling methods for skewed data cannot satisfy the strict optimality condition of defintion 2.

Theorem 1. *Suppose that $DA_u(q)$ and $DA_s(q)$ are the maximum number of page accesses per disk for uniform and skewed data to process query q respectively. Then,*

$$DA_u(q) < DA_s(q)$$

Proof. Let M be the number of disks and assume an optimal declustering algorithm. Then, the number of page accesses per disk for uniform data and skewed data to process query q is given as follows.

$$DA_u(q) = \lceil \frac{T_u(q)}{M} \rceil, \qquad DA_s(q) = \lceil \frac{T_s(q)}{M} \rceil$$

Since $T_u(q) < T_s(q)$, $DA_u(q) < DA_s(q)$. ■

This means that the number of tiles(disk pages), in other words storage utilization, is an important factor in declustering method in case of skewed data. In fact, we found a significant difference between T_s and T_u depending on data and the degree of skewedness from experiments.

These observations lead to a conclusion that it is very important to partition spatial objects in a way that reduces the number of tiles, in addition to find a good mapping function for allocating each tile to a disk number. We will focus on methods to improve the storage utilization in the next subsection.

3.2 An Efficient Declustering Method for Skewed Data

In this subsection, we propose a new declustering algorithm which is flexible to the distribution of data and results in a small number of pages in comparision with precedent declustering algorithms. The proposed algorithm is composed of the following three steps.

Step 1. Find Data Distribution
In this paper, we apply a spatial clustering algorithm to find the distribution of data. Up to now, several spatial clustering methods have been introduced[5,6, 9,10]. Among them, we apply SMTin as a spatial clustering algorithm. SMTin initially constructs delaunay triangulations for point set and extracts clusters from triangles whose distance is within a predefined threshold value. We can find the distribution in the underlying N objects by the time complexity of $O(N \log N)$. For more details, see [6].

Step 2. Split Overflow Clusters
After clustering step, there may be clusters whose number of elements exceeds disk page capacity. These clusters must be partitioned into several sub-clusters so that each of which can fit into one disk page. we applied an efficient partitioning method called STR proposed by Leutenegger, et al.[7] to split these clusters.

Step 3. Distribute Clusters onto Disk Page
After adjusting all of clusters so as to fit into one disk page, we calculate the center of minimum bounding rectangle enclosing cluster, sort them by the hilbert value of their center and then assign a disk number in a round robin fashion.

4 Outliers and Declustering

In data analysis, data with large dissimilarity with others may deteriorate result. Many researches have been done about these data called outlier in data mining area and various definitions of outlier have been made in the literature[11,12, 15]. But we give a differenct definition of outlier, which is based on SMTin as follows.

Definition 3. Outliers with Cluster Construction Threshold Value
Let CCT_{cs} be a cluster construction threshold value and $C_1, C_2, \ldots, C_n$ be clusters by the CCT_{cs}, then any object O' satisfying the following condition is outlier:

$$\forall O \in C_i, 1 \leq i \leq n, dist(O, O') > CCT_{cs}$$

In fact, we can control the number of outliers by means of CCT_{cs}. We will explain the effects of outliers and our solutions in the following subsections.

4.1 The Effect of Outliers on the Declustering

First, we illustrate the problems of outliers. After finding an initial cluster set, there can be some objects not included in any clusters depending on an initial cluster construction threshold value. We have to increase cluster construction threshold value to include them and the shape of cluster may be degenerated and minumum bounding rectangle enclosing cluster may be extended unnecessarily.

Another problem is that these clusters whose size is extremely smaller than maximum page size result in a low storage utilization. Although they may be regarded as a cluster, it is desirable to treat them as outliers.

4.2 An Efficient Method for Skewed Data with Outliers

In previous subsection, we showed that outliers may degenerate the performance and must be carefully treated. We may apply two approaches to handle them. The simplest approach is including them in the nearest cluster by force. Another solution is to regard outlier as a cluster whose size is extermely small and assign one disk page for it. However, these solutions result in a low storage utilization and a high disk access rate.

We propose to keep the outliers on an extra main-memory buffer. As outlier buffer size has a limitation, we keep a part of outliers in buffer and include the remained outliers in the nearest cluster by force. Figure 1 shows our proposed declustering algorithm.

```
Algorithm DC (Declustering Clusters to parallel disks)
Input P: set of points {p1,p2,...,pn}, M: number of disks available
      Bf_out: capacity of outlier buffer, Bf: disk blocking factor
      CCT_cs: cluster construction threshold value
Output {Ci,di} //Ci: i-th cluster, di: disk number assigned to Ci
Begin Algorithm
    C ← {};
    Construct initial clusters by CCT_cs;
    While (Card(outlier) > Bf_out)
        adjust CCT_cs;
        reconstruct clusters;
    End while
    For each cluster Si
        If Card(Si) > Bf
            {Si1,Si2,...,Sik } ← SplitCluster(Si, Bf);
            C ← C ∪ {Si1,Si2,...,Sik};
        End If
        Else
            C ← C ∪ {Si};
        End Else
    End For
    For each element Ci in C
        (xi,yi) ← center of cluster Ci;
        di ← H(xi,yi) mod M; // H(x,y) is Hilbert value of (x,y)
    End For
End Algorithm
```

Fig. 1. Description of Declustering by Clustering(DC) algorithm

5 Performance Evaluation

We performed several experiments to compare our method with previously proposed declustering algorithms. To do this, we generated synthetic skewed data to analyze the effect of data distribution on the performance of declustering. We also prepared two real data set extracted from the maps of Long Beach County and Seoul city. Figure 2 shows their distribution. For query set we generated two types of queries, which is uniformly distributed in data space and concentrated on a data area, and whose size is 0.1×0.1(small query) and 0.5×0.5(large query) of data space whose size is $[0,1]^2$.

Storage Utilization

We explained that the number of total disk pages has an effect on the performance. We found that tiling method occupy more disk pages than our proposed method. In detail, it occupy 1.6~3.7 times more disk pages than declustering

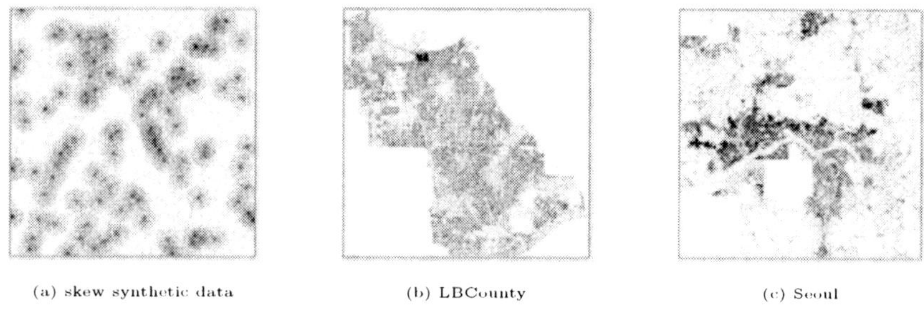
(a) skew synthetic data (b) LBCounty (c) Seoul

Fig. 2. Test data distribution

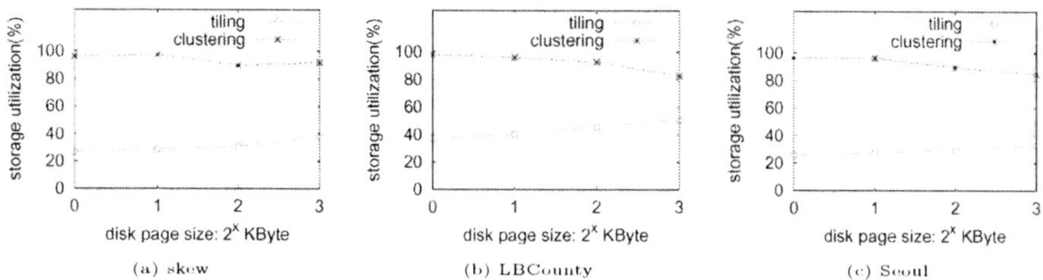

(a) skew (b) LBCounty (c) Seoul

Fig. 3. Storage utilization of tiling and clustered partition(outlier buffer is 1 KB)

by clustering algorithm. Figure 3 shows the storage utilization of tiling method and DC. It shows that tiling method is far from being optimal allocation but our method is nearly optimal as far as a storage utilization is concerned.

Scalability

We compared our algorithm only with Golden Ratio Sequence(GRS)[16] since it is known to be the best among tiling methods. Figure 4 shows the result of experiments. We see that our method gives a good performance regardless of data distribution and query size. Especially, when the number of disks is small and query size is large, enhancement of our method over GRS is significant. When query size is 25% of data space and the number of disks is 8, the declustering method by Golden Ratio Sequence accesses about 8 times more disk pages than DC for Seoul data. However, the performance improvement ratio over GRS become lower as the number of available disks increases.

We carried out a similar experiment with a set of queries concentrated on a downtown area rather than uniformly distributed. It is more realistic environment of experiment since queries tend to be located on specific regions. The experiment however shows very similar results with that of uniformly distributed queries.

The Effect of Outliers

We carried out an experiment to reveal the effects of outliers on the performance of declustering algorithm. If the size of outlier buffer is small, a cluster

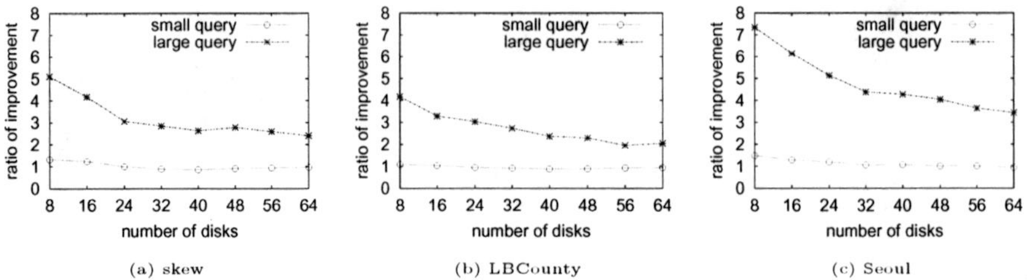

Fig. 4. Performance enhancement ratio of DC over GRS for uniformly distributed queries, where disk page size is 4 KByte and outlier buffer is 1KByte

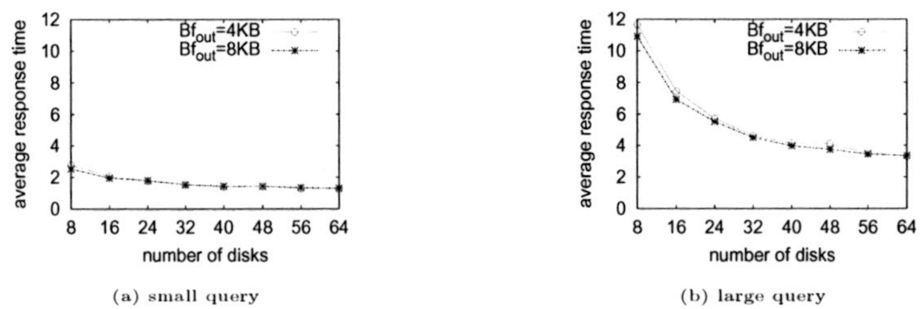

Fig. 5. Average response time by an outlier buffer size: disk page size is 1KByte

construction threshold value becomes large and the minimum bounding rectangle enclosing a cluster must be extended to include outliers. We found that the effect of outlier buffer is affected by a data distribution. It is of no use to increase outlier buffer exceeding a certain value which is related to the data distribution.

Figure 5 shows the effect of a outlier buffer on the performance of the proposed declustering algorithm for Seoul data. We gain more performance enhancement, though its effectiveness is trivial, by increasing the size of outlier buffer.

6 Conclusion

In this paper, we proposed a new declustering method for spatial objects. We investigated the effect of data distribution on the performance of declustering algorithm and showed that previously presented algorithms do not give a good performance for skewed and real data. We reviewed the definition of strict optimality proposed by Moon and Saltz and showed that tiling algorithms cannot be strictly optimal for skewed data.

Before declustering spatial objects onto multiple disks, we apply a spatial clustering algorithm to discover the data distribution. By doing so, our method is more flexible to the data distribution than tiling methods. In addition to this contribution, we showed the effects of outlier on the performance of declustering algorithm and proposed to store them separately.

Experimental results show that our method gives a high storage utilization and low disk access rate regardless of data distribution and query distribution.

Currently our works are limited to a static data set. In our future works, we will study on the dynamic clustering algorithm and show the effect of outliers more closely.

Acknowledgements. The author(s) wish(es) to acknowledge the financial support of the Korea Research Foundation made in the Program Year 1997.

References

1. Du, H.C., Sobolewski, J.S.: Disk Allocation for Cartisian Files on Multiple-Disk Systems. Int. J. ACM TODS, Vol. 7, No. 1, (1982) 82-102
2. Fang, M.T., Lee, R.C.T., Chang, C.C.: The Idea of De-Clustering and Its Applications. VLDB (1986) 181-188
3. Faloutsos, C., Metaxas, D.: Disk Allocation methods using error correcting codes. Int. J. IEEE Trans on Computers, Vol. 40, No. 8, (1991) 907-914
4. Faloutsos, C., Bhagwat, P.: Declustering using fractals. Parallel and Distributed Information Systems Conf (1993) 18-25
5. Zhang, T., Ramakrishnan, R., Livny, M.: BIRCH: An efficient data clustering methods for very large databases. SIGMOD (1996) 103-114
6. Kang, I.S., Kim, T.W., , Li, K.J.: A spatial data mining method by delaunay triangulation. Proc. ACM-GIS. (1997) 35-39
7. Leutenegger, S. T., Lopez, M.A., Edgington, J.M.: STR: A simple and efficient algorithm for r-tree packing. ICDE. (1997) 497-506
8. Abdel-Ghaffar, K., Abbadi, A. E.: Optimal allocation of two-dimensional data. ICDT (1997) 409-418
9. Sheikhleslami, G., Chatterjee, S., Zhang, A.:Wavecluster: A multi-resolusion clustering approach for very large spatial databases. VLDB (1998) 428-439
10. Guha, S., Rastogi, R., Shim, K.: CURE: An efficient clustering algorithms for large databases. SIGMOD (1998) 73-84
11. Knorr, E., Ng, R.: Algorithms for Mining Distance-Based Outliers in Large Datasets. VLDB (1998) 392-403
12. Barnett, V., Lewis, T.:Outliers in Statistical Data. Third Edition, John Wiley & Sons Ltd. (1998)
13. Moon, B. K., Saltz, J. H.: Scalability Analysis of Declustering Methods for Multidimensional Range Queries. Int. J. IEEE TKDE, Vol. 10, No. 2, (1998) 310-327
14. Prabhakar, S., Abdel-Ghaffar, K., El Abbadi, A.: Cyclic allocation of two-dimensional data. ICDE (1998) (94-101)
15. Ramaswamy, S., Rastogi, R., Shim, K.: Efficient Algorithms for Mining Outliers from Large Data Sets. SIGMOD (2000) (427-438)
16. Bhatia, R., Sinha, R.K., Chen, C.-M.:Declustering using golden ratio sequences. ICDE (2000) 271-280

A Retrieval Method for Real-Time Spatial Data Browsing

Yoh Shiraishi and Yuichiro Anzai

Department of Computer Science, Keio University,
223-8522, 3-14-1, Hiyoshi, Yokohama, Japan,
{siraisi, anzai}@ayu.ics.keio.ac.jp

Abstract. This paper presents a retrieval method for real-time spatial data browsing through a computer network. This method is designed based on "anytime algorithm" that improves a quality of the processing results over time. The retrieval method decomposes a region specified in a query into sub-regions and searches at each decomposed region using a spatial index. The searched data are kept as the intermediate results for the query and these results are incrementally sent to a client. Consequently, the client can incrementally browse spatial data for the query. We implemented this retrieval system using Java language and constructed a map browsing system as a sample application. Through some experiments, we discussed the effectiveness of our retrieval system.

1 Introduction

Providing spatial data such as map data and GIS data through a computer network is effective for location-oriented applications on the Internet. Especially, spatial data expressed by text data such as XML are more important in the point of view of standardization, interoperability and information integration [1]. However, it will take long response time in order to retrieve spatial data from remote databases and obtain a large quantity of spatial data via a network.

Therefore, we propose a retrieval method for real-time spatial data browsing through a computer network. Our method is inspired by "anytime algorithm" [2,3] that improves a quality of the processing results over time. It can provide spatial data incrementally to a client by controlling search and data transmission. This retrieval method executes a range query for a spatial database with a tree index such as R-tree and R*-tree, in order to collect spatial data within a region specified by a user. This method decomposes a region of the range query into sub-regions, and searches an index tree to find spatial data in each decomposed region. These searched data are kept as the intermediate results during the searching. These results are decomposed into packets and each packet is transmitted incrementally to the client.

The remainder of this paper is organized as follows. In Section 2, we mention the requirements of spatial data retrieval through a network. In Section 3, we present a retrieval method for real-time spatial data browsing. The implementation of this retrieval system is described in Section 4. In Section 5, we show

H.C. Mayr et al. (Eds.): DEXA 2001, LNCS 2113, pp. 460–469, 2001.

the experimental results and discuss the effectiveness of our retrieval method. Finally, we give conclusion in Section 6.

2 Real-Time Spatial Data Browsing through Internet

Our research aims to construct a system for browsing spatial data through a computer network. Spatial data are a large quantity of data that include various kinds of information such as map data and location attributes. However, when a user receives spatial data with large size for a query, the response time will be long. As the size of collected data is larger, data transmission time is longer. As a remote database has a larger data table, the data access cost will increase. Accordingly, spatial data browsing with real-time response is required.

In the field of artificial intelligence, "anytime algorithm" was proposed as an algorithm for problem solving under time constrained [2,3]. The algorithm improves the quality of the problem solving over time and can return some solutions whenever it is interrupted. On the other hand, "imprecise computation" was advocated in the field of real-time systems[4]. This concept is very similar to anytime algorithm. Both computational models have a monotonic improvement of the quality of the processing result, by keeping the intermediate results of the processing. There are some applications of imprecise computation[5,6]. An imprecise algorithm for image data transmission was proposed [5]. However, it cannot be applicable to text data transmission and spatial data retrieval. Also, "approximate query processing" is a query method for a real-time database based on the imprecise computation model [6]. This method gives the incremental output of the retrieval to a relational database, but applying into data retrieval via a network or spatial database systems was not discussed. Therefore, we apply "anytime algorithm" into spatial data retrieval.

3 A Retrieval Method for Spatial Data Browsing

In this paper, we regard a processing quality as the rate of collected data for spatial data retrieval and design the retrieval method that can improve the quality. The retrieval quality at time t is defined as follows:

$$q(t) = \frac{\text{the number of spatial data objects collected up to } t}{\text{the number of total data objects for the query}} \tag{1}$$

In order to improve this quality, our retrieval method keeps the intermediate results for the query and transmits these results incrementally. Our method consists of two processes: a process for search and a process for results transmission. The search process decomposes a region of a range query into sub-regions and searches a spatial index to find spatial data in each decomposed region. The transmission process decomposes the retrieval results into packets and supplies each packet to the client incrementally.

3.1 Spatial Index

We adopt R-tree[7] as a spatial index for data management. R-tree is the most popular spatial index based on the minimum bounding rectangle (MBR). The index structure is a balanced tree. Each node of the tree has some entries. An entry in a leaf node points to a data record that keeps a spatial data object and the MBR of the entry is defined as a region that covers the object. An entry in a non-leaf node points to a child of the node. The MBR of a node is calculated as a region that covers all entries of the node.

3.2 Query Expression

Finding spatial data in a region specified by a user is demanded frequently in spatial database systems and geographical information systems. Such a query is called a range query that is often used for spatial database systems. In this paper, we treat two kinds of range queries for retrieving two dimensional spatial data: a rectangle query and a circular query. A rectangle query has two ranges along each coordinate axis and has a rectangle region $R_{rect} =< x_{min}, y_{min}, x_{max}, y_{max} >$. On the other hand, a circular query is a query based on the distance between a query point and spatial data objects. The query region is represented as $R_{circle} =< x_{center}, y_{center}, radius >$. Our retrieval method collects all spatial data that overlap with a query region of these range queries.

3.3 Query Region Decomposition

Our method decomposes a region of a query into sub-regions that do not overlap one another. Namely, a query region R is expressed as a region that is covered by all disjointed regions.

$$R = r_1 \cup r_2 \cup ... \cup r_k = \bigcup_{i=1}^{k} r_i \tag{2}$$

$$\forall i, j \;\; r_i \cap r_j = \phi \;\; (i \neq j) \tag{3}$$

k is the number of decomposed regions. Each decomposed region r_i is defined by using two bounded regions: lower bounded region r_i^{lower} and upper bounded region r_i^{upper} (Fig.1).

$$r_i = \begin{cases} r_i^{upper} - r_i^{lower} & \text{for } i > 1 \\ r_i^{upper} & \text{for } i = 1 \end{cases} \tag{4}$$

$$r_i^{lower} = r_{i-1}^{upper} \tag{5}$$

These bounded regions must satisfy a condition $r_i^{lower} \subset r_i^{upper}$. Decomposed regions are ordered by the formula (5) and are kept as the ordered list *region_list*.

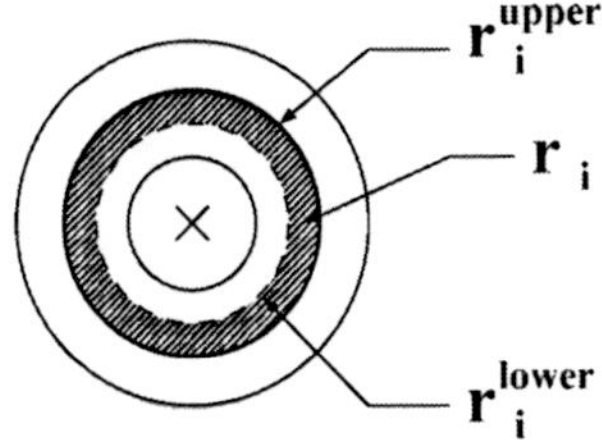

Fig. 1. Decomposing a region of a query

Since decomposed regions are searched in order of the list and the searched area is decided by r_i^{upper}, the area spreads with time.

Decomposing a query region must satisfy these conditions, but there are various kinds of ways to decompose a query region. In this paper, we use some parameters that decide how to extend the searched area. These parameters consist of the width that expresses the degree of the area enlargement and the base point of all decomposed regions (Fig.2).

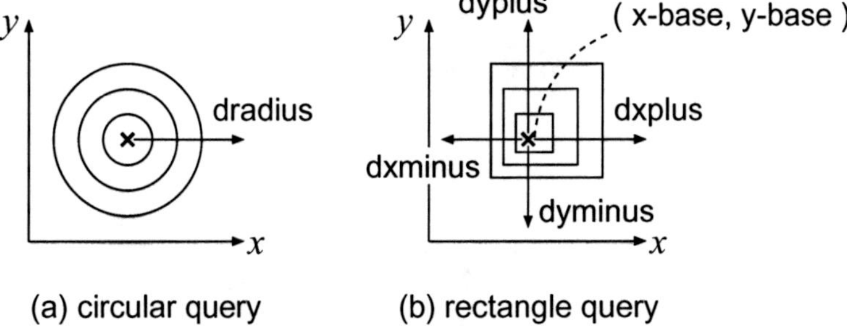

Fig. 2. The implementation of query region decomposition

A query region R_{circle} of a circular query is decomposed into sub-regions as shown in Fig.2 (a). d_{radius} decides the rate to extend a radius of decomposed regions. In this case, the base point is the center of the circle (x_{center}, y_{center}). The upper bounded region r_i^{upper} is calculated as follows:

$$r_i^{upper} = \begin{cases} < x_{center}, y_{center}, d_{radius} \times i > \text{for } 1 \leq i < k \\ < x_{center}, y_{center}, radius > \quad \text{for } i = k \end{cases} \tag{6}$$

On the other hand, a query region R_{rect} of a rectangle query is decomposed as shown in Fig.2 (b). The coordinate (x_{base}, y_{base}) expresses the base point of all decomposed regions. dx_{plus}, dx_{minus}, dy_{plus} and dy_{minus} decide the rate to extend regions along each coordinate axis. r_i^{upper} is calculated as follows:

$$r_i^{upper} = \begin{cases} < x_{base} + dx_{minus} \times i, y_{base} + dy_{minus} \times i, & \\ \quad x_{base} + dx_{plus} \times i, y_{base} + dy_{plus} \times i > & \text{for } 1 \leq i < k \\ < x_{min}, y_{min}, x_{max}, y_{max} > & \text{for } i = k \end{cases} \tag{7}$$

$$dx_{plus} \geq 0, \quad dy_{plus} \geq 0, \quad dx_{minus} \leq 0, \quad dy_{minus} \leq 0 \tag{8}$$

3.4 Search Algorithm

Our search algorithm behaves in the top down manner and the description is shown in Fig.3.

```
create region_list = ⟨r_1, ..., r_k⟩ by decomposing a query region R
create OPEN_LIST_i at each sub-region (r_i)
create RESULT_BUFFER_i for r_i
insert a root node into OPEN_LIST_1
for check each decomposed region (r_i) in order of region_list do
  while OPEN_LIST_i is not empty do
    pick up an element e from OPEN_LIST_i
    if e is an entry in a leaf node then
      if overlap(r_i, e.rect) ∧ overlap(r_i, o.geom) then
        insert e into RESULT_BUFFER_i
      else
        insert e into OPEN_LIST_{i+1}
      endif
    else
      if overlap(r_i, e.rect) then
        insert all children of e into OPEN_LIST_i
      else
        insert e into OPEN_LIST_{i+1}
      endif
    endif
  end
end
```

Fig. 3. A search algorithm based on region decomposition

Our method scans each decomposed region using a index tree in order of *region_list*. $OPEN\_LIST$ is a queue for searching and $RESULT\_BUFFER$ is a buffer to keep the searched result for each decomposed region. While an entry picked out from $OPEN\_LIST_i$ overlaps with the sub-region r_i, the entry is expanded using the $OPEN\_LIST_i$. Otherwise, the entry is inserted into $OPEN\_LIST_{i+1}$ for next decomposed region r_{i+1} as a candidate for the searching. Using entries in the $OPEN\_LIST_{i+1}$, the search for the next sub-region is executed. Our method does not start the search for each sub-region from scratch. Since an entry (e) of a leaf node points to a data object (o), this method evaluates whether the bounding box ($e.rect$) of the entry overlaps with r_i as well as whether the geometric attribute (*o.geom*) of the object overlaps with the region. If these conditions are satisfied, the entry is inserted into $RESULT\_BUFFER_i$. In this implementation, we manage entries in $OPEN\_LIST$ in the depth-first policy.

3.5 Transmitting Retrieval Results

The data transmission process marks up the retrieval results by XML and sends incrementally each result as a packet to a client. Since the transmission process keeps the results at each decomposed region using multiple buffers, it can supply the intermediate result to a client before the search finishes. Spatial data objects for each decomposed region are sent as packets. The process picks out these data objects from $RESULT\_BUFFER$ based on the maximum number (max_item) of data objects that a packet can include.

4 Implementation

We implemented a spatial data server based on our retrieval method using Java language (jdk1.2). This server executes a query requested by a client and supplies the retrieval results to the client. This retrieval system behaves as a TCP server. A search process and a transmission process are implemented as a thread using java.lang.Thread class. The search thread and the transmission thread behave concurrently and share the intermediate results through multiple buffers that the search thread keeps. Accordingly, the transmission thread can acquire the retrieval results from these buffers during the searching. We used the digital map data published by the Geographical Survey Institute [8] as sample data for our experiments and we composes a spatial database that includes line data and polygon data. As a spatial index for this database, we adopted R-tree with a quadratic splitting algorithm [7]. We use java.io.RandomAccessFile class in order to access data in a file. A DTD for XML expression of the retrieval result is shown in Fig.4.

```
<!ELEMENT spatial-data (line|polygon)*>
<!ELEMENT line (id?,((x,y),(x,y)))>
<!ELEMENT polygon (id?,((x,y),(x,y),(x,y)+))>
<!ELEMNET x (#PCDATA)>
<!ELEMENT y (#PCDATA)>
```

Fig. 4. A DTD for description of spatial data

Also, we implemented a map browsing system as a TCP client of this retrieval system. Through the TCP connection, the client requests a query to the server and receives the retrieval results from the server. This client parses spatial data from the results expressed by XML and draws a map based on the parsed data. We used SAX (Simple API for XML) as the XML parser.

5 Evaluation and Discussion

We have conducted some experiments to evaluate our method. A spatial data server and a map browsing client work on the different host (Sun Ultra-10 Workstation). The server host has 440 MHz CPU and 512 MB memory. The client host has 333 MHz CPU and 128 MB memory. These hosts are connected through 100 Mbps Ethernet.

5.1 The Improvement of the Retrieval Quality

First, we evaluated the basic performance of the implemented retrieval system. The response time (t_{wait}) of the retrieval system includes the search time (t_{search}), the XML tagging time (t_{tag}), the XML parsing time (t_{parse}), the drawing time (t_{draw}) and the rest (t_{etc}). t_{etc} includes the data transmission time. We measured these time using java.lang.System.currentTimeMillis() method. In this experiment, the data server manages 26745 line data objects that contain 53490 points.

We measured the response time when the client finishes the drawing for each received packet, and recorded the retrieval quality calculated by an expression (1). Fig.5 and Fig.6 show the performance for a circular query with $radius$ = 1500. The total number of collected line objects for the query is 6859.

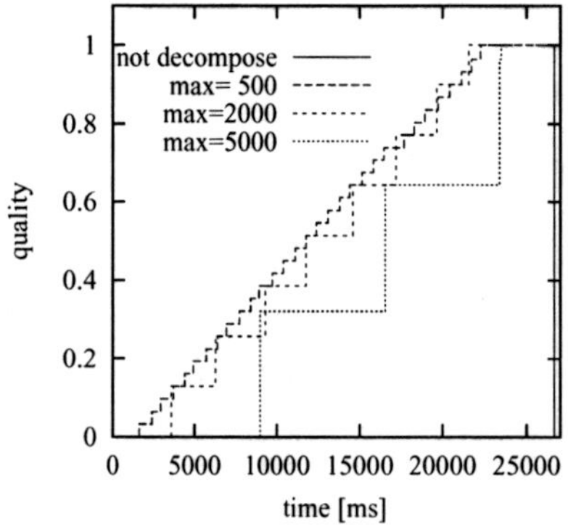

Fig. 5. The improvement of the retrieval quality for packet decomposition

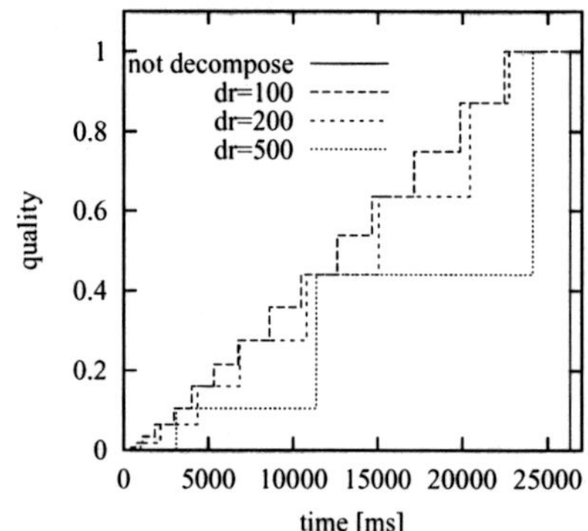

Fig. 6. The improvement of the retrieval quality by query region decomposition

Fig.5 shows the effect of packet decomposition based on the maximum number of data objects (max_item) when the server searches without region decomposition. This result shows the monotonic improvement of the retrieval quality. Also, the first response time becomes short by packet decomposition. The server can provide some fragments of the retrieval results before the search finishes completely.

Fig.6 shows the effect of region decomposition using d_{radius}. This result suggests that the retrieval quality improves monotonically, similar to the case using packet decomposition (Fig.5). As d_{radius} is smaller (namely, the number of decomposed regions is larger), the first response time is shorter and the quality improves smoothly.

5.2 Processing Cost

Next, we measured some processing costs for a circular query to collect line data object. The result is shown in Fig.7.

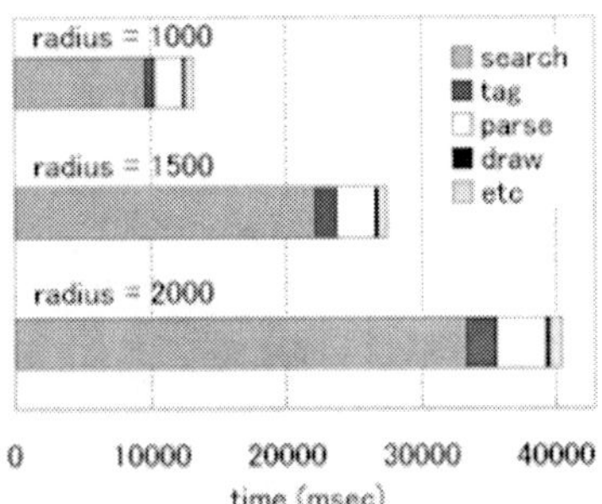

Fig. 7. Processing time

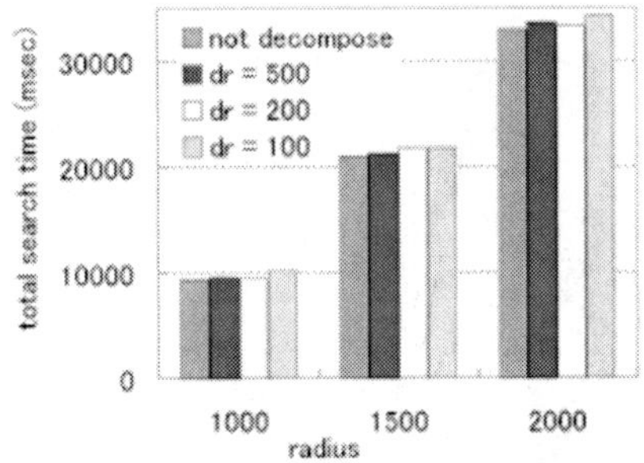

Fig. 8. Search cost

This result suggests that the search time makes up large percentage of the response time. Also, as a query range (*radius*) is longer (namely, the number of the collected data objects is larger), XML processing costs (t_{tag} and t_{parse}) are larger. These costs depend on the size of the transmitted data.

Also, Fig.8 shows the total search time when a client requests a circular query with $radius = \{1000, 1500, 2000\}$ and the server decomposes the query region by using $d_{radius} = \{100, 200, 500\}$. This result suggests that the total search time depends on the number of collected objects for the query and region decomposition has less overhead for the total search time. In addition to this, as the size of the last transmitted result is smaller by region decomposition and the XML processing time is shorter, the total response time is shorter. The tendency can be observed in Fig.6.

5.3 Map Browsing

We examined the drawing image when a client requests a rectangle query with $R_{rect} =< -52500, -18000, -49500, -14000 >$ and the server decomposes the query region using $\{x_{base} = -51000,\ y_{base} = -16000,\ dx_{plus} = dy_{plus} = 200,\ dx_{minus} = dy_{minus} = -200\}$. The server manages 1678 polygon objects that

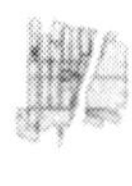

Fig. 9. The image ($t = 778msec$)

Fig. 10. The image ($t = 4398msec$)

Fig. 11. The last drawing image ($t = 14754msec$)

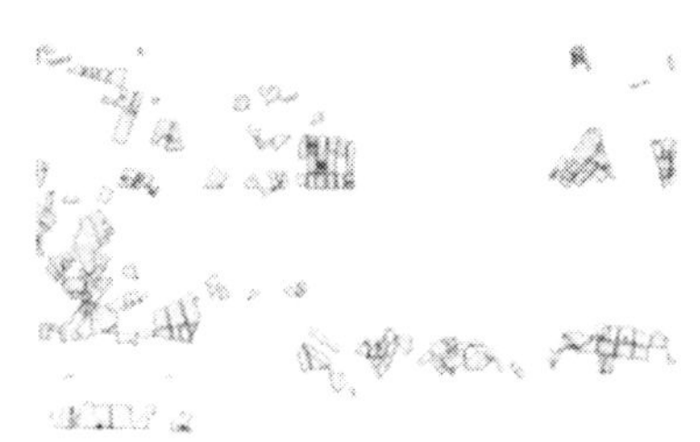

Fig. 12. The drawing image using packet decomposition

contain 28659 points. The case using region decomposition has a different drawing manner from the case using packet decomposition. The drawing images are shown in Fig.9, Fig.10, Fig.11 and Fig.12.

In both cases, the client can browse some spatial data before receiving all results from the server because the client draws incrementally the map data every time it receives packets. Fig.9 and Fig.10 are the drawing image based the intermediate results when the server searches using region decomposition. Fig.11 is the image based on all data objects collected for the query. These figures show that the region containing the collected objects spreads over time from the base point specified by the user. On the contrary, when the server transmits the retrieval results using packet decomposition, the client draws the map data sparsely (Fig.12).

5.4 Related Work

Incremental nearest neighbor algorithm for ranking spatial objects was proposed [9]. Using a priority queue, this algorithm ranks data objects while searching. It is more effective than a method using nearest neighbor query because it does not have to start the search from scratch. Generally, a search algorithm uses a queue, called an open list, and keeps candidate nodes based on a given policy. Our search method is depth-first approach, but the incremental algorithm is best-first approach based on the distance between spatial objects. Also, the algorithm can output the ranking results incrementally. In this point, this is very similar to our method. However, our goal is to browse spatial objects with real-time response, not to rank spatial objects. The incremental nearest neighbor algorithm exactly sorts using a single queue, but our method maintains multiple queues to control the search for each decomposed region. Our approach uses multiple queues for ordered sub-regions and roughly sorts spatial objects enough to realize real-time spatial data browsing.

6 Conclusion

We designed a retrieval method for real-time spatial data browsing through a computer network and implemented the retrieval system using Java language. Our retrieval method can supply incrementally the intermediate results for a query. These results are ordered by searching based on region decomposition and are decomposed into packets based on the number of data objects. Consequently, the client can incrementally browse spatial data for the query. Through some experiments, we showed that our method can monotonically improves the retrieval quality. Also, the experimental results suggested that our method can bring the first response with a short time and take the total response time with less overhead. Further consideration will include the refinement of the search algorithm and the construction of a framework for information integration based on spatial data infrastructure.

References

1. G-XML. http://gisclh01.dpc.or.jp/gxml/contents-e.
2. M. Boddy and T. Dean. Solving Time-Dependent Planning Problems. In *Proccedings of IJCAI 89*, pages 979–984, 1989.
3. S. Zilberstein and S. Russel. Optimal composition of real-time systems. *Artificial Intelligence*, 82(1-2):181–213, 1996.
4. K.-J. Lin, S. Natarajan, J. W.-S. Liu, and T. Krauskopf. Concord: A System of Imprecise Computation. In *Proccedings of COMPSAC 87*, pages 75–81. IEEE, 1987.
5. X. Huang and A. M. K. Cheng. Applying Imprecise Algorithms to Real-Time Image and Video Transmission. In *Proceedings of Real-Time Technology and Applications Symposium*, pages 96–101, 1995.
6. S. V. Vrbsky. A data model for approximate query processing of real-time databases. *Data & Knowledge Engineering*, 21:79–102, 1997.
7. A. Guttman. R-Trees: A Dynamic Index Structure for Spatial Searching. In *Proccedings of ACM SIGMOD Conference*, pages 47–57, 1984.
8. Geographical Survey Institute. http://www.gsi.go.jp/ENGLISH.
9. G. R. Hjaltason and H. Samet. Ranking in Spatial Databases. In *Advances in Spatial Databases :4th International Symposium, SSD '95 (LNCS-951)*, pages 83–95, 1995.

Designing a Compression Engine for Multidimensional Raster Data*

Andreas Dehmel

FORWISS
Orleansstraße 34
D-81667 Munich, Germany
dehmel@forwiss.tu-muenchen.de

Abstract. Multidimensional raster data appears in many application areas, typically in the form of sampled spatial or spatio-temporal analogue data. Due to the data volume and correlations between neighbouring samples usually encountered in this kind of data it has high potential for efficient compression, as can be seen by the wealth of specialized compression techniques developed for 2D raster images; other examples would be 1D time series, 3D volumetric or spatio-temporal data, 4D spatio-temporal data or 5+D data typically found in OLAP data cubes. Efficiently handling this kind of data often requires compression, be it to reduce storage space requirements or transfer times over low-bandwidth media. In this paper we present the design of the generic, tile-based compression engine developed for this purpose and implemented in the multidimensional array DBMS RasDaMan.

Keywords: Spatial and temporal databases, object-oriented databases, data compression

1 Introduction

Raster data of arbitrary dimensionality and base type, which we call *Multidimensional Discrete Data* or MDD for short, is an everyday phenomenon in digital data management. The most popular special cases of MDD are raster images, but in recent years digital audio and video data have also gained a substantial amount of exposure. The popularity and usability of this kind of data has been largely influenced by the development of dedicated compression methods, for instance JPEG, PNG, or the various MPEG standards, to name but a few, as only compression allows reducing the data volume enough to handle this data efficiently in everyday use.
Research done so far on compression in databases has mostly focussed on relational data and the impact of compression on overall performance as in [8]. The situation is very different for MDD, however, since MDD are both considerably

* Research funded by the European Commission under grant no. QLG3-CT-1999-00677 *NeuroGenerator*, see www.neurogenerator.org

H.C. Mayr et al. (Eds.): DEXA 2001, LNCS 2113, pp. 470–480, 2001.

bigger than relational data and have different properties. Compression in relational databases usually means a simple text compression method, whereas more advanced techniques developed for image- and video compression are a much more natural template for the development of MDD compression algorithms because both of these data types are just special cases of MDD themselves and exploit properties like spatial correlations which can be found in many types of MDD as well.
The problems in efficiently compressing MDD derive from their generic nature, i.e. neither the number of dimensions nor the structure of the base type may be restricted in any way. There is a huge amount of work done on compression for specific types of MDD like images, video and audio data, but to the best of our knowledge no work on *generic* MDD compression nor its integration into a DBMS kernel. That means that existing compression techniques may well serve as a design template but are much too restrictive "out of the box" to be of any use in the MDD context. We will list the requirements in more detail in Sec. 1.3 after a few introductory words on terminology and RasDaMan.

1.1 Terminology

Before taking a closer look at the requirements of MDD compression we will first establish the (RasDaMan) terminology used in the remainder of this paper. An MDD is a template for multidimensional raster data; the two template parameters are information about the geometry, encoded as a *spatial domain*, and about the *base type*. This leads to the following definitions:

Spatial Domain: a multidimensional interval spanned by two vectors l, h. We use the syntax $[l_1 : h_1, \ldots, l_d : h_d], \quad l_i, h_i \in \mathbb{Z}, l_i \leq h_i$ to represent a spatial domain in d dimensions. A point x lies within a spatial domain sdom if $\forall i : l_i \leq x_i \leq h_i \ (x \in \mathsf{sdom})$.

Cell: a cell is located at each position $x \in \mathsf{sdom}$ (dense data model). Its structure is determined by the *base type* of the MDD they belong to.

Base Type: describes the structure of a cell. There are atomic types as used in high level languages like C (e.g. `int`, `short`, ...) and arbitrary structured types which may consist of any combination of atomic types and other structured types.

1.2 RasDaMan

RasDaMan [2] is an array DBMS for MDD developed at FORWISS. In order to achieve finer access granularity, MDD are subdivided into sets of non-overlapping *tiles*, each of which is stored separately for efficient random access [1,3]. There is no restriction on base types except that all cells within an MDD must have constant size (which rules out e.g. variable-length strings); this allows fast calculation of cell addresses. All data within a cell is stored consecutively in memory which means that the values for the atomic types within a structured type are interleaved in order to achieve maximum speed when most type members are accessed together, which is typical for many queries.

1.3 Requirements for MDD Compression

There is a wealth of compression techniques for special data like images, audio and video data, which exploit intrinsic properties of these data types, a nice overview of which can be found in [7]. Images for instance are 2D MDD over a small number of possible base types, by far the most popular of which are 8bit (greyscale) and 24bit (true colour). Standard compression algorithms for generic MDD are lacking, however. There are a number of compression methods in common use today like the LZ series developed by Lempel and Ziv [9,10] which are generic in the sense that they interpret all data as an unstructured bytestream, but these naturally fail to exploit some of the structure inherent in MDD objects, such as

- correlations between neighbouring cells which will be lost at least in part if the multidimensional data is simply linearized into a bytestream as required for those compression methods. These correlations will not necessarily exist for all types of data, but many kinds of MDD like tomograms or the results of numerical simulations have a spatial and/or temporal interpretation which implies the presence of such correlations;
- the semantics of data belonging to structured base types. A satellite image with 9 spectral channels will often compress better if the values of each channel are compressed separately rather than all of them interleaved. This is even more true when the structured type consists of different subtypes, e.g. a mixture of `char`, `short` and `int`.

Please note that the performance of a compression method always depends heavily on the kind of data it is applied to; for instance if the values of a structured base type are the same within each cell, compressing the values for each atomic type separately will often compress worse than the interleaved approach. The standard approach is to separate the compression engine into a model layer at the top which transforms the data depending on its type into a format which allows more efficient compression, and a compression layer at the bottom which consists of traditional symbol-stream oriented compression techniques. The model layer for an image and an OLAP data cube will be completely different, but the compression layer is identical. There is also the important distinction to make between lossless and lossy compression modes, which will be resolved in the model layer as well. Although lossless mode is desirable especially in a DBMS, the entropy sets a hard limit on the maximum achievable rate; on the other hand in some situations the loss of some accuracy may well be worth the additional storage savings achieved by lossy compression.
Another aspect of the desired compression engine is that it should be usable for transfer compression as well, which means that it must be available on both the database server and the client and therefore machine-independent. Transfer compression can greatly reduce transfer times; when taking the compression / decompression overhead into account this is weakened somewhat in that only fast (and typically simple) compression techniques will perform well for transfer

compression unless the bandwidth between client and server is very low. In contrast, when storing data the reduction in size is usually more important than the computational overhead involved. For the compression engine this means that it must support a variety of compression methods with different time / compression rate properties.
All of the above indicates that a compression engine for multidimensional raster data should not be limited to one technique but rather be a modular collection of different approaches with individual strengths and weaknesses, where specific ones can be chosen according to the user's requirements.

2 Compression Engine Architecture

All compression functionality was isolated in a new module which is present on both client and server for maximum flexibility and efficient transfer compression. Modularity was a major factor when designing the compression engine, because there is no universal compression technique and therefore several methods have to be provided through a common interface. Because of RasDaMan's tile-based architecture it is natural to make compression tile-based as well. Each tile is compressed separately and the compression methods can differ between tiles, i.e. a compression method is a property of a tile, not of an MDD (see Fig. 2). The engine consists of two fundamental layers:

- the bottom layer corresponds to traditional stream-oriented compression techniques and is not aware of any MDD semantics but merely operates on a linear stream of symbols; therefore this layer can also be used outside of the tile context. An interface to this layer is provided by the class lincodecstream; it is described in more detail in Sec. 2.1;
- the top (=model) layer is MDD-aware and can therefore exploit characteristics like nD smoothness or base type structure. The interface for this layer is provided by the abstract class tilecompression which is at the root of an extensive class hierarchy. This layer can only operate on tiles and does not perform any compression itself, but merely transforms the data according to a data model before passing it on to an object of the bottom layer for actual compression. See Sec. 2.2 for a detailed overview of this layer.

2.1 The Lincodecstream Hierarchy

Figure 1 shows a skeleton of the bottom layer's class hierarchy. All classes derive from a common ancestor class linstream but are then split into separate class hierarchies for compression and decompression because these operations usually work very differently internally, e.g. in a compression operation the final size of the compressed data is unknown, whereas during decompression the size of both compressed and uncompressed data is usually known. When easy access to matching compression and decompression objects is required this can be achieved via the lincodecstream class that merges both branches. There are currently 3

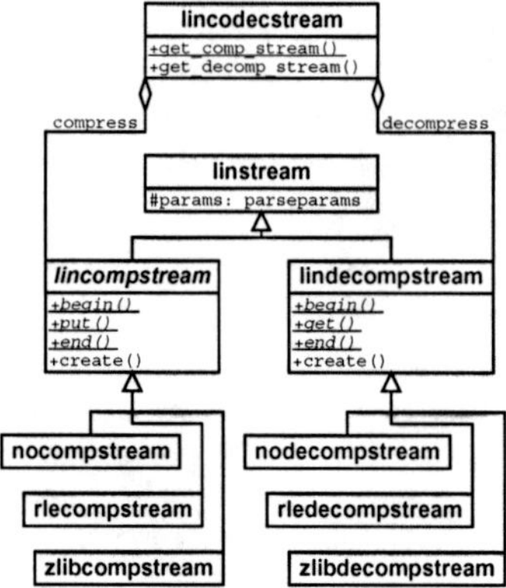

Fig. 1. Outline of the lincodecstream hierarchy in UML notation

compression streams available, which have very different weights on complexity- and compression factors:

None: no compression, the input stream is just copied.

RLE: an RLE algorithm based on the *PackBits* approach described in [13]. RLE algorithms decompose a data stream into tuples $(value, count)$ and thus provide fast and simple compression of sequences of identical symbols, which makes them attractive for both sparse data and transfer compression (the latter due to low complexity). *PackBits* was chosen because of its smart encoding of these tuples with a worst case data expansion by $\frac{1}{128}$th (in contrast to a primitive encoding which would double the size). The algorithm was further extended to operate on base types of size 1, 2, 4 and 8 to allow it to compress all atomic types as efficiently as possible[1].

ZLib: the well known, free standard compression library ZLib [12] was chosen because of its excellent compression properties on arbitrary binary data. ZLib compression is based on the LZ77 dictionary compression technique [9] which is far superior to RLE in terms of achievable compression, but also of considerably higher complexity.

Furthermore, due to their streaming properties lincodecstreams can be nested to any depth as a filter sequence of arbitrary length, they could even be composed dynamically on-the-fly.

2.2 The Tilecompression Hierarchy

The tilecompression layer is MDD-aware, i.e. it knows base type and spatial domain of the data and can use these to achieve better compression. The tile-

[1] If the algorithm worked only on bytes it would perform very badly when compressing data from larger base types: the sequence `<1,2,2,2,2>` over the type short corresponds to the byte sequence `<0,1,0,2,0,2,0,2,0,2>` on a little endian machine, which obviously wouldn't compress in RLE.

compression layer itself only performs transformations of the data and is coupled with classes of the lincodecstream layer for actual compression. The tilecompression class hierarchy consists of the following major branches (see Fig. 2):

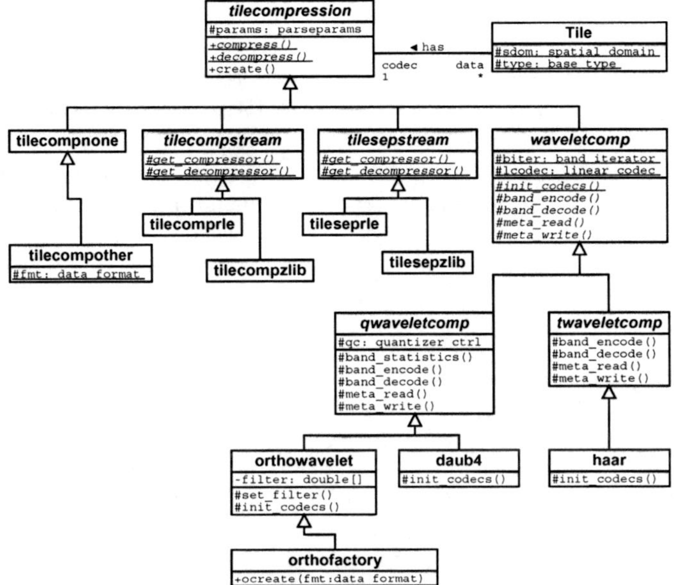

Fig. 2. Outline of the tilecompression hierarchy in UML notation

tilecompnone: no compression. This class is optimized for fast handling of uncompressed data and avoids copying operations that would have been necessary if it had been merged with another class of this hierarchy.

tilecompstream: the simplest variant of tile compression which does not use any MDD properties but merely reads/writes the linearized tile data from/to a lindecompstream/lincompstream. The (de)compression stream objects are provided by derived classes via `get_compressor()` / `get_decompressor()` methods, everything else is done in tilecompstream scope;

tilesepstream: a more sophisticated compression variant which uses the semantics of structured base types and compresses the values belonging to each atomic type separately. Thus an RGB image – which is a 2D MDD over the structured base type `struct {char red, char green, char blue}` – would be compressed by processing the `red`, `green` and `blue` values separately and concatenating the output. Like tilecompstream, the compression is based on lincodecstreams and uses the same interface to retrieve (de)compression objects from its derived classes. When applied to a tile over an atomic base type, tilecompstream and tilesepstream are equivalent;

waveletcompression: this is the most advanced compression algorithm currently supported by RasDaMan, which uses both base type semantics and spatial correlations. Section 2.3 deals with the architecture of this subclass in more detail.

Tile compression is integrated in RasDaMan's two communication layers, the one to the base DBMS for storage and retrieval of compressed tiles and the one to client applications for transfer compression.
One issue that hasn't been addressed yet is the specification of parameters for the various kinds of compression, but due to space restrictions this can't be covered in detail in this paper. A parameter string of the form `[key=value[,key=value]*]` is used for this purpose, which allows integer, floating point and string parameters. We provided the possibility to use parameters for decompression as well, but the policy is that the compression algorithm must store all parameters *necessary* for decoding the tile along with the data[2] so the decompressor can always return the correct result; thus decompression parameters are intended for optimization only.

2.3 Wavelet Compression

For the last couple of years, wavelets have received a huge amount of attention especially in the areas of data compression [19,20,18], including the upcoming *JPEG2000* standard [15], where they're used to transform a digital input signal into a representation better suited for compression; for example a sine wave has a rather complex spatial representation but a very simple one in the frequency domain. Wavelets are base functions with special properties such as (ideally) compact support; scaled and translated versions of the so-called *mother wavelet* are used to approximate functions at different resolution levels. What makes wavelets particularily attractive for lossy compression is that the transformed data can often be made very sparse and thus highly compressable without a noticeable degradation in the quality of the reconstructed signal [7]. In the discrete case, a 1D wavelet transform is performed by folding the input signal with matching (wavelet-specific) low-pass and high-pass filters to obtain average and detail coefficients, which can be used to reconstruct the original data during synthesis. Wavelet theory is a highly complex mathematical field far beyond the scope of this paper; the interested reader is referred to [16,17] for the profound theoretical background. Due to space restrictions we're unable to touch the subject here.

Wavelets in RasDaMan: Using wavelets for MDD compression requires the extension of the wavelet concept (typically given for the 1D case) to an arbitrary number of dimensions. The usual approach chosen in wavelet compression of images [18,19] is to perform 1D wavelet transformations first on rows, storing the average coefficients in the first and the detail coefficients in the second half of the rows, then doing 1D wavelet transformations on the columns of this transformed data, storing average and detail coefficients likewise. This partitions the original image into 4 areas, one where both transformations stored their averages (cc),

[2] e.g. subband levels and quantization steps when encoding wavelet coefficients etc.

one for the two possible mixtures of averages and details (cd, dc) and one for pure detail information (dd). This technique is then recursively applied to the cc region, see Fig. 3; the inverse procedure simply decodes columns, then rows, using 1D wavelet synthesis, starting at the coarsest resolution and doing the inverse recursion to finer resolutions.

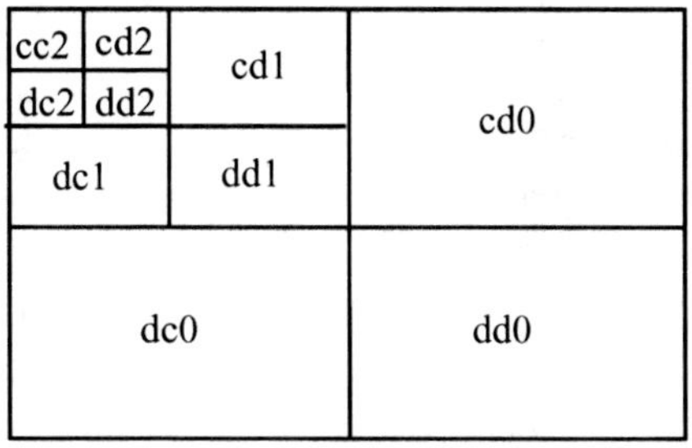

Fig. 3. Multiresolution wavelet decomposition in image compression

It is natural to extend this system for an arbitrary number of dimensions D, performing 1D decompositions of the MDD along dimensions $1, \ldots, D$ when encoding and 1D synthesis along dimensions $D, \ldots, 1$ when decoding. On each scale, this leads to 2^D regions $r_i = \{c, d\}^D$ where we recursively apply the same transformation to region $\{c\}^D$. Values belonging to an atomic type within a structured type are transformed separately.
When the values of an atomic type have been wavelet-coded, all of the above mentioned regions at all hierarchic levels are iterated over, quantized, and encoded with a linear stream. The iteration is done by a class banditerator which assigns the regions to bands and steps over the data band-wise. Currently the following band iterators are available:

isolevel: Each hierarchical level forms a band;

isodetail: All regions (in all hierarchical levels) with the same number of d in their identifiers form a band (e.g. `cd*` and `dc*` in Fig. 3);

leveldetail: All regions within a hierarchical level and with the same number of d in their identifiers form a band (e.g. `cd0` and `dc0` in Fig. 3).

The wavelet class itself is modular and consists of an abtract base class performing all the wrapper code like iterating over all atomic types in a structured base type. Its two abstract child classes twaveletcomp and qwaveletcomp implement lossless (transform only) and lossy (quantizing) wavelet compression. The only thing derived classes have to do is the actual wavelet analysis and synthesis. Due to space restrictions we're unable to present the architecture of the wavelet engine or the quantization in more depth here but give only a short overview over the following wavelet types:

Haar Wavelets: These are the oldest and most widely used wavelets, which is mostly due to their simplicity; they are also used (implicitly) in the S-transform [18,20]. Like all wavelet filter coefficients, the ones of the Haar wavelet are irrational numbers, but an equivalent transformation can be done in pure integer arithmetic where a pair (x_{2i}, x_{2i+1}) of input values is transformed into their arithmetic average $a_i = \frac{x_{2i}+x_{2i+1}}{2}$ and the difference $d_i = \frac{x_{2i}-x_{2i+1}}{2}$ during analysis and reconstructed using $x_{2i} = a_i + d_i$ and $x_{2i+1} = a_i - d_i$ during synthesis. Using some integer optimizations, we can make sure that the exact encoded data has the same type and number of bits as the original data which is not normally possible when using wavelets and makes Haar wavelets an attractive transformation technique for lossless compression of integer types. For floating point types, loss in the general area of the machine precision can't be avoided [19].

Generic Wavelet Filters: In the general case, a wavelet filter consists of real numbers which can only be approximated by floating point numbers on a computer system; folding a signal with such a filter naturally results in floating point coefficients too, in contrast to the Haar wavelets in Sec. 2.3. Uniting both concepts under one wavelet architecture was an important extension of the system. All wavelet filters currently supported are orthonormal with compact support (see Fig. 2).
Currently there exists a separate class for *Daubechies 4* wavelets [16] and an abstract class orthowavelet which can operate with arbitrary orthonormal wavelet filters with even length. The actual filter is initialized in the child class orthofactory which currently supports 20 filter types with lengths between 6 and 30 coefficients. The main reason for creating a special class for *Daubechies 4* was that the generic approach is less efficient the shorter the filter is. Biorthogonal wavelets as used in the upcoming *JPEG2000* standard [15] could simply be added as a brother class to orthowavelet.

3 Results

Although the engine isn't finished yet, it can already be used for data compression in RasDaMan. In this section we will present some preliminary results for several kinds of MDD typically stored in RasDaMan. The results are preliminary in that additional work is required for predictors and more efficient wavelet quantization, which is part of the future work. At the moment, wavelet coefficients are quantized with a user-defined number of bits per band, which unfortunately doesn't allow very high compression rates with acceptable distortion; still, careful bit assignment can already yield good results in many cases.
In the following examples, *RLE* and *ZLib* are lossless compression, whereas *Daub10* is lossy compression using the Daubechies 10-tap wavelet filter which can be found in e.g. [7] and a zlib stream for compressing the quantized coefficients. Compression factors denote the size of the compressed data relative to the uncompressed data size; for *Daub10* the best that could be found using the current quantization approach without noticeable degradation in quality are

given. These should improve substantially once zerotree quantization is available; detailed rate-distortion analysis will follow then. Here are the results for some 2D and 3D MDD over integer and floating point base types:

	sdom	type	size[kB]	RLE	ZLib	Daub10
tomo	$256 \times 256 \times 154$	`char`	9856	28.3589%	21.9568%	14.7853%
temp	$15 \times 32 \times 64$	`float`	120	100%	73.0924%	12.8507%
painting	727×494	`char`	351	98.2427%	75.7984%	24.4352%
tempsec	256×512	`float`	512	98.7696%	88.5839%	11.4721%

Even with the current suboptimal quantization, the wavelet engine can often compress data considerably better than the lossless approaches while keeping distortion low. Most noticeably, *Daub10* performs particularily well on floating point data where lossless compression achieves little to no gain. This is an important result for scientific applications which usually operate on floating point fields.

4 Conclusions and Future Work

We presented the design of a compression engine for generic MDD which has been implemented in the RasDaMan DBMS. This kind of data differs completely from traditional table data typically stored in relational DBMSs where mostly light-weight compression seems feasible due to small access granularity [8]. In contrast, MDD share many of the properties typically found in digital images, can become very large and have considerably coarser access granularity than table data, therefore the use of sophisticated compression techniques based mostly on work done in image compression is the most promising approach. The design of the compression engine allows using many different, extensible techniques side by side, so the best method can be chosen depending on the kind of MDD used and to cater for different future requirements.

There are two major issues left in the compression engine, one of which is more efficient wavelet quantization using a generalized zerotree [21] and the other are predictors. Predictors approximate cell values from the values of neighbouring cells and store the difference between the actual and the predicted value. This typically results in a reduction of the value range which in turn improves the compression performance. On one hand, there are inter-channel predictors where the values of a channel at a given position x are approximated by the values of the other channels at the same position. This is essentially what the RGB $\rightarrow$ YUV transformation does for colour images. Then there are intra-channel predictors which use values at neighbouring positions within the same channel to predict the value at position x. There may even be some potential of uniting both predictor types into one.

After these extensions, another important workpackage will be performing exhaustive tests on the effect of the available compression techniques on various types of MDD, be it in compression rates achieved or the impact on total execution times. In that context, the addition of a cost model for transfer compression to the query optimizer comes to mind as well.

References

1. P. Furtado, P. Baumann: *Storage of Multidimensional Arrays Based on Arbitrary Tiling.* In *Proc. of the International Conference on Data Engineering (ICDE)*, Sydney, Australia, 1999.
2. P. Baumann, A. Dehmel, P. Furtado, R. Ritsch, N. Widmann: *Spatio-Temporal Retrieval with RasDaMan (system demonstration)* . Proc. Very Large Data Bases (VLDB), Edinburgh, 1999, pp. 746-749.
3. P. Furtado: *Storage Management of Multidimensional Arrays in Database Management Systems.* PhD thesis, Technical University of Munich, 1999.
4. R. Ritsch: *Optimization and Evaluation of Array Queries in Database Management Systems.* PhD thesis, Technical University of Munich, 1999.
5. P. Baumann: *A Database Array Algebra for Spatio-Temporal Data and Beyond.* In *Proc. Fourth International Workshop on Next Generation Information Technologies and Systems (NGITS '99)*, Zikhron Yaakov, Israel, July 5-7 1999, LNCS 1649, Springer.
6. The International Organisation for Standardization (ISO): *Database Language SQL.* ISO 9075, 1992(E).
7. K. Sayood: *Introduction to Data Compression.* Morgan Kaufmann Publishers, Inc., San Francisco, CA, 1996.
8. T. Westmann, D. Kossmann, S. Helmer, G. Moerkotte: *The Implementation and Performance of Compressed Databases.* Reihe Informatik 3/1998.
9. J. Ziv, A. Lempel: *A Universal Algorithm for Data Compression.* IEEE Transactions on Information Theory, IT-23(3), 1977
10. J. Ziv, A. Lempel: *Compression of individual Sequences via Variable-Rate Coding.* IEEE Transactions on Information Theory, IT-24(5), 1978
11. R. Cattell: *The Object Database Standard: ODMG 2.0.* Morgan Kaufmann Publishers, San Mateo, California, USA, 1997.
12. ZLib homepage: `http://www.info-zip.org /pub/infozip/zlib/`
13. *TIFF Revision 6.0 Specification*, p42; Aldus Corporation, Seattle, 1992.
14. G.K. Wallace: *The JPEG Still Picture Compression Standard.* Communications of the ACM No.4, Vol 34, Apr 1991.
15. A.N. Skodras, C.A. Christopoulos, T. Ebrahimi: *JPEG2000: The Upcoming Still Image Compression Standard.* Proceedings of the 11th Portuguese Conference on Pattern Recognition (RECPA), 2000
16. I. Daubechies: *Ten Lectures on Wavelets.* CBMS-NSF Regional Conference Series in Applied Mathematics, CBMS 61, 1992.
17. C.K. Chui: *An Introduction to Wavelets.* Academic Press Inc., 1992.
18. N. Strobel, S.K. Mitra, B.S. Manjunath: *Progressive-Resolution Transmission and Lossless Compression of Color Images for Digital Image Libraries.* Image Processing Laboratory University of California, Santa Barbara 93106.
19. A. Trott, R. Moorhead, J. McGinley: *Wavelets Applied to Lossless Compression and Progressive Transmission of Floating Point Data in 3-D Curvilinear Grids.* IEEE Visualization, 1996.
20. A. Said, W.A. Pearlman: *An Image Multiresolution Representation for Lossless and Lossy Compression.* SPIE Symposium on Visual Communications and Image Processing, Cambridge, MA, 1993.
21. J. Shapiro: *Embedded Image Coding Using Zerotrees of Wavelet Coefficients.* IEEE Transactions on Signal Processing, Vol 41, 1993.

DrawCAD: Using Deductive Object-Relational Databases in CAD

Mengchi Liu and Shilpesh Katragadda

School of Computer Science, Carleton University, Ottawa, Canada K1S 5B6

Abstract. Computer-Aided Design (CAD) involves the use of computers in the various stages of engineering design. It has large volumes of data with complex structures that needs to be stored and managed efficiently and properly. In CAD, graphical objects with complex structures can be created by reusing previously created objects. The data of these objects have the references to the other objects they contain. Deductive object-relational databases can be used to compute the complete data of graphical objects that reuse other objects. This is the idea behind the development of the DrawCAD system. DrawCAD is a CAD system built on top of the Relationlog object-relational deductive database system. It facilitates the creation of graphical objects by reusing previously created objects. The DrawCAD system illustrates how CAD systems can be developed, using deductive object-relational databases to store and manage data and also perform the computations that are normally performed by the application program.

1 Introduction

Computer-Aided Design (CAD) is the use of computers, to assist in the creation, modification, analysis or optimization of an engineering design [1, 9, 12–14]. The design process is an iterative process involving many steps. CAD has a number of components that help in the various stages of the design process. The various components of a CAD system include a graphic package for visualization, a geometry manager for maintaining data structures that contain geometric information, numerical methods library to perform various numerical functions, an interface that connects the user and the system and a data manager that stores and maintains the large amount of CAD data.

CAD data has some unique characteristics that makes its management difficult. The design of a CAD object usually has a complex structure that involves large volumes of data. Also, in many CAD situations, the designed object has many aspects of data to be stored and may be updated later. It may also be used in the design of a more complex objects, and may in turn consist of lower level components. When a lower level component is changed, the higher level component that contained it should either be changed automatically or become invalid. All these different aspects of data need to be stored and dealt with properly in an integrated environment that can accessed by different CAD utilities so that the cost of storing, maintaining and accessing these objects is minimum.

H.C. Mayr et al. (Eds.): DEXA 2001, LNCS 2113, pp. 481–490, 2001.

Database systems, especially advanced database systems provide general purpose programs that can be used to access and manipulate large amount of data stored with complex structure in the database. They provide an independence between the program accessing data and the database. It is therefore important to use database systems to store CAD data in the most efficient manner for better management and easy retrieval. However, there are a number of such database systems, such as object-oriented database systems [3, 4, 10], object-relational database system [11], deductive database systems [7], and deductive object-oriented/object-relational database systems [2, 6, 5, 8]. The question is which is suitable for storing CAD data.

Based on our analysis, we believe that persistent deductive object-relational or object-oriented database systems are ideal for supporting CAD as they not only provide direct support for the effective storage and efficient access to large amounts of data with complex structures on disk, but also perform the inferences and computations.

This is the idea behind the development of the DrawCAD system. DrawCAD is a CAD system built on top of Relationlog, a persistent object-relational deductive database system [5]. It facilitates the creation of graphical objects by reusing previously created objects. The DrawCAD system illustrates how CAD systems can be developed, using advanced database techniques to store and manage data and also perform inferences and computations that are normally performed by the application program.

This paper is organized as follows. Section 2 discusses the design and implementation of DrawCAD. Section 3 illustrates the Relationlog database for DrawCAD. Section 4 shows some examples in DrawCAD. Section 5 provides the conclusions based on the current work done and some suggestions for future research.

2 DrawCAD Design and Implementation

DrawCAD is a CAD system built on top of the Relationlog object-relational deductive database system. It facilitates drawing on the computer screen, based on input from a mouse, and storing the graphic data in a Relationlog database. It can also read the data stored in the Relationlog database and display it. DrawCAD provides a two-way, user-friendly and continuous interaction with the Relationlog system. It is based on the idea of creation of blocks and their reuse. It facilitates creation of blocks by drawing primitives and grouping them. It also facilitates creation of a block by containing previously created blocks. So using DrawCAD, blocks can be created, their data stored in the Relationlog database and they can be reused in creating other blocks. It enables a continuous cyclic process of creation, persistent storage, querying and reuse of blocks, which illustrates the idea of designing parts by work specialization.

The design and implementation aspects of DrawCAD, not only involves the design and development of the graphical interface, but also the Relationlog aspects. The Relationlog system has been modified to facilitate interaction with

DrawCAD. Also the Relationlog database is designed in a special way to store and deduce data.

Programming environment DrawCAD is developed in TCL (Tool Command Language), using a graphical toolkit, TK, that comes with it. A TCL program or script is a bunch of commands like a batch file or a shell script. TCL is an interpreted language and needs an interpreter to execute the TCL scripts. The standard interpreter used is called *wish*. This interpreter is a set of TCL functions that interprets TCL commands.

TK is an add-on extension to TCL and provides extra TCL commands related to creating graphical interfaces. The main purpose of TK is to provide TCL commands to create and manipulate widgets. A *Widget* is a single component of the interface such as buttons, text boxes, check buttons etc. Widgets are placed in windows, which are the screens that show up when the TCL script is executed. Widgets perform different roles depending on their type.

The widgets that are used in DrawCAD, are mainly the button, entry box and canvas widgets. The entry box widget allows the user to input text information. The *canvas* widget allows drawing primitives to be drawn on it. Primitives like lines, ellipses and rectangles etc., can be drawn on the canvas based on certain mouse actions on it.

TCL allows a TCL interpreter (wish) to be embedded in C programs. This facilitates calling TCL commands from a C program. This way a graphical interface script, written in TCL, can be called from a C program. This is the method used to call DrawCAD from Relationlog.

DrawCAD Interface DrawCAD provides two windows: *design window* and *storage window*. The drawing primitives are drawn and blocks are created in the *design window*. This window has a canvas widget in which the drawing activity takes place. It also has a number of buttons which perform different functions. The *storage window* has a canvas widget that is used only for displaying the created blocks. Blocks can be selected, for reuse or deletion, from this window.

The blocks are created in the *design window* relative to the origin, which is the upper left corner of the canvas widget. Once the blocks are created they are moved to the *storage window*. DrawCAD has been designed this way so that the user has an empty *design window* whenever a new block is to be created. Also, the blocks that are to be reused can be selected from the *storage window*. The *storage window* acts as a repository for previously created blocks.

Interaction between DrawCAD and Relationlog The data that is input from DrawCAD, and stored in the Relationlog database, is of two kinds: *geometric data* and *block data*. The geometric data is the coordinate and color data of the drawing primitives. The block data includes the references to the different drawing primitives that form it, as well as the references to the sub-blocks and their locations in the block. The references to the drawing primitives are the unique identifiers of the drawing primitives, that form the block. The references to the sub-blocks are the unique drawing tags that are assigned to the blocks in the *storage window*.

The insertion and deletion of geometric and block data in the Relationlog database can be done through DrawCAD. Also, the Relationlog program has been so modified that it deduces the complete data of a block, when the block is inserted. The deduction of data is done as a result of querying the database. The data that is a result of the querying is made accessible to DrawCAD.

3 Relationlog Database for DrawCAD

The Relationlog database for DrawCAD stores the data input from DrawCAD. It is designed in a way that makes reuse of blocks possible. The schema of the database contains three parts: type definitions, relation definitions and rule definitions.

Type definitions Relationlog supports a number of primitive types such as *int*, *string*, and *float*, etc. It also supports user defined complex types using *tuple, set, list* constructs. DrawCAD mainly uses the following tuple types:

Point=[X: int, Y: int]
EntData=[Start: Point, End: Point, Color: Int]

The first type is for a point with X and Y coordinates. The second is for any entity type that has a start point and an end point and a color.

Relation definitions The relations used for DrawCAD are of two kinds: extensional relations that store the data input through DrawCAD, and intentional relations that store the data inferred using rules. The intensional relations combinedly store the complete data of the blocks.

The geometric data of the drawing primitives that form a block is stored in separate relations, one for each of the primitives. Their data cannot be stored as a part of a block relation, as each drawing primitives data is to be inserted as soon as it is drawn. This is to avoid making DrawCAD dependent on the main memory of the computer. The drawing primitive entities are referenced in the block relation. Retrieving the drawing primitive data of each block, involves simple rules that join the block relation to the different drawing primitive relations.

The following are the extensional relations:

(1) **Lines**: Stores the line ID and and the coordinate locations of the start point and end point of the line and its color.
(2) **Ellipses**: Stores the ellipse ID, the coordinate locations of the upper left corner and lower right corner of the rectangle that describes the ellipse and its color.
(3) **Rectangles**: Stores the rectangle ID, whether it is filled or not, and the coordinate locations of the upper left corner and the lower right corner and the color.

(4) **Polygons**: Stores the polygon ID, the number of sides, whether it is filled or not, the coordinate locations of the set of vertices that form the polygon, and its color.
(5) **Polylines**: Stores the polyline ID, the number of points, the coordinate locations of the series of points that form the polyline and its color.
(6) **Curves:** Stores the curve ID, the number of sides, the coordinate locations of the series of points that form the path of the curve, and its color.
(7) **Texts**: stores the text ID, the coordinate location of the text, the text matter and its color.
(8) **Blocks**: Stores the block ID, the set of references to the sub-blocks and their locations in the block, and the references to the different drawing primitives that form it. The references to the drawing primitives are the unique identifiers of the drawing primitives, that form the block. The references to the sub-blocks are the unique drawing tags that are assigned to the blocks in the *storage window.*

The following are the schemas for these extensional relations:

```
Lines (LID: int, Data: EntData)
Ellipse (EID: int, Data: EntData)
Rectangles (RID: int, Fill: int, Data: EntData)
Polygons (GID: int, Sides: int, Fill: int, Color: int, Vertices: {Point})
Polylines (PID: int, Sides: int, Color: int, Vertices: {Point})
Curves (CID: int, Sides: int, Color: int, Vertices: {Point})
Texts (TID: int, Data: [Loc: Point, Color:int, Text:String])
Blocks (BID: int,
        Sub_blocks:{[BID: int reference Blocks BID,
                     Base: {Point}]},
        Lines:{int} element reference Lines LID,
        Ellipses:{int} element reference Ellipses EID,
        Rectangles:{int} element reference Rectangles RID,
        Polygons:{int} element reference Polygons PID,
        Polylines:{int} element reference Polylines GID,
        Curves:{int} element reference Polylines CID,
        Texts:{int} element reference Texts CID)
```

There are two kinds of intensional relations in DrawCAD. The **Sub-blocks** relation is one of them. It contains the block IDs and all its sub-blocks and their base points. This relation stores the results of two recursive rules that identify all the sub-blocks of a block, down the composition hierarchy, and computes each sub-block's base-point. Its schema is shown below:

```
Sub_blocks(BID:int, {[BID:int, Base:Point]})
```

The other kind of relations, together, store the complete data of each block. For instance the **Block_Lines** relation stores the data regarding all the line entities that form each block. Its schema is shown below:

Block_Lines (BID:int, Lines:{[LID:int, Data:EntData]})

This relation stores the data of all the line entities that are referenced by a block and also the line entities referenced by its sub-blocks, computed relative to their base-points. See the rules below. The data of the other drawing entities are stored in similar relations.

Rule definitions The rules, which are a part of the schema, are used to deduce the complete data of each block, from the partial data that is stored in the database. The deduction of the complete data of a block is a three step process. The three steps and the rules associated with each step are discussed below:

1. **Direct Data of Blocks**: The direct data of a block is the data regarding the drawing entities referenced by the block. The direct data can be obtained by joining the block relation with the different drawing entity relations. This is to obtain the data of the drawing entities, referenced by a block, as part of the block's complete data. The rule shown below performs a join between the **Blocks** and the **Lines** relations. It deduces the data of lines, referenced by each block, as part of the block's data. The **Block_Lines** relation stores the intensional data of the lines of each block.

   ```
   Block_Lines (_BID, ⟨[_LID,_Data]⟩) :–
           Blocks (_BID,⟨_LID⟩),
           Lines (_LID,_Data])
   ```

   The rule states that if there is a reference to a line _LID in a block _BID, the data of this line, represented by the variable _Data is made a part of the **Block_Lines** relation. Each tuple in the **Block_Lines** relation has a Block's BID, together with all the lines it references: the LID of each line and the data of the line entity. Similar rules exist in the schema for deducing the data of the other drawing entities that form the blocks.

2. **Sub-blocks and Base-points** The following rules identify the identifiers of all the sub-blocks, of a particular block, down the sub-block hierarchy. They also compute the base points of each sub-block. The **Sub-blocks** relation stores the intensional data regarding all the sub-blocks of each block and their base-points.

   ```
   Sub_blocks (_BID, ⟨[_SubBID, ⟨[_X,_Y]⟩]⟩) :–
           Blocks (_BID,⟨[_SubBID, ⟨[_X,_Y]⟩]⟩)
   Sub_blocks (_BID, ⟨[_SubBID, ⟨[_X,_Y]⟩]⟩) :–
           Sub_blocks (_BID, ⟨[_SubBID′, ⟨[_X′,_Y′]⟩]⟩),
           Blocks (_SubBID′,⟨[_SubBID, ⟨[_X″,_Y″]⟩]⟩),
           _X=_X′+_X″,_Y=_Y′+_Y″
   ```

   The first rule states that if the block _BID has a reference to a sub-block _SubBID, and the sub-block location is [_X,_Y], then the **Sub-blocks** relation has a fact that states that the block _BID has a sub-block _SubBID with its base-point [_X,_Y]. The second rule states that if the block BID has a sub-block _SubBID' with its base-point is [_X',_Y']. in the **Sub-blocks** relation, and if the subblock _SubBID' has a reference to a sub-block _SubBID in the **Blocks** relation, then the block BID has a sub-block SubBID. This is due to the transitivity of the block and sub-block relationship. Also the base point of sub-block [_X,_Y], is calculated by adding its sub-block location [_X'',_Y''] to the base-point [_X',_Y'] of its super-block, This is represented by: _X=_X'+_X'', _Y=_Y'+_Y''.

3. **Data of Sub-blocks** The data of the drawing entities that are referenced by the sub-blocks is reused in representing the super-block. This is done by deducing the data of the sub-block, relative to the sub-blocks's base points by using rules to join the **Blocks** and **Sub_blocks** relations with the different drawing entity relations. The rule shown deduces the data of the lines that form the sub-blocks, of a block, as part of the complete data of the block.

   ```
   Block_Lines (_BID, ⟨[_LID, [[_X1,_Y1], [_X2,_Y2], _Color]]⟩) :-
           Sub_blocks (_BID, ⟨[_SubBID, ⟨[_X, _Y]⟩]⟩),
           Blocks (_SubBID, ⟨_LID⟩),
           Lines (_LID, [[_X1',_Y1'], [_X2',_Y2'], _Color]),
           _X1 = _X1' + _X, _Y1= _Y1' + _Y,
           _X2 = _X2' + _X, _Y2= _Y2' + _Y
   ```

   The rule states that if the block _BID has a sub-block _SubBID which has a reference to a line _LID, the data of the line, represented by the tuple [[_X1,_Y1], [_X2,_Y2], _Color] is added to the base-point [_X, _Y]. This is done by the clause _X1 = _X1' + _X, _Y1= _Y1' + _Y, _X2 = _X2' + _X, _Y2= _Y2' + _Y. The variables _X1, _Y1, _X2, _Y2, _Color computed is the data of the line, that forms the sub-block, computed as part of the block. Similar rules exist, in the database schema, for deducing the data of the other drawing entities of the sub-blocks of each block.

4 Sample Blocks in DrawCAD

In this section, we show some sample blocks in DrawCAD from the *fan-pulley problem*. These blocks illustrate the idea of reuse of blocks. Blocks are created for the *Nut*, *Cap screw*, *30305 Bearing* and a *30304 Bearing*. The *Shaft* is created using the *Nut* and the two *Bearings*, twice each. The *Shaft* is evolved into the *Inner-pulley*. The *Inner-pulley* is evolved into the block for the *Fan-pulley*, by using the *Cap-screw*, twice, and adding the external details of the pulley. Also, the *Inner-pulley* is evolved into the block for the *Wide-pulley* by adding different external details to it. Figure 1 shows the DrawCAD window with the different blocks of the *fan-pulley problem*.

This experiment shows how the blocks are evolved, starting from the basic components like the *Nut* and *Bearings* and ending with the two pulleys. The tuple in the **Blocks** relation for the Shaft entity is shown below.

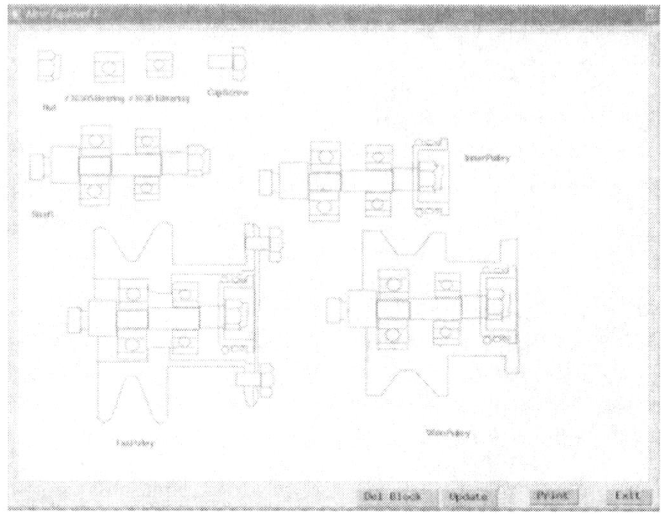

Fig. 1. Sample blocks created using DrawCAD

```
Blocks(
   BID: 5;
   Sub_blocks:{
      [BID: 1; Bases: {[X:235; Y:71]}];
      [BID: 2; Bases: {[X:79;  Y:40];
                       [X:77;  Y:110]}];
      [BID: 3; Bases: {[X:160; Y:47];
                       [X:159; Y:113]}]
   }
   Lines:{}; Ellipses:{}; Rectangless:{4; 5; 6; 7; 8};
   Polygons:{}; Polylines:{}; Curves:{7; 8}; Texts:{}
)
```

Block_Id	Block
1	Nut
2	30305 bearing
3	30304 bearing
4	Cap Screw
5	Shaft
6	Inner-pulley
7	Fan-pulley
8	Wide-pulley

Table 1. The Block IDs of the sample blocks

The Shaft entity has references to different drawing entities that form it. The sub-blocks attribute stores a set of tuples as its value. Each tuple in the set stores the int reference to a sub-block and its location. The Shaft entity has references to the following sub-blocks: Nut, 30305 bearing (two) and 30304 bearing (two). Also, the sub-block locations have been stored. The extract shows only the integer references to the sub-blocks. Table 1 shows the blocks correspond to these references.

The data, regarding the blocks, that is stored in the Relationlog database is only partial data. As shown in the database extract above, the Shaft entity only has references to the drawing entities and the sub-blocks that form it. The Relationlog system deduces the complete data of each block using the rules shown above.

5 Conclusions

The motivation behind the design and development of DrawCAD is to demonstrate a different approach to developing CAD systems, in which the advanced database system plays a major role, instead of the application program, in the functioning of the CAD system. In particular, we show how Relationlog, a deductive object-relational database system can be used to store CAD data and how its inference and computation mechanisms are useful to the CAD applications.

The sample blocks, created using DrawCAD, show how blocks can be created by specialisation. A block can reuse other blocks to represent its sub-parts. This not only reduces the database storage space but also the amount of work required to create parts of a block that exist as other blocks.

In the current problem, it is important that the database system have the capability of deducing the transitive closure of a relationship between blocks. In the problem of reuse of blocks, all the sub-blocks of a particular block have to be identified. This is achieved in Relationlog by using recursive rules. Also, the Relationlog system supports arithmetic functions that are used to compute the complete data of each block.

The design of the Relationlog database for storing the block data input from DrawCAD shows how data can be stored without redundancy. The blocks have only the references to the sub-blocks and Relationlog infers the data of the sub-blocks as part of its super-block. The problem of redundancy of data would occur if the data of the sub-blocks are duplicated in their super-blocks. The Relationlog database design for DrawCAD also helps during updates. If a block is deleted the data of its super-block is inferred after deletion to get the updated data of the super-block. But, if the data of a sub-block is duplicated in the super-block, deletion of a block will mean that its copy in the super-block has to be deleted too.

The current implementation of DrawCAD is not yet a full-fledged CAD system. In CAD, the user can perform certain operations on graphical objects, like blocks, such as scaling and rotation. The scaling operation can scale a block in either the X or Y directions, by a certain number of units, defined by the user.

The rotation operation can rotate a block by a certain rotation angle, defined by the user. These operations are performed at the time the block is inserted. The user inputs the values for the scale factor in both X and Y directions and the rotation angle of the block being inserted. Depending on the values, input by the user, the CAD application program performs some computations, based on the data of the block, and displays the transformed version of the block. These scaling and rotation operations involve complicated computations based on fundamental geometrical concepts. The scaling and rotation operations that are computed by the application program, can be performed by Relationlog using rules. The rules that represent the computations involved with scaling and rotating blocks, will be highly complicated. Also, the actual geometrical and mathematical steps involved with these operations needs to be investigated, if they are to be incorporated into DrawCAD. Incorporating these operations, in DrawCAD, will be considered in the future.

References

1. M.P. Groover and Jr E.W. Zimmers. *CAD/CAM Computer-Aided Design and Manufacturing.* Prentice-Hall,Inc., 1984.
2. M. Jarke, R. Gallersdorfer, M. Jeusfeld, M. Staudt, and Stefan Eherer. ConceptBase: A Deductive Object Base for Meta Data Management. *Journal of Intelligent Information System*, 4(2):167–192, 1995.
3. W. Kim. *Introduction to Object-Oriented Databases.* The MIT Press, 1990.
4. C. Lamb, G. Landis, J. Orenstein, and D. Weinreb. The ObjectStore System. *Communications of the ACM*, 34(10):50–63, 1991.
5. M. Liu. The Relationlog System. *Software – Practice and Experience*, 31(5):409–443, 2001.
6. M. Liu and M. Guo. ROL2: A Real Deductive Object-Oriented Database Language. In *Proceedings of the 17th International Conference on Conceptual Modeling (ER '98)*, pages 302–315, Singapore, Nov. 16-19 1998. Springer-Verlag LNCS 1507.
7. R. Ramakrishman and J. D. Ullman. A Survey of Deductive Database Systems. *Journal of Logic Programming*, 23(2):125–150, 1995.
8. R. Ramakrishnan, D. Srivastava, S. Sudarshan, and P. Seshadri. The CORAL Deductive System. *The VLDB Journal*, 3(2):161–210, 1994.
9. D. Ruland. A Data Model for Electronic CAD/CAM – Applications. In *Proceedings of the International Workshop on Graphtheoretic Concepts in Compututer Science*, pages 290–305, Anaheim, California, 1986.
10. V. Soloviev. An Overview of Three Commercial Object-Oriented Database Management Systems: ONTOS, ObjectStore, O2. *SIGMOD Record*, 21(1):93–104, 1992.
11. M. Stonebraker. *Object-Relational DBMSs: The Next Great Wave.* Morgan Kaufmann, 1995.
12. D.L. Taylor, editor. *Computer-Aided Design.* Addison Wesley., 1992.
13. W. Wilkes, P. Klahold, and G. Schlageter. Complex and Composite Objects in CAD/CAM Databases. In *Proceedings of the Fifth International Conference on Data Engineering*, pages 443–450, Los Angeles, California, USA, 1989. IEEE Computer Society.
14. Y-K. Yang. An Enhanced Data Model for CAD/CAM Database Systems. In *Proceedings of the 25th ACM/IEEE Conference on Design Automation*, pages 263–268, Anaheim, California, 1988.

A Statistical Approach to the Discovery of Ephemeral Associations among News Topics*

M. Montes-y-Gómez [1], A. Gelbukh [1], and A. López-López [2]

[1] Center for Computing Research (CIC), National Polytechnic Institute (IPN), 07738, Mexico.
mmontesg@susu.inaoep.mx, gelbukh@cic.ipn.mx

[2] Instituto Nacional de Astrofísica, Optica y Electrónica (INAOE), Puebla, Mexico.
allopez@inaoep.mx

Abstract. News reports are an important source of information about society. Their analysis allows understanding its current interests and measuring the social importance and influence of different events. In this paper, we use the analysis of news as a means to explore the society interests. We focus on the study of a very common phenomenon of news: the influence of the peak news topics on other current news topics. We propose a simple, statistical text mining method to analyze such influences. We differentiate between the *observable* associations—those discovered from the newspapers—and the *real-world* associations, and propose a technique in which the real ones can be inferred from the observable ones. We illustrate the method with some results obtained from preliminary experiments and argue that the discovery of the ephemeral associations can be translated into knowledge about interests of society and social behavior.

1 Introduction

The problem of analysis of large amounts of information has been solved to a good degree for the case of information that has fixed structure, such as databases with fields having no complex structure of their own. The methods for the analysis of large databases and the discovery of new knowledge from them are called data mining (Fayyad *et al.*, 1996, Han and Kamber, 2001). However, this problem remains unsolved for non-structured information such as unrestricted natural language texts.

Text mining has emerged as a new area of text processing that attempts to fill this gap (Feldman, 1999; Mladenić 2000). It can be defined as data mining applied to textual data, i.e., as the discovery of new facts and world knowledge from large collections of texts that—unlike those considered in the problem of natural language understanding—do not explicitly contain the knowledge to be discovered (Hearst, 1999). Naturally, the goals of text mining are similar to those of data mining: for instance, it also attempts to uncover trends, discover associations, and detect deviations in a large collection of texts.

In this paper, we focus on the analysis of a collection of news reports appearing in newspapers, newswires, or other mass media. The analysis of news collections is an interesting challenge since news reports have many characteristics different from the texts in other domains. For instance, the news topics have a high correlation with

* Work done under partial support of CONACyT, CGEPI-IPN, and SNI, Mexico.

H.C. Mayr et al. (Eds.): DEXA 2001, LNCS 2113, pp. 491–500, 2001.

society interests and behavior, they are very diverse and constantly changing, and also they interact with, and influence, each other.

Some previous methods consider: the trend analysis of news (Montes-y-Gómez *et al.*, 1999), the detection of new events on a news stream (Allan *et al.*, 1998), and the classification of bad and good news (García-Menier, 1998). Here, we focus on the analysis of a very common phenomenon of news: the influence of the peak news topics over other current news topics.

We define a peak news topic as a topic with one-time short-term peak of frequency of occurrence, i.e., such that its importance sharply rises within a short period and very soon disappears. For instance, the visit of Pope John Paul II to Mexico City became a frequent topic in Mexican newspapers when the Pope arrived to Mexico and disappeared from the newspapers in a few days, as soon as he left the country; thus this is a peak topic.

Usually, these topics influence over the other news topics in two main ways: a news topic induces other topics to emerge or become important along with it, or it causes momentary oblivion of other topics.

The method we proposed analyzes the news over a fixed time span and discovers just this kind of influences, which we call *ephemeral associations*.

Basically, this method uses simple statistical representations for the news reports (frequencies and probability distributions) and simple statistical measures (the correlation coefficient) for the analysis and discovery of the ephemeral associations between news topics (Glymour *et al.*, 1997).

Additionally, we differentiate between the *observable* ephemeral associations, those immediately measured by the analysis of the newspapers, and the *real-world* associations. In our model, the real-world associations in some cases can be inferred from the observable ones, i.e., for some observable associations its possibility to be a real-world one is estimated.

The rest of the paper is organized as follows. Section 2 defines ephemeral associations and describes the method for their detection. Section 3 introduces the distinction between the observable and the real-world associations and describes the general algorithm for the discovery of the real-world associations. Section 5 presents some experimental results. Finally, section 6 discusses some conclusions.

2 Discovery of Ephemeral Associations

A common phenomenon in news is the influence of a peak topic, i.e., a topic with one-time short-term peak of frequency, over the other news topics. This influence shows itself in two different forms: the peak topic induces some topics to emerge or become important along with it, and the others to be momentarily forgotten.

This kind of influences (time relations) is what we call ephemeral associations.[1] An ephemeral association can be viewed as a direct or inverse relation between the probability distributions of the given topics over a fixed time span. Figure 1 illustrates

[1] This kind of associations is different from the associations of the form $X \Rightarrow Y$, because they not only indicate the co-existence or concurrence of two topics or a set of topics (Ahonen-Myka, 1999; Rajman & Besançon, 1998; Feldman & Hirsh, 1996), but mainly indicate how these news topics are related over a fixed time span.

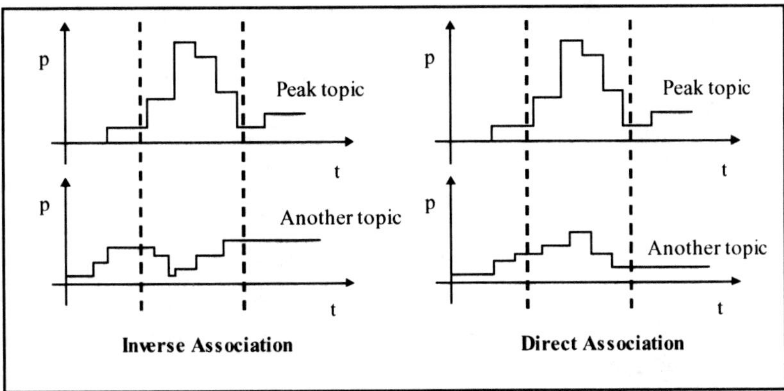

Fig. 1. Ephemeral associations between news topics

these ideas and shows an inverse and a direct ephemeral association occurring between two news topics. A direct ephemeral association indicates that the peak topic probably caused the momentary arising of the other topic, while an inverse ephemeral association suggests that the peak topic probably produces the momentary oblivion of the other news topic.

Thus, given a peak topic and the surrounding data, we detect the ephemeral associations in two steps:

1. Construction of the probability distribution for each news topic over the time span around the peak topic.
2. Detection of the ephemeral associations in the observed data set (if any).

These steps are described in the next two subsections.

2.1 Construction of the Probability Distributions

Given a collection of news reports corresponding to the time span of interest, i.e., the period around the existence of the peak topic, we construct a structured representation of each news report, which in our case is a list of keywords or *topics*. In our experiments we used a method similar to one proposed by Gay and Croft (1990), where the topics are related to *noun strings*. We apply a set of heuristic rules proper to Spanish and based on proximity of words that allow identifying and extracting phrases. These rules are guided by the occurrence of articles and some times by the occurrence of the prepositions *de* or *del* (of in English) along with nouns or proper nouns. For instance, given the following paragraph, the highlighted words are selected as keywords.

"La demanda de acción de inconstitucionalidad tiene como argumentos una serie de violaciones que el Congreso de Yucatán incurrió porque, de acuerdo con el PRD, hizo modificaciones a la ley electoral 90 días antes de que se lleven a cabo los comicios en ese Estado de la República".

Once this procedure is done, a frequency f_k^i can be assigned to each news topic. The frequency f_k^i is calculated as the number of news reports for the day i that mention the topic k. It is more convenient, however, to describe each news topic k by a probability distribution $D_k = \{p_k^i\}$ by the days i, where for a given day i, p_k^i expresses the probability for a news topic randomly chosen from the reports of that day to be the topic k:[2]

$$p_k^i = f_k^i \Big/ \sum_{j \in Topics} f_j^i \tag{1}$$

We will call the values p_k^i *relative probabilities*. A probability $p_k^i = 0$ indicates that the topic k was not mentioned on the day i. The relative probabilities p_k^i are advantageous for the discovery of the ephemeral associations mainly because they maintain a normalization effect over the news topics: for any day i,

$$\sum_{k \in Topics} p_k^i = 1$$

This condition holds for the whole period of interest and means that the increase of the relative probability of one news topic always is compensated by the decrease of probability of some other topics, and vice versa.

2.2 Detection of Ephemeral Associations

The ephemeral associations express inverse or direct relations between the peak topic and some other current news topics (see the figure 1). Let the peak topic be, say, the topic $k = 0$ and the other one we are interested in be, say, the topic $k = 1$. The statistical method we use to detect the observable associations is based on the correlation measure r between the topics $k = 0$ and $k = 1$(Freund and Walpole, 1990) defined as:

$$r = \frac{S_{01}}{\sqrt{S_{00} S_{11}}}, \quad \text{where} \quad S_{kl} = \sum_{i=1}^{m} \left(p_k^i p_l^i\right) - \frac{1}{m}\left(\sum_{i=1}^{m} p_k^i\right)\left(\sum_{i=1}^{m} p_l^i\right) \quad k,l = 0, 1. \tag{2}$$

Here, p_k^i are defined in the previous section and m is the number of days of the period of interest.

The correlation coefficient r measures how well the two news topics are related to each other.[3] Its values are between –1 and 1, where –1 indicates that there exists an exact inverse relation between the two news topics; 1 indicates the existence of an exact direct relation between the news topics, and 0 the absence of any relation at all.

Therefore, if the correlation coefficient between the peak topic and some other news topic is greater than a user-specified threshold u (i.e., $r < -u$) then there exists a *direct* ephemeral association between them. On the other hand, if the correlation

---

[2] This roughly corresponds to the percentage of the space the newspapers devoted to the topic k on the day i.

[3] The usual interpretation of the correlation coefficient is the following: $100\,r^2$ is the percentage of the variation in the values of one of the variables that can be explained by the relation with the other variable.

coefficient is less than the threshold $-u$ (i.e., $r < -u$) then there exists an *inverse* ephemeral association between the two topics.

There are two reasons for introducing the user-specified threshold u. First, it softens the criterion so that we can approximate the way a human visually detects the association. Second, to cope with the relatively small data sets in our application: since few data are available (a peak topic persists over few days), random variations of topic frequencies unrelated to the effect in question can greatly affect the value of the correlation coefficient. A typical value recommended for u is around 0.5.

3 Discovery of Real World Associations

Newspapers usually have a fixed size, and the editor has to decide what news to include in the day's number and what not to include. Thus, the frequencies of the news mentioned in a newspaper do not directly correspond to the number of events that happen in the real world on the same day.

In the next subsection, we explain this important difference between the real world news frequencies and the ones normalized by the fixed size of the newspaper. Then, we show how to estimate whether the observable associations are mainly due to the normalization effect or there is a possible real-world association component.

3.1 The Notion of Real World Associations

Since our ultimate goal is to discover the associations that hold in the real world, it is important to distinguish between two different statistical characteristics of the topics appearing in the newspapers. One characteristic is the real-world frequency: the frequency with which the corresponding news comes from the information agencies, for instance. Another characteristic is the observable frequency, expressed as the pieces of news actually appearing in the newspapers.

To illustrate this difference, let us consider two sources of information: say, a journalist working in Colombia and another one working in Salvador. Let the first one sends 30 messages each week and the second one sent 30 messages in the first week and 70 messages in the second week. These are the real-world frequencies: 30 and 30 in the first week, and 30 and 70 in the second one (i.e., there was something interesting happening in Salvador in the second week). However, the newspaper has a fixed size and can only publish, say, 10 messages per week. Then it will publish 5 and 5 messages from these correspondents in the first week, but 3 and 7 in the second week. These are the observable frequencies, since this is the only information we have from the newspaper texts.

Our further considerations are based on the following two assumptions.

Assumption 1: The newspapers tend to have a constant "size."[4]

Thus, the observable frequencies can be considered normalized, i.e., their sum is a constant, while the real world ones are not normalized. We assume that these two kinds of frequencies are proportional, being the proportion coefficient the normaliza-

[4] The "size" of a newspaper not only depends on its physical size (for instance, the number of pages) but also on the number of the journalists, the time required for editing, printing, etc.

tion constant. Thus, we define a real-world ephemeral association as an association that holds between the topics in the real world and not only in the observable (normalized) data, and we consider that an observable ephemeral association is a combination of two sources: a (possible) real-world ephemeral association and the normalization.

The normalization effect is always an inverse correlation effect. This means that the increase of probability of the peak topic is always compensated by the decrease of probability of some other topics, and vice versa. Thus, we can conclude that any *direct* observable ephemeral association is, very probably, a real-world association.

Assumption 2: The peak topic proportionally takes away some space from each current news topic.

First, this assumption implies that the relative proportions among the rest of the news topics do not change if we take away the peak topic and its related topics. Second, no topic completely disappears only as a consequence of the normalization effect.[5]

3.2 Detection of Real World Associations

As we have noted, all direct associations should be considered real-world ones, so we only need to analyze the inverse ones. The idea is to restore the original distribution of the topics by eliminating the normalization effect, and check if this distribution still correlates with that of the peak topic.

The Assumption 2 allows us to estimate the probability distribution $D'_k = \{p'^i_k\}$ of the topic k as it would be without the normalization effect, where the probability p'^i_k expresses the relative probability of occurrence of the topic k on the day i after we take away the peak topic and it related topics. This probability is calculated as follows:

$$p'^i_k = f^i_k \Big/ \sum_{j \notin Peak} f^i_j \tag{3}$$

Here the set *Peak* consists of the peak topic and its related topics (those with a direct association), while the frequency f^i_k indicates the number of news reports in the day i that mention the topic k.

Therefore, an inverse observable association between the peak topic and the news topic k is likely a real-world association if it remains after the normalization effect is eliminated from the topic k. In other words, if the correlation coefficient between the peak distribution and the corrected distribution D'_k is less than the user-specified threshold $-u$ (i.e., $r < -u$) then the inverse observable ephemeral association is likely a real-world one.

---

[5] Usually, newspaper editors design the newspaper format and contents in such a way that they expose all news of the day, even if briefly.

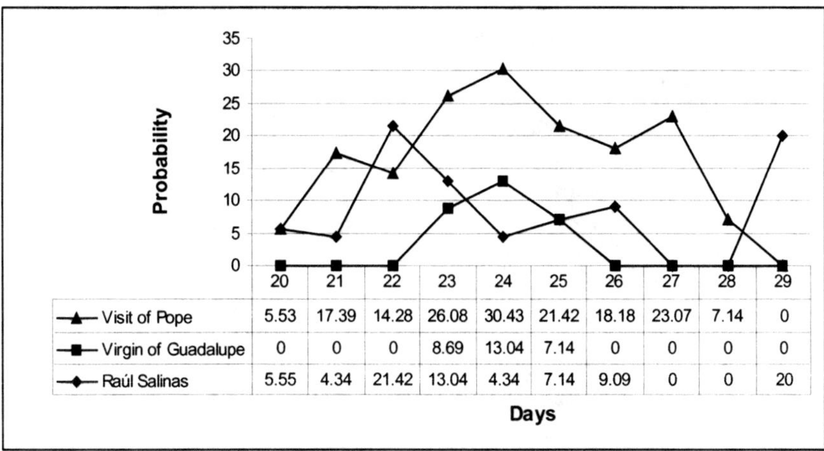

	20	21	22	23	24	25	26	27	28	29
Visit of Pope	5.53	17.39	14.28	26.08	30.43	21.42	18.18	23.07	7.14	0
Virgin of Guadalupe	0	0	0	8.69	13.04	7.14	0	0	0	0
Raúl Salinas	5.55	4.34	21.42	13.04	4.34	7.14	9.09	0	0	20

Fig. 2. Analysis of the peak topic "*Visit of Pope*"

Concluding, the our basic algorithm for the discovery of the real-world ephemeral associations among the news topics of a given period consists of the following steps:

1. Calculate the (observable) probabilities by the formula (1);
2. Calculate the (observable) correlations between the peak topic and the other ones by the formula (2);
3. Select the topics that strongly correlate with the peak one, using a threshold $u \approx 0.5$;
4. Determine which associations are real-world ones:
   a. All direct associations are real-world ones;
   b. For the inverse associations,
      i. Build the corrected distributions by the formula (3), using the knowledge obtained at the step 3;
      ii. Calculate the (real-world) correlations between the peak topic and the other ones using the formula (2) and the corrected distributions;
      iii. The topics for which this correlation is strong represent the real-world associations.

4 Experimental Results

To test these ideas, we used the Mexican newspaper *El Universal*.[6] We collected the national news for the ten days surrounding the visit of Pope John Paul II to Mexico City, i.e., from January 20 to 29, 1999, and looked for some ephemeral associations between this peak topic and the other topics.

One of the associations detected with our method (using the threshold $u = 0.6$) was a direct ephemeral association between the peak topic and the topic *Virgin of*

[6] http://www.el-universal.com.mx

Guadalupe.[7] The figure 2 illustrates this association. The correlation coefficient was $r = 0.959$ for the period between the 23 and 25 of January (stay of the Pope in Mexico), and $r = 0.719$ for the surrounding period between the 20 and 29 of January.

Since this association was a direct one, it had a high possibility for being a real-world one. This means that the topic *Virgin of Guadalupe* probably emerged because of the influence of the peak topic. Moreover, since this topic was the only one that had a direct association with the peak topic, we deduced that the visit of the Pope was strongly related with *Virgin of Guadalupe* (in fact, he has focused his discourse on this important Mexican saint).

Another interesting discovery was the inverse association between the peak topic and the topic *Raúl Salinas* (brother of the Mexican ex-president, Carlos Salinas de Gortari, sentenced in the 22 of January). The figure 2 also shows this association.

The correlation coefficient $r = -0.703$ between the 22 and 26 of January (period covering the *Visit of Pope* and the sentencing of *Raúl Salinas*) indicates the existence of an inverse observable ephemeral association.

In order to determine the possibility of this association for being a real-world one, we analyzed the normalization effect. First, we built the probability distribution of the topic *Raúl Salinas* without considering the peak topic and its related topics (the topic *Virgin of Guadalupe* in this case). The new probability distribution was:

$$D'_{Raul\ Salinas} = \{5.88,\ 5.26,\ 25,\ 17.64,\ 6.25,\ 9.09,\ 11.11,\ 0,\ 0,\ 20\}$$

Second, we recomputed the correlation coefficient between the peak topic and the topic *Raúl Salinas*. The new correlation coefficient $r = -0.633$ (between the 22 and 26 of January) indicated that it was very possible for this association to be real-world one. If this was true, then the topic *Raúl Salinas* went out of the attention because of the influence of the visit of the Pope to Mexico City.

As another example, we examined the peak topic *Death of Kennedy Jr.* This topic took place between the 18 and 24 of July of 1999. For the analysis of this peak topic, we used the news appearing in the national desk section of the newspaper *The New York Times.*[8] Among our discoveries, there were two inverse ephemeral associations. One of them between the peak topic and the topic *Election 2000*, with $r = -0.68$, and the other one between the peak topic and the topic *Democrats*, with $r = -0.83$. The figure 3 shows these associations.

Since these associations were both inverse ones, we analyzed their normalization effect. First, we built their probability distributions without considering the peak topic:

$$D'_{Election\ 2000} = \{0,\ 9.52,\ 0,\ 5.26,\ 0,\ 0,\ 0,\ 2.94,\ 11.11\}$$
$$D'_{Democrats} = \{11.53,\ 4.76,\ 0,\ 0,\ 0,\ 0,\ 0,\ 2.94,\ 7.4\}$$

Then, we recomputed their correlation coefficients. The probability distribution of the topic *Democrats* did not change (because of the zero probabilities of the topic

[7] A Mexican saint whose temple the Pope visited.

[8] The topics were extracted manually as opposed to the Spanish examples that were analyzed automatically.

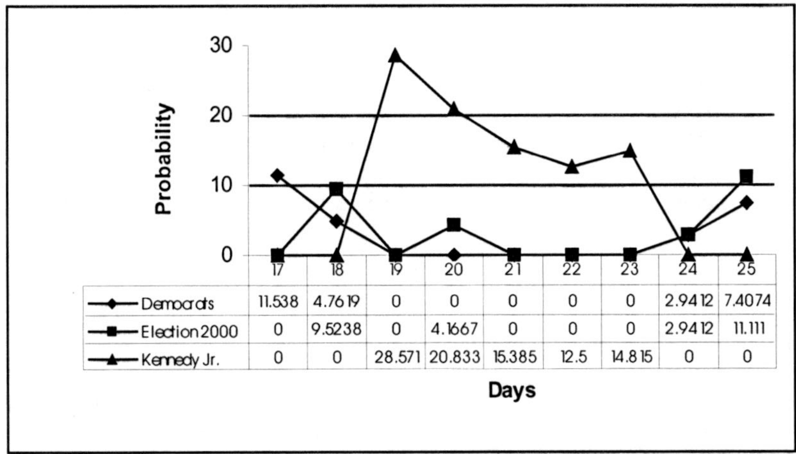

Fig. 3. Analysis of the peak topic "*Death of Kennedy Jr.*"

Democrats during the peak existence). Thus, the correlation coefficient was again $r = -0.83$ and we concluded that this association had a high possibility for being a real-world one.

On the other hand, the new correlation coefficient between the topic *Elections 2000* and the peak topic, $r = -0.534$, was not less than the threshold $-u$ (we used $u = 0.6$), therefore, there was not enough evidence for this association to be a real-world one.

5 Conclusions

We have analyzed a very frequent phenomenon in real life situations—the influence of a peak news topic on the other news topics. We have described a method for the discovery of this type of influences, which we explain as a kind of association between the two news topics and call *ephemeral associations*. The ephemeral associations extend the concept of typical associations because they not only reveal co-existence relations between the topics but also their temporal relations.

We distinguish between two types of ephemeral associations: the observable ephemeral associations, those discovered directly from the newspapers, and the real-world associations. We have proposed a technique with which the observable associations are detected by simple statistical methods (such as the correlation coefficient) and the real-world associations are heuristically estimated from the observable ones.

For the sources that do not have any fixed size, such as newswires, the observed frequencies of the news reports correspond to the real world ones. For such sources, the method discussed in this paper do not make sense. An easier way to discover the same associations in this case is not to normalize the frequencies in the formula (1), using $p_k^i = f_k^i$ instead and then applying the formula (2).

However, if it is not clear or not known whether the news source presents the normalization problem, then the method presented here can be applied indiscriminately. This is because in the absence of normalization effect, our method will give equally correct results, though with more calculations.

As future work, we plan to test these ideas and criteria under different situations and to use them to detect special circumstances (favorable scenarios and difficult conditions) that make the discovering process more robust and precise. Basically, we plan to experiment with multiple sources, and to analyze the way their information can be combined in order to increase the precision of the results.

Finally, it is important to point out that the discovery of this kind of associations, the ephemeral associations among news topics, helps to interpret the relationships between society interests and discover hidden information about the relationships between the events in social life.

References

1. Ahonen-Myka, Heinonen, Klemettinen, and Verkamo (1999), Finding Co-occurring Text Phrases by Combining Sequence and Frequent Set Discovery, Proc. of the Workshop on Text Mining: Foundations, Techniques and Applications, IJCAI-99, Stockholm, 1999.
2. Allan, Papka and Lavrenko (1998), On-line new Event Detection and Tracking, Proc. of the 21st ACM-SIGIR International Conference on Research and Development in Information Retrieval, August 1998
3. Fayyad, Piatetsky-Shapiro, Smyth and Uthurusamy (1996), Advances in Knowledge Discovery and Data Mining, Cambridge, MA: MIT Press, 1996.
4. Feldman, editor (1999), Proc. of The 16th International Joint Conference on Artificial Intelligence, Workshop on Text Mining: Foundations, Techniques and Applications, Stockholm, Sweden, 1999.
5. Feldman and Hirsh (1996), Mining Associations in Text in the Presence of Background Knowledge, Proc. of the 2nd International Conference on Knowledge Discovery (KDD-96), Portland, 1996.
6. Freund and Walpole (1990), Estadística Matemática con Aplicaciones, Cuarta Edición, Prentice Hall, 1990. (In Spanish)
7. García-Menier (1998), Un sistema para la clasificación de notas periodísticas, Simposium Internacional de Computación CIC-98, México, D.F., 1998.
8. Gay and Croft (1990), Interpreting Nominal Compounds for Information Retrieval, Information Processing and Management 26(1): 21-38, 1990.
9. Glymour, Madigan, Pregibon, and Smyth (1997), Statistical Themes and Lessons for Data Mining. Data Mining and Knowledge Discovery 1, 11-28, 1997.
10. Han and Kamber (2000), Data Mining: Concepts and Techniques, Morgan Kaufmann Publishers, 2001.
11. Hearst (1999), Untangling Text Data Mining, Proc. of ACL'99: the 37th Annual Meeting of the Association for Computational Linguistics, University of Marylnd, 1999.
12. Mladenić (2000), Proc. of the Sixth International Conference on Knowledge Discovery and Data Mining, Workshop on Text Mining, Boston, MA, 2000.
13. Montes-y-Gómez, López-López and Gelbukh (1999), Text Mining as a Social Thermometer, Proc. of the Workshop on Text Mining: Foundations, Techniques and Applications, IJCAI-99, Stockholm, 1999.
14. Rajman and Besançon (1998), Text Mining - Knowledge Extraction from Unstructured Textual Data, 6th Conference of International Federation of Classification Societies (IFCS-98), Rome, 1998.

Improving Integrity Constraint Enforcement by Extended Rules and Dependency Graphs

Steffen Jurk[1] and Mira Balaban[2]

[1] Cottbus Technical University of Brandenburg,
Dept. of Databases and Information Systems,
P.O.B. 101344, 03044 Cottbus, Germany
sj@informatik.tu-cottbus.de

[2] Ben-Gurion University,
Dept. of Information Systems Engineering,
P.O.B. 653, Beer-Sheva 84105, Israel
mira@cs.bgu.ac.il

Abstract. Integrity enforcement (IE) is important in all areas of information processing – DBs, web based systems, e-commerce. Beside checking and enforcing consistency for given data modifications approaches for IE have to cope with termination control, repair mechanisms, effect preservation and efficiency. However, existing approaches handle those problems in many different ways. Often the generation of repairs is too complex, termination of repairs is specified imprecise and effect preservation is insufficient. In this work we propose to extend integrity constraints by termination bounds and to represent the enforcement task by dependency graphs (DG) which allow efficient pre-processing without costly run-time evaluation of constraints. Further, we present an optimization technique by serializing DGs and a history approach for effect preservation. Our main contribution is an uniform framework that considers all relevant criteria for integrity enforcement and shows how termination control, effect preservation and efficiency can be designed to be used within modern database management systems.

1 Introduction

Integrity enforcement is important in all areas of information processing - DBs, web based systems, e-commerce, etc. Management of large data-intensive systems requires automatic preservation of semantical correctness. Semantical properties are specified by integrity constraints which can be verified by querying the information base. In dynamic situations, however, where operations can violate necessary properties, the role of integrity enforcement is to guarantee a consistent information base by applying additional *repairing actions*.

Integrity Enforcement (*IE*) is responsible for *selection* and *combination* of repairing actions, so that consistency for all constraints is achieved. Selection of a repairing action for a constraint depends on a *repairing policy*. The combination of repairing actions presents the three main problems in integrity enforcement: *Termination, effect preservation* and *efficiency*. The termination problem

H.C. Mayr et al. (Eds.): DEXA 2001, LNCS 2113, pp. 501–516, 2001.

is caused by repairing actions whose applications violate already enforced constraints, thereby leading to non-termination of the overall integrity enforcement process. The effect preservation problem arises when a repairing action achieves consistency by simply undoing the action being repaired. The efficiency problem deals with order optimization of the enforcement of the individual constraints. The optimization is possible since usually, the constraints are presented independently of each other, and an optimized ordering their enforcement might reduce repeated enforcements, or might lead to early detection of essential non-termination.

Termination control has been studied by many authors. The most common method is to describe constraints and their repairs as graphs, and detect cycles that might indicate potential non-termination. Yet, existing methods do not distinguish between desirable cyclic activations of repairing actions (finite cyclic activations) to non-terminating ones.

Effect preservation is the main motivation for the GCS work of Schewe and Thalheim [16]. The underlying idea is that an update is a change intended by its initiator. For example, the update $insert(a, e)$ intends that in the database state to which the update evaluates, the entity e is an element of the set a. In the context of Logic Programming the effects of updates have been studied by [9]. There, the effect of Prolog predicates depends on their positions in bodies of clauses and on the ordering of clauses in the program. Hence, changes resulting from updating primitives depends on the processing order which might cause different overall effects of an update.

In this paper we suggest an general approach for advanced database management, that combines ideas from *Rule Triggering Systems* (*RTS*s) [18] with compile-time oriented approaches, such as [16]. We suggest a uniform framework that considers the three relevant criteria of termination, effect preservation and optimization. Rather then providing a new approach, we understand our work as a uniforming approach were existing methods and ideas can be used and combined. The fundamental means of our work are *dependency graphs* which allow efficient pre-processing of database transactions, termination control and optimization.

With respect to selection of repairing actions, we claim that for each constraint, the desirable repairing policy (or policies) should be specified by the database developers. We underline the claim by showing the existence of multiple policies. With respect to termination, we suggest using termination bounds, that are provided by the database developers, as a powerful means for termination control. Our understanding of effect preservation is that every applied repair should not undo the initiated update. Finally, we show that the order is an important parameter for efficiency of enforcement, and present a method for optimizing the order towards avoiding unnecessary computational overhead caused by rollback operations.

The paper is organized as follows: Section 2 shortly describes related work and motivates our ideas on policies, termination bounds and optimizing the order of enforcement. As a result, we introduce our framework for integrity enforcement in section 3. Section 4 introduces dependency graphs as an essential means of the framework. Optimization of the order is discussed in section 5 and the history approach for effect preservation is presented in section 6. Section 7 concludes the paper.

2 The Right Task at the Right Time

The task of integrity enforcement attracted much work in the area of database management, particularly in the deductive database community. A classification of common approaches is given in [6]. In the GCS approach of [16], integrity with effect preservation is enforced by (static) update rewrite (*compile-time* integrity enforcement). Most approaches handle integrity enforcement at *run-time*, i.e., following an update application, relying on *design-time* analysis that is performed by the database developer. In general, hard problems like cycle detection for termination control and the finding of repairing actions, are done at design-time ([3]). Nevertheless, there is no uniform overall framework for controlling the relevant problems in integrity enforcement.

In this section we study the correlation in different approaches, between the relevant problems of IE (termination, consistency, effect preservation, optimization) to the level of time (design-, compile-, pre-processing- and run-time). Design-time (DT) covers activities of developers that specify the behavior and properties of a system. Compile-time (CT) activities cover methods that assist developers in verifying the design, e.g., cycle detection within active rules. In pre-processing-time (PT) an update is pre-processed into a new update that guarantees integrity. In a sense, we consider PT as pre-processing without evaluation of constraints and without execution of repairing actions. The run-time (RT) level is reached if a constraint is evaluated or a repair executed and only an expensive rollback operation can undo already performed changes. Table 1 shows that some related tasks, such as termination control, selection of repairing actions, or optimization, cannot be assigned to a unique level of integrity enforcement. In the next section we try to provide an answer to the question: "At which level the relevant tasks of IE should be handled?"

2.1 Repairing Mechanisms

As table 1 shows, there is no uniform treatment for repair mechanisms. Mayol [7,8] and MEER [1] compute repairs for each constraint at PT and RT. This is possible due to restrictions on the constraint language. MEER, for example, enforces only cardinality constraints of the ER model. The repairing actions are planned at PT, and the actual policy for selection among various alternatives is done at RT, by interaction with the user. The following example emphasizes the problem of alternative repairs:

Example 1. Consider the integrity constraint $a \subseteq b$ and an insert into the set a which might violate the constraint in case the new value is not a member of the set b. There exists three possible repairs, if the insert does not yield a consistent state: (1) *rollback* the whole transaction, (2) insert the new value into b, (3) only undo the insert. The latter repair only partially undoes the transaction, while the first one does rollback the whole transaction.

Table 1. Classification of a small range of existing approaches.

Approach	Task	Level
RTS	consistency (confluence)	DT/CT
	repairing actions (semi-automatic)	DT/CT
	termination (cycle detection)	DT/CT
	effect preservation (net effect)	DT/CT
	optimization (priorities, rule simplifications)	DT
	termination (by time-out, restrict nested rules)	RT
	optimization (rule execution)	RT
GCS	repairing actions (non-deterministic repairs possible)	DT
ACS	termination (restrict repeated updates)	CT
	effect preservation (specialization order)	CT
	consistency	CT
Mayol	termination (cycle detection)	PT
	repairing actions (automatic)	PT
	effect preservation	RT
	consistency	RT
MEER	repairing actions (fix repair policy by user interaction)	RT
	termination (restriction to cardinality constraint)	RT
	consistency	RT

In sum, generating repairs at PT or RT requires the consideration of different possible policies, and relies on interaction with the user for making an actual selection. The problem with that approach is that typical users cannot answer questions on repair policies. Therefore, the selection of appropriate repairing actions and its policies must be part of DT activities of application developers and can not be handled separately at PT or RT.

2.2 Termination Control

Termination control is a crucial requirement for integrity enforcement. The different methods can be categorized as follows: **(1) Bounds.** Some DBMSs provide time-out mechanisms that reject a transaction when a time bound set on a transaction is exceeded. Another approach is to restrict the maximal number of nested trigger activations. For example, Sybase imposes to cascade a trigger to a maximum of 16 levels. **(2) Restricted Constraints.** In database theory it is known that certain combinations of classes of constraints, e.g. functional and unary inclusion dependencies, guarantee termination. In MEER [1], termination proof for the suggested repairing updates relies on known results for testing if a database schema is strongly satisfiable [5]. **(3) Cycle Analysis.** The most common method is the detection of potential cycles within database schemata or sets of active rules. The work presented in this paper tries to combine the first and the third approaches.

An ultimate static method detects exactly all non-terminating applications: **(1)** It identifies all such cases (completeness). **(2)** It does not identify a terminating rule activation as non-terminating (soundness). However, in practice, most methods prefer completeness. That is, they identify all potentially non-terminating rule activations. The strength of a complete method stands in reverse correlation to the number of potential non-terminating activations that it detects. In the field of *Rule Triggering Systemss* [19], much effort have been devoted to termination control[1]. In these systems, static methods for termination analysis are used at CT. Consider, for example, two methods introduced in [3], where analysis is performed on activation or triggering graphs. Cycles in the graphs indicate potential non-termination. Figure 1 demonstrates two

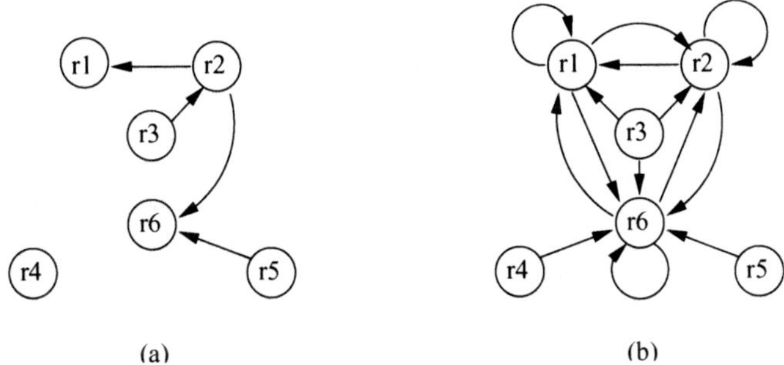

Fig. 1. (a) Activation graph and (b) Triggering graph

such graphs that result from the application of these methods to a set of rules $r_1, \cdots, r_6$ (consult [3] for details). Clearly, method (b) detects a high number of potential cycles, e.g., $r_1, r_6, r_2, r_1, \cdots$, while method (a) detects no cycle at all. Provided that both methods are complete, method (a) is stronger (it is also sound). That is, for complete methods, stronger methods detect less cycles[2].

The problem is that syntactic analysis is not sufficiently strong for distinguishing non-terminating rule sequences from the rest. Therefore, developers usually either avoid all detected cycles (thereby loosing the "good" ones that do not cause non-termination), or they leave cycle handling to the DBMS. Figure 2 shows desirable cycles (that the designer is aware of), that result from a recursively modeled hierarchy. A rule enforcing the salary-constraint would definitely be executed repeatedly along the hierarchy. The problem is how to distinguish terminating cycles from non-terminating ones.

In order to avoid strict cycle rejection we introduce, for every rule or constraint, a bound that restricts the number of executions within a cycle. For example, a rule that enforces the salary-constraint is bounded by the number of levels within the hierarchy. Assuming that the bound is known to the devel-

[1] Limitations of RTSs are studied in [15].

[2] This problem is closely related to the problem of *Integrity Constraint Checking* where syntactic analysis is used to identify updates that might cause violation of a given set of constraints.

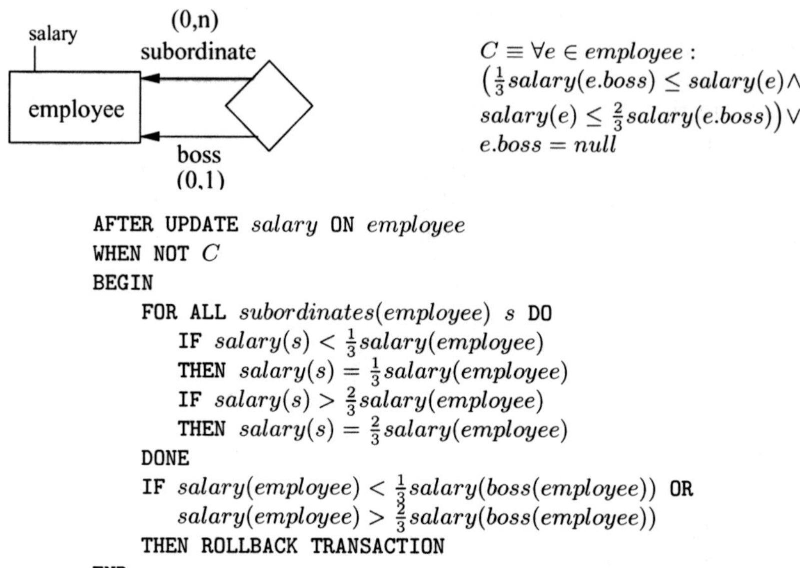

salary
(0,n)
subordinate
employee
boss
(0,1)
$C \equiv \forall e \in employee :$
$\left(\frac{1}{3}salary(e.boss) \leq salary(e) \wedge salary(e) \leq \frac{2}{3}salary(e.boss)\right) \vee e.boss = null$
AFTER UPDATE *salary* ON *employee*
WHEN NOT C
BEGIN
FOR ALL *subordinates*(*employee*) *s* DO
IF $salary(s) < \frac{1}{3}salary(employee)$
THEN $salary(s) = \frac{1}{3}salary(employee)$
IF $salary(s) > \frac{2}{3}salary(employee)$
THEN $salary(s) = \frac{2}{3}salary(employee)$
DONE
IF $salary(employee) < \frac{1}{3}salary(boss(employee))$ OR
$salary(employee) > \frac{2}{3}salary(boss(employee))$
THEN ROLLBACK TRANSACTION
END

Fig. 2. A recursively defined employee-boss hierarchy including a salary-restricting integrity constraint. The constraint is enforced by the given rule, that adapts the salary from subordinates but not from bosses.

oper means that the bound association belongs to the category of DT activities. Therefore, we propose the following rule extension:

Example 2. Extended rule syntax for using known boundaries.

```
CREATE TRIGGER <trigger name>
{ BEFORE | AFTER } <trigger event> on <table name>
[ REFERENCING <old or new values alias list> ]
[ FOR EACH { ROW | STATEMENT } ]
[ <trigger condition> ]
<trigger action>
BOUNDED BY <maximum of executions within a cycle>
```

The default bound, if no bound is given, is 1, which means to rollback a transaction if a cycle contains the rule more than once. The benefit is a meaningful restriction that is based on *natural bounds* of potential cycles, that helps developers to cope with termination problems. Termination can be enforced by pre-computing activation or triggering graphs and unfolding them according to the specified bounds. This is an important aspect of our approach.

2.3 Quality of Enforcement

The main task of IE is to enforce a set of integrity constraints $C_1, \cdots, C_n$. The order of enforcement is approach dependent, and provides a certain degree of freedom within the process of enforcement. Hence, the quality of enforcement can be understood as finding a "good" ordering.

Example 3. Let a, b, c be sets of integers with constraints $C_1 \equiv \forall t.(t \in a \Rightarrow t \in b)$ and $C_2 \equiv \forall t.(t \in a \Rightarrow t \notin c)$. C_1 is repaired by inserting missing elements into b or by propagating deletions in b to a. A rollback is performed if C_2 is violated. For an insert into a there are two possible enforcement orderings: Either $S_{12} \equiv insert_a(t); if\ t \notin b\ then\ insert_b(t); if\ t \in c\ then\ rollback$ or $S_{21} \equiv insert_a(t); if\ t \in c\ then\ rollback; if\ t \notin b\ then\ insert_b(t)$. Obviously, S_{21} is preferable, since in case of a rollback only $insert_a(t)$ has to be undone, whereas S_{12} requires to undo $insert_a(t)$ and $insert_b(t)$.

The example shows that rollback-optimized orders can improve the overall performance by avoiding undo operations. This is particularly important for large sets of rules and assertions. Note that both assertions and rules are part of current SQL:1999 standard, and are relevant for commercial database vendors.

Going back to the approaches introduced by table 1, optimization is usually not discussed in the literature. RTSs try to optimize rule sequences by applying priorities to rules (triggers) at DT. However, since a rollback operation can be artificially introduced (e.g. detection of a cycle, bound, violation of effects, etc.), static priorities are not sufficient. Furthermore, information about the amount of data and query costs can not be taken into account. Below, we propose optimization as part of PT or RT activities.

3 A DT-CT-PT-RT Framework for Integrity Enforcement

Following the observations presented above, we developed a framework for integrity enforcement that is based on extended rules and performs additional preparatory computations. We propose to split the relevant tasks as depicted in table 2. In this section we introduce extended rules, compares them to RTSs, and summarize the PT and RT activities of the framework.

Table 2. Suggested processing of the relevant tasks within our framework.

Task	Level
termination bounds (extended rules)	DT
repairing actions (extended rules)	DT/CT
termination (cut cycles according to bounds)	PT
optimization (find a "good" order)	PT
consistency (combine repairs)	PT
effect preservation (history)	RT

3.1 Extended Rules

Example 2 already introduced an extended version of the classical ECA rules. In this work we further extend the rule notion towards a constraint-centered rule that groups together several ECA-like repairing rules and a bound. The group includes rules that are relevant for the enforcement of a constraint.

Example 4. Extended rule as integrity constraints including repairing rules and a bound.

```
CREATE CONSTRAINT a-subset-b
AS NOT EXISTS ( SELECT t.* FROM a WHERE t.* IS NOT IN b )
AFTER INSERT ON a WHEN new NOT IN b THEN INSERT new INTO b
AFTER DELETE ON b WHEN old IN a THEN DELETE old FROM a
BOUNDED BY 1
```

Example 4 presents an inclusion dependency on two relations a and b. Inconsistencies are repaired by propagating insertions and deletions to a and b respectively. A bound is associated with each constraint in order to enforce termination. The repairing rules correspond to trigger definition of the SQL:1999 standard. Each rule is a semantic repair for the specified integrity constraint.

The designer has three responsibilities: **(1)** Ensure that each repairing rule is a semantic repair for the constraint. Formal definitions of repairs can be found in [4] and [2]. Approaches for deriving repairs with respect to given constraints can be found in [18,9]. **(2)** Derive bounds for constraint application, by analyzing the application domain. We hypothesize that for most practical applications, bound specification is feasible. **(3)** Show confluence of rules, e.g. [17,3].

3.2 Validating Integrity Enforcement

The constraint of example 4 includes redundancies, since the condition parts of the repairing rules can be derived from the constraint specification ($C \equiv a \subseteq b$ and $insert_a(t)$ imply that C is violated if $t \notin b$). However, for arbitrarily complex integrity constraints it is hard to derive such simplified and update-adapted conditions (an initial treatment is introduced in [18]). Further, the semantic verification of database behavior is limited to known classes of constraints. Therefore, we propose an alternative method for validating rules.

The framework can be run in a test mode, where the database is initially in a consistent state and after each rule execution the whole constraint (`AS` clause), is tested. In case the constraint does not hold the rule must be incorrect. Therefore, it is under the responsibility of the developer to assign test scenarios for each rule. We think that running a database in test mode is a pragmatic alternative for validating database applications, since existing methods of testing software can be used as well. Since testing is beyond the scope of this paper we omit any further details.

3.3 Compare to Rule Triggering Systems

In contrast to RTSs, termination can be controlled and enforced by using meaningful bounds. Note that in RTSs, even if cycles are detected, termination remains unclear. No optimization such as employing rule priorities at DT is necessary, and effect preservation is left for the DBMS responsibility. The following example demonstrates an update for which RTSs do not preserve the effects of the initial update.

Example 5. Consider a set x of integers and a set y of tuples (s,t) of integers. Let $\mathcal{I}_1 \equiv \forall z.(z \in y \Rightarrow z.t \in x)$ be an inclusion constraint and $\mathcal{I}_2 \equiv \forall z.(z \in y \Rightarrow z.s \notin x)$ be an exclusion constraint. The following ECA rules are obtained:

$$R_1 : \text{AFTER } insert_y((s,t)) \text{ WHEN } \neg\mathcal{I}_1 \text{ DO } insert_x(t)$$
$$R_2 : \text{AFTER } insert_y((s,t)) \text{ WHEN } \neg\mathcal{I}_2 \text{ DO } delete_x(s)$$
$$R_3 : \text{AFTER } delete_x(t) \text{ WHEN } \neg\mathcal{I}_1 \text{ DO } delete_y((*,t))$$
$$R_4 : \text{AFTER } insert_x(s) \text{ WHEN } \neg\mathcal{I}_2 \text{ DO } delete_y((s,*))$$

The wildcard $*$ denotes all values. The operation $T \equiv insert_y(i,i)$ on the empty database, might trigger either $R_1; R_4; R_2$ or $R_2; R_1; R_4$. Both executions lead to $insert_x(i)$ on the empty database which definitely does not preserve the effects of T. As long to tuple (i,i) is involved the effects are preserved, but in the general case (e.g. at CT) we have to assume that the set of rules does not preserve the effects. In section 6 we show how effects are preserved by our framework.

3.4 The Process of Integrity Enforcement

Based on a set of extended rules our framework is designed to handle all relevant problems of integrity enforcement, e.g. termination, effect preservation and optimization. All the constraint specifications are stored as meta data within a data repository of a DBMS. At PT a given update is prepared for its execution. In the first stage, a repair plan is built and termination is enforced by detecting and cutting potential cycles. Here the specified bounds help to enforce termination. Repair plans are based on dependency graphs which are introduced in section 4. In the second stage an order for constraint enforcement is fixed by applying certain optimization strategies as explained in section 5. In this work we discuss optimization on rollback operations only. At RT, the framework executes an optimized repair plan and preserves the effects by using the history of all previous database modifications. Details can be found in section 6.

4 Enforcement Plans and Dependency Graphs

This section introduces repair plans represented by dependency graphs (DGs). This work extends the DGs of Mayol [7]. We discuss the construction of dependency graphs, and how to enforce termination using DGs.

4.1 Static Integrity Constraint Checking

The computation of DGs at PT depends on an *interference* relationship between updates and integrity constraints. An update interferes with a constraint if its application might violate the constraint. Computing the interference relationship at PT requires detection of potential violations, without performing costly evaluations of the constraints.

In general, a PT computed interference relationship cannot guarantee RT violation, but it reduces the search space of an integrity enforcement procedure. Much work has been devoted to this problem in the field of integrity constraint checking [10,12,13,11]. Some methods perform simplifications that return a simplified condition that is left to test at RT [14]. In this work, we assume the existence of a predicate $interfere(S, C)$ that returns $false$ if S cannot violate C in any database state and $true$ otherwise.

Definition 1. *Let $\hat{R}$ be a set of rules and S an update.*

$$violate(S, \hat{R}) = \{r \mid r \in \hat{R} \wedge interfere(S, cond(r))\}$$

Clearly, a strong $interfere$ implies a small set of potential violations; the weakest $interfere$ is always true, implying $\hat{R}$ as the full set of violations. Henceforth, $event(r)$, $cond(r)$, $action(r)$ denote the event, condition and action of a rule r, respectively; $con(r)$ denotes the constraint of the extended rule that includes r, and $replace(r, newAction)$ denotes a replacement of the action of r.

4.2 Definition of Dependency Graphs

A dependency graph is defined by a tree structure. For a node n, $n.children$ denotes the set of child nodes of n. An update (sometimes called also *operation*) S is considered as a rule with $event(S) = cond(S) = null$.

Definition 2 (Dependency Graph - DG). *Let $\hat{R}$ be a set of rules and S an update. A dependency graph t for S is a tree whose nodes are labeled by rules, and satisfy the following:*

1. *$t = S$ (meaning the root node of t is labeled by S), and*
2. *for all nodes n of the tree t : $n.children = violate(action(n), \hat{R})$.*

In a sense, a DG reflects all possible constraint violations - the "enforcement space" or "worst case" - of the update. Note that a DG does not specify a concrete ordering for repairing. In order to derive a concrete transaction the paths of the DG must be serialized (sequenced). We elaborate on that point in section 5.

Example 6. Consider the database schema, constraints and rules in figure 3. A bank governs all customer data in a trust database. For each customer, a trust value is computed by a function f_{trust} that is stored in table trust. Further, customers need to be older than 20, earn more than \$5.000 per month, and their trust value must be at least 100. We omit bounds and provide only rules for insert updates. The given DG shows the worst case scenario for inserting a new person.

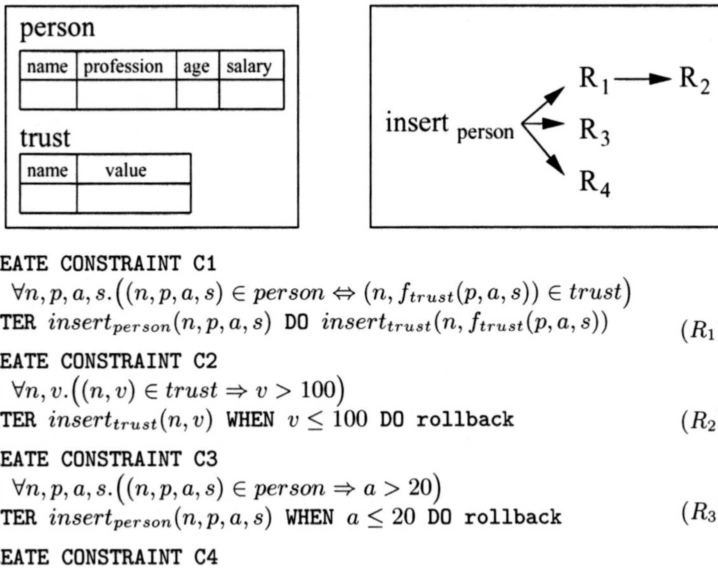

CREATE CONSTRAINT C1
AS $\forall n, p, a, s. \big((n, p, a, s) \in person \Leftrightarrow (n, f_{trust}(p, a, s)) \in trust\big)$
AFTER $insert_{person}(n, p, a, s)$ DO $insert_{trust}(n, f_{trust}(p, a, s))$ (R_1)

CREATE CONSTRAINT C2
AS $\forall n, v. \big((n, v) \in trust \Rightarrow v > 100\big)$
AFTER $insert_{trust}(n, v)$ WHEN $v \leq 100$ DO rollback (R_2)

CREATE CONSTRAINT C3
AS $\forall n, p, a, s. \big((n, p, a, s) \in person \Rightarrow a > 20\big)$
AFTER $insert_{person}(n, p, a, s)$ WHEN $a \leq 20$ DO rollback (R_3)

CREATE CONSTRAINT C4
AS $\forall n, p, a, s. \big((n, p, a, s) \in person \Rightarrow s > \$5.000\big)$
AFTER $insert_{person}(n, p, a, s)$ WHEN $s \leq \$5.000$ DO rollback (R_4)

Fig. 3. *Left:* the trust database; *Right:* dependency graph for an insert on person; *Bottom:* definition of constraints and rules

4.3 Termination

A DG might be infinite. A path in the graph represents a sequence of rules, such that the action of a rule in the sequence potentially violates the condition of the next rule. Non-termination is characterized by the existence of an infinite sequence (path) in the tree (analogous to the notion of cycles in an activation or a triggering graph). An infinite path must contain a rule that repeats infinitely often, since the total number of rules is finite. Termination can be enforced by restricting the number of enforcements for each rule on the path according to the bound that is specified for its constraint. If the bound is exceeded the path is cut and a rollback operation is used instead of the rule action. Consequently, a transaction based on a "truncated" DG always terminates.

However, static bounds do not exists, if the number of performed cycles depends on the update itself. For example, consider two sets and two constraints with cyclic dependencies, as in $C_1 \equiv \forall t.(t \in x \Rightarrow t \in y)$ and $C_2 \equiv \forall t.(t \in y \Rightarrow \sqrt{t} \in x)$, where x and y are sets of *integers*. Clearly, for inserting a value t into x the number of repeated enforcements for C_1 and C_2 depends on t. Therefore, the bound method is only useful, if appropriate bounds exist and can be specified by application developers.

4.4 Construction of Dependency Graphs

The construction of a dependency graph emerges naturally from Definition 2, and uses the bounds method. Let $\hat{R}$ denote the set of rules, and the array $count[C_i]$ with $C_i \in \hat{C}$ contain the bounds according to each constraint specification. The construction starts by applying $createDG(S, count)$ where the update S is taken as a rule to be repaired.

```
createDG(S, count)
  tree = S
  forall r ∈ violate(action(S), R̂) do
    if count[con(C_i)] = 0 then
      subTree = replace(r, rollback)
      tree = addChild(tree, subtree)
    else
      count[con(C_i)] = cou[const(C_i)] − 1
      subTree = createDG(r, count)
      tree = addChild(tree, subTree)
  return tree
```

The complexity of the algorithm depends on that of *violate*. In the worst case, the function *violate* tests for each rule $r \in \hat{R}$ whether r potentially violates S ($interfere(S, cond(r)) = true$). Under the assumption that rules do not change frequently, *violate* can be implemented efficiently, using indexing and caching techniques that avoid repeated computations. That is, rules sharing the same tables can be pre-computed, and already computed *interfere* values can be memorized. Consequently, for each database schema the appropriate dependency graph is computed only once, and is revised only when the specification of the constraints has been changed.

5 Serialization and Optimization

Dependency graphs (DGs) represent the general enforcement task. In order to derive an executable transaction a DG needs to be serialized. In this section we introduce a serialization procedure, and discuss its optimization.

Definition 3 (Serialization). *Let t be a DG. A serialization of t, denoted $ser(t)$, is a total ordering of the set of nodes (rules) of t.*

A *path serialization* of a dependency graph is a serialization that preserves the path ordering in the graph:

Definition 4 (Path Serialization). *Let t be a DG and $s = ser(t)$. The order s is a path serialization of t if for every two nodes t_1 and t_2 in s where $t_1 < t_2$, if t_1 and t_2 occur, both, in a single path in t, then t_1 occurs before t_2 in the path.*

Consider the DG in Figure 3. Some possible path serializations are:

$insert_{person}, R_1, R_2, R_3, R_4$	$insert_{person}, R_3, R_1, R_4, R_2$
$insert_{person}, R_1, R_2, R_4, R_3$	$insert_{person}, R_4, R_1, R_3, R_2$
$insert_{person}, R_3, R_4, R_1, R_2$	...

Definition 5 (Sequential Execution). *A finite serialization* $s \equiv r_1, \ldots, r_n$ *can be sequentially executed by the program* P_s : `for` $i = 1$ `to` n `do if` $cond(r_i)$ `then` $action(r_i)$. *The program* P_s *is called a sequential execution of* s

The following consistency theorem relies on the definition of path serializations (Definition 4). The proof appears in the full paper.

Theorem 1 (Consistency). *Let* t *be a finite DG (already truncated) with respect to an update* S *and a set of rules* $\hat{R}$. *Let* s *be a path serialization of* t. *Then the sequential execution of* s *yields a consistent database state.*

Since path serialization is not unique, there is room for optimization. As mentioned before, transaction processing within integrity enforcement can be improved, if rollback operations are performed as early as possible. Therfore, one idea for optimization is to identify possible rollback update in action parts of rules in the DG, and push this nodes to the beginning of the serialized DG.

Definition 6 (rollback optimization). *Let* s *be a path serialization of a DG* g *with* n *nodes, and* $f_s(i)$ *a weight function with* $1 \leq i \leq n$ *and*

$$f_s(i) = \begin{cases} i & \textit{i-th node of s contains no rollback operation} \\ 0 & \textit{otherwise} \end{cases}$$

Define

$$weight(s) = \sum_{i=0}^{n} f_s(i)$$

The sequence s *is rollback-optimized if* $weight(s) = max(weight(s'))$, *taken over all path serializations* s' *of* g.

We demonstrate optimization for the DG at figure 3 by the following path serializations and the result of its weight functions:
$s_1 = insert_{person}, R_1, R_2, R_3, R_4$ $\quad \sum f_{s1} = 1 + 2 + 0 + 0 + 0 = 3$
$s_2 = insert_{person}, R_3, R_1, R_4, R_2$ $\quad \sum f_{s2} = 1 + 0 + 3 + 0 + 0 = 4$
$s_3 = insert_{person}, R_3, R_4, R_1, R_2$ $\quad \sum f_{s3} = 1 + 0 + 0 + 4 + 0 = 5$

For the rules given in Figure 3 the serialization s_3 is a rollback-optimized one. Clearly, more sophisticated optimization techniques are possible. For example, if `BEFORE` rules and a modified notion of dependency graphs are used, the problem can be further optimized as shown by the following serialization (details are omitted):
$s_4 = R_3, R_4, insert_{person}, R_1, R_2$ $\quad \sum f_{s4} = 0 + 0 + 3 + 0 + 5 = 8$
which, indeed, avoids a rollback of $insert_{person}$.

The optimization method above assumes that all tests of conditions and executions of actions of rules have the same cost. Our framework also takes into account the average costs of testing conditions, and execution and rollbacks of actions. Costs can be collected by the running system, and reflect the specific behavior of the application. Since for a sequence of user transactions the order of rule enforcements is usually stable, we also employ temporal caching techniques to avoid computational overhead caused by optimization algorithms.

6 Run-Time and Effect Preservation

Theorem 1 guarantees that the sequential execution of a serialization yields a consistent database. In this section we consider the issue of effect preservation. We present a *run-time history* for achieving *effect preservation* (*EP*) under sequential execution.

Effect preservation is not often discussed in the literature. Rule triggering systems [18] use the notion of *net effect* of rules as a guard against, for example, deletions of inserted tuples in a single transaction. The notion of effect preservation generalizes the notion of net effect, since it amounts to disallowing undo operations. In particular, it implies that an inserted tuple can not be deleted, a deleted tuple can not be inserted again, and the update of a tuple can not be reversed. As shown by example 5, EP at CT is ambiguous and should therefore be handled at RT.

In order to support effect preservation, we consider an execution of a serialization $s \equiv r_1, \ldots, r_n$ as a single transaction that is associated with a *history* h_s of database modifications. Every new modification is checked against the history in order to find possible interferences of effects. The history considers insert, delete and update operations, where the latter one is represented as "delete existing value" and "insert a new value". Further, we distinguish between "real" inserts and deletes to "update caused" inserts and deletes.

Definition 7 (History). *The history h is a chronological collection of all database modifications within a transaction. Modifications are mapped to tuples of the history as follows:*

$$\begin{aligned} insert_{table}(value) &\mapsto (table, insert, value) \\ delete_{table}(value) &\mapsto (table, delete, value) \\ update_{table}(v_{old}, v_{new}) &\mapsto t_1 = (table, udelete, v_{old}) \text{ and} \\ & \quad\;\; t_2 = (table, uinsert, v_{new}) \\ & \quad\;\; \text{with } t_1 < t_2 \end{aligned}$$

Since h can be totally ordered, $t_1 < t_2$ means that t_1 is inserted to the history before t_2 (t_1 occurs before t_2).

Effect preservation is reduced to the problem of specifying modifications that are allowed according to previously executed modifications (history). Our understanding of EP is characterized by the following rules:

Definition 8 (Effect Preservation). *A modification insert, delete or update is accepted if its rule holds.*

$$\begin{aligned} Rule_{insert} &\equiv (table, delete, value) \notin h \\ Rule_{delete} &\equiv (table, insert, value) \notin h \\ Rule_{update} &\equiv (table, insert, v_{old}) \notin h \wedge (table, delete, v_{new}) \notin h \wedge \\ & \quad \neg\exists t_1, t_2.(t_1, t_2 \in h \wedge t_1 < t_2 \wedge t_1 = (table, udelete, v_{new}) \wedge \\ & \qquad t_2 = (table, uinsert, v_{old})) \end{aligned}$$

Consequently, $Rule_{update}$ avoids updates of newly inserted or newly deleted objects, and sanctions reversed updates, e.g., $x = x + 1; x = x - 1$.

Example 7. Recall example 5 and a modification $insert_y(i, i)$ on the empty database which yields an execution of R_2, R_1, R_4 and the following history:
$R_2 \rightarrow h = (y, insert, (i, i))$
$R_1 \rightarrow h = (y, insert, (i, i)), (x, insert, (i))$
$R_4 \rightarrow h = (y, insert, (i, i)), (x, insert, (i)), (y, delete, (i, i))$
Clearly, the last entry of h does not preserve the effects of the initial modification $insert_y(i, i)$. Therefore, the transaction is rejected.

Since database modifications usually affect only a few objects, the caused computational overhead is relatively low for each transaction. Yet, effect preservation at RT might cause rollback operations that have not been considered by the rollback optimization technique at PT. The design of PT effect preservation techniques is part of our planned future work.

7 Conclusion and Future Directions

In this paper we introduce a framework for integrity enforcement that improves existing rule triggering systems by extended rules. By using termination bounds we have shown that certain classes of termination problems can be fully shifted to design-time, provided that appropriate bounds can be specified by application developers. Furthermore, we have shown that optimization of the order of enforcement can be efficiently done by performing some preparatory work of the database system, so that assigning priorities at design-time can be avoided. The framework is based on *dependency graphs* which are a significant means for preprocessing database modifications. By assigning indexing and caching techniques additional computational overhead caused by processing dependency graphs can be avoided.

In the future, we plan to extend our work in the following directions: (1) Dependency graphs can be used for query result caching. That is, if within a rule sequence r_1, r_2 the conditions parts (SQL queries) of r_1 and r_2 share parts of their query execution plans, the latter rule can participate from the query evaluation of the previous rule. (2) Dependency graphs will serve for identifying parallel executable actions. (3) We would like to close the gap in our rollback optimization techniques. We plan to further develop the handling of effect preservation in the pre-processing stage of database modifications. (4) We plan to compare the efficiency of rule triggering systems and our framework, based on real world examples.

Acknowledgment. This research was supported by the DFG (Deutsche Forschungsgemeinschaft), Berlin-Brandenburg Graduate School in Distributed Information Systems (DFG grant no. GRK 316).

References

1. M. Balaban and P. Shoval. EER as an active conceptual schema on top of a database schema – object-oriented as an example. Technical report, Information Systems Program, Department of industrial Engineering and Management, Ben-Gurion University of the Negev, ISRAEL, 1999.
2. Mira Balaban and Steffen Jurk. The ACS Approach for Integrity Enforcement. Technical report, Ben Gurion University of the Negev, April 2000.
3. E. Baralis and J. Widom. An algebraic approach to static analysis of active database rules. In *ACM Transactions on Database Systems*, volume 25(3), pages 269–332, September 2000.
4. Steffen Jurk. The active consistent specializations approach for consistency enforcement. Master's thesis, Dept. of Computer Science, Cottbus Technical University, Germany, 2000.
5. M. Lenzerini and P. Nobili. On the satisfiability of dependency constraints in entity-relationship schemata. *Information Systems*, 15(4):453–461, 1990.
6. E. Mayol and Ernest Teniete. A survey of current methods for integrity constraint maintenance and view updating. In Chen, Embley, Kouloumdjian, Liddle, Roddick, editor, *Intl. Conf. on Entity-Relationship Approach*, volume 1727 of *Lecture Notes in Computer Science*, pages 62–73, 1999.
7. E. Mayol,E. Teniente. Structuring the process of integrity maintenance. In *Proc. 8th Conf. on Database and Expert Systems Applications*, pages 262–275, 1997.
8. E. Mayol,E. Teniente. Addressing efficiency issues during the process of integrity maintenance. In *Proc. 10th Conf. on Database and Expert Systems Applications*, pages 270–281, 1999.
9. F. Bry. Intensional updates: Abduction via deduction. In *Proc. 7th Conf. on Logi Programming*, 1990.
10. F. Bry,H. Decker,R. Manthey. A uniform approach to constraint satisfaction and constraint satisfiability in deductive databases. *Proceedings of Extending Database Technology*, pages 488–505, 1988.
11. H. Decker. Integrity enforcements on deductive databases. *Proceedings of the 1st International Conference on Expert Database Systems*, pages 271–285, 1986.
12. M. Celma,H. Decker. Integrity checking in deductive databases. the ultimate method? *Proceedings of 5th Australiasian Database Conference*, pages 136–146, 1995.
13. S.K. Das, M.H. Wiliams. A path finding method for constraint checking in deductive databases. *Data and Knowledge Engineering 3*, pages 223–244, 1989.
14. S.Y. Lee, T.W. Ling. Further improvement on integrity constraint checking for stratisfiable deductive databases. In *Proc. 22th Conf. on VLDB*, pages 495–505, 1996.
15. K.D. Schewe and B. Thalheim. Limitations of rule triggering systems for integrity maintenance in the context of transition specifications. *Acta Cybernetica*, 13:277–304, 1998.
16. K.D. Schewe and B. Thalheim. Towards a theory of consistency enforcement. *Acta Informatics*, 36:97–141, 1999.
17. van der Voort and A. Siebes. Termination and confluence of rule execution. In *In Proceedings of the Second International Conference on Information and Knowledge Management*, November 1993.
18. J. Widom and S. Ceri. Deriving production rules for constraint maintenance. In *Proc. 16th Conf. on VLDB*, pages 566–577, 1990.
19. J. Widom and S. Ceri. *Active Database Systems.* Morgan Kaufmann, 1996.

Statistical and Feature-Based Methods for Mobile Robot Position Localization

Roman Mázl[1], Miroslav Kulich[2], and Libor Přeučil[1]

[1]The Gerstner Laboratory for Intelligent Decision Making and Control
Faculty of Electrical Engineering, Czech Technical University
166 27 Prague 6, Technická 2, Czech Republic
{mazl, preucil}@labe.felk.cvut.cz

[2] Center for Applied Cybernetics
Faculty of Electrical Engineering, Czech Technical University
166 27 Prague 6, Technická 2, Czech Republic
kulich@labe.felk.cvut.cz

Abstract. The contribution introduces design and comparison of different-brand methods for position localization of indoor mobile robots. The both methods derive the robot relative position from structure of the working environment based on range measurements gathered by a LIDAR system. As one of the methods uses statistical description of the scene the other relies on a feature-based matching approach. The suggested localization methods have been experimentally verified and the achieved results are presented and discussed.

1 Introduction

In order to effectively explore a working environment and to autonomously build a map of the environment, a robot has to localize its position. Mobile robots are usually equipped with odometer or other dead-reckoning methods, which are capable to provide sufficient accuracy only in a short-term. Unfortunately, the position and orientation errors increase during time due to wheel slippage, finite encoder resolution and sampling rate, unequal wheel diameters, and other non-uniform influences, so that localization techniques have to be applied.

Localization methods can be divided into three basic categories:

- Landmark based methods
- Markov localization
- Scan matching approaches

The central idea of landmark localization is to detect and match characteristic features in the environment (landmarks) from sensory inputs. Landmarks can be *artificial* (for example Z-shaped, line navigation, GPS) or *natural* which are learned from a map of the environment [1], [2].

The Markov localization evaluates a probability distribution over the space of pos-

H.C. Mayr et al. (Eds.): DEXA 2001, LNCS 2113, pp. 517–526, 2001.

sible robot states (positions). Whenever the robot moves or senses the environmental entity the probability distribution is updated [3], [4].

The sensor matching techniques compare raw or pre-processed data obtained from sensors with an existing environment map or with previously obtained reference sensor data. The comparison in this sense denotes a correlation process of transitions and a rotation of the actual range scan with the reference range scans.

Sensor matching methods differ in a representation of the actual and reference scans, so the major types can be recognized like approaches matching particular entities as:

- Point-to-point
- Point-to-line
- Line-to-line

For the *point-to-point* method, both the reference and the actual scans are supposed to be raw sensor measurements (vectors of points) and the matching process consists of two steps: pairs of corresponding points are searched for in range scans followed by transitions and rotations to fit with a reference scan The procedure is guided by minimization of a distance function by the least-squares method [5]. A crucial part of this approach is retrieval of the corresponding pairs of points. This works properly only if the difference of the actual scan from the reference scan is sufficiently small. Furthermore, processing of a huge amount of points is time-consuming as the complexity is $O(n^2)$, where n is a number of measurement points.

These disadvantages lead to usage of the *point-to-line* algorithms. The main idea is to approximate the reference scan by a list of lines or to match the actual scan with visible lines of the map [6]. Similarly, two lists of lines representing the scans are matched in the *line-to-line* approach [7], [8].

Besides the previous matching techniques working directly with points (or point-based features as corners, line segments, etc.) there are also methods using statistical representations of the existing features. A fundamental work has been introduced by [9] and applies directional densities (histograms) to find correspondences in sensor data determining relative motions.

Moreover, the final performance and robustness of the most matching techniques can be additionally improved by using a Kalman filter [10], [11].

Therefore, the chapter 2 hereunder has been dedicated to a common algorithm for line segmentation from range data. Chapters 3 and 4 describe in particular the line-to-line (feature-based) and histogram–based (statistical) localization methods. Practical performance and brief discussion of the achieved results is given in chapters 5 and 6.

2 Range Measurement Segmentation

As the obtained range measurements are in the form of separate points (distances to rigid obstacles in the selected discrete direction) the processing requires input data segmentation into point sets belonging to particular boundary.

The used range-measurement segmentation applies two steps. For this purpose there has previously been developed a recursive interval-splitting approach [8] selecting the candidate points for a segment. The algorithm (step 1) takes the advantage of naturally angle-ordered points obtained from a laser range finder. Firstly, all the points are represented by a single segment, which is defined by boundary points from laser-scan (the first and the last point of the scan). Search for the most distant point from a segment is invoked afterwards. This point cracks the segment in question into two new segments. The whole process is applied recursively to both the new segments. Evaluation of the maximum curvature criterion followed by application of a LSQ (step 2) for optimal approximation points of the segment serves for the algorithm termination.

The less important and possibly incorrectly segmented elements are scratched in a post-processing filtration using heuristic rules like:

- *Low significance.* The segment is not build of less than certain number of points.
- *Minimum angular length.* The segment endpoints are not observed within a minimum angle interval. This filters adversely oriented and partially occluded segments.
- *Limited gap.* Two neighbouring points are within a chosen distance threshold. The rule partially handles multiple reflections, laser beam fading and improper segments originating from occlusions.
- *Gravity centre.* If gravity centres of a segment and of the original point set creating the segment in question are not matching, the found segment is omitted.

3 Line-to-Line Method

3.1 Corresponding Line Finding

The key part of the method is to find for each line from the actual scan a corresponding line from the reference scan (if such line exists). We say, that two lines correspond if and only if differences of their directions and positions are sufficiently small. To specify these conditions more precisely, lets denote x and y lengths of the lines, a, b, c, d distances between their vertices, and ϕ the angle between the lines.

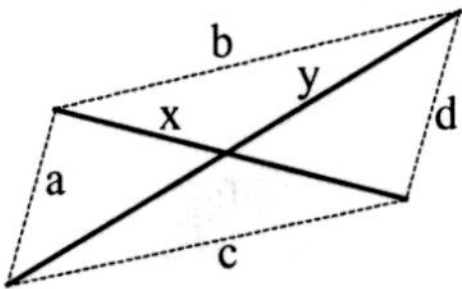

Fig. 1. Distance definition for evaluation of line correspondence.

The lines in question also have to satisfy the following two constrains given by expressions:

$$\phi < \Phi_{MAX} \tag{1}$$

$$\frac{\min(a,b)+\min(c,d)}{x+y} < K, \tag{2}$$

where Φ_{MAX} and K are thresholds saying how "close" the both lines have to be. For example, whenever two lines of a length 1 overlap, the common part is at least of a length equal to *1-K*.

3.2 Orientation Correction

The angle difference α between the scans is expected to be determined in this step. The leading idea behind is to evaluate the weighted sum of differences of particular corresponding lines:

$$\alpha = \frac{\sum_{i=1}^{n} \phi_i w_i}{\sum_{i=1}^{n} w_i} \tag{3}$$

where n is a number of pairs of the corresponding lines, ϕ_i is an angle between lines of the i-th pair, and w_i is the weight of the i-th pair. The weight is defined as a product of the lines' lengths, which prefers pairs containing long lines to pairs of short lines.

3.3 Position Correction

In order to correct the position of the actual scan, we express each line of the reference scan in a standard form:

$$a_i x + b_i y + c_i = 0 \tag{4}$$

$$\min_{p_x, p_y} \sum_{i=1}^{n} \sum_{j=1}^{2} (a_i(x_i^j + p_x) + b_i(y_i^j + p_y) + c_i)^2. \tag{5}$$

Simultaneously, each line of the actual scan is represented by its outer points $([x_i^1, y_i^1], [x_i^2, y_i^2])$ so that the shift $[p_x, p_y]$ of the actual scan can be determined by minimizing the penalty function for p_x and p_y following the expression (5).

3.4 Final Optimization

The localization problem can also be expressed as minimization of a penalty function respecting the position and orientation. As a suitable analytic solution does not exists suitable numerical solution has to be applied. The given problem uses the Nelder-Mead type simplex search method. The desired initial orientation and position can be derived and evaluated from separate optimization for rotation and shift obtained in the preceding steps.

4 Histogram-Based Correction Method

4.1 The Sensor Heading Correction

The other presented approach for correction of heading and position relies on similar method as used for the initial segmentation. The leading idea for angular refinement has been derived from [9] and applied to line segments instead of standalone point measurements. While the tangent line at each point location serves for construction of angle-histogram [9] in our approach we apply using direction of line segments.

The first step builds up a directional histogram comprising distribution of dominant directions in particular map image (obtained from a current range scan). Comparison of the current and the reference histograms is performed by a cross-correlation function:

$$c(j) = \sum_{i=1}^{n} h_1(i) * h_2(i+j) \qquad j \in \left(-n/2; n/2\right) \tag{6}$$

The angle s that is used to compensate the scene rotation is obtained for maximum of the $c(j)$. Usage of low number and sparse segments leads typically to directional histogram that does not have sufficiently smooth shape. This problem can be treated by the following procedure:

(a) A Gaussian core is assigned to each line segment (the set of its creating points):

$$f(x) = \frac{1}{\sqrt{2\pi}\sigma} \exp\left[-\frac{(x-\mu)^2}{2\sigma^2}\right] \tag{7}$$

Where μ stands for direction of the segment and σ denotes inverse number of points relevant to the segment.

(b) All the Gaussian cores are superimposed in order to obtain a smooth directional histogram.

4.2 Sensor Shift Correction

In principle, the x, y scan-to-scan translation of the sensor can be handled in a similar way as for the rotation case. The major modification is in definition of the histograms along two roughly orthogonal axes. Each axis is determined by direction of the most significant segments from reference range scan. Definition interval is required for ($-\infty$, $+\infty$), but can be restricted to finite case and simply omitting less important (= more distant) segments.

Particular Gaussian cores creating the histogram are defined by a mean value μ denoting projected position of the segment midpoint onto the used coordinate axis.

The σ depends on inverse number of points and mutual orientation of the segment with respect to the given axes. Segments parallel to each axis do not describe possible shifts along the axis, while their proper length is unknown. From this point of view is value of the σ increased for particular Gaussian cores that corresponds to segments parallel with coordinate axes.

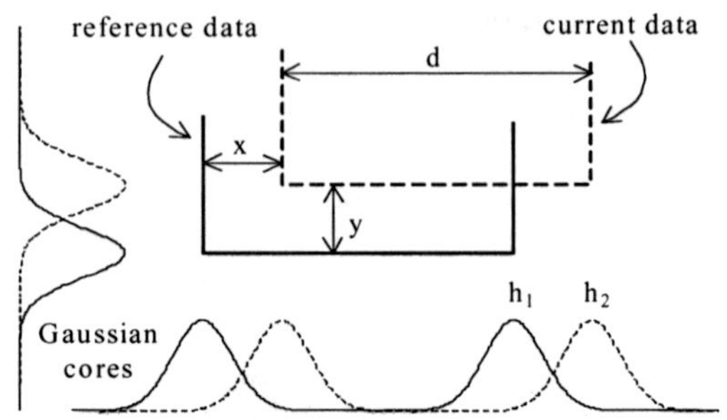

Fig. 2. Histogram generation for calculation of *x, y* shift values

Correlating the histograms h_1 and h_2 of the current and reference map images in both directions provides the desired translation j for maximised $c(j)$:

$$c(j)=\sum_{i=1}^{n} h_1(i) * h_2(i+j) \qquad j \in (-n/2; n/2) \tag{8}$$

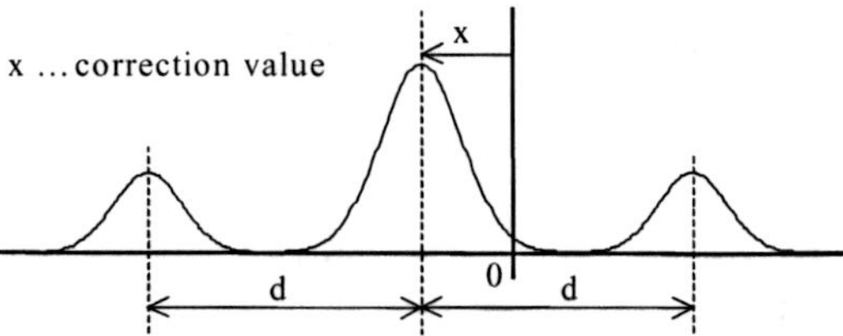

Fig. 3. Example of the resulting 1-D cross-correlation function along a single axis.

Two evaluated correction values (*a* and *b*) are composed into a single translation vector *T*. The following figure illustrates the situation with given dominant directions and calculation of the final direction for the sensor shift correction.

The largest segment defines the most significant direction; the other significant axis direction corresponds to the *i*-th segment, which maximizes the following formula:

$$\max_i \left(\frac{length(s_i)}{length(s_l)} * \frac{\left| direction(s_i) - direction(s_l) \right|}{\pi/2} \right) \tag{9}$$

where s_i is the candidate segment and s_l stands for the largest segment.

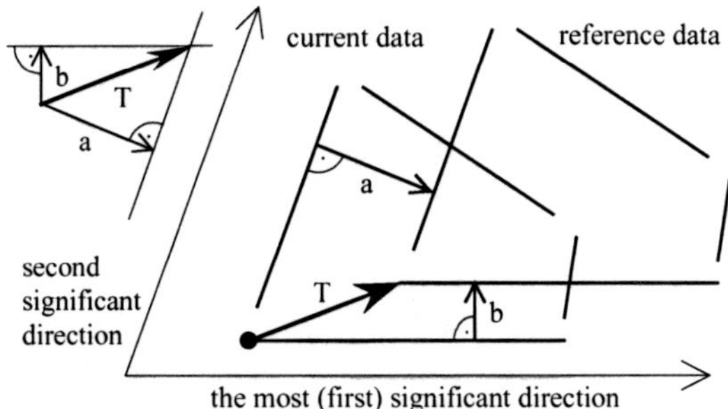

Fig. 4. Dominant directions *a, b* and derivation of the final translation *T* for correction.

5 Experiments

Both the described approaches were experimentally verified and tested with real data in indoor environments. The tests were setup and conducted with carefully chosen obstacles configuration and environment shape in order to point out their weaknesses in performance. The experimental evaluation has been designed mainly with respect to:

- Testing sensitivity to presence of dominant directions
- Evaluation of capability of the matching procedure to determine correct line-pairs
- Recognition and evaluation of the influence of the scene sampling density (with respect to maximal inter-scan changes)

From this point of view there have been built up scenes with significant dominant directions (see Fig. 6) on one hand beside scenes containing also boundary directions spread uniformly (e.g. referred often as random scenes, see Fig. 5) on the other. Another aspect being taken into consideration was the capability of the verified method to cope with dynamically changing scenes. This means that not all the obstacles determined in a single particular scene scan could be determined in the following frames. This means that the case tests robustness of the matching part of the algorithm itself. For the experiments, persons walking through a static environment have achieved this type of a scene setup.

6 Conclusion

The presented methods were mainly designed for self-localization of autonomous mobile robots in indoor environments. The introduced experiments were targeted on localization of relative motions only. This has been done via scan-to-scan comparison determining relative motions of the robot. Absolute positioning could be achieved by fitting the scene scans to a global map of the environment, what is straightforward.

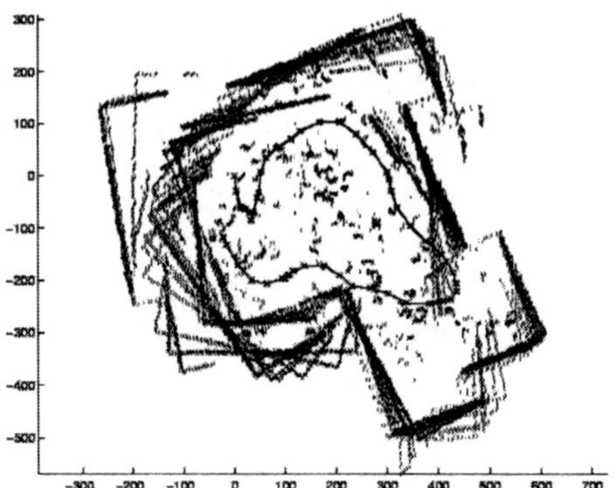

Fig. 5. Original scene with noisy data induced by walking persons.

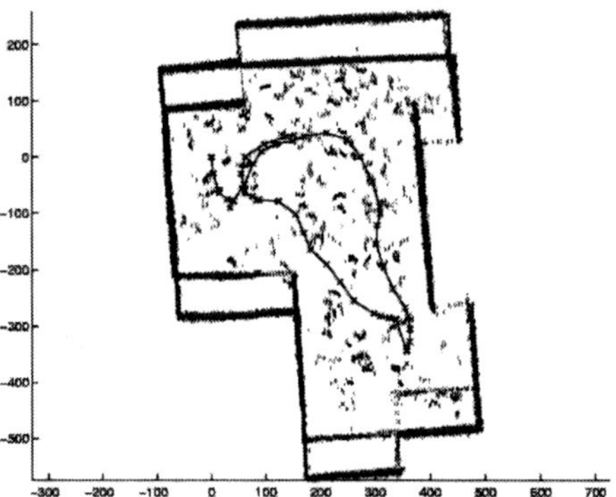

Fig. 6. Result of a position correction using the histogram-based method.

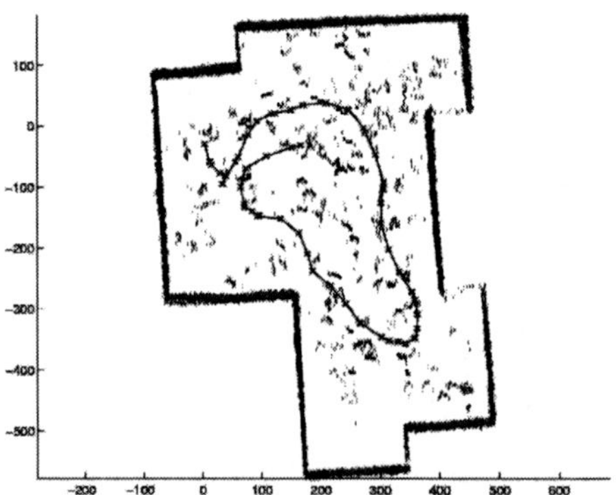

Fig. 7. Position correction using the line-to-line algorithm.

The experiments have brought a valuable recognition about the approach performance. The both of the methods were found to be quite comparable and robust in standard conditions. Although it could be expected that the histogram-based approach is likely to be more reliable in noisy scenes (because of integrating the sensor data into histograms) this is not very significant. Another weak point of the method stands in computational costs, which are about 3 times higher than for the other approach.

On the other hand the line-to-line matching approach might be suspicious for failures in noisy scenes. Not only pure lines are correlated and matched here but also complete rectangular structures (doubles of close-to-rectangular line segments) are used to create pairs. Using these "higher level features" for generating line pairs makes the method surprisingly robust to mismatches even for scenes with lots of randomly spread segments.

The maximal motion between two scans is the only remaining limitation determining the maximal distance for correspondence search. If not satisfied, the methods fail to create proper pairs and might crash from principle (see Fig. 7) by mismatching the line pairs in certain situations.

The presented comparison of the two methods introduces a new aspect for using low-level self-localization methods with a laser range measurements.

Acknowledgements. This research has been carried out being funded by the following grants: FRVŠ No. 1900/2001, MŠMT 212300013, and CTU internal grant No. 300108413. The work of Miroslav Kulich has kindly been supported by the MŠMT 340/35-20401 grant.

References

1. Leonard, J.J., Cox, I. J., and Hugh F. Durrant-Whyte: Dynamic map building for an autonomous mobile robot. In Proc. IEEE Int. Workshop on Intelligent Robots and Systems, pages 89-96, July 1990.
2. Borenstein J., Koren, Y.: Histogramic In-motion Mapping for Mobile Robot Obstacle Avoidance, IEEE Journal of Robotics and Automation, 7(4), pages 535-539, 1991.
3. Nourbakhsh, I., Powers, R., Dervish, S. B.: An Office-Navigating Robot, AI Magazine, 16(2), pages 53-60, 1995.
4. Fox, D., Burgard, W., Thrun, S.: Markov localization for mobile robots in dynamic environments. Journal of Artificial Intelligence, 11, pages 391-427, 1999.
5. Lu, F., Milios, E.,: Robot Pose Estimation in Unknown Environments by Matching 2D Range Scans, IEEE Computer Vision and Pattern Recognition Conference (CVPR), pages 935-938, 1994.
6. Gutmann, J. S., Burgard W., Fox, D., Konolige, K.:Experimental comparison of localization methods. International Conference on Intelligent Robots and Systems, Victoria, B.C. , 1998.
7. Gutmann, J., S., Weigel, T., Nebel B.: Fast, Accurate, and Robust Self-Localization in Polygonal Environments, Proceedings of the IEEE/RSJ International Conference on Intelligent Robots and Systems, 1999.
8. Chmelař,, B., Přeučil, L., Štěpán, P.: Range-data based position localization and refinement for a mobile robot. Proceedings of the 6th IFAC Symposium on Robot Control, Austria, Vienna, pp. 364-379, 2000.

9. Weiss, G., Puttkamer, E.: A map based on laserscans without geometric interpretation, In: U. Rembold et al. (Eds.): Intelligent Autonomous systems, IOS Press, pages 403-407, 1995.
10. Arras, K., O., Tomatis, N.: Improving Robustness and Precision in Mobile Robot Localization by Using Laser Range Finding and Monocular Vision, Proceedings of the 3rd European Workshop on Advanced Mobile Robots (Eurobot'99), Zurich, Switzerland, 1999.
11. Guivant, J., Nebot, E., Baiker, S.: Localization and map building using laser range sensors in outdoor applications, Journal of Robotic Systems, Volume 17, Issue 10, pages: 565-583, 2000.

Efficient View Maintenance Using Version Numbers

Eng Koon Sze and Tok Wang Ling

National University of Singapore
3 Science Drive 2, Singapore 117543
{szeek, lingtw}@comp.nus.edu.sg

Abstract. Maintaining a materialized view in an environment of multiple, distributed, autonomous data sources is a challenging issue. The results of incremental computation are effected by interfering updates and compensation is required. In this paper, we improve the incremental computation proposed in our previous work by making it more efficient through the use of data source and refreshed version numbers. This is achieved by cutting down unnecessary maintenance queries and thus their corresponding query results. The number of times of sending subqueries to a data source with multiple base relations are also reduced, as well as avoiding the execution of cartesian products. Updates that will not affect the view are detected and incremental computation is not applied on them. We also provide a compensation algorithm that resolve the anomalies caused by using the view in the incremental computation.

1 Introduction

Providing integrated access to information from different data sources has received recent interest from both the industries and research communities. Two methods to this data integration are the *on-demand* and the *in-advance* approaches.

In the on-demand approach, information is gathered and integrated from the various data sources only when requested by users. To provide fast access to the integrated information, the in-advance approach is preferred instead. Information is extracted and integrated from the data sources, and then stored in a central site as a materialized view. Users access this materialized view directly, and thus queries are answered immediately. Noting that information at the data sources do get updated as time progresses, this materialized view will have to be *refreshed* accordingly to be consistent with the data sources. This refreshing of the materialized view due to changes at the data sources is called *materialized view maintenance*. The view can be refreshed either by recomputing the integrated information from scratch, or through incrementally changing only the affected portion of the view.

It is inefficient to recompute the view from scratch. The deriving of the relevant portion of the view and then incrementally changing it is a preferred approach as a smaller set of data is involved.

H.C. Mayr et al. (Eds.): DEXA 2001, LNCS 2113, pp. 527–536, 2001.

In Section 2, we explain the working of materialized view maintenance, and its associated problems. In Section 3, we briefly discuss the maintenance algorithm proposed in [7]. The improvements to this algorithm is given in Section 4, and the changes to the compensation algorithm of [7] are given in Section 5. We compare related works in Section 6, and conclude our discussion in Section 7.

2 Background

In this section, we explain the view maintenance algorithm and its problems.

2.1 Incremental Computation

We consider the scenario of select-project-join view V, with n numbers of base relations $\{R_i\}_{1 \leq i \leq n}$. Each base relation is housed in one of the data sources, and there is a separate site for the view. The view definition is given as $V = \prod_{proj\_attr} \sigma_{sel\_cond} R_1 \bowtie ... \bowtie R_n$. A *count* attribute is appended to the view relation if it does not contain the key of the join relations $R_1 \bowtie ... \bowtie R_n$ to indicate the number of ways the same view tuple could be derived from the base relations. There are multiple, distributed, autonomous data sources, each with one or more base relations. There is communication between the view site and the data sources, but not between individual data sources. Thus a transaction can involve one or more base relations of the same data source, but not between different data sources. The view site does not control the transactions at the data sources. No assumption is made regarding the reliability of the network, i.e., messages sent could be lost or could arrive at the destination in a different order from what was originally sent out.

The data sources send notifications to the view site on the updates that have occurred. To incrementally refresh the view with respect to an update $\triangle R_i$ of base relation R_i, $R_1 \bowtie ... \bowtie \triangle R_i \bowtie ... \bowtie R_n$ is to be computed. The result is then applied to the view relation.

2.2 View Maintenance Anomalies and Compensation

There are three problems in using the incremental approach to maintain the view.

Interfering Updates. If updates are separated from one another by a sufficient large amount of time, incremental computation will not be affected by interfering updates. However, this is often not the case.

Example 1. Consider $R_1(\underline{A}, B)$ and $R_2(\underline{B}, C)$, and view $V = \prod_C R_1 \bowtie R_2$, with a count attribute added for the proper working of the incremental computation. R_1 contains the single tuple $(a1, b1)$ and R_2 is empty. Hence the view is also empty. Insert $R_1(a2, b1)$ occurs. The view receives this notification and the query $R_1(a2, b1) \rtimes R_2$ is sent to R_2. Let insert $R_2(b1, c1)$ occurs just before the view maintanance query for insert $R_1(a2, b1)$ reaches R_2. Thus, the tuple

$(b1, c1)$ would be returned. The overall result (without projection) is the tuple $(a2, b1, c1)$. The single projected tuple $(c1)$ is added to the view to give $(c1, 1)$. When the view receives the notification of insert $R_2(b1, c1)$, it formulates another query $R_1 \ltimes R_2(b1, c1)$ and sends it to R_1. The result $\{(a1, b1), (a2, b1)\}$ is returned to the view site. The overall result is $\{(a1, b1, c1), (a2, b1, c1)\}$ and this adds 2 more tuples of $(c1)$ to the view. The presence of interfering update (insert $R_2(b1, c1)$) in the incremental computation of insert $R_1(a2, b1)$ adds an extra tuple of $(c1)$ to the view relation, giving it a count value of 3 instead of 2.

Misordering of Messages. *Compensation* is the removal of the effect of interfering updates from the query results of incremental computation. Most of the existing compensation algorithms that remove the effect of interfering updates and thus achieve complete consistency [11] are based on the first-sent-first-received delivery assumption of the messages over the network, and thus will not work correctly when messages are misordered. A study carried out by [3] has shown that one percent of the messages delivered over the network are misordered.

Loss of Messages. The third problem is the loss of messages. Although the loss of network packets can be detected and resolved at the network layer, the loss of messages due to the disconnection of the network link (machine reboot, network failure, etc.) has to be resolved by the application itself after re-establishing the link. As the incremental computation and compensation method of the maintenance algorithm is driven by these messages, their lost would cause the view to be refreshed incorrectly.

3 Version Numbers and Compensation for Interfering Updates

The following types of version numbers are proposed in [7]. **Base relation version number** of a base relation. The base relation version number identifies the state of a base relation. It is incremented by one when there is an update transaction on this base relation. **Highest processing version number** of a base relation, and this number is stored at the view site. The highest processing version number is used to provide information to the maintenance algorithm on the updates of a base relation which have been processed for incremental computation. It indicates the last update transaction of a base relation which has been processed for incremental computation. **Initial version numbers** of an update. The initial version numbers of an update identify the states of the base relations where the result of the incremental computation should be based on. Whenever we pick a update transaction of a base relation for processing, the current highest processing version numbers of all base relations become the initial version numbers of this update. At the same time, the highest processing version number of the base relation of this update is incremented by one, which is also the same as the base relation version number of the update. **Queried version number** of a tuple of the result from a base relation. The queried version numbers of the result of incremental computation of an update indicate the states of the base relations where this result is actually generated. Base relation and highest processing version numbers are associated with the data source and view site respectively, while initial and queried version numbers are used only for the purpose of incremental computation and need not be stored permanently.

The different types of version numbers allow the view site to identify the interfering updates independent of the order of arrival of messages at the view site. The numbers in between the initial and queried version numbers of the same base relation are the version numbers of the interfering updates. This result is stated in Lemma 1, which was given in [7]. Once the interfering updates are identified, compensation can be carried out to resolve the anomalies. Compensation undoes the effect on the result of incremental computation caused by interfering updates. The formal definiton for compensating the interfering updates can be found in [7].

Lemma 1. *Given that a tuple of the query result from R_j has queried version number β_j, and the initial version number of R_j for the incremental computation of $\triangle R_i$ is α_j. If $\beta_j > \alpha_j$, then this tuple requires the compensation with updates from R_j of base relation version numbers β_j down to $\alpha_j + 1$. These are the* ***interfering updates*** *on the tuple. Otherwise if $\beta_j = \alpha_j$, then compensation on the query result from R_j is not required.*

4 Improved Incremental Computation

The view maintenance approach in [7] overcomes the problems caused by the misordering and loss of messages during transmission. However, efficiency in the incremental computation is not taken into consideration. Each sub-query only accesses one base relation, but generally a data source has multiple base relations. [7] uses the same strategy to incrementally compute the change for all updates. Since the view contains partial information of the base relations, we propose in this paper to involve the view in the incremental computation.

4.1 Querying Multiple Base Relations Together

Since a data source usually has more than one base relation, the sub-queries sent to it should access multiple base relations. This cuts down the total network traffic. It also reduces the time required for the incremental computation of an update, and results in smaller number of interfering updates. Using the join graph to determine the access path of querying the base relations, instead of doing a left and a right scans of the relations based on their arrangement in the relation algebra of the view definition, cuts down the size of the query results sent through the network by avoiding cartesian products.

Briefly, the incremental computation is handled as follows. Consider the join graph of the base relations of a view. The view maintenance query starts with the base relation R_i, $1 \leq i \leq n$, where the update has occurred. A sub-query is sent to a set of relations S, where $S \subset \{R_j\}_{1 \leq j \leq n}$, the relations in S comes from the same data source, R_i and the relations in S form a connected sub-graph with R_i as the root of this sub-graph. If there are more than one such set of base relations S, multiple sub-queries can be sent out in parallel. For each sub-query sent, we marked the relations in S as "queried". R_i is also marked as "queried". Whenever a result is returned from a data source, another sub-query is generated using the similar approach. Let R_k, $1 \leq k \leq n$, be one of the relations that have been queried. A sub-query is sent to a set of relations S, where $S \subset \{R_j\}_{1 \leq j \leq n}$, the relations in S comes from the same data source, none of the relations in S are marked "queried", and R_k and the relations in S form a connected sub-graph with R_k as the root of this sub-graph. Again, if there are more than one such set of base relations S, multiple sub-queries can be sent in parallel. The incremantal computation for this update is completed when all the base relations are marked "queried".

4.2 Identifying Irrelevant Updates

If a data source enforces the referential integrity constraint that each tuple in R_j must refer to a tuple in R_i, then we know that an insertion update on R_i will not affect the view and thus can be ignored by our view maintenance process. Similarly, deletion update on R_i will not affect the view if the data source further enforces that no tuple in R_i can be dropped when there are still tuples in R_j referencing it.

4.3 Partial Self-Maintenance Using Functional Dependencies

We proposed the involvement of the view relation to improve the efficiency of the maintenance algorithm by cutting down the need to access the base relations.

Additional Version Numbers. We propose the following additions to the concept of version numbers given in [7]. This enhancement would allow a data source to have more than one base relation, i.e., update transaction of a data source can involve any number of the base relations within it, and enable the maintenance algorithm to utilize the view in its incremental computation.

The two new types of version numbers are as follow. **Data source version number** of a data source. Since a data source usually has more than one base relation, it is not sufficient to determine the exact sequence of two update transactions involving non-overlapping base relations using the base relation version number alone. The data source version number is used to identify the state of a data source. It is incremented by one when there is an update transaction on the data source. **Refreshed version number** of a base relation, and this number is stored at the view site. If we want to use the view relation for incremental computation, we provide the refreshed version numbers to identify the states. The refreshed version number indicates the state of a base relation the view relation is currently showing.

The data source version number is used to order the update transactions from the same data source for incremental computation, and subsequent refreshing of the view. The base relation version number continues to be used for the identification of interfering updates. The refreshed version number is assigned to the queried version number of the tuples of the result when the view is used for incremental computation.

Accessing View Data for Incremental Computation. Lemma 2 uses functional dependencies to involve the view in the incremental computation. In the case where the view is not used, all tuples in μR_i (the query result of the incremental computation from R_i) need to be used to query the next base relation R_j. When conditions (1) and (2) of Lemma 2 are satisfied, only those tuples in μR_i that cannot be matched with any of the tuples in $V[R'_j, S']$ need to be used in accessing the base relations.

Lemma 2. *When the incremental computation of an update (insertion, deletion, and modification) needs to query base relation R_j, (1) if the key of R_j is found in the view, and (2) if R_j functionally determines the rest of the relations S that are to be queried based on the query result of R_j (denoted as μR_j), then the view can be accessed for this incremental computation and the refreshed version numbers are taken as the queried version numbers for the result. The view is first used for the incremental computation using $\mu R_j, S = \mu R_i \rtimes V[R'_j, S']$, where R'_j is the set of attributes of R_j in V, S' is the set of attributes of relations S in V, and $\mu R_j, S$ is the query result for R_j and the set of relations S. For the remaining required tuples are not found in the view, the base relations are next accessed.*

Example 2. Consider $R_1(\underline{A}, B, C)$, $R_2(\underline{C}, D, E)$ and $R_3(\underline{E}, F, G)$, with the view defined as $V = \prod_{B,C,F} R_1 \bowtie R_2 \bowtie R_3$. The following shows the initial states of the base and view relations.

$R_1(\underline{A}, B, C)$	$R_2(\underline{C}, D, E)$	$R_3(\underline{E}, F, G)$	$V(B, C, F, count)$
a1,b1,c1	c1,d1,e1	e1,f1,g1	b1,c1,f1,1
	c2,d2,e2	e2,f2,g2	

Let R_1 reside in data source 1, and R_2 and R_3 reside in data source 2. The base relation version numbers of R_1, R_2 and R_3 are each 1, and the data source version numbers of data sources 1 and 2 are also 1. The refreshed version numbers at the view site are $\langle 1, 1, 1 \rangle$ for R_1, R_2 and R_3 respectively.

Update transaction with data source version number 2 occurs at data source 1, and the updates involved are insert $R_1(a2, b2, c2)$ and insert $R_1(a3, b3, c1)$, which now has its base relation version number changed to 2. The view site receives this notification and proceed to handle the incremental computation. The highest processing version number of R_1 is updated to 2. Thus, the initial version numbers for the incremental computation of this update are $\langle 2, 1, 1 \rangle$. R_2 and R_3 are to be queried. Since the key of R_2, which is C, is in the view, and R_2 functionally determines the other base relations to be queried (only R_3 in this case), the view is first accessed for this incremental computation using the query $\{(a2, b2, c2), (a3, b3, c1)\} \rtimes V[R'_2, R'_3]$ (R'_2 contains attribute C, and R'_3 contains attribute F). It is found that the tuple (a3,b3,c1) can join with the tuple (c1,-,-) from R_2 and (-,f1,-) from R_3 ($C \to F$). Note the use of "-" for the unknown attributes values. The queried version numbers for both tuples are 1, taken from the refreshed version numbers for R_2 and R_3. Projecting the overall result over the view attributes adds one tuple of (b3,c1,f1) to the view. Thus the tuple (b3,c1,f1,1) is inserted into the view relation. The tuple (a2,b2,c2) that cannot retrieve any results from the view relation will have to do so by sending the view maintenance query $[\prod_C\{(a2, b2, c2)\}] \rtimes (R_2 \bowtie R_3)$ to data source 2. The result returned consists of the tuple (c2,d2,e2) from R_2 and (e2,f2,g2) from R_3, each with queried version number 1. Since the queried version numbers here correspond with the initial version numbers of both R_2 and R_3, there is no interfering update and compensation is not required. The tuple (b2,c2,f2,1) is inserted into the view.

Maintaining the View Without Querying All Base Relations. It is not necessary to know the complete view tuples before the view can be refreshed in some cases of modification or deletion updates. In this paper, modification update that involves the change of any of the view's join attributes will be handled as a deletion and an insertion updates because these update will join with different tuples of the other relations after the modification. Otherwise, the modification update will be handled as one type of update by our view maintenance algorithm. Applying Lemma 3 would also serve to reduce the overall size of queries and results transmitted.

Lemma 3. *For a modification or deletion update $\triangle R_i$, if the key of R_i is in the view, then maintenance can be carried out by modifying or deleting the corresponding tuples of $\triangle R_i$ in the view through using the key value of $\triangle R_i$, without the need to compute the complete view tuple.*

5 Compensation for Missing Updates

Lemma 1, which was proposed in [7], is used to identify interfering updates in the case where the base relations is queried for incremental computation. Using the view relation for incremental computation also creates the similar kind of problem, in that the view relation might not be refreshed to the required state when it is accessed. We called them *missing* updates to differentiate from the interfering updates.

Lemma 4. *Extending Lemma 1, the following is added. If $\beta_j < \alpha_j$, then this tuple (taken from the view relation) requires the compensation with updates from R_j of base relation version numbers $\beta_j + 1$ to α_j. These are the* ***missing updates*** *on the tuple.*

5.1 Resolving Missing Updates

The compensation of a missing insertion update is to add the tuples of this insertion into the query result. The compensation with a missing modification update is simply to update the tuples from the unmodified state to the modified state. These are given in Lemmas 5, 6 and 7 respectively.

Lemma 5. *Let μR_j be the query result from R_j (retrieved from the view) for the incremental computation of $\triangle R_i$. To compensate the effect of* ***missing deletion update*** *$\triangle R_j$ for the result of incremental computation of $\triangle R_i$, all tuples of $\triangle R_j$ that are found in μR_j are dropped, together with those tuples from the other base relations that are retrieved due to the original presence of $\triangle R_j$ in μR_j.*

Lemma 6. *Let μR_j be the query result from R_j (retrieved from the view) for the incremental computation of $\triangle R_i$, and μR_k be the query result from R_k. To compensate the effect of* ***missing insertion update*** *$\triangle R_j$ on the result of incremental computation of $\triangle R_i$, and assuming that μR_j is queried using the result from μR_k, all tuples of $\triangle R_j$ that can join with μR_k are added to μR_j, together with those tuples from the other base relations that should be retrieved due to the inclusion of $\triangle R_j$ in μR_j.*

Lemma 7. *Let μR_j be the query result from R_j (retrieved from the view) for the incremental computation of $\triangle R_i$. To compensate the effect of* ***missing modification update*** *$\triangle R_j$ (which does not involve any change to the view's join attributes), for the result of incremental computation of $\triangle R_i$, each old tuple (before the modification) of $\triangle R_j$ that occurs in μR_j has its values changed to the corresponding new tuple (after the modification).*

Note that for both missing deletion or modification update $\triangle R_j$, if the key of R_j is not in the view, then the relation R_k with its key that functionally determines the attributes of R_j will be used in applying Lemmas 5 and 7.

Theorem 1 gives the overall compensation process that is applied to resolve the maintenance anomalies.

Theorem 1. *Given α_1,...,α_n as the initial version numbers of incremental computation of update $\triangle R_i$, the compensation starts with those relations that are linked to R_i in the join graph, and proceed recursively to the rest of the relations in the same sequence as they are been queried. The compensation on the query result from R_j proceeds by first compensating with the missing updates of base relation version number $\beta_j^{min}+1$ to α_j, where β_j^{min} is the minimum queried version number of the tuples in the result from R_j, using Lemmas 5, 6 and 7. This is followed by the compensation with the interfering updates of base relation version number β_j^{max} down to α_j+1, where β_j^{max} is the maximum queried version number of the tuples in the query result from R_j, using the method discussed in [7].*

Theorem 2. *To achieve complete consistency, the view will be refreshed with the results of incremental computation in the same order as they have been queried.*

6 Comparison

Related works in this area are the Eager Compensation Algorithm (ECA and ECA^K) [10], the Strobe and C-Strobe Algorithms [11], the work of [2], the SWEEP and Nested SWEEP Algorithms [1], the work of [3], and the work of [7]. We compare these using a set of criteria, which are grouped into four categories.

The first criterion under the environment category is the number of data sources. All the approaches, except ECA, ECA^K and [2], cater for multiple data sources. The second criterion is the handling of compensation. ECA and C-Strobe send compensating queries to the data sources, while the other algorithms handle compensation locally at the view site. The latter method is preferred as compensating queries add to the overall traffic.

The first criterion under the correctness category is the correct detection of interfering updates. The compensation methods of ECA, ECA^K and Strobe are not through the detection of interfering updates, and hence they only achieve strong consistency [11]. C-Strobe does detect some interfering deletion updates which turn out to be non-interfering. The rest of the algorithms work by correctly detecting for the presence of interfering updates when messages are not misordered or lost. The next criterion is the network communication assumption. All the approaches, except [7] and the work of this paper, assume that messages are never lost and misordered. [3] also does not assume that messages are never misordered.

There are five criteria under the efficiency category. The first criterion is the number of base relations accessed per sub-query. Most of the approaches can only work by querying one base relation at a time. ECA and ECA^K can query all base relations of their single data source together. The method proposed in this paper is able to access multiple base relations within the same data source via the same query. The second criterion is the parallelism in the incremental computation of an update. Existing methods base their view maintenance querying on a left and right scan approach, and thus limit their parallelism to the two scans. In this paper, we use the join graph to guide the accessing of the base relations, and thus provide more parallelism. The third criterion is the parallelism in the incremental computation between different updates. ECA, ECA^K, Strobe and Nested SWEEP are able to process the incremental computation of different updates concurrently, but achieving only strong consistency. The rest of the methods have to process the incremental computation of different updates sequentially. [7] and the method in this paper can process the incremental computation concurrently and also achieve complete consistency. The fourth criterion is the use partial self-maintenance. ECA^K, Strobe and C-Strobe have a limited form of partial self-maintenance in that deletion update need not be processed for incremental computation. [2] can detect updates that will not affect the view. In this paper, we provide for more opportunity of partial self-maintenance. The fifth criterion is the handling of modification as one type of update. Only [7] and the method in this paper consider modification as one type of update.

The criteria under the application requirements category are the flexibility of the view definition, quiescence requirement and level of consistency achieved.

ECA^K, Strobe and C-Strobe require that the key of each base relation be retained in the view. The number of base relations in [2] is limited to two. The others have no such requirement. C-Strobe, [2], SWEEP, [3], [7] and our approach achieve complete consistency, and also do not require a quiescent state before the view can be refreshed. This does not apply to ECA, ECA^K, Strobe and the Nested SWEEP Algorithm.

7 Conclusion

The use of data source and refreshed version numbers in the maintenance algorithm allow for partial self-maintenance, as well as the accessing of multiple base relations residing at the same data source within a single query. Also, the accessing of the base relations for incremental computation are based on the join graph to avoid cartesian products. Using the join graph to determine the query path also results in more parallelism. Knowledge of referential integrity constraint imposed by the data source is used to eliminate irrelevant updates. Overall performance of the maintenance algorithm is improved by reducing the amount and size of messages sent over the network.

References

1. Agrawal, D., El Abbadi, A., Singh, A., Yurek, T.: Efficient View Maintenance at Data Warehouses. International Conference on Management of Data (1997) 417–427
2. Chen, R., Meng, W.: Efficient View Maintenance in a Multidatabase Environment. Database Systems for Advanced Applications (1997) 391–400
3. Chen, R., Meng, W.: Precise Detection and Proper Handling of View Maintenance Anomalies in a Multidatabase Environment. Conference on Cooperative Information Systems (1997)
4. Colby, L.S., Griffin, T., Libkin, L., Mumick, I.S., Trickey, H.: Algorithms for Deferred View Maintenance. International Conference on Management of Data (1996) 469–480
5. Griffin, T., Libkin, L.: Incremental Maintenance of Views with Duplicates. International Conference on Management of Data (1995) 328–339
6. Griffin, T., Libkin, L., Trickey, H.: An Improved Algorithm for the Incremental Recomputation of Active Relational Expressions. Knowledge and Data Engineering, Vol. 9 No. 3 (1997) 508–511
7. Ling, T.W., Sze, E.K.: Materialized View Maintenance Using Version Numbers. Database Systems for Advanced Applications (1999) 263–270
8. Qian, X., Wiederhold, G.: Incremental Recomputation of Active Relational Expressions. Knowledge and Data Engineering, Vol. 3 No. 3 (1991) 337–341
9. Quass, D.: Maintenance Expressions for Views with Aggregation. Workshop on Materialized Views: Techniques and Applications (1996)
10. Zhuge, Y., Garcia-Molina, H., Hammer, J., Widom, J.: View Maintenance in a Warehousing Environment. International Conference on Management of Data (1995) 316–327
11. Zhuge, Y., Garcia-Molina, H., Wiener, J.L.: The Strobe Algorithms for Multi-Source Warehouse Consistency. Conference on Parallel and Distributed Information Systems (1996)

α-Partitioning Algorithm: Vertical Partitioning Based on the Fuzzy Graph

Jin Hyun Son and Myoung Ho Kim

Div. of Computer Science, Dept. of EE & CS, KAIST
373-1 Kusong-dong Yusong-gu Taejon 305-701, Korea
{jhson,mhkim}@dbserver.kaist.ac.kr

Abstract. The issue of vertical partitioning was extensively studied with many proposed approaches, which can be applied to the areas where the match between data and transactions affects performance. Vertical partitioning is the process of producing groups of attributes, called fragments, which are composed of attributes with high affinity each other. Though a vertical partitioning method should be able to generate arbitrary n fragments as well as all meaningful fragments, previous methods have some limitations to support both of them. In this paper we propose an efficient and flexible vertical partitioning method based on a fuzzy graph. The method can not only generate all meaningful fragments at a time but also support n-ary partitioning without any complex mathematical computations.

1 Introduction

In distributed computing processing, the fragmentation of relations typically results in the parallel execution of a single query by dividing it into a set of subqueries that operate on fragments. Hence, fragmentation increases the level of concurrency and therefore the system throughput [1]. The partitioning of a data schema into fragments can be performed in two different ways: vertical partitioning and horizontal partitioning [1]. Vertical partitioning decomposes data attributes into groups which are composed of some attributes with high affinity each other, while horizontal partitioning subdivides data tuples into groups [1][5]. These partitioning schemes are based on data transaction (or query) patterns.

The concept of vertical partitioning can be applied to the areas where the match between data and transactions (or queries) affects performance, which includes partitioning of individual files in centralized environments, data distribution in distributed databases, dividing data among different levels of memory hierarchies, and so on [6]. Naturally, the objective of vertical partitioning is to improve both the performance of query execution and system throughput. For example, vertical partitioning for each database system in a single site can improve system performance by reducing the amount of unneeded information that is brought into main memory in block transfers from secondary storage [2][5][6]. For distributed information systems, it can also enhance overall system

H.C. Mayr et al. (Eds.): DEXA 2001, LNCS 2113, pp. 537–546, 2001.

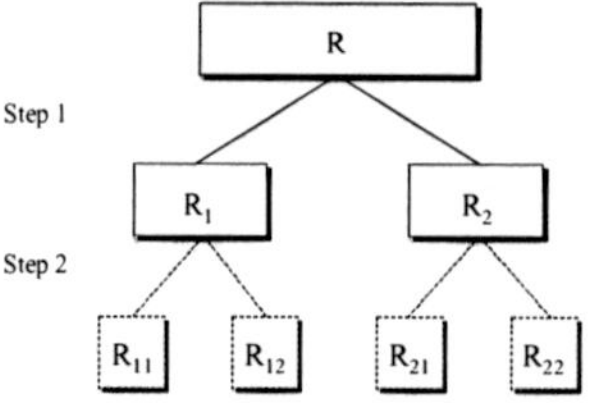

Fig. 1. Repetitive Use of Binary Partitioning

throughput by means of parallel query processing to attribute fragments located in different sites [1][3].

The "optimal" partitioning is inherently one that produces a partitioning scheme which minimizes the execution time of user applications that run on these groups of attributes, called fragments. In general, a vertical partitioning approach should be able to support two main functions: generating all meaningful fragments and providing n-ary partitioning. Previous vertical partitioning methods, however, have some limitations to support both of them.

There are many previous works on vertical partitioning. Because vertical partitioning basically stores together attributes that are frequently requested together by queries, [7] measured the affinity between pairs of attributes using the bond energy algorithm (BEA) of [8]. [4] proposed mechanisms that can automatically select a near-optimal attribute partition of a file's attributes, based on the usage pattern of the file and on the characteristics of the data in the file. On the other hand, [5] proposed a cluster algorithm and a binary partitioning algorithm using the bond energy algorithm (BEA). The rationale behind this algorithm is that the "optimal" solution is much close to the group composed of all attributes, which is opposite to [4]. The binary partitioning technique is required to be repeated until all meaningful fragments are determined, with complex computation of an empirical objective function. And, clustering is also repeated at each iteration after clustering two new affinity matrices corresponding to the newly generated fragments. To solve these limitations, [6] proposed a new vertical partitioning algorithm which has less computational complexity and generates all meaningful fragments simultaneously by using a graphical method.

The rest of the paper is organized as follows. In Section 2, we clear up our motivation for this topic. Section 3 illustrates our α-Partitioning algorithm of generating all meaningful fragments and Section 4 discusses a n-ary α-Partitioning algorithm. Finally, we conclude our paper with its contribution and further works in Section 5.

2 Motivation

As we mentioned, a general vertical partitioning method must support two important functions: an optimal or near-optimal solution generating all meaningful fragments and n-ary partitioning which can manage general vertical partitioning problems. In connection with these functions, we discuss two key reasons which can clarify our motivation of this topic. First, previous methods do not support efficiently both functions of a general vertical partitioning method. Most proposed methods are much concerned with support of generating all meaningful fragments heuristically. The function of n-ary partitioning, however, is necessary and useful to some system environments such as multiple levels of memory hierarchies. In addition, this function can also be applied to future new applications flexibly. Second, though the binary partitioning algorithm proposed in [5] can be extended to n-ary partitioning, it is not flexible and has some limitations. The binary partitioning algorithm would provide a n-ary partitioning solution by repetitively applying the binary partitioning. However, if the value of the objective function is not positive, the binary partitioning cannot proceed any more. In addition, there is no guideline in selecting which fragments to be further partitioned in each repetitive step. For example, when we want to obtain three attribute fragments from one relation schema, two consecutive binary partitioning must be performed as in Figure 1. However, because fragment A_1 and A_2 are independent to each other, there is no guideline in selecting which fragment to be further partitioned in Step 2 of Figure 1. Hence, the binary partitioning algorithm cannot support general n-ary partitioning.

In this paper we propose an efficient and flexible vertical partitioning algorithm, called α-Partitioning, based on the fuzzy graph. The algorithm generates all meaningful fragments at a time while minimizing the total degree of uncertainty within/between fragments. In addition, it supports flexible n-ary partitioning without any complex mathematical computations.

3 α-Partitioning Algorithm

3.1 Information Requirement

The major information required for vertical partitioning is related to data queries. When some attributes are usually accessed together in a query, vertical partitioning may place them in the same fragment. We, therefore, need to define the measure of the affinity between attributes. The affinity of attributes denotes how frequently any two attributes are commonly accessed by data queries, which can be represented with an Attribute Affinity Matrix (AAM).

Let $R = \{a_1, a_2, \cdots, a_n\}$ be a data schema composed of n attributes, $Q = \{q_1, q_2, \cdots, q_s\}$ be the set of user data queries that will run on data schema R, and $S = \{s_1, s_2, \cdots, s_m\}$ be the set of constituent sites of the system. Each query q_i invoked at site s_l may access a subset of R. Note that data schema R is the target of vertical partitioning that generates fragments which are composed of attributes with high affinity each other. The term *vertical partitioning* includes both the non-overlapping and overlapping cases. In general, non-overlapping fragments can not only cover most target applications but support overlapping fragments by replicating the non-overlapping fragments. In this paper we therefore propose a vertical partitioning algorithm to produce non-overlapping attribute fragments.

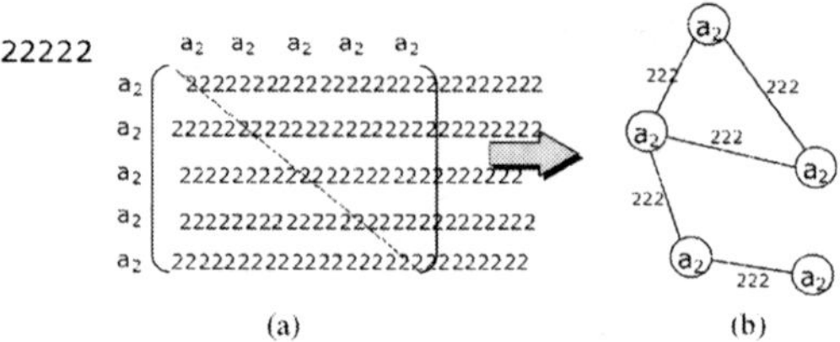

Fig. 2. AAM and its corresponding Fuzzy Graph

The following notations are used in computing the affinity of attributes.

$$use(q_i, a_j) = \begin{cases} 1 \text{ if attribute } a_j \text{ is referenced by query } q_i \\ 0 \ otherwise \end{cases}$$

$freq_l(q_k)$ = the frequency of query q_k generated at site s_l.

$$acc_l(q_k) = \begin{cases} 1 \text{ if } q_k \text{ is generated at site } s_l \\ 0 \ otherwise \end{cases}$$

In this paper the affinity between attributes a_i and a_j is defined as the ratio between the sum of the frequency of queries to access both a_i and a_j and the sum of the frequency of queries to access either a_i and a_j.

$$aff(a_i, a_j) = \frac{\sum_{k \ for \ use(q_k, a_i)=1 \ \wedge \ use(q_k, a_j)=1} \sum_{\forall \ s_l} freq_l(q_k) * acc_l(q_k)}{\sum_{k \ for \ use(q_k, a_i)=1 \ \vee \ use(q_k, a_j)=1} \sum_{\forall \ s_l} freq_l(q_k) * acc_l(q_k)}$$

Here, the value of $aff(a_i, a_j)$ denotes the degree of the affinity between attribute a_i and a_j, where $0 \leq aff(a_i, a_j) \leq 1$. The result of this computation is an $n \times n$ matrix, each element (i, j) of which has the value of $aff(a_i, a_j)$. We call this matrix the Attribute Affinity Matrix (AAM). Figure 2-(a) is an example of an AAM. This matrix is symmetric due to $aff(a_i, a_j) = aff(a_j, a_i)$. We can here easily convert the AAM into a fuzzy attribute affinity relation by means of defining the fuzzy membership function μ_X as follows:

$$X : R \longrightarrow R, \ where \ R = \{a_1, a_2, ..., a_n\}$$
$$\mu_X : R \times R \longrightarrow [0, 1]$$
$$\mu_X(a_i, a_j) = aff(a_i, a_j)$$

Here, $\mu_X(a_i, a_j)$ denotes a membership degree of element (a_i, a_j). From now on, we consider a fuzzy Attribute Affinity Matrix (AAM) with the fuzzy membership function μ_X.

3.2 Fuzzy α-Partitioning

With the fuzzy AAM generated at Section 3.1, we can depict its corresponding fuzzy graph as in Figure 2-(b). Each attribute in the matrix is to be a node in the fuzzy graph and the value of $aff(a_i, a_j)$ is to be the weight of the edge between node a_i and a_j.

In the fuzzy graph, we define two new terms which will be used as measures in determining whether attribute a_i and a_j belong to the same subgraph (i.e., fragment).

Definition 1. *The weight of the edge between attribute a_i and a_j in the fuzzy graph, i.e.,* $\mathbf{aff(a_i, a_j)}$ *is called the* ***cohesion certainty between*** $\mathbf{a_i}$ ***and*** $\mathbf{a_j}$, *simply* $\mathbf{Cohesion(a_i, a_j)}$.

Definition 2. *The value of* $\mathbf{1 - aff(a_i, a_j)}$ *in the edge between attribute a_i and a_j is called their* ***discohesion certainty,*** *simply* $\mathbf{Discohesion(a_i, a_j)}$.

It is clear that the sum of the cohesion certainty and the discohesion certainty for any two attributes is always 1. Hence, the closer the value of $aff(a_i, a_j)$ is to 1, the higher the value of $Cohesion(a_i, a_j)$ is and the lower the value of $Discohesion(a_i, a_j)$ is. Definition 3.1 and 3.2 can be further extended to the cohesion certainty within a fragment and the discohesion certainty between fragments, respectively, which will be addressed in the following.

We can now define the concept of the certainty between any two attributes which gives an important guideline to decide whether the two attributes may belong to the same fragment or not. Let $Certainty(a_i, a_j)$ denote the certainty between attribute a_i and a_j.

Definition 3. $Certainty(a_i, a_j) = Max\{Cohesion(a_i, a_j), Discohesion(a_i, a_j)\}$

We can notice a considerable fact that the value of $Certainty(a_i, a_j)$ is always greater than or equal to 0.5 from Definition 3.3. If the value of $aff(a_i, a_j)$ is close to 1 or 0, we can get more accurate information in deciding whether attribute a_i and a_j are assigned to the same fragment or not because the value of $Certainty(a_i, a_j)$ is close to 1. On the other hand, if the value of $aff(a_i, a_j)$ is close to 0.5, it is very ambiguous to determine it because the value of $Certainty(a_i, a_j)$ is close to 0.5. Eventually, our vertical partitioning algorithm divides the fuzzy graph into several subgraphs, which correspond to attribute fragments, using the concept of the certainty effectively.

In dividing the fuzzy graph, we use the concept of fuzzy α-cut. Doing α-cut in a fuzzy graph cuts all edges whose weight is less than or equal to α, resulting in several subgraphs. As an example, when we do α-cut ($\alpha = 0.6$) in Figure 3, two edges are cut and two fragments, i.e., $f_1 = \{a_1, a_2, a_5\}$ and $f_2 = \{a_3, a_4\}$ are generated. In consequence, the main function of our vertical partitioning called α-Partitioning is how to select the most proper α.

As a guideline for selecting the value of α, we use a simple objective function that indicates the total degree of uncertainty (D_α) within/between the candidate fragments. When we do α-cut in a fuzzy graph, a set of groups (or subgraphs) G_α is generated and the objective function D_α for G_α is defined as

$$D_\alpha = \sum_{\forall g} \sum_{a,b \in g} |a - b|$$

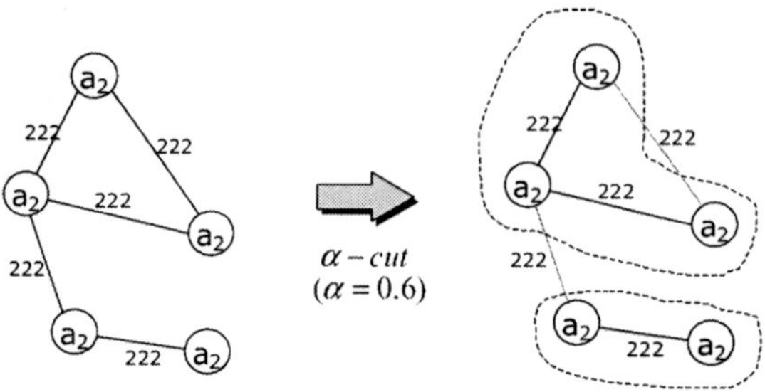

Fig. 3. α-cut in a fuzzy graph

α	g1	g2	g'	D_α
0	0.2, 0.6, 0.7, 0.8, 0.8			**2.8**
0.2	0.7, 0.6, 0.8	0.8	0.8	**0.4**
0.6	0.7, 0.8	0.8	0.8, 0.4	**0.5**
0.7	0.8	0.8	0.8, 0.4, 0.3	**1**
0.8			0.8, 0.4, 0.3, 0.2, 0.2	**2.8**

Cohesion Certainty *ciscohesion Certainty*

Fig. 4. An overall example of α-Partitioning

where $g \in G_\alpha$. Each generated group g from α-cutting is denoted by a set of edge weights between attributes which belong to its corresponding subgraph. Namely, two groups are generated by $\alpha(= 0.6)$-cut in Figure 3, $g_1 = \{0.7, 0.8\}$ and $g_2 = \{0.8\}$. In addition, a special group $g^{'}$ is generated. This group is composed of discohesion certainty values $1 - aff(a_i, a_j)$ of edges cut by α, i.e., $g^{'} = \{0.4, 0.8\}$ in Figure 3 because two edges with weight 0.2 and 0.6 are cut. Hence, the set $G_{0.6}$ in Figure 3 is $G_{0.6} = \{g_1, g_2, g^{'}\}$. The term $\sum_{a,b \in g} |a - b|$ in the function D_α means the Hamming distance for each group which has been used as a measure of fuzziness in a fuzzy set. Because the value of D_α, therefore, denotes the total fuzziness (i.e., uncertainty) raised by α-cutting of a fuzzy graph, our α-Partitioning algorithm should select the most proper α such that the objective function D_α is minimized in order to achieve the global optimality in the aspect of fuzziness. For $G_{0.6} = \{g_1, g_2, g^{'}\}$ mentioned above, the value of the Hamming distance in group g_1 and g_2 is related to the cohesion certainty within a fragment while the Hamming distance in group $g^{'}$ is connected to the discohesion certainty between fragments.

Figure 4 shows an overall example of our α-Partitioning. For each edge weight α, we generate a set of groups $G_\alpha = \{g_1, \cdots, g_n, g^{'}\}$. As we mentioned, we select α which minimizes the total degree of uncertainty D_α. This α value reversely

```
For (each α in a fuzzy graph) {
        - Apply α-cut to the fuzzy graph and generate a set of groups Gα.
        - Compute the total degree of uncertainty Dα.
}
- Select the minimum α value with Min(Dα) and
  generate all meaningful fragments by α-cutting the fuzzy graph.
```

Fig. 5. The α-Partitioning algorithm

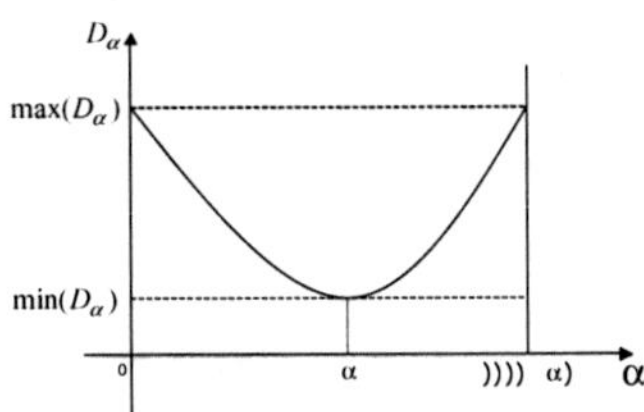

Fig. 6. The relationship between α and D_α

increases the cohesion certainty within a fragment g_i $(i = 1, \cdots, n)$ and the discohesion certainty between fragments represented by g'. Because $D_{0.2}$ is the minimum, we can finally get two fragments $f_1 = \{a_1, a_2, a_5\}$ and $f_2 = \{a_3, a_4\}$, which is the result of our α-Partitioning.

The α-Partitioning algorithm is described in Figure 5. The computational complexity of the algorithm is $O(n)$, where n is the number of distinct α values in a fuzzy graph. The analyses of the α-Partitioning algorithm give some noticeable properties as follows.

Lemma 1. *The value of D_0 is always equal to that of $D_{max(\alpha)}$.*

Proof) When a fuzzy graph is cut by $\alpha(=0)$, only one group g_0 (=\{ $aff(a_i, a_j)$ — a_i and a_j are nodes in the fuzzy graph\}) is generated. On the other hand, when the fuzzy graph is cut by $max(\alpha)$, only one graph g'(=\{ $1 - aff(a_i, a_j)$ — a_i and a_j are nodes in the fuzzy graph\}) is also generated. Hence,

$$\begin{aligned} D_0 &= \sum |aff(a_k, a_l) - aff(a_m, a_n)| \\ &= \sum |(1 - aff(a_k, a_l)) - (1 - aff(a_m, a_n))| \\ &= D_{max(\alpha)} \end{aligned}$$

Lemma 2. *If we select two α values with $\alpha_i \leq \alpha_j$, the number of fragments generated by α_i-cut is less than or equal to that of fragments generated by α_j-cut.*

Proof) When α_i is less than or equal to α_j, the number of edges cut by α_i is also less than or equal to the number of edges cut by α_j from the context of α-cut. Hence, it is natural that the number of fragments generated by α_i-cut is less than or equal to that by α_j-cut.

Step1: Find out the value α which generates the closest number of fragments m to n.
$A = \{\alpha|\ m\ fragments\ are\ generated\ by\ \alpha - cutting\}$
Step2: IF (n = m)
- Partition the fuzzy graph by the minimum α_i value in A.
Step3: ELSE IF $(n > m)$
- Partition the fuzzy graph by the maximum α_i value in A.
- Decomposition Phase
Step4: ELSE IF $(n < m)$
- Partition the fuzzy graph by the minimum α_i value in A.
- Composition Phase

Fig. 7. The n-ary α-Partitioning algorithm

Lemma 3. *There can be one or more α values with the same value of D_α.*

Proof) From Lemma 3.1, this lemma follows.

We can roughly depict the relationship between α and D_α as in Figure 6. The graph is composed of an increasing function and a decreasing function at the base of a point α which makes the minimum value of D_α. Because $\alpha(= 0)$-cut generates only a group g_1 representing the cohesion certainty and $\alpha(= max(\alpha))$-cut generates a group g' representing the discohesion certainty, all these D_α values are equal to $max(D_\alpha)$ as in Figure 6. There can generally exist several α values with the minimum value of D_α from Lemma 3.3. In this case, we select the minimum α value of them because the minimum value generates as less number of fragments as possible. The rationale behind this approach is that the "optimal" solution is much closer to the group composed of all attributes than to groups that are single-attribute fragments [5].

4 n-ary α-Partitioning Algorithm

It is known that if a non-overlapping n-ary partitioning is to be accomplished by an algorithm, the algorithm in general has the complexity $O(2^n)$ where n is the number of attributes [1][3][5]. In this paper we cover a simple and flexible n-ary α-Partitioning algorithm which is based on the α-Partitioning algorithm discussed in Section 3. Here, the number of fragments n is usually required by users.

The n-ary α-Partitioning algorithm is explained in Figure 7. With the expected number of fragments n, we first find out the value of α by which m number of fragments are generated, satisfying that m is the closest value to n. Because there can be several α values being able to generate the same number of fragments m, the set $A = \{\alpha|\ \alpha - cutting\ generates\ m\ fragments\}$ is defined in Step1 of the algorithm. Next, if the expected number of fragments n is equal to m, we select the minimum α_i value in A and generate n fragments by α-cutting. The rationale to select the minimum α_i value in A is based on the same reason mentioned in Section 3, namely, "the optimal solution is much closer to

Step1: Find the smallest value α' being greater than α_i.
Step2: Select an edge with weight α' and cut it, which generates the smallest Hamming distance of the fuzzy graph.
Step3: Repeat Step2 until there are n fragments.

Fig. 8. The Decomposition Phase

Step1: Find the biggest value α' being less than α_i.
Step2: Select and combine two groups g_i and g_j with the smallest increase of the Hamming distance in the fuzzy graph as well as $aff(g_i, g_j) = \alpha'$.
Step3: Repeat Step2 until there are n fragments.

Fig. 9. The Composition Phase

the group composed of all attributes than to groups that are single-attribute fragments [5]". If n is greater than m, we first partition the fuzzy graph with the maximum α_i value in A. Then, the decomposition phase is necessary in order to decomposing m fragments into n fragments. If n is less than m, the composition phase needs to compose m fragments into n fragments after we partition the fuzzy graph with the minimum α_i value in A.

The decomposition and composition phases are described in Figure 8 and Figure 9, respectively. During the decomposition phase, m fragments are further divided into $n(n > m)$ fragments. First, we find out in the fuzzy graph the smallest value α' that is greater than α_i mentioned in the above n-ary α-Partitioning algorithm, which is based on Lemma 3.2. In the groups, we select an edge with weight α' and cut it, which generates the smallest Hamming distance of the fuzzy graph. This step will be repeated until n fragments are generated.

Before discussing the composition phase, we need to define the affinity between two disjoint groups in a fuzzy graph as in Figure 10.

Definition 4. *When two groups g_i and g_j are connected by edges whose weights are $\alpha_1, \alpha_2, \cdots, \alpha_n$, the affinity* $\mathbf{aff}(\mathbf{g_i}, \mathbf{g_j})$ *between them is defined as*

$$\mathbf{aff}(\mathbf{g_i}, \mathbf{g_j}) = \mathbf{max}\{\alpha_1, \alpha_2, \cdots, \alpha_n\}$$

In the composition phase, we find out the biggest value α' which is less than α_i mentioned in the above n-ary α-Partitioning algorithm, which is also based on Lemma 3.2. In the groups generated by α_i-cutting, we, then, select and combine two groups g_i and g_j both whose affinity is $aff(g_i, g_j) = \alpha'$ and whose composition occur the smallest increase of the Hamming distance in the fuzzy graph. This step will be repeated until n fragments are generated.

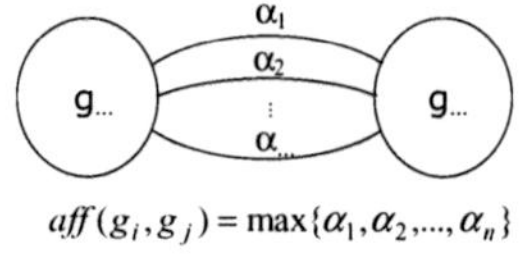

Fig. 10. The affinity between two disjoint groups

5 Conclusion

The role of vertical partitioning is to place some attributes in one fragment when they are usually accessed together by queries. Even though this concept has been mostly applied to the conventional database area so far, it can be extended to support many new applications such as parallel processing of transactions and workflow management systems. In this paper we have proposed a new efficient and flexible vertical partitioning algorithm which not only generates all non-overlapping fragments simultaneously but also supports general n-ary partitioning problem. The algorithm efficiently uses the fuzzy concept to reduce the vagueness which often occurs during grouping attributes. Further extension of this work will be in the direction of elaborating on in-depth performance evaluation compared to other existing techniques and finding out the actual applications in order to show the effectiveness of our proposed method.

References

1. M. Tamer Ozsu and Patrick Valduriez, *Principles of Distributed Database Systems*, Prentice Hall, 1999.
2. Wesley W. Chu and Ion Tim Leong, "A Transaction-Based Approach to Vertical Partitioning for Relational Database Systems," IEEE Transactions on Software Engineering, Vol. 19, No. 8, 804-812, August, 1993.
3. Ladjel Bellatreche and Ana Simonet, "Vertical Fragmentation in Distributed Object Database Systems with Complex Attributes and Methods," The Seventh International Workshop on Database and Expert Systems Applications, 15-21, 1996.
4. Michael Hammer and Bahram Njamir, "A Heuristic Approach to Attribute Partitioning," ACM SIGMOD, 93-101, 1979.
5. Shamkant Navathe, Stefano Ceri, Gio Wiederhold, and Jinglie Dou, "Vertical Partitioning Algorithms for Database Design," ACM Transactions on Database Systems, Vol. 9, No. 4, 680-710, December, 1984.
6. Shamkant B. Navathe and Minyoung Ra, "Vertical Partitioning for Database Design: A Graphical Algorithm," ACM SIGMOD, 440-450, 1989.
7. Hoffer, J.A., and Severance, D.G., "The use of cluster analysis in physical database design," In proceedings of first international conference on Very Large Database, 1975.
8. McCormick, W.T., Schweitzer, P.J., and White, T.W., "Problem decomposition and data reorganization by a clustering technique," Operation Research, Vol. 20, No. 5, 993-1009, September, 1972.

Using Market Mechanisms to Control Agent Allocation in Global Information Systems

I.N. Wang, N.J. Fiddian, and W.A.Gray

Department of Computer Science,
Cardiff University, Cardiff, Wales
{I.N.Wang, N.J.Fiddian, W.A.Gray}@cs.cf.ac.uk

Abstract. Multi-agent based global information systems present one of the broadest and most compelling areas for market-based control. Their inherently distributed and heterogeneous nature combined with their vast size makes traditional centralized control methods impractical. We use the 'invisible hand' of markets to guide agent decisions without centralized management. While most market-based studies impose auction mechanisms to drive market convergence, in our system the continual adaptation of the 'information economy' is an emergent effect, fuelled by competition between autonomous self-interested agents acting on locally gathered information. We argue that due to market-based competition an environment tailored to consumer requirements will emerge.
We focus on agents competing using mobility to adapt their location in response to consumer demand. In this modern version of the data allocation problem, we demonstrate that even simple decentralized mobility strategies can produce agent allocations comparable to centralized heuristic algorithms. Furthermore, we demonstrate that where agents implement competing strategies, due to market-based competition the agents that best satisfy consumer requirements will populate the emergent environment.

1 Introduction

The World Wide Web represents an unparalleled collection of unstructured and unintegrated data resources. It offers the potential for information discovery that would not be possible in a disconnected environment but is encumbered by its vast size and decentralized structure; the same structure that is responsible for its success. To harness the full potential of the web requires integrating and managing these resources while preserving a decentralized structure. Traditional centralized techniques for integration and management, such as global schemas and heuristic data allocation, impede local autonomy and scalability. We therefore look to database, agent and market-based control research to offer a more appropriate approach.

The future lies in a thoroughly decentralized 'information economy', with populations of autonomous self-interested agents selling and purchasing services and resources [12][11]. While autonomy is requisite due to the decentralized environment, self-interest refers to the agents' motivation to generate maximum

H.C. Mayr et al. (Eds.): DEXA 2001, LNCS 2113, pp. 547–556, 2001.

profit for themselves without regard for the effect on the system as a whole. Unlike narrower market-based systems that only feature price competition, information consumers will differentiate on broader criteria including response time, accuracy and reputation. Agents must therefore adopt competitive strategies in areas such as marketing and location as well as price, with their overall success being determined by a combination of their function and the quality of service delivered. Basically, as the consumer provides the money, the agents that best adapt to consumer requirements generate the most profit, and redundant agents go bankrupt. Through this 'natural' selection process the environment is tailored to meet the consumers' requirements, improving the quality of service the consumers experience.

Although not the focus of this paper, economic rationale may be requisite for the creation of truly global information systems in the first place. In the World Wide Web valuable resources are often hidden behind misleading advertising or subscription charges. Without financial incentive it is unlikely that such resources would be integrated into an information-filtering environment, and as a result the system would become a repository of worthless data. In addition, financial incentives promote the adoption of universal standards (e.g. common ontologies) as nonconformity discourages use and therefore revenue.

In this paper we concentrate on examining how in an environment where self-interested agents implement competing strategies, the emergent environment is adapted to meet consumer requirements. In particular we look at agents competing by utilizing mobility to adapt their location in response to changes in consumer demand. For example, if an agent observes a large increase in demand from London, through locating 'near' London it can reduce both communication costs and network delay and therefore increase its competitiveness. This is in some ways a decentralized version of the data allocation problem in that the aim is to distribute agents through the network so as to maximize the quality of service the consumers receive; we shall refer to it as the agent allocation problem.

This paper is ordered as follows. We look more closely at the agent allocation problem in section 2, reviewing related resource allocation approaches. In section 3 we outline the simple mobility strategies we have implemented and the experiments conducted with them, discussing the results in section 4. In section 5 we discuss our conclusions and future work in this area.

2 Market-Based Agent Allocation

From the outset of distributed information systems, research has been conducted into efficient methods for calculating near-optimal placements of data within networks, called the data/file allocation problem. However, like the management of these distributed information systems, these methods were generally centralized and static (see [6] for a survey), concentrating on network modelling and heuristic solutions. Such methods may be appropriate in confined systems but global information systems present too vast, dynamic and decentralized an environment as constructing a network model would be impractical, any such model would be instantly out-of-date, heuristic algorithms are doubtful to scale and autonomous entities are unlikely to accept a central solution. For global information systems a decentralized and dynamic approach is needed.

As mentioned earlier, we expect global information systems to be based on agent technology[1], and the data allocation problem will be recast as the agent allocation problem. Conveniently, as well as being the unit of allocation, agents also provide an ideal decentralized solution being autonomous, reactive and pro-active amongst others [15]. These properties combined with mobility, the ability to move across the network, allow each agent to determine its own placement (autonomy). An agent determines its placement based on its individual goals (pro-activity) and its local environment, dynamically responding to environmental changes (reactivity). For example, an agent located in London may decide to relocate to Tokyo based on changes in its usage pattern, thus altering the allocation of agents without central intervention.

While mobility provides the adaptation mechanism, it is market forces that give the self-interested agents incentive to move. The pursuit of profit encourages agents to locate close to their consumers, thereby improving the quality of service the consumers receive through reducing communications delay and cost. However, a counter-force is that superior sites are likely to be expensive, encouraging agents to distribute themselves at less congested locations. In centralized methods allocation decisions such as whether to minimize communication costs or maximize resource usage are made at design time, whereas in a market-based system the consumers dynamically drive these decisions through their preferences. Each consumer decides whether the benefit of utilizing an agent located at a superior site is worth any extra cost, and collectively these decisions generate market forces that steer the agents.

So far we have only mentioned an agent's ability to adapt its location, but the combination of mobility and market-based control introduces two additional adaptation considerations. Firstly, if an agent is generating sufficient revenue it may wish to expand its market share through launching a clone of itself or a sub-agent in a different location. Secondly, if an agent cannot generate enough income to support its continued existence (agents must pay for server hosting, advertising etc.) then it becomes bankrupt and should be removed from the system. Cloning causes an increase in the allocation of popular agents, while bankruptcy decreases the allocation of redundant agents. Combined with mobility, cloning and bankruptcy enable the agent allocation to be fully modified without central intervention.

Due to the decentralized environment, agents must make their mobility decisions based on locally gathered information. This information includes the value and content of the queries received from consumers and the path along which they were delivered. These local mobility decisions shape the global allocation and usually have knock-on effects for other agents. For example, an agent moving to a new location may attract some demand away from a competing agent,

[1] Multi-agent architectures for information integration have been proposed by a number of research projects, including InfoSleuth [1] and TSIMMIS [3].

possibly causing that agent to move or even go bankrupt. However while these effects will not always be globally desirable and the allocation is unlikely to be optimal, due to consumer-generated market-forces the allocation will be tailored towards consumer requirements. This effect is the market's 'invisible hand' associated with economist Adam Smith. Ensuring that agent decisions only produce desirable effects would require agents to have global network information and this is not feasible in global information systems, as we have explained previously. Even with global information it is unlikely that an optimal allocation can be found for all networks as the file allocation problem has been shown to be NP-complete [8].

There are various mobility strategies that an agent could adopt, from simple approaches such as always locating at the site of its most active user to more advanced strategies employing techniques such as machine learning. However in a competitive environment the strategy that best satisfies consumer requirements is likely to emerge as the dominant strategy in the system, and any new strategy will need to offer still greater advantages. So as well as stimulating the emergence of a consumer tailored system in the short-term, market-based control promotes further long-term development. Later on in this paper we present empirical evidence supporting these claims.

2.1 Related Work

With the continued emergence of multi-agent systems, researchers are increasingly viewing economic markets as offering solutions to complex and decentralized resource allocation problems; often called market-based control [5][14]. Market-based control methods have been applied in various guises to problems such as call routing [9], bandwidth assignment [16], factory scheduling [13], climate control [10][17] and, of particular relevance to our study, mobile agent distribution [2] and distributed information systems [7]; as well as more theoretical problems.

Many market-based studies employ some form of auction mechanism to coordinate market prices and ensure the system remains close to economic equilibrium, including work on mobile agent distribution [2] and distributed information systems [7]. Probably the most cited example is the WALRAS system [4], in which an auctioneer utilizes demand information received from agents to iteratively calculate equilibrium prices. The WALRAS system achieves competitive equilibrium under certain conditions, but there are aspects that make it and other auction mechanisms less applicable to totally decentralized models. As discussed in [11], the auctioneer is effectively a centralized entity working on global information, and therefore suffers similar problems with autonomy and scalability as the non-market-based centralized heuristics mentioned earlier.

In addition to centralization problems, auctions only model the supposed effects of markets rather than the mechanism through which they occur [11]. In real markets the 'invisible hand' is an emergent effect caused by competition between self-interested entities, while in auction-based systems it is imposed through the auctioneer. This limits markets to adapting within the scope of their auctions, which generally balance prices without quality of service considerations. In our system there is no price-balancing auctioneer, instead we rely on the 'invisible hand' effect to guide the market towards equilibrium, despite agents only acting on locally gathered information.

3 Strategies and Experiments

In earlier sections we outlined our decentralized market-based approach to agent allocation, where due to competition and market imposed restraints the emergent allocation is tailored to consumer requirements. To support this claim we implemented a simulation of a distributed multi-agent architecture (based on information integration architectures such as InfoSleuth [1] and TSIMMIS [3]) as an experimentation platform. Using this platform we examined the performance of two simple agent mobility strategies both individually and in competition, and compared their performance with allocations generated using centralized heuristic and random algorithms. In this section we describe the mobility strategies used and the experimental design.

3.1 Agent Strategies

As outlined earlier, agents compete to satisfy consumers through differing mobility strategies, and this causes the emergent environment to be tailored to consumer requirements. In order to test this theory we implemented two simple mobility strategies called Principal Consumer Mobility and Principal Neighbour Mobility, with both monitoring incoming queries to check if the income generated from remote sites warrants the agent relocating or launching a clone.

In Principal Consumer Mobility the following tests are performed to determine whether to relocate/clone:

- Clone test: `Is remote profit > fixed expenditure?`
- Mobility test: `Is income from site X > local income?`

The clone test checks whether the agent is generating enough profit to support a clone. If this is the case then a clone is launched at the site of the agent's principal consumer (the consumer generating the most income). The mobility test checks whether a remote site is generating more income than the local site, and if so then the agent relocates to this site.

In Principal Neighbour Mobility the following tests are performed to determine whether to relocate/clone:

- Clone test: `Is remote profit > fixed expenditure?`
- Mobility test: `Is income from connection X > local income + income from connection Y?`

These tests are similar to those for Principal Consumer Mobility except queries are grouped according to the network neighbour through which they

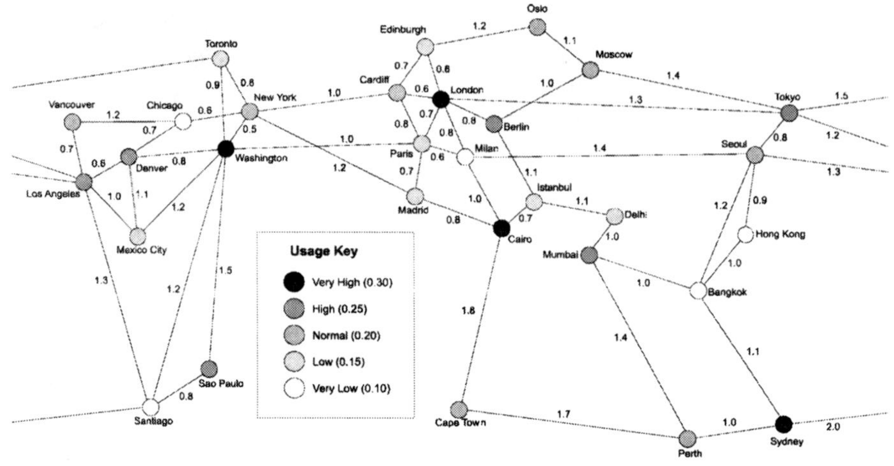

Fig. 1. Experimental network showing server usage and communication costs

were delivered. So rather than an agent cloning to the site of its principal user it clones to its principal neighbour and the same for moving. For example, referring to Figure 1, if an agent at Cardiff was receiving heavy traffic from Denver it might clone to New York, and then that clone may move to Denver via Chicago.

The benefit of Principal Consumer Mobility is that the agent moves directly to its main consumer, meaning it adapts quickly to changes in consumer requirements. However this strategy may not always be beneficial as the main consumer may sometimes be isolated from the main area of activity. Although Principal Neighbour Mobility is less responsive, it benefits from always heading towards the most active areas.

In our strategies we have introduced minimum thresholds for the clone and mobility tests to help prevent reactions to temporary blips in the usage pattern. However these thresholds also make the strategies less responsive to genuine changes. For our experimentation we compared two versions of Principal Consumer Mobility and Principal Neighbour Mobility, the standard version and the stable version. The difference between the two being that the stable version had considerably higher thresholds. The performance of these strategies both individually and in competition is discussed in Section 4.

3.2 Experimental Setup

We will briefly outline the basic network setup that was used for our experimentation. We simulated a network of thirty servers, shown in Figure 1. Although we envisage much larger networks, given that through moving and cloning an agent service can exist on any combination of servers, our simulated network still yields 2^{30} possible allocations per agent service, making agent allocation a non-trivial task. The value next to a network connection is the cost of communication along that connection, while a server's degree of shading corresponds to the usage level at that server (e.g. consumers at the London server generate 0.25 queries/unit of time). This is the average usage with inter-query times being calculated using the exponential distribution. The quality of service a consumer experienced was determined by their cost of purchasing a service from an agent, with consumers always preferring the cheapest option. Apart from differing usage all of the servers were homogeneous, supplying the same functions and charging the same price for hosting an agent. This ensured that the only method through which agents could improve the quality of service they delivered was by reducing consumers' network costs.

For our experiments we initialized agents implementing one of our mobility strategies at arbitrary locations in the network. We then left the agents for three hours to move and clone, and evaluated the emergent allocation. We tested how each strategy performed when it was the only strategy present, and when it was in competition with other strategies. In order that our experiments were fair the agents were identical in all respects except mobility strategy. Each agent adopted the same pricing strategy, which was to set its price so that it required one request per time period to cover its hosting costs and therefore avoid bankruptcy. If an agent received more than one request per time period then it would generate profit and could therefore launch clones.

For comparison we generated agent allocations with a hill-climbing algorithm using global information, and a random allocation algorithm. As with the market-based experiments these allocations were required to be sustainable, with each agent receiving at least one query per time period on average.

4 Results

The aim of our experimentation was to demonstrate two ideas: Firstly that autonomous agents implementing simple mobility strategies can produce agent allocations comparable to centralized heuristic algorithms; and secondly that due to market-based competition the emergent agent population will contain

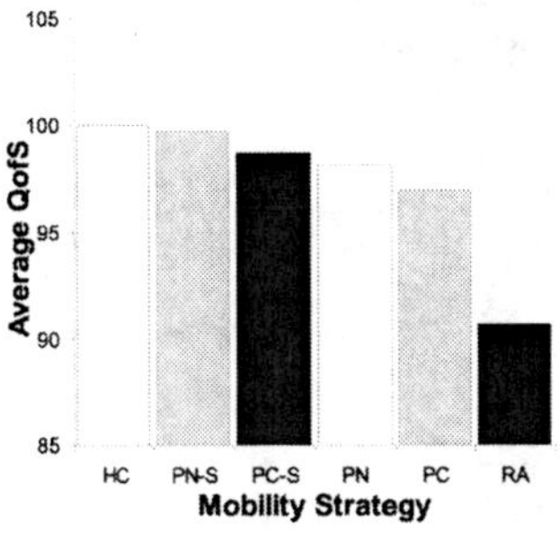

Fig. 2. Average quality of service produced by individual strategies and heuristics

those agents that best satisfy consumer requirements. We shall concentrate initially on the first idea by considering how individual mobility strategies perform without competition. From this we can then see whether those strategies that performed well individually emerge as successful when in competition with alternative strategies.

In Figure 2 we compare the average quality of service (QofS) experienced by consumers when individual strategies operate in the network, to that experienced with Hill-Climber and Random allocations. As expected given the relatively static environment the Hill-Climber algorithm delivered the highest quality of service, but then it does utilize global information. However, when decentralized agent strategies were used the average quality of service was not much lower. Of these strategies the stable versions perform best, with Principal Neighbour (stable) only 0.2% worse than Hill-Climber and Principal Consumer (stable) 1.3% worse. The Principal Consumer strategy fairs least well of the strategies, producing an average quality of service 3.1% worse than Hill-Climber. However this is considerably better than the average Sustainable Random allocation, which is 9.3% worse than Hill-Climber.

It is not surprising that the more stable versions of the agent strategies were more successful as the environment is relatively static. Their increased stability is achieved through higher thresholds for clone and mobility tests, helping prevent them from reacting to temporary blips in the usage pattern but also reducing their responsiveness to genuine usage changes. However, in more dynamic environments responsiveness may be more critical than stability and the standard versions may prove more successful.

We have shown that while individually our decentralized agent strategies can deliver a high quality of service, some perform better than others. If our second suggestion is correct then in a competitive environment those agent strategies that best satisfy consumer requirements will emerge dominant over less satisfactory strategies. To test this we initialised the network with two agents implementing competing strategies and waited (up to three hours) to see which strategy survived.

In Table 1 we show the results of our competitive testing. From this we can see that when agents implementing the Principal Neighbour (PN) and Principal Consumer (PC) strategies are initialised in the same network the Principal Neighbour strategy emerges dominant. However, when either of these strate-

Strategy v Strategy	Emergent Strategy
PC v PN	PN
PC v PC-S	PC-S
PC v PN-S	PN-S
PN v PC-S	PC-S
PN v PN-S	PN-S
PC-S v PN-S	Undetermined

Table 1. Emergent strategy from competition between two strategies

gies competes against one of our stable strategies (PN-S and PC-S) the stable strategy emerges dominant. These results agree with the strategies' individual performances as the stable strategies performed better individually than the standard strategies, and the Principal Neighbour strategy performed better individually than the Principal Consumer strategy. However, we have not determined the emergent strategy when Principal Neighbour (stable) (PN-S) and Principal Consumer (stable) (PC-S) compete, as this scenario tends to lead to a standoff with both strategies surviving. A possible reason is that not only do these policies make fewer bad decisions but they are also slower at capitalising on their opponents' bad decisions. Judging by the other results we would expect Principal Neighbour (stable) to emerge as the dominant strategy but this is likely to require longer than our imposed time limit.

With our results we have demonstrated two ideas: Firstly, that in a market-based system, autonomous agents implementing simple decentralized mobility strategies can generate agent allocations comparable to centralized heuristics; and secondly that due to market-based competition the emergent environment will usually be populated by the agents that best satisfy consumer requirements. By combining these results we can see that the market's 'invisible hand' guides the continual adaptation of the environment in both the short and long term, with consumers' requirements providing the motivating force.

5 Conclusion and Future Work

In this paper we have presented a market-based approach to agent allocation in global information systems. Unlike many other market-based agent systems that use centralized auction mechanisms, our approach is thoroughly decentralized relying on the market's 'invisible hand' to guide agent decisions. We considered an environment in which agents must purchase services and resources from other agents, including the right to reside on a server. By having agents adopt mobility strategies, we demonstrated that under market-based control even simple strategies based on locally gathered information could generate agent allocations comparable to centralized heuristic algorithms. Furthermore we showed that where agents adopted competing strategies the emergent population contained those that best satisfied the consumers' requirements.

We have only looked at emergent allocations generated by mediator agents adopting simple mobility strategies in a relatively static environment. There is enormous scope for future research into market-based control as a decentralized management technique for global information systems, including:

- Developing competitive strategies in other areas, such as price or marketing.
- Introducing techniques from machine learning and evolutionary programming to develop more intuitive strategies.
- Considering more dynamic environments where the speed of adaptation is important.
- Using competitive strategies at multiple agent levels (e.g. agents sub-contracting work to other agents).

In addition to these extensions there is considerable ongoing work in related areas such as mobile agents, information integration and electronic cash.

The ultimate goal is a global information system that responds to consumers' quality of service requirements without relying on centralized control. As a starting point, our results suggest that market-based competition could provide effective decentralized management for such a system.

References

1. R. Bayardo Jr., et al. InfoSleuth: Agent-based semantic integration of information in open and dynamic environments. In *Proc. of ACM SIGMOD Conference*, pages 195–206. Tucson, AZ, USA, May 1997.
2. J. Bredin, et al. Market-based resource control for mobile agents. In *Proc. of 2nd International Conference on Autonomous Agents*, pages 197–204. May 1998.
3. S. Chawathe, et al. The TSIMMIS project: Integration of heterogeneous information sources. In *Proc. of IPSJ Conference*, pages 7–18. Tokyo, Japan, 1994.
4. J. Cheng and M. Wellman. The WALRAS algorithm: A convergent distributed implementation of general equilibrium outcomes. *Computational Economics*, 12:1–24, 1999.
5. S. Clearwater, editor. *Market-Based Control: A Paradigm for Distributed Resource Allocation*. World Scientific, Singapore, 1995.
6. L. Dowdy and D. Foster. Comparative models of the file assignment problem. *ACM Computing Surveys*, 14(2):289–313, 1982.
7. E. Durfee, et al. Strategic reasoning and adaptation in an information economy. In M. Klusch, editor, *Intelligent Information Agents*. Springer Verlag, 1998.
8. K. Eswaran. Placement of records in a file and file allocation in a computer network. In *Proc. of IFIPS Conference*, pages 304–307. Stockholm, Sweden, 1974.
9. M. J. Gibney, et al. Market-based call routing in telecommunications networks using adaptive pricing and real bidding. In *Proc. of 3rd International Workshop on Multi-Agent Systems and Telecommunications (IATA-99)*, pages 50–65. Stockholm, Sweden, 1999.
10. B. Huberman and S. Clearwater. A multi-agent system for controlling building environments. In *Proc. of 1st International Conference on Multi-Agent Systems (ICMAS '95)*, pages 171–176. 1995.
11. P. Kearney and W. Merlat. Modelling market-based decentralized management systems. *BT Technology Journal*, 17(4):145–156, October 1999.
12. J. Kephart, et al. Price-war dynamics in a free-market economy of software agents. In *Proc. of ALIFE VI*. Los Angeles, CA, USA, June 1998.
13. W. Walsh, et al. Some economies of market-based distributed scheduling. In *Proc. of 18th International Conference on Distributed Computing Systems*, pages 612–621. 1998.
14. M. Wellman and P. Wurman. Market-aware agents for a multiagent world. *Robotics and Autonomous Systems*, 24:115–125, 1998.
15. M. Wooldridge and N. Jennings. Intelligent agents: Theory and practice. *The Knowledge Engineering Review*, 10(2):115–152, 1995.
16. H. Yamaki, et al. A market-based approach to allocating qofs for multimedia application. In *Proc. of 2nd International Conference on Multi-Agent Systems (ICMAS-96)*. Kyoto, Japan, December 1996.
17. F. Ygge and H. Akkermans. Decentralized markets versus central control: A comparative study. *Journal of Artificial Intelligence Research*, 11:301–333, 1999.

Query Integration for Refreshing Web Views

Haifeng Liu, Wee-Keong Ng, and Ee-Peng Lim

Centre for Advanced Information Systems, School of Computer Engineering
Nanyang Technological University, Singapore 639798, SINGAPORE
awkng@ntu.edu.sg

Abstract. As websites grow larger and become more sophisticated, organizations use structured database systems as a source of base data for information presented on the website. Thus, it has become critical to keep a very large website up-to-date in response to frequent changes to base data. This is particularly true for websites presenting fast changing information. The execution of a refresh query produces a *Web view* that forms the content of a portion of a Web page. As the execution of such queries involve database access, the execution time may affect the feasibility of timely refreshing a set of Web views contained in a website. In this paper, we focus on the problem of reducing database access and improving the feasibility of scheduling a set of refresh queries to timely refresh Web views. We propose an optimization technique, *query integration* to reduce the number of potential refresh queries. The technique seeks to integrate compatible queries into a single query. We illustrate the efficiency of this technique with empirical results.

1 Introduction

The World Wide Web is a huge information repository that continues to grow rapidly. The popularity of WWW has made it a prime vehicle for disseminating information. More and more corporations and individuals advertise themselves through websites in recent years. Compared to static and dynamic Web pages which are dynamically created by a CGI script at run-time, *semi-dynamic* Web pages are pages whose contents are extracted from some source database and which change in response to updates to the source database. An example of such a page can be found at `http://www.fish.com.sg` where a list of stock information is refreshed frequently with respect to updates to base data. A crucial problem arises when base data change frequently and there is a need to keep a large set of semi-dynamic pages up-to-date in response to source changes since no one is interested in stale data on the Web; an investor may suffer losses relying on obsolete stock price on the Web.

To perform timely updates on a website that hosts semi-dynamic Web pages, fresh data are "pulled" to the website by executing queries against the source database since the freshness cannot be guaranteed by "pushing" base data from the source database to the websites. To differentiate between the contents derived from base data and the *trivial* contents of a Web page, we refer to that portion of a page derived from base data as a *Web view*. Each view has an associated

H.C. Mayr et al. (Eds.): DEXA 2001, LNCS 2113, pp. 557–566, 2001.

refresh query. The task of refreshing a website is to schedule refresh queries to refresh the Web views in the website. In our approach, we collect and materialize all views of a website into a logical *viewbase*. A viewbase functions like a cache and provides fresh data whenever the Web pages must be re-generated. We have proposed a framework for timely refreshing a set of Web views, more details can be found at [5].

For each view in the viewbase, whenever a relevant update event occurred on the base data, a view *refresh request* is raised. A refresh request is *timely satisfied* if a single execution of the refresh query is started after the request has been raised and completed before the next request is raised; otherwise, the request is missed. We say a set of refresh queries is *feasible* enough to keep views in a viewbase fresh constantly if every refresh requests of the viewbase can be timely satisfied by scheduling the queries. Note that since a view may be derived from multiple base tables that are updated with different periods, the constant interval between the raised refresh requests for the view, called the *refresh period* of the view, is restricted to the minimal update period among all base tables. The base table having the minimal update period is called the *feature table* of the view.

The aim of the website refresh problem is to determine a feasible refresh query set for a viewbase. However, this is not easily achievable due to the *update pattern* of base data and the constraint of resources. We have presented some feasibility results in [3,4] for a given refresh query set when each base table in the source database is updated with finite frequency. From [3,4], a bottleneck for producing a feasible schedule of refreshing a website arises when too many refresh queries compete to occupy the scheduler. Fortunately, we observe that multiple views may be derived from the same base table(s) and their refresh queries have the similar structure. Thus, they can be refreshed by executing a single *complex* query instead of multiple *atomic* queries since the result of an atomic query covers only a single view. Therefore, if we can efficiently reduce the number of executed queries by *integrating* atomic queries into complex ones, we may easily produce a feasible schedule. Furthermore, reducing the number of executed queries can also decrease the workload on the source database which may be critical for a very large website.

The rest of the paper is organized as follows: We introduce some notations and formal definitions in Section 2. We introduce an optimization technique for query integration in Section 3. In Section 4, we apply query integration to the *candidate query set* of a website and propose an integration algorithm which may decrease the redundancy incurred by query integration. We show the benefit of query integration with empirical results in Section 5. We review some related work in Section 6 and conclude the paper in Section 7.

2 Notations and Definitions

To differentiate between the contents derived from base data and the *trivial* contents of a Web page, we refer to that portion of a page derived from base data as a *Web view*. The query producing the view is referred to the *refresh query* of the view. The task of refreshing a website is to schedule refresh queries to refresh the Web views in the website. In our approach, we collect and materialize all views of a website into a logical *viewbase*. A viewbase locating at the side of the Web server functions like a cache and provides fresh data whenever the Web pages must be re-generated.

Let $C = \{c_1, c_2, \ldots, c_n\}$ be a viewbase where for each view c_i, $1 \leq i \leq n$, there exists a refresh query q_i that yields c_i. Let $\Phi(q_i)$ denote the result set of query q_i. Then, $\Phi(q_i) = \{c_i\}$, $1 \leq i \leq n$, is singleton, and we say that q_i is *atomic*. We define a *complex* refresh query p as one whose result set has more than one element (i.e., $|\Phi(p)| \geq 1$). We emphasize here that the result of an atomic refresh query can be used to refresh only one view whereas the result of a complex query can be decomposed and distributed to refresh multiple views, i.e., the result of the complex query *covers* these views. In this work, we are not concerned with the detail of how the result of a complex query is distributed to multiple views. We assume that such a distribution can be performed with negligible cost.

Definition 1 (Candidate Query Set). *Given a viewbase C and a query set $Q(C)$, if the result of $Q(C)$ covers all views in C, i.e., $\Phi(Q(C)) = \bigcup_{q \in Q(C)} \Phi(q) = C$, we say $Q(C)$ is a candidate query set for C.* ∎

We refer to the initial refresh query set $Q_0(C) = \{q_1, q_2, \ldots, q_n\}$ of C where q_i's are atomic as a *trivial* candidate query set for C. To save database access and to reduce processor usage, the candidate query set should include as few elements as possible. Since the result of one complex query may cover multiple views, a candidate query set involving complex queries may have less elements than a trivial candidate query set. The task is to derive complex queries by integration of the current atomic queries.

3 Query Integration

In this section, we introduce the technique of integration of atomic refresh queries into complex queries. We define a refresh query as a SQL query since base data are all relational tables. In particular, we restrict it to a SPJ query. Thus, a refresh query q has the following form :

```
SELECT ⟨attributes⟩
FROM   ⟨tables⟩
WHERE  ⟨condition⟩
```

where we denote R_q as the set of tables involved in the query, π_q as the set of projected attributes in the query and σ_q as the selection condition that identifies tuples to be retrieved by the query. We begin by considering the class of SPJ queries whose WHERE clause is composed of comparison expressions that include join conditions but that exclude nested queries and set operators IN, IS NULL and so on. For our convenience, we divide the selection condition into two parts: *join condition* and *comparison condition*, denoted by σ_q^j and σ_q^c respectively. The join condition σ_q^j is an expression of the form $k_1 = k_2 = \cdots = k_u$ where each $k_i \in K_q$, $1 \leq i \leq |R_q|$, is a join attribute of one table in R_q. The join condition of q can also be written as $\sigma_q^j = join(K_q)$. The comparison condition σ_q^c is a sequence of *literals* connected by boolean operators '$\wedge$'. A literal is of the form $x\ op\ y + c$ or $x\, op\, c$ where $op \in \{=, >, >=, <=\}$, x, y are attributes of the table in R_q and c is a constant. We do not include negative literal here. Therefore, $\sigma_q = \sigma_q^j \wedge \sigma_q^c$.

Based on the mapping relationships between Web views and base data , we observe that multiple views (deriving from one base table or closely related) may be produced by performing one complex query rather than a set of atomic queries one at a time. The result of this complex query is stored as a virtual view in the viewbase. Thus, we may derive complex refresh queries following the two strategies below:

(i) Integrate views with the same base table into one virtual view.
(ii) Integrate complex views with different base tables that can be joined together into one virtual view.

3.1 Integration with Views from the Same Base Table

Suppose we have a set of Web views $C = \{c_1, c_2, \ldots, c_n\}$ where the corresponding base table set and refresh query of c_i are represented as T_i and q_i. In this case, the content of all views come from the same base table t, so $T_i = \{t\}$ for $1 \leq i \leq n$. Each refresh query q_i ($\Phi(q_i) = \{c_i\}$) has the form:

SELECT π_{q_i}
FROM t
WHERE σ_{q_i}

Our objective is to integrate queries in the refresh query set of C into a complex query p such that all tuples needed by views in C can be obtained by performing p, i.e., $\Phi(p) = C$. We achieve the goal by applying the following rules:

(i) $\pi_p = \bigcup_{i=1}^{n} \pi_{q_i}$
(ii) $R_p = t$
(iii) $\sigma_p = \sigma_{q_1} \vee \sigma_{q_2} \vee \cdots \vee \sigma_{q_n}$

Note that since views in C have the same base table, they have the same refresh frequency correspondingly, and the virtual view that has been determined by the integrated complex query also has the same refresh frequency.

3.2 Integration with Related Complex Views

In this section, we consider the integration of a complex query which covers multiple related complex Web views having multiple base tables.

Case I: Same Base Tables. We have a view set $C = \{c_1, c_2, \ldots, c_n\}$ where c_i ($1 \le i \le n$) is associated with base table set T_i and refresh query q_i. It is known that T_i is not singleton and $T_i = T_j = T$ for any i and j, and all refresh queries have the same join conditions; i.e., for any two refresh queries q_i and q_j, $R_{q_i} = R_{q_j} = T$ and $\sigma^j_{q_i} = \sigma^j_{q_j} = \sigma^j$. By applying the following integration rules, we can acquire a complex query p which covers the view set C. (i.e., $\Phi(p) = C$):

(i) $\pi_p = \bigcup_{i=1}^{n} \pi_{q_i}$
(ii) $R_p = T$
(iii) $\sigma_p = \sigma^j \wedge (\sigma^c_{q_1} \vee \sigma^c_{q_2} \vee \cdots \vee \sigma^c_{q_n})$

Note that all views, including derived virtual view, have the same base tables. Thus, they have the same refresh frequency. The following example illustrates this case:

Example 1. At the website `http://snoopy.asia1.com.sg/realstk` two Web views c_1, c_2 are all derived form the base tables Stock(counter, done, previous, volume, value) and Sesdaq(stockName, buy, sell, open, low, high) which stores all SESDAQ stocks' exchange information (see Fig. 1). Let refresh queries q_1 be

```
SELECT counter, done, buy, sell, open, low, high, volume
FROM   Stock, Sesdaq
WHERE (counter = stockName) AND (low > 0.2000);
```

and q_2 be

```
SELECT counter, done, buy, sell, open, low, high, volume
FROM   Stock, Sesdaq
WHERE (counter = stockName) AND (high < 0.4000);
```

Then p can be derived by integrating q_1 and q_2 as follows:

```
SELECT counter, done, buy, sell, open, low, high, volume
FROM   Stock, Sesdaq
WHERE (counter = stockName) AND ((low > 0.2000) OR (high < 0.4000));
```

∎

Case II: Different Base Tables but Same Join Fields. In this case, we have a set of complex views whose refresh queries may involve multiple base tables and base tables of views may be different each other. However, all these base tables have the same join field. Thus, for a set of views $C = \{c_1, c_2, \ldots, c_n\}$ with corresponding refresh query set $\{q_1, q_2, \ldots, q_n\}$, attributes in K_{q_i} ($1 \le i \le n$) (the set of join attributes of query q_i) are defined on the same attribute field.

Since all queries have the same join field, a new complex query can be integrated by joining all queries together on their attributes whose values are defined on the common join field. However, to guarantee that no tuples are lost during the process of joining all base tables of C, it is imperative to introduce the operation OUTER JOIN into the integrated complex query p. Thus, in the FROM clause of query p, a table called *joined table* resulting from a join operation is permitted to be specified. Therefore, p can be integrated as follows:

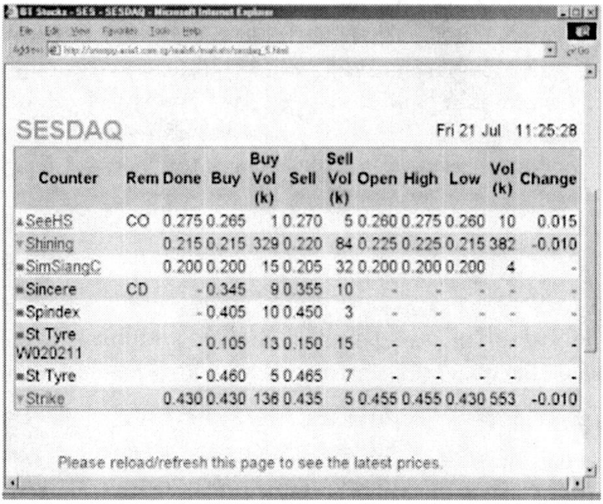

SESDAQ Fri 21 Jul 11:25:28

Counter	Rem	Done	Buy	Buy Vol (k)	Sell	Sell Vol (k)	Open	High	Low	Vol (k)	Change
SeeHS	CO	0.275	0.265	1	0.270	5	0.260	0.275	0.260	10	0.015
Shining		0.215	0.215	329	0.220	84	0.225	0.225	0.215	382	-0.010
SimSiangC		0.200	0.200	15	0.205	32	0.200	0.200	0.200	4	-
Sincere	CD	-	0.345	9	0.355	10	-	-	-	-	-
Spindex		-	0.405	10	0.450	3	-	-	-	-	-
St Tyre W020211		-	0.105	13	0.150	15	-	-	-	-	-
St Tyre		-	0.460	5	0.465	7	-	-	-	-	-
Strike		0.430	0.430	136	0.435	5	0.455	0.455	0.430	553	-0.010

Please reload/refresh this page to see the latest prices.

Fig. 1. A Web view derived from multiple base tables

(i) $\pi_p = \bigcup_{i=1}^{n} \pi_{q_i}$
(ii) $\sigma_p = \sigma^c_{q_1} \vee \sigma^c_{q_2} \cdots \vee \sigma^c_{q_n}$
(iii) R_p =OUTER JOIN ((OUTER JOIN (OUTER JOIN $(\cdots)$, JOIN$(R_{q_{n-1}})$ on $K_{q_{n-1}})$ on $(K_{q_1} \wedge K_{q_2} \wedge \cdots \wedge K_{q_{n-1}})$), JOIN$(R_{q_n})$ on $K_{q_n})$ on $(K_{q_1} \wedge K_{q_2} \wedge \cdots \wedge K_{q_n})$

Nevertheless, due to the introduction of OUTER JOIN operation, the derived complex query may contain a large amount of redundant data which is not covered by the original atomic queries. This redundancy may highly increase the workload of database server when the complex query is performed. Thus, it is not encouraged to perform query integration with OUTER JOIN involved.

4 Applying Query Integration

A side effect of query integration is that the virtual view produced by the integrated complex query may include redundant data. Therefore, when applying query integration to a viewbase with its trivial candidate query set, we impose one integration on a limited number of related queries rather than on all possible queries which can be integrated together into one query.

Given a viewbase $C = \{c_1, c_2, \ldots, c_n\}$ with trivial candidate query set $Q_0(C) = \{q_1, q_2, \ldots, q_n\}$, if views in C are distributed over the set of Web pages $P = \{w_1, w_2, \ldots, w_m\}$ $(w \geq n)$, then our strategy is to only integrate queries whose views are located in the same Web page into one single complex query. The detailed integration algorithm is proposed in Figure 2. The output of the algorithm is another refresh query set $Q_0(V)$ whose elements are either elements of $Q_0(C)$ or are integrated complex queries from elements of $Q_0(C)$,

```
V ← ∅, Q0(V) ← ∅;
foreach wi ∈ P
{
    Let Ci ⊂ C be collection of views contained in wi ;
    Let Qi ⊂ Q0(C) be collection of refresh queries of views in Ci;
    while (Ci ≠ ∅)
    {
        fetch a view ci,j ∈ Ci
        if qi,j ∈ Qi (Φ(qi,j) = ci,j) cannot be integrated with other queries in Qi
        {
            add ci,j into V;
            add qi,j into Q0(V);
            remove ci,j from Ci;
            remove qi,j from Qi;
        }
        else
        {
            Let Qi,j ⊂ Qi contains all queries which can be integrated with
                qi,j together into a complex query;
            integrate qi,j and queries in Qi,j into a complex query p
            add p into Q0(V);
            add v = Φ(p) into V;
            remove ci,j and all views yielded by queries in Qi,j from Ci;
            remove qi,j and all elements in Qi,j from Qi;
        }
    }
}
```

Fig. 2. A query integration algorithm for viewbase C with trivial candidate query set $Q_0(C)$

and another view set V whose elements are either elements of C or are virtual views produced by complex queries in $Q_0(V)$. Clearly, the result of $Q_0(V)$ is V and also covers C. That is, $Q_0(V)$ is the trivial candidate query set of V and also another candidate query set of C.

After obtaining derived virtual view set V and its trivial candidate query set $Q_0(V)$, we apply the traditional EDF (Earliest Deadline First) algorithm [2], which is optimal in most cases, to schedule queries included in $Q_0(V)$ and to materialize views in V. Note that if a virtual view $v \in V$ is integrated from a set of views $C_v \subset C$, then the refresh period of v is determined as the minimum refresh period among all views in C_v.

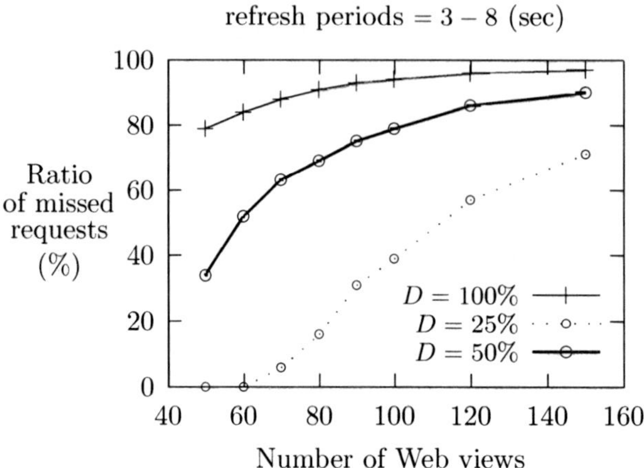

Fig. 3. Ratio of missed requests versus different number of views.

5 Simulation Results

We simulate the refresh of a set of Web views on a PC (pIII 550) with Red Hat 6.0. Sybase Adaptive Server Enterprise 11.9.2 provides the experimental database.

The input is a set of views $C = \{c_1, c_2, \ldots, c_n\}$ with trivial candidate query set $Q_0(C) = \{q_1, q_2, \ldots, q_n\}$ and refresh pattern set $R(C) = \{\langle T_{1,1}, U_1\rangle, \langle T_{2,1}, U_2\rangle, \ldots, \langle T_{n,1}, U_n\rangle\}$ where $T_{i,1}$ is the time instant when c_i raises the first refresh request and U_i is the refresh period of c_i to the EDF scheduler. Let the total number and missed number of raised refresh requests by views during the schedule be denoted r and r_m respectively. Then $M(C) = r_m/r \times 100\%$ is the percentage of the missed requests. We perform query integration on $Q_0(C)$ and obtain the derived view set V with candidate query set $Q_0(V)$. We feed V and $Q_0(V)$ to the scheduler to obtain the ratio $M(V)$ of missed requests during the schedule. We compare $M(C)$ and $M(V)$. It is expected that $M(V)$ be less than $M(C)$.

By varying the number of views in the original viewbase C and *integration ratio* $D = |V|/|C|$, we conduct a series of experiments to measure the ratio of missed refresh requests, the result is shown in Figure 3. All experiments use the same source database where 20 tables are stored and each table has 500 tuples. The update period of tables is constant and uniformly distributed in the range of between 3 and 8 seconds. The results indicate that the more views there are in the viewbase, (which implies the more number of refresh queries), the higher is the missing ratio. This supports our motivation to develop the technique of query integration. In addition, it is shown that the missing ratio of the refresh requests is greatly decreased after the query integration and lower integration ratio leads to lower missing ratio of the requests.

6 Related Work

Materializing and maintaining Web views have drawn attentions of researchers recently. In [8], an algorithm for incremental maintenance of hypertext views is proposed. [1] discussed the option of materializing a Web view inside the DBMS, at the Web serve, or not at all, always computing it on the fly. However, no previous work concerns "timeliness" when updating Web views while it is truly an important issue when base data change fast and is our focus.

The significant difference between query integration and multiple query optimization lies in that query integration does not search an optimal execution plan for a set of queries, which is exhaustive and explores a doubly exponential search space (some heuristic algorithms were proposed in [7] to improve efficiency). Instead, it derives a complex query to be executed to fetch the required data. Another work [6] on optimizing continuous queries shares the same idea with our work by grouping similar queries together. However, they focus on querying XML data sets using a query language like XML-QL while our refresh queries are more general SQL queries.

7 Conclusions

We have developed a query integration technique to reduce the number of executed refresh queries when refreshing a large website. To decrease the redundancy brought by query integration, we only integrate queries whose resultant views are located in the same Web page rather than all possible query pairs. M ore effective methods will be considered in our future work.

References

1. A. Labrinidis, N. Roussopoulos. WebView Materialization. In *Proceedings of the ACM SIGMOD International Conference on Management of Data*, Texas, USA, 2000.
2. C. L. Liu, J. Layland. Scheduling Algorithms for Multiprogramming in A Hard-Real-Time Environment. *Journal of the Association for Computing Machinery*, 20:46–61, 1973.
3. H. Liu, W. K. Ng, E.-P. Lim. Some preliminary results on the feasibility of website refresh queries. In *Proceedins of the 10th International Conference on Database and Expert System Applications (DEXA'99)*, pages 1076–1085, Florence, Italy, August 1999.
4. H. Liu, W.-K. Ng, E.-P. Lim. Keeping a Very Large Website Up-to-date: Some Feasibility Results. In *Proceedins of the 1th International Conference on Electronic Commerce and Web Technologies (EC-Web2000)*, Greenwich, UK, September 2000.
5. H. Liu, W.-K. Ng, E.-P. Lim. Model and Research Issues for Refreshing A Very Large Website. In *Proceedins of the 1th International Conference on Web-based Information Systems Engineering (WISE2000)*, Hong Kong, June 2000.

6. Jianjun Chen, D. J. DeWitt, Feng Tian, Yuan Wang. NiagaraCQ: A Scalable Continuous Query System for Internet Databases. In *Proceedings of 2000 ACM SIGMOD International Conference on Management of Data*, pages 261–272, Dallas, Texas, May 2000.
7. Prasan Roy, S. Seshadri, S. Sudarshan, Siddhesh Bhobe. Efficient and Extensible Algorithms for Multi Query Optimization. In *Proceedings of 2000 ACM SIGMOD International Conference on Management of Data*, pages 249–260, Dallas, Texas, May 2000.
8. G. Sindoni. Incremental Maintenance of Hypertext Views. In *Proceedings of the ACM SIGMOD Workshop on the Web and Databases (WebDB'98)*, Valencia, Spain, 1998.

Size-Adjusted Sliding Window LFU - A New Web Caching Scheme

Wen-Chi Hou Suli Wang

Department of Computer Science
Southern Illinois University at Carbondale
Carbondale IL 62901
hou@cs.siu.edu

Abstract. Web caching is a scalable and effective way to reduce network traffic and response time. In this study, we propose a new cache replacement policy for proxy and Web servers, the Size-Adjusted Sliding Window LFU (SSW-LFU). In this policy, we use the rates of recent accesses within a sliding window to estimate the probability of future document accesses. In addition, we take into account the variable sizes of documents. Simulations with real-life web access data are conducted to evaluate the performance. SSW-LFU outperformed other algorithms in hit ratio and had comparable byte hit ratio when compared with other algorithms such as LFU, LRU, Size, LRU-Min, etc.

1 Introduction

The Web has continued its exponential growth since its start in the early 1990s. As more and more information services are moved onto the Web, network congestion and server overloading have become the major problems of Web accesses. A scalable and effective way to improve the web performance is to use caches, where popular documents are stored either in local main memory or disks [1, 13, 10]. Web caching can reduce both the network traffic and the server load by migrating copies of popular documents from information servers closer to the clients. It can also reduce access latency by retrieving data from nearby proxy caches, instead of from remote data servers.

Caching can be implemented as client, proxy, or server caching at various points in the network. However, the types of traffic that a browser, a proxy, and a (Web) server cache manage may be quite different. A browser cache responds to exactly one client. As a client often visits the same documents repeatedly, relationships among the accesses may exist. A proxy cache, like the browser cache, caches worldwide documents; however, it normally responds to multiple clients who have little relationship. As for the server cache, it responds to worldwide clients like the proxy cache, but manages a relatively small number of documents that are only on that server. In this paper, we will concentrate ourselves on server and proxy caching as they both deal with accesses of little relations, which is quite different from program executions where notable localities of references often exist.

Most of the web cache replacement policies are inspired by techniques used in virtual memory systems. However, because of the unique characteristics of World Wide Web, traditional caching policies may not be able to handle web accesses efficiently. For example, instead of transferring a fixed-sized page, an entire web document, ranging

H.C. Mayr et al. (Eds.): DEXA 2001, LNCS 2113, pp. 567–576, 2001.

from hundreds of bytes to tens of megabytes, is transferred as a whole. Moreover, the popularity of documents on the web is highly diverse, generally assumed following the Zipf's Law [3, 5, 7]. Thus, when a new object enters a web cache, we must consider not only the relative frequency but also factors such as object sizes, transfer time costs, and expiration times.

Many replacement algorithms for web caching have been proposed in the literature [1, 2, 6, 7, 8, 12, 14]. In this paper, we propose a new cache replacement scheme. This policy is based on the least frequently used algorithm (LFU) as we recognize the importance of access frequency in web caching. Other factors such as the size and expiration time of the documents are also taken into account. Our simulation results show that the new algorithm has better or comparable performance when compared with other well-known algorithms.

The remainder of this paper is organized as follows. Section 2 is a brief review of previous work. Section 3 proposes the new caching replacement algorithm, the Size-Adjusted Sliding Window LFU (SSW-LFU). Section 4 is a comparison of different algorithms through trace simulation using real-life data. Section 5 is the conclusions.

2. Previous Work

Various cache replacement policies have been designed for web accesses. They can be roughly classified into one or more of the categories – Extensions of the traditional policies, Key-based policies, and Cost-based policies [2, 13]. Readers may refer to [2, 13] for details of these policies. Some of these policies are listed as follows.

(1) Extensions of Traditional replacement policies. Some of the well-known replacement strategies, such as Least Recently Used (LRU) and Least Frequently Used (LFU), have been extended to handle objects (or documents) of non-homogeneous sizes. The main problem with those policies is that they de-emphasize the fact that small documents are requested more often than large documents in web accesses.

(2) Key-based replacement policies. The main idea of this approach is to prioritize factors, e.g., size, frequency, etc., in determining the objects for replacement. Some notable policies are:

SIZE [14]: Objects are removed in order of size, with the largest object removed first.

LRU-MIN [1]: This policy tries to minimize the number of objects replaced, biased toward keeping smaller objects in the cache. Object with larger sizes are removed in LRU order until there is enough space in the cache

LRU-Threshold [9]: It is similar to LRU except that an object is never cached if it is larger than a certain threshold size.

Hyper-G [14]: This is a refinement of LFU by taking last access time and size into account.

(3) Cost/Function-based replacement policies. They employ weights to factors, such as the entry time of the object in the cache, last access time, cost of transfer, object expiration time, and so on.

Hybrid [15]: It employs a weighted exponential function to the access frequency, the size, and the latency. The document with the smallest value is then evicted.

Least Normalized Cost Replacement [12]: It employees a rational function to the access frequency the size, and the transfer time.

3. A Size-Adjusted Sliding Window LFU (SSW-LFU)

In this section, we propose a new replacement algorithm for proxy and server cache. The algorithm takes both the access patterns and sizes of documents into account, which are two main distinct features of proxy and server accesses. In addition, expiration time will also be considered.

The algorithm is based on the LFU strategy. With the incorporation of a sliding window scheme, the algorithm can adapts itself to changing access patterns. By taking into account the sizes of documents, better performance can be achieved.

3.1 Poisson Process

From a statistical point of view, a counting process $\{N(t), t \geq 0\}$, where $N(t)$ is the number of events that have occurred up to the time t, is said to be a Poisson process having a rate λ, $\lambda > 0$, if (i) $N(0) = 0$; (ii) the process has independent increments; (iii) the number of events in any interval of length t is Poisson distributed with a mean λt [11]. The above conditions assert that a Poisson process from any point on is independent of all that has previously occurred, and it also has the same distribution as the original process. So, at any given time, the expected waiting time w for a next event can be calculated as $w = 1/\lambda$. The smaller the expected waiting time, the higher the probability that another request will arrive in the near future.

As mentioned earlier, proxy and server caches serve requests from users with little relations. Therefore, the arrivals of requests for a document are quite independent from each other. Treating a request for a document as an event, the arrivals of requests in proxy and server caches can be approximated by a Poisson process. Note that the request arrival rate λ for a document is indeed the access frequency of that document.

In the real life, there may be periods of time during which certain documents are very popular, while not so in other periods. Therefore, we will later take into account the changing arrival rates of requests for documents in the design of the replacement policy.

3.2 LFU Algorithms

It evicts an object with the smallest reference count or frequency. A major problem with LFU is its inability of capturing the changes of the localities of references. As a result, LFU is usually not implemented in the conventional virtual memory systems.

Frequency reflects the popularity of a document and determines the expected period in which a next request will likely arrive in a Poisson process. Therefore, LFU may be most suitable for requests following Poisson distributions. Since objects are often accessed by unrelated users, LFU could have its place in proxy/server caching.

There are two versions of LFU in the literature for web caching: In-Cache-LFU [4] and Perfect-LFU [4]. Perfect-LFU remembers page counts even after a page is evicted from the cache, while the In-Cache-LFU discards the page counts together with the evicted pages. Perfect-LFU generally incurs large overheads and could not adjust to changing access patterns quickly. On the other hand, the In-Cache-LFU could lead to thrashing because objects with high counts will never be evicted (even though they will never used again) and the newly cached objects (which may become very popular later) may be evicted instantly because of their smaller counts. Note that In-Cache LFU is indeed the traditional LFU we generally refer to, therefore, we will use LFU and In-Cache LFU interchangeably hereafter.

3.3. The SSW-LFU Scheme

We attempt to retain documents that are likely to be used in the near future in the cache. While Perfect-LFU may have kept too long a history of accesses, In-Cache LFU may have discarded the history too soon. Here, we propose a Sliding Window scheme to capture the changing access patterns by keeping track of only a sufficient long history of accesses. A sliding window of size n contains the latest n accesses to the server. With an appropriate selection of the window size, latest access patterns can be captured precisely and the potential thrashing problem in In-Cache-LFU can be eliminated. The size of the window can be determined empirically by tracing previous accesses to the server.

A replacement policy not only should consider the temporal locality, but also the space utilization, which can affect the performance. LFU (and its variations) alone may not be able to achieve all these goals. As mentioned earlier, documents are of variable sizes. Purging larger documents can free more space than purging smaller ones and get better space utilization. Moreover, it has been shown [5] that smaller files are more popular than larger files, roughly following a Zipf's distribution. Therefore, we design a Size-adjusted Sliding Window LFU (SSW-LFU) algorithm that gives preference to smaller documents.

Let r be the number of references made to a given document within the window. Then, r/n is the access frequency of that document, where n is the window size. Based on the Poisson process model, the expected waiting time of the next access to the document is $1/\lambda$, where λ is r/n. To accommodate both the frequency and the size factors, we calculate the value $s\ /\ (r/n)$, here we call the ssw value, where s is the size of the document, to determine the document to be replaced. Since n is a constant, for simplicity, we will just use s/r for $s/(r/n)$ in our algorithm. Documents with the largest *ssw* values will be selected for replacement first when there is no enough space.

3.4 SSW-LFU Caching Algorithm

In Figure 1, we outline the actions to be taken when there is a cache miss. When there is not enough space, we first evict objects that have expired and then select objects with the largest ssw values for replacement until there is enough space. After each access, the window will shift forward and the access frequencies of documents will be updated.

4. Empirical Results

There are two commonly used performance metrics for caching. The Hit Ratio (HR) is the fraction of the documents that are found in the cache, and the Byte Hit Ratio (BHR) is the fraction of the number of bytes found in the cache. The hit ratio is calculated in terms of number of documents, while the byte hit ratio is in terms of number of bytes. The higher the hit ratio, the more often the requested documents are already in the cache, and thus the shorter the average response time for documents. On the other hand, the higher the byte hit ratio, the less the amount of data needed to be transferred, and the less the network traffic. The HR could favor policies that attempt to retain small documents in the cache, while the BHR could favor policies retaining large documents. The two metrics are somewhat conflicting. In this study, trace-driven simulations on real-life web and proxy servers are used to compare the performance of our algorithm with other popular algorithms such as LRU, (In-Cache) LFU, SIZE, LRU-Min, and Perfect-LFU.

```
Variables:  s_i;                                  // the  size of an newly requested object i
            ssw;                                  // the ssw value
            free-space;                           // the size of free space

if (object i is not in the cache)                 // a cache miss
{       if (free-space > s_i )
                cache the object i;
        else                                      // replacement required
        {       for each object j  in the cache do          // objects expiration time check
                {       if ( object j  has expired )  then
                        {       remove object j form  cache;  // remove related information
                                update free-space;  }          // update the size of free space
                }
                if (free-space < s_i)
                        remove objects with the largest ssw values  until free-space > s_i;
                cache the object i;
        }
        update free-space;
}
increment the frequency of object i;
decrement the frequency of the object whose reference has just drop out of the window.
```

Figure 1. SSW-LFU Algorithm.

4.1 Web Server Trace Simulation

The dataset used in this simulation is the log file collected from the Webstar http server of College of Science at SIUC dated from 07/29/99 to 08/19/99. Figure 2 illustrates the hit ratios of various web caching schemes. *MaxNeeded* is the cache size needed to contain all the documents requested. As observed, SSW-LFU outperforms all other algorithms in hit ratio. When the cache size is small, say, 0.5% to 2% of the MaxNeeded, the hit ratio of SSW-LFU is more than 30% higher than the closest LRU-MIN and Perfect-LFU schemes, and approximately 50% higher than SIZE algorithm. LRU has the worst performance, which might suggest that web accesses do not exhibit similar temporary locality as in the execution of ordinary programs.

Now, let us look at the performance from a byte hit ratio point of view. As shown in Figure 3, Perfect-LFU has the best performance in terms of BHR. The three algorithms favoring small size files, i.e. LRU-MIN, SIZE, and SSW-LFU, didn't perform as well because retaining small files in the cache does not contribute as much to BHR as large files. It was observed in the simulations that some median-sized documents were also very frequently referenced, while some small files were not. Since these algorithms (i.e., LRU-MIN, SIZE, and SSW-LFU) favor smaller files, larger files are more likely to be replaced, resulting in more bytes being purged. However, the performance of SSW-LFU is still comparable to LRU and LFU as the size is not the only factor determining the performance of SSW-LFU. Indeed, our algorithm is better than LFU and the same as LRU when the cache size is over 10% of the MaxNeeded. Although Perfect-LFU has the best performance in terms of BHR, it may not be a feasible approach in practice due to its overwhelming overheads.

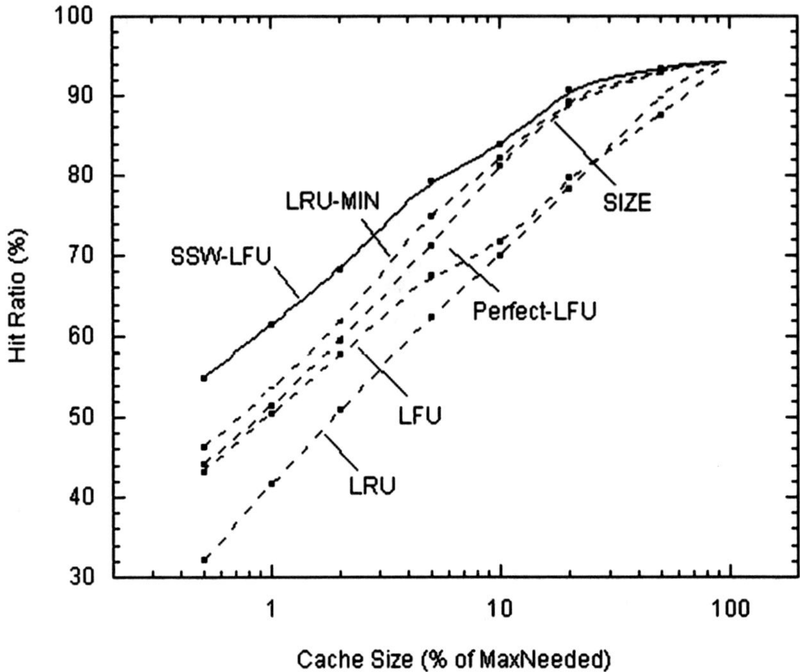

Figure 2. Hit Ratio of Different Caching Schemes for Web Trace.

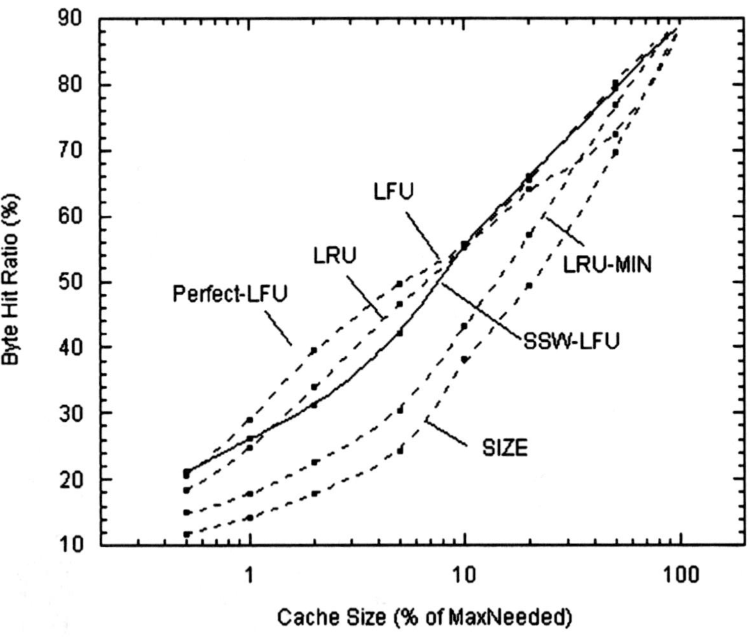

Figure 3. Byte Hit Ratio of Different caching Schemes for Web Trace.

In our experiments, we have experimented with a range of window sizes. As shown in Figure 4, the hit ratios remain quite stable when the window sizes are over 2,000 accesses. It indicates that we can pretty much grasp the access patterns using the last 2,000 accesses.

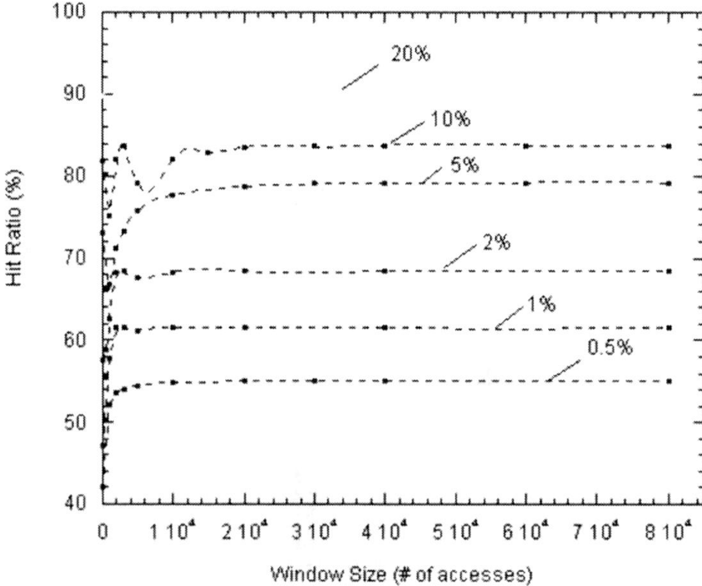

Figure 4. Hit Ratio of SSW-LFU with varying window sizes for web server trace.

4.2 Proxy Server Trace Simulation

Proxies are often used as client site portals through network firewalls and as helper applications for handling requests via protocols not implemented by the user agents. Since the files that clients request reside on different websites, it is not possible for a proxy server to cache all the websites involved. In reality, the proxy server only caches those files frequently requested by clients.

The log files used in the experiments are Digital's Web ProxyTraces [16]. We first use a program [17] to parse and encode all these fields as integers, and then generate the proxy trace data sets.

Just like the web trace simulation in the previous section, SSW-LFU outperforms all other web caching schemes in hit ratio, especially when the cache size is small (see Figure 5). Perfect-LFU is slightly poorer than SSW-LFU, but comparable with LRU-MIN, and clearly better than traditional caching schemes such as LFU and LRU.

As for the byte hit ratio, Perfect-LFU and LRU perform the best (see Figure 6). SSW-LFU is close to Perfect-LFU. But the performance of LRU-MIN degrades significantly although its hit ratio is high. Again, SIZE is the worst among all the caching schemes. As explained earlier, this is mainly due to the fact that certain median-sized files are also very popular. Since LRU-MIN and SIZE are strongly in favor of smaller files, their performances were affected adversely.

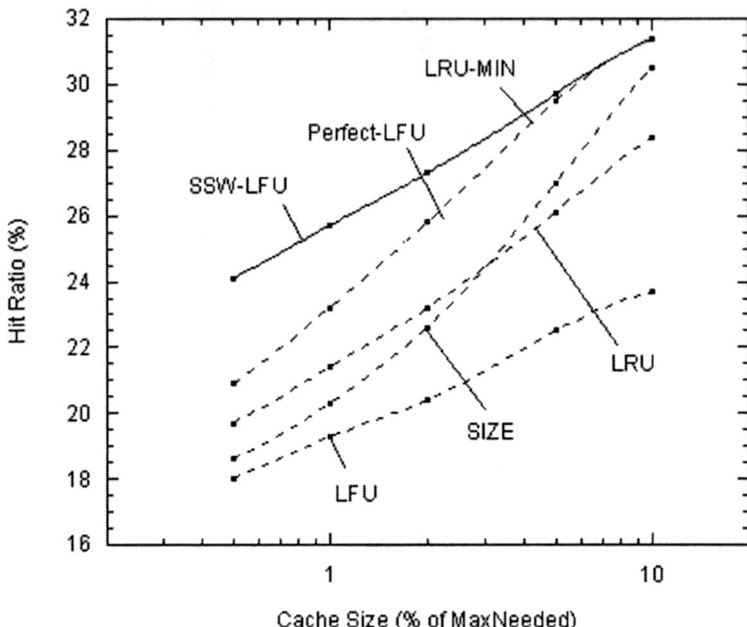

Figure 5: Hit Ratio of different caching schemes for proxy trace.

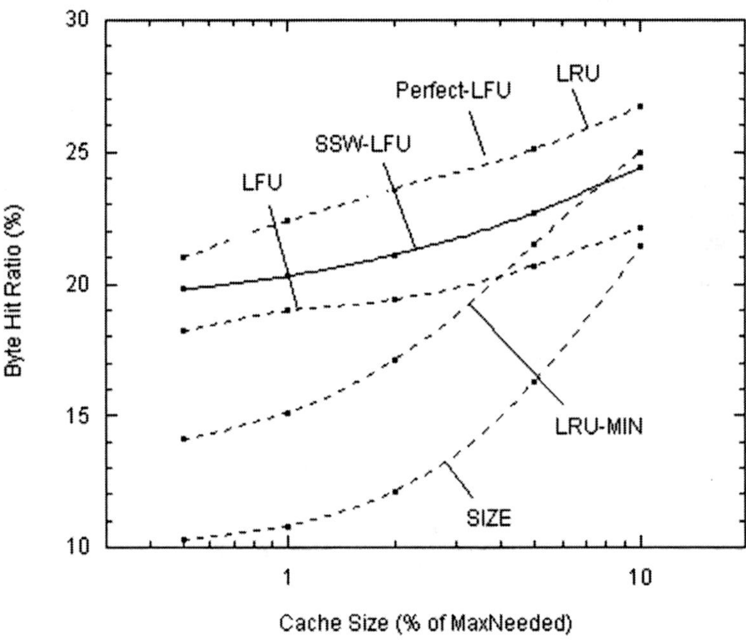

Figure 6: Byte Hit Ratio of Different Caching Schemes for Proxy Trace.

We have also experimented SSW-LFU with different window sizes. As shown in Figure 7, when the window size is over 2,000 accesses, the hit ratios pretty much remain the same. It suggests that using a windows size of 2,000 should be sufficient.

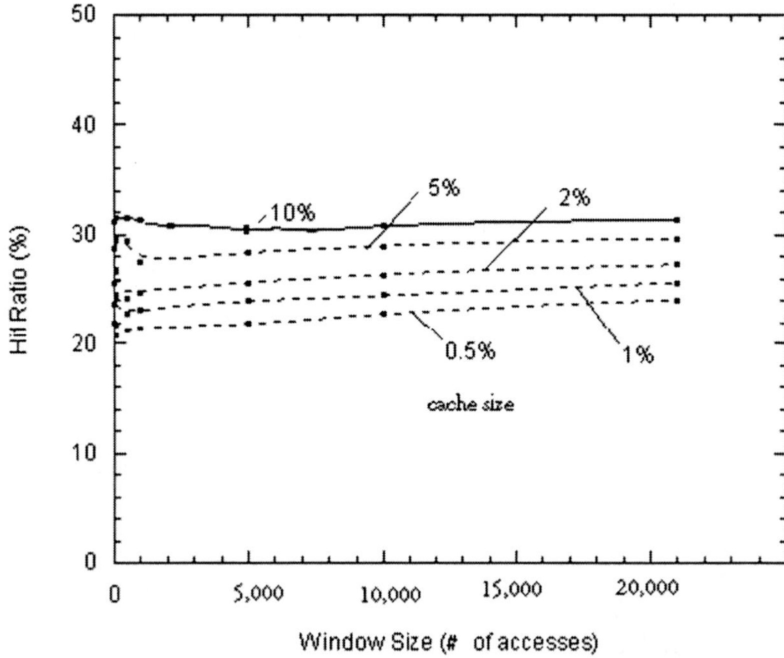

Figure 7: Hit Ratio of SSW-LFU with Varying Window Size for Web Server Trace.

4.3 Discussions

The experiments have shown that SSW-LFU has the best performance in hit ratio (HR) and reasonably good performance in byte hit ratio (BHR). SSW-LFU performs well in hit ratio because it takes into account the access frequencies of documents and attempts to retain small documents in the cache. However, since SSW-LFU gives preference to smaller documents, SSW-LFU could not perform as well as Perfect-LFU in the byte hit ratio. This is because large documents contribute more to BHR than small ones.

It is possible to improve the BHR of SSW-LFU by changing the formula of computing the ssw value or by adjusting the weight of the size of documents in the formula, however, probably at the price of lowering the HR performance.

5. Conclusions

In this study, we proposed a new algorithm, the Size-Adjusted Sliding Window LFU (SSW-LFU). In particular, we used the recent access rates of document within a sliding window to estimate the probability of future document accesses. The algorithm is based on the observation that web accesses to documents can be well modeled by Poisson processes due to the independence of users. We have also take the size of documents into account in the algorithm.

Simulations are conducted to compare our algorithm with some notable caching schemes. Two parameters, the hit ratio and the byte hit ratio, were used to evaluate the performance. The hit ratio is directly related to the web response time to the clients, while the byte hit ratio is related to the network traffic. Our algorithm has the best hit ratio and reasonably good byte hit ratio. Although Perfect-LFU has a slightly better byte hit ratio than ours, it may not be feasible in practice due to its overwhelming overhead. We have also found that with a window size of over 2,000, the access patterns can be captured very precisely.

References.

1. M. Abrams. C. Standridge, C. Abdulla, S. Wlliams, E. Fox, "Caching Proxies: Limitations and Potentials," Proc. Fourth Int'l World Wide Web Conf., Boston, 1995.
2. C. Agrawal, J. Wolf, P. Yu, Caching on the World Wide Web, IEEE Transactions on Knowledge and Data Engineering, Vol. 11, No.1, February 1999.
3. P. Barford, A. Bestavros, A Bradley, and ME Crovella, "Changes in Web client access patterns: characteristics and caching implications," World Wide Web, Special Issue on Characterization and Performance Evaluation. 1999.
4. L. Breslau, P. Cao, L. Fan, G. Phillips, S. Shenker, "Web Caching and Zipf-like Distributions: Evidence and Imnplications," Proceedings of IEEE Infocom, 1999.
5. C. Cunha, A. Bestavros, and M. Crovella, "Characteristics of www Client-Based Traces," Tech. Report TR-95-010, Computer Science Dept., Boston Univ., 1995.
6. P. Cao and S. Irani, "Cost-aware WWW proxy caching algorithms," Proceedings of the 1977 USENIX Symposium on Internet Technology and Systems, pages 193-206, December 1997.
7. S. Glassman, "A caching relay for the world wide web," Proc. First International World-Wide Web Conference, pages 69-76, May 1994
8. P. Lorenzetti, L. Rizzo, and L. Vicisano, "Replacement Policies for a Proxy Cache," 1998. http://www.iet.unipi.it/luigi/resarch.html.
9. E. Markatos, “Main Memory Caching of Web Documents”, Computer Networks and ISDN Systems, Vol. 28, pp. 893-905, 1996.
10. J. Pitkow and M. Recken, "A Simple Yet Robust Caching Algorithm Based on Dynamic Access Patterns," GVU Technical Report No. VU-GIT-94-39; also Proc. Second Int'l WorldWide Conf, Chicago, 1994.
11. S. Ross, "Introduction to Probability Models," Academic Press, 1980.
12. P. Scheuearmann, J. Shim, and R. Vingralek, "A Case for Delay-Conscious Caching of Web Documents," Proc. 6th Int. World Wide Web Conference, 1997.
13. J. Wang, “A Survey of Web Caching Schemes for the Internet”, ACM Computer Communication Review, 29 (5), 1999, 36-46.
14. S. Williams, M. Abrams, C.R. Standbridge, G.Abdulla and E.A. Fox, "Removal Policies in Network Caches for World-Wide Web Documents," Proceedings of the ACM Sigcomm96, Stanford University, August 1996.
15. R. Wooster and M. Abrams, "Proxy Caching that Estimates Page Load Delays," Proc. 6th Int. World Wide Web Conference, Santa Clara, CA, April 1998.
16. ftp://ftp.digital.com/pub/DEC/traces/proxy/webtraces.html.
17. ftp://ftp.digital.com/pub/DEC/traces/proxy/contrib/proxytrace2any.tar.gz.

ViDE: A Visual Data Extraction Environment for the Web

Yi Li   Wee Keong Ng   Ee-Peng Lim

School of Computer Engineering
Nanyang Technological University
Singapore 639798, SINGAPORE
wkn@acm.org

Abstract

With the rapid growth of information on the Web, a means to combat information overload is critical. In this paper, we present ViDE (Visual Data Extraction), an interactive web data extraction environment that supports efficient hierarchical data wrapping of multiple web pages. ViDE has two unique features that differentiate it from other extraction mechanisms. First, data extraction rules can be easily specified in a graphical user interface that is seamlessly integrated with a web browser. Second, ViDE introduces the concept of grouping which unites the extraction rules for a set of documents with the navigational patterns that exist among them. This paper describes our initial development of the system.

1 Introduction

With the Web becoming a major information repository, data extraction on the Web becomes increasingly important. Several major factors, among others, make data extraction on the Web a difficult task:

- Data on the Web is semistructured in the sense that the structure of the data is irregular and the schema of the data is not given in advance.
- Related information is distributed over many web pages on many web sites.
- Data on the Web is dynamic. Both the content and the representation of the data are subject to frequent changes.

ViDE (Visual Data Extraction) [8] is an interactive web data extraction environment that combines the flexibility of manual extraction and the productivity of automated extraction. Like many other systems, it uses a mediator-based architecture [6]. ViDE has some important features that facilitate efficient and effective extraction of a large number of web documents: the user interface is seamlessly integrated with a Web browser, in which all kinds of operations can be performed in an intuitive manner; data filtering and in-place refinement are used to help improve the accuracy and efficiency of extraction; document structure is combined with navigational patterns to extract multiple web documents.

H.C. Mayr et al. (Eds.): DEXA 2001, LNCS 2113, pp. 577–586, 2001.

This paper focuses on the graphical user interface of its working environment. [8] is a more complete account of ViDE on its core data structures and algorithms.

The paper is organized as follows: In Section 2, we discuss related work. Section 3 gives an overview of the whole system. Section 4 introduces the user interface. Section 5 is about single page extraction. Section 6 describes how multiple pages can be extracted. Section 7 demonstrates the power of ViDE by a non-trivial example. Finally, Section 8 concludes the paper.

2 Related Work

A considerable body of work has been done to research various aspects of dealing with semistructured data on the Web [12, 13, 9, 11]. Here we will only discuss those related to the development of visual interfaces for interactive systems.

BBQ [3] is a tool for browsing and querying XML data sources. The user interface supports working with multiple documents at the same time. A noticeable feature of BBQ is in-place query refinement, which allows the results of a query to serve as data sources of the subsequent queries.

W4F [10] has a unique data extraction mechanism that can extract an HTML document both as a plain text stream and as a tree defined by its HTML tags. This allows a great deal of flexibility in data extraction specification. Furthermore, an extraction wizard is used to give some hints on writing extraction rules. For HTML documents with complicated structures, the wizard is fairly primitive. Multiple-document extraction is possible but not well supported.

Extraction rules in ARANEUS [4, 5] is specified in a procedural language: EDITOR, which performs pattern matching, text copying, cutting and pasting to manipulate text streams. An obvious drawback of this approach is that wrappers are hard to specify and maintain.

XWRAP [2] is a wrapper code generation framework which provides a web browser-based interface for extraction specification. After the user specifies interesting regions in a web page, XWRAP uses some predefined heuristics or templates to derive extraction rules. This certainly simplifies the extraction rule specification process, but also leaves little space for customization.

NoDoSE [7] is in spirit very close to ViDE. Intended to extract general text files, it is inherently not strong on extraction rule specification. It totally depends on the user's discrimination for document structure analysis. Multiple-document extraction is achieved through document structure mining. Given a set of files, a well-designed interface allows the user to interactively decompose sample files into certain formats. This information is then used as the input of the structure mining algorithm to infer the grammar of all the files.

3 Overview

A complete web data extraction system involves many aspects of data technology: data extraction, data scrubbing, data integration, etc. However, our experience suggests that the difficulty in data extraction constitutes a major obstacle

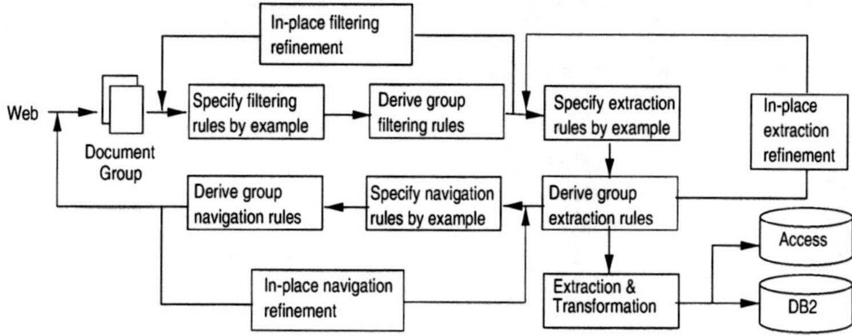

Fig. 1. The workflow in ViDE

against efficient web data utilization. Thus in the design and implementation of ViDE, we have made a considerable effort to resolve or alleviate this matter. In particular, answers to the following questions have had the most significant impacts on the overall design of ViDE:

- How to model HTML data? Similar to [2, 3, 10], in ViDE, a web page is treated as a tree defined by its HTML tags; hyperlinks serve as unidirectional links that glue these pages together.
- Should the data extraction process be interactive or automatic? We opt for an interactive approach for the following reasons: The Web is by its nature heterogeneous; online documents are becoming increasingly complicated; the distinction between useful data and useless data is highly context dependent.
- How to efficiently extract not just a few web pages, but as many as hundreds of or even thousands of web pages? Our approach relies on the assumption that similar web pages can be reached by systematically following certain navigation patterns(hyperlinks). Thus it is possible to organize similar web pages into document groups that can be processed efficiently.

The design of ViDE enables efficient data extraction on the web, but does not by itself provide it. Its power shines full while dealing with well organized web sitesils. Even with ill-formed HTML pages, the data exploration facility provided by ViDE is of great help in capturing the essence of the data at hand.

The process of data extraction in ViDE is iterative, as shown in Fig. 1. Three major stages round out a complete cycle of data extraction: filtering rule specification, extraction rule specification, and navigation rule specification. The new navigation rules specified at the end of each cycle will lead to the generation of new document groups from existing document groups, thus activating a new round of document group extraction activity. Another consequence of this procedure is that the document groups are hierarchically organized.

To bootstrap the whole process, the user starts with a root web page which is the only member of the root document group. Then the user iterates through the data extraction cycle, refining rule specifications along the way, until all the desired data has been included in the final data extraction hierarchy. Some

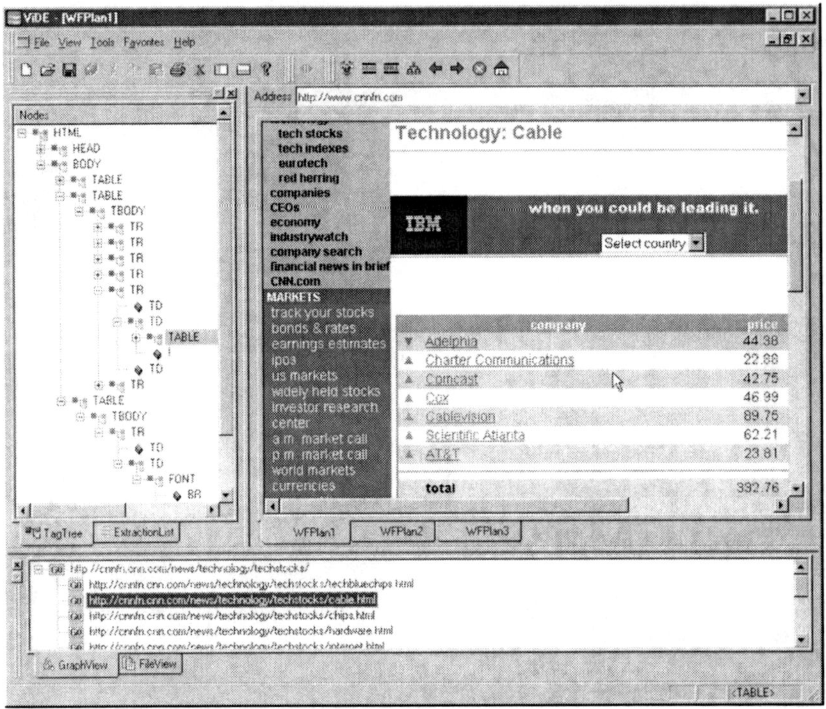

Fig. 2. The Main Window

concepts, such as document group and group rule derivation, will become clear after we introduce multiple web page extraction.

Once a data extraction plan has been specified, it can be scheduled for repeated execution. The extracted data can be cleaned and exported to relational database systems. ViDE provides all the necessary tools to perform these tasks.

4 The Graphical User Interface

Targeted at both professional and casual users, ViDE has a totally interactive interface. To extract data, there is no need for the user to work with a home-brewed little language, which often works well for small or regular web pages, but becomes awkward and clumsy for complicated web pages.

As in Fig. 2, the main window of ViDE has three major parts: the browser window on the top-right, the tag tree window on the top-left and the project window at the bottom. The browser window is a fully functional web browser with extensions to support interactive data extraction. The user uses this window to browse the Web exactly the same way as he does with the Internet Explorer. The user may open multiple browser windows at the same time. This may be convenient while extracting data from multiple web pages containing related information. The tag tree window shows the parsed tag tree of the current web page. The project window displays all the web pages to be extracted as a tree. The structure of the tree reflects the inter-document hierarchy of those web pages (see Section 6).

5 Extracting A Single Page

After the user specifies the URL of the web page to be loaded, ViDE displays the page in the browser window. Internally, the web page is parsed into a tag tree [1] that confirms to the syntax of HTML, i.e., each HTML tag pair forms a node in the tag tree and a tag pair contained in another tag pair becomes a child node of the containing tag.

The major activities involved in single page extraction include data selection, data filtering and data extraction.

5.1 Data Selection

Data selection is a critical factor that ultimately decides the efficiency of extraction rule specification. In ViDE, it is accomplished through *active nodes*. In the tag tree of a page, some nodes are *active*. Only active nodes can be selected for filtering or extraction. Selecting multiple active nodes is allowed. Extracting an active node results in the extraction of the whole sub-tree rooted at the node. An important property of active nodes is that the set of active nodes form a partition of the leaf nodes of the tag tree. This guarantees that wherever the mouse pointer is positioned, there will always be a unique active node with mouse focus.

As shown in Fig. 3, two operations are defined for an active node: drill down and bubble up. Drilling down an active node deactivates the node itself and activates all its direct children nodes, while bubble up activates the parent of the active node and deactivates all other active nodes in the subtree rooted at the parent node. This way, data extraction can be done at arbitrary granularity, from the whole tag tree to a single leaf node. The conformance of extraction to the internal structure of a web page is automatically enforced in this process.

Since the tag tree of a web page is often considerably more complicated that it appears to be, the drill down/bubble up operation may be quite counter-intuitive for some web pages. To mitigate this situation, the tag tree of a web page is displayed side by side with its browser view (Fig. 2). The tag tree view reveals the logical structure of a web page and helps the user make better decision on how the web page should be extracted.

Another facility in ViDE that may be of great help for specifying extraction rules is *indication highlighting*. Indication highlighting illuminate the range of an active node in the browser view so that the user can visually recognize the current data that may be extracted. This is best explained by the example in Fig. 4. Shown in the browser view is an HTML table that contains some stock statistics for different IT sectors. Since we are only interested in some specific sectors, we have drilled down that the `TABLE` tag that represents the table. The current

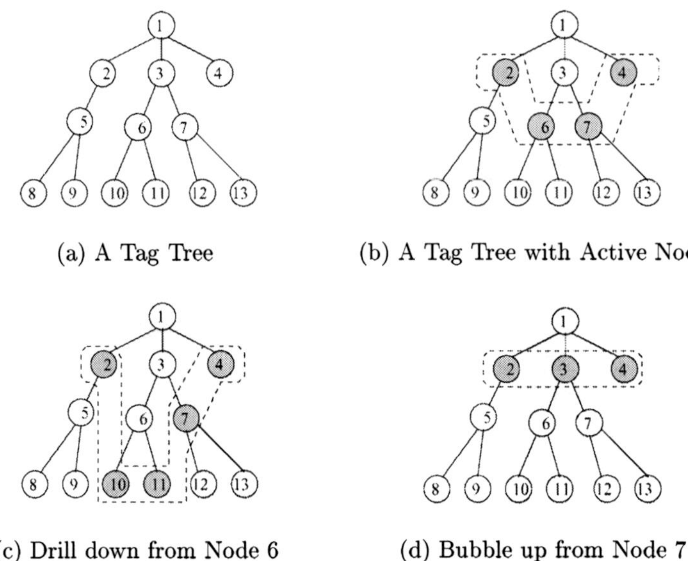

(a) A Tag Tree

(b) A Tag Tree with Active Nodes

(c) Drill down from Node 6

(d) Bubble up from Node 7

Fig. 3. Navigating the Tag Tree

sector	level	change	last update
tech blue chips	984.00	-27.12	7/28 16:03
cable	358.66	-24.59	7/28 16:02
chips	2223.69	-8.31	7/28 16:03
computers/peripherals	716.69	-14.06	7/28 16:03
internet	1093.72	-51.94	7/28 16:20
networking	617.06	-43.56	7/28 16:01
satellite	193.16	-4.50	7/28 16:02
software	1805.64	-75.19	7/28 16:02

Fig. 4. Indication Highlighting of an Active Node

active nodes are a set of `TR` (table row in HTML) tags. When the user moves mouse cursor over an active node, in this case, the chips sector, the background of the row is highlighted. With indication highlighting, the user can identify data extraction components easily and accurately.

5.2 Data Filtering

In ViDE, extraction is enhanced by data filtering and extraction, which is an indirect extraction technique that removes unrelated data from a web page. It is based on the observation that many well designed web sites adopt a uniform interface design across the whole web site. For example, it is common to use a horizontal bar on the top to show the logo of the company and a vertical bar on the left to list the content categories of the site. These parts of a web page generally do not contain interesting data and complicates the process of data extraction. Filtering not only simplifies extraction but also leads to resilient data extraction.

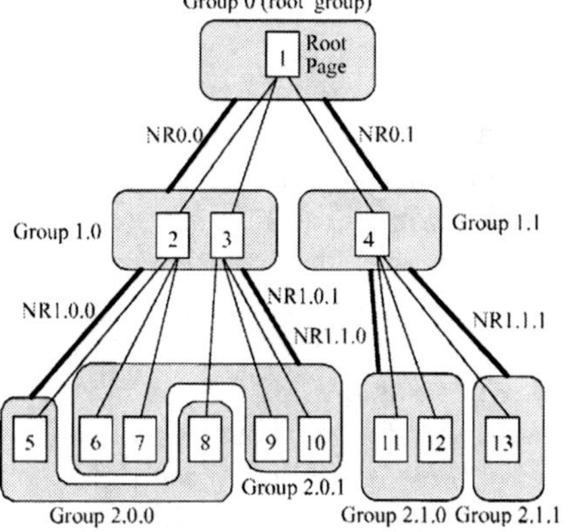

Source	*Navigation Rule*	*Derived*
0	NR0.0	1.0
0	NR0.1	1.1
1.0	NR1.0.0	2.0.0
1.0	NR1.0.1	2.0.1
1.1	NR1.1.0	2.1.0
1.1	NR1.1.1	2.1.1

Fig. 5. Document group hierarchy

6 Extracting Data from Multiple Pages

Most systems capable of extracting multiple document extraction have focused on extracting a set of documents with similar internal structures. This is inadequate when applied to the Web where information is often spread across many pages that are organized into a tree-like structure through hyperlinks. ViDE support extracting multiple web pages organized in this manner.

In ViDE, central to multiple-document extraction is the concept of *document grouping* that unites the extraction rules of a set of web pages and the navigational patterns that exist among them. Web pages can be either semantically similar, that is, they have similar internal representations, or navigationally similar, that is, they are accessed through similar hyperlinks. ViDE provide two cooperative mechanisms to support the grouping of web pages: navigation rule derivation by example and extraction rule derivation by example. Combined together, they provide a powerful data extraction mechanism.

6.1 Deriving Navigation Rules by Example

In ViDE, multiple document groups are constructed in a navigational manner to form a tree hierarchy, as shown in Fig. 5. In the figure, document groups are represented by shaded areas. The white boxes in a group are the member web pages of the group. The thick edge between two groups is a navigation rule that is explained below. The thin edge connecting two web pages represents a hyperlink from the parent node to its child node.

It is clear that there are indeed two hierarchies in ViDE: one for documents and one for document groups. To elaborate, we now step through the process of how these two hierarchies come into being. Our starting point is a single web page that eventually links to the web pages we are interested in. This page is not only the root of the web page hierarchy, but also the only member of the root group, which is the root of the document group hierarchy. We may now specify a navigation rule for the root page. The navigation rule of a web page dictates how we can navigate to other web pages by following some hyperlinks in that page. For instance, given an HTML table in a web page, a navigation rule can simply state that we should follow all the hyperlinks in the first column of the table. A document group may also have navigation rules. The navigation rule of a group is applied to every member of the group. The resulting web pages constitute a new group, which is a child group of the original group. In Fig. 5, after applying navigation rule NR0.0 to the root page (hence Group0, since it has only one member), two new web pages are obtained, which form a new group Group1.0. This can be repeatedly performed for the new groups until we have all the web pages we need. Also, a group may have multiple children groups in that multiple navigation rules may be specified for a group. The table in Fig. 5 summarizes the relationships between different document groups.

Given a group with multiple member web pages, the user does not have to specify navigation rules for every one of them. Since these web pages indeed have similar structures, ViDE is able to derive group navigation rules based on the examples given by the user.

In ViDE, URLs for individual web pages, except the root page, are never saved. To get at web pages to be extracted, we always start from the root page and evaluate all the navigation rules on the fly. This scheme works especially well for dynamically generated web pages.

6.2 Deriving Extraction Rules by Example

Extraction by example is also based on the document group hierarchy. Again, there are two types of extraction rules: a document extraction rule states how to extract data from a specific web page while a group extraction rule is applied to every member of the group for data extraction. Group extraction rules are derived from examples given by the user.

The hierarchy of document groups plays an important role in subsequent data integration activities that aggregate and consolidate the extracted data. This information is preserved through storing extracted data in a directory whose structure is identical to that of the document group hierarchy. All directories are named after the name of the corresponding group. The relationships between documents are embodied in file names that follow a certain naming convention.

6.3 In-place Refinement

The purpose of in-place refinement is to offset the *black-box effect* of the by-example approach, i.e., for the user the group rule derivation algorithm works like a black-box whose products are not immediately obvious. The result of an extraction rule may be a surprise for the user if the algorithm does not work the way as the user expected or the user did not pick up a proper web page as an example. In-place refinement gives the user a chance to inspect and improve the result of extraction before submitting it for final execution.

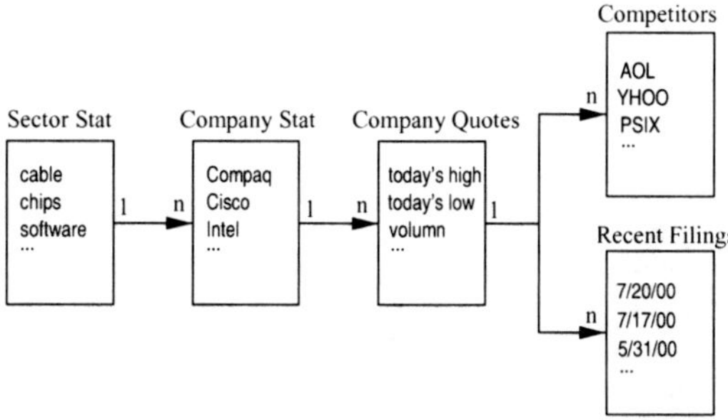

Fig. 6. Data at the CNN Financial Network Web Site

Table Name	*Pages extracted*	*No. of fields*	*No. of tuples*
SectorInfo	1	4	12
CompanyInfo	12	4	224
RecentFiling	214	3	3116
CompetitorInfo	230	3	15866

Table 1. Table Statistics for a Single Execution

7 Example

As an example, we use ViDE to extract some stock information from the CNN financial network [14]. A data extraction plan is specified with just a few mouse clicks, as shown in Fig. 6: We start from the root page of the technology stock (http://cnnfn.cnn.com/news/ technology/techstocks/), which has a table of stock statistics for twelve sectors of technology industries such as cables, blue tech chips, software etc. Each entry of the table links to a web page with stock statistics for all the companies in that sector, which again links to web pages with more detailed stock quotes on a specific company. From the company quotes page, hyperlinks for various types of information are available. In this example, we pick two of them: competitors and recent filings. In the final plan, there are a total of five document groups for which four navigation rules are specified: one for "Sector Stat", one for "Company Stat" and two for "Company Quotes".

The execution of the above extraction plan retrieved 704 web pages, in which 235 were for pure navigational purpose. In the 469 pages extracted, 457 were successful. A data transforming tool was used to export the extracted data into a Microsoft Access database. To better highlight the strength of ViDE, the information about these tables has been summarized in Table 1. Using an extraction scheduling tool to automate this task at 10AM everyday for a week, we were able to accumulate above 100000 records of stock information for more that 300 companies. As we can see, simple being the extraction plan, it does accomplish a non-trivial data extraction task with little human involvement.

8 Current Status and Future Work

ViDE is implemented on the Microsoft Windows platform. This is because ViDE needs a way to customize a web browser at a pretty low level, besides being tightly integrated with a web browser. This can be achieved with the Internet Explorer relatively easier than other browsers we have evaluated. There are plans to enhance the quality of extraction, for instance, it would be nice if the types of extracted data can be automatically discovered based on some heuristics. Also, we are interested in resilient data extraction based on tree pattern matching.

References

[1] Document Object Model(DOM) 1.0. W3C recommendation, 1998

[2] Ling Liu, Calton Pu, Wei Han. XWRAP: An XML-enabled Wrapper Construction System for Web Information Sources, Proceedings of the 16th International Conference on Data Engineering, San Diego CA, USA, 2000.

[3] Kevin D. Munroe, Yannis Papakonstantinou. BBQ: A Visual Interface for Integrated Browsing and Querying of XML. In *Visual Database Systems (VDB) 2000*

[4] G. Mecca, P. Atzeni, P. Merialdo, A. Masci, and G. Sindoni. From Databases to Web-Bases: The ARANEUS Experience. Technical Report RT-DIA-34-1998, Universita Degli Studi Di Roma Tre, May 1998

[5] P. Atzeni and G. Mecca. Cut and paste. In *Proceedings of 16th ACM SIGMOD Symposion on Principles of Database Systems*, 1997

[6] G. Wiederhold. Mediator in the Architecture of Future Information Systems. In *IEEE Computer 25*:3, pp. 38-49.

[7] B. Adelberg. NoDoSE - a tool for semi-automatic data extraction from text files. Technical Report, Computer Science Department, Northwestern University, 1998.

[8] Y. Li. Information Extraction and Integration on the Web: A Practical Approach. Technical Report, School of Computer Engineering, Nanyang Technological University, March 2000.

[9] Udi Manber, Mike Smith, Burra Gopal. WebGlimpse - Combining Browsing and Searching. *1997 Usenix Technical Conference*, Jan, 1997.

[10] Arnaud Sahuguet and Fabien Azavant. Building light-weight wrappers for legacy Web data-sources using W4F. In *Proc. of the Int. Conf. on Very Large Data Bases (VLDB)*, 1999

[11] Laks V. S. Lakshmanan, Fereidoon Sadri, and Iyer N. Subramanian. A declarative Language for Querying and Restructuring the Web. In *Proc. of 6th. Int. Workshop on Research Issues in Data Engineering, RIDE'96*, New Orleans, Feb, 1996.

[12] S. Chawathe, H. Garcia-Molina, J. Hammer, K. Ireland, Y. Papakonstantinou,J. Ullman, and J. Widom. The TSIMMIS Project: Integration of Heterogeneous Information Source. In *Proc. of the 100th IPSJ*, Tokyo, Japan, Oct, 1994.

[13] M. L. Barja, T. Bratvold, J. Myllymaki and G. Sonnenberger. Informia: a Mediator for Integrated Access to Heterogeneous Information Sourse. CIKM 98, Bethesda, MD USA

[14] http://cnnfn.cnn.com/news/technology/techstocks/

[15] http://www.w3.org/XML/

WebSCAN: Discovering and Notifying Important Changes of Web Sites*

Ma Qiang[1], Shinya Miyazaki[1], and Katsumi Tanaka[2]

[1] Graduate School of Science and Technology, Kobe University.
Rokkodai, Nada, Kobe 657-8501 Japan
{qiang, miyazaki}@db.cs.kobe-u.ac.jp http://www.db.cs.kobe-u.ac.jp
[2] Graduate School of Informatics, Kyoto University.
Yoshida Honmachi, Sakyo, Kyoto 606-8501,Japan
ktanaka@i.kyoto-u.ac.jp http://www.dl.kuis.kyoto-u.ac.jp

Abstract. In this paper, we propose a change monitoring/notification system *WebSCAN* (Web Sites Change Analyzer and Notifier) for Web, which monitors and analyzes the change of pre-registered Web sites and notifies *important changes* to users by a push-type delivery mechanism.

1 Introduction

The vast amount of information is available on the WWW. Usually, users use the bookmarks or automatic navigator software to access their favorite Web sites to acquire valuable information. However, the Web is dynamic[1], in other words, Web pages are changed and Web sites are created or disappear at any time and in arbitrary manner. Thus, it's not easy to acquire the fresh and valuable information timely.

In this paper, we propose a change monitoring and notification system *WebSCAN*(Web Sites Change Analyzer and Notifier) for Web sites, which monitors and analyzes the changes of Web sites to notify a user the important changes by a push-type delivery mechanism. In WebSCAN, the changes of Web sites are monitored periodically. The detected change is estimated by its content, browsing frequency and update frequency. While estimating, the structure of the Web site/pages and the content-based differences between changes and existing Web pages are also considered. Based on the estimated *change worth*, the important changes are then selected, which will be delivered to users automatically with the push technology.

Some works for the change detection over wrapped Web pages have been done at C3 project[2]. One of the main contributions of C3 project is to portray the changes between two structured data in a succinct and descriptive way:

* This research is partly supported by the Japan Ministry of Education, Culture, Sports, Science and Technology Grant-in-Aid for Scientific Research (Project No. 12680416), "Research for the Future" Program of Japan Society for the Promotion of Science under the Project "Advanced Multimedia Contents Processing" (Project No. JSPS-RFTF97P00501).

H.C. Mayr et al. (Eds.): DEXA 2001, LNCS 2113, pp. 587–598, 2001.

meaningful change detection[3]. They also consider the data structure to detect the changes. At the contrast, we are interested in estimating Web changes using their content and structure to pick up the valuable information, rather than change detection.

Netmind[4] is a typical URL changes monitor system that extends the Web search engines. Netmind also notifies users the change information using the push technology. WebGUIDE[5] is another system for exploring changes to Web pages and Web structure that supports recursive document comparison. The contribution of WebGUIDE is to support recursive document comparison and a difference viewing by a graphical navigator. However, the change semantics, such as freshness and popularity in our paper, are not considered in these conventional systems. In the nutshell, these systems just detect the changes, but not discover the important ones from massive changes.

WebCQ[6] is a system that discovers and detects the changes of the Web pages, and notifies user of interesting changes with personalized customization. Features of WebCQ include the capabilities for monitoring and tracking various types of changes, personalized delivery of page change notifications and personalized summarization of changes. However, as same as other conventional systems, the worth of Web page change is not considered at WebCQ. In addition, the notification is based on the user interests. This feature makes it necessary to specify user interests clearly. Since incoming information is not foreseeable and the Web is changed continuously, it's not easy to specify user profile to acquire the new valuable information.

In contrast to earlier works concerned with the *Web change notification*, the main contributions of WebSCAN proposed in this paper can be summarized into the following:

- **Content-based and Structure-based change analysis**
  To discover the higher worth information from the changed Web pages, the change worth is computed by considering both of content-based approach and structural approach. The former is based on computing the similarity/dissimilarity between newly added content and previous content. The latter is to consider the browsing frequency, update frequency, and the place of the changed Web page.
- **Semantics of Change Information: Freshness and Popularity**
  We compare the changed pages with the previous pages and compute their similarities/dissimilarities to evaluate the change worth: If the added information is not similar to previous pages, it will bring the *fresh* information. At the contrast, the added information that is similar to previous pages may bring *popular* information.
- **Push-type change notification with Personalization**
  One of the efficient ways to obtain new information is push technology[7]. In our approach, based on the change worth, the notification, which contains the selected change's information, is generated and delivered to the users automatically. Each user can use his own profile to filter and view the received notification in his original way.

The remainder of this paper is organized as follows: In section 2, we present the estimation of the change worth, which is used to select the important changes. We also show some experiment results in this section. In section 3, the push-type notification mechanism is discussed. A prototype system is reviewed in section 4. Finally, we conclude the paper with a summary in section 5.

2 Change Analysis

2.1 Comparison Scope

A *comparison scope* is a collection of web pages or page fragments to compare with the changed one for computing the change worth. Each member of a comparison scope has some relation to the change: similar, same topic, former version and so on. The Web changes have variant type, such as update, adding new page and so on. According to the change type, it's necessary to select the proper comparison scope (paragraphs, pages, directories and so on.) to compute change worth.

We choose the members of comparison scope based on the Web structure (analyzed by URL path) or the page structure (analyzed by Document Object Model). In most Web sites, the related pages are organized under one directory. In these cases, a directory is roughly regarded to represent a certain topic. Here, the directories of a Web site are analyzed based on URL paths. For example, the directory *foo* of Web site *www.foo.com* means the URL *http://www.foo.com/foo/*. With this assumption, the members of the comparison scope are selected as follows: at first, we represent a Web site as a tree based on analyzing its URL paths. Secondly, we select all of the change's siblings as the members of its comparison scope. Meanwhile, when a paragraph is added to an existing page (page modification), the previous existed paragraphs are collected as the members of its comparison scope.

(a) Page Modification. In the case of page modification, as **Fig. 1 (a)** shows, at first, we partition the modified page into some units at the same level as the change. These partitioned units are then collected into the comparison scope to compute the change worth.

(b) New Page. In the case of new page addition, the comparison scope is a collection containing all the siblings of the new page. Moreover, the descendants of its sibling are also contained in the comparison scope. For example, as **Fig.1(b)** shows, the comparison scope is composed of page $p1$, $p2$ and $p3$. [1]

(c) New topic. When a new topic (directory that contains some new pages) has been added, we can regard the added topic as a "virtual page" to select the comparison scope as same as a new page is added. For instance, as **Fig.1(c)** shows, the new topic st_{new} will be compared with the children ($p2$ and $p3$) of st_{old} and page $p1$ to compute its change worth.

[1] Hereafter ,as shown in **Fig.1(b)**, a Web site is represented as a tree based on the URL path analysis and each edge means the directory path.

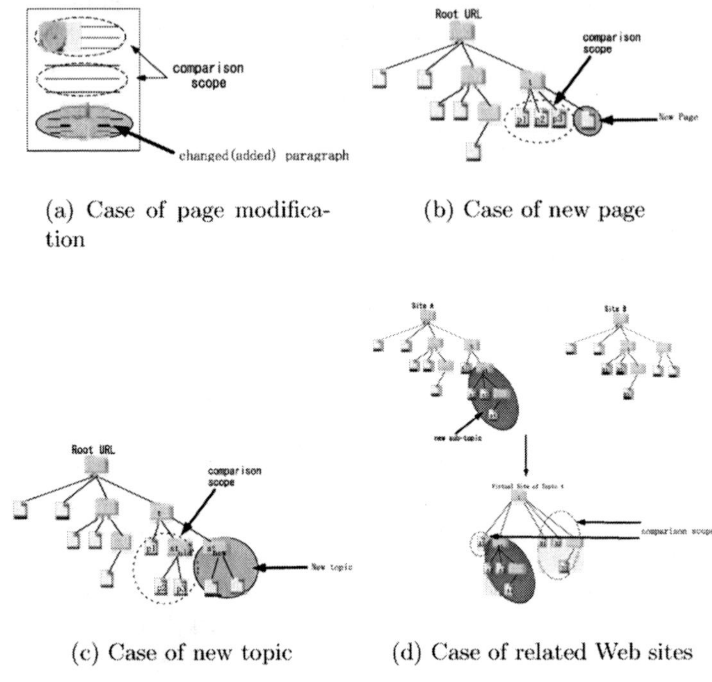

(a) Case of page modification

(b) Case of new page

(c) Case of new topic

(d) Case of related Web sites

Fig. 1. Comparison Scope

(d) Related Web sites. Since many Web sites deliver the similar information, the correlation of them should not be overlooked during the change analysis. Since these related sites have high similarities, it's possible to reorganize them to a virtual Web site per each topic. As shown in **Fig.1(d)**, our idea is to organize the related directories of different Web sites to one new virtual directory per each topic. After that, we can select the members of comparison scope as same as we doing at a single site.

2.2 Estimation of Change Worth

In WebSCAN, change worth is estimated by freshness, popularity[8], browsing frequency and update frequency. For simplicity, hereafter, we assume that the detected Web change is the new page's addition to compute the change worth. In the other change case, such as new topic, related Web sites and so on, the change worth can be estimated in the same way.

(a) Freshness. Intuitively, the changed page, which is quite different from previously existed pages due to containing much *new* information, would be often considered valuable. In other words, we can say that the new page has a high freshness or uniqueness. In this paper, the freshness is estimated based on the differences between the changed page and related ones. Here, we can define several measures of the freshness of page a by 1) the number of its similar pages in its comparison scope Ω denoted by $fresh_{num}(a, \Omega)$, 2) the dissimilarity among a and the pages in its comparison scope Ω denoted by $fresh_{cd}(a, \Omega)$, 3) the density of its similar pages in the comparison scope Ω denoted by $fresh_{de}(a, \Omega)$, and 4) the time intervals of a and its similar pages denoted by $fresh_{td}(a, \Omega)$, respectively. Furthermore, these freshness of a, can be integrated and denoted by the following $fresh_{\Omega}(a)$:

$$\begin{aligned} fresh_{\Omega}(a) &= w_1 \cdot fresh_{num}(a, \Omega) + w_2 \cdot fresh_{cd}(a, \Omega) \\ &+ w_3 \cdot fresh_{de}(a, \Omega) + w_4 \cdot fresh_{td}(a, \Omega) \\ & w_1 + w_2 + w_3 + w_4 = 1.0 \end{aligned} \tag{1}$$

where w_1, w_2, w_3, w_4 are the user definable weight values.

Hereafter, let ω be the set of a's similar pages in the comparison scope Ω, m be the number of pages in ω and n be the number of pages in Ω.

(a-1) Freshness based on the number of similar pages. If there is no (or few) page similar to a in Ω, we can say a is newer one containing much new information. Thus, its freshness is higher:

$$fresh_{num}(a, \Omega) = \frac{1}{log_2(2+m)} \tag{2}$$

(a-2) Freshness based on the content distance. The content distance of pages a and b can be defined as follows based on the vector space model:

$$dis(a, b) = 1 - sim(a, b) = 1 - \frac{v(a) \cdot v(b)}{\|v(a)\| \|v(b)\|} \tag{3}$$

where, $v(a)$, $v(b)$ are the keyword vectors of a and b.

The content distance means the dissimilarity of a and b. It also can represent that how much new information has been added to a comparing with previous page b. Therefore, the bigger the average content distance between a and its similar pages is, the higher freshness of a is:

$$fresh_{cd}(a, \Omega) = \frac{1}{m} \sum_{i=1, b_i \in \omega}^{m} dis(a, b_i) \tag{4}$$

where, b_i represents the similar page of a.

(a-3) Freshness based on the density of similar pages. The density d of a's similar pages in Ω is m/n. When d is small, a is rare one and its information value will be high:

$$fresh_{de}(a, \Omega) = log_2 \frac{n}{m} \tag{5}$$

(a-4) Freshness based on the time interval. Let's consider the following case: a series of reports for same event are updated at a Web site. Though that several pages are similar to page a in the comparison scope, the time intervals between a and its similar articles are big. It's thinkable that there appears some new trend represented by a, after a long no-update time. In this case, the follow-up report, page a, should have a high freshness. Therefore, the freshness based on the time interval is defined as follows:

$$fresh_{td}(a, \Omega) = \log(\frac{1}{m} \sum_{i=1, b_i \in \omega}^{m} (t(a) - t(b_i))) \quad (6)$$

where $t(a)$ is the update time of a. b_i is similar page of a.

(b) Popularity. In order to select valuable one from massive new pages, the similarity of the page with previous pages should be also evaluated. For instance, in user interesting topic, the new page that is quite similar to almost of the previous ones, would be often considered valuable.

The popularity of new page a can be estimated by 1) the density of its similar pages in comparison scope Ω, and 2) the time intervals of a and its similar pages in Ω. In short, if a has many similar pages in comparison scope and the time intervals among them is smaller, the popularity of a is higher. Consequently, we define the popularity of page a for a comparison scope Ω is defined as follows:

$$pop_{\Omega}(a) = w_5 \cdot e^{\lambda_1 d} + w_6 \cdot e^{-\lambda_2 t_d} \qquad w_1 + w_2 = 1.0 \quad (7)$$

where $w_5(>0), w_6(>0), \lambda_1(>0)$ and $\lambda_2(>0)$ are the weight values. $d = m/n$ is the density of similar pages, and t_d is the average time interval of a and its similar page $b_i(i = 1, ..., m)$:

$$t_d = \frac{1}{m} \sum_{i=1, b_i \in \omega}^{m} (t(a) - t(b_i)) \quad (8)$$

(c) Browsing Frequency. Usually, a Web site may have several topics, and posts related pages to the same directory. That's to say, topic is often organized per directory. The browsing frequency of each topic (directory) can signify the interest of user to that topic. A higher interesting topic may have higher browsing frequency. Therefore, the topic of higher browsing frequency should be high value to be notified due to higher user interest. Page a's change worth based on the browsing frequency is defined as follows:

$$V_{browsing}(a) = log(bf) \quad (9)$$

where, bf is the browsing frequency of the topic including a.

(d) Update Frequency. The Web sites on the Internet are changed arbitrarily. The update frequencies are also affecting the change worth. Our hypothesis is that, in freshness perspective, the longer the update time interval is, the bigger the change worth is. For instance, when a Web site has been updated after a long no-update time, the changes of this site will have high change worthies. At the contrast, in popularity perspective, the shorter the update time interval is, the smaller the change worth is. That's to say, when a Web site updates its pages frequently, there maybe some urgency or popular event occurred. Thus, these updated pages are valuable to be notified.

In the freshness perspective, the change worth based on the update time interval of change c is defined as follows:

$$V_{uf-fresh}(c,n) = log(ti(c,n)) \tag{10}$$

$$ti(c,n) = \frac{t(n)-t(n-1)+ti(c,n-1)\cdot(n-1)}{n} \tag{11}$$

where $t(n)$ is the time-stamp of a at the n-*times* update, n is the updated times and $ti(c,n)$ is (average)update time interval of c at n-*times* update.

On the other hand, in the popularity perspective, the change worth based on the update time interval is defined as follows:

$$V_{uf-pop}(c,n) = 1/V_{uf-fresh}(c,n) \tag{12}$$

Change Worth. Consequently, based on the freshness/popularity, browsing frequency and the update frequency, the change worth of change c $worth(c)$ is defined as an integrated form:

$$worth(c) = \begin{cases} worth_{fresh}(c) & \text{if user prefers to fresh information} \\ worth_{pop}(c) & \text{if user prefers to popular information} \end{cases} \tag{13}$$

where,

$$worth_{fresh}(c) = \alpha \cdot fresh(c,\Omega) + \beta \cdot V_{browsing}(c) + \gamma \cdot V_{uf-fresh}(c,n) \tag{14}$$

$$worth_{pop}(c) = \alpha \cdot pop(c,\Omega) + \beta \cdot V_{browsing}(c) + \gamma \cdot V_{uf-pop}(c,n) \tag{15}$$

$$\alpha + \beta + \gamma = 1.0, \alpha > 0, \beta > 0, \gamma > 0$$

where α, β, γ are user definable weight values.

If the change worth $worth(c)$ is bigger than the threshold value, we say c is an important one and notify it to users.

2.3 Preliminary Evaluation

In this subsection, we describe a preliminary evaluation of our approach for change worth estimation. Since we did not have access to a large crawl of the Web and we did not fully implement the proposed approach, it was not feasible

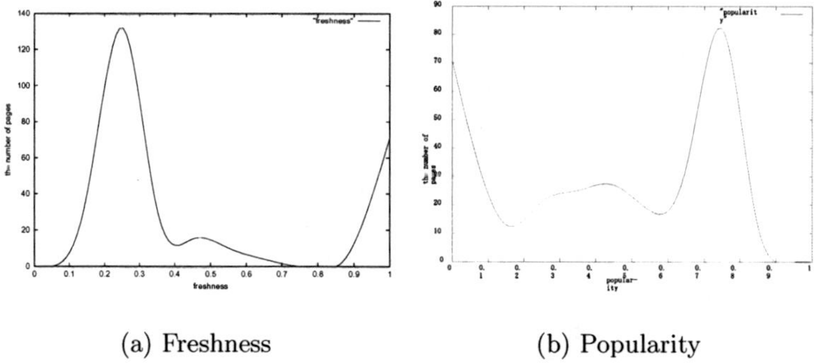

(a) Freshness (b) Popularity

Fig. 2. Distribution of Freshness and Popularity : Horizontal axis shows the value of freshness(or popularity). Vertical axis shows the number of added pages according to the freshness(or popularity) value.

Table 1. Experimental results

	Freshness	Popularity
Average	0.450	0.433
Recall Ratio	0.803	0.351
Precision Ratio	0.564	0.540

to do the full change worth computations. Instead, we implemented two simplified version of filters: freshness filter and popularity filter. Furthermore, we also adjust the values of freshness and popularity ranging from 0 to 1.0 at the preliminary evaluation.

- **freshness filter**
  Only the freshness is used to rank the changed pages. The filtering function is defined as follows:

$$\begin{aligned} worth_{fresh}(c) &= fresh(c, \Omega) \\ &= 0.4 \cdot fresh_{sum}(c, \Omega) + 0.4 \cdot fresh_{cd}(c, \Omega) \\ &+ 0.1 \cdot fresh_{de}(c, \Omega) + 0.1 \cdot fresh_{td}(c, \Omega) \end{aligned} \tag{16}$$

  If change c's worth $worth_{fresh}(c)$ is bigger than the threshold 0.25, it will be selected as the valuable change.
- **popularity filter**
  Popularity filter uses the popularity as the ranking measure. Its filtering function is defined as follows:

$$worth_{pop}(c) = pop(c, \Omega) = 0.5 \cdot e^{0.7d} + 0.5 \cdot e^{-0.3t_d} \tag{17}$$

  The threshold for choosing valuable changes is set to 0.75.

Fig. 2(a) and **Fig. 2(b)** illustrate the distribution of freshness and popularity based on our experiment results, respectively. Because that we estimate small number of changes, there are some changes have no similar page. In other words, the comparison scope is empty. In this case, we let its popularity be 0 and let freshness be 1.0. As shown, excluding these specially valued one, the distributions are similar to the regular distribution. Using this feature, we set the thresholds of freshness and popularity to 0.25 and 0.75 respectively, due to select half of the changed pages as the valuable ones, which will be regarded as the filtering results. As some early preliminary experiment, the parameters(w_1, w_2, w_3, w_4) for freshness computation are set to 0.4, 0.4, 0.1 and 0.1 respectively. Parameters(w_5, w_6, λ_1, λ_2) for popularity computation are set to 0.5, 0.5, 0.7 and 0.3 respectively. The threshold of similarity for deciding the similar pages is set to 0.6.

Further details of the preliminary evaluation are as follows:

- One Web site, Nikkan Sports (http://www.nikkansports.co.jp), is selected as the monitoring target.
- Web changes are limited to new page addition.
- Two days changes, about 299 pages, are detected from the Nikkan sports site that includes 6401 pages.

Tab. 1 shows the results of preliminary evaluation. For the freshness, precision ratio is 0.564 and recall ratio is 0.803. On the other hand, the precision and recall ratio for the popularity are 0.540 and 0.351, respectively. In addition, if we compute these ratios excluding the specially valued ones(as same as when we decide the threshold values), the precision and recall ratio of freshness are 0.65 and 0.718, respectively. The precision and recall ratios of popularity are 0.430 and 0.753, respectively. As our evaluation is a limited one, there are more improving works needed to do. Nevertheless, these results can confirm that the proposed notions, freshness and popularity, are useful for picking up the important information from massive changes.

As mentioned above, the comparison scope is constructed by the assumption that related pages are organized under same directory. In our preliminary evaluation, in each directory, about 77.6% pages belong to same topic. Though we estimated at only one site, at very least, this shows that the selected one is the kind of comparison scope we are after.

3 Push-Based Change Notification

One of the notable features of push technology is that the same information is delivered to users. In other words, user is limited to browse information as same as the others. On the other hand, more and more users require personalized information. This is one of conflicts of popularization and personalization[9].

Our approach is to separate the personalization method from the popularized notification. As same as the typical systems, same notification is delivered to all registered users. When a user received the notification, he(she) can use his/her profile to filter and fetch his/her original notification from the delivered one. The filtered notification would be translated to an HTML file, whose layout is also specified by each user. This means that the delivered notification can be viewed in variant ways.

Since the Web sites are changed dynamically, notification timing is also important for assisting user to obtain the right information at the right time. WebSCAN has two options to delivery the notification, real-time mode and periodic mode. At the real-time mode, the important changed information will be delivered immediately. On the other hands, the notification will be delivered periodically in the periodic mode.

The notification contains the changes since last-time delivery. The added information of each change, such as URL, summary, freshness, popularity, changeworthies based on browsing frequency and update frequency, are also included.

The summary of each change is simply generated from its title, top sentences and the URLs of its images files(if there are some). With the summary, user can gain some pre-knowledge of the changes to easily judge which is valuable for reading or not, than just be notified the fact that there are some changes.

Typical change notification systems usually use the one-to-one push model to deliver change information due to satisfy the user's variant demands. It's necessary to deliver everyone his/her own notification in these systems. Moreover, it's not easy to often modify one's own profile for fetching some different information. Our approach is using the one-to-n model to deliver change notification to registered users. Each user uses his/her own profile, which is maintained by himself/herself at the client side, to acquire his favorite information and view it in his/her favorite way.

The personalization method of WebSCAN means that each user can

- **(1) specify his/her favorite Web sites and topics**:
  Usually, a user has his/her own interests differenced from others. In WebSCAN, each user can pre-defined his/her favorite Web sits and topics in his/her profile to fetch his/her interesting changes. In other words, the specified Web sites and topics are one of the factors for filtering the notification.
- **(2) compute his/her own change worth**:
  In WebSCAN, the change worth is computed at the user's side using **Function (13)**. User then can set the parameters according to his/her interests. For example, if a user prefers to fresh changes, he/she can set the weight values of the freshness higher. Moreover, each user also can specify the threshold of change worth to fetch the valuable information.
- **(3) define the layout of presentation**:
  Filtered information is translated to a HTML file and presented to user via browser, such as IE, Netscape and so on. In WebSCAN, a user himself/herself can specify the layout of the outcome HTML file. WebSCAN also provides some default styles for user selecting, such as hanging-poster like style, newspaper like style and so on.

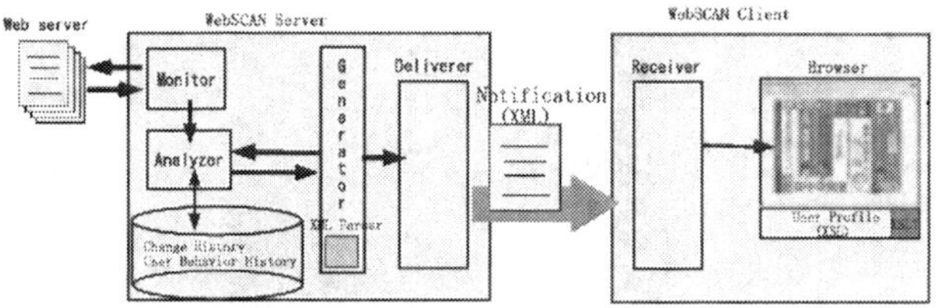

Fig. 3. Prototype System Model

```
....
<NOTIFICATION>
<SITE>
  <URL>http://www.usatoday.com</URL>
  <DIR>
    <URL>BASEBALL</URL>
    <PAGE>
     <URL>hphoto.htm</URL>
     <CHANGE-WORTH>
      <FRESHNESS>0.345</FRESHNESS>
      <POPULARITY>0.673</POPULARITY>
     </CHANGE-WORTH>
     <TITLE>USATODAY.com</TITLE>
     <INDEX>Bush to dedicate ...</INDEX>
     <IMG src="memorial.jpg"/>
    </PAGE>
     ....
  </DIR>
</SITE>
...
</NOTIFICATION>
....
```

(a) Notification

```
....
<xsl:template match="/">
...                 filtering(specified site)
<xsl:if test="
  NOTIFICATION/SITE[URL='http://www.usatoday.com']">
....
<xsl:apply-templates select=
  "/NOTIFICATION/SITE//DIR[URL='BASEBALL']//PAGE" >
...
<xsl:script language="JavaScript"><![CDATA[
w1=0.35; w2=0.65;
function totalworth(p){
  fresh=p.selectNodes("//CHANGE-WORTH/FRESHNESS");
  pop=p.selectNodes("//CHANGE-WORTH/POPULARITY");
.....
}
]]></xsl:script>
.....   change-worth compute method
filtering(specified topic)
```

(b) User Profile

Fig. 4. Examples of Notification and User profile

4 Prototype System

A prototype system was implemented using Perl and Visual Basic at Windows 2000 platform. The push-type notification mechanism is implemented using the XML/XSLT technology. The XML[10] formatted notification is generated based on the estimated change worth and delivered to the registered users. Each user uses his/her own profile, which is represented as an XSL[11] file, to filter and present the notification.

As illustrated in **Fig.3**, the current prototype system has a three-tier structure including(1)*Monitored Web site*, (2) *WebSCAN Server* and (3) *WebSCAN Client.*

WebSCAN server is composed of *Monitor*, *Analyzer*, *Generator* and *Deliverer*. A database for user behavior history and a snapshot of previous Web sites are also used.

The monitor watches the time-stamp and size of all pages in a Web site. When some changes are detected, monitor will fetch the changed information and invoke the analyzer to analyze the changes. The analyzer compares the detected change with its comparison scope to estimate its change worth. After the analysis, the generator selects the important changes to generate the notification. The deliverer then delivers this notification to the registered users.

The client of WebSCAN is composed of *Receiver* and *Browser*. The receiver is used to receive the notification delivered by the server. The browser filters and presents the received notification using an XSL file, which represents user profile. **Fig. 4(a)** shows part of a sample notification. Part of sample XSL formatted profile is shown in **Fig. 4(b)**.

5 Conclusion

WebSCAN, which is proposed in this paper, is a system that monitors and analyzes the changes of Web sites to notify user the important changes by a push-type delivery mechanism. In contrast to earlier works, the important change is picked up based on its change worth estimated by considering both the change content and the Web structure. Moreover, the notification for important changes is delivered to the users by a push-type mechanism, which separates the user customize method from the notification to integrate the popularization and personalization. In our current work, the change worth is estimated based on the content and structure. The change semantics based on other factors, such as hyperlinks will be done as our future works.

References

1. Brian E. Brewingtion and George Cybenko. How dynamic is the web? In *Proc. of WWW9*, pp. 264–292 (2000).
2. C3 Project. http://www-db.stanford.edu/c3/c3.html.
3. Sudarshan S. Chawathe and Hector Garcia-Molina. Meaningful change detection in structured data. In *Proc. of SIGMOD'97*, pp. 26–37 (1997).
4. NetMind. http://www.netmind.com.
5. Fred Douglis, Thomas Ball, Yih-Farn Chen, and Eleftherios Koutsofios. WebGUIDE: Querying and navigating changes in web repositories. In *Proc. of WWW5*, pp. 1335–1344 (1996).
6. Ling Liu, Calton Pu, and Wei Tang. WebCQ-detecting and delivering information change on the web. In *Proc. of CIKM'00* (2000).
7. Demet Aksoy, Mehmet Altinel, Rahul Bose, Ugur Cetintemel, Michael Franklin, and Stan Zdonik. Research in data broadcast and dissemination. In *Proc. of 1st International Conference on Advanced Multimedia Content Processing (AMCP'98)*, pp. 196–210 (1998).
8. Ma Qiang, Kazutoshi Sumiya, and Katumi Tanaka. Information Filtering Based on Time-series Features for Data Dissemination Systems(in Japanese). In *Trans. of IPSJ*, Vol.41, No. TOD7, pp. 46–57 (2000).
9. Swarup Acharya, Michael Franklin, and Stanley Zdonik. Balancing push and pull for data broadcast. In *Proc. of ACM SIGMOD '97*, pp. 183–194 (1997).
10. W3C. eXtensible Markup Language(XML) 1.0. http://www.w3.org/TR/REC-XML.
11. W3C. eXtensible Stylesheet Language(XSL). http://www.w3.org/TR/xsl.

Knowledge Base Maintenance through Knowledge Representation

John Debenham

University of Technology, Sydney,
Faculty of Information Technology,
PO Box 123, NSW 2007, Australia
debenham@it.uts.edu.au

Abstract. The problem of maintaining a knowledge base is substantially concerned with keeping track of rules that share common wisdom. A knowledge representation is described in which a collection of rules that are based on common wisdom are represented as a single 'item'. For items, maintenance hazards, caused by one item being partially hidden within another, still remain. 'Objects' are introduced as item building operators so enabling these hidden links to be identified and made explicit. A single operation for objects enables some of these hidden links to be removed thus simplifying maintenance.

1. Introduction

Maintaining the integrity of a knowledge base is a complex practical problem. A *rule* is a chunk of knowledge in an if-then form. If knowledge is represented as rules then maintenance hazards occur when wisdom embedded in one rule is also embedded in another. A knowledge representation is described in which a collection of rules that are based on common wisdom are represented as a single 'item'. So a single item encapsulates a set of declarative rules, and in turn each rule encapsulates a set of imperative programs. The item representation makes no distinction between data, information and knowledge things [1]. The *data* things in an application are the fundamental, indivisible things. Data things can be represented as simple constants or variables. If an association between things *cannot* be defined as a succinct, computable rule then it is an *implicit* association. Otherwise it is an *explicit* association. An *information* thing in an application is an implicit association between data things. Information things can be represented as tuples or relations. A *knowledge* thing in an application is an explicit association between information and/or data things. Items make it difficult to analyse the structure of a whole application. To make the structure clear, 'objects' are introduced as item building operators. Objects are an abstraction representing the structure of knowledge. Items are *either* represented informally as "i-schema" *or* formally as λ-calculus expressions [2]. The i-schema notation is used in practice. Items contain two classes of constraints that apply equally to knowledge and to data. In [3] these constraints are generalised to fuzzy acceptability measures of knowledge base integrity.

For items, maintenance hazards, caused by one item being partially hidden within another, still remain [4]. The use of objects enables these maintenance links to be made explicit. A single rule for item and object decomposition enables some of these

H.C. Mayr et al. (Eds.): DEXA 2001, LNCS 2113, pp. 599–608, 2001.

links to be removed so simplifying maintenance [5]. Classical database normalisation [6] is a special case of the application of that single rule. In the 1980s there was considerable interest in building expert systems. At that time declarative formalisms, in particular if-then formalisms such as logic programming, provided one way of computing with knowledge that was far easier to use than imperative formalisms. The comparative ease of use of if-then formalisms was responsible for a misapprehension that knowledge should be thought of as "if-then stuff". In a sense this is true because even if a chunk of knowledge has a number of if-then interpretations then it is unlikely that more than one of those interpretations will be useful in a particular application. One consequence of this misapprehension is that changes in the validity of a single rule that may not even been identified may have subtle and serious implications for the validity of a number of chunks of knowledge that have been identified and represented. So a knowledge representation with the property that a single chunk of knowledge, which may have a number of if-then interpretations, can be represented as a single entity should be a superior practical formalism for knowledge base design. The unified knowledge representation has this property. The unified representation is at a level of abstraction that is far closer to 'reality' than traditional declarative formalisms. This is shown by the hierarchy: a real chunk of knowledge is represented as a single "item". Each item has a number of interpretations as if-then forms. Each if-then form, or rule, has a number of interpretations as imperative programs.

2. Declarative, Rule-Based Formalisms

In a *declarative formalism* an if-then interpretation of a knowledge thing is represented as an "if-then" form as a rule. Two difficulties with declarative formalisms are illustrated using Horn clause logic as the representation formalism [7]. Logic is chosen because it is a widely understood notation, and *not* for any practical reason.

Consider the chunk of knowledge: [K1] "The sale price of a part is the cost price of that part marked up by the markup rate for that part". This single chunk is a simple statement of fact: it is *not* in an if-then form. Under a reasonable understanding of the meaning of chunk [K1] it admits three different if-then interpretations:

part/sale-price(x, y) ← part/cost-price(x, z),
  part/mark-up(x, w), $y = (z \times w)$ [C1.1]
part/cost-price(x, z) ← part/sale-price(x, y),
  part/mark-up(x, w), $y = (z \times w)$ [C1.2]
part/mark-up(x, w) ← part/sale-price(x, y),
  part/cost-price(x, z), $y = (z \times w)$ [C1.3]

For the third of these if-then interpretations—with "part/mark-up" as its head—there is a possibility of round-off error. The three clauses [C1.1]—[C1.3] are a rather inconvenient representation of the single chunk [K1] because *one* statement of fact has been represented as *three* logical statements. Consider another chunk of knowledge: [K2] "The profit on a part is the difference between the sale price of that part and the cost price of that part." As for [K1], the chunk [K2] is not in an if-then form. Under a reasonable understanding of its meaning, it also admits three if-then interpretations:

part/profit(x, y) ← part/sale-price(x, z),
  part/cost-price(x, w), $y = z - w$ [C2.1]
part/sale-price(x, z) ← part/profit(x, y),
  part/cost-price(x, w), $y = z - w$ [C2.2]
part/cost-price(x, w) ← part/sale-price(x, z),
  part/profit(x, y), $y = z - w$ [C2.3]

The six Horn clauses [C1.1]—[C2.3] may be combined using resolution to give additional potentially useful clauses:

part/profit(x, y) ← part/cost-price(x, w),
  part/mark-up(x, u), $z = (w \times u)$, $y = z - w$ [C3.1]
part/profit(x, y) ← part/sale-price(x, z),
  part/mark-up(x, u), $z = (w \times u)$, $y = z - w$ [C3.2]
part/mark-up(x, w) ← part/sale-price(x, y),
  part/profit(x, u), $u = y - z$, $y = (z \times w)$ [C3.3]

as well as some rather useless clauses such as:

part/sale-price(x, y) ← part/sale-price(x, v), part/profit(x, u), $u = v - z$,
  part/mark-up(x, w), $y = (z \times w)$ [C3.4]

A danger with all of [C3.1]—[C3.4] is that they are assembled from particular if-then interpretations of two chunks of knowledge, namely [K1] and [K2]. If the meaning of either of those two chunks should change then [C3.1]—[C3.4] may all have to be changed as well. This is not a problem if the relationships between [C3.1]—[C3.4] and both [K1] and [K2] are represented. But in the declarative representation, it is not clear that the meanings of [K1] and [K2] are buried in the four clauses [C3.1]—[C3.4]. So [C3.1]—[C3.4] and any other clauses derived from the original six clauses above, are potential maintenance hazards [10]. Given the six original clauses [C1.1]—[C2.3] there is no reason to combine them as illustrated in [C3.1]—[C3.4]. But clauses such as [C3.1]—[C3.4] are valid and could have been constructed by a knowledge engineer as part of a knowledge base. If they form part of a knowledge-based implementation then they may constitute a maintenance hazard [8].

Two problems with declarative formalisms have been identified. First, they have insufficient expressive power to represent all that a single chunk of knowledge has to say. Second there is no mechanism to prevent rules from being constructed whose validity relies on the validity of unrepresented sub-rules so leading to a potential maintenance hazard [9].

3. Items

Consider again the chunk of knowledge [K1]. Suppose that that chunk is represented as a thing—which we will call an *item*—with the name *[part/sale-price, part/cost-price, part/mark-up]*. The data associated with this item may be presented as a rather messy relation; such a relation is called the *value set* of the item, a possible value set is shown in Fig. 1. The meaning of an item *A*—called its *semantics* S_A—

part/sale-price		*part/cost-price*		*part/mark-up*	
1234	1.44	1234	1.20	1234	1.2
2468	2.99	2468	2.30	2468	1.3
3579	4.14	3579	3.45	3579	1.2
1357	10.35	1357	4.50	1357	2.3
9753	12.06	9753	6.70	9753	1.8
8642	12.78	8642	8.52	8642	1.5
4321	5.67	4321	2.70	4321	2.1

Fig. 1. Value set for a knowledge item.

is an expression that recognises the members of that item's value set. For the item considered above the semantics could be:

$$\lambda uvwxyz\bullet[\ S_{part/sale\text{-}price}(u, v) \wedge S_{part/cost\text{-}price}(w, x) \wedge S_{part/mark\text{-}up}(y, z) \wedge (u = w = y) \wedge (v = x \times z)\ ]\bullet$$

where $S_{part/sale\text{-}price} = \lambda xy\bullet[\ S_{part}(x) \wedge S_{sale\text{-}price}(y) \wedge \text{sells-for}(x, y)\ ]\bullet$
and where $S_{part} = \lambda x\bullet[\text{is-a}[x:P]]\bullet$ for some suitable domain P where:

$$\text{is-a}[x:P] \begin{cases} = \mathbf{T} & \textit{if } x \text{ is in } P \\ = \mathbf{F} & \textit{otherwise} \end{cases}$$

In this example the knowledge represented by the item is very simple. The components of this knowledge item are *part/sale-price*, *part/cost-price* and *part/mark-up*. These components each occur once in the value set shown in Fig. 1. The value sets of some knowledge items have multiple occurrences of some components to enable complex item semantics to be expressed. For example, consider the rule whose meaning is defined by the pair of recursive clauses:

$$P(w, x) \leftarrow P(y, z),\ P(u, v),\ Q(w, y, u),\ R(x, z, v),\ x > 5$$
$$P(w, x) \leftarrow Q(w, x, x),\ x \leq 5$$

The semantics of any item that represents this rule will employ multiple occurrences of the component P. The value set of any such item will also contain multiple occurrences of the component P. The semantics of complex, recursive knowledge items are represented in this way. The semantics of *all* knowledge items is λ-calculus "recognising functions" for the items' values sets.

Items are a single formalism for describing data, information and knowledge. Items may be presented informally as i-schema; that is, as they are employed in practice. Items may also be presented formally in the λ-calculus. Items have three important properties: items have a uniform format no matter whether they represent data, information or knowledge things; items incorporate two powerful classes of constraints, and a single rule of 'decomposition' can be specified for all items. Item 'decomposition' is a process which can be applied to the conceptual model to make it 'maintainable' in a precise sense. In particular, item decomposition removes potential maintenance hazards of the type illustrated above.

name		item name
name1	*name2*	item components
x	y	dummy variables
meaning of item		item semantics
constraints on values		value constraints
set constraints		set constraints

part/cost-price	
part	*cost-price*
x	y
costs(x,y)	
x<1 999 → y≤300	
∀	
----------------	O

Fig. 2. i-schema

An *item* consists of: an item name, item components, item semantics, item value constraints, and item set constraints. The *item name* is usually written in italics, *A*. The *item components* is a set of the names of items which this item represents some association between. The *item semantics* is an expression which recognises the members of the value set of this item, S_A. The *item value constraints* is an expression which must be satisfied by all members of the value set of this item, V_A. The *item set constraints* are constraints on the structure of this item's value set, C_A. The i-schema format for items is shown in Fig. 2. If two items have the property that the semantics of one logically implies the semantics of the other then the first item is a *sub-item* of the second. If two items have the property that they are both sub-items of each other then those two items are said to be *equivalent*.

For example, in an application there are 'parts' represented by the *part* data item. Each 'part' is identified by a 'part-number'. The value constraint for *part* requires that part numbers should lie in the range (1 000, 9 999). The set constraint for *part* requires that there are less than 100 different part numbers. Further there are 'costs' represented by the *cost-price* data item. Each *part* is associated with a *cost-price*. This association is represented by the information item *part/cost-price*. That item is subject to the "value constraint" that parts whose part-number is less that 1 999 will be associated with a cost price of no more than $300. That item is subject to the "set constraints" that every part must be in this association, and that each part is associated with a unique cost-price. The i-schema for the *part/cost-price* item is shown in Fig. 2; it contains two set constraints. The '∀' in the *part* component column specifies a *universal constraint*; denoted by "Uni" in the formal λ-calculus representation. This universal constraint requires that all members of the value set of *part* must be in the value set of *part/cost-price*. The horizontal line in the *part* column and the '**O**' in the *cost-price* column specifies a candidate constraint; denoted by "Can" in the formal λ-calculus representation. This candidate constraint requires that members of the value set of *part* functionally determine the members of the value set of *cost-price* in this item—in traditional database jargon, part is a potential key of the part/cost-price relation. In general, the horizontal lines identify a set of components whose value sets functionally determine the value set of the single component identified by '**O**'. Candidate constraints for a knowledge item identify potential if-then interpretations of that item.

Items are a universal formalism in that they can describe knowledge just as naturally as information (ie relations) or data. For example, consider the chunk of knowledge [K1]. [K1] is represented as the knowledge item *[part/sale-price, part/cost-price, part/mark-up]* whose i-schema is shown in Fig. 3. That i-schema has four set constraints. The last three of those set constraints identify the three if-then

[part/sale-price, part/cost-price, part/mark-up]		
part/sale-price	*part/cost-price*	*part/mark-up*
(w, x)	(w, y)	(w, z)
$x = y \times z$		
$\rightarrow x > y$		
∀	∀	
o	----------	----------
----------	----------	o
----------	o	----------

[part/profit, part/sale-price, part/cost-price]		
part/profit	*part/sale-price*	*part/cost-price*
(y, v)	(y, x)	(y, z)
$(v = x - z)$		
$\rightarrow v > 0$		
∀	∀	
o	----------	----------
----------	----------	o
----------	o	----------

Fig. 3. Knowledge items for [K1] and [K2]

interpretations represented above as the clauses [C1.1]—[C1.3]. So the item shown in Fig. 3 represents *all* that the chunk of knowledge [K1] says. Items appear to have resolved the first difficulty with rules identified above. Items are more than a convenient way of representing a set of rules; they can be manipulated, combined and decomposed. Computing with a collection of items amounts to computing with the set of rules represented within those items. Manipulating items present no greater level of computational complexity than rule-based formalisms.

The i-schema for the chunk of knowledge [K2] is shown in Fig. 3. Item join is an operation that may be applied to two items *A* and *B* that share a set of common components E to construct a third item called the *join* of *A* and *B* on E, and denoted by: $A \otimes_E B$. Item join is defined formally below [2]. The following is an example of the use of the join operator:

[part/profit, part/sale-price, part/cost-price, part/mark-up] =
[part/sale-price, part/cost-price, part/mark-up] $\otimes_{\{part/sale\text{-}price,\ part/cost\text{-}price\}}$
[part/profit, part/sale-price, part/cost-price]

The i-schema for this item is shown in Fig. 4. The i-schema for a sub-item of this item is shown in Fig. 5. Each candidate constraint in an item identifies an if-then interpretation of that item. The if-then interpretation of the sub-item in Fig. 5 identified by the third row from the bottom of that i-schema is the rule [C3.1]. That i-schema also contains two other if-then interpretations—identified by the last two

[part/profit, part/sale-price, part/cost-price, part/mark-up]			
part/profit	*part/sale-price*	*part/cost-price*	*part/mark-up*
(y, v)	(y, x)	(y, z)	(y, w)
$(v = x - z) \wedge (x = z \times w)$			
$\rightarrow ((x > z) \wedge (v > 0))$			
∀	∀	∀	
O	------------------------	------------------------	
------------------------	------------------------	O	
------------------------	O	------------------------	
	O	------------------------	------------------------
	------------------------	------------------------	O
	------------------------	O	------------------------

Fig. 4. Join of items for [K1] and [K2] on {*part/sale-price, part/cost-price*}

[part/profit, part/cost-price, part/mark-up]		
part/profit	*part/cost-price*	*part/mark-up*
(y, v)	(y, z)	(y, w)
$(v = z \times (w - 1))$		
$\rightarrow v > 0$		
∀	∀	
O	------------------------	------------------------
------------------------	------------------------	O
------------------------	O	------------------------

Fig. 5. Sub-item of item in Fig. 4

rows of that i-schema—that have not been expressed here [2]. Using the rule of composition ⊗, knowledge items, information items and data items may be joined with one another regardless of type [11]. For example, the knowledge item:

[cost-price, tax] [$\lambda xy \bullet [x = y \times 0.05] \bullet$, $\lambda xy \bullet [x < y] \bullet$,
(Uni(*cost-price*) ∧ Can(*tax*, {*cost-price*}))$_{[cost\text{-}price,\ tax]}$]

can be joined with the information item *part/cost-price* on the set {*cost-price*} to give the information item *part/cost-price/tax*. In other words:

[cost-price, tax] $\otimes_{\{cost\text{-}price\}}$ *part/cost-price* =
part/cost-price/tax[$\lambda xyz \bullet [costs(x, y) \wedge z = y \times 0.05] \bullet$,
$\lambda xyz \bullet [((1000<x<1999) \rightarrow (0<y \leq 300)) \wedge (z<y)] \bullet$,
(Uni(*part*) ∧
Can(*cost-price*, {*part*}) ∧ Can(*tax*, {*cost-price*}))$_{part/cost\text{-}price/tax}$]

name		object name
type1	type2	argument type
x	*y*	dummy variables
meaning of object		object semantics
constraints on values		object value constraints
set constraints		object set constraints

costs	
D^1	D^1
x	y
costs(x,y)	
x<1999 → y≤300	
∀	
------------	O

Fig. 6. o-schema format and the object '***costs***'

In this way items may be joined together to form more complex items [12]. Alternatively, the ⊗ operator may form the basis of a theory of decomposition in which each item may be replaced by a set of simpler items. An item I is *decomposable* into the set of items $D = \{I_1, I_2,..., I_n\}$ if:

- I_i has non-trivial semantics for all i,
- $I = I_1 \otimes I_2 \otimes ... \otimes I_n$, where
- each join is *monotonic*; that is, each term in this composition contributes at least one component to *I*.

If item *I* is decomposable then it will not necessarily have a unique decomposition. So items can be combined using the ⊗ operator. The ⊗ operator also forms the basis of a theory of decomposition that removes hidden relationships from the represented knowledge. So items overcome the second difficulty described above for rules.

Items are a universal formalism for knowledge representation but make it difficult to analyse the structure of the whole application. For example, two chunks of knowledge that share the same basic wisdom may be expressed in terms of quite different components; this could obscure their common wisdom [13]. To make the inherent structure of items clear 'objects' are introduced as item building operators [4].

4. Objects

The introduction of objects enables the structure of the conceptual model to be analysed. In [4] it is shown that objects support a formal structure which may be used to manage maintenance. Objects are item building operators which have four important properties: objects have a uniform format no matter whether they represent data, information or knowledge things; objects incorporate powerful classes of constraints; objects enable items to be built in such a way as to reveal their inherent structure, and a single rule of 'decomposition' can be specified for objects such that if a 'decomposed' set of object operators is applied to a 'decomposed' set of 'base' items then the resulting conceptual model will contain only 'decomposed' items and will thus be maintainable. As for items, objects may either be represented informally as "o-schema" or formally as λ-calculus expressions. Object names are written in bold italic script. For example, suppose that ***costs*** is an operator that generates the information item *part/cost-price* from its components *part* and *cost-price*; that is:
part/cost-price = ***costs***(*part, cost-price*)

Further, suppose that the object ***mark-up-chunk*** is an operator which generates the knowledge item *[part/sale-price, part/cost-price, part/mark-up]* from its components; that is:

[part/sale-price, part/cost-price, part/mark-up] =
mark-up-chunk(*part/sale-price, part/cost-price, part/mark-up*)

In general, an n-adic object is an operator which maps n given items into another item for some value of n. Further, the specification of each object will presume that the set of items to which that object may be applied are of a specific "type". The *type* of an m-adic item is determined both by whether it is a data item, an information item or a knowledge item and by the value of m. The type is denoted respectively by $\mathbf{D}^m$, $\mathbf{I}^m$ and $\mathbf{K}^m$; unspecified, or free, type which is denoted by $\mathbf{X}^m$ is also permitted. The definition of an object is similar to that of an item. An *object* consists of: an object name, argument types, object semantics, object value constraints, and object set constraints. The *object name* is usually written in bold italics. The *argument types* are a set of types of items to which that object operator may be applied. The *object semantics* is an expression which recognises the members of the value set of any item generated by the object. The *object value constraints* is an expression which must be satisfied by all members of the value set of any item generated by the object. The *object set constraints* are constraints on the structure of the value set of any item generated by the object. The o-schema format for objects is shown in Fig. 6. If two objects have the property that the semantics of one logically implies the semantics of the other then the first object is a *sub-object* of the second. If two objects have the property that they are each sub-objects of each other then those two objects are said to be *equivalent*.

For example, the o-schema for the ***costs*** object is shown in Fig. 6. The o-schema for the ***costs*** object contains two set constraints. The '$\forall$' symbol has the obvious extension of meaning to its use for items; likewise for the horizontal line and the '**O**' symbol. Data objects provide a representation of sub-typing.

For example, the ***costs*** object in its λ-calculus form is:

$$\textbf{\textit{costs}}[\lambda P{:}\mathbf{X}^1 Q{:}\mathbf{X}^1{\bullet}\lambda xy{\bullet}[\ S_P(x) \wedge S_Q(y) \wedge \text{costs}(x,\ y)\ ]{\bullet\bullet},$$
$$\lambda P{:}\mathbf{X}^1 Q{:}\mathbf{X}^1{\bullet}\lambda xy{\bullet}[\ V_P(x) \wedge V_Q(y) \wedge ((1\,000 < x < 1\,999) \rightarrow (y \leq 300))\ ]{\bullet\bullet},$$
$$\lambda P{:}\mathbf{X}^1 Q{:}\mathbf{X}^1{\bullet}[C_P \wedge C_Q \wedge (\text{Uni}(P) \wedge \text{Can}(Q,\ \{P\}))_{\vee(\textbf{\textit{costs}},P,Q)}\ ]{\bullet}]$$

and the λ-calculus for the ***mark-up-chunk*** object is:

$$\textbf{\textit{mark-up-chunk}}[\lambda P{:}\mathbf{X}^2 Q{:}\mathbf{X}^2 R{:}\mathbf{X}^2{\bullet}\lambda x_1x_2y_1y_2z_1z_2{\bullet}[\ S_P(x_1,x_2) \wedge S_Q(y_1,y_2)$$
$$\wedge\ S_R(z_1,z_2) \wedge ((\ x_1 = y_1 = z_1\ ) \rightarrow (x_2 = z_2 \times y_2))\ ]{\bullet\bullet},$$
$$\lambda P{:}\mathbf{X}^2 Q{:}\mathbf{X}^2 R{:}\mathbf{X}^2{\bullet}\lambda x_1x_2y_1y_2z_1z_2{\bullet}[\ V_P(x_1,x_2) \wedge V_Q(y_1,y_2) \wedge V_R(z) \wedge$$
$$((\ x_1 = y_1 = z_1\ ) \rightarrow (\ x_2 > y_2\ ))\ ]{\bullet\bullet},$$
$$\lambda P{:}\mathbf{X}^2 Q{:}\mathbf{X}^2 R{:}\mathbf{X}^2{\bullet}[C_P \wedge C_Q \wedge C_R \wedge (\text{Uni}(P) \wedge \text{Uni}(Q) \wedge \text{Can}(P,\ \{Q,\ R\})$$
$$\wedge\ \text{Can}(Q,\ \{P,\ R\}) \wedge \text{Can}(R,\ \{P,\ Q\}))_{\vee(\textbf{\textit{mark-up-chunk}},P,Q,R)}\ ]{\bullet}\ ]$$

The ***mark-up-chunk*** knowledge object represents the essence of the knowledge within the knowledge chunk [K1] without any reference to the components of that chunk. Objects represent abstract knowledge. Objects also represent value constraints and set constraints in a uniform way. A "join" operation for objects is defined in a similar way [4] to the join operation for items described above. If a set of objects have been decomposed using the object join operator then items generated by those objects will also be in a decomposed form.

Data objects provide a representation of sub-typing. Knowledge is quite clumsy when represented as items; objects are a more compact representation. For example, consider the *[part/sale-price, part/cost-price, part/mark-up]* knowledge item which represents the chunk of knowledge [K1]. This item can be built by applying a knowledge object ***mark-up-chunk*** of argument type ($\mathbf{I}^2$, $\mathbf{I}^2$, $\mathbf{I}^2$) to the items *part/sale-price*, *part/cost-price* and *part/mark-up*.

References

1. Barr, V. (1999). "Applying Reliability Engineering to Expert Systems" in *proceedings 12th International FLAIRS Conference*, Florida, May 1999, pp494-498.
2. Debenham, J.K. "*Knowledge Engineering*", Springer-Verlag, 1998.
3. Debenham, J.K. "The Degradation of Knowledge Base Integrity", in *proceedings 13th International FLAIRS Conference FLAIRS-2000*, Orlando, Florida, May 2000, pp113-117.
4. Debenham, J.K. (1999). "Knowledge Object Decomposition" in *proceedings 12th International FLAIRS Conference*, Florida, May 1999, pp203-207.
5. Debenham, J.K. "Representing Knowledge Normalisation", *in proceedings Tenth International Conference on Software Engineering and Knowledge Engineering SEKE'98*, San Francisco, US, June 1998.
6. Date, C.J., "*An Introduction to Database Systems*" (4th edition) Addison-Wesley, 1986.
7. Mayol, E. and Teniente, E. (1999). "Addressing Efficiency Issues During the Process of Integrity Maintenance" i*n proceedings Tenth International Conference DEXA99*, Florence, September 1999, pp270-281.
8. Ramirez, J. and de Antonio, A. (2000). "Semantic Verification of Rule-Based Systems with Arithmetic Constraints" in *proceedings 11th International Conference DEXA2000*, London, September 2000, pp437-446.
9. Katsuno, H. and Mendelzon, A.O., "On the Difference between Updating a Knowledge Base and Revising It", in *proceedings Second International Conference on Principles of Knowledge Representation and Reasoning, KR'91*, Morgan Kaufmann, 1991.
10. Johnson, G. and Santos, E. (2000). "Generalizing Knowledge Representation Rules for Acquiring and Validating Uncertain Knowledge" in *proceedings 13th International FLAIRS Conference*, Florida, May 2000, pp186-2191.
11. Werner, E. "Logical Foundations of Distributed Artificial Intelligence" in O'Hare, G.M.P. & Jennings, N.R. (Eds) "*Foundations of Distributed Artificial Intelligence*", pp57-118, Wiley, 1996.
12. Darwiche, A. (1999). "Compiling Knowledge into Decomposable Negation Normal Form" in *proceedings International Joint Conference on Artificial Intelligence, IJCAI'99*, Stockholm, Sweden, August 1999, pp 284-289.
13. Jantke, K.P. and Herrmann, J. (1999). "Lattices of Knowledge in Intelligent Systems Validation" in *proceedings 12th International FLAIRS Conference*, Florida, May 1999, pp499-505.

ANKON: A Multi-agent System for Information Gathering

Claudia Diamantini and Maurizio Panti

Computer Science Institute, University of Ancona
via Brecce Bianche, 60131 Ancona, Italy
{diamanti,panti}@inform.unian.it

Abstract. The global information management scenario requires support systems which help the user in discovering interesting information contained in heterogeneous sources spread through all over the world. In the present paper, we introduce the notion of hierarchical global concepts to support the flexible management of imprecise and heterogeneous representation of information. In particular, we show how the characteristics of a cluster hierarchy can be exploited in the query reformulation phase in order to comply with the user imprecise and uncertain information requirements. The technique has been implemented in a FIPA compliant multi-agent system, with a mediator-like architecture.

1 Introduction

The global information systems scenario, with the large amount of autonomous information sources spread all over the world, and the management of semistructured data, makes the access to information a quite different task with respect to the traditional query specification.

Traditionally, users define themselves the structured sequence of actions that must be performed to solve a given task. In the new scenario, the hypothesis on the user awareness of sources schemes and consciousness of what and how to search to satisfy a precise need is no longer actual. Rather, we have to assume that the user has a generic domain knowledge, but neither a knowledge of available information sources, nor their scheme, content, and location. As a consequence, the most common way to access information, typical for example in Web search engines, follows the Information Retrieval paradigm, where a few words are used to represent the user need, which are then matched against very large numbers of informative elements, for example, web pages. The results are often unsatisfactory, mainly because of the very poor user/information model: two people may have very different needs but use the same, typically few, words in the query. The same piece of information can be given different representations in different sources. The complexity of today's information systems could be lowered by a cooperative support to query specification. To meet this condition, the system should be able to pro-actively support the uniform access to multiple information sources, addressing, on the one hand, the personal background of each single user, and matching it against source specific capabilities

H.C. Mayr et al. (Eds.): DEXA 2001, LNCS 2113, pp. 609–620, 2001.

on the other. Since users/sources views of information can be only partially unified, exact matching rules are better replaced by partial matchings and degrees of similarity. This involves uncertainty and imprecision management both in information representation and query processing.

Uncertainty and imprecision are the main concern of ANKON, presented in this paper in the framework of heterogeneous databases. It is capable to manage approximate queries, and to pro-actively guide the user in the progressive specification of its needs. These features are the result of a novel approach to knowledge representation and management, where the core knowledge is a hierarchy of concepts at different levels of abstraction, automatically induced by a hierarchical clustering algorithm. The system maintains an intensional description of concepts which allows to merge the notion of approximate query processing [6] and the notion of conceptual query processing [7]. In particular, by relating quality measures for approximate query answering, like precision and recall, to concept abstraction, the system is capable to bind query terms to concepts at query processing time, rather than at knowledge definition time, giving the user a better capability to specify its information needs.

This approach to knowledge representation and management is instantiated in a mediator-like architecture, and implemented in a multi-agent system platform, conforming to FIPA specifications, so to meet the general requirements of a cooperative information system: the mediator architecture [23] is almost universally recognized as the reference architecture to manage autonomous, heterogeneous sources. The multi-agent FIPA platform defines the physical infrastructure which enables the interoperability between software agents. Furthermore, It provides for coordinator agents which standardize some cooperation facilities, such as brokering services.

The rest of the paper is organized as follows. In section 2 we briefly review related researches. In section 3 we first formulate the problem of approximate query management, then we describe the representation of knowledge in ANKON, and discuss how it enables the flexible management of approximate queries. Section 4 presents the whole system architecture and implementation. Section 5 concludes the paper.

2 Related Works

One of the major tasks in the development of systems supporting the uniform access to multiple information sources, is that of managing semantic heterogeneity of data. The problem has been addressed in the traditional areas of database and information retrieval, to manage structured and unstructured data [19,17, 12,24] and in the overlapping and emerging area of Web research [13,14]. The solution to this problem is typically provided by some kind of domain ontology. We use the term "ontology" with the broad meaning of a system of mappings which relate different representations of domain concepts, thus giving an abstract (i.e. representation independent) definition of concepts and concepts properties, and enabling "comprehension" among autonomous systems, being either human or software agents, thanks to the mapping between individual's concepts [15]. Most of the approaches to the definition of an ontology are declarative in nature. Declarative approaches are concerned with the development/exploitation of formal models and graph-based languages for declarative specification of mapping rules [1,2,11,14,20,21]. Although almost accurate domain ontologies can be constructed in this way, these approaches are hardly generalizable and scalable to huge amounts of information sources.

Generalizability and scalability can be improved by semi-automatic ontology induction. It basically relies on clustering techniques and neural networks [4,10, 16]. Data coming from local sources are clustered together, on the basis of some similarity notion, to form equivalence classes at some abstraction level. In this respect the generic cluster, in that it contains data considered equivalent, can be interpreted as an extensional definition of a concept in the unified domain ontology.

These works can be seen to extend the traditional database design methodology in the context of multiple sources management[1]. As such, they typically present two main draw-backs: first, the intensional description of the ontology still relies on human intervention, in order to establish global terms, which has to be used in the queries. This forces the user to have a sort of global scheme knowledge. Second, they do not introduce any facility for the management of concepts abstraction, and hence of uncertainty and imprecision.

Uncertainty and imprecision issues has been considered in [3,6,7,18]. In [18], users which are unaware of attribute names can resort to a "semantic integration procedure", based on neural networks, to find similar attributes up to a similarity threshold value. In the context of approximate queries, Chang and Garcia-Molina [6] define a framework based on precision and recall measures, to evaluate the quality of a "semantic translation rule" system. Chu et alii [7] perform query relaxation by the so called *Type Abstraction Hierarchy* structure, which represents attribute values at different levels of abstraction. All these works have some ideas in common with the present paper. However, they consider the attributes domain level, not the conceptual level. Thus, limited or no support is given to the user in the specification of query terms. Furthermore, no explicit relation is established between the abstraction level at which translations happen and the properties of the answer, so such properties cannot be decided by users. [3,5] exploit a taxonomy of terms to match user's terms to the semantically closest available system terms. Semantic closeness is established as a function of linguistic relations (hypernyms, synonyms) between terms which are defined by the help of a thesaurus (Roget's thesaurus, WordNet). These approaches suffers from a general-purpose, linguistic assignment of semantics to terms. In particular, they do not provide support to disambiguation by contextualization. Furthermore, they do not relate intensions (the terms) and extensions (the instances in the databases), so it is impossible to fully exploit the taxonomy to decide at query time the desired answer properties.

[1] And, in fact, scheme integration is one critical step in the bottom-up design strategies.

3 A Principled Approach to Approximate Query Management

Let us consider the four information sources given in Fig. 1, containing various kind of information about science and arts. The sources are uniformly described by means of ER schemes, nevertheless they can be databases with any logical structure. Let us now suppose that an user wants to formulate a query over

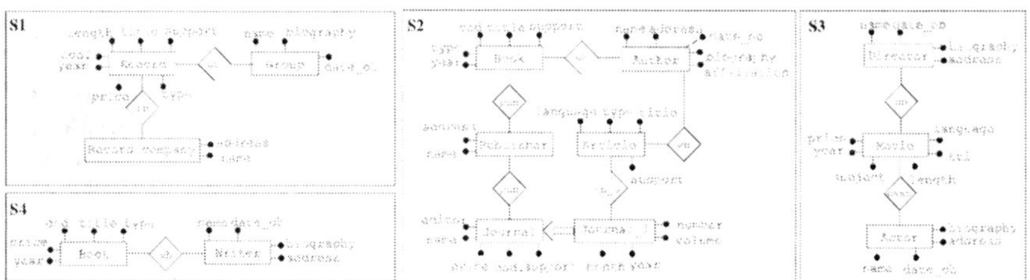

Fig. 1. The schemes of four information sources

these sources to know about the titles of artistic productions. In the classical framework, where the user knows sources and sources scheme, a possible query would look like: SELECT ttl, title FROM record@S1, movie@S3, book@S4. This would produce all and only the requested information to the user. Unfortunately, this is not the case, as the user knows neither which sources he can query, nor their scheme. So his query should be bases only on his general domain knowledge, for instance on terms like title and arts. In this case, no answer could be given in the classical framework, since an exact matching between terms does not exist. An intelligent system should be able to gracefully degrade its performance, by finding suitable approximations of the original query, when exact term matching is not possible. Query approximation implies that a non perfect answer to the original query can be given: in general, some interesting information will be missed, while some non interesting information will be introduced. The notions of *precision* and *recall* can be borrowed from Information Retrieval (IR) [22] to measure these errors. This idea was introduced by the present authors in [9]. Recently, Chang and Garcia-Molina proposed a closeness metric based on precision and recall to manage approximate queries in the framework of rule-based systems [6]. Denoting by A_q the set of relevant information for a query q, and by B some other set of information, recall and precision of B with respect to q can be defined as: $Rec(B,q) = \frac{|A_q \cap B|}{|A_q|}$, $Prec(B,q) = \frac{|A_q \cap B|}{|B|}$.

We like to point out the tight relation existing between query approximation and the notion of "conceptual query" processing [7]. In fact, in query approximation term matching is substituted by concept matching, in the sense that terms can be seen to denote concepts, which are then mapped to the closest available concept. In the example, the concept of arts could be matched with the concept with extension {book, record, movie}.

Answer precision and recall is modified by matching concepts at different levels of abstraction: if we match the concept of arts with the more general concept of intellectual production, the concept with extension {book, record, movie, article}, then article titles will be included in the answer, which would lower precision. If it is matched with the more specific concept of, say, multimedia artistic production, i.e. the concept with extension {record, movie}, then recall is lowered.

In general, the performance required to a system by users varies from one query session to another as a function of user's information needs: in some cases a precise object is needed, in other cases fast retrieval of few key objects will suffice, while in certain situations user is interested in retrieving as much as possible of the total objects relevant to the subject of his query, trading completeness with precision and response time, that is accepting some unrelevant objects, and accepting to wait. Thus, equipping the system with the capability to deal with concepts at different levels of abstraction is fundamental to give it flexibility in approximate query management.

3.1 Concept Representation

In ANKON, domain knowledge is induced from meta-data information coming from the sources, by means of clustering algorithms. For notational purposes, we follow the relational terminology, describing meta-data information in terms of attributes and tables. The knowledge base is formed by two linked cluster structures: the first one groups local attributes into semantically equivalent classes, to define a set of *global attributes*. The second one groups local tables into semantically equivalent classes, on the basis of global attributes sharing among tables. We term these classes as *global concepts*, since they aim to represent a reconciliation of local views over the same concept. The set of global concepts defines a generalization hierarchy. We introduce a novel representation of a concept hierarchy, that is strictly related to the hierarchical clustering criterion called *Entropic Criterion for Conceptual Clustering* (EC^3), where entropic measures define a binary counterpart of two properties, generally accepted as the fundamental properties of a "good" clustering policy, namely the *cohesion* or minimum volume of a cluster and the *separation* or minimum overlap among clusters [9]. Conditional probabilities involved in the criterion can be exploited to give an *intensional representation* of global concepts.

Let us denote by Y the set of global attributes, and by T the set of local tables.

Definition 1. *Given a cluster* $C \subseteq T$ *and a (global) attribute* $y \in Y$, *the* relevance degree of y in the intension of C *is the conditional probability* $P(y = 1|c = C)$ *and the* relevance degree of $\neg y$ in the intension of C *is the conditional probability* $P(y = 0|c = C)$.

Definition 2. *The intension of a cluster $C \in T$ is the set of all predicates y_i, $\neg y_i$, $y_i \in Y$, weighted by their intensional relevance degree:*

$$I(C) = \sum_{y_i \in Y} P(y_i = 1|c = C)y_i \oplus P(y_i = 0|c = C)\neg y_i \ ,$$

where $\oplus$ denotes a formal sum.

This definition of intension can be interpreted from two points of view. On the one hand, it is a soft (or weighted) version of the traditional hard notion of concept intension. Usually, when we intensionally describe a concept, the properties which are shared by the largest part of the concept instances are taken as properties of the concept itself, forgetting exceptions. The above definition of intension gives, for each property expressed by an attribute, a quantitative measure of the accuracy, or degree of correctness, we have when we describe the cluster in terms of this property. This accuracy is simply the fraction of cluster elements possessing the property, over the total number of cluster elements, which defines exactly the value of $P(y|c)$. On the other hand, each $P(y|c)$ expresses a measure of the *precision* of the cluster in exemplifying the property.

A dual notion of relevance degree is recall capability.

Definition 3. *Given a cluster $C \subseteq T$ and an attribute $y \in Y$, the* recall capability of C by y *is the conditional probability $P(c = C_j|y = 1)$ and the* recall capability of C by $\neg y$ *is the conditional probability $P(c = C_j|y = 0)$.*

The recall capability of an attribute gives us a measure of the connection strength between the cluster and the property expressed by the attribute, measuring how many domain elements which possess the property are actually elements of that cluster.

The global concept hierarchy is represented by retaining, for each node C, its intension in the form of a vector $< N_{y_1}, \ldots, N_{y_r}, N_C, ptr, b >$, where N_{y_j} is the number of instances in the cluster possessing the attribute y_j, N_C is the cluster cardinality, and *ptr* is a pointer to the list of children nodes. b is a bit flag set to one for leaf nodes. This representation allows to calculate quickly both intensional relevance degree and recall capability for each attribute and cluster. Furthermore, it is simple to update, if some instance has to be added to or removed from a node. Leaf nodes correspond to sets of identical instances, so $N_{y_j} = N_C$, or $N_{y_j} = 0$. In a leaf node, *ptr* points to the list of table names and wrapper addresses.

3.2 Approximate Query Management

As previously stated, the performance required to a system by users varies from one query session to another as a function of user's information needs. The present system has been designed to allow users to specify such needs in terms of precision and recall of the answer. Hence, queries are formed by a set of global attributes together with the constraints on the lower bound values of precision and recall. This information is processed by the system in two main steps: first, the concept hierarchy is searched in order to determine the concepts which best match the user query. Second, on the basis of the selected global concepts, the original query is reformulated into a set of local queries for each interested source.

Considering simple queries where a unique attribute y is specified, and defining the set of tables which are relevant for y as: $T_y = \{t \in T | y \text{ exists in the scheme of } t\}$, it is straightforward to notice that the precision and recall of a global concept C w.r.t. y are defined by: $Prec(C, y) = P(y = 1|C)$, $Rec(C, y) = P(C|y = 1)$. For compound queries, we assume a Boolean model, that is a model where the query is a logical combination of terms by means of AND, OR, NOT operators. It is immediate to extend the above notion of relevance to this kind of queries, and calculate precision and recall of a global concept C w.r.t. compound queries, exploiting the well-known relations between Boolean operators and probabilities. For example, it turns out that $Prec(C, y_1 \wedge y_2) = P(y_1 = 1|C) \cdot P(y_2 = 1|C)$.

The global concept hierarchy can then be visited in order to find the concept whose intension best matches the query. Properties of well-formed cluster hierarchies with respect to the notions of intensional relevance degree and recall capability, guarantees that such a matching can be found (if it exists) without exhaustive search. For instance, since recall capability lowers from the root to the leafs, if the required recall is greater than a concept recall capability, the whole concept subtree can be pruned.

Since precision and recall are conflicting measures, the matching cannot always be found. Different search strategies have been devised to cope with this situation. The basic strategy considers both constraints as mandatory, reporting a failure if they cannot be completely satisfied. The second and third one allow for suboptimal solutions, satisfying the precision constraint only, or the recall constraint only, depending on user needs. The last strategy allows the system to pro-actively guide the user in a step-by-step construction of his query. When the query is underspecified, the system finds multiple candidate paths in the hierarchy. In this case, it can select from the intension of each candidate global concept the attributes with the greatest relevance degree, and ask the user to choose one. Note that this procedure is different from the immediate provision of all the attributes by users in a couple of ways: first, additional attributes are exploited only locally to global concepts, second, the terms proposed to the user are known terms for the mediator, and this gives to the user and idea of the mediator knowledge. Since the user knowledge is likely to be larger than the mediator knowledge, it is simpler for the user to recognized the meaning of these terms, than it is for the mediator to recognize user terms. This allows to prevent oneself from wasting time with queries the system cannot correctly understand.

After the suitable level of the hierarchy has been reached, the system can resort to the extensional definition of the concept to reformulate the query. This involves, for each global concept, reaching the leaf nodes under it, accessing the information about tables name and address, and calculating the correspondence between global and local attributes, to substitute to each occurrence of a global attribute the attribute name appearing in the local tables.

Summing up, by the presented approach, the user is relieved from knowing both at which sources the searched information resides, and the exact names of local tables, as they are calculated by the system. Furthermore, terms are bound to concepts at query processing time, rather than at knowledge definition time, giving the user a better capability to specify its information needs. At this stage, the user still need to know global attributes names. This limit will be overcome by the introduction of user agents, which can "learn" a set of mappings among the terms preferred by the user and the global attributes names.

4 Implementation

ANKON is implemented in Java, as an open, multi-agent platform conforming to FIPA specifications. The multi-agent platform defines the physical infrastructure which enables the interoperability between agents registered at the platform. It defines a standard message-based communication protocol between agents, based on the communication language FIPA-ACL. It also introduces coordinator agents which standardize the major cooperation facilities, like the Agent Management System, which manages agents registration and physical addresses, and the Directory Facilitator, which keeps track of the type of services given by the agents, acting as a sort of "yellow page", or brokering service. We refer to the original FIPA documentation for details, available at `http://www.fipa.org`.

Information agents on the platform are functionally organized in a three-layer architecture, sketched in Fig. 2. At the front-end, user agents define the interface

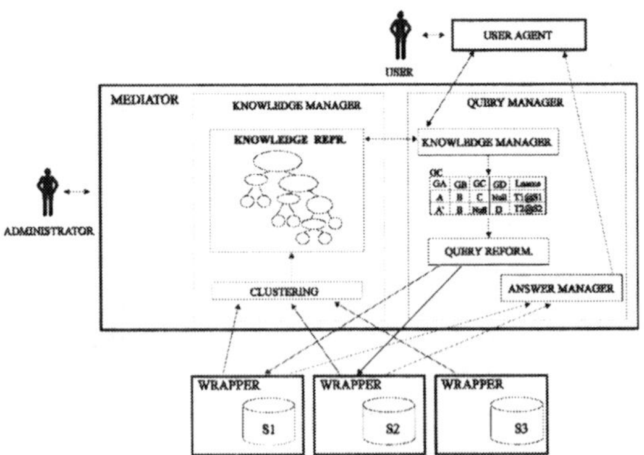

Fig. 2. Functional organization of information agents

to the system for a specific user, implementing a set of facilities. First, they maintain a set of mappings between user and system preferred terms. Second, they allow multiple searches to be done in parallel, collecting results in log files for subsequent analysis. Third, they allow the specification of precision and recall values, either by inserting numeric values in a dialog window, or by the use of qualitative indicators like 'high' and 'low'. Last, they allow to choose the preferred search strategy. The user input is then interpreted, and the query inserted in an ACL message and sent to the mediator.

At the back-end, wrapper agents define the interface to the system for a specific source. They receive a request coming from the mediator in the ACL language, and translate it in the source query language, starting the local query manager. The response of the source is then inserted into an ACL message and sent back to the mediator.

In the mediator architecture, we can recognize two main modules, the Knowledge Manager (KM), and the Query Manager (QM). The KM is responsible of both the construction and updating of knowledge. It includes a clustering algorithm to induce global attributes, and an incremental hierarchical clustering algorithm based on EC^3 to induce global concepts. The latter algorithm allows the fast, incremental updating of the cluster hierarchy in the case of source modification but, like any incremental algorithm, the results depends on the order of presentation of instances, and by the right setting of a scale parameter λ, producing hierarchies which can be suboptimal with respect to the EC^3 criterion. Thus, the system implements a set of functionalities which allows the analysis and tuning of the knowledge base by the system administrator. In the performed experiments, we noticed that the algorithm is always capable of recognizing the main domain concepts (the high levels of the hierarchy) without human intervention, moving only few instances from their best position. Other functionalities allows the administrator to register the mediator to a platform, and to define the set of wrapper agents (and hence of sources) visible to the mediator. Once the set of wrappers forming the mediator's domain is selected, the KM module send them a meta-data request message. These messages are interpreted by the wrappers, which then query the local Data Dictionaries and send back scheme information to the mediator. Mediators are multi-threaded and implements a time-out strategy to recognize a communication failure with wrapper agents. The receipt of meta-data information automatically starts the construction of the knowledge base. A maintenance method allows the mediator to periodically ask the wrappers, in order to know about some changes in source structure. Figure 3 shows the mediator management window, where both the intension and extension of concepts in the hierarchy can be analyzed, as well as the set of messages exchanged by the mediator with other agents.

The QM receives queries from the user agent. It exploits the knowledge base in order to perform query reformulation, interacting with the user through the user agent when necessary. Reformulated queries are then sent to the relevant wrappers, and answers collected and sent back to the user. Figure 4 shows a snapshot of a system-user interaction session. The query starts with the user term *subject*, which is assumed to be a characterizing term of any artistic production (the equivalent of sources term *type*). In response, the system proposes a set of terms. After an unsatisfactory search continued with the term *author*, the user

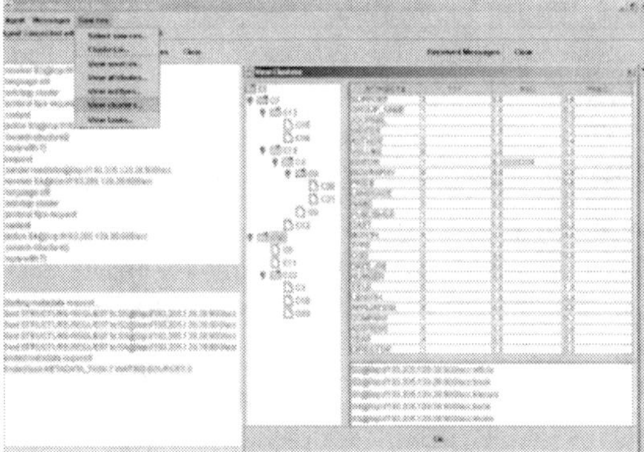

Fig. 3. The mediator management window and the induced concept hierarchy

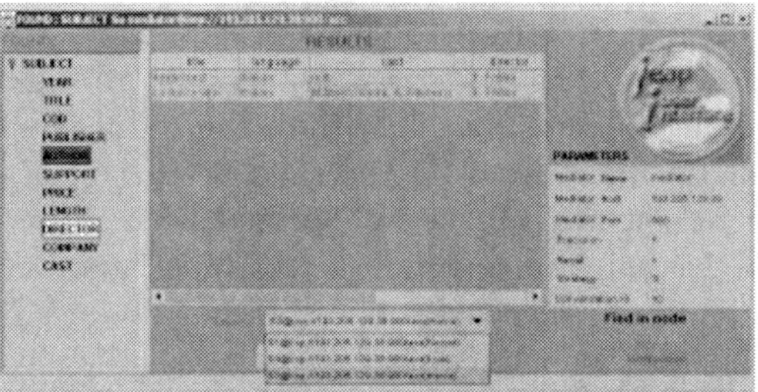

Fig. 4. Results after system-user interaction

back-tracks the search, and tries the term *director*. This produces as answer all and only information about artistic productions.

5 Conclusions

The paper presented a multi-agent system for information gathering in open environments. The multi-agent architecture enables transparency and interoperability in the following ways: (1) as a FIPA compliant multi-agent architecture, it facilitates the interoperability between FIPA software agents registered at any platform; (2) as it implements a mediator model, it guarantees logical heterogeneity transparency, through the wrappers. This means that differences in data models and languages for the various sources are hidden to the user. It also guarantees conceptual heterogeneity transparency, since the mediators maintain for the user an unified view of the conceptual structure of different sources, so that the user need not to have a conceptual scheme knowledge, but only a generic domain knowledge; (3) the introduction of user agents allows to enhance transparency. In fact, adapting to the user vocabulary, it defines an user-tuned interface. In the present implementation, the adaptation is simply a set of manually defined mappings. Future developments will endow the agent with the capability to automatically learn these mappings. Enhancements also include the learning of other user profile characteristics, in order to automatically set query constraints, and to select the appropriate mediators, exploiting the information collected by the DF and its own information.

Beside transparency, characterizing features of the architecture are the capability of managing approximate queries, and the capability to guide the user in the progressive specification of its needs. These features are the result of a novel approach to knowledge representation and management at the mediator, which allows to merge the notions of approximate query processing and the notion of conceptual query processing. This is done by relating quality measures for approximate queries answering, like precision and recall, to concept abstraction, which allows to devise strategies to bind query terms to concepts at query processing time, rather than at knowledge definition time, giving the user a better capability to specify its information needs. Of course, the effectiveness of the whole system strongly relies on the quality of the generated ontology. Some preliminary evaluation of the performance of the EC^3 criterion have been presented in [8,9]. Furhtermore, it is known that, independently from the specific algorithm adopted, a semantic clustering procedure would benefit from the exploitation of more semantic information. In particular, we plan to study the exploitation of application contexts.

References

[1] Abasolo, G.M., Gomez, M.: MELISA. An ontology-based agent for information retrieval in medicine. In *Proc. ECDL 2000 Workshop on the Semantic Web*, Lisbona, Portugal, Sep. 2000.

[2] Braga, R.M.M., Werner, C.M.L., Mattoso, M.: Using ontologies for domain information retrieval . In AAAI Press, editor, *Proc. 11th Int. Work. on Database and Expert Systems Applications*, pages 836 – 840, 2000.

[3] Bright, M.W., Hurson, A.R., Pakzad, S.: Automatic Resolution of Semantic Heterogeneity in Multidatabases. *ACM Trans. on Databases Systems*, June 1994.

[4] Castano, S., De Antonellis, V.: A Schema Analysis and Reconciliation Tool Environment for Heterogeneous Databases. In *Proc. Int. Symp. on Database Engineering and Applications (IDEAS'99)*, pages 53–62, 1999.

[5] Cazalens,S., Desmontils, E., Jacquin, C., Lamarre, P.: A Web site indexing process for an Internet information retrieval agent system. In *Proc. 1st International Conference on Web Information Systems Engineering*, pages 254 – 258 vol.1, 2000.

[6] Chang, C.K., Garcia-Molina, H.: Approximate Query Translation Across Heterogeneous Information Sources. In *26th International Conference on Very Large Databases (VLDB'00)*, pages 566–577, Cairo, Egypt, 2000.

[7] Chu, W.W., Yang, H.,Chiang, K., Minock, M., Chow, G., Larson, C. : CoBase: A Scalable and Extensible Cooperative Information System. *Jour. of Int. Info. Sys.*, 6(1), 1996.

[8] Diamantini, C., Panti, M. : A Conceptual Indexing Method for Content-Based Retrieval. In R.R. Wagner A.M. Tjoa, A. Cammelli, editor, *Proc. 10th Int. Work. on Database and Expert Systems Applications*, pages 192–197, Firenze, Italy, Sept. 1999. IEEE Press.

[9] Diamantini, C., Panti, M.: Exploiting Hierarchical Global Views for Query Reformulation. In *Proc. 3rd IEEE Know. and Data Eng. Exch. Workshop (KDEX'99)*, Chicago, U.S.A., Nov. 1999. IEEE Press.

[10] Ellmer, E., Huemer, C., Merkl, D., Pernul, G.: Neural Network Technology to Support View Integration. In M. Papazoglou, editor, *Proc. 14th International Conference on Object-Oriented and Entity-Relationship Modeling (OOER95), LNCS n. 1021*, pages 181–190, 1985.

[11] Fensel, D., Horrocks, I., Van Harmelen, F., Decker, S., Erdmann, M., Klein, M.: OIL in a Nutshell. In R. Dieng et al., editor, *Proc. of the European Knowledge Acquisition Conference (EKAW-2000), LNAI.* Springer-Verlag, Oct. 2000.

[12] Garcia-Molina, H., Papakonstantinou, Y., Quass, D., Rajaraman, A., Sagiv, Y., Ullman, J.V., Vassalos, Widom,J.: The TSIMMIS approach to mediation: data models and languages. *Journ. of Int. Info. Sys.*, 8:117–132, 1997.

[13] Gravano, L., Papakonstantinou, Y.: Mediating and Metasearching on the Internet. *Bulletin of the Technical Committee on Data Engineering*, 21(2):28–36, June 1998.

[14] Guarino, N., Masolo, C., Vetere, G.: OntoSeek: content-based access to the Web. *IEEE Intelligent Systems*, 14(3):70–80, 1999.

[15] Gruber, T: The role of a common ontology in achieving sharable, reusable knowledge bases. In *Proc. 2nd Int. Conf. on Principles of Knowledge Representation and Reasoning*, Cambridge, CA, 1991.

[16] Li, W., Clifton, C.: Semantic Integration in Heterogeneous Databases Using Neural Networks. In *Proc. of the 20th Int. Conf. on Very Large Databases (VLDB'94)*, Santiago, Chile, September 1994.

[17] Ram, S.: Special issue on heterogenous distributed database systems. *IEEE Computer Magazine*, 24(12), December 1991.

[18] Scheuermann, P., Li, W.S., Clifton, C.: Dynamic Integration and Query Processing with Ranked Role Sets. In *Proc. 1st IFCIS Int. Conf. on Coop. Info. Sys. (CoopIS'96)*, pages 157–166, Brussel, Belgium, June 19–21 1996. IEEE Press.

[19] Sheth, A., Larson, J.: Federated database systems for managing distributed, heterogeneous, and autonomous databases. *ACM Computing Surveys*, 22(3):183–236, 1990.

[20] Staab, S., Erdmann, M., Maedche, A., Decker, S.: An Extensible Approach for Modeling Ontologies in RDF(S) . In *Proc. of ECDL 2000 Workshop on the Semantic Web*, Lisbona, Portugal, Sep. 2000.

[21] Visser, P.R.S., Jones, D.M., Beer, M.D., Bench-Capon, T.J.M, Diaz, B.M., Shave, M.J.R: Resolving Ontological Heterogeneity in the KRAFT Project. In A.M. Tjoa T. Bench-Capon, G. Soda, editor, *Proc. 10th Int. Conf. on Database and Expert Systems Applications (DEXA'99)*, pages 668–677, Florence, Italy, Sept. 1999. Springer-Verlag.

[22] Van Rijsbergen, C.J.: *Information Retrieval.* Butterworths, 1997.

[23] Wiederhold, G.: Mediators in the Architecture of Future Information Systems. *IEEE Computer Magazine*, 25:38–49, March 1992.

[24] Yu, C., Sun, W., Dao, S., Keirsey, D.: Determining Relationships Among Attributes for Inter-Operability of Multi-Database Systems. In *Proc. 1st Int. Work. on Interoperability in Multidatabase Sys.*, Los Alamitos, CA, 1991. IEEE Press.

Mining Astronomical Data

Bruno Voisin[1,2]

[1] SIS Computer Science Team, Université de Toulon et du Var, Avenue de l'Université, BP 132, 83957 La Garde Cedex, FRANCE
[2] Laboratoire d'Astronomie Spatiale, Traverse du Siphon, Les Trois Lucs, 13012 Marseille, FRANCE
voisin@univ-tln.fr

Abstract. Astronomy is among those sciences that, with time and technology, has found itself producing more and more data. Now, dealing with so many data is a major problem, and standard query techniques become insufficient. This paper raises the relevance of data mining techniques in such cases, through a complete example of application to real astronomical data. The approach, the implementation and the results are analysed. The stake of such works is to give modern sciences a new way to use data, while keeping concerned with the fact that the majority of users are non-experts in knowledge engineering.

1 Introduction

With the improvements of instrumentation and storage technologies, astronomy is a science that produces more and more data, and lacks an efficient way to use it. This is why astronomical conferences like *Mining the Sky*[1] or *Astronomical Data Analysis*[2] have recently been organised to discuss of new techniques to deal with stellar data. Knowledge discovery in databases (KDD)[FPSSU96], and more precisely data mining, deal with methods and heuristics that allow to explore massive amounts of data, and to discover the 'laws' that rule the dataset. Such techniques may prove extremely useful for sciences, such as astronomy, that generate increasing amounts of data.

This paper presents the results and the teachings of the use of knowledge discovery techniques on astronomical data. After the presentation of the context (astronomy) and the data main properties (continuous and heterogeneous), we will focus on a particular problematic, *the cross-referencing*, which aims at discover, among a great number of light sources, which ones are produced by a same stellar entity. We will show the limits of "standard" data analysis, which consists into the comparison of a few common attributes : coordinates. We will then present the KDD approach we implemented, using decision trees, its results, and we will discuss its benefits.

This paper is organised as follows : section 2 gives prominence to astronomical data characteristics, and the discovery challenge to deal with. Section 3 briefly

[1] http://ibm-2.mpa-garching.mpg.de/~cosmo/
[2] http://www.stat.uconn.edu/~patrick/imsdec00/imsdec00/node47.html

H.C. Mayr et al. (Eds.): DEXA 2001, LNCS 2113, pp. 621–631, 2001.

describes the actual solution used by the astronomers, and shows its limits. Section 4 presents our KDD approach, its generic principles, and its specificities in this applicative context. Results obtained are then discussed. Section 5 discusses about other existing KDD approaches, some similar, and some showing nice research perspectives we intend to focus on. Section 6 concludes.

2 Problematic

Data: light and stars. Data comes from the processing of sky images and are in a table format. A standard astronomical image is a dark photographic plate with a lot of light sources of different sizes and shapes, many of them produced by stars, galaxies and other stellar entities. Other light sources are nothing but noise due to the physical photographic process. This is very noisy data, due to telescopes optical disturbances, and the lot of stellar entities that can be found in the sky. While it is possible to recognise the brightest stars from an astronomical survey to another, this is harder for the darker ones, as there are a lot of them, and their coordinates may vary depending on the survey.

Multi-wavelength: Optical $\neq$ Ultraviolet. While astronomy traditionally involved working in the *optical* wavelength (human visible light), technological improvements allowed works in other wavelengths. It soon became interesting to study the seeming of some particular stellar entities under different wavelength. This is called *multi-wavelength* astronomy. In our context, data come from an ultraviolet wavelength experiment. It gives informations to astronomers, which allow them to study galaxy formation. However, since ultraviolet surveys are not so common, differences between optical and ultraviolet images of the same location render it hard to correlate them. Indeed : morphological differences, brightness variations and different image processing techniques make it hard to compare light sources from two different wavelengths (Fig 1). Therefore, the task is to establish whether a light source on a survey corresponds to another source, on another survey. This difficulty comes from many causes such as telescopes different resolutions, telescopes optical distortions, atmospheric disturbances, and morphological differences between optical and ultraviolet seeming of a same stellar entity.

Problem: find who is who. This task is called *cross-referencing*. It consists in correlating one of the optical catalogs of known stellar entities with the list of light sources observed in a recent survey, that we want to identify. Traditionally done on the comparison of light sources coordinates, the resulting associations of light sources get disturbed by the noisy nature of astronomical data. This results in many "possible" associations of light sources. It is up to the astronomer to pick "by hand" those he estimates to be the most probable. But it sometimes happens that none of the light sources of a survey A corresponds better than another to a light source of a survey B. This is the typical case when dealing with surveys in different wavelengths. This is even worse since several light sources in a wavelength may result in only one big light source in another wavelength. That's when morphological similarities cease to help cross-referencing. This paper focus

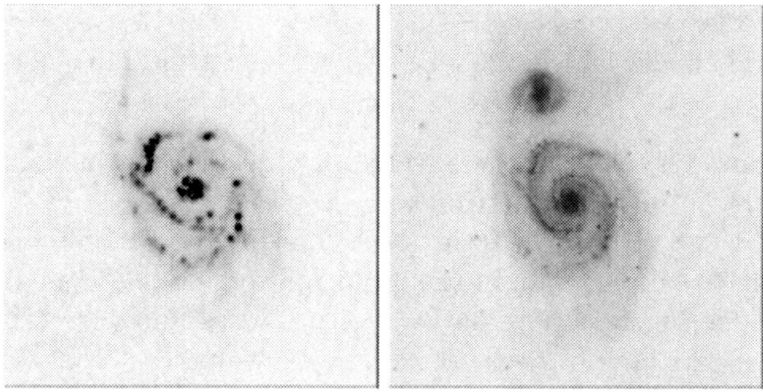

Fig. 1. UV and Optical seeming of the M51 galaxy

on those problems which make cross-referencing a hard task, and thus, do not ease its automation. Our context is the correlation of optical data of the DPOSS catalog with ultraviolet data of the FOCA[3] experiment.

3 Standard Approach

Classical cross-referencing is done by proximity search, that is : associate to each of the new survey light source those of the reference catalog whose coordinates are the closest. This is a classical data analysis, consisting in the comparison of two tuples, on the basis of their only comparable attributes.

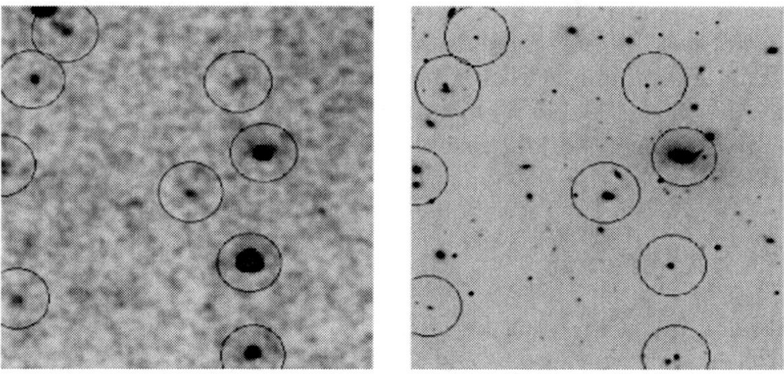

Fig. 2. A FOCA ultraviolet image and its DPOSS optical counterpart

First, the (x, y) pixel coordinates on the source image are converted into (α, δ) standard astronomical coordinates. Then, all catalog entries in an r radius around this point are considered matching candidates (Fig. 2), r depending on the optical particularities of the telescopes which produced the surveys. Finally,

[3] http://www.astrsp-mrs.fr/private/foca/

if a more precise answer is needed, it comes to the astronomer to study the candidates and choose which one seems to be the better. This method has several advantages :

- except some very special cases, celestial objects don't move, and their coordinates are an invariant attribute,
- intuitively, two objects with the same coordinates are only one entity, unless they come to be perfectly in the alignment of the telescope observing line,
- even considering telescope optical disturbances and correcting them, these are light algorithms in terms of computer resources.

However, distance-only research has several limitations :

- optical observing instrument disturbances may never be fully corrected. So, every coordinates contain computation errors. Worse, optical disturbances are not uniform on a single image,
- when dealing with complex morphology objects such as galaxies, coordinates are less significant, since they only correspond to an *approximative* center of the object,
- differences in resolution between image and catalog will augment the number of possible associations between light sources. In our case, FOCA is a really low level resolution dataset compared to the DPOSS survey (Fig. 2),
- in the case of several matching candidates, it is also possible for the studied light source to be the combination of more than one of its matching candidates. Choosing one of the candidates as the "true" one is then unacceptable.

It is noticeable that these problems are quite hard to resolve, and so, it relies on astronomers themselves to choose among the possible associations which ones are the most probable. Due to the great number of light sources in the sky, such a work is not possible on a large scale such as the terabytes produced by modern surveys. As an example, it took a full month to establish cross-references on a single FOCA image. These observations show that coordinates are insufficient for cross-referencing celestial objects, especially in the case of multiple matching candidates.

4 KDD Approach

The classical approach being insufficient, as we have a large amount of data attributes unused, we came to consider a knowledge discovery oriented cross-referencing. The goal was to explore the many attributes of stellar entities to obtain a more precise cross-referencing process, thus reducing the manual work needed.

4.1 Generic Principle

Considering the coordinates to be an insufficient attribute in the field of cross-referencing, an intuitive method would be to compare every attributes of the studied light source to the reference catalog entries attributes.

While this may seem easy, it is not in the case of different wavelength readings, since attributes computed from ultraviolet surveys differ greatly from the ones of optical surveys. And as the commonly known reference catalogs are processed from optical wavelength surveys, this implies many difficulties for cross-referencing FOCA's ultraviolet light sources.

The search for links between ultraviolet/optical attributes is even one main goal of cross-referencing, as it allows a better understanding of stellar entities properties, for it is obvious that there must be a link between visible and ultraviolet counterparts of a same celestial entity. The problem is to find it.

The main goal of KDD is basically to discover rules into huge amount of data[Man97][FHS96]. There are two main approaches to achieve this : **unsupervised discovery** is done through heuristics of data exploration, in order to find all rules that can be found in the data. This is a search without a priori. **Supervised discovery** is derived from AI and machine learning techniques. It aims at finding a smaller set of particular rules, from a smaller "learning set" of data.

In our context, we aim at establishing whether two light sources - one optical, the other ultraviolet - come from a same stellar entity. Let X and Y respectively be the optical and ultraviolet light sources and $\{X\}, \{Y\}$ their attributes, we seek f_i rules like : $f_i(\{X\}, \{Y\}) = \{0, 1\}$ so that $f_i = 1$ if X and Y come from the same entity, else $f_i = 0$. Due to the precise goal of our rules, a supervised discovery approach seems appropriate.

4.2 Decision Trees

Our work relies on decision trees [Qui86][Qui93], a supervised discovery technique. This choice has two main reasons :

- decision trees are easy to compute. One of the goal of this work, in an astronomical context, is to find out whether data mining could help processing astronomical data. Quick implementation of decision trees allowed fast results and thus confirmed the interest of such methods to astronomers,
- decision trees are easy to understand, especially for a non-expert user. While it is nice to find knowledge, it is better to be able to understand it. In our case, it is extremely important for astronomers to be able to understand the results of the mining process.

A decision tree is a tuple classifying graph. The root of the tree "contains" all the tuples of the dataset, and classify them into the set of its children nodes, depending on the value of one particular attributes. Each of those nodes will subsequently classify the tuples it contains into its own children nodes on the basis of another attribute. Such classification aims to create an arborescent structure, whose leaves will contain only tuples whose *class attribute* has the same value for all tuples in a single leaf. The choice of the class attribute depends which kind of knowledge is seeked. It is therefore possible to build a decision tree for each attribute of data.

Then, for a tuple whose class attribute is unknown, we can establish a path in the tree, starting from the root, and descending into children nodes depending on the values of attributes of our particular tuple. The final leaf we will obtain will so give us a probable value for the class attribute.

So, we can establish that each path from the root of the tree to a leaf corresponds to a rule of the dataset, which allow the prediction of the class attribute.

4.3 Learning and Inducing

In order to build a decision tree, we need to select, for each node of the tree, which attribute/value pair leads to a better class attribute classification of the tuples. This is done through the informational measure of *entropy*, introduced by Shannon[SW49]. It is basically a measure of "chaos" into the data. The chaos here, means that we have tuples with many different values of the class attribute. So, the more a node will be "pure" (ie. contains only tuples with the same value of the class attribute), the lesser its entropy will be, with a value of 0 for a pure leaf. On the contrary, a node containing n tuples of each possible class attribute value would have a maximum entropy.

This measure permits the comparison between a node's entropy and the one of its children set. The difference between these measures gives a value called *informational gain*. The more important this value is, the lesser the entropy of the children is in comparison to their father's, the more powerful is the classification obtained.

Due to the continuous nature of most attributes we had to deal with in the astronomical context, our algorithm builds binary trees, maximising the informational gain at each level using Shannon entropy measurement.

The dataset we use consists of more than 1500 ultraviolet/visible light sources couples. Each couple is defined by over 40 information fields describing its two seemings. These couples were generated by a standard cross-referencing method, based on light sources proximity. Thus, the set of "good" couples (those for which the two seemings come from a same stellar entity) is a subset of the learning set we built.

Still, in order for the trees to be computed, we needed to classify these couples, determining which among them are "good", and which are "bad". This goodness will be our class attribute. Figure 3 shows the couples distribution depending on distance between their two seemings (ultraviolet/optical) :

- the abscissa axis indicates the angular distance in seconds between the ultraviolet and the visible counterparts of a couple,
- the ordinate axis indicates the number of couples in the learning set.
- the Space Density function represents the average number of optical light sources to be found "at random" in a circle of radius x''. Each of these light sources randomly present will generate a wrong couple.

The distribution and the space density show that in a radius of $3''$ around an ultraviolet light source, the probability for an optical light source to be found

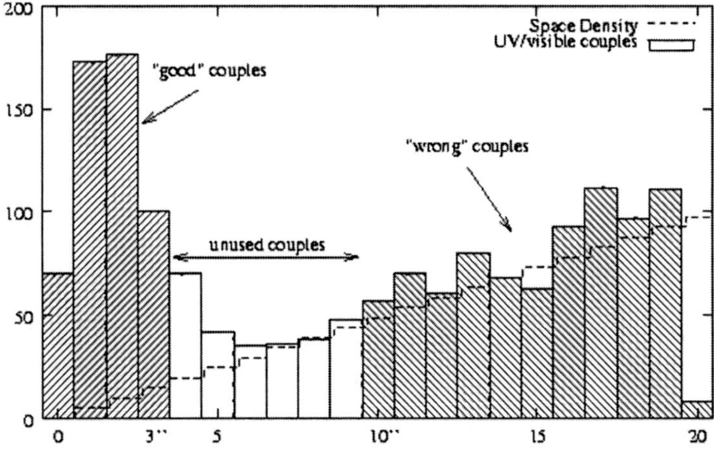

Fig. 3. Learning set distribution, sorted by counterparts distance on the abscissa axis.

"at random" is very feeble. Most of the optical light sources found will then probably be counterparts of the ultraviolet source. In a radius of 10″ and more, it is the contrary : the number of optical light sources found corresponds to the number we should find because of the space density. Between 3″ and 10″, it is hard to establish whether couples are probably good or wrong.

In order to compute our decision tree, after discussion with the astronomers, it was chosen to consider only couples whose seemings are distant by less than 3″ or more than 10″. The first are classified as good, and the others as wrong. A good couple means that its two seemings (light sources) represent the same celestial entity.

Of course, this method has a side effect : some real good couples are classified as wrong, and some real wrong ones are classified as good. The consequences of this biased learning set are discussed in section 4.4. Figure 4 show one of the trees obtained.

It is to notice that none of the position/coordinates/distance attribute has been used for building the tree, since we look for links between data, other than distance between light sources.

FOCA/DPOSS couples have more than 60 attributes, of which more than 20 are coordinates-like. This leaves us with 40 attributes to build the decision tree. Table 1 describes the ones used in the example. Let's notice that the *AreaJ* attribute, which was found to be of great significance, was a surprise for astronomers, which intuitively would have used magnitude to classify candidates. So this parameter is in a way the "gold nugget" of our mining process...

4.4 Validating

Statistical evaluation. Accuracy of the decision trees was measured through a *cross-validation* process. It consists in selecting 10 random samples of the

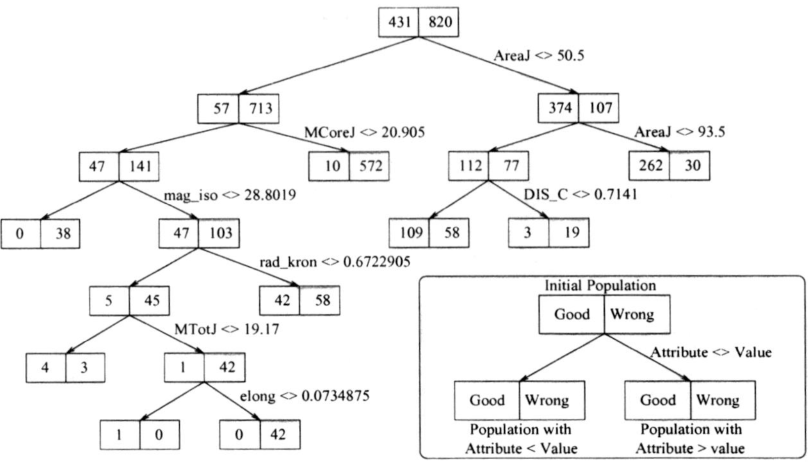

Fig. 4. A decision tree for FOCA / DPOSS cross-referencing

Table 1. Definition of the attributes used in the decision tree of figure 4

AreaJ	Pixel-related size of the light spot on the POSS image
DIS_C	Distance to the center of the image (implies much more noise)
MCoreJ	Visible magnitude of the light spot core
mag_iso	Ultraviolet 'isophotal' magnitude
rad_kron	Radius covered by the ultraviolet light source
MTotJ	Overall visible magnitude
elong	Computed elongation of elliptic light sources

dataset, each one being 80% of the full dataset. Trees are generated, being each time tested on the 20% remaining data. The average accuracy obtained (Table 2) gives an idea of the efficiency of trees that may be generated on data.

Learning from wrong. These statistical evaluations are encouraging. Moreover, figure 5 shows the results of a study of the distribution of couples classified as "wrong" by the decision tree. It shows the number of such couples depending of the distance between the couple's two seemings.

Let's observe three particularities of this graphic :

- the number of wrong couples nicely correlates with the number that should be produced at random due to space density. This is even more interesting since space density *was not known* of the data mining algorithm. This is a discovered information,
- a small number of good couples of the learning set (seemings distanced by less than 3″) are classified as wrong by the tree,
- a small number of wrong couples of the learning set (seemings distanced by over 10″) are classified as good by the tree.

Table 2. This table shows results of validation tests of trees built from data of a FOCA/DPOSS subset (rows), and tested on other sets (rows). Q and M are respectively two different telescopes used in the FOCA experiment.

	Q030	Q067	Q089	M030	M067	Average
Q030	91%	87%	80%	85%	92%	87%
Q067	88%	93%	83%	86%	91%	88%
Q089	87%	90%	91%	86%	90%	89%
M030	81%	76%	70%	84%	87%	80%
M067	78%	78%	70%	80%	91%	79%
All	89%	92%	88%	86%	89%	89%

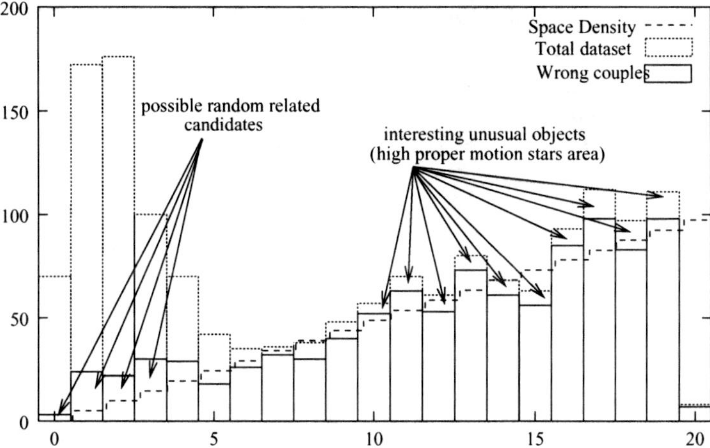

Fig. 5. Distribution of "wrong" tree-classified couples, depending of the distance between each couple optical/ultraviolet seemings.

While the first observation confirms the tree accuracy, the two others show the deficiencies of the automatic classification. But let's have a closer look at these errors. The first set of errors contains "a priori" good couples that are left in a tree leaf containing mostly wrong couples. So these "a priori" good couples mostly look like they are wrong, even if their seemings are very close each other.

This turned to be a precious information for astronomers. Indeed, if such couples necessarily exists, due to space density, it is impossible to plot them simply by seemings distance observation (standard cross-referencing). This is a new information provided by our approach.

Moreover, the other set of badly classified couples are "a priori" bad couples that the tree finds mostly good-looking. These are ideal subjects for studies, as if the tree turned out to be right (the two light sources of the couple coming from the same stellar entity), this would imply very interesting properties of an unusual stellar entity, like for example *high proper motion* stars.

Of course, the tree should not be considered as omniscient, and most of its classification errors are due to the noisy and imperfect learning set. Anyway, its deficiencies allow to plot very reduced interesting subsets of data, easier to work on for the astronomers than the full, unprocessed dataset.

5 Related Works

While in our applicative context, the discovery process used is based upon decision trees, there are many others data mining techniques. We will here discuss of our approach in comparison of some of these, in order to show their similarities/differences, and their usefulness for astronomical data.

Neural networks are based upon a fixed topology network, whose entries corresponds to the attributes of the tuples of the learning set. The network returns a value basically equivalent to the class attribute we define when using decision trees. The learning set is used to compute the network result for each tuple, and each time, weights changes on the network nodes lead to a reduction of the errors, and finally, to a nice prediction network for the class attribute. This is basically the same kind of knowledge obtained by decision trees. However, it is harder to extract rules from the final net, and so it seems less fitted to our context, where astronomers had to be able to understand intuitively the knowledge discovered. This is why, despise the neural net increased accuracy with continuous data, we chose to work with decision trees.

Frequent itemsets are one of the most known data mining technique. It is based upon a huge dataset containing a number of variable length tuples, each one containing a finite number of discrete items. The algorithms aim to explore the dataset to extract all itemsets frequently found, which is algorithmically challenging, due to the size of datasets used. `Apriori`[AS94] and `Close` [Pas00] are typical examples of such algorithms. But the continuous nature of astronomical data doesn't allowed an easy use of such techniques.

Genetic algorithms[Dav91] may lead to an interesting unsupervised discovery technique [RS94]. Basically a problem optimisation heuristic, genetic algorithms imply to model all problem possible solutions into a data vector. Then, the algorithm generates random solutions into a *population* and evolves it according to Darwinian evolution theories. Solution vectors are modified, mixed, and the final population is as close as possible of an optimal solution. A correct modelling of a "data rule" would allow a genetic approach of discovery. The algorithm would then explore data, and extract the best rules that could be found. This is one of our future prospects.

6 Conclusion

With the increasing, huge amount of data produced by astronomy, it is becoming crucial to provide the astronomers a new way to process and explore information. Huge datasets of noisy, continuous data, and non-experts users in knowledge engineering thus characterise an original domain where the discovery of numeric rules could lead to a better understanding of our universe.

In this context, we presented a knowledge discovery work upon astronomical data, that is part of a Ph.D. thesis. We first described data and their linked problematic. Then, we studied a KDD approach, based upon decision trees, and shown its benefits towards a standard data analysis process, even in a non-discrete data context, "a priori" not favourable to data mining. An important benefit of decision trees in this context was to provide an *understandable* and *usable* technique for astronomers, even though few trained to knowledge engineering.

Results obtained, being statistically validated and encouraging, are actually studied in depth by astronomers, that discover a "global view" of their own data, thus allowing new studies. Genericity of the process should also result soon in its application to other astronomical problematics, like *redshift*.

In parallel to these works and the development of the discovery software *Mélusine*[4], studies are made on a genetic approach of unsupervised discovery for astronomical data.

References

[AS94] R. Agrawal and R. Srikant. Fast algorithms for mining association rules in large databases. In *Proc. VLDB conf.*, pages 478–499, September 1994.

[Dav91] Lawrence Davis. *Handbook of Genetic Algorithms.* Van Nostrand Reinhold (New York), 1991.

[FHS96] Usama Fayyad, David Haussler, and Paul Storloz. Kdd for science data analysis: Issues and examples. In *Proceedings of the Second International Conference on Knowledge Discovery and Data Mining (KDD-96).* AAAI Press, August 1996.

[FPSSU96] U. M. Fayyad, G. Piatetsky-Shapiro, P. Smyth, and R. Uthurusamy. *Advances in Knowledge Discovery and Data Mining.* AAAI Press, 1996.

[Man97] Heikki Mannila. Methods and problems in data mining. In Afrati and P. Kolaitis (ed.), editors, *International Conference on Database Theory.* Springer-Verlag, January 1997.

[Pas00] Nicolas Pasquier. Extraction de bases pour les règles d'association à partir des itemsets fermés fréquents. In Inforsid, editor, *Actes du XVIIIème congrès Inforsid*, pages 56–77, Mai 2000.

[Qui86] J.R. Quinlan. Induction of decision trees. *Machine Learning*, 1:81–106, 1986.

[Qui93] J.R. Quinlan. *C4.5 : Programs for Machine Learning.* Morgan Kaufmann, 1993.

[RS94] Nicholas J. Radcliffe and Patrick D. Surry. Co-operation through hierarchical competition in genetic data mining. In *Parallel Problem Solving From Nature*, 1994.

[SW49] Claude E. Shannon and Warren Weaver. *The mathematical theory of communication.* University of Illinois Press, 1949.

[4] available at http://sis.univ-tln.fr/˜voisin/melusine.html

Integration of WWW Applications Based on Extensible XML Query and Processing Languages

Norihide Shinagawa[1], Kouichi Kuragaki[2], and Hiroyuki Kitagawa[3]

[1] Center for Environmental Remote Sensing, Chiba University
1-33 Yayoi, Inage, Chiba 263-8522, Japan
siena@cr.chiba-u.ac.jp
[2] Doctoral Program in Engineering, University of Tsukuba*
[3] Institute of Information Sciences and Electronics, University of Tsukuba
1-1-1 Tennohdai, Tsukuba, Ibaraki 305-8573, Japan
{kitagawa,kuragaki}@kde.is.tsukuba.ac.jp

Abstract. The rapid advance of the Internet has brought with it a variety of WWW applications. Integration of these WWW applications, which implies development of meta level applications (shortened to meta-applications), is an important research issue. In the Internet context, XML has attracted a great deal of attention and will be used as a standard data format in WWW applications. This paper proposes a scheme to develop meta-applications on top of XML-based WWW applications. Our approach uses an XML query language called X^2QL to manipulate XML instances. X^2QL features the inclusion of user-defined foreign functions so that we can define functions specific to WWW application integration, such as submitting forms and following hyperlinks. In addition, we propose X^2PL, which is an extensible XML processing language. In X^2PL, processing flows composed of embedded X^2QL queries are specified. This paper also describes an integration example and the development of a prototype system.

1 Introduction

The rapid advance of the Internet has brought with it a variety of WWW applications (shortened to *applications*). These applications include WWW page search services and electronic commerce applications. Integration of such WWW applications, which implies the development of meta level applications (shortened to *meta-applications*), is an important research issue [1] [2] [3] [4].

In the Internet context, XML has attracted a great deal of attention. XML has been widely used to code WWW pages and application data. It will soon become a standard data format for representing data exchanged with WWW applications.

* Current Affiliation: SECOM CO., LTD.

H.C. Mayr et al. (Eds.): DEXA 2001, LNCS 2113, pp. 632–645, 2001.

This paper proposes a scheme to develop meta-applications on top of XML-based WWW applications. Our approach uses XML as a canonical data representation form, and an XML query language called X^2QL [5] is employed to manipulate XML instances. Query expressions are non-procedural and declarative. Therefore, they are easier to develop and maintain than programming language code. However, XML query languages are usually not powerful enough to deliver complete meta-application specifications. In addition to XML data selection and restructuring supported by XML query languages, we need (1) to specify interactions with WWW sites, such as sending requests through forms and receiving responses, and (2) to specify control and processing flows in meta-applications. X^2QL is an extensible XML query language, and features the inclusion of user-defined foreign functions [5]. Requirement (1) is met by defining functions specific to WWW application integration, such as submitting forms and following hyperlinks based on this extensibility. To meet requirement (2), we propose X^2PL, which is an extensible XML processing language. In X^2PL, processing flows composed of embedded X^2QL queries are specified. The role of X^2PL for X^2QL is somewhat similar to that of a language like PL/SQL and Transact-SQL for SQL in the context of RDB application development. This paper also describes an integration example and the development of a prototype system.

The remaining part of this paper is organized as follows. Section 2 shows an example scenario integrating two applications. Section 3 explains X^2QL, which is an extensible XML query language developed by our research group. Section 4 explains X^2PL, which is an extensible XML processing language proposed in this paper. Section 5 shows example descriptions in X^2PL. Section 6 describes the architecture of the X^2PL processing system. Section 7 mentions related work. Finally, Section 8 summarizes the main points of this paper.

2 Integration Example

This section presents an example of application integration. First, we show underlying applications, their input forms, and their resulting XML instances. We then show a scenario integrating those applications.

2.1 WWW Applications

Suppose the following two applications: an online book search site such as amazon.com and an OPAC (Online Public Access Catalog) site of a library. Their input pages include forms written in XHTML, and output pages are written in XML. Both the input and output pages of most applications are presently written in HTML. However, they will soon come to be written in XML, so we can suppose the above situation.

In the online book search site, we input keywords to search books using the form with an `input` element whose `name` attribute value is `keys`. Suppose the `input` is a child of the `form` element. The result is provided by an XML instance whose DTD is shown in Figure 1. This includes at most N `book` elements and an optional `anchor` element. A `book` consists of its `title`, `author` and `price`, and an `anchor` describes the URL of the page listing the remaining books.

```
<!DOCTYPE result [
<!ELEMENT result (book*,anchor?)>
<!ELEMENT book   (title,
                  author,price)>
<!-- the content models of the other
      element types are #PCDATA -->
]>
```

Fig. 1. DTD of the book search result.

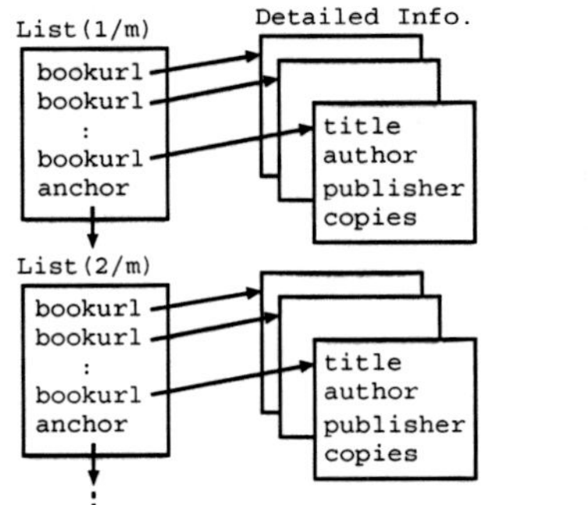

Fig. 2. Structure among result pages.

```
<!DOCTYPE result [
<!ELEMENT result  (bookurl*,
                   anchor?)>
<!ELEMENT bookurl #PCDATA>
<!ELEMENT anchor  #PCDATA>
]>
```

Fig. 3. DTD of the OPAC result.

```
<!DOCTYPE result [
<!ELEMENT result  (title,author,
                   publisher,copies)>
<!ELEMENT publisher (address,
                     name,date)>
<!ELEMENT copies  (copy+)>
<!ELEMENT copy    (place,state)>
<!-- the content models of the other
      element types are #PCDATA -->
]>
```

Fig. 4. DTD of detailed information.

On the other hand, in the OPAC site of the library, we must give at least one of a book title, an author name and keywords using the form with `input` elements whose `name` attribute values are `title`, `author` and `keys`, respectively. The result is also a set of XML instances, as shown in Figure 2, whose DTD are shown in Figures 3 and 4. It includes at most M `bookurl` elements and an optional `anchor` element linking to the remaining book list. A `bookurl` describes the URL of the corresponding book information, and the page consists of `title`, `author`, `publisher` and `copies` elements. A `copies` includes `copy` elements, which contain information about the corresponding copies. A `place` shows where the book is located, and `state` shows whether it is on loan.

2.2 WWW Application Integration Scenario

Suppose we want to know if published books related to certain keywords are available in the library. To accomplish this scenario, we should perform the following tasks: First, we search books by the online book search site. We then check each book by the library OPAC site. Finally, we collect useful information from detailed pages linked from the result. In these steps, we should manipulate input and output data manually. This becomes unrealistic when the intermediate result is huge.

2.3 Meta-application

Developing a meta-application makes it possible to automate most of the above steps. Individual users can then get the final result by giving only the first keywords. The meta-application that makes our example reality is shown in Figure 5. In our context, the meta-application sends requests to and receives responses from underlying applications, and selects and restructures resulting XML instances. These are coded in X^{2}QL, which is explained in Section 3. Additionally, the meta-application controls the processing flows. It is coded in X^{2}PL, which is explained in Section 4.

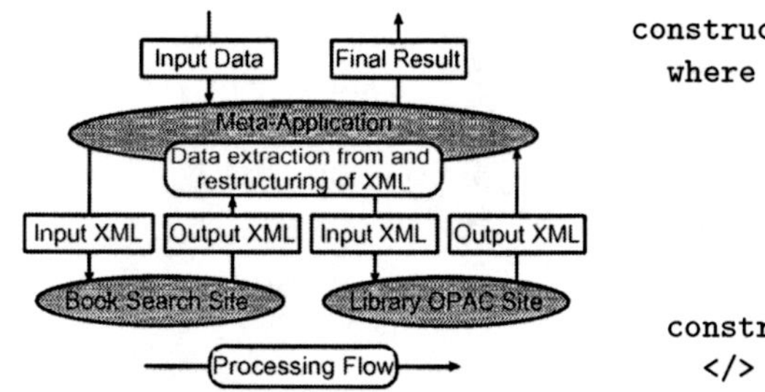

Fig. 5. Example of application integration.

```
construct <booklist>
  where    <result>
             <book>
               <title/>  element_as $t
               <author/> element_as $a
             </>
           </> in "BookstoreResult.xml"
  construct <book> $t $a </>
    </>
```

Fig. 6. Example of an X^{2}QL query.

3 X^{2}QL: Extensible XML Query Language

X^{2}QL [5] is based on XML-QL [6]. However, X^{2}QL features user-defined foreign functions, whose implementation is written in general programming languages. First, we give the syntax of X^{2}QL in Subsection 3.1. We then explain foreign functions in Subsection 3.2.

3.1 Query Syntax

The basic syntax of an X^{2}QL query is as shown below.

> **where** *patterns* **in** *source* [, *patterns* **in** *source*]* [, *predicate*]*
> **construct** *each output structure*

`Where` clause binds variables according to specified conditions. A variable can be bound to either an element, the content of an element, an element name, an attribute name, or an attribute value. The expression `element_as $e` binds the variable `$e` to the preceding element, and the expression `content_as $c` binds `$c` to the content of the preceding element. `Construct` clause specifies the structure of the output constructed from each set of variable bindings. The query result is a sequence of their outputs. Note that the outermost `where` clause can be omitted, and `construct` clauses can have nested sub-queries.

For instance, a query for a resulting XML instance from the online book search site shown in Subsection 2.1 can be specified as shown in Figure 6. This query specification creates a `booklist` element, whose content is the result of the inner subquery. The subquery binds variables `$t` and `$a` to `title` and `author` from each `book`, and then creates a `book` element, which consists of `title` and `author` given by `$t` and `$a`.

3.2 Foreign Function

In the current version of X^{2}QL, users can define foreign functions whose implementation is given as external programs written in Java. This extensibility allows users to introduce various processing capabilities into X^{2}QL. Foreign functions are classified into *general functions*, which are normal-style functions, and *element methods*, which are associated with specific element types. Foreign functions are defined by the following syntax. The definition of a foreign function specifies the data types of arguments and return values.

`function` *type-name general-function-name*(*argument-list*)
`defined-by` "*URI of the implementation*"

`function` *type-name element-type-name*.*element-method-name*(*argument-list*)
`defined-by` "*URI of the implementation*"

argument-list `::=` *type-name argument-name*[, *type-name argument-name*]*

The data types `string`, `number`, `boolean`, `content`, `element` and any element types are allowed. Variables bound by `element_as` and `content_as` are associated with the `element` and `content` values. Each element type is treated as a subtype of `element`. The types of element names, attribute names and attribute values are `string`, or `number` if possible.

3.3 Foreign Functions for Application Integration

This subsection introduces the capabilities needed to develop meta-applications as foreign functions. The first foreign function is used to submit forms, and the second foreign function is used to get destination pages of a hyperlink.

Submiting Forms. In applications, forms written in (X)HTML are generally used to input conditions and to get the result after submission. This task is done manually using WWW browsers. To automate this task, we introduce the `submit()` method of `form` element type; it is defined as follows:

```
function   element form.submit( inputdata arg )
defined-by "http://..."
```

where the argument `arg` is an `inputdata` element, which contains values to fill in the `form`. The child elements of `inputdata` have names that match `name` attribute values in the `form`.

The implementation of `submit()` associates fields in the `form` with the corresponding values given by `inputdata`. It then encodes the processing request into an HTTP request and sends it to the application using GET or POST HTTP methods. It then receives the resulting XML instance as the HTTP response. Finally, it returns the root element of the XML instance.

Following Hyperlinks. To follow hyperlinks, we introduce the `follow()` method of `anchor` element type; it is defined as follows:

```
function   content anchor.follow( string path )
defined-by "http://...".
```

The implementation of `follow()` begins from the URL in the `anchor`, follows paths that match the given regular path expression, and collects the destination pages. It returns a `content` value which is a sequence of the root elements of the collected pages.

4 X²PL: Extensible XML Processing Language

X²QL allows data extraction from XML instances and allows them to be restructured. However, procedural processing flows required in application integration cannot be written in X²QL. We therefore introduce X²PL to develop meta-applications. Subsection 4.1 explains types in X²PL, and Subsection 4.2 describes the syntax.

4.1 Data Types

In X²PL, all the types in X²QL can be used. The result of an embedded query is `content` value. We call them *basic types.* In the following explanations, *values* refer to these types of values. Data type conversion among them is defined in X²QL [5], and X²PL follows the same rule. Its details are omitted here because our example does not need this feature.

In addition to basic types, X²PL introduces `list` and `cursor` types. A list is a collection that can contain any values. A cursor is an object to sequentially access each result generated by a query. Lists and cursors are associated with names and handled by the names in scripts.

4.2 Basic Constructs

We call X²PL code *scripts*, and each script is a sequence of *statements.* X²QL queries are embedded into X²PL scripts. The syntax is shown in Figure 7.

```
script          ::= (statement)*
block           ::= "{" (statement)* "}"
statement       ::= assign-stmt | add-stmt | assignlist-stmt | addlist-stmt
                    | remove-stmt | insert-stmt | permute-stmt
                    | cursor-stmt | open-stmt | close-stmt | for-stmt | while-stmt
                    | if-stmt | try-stmt | return-stmt | parallel-stmt | timeout-stmt
                    | stdin-stmt | stdout-stmt | stderr-stmt

assign-stmt     ::= "assign" variable expression
add-stmt        ::= "add" variable expression

assignlist-stmt ::= "assignlist" list-name ("eachof")? expression
addlist-stmt    ::= "addlist" list-name ("eachof")? expression
remove-stmt     ::= "removeItemAt" list-name arith-expr
insert-stmt     ::= "insertItemAt" list-name arith-expr expression
permute-stmt    ::= "replaceItemAt" list-name arith-expr expression
getItemAt-expr  ::= "getItemAt(" list-name "," arith-expr ")"
getSize-expr    ::= "getSize(" list-name ")"

cursor-stmt     ::= "cursor" cursor-name expression
open-stmt       ::= "open" cursor-name
close-stmt      ::= "close" cursor-name
for-stmt        ::= "for(" cursor-name "," variable ")" block
fetch-expr      ::= "fetch" cursor-name

while-stmt      ::= "while(" boolean-expr ")" block
if-stmt         ::= "if(" boolean-expr ")" block ("else" block)?
try-stmt        ::= "try" block ("catch(" exception-name ")" block)+ "finally"
                    block
return-stmt     ::= "return" expression
parallel-stmt   ::= "parallel("arith-expr ")" (block)+
timeout-stmt    ::= "timeout(" arith-expr ")" block

stdin-stmt      ::= "stdin" variable
stdout-stmt     ::= "stdout" expression
stderr-stmt     ::= "stderr" expression

expression      ::= "[" query "]" | "{" arith-expr "}" | string-expr | boolean-expr
                    | variable | foreign-func-expr | getItemAt-expr | getSize-expr
                    | fetch-expr
```

Fig. 7. Syntax of X^2PL.

Value Manipulation. In X^2PL scripts, two kinds of variables with different scopes are used. Variables that start with single '$' are available only in a query. Variables with '$$' are available in the given script and can be accessed from queries. Both kinds of variables can be bound to values. In the following explanations, *variables* are the variables with the script scope. An **assign** statement assigns the value given by *expression* to the *variable*, and an `add` statement adds the given value to the value assigned to the *variable*.

List Manipulation. Two functions are defined for the `list` type. Function `getSize` returns the number of items in the specified list. Function `getItemAt` returns the n-th item of the specified list where n is $0 = n <$ `getSize(`*list-name*`)`. An `assignlist` statement creates a list from the given *expression* and names it by the given *list-name*. An `addlist` statement appends the list generated from the given *expression* to the list named *list-name*. When the *expression* is a *query* and `eachof` is specified, the list contains all the individual outputs from the `construct` clause. Otherwise, the list contains the whole value. A `removeItemAt` statement removes the n-th item from the specified list. An `insertItemAt` statement inserts the given value before the n-th item of the specified list. An `replaceItemAt` statement replaces the n-th item of the specified list by the given value. In these statements, the available range of n is $0 = n <$ `getSize(`*list-name*`)`.

Cursor Manipulation. A `cursor` statement defines a cursor and associates it with the given *cursor-name*. `open` and `close` statements begin and finish use of the cursor. Function `fetch` returns the current value of the specified cursor, and advances the cursor to the next value. A `for` statement begins the specified cursor, iterates its following block for each value on the cursor, and finishes it.

Processing Flow Control. X^2PL allows `while` statement for iteration, `if` statement for conditional processing, `try` statement for exception handling and `return` statement for resulting a value. In addition to them, X^2PL allows statements to control interaction with applications. A `parallel` statement begins to process all the following blocks concurrently, and finishes them when n blocks or all have finished. When zero is specified, this statement does not finish until all blocks have finished. A `timeout` statement forces finish of the following block at the specified interval. The interval is specified in milliseconds.

Input and Output. An `stdin` statement inputs a string from the standard input and assigns it to the specified variable. `stdout` and `stderr` statements output the given value into the standard and error output, respectively.

5 Specification of Meta-applications

Using X^2PL and the foreign functions introduced in Subsection 3.3, we can write the meta-application shown in Section 2 as shown in Figure 8. Note that the same meta-application can be specified in different ways. For example, cursors could be used instead of lists.

Lines 1–9 Define foreign functions.

```
function element Form.submit(
          element inputdata)
defined-by
   "http://localhost/src
    /x2pl.x2qlff.Form#submit"
function content Anchor.follow()
defined-by
   "http://localhost/src
    /x2pl.x2qlff.Anchor#follow"

stdin($$keys)
assign $$bs_input
 [ construct <inputdata>
               <keys>$$keys</>
             </> ]

assign $$bs_result
 [ where <html> <body>
           <form/>
             element_as $f
         </> </>
         in "http://books/..."
   construct
         $f.submit($$bs_input) ]

assign $$num {0}
while($$num < 50
   && $$bs_result != null) {
  addlist bs_books eachof
   [ where <result>
             <book>$book</>
           </> in $$bs_result
     construct
           <inputdata>
             $book
           </> ]

  assign $$num getSize(bs_books)

  assign $$bs_result
   [ where <result>
             <anchor>$url</>
           </> in $$bs_result
     construct
           $url.follow() ]
}

assign $$limit getSize(bs_books)
if($$limit > 50) {
  assign $$limit {50}
}
assign $$num {0}
while($$num < $$limit) {
  assign $$l_input
     getItemAt(bs_books, $$num)
  assign $$num  {$$num + 1}
  addlist l_bookurls eachof
   [ where
         <html><body>
           <form/> element_as $f
         </></>
         in "http://opac/...",
         <result>
           <anchor/>
              element_as $a
         </>
         in $f.submit($$l_input)
     construct
         $a ]
}

assign $$limit getSize
                   (l_bookurls)
assign $$num {0}
while($$num < $$limit) {
  assign $$url
     getItemAt(l_bookurls, $$num)
  add $$result
   [ where
         <result>
           <title/>  element_as $t
           <author/> element_as $a
           <copies/> element_as $c
         </> in $$url.follow()
     construct
         <book> $t $a
        where
           <copies>
             <copy/> element_as $v
           </> in $c
        construct
           $v
         </> ]
  assign $$num {$$num + 1}
}
assign $$result
 [ construct <finalresult>
               $$result
             </> ]
return $$result
```

Fig. 8. Example of a script.

Lines 10–14 Get keywords from standard input and assign them to `$$keys`, then construct an `inputdata` element and assign it to `$$bs_input`. This is used to fill in the form of the online book search site.

Lines 15–22 Bind `$bs_form` to the form of the online book search site, then submit it with the value of `$$bs_input` using the `submit()` method. Finally, assign the result to `$$bs_result`.

Lines 23–33 Create a list named `bs_books`, which consists of `book` elements in the `$$bs_result`.

Line 34 Get the number of items in the list `bs_books`.

Lines 35–41 Extract the URL of the next page including the remaining book list, then extract the root element of the next page using the `follow()` method. Finally, assign the result to `$$bs_result`.

Lines 42–64 Get URLs of detailed book information from the library OPAC site by submitting the form with each of the first fifty searched books.

Lines 65–92 Get detailed book information and restructure it into the final result. Then return it.

6 X²PL Processing System

We have developed an X²PL processing system. This section describes the development.

6.1 System Overview

This processing system translates scripts into Java code, then executes the code, which simplifies the implementation. By using scripts, users give only their initial inputs to get the final results.

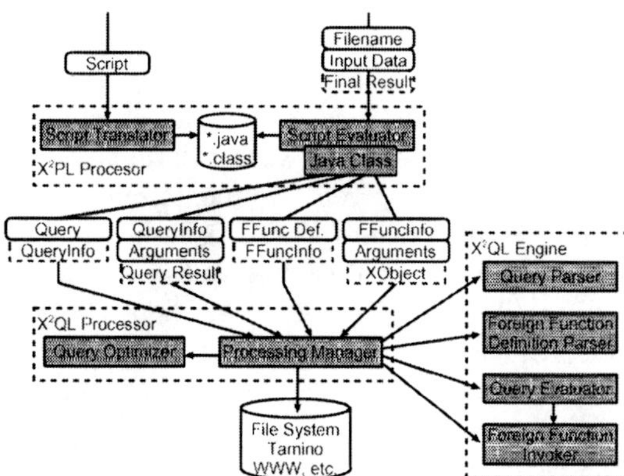

Fig. 9. System architecture.

As Figure 9 shows, X^2PL processing system consists of three modules: *X^2PL Processor*, *X^2QL Processor* and *X^2QL Engine*. They are indicated by boxes enclosed in dashed lines. Each module has submodules. Arrows show dependencies of modules with data flows. Solid ovals indicate arguments and dashed ovals indicate results. Details are explained in Subsection 6.2.

First, X^2PL Processor generates and compiles Java programs. Queries and foreign function calls within the script are processed using the Java API of X^2QL Processor. X^2QL Processor then internally uses X^2QL Engine to parse queries, evaluate them, and invoke foreign functions. The results are, finally, returned to the users.

6.2 System Modules

X^2PL Processor module has *Script Translator* and *Script Translator* submodules. Script Translator receives script files and translates them into Java code, then compiles them into Java classes. Script Translator calls the entry point of the generated Java code.

X^2QL Processor module has *Processing Manager* and *Query Optimizer* submodules. Processing Manager provides four services as the Java API of the X^2QL engine: (1) Parse a given query into a QueryInfo object, which is the internal representation of a query, using Query Parser. (2) Evaluate a query in a QueryInfo by Query Evaluator, then return a QueryResult object, which is the result of query processing. (3) Parse given foreign function definitions into an FFuncInfo object, which is a set of the internal representation of them, using Foreign Function Definition Parser. (4) Invoke a foreign function in an FFuncInfo object by Foreign Function Invoker, then return an object corresponding to the return value. Query Optimizer plans query processing and simplifies a given query. X^2QL Processor fetches instances needed in query processing. When XML instances are managed by a document database system such as Tamino [7], XML instances can be filtered by querying in the database system. Filtered XML instances may always satisfy some conditions in the query. In such cases, the query can be simplified by removing redundant conditions.

X^2QL Engine module has *Query Parser*, *Query Evaluator*, *Foreign Function Definition Parser* and *Foreign Function Invoker* submodules. Query Parser parses a given query into a QueryInfo. Query Evaluator evaluates a specified query in a given QueryInfo with given arguments, and returns a QueryResult. Internally, queries are translated into XSLT stylesheets, then processed by the XSLT processor [5]. Foreign Function Definition Parser parses given foreign function definitions into an FFuncInfo. Foreign Function Invoker invokes a specified foreign function with the arguments, then returns an object of the result value. Foreign function calls within queries are also invoked using this submodule.

6.3 Experiment with the Script

In an experiment with the processing system, X^2PL Processor could translate our example script into about 150 statements in Java. This Java code uses the Java

API of X^2QL Processor. X^2QL Evaluator translates given queries into XSLT stylesheets. The generated XSLT stylesheets are 33 to 43 lines, and the total is 246 lines. The script can work with amazon.com, which is a well known online book search site, and the OPAC site of the library of University of Tsukuba using wrapper programs. This result allows us to determine that we have been able to write the meta-application in a small script.

7 Related Work

This section briefly covers related work. Serveral integration schemes for WWW applications have been proposed.

Application Manifold (AM) [8] has been proposed as an integral solution to integrate and customize applications. It is in a sense an adaptation of Information Manifold [9], for data integration, to the context of application integration. In AM, available data in *global applications*, corresponding to meta-applications in our context, are expressed in XML, actors in them are modeled as classes, and their activities are specified in State Charts of UML. *Local applications*, corresponding to applications, are described in the same way, and some of their variables are given as views written in XML-QL over variables of the global application. Global variables originating from local variables are derived by *inverse queries* of corresponding views. AM rewrites state chates describing global applications into processing flow in terms of the local applications, then processes them. AM allows to extract data from XML instances, to restucture them, and to interact with local applications. It cannot however process elements via functions specific to their element types, because it does not feature extensibility.

In some studies, general programming languages are used to extract data from WWW pages and integrate data sources on the WWW. WebL [10] is a programming language for WWW scripting, featuring service combinators and markup algebra. When an access to a page fails, service combinators provide a feasible way to access the page by simulating the application using a copy stored in the local storage in a past access. Markup algebra enables calculation over a set of elements given by markups. Users can develop meta-applications using these features. However, it is not easy to write code in programming languages. Our approach uses X^2QL, which allows high-level and declarative descriptions, and the queries are combined in X^2PL scripts. This approach can cope with high-level descriptions, as well as flexible and detailed descriptions.

Davulcu and others [1] and Konopnicki and Shmueli [4] have proposed schemes based on query languages. Davulcu and others model each application as a relation, and provide multi-layered schema similar to the ANSI/SPARC model. This approach enables users to develop meta-applications as relational database applications. Konopnicki and Shmueli model WWW data in an object-oriented data model called *Quom*, analyzing HTML and XML instances using a rule-based language called *Quodl*. Data extraction by *Quodl* is specified using XSLT or regular expressions. Our approach, on the other hand, treats XML instances directly, and extracts data from them by X^2QL. Therefore, the specification can be made in a more straightforward style.

Some researchers propose to extract data from applications by query language; for instance, WebOQL [11] and WebSQL [12]. WebOQL and WebSQL automate hyperlink navigation from a given page. However, these do not support the coding of processing flows, which means they are insufficient for developing meta-applications.

Wrapper generation schemes such as Jedi [13], W4F [14] and WIDL [15] are used to make it easy to develop meta-applications. These map HTML documents to other data structures. In this paper, we assume XML instances as the vehicle for data exchange. Using their approaches, we can regard applications that are HTML data sources as XML data sources.

SOAP [16] supports application integration using a common protocol between applications. SOAP protocol is written in XML, and our approach may be applicable to SOAP applications.

8 Conclusion

The rapid advance of the Internet has increased the importance of WWW application integration. In this paper, we have proposed an application integration scheme based on an XML query language. Our approach uses X^2QL to manipulate XML instances and introduces X^2PL to control processing flow. Foreign functions enable interaction with WWW applications in queries. We have also developed the X^2PL processing system and meta-applications on top of the processing system.

Future research issues includes support for WWW standard technologies. This involves XQuery [17], XLink [18], XPointer [19], XML Schema [20] [21], XForms [22], which is a form specification in XML, and others. We are planning to improve features of X^2PL and its processing system by applying our scheme to various meta-application development projects. In addition, optimization schemes for script processing, performance analysis, and performance comparison with other approaches are also interesting future research issues.

Acknowledgment. This research was supported in part by the Grant-in-Aid for Scientific Research from the Ministry of Education, Sports, Culture, Science and Technology, Japan.

References

1. H. Davulcu, J. Freire, M. Kifer, and I. V. Ramakrishnan. A Layered Architecture for Querying Dynamic Web Content, *Proc. ACM SIGMOD Conf.*, pp. 491–502, 1999.
2. D. Konopnicki, L. Leiba, O. Shmueli, and Y. Sagiv. A Formal Yet Practical Approach to Electronic Commerce, *Proc. 4th IFCIS International Conference on Cooperat Information Systems (CoopIS 1999)*, pp. 197–208, 1999.
3. H. Kitagawa, A. Morishima, and H. Mizuguchi. Integration of Heterogeneous Information Sources in InfoWeaver, *Advances in Databases and Multimedia for the New Century — A Swiss/Japanese Perspective —*, World Scientific Publishing, pp. 124–137, 2000.

4. D. Konopnicki, and O. Shmueli. A Comprehensive Framework for Querying and Integrating WWW Data and Services, *Proc. 4th IFCIS International Conference on Cooperat Information Systems (CoopIS 1999)*, pp. 172–183, 1999.
5. N. Shinagawa, H. Kitagawa, and Y. Ishikawa. X^2QL: An eXtensible XML Query Language Supporting User-defined Foreign Functions, *Proc. 2000 ADBIS-DASFAA Symposium on Advances in Databases and Information Systems*, LNCS 1884, pp. 251–264, 2000.
6. A. Deutsch, M. Fernandez, D. Florescu, A. Levy, and D. Suciu. A Query Language for XML, *Proc. 8th International World Wide Web Conference (WWW8)*, Computer Networks 31 (11–16), pp. 1155–1169, 1999.
7. Software AG, Tamino platform, http://www.softwareag.com/taminoplatform/.
8. A. Eral, and T. Milo. Integrating and Customizing Heterogeneous E-Commerce Applications, *Workshop on Technologies for E-Services (in Cooperation with VLDB 2000)*, 2000.
9. A. Y. Levy, A. rajaraman, and J. J. Ordille. Querying Heterogeneous Information Sources Using Source Descriptions. *Proc. 22th International Conference on Very Large Data Bases (VLDB '96)*, pp. 251–262, 1996.
10. T. Kistler, and H. Marais. WebL - A Programming Language for the Web, *Proc. 7th International World Wide Web Conference (WWW7)*, Computer Networks 30 (1–7), pp. 259–270, 1998.
11. G. O. Arocena, and A. O. Mendelzon. WebOQL: Restructuring Documents, Databases and Webs, *Proc. International Conference on Data Engineering*, pp. 24–33, 1998.
12. G. O. Arocena, A. O. Mendelzon, and G. A. Mihaila. Applications of a Web Query Language, *Proc. 6th International World Wide Web Conference (WWW6)*, Computer Networks 29 (8–13), pp, 1305–1315, 1997.
13. G. Huck, P. Fankhauser, K. Aberer, and E. J. Neuhold. Jedi: Extracting and Synthesizing Information from the Web, *Proc. 3rd IFCIS International Conference on Cooperat Information Systems (CoopIS 1998)*, pp. 32–43, 1998.
14. A. Sahuguet, and F. Azavant. WysiWyg Web Wrapper Factory (W4F), http://db.cis.upenn.edu/DL/WWW8/.
15. P. Merrick, and C. Allen. Web Interface Definition Language (WIDL), http://www.w3.org/TR/NOTE-widl, 1997.
16. D. Box, D. Ehnebuske, G. Kakivaya, A. Layman, N. Mendelsohn, H. F. Nielsen, S. Thatte, and D. Winer. Simple Object Access Protocol (SOAP) 1.1, http://www.w3.org/TR/SOAP/, 2000.
17. D. Chamberlin, D. Florescu, J. Robie, J. Simeón, and M. Stefanescu. XQuery: A Query Language for XML, http://www.w3.org/TR/xquery, 2001.
18. S. DeRose, E. Maler, and D. Orchard. XML Linking Language (XLink) Version 1.0, http://www.w3.org/TR/xlink, 2000.
19. R. Daniel Jr., S. DeRose, and E. Maler. XML Pointer Language (XPointer) Version 1.0, http://www.w3.org/TR/xptr, 2000.
20. H. S. Thompson, D Beech, M. Maloney and N. Mendelsohn. XML Schema Part 1: Structures, http://www.w3.org/TR/xmlschema-1/, 2001.
21. P. V. Biron and A. Malhotra. XML Schema Part 2: Datatypes, http://www.w3.org/TR/xmlschema-2/, 2001.
22. M. Dubinko, J. Dietl, R. Merrick, D. Raggett, T. V. Raman, and L. B. Welsh. XForms 1.0, http://www.w3.org/TR/xforms, 2000.

Incorporating Dimensions in XML and DTD*

Manolis Gergatsoulis[1], Yannis Stavrakas[1,2], and Dimitris Karteris[1]

[1] Institute of Informatics & Telecommunications,
National Centre for Scientific Research (N.C.S.R.) 'Demokritos',
153 10 Aghia Paraskevi Attikis, Greece.
[2] Knowledge & Database Systems Laboratory
National Technical University of Athens (NTUA), 157 73, Athens, Greece.
{manolis,ystavr}@iit.demokritos.gr
dkart@tee.gr

Abstract. In this paper we investigate various aspects of representing multidimensional information in the frame of the WWW. *Multidimensional XML* (MXML) is an extension of XML suitable for representing data that assume different facets, having different value or different structure, under different *contexts*. In Multidimensional XML, elements and attributes may depend on a number of *dimensions*, that define worlds under which variants of those elements or attributes hold. Moreover, we propose an extension of DTD that takes dimensions into account and is suitable for describing the logical structure of MXML documents. We also present a graph data model for MXML, and show how MXML can be reduced to conventional XML for a given world.

Keywords: Multidimensional Languages, Semistructured Data, XML, Web Databases.

1 Introduction

XML is a markup language suitable for data representation and exchange over the Web [3]. XML resembles HTML, but unlike HTML, it focuses on the structure of data rather than on presentation. XML can be seen either from a document-centric perspective or from a data-centric one. The document-centric view originates from SGML, the markup language that inspired the design of XML, and sees XML as a way to embed in a Web document information about its structure. The data-centric perspective has been adopted by those that perceive XML as a data exchange language over the Web. From this perspective the emphasis is on querying and on describing the relationships between pieces of data, in a way similar to a database schema.

Although the main characteristic of XML is its extensibility in terms of defining new element types at will, it falls short when it comes to representing *multidimensional information*, that is, information that presents different facets under

* This work has been partially supported by the Greek General Secretariat of Research and Technology under the project "Executable Intensional Languages and Intelligent Applications in Multimedia, Hypermedia and Virtual Reality" of ΠΕΝΕΔ'99.

H.C. Mayr et al. (Eds.): DEXA 2001, LNCS 2113, pp. 646–656, 2001.

different contexts. As a simple example imagine a report that needs to be represented at various degrees of detail and in various languages. A solution would be to create a different XML document for every possible combination. Such an approach is certainly not practical, since it involves excessive duplication of information. What is more, the different variants are not associated as being parts of the same entity. The problem of varying entities is especially present in the frame of the WWW, where information providers cannot assume too much about the background *context* of the information consumers. Therefore, there is need for data models and languages suitable for representing and exchanging multidimensional data over the Web.

Ideas on how this problem can be handled are given in [11,10], where a formalism, called Multidimensional XML (MXML), is presented. MXML extends XML by allowing *context specifiers* to qualify elements and attribute values, and specify the contexts under which the document and its components have meaning. MXML was influenced by *Intensional HTML* (IHTML) [12], a Web authoring language, based on and extending ideas proposed for a software versioning system [9]. IHTML allows a single Web page to have different variants and to dynamically adapt itself to a given context.

In this paper, a) we motivate the use of and specify MXML syntax and semantics by reviewing and further extending the formalism presented in [11,10], b) we clarify how the structure and the content of MXML elements and attributes depend on dimensions, c) we propose an extension of Document Type Definition (DTD) that takes into account dimensions and can be used to describe the logical structure of MXML documents, d) we present a data model for MXML, called MXMLGraph (MXMLG in short) and discuss some properties of MXML, and e) we show that, given a specific world, it is possible to obtain a conventional XML document, which constitutes the facet of the MXML document under that specific world.

2 Incorporating Dimensions in XML Documents

In a *multidimensional XML document* (*MXML document* in short), dimensions may be applied to elements and attributes. An element whose content depends on one or more dimensions is called *multidimensional element*. An attribute whose value depends on one or more dimensions is called *multidimensional attribute*.

2.1 Dimensions and Worlds

The notion of *world* is fundamental in MXML. A world represents an environment under which data in a multidimensional document obtain a meaning. A world is determined by assigning values to a set of *dimensions*.

Definition 1. *Let $\mathcal{S}$ be a set of dimension names and for each $d \in \mathcal{S}$, let $\mathcal{D}_d$, with $\mathcal{D}_d \neq \emptyset$, be the domain of d. A* **world** *W is a set of pairs (d, u), where $d \in \mathcal{S}$ and $u \in \mathcal{D}_d$ such that for every dimension name in $\mathcal{S}$ there is exactly one element in W.*

MXML uses *context specifiers* that specify sets of worlds. Context specifiers qualify the variants (or *facets*) of multidimensional elements and attributes, relating each variant to the set of worlds under which the variant becomes the holding one for the corresponding multidimensional entity. Two context specifiers are called *mutually exclusive* if they specify disjoint sets of worlds.

2.2 The Syntax of Multidimensional XML

The syntax of XML is extended as follows in order to incorporate dimensions. In particular, a multidimensional element has the form:

```
<@element_name attribute_specification>
   [context_specifier_1]
      <element_name attribute_specification_1>
         element_content_1
      </element_name>
   [/]
   . . .
   [context_specifier_N]
      <element_name attribute_specification_N>
         element_content_N
      </element_name>
   [/]
</@element_name>
```

A multidimensional element is denoted by preceding the element name with the special symbol "`@`", and encloses one or more *context elements* that constitute facets of that multidimensional element, holding under specific worlds specified by the corresponding *context specifier*. Context elements have the same form as conventional XML elements. All context elements of a multidimensional element have the same name which is the name of the multidimensional element.

To declare a multidimensional attribute we use the following syntax:

```
attribute_name = [context_specifier_1] attribute_value_1 [/] . . .
                 [context_specifier_n] attribute_value_n [/]
```

Therefore, a multidimensional attribute is assigned a set of context-value pairs. Each context-associated value becomes the holding value of the attribute under the worlds specified by the corresponding context specifier.

A *context specifier* is of the form:

```
dimension_1_specifier, ..., dimension_m_specifier
```

where `dimension_i_specifier`, $1 \leq \mathtt{i} \leq \mathtt{m}$, is a *dimension specifier* of the form:

```
dimension_name  specifier_operator  dimension_value_expression
```

A *specifier_operator* is one of $=$, $!=$, `in`, `not in`. If the *specifier_operator* is either $=$ or $!=$, the *dimension_value_expression* consists of a single dimension value. Otherwise, if the *specifier_operator* is either `in` or `not in`, the *dimension value expression* is a set of values of the form $\{\mathtt{value}_1, \ldots, \mathtt{value}_\mathtt{k}\}$.

A context specifier may also be the reserved word "`default`", where `[default]` represents all worlds not covered by the context specifiers of the same entity. Finally, the context specifier [ ] represents the set of all possible worlds.

Example 1. A part of an imaginary menu of a restaurant described in MXML.

```
<restaurant>
  <menu>
    <salad name = "Chef's salad" vegetarian = [season = summer]"yes"[/]
                                              [season != summer]"no"[/] >
      <@comment>
        [language = English, detail = low]
          <comment> A traditional salad. </comment>
        [/]
        [language = English, detail = high]
          <comment>
            A salad, with a long history which
            is connected with the tradition of the town.
          </comment>
        [/]
        [language = French, detail in {low, high}]
          <comment> Une salade regionale traditionelle. </comment>
        [/]
      </@comment>
      <@price>
        [season = summer] <price> 3 USD </price>
      [/]  [default] <price> 4 USD </price> [/]
      </@price>
      <ingredient> tomato </ingredient>
      <@ingredient>
        [season != summer] <ingredient> bacon </ingredient> [/]
      </@ingredient>
      <ingredient> olive oil </ingredient>
      <@ingredient>
        [occasion = special]
          <ingredient special_supplier=[season in {spring, summer}]"sp1"
                                       [/] [default]"sp2"[/] >
            <name> special sauce </name>
            <remarks> Must order three days in advance </remarks>
          </ingredient>
        [/]
        [default] <ingredient> normal sauce </ingredient> [/]
      </@ingredient>
    </salad>
  </menu>
  <supplier scode="sp1">
    <name> John Smith </name> <address> 234 XYZ Street </address>
  </supplier>
  <supplier scode="sp2"> ...  </supplier>
<\restaurant>
```

2.3 Dimensions Applied to Elements

While multidimensional elements can only contain context elements, context elements may contain other multidimensional elements, conventional elements, or any combination of the two in an arbitrary depth. Context elements of the same multidimensional element are not required to have the same content, or even to conform to the same structural constraints. Therefore, dimensions can affect the content of an element in every aspect, be it its structure or its value.

The effect of context in element value: Consider the element comment in Example 1, which is a multidimensional element whose value depends on the dimensions language and detail. The context specifier of the third context element of comment is [language = French, detail in {low, high}], and represents possible worlds where language = French and detail = low or language = French and detail = high. In all these worlds, the value of comment is "Une salade regionale traditionelle".

The effect of context in element structure: Context specifiers also affect the element structure. For example, the fourth ingredient element in Example 1 contains the subelements name and remarks for the context [occasion=special], but for all the other contexts, i.e. for all other possible values of the dimension occasion (implied by [default]), it contains no subelements.

Notice that it is not necessary for a multidimensional element to have context elements for every possible world. For example, the multidimensional element

```
<@ingredient>
      [season != summer] <ingredient> bacon </ingredient> [/]
</@ingredient>
```

in Example 1, has no facet for the context [season = summer].

Finally, a multidimensional element or attribute whose only facet holds under every possible world, can be substituted by a conventional element or attribute.

2.4 Dimensions Applied to Attributes

Each context element can have its own (conventional or multidimensional) attributes, exactly as it can have its own (conventional or multidimensional) child elements. Within the same multidimensional element, context elements may have different attributes, exactly as they may have different child elements. Notice that in Example 1, a salad ingredient has the attribute special_supplier for the context [occasion=special], but for any other context (denoted by [default]) ingredient has no attributes.

Attributes of type "ID", "IDREF" and "IDREFS" can be attached to context and conventional elements. By using attributes of types "IDREF" and "IDREFS", context and conventional elements are able to point to multidimensional, conventional, or context elements. Multidimensional elements can be attached only attributes of type "ID"; hence, although multidimensional elements can be pointed to by IDREF attributes, they cannot themselves point to other elements.

The IDREF attribute special_supplier in the fourth ingredient of Example 1, has the value "sp1" for the context [season in {spring, summer}] and the value "sp2" for all the other contexts (represented by [default]), thus pointing to different elements depending on the value of the dimension season.

2.5 Well-Formed MXML

The notion of *well-formed* MXML is an extension of the notion of well-formed XML. In addition, to the XML well-formedness criteria an MXML document must also exhibit the property of *context well-formedness*, which is defined below.

Definition 2. *An MXML document D is said to be* context-deterministic *iff for every multidimensional element (attribute) M in D the following condition holds: If* $c_1, c_2, \ldots, c_n$ *are the context specifiers qualifying the context elements (attribute values) of M then* c_i *is mutually exclusive with* c_j *for all* $i \neq j$.

In a context-deterministic MXML document each multidimensional element or attribute has at most one holding facet under any specific world.

Definition 3. *An MXML documents D is said to be* context well-formed *iff it is context deterministic and the following conditions hold: 1) For every multidimensional element there exists at least one context element, and 2) For every multidimensional attribute there exists at least one facet of that attribute.*

Context well-formedness ensures that for every multidimensional entity there is at least one world under which this entity has meaning (a holding facet).

3 Multidimensional DTD

In XML, a *Document Type Definition* (DTD) [3] is used for defining constraints on the logical structure of a document. In this section, we propose an extension of DTD, called *Multidimensional DTD*, that takes dimensions into account and is suitable for describing the logical structure of MXML documents.

Dimension Declarations: Dimensions are declared in MDTD through *dimension declarations* of the form:

```
<!DIMENSION dimension_name dimension_domain>
```

Using dimension declarations we can declare a dimension and associate with it a set of possible values. For example, the declaration

```
<!DIMENSION language {English, French}>
```

denotes that '`language`' is a dimension name and constraints its possible values to elements of the set {`English, French`}.

In the frame of this paper we assume finite dimension domains, described by enumerating their elements. Other ways of representation, as well as infinite domains, may also be useful, however they fall out of the scope of this paper.

Multidimensional Element Declarations: *Element declarations* of conventional DTD are also used in MDTD for conventional elements. Another construct, called *multidimensional element declaration*, is introduced, to deal with context dependent elements. The syntax of the new construct is:

```
<!MULTIELEMENT element_name associated_dimensions type_decl>.
```

The dimensions on which a multidimensional element depends on are declared in '`associated_dimensions`'. For example, in the following declaration:

```
<!MULTIELEMENT comment {language, detail} (#PCDATA)>
```

comment is declared to be a multidimensional element which depends on the dimensions language and detail.

Multidimensional element declarations allow separate constraints for the context elements of a multidimensional element. For example in:

```
<!MULTIELEMENT ingredient {season, occasion}
       [occasion = special] ((name, remarks?) | #PCDATA) [/]
       [default] (#PCDATA) [/]>
```

the type of the element ingredient is declared to be either (name, remarks?) or (#PCDATA) whenever the value of the dimension occasion is special; in any other case, the type of the element ingredient is declared to be (#PCDATA).

Attribute Declarations: *Attribute declarations* have been extended to take into account multidimensional attributes. In the declaration

```
<!ATTLIST salad name CDATA #REQUIRED
       vegetarian {season} CDATA #IMPLIED>
```

the element salad is declared to have two attributes, namely name and vegetarian. The value of the attribute name does not depend on dimensions, while the value of the attribute vegetarian depends on the dimension season.

Attribute declarations allow to declare that an attribute is present under some contexts, while it is absent under other contexts. For example, in

```
<!ATTLIST ingredient
     [occasion=special] special_supplier {season} IDREF #REQUIRED [/]>
```

the element ingredient is declared to have the attribute special_supplier only for the contexts where the value of the dimension occasion is special; in this case, the attribute must exists for every possible value of the dimension season. In all other contexts the element ingredient has no attributes.

Example 2. A MDTD for the MXML document of Example 1.

```
<!DOCTYPE restaurantDTD [
<!DIMENSION language  {English, French}>
<!DIMENSION detail    {low, high, exhaustive}>
<!DIMENSION season    {spring, summer, fall, winter}>
<!DIMENSION occasion  {special, normal}>
<!ELEMENT restaurant  (menu | supplier)*>
<!ELEMENT menu  (salad+, first+, maindish+, dessert+)>
<!ELEMENT salad (comment?, price, ingredient*)>
<!ATTLIST salad name CDATA #REQUIRED
             vegetarian {season} CDATA #IMPLIED>
<!MULTIELEMENT comment {language, detail} (#PCDATA)>
<!MULTIELEMENT price {season} (#PCDATA)>
<!MULTIELEMENT ingredient {season, occasion}
     [occasion = special] ((name, remarks?) | #PCDATA) [/]
     [default] (#PCDATA) [/]>
<!ATTLIST ingredient
     [occasion = special] special_supplier {season} IDREF #REQUIRED [/]>
<!ELEMENT name    (#PCDATA)>
<!ELEMENT remarks (#PCDATA)>
<!ELEMENT supplier (name, address)>
<!ATTLIST supplier scode ID #REQUIRED>  ]>
```

4 A Data Model for MXML

Graph based data models are often used to represent XML data [1,5,4,6]. In this section, we propose a data model, called *Multidimensional XML Graph* (or *MXMLG*), suitable for modelling MXML documents. MXMLG provides nodes and edges of appropriate type for representing multidimensional information.

Definition 4. *Let $\mathcal{CS}$ be a set of context specifiers and $\mathcal{D}_e$, $\mathcal{D}_a$, $\mathcal{T}$ be three sets called* element names, attribute names, *and* text values *respectively. A* multi-dimensional XML graph *$G = (N, E, r, \mathcal{CS}, \mathcal{D}_e, \mathcal{D}_a, \mathcal{T})$ is a finite directed edge-labelled graph such that:*
1) $N = N_{me} \cup N_{ce} \cup N_{ma} \cup N_a \cup N_t$ where N_{me}, N_{ce}, N_{ma}, N_a and N_t are disjoint sets of nodes, called multidimensional element nodes, context element nodes, multidimensional attribute nodes, (context) attribute nodes, *and* text nodes *respectively.*
2) $E = E_e \cup E_a \cup E_{ec} \cup E_{ac} \cup E_r \cup E_t$ where $E_e \subseteq N_{ce} \times \mathcal{D}_e \times (N_{ce} \cup N_{me})$ is a set of edges called element edges, *$E_a \subseteq (N_{ce} \cup N_{me}) \times \mathcal{D}_a \times (N_a \cup N_{ma})$ is a set of edges called* attribute edges, *$E_{ec} \subseteq N_{me} \times \mathcal{CS} \times N_{ce}$, is a set of edges called* element context edges, *$E_{ac} \subseteq N_{ma} \times \mathcal{CS} \times N_a$ is a set of edges called* attribute context edges, *$E_r \subseteq N_a \times (N_{ce} \cup N_{me})$ is a set of edges called* attribute reference edges, *and $E_t \subseteq (N_a \cup N_{ce}) \times N_t$ is a set of edges called* text edges.
3) $L_t : N_t \to \mathcal{T}$ is a labeling function for text nodes.
4) r is a specific node in N_{ce}, called the root node *such that: a) Each node in the graph is reachable from r, and b) $G' = (N, E_e \cup E_a \cup E_{ec} \cup E_{ac} \cup E_t)$ is a tree rooted at r.*

MXMLG can also represent conventional XML documents since XML can be considered as a special case of MXML.

The MXMLGraph for the document of Example 1 is shown in Figure 1.

5 Properties of MXML

Context Propagation: A context specifier gives the *explicit context* of the entity that qualifies. When element or attributes are combined to form an MXML document, the explicit context of an entity does not alone determine the worlds under which that entity holds, since when an entity e_2 is part of another entity e_1, then e_2 can have substance only under the worlds that e_1 has substance. This can be conceived as if the context under which e_1 holds is inherited to e_2. The context propagated in that way is combined with (constraint by) the explicit context of each element to give the *inherited context* for that element. For determining the inherited context of an attribute, the explicit context of the attribute is used to constrain the inherited context of the element that contains the attribute. The inherited contexts can be considered as the "real" contexts for elements and attributes in the frame of the document where they occur.

Reducing MXML to XML: Each MXML document represents in fact a set of conventional XML documents. Given a world w, an MXML document can be

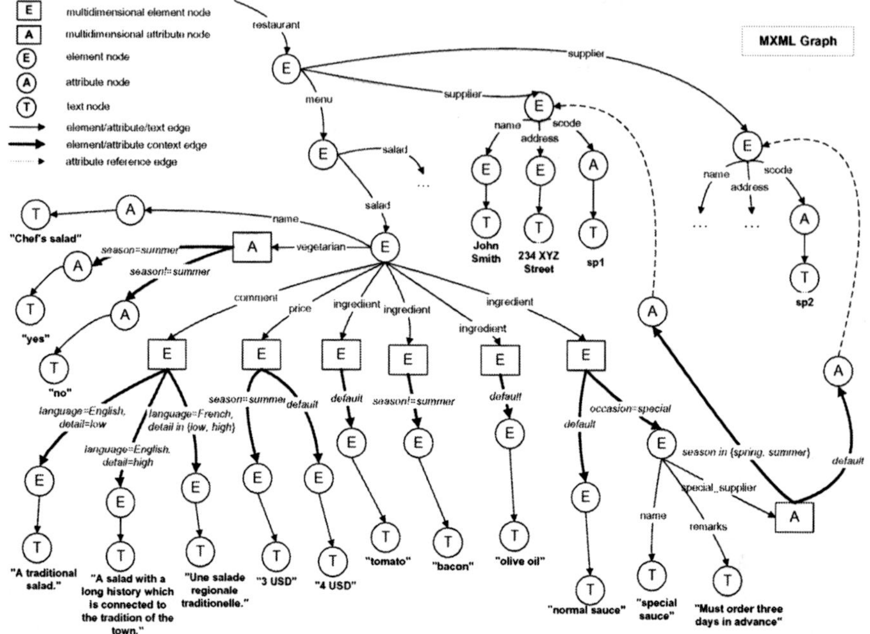

Fig. 1. The Multidimensional XML Graph for Example 1.

reduced to a conventional XML document which is the facet of the multidimensional document under w. The reduction process is defined in the procedure that follows, where for convenience we consider the MXMLG graphs G and G' that correspond to the MXML and XML documents respectively.

Procedure reduceMXMLG(G, w, G')

Step 1: Remove all context edges (e, C, e') from G for which $v \notin U_C$ where $(d, v) \in w$ and $(d, U_C) \in C$. Then remove all subgraphs not accessible from r.
Step 2: For every element/attribute context edge of the form (p, C, q), in the graph G' obtained in step 1, do the following: Let $(e_1, l_1, p), \ldots, (e_k, l_k, p)$ be all edges in G leading to p. Then replace each (e_i, l_i, p), for $i = 1, \ldots, k$ by an edge (e_i, l_i, q) of the same type. Remove the edge (p, C, q) and the node p.
Step 3: Prune all subtrees which have no text leaf node.

A system that implements the above process and demonstrates a number of examples is presented in [7].

Validity of MXML Documents: The validity of an MXML document is defined with respect to an MDTD, and is an extension of the notion of validity for conventional XML documents. Given a world w, it is possible to apply a process similar to the one presented above, and reduce an MDTD to a conventional DTD that holds under w. An MXML document M is *valid with respect to an MDTD under a world* w, if the conventional XML document D obtained by reducing M for that particular world w is valid with respect to the DTD that is the MDTD facet under w. An MXML document is *valid with respect to an MDTD* if it is valid with respect to that MDTD under every possible world.

6 Discussion and Motivation for Future Work

Investigating potential applications of MXML is an interesting direction. The representation of time-dependent information using MXML is promising [8], since various notions of time can be seen as MXML dimensions. The use of MXML to encode geographical information, where objects depend on dimensions like `scale` and `theme` is another area that we examine. Other schema languages for MXML, could also be investigated. Research on query languages for XML is especially active [1,2,5], however, in this paper we do not consider query languages for MXML. A query Q on an MXML document D can be seen as a pair (Q_w, w) where Q_w is a query on the conventional XML document which is the facet of D under the world w. The development of a "multidimensional query language" especially designed for the MXML data model is in our immediate plans.

References

1. S. Abiteboul, P. Buneman, and D. Suciu. *Data on the Web: From Relations to Semistructured Data and XML*. Morgan Kaufmann Publishers, 2000.
2. A. Bonifati and S. Ceri. Comparative analysis of five XML query languages. *SIGMOD Record*, 29(1), March 2000.
3. T. Bray, J. Paoli, and C. M. Sperberg-McQueen. Extensible markup language (XML) 1.0 (second edition). http://www.w3.org/TR/REC-xml, October 2000.
4. J. Clark and S. DeRose. XML Path Language (XPath), Version 1.0 (W3C Recommendation). http://www.w3.org/TR/xpath, 1999.
5. A. Deutch, M. Fernández, D. Florescu, A. Levy, and D. Suciu. XML-QL: A query language for XML. http://www.w3.org/TR/NOTE-xml-ql, 1999.
6. M. Fernandez and J. Robie. XML Query Data Model (W3C Working Draft 11 May 2000). http://www.w3.org/TR/query-datamodel, 1999.
7. M. Gergatsoulis, Y. Stavrakas, D. Karteris, A. Mouzaki, and D. Sterpis. A Web-based System for Handling Multidimensional Information through MXML. *It will be presented at 5th East-European Conference on Advances in Databases and Information Systems (ADBIS), Vilnius, Lithuania, September 2001.*
8. T. Mitakos, M. Gergatsoulis, Y. Stavrakas, and E. V. Ioannidis. Representing time-dependent information in multidimensional XML. *Proc. of the 23rd Int. Conf. "Information Technology Interfaces" (ITI'01), Pula, Croatia, June 2001.*
9. J. Plaice and W. W. Wadge. A New Approach to Version Control. *IEEE Transactions on Software Engineering*, 19(3):268–276, 1993.
10. Y. Stavrakas, M. Gergatsoulis, and T. Mitakos. Representing context-dependent information using Multidimensional XML. In J. Borbinha and T. Baker, editors, *Research and Advanced Technology for Digital Libraries (ECDL'00), Proceedings*, Lecture Notes in Computer Science (LNCS) 1923, pages 368–371. Springer, 2000.

11. Y. Stavrakas, M. Gergatsoulis, and P. Rondogiannis. Multidimensional XML. In P. Kropf, G. Babin, J. PLaice, and H. Unger, editors, *Distributed Communities on the Web, Third International Workshop (DCW'2000)*, Lecture Notes in Computer Science (LNCS) 1830, pages 100–109. Springer-Verlag, 2000.
12. W. W. Wadge, G. D. Brown, M. C. Schraefel, and T. Yildirim. Intensional HTML. In *Proc. of the 4th Int. Workshop on Principles of Digital Document Processing (PODDP '98)*, LNCS 1481, pages 128–139. Springer, March 1998.

Keys with Upward Wildcards for XML

Wenfei Fan[1], Peter Schwenzer[2], and Kun Wu[3]

[1] Bell Laboratories and Temple University
wenfei@acm.org
[2] Temple University Health System
schwenp@tuhis.temple.edu
[3] Motorola Inc.
akw037@motorola.com

Abstract. The paper proposes a key constraint language for XML and investigates its associated decision problems. The language is defined in terms of regular path expressions extended with downward and upward wildcards, which can not only move down XML document trees, but also upwards. In a uniform syntax it is capable of expressing both absolute keys and relative keys, which are important to hierarchically structured data. In addition, keys defined in the language can be reasoned about efficiently. The paper provides a sound and complete set of inference rules and a cubic time algorithm for determining implication of the keys.

1 Introduction

As XML [5] is increasingly used in data exchange, data integration and modeling Web data [1], the importance of keys for XML is being recognized: for specifying the semantics of the data, preserving information in data exchange and integration, preventing update anomalies, indexing and archiving the data, and for formulating and optimizing XML queries. Several key specifications have been proposed for XML (e.g., [20]). These proposals, however, have a number of limitations. This highlights the need to provide a key specification language for XML that is capable of expressing important semantics of XML data and is simple enough to be reasoned about efficiently.

In a relational database, we define a key for a relation (a set of tuples) by providing a set of attributes that uniquely identifies tuples in the relation. Along the same lines, to define a key for XML data we specify a pair (Q, S), where

- Q is a path expression that identifies a set of XML elements on which the key is defined, denoted by $[\![Q]\!]$ and called the *target set*; and
- S is a set of path expressions that provides identification for elements in $[\![Q]\!]$, called the *key paths*.

Since XML data is typically modeled as a tree, $[\![Q]\!]$ represents a set of nodes in an XML document tree, and S specifies another set of nodes whose values identify nodes in $[\![Q]\!]$. As observed by [7], two forms of keys are particularly important to hierarchically structured data, such as XML documents and scientific databases. The first is *absolute key*, which identifies a node x in $[\![Q]\!]$ with the values of some

H.C. Mayr et al. (Eds.): DEXA 2001, LNCS 2113, pp. 657–667, 2001.

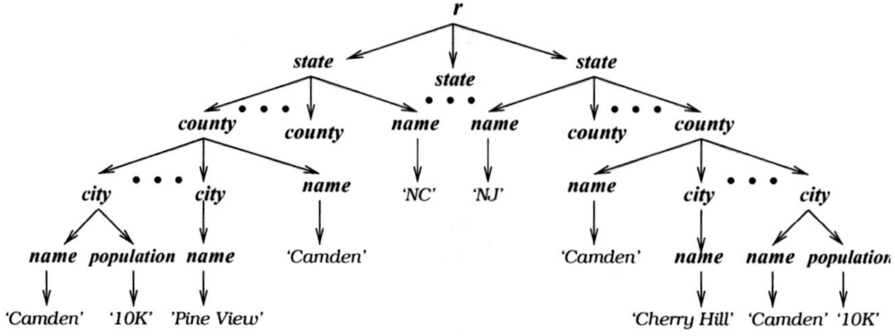

Fig. 1. An XML tree

nodes in the subtree rooted at x. That is, S consists of paths that lead to nodes in the subtree of x. The second is *relative key*, which, to identify a node y in $[\![Q]\!]$, needs to refer to ancestors of y, as opposed to an absolute key specification. In other words, S consists of not only paths leading to nodes in the subtree of y, but also paths that refer to nodes in the subtrees of some ancestors of y. This is analogous to a key for a weak entity in a relational database, which is composed of a key of its "parent" entity and some additional identification [18].

Example. To illustrate absolute and relative keys, let us consider an XML document that contains information about states, counties and cities in the U.S. The document is represented as a tree in Fig. 1. A state has a number of counties, and a county in turn has a number of cities. One wants to define keys for `state`, `county` and `city` elements. A key of `state` is specified with the `name` of `state`:

$$(\_* .state,\ \{name\}).$$

Here $\_*$ is a combination of a (downward) wildcard '_' and the Kleene star '$*$', which matches any path. The path expression $\_*.state$ starts from the root r and identifies the target set, which consists of all `state` nodes in the tree no matter where they occur. Of these `state` nodes, `name` is defined to be a key. It asserts that two distinct `state` nodes cannot have `name` subelements with the same value. That is, the value of a `name` subelement uniquely identifies a `state` node. This is an *absolute key* since it does not need to refer to any ancestor of `state`. Observe that two different notions of equality are used: *value equality* when comparing the values of nodes reached by following the key path `name`, and *node identity* when comparing `state` nodes in the target set. The equality issue is important to XML keys since XML trees do not allow sharing of nodes. In contrast, only value equality is needed when defining relational database keys.

When it comes to a key for `county` nodes, the story is more complicated. The `name` of a `county` uniquely identifies the `county`, but only within a `state`. For example, both NJ (New Jersey) and NC (North Carolina) have a unique county named 'Camden', but with only the county name one cannot distinguish between the two different counties in the two states. In other words, `name` of `county` is a key of `county` nodes *relative to* `state`. To uniquely identify a `county` in the document, one needs not only `name` of `county`, but also `name` of the `state` that the `county` belongs to. To capture this semantics, we specify a *relative key*:

$$(\_* .state.county, \ \{name, \ \widehat{up}.name\}).$$

Here $\widehat{up}$ is the upward wildcard symbol that means "moving up to the parent node" in an XML tree. This is a relative key because it needs `name` of the `state`, i.e., it is relative to an ancestor of `county`.

Similarly, to uniquely identify `city` nodes we need to specify a relative key. Indeed, the 'Camden' counties in NJ and NC both have a city also named by 'Camden'. The relative key consists of `name` of the `city`, `name` of the `county` in which the `city` is, and `name` of the `state` where the `county` is located. That is:

$$(\_* .state.county.city, \ \{name, \widehat{up}.name, \widehat{up}.\widehat{up}.name\}).$$

These are keys in our key constraint language for XML, denoted by $\mathcal{K}$.

There are two important questions associated with keys for XML. One concerns *satisfiability* of keys: given a finite set of keys, is there an XML document that satisfies these keys? In other words, are these keys meaningful? The second question concerns *implication* of keys: suppose it is known that an XML document satisfies a finite set of keys, does it follow that the document must also satisfy some other key? These are the classical decision problems studied in relational dependency theory [2]. They are equally important to XML data. For example, in data integration, it is increasingly common to use XML as a uniform data format for mediators [4]. One may want to know whether a key φ holds in a mediator interface. However, this cannot be verified directly since the mediator interface does not contain data. One way to verify φ is to show that it is implied by keys that are known to hold [15].

Contributions. The main contributions of the paper are the following:

1. We propose a key constraint language $\mathcal{K}$ for XML. The language is defined in terms of regular path expressions extended with two forms of wildcards: a wildcard '_' that can move down XML trees as commonly used in XML query languages [1], and an *upward wildcard* $\widehat{up}$ that moves up XML trees. With these wildcards, $\mathcal{K}$ is capable of expressing both absolute and relative keys uniformly, using the same syntax. The key specification is independent of any DTD and other schema specifications.
2. We show that keys defined in the language $\mathcal{K}$ can be reasoned about efficiently. More specifically, we demonstrate that any keys of $\mathcal{K}$ are always satisfiable, and for implication of keys, we provide a sound and complete set of inference rules and a cubic time algorithm.

Related work. Keys and the more general functional dependencies have been well studied for relational and object-oriented databases (see [2] for a survey and [16,17,19] for recent work). As observed by [8,7], these constraint specifications are not appropriate for XML data and the complexity results in connection with reasoning about these constraints no longer hold in the XML setting [9,12].

Key specifications for XML have been proposed in the XML standard (DTD) [5], XML Schema [20] and in a recent proposal [7]. One can view ID attributes in a DTD as keys. This key specification is rather weak. First, IDs can only be specified in DTDs and thus do not help documents without a DTD. Second, IDs are unique within the entire document rather than among a "class" of elements. Because of this, IDs cannot capture keys in relational databases. Third, "keys" can only be defined with attributes. In practice, one may want to define keys with complex structures. Fourth, with ID attributes one can only specify unary and primary keys, i.e., at most one ID attribute can be specified for each element type. Our key specification overcomes these limitations.

XML Schema specifies keys with XPath [11] expressions. XPath provides a (downward) wildcard and a "parent" function that is similar to our upward wildcard. Thus our $\mathcal{K}$ constraints can be expressed in XPath syntax. However, as observed by [7], XPath is too complicated to be reasoned about efficiently. It is still open whether the decision problems are decidable or not for keys defined with XPath. Another technical issue is value equality. XML Schema restricts equality to text, but in many situations keys are not so restricted.

Closer to our work is the key specification of [7]. In [7], a general notion of value equality and the notions of absolute and relative keys were introduced. However, [7] did not consider the upward wildcard and thus to identify an element in an XML document, it may require a chain of (relative) keys. In contrast, in our key language $\mathcal{K}$, a single key suffices for this purpose. As upward wildcards are supported by XPath and XSL [10], one may also want to use them to express XML keys and to develop a better understanding of XML key analysis in their presence. This paper investigates the impact of upward wildcards on the decision problems associated with absolute and relative keys for XML. These problems for absolute keys were studied in [6] (in the absence of upward wildcards).

Implication problems associated with a class of simple XML keys (and foreign keys) were investigated in [14,12]. The keys considered in those papers are defined with XML attributes and are not as expressive as keys studied here.

Organization. The rest of the paper is organized as follows. Section 2 defines the key constraint language $\mathcal{K}$ for XML. Section 3 studies satisfiability and implication of keys in $\mathcal{K}$. Section 4 identifies directions for further research. The proofs are given in the full version of the paper [13].

2 Regular Path Expressions and Key Constraints

In this section, we first present the notions of XML trees and value equality on XML trees. We then introduce two classes of extended regular path expressions and define the key constraint language $\mathcal{K}$ in terms of these path expressions.

2.1 XML Trees

A tree model. Along the same lines of XML APIs (DOM [3]), query languages (XSL [10]) and specifications (XML Schema [20], XPath [11]), we define an XML document tree as follows. Assume a countable set $\mathbf{E}$ of element labels (tags), a countable set $\mathbf{A}$ of attribute names, and a symbol $\mathtt{S}$ indicating text (e.g., PCDATA in XML [5]). Assume that $\mathbf{E}$, $\mathbf{A}$ and $\{\mathtt{S}\}$ are pairwise disjoint.

An *XML tree* T is defined by (V, *lab*, *ele*, *att*, *val*, r). Here V is the set of *nodes* of T and *lab* is a function that labels each node with a symbol in **E**, **A** or with S. A node v is called an *element* (resp. *attribute* or *text* node) if $lab(v)$ is in **E** (resp. $lab(v) \in$ **A** or $lab(v) =$ S). Elements may have children, whereas attributes and text nodes are leaves of T. More specifically, if v is an element, then the mappings *ele* and *att* define the *children* of v: $ele(v)$ is a list of elements of V called the *subelements* of v, and $att(v)$ is a set of attributes with distinct labels, called the *attributes* of v. There is a parent-child *edge* from v to each of its children. Observe that the subelements are ordered (a list), while the attributes are not (a set). Attributes and text nodes carry string values. The mapping *val* assigns a string value to each attribute and text node x, i.e., $val(x)$ is a string. Finally, r is a distinguished node in V and is called the *root* of T.

An XML tree has a tree structure, i.e., for each node $v \in V$, there is a unique path of parent-child edges from the root r to v. An XML tree is called *finite* if V is finite. We only consider *finite* XML trees in this paper.

For example, Fig. 1 depicts an XML tree.

Value equality. This notion is central to a definition of keys. To check keys in relational databases, one needs only to compare atomic values, e.g., integer, real and string values. An XML tree has a hierarchical structure and it is no longer trivial to compare the values of two XML trees (subtrees).

Let T = (V, *lab*, *ele*, *att*, *val*, r) be an XML tree. Two nodes v, v' in V are *value equal*, denoted by $v =_v v'$, iff the following conditions are satisfied: (1) $lab(v) = lab(v')$, i.e., they have the same label; (2) if they are text or attribute nodes then $val(v) = val(v')$, i.e., they have the same string value; (3) if they are element nodes, then their children are pairwise value equal, i.e., for any $v_1 \in att(v)$, there is $v_2 \in att(v')$ such that $v_1 =_v v_2$ and vice versa, and moreover, if $ele(v) = [v_1, ..., v_k]$, then $ele(v') = [v'_1, ..., v'_k]$ and for all $i \in [1, k]$, $v_i =_v v'_i$.

For example, in Fig. 1 the leftmost `city` node (Camden in NC) and the rightmost `city` node (Camden in NJ) are value equal: they have the same label (`city`) and all their children (`name`, `population`) are pairwise value equal.

2.2 Extended Regular Path Expressions

A key φ of $\mathcal{K}$ is specified by (Q, S), where Q is a path expression called the *target path*, and S is a set of path expressions called the *key paths* of φ. The target path identifies a set of nodes in an XML tree on which the key is defined, denoted by $[\![Q]\!]$. The key paths provide identification for the nodes in $[\![Q]\!]$. As pointed out by [7], the language for specifying key paths could be simpler than the one for describing target paths. As mentioned earlier, XPath is too complex for one to reason about keys. Here we present two regular path languages, denoted by TL and KL, for specifying target paths and key paths, respectively. These languages are both powerful enough to specify important keys and simple enough to yield low complexity for reasoning about keys defined with these languages.

The path language TL. This language will be used to specify target paths in $\mathcal{K}$ constraints. A path expression of TL is syntactically defined as follows:

$$Q \ ::= \ \epsilon \ | \ l \ | \ Q.Q \ | \ \_*$$

where ϵ is the empty path, node label $l \in \mathbf{E} \cup \mathbf{A} \cup \{\mathtt{S}\}$, "." is the concatenation operator, "_" is the downward wildcard symbol that matches any label and "_*" is the combination of the wildcard and Kleene closure that represents any path. For example, $\_*.state$ and $\_*.state.county$ are path expressions in TL.

A *(simple) path* ρ is a TL expression without _*. In an XML tree T, ρ represents a parent-child path: we write $T \models \rho(v_1, v_2)$ iff there is a parent-child path from node v_1 to v_2 whose sequence of node labels is ρ. Recall that attribute and text (S) nodes are leaves and do not have outgoing edges. Hence we assume that if ρ contains attribute or S, then the label must be the last symbol in ρ.

A path expression Q of TL defines a regular language of paths. We use $\rho \in Q$ to denote that path ρ is in the language defined by Q. Let T be an XML tree, and v_1, v_2 be nodes in T. We say that v_2 is *reachable by following* Q *from* v_1, denoted by $T \models Q(v_1, v_2)$, iff there is a path $\rho \in Q$ such that $T \models \rho(v_1, v_2)$. In particular, $T \models \_*(v_1, v_2)$ if there is a (possibly empty) parent-child path ρ from v_1 to v_2, no matter what the path is. Intuitively, this means moving down from a node to an arbitrary depth. We use $[\![Q]\!]$ to denote the set of nodes in T that is reachable by following Q from the *root* r: $[\![Q]\!] = \{v \mid T \models Q(r, v)\}$.

The path language KL**.** This language is used to express key paths. A path expression P of KL has the form $\varrho.\rho$, where ϱ is a (possibly empty) sequence of $\widehat{up}$ symbols and ρ is a *nonempty* (simple) path. Here $\widehat{up}$ is the *upward wildcard* that matches any node label upwards. We call ϱ the *upward prefix* of P and denote it by P^u. For example, $\widehat{up}.name$ and $\widehat{up}.\widehat{up}.name$ are KL expressions.

In an XML tree T, $\widehat{up}$ indicates moving from a child node up to its parent. More specifically, let v_1 and v_2 be nodes in T. We write $T \models \widehat{up}(v_2, v_1)$ iff v_2 is a child of v_1 no matter what label v_1 has. In general, given any KL expression $P = \varrho.\rho$ with ϱ being the upward prefix of P, we say that v_1 is *reachable by following* P *from* v_2, denoted by $T \models P(v_2, v_1)$, iff there is a node v in T such that v is reached by moving up k levels from v_2 and $T \models \rho(v, v_1)$, where k is the number of $\widehat{up}$ symbols in ϱ. Observe that there exists at most one v reachable by moving up k levels from v_2. Note that nonempty (simple) paths are also KL expressions, i.e., when their upward prefixes are the empty path.

Let n be a node in T and P be a KL expression. We use $n[\![P]\!]$ to denote the set of nodes reachable from n by following P: $n[\![P]\!] = \{v \mid T \models P(n, v)\}$.

Notations. The *length* of a path ρ, denoted by $|\rho|$, is the number of node labels in ρ. Let ϱ be a sequence of upward wildcard symbols. We use $|\varrho|$ to denote the number of the $\widehat{up}$ symbols in ϱ. Thus for any KL expression P, $|P^u|$ denotes the number of the $\widehat{up}$ symbols in P. For example, let $P = \widehat{up}.\widehat{up}.name$ then $|P^u| = 2$.

Let Q_1, Q_2 be in TL (resp. KL). We say that Q_1 is a *prefix* of Q_2, denoted by $Q_1 \preceq_p Q_2$, if there exists Q in TL (resp. KL) such that $Q_2 = Q_1.Q$. Similarly, Q_1 is called a *suffix* of Q_2, denoted by $Q_1 \preceq_s Q_2$, if there is Q such that $Q_2 = Q.Q_1$. For example, $\_*.state \preceq_p \_*.state.county$ and $county \preceq_s \_*.state.county$.

2.3 A Key Constraint Language for XML

In terms of TL and KL, we define key constraints of $\mathcal{K}$ as follows.

Definition 2.1: A *key constraint* φ of $\mathcal{K}$ is an expression of the form

$$(Q, \{P_1, \ldots, P_k\}),$$

where Q is a TL expression, called the *target path* of φ; P_1, ..., P_k are KL expressions, called the *key paths* of φ, with $k \geq 1$. In addition, Q has a suffix Q_s such that Q_s is a path (i.e., it does not contain '$\_*$') and for each $i \in [1, k]$, $|Q_s| \geq |P_i^u|$, where P_i^u is the upward prefix of P_i.

An XML tree T *satisfies* φ, denoted by $T \models \varphi$, iff for any n_1, n_2 in $[\![Q]\!]$, if for all $i \in [1, k]$ there are $x \in n_1[\![P_i]\!]$ and $y \in n_2[\![P_i]\!]$ such that $x =_v y$, then $n_1 = n_2$; that is, $\forall\, n_1\, n_2 \in [\![Q]\!]\ (\bigwedge_{1 \leq i \leq k} \exists\, x \in n_1[\![P_i]\!]\ \exists\, y \in n_2[\![P_i]\!](x =_v y) \rightarrow n_1 = n_2)$.

A key φ is called an *absolute key* if for each $i \in [1, k]$, P_i does not contain an upward wildcard, i.e., $|P_i^u| = 0$. Otherwise it is called a *relative key*. ■

For example, the three constraints we have seen in Sect. 1 are keys of $\mathcal{K}$. More specifically, the key for `state` nodes is an absolute key, and the other two are relative keys. Other examples of $\mathcal{K}$ constraints include:

$$(\_*.book,\ \{name\}), \quad (\_*.book.chapter,\ \{number,\ \widehat{up}.name\}).$$

The first one is an absolute key, which says that `name` is a key for all the `book` nodes in a document. The second one is a relative key, which states that `number` is a key for `chapter`, but only within the `book` that contains the `chapter`. To uniquely identify a `chapter` in the document, one needs the `number` of the `chapter` as well as the `name` of the `book`.

In a key φ, the target path Q starts at the root of an XML tree T. We require $|Q_s| \geq |P_i^u|$ to ensure that the sequence P_i^u of $\widehat{up}$ symbols does not seek the "parent" of the root of T. Intuitively, the (nonempty) set of key paths of φ provides identification for the nodes in $[\![Q]\!]$. If two nodes n_1, n_2 of $[\![Q]\!]$ have all the key paths and agree on them, then they must be the same node. In other words, the key requires that if two nodes in $[\![Q]\!]$ are distinct, then the two sets of nodes reached on some P_i must be disjoint up to value equality. Note that we do not require $n_1[\![P_i]\!]$ and $n_2[\![P_i]\!]$ to be singleton sets. That is, there may be multiple nodes reachable from n_1 or n_2 by following P_i. In particular, if P_i is missing at either n_1 or n_2 then $n_1[\![P_i]\!]$ and $n_2[\![P_i]\!]$ are disjoint up to value equality and the key is satisfied. This definition of keys takes into account the semistructured nature of XML data [1]. Observe that P_i starts from nodes in $[\![Q]\!]$. Recall that attribute and text nodes do not have outgoing edges. Thus we only consider paths $\rho \in Q$ such that ρ does not contain any attribute or `S`.

For example, $(\_*.state.county.city,\ \{name, \widehat{up}.name, \widehat{up}.\widehat{up}.name\})$ is satisfied by the XML tree in Fig. 1 since no two distinct `city` nodes agree on all the key paths up to value equality. However, the tree does not satisfy the key $(\_*.state.county.city,\ \{name\})$, because the `city` of Camden in the `county` of Camden of NC and the `city` of Camden in the `county` of Camden of NJ agree on `name`, but they are different cities.

Observe that two notions of equality is used to define keys: *value equality* ($=_v$) when comparing nodes reached by following key paths, and *node identify* ($=$) when comparing two nodes in the target set. Also note that our key specification is independent of DTDs and other schema specifications.

3 Decision Problems for $\mathcal{K}$ Constraints

We next investigate the satisfiability and implication problems associated with key constraints of $\mathcal{K}$. We should remark that we consider *finite* XML trees only.

Let Σ be a finite set of $\mathcal{K}$ constraints and T an XML tree. We use $T \models \Sigma$ to denote that T *satisfies* Σ. That is, for any $\psi \in \Sigma$, $T \models \psi$. Let $\Sigma \cup \{\varphi\}$ be a finite set of $\mathcal{K}$ constraints. We use $\Sigma \models \varphi$ to denote that Σ *implies* φ, that is, for any XML tree T, if $T \models \Sigma$, then $T \models \varphi$.

The *satisfiability problem* for $\mathcal{K}$ is to determine, given any finite set of key constraints Σ of $\mathcal{K}$, whether there exists an XML tree T such that $T \models \Sigma$.

The *implication problem* for $\mathcal{K}$ is to determine, given any finite set of key constraints $\Sigma \cup \{\varphi\}$ in $\mathcal{K}$, whether $\Sigma \models \varphi$.

For example, let $\Sigma_0 = \{(\_*, \{ID\})\}$ and $\varphi_0 = (\_*.person, \{ID, name\})$. Then $\Sigma_0 \models \varphi_0$ is an instance of the implication problem for $\mathcal{K}$.

3.1 Satisfiability of Keys

Given a key constraint language for XML, it is important to be able to decide whether keys expressed in the language can be satisfied by any XML trees at all. Better still, it is desirable if all keys are meaningful, i.e., given any finite set of keys, one can always find a finite XML tree that satisfies the keys. Some key specifications do not have this finite model property. For example, keys proposed in XML Schema [20] and the strong keys defined in [7] may not have any finite XML tree that satisfies them (see [6] for examples).

In relational databases, given any keys (and foreign keys) over a schema, there is always a nonempty finite instance of the schema that satisfies the constraints. Keys of $\mathcal{K}$ are also always satisfiable. Indeed, given any finite set Σ of keys in $\mathcal{K}$, one can always find an XML tree T such that $T \models \Sigma$. In particular, the tree consisting of a single node (the root) satisfies any keys in $\mathcal{K}$.

3.2 Implication of Keys

For implication of $\mathcal{K}$ constraints we establish the following:

Theorem 3.1: Implication of $\mathcal{K}$ constraints is finitely axiomatizable and is cubic-time decidable. ∎

A proof sketch is given as follows. It involves containment of path expressions, a finite set of inference rules and an algorithm for determining key implication.
Containment of path expressions. As will be seen shortly, for inference of $\mathcal{K}$ constraints we need to determine *containment of path expressions*.

Let Q_1, Q_2 be path expressions in TL (resp. KL). We say Q_1 is *contained* in Q_2, denoted by $Q_1 \subseteq Q_2$, if for any XML tree T and any nodes x and y in T, if $T \models Q_1(x, y)$ then $T \models Q_2(x, y)$. We write $Q_1 \equiv Q_2$ if $Q_1 \subseteq Q_2$ and $Q_2 \subseteq Q_1$.

Given the definition of KL expressions one can show the following: for any path expressions P_1, P_2 in KL, $P_1 \subseteq P_2$ iff P_1 and P_2 are (syntactically) equal (i.e., $P_1 = P_2$). This can be easily verified by induction on the number of upward wildcard symbols in P_1, i.e., on $|P_1^u|$. This simplifies our inference rules for $\mathcal{K}$ constraint implication. As a result, containment of KL expressions can be decided in linear time. As an example, observe that $\widehat{up}.name \not\subseteq \widehat{up}.\widehat{up}.foo.name$ and $\widehat{up}.\widehat{up}.foo.name \not\subseteq \widehat{up}.name$ for any label foo.

For TL expressions, we have shown the following in [6].

Lemma 3.2: Containment of TL expressions is decidable in quadratic time. ■

A sound and complete set of rewriting rules has been developed for determining containment of TL expressions. In particular, for any TL expressions Q_1, Q_2 and Q, the following holds: $Q_1.Q.Q_2 \subseteq Q_1.\_*.Q_2$. See [6] for the proof.

Finite axiomatizability. We next present a set of inference rules for implication of key constraints of $\mathcal{K}$, denoted by $\mathcal{I}$, as follows:

– superkey:
$$\frac{(Q,\ S), \quad P \in KL}{(Q,\ S \cup \{P\})}$$

– subnode:
$$\frac{(Q.\rho,\ \{\varrho.P_1, ..., P_l', ..., \varrho.P_k\}), \quad P_l' \text{ is either } \rho' \text{ or } \varrho.P_l \qquad \rho, \rho' \text{ are paths}, \quad \varrho \text{ is a sequence of } \widehat{up}\text{'s and } |\varrho| = |\rho|, \quad P_l = \rho.\rho'}{(Q,\ \{P_1, ..., P_l, ..., P_k\})}$$

– containment:
$$\frac{(Q,\ S), \quad Q' \subseteq Q}{(Q',\ S)}$$

– empty-path:
$$\frac{S \subseteq KL, \quad S \text{ is nonempty}}{(\epsilon,\ S)}$$

We briefly illustrate these rules as follows.
(1) *superkey*. It should be mentioned that this rule also holds for keys in relational databases. It states that if S is a key for $[\![Q]\!]$, then so is any superset of S.
(2) *subnode*. Consider two nodes $n_1, n_2 \in [\![Q]\!]$. Suppose that for all $i \in [1, k]$ there exist $x_i \in n_1[\![P_i]\!]$ and $y_i \in n_2[\![P_i]\!]$ such that $x_i =_v y_i$. Then since ρ is a prefix of P_l, there must be distinct nodes $n_1', n_2' \in [\![Q.\rho]\!]$ such that $n_1' \in n_1[\![\rho]\!]$ and $n_2' \in n_2[\![\rho]\!]$. Observe that $x_l \in n_1'[\![P_l']\!]$ and $y_l \in n_2'[\![P_l']\!]$, and moreover, for any $i \in [1, k]$, if $i \neq l$ then $x_i \in n_1'[\![\varrho.P_i]\!]$ and $y_i \in n_2'[\![\varrho.P_i]\!]$. Since $(Q.\rho,\ \{\varrho.P_1, ..., P_l', ..., \varrho.P_k\})$ is a key, we must have $n_1' = n_2'$. Hence $n_1 = n_2$ since n_1, n_2 are ancestors of n_1', n_2', respectively, and because XML trees do not allow sharing of nodes. Thus $(Q,\ \{P_1, ..., P_l, ..., P_k\})$ is also a key. Note that if $\rho = \epsilon$, then the key in the precondition and the one in the consequence of the rule are the same.
(3) *containment*. This rule holds because $[\![Q']\!] \subseteq [\![Q]\!]$ given $Q' \subseteq Q$ and moreover, a key for $[\![Q]\!]$ is also a key for any subset of $[\![Q]\!]$.
(4) *empty-path*. It is sound because $[\![\epsilon]\!]$ consists of a single node, i.e., the root.

Note that containment of path expressions is used in the inference rules.

Given a finite set $\Sigma \cup \{\varphi\}$ of $\mathcal{K}$ constraints, we use $\Sigma \vdash \varphi$ to denote that φ is provable from Σ using $\mathcal{I}$. That is, there is an $\mathcal{I}$-proof of φ from Σ.

For example, recall Σ_0 and φ_0 given earlier. We show $\Sigma_0 \vdash \varphi_0$ as follows. By $\_*.person \subseteq \_*$ and the containment rule, $\Sigma_0 \vdash (\_*.person,\ \{ID\})$. By the superkey rule, $\{(\_*.person,\ \{ID\})\} \vdash (\_*.person,\ \{ID,\ name\})$. Thus $\Sigma_0 \vdash \varphi_0$.

Lemma 3.3 asserts that $\mathcal{I}$ is indeed a finite axiomatization. That is, given any finite set $\Sigma \cup \{\varphi\}$ of $\mathcal{K}$ constraints, $\Sigma \models \varphi$ iff $\Sigma \vdash \varphi$. See [13] for the proof.

Lemma 3.3: The set $\mathcal{I}$ of inference rules is sound and complete for implication of $\mathcal{K}$ constraints. ∎

For example, we have shown $\Sigma_0 \vdash \varphi_0$. By Lemma 3.3, we have $\Sigma_0 \models \varphi_0$.

A similar result was shown in [6]. However, keys considered in [6] do not contain the upward wildcard $\widehat{up}$. The presence of $\widehat{up}$ complicates the proof.

Complexity. Finally, we show that keys of $\mathcal{K}$ can be reasoned about efficiently.

Lemma 3.4: The implication problem for $\mathcal{K}$ is decidable in cubic time. ∎

A cubic-time algorithm for determining implication of $\mathcal{K}$ constraints is given in [13]. The algorithm is developed based on the inference rules of $\mathcal{I}$.

Lemmas 3.3 and 3.4 suffice to prove Theorem 3.1.

4 Conclusion

We have proposed a key constraint language for XML defined in terms of regular path expressions extended with downward and upward wildcards. Despite the simple syntax of the language, it is capable of expressing both absolute and relative keys, which are important to hierarchically structured data including XML documents. We have shown that any keys expressed in the language can be satisfied by an XML document. We have also shown that the implication problem for the key language is finitely axiomatizable and cubic-time decidable.

A number of questions remain open. First, the decision problems are investigated in the absence of DTDs. Keys may interact with DTDs and the interaction may complicate reasoning about keys [12,9]. This issue needs further investigation. Second, keys help information preservation in data exchange and integration. An important project is to study how to achieve this in practice. Third, keys may lead to efficient storage and access methods for XML data. This practical issue deserves further research.

Acknowledgments. We thank Peter Buneman for helpful discussions.

References

1. S. Abiteboul, P. Buneman, and D. Suciu. *Data on the Web: From Relations to Semistructured Data and XML.* Morgan Kaufman, 2000.
2. S. Abiteboul, R. Hull, and V. Vianu. *Foundations of Databases.* Addison-Wesley, 1995.
3. V. Apparao et al. *Document Object Model (DOM) Level 1 Specification.* W3C Recommendation, Oct. 1998. `http://www.w3.org/TR/REC-DOM-Level-1`.
4. C. Baru et al. XML-based information mediation with MIX. In *Proc. ACM SIGMOD Conf. on Management of Data*, 1999.

5. T. Bray, J. Paoli, and C. M. Sperberg-McQueen. Extensible Markup Language (XML) 1.0. W3C Recommendation, Feb 1998. `http://www.w3.org/TR/REC-xml`.
6. P. Buneman, S. Davidson, W. Fan, C. Hara, and W. Tan. Reasoning about keys for XML. Technical Report TUCIS-TR-2000-005, Temple University, 2000.
7. P. Buneman, S. Davidson, W. Fan, C. Hara, and W. Tan. Keys for XML. In *Proc. 10th Int'l World Wide Web Conf. (WWW'10)*, 2001.
8. P. Buneman, W. Fan, J. Siméon, and S. Weinstein. Integrity constraints for semistructured data and XML. *SIGMOD Record*, 30(1), Mar. 2001.
9. P. Buneman, W. Fan, and S. Weinstein. Interaction between path and type constraints. In *Proc. ACM Symp. on Principles of Database Systems (PODS)*, 1999.
10. J. Clark. *XSL Transormations (XSLT)*. W3C Recommendation, Nov. 1999. `http://www.w3.org/TR/xslt`.
11. J. Clark and S. DeRose. *XML Path Language (XPath)*. W3C Recommendation, Nov. 1999. `http://www.w3.org/TR/xpath`.
12. W. Fan and L. Libkin. On XML integrity constraints in the presence of DTDs. In *Proc. ACM Symp. on Principles of Database Systems (PODS)*, 2001.
13. W. Fan, P. Schwenzer, and K. Wu. Keys with upward wildcards for XML. Technical Report TUCIS-TR-2000-007, Temple University, 2000. `http://www.cis.temple.edu/~fan/papers/xml/upward.ps.gz`.
14. W. Fan and J. Siméon. Integrity constraints for XML. In *Proc. ACM Symp. on Principles of Database Systems (PODS)*, 2000.
15. D. Florescu, L. Raschid, and P. Valduriez. A methodology for query reformulation in CIS using semantic knowledge. *Int'l J. Cooperative Information Systems (IJCIS)*, 5(4):431–468, 1996.
16. C. Hara and S. Davidson. Reasoning about nested functional dependencies. In *Proc. ACM Symp. on Principles of Database Systems (PODS)*, 1999.
17. M. Ito and G. E. Weddell. Implication problems for functional constraints on databases supporting complex objects. *J. Computer and System Sciences (JCSS)*, 50(1):165–187, 1995.
18. R. Ramakrishnan and J. Gehrke. *Database Management Systems.* McGraw-Hill Higher Education, 2000.
19. Z. Tari, J. Stokes, and S. Spaccapietra. Dependency constraints and normal forms for object-oriented schemata. *ACM Trans. on Database Systems*, 22(4), 1997.
20. H. S. Thompson, D. Beech, M. Maloney, and N. Mendelsohn. *XML Schema Part 1: Structures.* W3C, Apr. 2000. `http://www.w3.org/TR/xmlschema-1/`.

A Framework for the Classification and Description of Multidimensional Data Models

Alberto Abelló[1], José Samos[2], and Fèlix Saltor[1]

[1] U. Politècnica de Catalunya (UPC), Dept. de Llenguatges i Sistemes Informàtics
{aabello,saltor}@lsi.upc.es
[2] U. de Granada (UGR), Dept. de Lenguajes y Sistemas Informáticos
jsamos@ugr.es

Abstract. The words On-Line Analytical Processing bring together a set of tools, that use multidimensional modeling in the management of information to improve the decision making process. Lately, a lot of work has been devoted to modeling the multidimensional space. The aim of this paper is twofold. On one hand, it compiles and classifies some of that work, with regard to the design phase they are used in. On the other hand, it allows to compare the different terminology used by each author, by placing all the terms in a common framework.

1 Introduction

In the last years, multidimensional modeling has gained attention of the research community. It is a powerful conceptualization technique used in On-Line Analytical Processing (OLAP) applications. As explained in [CD97], OLAP tools, by means of multidimensional modeling, facilitate complex analysis and visualization of data for decision making processes. Its main advantages are its proximity to the analysts way of thinking, and facility to improve query performance.

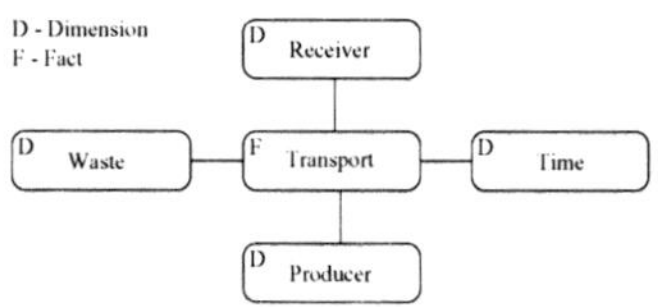

Fig. 1. Multidimensional scheme example

This technique is based on the concept of a hypercube (we will misuse the term "cube" from here on) containing the data cells of interest to the analysis. Every one of these data cells is identified by a coordinate in each analysis dimension. For instance, as depicted in figure 1, in a waste transport business, we would analyze fact "Transport" involving the transported "Waste", the "Time" the transport takes place, the "Producer" it is transported from, and the "Receiver" it is transported to. Therefore, we would have a 4-dimensional space

H.C. Mayr et al. (Eds.): DEXA 2001, LNCS 2113, pp. 668–677, 2001.

where each point represents transport data, and is identified by a waste, a point in time, a waste producer, and a waste receiver.

In this paper, we classify the huge amount of efforts devoted to modeling the cube into four groups based on the design phase for which they are, from our point of view, more suitable. Moreover, a framework is also defined to be able to compare their modeling constructs. Section 2 briefly reviews previous work on classifying multidimensional models. Sections 3.1 and 3.2 define the framework that will allow us to describe and classify the different models; while section 4 contains a brief comparison of some models. These models are sorted out in four different subsections based on the modeling level that we think they are in. Section 5 presents some conclusions, followed by acknowledgements and bibliography.

2 Related Work

In [BSHD98], a list of requirements for a multidimensional model in order to be suitable for OLAP applications, is used to analyze seven models, that are chosen because they contain some kind of formalism. Among those seven we find [AGS97], [GL97], [CT98], [Vas00], and [Leh98]. Those requirements were derived from general design principles, and from characteristics of OLAP applications.

[Ped00] presents eleven requirements (found in clinical data warehousing) for multidimensional data models, and evaluates twelve preexisting data models against them. Those presented in [AGS97], [Dyr96], [Kim96], [GL97], [CT98], [Leh98], and [Vas00] are among those twelve. An statistical model, and a commercial system are also included. Moreover, it presents a new data model which does address all those requirements.

[Vas00] gives yet another classification of multidimensional models. Among others, it pays attention to [GL97], [AGS97], [CT98], [Leh98], some industrial standards, and a couple of statistical models.

3 A Classification and Description Framework

The following sections introduce two sets of classification and description levels for multidimensional models. These levels are orthogonal. Thus, a model can be classified as either *Conceptual*, *Logical*, *Physical*, or *Formalism*; and contain constructs at any of the three detail levels, i.e. *Upper*, *Intermediate*, or *Lower*.

3.1 Design Levels

A data model is a set of concepts that can be used to describe the structure of a database. We propose to distinguish different multidimensional data models attending to the kind of constructs/concepts they provide and the multidimensional design phase they are used in.

As shown in figure 2 (left), from [UW97], in an On-Line Transactional Processing (OLTP) environment, during the first design step, at *Conceptual* level,

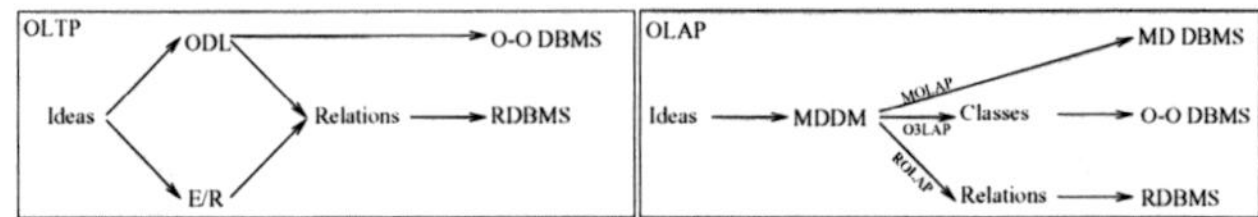

Fig. 2. Modeling and implementation process in OLAP vs OLTP environments

we would use Entity-Relationship (E/R) or Object Definition Language (ODL) to represent user ideas; in the next step, at *Logical* level, we would usually use the Relational model, but we could also use Hierarchical, or Network models (not depicted in the figure); and in the last step, at *Physical* level, the implementation would depend on a specific DBMS (i.e. Oracle, Informix, ObjectStore, etc.). In a similar way, in our proposal for an OLAP environment, in figure 2 (right), we would have the Multidimensional Data Model (MDDM) at *Conceptual* level, and, depending on the approach (i.e. Relational -ROLAP-, Object-Oriented -O3LAP-, or pure Multidimensional -MOLAP-), we would use a different model at *Logical* level, and a different DBMS for the implementation.

We adopted the terminology in [BCN92], that considers models at *Conceptual* level that are close to the user and independent of the implementation; those at *Logical* level depending on the kind of Database Management System (DBMS) used in the implementation, but still understandable by end users; and finally, those at *Physical* level depending on the specific DBMS used, and conceived to describe how data is actually stored. In [EN94], we find a similar categorization of data models into "High-level" or "conceptual", if they provide concepts that are close to the way users perceive data; "Low-level" or "physical", if they provide concepts that describe the details of how data is stored in the computer; and "Implementation", if they provide concepts that can be understood by end users, but that are not too far removed from the way data is organized within the computer.

Besides these three mentioned above, we found another set of models (let us say they are *Formalisms*) whose concepts would not be used at any database design phase, but on giving a theoretical framework. They include an algebra or calculus. In an OLTP environment, a formalism would be the Relational Algebra.

3.2 Detail Levels

Each one of the papers mentioned in section 2, begins by defining a list of specific requirements for a multidimensional model in order to evaluate all those models already existing. We are not giving such a list. Each one of the models compiled in this paper uses its own terminology and defines a specific set of design elements. In this sense, we are going to use different *detail levels* to classify the constructs of the models, to be able to compare them, and examine the expressive power of every model.

In a multidimensional model, conceptually, we distinguish three different detail levels:

Upper Level (UL): At this level, we find *Dimensions* (D) and *Facts* (F). The dimensions are used to characterize the facts, and show the viewpoints the facts will be analyzed from. By relating a set of dimensions to a fact, we obtain a star shape scheme. The possibility of navigating from a star to another one is shown by relating dimensions.

Intermediate Level (IL): *Dimensions* and *Facts* are decomposed into *Dimension Levels* (DL), and *Fact Cells* (FC) respectively. The different *Dimension Levels* in a *Dimension* form an aggregation hierarchy. Each *Fact Cell* contains data at a given *Dimension Level* for each *Dimension* its *Fact* is related to.

Lower Level (LL): The last level shows the set attributes of the *Dimension Levels* and *Fact Cells*. That is *Classification Attributes* (CA), and *Measures* (M) respectively.

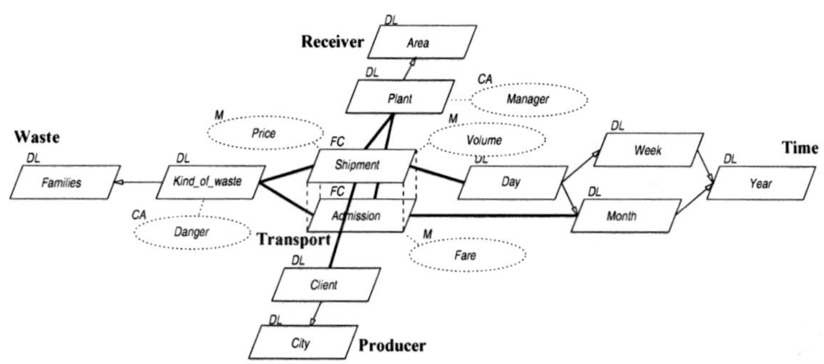

Fig. 3. Further detailed multidimensional scheme example

Going back to our example in figure 1, which represents a multidimensional scheme at *Upper Level*, as composed by a *Fact* ("Transport"), and four *Dimensions* ("Waste", "Producer", "Receiver", and "Time"); figure 3 represents the same multidimensional scheme at lower detail levels. Each one of the *Dimensions* is further described by a hierarchy of different *Dimension Levels*. For instance, "Time" *Dimension* contains "Day", "Week", "Month", and "Year" *Dimension Levels*. Moreover, if we were interested in the benefits of a transport, we would need to analyze data that would belong to different kinds of cube cells (price of the shipment that we charge to our client, minus admission fare that a processing plant charges to us). On one hand, we can see a "Shipment" *Fact Cell* containing data about our shipments which depends on the lower level of each one of the four dimensions. On the other hand, data about "Admission" of "Waste" in a "Plant" do not depend on our clients, nor on "Day" level of "Time" dimension (it depends on "Month" level). Therefore, "Admission" and "Shipment" are different kinds of *Fact Cells*, but belong to the same *Fact* we want to analyze. Finally, drawn with dotted lines, we can see constructs at *Lower Level*. Some *Dimension Levels* have *Classification Attributes* associated (for instance, a "Plant" has a "Manager"). Besides, *Fact Cells* have associated *Measures* (for instance, an "Admission" has a "Fare") that we want to analyze.

4 Application of the Framework to Some Relevant Models

This section contains a set of multidimensional data models classified in four different subsections. Each one of these four subsections contains proposals at a given design level (i.e. *Conceptual*, *Logical*, *Physical*, and *Formalisms*).

Table 1. Summary table of the different models presented

Authors (Model)	Reference	Design Level	Upper Level			Intermediate Level			Lower Level		
			F	D	Rel.	FC	DL	Rel.	M	CA	Rel.
Lehner (NMDM)	[Leh98]	C	–	√	–	–	√	√	–	√	√
Cabibbo and Torlone (*MD*)	[CT98]	C/F	√	√	√	–	√	√	√	√	√
Golfarelli et al. (DFM)	[GMR98]	C	–	√	–	√	√	√	√	√	√
Sapia et al. (MERM)	[SBHD99]	C	√	√	√	√	√	√	√	√	√
Tryfona et al. (starER)	[TBC99]	C	–	√	–	√	√	√	√	√	√
Kimball	[Kim96]	L	–	√	√	√	–	√	√	√	√
Buzydlowski et al. (O3LAP)	[BSH98]	L	–	√	√	√	√	√	√	√	√
Gopalkrishnan et al. (ORV)	[GLK99]	L/P	–	√	√	√	–	√	√	√	√
Mangisengi et al. (NR)	[MTW99]	L	√	–	–	√	–	√	√	–	√
Mangisengi et al. (ER)	[MTW99]	L	–	√	√	√	√	√	√	√	√
Dyreson	[Dyr96]	P	–	√	–	–	√	√	–	–	–
Agrawal, Gupta, and Sarawagi	[AGS97]	F	–	–	–	√	–	–	–	√	√
Hacid and Sattler	[HS97]	F	–	√	–	–	√	√	√	√	√
Gyssens and Lakshmanan	[GL97]	F	–	–	–	√	√	√	√	√	√
Vassiliadis	[Vas00]	F	–	√	√	√	√	√	√	–	√
Pedersen (EMDM)	[Ped00]	F	√	√	√	–	√	√	√	–	–

Table 1 contains a summary of elements and relationships among them that we found at each model. Notice we are not showing information about neither instances nor instantiation relations. As pointed out by [BSHD98], some multidimensional models do not separate cube structure and contents. Only those concepts represented at schema level are considered. A tick means something is captured by the model, while a hyphen means that the authors of the model either say something not to be modeled or just do not say how to model it.

A hyphen in the column corresponding to:

Measure (M) means that nothing can be represented in the scheme about measures. Maybe, there are only pure numerical values stored in the cube (without any meaningful domain).

Classification Attribute (CA) means dimensions do not have attributes describing their different entities. All the information is kept in the form of classification hierarchies at the most.

LL Relationships means there is no way in the model to represent relationships among *Measures* and/or *Classification Attributes*.

Dimension Level (DL) means there are not explicit levels in the dimensions.

Fact Cell (FC) means that either the *Measures* are not grouped, or they are not related to a specific set of *Dimension Levels*, but to dimensions as a whole (usually reflected as relating the measures to the lowest level in the classification hierarchy).

IL Relationships means there is no way in the model to represent relationships among *Fact Cells* and/or *Dimension Levels*. For instance, it implies that there is not the possibility of explicit dimension hierarchies.

Fact (F) means that the different *Fact Cells* can not be grouped with the intention to relate *Measures* that, even though are defined at different granularities, are used together in a given decision making process.

Dimension (D) means that either there is only the possibility of modeling one *Dimension Level*, or if it is possible to model more than one, they cannot be grouped into another element of the model.

UL Relationships means there is no way in the model to represent relationships among *Facts* and/or *Dimensions*.

4.1 At Conceptual Level

In this section we place those models that contain concepts which are closer to the user than to the actual computer implementation. They try to represent how users perceive a multidimensional cube.

[Leh98] is rather a presentation-oriented model, conceived to ease navigation through data. It proposes the existence of two levels in order to improve the power and flexibility of the analysis process. The first level (called "Primary Multidimensional Object") contains the *Dimension Levels* at which the facts are, and the second level (called "Secondary Multidimensional Object") shows *Classification Attributes* that select the desired facts. The main characteristic of this model is that different instances in the same class might have different attributes. All schema constructs in this model refer to dimensions.

The model in [CT98] is qualified as "logical". However, they say that it is independent of any specific implementation, and present a design methodology to obtain a multidimensional scheme from an E/R one. Moreover, it is also said that their model is at a higher level of abstraction than a star scheme consisting of relational tables. Therefore, we classify it as *Conceptual*, in spite of it also provides a strong formal foundation (including a calculus). Each *Dimension* is organized in a hierarchy of *Dimension Levels* corresponding to data domains at different granularity. In turn, a *Dimension Level* can have *Classification Attributes* associated with it. The *Facts* are functions from *Dimension Levels* to *Measures*.

[GMR98] presents a graphical model besides a methodology to obtain a multidimensional scheme from the operational schemes (either E/R or Relational). Contrary to what is said for some *Formalisms*, the authors claim that it is important to clearly distinguish between dimensions and measures. A scheme is composed by a set of *Fact Cells*, and *Dimensions* with hierarchies of *Dimension Levels* forming a "quasi-tree". *Fact Cells* contain *Measures*, while *Dimension Levels* contain two kinds of *Classification Attributes*: those defining aggregation hierarchies, and the others, that are only used to select data. A special relation between two schemes is also defined (called "compatibility" and "strict compatibility"), which indicates and restricts when a query can be formulated including *Measures* in both schemes. Roughly, two schemes are "compatible" when they have, at least, one common *Dimension Level*.

[SBHD99] argues that the E/R model is not suited for multidimensional conceptual modeling. Thus, a specialization is defined, and its usage exemplified.

Dimension Level is a specialization of Entity, while Relationship is specialized into *Fact*, and roll-up relations between *Dimension Levels*. *Measures* and *Classification Attributes* are, respectively, "relationship", and "entity" attributes.

[TBC99] is also based on the well known E/R. This model distinguishes three kinds of *Measures*, i.e. "stock", "flow", and "value-per-unit". Moreover, it also allows to represent different kinds of relationships among *Dimension Levels* and *Fact Cells* (i.e. "Specialization/Generalization", "Aggregation", and "Membership"). For instance, aggregation hierarchies in *Dimensions* are defined by means of "Membership" relationships. Moreover, cardinality between a *Dimension Level* and a *Fact Cell* is not restricted to 1:N (as it is in other models), but N:M is also allowed.

4.2 At Logical Level

This section contains those papers describing a model neither *Conceptual*, nor *Physical*. Their constructs are clearly oriented to a given kind of DBMS. Nevertheless, they are not that far from users conceptions.

Doubtless, the most prominent work at this design level is [Kim96]. It describes the implementation of the multidimensional model on a Relational DBMS. In this book, Ralph Kimball presents some multidimensional design patterns, and describes how they could be tackled. A huge Relational table represents every *Fact Cell*, and smaller tables, corresponding to its *Dimensions*, surround each one of them. *Dimension Levels* are implicit in the values of attributes in *Dimensions*, while foreign keys are defined from each *Fact Cell* to its *Dimensions*. This is known as a "star join schema".

Some efforts have been done to improve Kimball's work. We can see [BSH98], or [GLK99], for two Object-Oriented approaches.

[MTW99] introduces and compares two different approaches to multidimensional modeling (notice that there are two entries in the summary table for these authors). The ideas of those approaches are based on "nested relations" (Non-First Normal Form Relations), and the extension to the Relational model introduced in [Cod79]. By means of "nested relations", it is possible to have *Measures* into *Fact Cells*, and these nested into *Facts*. On the other hand, using Codd's extension allows to introduce "object identifiers" (OIDs), "associations", and "object types". This facilitates to relate *Fact Cells* and *Dimensions*, and define aggregation hierarchies among *Dimension Levels*.

4.3 At Physical Level

In this section, we place those proposals that explain how a data cube could be implemented (i.e. stored, and/or retrieved). The proposals at this level do not only depend on the kind of DBMS, but also present which specific mechanisms it should implement.

At this level, we found only one paper about modeling. This fact could be surprising; however, at *Physical* level, proposals must be devoted to specific storage techniques instead of providing a true data model. Since modeling is a conceptualization by means of a given set of constructs, it is more suitable the closer to the user we are. We did not expect to find any work in this section, however, this one expresses how data should be stored besides some concepts to understand it.

[Dyr96] explains how a sparse cube could be implemented in a MOLAP database by means of disjoint, complete "cubettes". A "cubette" is defined as containing data about a given subset chosen from the domain of interest. An algorithm to retrieve an aggregate value from the incomplete data cube is described, besides another algorithm to remove redundant "cubettes".

4.4 Formalisms

In this section, we place those models mainly devoted to the definition of a multidimensional algebra and/or calculus. They do not pay too much attention to facilitate the capture of the specific user concepts. Since their focus is not in conceptualizing users ideas, we can see, in the summary table, that they do not offer as much constructs as other models. However, if we would take into account the expressiveness of the algebras, they could be as semantically rich as conceptual are. We only take into account modeling constructs, studying the expressiveness of the operations is out of the scope of this paper.

[AGS97] presents one of the first multidimensional models, and probably, one of the most referenced ones. In spite of its qualification as "logical" by the authors, since its focus is on presenting an algebra as powerful as Relational algebra, we consider it a formalism. It does not offer too many conceptual elements to model a multidimensional scheme. Actually, it just provides *Classification Attributes* without any possibility of even grouping them into different *Dimensions.* At most, we could consider that it allows to group *Measures* into tuples giving rise to *Fact Cells.* An important feature is that allows symmetric treatment of *Measures* and *Classification Attributes* by providing a conversion operation.

[HS97] uses Description Logics to describe the cube. It is represented as a relationship among cells, which keeps coordinates and measures. It is not explicitly said, but *Dimensions* could be modeled as the set of concepts participating in classification hierarchies, which are composed by *Dimension Levels* related through Part-Whole relationships.

[GL97] proposes a Relational approach defining an "n-dimensional table scheme" as a triple containing a dimension names set; an attributes set; and a function from dimension names to attribute set, showing the attributes of each dimension. This allows to represent *Measures*, *Classification Attributes*, and *Dimension Levels.* If we subtract the *Classification Attributes* from the set of all attributes in the cube, we could also consider implicitly defined a *Fact Cell.*

[Vas00] presents a complete and sound algebra. It defines a *Dimension* as a lattice of *Dimension Levels*, that do not contain *Classification Attributes. Fact Cells* are implicitly said to be tuples of *Measures*, and always defined at the bottom level of the *Dimensions.*

Finally, [Ped00] provides a formalism and an algebra that is closed and, at least, as strong as Relational algebra with aggregation functions. It defines *Facts*, and *Dimensions* containing different *Dimension Levels*. However, we do not consider the model allows to show *Fact Cells*. Data in the *Facts* can be related to any *Dimension Level*, but this information cannot be shown in the scheme. *Classification Attributes* can neither be related to *Dimension Levels*, while *Dimension Levels* are used as *Measures* (by treating symmetrically dimensions and facts).

5 Conclusions

This paper has presented a framework that allows us to classify and compare multidimensional models. It has been exemplified by studying some representative models. Classification and description of other models has been left out just because of space limitations. There exist previous studies comparing different multidimensional models (see section 2). However, those studies did it just to show their lacks against a given list of requirements, and models for absolutely different purposes were put into the same bag. On the contrary, we have classified them in different levels (i.e. *Conceptual*, *Logical*, *Physical*, and *Formalisms*) based on their usage in the multidimensional design process. Furthermore, we have given a framework to compare the terminology used by different authors for the constructs of their models.

It seems that *Conceptual* models offer the possibility of representing much more semantics that models at other levels. Indeed, *Conceptual* models do have to provide a rich set of semantic constructs in order to capture user ideas. In turn, *Formalisms* are those that offer less conceptual constructs. However, notice they do offer an algebra whose expressiveness was not considered in this paper, because our focus was on modeling constructs. At *Physical* level, we find storage techniques instead of true data models.Thus, just one *Physical* model was found. Moreover, there was not found a great variety of models at *Logical* level.

The more recent the models are, they use to capture more semantics. This can be interpreted as a trend to semantically enrich multidimensional models. However, having models that provide constructs at every detail level does not mean they capture all possible semantics. We have found neither a model encompassing the semantic constructs of the rest, nor a consensus or standard stating what should be represented in a multidimensional scheme.

Acknowledgements. This work has been partially supported by the Spanish Research Program PRONTIC under projects TIC2000-1723-C02-01 and TIC2000-1723-C02-02, as well as the grant 1998FI-00228 from the Generalitat de Catalunya.

References

[AGS97] R. Agrawal, A. Gupta, and S. Sarawagi. Modeling multidimensional databases. In *Int. Conf. on Data Engineering (ICDE)*. IEEE Press, 1997.

[BCN92] C. Batini, S. Ceri, and S. Navathe. *Conceptual Database Design- an Entity-Relationship Approach.* Benjamin/Cummings, 1992.

[BSH98] J. W. Buzydlowski, I. Song, and L. Hassell. A Framework for Object-Oriented On-line Analytical Processing. In *Int. Workshop on Data Warehousing and OLAP (DOLAP).* ACM, 1998.

[BSHD98] M. Blaschka, C. Sapia, G. Höfling, and B. Dinter. Finding your way through multidimensional data models. In *Int. Conf. on Database and Expert Systems Applications (DEXA)*, number 1460 in LNCS. Springer, 1998.

[CD97] S. Chaudhuri and U. Dayal. An overview of data warehousing and OLAP technology. *SIGMOD Record*, 26(1), 1997.

[Cod79] E. F. Codd. Extending the relational model to capture more meaning. *ACM Transactions on Database Systems*, 4(4), 1979.

[CT98] L. Cabibbo and R. Torlone. A logical approach to multidimensional databases. In *Advances in Database Technology - EDBT'98*, number 1377 in LNCS. Springer, 1998.

[Dyr96] C. Dyreson. Information retrieval from an incomplete data cube. In *Int. Conf. on Very Large Data Bases (VLDB).* Morgan Kaufmann, 1996.

[EN94] R. Elmasri and S. B. Navathe. *Fundamentals of Database Systems, 2nd Ed.* Benjamin Cummings, 1994.

[GL97] M. Gyssens and L. V. S. Lakshmanan. A foundation for multi-dimensional databases. In *Int. Conf. on Very Large Data Bases (VLDB).* Morgan Kaufmann, 1997.

[GLK99] V. Gopalkrishnan, Q. Li, and K. Karlapalem. Star/snow-flake schema driven object-relational data warehouse design and query processing strategies. In *Int. Workshop on Data Warehousing and Knowledge Discovery (DaWaK)*, number 1676 in LNCS. Springer, 1999.

[GMR98] M. Golfarelli, D. Maio, and S Rizzi. The Dimensional Fact Model: a Conceptual Model for Data Warehouses. *Int. Journal of Cooperative Information Systems*, 7(2&3), 1998.

[HS97] M.-S. Hacid and U. Sattler. An object-centered multi-dimensional data model with hierarchically structured dimensions. In *IEEE Knowledge and Data Exchange Workshop (KDEX).* IEEE Computer Society, 1997.

[Kim96] R. Kimball. *The Data Warehouse toolkit.* John Wiley & Sons, 1996.

[Leh98] W. Lehner. Modeling large scale OLAP scenarios. In *Advances in Database Technology - EDBT'98*, volume 1377 of *LNCS.* Springer, 1998.

[MTW99] O. Mangisengi, A M. Tjoa, and R. R. Wagner. Multidimensional Modeling Approaches for OLAP Based on Extended Relational Concepts. In *Int. Database Conf. on Heterogeneous and Internet Databases (IDC)*, 1999.

[Ped00] T. B. Pedersen. *Aspects of Data Modeling and Query Processing for Complex Multidimensional Data.* PhD thesis, Faculty of Engineering and Science, 2000.

[SBHD99] C. Sapia, M. Blaschka, G. Höfling, and B. Dinter. Extending the E/R model for the multidimensional paradigm. In *Int. Workshop on Data Warehouse and Data Mining (DWDM)*, number 1552 in LNCS. Springer, 1999.

[TBC99] N. Tryfona, F. Busborg, and J. G. B. Christiansen. starER: A conceptual model for data warehouse design. In *Int. Workshop on Data Warehousing and OLAP (DOLAP).* ACM, 1999.

[UW97] J. Ullman and J. Widom. *A First Course in Database Systems.* Prentice-Hall, 1997.

[Vas00] P. Vassiliadis. *Data Warehouse Modeling and Quality Issues.* PhD thesis, Department of Electrical and Computer Engineering, 2000.

Range Top/Bottom *k* Queries in OLAP Sparse Data Cubes

Zhong Wei Luo, Tok Wang Ling, Chuan Heng Ang, Sin Yeung Lee, and Bin Cui

School of Computing, National University of Singapore
{luozhong, lingtw, angch, jlee, cuibin}@comp.nus.edu.sg

Abstract. A range top *k* query finds the top *k* maximum values over all selected cells of an OLAP data cube where the selection is specified by the range of contiguous values for each dimension. In this paper, we propose a partition-based storage structure, which is capable of answering both range top and bottom *k* queries in OLAP sparse data cubes. This is achieved by partitioning a multi-dimensional sparse data cube and storing it in partition-major order into two one-dimensional arrays: one is for the dense partitions and the other one is for the sparse partitions. This algorithm supports both single cell update and bulk batch update. Nevertheless, the update cost for a set of cells in a partition is similar to the update cost of a single cell update, i.e. extra 2 I/Os in the most cases and the worst is extra 5 I/Os in some very rare cases. Our approach also reduces the storage cost of sparse data cubes.

1 Introduction

The data cube [4], also known as the multidimensional database (MDDB) in the On-Line Analytical Processing (OLAP) system, is designed to provide aggregate information for data analysts of various levels of summary information in the database and data warehouse. In a data cube, attributes are categorized into *dimension attributes* and *measure attributes*. The measure attributes of those records with the same functional attributes values are combined (e.g. summed up) into aggregate value. Thus, a MDDB can be viewed as a *d*-dimensional array, indexed by the values of the *d* dimension attributes, whose cells contain the values of the measure attributes for the corresponding combination of dimension attributes.

Using the data cube model, we can formulate many range queries. In particular, we propose a new pre-computation approach for a class of OLAP queries called Range Top/Bottom *k* Queries, which is capable of finding both top *k* maximum and bottom *k* minimum values with just one storage structure. A Range Top *k* Query finds the top *k* maximum values over all selected cells of an OLAP data cube where the selection is specified by a range of contiguous values for each dimension. For example, finding the top 10 sales of stationary items (each has an item code ranging from 1200 to 1258) between day 130 and 131 in the western outlets (branch-no ranging from 45 to 89) is a range top *k* query. It can be realized using the following SQL-like statement:

SELECT TOP(amount, 10) FROM sales WHERE
$(1200 \le \text{item} \le 1258)$ AND $(130 \le \text{day} \le 131)$ AND $(45 \le \text{branch} \le 89)$;

H.C. Mayr et al. (Eds.): DEXA 2001, LNCS 2113, pp. 678–687, 2001.

Previous Work on MAX/MIN. To handle range MAX/MIN query efficiently, considerable research has been done in the database community [5, 6, 7, 8].

In [5], a balanced hierarchical tree-based algorithm was presented. In this method, a generalized quad-tree is constructed on the data cube and in each tree node the index of the maximum value in the region covered by that node was stored. Then a branch-and-bound[10]-like procedure was used to speed up the queries.

[6] proposed the concept of maximal cover, which represents the data distribution with respect to range MAX processing. Thus, the problem of processing range MAX is transformed into the problem of finding an appropriate maximal cover. To speed up the search process, the authors proposed the maximal cover network, which is a search structure based on the containment relation between two maximal covers.

[8] presented a Block-based Relative Prefix Max Approach, which uses Block Pre-computed max Cube (*BPC*) and Location Pre-computed Cube (*LPC*) as auxiliary information to answer range max queries. *BPC* partitions the given data cube and stores the maximum values, which are in the range of the cell with the lowest dimension index to the current cell in the partition, whereas *LPC* stores pre-computed max over partitions and location of the max.

On the other hand, the Hierarchical Compact Cube Approach [7] uses a hierarchical structure which stores the maximum value and its location of all the children sub-cubes. The storage requirement is much less than the block-based approach. Furthermore, the average query time of this approach is bounded by a constant independent on the number of data in the data cube.

However, the above-mentioned work has the following weaknesses:

1. These approaches cannot be directly applied to range top/bottom *k* queries.
2. The data accesses in these approaches are based on cell accessing. It does not reflect the real processing time, because the basic unit of I/O operations associated with a disk is a block instead of a cell.
3. [6, 7, 8] do not take sparse data cubes into consideration. However, in many applications with large number of dimensions, typically, only 20% of data in the data cube is non-empty [2].

Our approach can solve the above-mentioned problems. We partition the data cube and store it as one-dimensional array in partition-major order, thus making it suitable to be accessed based on blocks. Our new storage structure can be applied to other pre-computed partition-based range queries, such as range SUM and MAX/MIN. Moreover, our new storage structure is capable of handling both range top and bottom *k* queries. In the following, we only process range top *k* queries for simplicity. Our approach also reduces the storage cost for sparse data cubes.

2 The Data Structure

To reduce the storage cost of sparse data cubes and the disk I/O cost for the range top *k* queries, we propose a new storage structure for the data cube and use an auxiliary pre-computed data cube called *LPC* (Location Pre-computed Cube), which is the index of the original data cube. The original data cube is denoted as *DC*.

2.1 Physical Data Cube (*PDC*)

A Data Cube *DC* of d dimension is a d-dimensional array. For each dimension, the index can range from 0 to n_i-1 (n_i denotes the size of the ith dimension). Hence, a cell in *DC* can be expressed in the following form: $DC[x_1,\ldots,x_d]$, where $0 \le x_i \le n_i-1$.

Example 2.1. Fig. 1 shows a 2-dimensional data cube. The range of the top k query is expressed as (0:6,1:5) and it is depicted by the shaded area.

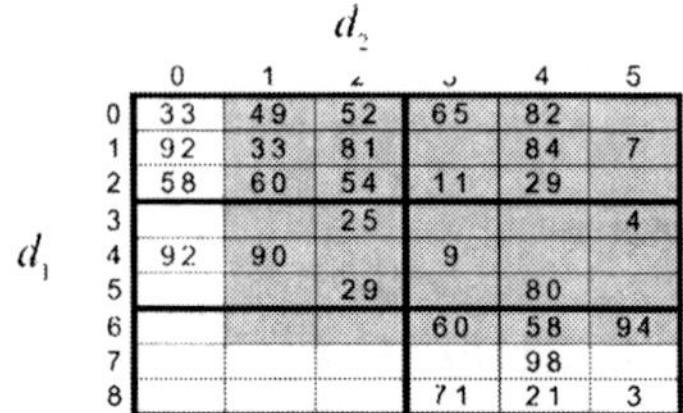

Fig. 1. A 2-dimensional data cube *DC*

Given a d-dimensional *DC*, and d integers $b_1,\ldots,b_d$ called **partition factors**, we divide the *DC* into a number of partitions by applying partition factor b_i on i^{th} dimension. In order to reduce the storage cost for sparse data cubes, we classify these partitions into 3 types: **empty partitions**, **sparse partitions** and **dense partitions** and store sparse partitions and dense partitions in different storage structures. Let p and m denote the number of cells in the partition and the number of non-empty cells in the partition, respectively. If m=0, this partition is an **empty partition**. If $m \le \lceil p\times\delta \rceil$, this partition is a **sparse partition**, otherwise it is a **dense partition**, where δ is the **density threshold** to determine if the partition is dense or sparse and $0<\delta<1$, e.g. 30%.

In Fig. 1, p=3×3=9 and we set δ to 50%, then the partition (6:8, 0:2) is an empty partition, the partitions (3:5, 0:2) and (3:5, 3:5) are sparse partitions, whereas the partitions (0:2, 0:2), (0:2, 3:5) and (6:8, 3:5) are dense partitions.

To reduce the storage requirement of a sparse data cube and disk I/O for the range top k queries, each sparse partition is stored into one or two physically adjacent blocks. In order to avoid the frequent changing of partitions from dense partitions to sparse partitions or vice versa caused by insertions or deletions of cells, we do not choose $\lceil p\times\delta/2 \rceil$ as the block size. Instead, each block has the extra space in the initial loading of sparse partitions, i.e. the block size of $\lceil p\times\delta(1+\mu)/2 \rceil$, where μ denotes the **tolerant factor** ($0<\mu<1$). If $m \le \lceil p\times\delta/2 \rceil$, the non-empty cells of the partition are stored into one block, otherwise they are evenly distributed into two physically adjacent blocks. For the same reason, if $m < \lceil p\times\delta(1-\mu) \rceil$ after many deletions in a dense partition, the partition is moved to two physically adjacent blocks as a sparse partition. On the other hand, if $m > \lceil p\times\delta(1+\mu) \rceil$ after many insertions in a sparse partition, the partition is moved to a dense partition.

To reduce the disk I/O, we consecutively store the cells of a partition into the disk, thus partitions appear physically in partition-major order. For example, all of the 9 cells of the partition (0:2, 0:2) are consecutively stored on the disk.

Definition 2.1. Given a d-dimensional *DC*, and d partition factors $b_1,\ldots,b_d$, the dense and sparse Physical Data Cubes, denoted as **dense** *PDC* and **sparse** *PDC*, respectively, are two data cubes such that:

1. They are one-dimensional arrays stored on the disk, whereas the *DC* is the logical representation of the dense and sparse *PDC*.
2. The dense partitions and sparse partitions of *DC* are stored in dense *PDC* and sparse *PDC*, respectively.
3. Each partition in dense *PDC* contains
   - the number of empty cells in the partition.
   - the measure values of the cells in the partition.
4. Each partition in sparse *PDC* contains
   - the measure values and their locations of the non-empty cells in the partitions are stored in descending order by their measure values.
   - the number of empty cells in each block.

We use the above-mentioned method to implement the dense and sparse *PDC*. And, the analysis of the suitable values of δ and μ is given in Section 5.

Example 2.2. Fig. 2 shows the dense and sparse *PDC* of the *DC* in Fig. 1. δ and μ are set to 50% and 20%, respectively, i.e. the block size of the sparse *PDC* is $\lceil 9\times 50\%(1+20\%)/2 \rceil = 3$.

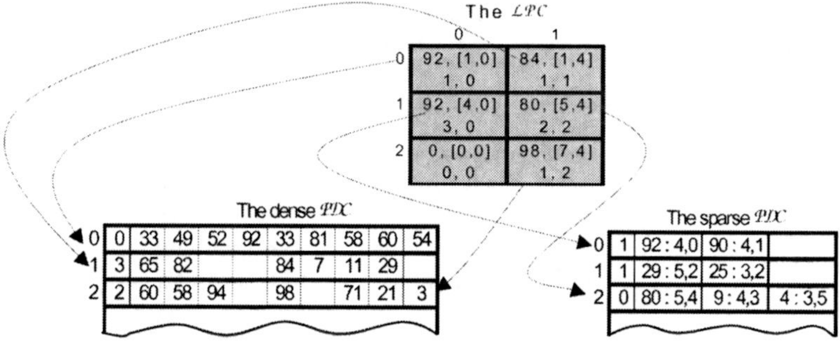

Fig. 2. *PDC* and *LPC* of *DC* in Fig. 1

2.2 Location Pre-computed Cube (*LPC*)

Definition 2.2. Given a d-dimensional *DC*, d partition factors $b_1,\ldots,b_d$ and the corresponding *PDC*, the **Location Pre-computed Cube**, denoted as *LPC*, is another data cube such that:

1. It has the same dimension d and
2. If the size of the ith dimension in *DC* is n_i, i.e. it ranges from 0 to n_i-1, then the dimension i in *LPC* will be ranged from 0 to $\lceil n_i/b_i \rceil$-1.
3. Each element *LPC*$[x_1, \ldots, x_d]$ in *LPC* is corresponding to one partition in *DC* and stores four items:

   Max: The maximum value of all the cells *DC*$[j_1, \ldots, j_d]$ in the partition where $bx_i \le j_i < \min(b(x_i+1), n_i)$ for i=1,...,d and

   Index: The location of the maximum value.

   Flag: A status flag indicating the type of the partition. 0, 1, 2 and 3 represent the partition is empty, dense, sparse with one block, and sparse with two blocks, respectively.

No: The partition number, if the partition is dense or the block number, if the partition is sparse.

For processing range bottom *k* queries, minimum values and their indexes in each partition also need to be stored in *LPC*, but no changes are needed for *PDC*. Fig. 2 shows the *LPC* of the *DC* in Fig. 1. Note that the partition (3:5, 0:2) is stored in two blocks of the sparse *DC* indicated by *LPC*[1,0].*Flag*=3.

3 Block-Based Range Top *k* Query Algorithm

Instead of accessing the data cube directly to find the top *k* maximum values, we will first load the elements of *LPC*, which are overlapped by the query range *Q*, into memory and store them in a priority queue, called *PH*, implemented using implicit heap such that the largest maximum value of the element can be immediately available in the front of the queue. Note that as we are using heap structure, we do not need all the elements in the queue completely sorted. And then, using a loop to dequeue the elements from *PH* and read the corresponding partition of *PDC* to find the top *k* maximum value candidates, until we confirm the top *k* maximum values have been found.

Block-Based Range Top *k* Query Algorithm
Input: *k*, *PDC*, Query Range *Q*
Output: *Top*[*i*], whose values are in descending order, where *i*=0, 1,…, *k*-1.
Declaration:

PH: a priority queue to store the elements in *LPC*, which are overlapped by query range *Q*. *PH* stores elements of the form <*Max*, *Index*, *Flag*, *No*> as described in the definition 2.2.
#Found: the number of the top maximum values that have been found.
PDC[]: array to store the cells in the partition of *PDC*.
P_{root}: the pointer all the time pointing to the root of *PH*.

begin
step 1: Initialization
Load each element of *LPC*, which is overlapped by *Q*, into *PH*;
#Found := 0;
step 2: Main Loop to find the top *k* maximum values.

While (*#Found* < *k*) **do**
e := dequeue the element from *PH*;
Read the partition to *PDC*[] according to *e.Flag* and *e.No*;
Find the top (*k* - *#Found*) maximum values in *PDC*[], whose locations are in *Q* and update the entries from *Top*[*#Found*] to *Top*[*k*-1] accordingly;
#Found := The number of values in *Top*[], which are not less than P_{root}→*Max*;

end

Note that P_{root}→*Max* is the maximum value of uninvestigated cells in the partitions overlapped by query range *Q*. Hence, the values in *Top*[] which are not less than P_{root}→*Max* are the top maximum values that have been found already.

4 Deletions, Insertions, and Updates

Cells may be deleted, inserted or their measure values may be updated. To reduce the storage cost of *PDC* and guarantee good performance, partitions may be switched between the dense and sparse *PDC* caused by cell insertions and deletions. Switching partitions will produce empty partitions in the dense *PDC* and empty blocks in the sparse *PDC*. The partition numbers of these empty partitions and block numbers of these empty blocks are stored in a file, called *free_list*, for reuse.

Deletions, Insertions, and Updates in dense *PDC*

In deletions, there is a threshold, i.e. $\delta(1\text{-}\mu)$, to determine if the dense partition should be moved to the sparse *PDC*, which is different from the density threshold, δ. This is to avoid frequently switching partitions between the dense and sparse *PDC* caused by frequent insertions and deletions. If $m > \lceil p \times \delta(1\text{-}\mu) \rceil$, the cell is simply deleted. Otherwise, after deleting the cell in memory, get the block number of two physically adjacent empty blocks from *free_list* and move the partition to the sparse *PDC*.

The insertions and updates in dense *PDC* are simple. The corresponding cell in the dense *PDC* is accessed to insert the cell or update its measure value.

Deletions, Insertions, and Updates in sparse *PDC*

For the deletion, insertion or update of a cell in sparse *PDC*, we load the corresponding whole sparse partition into memory and use binary search to delete, insert the cell or update its measure value, because the cells are in descending order by their measure values in the sparse partition.

In deletions, if the sparse partition becomes empty, the block numbers of this sparse partition is stored to *free_list* and its status flag in *LPC* will be updated.

For insertions, there are 4 cases before the insertion:

Case 1: The partition is not full. Insert the cell in descending order.

Case 2: The partition is empty. Allocate one empty block and insert the cell.

Case 3: The sparse partition, which has one block, is full. Allocate two physically adjacent blocks, insert the cell and evenly distribute these non-empty cells into the two blocks.

Case 4: The sparse partition, which has two blocks, is full. Insert the cell in memory, allocate an empty partition and move the partition to dense *PDC*.

In updates, the sparse partition is read into memory, the measure value of the cell is updated, re-arrange it in descending order, then the partition is written to disk.

To reduce the update cost further, we can use bulk batch update. The cells of *PDC* which we want to delete, insert or update are grouped by partitions and updated partition by partition. Thus, the update cost for a set of updates is similar to the update cost of a single cell update. When we delete, insert or update a cell in *PDC*, we may also need to update *LPC*. Updating the corresponding element in *LPC* is simple and constrained to one element access.

Usually, the partition size is less than the size of one physical block of disk for getting the good performance of range top *k* queries. This can be proved from our experiment results in Section 6. In most cases, the update cost of a cell in *PDC* is 3 disk I/Os including reading the element from *LPC* and reading and writing the partition, i.e. 2 extra I/Os compared with storing the original *DC* along dimensions. Occasionally, 1 more extra I/O is needed to update the *LPC*, when the maximum value has been changed in a partition. In some very rare cases, partition switching between sparse and dense *PDC* and block moving in sparse *PDC* are needed after many deletions and insertions of cells. For example, to move a partition from the dense *PDC* to the sparse *PDC*, we need to read one partition from the dense *PDC*, write two blocks to the sparse *PDC*, read and write one element in *LPC* and read and write *free_list* once. Hence, in the worst case, 5 extra I/Os are needed.

5 Disk Storage Cost for *LPC* and *PDC*

In order to reduce the disk storage cost of *LPC* and the sparse *PDC*, we use a one-dimensional index, denoted as **Relative Location,** ranged from 0 to $\prod_{i=1}^{d} b_i - 1$, to represent the position of a cell in the partition of the *DC*.

Definition 5.1. Given a d-dimensional *DC*, and d partition factors $b_1,\ldots,b_d$, the **Relative Location** of $DC[x_1,\ldots,x_d]$, denoted as $RL[x_1,\ldots,x_d]$, where $0\le x_i \le n_i-1$, is an integer which represents the index of $DC[x_1,\ldots,x_d]$ within the partition and has the value of $\sum_{i=1}^{d}((x_i \bmod b_i)\times\prod_{j=i+1}^{d} b_j)$.

Example 5.1. Fig. 3 shows the relative locations in a partition, e.g. (3:5, 0:2), of the given *DC* in Fig. 1.

relative index	0	1	2
0	0	1	2
1	3	4	5
2	6	7	8

Fig. 3. The relative locations in a partition

As the size of a partition in *PDC* is b^d (without loss of generality, we assume partition factors $b=b_1=\ldots=b_d$), the range of the values of the relative locations is from 0 to b^d-1. Hence, the number of bytes needed to represent a relative location is $\lceil (d\log_2 b)/8\rceil$. Let s denote the number of bytes that each cell occupies in *DC*. In each element of *LPC*, *Max* and *Index* need s and $\lceil (d\log_2 b)/8\rceil$ bytes, respectively. And, *Flag* needs 2 bits, so we store *Flag* and *No* together using 4 bytes. Hence, the storage cost for *LPC* is $(\prod_{i=1}^{d}\lceil n_i/b\rceil)\times(s+\lceil(d\log_2 b)/8\rceil+4)$ bytes. The number of empty cells in each dense partition also needs $\lceil (d\log_2 b)/8\rceil$ bytes. It is negligible compared with the partition size $b^d\times s$. Hence, if we store the *DC* as a dense *PDC*, the storage cost of the *PDC* is about $(\prod_{i=1}^{d} n_i)\times s$ bytes.

Example 5.2. Consider a 5-dimensional *DC* whose size of each dimension is 64. Each cell occupies 4 bytes, and the partition factor b is set to 4. Thus, the storage cost of the dense *PDC* is about $(\prod_{i=1}^{5} 64)\times 4$, i.e. 4GB, whereas the *LPC* needs only

$(\prod_{i=1}^{5}\lceil 64/4 \rceil)\times(4+\lceil(5\log_2 4)/8\rceil+4)$, i.e. 10MB. Given suitable partition factors, it may be feasible to keep all the elements of *LPC* in main memory when answering ad hoc range top *k* queries at run time.

Each cell in the sparse *PDC* needs $(s+\lceil(d \log_2 b)/8\rceil)$ bytes. In the worst case, each partition in the sparse *PDC* needs two blocks with the block size of $\lceil p\times\delta(1+\mu)/2\rceil$, where δ and μ are density threshold and tolerant factor, respectively. Hence, the maximum storage cost for a partition in the sparse *PDC* is about $(s+\lceil(d\log_2 b)/8\rceil)\times\lceil p\times\delta(1+\mu)/2\rceil\times 2$ bytes, whereas the dense partition needs $p\times s$ bytes. Hence, in the worst case, the percentage of the storage cost we can reduce is about $1-(1+\lceil(d \log_2 b)/8\rceil/s)\times\delta(1+\mu)$. The selection of μ depends on the frequency of insertions and deletions. If insertions and deletions are frequent, μ should be larger to avoid frequently partition switching or block moving. However, when μ is large, much storage space will be wasted in each block. The choice of δ depends on the data distribution. If δ is too small, few partitions are put in the sparse *PDC*. If δ is too large, each block wastes much storage space.

In example 5.2, the percentage of saving in storage is $1-1.5\times\delta(1+\mu)$. From Fig. 4, it is reasonable to choose δ from 0.2 to 0.3 and μ from 0.1 to 0.3.

benefit	δ=0.2	δ=0.3	δ=0.4	δ=0.5
μ=0.1	0.67	0.505	0.34	0.175
μ=0.2	0.64	0.46	0.28	0.1
μ=0.3	0.61	0.415	0.22	0.025
μ=0.4	0.58	0.37	0.16	-0.05
μ=0.5	0.55	0.325	0.1	-0.125

Fig. 4. The percentage of storage cost reduced in the sparse partitions.

6 Experiments and Performance Analysis

The following figures show our experiment results. A set of data cubes with various data sizes, partition factors and dimensionalities are randomly generated. Without loss of generality, we assume data cubes *DC* with equal size for each dimension and equal partition factor. Data values are ranged from 1 to 65535. Accordingly, we constructed *PDC*, and *LPC*. We then generated 1000 queries of random range and measured the average response times. The experiments are run in Windows NT 4.0 on Pentium III with 668MHZ CPU and 128MB RAM. Let *d*, *n*, *b* and *k* represent the dimensionality, the dimension size, the partition factor and the top maximum values queried, respectively. We make several observations from these experiments:

1. Fig. 5 shows the percentage of the storage cost of the *PDC* and the *LPC* compared with the original 3-dimensional *DC*, which has randomly distributed 20% non-empty cells. When δ and μ are set to 30% and 20%, respectively, about 50% storage space of the original *DC* is reduced by the *PDC*, whereas the storage cost of *LPC* is negligible in the most cases of various partition factors.
2. From Fig. 6, it can be observed that the partition factors have become more crucial to the query performance with the dimensionality increasing for our method. The best partition factors for the 3-dimensional *DC* and 4-dimensional *DC*

with each dimension size of n=100 for range top 20 queries are 6 and 5 respectively, which is different from the range max/min queries [8]. The algorithm in [8] shows the best for range max/min queries when $b \approx \sqrt{n}$.

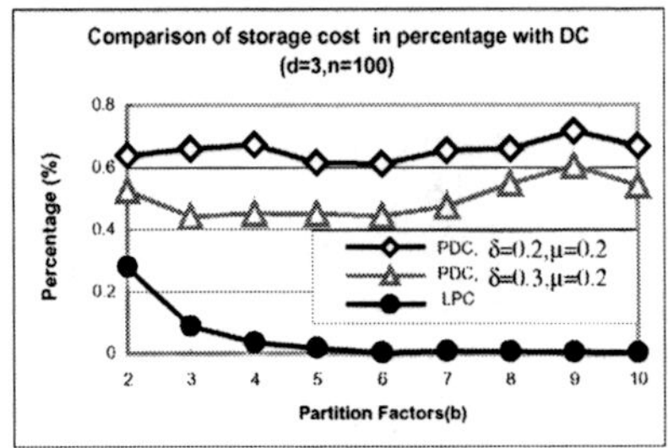

Fig. 5. The percentage of storage cost compared with the original data cube.

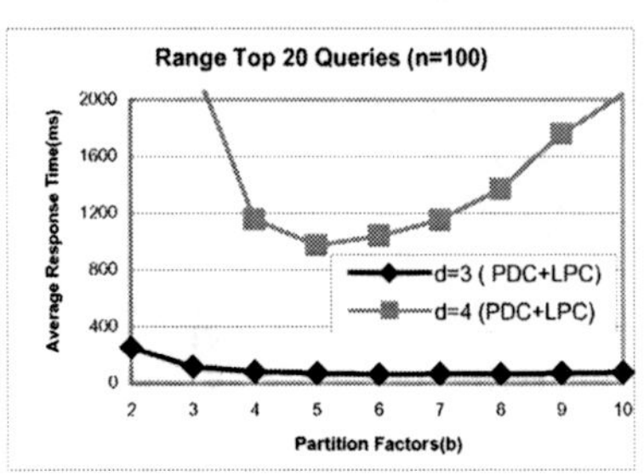

Fig. 6. Range Top 20 Queries using various partition factors

3. Fig. 7 and Fig. 8 show the average response time per query for range top 20 queries for d=3 and d=4, respectively. When the number of partitions overlapped by the query range increases, the average response time of our method increases very slowly and it becomes much more efficient than the naïve method, i.e. scanning the cells in the original data cube. For example, when d=3 and 20 partitions are overlapped by the query range, the average response time of our method is 33.1% of the naïve method, i.e. 0.023 second, whereas when d=3 and 200 partitions are overlapped by the query range, the average response time of our method is only 7.7% of the naïve method, i.e. 0.048 second.

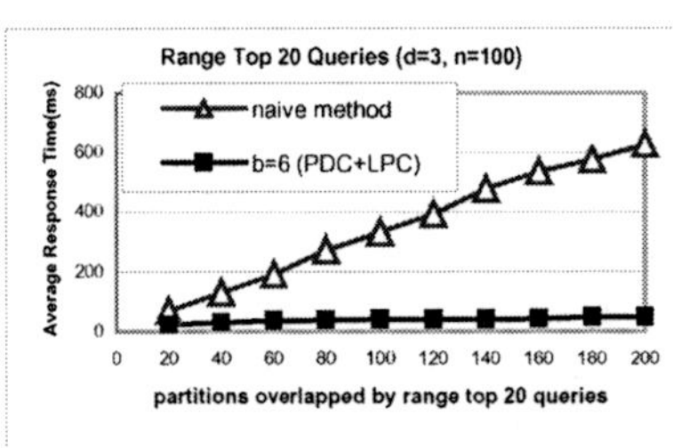

Fig. 7. The average response time vs. partitions for 3-dimensional data cube

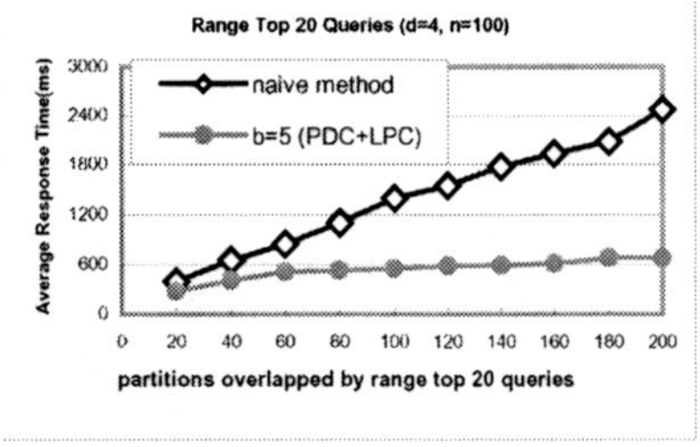

Fig. 8. The average response time vs. partitions for 4-dimensional data cube

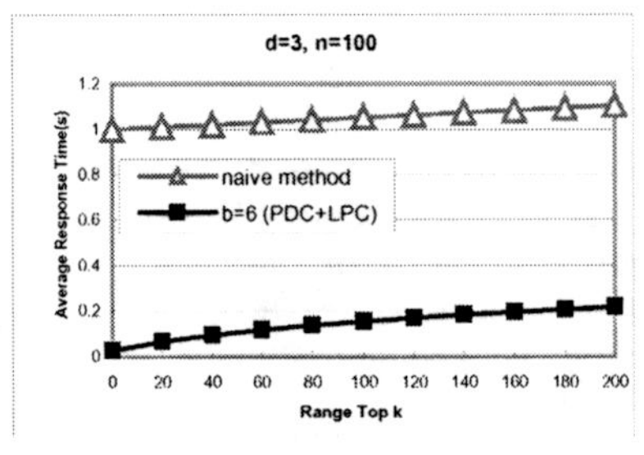

Fig. 9. The average response time vs. k for d=3

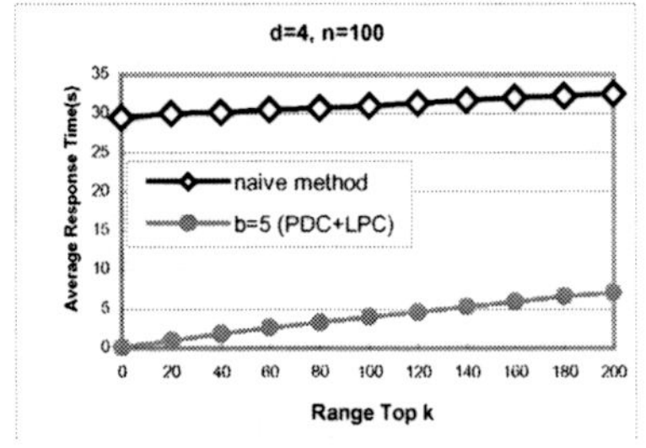

Fig. 10. The average response time vs. k for d=4

4. Fig. 9 and Fig. 10 show that the average response time of our method increases slowly with *k* increasing. Even for the large value of *k*, e.g. *k*=200, our method still provides good performance. For *k*=200, *b*=5, *n*=100 and *d*=4, the average response time of our method is 21.8% of the naïve method, i.e. 7.094 seconds.

7 Conclusion

Several pre-computations techniques have been developed to answer range max/min queries efficiently, but these methods may not be able to apply to range top/bottom *k* queries. In this paper, we propose a new storage structure for sparse data cubes, which reduces the storage cost of original *DC* and significantly reduces disk I/O cost when answering range top/bottom *k* queries. The extra storage needed for *LPC*, the index of the original *DC*, is negligible. As shown in the experiment, about 50% storage space can be saved for a 3-dimensional *DC* with randomly distributed 20% non-empty cells. And our method outperforms the naïve method by a large margin, especially when the query range is large. For example, for *d*=3 and 200 partitions overlapped by the query range, the average response time of our method is only 7.7% of the naïve method.

To speed up the range top *k* query, we can store some pre-computed maximum values with the corresponding locations for the dense partitions, thus reducing the chance to access the dense partitions. Details of this study can be found in [9].

References

[1] C. Y. Chan, Y.E. Ioannidis. "Hierarchical Cubes for Range-Sum Queries". Proceedings of the 25th VLDB Conference, pages 675-686, 1999.

[2] G. Colliat, "OLAP, *relational and multidimensional database systems*", SIGMOD Record 25, pages 64-69, 1996.

[3] S. Geffner, D. Agrawal, A.E. Abbadi, T. Smith. "Relative Prefix Sum: An Efficient Approach for Querying Dynamic OLAP Data Cubes". In Proceedings of the 15th International Conference on Data Engineering, pages 328-335, 1999.

[4] J. Gray, A. Bosworth, A. Layman, H. Pirahesh. "Data cube: A relational aggregation operator generating group-by, cross-tabs and sub-totals". In Proc. of the 12th International Conference on Data Engineering, pages 152-159, 1996.

[5] C. Ho, R. Agrawal, N. Megiddo, R. Srikant. "Range Queries in OLAP Data Cubes". In Proc. of the ACM SIGMOD Conference on the Management of Data, pages 77-88, 1997.

[6] D. W. Kim, E. J. Lee, M. H. Kim, Y. J. Lee. "An efficient processing of range-MIN/MAX queries over data cube". Information Science, pages 223-237, 1998.

[7] S. Y. Lee, T. W. Ling, H.G. Li. "Hierarchical Compact Cube for Range-Max Queries". In Proc. of the 26th International Conference on Very Large Databases, 2000.

[8] H. G. Li, T. W. Ling, S.Y. Lee. "Range-Max/Min Query in OLAP Data Cube". In Proc. of the 11th International Conference on Database and Expert Systems Applications, 2000.

[9] Z. X. Loh, T. W. Ling, C. H. Ang, S. Y. Lee, H. G. Li. "Adaptive Pre-computed Partition Top Method for Range Top-*k* Queries in OLAP Data Cubes". Submitted for publication.

[10] L. Mitten. "Branch and bound methods: General formulation and properties". Operations Research ,18:24-34, 1970.

On Formulation of Disjunctive Coupling Queries in WHOWEDA

Sourav S. Bhowmick[1], Wee Keong Ng[1], and Sanjay Madria[2]

[1] School of Computer Engineering, Nanyang Technological University, Singapore 639798
{assourav, awkng}@ntu.edu.sg
http://www.ntu.edu.sg/home/assourav

[2] Department of Computer Science, University of Missouri-Rolla, Rolla MO 65409
{madrias}@umr.edu

Abstract. We describe how to formulate *coupling query* to glean relevant Web data in the context of our web warehousing system called WHOWEDA (*W*are*h*ouse *O*f *We*b *Da*ta). One of the important feature of our query mechanism is the ability to express disjunctive query conditions compactly. We describe how to formulate coupling queries in text form as well as pictorially using *coupling text* and *coupling graph*. We explore the limitations of coupling graph with respect to coupling text. We found out that AND, OR and AND/OR-coupling graphs are less expressive than their textual counterparts. To address this shortcoming we introduced another query formulation technique called *hybrid graph* which is a special type of *p*-connected coupling graph.

1 Introduction

Due to irregularity and semistructured nature of Web data, it is important for a query language to express disjunctive form of web query. Sometimes query evaluation is relatively less expensive if a query is formulated and evaluated using disjunctive constraints rather than repeated evaluation of each query in the equivalent conjunctive query set. Also, expressing all possible set of conjunctive query accurately for a disjunctive condition incurs significant cognitive overhead which may result in erroneous query. Finally, a disjunctive query can be expressed compactly using regular expression. Expressing all possible set of conjunctive queries can be quite cumbersome. In spite of these benefits, most of the web query systems supports very limited form of disjunctive conditions, if any. W3QS [8] has a limited form of disjunctive condition which involves the variability of the depth of traversal of a query can be expressed by these languages. Query systems for semistructured data and XML query languages such as XML-QL [6], Lorel [7], support limited form of disjunctive conditions. However, whether these languages can express disjunctive conditions on the hyperlink structure of Web documents are not evident in [1,6,7].

H.C. Mayr et al. (Eds.): DEXA 2001, LNCS 2113, pp. 688–698, 2001.

A web query may take both textual and pictorial forms. Textual formulation of web query enables us to express any complex web query accurately. However, text-based queries has some disadvantages. To express such queries, a user must be completely familiar with the syntax of the query language, and must be able to express his/her needs accurately in a syntactically correct form. For instance, query languages such as XML-QL, Lorel, and WebOQL [2] although are powerful languages, but is definitely not easy to formulate in textual form. Although, it is possible to apply syntactic sugar on these languages, but issues involved with such effort are not discussed in [6,7,2].

In this paper, we introduce the notion of *coupling query* to express a web query and show how it addressses the above limitations in the context of our web warehousing system, called WHOWEDA (*W*are*h*ouse *O*f *We*b *Da*ta) [4].

2 Coupling Query

We now formally introduce the notion of a *coupling query*. We begin by briefly describing the underlying data model of our web warehousing system. For detailed treatment, please refer to [4].

The *WareHouse Object Model* (WHOM) [4] serves as the basic data model for our web warehousing system. Informally, our web warehouse can be conceived of as a collection of *web tables*. A set of *web tuples* is materialized in a web table. A web tuple is a directed graph consisting of sets of *node* and *link objects* (hereafter, referred to as *nodes* and *links* respectively for brevity). In WHOWEDA, *nodes* and *links* are instances of *node type* and *link type* respectively. Intuitively, a *node* represents the metadata associated with a Web document and the content and structure of the document (excluding hyperlinks in the document). Specifically, it consists of two components: a set of *node metadata trees* to represent values of different metadata associated with the document and a *node data tree* (directed labeled tree) to represent the content and structure of the document. Similarly, a *link* consists of a set of link meta-attribute/value pairs (such as `target URL`, `source URL` and `link_type`) represented as *link metadata trees*, a *link data tree* and an unique reference identifier. Link data tree is a directed labeled tree to represent the structure and content of a HTML or XML link [1]. The reference identifier is used to associate the *location* of links in a particular Web document or node. Observe that although a hyperlink is embedded in a Web document, we logically separate hyperlinks from Web documents while modeling HTML and XML data in WHOM. The reader may refer to [4] for complete discussion on how Web data is represented in the warehouse.

Informally, a coupling query consists of five components, *sets of node* and *link type identifiers*, set of *predicates*, set of *coupling query predicates* and a set of *connectivities*. We illustrate the components of a coupling query by formulating a web query. Consider the NCI Web site at `rex.nci.nih.gov`. Suppose a user wishes to retrieve information related to

[1] We only consider simple and extended XML links.

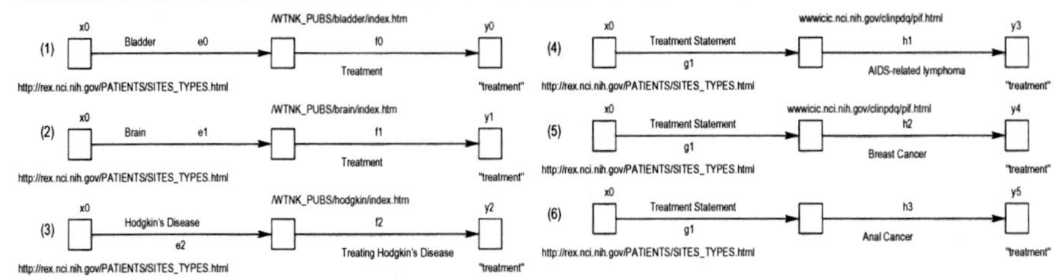

Fig. 1. Results of the query

treatment of different types of cancer. This site provides information about specific types of cancer, including information about diagnosis, staging, treatment, follow-up care and coping. Specifically, the links in the web page at `rex.nci.nih.gov/PATIENTS/SITES_TYPES.html` provide links to information related to different types of cancer. The link “treatment statement” points to `cancernet.nci.nih.gov/pdq/pdq_treatment.shtml` containing a list of links to cancer-related diseases. Each of these links point to a page containing information on diagnosis, treatments etc. of a particular disease. There are also hyperlinks labeled “bladder”, “brain” etc. in `rex.nci.nih.gov/PATIENTS/SITES_TYPES.html` which directly connects to a page containing details of these diseases. Observe that some of the links such as “AIDS-related lymphoma”, “Anal Cancer” etc. in `pdq_treatment.shtml` are not available in `SITES_TYPES.html`. Similarly, the links related to “Non-Hodgkin's Lymphoma”, “Hodgkin's Disease”, in `SITES_TYPES.html` are not listed in `pdq_treatment.shtml`. Therefore, in order to retrieve a complete list of treatment details of various types of cancer we need to navigate the link “treatment statement” and the links related to different cancers in the Web page. In order to express this query, we need: (1) A starting point for the search (Web page at `rex.nci.nih.gov/PATIENTS/SITES_TYPES.html`) and (2) to scan the pages accessible from the starting page by following links having the specific characteristics as described above.

Therefore, we search for a path in the Web hypertext structure, beginning at the Web page at `rex.nci.nih.gov/PATIENTS/SITES_TYPES.html` and ending at a page containing the keyword “treatment” by following only hypertext links that satisfies the above conditions. Such hypertext path can be expressed in the coupling query by the *connectivity* $x\langle(ef)|(gh)\rangle y$. Here x, y are *node type identifiers*, e, f, g and h are *link type identifiers* and $(ef)|(gh)$ is called a *link path expression* which is essentially a sequence of link type identifiers which may include regular expressions. Each type identifier represents a set of documents or hyperlinks. The angled brackets are used for delimitation purposes only. A connectivity element is categorized into two types—*simple* and *complex*. A *simple* connectivity contains only *simple* link path expression. By simple link path expression we mean that there is no regular expressions defined over it. On the other hand, in a complex connectivity, the link path expression may contain regular expressions. Observe that the above connectivity is of complex type and the expression $(ef)|(gh)$ enables us to express disjunctive conditions in a coupling query, i.e., either follow the links of types e and f or follow the links of types g and h.

Instances of x is the first vertex of the path and corresponds to the page at `rex.nci.nih.gov/PATIENTS/SITES_TYPES.html`. Coupling query allows the mapping of specific pages to a node type identifier. This is written in the form of a *predicate*:

$p_{1_1}(x) \equiv$ `METADATA::x[url] EQUALS`
`"http://rex[.]nci[.]nih[.]gov/PATIENTS/SITES_TYPES[.]html"`

The link type identifiers e, f, g and h must satisfy the above conditions. These conditions are expressed as following predicates:

$p_{1_3}(f) \equiv$ `STRUCTURE::f[A] EXISTS_IN "body.p"`
$p_{1_4}(e) \equiv$ `CONTENT::e[A] NON-ATTR_ENCL "Treatment Statements"`
$p_{1_5}(h) \equiv$ `CONTENT::h[A] ATTR_CONT`
`"{(href, MATCH(:BEGIN_WORD: + treat.* + ;END_WORD:)}"`
$p_{1_6}(g) \equiv$ `STRUCTURE::g SATISFIES "A"`
$p_{1_7}(g) \equiv$ `STRUCTURE::g[A] EXISTS_IN "table(.%)+.p"`

Note that similar to node type identifier, specific hyperlinks are mapped to a link type identifier. Also, observe that the predicates allow us to impose constraints on specific portions of Web documents or hyperlinks, on attributes associated with HTML or XML elements and on the hierarchical structure of Web documents based on partial knowledge of the structure of the documents.

The last vertex y must contain the keyword "treatment" anywhere in the document and is expressed by the following predicate:

$p_{1_2}(y) \equiv$ `CONTENT::y[html(.%)+] NON-ATTR_CONT`
`":BEGIN_WORD: + treatment + :END_WORD:"`

We also want to make sure that all the documents retrieved by the search belongs to the Web site of NCI. This is done by defining the following *coupling query predicates*:

$q_2(G_1) \equiv$ `COUPLING_QUERY::`G_1`.host EQUALS "rex.nci.nih.gov"`

Note that coupling query predicates enables us to control the execution of a query.

The set of query results is shown in Figure 1. Observe that the results are directed connected graph and preserves the hyperlinked structure of the relevant documents that satisfies the query conditions. We now formally define a coupling query.

Definition 1. *A* **coupling query** *is a 5-tuple* $G = \langle X_n, X_\ell, C, P, Q\rangle$ *where* X_n *is a set of node type identifiers,* X_ℓ *is a set of link type identifiers,* C *is* *a set (possibly empty) of connectivities defined over* X_n *and* X_ℓ*,* P *is a set of predicates defined over* X_n *and* X_ℓ *and* Q *is a set (possibly empty) of coupling query predicates such that the following conditions are true: (1)* $X_n \neq \emptyset$*,* $P \neq \emptyset$*,* $X_n \cap X_\ell = \emptyset$*; (2) If* $|X_n| = 1$ *then* $X_\ell = \emptyset$*,* $C = \emptyset$ *and* $P \neq \emptyset$*; (3) Let* X_{nc} *and* $X_{\ell c}$ *be the set of node and link type identifiers in* C *respectively. Then* $X_{nc} = X_n$ *and* $X_{\ell c} = X_\ell$*; (4) There must not exist conjunctive connectivity set* $C_a \equiv k_{a1} \wedge k_{a2} \wedge \cdots \wedge k_{an}$ *and* $C_b \equiv k_{b1} \wedge k_{b2} \wedge \cdots \wedge k_{bn}$ *such that* $C_a \vee C_b$ *and* $k_{ax} = k_{bx}$ $\forall\ 0 < x \leqslant n$*; (5) Let* $p(x) \in P$*. Then* $x \in (X_n \cup X_\ell)$*; (6) Let* $G(C)$ *be the graphical representation of* C*. Then* $G(C)$ *must be a directed connected acyclic graph with single source vertex. Further, let* x *be the identifier of the source vertex in* $G(C)$*. Then, there must exist a non-trivial predicate* $p(x) \in P$*.* ∎

3 Canonical and Non-canonical Coupling Queries

A coupling query is categorized into two types: *canonical* and *non-canonical.* We say that a coupling query is *canonical* if it contains a set (possibly empty) of simple connectivities in Disjunctive Normal Form (DNF). For example, if $G = \langle X_n, X_\ell, C, P, Q\rangle$, $C \equiv C_1 \vee C_2$ where $C_1 \equiv k_1 \wedge k_2$, $C_2 \equiv k_3$ $k_1 \equiv x\langle e\rangle y$, $k_2 \equiv y\langle f\rangle z$ and $k_3 \equiv x\langle e\rangle z$ then G is a canonical coupling query. C_1 and C_2 are called *conjunctive connectivity sets*. Based on the above definition of canonical coupling query, we classify canonical queries into the following five types. Let $G_c = \langle X_n, X_\ell, C, P, Q\rangle$ be a canonical coupling query. Then,

- **Type 1:** G_c does not contain any connectivities. That is, $|X_n| = 1$, $X_\ell = \emptyset$ and $C = \emptyset$. Note that this is the simplest form of coupling query.
- **Type 2:** G_c contains a single simple connectivity. That is, $|X_n| = 2$, $|X_\ell| = 1$, $C \equiv k$ where k is a simple connectivity.
- **Type 3:** G_c contains more than one simple connectivities and these connectivities are in conjunction. That is, $C \equiv k_1 \wedge k_2 \wedge \cdots \wedge k_r$ where k_i is a simple connectivity for all $1 < i \leqslant r$.
- **Type 4:** G_c contains more than one simple connectivities and these connectivities are in disjunction. That is, $C \equiv k_1 \vee k_2 \vee \cdots \vee k_r$ where k_i is a simple for all $1 < i \leqslant r$.
- **Type 5:** G_c contains more than one simple connectivities and these connectivities are in DNF. That is, $C \equiv C_1 \vee C_2 \vee \cdots \vee C_r$ where C_i is a conjunctive connectivity set for all $1 < i \leqslant r$.

A *non-canonical coupling query*, on the other hand, may contain simple or complex connectivities and these connectivities may not be in DNF. For instance, if $C \equiv k_1 \wedge k_2$, $k_1 \equiv x\langle e|f\rangle y$ and $k_2 \equiv y\langle g\rangle z$ then G is a non-canonical coupling query. We classify non-canonical queries into the following four types. Let $G_{nc} = \langle X_n, X_\ell, C, P, Q\rangle$ be a non-canonical coupling query. Then,

- **Type 1:** G_{nc} contains a single complex connectivity. That is, $|X_n| = 2$, $X_\ell \neq \emptyset$, $C \equiv k$ where k is a complex connectivity.

- **Type 2:** G_{nc} contains more than one connectivity and at least one of them is complex. Further, these connectivities are in conjunction. That is, $C \equiv k_1 \wedge k_2 \wedge \cdots \wedge k_r$ where k_i is complex for $1 < i \leqslant r$.
- **Type 3:** G_{nc} contains more than one connectivity and at least one of them is complex. Further, these connectivities are in disjunction. That is, $C \equiv k_1 \vee k_2 \vee \cdots \vee k_r$ where k_i is complex for $1 < i \leqslant r$.
- **Type 4:** G_{nc} contains more than one simple or complex connectivities and these connectivities are in conjunction and in disjunction to one another.

A *valid* canonical coupling query is necessary for generating *web schemas* of a set of web tuples retrieved from the Web [5]. Moreover, this form is also necessary for *global web coupling* operation [4]. Informally, a canonical coupling query is valid if each conjunctive connectivity set in the query represents a directed connected acyclic graph with single source vertex. Also, every non-canonical coupling query can be transformed to a valid canonical coupling query [3].

4 Coupling Query Formulation

By default, a coupling query is formulated in text form. It may also be formulated graphically. The textual representation of the query is called *coupling text* and the pictorial representation of a coupling query is called *coupling graph*. In coupling text, the user specifies the five components X_n, X_ℓ, C, P and Q in a GUI. In the remaining portion of this paper we shall use coupling text and coupling query interchangeably. Note that, unless explicitly stated otherwise, a canonical coupling query indicates a valid canonical query.

4.1 Definition of Coupling Graph

Informally, a coupling graph is a directed connected acyclic graph. This mechanism enables a user to specify a coupling query by drawing a graph. The label of vertices of the graph are node type identifiers and predicates, if any, defined over these identifiers. The label of the edges of the graph are link type identifiers and predicates on these link type identifiers (if any). The edges between the vertices specifies the connectivity constraints. The set of coupling query predicates is specified by clicking on the entire coupling graph. A coupling graph is used to express queries containing simple connectivities only.

4.2 Types of Coupling Graph

We classify coupling graphs into three categories, i.e., *AND-coupling graph*, *OR-coupling graph* and *AND/OR-coupling graph*.

In an *AND-coupling graph* all the edges are AND together. It is used to express pictorially a coupling query containing a set of simple connectivities in conjunction to one another (canonical queries of Types 2 and 3). Formally, let

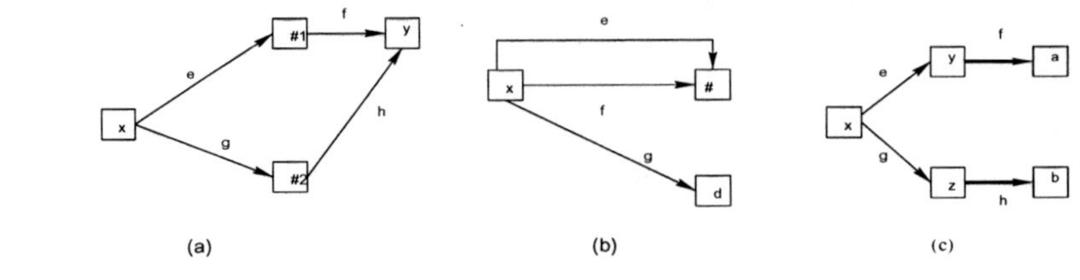

Fig. 2. Coupling graphs.

$G_{cg} = (V_q, E_q)$ be a coupling graph. Then G_{cg} is an AND-coupling graph if $e_{qi} \in E_q$ and $e_{qj} \in E_q$ and $e_{qi} \wedge e_{qj}$ $\forall\, 0 < (i,j) \leqslant |E_q|$ and $i \neq j$. Note that the graphical representation of canonical form of coupling text (of Types 2 and 3) is identical to the corresponding AND-coupling graph. For example, Figures 2(a) is an example of AND-coupling graph expressing the set of simple connectivities $(x\langle e\rangle\#_1 \wedge \#_1\langle f\rangle y \wedge x\langle g\rangle\#_2 \wedge \#_2\langle h\rangle y)$.

An *OR-coupling graph* is used to formulate pictorially coupling queries in which the connectivities are simple and are in disjunction to one another. In an *OR-coupling graph* all the edges are OR'd together. As we only allow coupling graphs with single source vertex, OR-coupling graphs must not have more than one vertex with no incoming edges. Consequently, OR-coupling graph pictorially represents queries containing a set of simple connectivities having identical source identifier. As we disregard formulation of non-canonical coupling queries using coupling graphs, an OR-coupling graph is a pictorial representation of a canonical form of Type 4-coupling text. Formally, let $G_{cg} = (V_q, E_q)$ be a coupling graph. Then G_{cg} is an OR-coupling graph if $e_{qi} \in E_q$ and $e_{qj} \in E_q$ and $e_{qi} \vee e_{qj}$ $\forall\, 0 < (i,j) \leqslant |E_q|$ and $i \neq j$. For example, Figure 2(b) is an example of OR-coupling graph expressing connectivities $(x\langle e\rangle\# \vee x\langle f\rangle\# \vee x\langle g\rangle d)$.

Informally, an AND/OR-coupling graph represents coupling queries in which the connectivities are in conjunction as well as in disjunction to one another. We first define the notion of *AND-edges* and *OR-edges* in order to elaborate on this type of coupling graph. In a coupling graph, an edge (v_1, e, v_2) is an *AND-edge* if the out-degree and in-degree of v_1 and v_2 respectively is equal to one. Otherwise, the edge is called an *OR-edge*. Now we define AND/OR-coupling graph. Let $G_{cg} = (V_q, E_q)$ be a coupling graph. Then, G_{cg} is an AND/OR graph if any one of the following conditions is true: (1) If all edges are OR-edges then the depth of the graph must be greater than one. This is because if the depth is equal to one then the graph is an OR-coupling graph and (2) G_{cg} must contain AND and OR-edges. Note that in an AND/OR-coupling graph all the outgoing or in-coming OR-edges to a vertex is OR'd together. Furthermore, connectivities in each level in the graph is AND together with the connectivities in the next level. For example, Figure 2(c) shows an AND/OR-coupling graph and the edges e and g are OR-edges and f and h are AND-edges. Hence, it expresses a coupling query with the following connectivities: $(x\langle e\rangle y \wedge y\langle f\rangle a) \vee (x\langle g\rangle z \wedge z\langle h\rangle b)$.

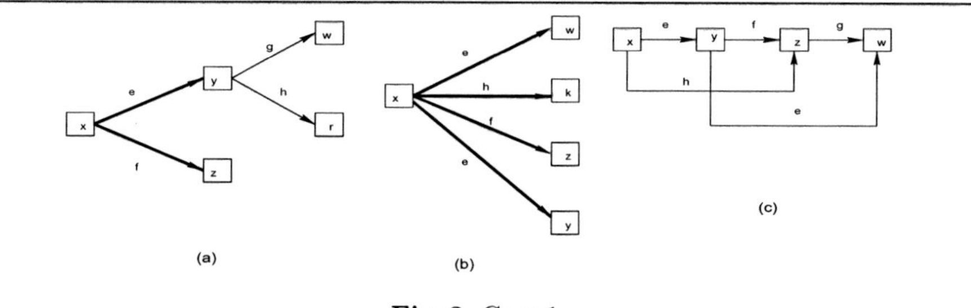

Fig. 3. Case 1.

An AND/OR-coupling graph can be used to pictorially represent *some types* of canonical coupling text of Type 5, but not all. This is due to the inherent limitations of drawing an AND/OR-coupling graph to represent a unique coupling query. We discuss this issue in detail in the next subsection.

4.3 Limitations of Coupling Graphs

In this section we explore the limitations of coupling graphs in expressing canonical coupling queries compared to its textual counterpart. We begin with AND-coupling graphs. Edges in an AND-coupling graph represents a set of simple connectivities AND together. This is equivalent to a set of simple connectivities in conjunction to one another in a canonical form of Types 2 and 3-coupling text. Hence, any query that can be expressed by canonical form of Types 2 or 3-coupling text can also be formulated using an AND-coupling graph.

An OR-coupling graph represent a set of simple connectivities in disjunction to one another. This is equivalent to the canonical form of Type 4-coupling text. Observe that each connectivity in the coupling query must represent a path from the source vertex to a leaf vertex in the OR-coupling graph. Hence, an OR-coupling graph cannot express those simple connectivities which represents a path other than those between the source vertex and leaf vertices in the graphical representation of the connectivities. We elaborate on this with an example. Consider the connectivities $C \equiv k_1 \vee k_2 \vee k_3$ where $k_1 \equiv x\langle e\rangle y$, $k_2 \equiv y\langle f\rangle z$ and $k_3 \equiv x\langle g\rangle z$. A query containing these connectivities can be expressed by a canonical form of Type 4-coupling text. However, this query cannot be composed using an OR-coupling graph as k_2 represents a path between an interior vertex and a leaf vertex. Typically, an OR-coupling graph is only capable of expressing simple connectivities with identical source identifiers. Consequently, we may conclude that the expressiveness of OR-coupling graph is not equivalent to that of the canonical form of Type 4-coupling text.

We now identify the limitations of AND/OR-coupling graphs and illustrate them with examples. We begin with the first limitation.

Case 1. If $C \equiv C_1 \vee C_2 \vee \cdots \vee C_n$ be a set of connectivities in a coupling query G and if G_{cg} be the AND/OR-coupling graph of G then $C_1, C_2, \ldots, C_n$

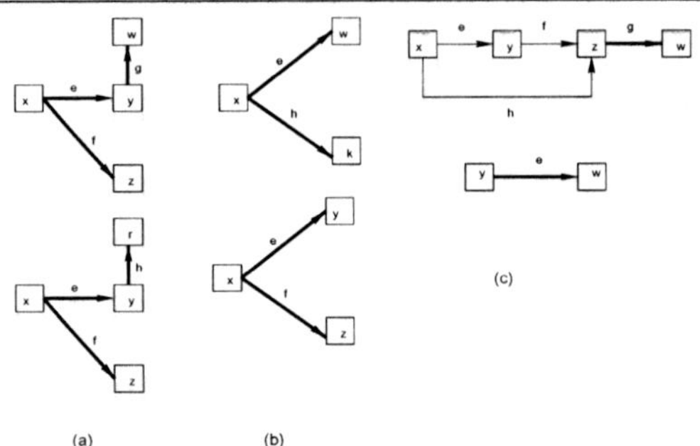

Fig. 4. Hybrid graphs.

represents such paths in G_{cg}. This indicates that an AND/OR-coupling graph fails to express a set of connectivities that can be visualized as a non-linear structure, i.e., tree or a graph. For instance, an AND/OR-coupling graph cannot express the following connectivities: $C_3 \equiv C_{31} \vee C_{32}$ where $C_{31} \equiv x\langle e\rangle y \wedge x\langle f\rangle z \wedge y\langle g\rangle w$ and $C_{32} \equiv x\langle e\rangle y \wedge x\langle f\rangle z \wedge y\langle h\rangle r$.

It may seem that by relaxing the definition of an AND/OR-coupling graph it may be possible to resolve this limitation. For example, consider the graph in Figure 3(a). Let edges with identifiers e and f be AND-edges in lieu of OR-edges. Then C_3 in the above example can be expressed by this AND/OR-coupling graph. Now consider the connectivities $C_5 \equiv C_{51} \vee C_{52}$ where $C_{51} \equiv x\langle e\rangle w \wedge x\langle h\rangle k$ and $C_{52} \equiv x\langle f\rangle z \wedge x\langle e\rangle y$. The coupling graph of a query involving C_5 is shown in Figure 3(b). However, since all the edges are AND-edges, this graph actually express $(x\langle e\rangle w \wedge x\langle h\rangle k \wedge x\langle f\rangle z \wedge x\langle e\rangle y)$. This connectivity constraint cannot be expressed even by relaxing the definition of AND-edges. Hence, allowing such flexible definition of AND-edges may generate an AND/OR-coupling graph which may not represent the intended connectivities when transformed to its textual form. Due to this problem, we disallow AND-edges from vertices whose in-degree or out-degree is more than one.

Case 2. This shortcoming is similar to the one discussed in the context of OR-coupling graph. An AND/OR-coupling graph, similar to OR-coupling graph cannot express connectivity that represents a path in the graph other than those from the source vertex to leaf vertices. For example, consider the connectivities $C_6 \equiv C_{61} \vee C_{62} \vee C_{63}$ where $C_{61} \equiv x\langle e\rangle y \wedge y\langle f\rangle z \wedge z\langle g\rangle w$, $C_{62} \equiv x\langle h\rangle z \wedge z\langle g\rangle w$ and $C_{63} \equiv y\langle e\rangle w$. The graphical representation of these connectivities is shown in Figure 3(c).

4.4 Hybrid Graph

We now introduce the notion of *hybrid graph* to resolve the limitations of OR and AND/OR-coupling graphs discussed in the preceding section. Informally, a *hybrid* graph is composed by drawing a p-connected coupling graph for $p > 1$

such that (1) Each connected component is an AND, OR or AND/OR-coupling graph, (2) the connected components are in disjunction to one another and (3) If $G_i = (V_i, E_i)$ and $G_j = (V_j, E_j)$ be two connected components then $V_i \cap V_j \neq \emptyset$.

Resolution of Case 1. AND-coupling graph can express connectivities which can be visualized as trees or graphs. Hence, the limitations discussed in Case 1 of AND/OR-coupling graph can be eliminated by drawing a hybrid graph containing AND-coupling graph. For instance, consider the connectivities C_3 of Case 1. Queries containing these connectivities can be expressed by the hybrid graph in Figure 4(a). Observe that this graph is a 2-connected graph where all the components are AND-coupling graphs. Further, in each hybrid graph the AND-coupling graphs are in disjunction to one another. Similarly, the query containing the connectivities C_5 can be expressed by the hybrid graph in Figure 4(b).

Resolution of Case 2. We consider the case which is a limitation for both OR-coupling graph and AND/OR-coupling graph. Consider the query containing the connectivities C_6 as described in Case 2. This can be expressed by a 2-connected hybrid graph as depicted in Figure 4(c). Notice that it consist of an AND/OR and an AND-coupling graph.

Observe that in all the above cases the connected components are in disjunction to one another. Also, a pair of connected components always share some vertices with identical identifiers.

5 Future Work

Currently, coupling queries are directed connected acyclic graphs having single source vertex. As part of our future work, we wish to generalize the coupling query into cyclic graphs with multiple source vertices. Also, we wish to augment coupling queries by allowing to impose conditions based on negation. Note that the inclusion of cycles and negation introduces interesting challenges with respect to the computability of the coupling query. Finally, in this paper we have ignored how to formulate query for processing of forms in the Web. We wish to extend our notion of coupling query to be able to autonomously fill out form and retrieve results by submission of the forms and manipulate these results further.

References

1. S. ABITEBOUL, D. QUASS, J. MCHUGH, J. WIDOM, J. WEINER. The Lorel Query Language for Semistructured Data. *Journal of Digital Libraries*, 1(1):68-88, April 1997.
2. G. AROCENA, A. MENDELZON. WebOQL: Restructuring Documents, Databases and Webs. *Proceedings of ICDE 98*, pp. 24-33, Orlando, Florida, February 1998.
3. S. S. BHOWMICK, W. K. NG, S. MADRIA. Imposing Disjunctive Constraints on Inter-Document Structure Using Coupling Queries. *Proceedings of the 12th International Conference on Database and Expert System Applications (DEXA'01)*, Munich, September, 2001.

4. S. S. Bhowmick. WHOM: A Data Model and Algebra for a Web Warehouse. *PhD Dissertation*, School of Computer Engineering, Nanyang Technological University, Singapore, 2001. Available at `www.ntu.edu.sg/home/assourav/`.
5. S. S. Bhowmick, W.-K. Ng, S. Madria. Web Schemas in Whoweda. *3rd ACM International Workshop on Data Warehousing and OLAP (DOLAP'00) (In conjunction with ACM CIKM' 00)*, Washington D.C., November, 2000.
6. A. Deutsch, M. Fernandez, D. Florescu, A. Levy, D. Suciu. A Query Language for XML. *Proceedings of the 8th World Wide Web Conference*, pp. 1155-1169, Toronto, Canada, May 1999.
7. R. Goldman, J. McHugh, J. Widom. From Semistructured Data to XML: Migrating the Lore Data Model and Query Language. *Proceedings of WebDB '99*, pp. 25-30, Philadelphia, Pennsylvania, June 1999.
8. D. Konopnicki, O. Shmueli. Information Gathering in the World-Wide Web: The W3QL Query Language and the W3QS System. *Theory of Database Systems (TODS)* , 23(4):369-410, 1998.

Topic-Centric Querying of Web Information Resources†

İ.S. Altıngövde[1], S.A. Özel[1], Ö. Ulusoy[1], G. Özsoyoğlu[2], and Z.M. Özsoyoğlu[2]

[1]Department of Computer Engineering, Bilkent University, Ankara, Turkey
(ismaila, selma, oulusoy)@cs.bilkent.edu.tr
[2]Department of Electrical Engineering and Computer Science, Case Western Reserve University, Cleveland, Ohio 44106
(tekin, meral)@eecs.cwru.edu

Abstract. This paper deals with the problem of modeling web information resources using expert knowledge and personalized user information, and querying them in terms of topics and topic relationships. We propose a model for web information resources, and a query language SQL-TC (Topic-Centric SQL) to query the model. The model is composed of web-based information resources (XML or HTML documents on the web), expert advice repositories (domain-expert-specified metadata for information resources), and personalized information about users (captured as user profiles, that indicate users' preferences as to which expert advice they would like to follow, and which to ignore, etc).

The query language SQL-TC makes use of the metadata information provided in expert advice repositories and embedded in information resources, and employs user preferences to further refine the query output. Query output objects/tuples are ranked with respect to the (expert-judged and user-preference-revised) importance values of requested topics/metalinks, and the query output is limited by either top n-ranked objects/tuples, or objects/tuples with importance values above a given threshold, or both.

1 Introduction

The web today hosts very large information repositories containing huge volumes of data. However, due to the lack of a centralized authority governing the web and a strict schema characterizing the *data* on the web, finding relevant information on the web is a major struggle.

We propose using metadata for an improved searching/querying paradigm. To illustrate our approach, assume that we want to locate movies listed at www.movie-bank.com, related to the novel "Carrie", written by the novelist Stephen King, and are rated at least "very good" (i.e., with an importance value above 0.7 in a scale of 0 to1) by the movie critic (expert) Joe Siegel. Presently, such a task can be performed by browsing the movie pages or by a keyword-based search on a web search engine followed up by a lookup of (some of) the resulting hits, which may be ineffective as well as time-inefficient. Assume that we have an expert that provides a data model for this web site, where "novel", "Carrie", and "Stephen-King" are topics, *RelatedTo* and *WrittenBy* are relationships among topics (called *associations* in the topic map standard, and, in this paper, referred to as *topic metalinks*), and for each topic, there are, perhaps X-Pointer-like pointers pointing to web documents containing "occurrences" of that topic, called *topic sources.* Then, we could formulate and

† This research is supported by a joint grant from TÜBİTAK (grant no. 100U024) of Turkey and the National Science Foundation (grant INT-9912229) of the USA.

H.C. Mayr et al. (Eds.): DEXA 2001, LNCS 2113, pp. 699–711, 2001.

evaluate the query "find movies *RelatedTo* novel Carrie, *WrittenBy* Stephen King, and rated above 0.7 by Joe Siegel" against the data model of the information source, and satisfy the user's request.

In this paper, we describe a "web information space" data model for web information resources, and the query language SQL-TC, where TC stands for topic-centric, to query the data model and web information resources in an integrated manner. The information space is composed of: *i*) Web-based *information resources*, which are XML [6] or HTML documents. *ii*) Independent *expert advice repositories* that contain domain expert-specified model of information resources. We assume that the expert advice, modeled as topic maps, is stored and maintained as XTM [22,23,24] documents. *iii*) *Personalized information* about users, captured as user profiles, that contain users' preferences as to which expert advice they would like to follow, and which to ignore, etc., and users' knowledge about the topics that they are querying. We maintain user profiles as XML documents.

In this model, topics and topic metalinks are the fundamental concepts through which information resources are modeled and queried. It is important to note that the expert advice repository is a *metadata* model, designed independently from the associated information resources (with the exception of topic source specifications) to model possibly multiple information resources, and capturing the expertise of a domain expert in a lasting manner. Therefore, the expert advice repository is *stable* (i.e., changes little), stays relevant (with the exception of topic sources) even when the information resource changes over time, and is much smaller than the information resource that it models. Finally, SQL-TC query output objects/tuples are ranked with respect to the (domain-expert-judged and user-preference-revised) importance values of requested topics/metalinks. The SQL-TC query output sizes are kept small by returning either (a) top n importance value-ranked objects/tuples, or (b) objects/tuples with importance values above a given threshold, or (c) both.

Thus, the main advantages of our proposal for web search and querying are (a) incorporating expert advice and personalized information, and (b) controlled delivery of query outputs in terms of top-ranking objects/tuples above a given importance value threshold. The disadvantage is the cost of creating and maintaining expert advice and personalized user information. Note that the expert advice, being stable over time, is a one-time effort to create, amortized by its use over time and fast response to user queries.

The query language SQL-TC allows users to query both expert advice repositories, and the associated information resources. Thus, querying resources with respect to multiple expert advices, coupled with the incorporation of personalized information, is expected to produce highly relevant and semantically related responses to users' queries within short time spans.

Next section discusses topic maps and the related standard. Section 3 is devoted to the web information space model with expert advice and user profiles. In Section 4, SQL-TC query language syntax and its features are covered, along with a number of examples.

2 Related Work

We summarize the Topic Map data model, as described in [3, 5, 8, 11, 15]. Definition of a topic is very general: a topic can be anything about which anything can be asserted by any means. As an example, in the context of Encyclopedia, the country Spain, or the city Rome are topics. Topics are *typed,* (e.g., type of the topic Rome is city), and have names. Topic names are also typed; e.g., base name (required), display name (optional), etc. Topic names have *scopes,* e.g., language, style, domain, etc. Topics have *occurrences* within addressable information resources. For example, a topic can be *described* in a monograph, *depicted* in a video or a picture, or *mentioned* in the context of something else. Moreover, each occurrence is typed using the notion of *occurrence role.* A *topic association* specifies a relationship between two or more topics. For example, topic Rome *is-in* topic Italy; topic Tom Robbins *was-born-in* topic USA, etc. A *topic map* is a structure, perhaps a file or a database or an XML document, which contains a topic data model, together with occurrences, types, contexts, and associations. A number of topic map examples and applications are provided in [4, 9, 13, 16, 17, 18, 19, 20].

XTM (XML Topic Map) is an effort to represent topic maps as XML documents. The proposals and DTDs for XTM are publicly available in [22, 23]. An XTM Processing Model is provided in [24].

3 Web Information Space Model

The three components of the model are information resource model, expert advice model, and user profile model.

3.1 Information Resource Model

Information resources are web-based documents, containing multimedia data of any arbitrary type. For the purposes of this research, we assume that information resources are in the form of XML/HTML documents.

Topic source represents an occurrence of a topic within an information resource. For example, the topic (with name) "Van Gough" occurs multiple times as HTML documents within the documents of the information resource "Online Collections of the Smithsonian Institution" [14], and each such HTML document occurrence constitutes a topic source. The expert advice model, discussed next, has an entity, called Topic Source Reference, which contains (partial) information about a topic source (such as its web address, etc).

3.2 Expert Advice Model

3.2.1 Topic and Topic Source Reference Entity Types

We assume that the experts in the web information space model are registered and known either through the user profiles or specified in each query explicitly. Each domain expert E_i, $1 \leq i \leq n$, models an information resource in terms of topic and topic source reference entities and, metalink relationships. We start with the topic entity, which constitutes metadata, and has the following attributes.

- *T(opic-)Name* (of type string) contains either a single word (i.e., a keyword) or multiple words (i.e., a phrase). Topic names characterize the data (real-world subjects [22]) in information resources. Example topic names are "database" (a keyword) and "United Nation's International Policies" (a phrase). Topic names are defined by domain experts, and can be arbitrarily specified phrases or words. Therefore, the issue of similarity between topic names is addressed. To check for the similarity of two topics on the basis of their names, we employ SimTName( ) function, which returns the name similarity of two topics with arbitrarily long topic names as a real value within the range [0, 1].

- *T(opic-)Type* and *T(opic-)Domain* attributes specify, respectively, the type of the topic and the domain within which the topic is to be used. For example, the topic "Hamlet" is of type "character" in the domain of "plays". The topic "Paris" may be of type "Greek god" in the domain of "mythology", whereas it is of type "city" in the domain "geography". And, the topic "diabetes" may be of type "chronic disease" in the domain of "medicine". Again, we allow different experts to use different words/phrases for topic types and topic domains.
- *T(opic-)Author* attribute defines the expert (name or id or simply a URL that uniquely identifies the expert) who authors the topic.
- *T(opic-)MaxDetailLevel.* Each topic can be represented by a topic source in the web information resource at a different *detail level*. Therefore, each topic entity has a maximum detail level attribute. As an example, assume that levels 1, 2 and 3 denote levels “beginner”, “intermediate”, and “advanced”. Note that the detail level value of a topic source must be less than or equal to the maximum detail level attribute of the topic.
- *T(opic-)id.* Each topic entity has a T(opic-)id attribute, whose value is an artificially generated identifier, internally used for efficient implementation purposes, and not available to users.
- *T(opic-)SourceRef.* Each topic entity has a T(opic-)SourceRef attribute which contains a set of Topic-Source-Reference entities as discussed below.
- Topics also have other attributes such as roles, role-playing, etc.

The attributes (TName, TType, TDomain, TAuthor) constitute a key for the topic entity. And, the Tid attribute is also a key for topics.

The expert E_i, $1 \leq i \leq n$, states his/her advice on topics as a Topic-Advice function TAdvice() that assigns an *importance value* to topics from one of $[0, 1] \cup \{$No, Don’t-Care$\}$. The importance value is a measure for the importance of the topic, except for the cases below.

a) When the value is “No”, for the expert, the topic is rejected (which is different than the importance value of zero in which case the topic is accepted, and the expert attaches a zero value to it), and
b) When the importance value is “Don’t-Care”, the expert does not care about the use of the topic (but will not object if other experts use it), and chooses not to attach any value to it. Don’t-Care value is used when merging multiple expert advices.

Example 1. Assume that the expert E assigns the following topic advice:
TAdvice(E, TType=”Diabetes”, TName=“*Diabetes Surgeries*”, TDomain=“New Patient Training”) = 0.3
where * denotes a wildcard character that matches any string. This topic advice states that, for training new patients, a topic of type diabetes and with a name containing the phrase “Diabetes Surgeries” is of low importance value.

For the topic advice function TAdvice(), we use the Closed World Assumption with the “No” (or the “Don’t’-Care”) option, denoted as CWA-No (or CWA-Don’t’-

Care) that states that any TAdvice() choice that is not explicitly specified has the value "No" (or "Don't-Care", respectively).

T(opic-)S(ource-)Ref(erence), also an entity in the expert advice model, contains additional information about topic sources. A topic source reference entity has the following attributes.

- *Topics* (set of Tid values) attribute that represents the set of topics for which the referenced source is a topic source.
- *Web-Address* (URL) of the document that contains the topic source.
- *Detail level* (sequence of integers). Each topic source reference has a *detail level* describing how advanced the level of the topic source is for the corresponding topic. The detail levels are ordered using the same ordering of the corresponding topics in the attribute Topics.
- Other attributes such as *Mediatype, Role, Last-Modified, Last-Visited* etc.

The expert E_i states his/her advice on topic sources as a Source-Advice function SAdvice() that assigns an importance value to topic sources from one of $[0, 1] \cup$ {No, Don't-Care}.

In addition to comparing topic entities by their names (as strings), we compare topics by their topic sources using the function SimTopicSource( ), which returns the similarity of two topics by their topic sources as a real value within the range [0, 1].

3.2.2 Metalink Types and Topic Closures

Topic Metalinks represent relationships among topics. Metalink attributes include types, roles, domains, etc. As an example, consider learning-related metalink type *Prerequisite*, and the metalink instance "Diabetes Complications^2→ *Prerequisite* Diabetes^1" stating that "The prerequisite to understanding/learning the topic Diabetes Complications at level 2 is an understanding of the topic Diabetes at level 1 (or higher). The notation →*Prerequisite* represents an instance of the metalink type *Prerequisite.* Within the context of electronic books, we gave [12] a sound and complete set of axioms for the *Prerequisite* relationship. Any relationship involving topics deemed suitable by an expert in the field can be a topic metalink. For instance, *SubTopicOf* and *SuperTopicOf* metalink types together would represent a topic composition hierarchy.

Metalinks represent relationships among topics, not topic sources. Therefore, they are "meta" relationships, hence our choice of the term "metalink". And, metalink types are usually recursive relationships.

The expert E_i states his/her advice (i) on metalink type signatures as the set *Metalinks,* and (ii) on metalink instances as a Metalink-Advice function MAdvice() that assigns an importance value to a metalink from one of $[0, 1] \cup$ {No, Don't-Care}. E_i.Metalinks denote the set of metalink instances (of possibly different types) defined by the expert E_i. Similarly, E_i.Topics denote the set of topics defined by the expert E_i.

Example 2. Assume that the expert E states the following metalink signatures: E.Metalinks = {*RelatedTo:* topic → topic, *Prerequisite*: SetOf topic→ SetOf topic } where the first signature states that the *RelatedTo* metalink type takes two topics of any type as arguments, and the second signature states that the *Prerequisite* metalink type takes two sets of topics of any type as arguments. For instance, the expert E states the following metalink instance as an advice: MAdvice (E, Diabetes Care^1 →*RelatedTo* Diabetes Complications^1) = 0.8

This metalink states that the importance value of the metalink "the topic Diabetes Care at the beginner level (1) is related to Diabetes Complications at the beginner level" is reasonably high (0.8) (There may be other causes for diabetes complications).

We assume that different experts specify (a) possibly different topic entities with similar names, (b) overlapping topic sources, and (c) possibly different metalink types and instances. Thus, the system may need to merge the advices from multiple experts and resolve conflicts among advices. An example illustrating this situation along with a user preference-based solution attempt is provided in Example 6 of Section 4.

In this work, we assume that the expert advice described here may either be embedded in information resources or stored independently; in which case, we assume that the expert advice is in the form of an XTM document. A prototype system is developed (but not reported here, due to space considerations) using XTM documents as expert advice repositories.

As stated before, metalink types are usually recursive. For example, *RelatedTo* is both transitive and reflexive. *IsIn* is transitive, but not reflexive; *SubTopicOf* is transitive. Therefore, when a user lists a set X of topics, and asks for topic sources of topics in X as well as others that are *RelatedTo* topics in X, we need to take the "topic closure" of the topic set X with respect to the recursive metalink type *RelatedTo.* We emphasize the notion of *Topic Closures* with respect to recursive metalink types, in order for queries to return results that satisfy all the axioms of the associated metalink types. Given a set X of topics, the query response will include the topic closure X^+, which is formed of all topics that are logically implied by the initial set X.

Clearly, computing topic closures requires a sound and complete set of axioms for the metalink types deployed by the expert E, and a polynomial-time algorithm that computes the topic closure using the axioms. As an example, in our earlier work [12], we gave a sound and complete axiomatization for the *Prerequisite* metalink type. For each new metalink type added into the expert advice model, sound and complete axioms for all metalink types, including those that apply to multiple metalink types are found. To illustrate this, consider the *RelatedTo* metalink type and the cyclic and nondecomposable *Prerequisite* metalink type. Note that, from its signature, all *RelatedTo* metalink instances have a single topic in the LHS and the RHS. Then we have the following axioms:

RelatedTo Axioms:

- Reflexivity. If A →*RelatedTo* B then B →*RelatedTo* A
- Transitivity. If A →*RelatedTo* B and B →*RelatedTo* C then A→*RelatedTo* C

Prerequisite Axioms: Armstrong's axioms.

RelatedTo and *Prerequisite* mixed axioms:

- If X →*Prerequisite* A and A →*RelatedTo* B then C →*RelatedTo* B, ∀ C where C ∈ X.
- If X → *RelatedTo* A and A →*Prerequisite* B then C →*RelatedTo* B, ∀ C where C ∈ X.

With these axioms, one can find the topic closure X^+ of a set X of topics by using the O (n.t) closure algorithm, where n is the number of *Prerequisite* and *RelatedTo* metalinks, and t is the max length of the encoding for a *Prerequisite* or a *RelatedTo* metalink.

3.3 Personalized Information Model: User Profiles

3.3.1 User Preferences

Along the lines of [1], the user U specifies his/her preferences as an ordered set of Accept-Expert, Accept-Expert-Metalink-Importance-Threshold, etc. statements. For the sake of saving space, we illustrate preference functions with an example.

Example 3. Assume that we have three experts W-Clinton, A-Gore, and GW-Bush. The user John-Doe specifies the following preferences:

Expert (John-Doe) = <GW-Bush, W-Clinton>
(Accept the advices of GW-Bush and W-Clinton; reject any advice from A-Gore)

TImportance (John-Doe) = {(GW-Bush, 0.5), (W-Clinton, 0.9)}
(Accept the topics from GW-Bush if GW-Bush-assigned importance is above 0.5; accept the topics from W-Clinton if W-Clinton-assigned importance is above 0.9)

MImportance (John-Doe) = {(W-Clinton, 0.9)} (Always accept the metalinks from GW-Bush; accept the metalinks from W-Clinton if W-Clinton-assigned importance is above 0.9)

SImportance (John-Doe) = {(GW-Bush, 0.5)} (Always accept the sources from W-Clinton; accept the sources from GW-Bush if GW-Bush-assigned importance is above 0.5)

Reject-Topic(John-Doe)={name="*Lewinski*",<W-Clinton, Name="Gift-Taking">}
(Always reject topics with names containing the word "Lewinski" (regardless of the expert); reject advice from W-Clinton on a topic with name "Gift-Taking")

Reject-Source (John-Doe) = {Web-Address=www.dirtypolitics.com}

Conflict-Resolution = Ordered-Accept (Follow the order as specified by "expert": always accept the advice of GW-Bush; accept the advice of W-Clinton only when it does not conflict with the advice of GW-Bush. The other alternative choices include "Accept-and-Merge-All-Advice")

3.3.2 User Knowledge

For a given user and a topic, the knowledge level of the user on the topic (zero, originally) is a certain detail level of that topic. The set *U-Knowledge (U)* = {(topic, detail-level-value)}

contains users' knowledge on topics in terms of detail levels. As in other specifications, topics may be fully defined using the three key attributes TName, TType and TDomain, or they may be partially specified in which case the user's knowledge spans a set of topics satisfying the given attributes.

Besides detail levels, we also keep historical information for each topic source that the user has visited, which include web addresses (URLs) of topic sources, first/last visit dates and the number of times the source is visited. We use the information on user's knowledge while evaluating query conditions and computing topic closures, in order to reduce the size of the information returned to the user. In the absence of a user profile, the user is assumed to know nothing about any topic. See Appendix B for an example.

4 Topic-Centric Query Language: SQL-TC

We specify the syntactic constructs of SQL-TC. The formal syntax in an extended Backus-Naur format is given in [2].

select [*topic* {*.attribute*} | *metalink* {*.attribute*}] **as** *T* **from resources** *XML: url1,*

using experts *Topic Map1: url1, ...* **as** E1, ... **with user profile** *XML: URL* **as** *U*
where (i) conditions on topics and metalinks of experts; (ii) content-based conditions on sources, (iii) conditions on user profile information
order by [topic] **importance**
stop after n **most important**| **when importance below** m
| **after** n **most important and when importance below** m

Variables are prefixed by the $ symbol, constants are in quotes, and metalinks are in italics. **Stop after** clause is adapted from [7].

4.1 Querying Web-Based Information Resources

We assume that we have two experts whose advices are at www.sql-tc.com/king.xtm (expert E1) and horror-books.com/books.xtm (expert E2), respectively. The information resources are at www.stephenkinglibrary.com and www.stephen-king.net. As the expert advice and the user profile information, we use the instances provided in Appendices A and B, respectively.

Example 4. (*Topic and source variables, and detail levels*) Using only the advice at www.sql-tc.com/king.xtm, find two highest-ranked novels that are written by the novelist Stephen King, and the novels' detail level 4 reviews from the two information resources.

select [$topic.name, $sourceRef.web-address] **as** T
from resources www.stephenkinglibrary.com, www.stephen-king.net
using experts www.sql-tc.com/king.xtm **as** E
where *WrittenBy* **in** E.Metalinks **and**
$topic = **any** (*WrittenBy* ("Stephen King", "novelist", "literature", E)) **and**
$sourceRef = **any** SourceOf($topic, 4, E) **and** "review" **in** $sourceRef.roles
order by $topic **importance**
stop after 2 **most important**

Novel names are topic names, and the novel reviews constitute topic sources. The result of the query is a 2-column table with 2 tuples. The first atomic formula in the where clause states that *WrittenBy* is a metalink type declared by expert E. Assume that the metalink type *WrittenBy* has the signature: *WrittenBy*(E): SetOf author → novel

In the second where clause statement, the variable $topic is instantiated by one of the novel entities returned by the *WrittenBy()* metalink where each selected novel is authored by the topic that has TName of "Stephen King", TType of "novelist" and TDomain of "literature", and specified by the expert E. This query illustrates two types of variables, namely, $topic which is a topic variable, and $sourceRef which is a topic source reference variable. SourceOf() is a function that takes in the triple <topic entity, detail level, expert>, and returns a set of topic source reference (TSRef) entities at the given detail level as specified by the given expert. Thus, in the above query, the value of $sourceRef.web-address expression is, according to expert E, the web addresses of topic sources at detail level 4 obtained from the topic reference entities for the topic $topic.

Using the expert advice in Appendix A, this query produces 4 tuples; however, only the two highest ranked tuples (one for Carrie with importance value of 1, and another for the Stand with the importance value of 0.8) are returned as shown in Table1.

Table 1. Output of the SQL-TC query in Example 4

Tname	SourceRef.Web-address
"Carrie"	www.critics.com/carrie.html
"The Stand"	www.critics.com/stand.html

Example 5. (*Topic closure computation and user profiles*) Using only the advice of expert E and excluding the novels read by the user, find the highest ranked novel and its detail level 4 reviews where the novel is written by Stephen King and related to the novel "Wizard and The Glass".

select [$topic.name, $sourceRef.web-address] **as** T
from resources www.stephenkinglibrary.com, www.stephen-king.net
using experts www.sql-tc.com/king.xtm **as** E
with user profile www.myprofile.com
where *WrittenBy, RelatedTo* **in** E.Metalinks **and**
$topic = **any** (*WrittenBy* ("Stephen King", "novelist", "literature", E)
and *RelatedTo** ("Wizard and The Glass", ,"literature", E)) **and**
$sourceRef = **any** SourceOf($topic, 4, E) **and** "review" **in** $sourceRef.roles
and
$topic **not in** GetTopics(U.UserKnowledge)
order by importance
stop after 1 **most important**

We assume for this query that the metalink type *RelatedTo* of expert E has the signature *RelatedTo*(E): novel → novel. Note that in this query the user asks for the highest-valued tuple, not the highest-valued novel. Derived importance value computation of output tuples [2] takes place, and the tuple in Table 2 is chosen. Let us discuss the interpretation of this query using the expert advice repository and user profile instances in the Appendices. The novels that are related to the novel "Wizard and The Glass" are recursively located. From Appendix B, the output returns only those novels that are not known by the user. For instance, according to the expert advice in Appendix A, the topics that are related to "Wizard and The Glass" are "The Wasteful Lands", "Drawings of Three" and "Dark Tower". However, since the novel "Dark Tower" is already known according to the user profile (given in Appendix B), it is not included in the final result, and the tuple (NOT the novel) with the highest importance value is selected.

Table 2. Output of the SQL-TC query in Example 5

Tname	SourceRef.Web-address
"The Wasteful Lands"	www.critics.com/dark3.html

Example 6. (*User preferences, user knowledge and multiple experts*) Using first the expert www.sql-tc.com/king.xtm, and then, if there are no conflicts, the expert www.horror-books.com/books.xtm, find all novels and their summaries such that the main characters of the selected novels are influenced from "Jack Park", the main

character of the novel "The Stand", and retrieve only those sources that have not been visited by the user in the last 30 days.

select [$topic.name, $sourceRef.web-address] **as** T
from resources www.stephenkinglibrary.com, www.stephen-king.net
using experts www.sql-tc.com/king.xtm **as** E1, www.horror-books.com/books.xtm **as** E2
with user profile www.myprofile.com as U
where *NovelsOfNovelCharacters*, *InfluencedBy* **in** (E1, E2). Metalinks **and**
$topic=**any** *NovelsOfNovelCharacters* (
*InfluencedBy** ("Jack Park", hero, novel characters,),) **and**
$sourceRef= **any** SourceOf($topic, ,) **and** "summary" **in** $sourceRef.roles **and**
$sourceRef.web-address **in** GetSourceAddresses (U.UserKnowledge) **and**
GetLastVisitedDays (U.UserKnowledge, $sourceRef.web-address) > "30"

The second where clause assigns a novel to the topic variable $topic where the novel has a main character influenced by "Jack Park", in the domain of "literature". For both experts, we assume that the signatures of the metalink types *InfluencedBy* and *NovelsOfNovelCharacters* are the same, and each is defined as

InfluencedBy (E): novel-character → novel-character and
NovelsOfNovelCharacters (E): novel-character → SetOf novel

where E denotes either of the two experts. Note that, in the query, the selection of the expert for the above metalinks (and the expert of the function SourceOf()) is not specified in the query, and deferred to the user's preferences. Also, in the SourceOf() function, a topic source at any detail level is accepted.

For this example, we assume that the *InfluencedBy* metalink is binary, transitive, and cyclic, and we apply the corresponding topic closure computation algorithm for this case. According to the advice of expert www.sql-tc.com/king.xtm (E1 in Appendix A), "Jack Park", influences the character "John Smith". As "John Smith" is claimed to be the main character of the novels "Scream" and "Maniac" by expert www.horror-books.com/books.xtm (E2 in Appendix A), the topic closure computation will bind each of "Scream" and "Maniac" to the $topic variable. Thus, $sourceRef.web-addresses will be assigned to the corresponding sources www.books.com/scream.html and www.books.com/maniac.html. The function GetSourceAddresses() returns addresses of visited sources and the function GetLastVisitedDays() retrieves the days since the last-visit of a given source from the user profile database U (in Appendix B). Subsequently, the entire query will return www.books.com/maniac.html as it is the only source that is visited by the user and not in the last thirty days.

Note that this query employs more than one expert advice, and the issue of conflicts among different expert advice comes up. In the user preferences (given in Appendix B), first the advice of E1 and then, if there are no conflicts, the advice of E2 are to be accepted. Assume that the following metalink advice instances are encountered during the topic closure computation with respect to the *InfluencedBy* metalink type:

MAdvice(E1, "John Smith" →*InfluencedBy* "Jack Park") = 0.8
MAdvice (E2, "John Smith" →*InfluencedBy* "Jack Park") = "No"

The query evaluation relies first on E1 and includes the character "John Smith" in the closure set, or relies on E2 and discards the character "John Smith" (and thus all other topics that may possibly be added to the closure because of the inclusion of "John Smith") from the closure. To resolve the conflict, the query engine consults the metalink-importance-threshold statements declared in the user preferences, and discards the advice with a lower importance value than the given threshold. The user preferences (of Appendix B) declare threshold values 0.5 and "Don't-Care" for experts E1 and E2 respectively. And, the conflict-resolution statement of the user's preferences declares an ordered acceptance of advices. Thus, we add "John Smith" into the topic closure set.

4.2 Querying Expert Advice Repositories

Example 7. (*Metalink attributes*) Find top 30-ranked metalinks in the domain of literature and having an importance value of at least 0.7 for the expert www.sql-tc.com/king.xtm such that, in each such metalink, Stephen King is a participator.
select [$metalink.type] **as** T
using experts www.sql-tc.com/king.xtm **as** E
where $metalink **in** E.Metalinks **and**
    $metalink= **any** (MetalinksWithTopic ("Stephen King", , , E)) **and**
    $metalink.domain = "literature"
order by importance
stop after 30 **most important and when importance below** 0.7

The function MetalinksWithTopic() takes a topic (either fully identified by TName, Ttype, TDomain, and TAuthor in the given order, or partially identified), and returns metalink instances. According to Appendix A, the query output includes the "*WrittenBy*" metalink type.

References

[1] Agrawal, R., Wimmers, E.L., "A Framework for Expressing and Combining Preferences", ACM SIGMOD Conf., pp. 297-306, 2000.
[2] Altıngövde, I.S., Ozel, S.A., Ulusoy, O., Ozsoyoglu, G., Ozsoyoglu, Z.M., SQL-TC: A Topic-Centric Query Language for Web-Based Information Resources, manuscript in preparation, 2001.
[3] Biezunski, M., "Topic Maps at a glance", at http://www.infoloom.com/tmsample/bie0.htm
[4] Biezunski, M, "A Topic Map of This Conference's Proceedings", Proc. of GCA, 1996, http://www.infoloom.com/IHC96/mb214.htm
[5] Biezunski, M., Bryan, M., Newcomb, S., editors, ISO/IEC 13250, Topic Maps, available at http://www.ornl.gov/sgml/sc34/document/0058.htm.
[6] Bray, T., Paoli, J., Sperberg-McQueen, C. M., "Extensible Markup Language 1.0 Specification". World Wide Web Consortium (W3C), February 1998.
[7] Carey, M.J., Kossmann, "On Saying "Enough Already" in SQL", ACM SIGMOD 1997.
[8] ISO 13250 Topic Map Standard available at http://www.w3c.com
[9] Ksiezyk, R., "Answer is Just a Question [of matching Topic Maps], Proc. of XML Europe 2000, GCA, Alexandria, VA, 2000.

[10] Microsoft MSDN Online Support, available at http://support.microsoft.com/servicedesks/msdn.
[11] Newcomb, S., Biezunski, M., "Topic Maps go XML", XML Europe 2000, June 2000.
[12] Ozsoyoglu, G., Balkir, N.H., Cormode, G., Ozsoyoglu, Z.M., "Electronic Books in Digital Libraries", IEEE Advances in Digital Libraries Conf., Washington, D.C., May 2000.
[13] Ontopia Topic Map Technology, available at www.ontopia.net
[14] Online Collections of the Smithsonian Institution, available at http://www.si.edu.
[15] Pepper, S., "Euler, Topic Maps, and Revolution", available at http://www.infoloom.com/tmsample/pep4.htm
[16] Rath, H.H., "Topic Maps Self Control", Extreme Markup Lang. 2000, Montreal, PQ, Canada, 2000.
[17] The K42 Topic Map Engine, available at http://k42.empolis.co.uk
[18] Topic Maps available at www.infoloom.com
[19] Topic Map Samples, available at http://www.techquila.com/tmsamples/
[20] tmproc: A Topic Maps implementation, available at http://www.ontopia.net/software/tmproc/index.html
[21] XML Pointer Language (XPointer) version 1.0, available at http://www.w3.org/TR/xptr/
[22] XML Topic Maps (XTM) 1.0 available at http://www.topicmaps.org/xtm/1.0
[23] XTM: XML Topic Maps- working documents, available at http://www.doctypes.org/xtm/home.html
[24] XTM Processing Model 1.0, TopicMaps.Org AG Review Specification, 4 Dec 2000, available at http://topicmaps.org/xtm/1.0/xtmp1.html

Appendix A: Expert Advice Repositories

In the following, we provide expert advices as list for the ease of illustration. Clearly, the expert advice repositories may be in the form of text files, XML files and/or tables/objects of any conventional databases.

To save space, we only provide topics, sources and metalinks that are illustrated in the examples throughout the paper.

A.1 Expert Advice Provided in www.sql-tc.com/king.xtm (Expert E1)

Each topic of the expert advice is specified in the form of tuple: <Tid, TDetail level, Ttype, Tname, Tdomain, T-Advice, Source>.

Topics (E1) = {<T1, -, novelist, "Stephen King", literature, 1, S1>, <T2, -, novel, "Carrie", literature, 1, {S2, S3}>, <T3, -, novel, "The Stand", literature, 0.8, S4>, <T4, 4, novel, "Wizard and The Glass", literature, 0.3, ->, <T5, 3, novel, "The Wasteful Lands", literature, 0.4, S5>, <T6, 2, novel, "Drawings of Three", literature, 0.6, S6>, <T7, 1, novel, "Dark Tower", literature, 0.8, ->, <T8, -, hero, "Jack Park", novel characters, -, ->, <T9, -, character, "John Smith", novel characters, -, ->}

Similarly, each metalink of the expert advice is specified in the form of tuple: <Mid, Mtype, Mdomain, Antecedent players, Consequent players, M-advice>.

Metalinks (E1) = { <M1, WrittenBy, {literature, horror}, T2, T1, 1>, <M2, WrittenBy, {literature, horror}, T3, T1, 0.6>, <M3, WrittenBy, {literature, horror}, T4, T1, 0.6>, <M4, WrittenBy, {literature, horror}, T5, T1, 0.6>, <M5, WrittenBy, {literature, horror}, T6, T1, 0.6>, <M6, WrittenBy, {literature, horror}, T7, T1, 0.6>, <M7, RelatedTo, -, T7, T6, 0.6>, <M8, RelatedTo, -, T6, T5, 0.5>, <M9, RelatedTo, -, T5, T4, 0.3>, <M10, InfluencedBy, -, T9, T8, 0.8>}

Note that, in the above list, the attributes of tuples may be set-valued. Although we refer the player topics by their internal ids (as in the prototype implementation) for the sake of saving space, the player topics could also be specified by the quadruples of the form TName, TType, TDomain, TDetail-level.

A source element of the expert advice is specified in the form of tuple: <Sid, Web-address, Role, MediaType, LastUpdated, Detail level, S-Advice>.

Sources(E1) = { <S1, www.king.com/, Website, multimedia, 16.01.2001, -, 1>, <S2, www.books.com/carrie.html, Summary, Text, -, -, 0.5>, <S3, www.critics.com/carrie.html, Review, Text, -, 4, 0.8>, <S4, www.critics.com/stand.html, Review, Text, -, 4, 0.7>, <S5, www.critics.com/dark3.html, Review, Text, -, 4, 0.8>, <S6, www.critics.com/dark2.html, Review, Text, -, 4, 0.3>}

A.2 Expert Advice Provided in www.horror-books.com/books.xtm (Expert E2)

Similarly, the metadata that is specified by expert E2 is given in the below.

Topics(E2) ={<T10, -,novel, "Scream", literature, 0.3, S7>, <T11, -, novel, "Maniac", literature, 0.4, S8>, <T12, -, hero, "Jack Park", novel characters, -, ->, <T13, -, character, "John Smith", novel characters, -, ->}

Metalinks(E2) = { <M11, InfluencedBy, -, T13, T12, No>, <M12, NovelsOfNovelCharacters, -, T13, T10, 0.6>, <M13, NovelsOfNovelCharacters, -, T13 , T11, 0.2>}

Sources(E2) = {<S7, www.books.com/scream.html, Summary, text, 12.02.2001, -, 0.6>, <S8, www.books.com/maniac.html, Summary, text, 13.02.2001, -, 0.7>}

Appendix B: Personalized Information for User U

In the following, we provide personalized information in terms of user preferences and user knowledge for a typical user U. Assume that user profile is kept in the virtual web location **www.myprofile.com**.

User-Preferences (U) contains a set of statements as follows:

Expert (U) = <www.sql-tc.com/king.xtm, www.horror-books.com/books.xtm>
TImportance(U) = { (www.sql-tc.com/king.xtm, 0.5), (www.horror-books.com/books.xtm, 0.3)}
Mimportance(U) = {(www.sql-tc.com/king.xtm, 0.5), (www.horror-books.com/books.xtm, "Don't-Care")}
Simportance(U) = {(www.sql-tc.com/king.xtm, 0.5), (www.horror-books.com/books.xtm, 0.3)}
Reject-S (U) = {www.sking-fanatics.com}
Conflict-R (U) = Ordered-Accept

User-Knowledge (U)

User knowledge is specified in the form of tuple: <TName, DetailLevel, Source-address, Sourcerole, Sourcemediatype, FirstVisit, Last visit,Visit No>

User-Knowledge (U) = {<"Scream", -, www.books.com/scream.html, summary, text, -, 12.02.2001, 2>,
<"Maniac", -, www.books.com/maniac.html, summary, text, -, 13.02.1999, 3>,
<"Dark Tower", 1, www.books.com/dark1.html, review, text1, -, -, 3>}

WebCarousel: Automatic Presentation and Semantic Restructuring of Web Search Result for Mobile Environments *

Akiyo Nadamoto[1], Hiroyuki Kondo[1], and Katsumi Tanaka[2]

[1] Graduate School of Science & Technology, Kobe University, Rokkodai, Nada, Kobe 657, Japan
{nadamoto, kondo}@db.cs.kobe-u.ac.jp
http://www.db.cs.kobe-u.ac.jp

[2] Department of Social Informatics, Graduate School of Informatics, Kyoto University, Yoshida Honmachi, Sakyo, Kyoto 606-8501,Japan
ktanaka@i.kyoto-u.ac.jp

Abstract. In the present paper, we propose a new way of organizing Web search results and a way of viewing those results passively in the mobile environment which has limited display and limited interaction. The system makes a 'carousel' of 'carousel components', each of which consists of images and voice extracted from a searched Web page. The carousel components of a carousel are displayed automatically and repeatedly in the mobile environment. When a user issues a request during viewing a carousel component, the system automatically computes sets of similar, different, more-detailed, and more-summarized pages, which are also organized as carousels. We also describe our prototype system called WebCarousel. The characteristic of WebCarousel is as follows: (1) Web search results are shown by synthesized speech synchronized with related images in a repeated manner by carousels. (2) Dynamic reorganization of search results into carousels is done by discovering 'semantic' relationships between Web pages.

1 Introduction

Recently, much attention has been focused on the Internet content acquisition in mobile environments (ex. Cellular phone, PDA). In particular, we pay attention to a more effective way that acquires and presents Web contents in mobile environments. It is difficult for mobile equipments to display ordinary Web contents on the Internet. Because most mobile equipments have narrow and poor display, and they don't have full keyboards. Therefore, many restrictions are imposed on content presentation and users' interactions.

* This research is partly supported by the cooperative research project with NTT DoCoMo, the research for the Future Program of Japan Society for the Promotion of Science under the project: Researches on Advanced Multimedia Contents Processing, and the grant of Scientific Research (12680416) from Ministry of Education, Science, Sports and Culture of Japan.

H.C. Mayr et al. (Eds.): DEXA 2001, LNCS 2113, pp. 712–722, 2001.

In this paper, we propose a new way of organizing Web search results and a way of viewing those results passively in the mobile environments. In conventional Web-browsing environments, we usually have to read, scroll and click contents on a PC. It is, however, difficult for us to read, scroll and click Web contents in mobile environments, specially in the case of browsing search results from search engines. So, we believe it is necessary to provide a new browsing facility that enables watching and listening search results on mobile environments. The next generation cellular phone technology, such as IMT2000, will accelerate it very much since the IMT2000 will make it possible to send synchronized multimedia content.

In order to cope with the problem, we introduce a new way of restructuring web search results for passive viewing. Our restructuring method is to classify search results dynamically for user-interested pages into several groups, called ***carousels***. By analyzing Web pages, it divides the web pages of search results into four groups, based on similarity, difference, detail, summary relationships. User can select a carousel and transit among carousels by a few interactions. For each carousel, the Web pages are presented automatically and repeatedly(see Fig. 1).

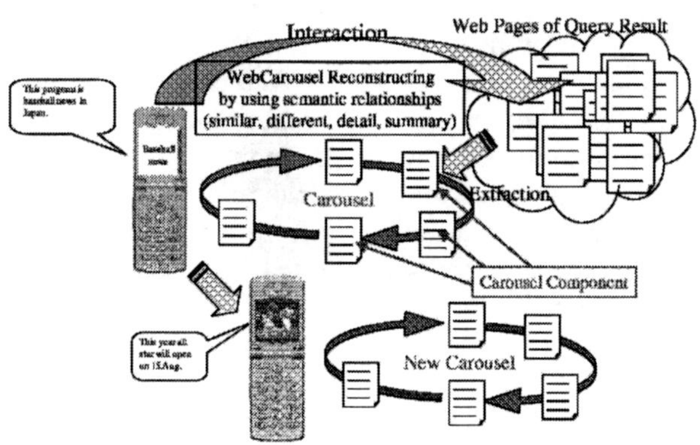

Fig. 1. WebCarousel

2 Related Work

According to the rapid progress of mobile equipments, much attention has been focused on the ***Web adaptation*** technology. The Web adaptation is to transform Web content for several browsing equipments. Hirakawa et al.[1] proposed a way of the Web adaptation using a proxy server to transform ordinary Web pages for mobile equipments. This proxy server changes a view of a Web page including colors and sizes in proportion to the ability of each mobile equipment such as cellular phone or PDA or car navigation equipment. The Stanford

Power Browser project[2] developed a new browsing manager which automatically transforms Web pages for viewing them by PDAs. Furthermore, in order to support pen-based search and navigation by PDAs, they explored support tools for keyword compensation and anchor view generation. That is, their system complements the input keyword in order to assist the pen input. Hori et al.[3] proposed an annotation-based system for Web content conversion. Their approach is based on the usage of additional annotation file, which describes how the corresponding Web page should be displayed for each browsing equipment. The linkage between original Web pages and their annotation files are realized by XPOINTER/XLINK of XML.

Another approach is the usage of markup languages desicated for mobile equipements. Compact HTML is one of a subset of HTML, and it is used to display Web pages on mobile environments. It doesn't need a proxy. It describes Web pages for exclusive use, so users can't get all the Web page on the Internet by using mobile environments. 'i-mode'[4] is representative using Compact HTML in Japan. WML[5] is a markup language used for WAP and based on XML. WML is intended for use in specifying content and user interface for narrowband devices, including mobile environments.

As the third approach, we proposed a way to browse Web pages in a more passive style. The watch and listen Interface[6][7][8][9][10]is our solution for this objective. Once a user specifies a URL, the Web page corresponding to the URL is shown such as a TV-program, which the user can watch and listen to it. The interface presents the content of the corresponding Web page like a TV program, in which some animation characters speak the text in the original page like lines, and the images contained in the Web page are presented consecutively one by one by synchronizing with characters' speech and behaviors. This technique is effective in mobile environments.

3 Carousel-style Presentation of Search Results

The members of a carousel are not always whole Web pages, but some portions of Web pages. Each member of a carousel is called a *carousel component*. In order to extract a carousel component corresponding to a Web page, we need to discover a portion of the Web page that is regarded as the representative portion of the page. In order to find a carousel component for each Web page, we need to look for images or videos that should be presented simultaneously when the sentences of the carousel component are spoken by synthesized speech.

A carousel component, say CC, for a Web page P is defined to consist of the following three elements:

$$CC = (C_{head}, C_{voice}, C_{visual})$$

C_{head} Header component: A title of P. It's presented for display.
C_{voice} Voice component: A textual portion of P. It's synthesized speech.
C_{visual} Visual component: An image of P. It's presented for display.

A HTML document has a tree structure, in which each non-leaf node corresponds to a tag and each leaf node corresponds to a text or an image or a video. We analyze HTML tag structure to find a carousel component for each Web page by using structural tags. Structural tags are used to denote the document structure. These are P, BLOCKQUOTE, DIV, VL, OL, DL, TABLE tags.

In the following, we show an algorithm to create a carousel component from its corresponding Web page. The input of the algorithm are (1) a Web page P, (2) the maximum size MAX_c of text, which will be presented by voice presentation and (3) search keywords $Q = k_1, k_2, \cdots, k_n (n \geq 1)$. The output of the algorithm is a carousel component CC_P corresponding to the given page P. Roughly, the following algorithm parses the given Web page, finds fragments of P that contains all the specified keywords, adjusts and determines an appropriate fragment for voice presentation, finds an appropriate image or video that should be presented synchronized with selected text fragment, and composes a carousel component.

(STEP 1)Generation of a header component C_{header}

A header component C_{header} is a title of the Web page P. The region between $< TITLE >$ and $< /TITLE >$ is C_{header}.

(STEP2)Discovery of a voice component C_{voice}

A voice component C_{voice} is a minimal contiguous portion of a Web page that includes all user-specified keywords $Q = (k_1, k_2, \cdots, k_n)$. As shown in Fig. 2, we find candidates of C_{voice} by traversing the page's tag structure in the breadth-first search manner.

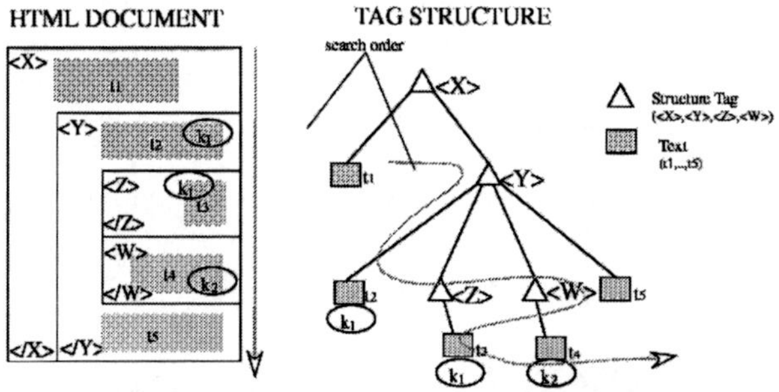

Fig. 2. Extraction of Voice Component

(STEP3)Extraction of a visual component C_{visual}

Visual component C_{visual} consists of a single image or video which is synchronized with C_{voice} during the carousel component presentation. If there isn't image which can be synchronized with C_{voice}, the texts in C_{voice} which are surrounded by tags for emphasizing becomes C_{visual}. In order to find the visual component, we find ***minimal*** tagged regions[1] each of which contains the voice component and at least one image or video in the HTML tree structure. Then, the selected image or video becomes the visual component.

4 Dynamic Generation of Carousels

4.1 Initial Carousel Generation

If a carousel is composed of all the pages of a search result, it becomes a huge carousel and users can't watch and listen to all the carousel components. So, we generate the initial carousel by top 10 pages ranked by the searchengine. While viewing the initial carousel, users can do a few interactions. Especially, users can issue a request to obtain another carousel consisting of carousel components each of which is ***similar to, different from, more detailed than*** or ***more summarized than*** the present carousel component of current presentation.

4.2 Carousel Generation by Semantic Relationships

By using vector space model, for each user-specified searched page P, the Web search result (a collection of searched Web pages) is dynamically organized into four types of group as follows:

- $Similar(P)$ denotes a group consisting of pages that contain the similar content as the user-specified page P.
- $Different(P)$ denotes a group consisting of pages that contain different content compared with P.
- $Detailed(P)$ denotes a group consisting of pages that contain the similar and more detailed content compared with P.
- $Summarized(P)$ denotes a group consisting of pages that contain the similar simpler content compared with P.

The keyword feature vector of Web page P_i is denoted by $\mathbf{F}(P_i)$ and is defined as follows:

$$\mathbf{F}(P_i) = (w_1^i, \cdots, w_n^i) = \frac{1}{N_i}(f_1^i, \cdots, f_n^i)$$

$f_j^i, j \in (1, \cdots, n)$ is a word frequency of word w_j in Web page P_i.
N_i denotes the total number of words in P_i.
w_j^i denotes the weight of word W_j in page P_i.

We propose a way to compare keyword feature vectors between two pages. The following calculates the degree of similarity, difference, detailed, summarized relationships of page P_1 for page P_0, and it decides the type of P_1.

[1] Here, a tagged region denotes a contiguous area surrounded by $< X >$ and $< X >$ for arbitrary X.

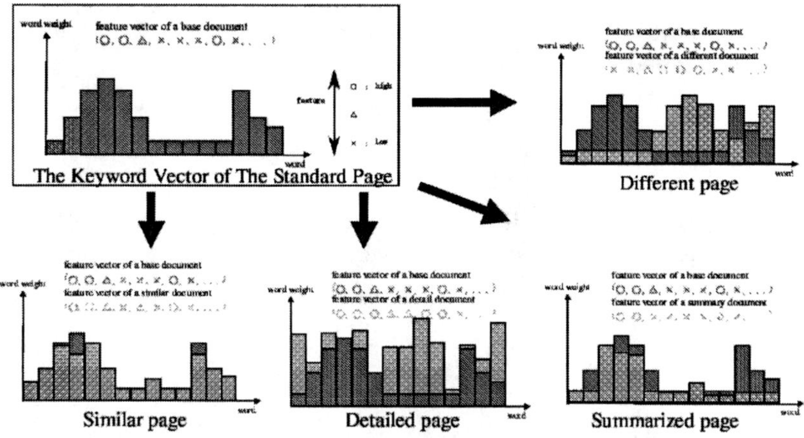

Fig. 3. The Keyword Vector

1. For a user-specified page P_0 and the compared page P_1, the similarity degree λ_{sim} is obtained by taking inner product value $\mathbf{S}(P_0, P_1)$ of keyword vectors of P_0 and P_1. λ_{sim} is defined as:

$$\lambda_{sim} = \mathbf{S}(P_0, P_1) = \frac{\mathbf{F}(P_0) \cdot \mathbf{F}(P_1)}{||\mathbf{F}(P_0)|| \cdot ||\mathbf{F}(P_1)||}$$

   If λ_{sim} is high, P_1 is regarded to be similar to P_0 (see Fig. 3.)
2. As shown in different page of Fig. 3, intuitively if the histogram pattern of $\mathbf{F}(P_1)$ is ***opposite*** to that of $\mathbf{F}(P_0)$, then page P_1 is regarded to contain different topics. The degree of difference λ_{diff} is defined as:

$$\lambda_{diff} = 1 - \mathbf{S}(P_0, P_1)$$

   If λ_{diff} is high, P_1 is regarded as describing different topic from P_0.
3. We assume that the 'more detailed' page has more additional information than the given page. Intuitively, we consider that almost all the word's weights of the 'more detailed' page vector are greater than or equal to those of a given pages' vector (see detailed page of Fig. 3). Lot the keyword vector of a user-specified page be:

$$\mathbf{F}(P_0) = (w_1^0, w_2^0, \cdots, w_i^0, \cdots, w_n^0)$$

   Also, let the keyword vector of a compared page be:

$$\mathbf{F}(P_1) = (w_1^1, w_2^1, \cdots, w_i^1, \cdots, w_n^1)$$

   Without loss of generality, we assume the following:
   - For each k in $\{1, \cdots, i\}$, $w_k^0 > \theta_0$ and $w_k^1 > \theta_0$, and $|w_k^1 - w_k^0| \leq \theta_1$
   - For each k in $\{i+1, \cdots, j\}$, $w_k^0 < \theta_0$ and $w_k^1 < \theta_0$

In the above cases, we make w_k^0 and w_k^1 to be 0. That is, let $\mathbf{F}'(P_0)$ and $\mathbf{F}'(P_1)$ are defined as follows

$$\mathbf{F}'(P_0) = (\underset{0}{0}, \cdots, \underset{i}{0}, \underset{i+1}{0}, \cdots, \underset{j}{0}, w_{j+1}^0, \cdots, w_n^0)$$
$$\mathbf{F}'(P_1) = (\underset{0}{0}, \cdots, \underset{i}{0}, \underset{i+1}{0}, \cdots, \underset{j}{0}, w_{j+1}^1, \cdots, w_n^1)$$

The degree of 'more detailed' relationship of P_1 compared with P_0 is denoted by λ_{detail}. It is expressed with an average of the difference of each element of vectors $\mathbf{F}'(P_0)$ and $\mathbf{F}'(P_1)$, is defined by

$$\lambda_{detail} = \mathbf{D}(P_0, P_1) = \frac{1}{n-j} \sum_{k=j+1}^{n} (w_k^1 - w_k^0)$$

If λ_{detail} is high, P_1 is regarded to have 'more detail' relationships with P_0.

4. The degree of the summarization relationship is intuitively opposite to the degree of the 'more detailed' relationship. The degree of 'more summarized' relationship of P_1 compared with P_0 is denoted by λ_{summ} , and is defined by

$$\lambda_{summ} = \mathbf{D}(P_1, P_0) = \frac{1}{n-j} \sum_{k=j+1}^{n} (w_k^0 - w_k^1)$$

If λ_{summ} is high, P_1 is regarded to have 'more summarized' relationship with P_0.(See summarized page of Fig. 3)

We experimented in order to test the usefulness of the above degrees of relationships. Before we start the experiment, we make a query for the search engine, and for each page we examined to which group every other page belongs by hand.
We used search result data from 100 to 500 pages, and used 5 keywords. The top 10 ranking list is returned as answer of the system. Table 1 shows the precision ratio of each relationship.

Table 1. Result of the experiment (precision %)

Number of search results	similarity	difference	detail	summary
100	90%	-	73%	30%
200	82%	-	70%	30%
300	82%	-	59%	21%
500	73%	-	45%	17%

4.3 Generating Carousel Components After Interaction

As stated previously, WebCarousel uses a top 10 Web pages retrieved by a search engine to create the initial carousel. For obtaining carousel components of the initial carousel, WebCarousel finds a minimal contiguous region that contains all the given keywords. Once the initial carousel is generated, users can start their interactions. Users select a carousel component, and can issue a request to obtain next carousel of carousel components that are ***similar to***, ***different from***, ***more detailed than*** or ***more summarized than*** the user-selected page.

To compute the carousel components of the next carousel, we use a set K' of ***related keywords*** as well as searched keywords $K = \{k_1, k_2, \ldots, k_n\}$. Let p and p' be a user-selected page and a new carousel component page, respectively. Also, let $F(p)$ and $F(p')$ denote their keyword feature vectors, respectively. Then, the ***related keywords*** for page p are defined as follows:

- **similar to** relationship
  K' is defined to be a set of keywords whose weights is higher than a predefined threshold in both of $F(p)$ and $F(p')$.
- **different from** relationship
  K' is defined to be a set of keywords whose weight is higher than a predefined threshold in $F(p')$ and whose weight is lower than a predefined threshold in $F(p)$.
- **more detailed than** relationship
  K' is defined to be a set of keywords whose weight is higher than a predefined threshold in $F(p')$ and whose weight is lower than a predefined threshold in $F(p)$.
- **more summarized than** relationship
  K' is defined to be a set of keywords whose weights is higher than a predefined threshold in both of $F(p)$ and $F(p')$.

When finding candidates of C_{voice} of carousel components of carousels except initial carousel, the system finds a minimal contiguous area of a page that contains all the related keywords as well as original search keywords. That is, $K \cup K'$ is used to find C_{voice}. If the playing time of C_{voice} is limited, the following priority is used to find C_{voice}:

1. Keywords appearing in both of K and K'.
2. Keywords that appear in K, but does not appear in K'.
3. Keywords that appear in K', but does not appear in K.

5 WebCarousel Bookmark

It is necessary for users to save carousel components, carousels and the user's behavior during the usage of WebCarousel. So, we provide bookmarking functions for WebCarousel, we call this bookmarking is *WebCarousel Bookmark*.

WebCarousel Bookmark has the following features:

- Memorizing current carousel component.
- Memorizing current carousel.
- Memorizing the history of the user's behavior.

We provide new XML tags to describe WebCarousel Bookmark. WebCarousel Bookmark uses namespace of XML, and each tag has discriminated name space of "*wc*". The definitions and meanings of WebCarousel Bookmark tags are as follows:

– **< webcarousel >** : Root element of bookmark. This element includes search keyword and history of bookmark.
– **< keyword >** : This tag denotes search keywords. Keyword tag has attributes: keyword ID and the keyword's input order.
– **< bookmark – component >**, **< bookmark – carousel >**, **< bookmark – interaction >** : These tags are bookmark types, and include elements of *< component >*, *< carousel >*, *< interaction >*.
– **< component >**, **< carousel >**, **< interaction >** : These tags denote stored carousel components, stored carousels, and stored interactions, respectively.

Fig. 4 shows an example of the WebCarousel bookmark description is shown as follows.

```
<?xml version="1.0" encoding="UTF8" ?>
<xml:schema>
  <namespaceDcl href="http://www.db.cs.kobe-u.ac.jp/~kondo/WC/" name="wc"/>
</xml:schema>

<!DOCTYPE webcarousel PUBLIC "-//TanakaLab//DTD book//JA"
"http://www.db.cs.kobe-u.ac.jp/~kondo/WC/webcarousel.dtd">

<xml:data>
<wc:webcarousel>
  <wc:keyword id="k1" number="1"> Baseball </wc:keyword>
  <wc:keyword id="k2" number="2"> Allstar </wc:keyword>

 <wc:bookmark-component id="bco1" number="1">
    <wc:componet id="c1" number="1">
     http://gotcha.mycom.co.jp/column/sports/1999/07/23/
    </wc:componet>
 </wc:bookmark-component>

 <wc:bookmark-interaction id="bin1" number="2">
  <wc:carousel id="C1" number="1">
    <wc:componet id="c1" number="1">
     http://gotcha.mycom.co.jp/column/sports/1999/07/23/
    </wc:componet>
    <wc:componet id="c1" number="2">
     http://www.kobe-np.co.jp/2000/07/24/sports4.html
    </wc:componet>
    <wc:componet id="c1" number="3">
     http://www.asahi.com/paper/sports/baseball/allstar02.html
    </wc:componet>
  </wc:carousel>
  ............
  <wc:intereaction id="i1" number="k2" basepage="C1c2" type="similarity"/>
 <wc:bookmark-interaction>
</wc:webcarousel>
</xml:data>
```

Fig. 4. Example of WebCarousel Bookmark

6 WebCarousel Prototype

We develop WebCarousel prototype system, which emulates a cellular phone on a PC. The following shows how to work this prototype system.

1. Get search result data from a Web search engine[2].
2. Construct the first carousel from searched Web pages, which consists of the top ten list of search results.
3. The system shows the carousel component to a user. The carousel component comes up to be displayed it's title and images with synthesized speech.
4. If there is an interaction, that select the one of carousel and push a *similar to* button or *different from* button or *more detailed than* button or *more simplified than* button, the system makes a new carousel dynamically and shows it to the user.
5. When the user pushes the save button, the system invokes the WebCarousel Bookmark, and memorize current carousel component, current carousel or the history of the user's behavior.

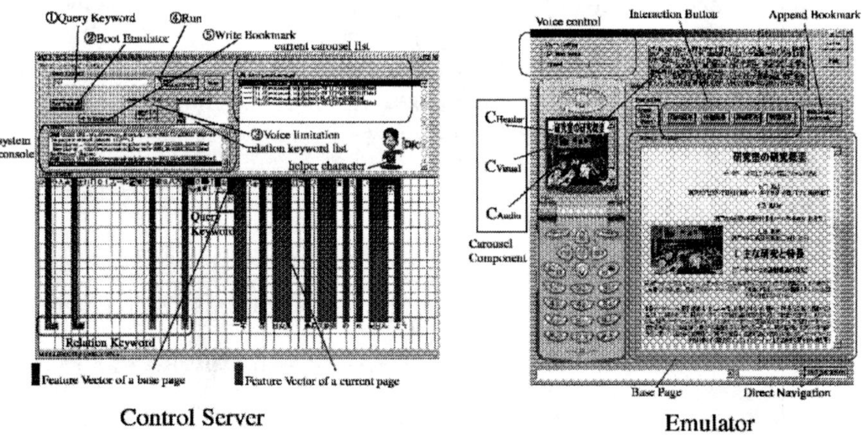

Fig. 5. Display of WebCarouel Control Server and Emulator

We implemented our WebCarousel prototype system on Windows platform. We used Microsoft Visual C++, Microsoft Speech API and NEC Smart-voice for speech synthesis to implement the prototype system. Fig. 5 shows the screen images of WebCarousel. The left side of Fig. 5 shows the WebCarousel, which caluclate several semantic relationships by comparing feature vectors of Web pages, and creating new carrousels. The right side of Fig. 5 shows the screen image of emulator. The right subwindow shows a searched Web page, and the left subwindow emulates a cellular phone's presentation of the corresponding carousel component. The carousel component is presented by speech synthesis speech synchronized with related image.

[2] We have also implemented and use our own search engine for WebCarousel. Our search engine makes generating a ranked list of searched Web pages like ordinary search engines. Of course, it is possible to use conventional Web search engines instead of our own search engine.

7 Concluding Remarks

In this paper, we proposed the concept of the automatic carousel-style presentation of Web search results and semantic restructuring of carousels based on several semantic relationships among Web pages. Also, we showed our prototype implementation called WebCarousel, which emulates a cellular phone environment. These concepts and the prototype are shown to be helpful to relax a lot of restrictions enforced on mobile environments, such as narrow screen, poor interaction environment. Our contributions of the present paper are summarized as follows:

– A new "passive" browsing method for Web search results by cellular phones using:
  - Synthesized speech synchronized with related images
  - Automatic and repeated presentation by carousels (groups of Web pages)
  - Transitions among carousels by simple interactions.
– Dynamic reorganization of search results into carousels using by discovering 'semantic' relationship between Web pages
– Dynamic reorganization of carousel components
– Generate of WebCarousel bookmarks

References

1. Y.Hirakawa, E.Endoh, K.Yasuda, M.Ishikawa, T.Asada, T.hagino: Web System of Next Generation Mobile, YRP Smposium (2000)
2. O.Bukukkokten, H.Garcia-Molina, A.Paepcke: Focused Web Searching with PDAs, WWW9 Conference Amsterdam (May 2000)
3. M.Hori, G.Kondoh, K.Ono, S.Hirose, and S.Singhal, Annotation-Based Web Content Transcoding: WWW9 Conference Amsterdam (May 2000)
4. i-mode Available at http://www.nttdocomo.co.jp/.
5. WAP. Available at http://www.webtv.com/.
6. T.Hattori, K.Sumiya, A.Nadamoto, M.Kusahara, K.Tanaka: User-Adaptable Web Presentation by TV-program Metaphors, Technical report, IPSJ SIGDBS Technical Report, Okinawa, Vol.99, No.61 99-DBS-119-69 (July 1999)
7. A.Nadamoto, T.Hattori, H.Kondo, I.Sawanaka, M.Kusahara, K.Tanaka: Authoring Mechanism for presenting Web-Information based on TV-Program metaphors, Technical report, IPSJ, Kobe Vol.2000, No.10 00-DBS-120-14 pp.99-106 (January 2000)
8. T.Hattori, I.Sawanaka, A.Nadamoto, K.Tanaka: Discovering Synchronizable Regions and A Scripting Markup Language S-XML for Passive Web Browsing, Technical report, IPSJ, Tokyo, Vol.2000, No.44 00-DBS-121-2, pp.9-16 (May 2000)
9. K.Tanaka, A,Nadamoto, M.Kusahara, T.Hattori, H.Kondo, and K.Sumiya: Back to the TV: InformationVisualization Interfaces Based onTV-Program Metaphors, ICME2000, pp.1229-1232 (Aug. 2000)
10. A.Nadamoto, T.Hatori, H.Kondo, I.Sawanaka, K.Tanaka: Automatic Conversion and a Scripting Markup Language for Passive watching and listening of the Web contents, IPSJ Database Vol.42 No.SIG1 (TOD8) pp.103-116 (Jan. 2001)

Imposing Disjunctive Constraints on Inter-document Structure

Sourav S. Bhowmick[1], Wee Keong Ng[1], and Sanjay Madria[2]

[1] School of Computer Engineering, Nanyang Technological University, Singapore 639798
{assourav, awkng}@ntu.edu.sg
http://www.ntu.edu.sg/home/assourav

[2] Department of Computer Science, University of Missouri-Rolla, Rolla MO 65409
{madrias}@umr.edu

Abstract. Most of the contemporary web query systems has limited capabilities in imposing disjunctive constraints on the hyperlinked structure of Web documents. Such query facility is important because it gives us an opportunity to overcome the irregular and semistructured nature of the inter-document structure in the Web. In this paper, we describe a query mechanism called *coupling query* to address this issue in the context of our web warehousing system called WHOWEDA (*W*are*h*ouse *O*f *We*b *Da*ta). We describe the syntax and semantics of the *connectivities* in a coupling query which enables us to impose disjunctive constraints on the inter-document structure. We describe two flavours of coupling query, i.e., *canonical* and *non-canonical*, and show how a non-canonical query can be transformed to a *valid* canonical query. Such transformation is useful for query evaluation.

1 Introduction

Due to the irregular and semistructured nature of Web data, it is important for a web query language to express disjunctive constraints on the hyperlinked structure compactly. First, disjunctive queries allow us to overcome the limitations of irregular structure of inter-linked Web documents and pose meaningful queries over it. Second, sometimes query evaluation is relatively less expensive if a query is formulated and evaluated using disjunctive constraints rather than repeated evaluation of each query in the equivalent conjunctive query set. Third, expressing all possible set of conjunctive query accurately for a disjunctive condition incurs significant cognitive overhead which may result in erroneous query. Finally, a disjunctive query can be expressed compactly using regular expression. Expressing all possible set of conjunctive queries can be quite cumbersome and frustrating.

Although the importance of imposing disjunctive constraints on inter-document structure is undeniable, most of the web query systems support very

H.C. Mayr et al. (Eds.): DEXA 2001, LNCS 2113, pp. 723–733, 2001.

limited [5,6,7,2] form of disjunctive constraints, if any, on the inter-document structure of the Web. For instance, W3QS do not address the issue of such constraints on interlinked documents extensively. A limited form of disjunctive condition which involves the variability of the depth of traversal of a query can be expressed by these languages. Query systems for semistructured data and XML query languages such as XML-QL, Lorel, also support limited form of disjunctive constraints on the inter-linked structure of Web documents. Query languages for semistructured data such as Lorel [1] were not specifically developed for the Web, and do not distinguish between graph edges that represent the connection between a document and one of its parts and edges that represent a hyperlink from one Web document to another. On the other hand, XML-QL, YAT_L and Lorel are designed specifically for XML and does not scale up well with HTML documents.

In this paper, we address the above issue by introducing the notion of *coupling query* to express a web query in the context of our web warehousing system, called WHOWEDA (*W*are*h*ouse *O*f *We*b *Da*ta) [3].

2 Coupling Query

We now introduce the notion of *coupling query*. We begin by briefly describing the underlying data model of our web warehousing system. The *Ware*H*ouse* O*bject* M*odel* (WHOM) [3] serves as the basic data model for our web warehousing system. Informally, our web warehouse can be conceived of as a collection of *web tables*. A set of *web tuples* is materialized in a web table. A web tuple is a directed graph consisting of sets of *node* and *link objects* (hereafter, referred to as *nodes* and *links* respectively for brevity). In WHOWEDA, *nodes* and *links* are instances of *node type* and *link type* respectively. Intuitively, a *node* represents the metadata associated with a Web document and the content and structure of the document (excluding hyperlinks in the document). Similarly, a *link* represents the metadata, structure and content of a HTML or XML link [1]. The reader may refer to [3] for complete discussion on how Web data is represented in the warehouse.

2.1 Connectivities

Coupling query can be used for querying both HTML and XML documents and may be visualized as a directed connected acyclic graph [3,4]. Some of the important features of our query mechanism are ability to query metadata, content, internal and external (hyperlink) structure of Web documents based on *partial* knowledge, ability to express constraints on tag attributes and tagless segment of data, ability to express conjunctive as well as disjunctive query conditions compactly, ability to control execution of a web query and preservation of the topological structure of hyperlinked documents in the query results.

[1] We only consider simple and extended XML links.

Informally, a coupling query consists of five components, *sets of node* and *link type identifiers*, set of *predicates*, set of *coupling query predicates* and a set of *connectivities*. Each *node* and *link* type identifiers represent a set (possibly empty) of documents and hyperlinks respectively. The predicates are associated with some of the node and link type identifiers and are used to impose conditions that must be satisfied by the relevant documents and hyperlinks of the corresponding identifiers. Coupling query predicates are used to control the execution of the query for retrieving relevant data.

A *connectivity* is a predicate on the inter-document relationship of a one or two classes of Web documents and helps us to impose disjunctive constraints on the hyperlinked structure. To define a connectivity element, one first categorizes the set of documents and hyperlinks into different types by using a set of predicates. Then it is defined by using the type identifiers of these documents and hyperlinks. A connectivity k is an expression of the form: $k \equiv \texttt{s}\langle\rho\rangle\texttt{t}$ where $\texttt{s}$ is the *source node type identifier* (*source identifier* in short), $\texttt{t}$ is the *target node type identifier* (*target identifier* in short) and ρ is called a *link path expression* which is essentially a sequence of link type identifiers which may include regular expressions, e.g., e, efg, $ef\{1,3\}$. The node type identifiers are used to nominally identify the set of node and link objects respectively sharing some common properties (defined by predicates). They may also represent nodes which are not bound by any predicate, i.e., *free identifier*. Such identifier is denoted by the symbol #. The angle brackets around ρ are used for delimitation purposes only. Note that the connectivity $\texttt{s}\langle\rho\rangle\texttt{t}$ specifies how the instances of $\texttt{s}$ are connected to the instances of $\texttt{t}$.

We now elaborate on the *link path expressions* which plays pivotal role in expressing disjunctive constraints. A link path expression specifies how a set of documents are connected to another set of documents. We begin by defining *simple* and *complex link components* which are used for defining link path expression. A *simple link component* is a link type identifier that represents a set of hyperlink instances. Like source and target node type identifier, it can be bound or free. We use the symbol '-' to denote a free link component. A *complex link component* contains regular expressions defined over simple link components. Let ℓ_1 and ℓ_2 be two simple link components. Then, (1) $\ell_1?$, $\ell_1|\ell_2$, $\ell_1\ell_2$ and $\ell_1\{m,n\}$ are complex link components where $m \geqslant 0$, $n > 1$ and $m < n$. The existence of m is optional. (2) If c_1 and c_2 are simple or complex link components then c_1c_2, $c_1?$, $c_1|c_2$ and $c_1\{m,n\}$ are complex link components. (3) Nothing else is a complex link component. Examples of complex link components are efg, $e?$, $e|f$, $e\{1,4\}$. Based on these two types of link components, A link path expression is *simple* if the path expression contains only a simple link component. Otherwise, it is a *regular* link path expression.

A connectivity can be classified into two types i.e., *simple* and *complex*. A connectivity $k \equiv x\langle\rho\rangle y$ is *simple* if ρ is a simple link path expression. Examples of simple connectivity are as follows: $k_1 \equiv x\langle e\rangle y$, $k_2 \equiv \#_1\langle f\rangle\#_2$, $k_3 \equiv \#_1\langle \text{-}\rangle\#_2$. A connectivity $k \equiv x\langle\rho\rangle y$ is *complex* if ρ is a regular link path expression. The following are examples of complex connectivities: $k_1 \equiv x\langle efgh\rangle y$ and $k_2 \equiv$

$x\langle e\text{-}\{1,5\}\rangle z$. The first expression specifies that starting from a node of type x, one may reach a node of type y by following the link instances of type e, f, g and h. The next connectivity specifies that from an instance of x, there must exist a link of type e followed by at most five arbitrary links that connects to a document of type y. In this case, the properties of the links following e are not defined by any predicate.

We now identify the four basic cases of complex connectivities which we will be using in our subsequent discussions.

- **Case 1:** Connectivity containing link path expression of the form $\ell_1\ell_2\cdots\ell_n$. This type of connectivity can be reduced to a set of simple connectivities adjacent to one another, i.e., $x\langle\rho\rangle y \equiv x\langle\ell_1\rangle\#_1 \wedge \#_1\langle\ell_2\rangle\#_2 \wedge \cdots \wedge \#_{n-1}\langle\ell_n\rangle y$. Observe that the identifiers # represents any arbitrary collection of node objects. For instance, the connectivity $k \equiv x\langle e\text{-}g\rangle y$ can be transformed to the following set of simple connectivities in conjunction to one another: $x\langle e\rangle\#_1 \wedge \#_1\langle\text{-}\rangle\#_2 \wedge \#_2\langle g\rangle y$.
- **Case 2:** Connectivity containing '|' and '?' regular expression operators in the link path expression.
- **Case 3:** Connectivity containing '{m , n}' operator in the link path expression.
- **Case 4:** Connectivity containing '|', '?' and '{m , n}' operators in the link path expression. Observe that it is the combination of the above cases.

A coupling query may contain a set of simple or complex connectivities. They are used to specify that the hyperlinked structure of a set of relevant documents must conform to this connectivity constraint in order to match the query. Consider the following connectivities: $C_2 \equiv x\langle ef?\rangle y \vee x\langle e\rangle b$ and $C_3 \equiv x\langle e\{1,2\}\rangle y \wedge x\langle f\{2,3\}\rangle z$. C_2 specifies that the hyperlink structure of documents satisfying the coupling query must conform to any one of the following structure: (1) node objects of type x are connected to node objects of type y via the links of type e, followed by optional links of type f; or (2) node objects of type x are connected to those of type b via links of type e. Finally, the last set of connectivities C_3 specifies that the node objects of type x are connected to node objects of type y and z via at most two hyperlinks of type e and at least two and at most three links of type f respectively. Note that these connectivity elements may be in conjunction or in disjunction to one another.

We now formally define a coupling query. A simple example on how to specify the above components of a coupling query step-by-step is given in [4].

Definition 1. *A* **coupling query** *is a 5-tuple $G = \langle X_n, X_\ell, C, P, Q\rangle$ where X_n is a set of node type identifiers, X_ℓ is a set of link type identifiers, C is a set (possibly empty) of connectivities defined over X_n and X_ℓ, P is a set of predicates defined over X_n and X_ℓ and Q is a set (possibly empty) of coupling query predicates such that the following conditions are true: (1) $X_n \neq \emptyset$, $P \neq \emptyset$, $X_n \cap X_\ell = \emptyset$; (2) If $|X_n| = 1$ then $X_\ell = \emptyset$, $C = \emptyset$ and $P \neq \emptyset$; (3) Let X_{nc} and $X_{\ell c}$ be the set of node and link type identifiers in C respectively. Then $X_{nc} = X_n$ and $X_{\ell c} = X_\ell$; (4) There must not exist conjunctive connectivity set*

$C_a \equiv k_{a1} \wedge k_{a2} \wedge \cdots \wedge k_{an}$ and $C_b \equiv k_{b1} \wedge k_{b2} \wedge \cdots \wedge k_{bn}$ such that $C_a \vee C_b$ and $k_{ax} = k_{bx} \; \forall \, 0 < x \leqslant n$; (5)Let $p(x) \in P$. Then $x \in (X_n \cup X_\ell)$; (6) Let $G(C)$ be the graphical representation of C. Then $G(C)$ must be a directed connected acyclic graph with single source vertex. Further, let x be the identifier of the source vertex in $G(C)$. Then, there must exist a non-trivial predicate $p(x) \in P$. ∎

Informally, the results of a coupling query is a set of directed connected acyclic graph containing node and link objects. These graphs are called *web tuples*. The set of documents and hyperlinks in a web tuple satisfies the connectivities and predicates defined in a coupling query.

3 Canonical and Non-canonical Coupling Queries

In this section, we categorize a coupling query into two types: *canonical* and *non-canonical*. The justification for this classification is that as we shall see in Section 4, it is necessary to reduce a *non-canonical* query into a *valid canonical* form in order to evaluate it.

We say that a coupling query is *canonical* if it contains a set (possibly empty) of simple connectivities in Disjunctive Normal Form (DNF). For example, if $G = \langle X_n, X_\ell, C, P, Q \rangle$, $C \equiv C_1 \vee C_2$ where $C_1 \equiv k_1 \wedge k_2$, $C_2 \equiv k_3$ $k_1 \equiv x\langle e \rangle y$, $k_2 \equiv y\langle f \rangle z$ and $k_3 \equiv x\langle e \rangle z$ then G is a canonical coupling query. C_1 and C_2 are called *conjunctive connectivity sets*. Based on the above definition of canonical coupling query, we classify canonical queries into the following five types. Let $G_c = \langle X_n, X_\ell, C, P, Q \rangle$ be a canonical coupling query. Then,

- **Type 1:** G_c does not contain any connectivities. That is, $|X_n| = 1$, $X_\ell = \emptyset$ and $C = \emptyset$. Note that this is the simplest form of coupling query.
- **Type 2:** G_c contains a single simple connectivity. That is, $|X_n| = 2$, $|X_\ell| = 1$, $C \equiv k$ where k is a simple connectivity.
- **Type 3:** G_c contains more than one simple connectivities and these connectivities are in conjunction. That is, $C \equiv k_1 \wedge k_2 \wedge \cdots \wedge k_r$ where k_i is a simple connectivity for all $1 < i \leqslant r$.
- **Type 4:** G_c contains more than one simple connectivities and these connectivities are in disjunction. That is, $C \equiv k_1 \vee k_2 \vee \cdots \vee k_r$ where k_i is a simple for all $1 < i \leqslant r$.
- **Type 5:** G_c contains more than one simple connectivities and these connectivities are in DNF. That is, $C \equiv C_1 \vee C_2 \vee \cdots \vee C_r$ where C_i is a conjunctive connectivity set for all $1 < i \leqslant r$.

A *non-canonical coupling query*, on the other hand, may contain simple or complex connectivities and these connectivities may not be in DNF. Observe that a non-canonical coupling query enables us to express disjunctive constraints compactly. For instance, if $C \equiv k_1 \wedge k_2$, $k_1 \equiv x\langle e|f \rangle y$ and $k_2 \equiv y\langle g \rangle z$ then G is a non-canonical coupling query. We classify non-canonical queries into the following four types. Let $G_{nc} = \langle X_n, X_\ell, C, P, Q \rangle$ be a non-canonical coupling query. Then,

- **Type 1:** G_{nc} contains a single complex connectivity. That is, $|X_n| = 2$, $X_\ell \neq \emptyset$, $C \equiv k$ where k is a complex connectivity.
- **Type 2:** G_{nc} contains more than one connectivity and at least one of them is complex. Further, these connectivities are in conjunction. That is, $C \equiv k_1 \wedge k_2 \wedge \cdots \wedge k_r$ where k_i is complex for $1 < i \leqslant r$.
- **Type 3:** G_{nc} contains more than one connectivity and at least one of them is complex. Further, these connectivities are in disjunction. That is, $C \equiv k_1 \vee k_2 \vee \cdots \vee k_r$ where k_i is complex for $1 < i \leqslant r$.
- **Type 4:** G_{nc} contains more than one simple or complex connectivities and these connectivities are in conjunction and in disjunction to one another.

For brevity, different types of canonical and non-canonical coupling queries are denoted as G_c^t or G_{nc}^t respectively where $0 < t \leqslant 5$ and indicates G_c or G_{nc} is of Type t.

4 Valid Canonical Query Generation

In this section, we discuss how to transform a coupling query specified by a user to a *valid* canonical coupling query. Informally, a canonical coupling query is valid if each conjunctive connectivity set in the query represents a directed connected acyclic graph with single source vertex. Observe that a user may express a canonical or non-canonical coupling query. However, in order to evaluate such a query it is necessary to transform non-canonical query into its canonical form. The valid canonical coupling query generation process can be best explained by dividing it into the following two phases: *coupling query reduction phase* and *validity checking phase*. In the following subsections we elaborate on these phases in turn. Due to space constraints, the proofs of all the propositions discussed here are given in [3].

4.1 Phase 1: Coupling Query Reduction

In this phase we transform a non-canonical form of coupling query into a canonical form. To transform any non-canonical coupling query $G_{nc} = \langle X_n, X_\ell, C, P, Q\rangle$ to a canonical form $G_c = \langle X'_n, X'_\ell, C', P', Q\rangle$ the following steps need to be performed: (1) Reduce the set of connectivities C into a set of simple connectivities in DNF (denoted as C') [3]. Note that this reduction involves transformation of complex connectivities into simple form. Formally, let k be a complex connectivity. Then, $k \equiv C_1 \vee C_2 \vee \cdots \vee C_n$ where $C_i \equiv k_{i_1} \wedge k_{i_2} \wedge \cdots \wedge k_{i_r}$, $\forall\, 0 < i \leqslant n$ and k_{i_j} is a simple connectivity $\forall\, 0 < j \leqslant r$. (2) Identify the set of node and link type identifiers in C' and generate the set of node and link type identifiers X'_n and X'_ℓ respectively of G_c. Note that the complex connectivities in C are compact expression for specifying connectivity involving a set of node and link type identifiers. Hence, reduction of these complex connectivities into simple form generates additional node or link type identifiers that need to be incorporated in X'_n or X'_ℓ respectively. (3) Finally, the components P and Q of G_{nc} are assigned as the corresponding components of G_c without any modification.

Observe that the major step in reducing non-canonical coupling query to its canonical form is to convert the set of connectivities in G_{nc} to a set of simple connectivities in DNF. Subsequent generation of X'_n, X'_ℓ and the other components is straight forward. Hence, in the following discussion we describe the reduction of C to C' for non-canonical coupling query of Types 1 to 4.

Reduction of Type 1 and 2 Non-canonical Coupling Query. We begin with non-canonical coupling query of Types 1 and 2. Let the function *Transform*(G_{nc}) takes as input a non-canonical coupling query and returns as output the canonical form of the query (if possible). In a non-canonical Type 1 or 2-coupling query one or more connectivities are in complex form. Each complex connectivity in C of G_{nc} can be replaced by a set of simple connectivities in DNF. Observe that such set of simple connectivities may be in conjunction with another set of simple connectivities in the coupling query. Consequently, these simple connectivities can be further reduced to a set of simple connectivities which are in DNF. In fact, any non-canonical Type 1 or 2 coupling query can be reduced to a canonical form of Type 3 or 5.

Proposition 1. *Let G^t_{nc} be a non-canonical coupling text where $t \in [1, 2]$. Then, $G^y_c = \text{Transform}(G^t_{nc})$ where $y \in [3, 5]$.* ∎

Reduction of Non-canonical Type 3-Coupling Query. A non-canonical Type 3-coupling query contains one or more complex connectivities which are in disjunction to one another or to a simple connectivity. Since, a complex connectivity can be transformed to a set of simple connectivities in DNF, the non-canonical form of Type 3-coupling query can be reduced to a canonical form of Type 5.

Proposition 2. *Let G^3_{nc} be a non-canonical coupling text of Type 3 category. Then, $G^5_c = \text{Transform}(G^3_{nc})$.* ∎

Reduction of Non-canonical Type 4-Coupling Query. Recall that a Type 4-coupling query may be non-canonical for two reasons: First, the connectivities in the query are all simple but they are not in DNF. For example, a query containing the connectivity $C \equiv ((x\langle e\rangle y \vee x\langle z\rangle k) \wedge y\langle s\rangle t) \wedge t\langle\text{-}\rangle q$ is an example of such non-canonical Type 4-coupling query. Second, there may exist one or more complex connectivities in the coupling query. Hence, we discuss how to reduce these two categories of non-canonical Type 4-coupling query into their canonical form. We begin our discussion be introducing some terms which we will be using subsequently.

Let $K = \{k_1, k_2, k_3, \ldots, k_n\}$ be a set of simple connectivities. Then $con(K) \equiv k_1 \wedge k_2 \wedge \cdots \wedge k_n$ and $dis(K) \equiv k_1 \vee k_2 \vee \cdots \vee k_n$ where $n > 0$ and $n > 1$ for $con(K)$ and $dis(K)$ respectively.

Category 1: Non-canonical Type 4-Coupling Query with Simple Connectivities. The set of simple connectivities in this type of G_{nc} can be nested. At the lowest level of nesting the connectivities can take any of the following four forms:

- Case 1: $con(K_1) \vee con(K_2)$. For example, $((x\langle e\rangle y \wedge y\langle f\rangle z) \vee (x\langle f\rangle g)) \wedge y\langle f\rangle t$.
- Case 2: $dis(K_1) \wedge dis(K_2)$. For example, $((x\langle e\rangle y \vee x\langle f\rangle z) \wedge (x\langle f\rangle g \vee x\langle r\rangle g)) \wedge z\langle f\rangle t$.
- Case 3: $con(K_1) \vee dis(K_2)$. For example, $((x\langle e\rangle y \wedge y\langle f\rangle z) \vee (x\langle f\rangle g \vee x\langle r\rangle g)) \wedge y\langle f\rangle t$.
- Case 4: $dis(K_1) \wedge con(K_2)$. For example, $((x\langle e\rangle y \vee x\langle f\rangle z) \wedge (x\langle f\rangle g)) \wedge y\langle f\rangle t$.

Consequently, to reduce the set of connectivities in G_{nc} it is imperative to transform any of the above four cases to a set of simple connectivities in DNF at every level of nesting. Hence, the steps for reduction of the connectivities in a non-canonical Type 4-coupling query of Category 1 type are as follows: (1) Reduce the set of connectivities which can take any of the above four form in the lowest level of nesting into a set of simple connectivities in DNF, i.e, $con(K_1) \vee con(K_2) \vee \cdots \vee con(K_n)$. (2) These reduced set of connectivities will again be in disjunction or in conjunction with another set of simple connectivities in the next level. These connectivities can again be expressed as any of the four forms and consequently reduced to DNF. (3) The above steps are repeated till the highest level of the nested expression is reduced to DNF. We illustrate these steps with an example. Consider the connectivity $C \equiv ((x\langle e\rangle y \vee x\langle z\rangle k) \wedge y\langle s\rangle t) \wedge t\langle \text{-}\rangle q$. Observe that at the lowest level of nesting the connectivities are of type Case 4, i.e., $dis(K_1) \wedge con(K_2)$. This can be reduced to the following set of simple connectivities in DNF: $((x\langle e\rangle y \wedge y\langle s\rangle t) \vee (x\langle z\rangle h \wedge y\langle s\rangle t))$. This expression is in conjunction with the connectivity $t\langle \text{-}\rangle q$ in the next level of nesting. Hence, this can again be reduced to a set of simple connectivities in DNF as follows: $((x\langle e\rangle y \wedge y\langle s\rangle t \wedge t\langle \text{-}\rangle q) \vee (x\langle z\rangle h \wedge y\langle s\rangle t \wedge t\langle \text{-}\rangle q))$.

Proposition 3. *Let $con(K)$ and $dis(K)$ represents a set of simple connectivities in conjunction and disjunction respectively. Then the following expressions can be reduced to a set of simple connectivities in DNF: (1) $con(K_1) \vee con(K_2)$ (2) $dis(K_1) \wedge dis(K_2)$ (3) $dis(K_1) \vee con(K_2)$ and (4) $dis(K_1) \wedge con(K_2)$.* ∎

Category 2: Type 4 Non-canonical Coupling Query Containing Complex Connectivities. To facilitate our discussion we classify this non-canonical query into three types based on the nature of the complex connectivities in the query. Let G_{nc} be a non-canonical Type 4-coupling query. Then,

- **Class 1:** C contains complex connectivities of Case 1 type only.
- **Class 2:** C contains complex connectivities of any type except Case 1.
- **Class 3:** C contains Case 1 and any remaining types of complex connectivities.

The steps for reducing Category 2 non-canonical coupling query are as follows: (1) Reduce the complex connectivities into set of simple connectivities in DNF. (2) The reduced connectivities are in any of the four forms described in Category

1. Therefore, the problem is now reduced to the reduction of a non-canonical query containing simple connectivities. Hence, execute the steps described in Category 1 to generate a set of simple connectivities in DNF. We now discuss the reduction of complex connectivities in detail. The connectivities in G_{nc} of Classes 1 and 2 may contain complex connectivities that may exist in any of the following six forms. Let k_c be a complex connectivity of Class 1 or 2 then k_c may occur in any of the following ways:

- Case 1: $k_c \vee con(K)$. For example, $x\langle efg\rangle y \vee (x\langle r\rangle z \wedge z\langle f\rangle t)$.
- Case 2: $k_c \vee dis(K)$. For example, $x\langle ef|g\rangle y \vee (x\langle r\rangle z \vee x\langle f\rangle t)$.
- Case 3: $k_c \wedge con(K)$. For example, $x\langle ef\{1,3\}\rangle y \wedge (x\langle r\rangle z)$.
- Case 4: $k_c \wedge dis(K)$. For example, $x\langle efg\rangle y \wedge (x\langle r\rangle z \vee x\langle f\rangle t)$.
- Case 5: $k_{c1} \wedge k_{c2}$. For example, $x\langle ef\rangle y \wedge y\langle rs\rangle z$.
- Case 6: $k_{c1} \vee k_{c2}$. For example, $x\langle e|f\rangle y \vee x\langle e\{1,3\}\rangle t$.

For coupling query of Class 3, there are additional two possible cases:

- Case 7: $k_{c1} \wedge k_{c2}$ where k_{c1} is a complex connectivity of Case 1 type and k_{c2} is of a type other than Case 1. For example, $x\langle ef\rangle y \wedge y\langle r|s\rangle z$.
- Case 8: $k_{c1} \vee k_{c2}$ where k_{c1} and k_{c2} are of the above types. For example, $x\langle e|f\rangle y \vee x\langle eg\rangle t$.

Note that all the above cases can be reduced to any one or more of the four cases as described in Category 1 [3]. Hence,

Proposition 4. *Let C be a set of connectivities containing one or more complex connectivities in a non-canonical Type 4-coupling query. Then C can be reduced to a set of simple connectivities in DNF.* ∎

Therefore, based on Propositions 3 and 4 we can say that any non-canonical Type 4-coupling query can be reduced to a Type 5 canonical coupling query.

Proposition 5. *Let G^4_{nc} be a non-canonical coupling text of Type 4 category. Then, $G^5_c = \text{Transform}(G^4_{nc})$.* ∎

Consequently, the following theorem holds:

Theorem 1. *Any non-canonical coupling query can be reduced to its canonical form.* ∎

The proof for above theorem is straight forward and can be deduced from Propositions 1, 2 and 5.

4.2 Phase 2: Validity Checking

In this phase the canonical coupling query generated from the previous phase is inspected to determine if it represents a valid query. Hence, we check whether each conjunctive connectivity set represents a directed connected acyclic graph with single source vertex. If G_c is not valid query then the invalid conjunctive connectivity set is either eliminated from the coupling query autonomously or the query is modified by the user. Specifically, if a invalid canonical coupling query $G_c = \langle X_n, X_\ell, C, P, Q\rangle$ is modified autonomously then the following steps are executed: (1) Remove each invalid conjunctive connectivity set C_i from C in G_c; (2) For each C_i, the corresponding node and link type identifiers which do not occur in C_j where $j \neq i$ and $0 < j \leqslant n$ are removed from X_n and X_ℓ respectively. (3) The predicates defined over these identifiers, if any, are also removed from P. For instance, consider a non-canonical coupling query containing the following connectivities $C \equiv (x\langle e\rangle y \vee x\langle h\rangle w) \wedge (y\langle f\rangle z \vee y\langle g\rangle w)$. Graphically, it is a directed connected acyclic graph with single source vertex. This query can be transformed into a canonical form as shown below:

$$\begin{aligned} C &\equiv ((x\langle e\rangle y \vee x\langle h\rangle w) \wedge y\langle f\rangle z) \vee ((x\langle e\rangle y \vee x\langle h\rangle w) \wedge y\langle g\rangle w) \\ &\equiv (x\langle e\rangle y \wedge y\langle f\rangle z) \vee (y\langle f\rangle z \wedge x\langle h\rangle w) \vee (x\langle e\rangle y \wedge y\langle g\rangle w) \vee (x\langle h\rangle w \wedge y\langle g\rangle w) \end{aligned}$$

Observe that the second conjunctive connectivity set represents a disconnected graph. Further, the fourth conjunctive connectivity set represents a graph with multiple source vertices. Hence, this query is not valid.

Once a valid query is generated, we can proceed to execute the query on the Web and a set of web tuples satisfying the query is retrieved and materialized in a web table in the web warehouse.

5 Future Work

Currently, we have implemented a preliminary version of the coupling query. As part of our future work, we wish to generalize the coupling query into cyclic graphs with multiple source vertices. Also, we wish to augment coupling queries by allowing to impose conditions based on negation. Note that the inclusion of cycles and negation introduces interesting challenges with respect to the computability of the coupling query. Furthermore, we wish to develop a mechanism to estimate the evaluation cost of a coupling query over the Web. Finally, we are exploring techniques for generating query execution plan and rewriting rules for coupling query.

References

1. S. Abiteboul, D. Quass, J. McHugh, J. Widom, J. Weiner. The Lorel Query Language for Semistructured Data. *Journal of Digital Libraries*, 1(1):68-88, April 1997.
2. G. Arocena, A. Mendelzon. WebOQL: Restructuring Documents, Databases and Webs. *Proceedings of ICDE 98*, pp. 24-33, Orlando, Florida, February 1998.
3. S. S. Bhowmick. WHOM: A Data Model and Algebra for a Web Warehouse. *PhD Dissertation*, School of Computer Engineering, Nanyang Technological University, Singapore, 2001. Available at `www.ntu.edu.sg/home/assourav/`.
4. S. S. Bhowmick, W. K. Ng, S. Madria. On Formulation of Disjunctive Coupling Queries in Whoweda. *Proceedings of the 12th International Conference on Database and Expert System Applications (DEXA'01)*, Munich, September, 2001.

5. A. Deutsch, M. Fernandez, D. Florescu, A. Levy, D. Suciu. A Query Language for XML. *Proceedings of the 8th World Wide Web Conference*, pp. 1155-1169, Toronto, Canada, May 1999.
6. R. Goldman, J. McHugh, J. Widom. From Semistructured Data to XML: Migrating the Lore Data Model and Query Language. *Proceedings of WebDB '99*, pp. 25-30, Philadelphia, Pennsylvania, June 1999.
7. D. Konopnicki, O. Shmueli. Information Gathering in the World-Wide Web: The W3QL Query Language and the W3QS System. *Theory of Database Systems (TODS)* , 23(4):369-410, 1998.

A Semi-automatic Technique for Constructing a Global Representation of Information Sources Having Different Formats and Structure

Domenico Rosaci, Giorgio Terracina, and Domenico Ursino

Dipartimento di Informatica, Elettronica, Matematica e Trasporti
Università degli Studi "Mediterranea" di Reggio Calabria
Via Graziella, Località Feo di Vito, 89100 Reggio Calabria, Italy
{rosaci,terracina,ursino}@ing.unirc.it

Abstract. In this paper we propose a semi-automatic technique for constructing a global representation of information sources having different formats and structures. The proposed technique exploits a conceptual model, called SDR-Network, for both uniformly representing and deriving the semantics of involved information sources. The global representation is enriched with two support structures which improve access transparency to stored information, namely a global semantic catalogue (or Metascheme) and a Set of Mappings, encoding the transformations carried out during the construction of the global representation.

1 Introduction

The enormous development of the Internet, in general, and of the Web, in particular, led to great challenges in the fields of information management and exploitation. Some system architectures have been proposed in the past to let different heterogeneous information sources to cooperate [5,6,9,14]. The heterogeneity of the involved information sources concerned their data models, their query and manipulation languages and their management systems. However, such architectures handled only structured information sources, i.e., for a given information source, all instances relative to the same concept had the same structure. Nowadays existing information sources are not only heterogeneous in their data models, query and manipulation languages and management systems, but they also show quite different structures, some of them being well structured (e.g., relational databases), other ones being semi-structured (e.g., XML documents) and other ones being unstructured (e.g., texts).

In addition, the development of computer networks increased the need of some kinds of interaction between different information sources. In order to make this task easier, the necessity arises of guaranteeing access transparency to stored data; in its turn, this requires the definition of a global representation of all involved information sources. Since the number and the sizes of the involved information sources are large, any proposed technique for obtaining the

H.C. Mayr et al. (Eds.): DEXA 2001, LNCS 2113, pp. 734–743, 2001.

global representation and the support structures should be (semi-)automatic. In addition, for obtaining high quality results, it must take into account both the structure and the semantics of the involved information sources [4].

In this paper we propose a semi-automatic technique for constructing a global representation of information sources having different formats and structures.

In order to handle the heterogeneity of the involved information sources, we exploit a particular conceptual data model, called SDR-Network. Given an information source IS, the corresponding SDR-Network is a rooted labeled graph $Net(IS) = \langle NS(IS), AS(IS) \rangle$ [13]. Here, $NS(IS)$ is a set of nodes, each one representing a concept of IS. $AS(IS)$ denotes a set of arcs; an arc represents a relationship between two concepts. More specifically, an arc from S to T, labeled L_{ST} and denoted by $\langle S, T, L_{ST} \rangle$, indicates that the concept represented by S is semantically related to the concept denoted by T. S is called the "source node", whereas T is the "target node" of the arc. L_{ST} is a pair $[d_{ST}, r_{ST}]$, where both d_{ST} and r_{ST} belong to the real interval $[0, 1]$. d_{ST} is the *semantic distance coefficient*; it indicates how much the concept expressed by T is semantically close to the concept expressed by S; this depends from the capability of the concept associated to T to characterize the concept associated to S. As an example, in an XML document, a sub-element E_1 of an element E, is closer to E than another element E_2 which E refers by an $IDREF$ attribute. r_{ST} is the *semantic relevance coefficient*, representing the fraction of instances of the concept denoted by S whose complete definition requires at least one instance of the concept denoted by T.

Note that, basically, any information source can be represented as a set of concepts and a set of relationships among concepts. Since the SDR-Network nodes and arcs are well suited to represent both concepts and their relationships, the SDR-Network can be used to uniformly model most existing information sources. In this respect, semantic preserving translations have been provided from some interesting source formats, such as XML, OEM and E/R, to SDR-Network [13].

In order to construct the global representation of heterogeneous information sources, it is necessary to define their semantics [4]; an important support for carrying out this task consists in the knowledge of *inter-source properties*, i.e., terminological and structural properties (such as synonymies, homonymies and sub-source similarities) relating object classes belonging to different information sources [2,3,4,7,8,10,12]. Our technique for constructing the global representation can exploit inter-source properties derived by any of the approaches proposed in the literature, such as [2,3,4,7,8,12]. However, we have defined our own approach, based on the exploitation of the SDR-Network, in particular of the semantic distance and relevance coefficients, for deriving such a kind of properties [13].

The technique we propose here stores all necessary information in an *Intensional Information Base (IIB)*, consisting of both a *Metascheme* $IIB.M$ and a set of *Meta-Operators*. The Metascheme stores all information about involved sources, their object classes, properties existing among object classes, etc. Insertions, deletions and modifications of both object classes and their properties, carried out by the integration algorithm, are realized by modifying the content of the Metascheme. The Meta-Operators are predefined procedures which allow to either modify or query the Metascheme. They are the only means to access the Metascheme. The Metascheme contains also a *Set of Mappings* (hereafter denoted by $IIB.M.SoM$), describing the way an object class belonging to the global SDR-Network has been obtained from one or more object classes belonging to input SDR-Networks, and a *Set of Views* (hereafter called $IIB.M.SoV$), allowing to obtain instances of object classes of the global SDR-Network from instances of the object classes of the input SDR-Networks.

Observe that the Set of Mappings and the Set of Views allow our technique to describe modifications performed on involved information sources during the integration process by using both input and output information sources and the set of operations which led to the output information source; in our case, maintaining both such representations is cheap, automatic and does not require a large amount of storing resources, as shown in the following. We argue that this characteristic is particularly interesting; indeed, in the literature, generally, each transformation carried out on information sources for the purpose of integration is described by providing either its input and its output or its input and the set of operations performed during the transformation [1]. However, it is difficult to obtain the description of performed operations if the former representation is adopted. Similarly, it is expensive to derive the output if the latter representation is assumed.

The plan of the paper is as follows: the Intensional Information Base is described in details in Section 2, whereas technical details concerning the algorithm for obtaining the global representation are presented in Section 3. Finally, in Section 4 we draw our conclusions.

2 Support Intensional Information Base

Our approach exploits an Intensional Information Base (IIB) as a support for storing information about input SDR-Networks, the global SDR-Network and the set of transformations carried out on input SDR-Networks for obtaining the global one. In particular, *IIB* includes a *Metascheme M* (storing the information relative to involved sources, their object classes and inter-source properties among classes) and a set of *Meta-Operators* for modifying and querying the Metascheme.

2.1 The Metascheme

The Metascheme we exploit is shown in Figure 1. The most important entities in the Metascheme are the entity *Node* and the entity *Arc*. The relationship *Participates* represents the participation of a node into an arc; its attribute *Type* indicates if the node is either the source or the target node of the arc. A node can be synonym with other nodes; in the Metascheme, synonymies (resp., homonymies) are represented by the relationship *Synonym* (resp., *Homonym*);

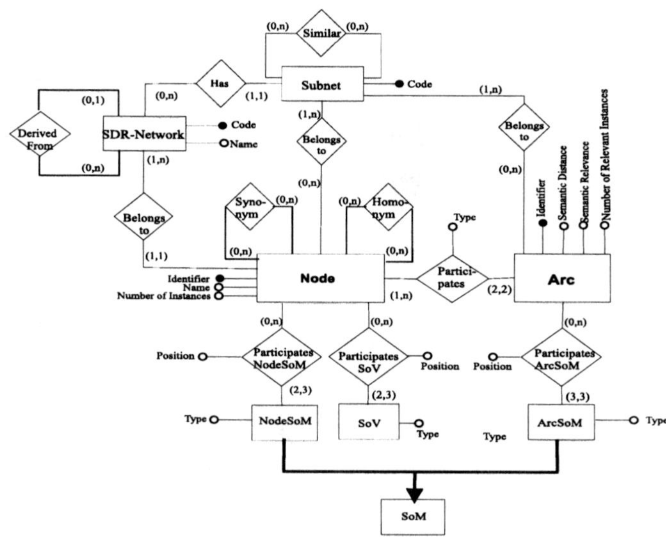

Fig. 1. The Metascheme of the Intensional Information Base

this relationship is used for representing the Synonymy Dictionary SD (resp., the Homonymy Dictionary HD); each tuple of SD (resp., HD) has the form $\langle N_1, N_2 \rangle$, where N_1 and N_2 are the synonym nodes (resp., the homonymy nodes).

An SDR-Network can be derived from more SDR-Networks (this happens when it is the global SDR-Network obtained by integrating the SDR-Networks provided in input). A sub-net is a portion of an SDR-Network and consists of a set of nodes and a set of arcs. A sub-net can be similar to one or more sub-nets. This situation is represented by the relationship *Similar*; this relationship is used for representing the Sub-net Similarity Dictionary *SSD*, whose tuples have the form $\langle S_1, S_2 \rangle$, where S_1 and S_2 are the involved sub-nets; Sub-net Similarities correspond, in the SDR-Network conceptual model, to Sub-scheme similarities.

The entity *SoM* stores the Set of Mappings; it can be looked at as to store the way either a node or an arc of a global SDR-Network has been obtained from nodes or arcs of other SDR-Networks by the integration algorithm. *SoM* includes an entry for each creation or modification of either a node or an arc carried out by the algorithm for constructing the global representation. The Set of Mappings includes two subsets, namely the Set of Mappings relative to nodes (*NodeSoM*) and the Set of Mappings relative to arcs (*ArcSoM*). This distinction is expressed by the generalization hierarchy shown in Figure 1. Tuples of *NodeSoM* are of the form:

- $\langle N_p, N_q, N_{pq}, NodeMerge \rangle$, indicating that the nodes N_p and N_q are merged into the node N_{pq};
- $\langle N_p, -, N_q, NodeRename \rangle$, indicating that the node N_p is renamed and transformed into the node N_q;

- $\langle R_1, R_2, R, RootCreate\rangle$, indicating that a node R is added in the same SDR-Network which R_1 and R_2 belong to. Here, R_1 and R_2 are the roots of two sub-nets and R becomes the "global" root of those two sub-nets (see below).

Analogously, tuples of *ArcSoM* are of the form:

- $\langle A_p, A_q, A_{pq}, ArcMerge\rangle$, indicating that arcs A_p and A_q are merged into the arc A_{pq};
- $\langle A_p, -, A_q, ArcChangeCoeff\rangle$, indicating that the arc A_q substitutes A_p in the corresponding SDR-Network. A_q has the same source and target nodes as A_p but can differ from it for the semantic distance and the semantic relevance coefficients.

The attribute *Type* of the entity *NodeSoM* (resp., *ArcSoM*) specifies the kind of the mapping. A node (resp., an arc) can participate to one or more tuples of *NodeSoM* (resp., *ArcSoM*); in each tuple it participates, it can be the first, the second or the third node (resp., arc) of the tuple. The relationship *ParticipatesNodeSoM* (resp., *ParticipatesArcSoM*) and its attribute *Position* store this information.

The entity *SoV* encodes the Set of Views. It stores a tuple for each node creation or modification carried out during the integration process (and, therefore, a tuple for each tuple of $NodeSoM$). Each view allows to obtain instances of a node from instances of nodes it derives from. Since instances are associated only to nodes, there is no necessity to have a Set of Views relative to arcs.

Views are defined using a "template" language, independent from conceptual and logic scheme model, whose basic operators are parametric procedures that, once instantiated and translated into procedures valid for the management system of the information source storing data which they operates upon, compute derived data instances from input data instances. In other words, each view is an instance of one among a set of parametric views expressed using a meta-language, and is obtained (*i*) by substituting formal parameters with actual ones, according to *SoM* entries; (*ii*) by translating the obtained view from the original meta-language, which it was expressed in, to the language of the management system storing the information which the view operates upon. The set of parametric views are the following:

- $D\_NodeMerge(N_p, N_q, N_{pq})$: it is associated to merging nodes N_p and N_q into the node N_{pq} and derives instances of N_{pq} from instances of both N_p and N_q;
- $D\_NodeRename(N_p, N_q)$: it is associated to renaming the node N_p into the node N_q and derives instances of N_q from instances of N_p;
- $D\_RootCreate(R_1, R_2, R)$: it is associated to creating a root R for R_1 and R_2 (see the corresponding $NodeSoM$ entry); it derives the instances of R from those of R_1 and R_2.

2.2 The Meta-operators

The Intensional Information Base is provided with a set of Meta-Operators; they can be classified into *Meta-Procedures*, that allow to manipulate the information stored in the Metascheme, and *Meta-Functions*, that can be used for querying the Metascheme. As an example, some Meta-Procedures are:

- $Add\_Node(S, N)$, which receives an SDR-Network S and a node N and adds N to S.
- $Delete\_Node(N)$, which takes a node N as input and deletes it from the SDR-Network it belongs to.
- $Transfer\_Incoming\_Arcs(N_x, N_y)$, which receives two nodes N_x and N_y and transfers the incoming arcs of N_x to N_y.
- $Transfer\_Outgoing\_Arcs(N_x, N_y)$, which receives two nodes N_x and N_y and transfers the outgoing arcs of N_x to N_y.
- $Set\_Node\_Inst\_Number(N, n_i)$, which receives a node N and an integer n_i and lets n_i to be the number of instances associated to N.

Some Meta-Functions are:

- $Get\_Node\_Inst\_Number(N) \rightarrow n$, which receives a node N and returns the number of instances associated with N.
- $Get\_Arcs(N_S, N_T) \rightarrow AS$, which takes two nodes N_S and N_T as input and returns the set AS of arcs having N_S as the source node and N_T as the target node.
- $Get\_Nodes(S) \rightarrow NS$, which receives an SDR-Network S and returns the set NS of its nodes.
- $Get\_SDR\_Root(S) \rightarrow R$, which receives an SDR-Network S and returns its root R.
- $Get\_Sub\text{-}net\_Root(SN) \rightarrow R$, which takes a sub-net SN as input and yields its root R as output.

3 Construction of the Global Representation

The construction of the global representation of a group of SDR-Networks is carried out by an integration algorithm. This receives a support Intensional Information Base IIB and two SDR-Networks and integrates them for obtaining a global SDR-Network SDR_G. During the integration process the Metascheme of IIB ($IIB.M$) is modified accordingly to the performed transformations.

The algorithm first constructs the Synonymy Dictionary SD, the Homonymy Dictionary HD and the Sub-net Similarity Dictionary SSD, relative to the SDR-Networks given in input, by examining the relationships *Synonym*, *Homonym* and *Similar* of $IIB.M$. SD (resp., HD, SSD) is composed by a set of pairs of the form $\langle N_x, N_y \rangle$ (resp., $\langle N_x, N_y \rangle$, $\langle SS_x, SS_y \rangle$), where N_x (resp., N_x, SS_x) and N_y (resp., N_y, SS_y) are synonym nodes (resp., homonym nodes, similar sub-nets).

Then, involved SDR-Networks are juxtaposed for obtaining a (temporarily redundant and, possibly, ambiguous) global SDR-Network SDR_G. In order to normalize SDR_G, by removing its inconsistencies and ambiguities, several transformations must be carried out on it.

The first step of SDR_G normalization consists of deriving its root[1]. In particular, if the roots of the two SDR-Networks in input are synonym, they must be merged; otherwise, a new root node is created and connected to the roots of the two SDR-Networks.

[1] Remember that SDR-Networks are rooted labeled graphs.

The second step of the normalization of SDR_G consists of exploiting node synonymies, node homonymies and sub-net similarities for determining which nodes of SDR_G must be assumed to coincide, to be completely distinct or to be renamed. The second step is, in its turn, composed by the following sub-steps:

- *SDR-Network node examination.* First the Synonymy Dictionary SD is taken into account; for each pair $\langle N_x, N_y \rangle$ of nodes belonging to SD, N_x and N_y must be assumed to coincide in SDR_G and, therefore, must be merged into a new node N_{xy}. Then the Homonymy Dictionary HD is examined; for each pair $\langle N_x, N_y \rangle$ of nodes belonging to HD, N_x and N_y must be considered distinct in SDR_G and, consequently, at least one of them must be renamed.
- *SDR-Network arc examination.* For each pair of nodes $[N_S, N_T]$ such that N_S derives from a merge process, it must be checked if N_S is connected to N_T by two arcs[2] and, in the affirmative case, they must be merged into a unique one. If only one arc exists between N_S and N_T, the corresponding coefficients must be updated.
- *Sub-net examination.* First the Sub-net Similarity Dictionary SSD is considered; for each pair $\langle S_x, S_y \rangle$ of sub-nets belonging to SSD, S_x and S_y must be "merged" (the way this is done is described in the following). The merge of sub-nets could lead to the presence of two arcs connecting the same pair of nodes; if this happens, the two arcs must be merged.

The set of transformations the algorithm carries out is stored in $IIB.M.SoM$ and the corresponding views are stored in $IIB.M.SoV$. The complete algorithm for obtaining the global representation of two SDR-Networks is as follows:

Algorithm for constructing the global representation of two SDR-Networks

Input: a pair $SP = \{SDR_1, SDR_2\}$ of SDR-Networks; a support Intensional Information Base IIB;

Output: a global SDR-Network SDR_G; a modified Intensional Information Base IIB;

```
var
    Merged, NSet: a set of nodes; AS: a set of arcs;
    N_xy, N_s, N_t, R_1, R_2: a node; S_1, S_2: a sub-net;
begin
    [IIB.M.SD, IIB.M.HD, IIB.M.SSD] :=
                                Extract_Interesting_Properties(SP);
    SDR_G := Juxtaposition(IIB, SP);
    R_1 := IIB.Get_SDR_Root(SDR_1); R_2 := IIB.Get_SDR_Root(SDR_2);
    if ⟨R_1, R_2⟩ ∉ IIB.M.SD then Create_Root(IIB, R_1, R_2, SDR_G);
    Merged := ∅;
    for each ⟨N_x, N_y⟩ ∈ IIB.M.SD do begin
        N_xy := Merge_Nodes(IIB, N_x, N_y, SDR_G);
        Merged := Merged ∪ {N_xy};
    end;
    for each ⟨N_x, N_y⟩ ∈ IIB.M.HD do Rename_Nodes(IIB, N_x, N_y);
    NSet := IIB.Get_Nodes(SDR_G);
```

[2] Note that this situation could happen only if also N_T derives from a merge process.

```
    for each N_s ∈ Merged do
        for each N_t ∈ NSet such that N_t ≠ N_s do begin
            AS := IIB.Get_Arcs(N_s, N_t);
            if (AS = {A_1, A_2}) then Merge_Arcs(IIB, A_1, A_2, SDR_G);
            else if (AS = {A_1}) then Update_Coefficients(IIB, A_1, SDR_G);
        end;
    for each ⟨S_1, S_2⟩ ∈ IIB.M.SSD such that
    ⟨IIB.Get_Sub-net_Root(S_1), IIB.Get_Sub-net_Root(S_2)⟩ ∉ IIB.M.SD do
        Merge_Sub-nets(IIB, S_1, S_2, SDR_G);
    for each N_s ∈ NSet do
        for each N_t ∈ NSet such that N_t ≠ N_s do begin
            AS := IIB.Get_Arcs(N_s, N_t);
            if (AS = {A_1, A_2}) then Merge_Arcs(IIB, A_1, A_2, SDR_G);
        end
end
```

The function *Extract_Interesting_Properties* takes a pair SP of SDR_Networks as input and derives the Synonymy Dictionary, the Homonymy Dictionary and the Sub-net Similarity Dictionary of the Metascheme. The function *Juxtaposition* receives an Intensional Information Base IIB and a pair SP of SDR-Networks and juxtaposes them for obtaining a (temporarily redundant and, possibly, ambiguous) global SDR-Network SDR_G. The procedure *Create_Root* creates a root for SDR_G and links it to the roots of the two SDR-Networks which have been juxtaposed. The function *Merge_Nodes* receives a support Intensional Information Base IIB, two nodes N_x and N_y and the global SDR-Network SDR_G and merges N_x and N_y for obtaining a unique node N_{xy}. The procedure *Rename_Nodes* receives a support Intensional Information Base IIB and two nodes N_x and N_y and renames at least one of them; it may require the support of the human domain expert for deciding which nodes must be renamed as well as the new names. The procedure *Merge_Arcs* receives a support Intensional Information Base IIB, two arcs A_1 and A_2 and a global SDR-Network SDR_G and merges A_1 and A_2 for obtaining a unique arc. The procedure *Update_Coefficients* receives a support Intensional Information Base IIB, an arc A_1 and the corresponding SDR-Network SDR_G and updates the semantic relevance coefficient associated to A_1. The procedure *Merge_Sub-nets* receives a support Intensional Information Base IIB, two sub-nets S_1 and S_2, a global SDR-Network SDR_G and merges S_1 and S_2 for obtaining a unique sub-net.

Due to space constraints, in the following subsection, we provide only the detailed description of the procedure *Merge_Nodes*.

3.1 Function Merge_Nodes

The function *Merge_Nodes* takes in input a support Intensional Information Base IIB, two nodes N_x and N_y and a global SDR-Network SDR_G and merges N_x and N_y into a node N_{xy}. It first adds a new node N_{xy} to SDR_G and then derives the name, the number of instances and the arcs of N_{xy} from the corresponding ones of both N_x and N_y. Finally, it deletes N_x and N_y and adds suitable entries to both the Set of Mappings and the Set of Views. The function is defined as follows:

Function *Merge_Nodes*(**var** IIB: a support Intensional Information Base; N_x, N_y: a node; SDR_G: an SDR-Network): a node;
var
N_{xy}: a node; n_1, n_2: Integer;
begin
$IIB.Add\_Node(SDR_G, N_{xy})$;
$IIB.Set\_Node\_Name(N_x, N_y, N_{xy})$;
$n_1 := IIB.Get\_Node\_Inst\_Number(N_x)$;
$n_2 := IIB.Get\_Node\_Inst\_Number(N_y)$;
$IIB.Set\_Node\_Inst\_Number(N_{xy}, n_1 + n_2)$;
$IIB.Transfer\_Incoming\_Arcs(N_x, N_{xy})$;
$IIB.Transfer\_Outgoing\_Arcs(N_x, N_{xy})$;
$IIB.Transfer\_Incoming\_Arcs(N_y, N_{xy})$;
$IIB.Transfer\_Outgoing\_Arcs(N_y, N_{xy})$;
$IIB.Delete\_Node(N_x)$; $IIB.Delete\_Node(N_y)$;
$IIB.M.NodeSoM := IIB.M.NodeSoM \cup \{\langle N_x, N_y, N_{xy}, NodeMerge \rangle\}$;
$IIB.M.NodeSoV := IIB.M.NodeSoV \cup \{D\_NodeMerge(N_x, N_y, N_{xy})\}$;
return N_{xy};
end

It is worth pointing out that the deletion of either a node or an arc from an SDR-Network does not imply the removal of that object from the Metascheme. Indeed, the deleted object remains in the Metascheme and the information relative to its deletion from the SDR-Network is added. This is done in order to guarantee the capability of reconstructing the sequence of operations performed to obtain the global SDR-Network.

4 Conclusions

In this paper we have proposed a semi-automatic technique for the construction of a global representation of information sources having different formats and structures. The proposed technique is based on the SDR-Network conceptual model which *(i)* uniformly represents information sources of different nature and *(ii)* allows the reconstruction of the semantics of involved information sources. The global representation is enriched with two support structures which improve access transparency to stored information, namely, *(i)* a global semantic catalogue, storing information about involved information sources, their global representation, object classes belonging to both input information sources and their global representation, and inter-source properties; *(ii)* a Set of Mappings, which stores transformations carried out during the construction of the global-level representation.

As for some future developments of our activity, we plan to apply the same guidelines (i.e., the exploitation of both SDR-Networks and the Intensional Information Base) for implementing other kinds of transformations on information sources (e.g., the abstraction of a global information source [11]). In addition, we plan to insert the proposed technique as a part of a more general framework which takes in input a group of heterogeneous information sources and realizes new forms of "mediators" allowing for the cooperation and the querying of information sources having different formats and structures.

References

1. C. Batini, S. Castano, V. De Antonellis, M.G. Fugini, and B. Pernici. Analysis of an inventory of information systems in the public administration. *Requirement Engineering Journal*, 1(1):47–62, 1996.
2. C. Batini and M. Lenzerini. A methodology for data schema integration in the entity relationship model. *IEEE Transactions on Software Engineering*, 10(6):650–664, 1984.
3. S. Castano and V. De Antonellis. Semantic dictionary design for database interoperability. In *Proc. of International Conference on Data Engineering (ICDE'97)*, pages 43–54, Birmingham, United Kingdom, 1997. IEEE Computer Society.
4. P. Fankhauser, M. Kracker, and E.J. Neuhold. Semantic vs. structural resemblance of classes. *ACM SIGMOD RECORD*, 20(4):59–63, 1991.
5. S. Flesca, L. Palopoli, D. Saccà, and D. Ursino. An architecture for accessing a large number of autonomous, heterogeneous databases. *Networking and Information Systems Journal*, 1(4-5):495–518, 1998.
6. H. Garcia-Molina, Y. Papakonstantinou, D. Quass, A. Rajaraman, Y. Sagiv, J. Ullman, V. Vassalos, and J. Widom. The TSIMMIS approach to mediation: Data models and languages. *Journal of Intelligent Information Systems*, 8:117–132, 1997.
7. W. Gotthard, P.C. Lockemann, and A. Neufeld. System-guided view integration for object-oriented databases. *IEEE Transactions on Knowledge and Data Engineering*, 4(1):1–22, 1992.
8. J.A. Larson, S.B. Navathe, and R. Elmastri. A theory of attribute equivalence in databases with application to schema integration. *IEEE Transactions on Software Engineering*, 15(4):449–463, 1989.
9. A. Levy, A. Rajaraman, and J. Ordille. Querying heterogeneous information sources using source descriptions. In *Proc. of 22th International Conference on Very Large Data Bases (VLDB'96)*, pages 251–262, Bombay, India, 1996. Morgan Kaufmann.
10. L. Palopoli, L. Pontieri, G. Terracina, and D. Ursino. Intensional and extensional integration and abstraction of heterogeneous databases. *Data & Knowledge Engineering*, 35(3):201–237, 2000.
11. L. Palopoli, L. Pontieri, and D. Ursino. Automatic and semantic techniques for scheme integration and scheme abstraction. In *Proc. of International Conference on Database and Expert Systems Applications (DEXA'99)*, pages 511–520, Firenze, Italy, 1999. Lecture Notes in Computer Science, Springer-Verlag.
12. S. Spaccapietra and C. Parent. View integration: A step forward in solving structural conflicts. *IEEE Transactions on Knowledge and Data Engineering*, 6(2):258–274, 1994.
13. G. Terracina and D. Ursino. Deriving synonymies and homonymies of object classes in semi-structured information sources. In *Proc. of International Conference on Management of Data (COMAD 2000)*, pages 21–32, Pune, India, 2000. McGraw Hill.
14. G. Wiederhold. Mediators in the architecture of future information systems. *IEEE Computer*, 25(3):38–49, 1992.

Integration of Topic Maps and Databases: Towards Efficient Knowledge Representation and Directory Services

Thomas Luckeneder, Knud Steiner, and Wolfram Wöß

Institute for Applied Knowledge Processing (FAW)
Johannes Kepler University Linz, Austria
{tluckeneder, ksteiner, wwoess}@faw.uni-linz.ac.at

Abstract. In the field of artificial intelligence there is a well established knowledge representation technique called a semantic network. A semantic network is created using a structure consisting of nodes and links.
Beside semantic networks, especially for knowledge representation and knowledge interchange over the Word Wide Web the international Topic Map ISO standard was developed. It defines a syntax that allows the creation of a strongly typed, linked model of an area of knowledge. Although Topic Maps are being embraced by a wide number of organizations and companies there is still a lack of software that supports the Topic Map standard.
In this paper a meta data structure is introduced, which allows to make a Topic Map persistent within a relational database. To make integrity checks within Topic Maps possible, several constraint mechanisms are introduced. Additionally, for building world wide Internet directory services a multi-language component is included.
The presented concept is realized in the form of a three layer architecture including also an Admin-/Editorshell. This development is the result of a cooperation with one of the largest Internet sites in Austria, covering content and commerce.

Keywords. Topic maps, knowledge representation, directory services, relational databases.

1 Introduction

In the AI (artificial intelligence) area there is a knowledge representation technique called a semantic network [1]. A semantic network is created using a structure consisting of nodes and links. Nodes represent objects, concepts, or situations within a specific domain. Links represent and define relationships between the nodes. Semantic networks are often used to represent the knowledge of human experts in AI applications called inference engines or expert systems [2].

In 1999 the international Topic Map ISO standard [3] has been developed. It essentially defines a syntax, that allows the creation of a strongly typed, linked model of an area of knowledge. This model is a representational device, separate to any number of individual information objects of a knowledge domain. It can be used to

H.C. Mayr et al. (Eds.): DEXA 2001, LNCS 2113, pp. 744–753, 2001.

provide navigational access to that knowledge domain and to help to describe the routes or links, that connect together related parts of it. Also, because the syntax of the model is defined by SGML (Standard Generalized Markup Language), HyTime (Hypermedia Time-based Structuring Language [4]) and XML DTDs (eXtensible Markup Language Document Type Definitions), it is an *open* model that can be shared with others [5].

Basically, the WWW (Word Wide Web) can be described as hypergraph or hypertext system. Objects called nodes (documents, images, etc) are connected through oriented links. The resulting global geometry is locally defined by the link structure. One important aspect that has to be considered is that links do not reflect any content and that they are independent from the information which they are connecting. As a consequence, Web links are far from generally conform to those in semantic fields, which imply typed meaning (like generalization, previous- and next relationships, opposite, extension, ...). Exceptions are structured Web-sites, like directories or educational databases or sometimes well designed commercial portals.

Topic Maps provide a very promising possibility to semantically enrich existing Web-sites. This is a main reason why Topic Maps are being embraced by a wide number of organizations throughout the world. Companies and individuals have realized that the power of Topic Maps can help them to solve their information access problems. However, in order to make the vision reality there must be software that supports the Topic Map standard [6].

In this paper a meta data structure is introduced, which allows to make a Topic Map persistent within a relational database. To make integrity checks within Topic Maps possible, several constraint mechanisms are introduced. Additionally, for building world wide Internet directory services a multi-language component is included.

The paper proceeds as follows: Section 2 starts with a general discussion of Topic Maps as a new Web paradigm comparing them with hierarchy classification. Beside this, Section 2 gives an overview of the basic elements of Topic Maps. In Section 3 concept and architecture of the Topic Map based Internet directory service are introduced. Section 4 concludes and gives an outlook on further research.

2 Topic Maps – A New Web Paradigm

Semantic networks are frequently used to model the knowledge stored within expert systems. Expert systems use facts and rules to analyze a complex set of data and make inferences based on the data and other input. The elements of knowledge that are stored within a semantic network are combined in a way that allows to infer new information about a node by following the links within the network.

Different to semantic networks, Topic Maps, as defined in ISO/IEC 13250, focus more the organization of information in such a way that can be optimized for navigation. Because of information is not useful if it can not be retrieved or combined (linked) Topic Maps have been designed to solve the management problem of large quantities of unorganized information

Topic Maps are built up with units called topics which can have links that refer to all their occurrences. A topic link aggregates every part of information that is about a given subject within a given information set.

The above (brief) description allows to derive the following *structural similarities* between Topic Maps and semantic networks [2]:

- Both Topic Maps and semantic networks are organized as a network of information nodes or modules.
- Both Topic Maps and semantic networks allow the user to model links between nodes.
- Both Topic Maps and semantic networks allow the user to attach semantic information to nodes and links.

There is also a *basic difference*: Topic Maps focus more on the navigation between topics than on their associations. Semantic networks focus on the links between nodes and the knowledge that is represented by linked nodes.

2.1 Hierarchy Classification versus Topic Maps

The Topic Maps model allows to classify information objects as occurrences of particular topics. In this way a *topic* represents a meta category for a group of documents, but in the other way it is completely defined by the set of its occurrences.

Topics may be associated with other topics. Such associations are expressed by a link. Topics and associations may have assigned topic types and association types respectively.

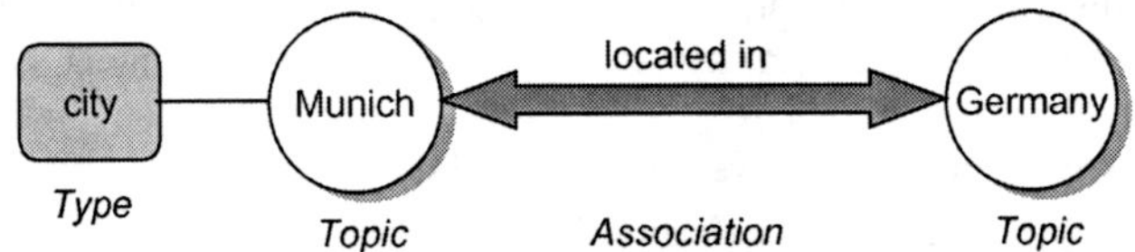

Fig. 1. Association between the topics Munich and Germany.

For example, in Figure 1 the topic "Munich" of the type "city" may be defined categorizing an encyclopedia article and some photographs. The topic "Munich" is in relation with another topic "Germany" defined by a "located in" association [7].

Hierarchy classification means that properties are assigned to objects in a tree-like structure. One root category is divided into more specific subcategories (branches). Today most of the information classification and presentation methods are based on the tree paradigm. The basic methods of science are analysis and synthesis which reflect tree-like decomposition of a problem to sub-problems finding the partial solutions recursively. A major advantage of a tree-like decomposition is inheritance of properties over different hierarchy levels. This establishes abstraction instead of an unordered variety.

For structuring well defined fields of knowledge a hierarchical structure is a proper organization. But for more unstructured and general knowledge it is not efficient enough. Therefore one of the main driving forces behind development of Topic Maps was the requirement to have more flexible categorization schemes than only hierarchical ones. If it is necessary to preserve this in Topic Maps, rules for tree-like parameterization of the map are required.

In Topic Maps everything may be identified as a topic. This mechanism makes Topic Maps very powerful, since everything may be modeled from scratch using just topic and link constructs, not necessarily being predefined in the standard. A further aspect is simplicity in software design because every construct in Topic Maps may be processed in the same way – as a topic. Such a homogeneity promises to be very effective in user interface design.

It is important to note that if the exploration of a Topic Map like in Figure 2 is started from a single topic, the rest of the map becomes a tree. The only exception are loops in the navigation path. Such loops may cause infinite traces, but still make sense in case of pursuing information and knowledge.

2.2 Basic Elements of Topic Maps

The international standard for Topic Maps provides a notation representing information about the structure of information resources by defining topics and the relationships between topics. A set of one or more interrelated documents that correspond to the notation defined by this standard is called *Topic Map*. The basic elements defined by the Topic Map standard are:

- Topic and topic type,
- Topic occurrence and occurrence role type,
- Topic association, association type and association role type.

A *topic* is the basic element of the Topic Map model. Every other element of the Topic Map model described below may also be expressed as a topic. This model-inherent "topic recursion" enables Topic Map designers to create self-describing and self-documenting Topic Maps.

Topics can be grouped into classes called *topic types* whereas a topic may have zero, one or several types. A topic type is defined recursively as a topic. It represents a subject that is suitable for establishing a class-instance relationship between the typing subject (class) and the subjects represented by topics being typed (instances).

Any particular topic may be described in detail by a set of characteristics. The Topic Map standard comprises three kinds of topic characteristics:

- *Topic names* are name characteristics primarily consisting of a base name element. This acts as default designator and provides the default value for both display and sorting purposes. In addition each topic may have a display name and a sort name. The display name is presented within the user interface of a Topic Map processing application. The sort name is useful as a sort key.
- A *topic occurrence* represents a set of typed links (or references) to addressable information objects/resources that are relevant to the subject of a particular topic. Such occurrences are generally outside the Topic Map document itself (although some of them could be inside it). Occurrences are pointed at using whatever mechanisms the system supports, typically HyTime addressing or XPointers. The sense/meaning in which the set of all information objects that are addressed by any given occurrence element are relevant to the containing topic is expressed by its occurrence role type. In addition, information objects may have properties as well as values for those properties assigned to them externally. *Facets* provide a means

for annotating information objects pointed at by topic occurrences with simply structured meta-data (property/value pairs). Both properties and property values are expressed by means of topics (*facet types* and *facet value types*).

- An essential aspect of the Topic Map model is to provide a mechanism to express relationships between the concepts which are modeled. A *topic association* groups one or more participating topics by one ore more association roles (association role types). The global meaning of the association is specified by its association type whereas each association role specifies the role of the topics assigned to it.

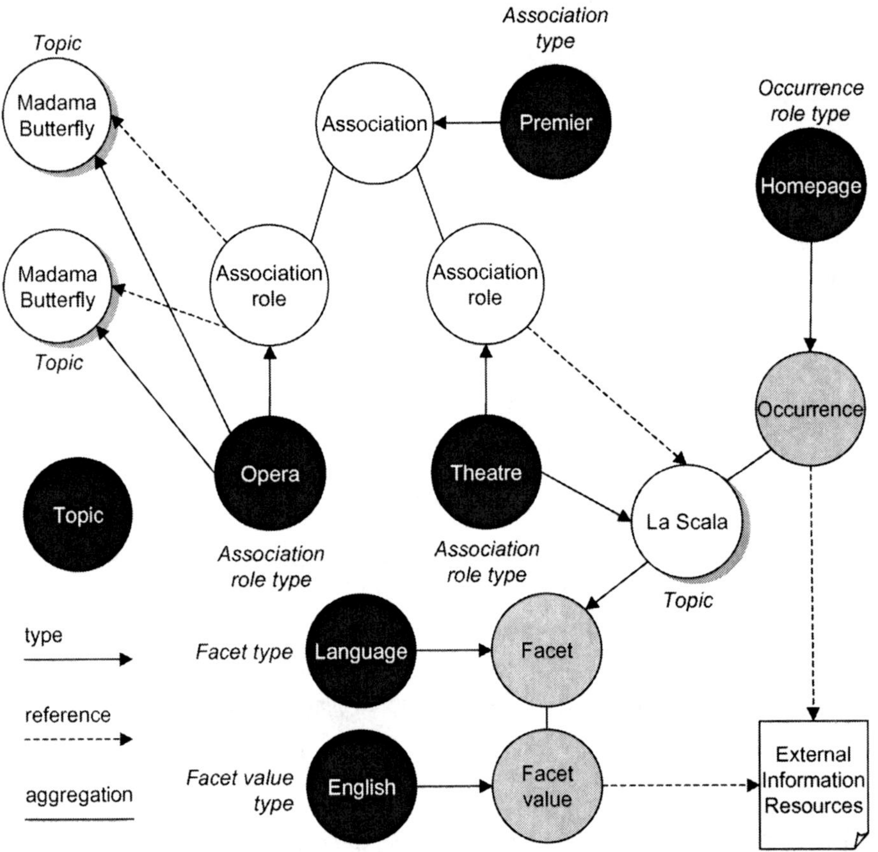

Fig. 2. Example of a Topic Map.

Figure 2 shows an example of a Topic Map. The topic "Premier" is the type of the association which is the aggregation of two association roles. The topics "Opera" and "Theatre" are the types of these association roles. The association role of the type "Opera" references two operas: "Madama Butterfly" and "La Traviata". Both operas are of the type "Opera". Analogous to "Opera" the association role of the type "Theatre" references the topic "La Scala" which itself references an occurrence of the type "Homepage". Furthermore, the facet element is of the type "Language" with the assigned facet value type "English". The occurrence as well as the faces value reference the external information resource.

The base notation of Topic Maps is SGML. An interchangeable Topic Map always consists of at least one SGML document and it may include and/or refer to other kinds of information resources. A set of information resources that comprise a complete interchangeable Topic Map can be specified using the bounded object set (BOS) facility which is defined by the HyTime architecture in ISO/IEC 10744 [4]. XML as subset of SGML may also be used as a base notation for Topic Maps.

Topic Maps enable multiple, concurrent views of sets of information objects. The structural nature of these views is unconstrained – they may reflect an object oriented approach, or they may be relational, hierarchical, ordered, unordered or any combination of the foregoing. Moreover, an unlimited number of Topic Maps may be overlaid on a given set of information resources.

3 A Topic Map Based Internet Directory Service

As discussed in Section 1 and 2, Topic Maps are being embraced by a wide number of organizations and companies. But there is still a lack of software that supports the Topic Map standard. In this paper an Internet directory service is introduced, which is based on a Topic Map using the advantages of semantic networks in this field consequently. A key point for a useful and efficient application is the possibility to make the Topic Map persistent within a relational database and to establish integrity check mechanisms. Additionally, to provide world wide access a multi-language component is important. Concept and architecture of the Topic Map based Internet directory service are described in this section.

3.1 Components of the Topic Map Based Internet Directory

In order to increase both maintainability and extensibility, the application for managing the content of the Internet directory service is divided into six components (Figure 3):

- *Admin-/Editorshell* and *Web-Presentation*. These two modules cover all necessary Tango-scripts for the Admin-/Editorshell and the Web-Presentation. Tango is a Web-application software which enables a dynamic generation of Web-pages whose content results from a database query. In this application Tango-scripts are not used for the implementation of the business logic of the Topic Map management and administration in general, but for the realization of the user and context dependent user interface. Database write operations are separated from these scripts and implemented as stored procedures within the Directory.Maps module. Data exchange is done using well defined interfaces with the advantage that a module can be changed without effecting any other module.

- *Directory.Maps*. The essential business logic for the Internet directory service is part of the Directory.Maps module. It is implemented in Oracle mainly using stored procedures.
- *Topic Map Engine*. This module contains Oracle stored procedures with basic database access operations. Database operations are independent from the business logic in the Directory.Maps module.
- *DirectoryData* and *OtherSiteData*. DirectoryData includes the database schema for storing a Topic Map in a relational database as well as the actual content of the Internet directory service. The content is visualized via the Web-Presentation module. In most cases an Internet directory service is embedded in a large and comprehensive Web site, which is characterized by heterogeneous data structures and a large database. Due to the fact data concerning Topic Maps (DirectoryData) is separated from other data on this site. This kind of data is stored in OtherSiteData.

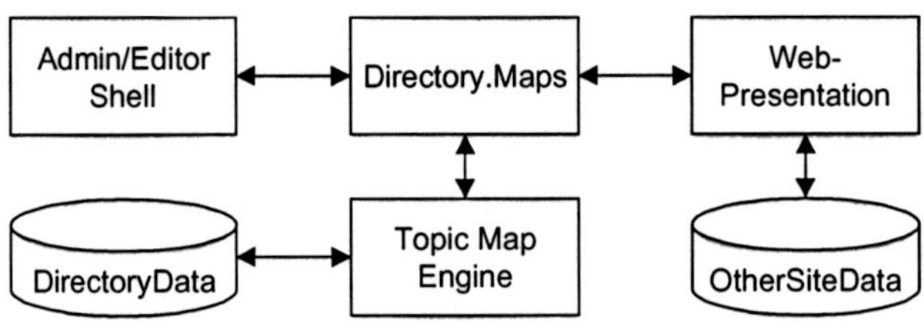

Fig. 3. Components of the Topic Map based Internet directory.

3.2 Three Layer Architecture

To establish a well structured architecture, Topic Maps are logically organized in three layers:

- Within the *meta layer* all Topic Map meta types are specified. They are directly derived from the Topic Maps standard. Meta types are used to control the internal business logic of the Directory.Maps module. Furthermore, the advanced concepts for Topic Maps [8] are also mapped to meta types in this layer (see Section 3.3).
- The *schema layer* represents the schema of the Internet directory service. The schema is primarily used to guarantee consistency and integrity of the content of the directory which is stored within the instance layer. Consistency and integrity checks are implemented using constraints which are specified within the Directory.Maps module.
- The *instance layer* contains the actual content of the directory service based on the defined schema topics which are stored within the schema layer.

3.3 Meta Types and Constraints

To make integrity checks within Topic Maps possible, in this approach several constraint mechanisms are introduced. The implementation of the meta types within the meta layer is based on both the basic concepts of the Topic Maps standard as well as the advanced concepts for building Topic Map applications. In detail, the implemented and used meta types are:

- *Topic type (tt)*, *Association type (at)*, *Association role type (art)*, *Occurrence role type (ort)*.
- *Facets*. In this approach it is distinguished between discrete and non-discrete facet types (ftd and ftnd) as well as discrete and non-discrete facet value types (fvtd and fvtnd). Discrete facet types and facet value types are supposed to be frequently used facets with a limited range of values. In contrast to discrete facets, the range of values of non-discrete facets is not limited. Non-discrete facet value types are arbitrary strings and mostly used only once. Both types are treated and processed as topics.

Furthermore, the introduced concepts in [8] and [9] resulted in the following meta constraints. Each constraint is internally implemented as association and belongs to the schema layer:

- *Association constraint (ac)*. Within the schema layer a concrete association constraint defines for an association type which association role types and which topic types (a regular topic of the associated topic type respectively) may be associated at the instance layer. For example, an association constraint for the association type "contains" defines that it is only allowed to associate regular topics of the topic type "country" within the association role type "container". In addition, it defines that it is only allowed to associate regular topics of the topic type "state" within the association role type "containee".
- *Occurrence constraint (oc)*. Analogous to an association constraint, an occurrence constraint determines which occurrence role type(s) are permitted to be assigned to regular topics of a specific topic type.
- *Facet constraint (fc)* and *facet value constraint (fvc)*. According to the distinction of discrete and non-discrete facet types and facet value types there is an analogous distinction between discrete and non-discrete facet constraints and facet value constraints. A facet constraint defines which facet types (no matter discrete or non-discrete) are permitted to be associated to a certain occurrence role type. Furthermore, a facet value constraint defines which facet value types are permitted to be associated with a facet type.

3.4 The Multi-language Component

Especially in the context of building a world-wide Internet directory service the use of multi-languages for the content of the directory service is a key aspect.

The Topic Map standard includes a general concept for using scopes. Scopes are used to limit the validity of topics or the name characteristics of certain topics (e.g., the topic "Paris" is only valid within the scope "Countries" or a concrete base name of a topic is only valid within the scope "Language: English").

Basically, all Topic Map elements with name characteristics are allowed to be used for multi-languages. In particular, this includes the following topics at the schema layer: topic type, association type, association role type, occurrence role type, discrete and non-discrete facet type and facet value type. It also includes the following topics at the instance layer: regular topic and locator-alias.

Editors who are responsible for the content of the Internet directory service are supported in managing and maintaining different language versions of topics by the Admin-/Editorshell. Using scopes offers the advantage that each topic exists only once, but their name characteristics (which express their textual and also semantic representation) exists for each language scope. To achieve this, for each topic editors have to specify different terms according to the required languages at schema and instance layer. The Web-Presentation module visualizes the language dependent name characteristics of a concrete topic according to the language scope that is set by the user who is browsing within the Internet directory service.

A locator is assigned to an occurrence and represents a hyperlink to an information resource. The locator-alias is the textual representation of a locator which is visualized by the Web-Presentation module. Analogous to topics, different locator-alias terms have to be specified according to the required languages.

3.5 User Authorization

Corresponding to the three layer architecture of the main system the authorization system considers three different user groups:

- A *system user* is permitted to change (read and write access) each topic from each layer (meta-, schema- and instance-layer).
- An *administrator* has full access to topics at the instance- and schema-layer and only read access to topics at the meta-layer. An administrator is responsible for the schema of a Topic Map.
- *Editors* have full access to topics at the instance-layer and only read access to topics at the schema- and meta-layer. Editors are responsible for the content maintenance of the directory service.

The assignment of a user to a user group is the result of the login process which requires username and password.

4 Conclusions

Developed first as a tool for knowledge representation and resources indexing, the Topic Map technology seems bound to become a more pervasive tool, pertinent wherever one needs to tackle complexity. Given the technology is still young, it has to be confronted to a variety of use cases in order to be refined and validated.

Topic Maps provide a promising possibility to semantically enrich existing Web-sites. This is a main reason why Topic Maps are being embraced by a wide number of organizations throughout the world. Companies and individuals have realized how the power of Topic Maps can help them to solve their information access problems. However, in order to make the vision reality there must be software that supports the Topic Map standard.

In this paper a meta data structure is introduced, which allows to make a Topic Map persistent within a relational database. To make integrity checks within Topic Maps possible, several constraint mechanisms are introduced. Additionally, a multi-language component is included. The mentioned components are very important for the efficient implementation of an Internet directory services. Furthermore, the presented approach also focuses the graphical design of the Web presentation. The user interface has to correspond to the concepts of Topic Maps to allow an appropriate navigation within the knowledge structure.

The introduced Topic Map based Internet directory service is the result of a cooperation with one of the largest Internet sites in Austria. Currently, the project partner fills up and completes the content of the Internet directory service with the intention to go online as soon as possible.

Further work will start with the improvement of the system performance. Especially if HTML-pages are generated dynamically based on database query result sets, runtime is a very crucial aspect for a Web-site. It is intended to use the materialized views technology (Oracle 8i) to improve the performance of queries containing "expensive" join operations.

Another focus of interest will be the implementation of an improved graphical presentation of the Topic Map. That topic which is currently visited by a user is positioned in the center of the graphical representation. Semantically relevant topics are connected via lines and arranged around the center topic. The length of such a line represents the semantic relevance of each topic in relation to the current topic. Users control the number of shown topics by changing the relevance distance value.

References

1. Griffith, R. L.: Three Principles of Representation for Semantic Networks. ACM Transactions on Database Systems, Vol. 7, No. 3, pp. 417-442 (1982)
2. Freese, E.: Using Topic Maps for the representation, management & discovery of knowledge. Proceedings of XML Europe 2000 Conference, http://xtech.org/papers/xmleurope2000/pdf/s22-01.pdf (2000)
3. Topic Map ISO/IEC 13250: Topic Maps, Information Technology, Document Description and Processing Languages. Eds.: Biezunski Michel, Bryan Martin, Newcomb Steve, http://www.y12.doe.gov/sgml/sc34/document/0129.pdf (03.12.1999)
4. HyTime ISO/IEC 10744: Hypermedia/Time-based Structuring Language (HyTime), 2nd Edition. Eds.: Goldfarb Charles, Newcomb Steve, Kimber Eliot, Newcomb Peter, http://www.ornl.gov/sgml/wg8/ docs/n1920/html/n1920.html (1997)
5. Baird, C.: Topic Map Cartography – a discussion of Topic Map authoring. Proceedings of XML Europe 2000 Conference, http://www.topicmaps.com/machinery/intermediary.asp?file=../content/resources/resolved\tmcartography.xml (2000)
6. Moore, G.: Topic Map Technology – The State of the Art. Proceedings of XML Europe 2000 Conference, http://www.topicmaps.com/machinery/intermediary.asp?file=../content/resources/resolved\final2.xml (2000)
7. Ksiezyk, R.: Trying not to get lost with a Topic Map. Proceedings of XML Europe 1999 Conference, http://www.topicmaps.de/content/resources/xmleur99/rak.htm (1999)
8. Rath, H. H.: Mit Topic Maps intelligente Informationsnetze aufbauen – Mozart und Kugeln. iX Magazin No.12 (1999)
9. Rath, H. H.: Making topic maps more colorful. Proceedings of XML Europe 2000 Conference, http://xtech.org/papers/xmleurope2000/pdf/s29-01.pdf (2000)

A Spatial Hypermedia Framework for Position-aware Information Delivery Systems

Haruhiko HIRAMATSU † Kazutoshi SUMIYA ‡ Kuniaki UEHARA ‡

† Graduate School of Business Administration, Kobe University
hiramatu@kobe-u.ac.jp
‡ Division of Advanced Information Processing for Wide Area Networks, Research Center for Urban Safety and Security, Kobe University
{sumiya,uehara}@ai.cs.kobe-u.ac.jp

Abstract. In this paper, we propose a spatial hypermedia framework for position-aware information delivery systems. In our proposed method, position information of contents are mapped to logical space which is one virtual space according to features of information, and then, links are generated according to not only the geographical position relation of real space but also the position relation to logical space. Therefore, we can generate links between spatial information which spread in real space dynamically. We have implemented the prototype system based on the propagation link to propose using XML, and evaluate the validity.

1 Introduction

Recently, position-aware information delivery services have become widespread with the popularization of mobile devices such as a cellular phones and PDAs. J-station [1], iMapFan[2] and others are examples. These existing position-aware information delivery services connect to the Internet and provide information. Moreover, there is much research which uses position information, such as, OpenGIS[3], G-XML[4], SpaceTag[5] and ActiveGIS[6].

The information treated with position-aware information delivery systems is not only text but a hypertext and hypermedia. Various information is associated by the hyperlink. The static link generally used by the WWW has the problem of dangling links[7], in which a linked content(or a linking content) does not exist, when informational updating frequency is high. Therefore, the dynamic link[8][9] which generates links by calculation is effective for the position-aware information delivery system.

In the existing position-aware information delivery system, the dynamic link is used also; however, there are the following problems.

- These systems cannot associate the information when the position relation in real space is not filled, because the existing position-aware information delivery system uses the fixed position relation in real space.
- It is difficult to treat information, such as typhoon information, which moves and changes its content according to time.

H.C. Mayr et al. (Eds.): DEXA 2001, LNCS 2113, pp. 754–763, 2001.

– Existing position-aware infromation delivery systems are built with their own techniques; therefore, there is no framework which treats the spatial hypermedia.

In this paper, we propose a spatial hypermedia framework for position-aware information delivery systems. Our proposed framework consists of a dynamic link mechanism which is based not only on the geographical position relation of real space but also on the position relation of logical space, which is one of virtual space. The position relation of logical space is reconstructed from the geographical position relation according to features of information which are determined by the definition embedded to a link beforehand. It is possible to generate links between the information which spreads in real space. This dynamic link mechanism is called a propagation link mechanism in this paper. A propagation link mechanism can build various kinds of links by setting up of spatial conditions and temporal conditions; therefore, it is possible to use other existing position-aware information systems.

This paper is organized as follows: In section 2 we describe our approach. In section 3 we explain our proposed link management mechanism called the propagation link. In section 4 we explain spatial hypermedia using our proposed link mechanism and in section 5 we explain a prototype system based on our proposed method. Finally, we give a conclusion in section 6.

2 Motivation and Our Approach

2.1 Dynamic Link of Information Delivery Systems

In the WWW, contents are mutually connected by links. The linking contents are called *Sources*, and the linked contents are called *Destinations*. It is possible to get much information easily by following links on the WWW. The static link is embedded into contents in advance. Therefore, the rightness of a link may be lost when information is updated frequently. This is the case where the linking content exists but the linked content was deleted, leaving a dangling link. So a dynamic link is effective for this problem because the destination (or source) is dynamically set up by a calculation according to the situation.

We have proposed the Mille-feuille[10], which is a valid time dependent dynamic link mechanism which introduces time into the content and the anchor. In Mille-feuille, contents and links are separated like the Dexter hypertext reference model[11]. However, in a position-aware information delivery system, we must take into consideration not only time but also position.

2.2 Relations in Real Space and Logical Space

Many contents in real space have position information and an area in which the content has a meaning. Existing position-aware information delivery systems are based on a position relation in real space using this geographical position information. Regardless of the features of the information, links are dynamically generated between contents which have a fixed geographical position relation, such as inclusion, neighboring and continuity, in real space. However, a link between information which has changed the position relation according to time and position, such as the information which spreads into space like typhoon information, is not generated. The problem is the information which should be delivered to users is missing. That is, the information is not spread using a position relation in real space. Therefore, a dynamic link mechanism, based on the position relation according to features of the information, is needed.

2.3 Our Approach

The spatial hypermedia framework proposed in this paper is a position-aware dynamic link mechanism where the *Source* and *Destination* are determined by time information and position relation in logical space, which is one of virtual space. In this dynamic link mechanism, position information and time information are added to contents, and links are managed separately from contents. The position information of a content is mapped to a logical space according to the spatial conditions which are defined in the link definition beforehand, and a position relation is reconstructed in logical space. When a position relation between contents in logical space fulfills the space conditions, a propagation link is generated in logical space and a position-aware dynamic link corresponding to a propagation link is generated in real space.

Fig. 1 shows the concept of our proposed link mechanism. Rectangle O, A, B, C, D, E express contents. The position information of each content is mapped to logical space according to the spatial conditions. As a result, the position relation in real space changes and propagation links are generated between O and A, B and E. A user can get A, B and E as the nearest information.

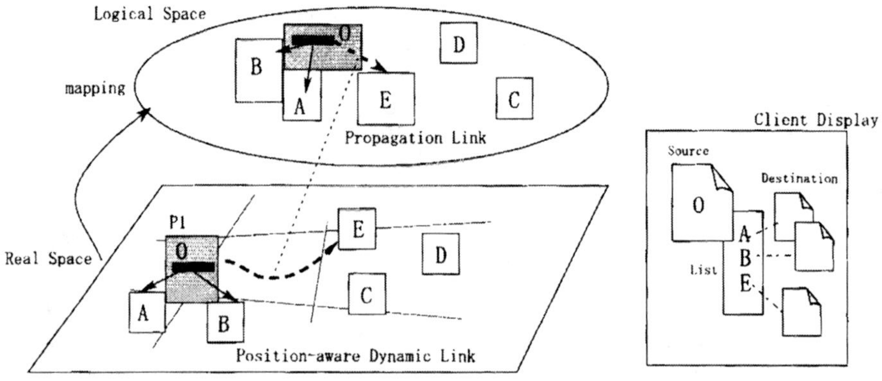

Fig. 1. A concept of our proposed propagation link mechanism.

3 Propagation Link

3.1 Content and Propagation Link Definition

There are various contents in real space. All of the contents have position information. Therefore, a content C is expressed as follows:

$$C = (ID, VER, G) \tag{1}$$

where ID is the identifier. VER is the version which means the number of times of updating. G expresses the position information of the content in real space, which, in this paper, is treated as a rectangular area. The position information of contents in real space is mapped to logical space which is one of virtual space according to the spatial condition S defined arbitrarily. Links are generated in logical space between contents which fulfill the spatial condition S. These are what we call propagation links in this paper, and the link in real space corresponding to the propagation link is called the position-aware dynamic link. A propagation link L is expressed as follows:

$$L = (C_S, C_D, S, T) \tag{2}$$

where C_S is the *Source* content which contains the anchor, C_D is the *Destination* content which contains the anchor, T expresses a temporal condition and S expresses a spatial condition. A propagation link is determined by T and S.

3.2 Spatial Conditions of a Propagation Link

Spatial condition S of a propagation link is the rule expressing the relation between contents defined in advance. The rule consists of the following:

- Features of information in real space.
- Spatial effective condition F of a link by the position relation in logical space.

The position information of a content is mapped, by the rule corresponding to a feature, to logical space from real space. When a position relation in logical space fulfills the effective condition F, a link is generated between contents.

For example, the position information of contents C_1, C_2 are G_1, G_2, and the feature of information is a typhoon. G_1, G_2 are mapped to G'_1 and G'_2 in logical space according to mapping rules corresponding to the feature of information. The spatial effective condition F consists of the following:

- The function $AdminArea(x, y)$ judges that x, y are an administrative district region.
- The function $Neighbor(x, y)$ shows the contiguity of x and y.

When a position relation between G'_1 and G'_2 fulfills the following equations, a propagation link between C_1 and C_2 is generated in logical space.

$$AdminArea(G'_1, G'_2) = true \tag{3}$$

$$Neighbor(G'_1, G'_2) = true \tag{4}$$

At the same time, a position-aware dynamic link is generated in real space.

3.3 Temporal Conditions of a Propagation Link

The temporal condition T of a propagation link specifies the version of contents. For example, in the case of generating a link between the newest version of contents C_1, C_2, the temporal condition T is expressed as the following equation.

$$Newest(C_1, C_2) = true \tag{5}$$

Moreover, the valid time of contents is evaluated apart from the temporal condition T; that is, both the *Source* contents and the *Destination* contents must be effective in present time. The temporal validity of dynamic links are discussed in Mille-feuille[10].

3.4 Creation and Expiration of a Propagation Link

A propagation link is generated according to a definition of formula 2. It searches for the contents of Destination which fulfill S defined by the link of a *Source* in logical space. The contents which fulfill conditions are chosen as a Destination, a propagation link is generated in logical space, and a position-aware dynamic link is generated in real space. Two or more propagation links may be generated since links are generated between contents which fullfill S.

When the position information of contents changes, in the contents with the same ID, it investigates whether it is effective. When effective, it is determined as a Destination or a *Source*. If its effective time is over, no contents which fulfill S in a definition of a propagation link to be, a propagation link expires.

4 Spatial Hypermedia using Propagation Link

We can generate various kinds of propagation links by the spatial condition S and the temporal condition T. In this paper, we use $Neighbors$, $Contains$ and $Overlaps$ as an example showing a spatial condition F in logical space. These position relation are shown in Fig. 2 and each function which expresses these relations is expressed in the following formulas.

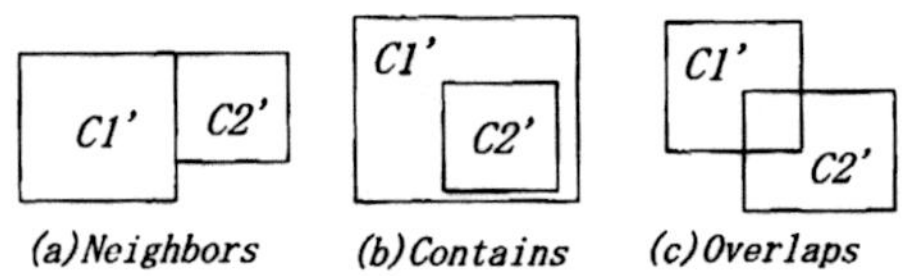

Fig. 2. Examples of the position relation in logical space.

$$Neighbors(C_1', C_2') = true \tag{6}$$

$$Contains(C_1', C_2') = true \tag{7}$$

$$Overlaps(C_1', C_2') = true \tag{8}$$

It is the function with which a domain judges whether the boundary of contents has touched, as in an administrative district region in $Neighbors$. $Contains$ shows whether one part is completely contained on another part. The relation, for example, between a state and a city applies here. $Overlaps$ evaluates whether a part of the domain overlaps.

As examples of propagation link shown in Fig. 3, *Newest-nearest* link, *Connection* link and *Unexplored-uncoming* link are explained below. In addition, as in the spatial condition S, features of information are not specified but only spatial effective conditions between contents are explained.

4.1 Newest-nearest link

A newest-nearest link is generated automatically between the newest and nearest contents. This link is effective when a content is updated or moved frequently; that is, it is a function in which a user does not perform navigation manually in request of the newest and the nearest contents, but the system performs navigation automatically.

The spatial condition S is shown in equations(6), (7) or (8). The temporal condition T is the function which expresses both the *Source* and *Destinations* that are the newest version.

$$T = Newest(C_1, C_2) \tag{9}$$

where $Newest()$ is a function showing the newest contents.

An example is shown in Fig. 3-(a). In Fig. 3-(a), a position relation between C_1' and C_4' does not fulfill one of the equations(6)(7)(8), so a propagation link is not generated between these contents.

4.2 Connection link

The connection link has a function which generates a link between contents which are not in an inclusion relation. S is explained using Fig. 3-(b).

In Fig. 3-(b), the position relation in logical space between C_1' and C_2' must fulfill one of the equations(6)(7)(8). The position relation in logical space between C_2' and C_3' must fulfill one of the equations(6)(7)(8). The position relation in logical space between C_1' and C_3' must fulfill none of the equations(6)(7)(8). A connection link is generated between C_1' and C_3' via C_2'.

4.3 Unexplored-uncoming link

An unexplored link is processed by the dynamic link mechanism which waits to display a link to the contents to which it does not arrive spatially and in time. In the following cases, we can use this link.

- time condition T is the future. That is, it is set up so that the contents will appear after the present time.

– there are no contents which fulfill spatial condition S and which can be chosen.

That is, the temporal condition T fulfills equation(10) or the spatial condition S is not fulfilled at the present time t_{now}.

$$Future(C'_1, C'_2) = true \tag{10}$$

where $Future()$ is the function showing future time.

While waiting for the generation of a link, when a link is not displayed to a user but a content arrives, it displays automatically. However, it may not be released from the restriction but may be in a waiting state eternally. Fig. 3-(c) shows that if C'_2 does not appear in t_{now}, a server waits for the generation of a link.

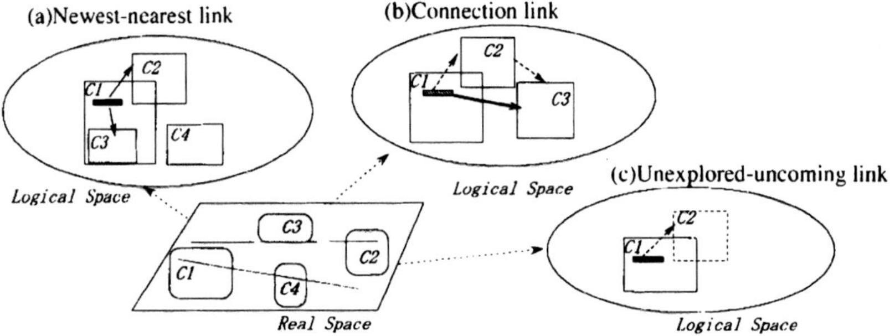

Fig. 3. Examples of a propagation link.

4.4 An example of operation

Figures 4 shows examples of a link's behavior. In Fig. 4, a rectangle expresses a content, the arrow of a solid line indicates a link to be, and the underlined text expresses the anchor. In this example, it is a link from "typhoon information" to "warning information", and S is set up based on the influence area of a typhoon.

1. **[9/1 00:00]** The contents which contain the anchor "Typhoon Information" are in position P_1. The position relation between P_1 and P_3 becomes a neighboring relation in logical space by the influence area of a typhoon. A link from "Typhoon Information" to "Heavy Rain Warning" is generated.
2. **[9/1 02:00]** An anchor "Typhoon Information" appears into the contents of P_2 because a typhoon moves. At this time, P_1, P_2 and P_3 fulfill a neighboring relation in logical space. A new link from "Typhoon Information" to "Gale Warning" is generated. Moreover, the contents of P_3 is updated to a new version "Flood Warning"; therefore, the link from P_2 is changed into the content of a new version.
3. **[9/1 04:00]** Furthermore, a typhoon moves. The position relation between P_1, P_2 and P_3 does not fulfill the spatial conditions. An anchor "Typhoon Information" becomes a waiting state because there are no contents which fulfill the conditions.

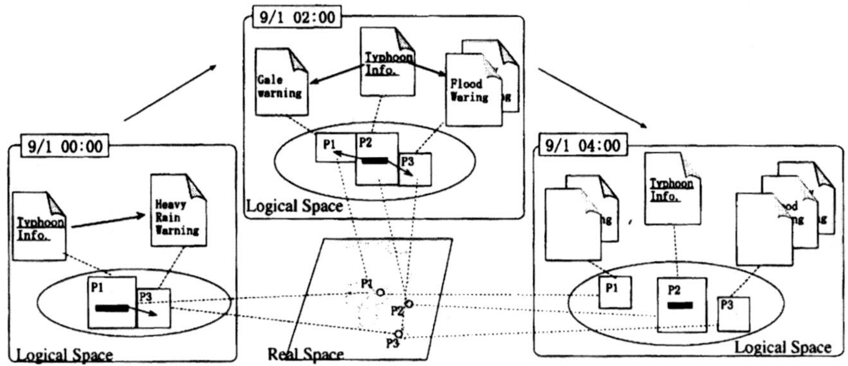

Fig. 4. An example of weather information.

5 Prototype System

5.1 System Architecture

We have been developing a prototype system. The system was implemented by Java[12]. Futhermore, Servlet and JSP(Java Server Pages) are used, so it can be displayed on general Web browsers.

System architecture is shown in Fig. 5-(a). This prototype system consists of contents database, link manager, spatial condition database, temporal condition database and translator. Clients can be connected to general Web browsers, as stated above. A screen image of the prototype system is shown in Fig. 5-(b). This screen consists of log, list of available contents, Input form of XML files for control, list of *Source* contents, list of *Destination* contents and the *Destination* display. In the prototype system of the proposed propagation link mechanism,

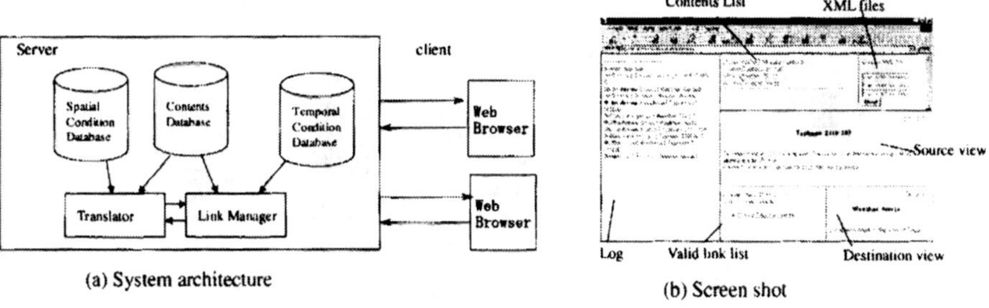

Fig. 5. System architecture and screen image of our prototype system.

XML[13] is used. XML is a subset of SGML and is the language which adds the extended function to HTML. The propagation link can be realized by XLink which is the extended link mechanism of XML since contents and links are separated.

5.2 Usage of Position-aware Information Delivery Systems

Fig. 6 shows a screen image of our prototype system, and Fig. 7 shows examples of the operation of the system. These examples show that links are generated between the typhoon information and the alarm information.

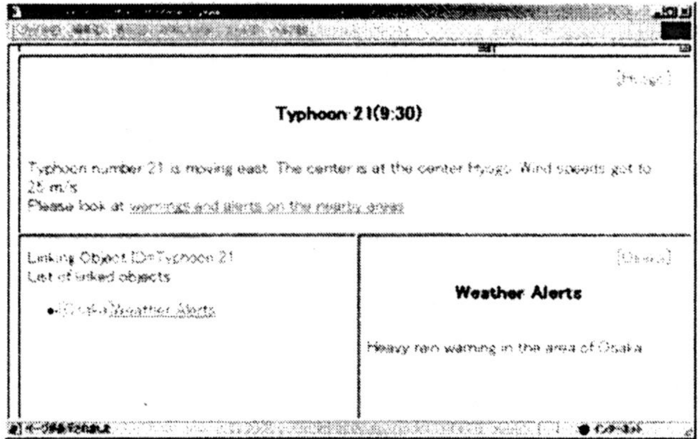

Fig. 6. Screen image of weather information delivery service.

1. If a valid destination content is chosen from a list, contents will be displayed. At this time, the link is generated to effective contents as a Destination.
2. When the contents of the *Source* become invalid and a new version does not arrive, then the anchor becomes a waiting state by the *Unexplored-uncoming* link.
3. If the new contents of the *Source* appear, the list of effective contents will be changed by the *Newest-nearest* link. All contents are displayed in the list view.

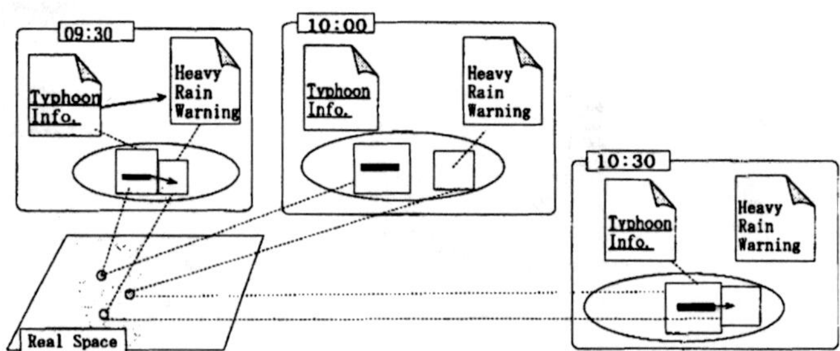

Fig. 7. Operations of weather information delivery service.

Thus, links are automatically generated according to position and time. Moreover, a propagation link mechanism can generate a link between contents which is not generated by other existing position-aware information systems.

6 Conclusions

This paper described the framework of the spatial hypermedia for position-aware information delivery systems; especially, the link mechanism was described. We proposed a propagation link which is the dynamic link mechanism based on position relation in logical space. Moreover, we explained that the propagation link was generated according to spatial conditions and temporal conditions, and examples of typical propagation links were shown. Finally, we discussed the prototype system which uses XML, and that the propagation link mechanism is realized by the existing hypermedia. It is shown that more effective position-aware information delivery becomes possible by our proposed framework.

Acknowledgments

This research was supported by the Research for the Future Program of Japan Society for the Promotion of Science under the project "Researches on Advanced Multimedia Contents Processing(JSPS-RFTF97P00501)".

References

1. J-Station. http://www.j-phone-west.com/.
2. Mapfan Web. http://www.mapfan.com/.
3. Open GIS Consortium. http://www.opengis.org/.
4. G-XML HomePage. http://gisclh.dpc.or.jp/gxml/contents/.
5. H. Tarumi, K. Morishita, M. Nakao, and Y. Kambayashi. Space Tag: An Overlaid Virtual System and its Applications. *In proc. of International Conference on Multimedia Computing and Systems (ICMCS'99)*, pages 207–212, 1999.
6. T. Terada, M. Tsukamoto, and S. Nishio. A Geographical Information System Using Active Database Systems(in Japanese). *Journal of Information Processing Society of Japan*, 41(11):3103–3113, Nov 2000.
7. J. E. Ptkow. and R. K. Jones. Supporting the web: A distributed hyperlink database system. *In Proc. of 5th Inernational World Wide Web Conference*, May 1996.
8. Q. Qian, M. Tanizaki, and K. Tanaka. Abstraction and Inheritance of HyperLinks in an Object-Oriented Hypertext Database System TextLink/Gen. *IEICE Transactions on Information and Systems*, E78-D(11):1343–1353, 1995.
9. K. Tanaka, N. Nishikawa, S. Hirayama, and K. Nanba. Query Pairs As Hypertext Links. *In Proc. of 7th IEEE Data Engineering Conference*, pages 456–463, 1991.
10. K. Sumiya, R. Noda, and K Tanaka. A Temporal Link Mechanism for Hypermedia Broadcasting (in Japanese). *The Transaction of the Institute of Electronics, Information and Communication Engineers*, J82-D-I(1):291–302, January 1999.
11. F. Halasz and M. Schwartz. The dexter hypertext reference model. *Communications of the ACM*, 37(2):30–39, Feb 1994.
12. The Source for Java Technology. http://java.sun.com/.
13. EXtensible Markup Language (XML). http://www.w3c.org/xml/.

Ariadne, a Development Method for Hypermedia

Paloma Díaz, Ignacio Aedo, and Susana Montero

Laboratorio DEI. Departamento de Informática. Universidad Carlos III de Madrid
Avda. de la Universidad 30. E-28911 Leganés (Spain)
{pdp@inf, aedo@ia, smontero@inf}.uc3m.es

Abstract. Hypermedia development poses very specific problems such as the need for mechanisms to model sophisticated navigational structures, interactive behaviours and usable multimedia compositions. Moreover, since the majority of hypermedia applications are accessed by different users, security becomes a key feature. In this context, we present a development method called Ariadne which offers a number of tools to create hypermedia applications in an progressive and integrated way.

1 Introduction

Hypermedia development poses very specific problems that do not appear in other software applications [13,10,5], such as the need for mechanisms to model sophisticated navigational structures, some of which can be ephemeral, interactive behaviours and multimedia compositions which have to be usable and harmonic at the same time. Although experience and modelling skills can be borrowed from existing design methods such as object oriented modelling, hypermedia developers need intellectual mechanisms to analyse and design using abstractions and design entities related to the hypermedia domain (e.g. nodes, links, anchors and synchronisms). In fact, there are some hypermedia methods which provide designers with hypermedia specification tools including HDM [10], RMM [11] and OOHDM [16]. Moreover, since the majority of hypermedia applications, and particularly those implemented as web environments, are accessed by different users with different purposes, security becomes a key feature to be taken into account. Hypermedia methods should provide mechanisms to deal with all the features of any hyperdocument, including security, in an progressive and integrated way.

In this context, we present a development method for hypermedia applications, called Ariadne, that is aimed at providing an integrated framework to specify all the static and dynamic features of any hyperdocument. The method applies an iterative process based on the evaluation of design solutions with potential users to determine their utility and usability. Compared to similar methods, Ariadne improves three significant aspects: it provides a mechanism to define time- and space-based constraints among contents; it offers a product

H.C. Mayr et al. (Eds.): DEXA 2001, LNCS 2113, pp. 764–774, 2001.

to model the users structure based on roles and teams; and it includes a security model to define the policy that will be applied during the hyperdocument operation.

2 Principles of Hypermedia Modelling

Modelling hypermedia applications involves several complementary views which have to be properly addressed by a development method [5], including navigation, presentation, control, security, processes and data, that are discussed below.

Navigation design. One of the most important tasks in hypermedia modelling is the design of the browsing structure made up of nodes and links, that should not be confounded with structural relationships such as a part-whole relation. Most hypermedia design methods propose mechanisms to specify browsing capabilities [10,11,16,12,15].Moreover, hypermedia authors tend to include some navigation tools such as visual maps, active indexes, guided tours, marks, footprints and backtracking mechanisms [14]. Thus, hypermedia methods should also provide elements to model such navigation aids. Finally, navigation modelling has to deal not only with declarative but also with event-based specifications. For instance, RMM includes conditional guided tours and indexes whose components are calculated applying a rule specified by the designer.

Presentation design. Another basic feature of hypermedia concerns presentation issues, since nodes include multimedia contents that need to be organised and harmonised in different dimensions such as time and space. In fact, the way and rhythm used to deliver the contents to the user determines to a great extent the hyperdocument usefulness.

Control design. Control design provides a behavioural specification describing how particular events affect to the system. Hypermedia systems are highly interactive and, therefore, modelling the system reaction to particular events is a relevant design concern [5].

Security design. The increasing popularity of hypermedia systems, mainly due to the proliferation of web applications, has put stress on the need for preserving the security of the information they hold [6]. Security rules have to be analysed and formally specified in terms of entities of the domain, for which high-level models are required [8,4]. A security model for hypermedia has to provide elements to formalise security policies using components and services of the hypermedia technology (e.g. nodes, links, link traversal and so on).

Processes modelling. Processes modelling is oriented towards defining how the system works. The main function of a hypermedia system is the hypertext navigation, that cannot be represented by means of process models such as DFDs. However, complex hypermedia systems include more and more no-navigation functions that can profit from the use of process oriented methods. For instance, Java applets or search engines can be specified using an appropriate processing modelling technique.

Data design. Data design methods describe the system in terms of data entities and structural relationships. Although nodes needn't be structured, some hyperdocuments such as books, dictionaries, digital libraries and so on, have an intrinsic hierarchical structure which can be defined using abstractions borrowed from data models. In fact, paradigms like entity-relationship, semantic and object-oriented modelling have been applied in the hypermedia field or used as the application structural schema in different works, such as [11] in E-R models, [15] in semantic modelling and [10,16,12] in object-oriented modelling.

3 Ariadne: A Method for Developing Hypermedia Systems

Ariadne proposes a systematic approach to produce hypermedia applications. Compared to other hypermedia design methods such as HDM, OOHDM or RMM, Ariadne shares a number of similarities concerning the specification of the logical structure, navigation and interface layouts but it also improves or introduces mechanisms to deal with the six design views in an integrated way. In particular, the main contributions of Ariadne are: the introduction of a specific mechanism to establish space and time-based relationships among contents, called alignments and synchronisations respectively; the inclusion of elements to define a users structure that can be used not only for security purposes (e.g. to define adaptive accesses); and, finally, the inclusion of a high-level security model which makes possible to specify a role-based security policy, simpler and easier to maintain than group-based policies [9], using the same design entities than those used to specify other hypermedia features such as the hypertext structure.

This method proposes a development process consisting of three phases: Conceptual Design, Detailed Design and Evaluation. Each of them generates a number of products covering the six design views presented in the previous section. Although some of these products were first introduced in [5], in this paper we describe the method itself, which is summarised in figure 1. The outer boxes are the three design phases and inside each box, the different activities that have to be carried out as well as the products generated can be found. Arrows represent a sequence which is not unique but has been shown very helpful in different developments. Ariadne assumes an iterative process where the evaluation of prototypes is used to gather information to improve the design, whether conceptual or detailed. The method is explained below using the design of a research group web site as an example.

3.1 Conceptual Design Phase

At this point, the application is approached from a high level of abstraction so that solutions are expressed in terms of expected types of elements. With this purpose, the Labyrinth hypermedia model [3,7] is assumed to describe the elements and functions of any hyperdocument. The steps to be completed are represented in the five inner boxes included in the Conceptual Design in figure 1.

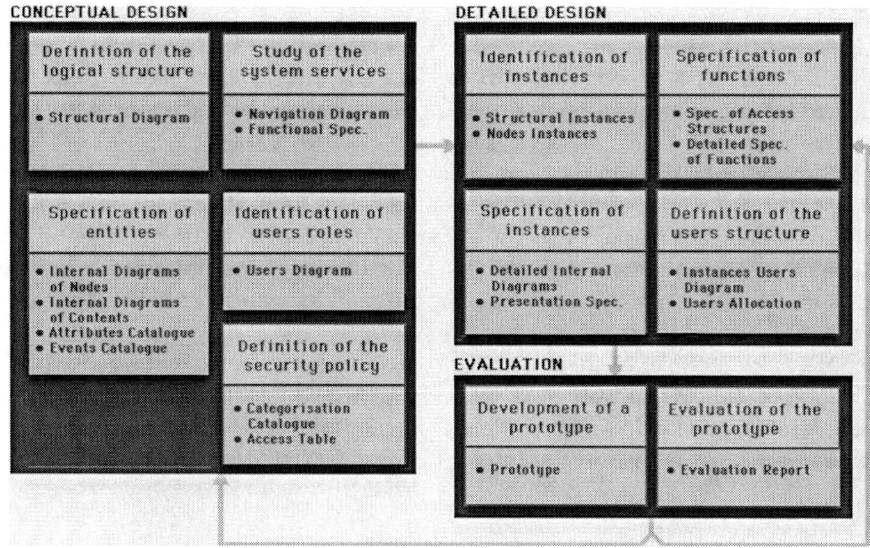

Fig. 1. The Ariadne method

There are a number of validation rules among diagrams to guarantee consistency and completeness [5].

Definition of the Logical Structure. The objective of this step is to define structural relationships. The hyperdocument structure is represented by means of composite nodes connected to their components (simple or composite nodes) by means of two possible relationships: aggregation which is a mechanism to refer to a set of nodes as a whole; and generalisation that represents an inclusion relation involving inheritance mechanisms. Moreover, references to external elements (e.g. related web pages), can be included as external nodes. Figure 2 shows the logical structure of the example using UML notation [2].

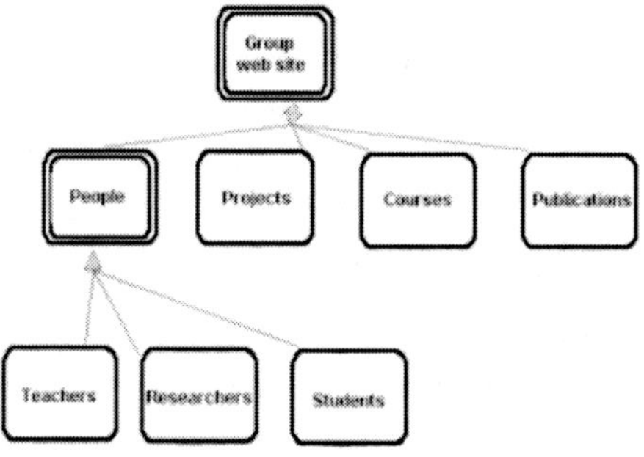

Fig. 2. Example of Structural Diagram

Study of the System Services. This step is oriented towards describing the services of the application. Two products are generated: the Navigation Diagram, that represents the navigation options; and the Functional Specifications, that gather information concerning other services (e.g. validating input data in an on-line form).

Navigation paths and tools are specified in the Navigation Diagram. Navigation paths are settled among nodes using labelled links which can be n-ary and bi-directional. For instance, the link that makes possible to browse the publications of each member is represented with the bi-directional link `writes` in figure 3. Since `People` is a generalization composite, all its components (i.e. `Teachers`, `Students` and `Researchers`) inherit this link.

Navigation tools are represented in this Diagram as nodes tagged with an "NT" (see the `Group web site` node in figure 3). At this conceptual stage, no distinction is made among different navigation tools. Their behaviours and appearances are defined in the Internal Diagrams (see description below).

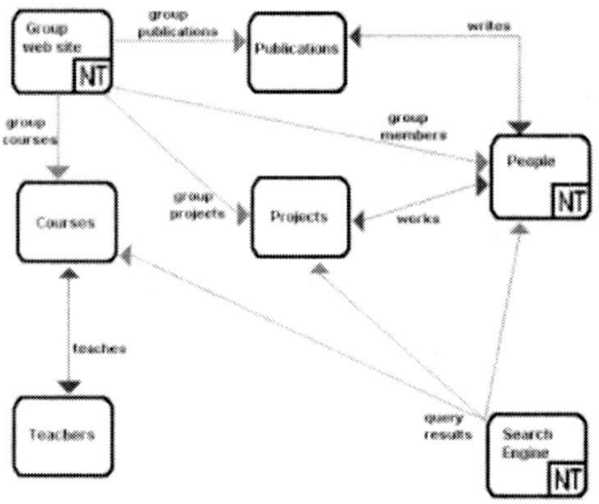

Fig. 3. Example of Navigation Diagram

Virtual links, whose source or target is procedurally defined, are not different from other links at this stage since anchors are not established yet. In the Internal Diagrams of nodes and contents (see below) virtual links are associated with an event to calcute their source or target (e.g. the links `writes` or `works`).

The other product of this activity is the set of Functional Specifications, which consists of a series of documents generated using a top-down approach. Each process is decomposed into a number of subprocesses till the lowest level of definition, made up of Labyrinth events [3,7], is achieved. A Functional Specification document is generated for each process and subprocess, including: a unique process identifier; a descriptive name; a type of function (personalisation, edition, communication and unclassified); a description of the actions performed by the process, which can be expressed using any process or control-oriented modelling technique (e.g. Data Flow Diagrams, State Transition Diagrams, Petri Nets, etc.); references to related functions and events, which provide both a forward and backward traceability mechanism.

Specification of Entities. In this step, more information about types of nodes and contents is provided in the Internal Diagrams.

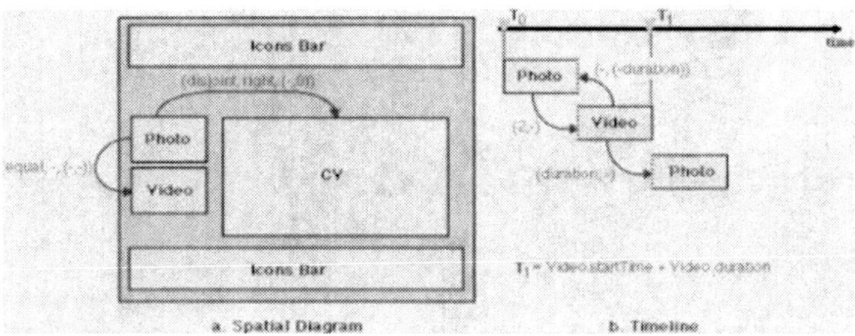

Fig. 4. Internal Diagram of node People

An Internal Diagram is created for each node in the Structural and Navigation Diagrams to specify: the type of contents it includes; its attributes (e.g. a background colour); the events that model its behaviour, and the anchors that make up the links coming/leaving to/from the node. The Internal Diagram consists of two subdiagrams where contents, anchors and events can be placed: the Spatial Diagram, which is a two dimensional space representing the node visualisation area (see figure 4.a); and the Timeline, which represents how the node evolves throughout a time interval (see figure 4.b). At this conceptual stage, specific positions are not defined, but it is possible to logically specify the appearance of a node by placing some holes that will contain kinds of contents. For instance, in the `People` node we can decide that the photo will always be placed to the left and personal data to the right (see figure 4.a). Since this layout is inherited by all the nodes generalised by the node `People`, this diagram forces to maintain a certain degree of consistency in the interface of the members pages.

Positions in the Spatial Diagram and the Timeline can be defined using logical units of space/time (e.g. T0 in figure 4.b represents the moment when the node is conveyed to the user). However to create more harmonic and dynamic presentations, space and time-based relationships can be set among contents, called alignments and synchronisations respectively [3,7]. Both relationships are depicted through directed arcs labelled to describe which constraint has to be fulfilled. In the case of aligments, that label is a triple of values (topology, direction, distance) being the latter a pair representing displacements in the X and Y axes. For instance, we can establish that the photo and curriculum vitae have to be aligned by the top and, with this purpose, an alignment arc is set between these two contents within the `People` node (see figure 4.a). Synchronisations are labelled with a tuple (start, end) representing delays in the beginning/end of the target content. Both delays can assume a predefined value (duration and startTime) or a logical unit of time. For example to model the following situation "the photo is initally shown, two units after it is replaced by a video and when the video ends the photo turns to its initial position" several relationships are defined: an alignment in figure 4.a and three synchronisation arcs in figure 4.b. More details on the alignment and synchronisation mechanisms can be found in [3,7]. Finally, events can be associated to a particular moment in the Timeline so that they are evaluated when such moment is reached.

Fig. 5. Internal Diagram of the Content Icons Bar

Contents placed in the nodes have their own Internal Diagrams where anchors, events and attributes are defined (see figure 5). Composite contents can also be defined. For instance, an icons toolbar can be modelled as an aggregated content referred to by means of a unique element: the composite `Icons Bar`. Placing this aggregation at the top and at the bottom of each node (see figure 4.a) all the icons will be presented in the same way they are organised in the `Icons Bar`. Contents that act as anchors are marked using an striped pattern and the corresponding link is associated to them. For instance, `Projects Icon` and `Publications Icon` in figure 5 are the sources of the links `works` and `writes` respectively, both of which were introduced in the Navigation Diagram (figure 3). Virtual links have an event whose entry in the Events Catalogue includes the process to derive them. For instance, the targets of the two links represented in figure 5 are calculated at runtime by means of the E13 and E14 events.

Attributes and events associated to the elements in their Internal Diagrams are fully specified in the Attibutes and Events Catalogues, which are repositories where these elements are held. For each attribute there is an entry including the property's name, its default value and the list of associated elements. For each event there is an entry including: the event unique identifier; the Condition that enables the event (the link works has been selected); the Actions performed by the event; the list of elements the event is tied to and the list of Functional Specifications that describe the event from a higher level of abstraction.

Identification of users roles. The users structure is represented by means of the Users Diagram. Such structure sets the basis of the security policy defined in the Access Table (see below) and makes possible to define user-dependent presentations as well as hyperdocument personalisations. The main purpose of this activity is to analyse which are the expected types of users of our application and, consequently, no individual users are identified but roles. A role represents

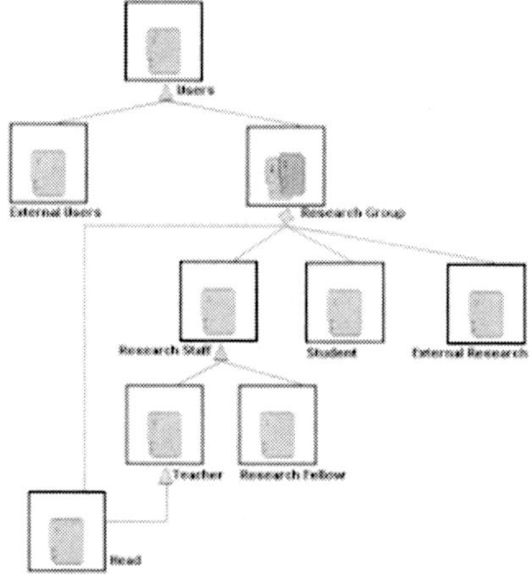

Fig. 6. Example of Users Diagram

a job function or responsibility (e.g. undergraduate and postgraduate students, teachers and so on). Roles can be specified as hierarchical structures, where specific roles are grouped into more general roles by means of generalization relationships (see the figure 6). Roles can also be grouped into teams that work together. In this case, composition reflects an aggregation relationship. While a role identifies a job function or responsibility, a team is a group of roles or users which will have some common goal without functional implications. For instance, the `Research Group` in figure 6 is a team grouping a number of people that cooperates, including `Research Staff`, `Students` and `External Researchers`. Teams are used to provide cooperating users with private work spaces.

Definition of the security policy. This step is intended for defining which actions are permitted to each user role. Two products are generated: the Categorisation Catalogue, where each content and node is assigned a security category defining the most permissive kind of operation the object can undergo; and the Access Table that implements the security model presented in [4,6]. This model uses security categories (Browsing, Personalising and Editing) to control the kind of actions users can perform on a hyperdocument and it assumes a RBAC (Role Based Access) policy [9]. Each role is allocated a manipulation category for each node and content in the hyperdocument although a default value can be used to simplify the design task. Access permissions are inherited from general roles and their values can be overriden. Private views of the hyperdocument can also be defined for each user role using a mechanism of explicit denial of access.

3.2 Detailed Design

During this phase, the abstract entities and functions specified in the previous phase are instantiated into concrete elements. Thus, while the Conceptual Design can be considered as an authoring-in-the-large process where the hyperdocument features are faced from a high level of abstraction, the Detailed Design is an authoring-in-the-small activity where the hyperdocument that will be delivered to the users is fully specified. The activities of this phase (see figure 1) are presented below.

Identification of instances. Structures defined in the Structural Diagram are instantiated to create similar hyperdocuments. For instance, the structure shown in figure 2 can be replicated to define the web sites of different research groups. Moreover, nodes identified in the previous phase are also instantiated. Thus, the node `Teacher` is replicated as many times as needed to represent all the teachers in the group.

Specification of functions. Both the Navigation Diagram and the Functional Specifications created in the Conceptual Design are now fully specified. In the first case, a Specification of Access Structures is created for each navigation tool to determine which kind of navigation aid it implements. The functions are also specified in the Detailed Specification of Functions where a low-level description of each function is provided.

Specification of instances. All the nodes and contents are described in their Detailed Internal Diagrams. The objective is to gather detailed information to create a prototype and even to fully or partly automate this process. For example, in each instance of the `Teacher` node, the holes put in its Internal Diagram representing types of contents are associated now a concrete content, whether as a text or as a reference to a file. Both contents and nodes have Presentation Specifications where details on how to convey information to the user are established. For instance, nodes can be assigned a size or they can be associated to a kind of window (full-screen, pop-up, etc.). Contents will have presentation properties that depend on their nature.

Definition of the users structure. Concerning the users structure, teams are instantiated in the Instanced Users Diagram to create as many groups as required (e.g., several research groups with the same composition). The next step is to assign specific users to the existing roles producing the Users Allocation. Thus, users will be able to exercise the abilitites specified for the roles they belong to according to the principles of RBAC. A user can be associated to more than one role and then the most permissive clearance is always applied during the hyperdocument operation.

3.3 Evaluation

Since hypermedia systems are highly interactive, the development method has to be a user-centred process where the different interface solutions have to be evaluated. Thus, prototyping and evaluation become two key activities.

Development of a prototype. Prototypes can be easily generated from the detailed design products created in the previous phase, whether using authoring tools (e.g. Authorware), mark-up languages (e.g. XML) or programming languages (e.g., Java).

Evaluation of the prototype. Evaluation is primarily aimed at providing information about the potential usability of a system in order either to improve features and functionalities within an interface or to assess a completed interface. Evaluation can be carried out using different methods including analytic, expert, empirical and experimental techniques [1]. In any case, evaluation has to be carefully prepared and planned since its results are used to modify the conceptual or detailed design to better gather the users needs.

3.4 Validation and Verification Rules

Ariadne provides a number of integrated products to specify the features of any hypermedia application. Such integration is achieved due to the inclusion of cross-references among related products and a number of inter- and intra-validation rules which ensure that each entity is fully and correctly described. For example, during the Conceptual Design, Functional Specifications refer to the corresponding entries in the Events Catalogue and vice versa, increasing both the forward and backward traceability of the processes and reactions specifications. In the same phase, an example of inter-validation rule is the one that ensures that there is an Internal Diagram for each node identified in the Structural or in the Navigation Diagram and an intra-validation rule detects if there is any overlapping among the anchors or contents specified in an Internal Diagram.

Moreover, once a product has been generated a verification procedure has to be executed to analyse if it complies the requirements of the application. The last phase of Ariadne, the evaluation, provides empirical evidence on how well requirements have been addressed since the prototype is used to collect subjective and objective data about the product utility and usability.

4 Conclusions

Hypermedia development requires very specific methods dealing with a number of design views, including navigation, presentation, data or structure, processes or function, control or interaction and security. Knowledge and experience can be borrowed from data, processes and event models but specific tools to specify navigation paths and tools and multimedia presentations are needed. In this paper we introduced Ariadne, a method aimed at gathering the peculiarities of hypermedia applications and dealing with the six design views aforementioned.

Acknowledgements. Ariadne is supported by "Dirección General de Investigación del Ministerio de Ciencia y Tecnología" (TIC2000-0402).

References

1. Benyon, D., Davies, G., Keller, L., Preece, J. and Rogers,Y.: A Guide to Usability - Usability Now!. Milton Keynes: The Open University (1990).
2. Booch, G., Jacobson, I. and Rumbaugh, J.: The Unified Modeling Language. Addison-Wesley (1998).

3. Díaz, P., Aedo, I. and Panetsos, F.: Labyrinth, an abstract model for hypermedia applications.Description of its static components. Information Systems **22**(8) (1997) 447–464.
4. Díaz, P., Aedo, I., Panetsos, F. and Ribagorda, A.: A security model for the design of hypermedia systems. Proc. of the 14th Information Security Conference (SEC98). Vienna and Budapest (September 1998) 251–260.
5. Díaz, P., Aedo, I. and Panetsos, F.: A methodological framework for the conceptual design of hypermedia systems. Proc. of the Fifth Conference on "Hypertexts and Hypermedia: Products, Tools and Methods" (H2PTM 99). Paris (September, 1999) 213–228.
6. Díaz, P., Aedo, I. and Panetsos, F.: Definition of integrity policies for hypermedia systems. In: van Biene-Hershey; M., Strous, L.A. (eds.): Integrity and Internal Control in Information Systems Strategic Views on the Need for Control. Kluwer Academic Publishers (2000) 85–98.
7. Díaz, P., Aedo, I. and Panetsos, F.: Modelling the dynamic behaviour of hypermedia applications. IEEE Transactions on Software Engineering **27** (6) (2001) 550–572.
8. Fernández, E.B., Krishnakumar, R.N., Larrondo-Petrie, M. M. and Xu, Y.: High-Level Security Issues in Multimedia/Hypertext Systems. In: Horster, P. (ed.): Communications and Multimedia Security II. Champman & Hall (1996) 13–24.
9. Ferraiolo, D.F., Barkley, J.F. and Kuhn, D.R.: A Role-Based Access Control Model and Reference Implementation within a Corporate Intranet. ACM Trans. on Information and Systems Security **2**(1) (February, 1999) 34–64.
10. Garzotto, F., Paolini, P. and Schwabe D.: HDM - A Model-Based Approach to Hypertext Application Design. ACM TOIS **11**(1) (January, 1993) 1–26.
11. Isakowitz, T., Stohr, E.A. and Balasubramanian, P.: RMM: A Methodology for structured hypermedia design. Comm. of the ACM **38**(8) (1995) 34–44.
12. Lange, D. B.: An object-oriented design method for hypermedia information systems. Proceedings of the 27th Annual Hawaii International Conference on System Sciences (1994) 366-375.
13. Lowe, D. and Hall, W.: Hypermedia and the web: an engineering approach. John Wiley & Sons. (1999).
14. Nielsen, J.: Multimedia and Hypertext: the Internet and beyond. Academic Press, Inc. (1995).
15. Schnase, J.L., Leggett, J.J., Hicks, D.L., and Szabo, R.L.: Semantic Data Modelling of Hypermedia Associations. ACM TOIS **11**(1) (1994) 27–50.
16. Schwabe, D. and Rossi, G.: Developing Hypermedia Applications using OOHDM. Workshop on Hypermedia Development Processes, Methods and Models, Hypertext'98, Pittsburgh (1998).

A General Approach to Compression of Hierarchical Indexes

Jukka Teuhola

Turku Centre for Computer Science (TUCS), Univ. of Turku
Lemminkäisenkatu 14 A, FIN-20520 Turku, FINLAND
Email: teuhola@cs.utu.fi

Abstract. Tree-structured indexes typically restrict the search domain level by level, which means that the search information can be encoded more and more compactly on the way down. This simple observation is here formulated as a general principle of index compression. Saving storage space is one advantage, but more important is reduction of disk accesses, because more entries can be packed into a page. The index fan-out can be increased, reducing the average height of the tree. The applicability of compression is studied for several popular one- and multi-dimensional indexes. Experiments with the well-known spatial index, R*-tree, show that with modest assumptions and simple coding, 30-40% reduction of disk accesses is obtainable for intersection queries. Compression of index entries can be used together with other index compaction techniques, such as quantization and pointer list compression.

1 Introduction

Traditionally, data compression has been regarded mainly as a way of reducing the external storage costs of data. However, today *transfer time* is a more important reason for compression. It is true that disk technology has progressed, and access times improved, but not as much as processor speeds. Therefore, it has become more and more practical to trade disk accesses for compression/decompression procedures.

New application areas of databases, such as CAD, multimedia, GIS, data warehouses, digital libraries, office documents, etc. store vast amounts of data. Compression is commonly used in these areas, and standard techniques e.g. for text and images can be applied. However, the stored datasets are most often equipped with various kinds of indexes, in order to support fast retrieval. A large part of the access cost can be attributed to accessing the indexes, and thus index compression can bring similar advantages as compression of data itself. For complex data types, also indexes are complex; *multidimensional* indexes are a challenging target for compression.

Index compression can be divided into two main categories:

1. Compression of search information (e.g. keys)
2. Compression of pointers to data

H.C. Mayr et al. (Eds.): DEXA 2001, LNCS 2113, pp. 775–784, 2001.

For simple indexes, the gains of these techniques depend on the uniqueness of keys: For primary indexes, the former is most applicable, whereas for secondary indexes the latter can bring large benefits [18]. Here we suggest general guidelines for compressing search information in hierarchically structured indexes. There are two orthogonal ways of reducing the size of search-directing items:

1. *Approximation*, also called *quantization*, usually omits the least significant bits of the search-directing entries, see e.g. [5]. This is often *lossy*, increasing the number of 'false drops'.
2. *Compression* applies a *lossless* coding scheme, based on a *model* of data distribution. The precision of the model dictates the gain obtained.

By applying both approximation and compression, we can squeeze the index entries to a fraction of the original size. In this paper we study only (lossless) compression, adapted to various kinds of indexes. Especially, we restrict ourselves to *one-pass*, adaptive schemes, where the model is built on the fly, on the basis of the processed part of the index. Then, there is no need to store the model.

The key idea in developing a compression method is to take advantage of *clustering* of data, which is a natural property of all indexes: they try to reduce the search space by partitioning the data set into local subsets. A cluster with tight bounds enables compact representation of the cluster elements. Based on this observation, we first present the general compression scheme in Section 2. Thereafter we adapt the scheme to specific types of indexes.

2 General Index Compression Scheme

Assume that we have a paged, hierarchical index, with a number of entries per page (node), restricting the values of entries in the child pages. We have at least two possible bases for compressing an entry x:

1. entries in the parent (more generally ancestors) of x,
2. entries processed before x on the current page.

Either or both of these can be missing (for root entries, and the first entry of a page), but default values can then be applied. Using the parent entries, we get some kind of boundaries for x, enabling more compact coding since there are fewer alternative values. If not more is known, a uniform distribution withing the bounds can be assumed for x, resulting in a simple fixed-length code for each alternative value. Notice, however, that the code length is only *locally* fixed: A certain range implies a related length, but different ranges produce different lengths. Fixed-length coding can be somewhat improved by the *phasing* technique [3] if the range is not a power of two.

By taking advantage of the processed entries in the current index node, further compression can be achieved. Assuming that the entries are somehow *ordered*, at least two possible approaches can be taken:

1. *Neighbor coding*: The predecessor p_x of entry x is assumed to be the closest to x among processed entries. Then we can represent x as $p_x + \Delta x$, where '+' should be understood generally. Now it is sufficient to store Δx, which probably has a very skew distribution, and can be coded efficiently, possibly by a variable-length code. The bounds obtained from ancestors are also utilized in choosing the coding scheme.
2. *Interpolative coding*: Assume that the entries on the page constitute a well-ordered sequence of values. The middle element *mid* is encoded first within the inherited/default range *lower..upper*. Then, the middle element mid_1 of the first half is encoded within *lower..mid*, and the middle element mid_2 of the second half is encoded within *mid..upper*, etc. This simple and effective coding scheme was suggested in [13] for compressing inverted lists. As in binary search, the page entries constitute an implicit binary tree, where each node further restricts the range of its descendants.

All the information needed in coding is obtained along the access path, which is followed anyway during search and update.

The neighbor-based compression scheme often involves coding of small numbers from a skew distribution. If we know the distribution, adaptive *entropy coding*, such as *arithmetic coding* [15] can be applied, which gets close to the information-theoretic lower bound (*entropy*). However, often we do not know the precise distribution, or we cannot afford to use much time for en-/decoding. A *universal coding scheme* is then one alternative, see [9]. If an exponential distribution is assumed, γ-*coding* is a good choice.

Interpolative coding [13] is mainly applicable to increasing sequences of values on a page. We can also view it as a coding technique of deltas in the special case that all delta-values are positive.

Compression of index pages results in a higher number of entries per page, and thereby in a larger fan-out of nodes. Thus, not only is the page count reduced, but possibly also the tree height. These are the main goals of compression, and enable more effective index processing.

We summarize the general guidelines for index compression:

1. Determine the global bounds of the indexed domain.
2. Use ancestor (or global) information to set local bounds for the entries on the current page.
3. Encode the page entries one by one, so that the processed entries are used to further restrict the bounds or distribution of the next entry to be encoded.

As for related work, we want to mention the index compression techniques of Goldstein et al. [10]. Their emphasis was in maximizing the decompression speed, by storing in-page code tables. Our main goal, instead, is a high compression ratio. Another interesting reference is *GiST* [12], a generalized index structure defined as an extensible data type, having abstract methods also for compression and decompression. These must be tailored for each 'instantiation' of GiST; our approach could be useful in this job.

3 Compression of B-Trees

The delta-technique described above is well-known in B-tree indexes, especially with alphabetic keys. It goes by the name of *front compression*, where we encode the number of prefix characters that are common with the predecessor. For example, for successive keys "COMMON" and "COMPUTER", the latter can be represented as 3-PUTER, where number 3 is encoded for example as a byte (i.e. fixed-length code), restricting the prefix size to 255.

In B^+-trees, another compaction scheme is useful, namely *tail compression*, where only a sufficient number of characters is stored to delimit the key from predecessors and successors. Combined front and tail compression is used e.g. in IBM's VSAM method. If tail compression is used on the leaf level of a dense index, *false drops* may occur in queries. Thus, tail compression belongs to approximation methods, and we do not discuss it further.

Let us take an example of the parent-neighbor scheme for integer keys. Assume that we know from the parent node that the range of keys on a page is 12..34. Assume further that there are three keys, namely {21, 28, 31} to be encoded. Using fixed-length coding within *lower..upper*, the number of bits is $\lceil \log_2(upper - lower + 1) \rceil$ per entry. The example codes are derived as follows.

Key	Delta	Range size	#Bits	Code
21	$21 - 12 = 9$	$34 - 12 + 1 = 23$	5	01001
28	$28 - 21 = 7$	$34 - 21 + 1 = 14$	4	0111
31	$31 - 28 = 3$	$34 - 28 + 1 = 7$	3	011

Using only the parent-based information (range 12..34), we would need $3 \cdot 5 = 15$ bits, instead of 12.

With compressed keys, the B^+-tree can be condensed, and the fan-out increased, resulting possibly in reduced tree height. In fact, the definition of the B^+-tree must be changed, somewhat: We cannot set a fixed order for the tree, to set limits to the node fan-out. Overflow can be handled normally: the page is split into two halves with an equal (± 1) number of entries in both. However, detection of underflow must be based on the space utilization of the page. A constant (probably between 40 and 50 %) threshold must be set.

4 Compression of Multidimensional Point Indexes

Multidimensional data structures are usually divided into *point access methods* (PAMs) and *spatial access methods* (SAMs). PAMs are often used for indexing multiattribute data, *feature vectors* of complex objects, *data cubes* in data warehouses, etc. SAMs store objects having spatial extent, application areas being computer-aided design, geographic information systems, image and multimedia databases, etc. Spatial access methods are applicable to points, as well. There exist a large number of PAMs, so we take only a few representatives and consider, how the general compression scheme can be applied to them.

4.1 Space-Filling Curves

The simplest approach to organize a set of multidimensional points is to make a transformation to 1-dimensional space. *Z-curve* [14] and Peano-Hilbert curve are linearizations of point sets into locality-preserving sequences. A one-dimensional index is sufficient to support their accessing, as exemplified by the *UB-tree* [1]. Thus, the B$^+$-tree compression described above is directly applicable.

4.2 K-d-Tree Family

K-d-tree [4] is a binary search tree for k dimensions. For each node, we know a *box* (hyper-rectangle), within which all descendants reside. The node key splits the box into two, according to one dimension. The halves are then related to subtrees. The choice of split dimension is done in alternating order. The split point is typically the *median* of the point coordinates, for balancing.

There have occurred many generalizations of the k-d-tree for external memory, such as *K-D-B-tree* [16]. In principle, the binary tree must be partitioned into pages. However, we can use the virtual binary tree as the basis of compression. Assume that a node to be compressed contains a certain split value x in dimension d. Having descended to that node, zero or more splits according to d have been made, either in ancestors, or on the current page. These splits determine an interval, where x must be located. The representation of x takes at most $\lceil \log_2(\mathit{interval\ length}) \rceil$ bits. This is thus a generalization of B$^+$-tree compression.

4.3 Metric Trees

Metric index structures apply to a more general class of domains, where *distances* between stored objects are available, but they are not necessarily coordinate-based Euclidean distances, see [17]. An example is the *M-tree* described in [7], where entries in an index node are enclosed in a *hypersphere*, with a certain center and radius. Child spheres are located inside the parent sphere. The goal is to make the spheres as disjoint as possible, and to minimize their radii.

The success of M-tree compression depends on the possibility of compactly representing the delta information, i.e. difference of the object from either the page center or the nearest neighbor within the page. Since the neighbor must be encoded first, the neighbor relationships constitute a virtual tree structure, and the *minimum spanning tree* is an obvious choice to minimize the deltas (cf. [6]). To avoid representing the spanning tree, we can use just a linear order for the entries within page. To minimize the deltas, we should find the minimum *Hamiltonian path* through the entries. This is closely related to the *traveling salesman problem*, which is NP-hard, but numerous good heuristics exist.

We conjecture that in most applications, clustering of objects in metric trees ensures that the delta-technique is effective. However, tailoring is needed for each specific space and metric. As an example, we consider the *S-tree* [8], which is an index structure for *signatures*, i.e. bit vectors generated by randomization from attributes of complex objects. Signatures act as filters in multiattribute retrieval. The natural distance measure is the *Hamming distance*, i.e. number of differing bit positions. S-tree is a kind of metric tree, but it does not store explicit centers and radii. The actual object signatures reside on leaf pages. The parent contains the *bitwise OR* of the signatures on each child page. An upper bound to the Hamming distance between parent and child is known: If the parent signature contains a 0-bit, then the child contains it also, and the child 0-bit can be omitted. This represents the parent-based compression of our general scheme. If we additionally want to apply the delta technique, we can proceed as follows.

1. Arrange the signatures of the page into linear order, trying to minimize the sum of Hamming distances of adjacent signatures, e.g. by applying traveling salesman heuristics.
2. Store the first signature as such. For the rest, compute the *exclusive OR* with the left neighbor and compress the created *sparse* bit vector using some of the well-known techniques [18].

The original signature can be recovered by XORing because the neighbor will be decoded first (cf. [6]). Similarly, the suppressed zeroes can be copied from the parent to the child signature, because the parent is decoded first.

5 Compression of Spatial Indexes

Of the various spatial index structures, we restrict our study to the well-known *R-tree* [11], and its variant, *R*-tree* [2], but the ideas can be generalized. R-tree utilizes the typical spatial construct: *minimum bounding (hyper-)rectangle, MBR*, called also *bounding box*. The MBRs of spatial objects are represented on the leaf level of the R-tree. For each page (except the root), the MBR of all rectangles on that page is stored in the parent, to serve searching. The structure is thus organized hierarchically into *nested* MBRs, where each level of nesting corresponds to a level in the R-tree. A small 2-dimensional example is given in Fig. 1.

The goal in building the R-tree is to minimize the overlap between MBRs of different branches, and hereby minimize the number of paths to be followed in queries. In this job, R*-tree usually works better than the basic R-tree.

It is rather easy to apply our general compression approach to R-trees. The parent MBR gives bounds to the MBR of the child rectangles. Thus, for each dimension d, we know the lower and upper bounds (denote l_d^{MBR} and u_d^{MBR}), within which we can compactly represent the bounds (denote l_d^{cur} and u_d^{cur}) of the current rectangle in dimension d, in the same way as for the 1-dimensional B^+-tree above. A simple improvement to this is based on the observation that when encoding u_d^{cur}, we know that it is in the interval $[l_d^{cur}, u_d^{MBR}]$, which is tighter than the parent interval $[l_d^{MBR}, u_d^{MBR}]$, and gives better compression.

For neighbor-based enhancement of compression, an obvous solution is as follows. Choose one dimension (d) and sort the rectangles of the page according to l_d. When encoding l_d^{cur}, encode it relative to l_d^{prev} of the previous rectangle, instead of l_d^{MBR} of the parent. However, only one dimension can be taken advantage of in this approach.

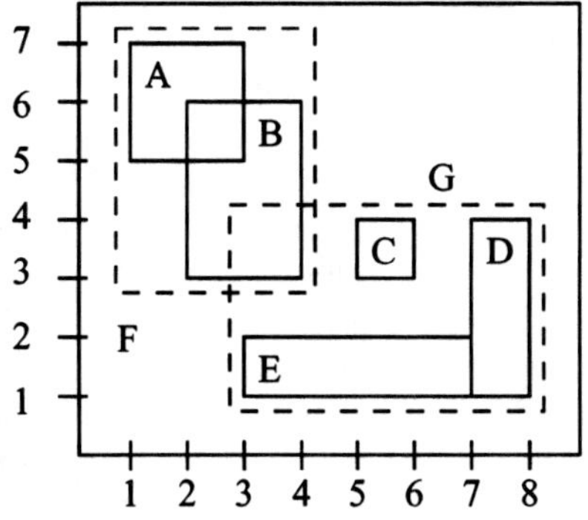

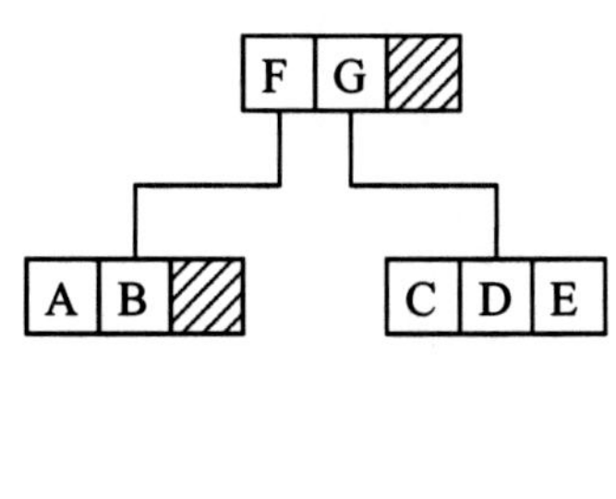

Box	Parent	l_x			u_x			l_y			u_y		
		Val	Range	Bits	Val	Range	Bits	Val	Range	Bits	Val	Range	Bits
A	F	1	1..4	2	3	1..4	2	5	3..7	3	7	5..7	2
B	F	2	1..4	2	4	2..4	2	3	3..7	3	6	3..7	3
C	G	5	3..8	3	6	5..8	2	3	1..4	2	4	3..4	1
D	G	7	3..8	3	8	7..8	1	1	1..4	2	4	1..4	2
E	G	3	3..8	3	7	3..8	3	1	1..4	2	2	1..4	2
F		1	1..8	3	4	1..8	3	3	1..8	3	7	3..8	3
G		3	1..8	3	8	3..8	3	1	1..8	3	4	1..8	3
Bitsum				19			16			18			16

Fig. 1. Coding of nested rectangles in a sample R-tree

6 Experiment: Compression of R*-Trees

In order to get concrete results to support our claims, we performed some practical experiments. For that, we chose the R*-tree structure [2], because of its usefulness and popularity in low-dimensional spaces, both as a point and spatial index. We used the simple version of our compression scheme, as in Fig. 1: A lower value l_d^{cur} of the current rectangle in dimension d is restricted by l_d^{MBR} and u_d^{MBR} of the parent, and the upper value u_d^{cur} is restricted by l_d^{cur} and u_d^{MBR}.

We used a synthetic set of 2-dimensional rectangles, uniformly distributed in an $M \times M$ square. Side lengths were uniformly distributed integers. This represents the worst case for compression; higher gains can be expected for non-uniform distributions, cf. [10]. The parameters and their default values were:

- P = page size (4 Kbytes)
- N = number of data rectangles (10^5)
- M = side length of the total space (10^6)
- S = average side length of rectangles (10^4)
- Minimum page load for results of split (40%)
- Proportion of re-inserts at overflow (30%)

The last two are general recommendations for the R*-tree. The pages were compressed when written to disk and uncompressed when read from disk. A 'sufficient' buffer size was reserved for pages, because when uncompressed, they take more that P bytes. Overflow at insert was determined by the bit count after encoding (before writing). Because the compression ratio varies, the number of entries per page is also variable. Special buffering techniques were not considered in our experiments. We counted *logical* reads and writes (= buffer or disk I/O).

Fig. 2(a) shows the number of pages required by the normal and compressed R*-trees for N up to 10^5. Here we used 32 bits for the uncompressed coordinates. The pointers (also 32 bits) were not compressed in either version, setting a limit to the compression ratio. With the chosen parameters, almost 40% saving in space is obtained. For $M = 10^5$ and $S = 10^3$, already 49% saving is obtained.

The number of logical (buffer or physical) disk accesses for building the R*-tree by repeated inserts is depicted in Fig. 2(b), showing a reasonable reduction of accesses. The somewhat irregular behavior of the curves results from the integral number of tree levels. The growth of tree heights is illustrated in Fig. 2(c) where the page size P was exceptionally chosen to be only 256 bytes, to get a better conception of the general behavior.

Perhaps the most interesting results are given in Fig. 2(d), reporting the number of page accesses in *intersection queries*. The results are averages of 1000 queries. We used our largest test case of $N = 10^5$ rectangles, and varied the average side length of the query rectangle up to half of the domain interval. For large query rectangles, the saving of accesses varies between 35–37%; for smaller, the relative gain is also smaller.

There is a trade-off between compression time and disk access time. We executed the experiments on a two-processor 400 MHz Pentium II, with 512 MB main memory. The average CPU time for rectangle insert was 0.00027 sec for the uncompressed, and 0.00334 sec for the compressed R*-tree. This 1:12 ratio is more than compensated by the smaller number of disk accesses in the compressed version. For intersection queries, the ratios of CPU times varied between 1:5 (for large query rectangles) and 1:12 (for small query rectangles). Again, the compression overhead is only a fraction of the total time. Assuming a 'cold' situation with an empty buffer at the start, and a typical value of 10 msec per disk access, the net time saving with our compressed R*-tree is still more than 30% for large query rectangles.

Though restricted, the experiments give a strong indication of the potential benefits that can be obtained by index compression, in general. Enhancement of the coder and tailoring to other index types are left for future work.

7 Conclusion

With new data-intensive and multidimensional applications of databases, different kinds of indexes play a central role in making the processing more effective. We suggested that sophisticated compression is one way to improve the indexing performance. We studied only tree-structured indexes, where the path from root

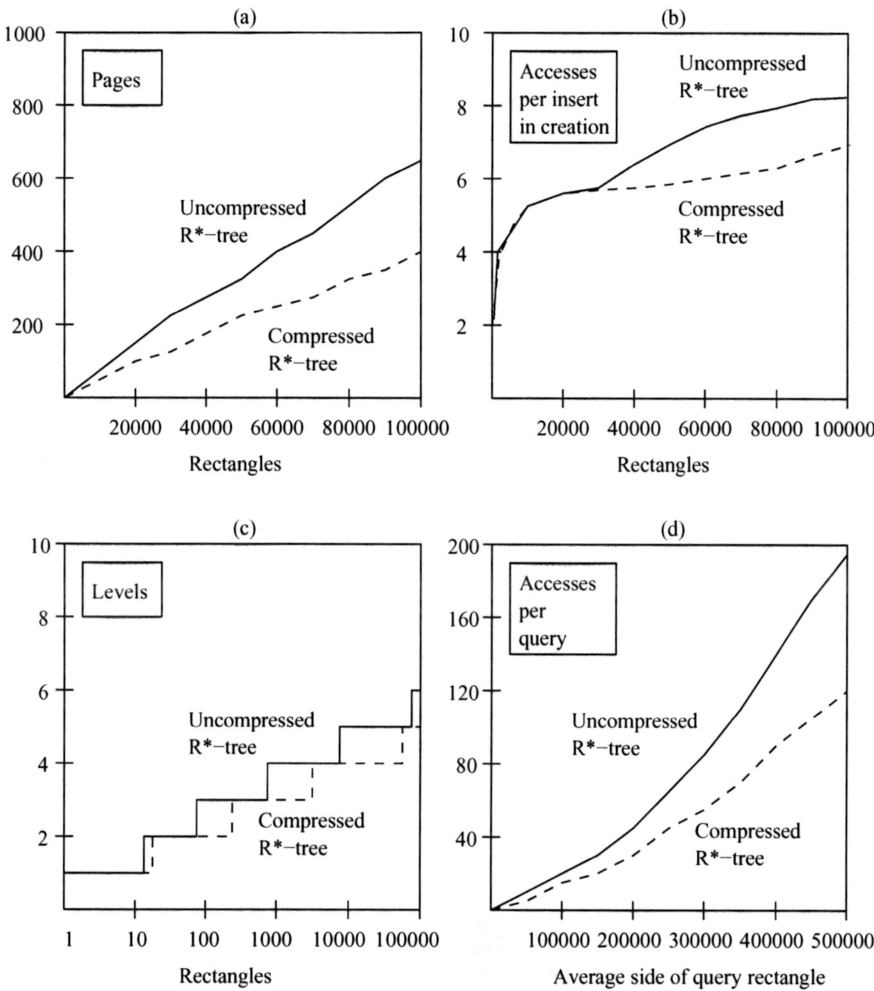

Fig. 2. Compression results for R*-tree

to leaf represents a stepwise restriction of the domain, enabling more compact representation of lower levels.

The purpose of this paper was mainly to reveal the potential of compression. Therefore, we gave only rather general descriptions of possible approaches for a few types of hierarchical indexes. The final tailoring must be done for each index type separately. Our experiments with R*-trees revealed that a very simple compression scheme can easily bring a saving of 30–40% both in space and time. Due to more and more powerful processors, the processing time required for compression and decompression is negligible compared to disk access time. Thus it becomes affordable to apply also more sophisticated coding techniques.

Index compression can in many cases be combined with index approximation. Together, they can reduce heights of index trees and increase their fan-out. This is especially beneficial in high-dimensional cases, where large parts of the index must often be scanned in solving queries. Compression is thus one way of fighting against the so called 'curse of dimensionality', which tends to reduce the usefulness of hierarchical indexes.

References

1. Bayer, R.: The Universal B-Tree for Multidimensional Indexing, Technical Rep. TUM-19637, Technische Universität München (1996).
2. Beckmann, R., Kriegel, H.-P., Schneider, R., and Seeger, B.: "The R*-tree: An Efficient and Robust Access Method for Points and Rectangles", Proc. ACM SIGMOD Conf., Atlantic City, NJ (1990) 322–331.
3. Bell, T.C., Cleary, J.G., and Witten, I.H.: "Text Compression", Prentice-Hall (1990).
4. Bentley, J.L.: "Multidimensional Binary Search Trees in Database Applications", *IEEE Trans. on Software Eng.*, Vol. SE-5, No. 4 (1979) 333–340.
5. Berchtold, S., Böhm, C., Jagadish, H.V., Kriegel, H.-P., and Sander, J,: "Independent Quantization: An Index Compression Technique for High-Dimensional Data Spaces", Proc. 16th ICDE Conf., San Diego, CA (2000) 577–588.
6. Bookstein, A., and Klein, S.T.: "Compression of Correlated Bit-Vectors", *Inf. Systems*, Vol. 16, No. 4 (1991) 387–400.
7. Ciaccia, P., Patella, M., and Zezula, P.: "M-tree: An Efficient Access Method for Metric Spaces", Proc. 23rd VLDB Conf., Athens, Greece (1997) 426–435.
8. Deppisch, U.: "S-Tree: A Dynamic Balanced Signature Index for Office Retrieval", Proc. ACM Conf. on Res. and Dev. in Inf. Retrieval, Pisa, Italy (1986) 77–87.
9. Elias, P.: "Universal Codeword Sets and Representations of the Integers", *IEEE Trans. Information Theory*, Vol. IT-21, No. 2 (1975) 194–203.
10. Goldstein, J., Ramakrishnan, R., and Shaft, U.: "Compressing Relations and Indexes", Proc. 14th ICDE Conf., Orlando, FA (1998) 370–379.
11. Guttman, A.: "R-trees: A Dynamic Index Structure for Spatial Searching", Proc. ACM SIGMOD Conf., Boston, MA (1984) 47–57.
12. Hellerstein, J.M., Naughton, J.F., and Pfeffer, A.: "Generalized Search Trees for Database Systems", Proc. 21st VLDB Conf., Zurich, Switzerland (1995) 562–573.
13. Moffat, A., and Stuiver, L.: "Exploiting Clustering in Inverted File Compression", Proc. 6th Data Compression Conf. (DCC), Snowbird, UT (1996) 82–91.
14. Orenstein, J.A., and Merrett, T.H.: "A Class of Data Structures for Associative Searching", Proc. 3rd ACM SIGACT-SIGMOD-SIGART Symp. on Principles of Database Systems, Waterloo, Ontario, Canada (1984) 181–190.
15. Rissanen, J.J.: "Arithmetic Coding", *IBM J. Res. Develop.*, Vol. 23, No. 2 (1979) 149–162.
16. Robinson, J.T.: "The K-D-B-Tree: A Search Structure for Large Multidimensional Dynamic Indexes", Proc. ACM SIGMOD Conf., Ann Arbor, MI (1981) 10–18.
17. Uhlmann, J.K.: "Satisfying General Proximity/Similarity Queries with Metric Trees", *Inf. Proc. Letters*, Vol. 40, No. 4 (1991) 175–179.
18. Witten, I.H., Moffat, A., and Bell, T.C.: "Managing Gigabytes – Compressing and Indexing Documents and Images", Morgan Kaufmann Publ. (1999).

Index and Data Allocation in Mobile Broadcast

Chen Qun, Andrew Lim, Zhu Yi

Department of Computer Science
National University of Singapore
3 Science Drive 2, Singapore 117543
Email: {chenqun,alim,zhuyi}@comp.nus.edu.sg

Abstract. In mobile computing, a periodic broadcast of frequently requested data can reduce the workload of up-link channel, decreasing the energy consumption dramatically. Many indexing and scheduling techniques have been considered for wireless data broadcast. In this paper, we propose an efficient algorithm for the Optimal Index and Data Allocation problem, which minimizes the access latency.

1 Introduction

Rapid advances in computer software/hardware and wireless network technologies have led to the popularity of wireless computing. Trends are moving towards mobile users carrying small, battery powered palmtops with wireless connections. Organizing and accessing data on wireless communication channels becomes a challenge. There are two fundamental modes providing users with information:

1. *Broadcasting Mode.* Data is periodically broadcast on the downlink channel. Accessing broadcast data does not require uplink transmission and is "listen only". Querying involves simple *filtering* of the incoming data stream according to a user specified "filter".
2. *On-Demand Mode.* The client requests a piece of data on the uplink channel and the server responds by sending this data to the client on the downlink channel.

In practice, both modes are used. The most frequently accessed pieces of data will be broadcasted. Since the cost of broadcasting does not depend on the number of users, this method scales with the number of users. The disadvantage of data broadcasting is that data can only be broadcast sequentially. So users need to wait for the required data to appear on the broadcast channel.

Imielinski et al. [1] described two index methods to broadcast data, *(1,m) indexing* and *Distributed Indexing*, where each data item is considered to have the same access frequency. The *access time*(the time elapsed from the moment a user poses a request to the moment the result is downloaded by the user) and *tuning time*(the time spent by the user listening to a channel) are used to estimate the response time and the power consumption for a data request. If each data item has different access frequencies, two possible approaches may be

H.C. Mayr et al. (Eds.): DEXA 2001, LNCS 2113, pp. 785–794, 2001.

adopted. One is to broadcast the popular data more often, which minimizes the average access time ([2, 3]).

The other is to construct a skewed index tree with the popular data having a shorter path from the root of the index tree; This minimizes the average tuning time ([4, 5]). The construction of this index tree is analogous to that of the Huffman code, which is pointed out in [5]. However, users may fail to find a desired data item by traversing the Huffman tree. Another class of Huffman trees termed *alphabetic Huffman tree* was proposed in [6], which functioned as a binary search tree. This was extended to k-ary search trees in [5] such that by adjusting the fanout of the tree, a tree node can fit in a wireless packet of any size. In this paper, we consider this k-ary search tree as our index tree and discuss the Optimal Index and Data Allocation Problem.

Shou-Chih Lo *et al.*[7] proposed a solution to find the optimal index and data problem. In [7], all possible allocations were represented as a tree in which the optimal solution was searched; then a pruning strategy was proposed to reduce the search space greatly based on some properties. However, the pruning algorithm applies only to problems with small input size. When the size of the broadcast data is large, two heuristics *Index Tree Shrinking* and *Index Tree Sorting* are offered to solve the same problem. Their experiments showed that when the access frequency varies greatly among data nodes, these two heuristics perform badly.

2 Problem Description

Each periodic broadcast constitutes a broadcast cycle. The server will adjust the content of each broadcast cycle to satisfy the current needs from clients. The logic unit of a broadcast is the bucket. Each bucket in the broadcast can accommodate an index node or a data node. The size of an index tree is assumed to be equal to the size of a data node. The user has to first tune in to the broadcast channel to get the bucket containing the root of the index tree and then continues the data access. Thus the access time can be divided into two parts: *probe wait* and *data wait.* The *probe wait* is the time to get the bucket containing the root of the index tree; The *data wait* begins at the time after the *probe wait* and ends at the moment when the required data item is retrieved. Optimal Index and Data Problem is about minimizing the data wait.

In [7], the **Multi-Channels Index and Data Allocation Problem** is defined as follows:

Definition 1. *We are given multiple broadcast channels and an index tree T. Let the broadcast channels be $C = \{C_1, C_2, \cdots, C_k\}$, the set of index nodes in the index tree be $I = \{I_1, I_2, \cdots, I_m\}$, and the set of data nodes in the index tree be $D = \{D_1, D_2, \cdots, D_n\}$. Each data node D_i is associated with a weight $W(D_i)$ indicating the average data access frequency for the node. Assume that one bucket is transmitted in one slot of the broadcast channel in one time unit. Then, an index and data allocation can be represented as a mapping function* *f:I* $\cup$ *D* $\longrightarrow$ *C* $\times$ *S, where S denotes the domain of channel slots. A feasible allocation has to satisfy the condition in which a child node should be broadcast after its parent node in the index tree. Let* $N(D_i)$ *denote the offset in terms of channel slots between the first bucket of a broadcast cycle and data node* D_i*. The average* data wait *for accessing the data nodes can be obtained by:*

$$ADW(T) = \frac{\sum_{D_i \in D} W(D_i) \cdot N(D_i)}{\sum_{D_i \in D} W(D_i)} \tag{1}$$

We now focus on the example index tree in Figure 1. The data wait for the allocation shown in figure 1 is $\frac{(20\times3+8\times4+18\times6+6\times7)}{(20+8+18+6)} = 4.65$.

Our goal is to find an optimal allocation which minimizes formula(1). There may be more than one optimal allocation for a given index tree. In this paper, we first consider the index and data allocation on one channel, then extend our algorithm to handle the multiple channel situation.

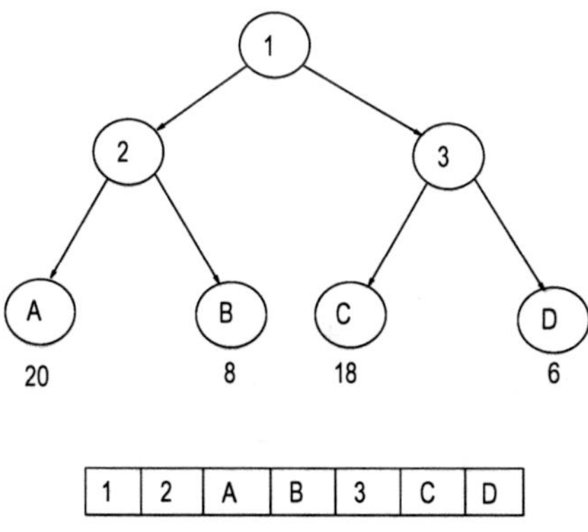

Fig. 1. An Example Index Tree and One-Channel Allocation

3 Preliminaries

In this section, we introduce some definitions and lemmas used in designing the algorithm.

Definition 2. *For an allocation segment S consisting of index and data nodes, we define the segment S's* **priority** *as* $P(S) = \frac{\sum W(D_i)}{N(S)}$*, in which* $\sum W(D_i)$ *means the total weight of data nodes in S, and where N(S) is the total number of nodes in S.*

Lemma 1. *For two allocation segments S_1 and S_2, we assume that $P(S_2) \leq P(S_1)$, and S is the resulting segment of combining S_1 and S_2, $S = \{S_1, S_2\}$ or $S = \{S_2, S_1\}$, then $P(S_2) \leq P(S) \leq P(S_1)$.*

Proof: $W(S)$ denotes the total weight of data nodes in segment S; $N(S)$ denotes the total number of nodes in S.

$$\begin{aligned} & P(S_2) \leq P(S) \\ \Longleftrightarrow \quad & \frac{W(S_2)}{N(S_2)} \leq \frac{W(S_1)+W(S_2)}{N(S_1)+N(S_2)} \\ \Longleftrightarrow \quad & W(S_2)N(S_1) \leq W(S_1)N(S_2) \\ \Longleftrightarrow \quad & P(S_2) \leq P(S_1) \end{aligned}$$

Similarly, we can prove that $P(S) \leq P(S_1)$.

Intuitively, when allocating nodes in an index tree, we prefer to allocate segments with higher priority before segments with lower priority. This is illustrated by the following lemma.

Lemma 2. *There are two allocation segments S_1 and S_2; and $S = \{S_1, S_2\}$ and $S' = \{S_2, S_1\}$ are both feasible allocations. It means that there is no index node in S_1 that is the ancestor of nodes in S_2; similarly there is no index node in S_2 that is the ancestor of nodes in S_1. If $P(S_1) > P(S_2)$, then S is a better allocation than S' in terms of the objective function of the OIDA problem.*

Proof: The objective function of the OIDA problem is formula(1); Because $\sum W(D_i)$ in any feasible allocation that remains unchanged, and our goal is to minimize $\sum(W(D_i)N(D_i))$, which is denoted as $TW(S)$.

When we exchange positions of S_1 and S_2, the relative positions of nodes in S_1 and S_2 remain unchanged. So

$$\begin{aligned} & TW(S) - TW(S') \\ & \quad = W(S_2)N(S_1) - W(S_1)N(S_2) \\ & \quad < 0, since P(S_2) < P(S_1) \end{aligned}$$

So, $TW(S) < TW(S')$; S is a better allocation than S'.

Definition 3. *For an index and data node allocation $S = \{N_1, N_2, \cdots, N_k\}$, in which N_i is an index or data node, there are k prefix segments $S_1, S_2, \cdots, S_k$. $S_i = \{N_1, N_2, \cdots, N_i\}$, for all $1 \leq i \leq k$; If $P(S_j) = max\{P(S_i)$, for all $1 \leq i \leq k\}$, we call S_j the* **Most Profitable Prefix Segment** *(simplified as* **MPPS***) of S.*

There may be more than one **MPPS** for an allocation S. Another fact we noticed is that **MPPS** always ends with a data node. Otherwise, it ends with an index node. Then we can get a prefix segment with higher priority by deleting the index node from the **MPPS**. This is a contradiction.

Definition 4. *Among all* **MPPS** *of an allocation S, the one with the maximal node number is called the* **Longest Profitable Prefix Segment** *(simplified as* **LMPPS***).*

LMPPS is important because it is uninterruptible when merging separate allocations into one. This is shown in the following theorem.

Definition 5. *For an index and data allocation S, we find its* **LMPPS***, denoted as* S_1*; We specify* $S = S - S_1$*, and repeat the above procedure until* $|S| = 0$*. At last, we get a series of* **LMPPS***,* $S_1, S_2, \cdots, S_k$*. Obviously* $S = \{S_1, S_2, \cdots, S_k\}$*. We call segments* $(S_1, S_2, \cdots, S_k)$ *S'* **Profit Segments***.*

Lemma 3. *For an index and data allocation S, if* $S = \{S_1, S_2, \cdots, S_k\}$*, in which* $S_1, S_2, \cdots, S_k$ *are S's profit segments, then* $P(S_1) > P(S_2) \cdots > P(S_k)$*.*

Proof: By contradiction. If $P(S_1) \leq P(S_2)$, then $P(S_1) \leq P(\{S_1, S_2\})$(according to **Lemma 1**).This is contradictory to the fact that S_1 is the **LMPPS** of S. Similarly we can prove that $P(S_i) > P(S_i + 1)$, for $2 \leq i \leq k - 1$.

4 Merge-Allocation Theorem

Now we are ready to introduce an important theorem.

Theorem 1. *(***Merge-Allocation Theorem***) There are two separate allocations* S_1 *and* S_2*. There is no index node in* S_1 *that is the ancestor of nodes in* S_2*; Similarly there is no index node in* S_2 *that is the ancestor of nodes in* S_1*. And* $S_1 = \{S_{11}, S_{12}, \cdots, S_{1m}\}$*, in which segments* $S_{11}, S_{12}, \cdots, S_{1m}$ *are* S_1*'s profit segments;* $S_2 = \{S_{21}, S_{22}, \cdots, S_{2n}\}$*, in which segments* $S_{21}, S_{22}, \cdots, S_{2n}$ *are* S_2*'s profit segments.*

We want to merge S_1 *and* S_2 *into one allocation. We denote the set composed of all feasible merged allocations in which the relative positions of nodes in* S_1 *and* S_2 *remain unchanged as* **MergeSet***. We assume that S' is an element in* **MergeSet***. Then if node* N_i *is positioned before* N_j *in* S_1*, then* N_i *should still be positioned before* N_j *in S'; Similarly, if node* N_i *is positioned before* N_j *in* S_2*,* N_i *should still be positioned before* N_j *in S'.*

In the set **MergeSet***, there is one optimal allocation(described as follows) in terms of the objective function of OIDA.* $S_1 = \{S_{11}, S_{12}, \cdots, S_{1m}\}$

$S_2 = \{S_{21}, S_{22}, \cdots, S_{2n}\}$

we arrange these (m+n) profit segments in non-increasing order according to their priority as $S'_1, S'_2, \cdots, S'_{m+n}$*, in which* S'_i *is a profit segment of* S_1 *or* S_2 *and* $P(S'_i) \geq P(S'_{i+1})$ *for all* $1 \leq i \leq m + n - 1$*.*

Then we can conclude that $S' = \{S'_1, S'_2, \cdots, S'_{m+n}\}$ *is the optimal allocation in* **MergeSet***.*

Proof: First we show that S' is an element in MergeSet. According to Lemma 3,

$$P(S_{11}) > P(S_{12}) \cdots > P(S_{1m})$$
$$P(S_{21}) > P(S_{22}) \cdots > P(S_{2n})$$

The relative positions of nodes in S_1 and S_2 remain unchanged in S'. So S' is an element of **MergeSet**.

It remains to be seen that S' is optimal among all allocations in **MergeSet**. We will show that there is one optimal allocation that begins with S_1'. Then we will conclude that it is S'.

We assume that the allocation $S"$ is the optimal allocation in **MergeSet**. And S_1' is the profit segment of S_1(if S_1' is in S_2, the proof is the same). We consider the prefix segment $S"_1$ of $S"$ ending with the last node in S_1'.

If $S"_1$ only includes nodes from S_1', S" begins with S_1', done.

Otherwise, $S"_1$ includes nodes from S_1' and nodes from S_2, because other nodes in S_1 cannot be positioned before the last node in S_1'. So nodes in $S"_1$ can be divided into two parts: one part from S_1', the other from S_2. There are two situations to be considered.

First, if $S"_1$ begins with a node in S_1', then $S"_1$ can be represented as follows: $\{S"_{11}, S"_{21}, S"_{12}, S"_{22}, \cdots, S"_{1(k-1)}, S"_{2(k-1)}, S"_{1k}\}$

$S"_{1i}$ consists of nodes from S_1', for all $1 \le i \le k$; S_{2i} consists of nodes from S_2, for all $1 \le i \le k-1$. Because positions of $S"_{11}$ and $S"_{21}$ can be exchanged and S" is the optimal allocation, according to Lemma 2, $P(S"_{11}) \ge P(S"_{21})$. Similarly we can conclude that

$$P(S"_{11}) \ge P(S"_{21}) \cdots \ge P(S"_{1(k-1)}) \ge P(S"_{2(k-1)} \ge P(S"_{1k})$$
$$\Longrightarrow \qquad P(S"_{11}) \ge P(S"_{12}) \cdots \ge P(S"_{1(k-1)}) \ge P(S"_{1k})$$

$S_1' = \{S"_{11}, S"_{12}, \cdots, S"_{1(k-1)}, S"_{1k}\}$. Because S_1' is the **LMPPS** of S_1, $P(S"_{11}) \le P(S_1')$. So, according to Lemma 1,

$$P(S"_{11}) = P(S"_{12}) \cdots = P(S"_{1(k-1)}) = P(S"_{1k})$$
$$\Longrightarrow P(S"_{11}) = P(S"_{21}) \cdots = P(S"_{1(k-1)}) = P(S"_{2(k-1)}) = P(S"_{1k})$$

So, $S"_1$ can be permuted as $\{S"_{11}, S"_{12}, \cdots, S"_{1k}, S"_{21}, S"_{22}, \cdots, S"_{2(k-1)}\}$ while remaining optimal. Now $S"$ begins with $\{S"_{11}, S"_{12}, \cdots, S"_{1k}\} = S_1'$.

Secondly, if $S"_1$ begins with a node in S_2, the proof is similar to the first situation. $S"_1$ then can be represented as follows:

$$\{S"_{21}, S"_{11}, S"_{22}, S"_{12}, \cdots, S"_{2k}, S"_{1k}\}$$

$S"_{1i}$ consists of nodes from S_1', for all $1 \le i \le k$; $S"_{2i}$ consists of nodes from S_2, for all $1 \le i \le k$. Because segments $S"_{21}$ and $S"_{11}$ can be exchanged and S" is the optimal allocation, according to Lemma 2, $P(S"_{21}) \ge P(S"_{11})$; Similarly we can conclude that

$$P(S"_{21}) \ge P(S"_{11}) \cdots \ge P(S"_{2k}) \ge P(S"_{1k})$$
$$\Longrightarrow P(S"_{11}) \ge P(S"_{12}) \cdots \ge P(S"_{1(k-1)}) \ge P(S"_{1k})$$

$S_1' = \{S"_{11}, S"_{12}, \cdots, S"_{1k}\}$. Because S_1' is the **LMMPS** of S_1, $P(S"_{11}) \le P(S_1')$. According to Lemma 1,

$$P(S"_{11}) = P(S"_{12}) \cdots = P(S"_{1k})$$
$$\Longrightarrow P(S"_{11}) = P(S"_{22}) = P(S"_{12}) \cdots = P(S"_{2k}) = P(S"_{1k})$$

So, $S"_1$ can be permuted (while remaining optimal) as

$$\begin{aligned} & \{S"_{21}, S"_{11}, S"_{12}, \cdots, S"_{1k}, S"_{22}, \cdots, S"_{2k}\} \\ = & \{S"_{21}, S'_1, S"_{22}, \cdots, S"_{2k}\} \end{aligned}$$

Because $S"_{21}$ is a prefix segment of S_2, $P(S"_{21}) \leq P(S'_1)$. So according to Lemma 2, $S"_1$ can be further permuted to $\{S'_1, S"_{21}, S"_{22}, \cdots, S"_{2k}\}$ while remaining optimal. Again $S"_1$ can be permuted to begin with S'_1.

Until now, we have proved that there is an optimal allocation in **MergeSet** which begins with S'_1. We denote this optimal allocation as S. Because S is optimal, the sub-allocation $S_1 = (S - S'_1)$ is also optimal. Following the same proof as above, we can conclude that S_1 begins with S'_2. Continuing this process, we can conclude that $S = S' = \{S'_1, S'_2, \cdots, S'_{n+m}\}$. So S' is an optimal allocation in **MergeSet**.

We can notice that the **Merge-Allocation Theorem** also applies when merging more than two separate allocations into one. Our algorithm is based on the **Merge-Allocation Theorem.**

5 Algorithm for OIDA Problem

We now describe our algorithm for the OIDA problem in one channel. Our algorithm uses the bottom-up strategy. Given an index tree with depth L(we assume that the root is level 0), we compute the sub-allocations of sub-trees rooted at nodes at Level L; Based on the previous step's results, we compute the sub-allocations of sub-trees rooted at nodes of level (L-1) by merging its children's sub-allocations. We continue this procedure until the whole index tree's allocation is computed.

Apply the **Merge-Allocation Theorem** when computing the allocation of an index subtree rooted at N_i, we first divide the allocation of the subtrees rooted at N_i's children(computed at the previous step) into profit segments, arranging them in the non-increasing order, then merging them together. Then lastly, we add the node N_i to the head of the merged allocation. The resulting allocation is the allocation of subtree rooted at N_i.

Algorithm for OIDA Problem

- *For* $i = L$ *to 0* // L is the depth of the index tree
  - *For every node* N_j *in Level* i
    - *If* N_j *has no child then*
      - *The resulting allocation of the subtree rooted at* N_j *is* $\{N_j\}$;
    - *Else*
      1. *Divide every allocation of subtrees rooted at* N_j*'s children into profit segments;*
      2. *Arrange all profit segments in the non-increasing order and merge them together;*

3. *Add node N_j to the head of the merged allocation; The resulting allocation is the allocation for the subtree rooted at N_j;*

  * *End-If*
- *End-For*
- *End-For*

Analysis of the time complexity of this algorithm: We assume that the number of nodes in the index tree is n. This algorithm computes allocations of subtrees rooted at any node in the index tree. In computing the allocation of the sub-tree rooted at one single node, step(1) requires at most $O(n^2)$ time; Step(2) requires at most $O(n)$ time; Step(3) requires $O(1)$ time. Therefore, this algorithm's time complexity is $O(n^3)$.

For the k-channel situation, we first compute the one-channel sequence of the index tree using the above algorithm. Then we use a simple procedure similar to the one used in [8] to allocate the sequence into any k broadcast channels: for every node from left to right in the resulting sequence, we allocate it to a position in k channels which is after its parent node and nearest to the first channel slot.

6 Algorithm Performance and Experimental Results

There is one heuristic available for OIDA:*Index Tree Sorting*, which was proposed in [7]. In the *Index Tree Sorting* heuristic, for every node in the index tree, its children are sorted from left to right in descending order by their priority. After all nodes are sorted, the index tree is traversed in preorder to produce the broadcast. In our experiments, we will compare our new algorithm with the *Index Tree Sorting* heuristic in the single-channel and multi-channel situation.

We choose three types of index trees in our experiments:(1) full-balanced trees;(2) imbalanced trees with the same fanout;(3) imbalanced trees with different fanouts. The access frequencies of data nodes are generated using normal distribution $N(\mu, \sigma)$. We select $\mu = 100, \sigma = 20, 30, 40$ or 50. The detailed results are shown in Table 1, 2, 3 (the one-channel situation), and Table 4, 5, 6 (the three-channel situation). The real numbers in tables are data waits.

Algorithm	$\sigma = 20$	$\sigma = 30$	$\sigma = 40$	$\sigma = 50$
Sorting	21.47	20.44	19.92	20.11
New	21.37	19.67	18.72	18.58
Improvement	0.10	0.77	1.20	1.53

Table 1. Allocating 3-ary full-balanced index trees with depth 3 in one channel

From these experiments, we can see the evident improvement of our algorithm over the Index Tree Sorting heuristic. When σ is greater, which means that the access frequencies of data nodes vary more greatly, the improvement is greater.

Algorithm	$\sigma = 20$	$\sigma = 30$	$\sigma = 40$	$\sigma = 50$
Sorting	21.11	19.68	20.98	20.95
New	20.99	19.46	20.38	20.23
Improvement	0.12	0.22	0.60	0.72

Table 2. Allocating imbalanced index trees with fanout 3 and 40 nodes in one channel

Algorithm	$\sigma = 20$	$\sigma = 30$	$\sigma = 40$	$\sigma = 50$
Sorting	19.55	21.88	21.03	22.10
New	19.39	21.66	20.45	20.98
Improvement	0.16	0.22	0.58	1.12

Table 3. Allocating imbalanced index trees with different fanouts(2-4) in one channel

Algorithm	$\sigma = 20$	$\sigma = 30$	$\sigma = 40$	$\sigma = 50$
Sorting	22.26	22.24	21.72	21.28
New	21.65	21.40	20.65	19.83
Improvement	0.61	0.84	1.07	1.45

Table 4. Allocating 3-ary full-balanced index trees with depth 4 in three channels

Algorithm	$\sigma = 20$	$\sigma = 30$	$\sigma = 40$	$\sigma = 50$
Sorting	21.84	21.04	21.51	20.80
New	21.41	20.17	20.43	19.00
Improvement	0.43	0.87	1.08	1.80

Table 5. Allocating imbalanced index trees with fanout 4 and 120 nodes in three channels

Algorithm	$\sigma = 20$	$\sigma = 30$	$\sigma = 40$	$\sigma = 50$
Sorting	22.85	22.20	21.53	21.83
New	22.40	21.69	20.63	20.15
Improvement	0.45	0.51	0.90	1.78

Table 6. Allocating imbalanced index trees with different fanouts(2-4) in three channels

This coincides the fact shown in [7] that when σ is greater, the sorting heuristic deviates more from the optimal allocation.

7 Conclusion

In mobile computing, broadcast index trees are usually large. It is unrealistic to use the exhaustive search to solve the optimal index and data allocation problem. Therefore, heuristics are needed to produce near-optimal solutions. In this paper, we proposed a new algorithm based on the **Merge-Allocation Theorem** for OIDA. We proved that merged allocation is optimal if the relative positions of nodes in sub-allocations remain unchanged. Our experiments showed that our new algorithm performs well.

References

1. T.Imielinski, S.Viswanathan, and B.R.Badrinath, *Data on Air: Organization and Access*,IEEE Trans. on Knowledge and Data Engineering, Vol.9, No 3, pp 353-372, May/June 1997.
2. S. Acharya, R. Alonso, M. Franklin, and S. Zdonik, *Broadcast Disks: Data Management for Asymmetric Communication Environments*, Proc. ACM SIGMOD Conf., pp 199-210, San Jose, CA, May 1995.
3. T. Imielinski and S. Viswanathan, *Adaptive Wireless Information Systems*, Proc. Special Interest Group on Database Systems(SIGDBS) Conf., pp 19-41, Tokyo, Japan, October 1994.
4. M. Chen, P. Yu, and K. Wu, *Indexed Sequential Data Broadcasting in Wireless Mobile Computing*, 17th IEEE International Conference on Distributed Computing Systems, pp 124-131, Baltimore, Maryland, May 1997.
5. N.Shivakumar and S. Venkatasubramanian, *Energy-Efficient Indexing For Information Dissemination in Wireless Systems*, ACM, Journal of Wireless and Nomadic Application, 1996.
6. T. C. Hu and A. C. Tucker, *Optimal Computer Search Trees and Variable-length Alphabetic Codes*, SIAM J. Appl. Math., 21(4):514-532, 1971.
7. Shou-Chih Lo and Arbee L.P.Chen, *Optimal Index and Data Allocation in Multiple Broadcast Channels*, IEEE trans. on....
8. S.C.Lo and A.L.P. Chen, *Optimal Index and Data Allocation in Multiple Broadcast Channels*, Technical Report, Tsing Hua University,Taiwan

Modeling and Transformation of Object-Oriented Conceptual Models into XML Schema

Renguo Xiao[1], Tharam S. Dillon[1], E. Chang[2], and Ling Feng[3]

[1] Dept. Of Computing, Hong Kong Polytechnic University, China
{csrxiao, csdillon}@comp.polyu.edu.hk
[2] Dept. of Computer Science & Software Engineering, University of Newcastle, Australia
[3] Infolab, Tilburg University, The Netherlands, ling@kub.nl

Abstract. EXtensible Markup Language (XML) is fast emerging as the dominant standard for describing data and interchanging data between various systems and databases on the Internet. It offers the Document Type Definition (DTD) as a formalism for defining the syntax and structure of XML documents. The XML Schema definition language as a replacement of DTD provides more rich facilities for defining and constraining the content of XML documents. However, to enable efficient business application development in large-scale e-Commerce environments, XML lacks sufficient power in modeling real-world data and their complex inter-relationships in semantics. Hence, it will inevitably be necessary to use other methods to describe data paradigms and develop a true conceptual data model, and then transform this model into an XML encoded format, which can be treated as a logical model. In this paper, we present the way to model XML and to transform the Object Oriented (OO) conceptual model into XML Schema. We choose the OO conceptual model because of its expressive power for developing a combined data model. The paper first discusses the modeling of XML and why we need the transformation. Then, several generic transforming rules from the OO conceptual model to XML schema, with the emphasis on the transformations of generalization and aggregation relationships, are presented. Different perspectives regarding these conceptual relationships (e.g., *ordered* and *homogeneous composition* in aggregation relationships, *inheritance* and *overriding* in generalization relationships) and their transformations are particularly discussed.

1 Introduction

XML is fast emerging as the dominant standard for describing data and interchanging data between various systems and databases on the Internet. As a new markup language that supports user-defined tags, and encourages the separation of document content from its presentation, XML is able to automate web information processing in particular for data exchange and interoperability which are major issues in B to B e-Commerce. An XML document contains special instructions called tags, which usually enclose identifiable parts of the document. In data exchange applications, whenever composite data must be exchanged between two programs, XML serves as a suitable format for making the data self-describing. Besides, XML separates data

H.C. Mayr et al. (Eds.): DEXA 2001, LNCS 2113, pp. 795–804, 2001.

from presentation, making it reusable. Currently, XML offers the Document Type Definition (DTD) as a formalism for defining the syntax and structure of XML documents. The XML Schema definition language as a replacement of DTD provides more rich facilities for defining and constraining the content of XML documents. However, to enable efficient business application development in large-scale e-Commerce environments, XML lacks the power in modeling real-world data and their complex inter-relationships in semantics. Hence, it will inevitably be necessary to use other methods to describe data paradigms and develop a true conceptual data model, and then transform this model into an XML encoded format, which can then be treated as a logical model.

In this paper, we will introduce a solution for modeling XML and the transformation from OO conceptual models to XML Schema, as depicted in Figure 1. The aim of this work is to present a coherent way to integrate OO conceptual models and XML, making it easier to create, manage and retrieve XML documents.

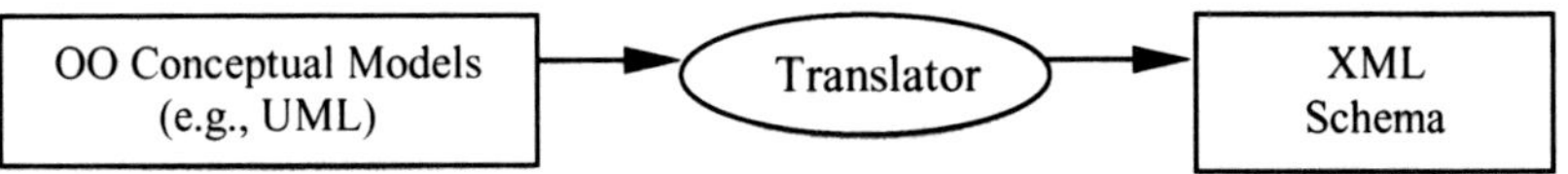

Fig. 1. Transformation from OO conceptual models to XML Schema

The remainder of the paper is organized as follows. Section 2 reviews some closely related work. Section 3 presents several generic transforming rules from the OO conceptual model to XML schema, with the emphasis on the transformations of generalization and aggregation relationships. Different perspectives regarding these conceptual relationships and their transformations are particularly discussed. Section 4 concludes the paper.

2 Related Work

XML bears a close correspondence to semi-structured data models [1,2,3]. The current trend in the literature on the modeling of semi-structured and unstructured data is to propose graph or tree models. The Object Exchange Model (OEM) is a simple, self-describing object model which represents semi-structured data by a labeled graph [1,4]. The nodes in the graph represent objects and the labels on the edges convey semantic information about the relationships between objects. The leaf nodes (nodes without outgoing edges) represent atomic objects and have values associated with them. The other nodes represent composite objects.

Another model for XML is the Document Object Model (DOM), which well documented in the W3C specification. It's also a tree model for XML documents. When an XML parser loads a document, it scans the document, looks for elements, attributes, and texts, and constructs a hierarchical tree based on these items. When the parser encounters an element in the source document, it creates a new node in the tree containing a representation of that element. As DOM aims to provide a set of implementation neutral and language independent programming interfaces for accessing nodes in a document tree, and for reading, writing, and modifying individual nodes or entire fragments of the tree, it can be viewed more as an Application Program Interface (API) rather than a conceptual model.

Recently, Conrad *et. al.* proposed to conceptually model XML DTDs using UML [6]. The idea is to use essential parts of static UML to model XML data schemata. The mapping between the static part of UML (i.e., class diagrams) and XML DTDs was developed. To take advantage of all facets that DTD concepts offer, the authors further extended the UML language in an UML-compliant way. The work reported in this paper distinguishes from this work in the following three aspects. First, we focus on conceptual modeling at XML Schema level instead of XML DTD level. Second, our transformations target at the general OO features, and is not limited to UML. In particular, we take different perspectives of OO structural relationships into consideration (e.g., *ordered* and *homogeneous composition* in aggregation relationships, *inheritance* and *overriding* in generalization relationships) and examine how they can be explicated by XML Schema.

3 Transformation from OO Conceptual Models into XML Schema

In the following, we use XML Schema as the logical structure to interpret the aggregation and generalization relationships in OO conceptual models.

3.1 Transformation of the Aggregation Relationship

The aggregation relationship represents a "part-of" relationship, indicating that a "whole" object consists of "part" objects [7]. This kind of relationships exists commonly in XML documents. XML assumes that data is hierarchically structured. One element may contain sub-elements, which may in turn contain other sub-elements. Therefore, we can easily map aggregation relationships in an OO conceptual model onto XML Schema. To specify a generic transformation rule for aggregation relationships, let us look at a two-layered aggregation relationship example shown in Figure 2. Class C is a composite class, consisting of n component classes C_1, ..., C_n. The component class C_i is also a composite class because it itself consists of m component classes from C_{i1}, ..., C_{im}. We call a component class containing no other component classes a *leaf class*. C_1 is a leaf class in this example. Basically, a component class can be 1) a leaf class if it contains no other component classes; or 2) a composite class consisting of other component classes.

The following steps generate an XML Schema segment for aggregation relationships in OO conceptual models.

[Step 1] For an aggregation relationship rooted at a composite class C, create an element named C with a ComplexType *CType* (<xsd:element name="*C*" type= "*CType*">).

[Step 2] For each component class C_i of C, create a sub-element named C_i within the ComplexType *CType* (<xsd:element name="C_i" type= "...">). If the component class C_i is a leaf class, then C_i has an internal type of the XML Schema. If the component class C_i is a composite class, repeat Step 1 and 2 to transform another aggregation relationship rooted at C_i.

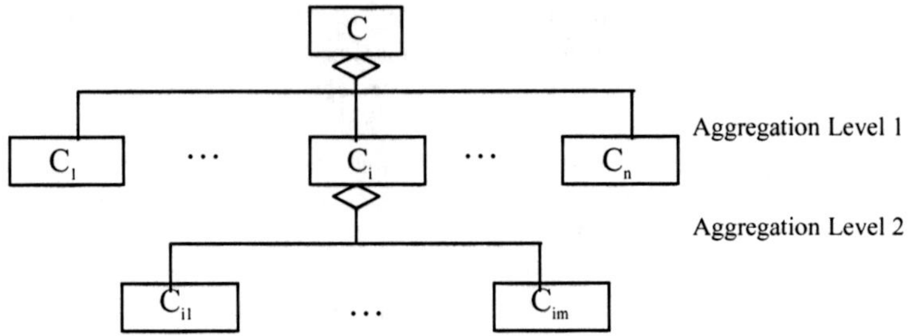

Fig. 2. A two-leveled aggregation relationships rooted at *C*

Figure 3 gives a running example where the *Invoice* class consists of classes *Heading, Contact_Person, Items_Ordered* and *Total_Price*, and class *Contact_Person* further consists of classes *Name, Address* and *Phone_No*. Following the above transformation steps, we can derive the corresponding XML Schema segment.

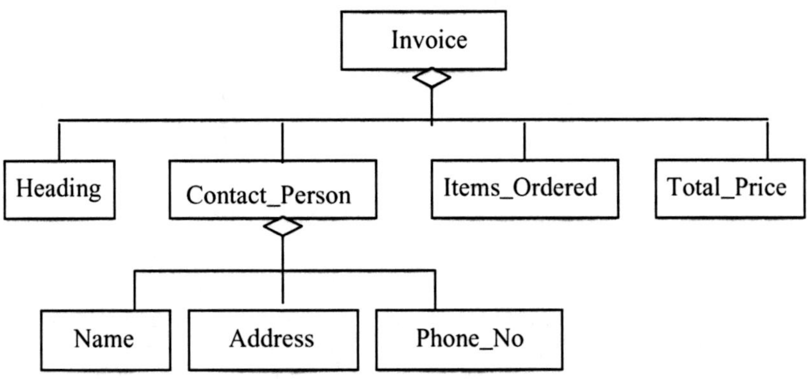

Fig. 3. An aggregation relationship example

```
<xsd:element  name= "Invoice"  type="InvoiceType"/>

<xsd:complexType  name="InvoiceType">

   <xsd:sequence>

      <xsd:element name="Heading" type="xsd:string"/>

      <xsd:element name="Contact_Person"
                   type="ContactPersonType"/>

      <xsd:element name="Items_Ordered"
                   type="xsd:string"/>

      <xsd:element name="Total_Price"
                   type="xsd:decimal"/>
```

```
    </xsd:sequence>
  </xsd:complexType>
  <xsd:complexType name="ContactPersonType">
    <xsd:sequence>
      <xsd:element name="Name" type="xsd:string"/>
      <xsd:element name="Address" type="xsd:string"/>
      <xsd:element name="PhoneNo" type="xsd:decimal"/>
    </xsd:sequence>
  </xsd:complexType>
```

Note that the sub-elements of *Invoice* and *Contact-Person* are embraced within <xsd:sequence> and </xsd:sequence>, respectively. It captures the *ordered composition* semantic. On the contrary, we can translate aggregation relationships into the XML Schema using the "all" group, stating that all the sub-elements in the group may appear once or not at all, and they may appear in any order. For example, <xsd:all> <xsd:element name="a" …> <xsd:element name="b" …> </xsd:all> implies that "a" can appear before "b" or after "b".

After generating the XML Schema, we can use it to assess the validity of the instance documents. One instance document that conforms to the above XML Schema is shown below:

```
  <Invoice>
    <Heading> This is Invoice 1</Heading>
    <Contact_Person>
      <Name> This is John </Name>
      <Address> This is address of John </Address>
      <PhoneNo> 27667313 </PhoneNo>
    </Contact_Person>
    <Items_Ordered>Ordered items are … </Items_Ordered>
    <Total_Price> 32000 </Total_Price>
  </Invoice>
```

When a "whole" object consists of some "part" objects, and all the "part" objects are of the same type, we call it *homogenous composition*. For example, a *Daily_Program* in Figure 4 consists of several *Programs*. We can generate an XML Schema for the homogenous aggregation relationship as follows.

[Step 1] For a homogenous aggregation relationship rooted at a composite class *C*, create an element named *C* with a ComplexType *CType* (<xsd:element name="*C*" type= "*CType*">).

[Step 2] For the component class *C'* of *C*, create a sub-element named *C'* within the ComplexType *CType* (<xsd:element name=" *C'* " type= "…" minOccurs= "…" maxOccurs= "…">), where *minOccurs* and *MaxOccurs* indicates the number of component objects of the same type that occur as sub-elements of *C*. If the component class is a leaf class, then *C'* has an internal type of the XML Schema; otherwise, repeat Step 1 and 2 to transform another aggregation relationship rooted at *C'*.

In general, an element is required to appear when the value of *minOccurs* is 1 or more. The maximum number of times an element may appear is determined by the value of *maxOccurs* attribute in its declaration. This may be a positive integer value or the term unbounded to indicate there is no maximum number of occurrences. The default value for both the minOccurs and the maxOccurs attributes is 1. Be sure that if we specify a value for only the minOccurs attribute, it is less than or equal to the default value of maxOccurs, i.e. it is 0 or 1. Similarly, if we specify a value for only the maxOccurs attribute, it must be greater than or equal to the default value of minOccurs, i.e. 1 or more. If both attributes are omitted, the element must appear exactly once [5].

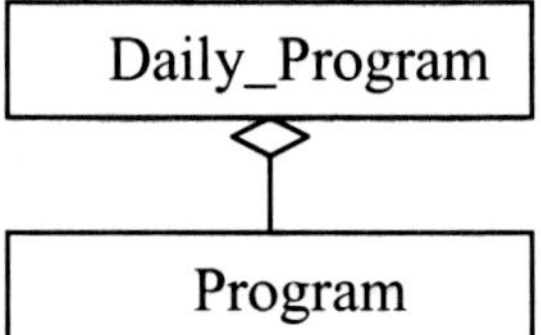

Fig. 4. A homogeneous composition example

According to the above transformation procedure, we can translate the homogeneous aggregation relationship shown in Figure 4 into the following XML Schema segment.

```
<xsd:element name="Daily_Program"
             type="DailyProgramType"/>

<xsd:complexType name="DailyProgramType">

   <xsd:element name="Program" type="xsd:string"
                minOccurs="1" maxOccurs="unbounded"/>

</xsd:complexType>
```

It declares that the *Daily_Program* element consists of at least one or more *Program* sub-elements which are of the same type. Obviously, the following instance document conforms to this definition because all the sub-elements are homogeneous.

```
<Daily_Program>
    <Program> This is Program1… </Program>
    <Program> This is Program2… </Program>
    <Program> This is Program3… </Program>
</Daily_Program>
```

3.2 Transformation of the Generalization Relationship

Generalization is another important mechanism in OO conceptual models for modeling the real world. It organizes classes in taxonomies by their similarities and differences, structuring the description of objects. The superclass hold common properties, while the subclasses add specific properties. For example, class *SavingAccoun*t and class *CurrentAccount* in Figure 5 are more specific compared to their generic class *Account.*

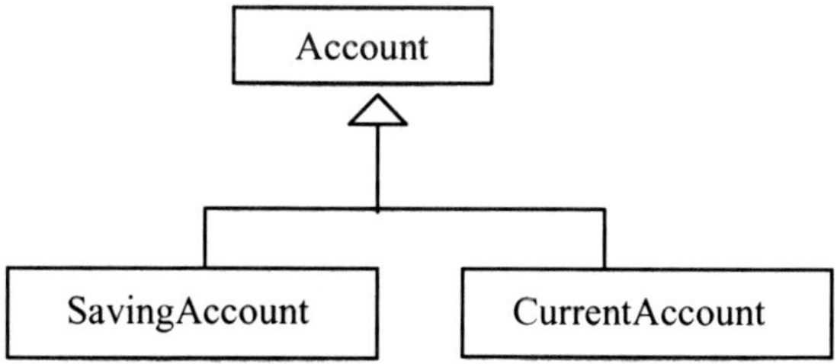

Fig. 5. A generalization example

Generalization is the structural relationship that permits the inheritance mechanism to occur. A specialized subclass inherits properties of its superclass. Inherited properties can be reused from a superclass or overridden in the subclasses. New properties can be added to the subclasses. All these nice OO modeling features can be carried to XML documents due to the flexible and powerful type creation facilities offered by the XML schema. There are basically three ways to construct a type from existing types at XML Schema level [5].

Deriving types by extension. A *newly* derived complex type contains all the elements of the original type plus additional elements that are specific in the new type. For example, from an existing type *AccountType*, two new types, *SavingAccountType* and *CurrentAccountType*, can be defined according to the following XML Schema segment.

```
<xsd:complexType  name="AccountType"/>
  <xsd:sequence>
```

```
      <xsd:element name="AccountNo" type="xsd:integer"/>
      <xsd:element name="Name" type="xsd:string"/>
      <xsd:element name="Balance" type="xsd:decimal"/>
    </xsd:sequence>
  </xsd:complexType>

  <xsd:element name="SavingAccount"
               type="SavingAccountType"/>
  <! --- new type derived from the basic AccountType --->
  <xsd:complexType  name="SavingAccountType"/>
    <xsd:complexContent>
      <xsd:extension base="AccountType">
        <xsd:element name="InterestRate"
                     type="xsd:decimal"/>
      </xsd:extension>
    </xsd:complexContent>
  </xsd:complexType>

  <xsd:element name="CurrentAccount"
               type="CurrentAccountType"/>
  <xsd:complexType name="CurrentAccountType"/>
    <xsd:complexContent>
      <xsd:extension base="AccountType">
        <xsd:element name="OverDraftLimite"
                     type="xsd:decimal"/>
      </xsd:extension>
```

```
    </xsd:complexContent>
  </xsd:complexType>
```

Based on the XML Schema segment, we can have the following valid instance document segment. As shown, both *SavingAccount* and *CurrentAccount* inherit the sub-elements *AccountNo, Name,* and *Balance* from *AccountType*. Besides, each of them has its own specific sub-element, i.e., *InterestRate* for *SavingAccount* and *OverDraftLimit* for *CurrentAccount*.

```
  <SavingAccount>
     <AccountNo> 123999011 </AccountNo>
     <Name> John Smith </Name>
     <Balance> 10000 </Balance>
     <InterestRate> 0.05 </InterestRate>
  </SavingAccount>


  <CurrentAccount>
     <AccountNo> 123999011 </AccountNo>
     <Name> John Smith </Name>
     <Balance> 10000 </Balance>
     <OverDraftLimit> 5000 </OverDraftLimit>
  </CurrentAccount>
```

Deriving types by restriction. A complex type derived by restriction is similar to its base type, except that its declarations are more limited than the corresponding declarations in the base type, and the values represented by the new type are a *subset* of the values represented by the base type. Therefore, the types derived by restriction must have the same structure and repeat all the components of the base type definition.

Redefining types. This mechanism allows one to redefine an *existing* simple/complex type that is obtained from an external schema file. The resulting definition has the same type name as the original one to be modified, and becomes the only definition of this type in the corresponding namespace.

To transform a generalization relationship in OO models into XML Schema, we can simply take the following steps:

[Step 1] For the superclass C in the generalization relationship, create an element named C, whose sub-elements describe the common properties of its specific subclasses.

[Step 2] For each subclass C_i of C, use the "*deriving types by extension*" mechanism to create a new element C_i, with some newly defined specific sub-elements. If C_i also overrides certain properties inherited from the superclass C, then use the "*deriving types by restriction*" and "*redefining types*" mechanisms to modify C_i's type definition to generate another new element C_i'.

4 Conclusion

XML becomes an increasingly important data format for storing structured and semi-structured text intended for dissemination and ultimate publication on a variety of media. It is a markup language that supports user-defined tags and encourages the separation of document content from presentation. On the other hand, with the wide acceptance of the OO conceptual models, more and more systems are initially modeled and being expressed with OO notations. This situation suggests the necessity to integrate the OO conceptual models and XML. The goal of this work is to present a coherent way to integrate the OO conceptual models and XML documents. We discuss the transformation from the OO conceptual models into XML Schema, with the emphasis on the transformation of aggregation and generalization relationships, in order to help people conveniently and automatically generate XML documents. In the future, we plan to incorporate dynamic behavior of objects into XML documents. The transaformation from XML Schema into the OO conceptual model is also an interesting topic deserving of further investigation.

References

1. R. Goldman and J. Widom, Dataguides: Enabling Query Formulation and Optimization in Semistructured Databases. Proc. of Intl. Conf. Very Large Data Bases, pages 436-445, 1997.
2. P. Buneman, S. Dacidson, G. Hillebrand, and D. Suciu, A Query Language and Optimization Techniques for Unstructured Data, Proc. of the ACM SIGMOD Intl. Conf. Management of Data, pages 505-516, 1996.
3. N. Bradley, The XML companion, Addison-Wesley, 1998.
4. J. McHugh, S. Abiteboul, R. Goldman, D. Quass and J. Widom, Lore: A Database Management System for Semistructured Data. SIGMOD Record, 26(3):54-66, 1997.
5. XML Schema Part 0: Primer W3C Candidate Recommendation 24 October 2000, http://www.w3.org.
6. R. Conrad, D. Scheffner and J.C. Freytag, XML Conceptual Modeling using UML, Proc. of Intl. Conf. on Conceptual Modeling, pages 558-571, USA. 2000.
7. T. Dillon and Tan PL, Object Oriented Conceptual Models, Prentice Hall, 1993.

Adding Time to an Object-Oriented Versions Model[1]

Mirella Moura Moro, Silvia Maria Saggiorato, Nina Edelweiss, and Clesio Saraiva dos Santos

Instituto de Informática - Universidade Federal do Rio Grande do Sul
Av. Bento Gonçalves, 9500 - Bloco IV - Porto Alegre, RS, Brazil
CEP 91501-970 - Caixa Postal: 15064
{mirella, silviams, nina, clesio}@inf.ufrgs.br

Abstract. In this paper, we propose an object-oriented version model which presents temporal concepts to store not only the object lifetime but also the history of dynamic attributes and relationships defined in the versioned objects and versions. One of the main features of our model is the possibility of having two different time orders, branched time for the object and linear time for each version. The model supports integration with existing databases, by allowing the modeling of normal classes among the temporal versioned classes. Finally, an approach to its implementation on top of a commercial database is presented.

1 Introduction

The information stored in a database evolves with time and, very often, it is necessary to keep track of such evolution. This fact led to researches concerning temporal database systems [4,14,20], which keep the evolution of data by associating timestamps to them. In the last 20 years several temporal data models were proposed by extending traditional data models in a way to capture also temporal features [5,8,11,12,15,19]. However, very few implemented temporal systems are available. A feasible way of implementing a temporal database is to map the temporal data model to a conventional commercial database [3,16,17,18,20].

On the other hand, non-conventional applications, as CAD and CASE tools, often demand the support of many database states as design alternatives. To fulfill such requirement, many works have focused the question of versions support [6,10,13,19]. The versioning of objects helps not only to keep track of the evolution of the objects but also to store the data corresponding to a specific context. Although some design alternatives are stored as versions, not all the history of the changes on data is recorded. Some important modification may have occurred whose values were not registered. The full history is only accessible if a temporal model is used.

The objective of this paper is to present a temporal object-oriented versions model, which brings together the features of a version model and a temporal model, called *Temporal Versions Model* (TVM). It allows the storage of all the versions of an object and, for each version, the history of the changes made in the values of its dynamic attributes and relationships. An approach to implement the TVM model on top of a commercial database is also presented.

---

[1] This work is partially sponsored by IBM, Solectron, CNPq, CAPES

H.C. Mayr et al. (Eds.): DEXA 2001, LNCS 2113, pp. 805–814, 2001.

The paper is structured as follows. Section 2 briefly reviews the basic version and temporal concepts. Section 3 presents the Temporal Versions Model. Section 4 illustrates the use of TVM using a simple modeling example. An approach to implement TVM on a commercial database is presented in section 5. Finally, section 6 summarizes the main ideas of the paper and presents future works.

2 Versions and the Temporal Dimension

The concept of version enables the user to keep different design alternatives. *Versions* can be defined as distinct snapshots of an object under design, in different states, which share some identifiable common characteristics [1]. Talens defines two types of version [13], according to the level were the versioning is applied: *class versioning* (evolution of classes) and *instances versioning* (modifications of the properties inside the instances). Only the second type of versioning is considered in this paper. The addition of the temporal dimension to class versioning is currently under analysis, and will be presented in a future work.

Instances versioning implies that different versions of the same object differ only in the values of some of their properties. Not all the history of the instances associated values is kept, only those values that are identified explicitly by the user as a new instance version. The addition of the temporal dimension enables to store the whole evolution of attributes and relationship values of these instances. Hence, the proposed model (TVM) is based on the concepts of instance version and time, allowing the storage of object versions and, for each version, its lifetime and the history of all the changes made on its elements.

This paper supposes that the reader is familiar to the basic temporal and version definitions. The most important concepts concerning the temporal dimension used here are: time order (*linear* and *branched*), time nature (*continuous* and *discrete*), timestamp types (*instant*, *temporal interval*, *temporal element*), time dimension (*valid* and *transaction times*) [7,14]. Concerning versioning, the concepts are: *versioned object* [6,10], *version history* and *version graph* [1,6,9], *current version*, *state* or *status* of the data stability contained in the versions and the operations which can be done over them [1,2,6,13], *static* and *dynamic references* [6,10].

3 The Temporal Versions Model

With the purpose of defining a data model that links versions and time concepts, Golendziner's *Versions Model* [6] was extended by adding the temporal dimension. The main features of the resultant data model are presented here.

3.1 Temporal Representation in TVM

Time is associated to objects, versions, attributes and relationships, allowing a better and more flexible modeling of reality. An object has a timeline for each of its versions. Several versions of an object may be available at the same time, which leads to the possibility of two different time orders: (i) branched time for an object, due to its different versions timelines, and (ii) linear time within each version. Time varies in a discrete way, and temporality is represented in the model through temporal intervals and bitemporal timestamps (transaction and valid times).

The attributes *start* and *end* (related to the initial and final times of lifetime respectively) are pre-defined. The object attributes and relationships can be defined as *static* (when they do not have the values variation stored) or *temporal* (all the values changes are stored creating their histories). The act of classifying attributes and relationships as temporal is under the user's responsibility during the database modeling. A class may present attributes and relationships of both types.

The temporal attributes and relationships values are associated with the pre-defined properties *vTimei*, *vTimef*, *tTimei*, *tTimef* which represent, respectively, the initial and final valid times, and the initial and final transaction times. The lifetime of a version must be contained within the versioned object's lifetime. And the values stored for temporal attributes and relationships must present timestamps contained within the correspondent version's lifetime.

3.2 Versioning Features

Versioning is associated to objects and not to classes. When a version is created from an object yet without versions, this object becomes the first version and the new version is derived from it (*implicit versioning*). *Explicit versioning* corresponds to the creation of a versioned object by the specific method (*Create_versioned_object*).

Version States. A version changes its status during its lifetime (Fig. 1). A version is created in the status *working*. In this status the version is essentially temporary and can be derived, modified, queried, and removed. When a version is derived from another one, its predecessor is automatically promoted to *stable*, avoiding modifications on versions that are important from the historical point of view. In this status the version cannot be modified, but can be derived, promoted to *consolidated*, queried, and removed. In the *consolidated* status the version can be queried and derived, but cannot be modified nor removed. TVM assumes only logical removals, when the version is moved to the *deactivated* status and has its lifetime finished. In this status can only be queried, or restored.

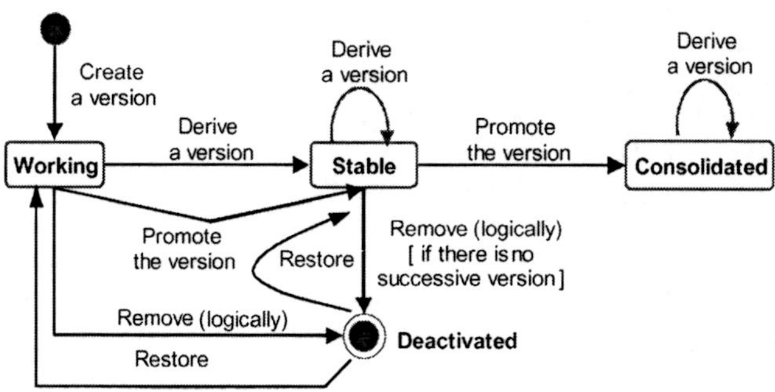

Fig. 1. The status and the events that cause transitions represented in a state diagram

Classes Hierarchy. Golendziner's class hierarchy was adapted to add the temporal dimension, as illustrated in Fig. 2.

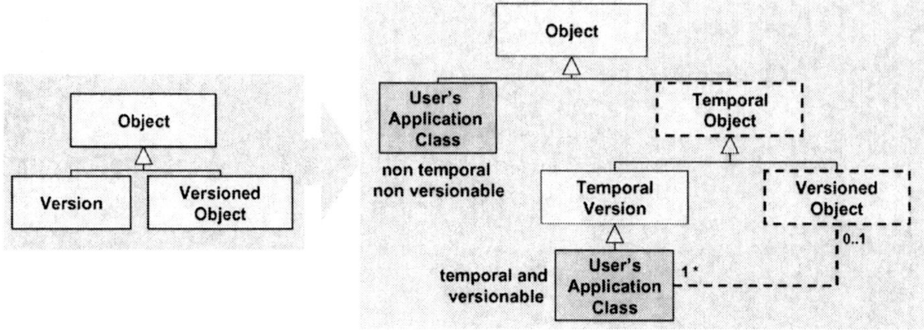

Fig. 2. Golendziner's class hierarchy at left and the TVM's class hierarchy with the user's application classes at right. The dashed lines inform the parts that are transparent to the user, managed by the system control.

The class *TemporalObject* represents the temporal aspects of the model. This class has the attributes *start* and *end* defined. The attributes *start* and end are defined in this class, storing the transaction time value at the object creation and exclusion.

Two types of application classes may be defined:

- *Non temporal nor versionable application class*, defined as *Object* subclass. Its modeling is used to consider classes which represent either objects of an existing model or auxiliary classes in which concepts of time and version are not necessary;
- *Temporal and versionable application class* defined as subclass of *TemporalVersion*. It has an association relationship with the *VersionedObject* class. Its attributes and relationships can be defined as *static* or *temporal*, its instances are versions with the timestamps associated to the temporal attributes and relationships, and it inherits the attributes *start* and *end* from *TemporalObject* as well.

The class *Object* has methods to manage objects. The class *TemporalVersion* has the version attributes *configuration* and *status* (which informs if the version belongs to a configuration and its status, respectively) and the navigation attributes *ascendant*, *descendant*, *predecessor*, and *successor*. This class has methods to get all its attributes, as well as to derive and promote versions.

Finally, the class *VersionedObject* has the attributes to inform the current version, the number of configurations and versions, the first and last versions, the next version number, and whether the user has specified a current version or not. This class has methods to get all its attributes, and to change the current version. The user defines the application class as subclass of *Object* or *TemporalVersion*, while the classes *TemporalObject* and *VersionedObject* are managed by the system.

OID structure. A version is a first class object, having an object identifier (OID), which allows the object to be directly manipulated or queried. The OID structure is composed as follows:

< Entity identifier, Class identifier, Version number >

The version number is represented by integer values created sequentially. These numbers cannot be reused in case of exclusion. The following features distinguish among the different types of objects with these OID structure:

- *Versioned object* with no versions: there is no reference to a versioned object;
- *Versioned object* with versions: there is a reference to a versioned object;
- *Version*: there is a reference to the versioned object to which it belongs.

A non-versioned object and the first version have the same version number. Therefore, the evolution of a non-versioned object to a versioned one creates an instance of *VersionedObject*, without changing its version number.

4 Modeling Example

To illustrate the different concepts of TVM, this model is used to model a simple application – a websites design company. Beyond its client's sites, the company keeps the professional pages of its employees. In order to simplify and make clear the concepts, only the nucleus of the model is presented.

Each website is composed by one or more pages, one of them being the initial or main page. Each page is associated to a page pattern, which defines the background color and image, a banner, and the default font specification. The pattern is used as a standard for the employees' page layout. According to the company instruction, this pattern varies according to the seasons of the year and commemorative dates. For instance, during the company's anniversary month, the background image presents a cake with lighted candles, and the banner offers special discounts.

The features of version and time are used in:

- The *WebSite*, *WebPage*, and *PagePattern* classes - all the alternatives of the site, its pages and pattern, as well as the temporal attributes values are stored;
- The relationship *associatedWith* - the main relationship of the model through which the company changes the website pattern of its employees;
- The attribute *banner* - each pattern can be associated with the website for a long time, hence several banners can be used during the same period;
- Relationship *initialPage* - the evolution of the initial or main page is also stored;

Special symbols were defined to represent graphically, in a class diagram, the TVM temporal relationships and attributes, as well as the versionable classes (Table 1). Using this representation, the class diagram corresponding to this example is presented in Fig. 3.

Table 1. Special symbols for graphical representation in a class diagram

Symbol	Meaning
^{T}V	The associated class is temporal and versionable
<<Temporal>>	The associated relationship is temporal
<<T>>	The associated attribute is temporal

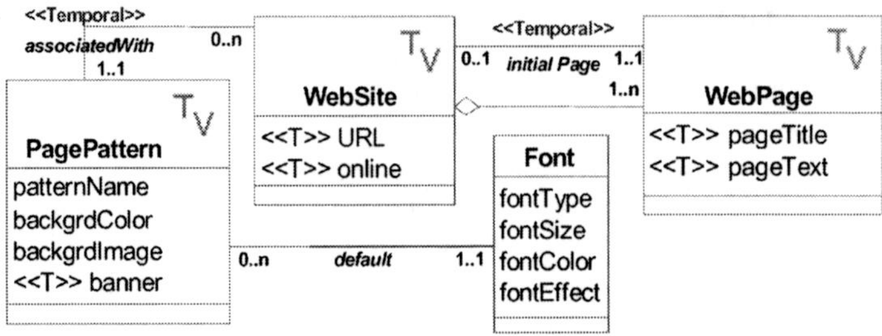

Fig. 3. Class diagram for the example

Fig. 4 illustrates the *PagePattern* class with its versioned objects *Autumn*, *Winter*, *Spring*, and *Summer*. The versioned object *Winter* is detailed with its five versions: the first one (2,15,1) is the default page for the Winter, the second (2,15,2) and the third (2,15,3) ones were derived as alternatives for the Christmas, the fourth (2,15,4) was derived as version for the new year, and the last one (2,15,5) was derived from the new year as the new millennium version. Fig. 5 presents graphically the evolution of the *associatedWith* relationship for one employee's website. The *WebSite* version is always the same one (2,8,1), while the association with the pattern changes in accordance with the commemorative date inside the Winter period.

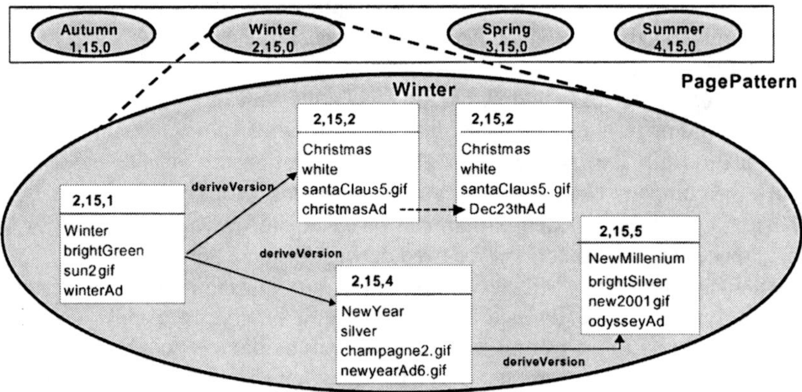

Fig. 4. Graphical representation of one versioned object. The change in the attribute value of *banner* (*christmasAd* to *Dec23thAd*) does not create a new version, only gives birth to one more value in its history

5 Implementing TVM

The use of a powerful temporal data model does not require a specific database management system that supports it to implement an application. Existing commercial DBMSs can be used for this purpose as long as a proper mapping from the temporal data model to the data model underlying the adopted DBMS is provided. In order to

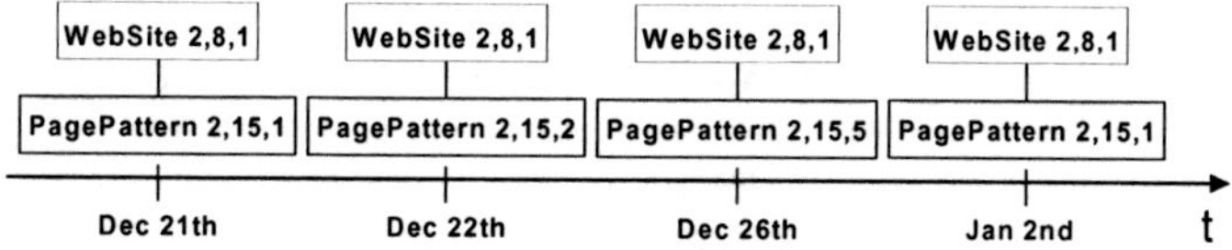

Fig. 5. Temporal relationship *associatedWith* timeline, in the Winter period, for one website

test the feasibility of this approach, TVM was mapped to a commercial database. The database DB2 was chosen because it presents support of temporal data types similar as the standard SQL-92 [20]. The mapping is divided in two parts: the representation of the model's hierarchy, and the mapping of the application classes.

5.1 The Model Hierarchy Mapping

The class hierarchy is mapped to an equivalent type hierarchy of DB2, in which some methods can be executed through SQL commands and queries. Fig. 6 shows the attributes and methods defined for the model hierarchy. Basically, only the methods related to the time and version features need to be translated.

Object
Create_object Create_specialized_object Delete_object Get_complete_object Get_object Modify

TemporalObject
end start
Delete_version

VersionedObject
Configuration_count Current_version Version_count First_version Last_version Next_version_number User_current_flag
Change_current Create_specialized_versioned_object Create_versioned_object Get_configuration_count Get_current_version Get_first_version Get_last_version Get_version_count

TemporalVersion
Ascendant Configuration Descendant Predecessor Status Successor
Derive_Version Get_ascendant Get_configuration Get_descendant Get_versioned_object Get_predecessor Get_successor Get_status Promote

Fig. 6. The classes of the hierarchy with their attributes and methods

The class *Object* is mapped to a not instantiable structured type without attributes. The methods of creating and modifying objects are equivalent to the SQL INSERT and UPDATE, respectively. The methods of getting objects and complete objects can be executed through SQL SELECT commands.

The class *TemporalObject* is mapped to a not instantiable structured type with the attributes *start* and *end*, both of the type TIMESTAMP. This class presents a method *Delete_version* which is mapped to a stored procedure that receives the OID and executes the logical exclusion by changing the status to *deactivated*, registering the attribute *end* value as the present instant.

The class *TemporalVersion* is mapped to a not instantiable structured type. The attributes *descendant* awhich and *successor* are not mapped because the DBMS does not have a type to implement collections. However, these information can be obtained by the methods *Get_descendant* and *Get_successor*, respectively. The attribute *predecessor* is mapped to a VARCHAR attribute. The attributes *status* and *configuration* are mapped to CHAR attributes with pre-defined values.

Concerning the methods of *TemporalVersion*, *Get_descendant* is mapped to a stored procedure that receives the object OID and returns the set of OIDs from the descendants; *Derive_version* and *Get_configuration* are mapped to stored procedures that generate a new version and a configuration, respectively, according to the parameters informed; *Get_versioned_object* is mapped to a user defined function that receives an OID and returns the OID from the versioned object to which the version belongs; *Get_successor* is mapped to a stored procedure that receives the version OID and returns the set of OIDs from its successor versions; *Get_predecessor* and *Get_status* do not need to be mapped because DB2 creates, for each attribute, one method *Observer* with equivalent functions; and *Promote* is mapped to a stored procedure that promotes the version to its next *status*, according to Fig. 1.

The class *VersionedObject* is mapped to a structured type. The attributes *Version_count*, *Configuration_count*, and *Next_version_number* receive the type INTEGER. The attributes *First_version*, *Last_version*, and *Current_version* receive the type VARCHAR. And the *User_current_flag* receives the type CHAR.

The *VersiondObject* methods are mapped as follows: *Create_versioned_object* and *Create_specialized_versioned_object* are executed by SQL INSERT commands; *Get_version_count*, *Get_configuration_count*, *Get_first_version*, *Get_last_version*, and *Get_current_version* do not need to be mapped because DB2 creates, for each attribute, one method *Observer* with equivalent functions; and *Change_current* is mapped to a stored procedure that changes the current version of the object informed in the parameter. The information related to the versioned objects is stored in only one table called *VersionedObjetcs*, which is created based on the structured type *VersionedObject* described above.

Complementary mappings. Concerning the *OID mapping*, the three parts of the OID (entity id, class id, version number) are stored in one VARCHAR attribute separated by commas. For instance, the OID '101,20,5' identifies the fifth version of the entity 101 in the class 20. The entity and class identifiers are generated by the system. The version number is managed by the attribute *Next_version_number* of the class *VersionedObject*.

Metadata needs also to be mapped. One extra table, called *CONTROL_CLASS*, is created in order to store some information related to the application classes for each schema. It has the following attributes: *ID_CLASS* stores the identifier from each class, *CLASS* stores the class names, *VERSIONED* informs whether a class is versionable or not, *IS_ROOT* identifies the schema classes which are hierarchy roots, *ASCENDANT* stores the superclass identifier for each subclass.

The *temporal label* is mapped to a not instantiable structured type called *TEMPORALSTAMP*, which has the attributes *vTimei*, *vTimef*, *tTimei*, *tTimef* with type TIMESTAMP.

5.2 The Application Classes Mapping

As DB2 does not implement collections, this part of the mapping requires that the class model is in the first normal form. For each normal class (non-versionable and non-temporal) the following objects must be created in the database: (1) a structured type with the same class structure, which is added to the attribute *ascendant* in case the class is a subclass; and (2) a table to store the class instances, called *main table*. If this last table stores the instances of a subclass, two triggers shall be associated to the *insert* operation. The first one verifies if the ascendant value corresponds to a valid OID, and the second one forbids the user to inform values to the inherited attributes.

For each temporal and versionable class, the same structured type and table mentioned above and the following objects must be created:

- A table for each temporal attribute and relationship to store the historic;
- A trigger, associated to the temporal attribute and relationship updates, which stores the old values in its respective auxiliary table. For each new value inserted in the auxiliary table, (1) if the initial valid time (of the new value) is not informed by the user, as usual, it assumes the present moment; and (2) the final valid time (of the old value) receives the initial valid time (of the new value) minus one instant;
- A trigger, associated to the operation *update*, which allows the user modifies only versions in the status *working*;
- A trigger, associated to the operation *update* of the *VersionedObject* attributes, which do not allow the user modifies the attributes manually.

Static and Dynamic References. Static and dynamic references are allowed in complex objects. However, in this implementation of TVM these references are not available in association relationships because the mapping is done to a database in which the concept of aggregation does not exist. Therefore, when there is relationship between two classes, it may have both types of references between their objects.

In order to distinguish between the types of references, the following features must be considered: (i) *static reference*: the object references another one whose OID has the version number different from zero, which means the referenced object is either a version or a non-versioned object; (ii) *dynamic reference*: the object references another one whose OID has the version number zero, a versioned object.

6 Summary and Concluding Remarks

This paper proposes the Temporal Versions Model (TVM) to be used as a database modeling technique. The model is an extension of an object-oriented versions model, by adding the temporal dimension to the instance versioning level. Indeed, the designer may model the database considering the design alternatives as well as the data evolution. It is important to notice that the presented model does not require all classes to be temporal and versionable, allowing the integration with existing applications.

TVM allows the storage of different designed versions together with all the updates in the values of those attributes and relationships defined as temporal. Therefore, different versions coexist, representing branched time order, which it is not usual in the models found on the literature in which the time order is almost always linear. Within a version, the updates of temporal attributes and relationships vary in linear order.

This work is part of a project that aims to implement an integrated environment software for class specification, object versioning, versions management, query, and visualization. TVM is being used as the base for the definition of a schema evolution model, thus adding the temporal dimension also to the class versioning level.

References

1. Ahmed, R., Navathe, S.B.: Version Management of Composite Objects in CAD Databases. Proc. ACM SIGMOD Int. Conf. on Management of Data, Denver (1991) 218-227
2. Chou, H.T., Kim, W.: A Unifying Framework for Version Control in a CAD Environment. Proc. 12th Conf. on Very Large Data Bases (1986) 336-344
3. Edelweiss, N, Hübler, P., Moro, M.M., Demartini, G.: A Temporal Database Management System Implemented on Top of a Conventional Database. Proc. 20th Int. Conf. of the Chilean Computer Science Society, Santiago, Chile (2000) 58-67
4. Etzion, O, Jajodia, S., Sripada, E. (eds.): Temporal Databases: Research and Practice. Lecture Notes in Computer Science, Vol. 1300. Springer-Verlag, Berlin Heidelberg, (1998)
5. Gadia, S.K., Yeung, C.S.: A Generalized model for a relational temporal database. Proc. ACM SIGMOD Int. Conf. on Management of Data, Chicago (1988) 251-259
6. Golendziner, L.G., dos Santos, C.S.: Versions and configurations in object-oriented database systems: a uniform treatment. Proc. 7th Int. Conf. Manag. of Data, Pune, India (1995) 18-37
7. Jensen, C.S. et al.: The Consensus Glossary of Temporal Database Concepts - February 1998 Version. In: Etzion, O., Jajodia, S., Sripada, S. (eds.): Temporal Databases Research and Practice. Springer-Verlag, Berlin Heidelberg (1998) 367-405
8. Käfer, W., Schöning, H.: Realizing a temporal complex-object data model. Proc. ACM SIGMOD Int. Conf. on Management of Data, San Diego (1992) 266-275
9. Katz, R.H., Chang, E., Bhateja, R.: Version Modeling Concepts for Computer-Aided Design Databases. Proc. ACM SIGMOD Conference, Washington (1986) 379-386
10. Kim, W., Bertino, E., Garza, J. F.: Composite objects revisted. Proc. ACM SIGMOD Int. Conf. on Management of Data, Oregon (1989) 337-347
11. Loucopoulos, P., Theodoulidis, C., Wangler, B.: The entity relationship time model and conceptual rule language. Proc. 10th Int. Conf. on ER Approach, S. Mateo (1991)
12. Snodgrass, R.: The Temporal query language Tquel. ACM Transactions on Database Systems, 12(2) (1987) 247-298
13. Talens, G., Oussalah, C.: Versions of Simple and Composite Objects. Proc. 19th Int. Conf. on Very Large Data Bases, Dublin (1993) 62-72
14. Tansel, C.G. et al. (eds): Temporal Databases - Theory, Design and Implementation. Benjamin/Cummings, Redwood City (1993)
15. Tauzovich, B.: Towards Temporal Extensions to the Entity-Relationship Model. Proc. Int. Conf. on the Entity Relationship Approach, San Mateo (1991) 163-179
16. Theodoulidis, B.: The ORES temporal databases management system. SIGMOD Record, 23(2) (1994) 511-511
17. TIME DB: A Temporal Relational DBMS. ©TimeConsult. Available at: http://www.timeconsult.com/Software/Software.html (1999)
18. TOOBIS: Temporal Objects-Oriented Databases in Information Systems. Available at: http://www.di.uoa.gr/~toobis/ (2000)
19. Wuu, G.T.J, Dayal, U.: A Uniform Model for Temporal and Versioned Object-Oriented Databases. In: Tansel, A. et al (eds.): Temporal Databases: Theory, Design, and Implementation. Benjamin/Cummings, Redwood City (1993) 230-247
20 Snodgrass, R.T.: Developing Time-Oriented Database Applications in SQL. Morgan Kaufmann (2000).

Cache Conscious Clustering C3

Zhen He and Alonso Marquez

Department of Computer Science, The Australian National University
Canberra, ACT 0200, Australia
{zhen, alonso}@cs.anu.edu.au

Abstract. Despite over 10 years of research into OODBMS design, performance remains as one of the major problems. I/O reduction has proven to be one of the most effective ways of enhancing performance. Two techniques of improving I/O performance of OODBMS are *clustering* and *buffer replacement*. *Clustering* places objects that are likely to be accessed together onto the same disk page and thus reduces I/O. *Buffer replacement* involves the selection of a page to be evicted, when the buffer is full. The page evicted ideally should be the page needed furthest in the future. Selection of the correct page for eviction results in a reduction in the total I/O generated by the system. These two techniques effect the likelihood of a requested object being memory resident in an interdependent way. This fact has been acknowledged in the existing literature. However despite this acknowledgement no existing work investigates this interdependency. This paper makes the first investigation into this interdependency by exploring the effects of ten different buffer replacement algorithms on the performance of two different clustering algorithms. We developed a new family of clustering algorithms that incorporate cache behavior when performing clustering. We term this new family of clustering algorithms, *cache conscious clustering (C3)*. A particular C3 algorithm (GPC3) was tested against a well known and highly competitive clustering algorithm GGP, and the results show GPC3 outperforms GGP by upto 40% for popular buffer replacement algorithms such as LRU and CLOCK. These results show for the first time clustering should be approached from a cache conscious point of view.

1 Introduction

The current rate of performance improvement for CPUs is much higher than that for memory or disk I/O. CPU performance doubles every 18 months while disk I/O improves at only 5-8 % per year. In addition, cheap disks mean object databases will become bigger as database designers realise that more data can be stored [9]. A consequence of these facts is that disk I/O is likely to be a bottleneck in an increasing number of database applications. It should also be noted, memory is also becoming a more prevalent source of bottleneck on modern DBMS [1]. However their study was conducted on relational DBMS. We believe for object-oriented DBMS where navigation is common, I/O may be a more common source of bottleneck.

H.C. Mayr et al. (Eds.): DEXA 2001, LNCS 2113, pp. 815–825, 2001.

The question now is what is the best way of reducing the effect of I/O in an OODBMS? We believe the answer lies in taking advantage of the synergy that exists between the optimisation techniques, *clustering*, and *buffer replacement*. *Clustering* is the arrangement of objects into pages so that objects accessed close to each other temporally are placed into the same page. This in turn reduces the total I/O generated. *Buffer replacement* involves the selection of a page to be evicted, when the buffer is full. The page evicted ideally should be the page needed furthest in the future. Selection of the correct page for eviction results in a reduction in the total I/O generated by the system. This paper will show that synergy does indeed exists between the two techniques. In addition, exploitation of that synergy results in improvements in performance. In one of the most fundamental papers on clustering [14], Tsangaris and Naughton stated that, "A clustering strategy will depend much on the cache management policy.". However despite this statement they chose not to explore this dependency, stating as the reason, "having to deal with the cache policy makes clustering an even more difficult problem." [14]. The paper then goes on to state the aim of clustering should therefore be to "enhance locality of the client reference stream, using a metric independent of the cache management policy." Finally the paper proposes the *graph partitioning* family of algorithms as the best way to cluster objects for enhanced locality.

This paper proposes a new family of clustering algorithms termed cache conscious clustering (C3). Cache conscious clustering algorithms exploit the synergy between clustering and buffer replacement. In order to evaluate the performance of C3, we conducted experiments involving GPC3 and Greedy Graph Partitioning (GGP) [7]. GPC3 is a concrete example of a C3 algorithm. GGP is a member of the graph partitioning family of clustering algorithms. Up to now graph partitioning has been shown to give the best quality [1] of clustering [13,7]. GPC3 was found to outperform GGP in a variety of situations.

There are three main contributions made by this paper. The first contribution is restating the clustering problem to incorporate caching. The second, is proposal of a new family of clustering algorithms that incorporate caching. We then give a concrete example of a new clustering algorithm that falls within this new family of clustering algorithms. This new clustering algorithm is evaluated in a simulation study. It should be noted this algorithm is the first static clustering [2] algorithm that exploits the dependency between clustering and cache management. The third contribution is a simulation study of the dependency between clustering and cache management.

[1] By quality of clustering we mean the ability to minimise I/O in perfect conditions. Perfect conditions occur when the pattern of object access used for training and evaluation are exactly the same.

[2] By static clustering, we mean a clustering algorithm that rearranges the object base when the database is off-line.

2 Related Work

There has been a number of existing studies on static clustering algorithms [13, 7]. The simplest static clustering algorithm is the Probability Ranking Principle (PRP) algorithm[13]. PRP just involves placing the objects in the object graph in decreasing heat (where 'heat' is simply a measure of access frequency). This simple approach groups objects of similar heat into the same page. When the buffer is large and the working set of the database completely fits into memory this algorithm provides the optimal solution.

Graph partitioning clustering algorithms consider the object placement problem as a graph partitioning problem in which the min-cut criteria is to be satisfied for page boundaries. The edges of the graph are weighted using tension [3]. The latest studies on static clustering [13,7], reveal graph partitioning algorithms as the family of clustering algorithms, providing the best quality of clustering. It is for this reason that we have chosen to use greedy graph partitioning (GGP) [7] as the algorithm of comparison.

A large range of buffer replacement algorithms were used in the this study and they include: Least Recently Used (LRU); First In First Out (FIFO); Least Frequently Used (LFU); LRU-K (extends basic LRU by using historical information) [11]; GCLOCK (extension of CLOCK by using training data to help make eviction choices) [10]; belady's optimal buffer replacement algorithm [2].

3 Problem Statement

Given an object base, a set of workloads that operate on the object base and a buffer replacement algorithm, we are interested in improving the throughput [4] of the system by reducing the total I/O generated. Periodic rearrangement of objects is permitted as a means of reducing I/O. Database activity may be suspended when rearrangement is taking place. The following assumption can be made: the pattern of object access between successive periods of database operation [5] bares some degree of similarity.

4 The Case for Cache Conscious Clustering

Traditionally clustering has been formulated as a locality enhancement problem [14]. The metric used for locality is the working set size [6]. The working set size for M consecutive page requests is computed as follows: take M consecutive page requests, eliminate duplicates and then compute the cardinality of the resulting set. Smaller resulting cardinality means higher locality. The best existing clustering algorithm resulted from finding a heuristic [6] solution to minimising

[3] Tension uses simple markov chains to compute the probability that two objects can be accessed one after the other.

[4] Long term average performance.

[5] Before and after every rearrangement.

[6] Since the problem was found to be NP complete.

working set size of M = 2. This means given two consecutive page requests the aim of clustering is to confine both requests to the same page. This formulation allows clustering to be optimised for cache sizes of *one* page. However, typically caches can hold more than one page.

The fundamental difference between our approach and that of Tsangaris and Naughton's [13] is that we cluster for a cache of N pages, where N is greater than or equal to one. There are two consequences of clustering for a larger cache. The first is a request for an object on a *different* page *in memory* is now considered to cost the same as a request to an object of the *same* page [7]. Clustering changes from a problem of, how do I prevent the object graph traversal from leaving this page? To one of, how do I prevent the object graph traversal from leaving memory? The second consequence of clustering for a larger cache is that clustering must be buffer replacement aware.

Clustering for cache sizes of greater than one page should meet the following two objectives:

- confine traversals to in memory pages.
- cluster objects that are going to be used furthest away in the future together into the same page.

The first objective is a natural consequence of the fact a request to an object on a *different* page *in memory* is considered equally as good as a request to an object on the *same* page. The second objective is due to the aim of buffer replacement algorithms: to evict the page that is going to be referenced furthest away in the future. Ideally at every eviction the furthest away in memory objects should be clustered together.

5 Cache Conscious Clustering (C3)

This section details the new cache conscious family of clustering algorithms (C3). C3 was arrived at due to the following observation: the first objective outlined in section 4, namely that of confining traversals to in memory pages can be further divided into two sub-objectives. The two sub-objectives are:

- maximise the number of hot [8] objects in memory.
- minimise the number of pages that a traversal touches.

The first sub-objective increases the number of buffer hits and thus increases the chances of confining a traversal to in memory pages. The second sub-objective increases the probability that the pages involved in a traversal are memory resident [9]. It is important to note that the two sub-objectives can potentially conflict.

[7] For simplicity, we neglect the effects of CPU caches.

[8] Where 'heat' is simply a measure of access frequency.

[9] Provided that the working set of the application does not fit in memory. Thus only one portion of pages used by the application can fit in memory at any one time.

For example a hot object may reference many cold objects and thus clustering the hot objects with its cold objects better satisfies the second sub-objective. However the first sub-objective is best met when hot pages are purer in terms of hot objects contained [10].

C3's way of meeting the two sub-objectives is to break clustering into two phases. The first phase attempts to satisfy the first sub-objective by dividing objects into regions of similar probability of reference (heat). The second phase attempts to meet the second sub-objective by further dividing objects of each region into pages based on relationships between objects.

Figure 1 gives a diagrammatic representation of one example of the application of our two phased approach. The example shows the first phase dividing the object base into two regions of contrasting heat. The second phase is shown to cluster related objects further into pages.

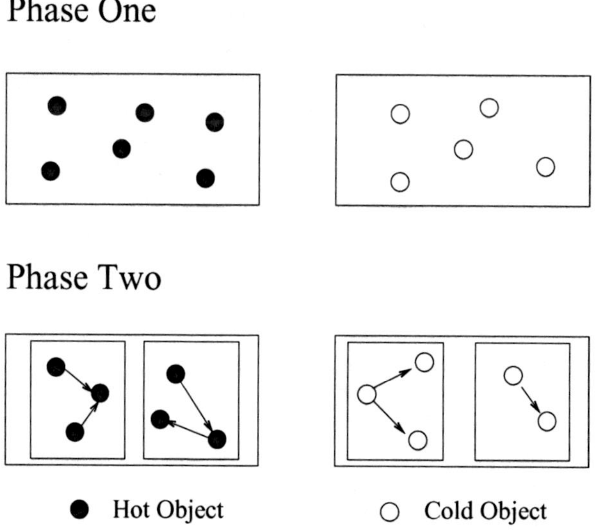

Fig. 1. Diagrammatic description of the two phases of C3. The first phase of this example only divides the objects into two regions of contrasting heat. However in general the first phase of C3 allows the object base to be divided into N regions.

The first phase is accomplished by sorting the objects into decreasing heat. The sorted sequence is then cut at N - 1 places to form N regions of more homogeneous heat. The places at which the N - 1 cuts occur is a property of the particular C3 algorithm. See section 6 for an example. The way the sorted sequence of objects is cut into regions has a large effect on the performance of the clustering algorithm. Cutting the sorted sequence into smaller regions has

[10] Since most buffer replacement algorithms try to keep hot pages in memory.

the following consequences: regions with objects of more homogeneous heat are created; the probability that two related objects are placed into the same region is decreased. The first consequence is beneficial to the first sub-objective, since it creates purer hot pages. However the second consequence runs counter to the second sub-objective, since related objects of one traversal are more likely to be assigned to different pages. Therefore, the sorted sequence must be cut carefully.

The second phase further clusters each heat region into pages using any clustering algorithm that clusters based on some notion of relatedness between objects. Clustering algorithms that can be used in the second phase include algorithms that use the following statistics to model user behavior: structural relationships between objects [12,3]; weighted structural relationships [12]; tension [13,7].

Both phases of C3 contribute to C3 satisfying the second objective of section 4, namely clustering objects that are going to be used furthest away in the future together into the same page. The first phase of C3 removes potential hot objects from cold pages [11]. This is beneficial since hot objects are potentially more likely to be used in the near future. Thus there removal from cold pages increases the probability that cold pages are referenced further away in the future. The second phase further groups cold objects that are likely to be used in the same time interval, together. Thus the combination of the two phases results in cold pages with many cold objects that are likely to be used in the same time interval, being placed together. This allows buffer replacement algorithms to select pages that contain a larger fraction of the furthest referenced objects, when performing eviction.

6 GPC3 a Concrete Example of C3

This section outlines the GPC3 clustering algorithm. GPC3 is a concrete example of a C3 clustering algorithm. In the first phase GPC3 divides the object base into two regions of contrasting heat. The cut occurs at the point that results in all objects in the hot region just fitting in memory. The second phase of C3 uses the graph partitioning algorithm GGP [7] to further divide the objects in each region into pages.

The second phase of GPC3 is particularly effective for reducing I/O of the cold region. Graph partitioning the cold region increases the locality of reference of cold pages. Since cold pages are not expected to stay in memory long it is appropriate to formulate the clustering of cold objects as a WSS with M = 2, minimisation problem. This effectively means objects belonging to the cold region are clustered for a cache of size one. Graph partitioning algorithms are the best algorithms for solving the WSS with M = 2, minimisation problem [13, 7].

[11] Cold pages are more likely to be targeted for eviction, since "the purpose of buffer replacement algorithms is to keep popular pages memory resident" [11].

7 Experimental Results

In this section we present results of experiments conducted with the Object Clustering Benchmark (OCB) [4] using the Virtual Object Oriented Database simulator, (VOODB) [5]. VOODB is based on a generic discrete-event simulation framework. Its purpose is to allow performance evaluations of OODBMs in general, and optimisation methods like clustering in particular.

OCB is designed to benchmark OODBM systems and clustering polices in particular. The OCB database has a variety of parameters which make it very user-tunable. A database is generated by setting parameters such as total number of objects, maximum number of references per class, base instance size, number of classes, etc... Once these parameters are set, a database conforming to these parameters is randomly generated. The database consists of objects of varying sizes. In the experiments conducted in this paper the objects varied in size from 50 to 1200 bytes and the average object size was 268 bytes. A total of 20, 000 objects were used, resulting in a database size of 5.3 MB. The default OCB parameters were used, with the only exception being the number of classes was set to 50. The changes to the default parameters of VOODB, include: system class set to centralised; multiprogramming level set to 1; object initial placement set to sequential.

The results were generated via three steps. The first *training* step runs the database and collects statistical data of object access. The second *clustering* step uses the training data with the clustering algorithm to rearrange objects. The third *evaluation* step measures I/O generated from running the workload on the newly clustered database.

Our experiments compare the performance of two clustering algorithms, Greedy Graph Partitioning (GGP) and GPC3. In the experiments the point at which our implementation of GPC3 cuts the object graph [12] was set at three different places. These places were 60%, 90% and 120% of buffer size. This was done to test the sensitivity of GPC3 to variation of hot region size. 90% was chosen instead of 100% since it was found to give better results. This gives a indication of the sensitivity of GPC3 to its hot region size setting. As further work we plan to develop and test ways of generating the optimal hot region size setting, using information gathered in the training step.

The OCB workload used in this study included simple traversals, hierarchical traversals and stochastic traversals [4]. The depth of the traversals were 2, 4, and 6 respectively. 10000 transactions [13] were run for every result reported in this paper.

We introduced skew into the way in which roots of traversals were selected. Roots were broken up into hot and cold regions. In all experiments the hot region was set to 2 % size of database and had a 98 % probability of access [14]. However

[12] During phase one of GPC3 algorithm.

[13] Each transaction involved execution of one of the three traversals.

[14] That is there was a 98 % probability that the root of a traversal is from the hot region.

the number of hot objects generated by this pattern of access is greater than 2 % of database size since each traversal accesses more objects than just the root.

7.1 Dependency between Clustering and Buffer Replacement

In this section we explore the performance of GGP and GPC3 on ten different buffer replacement algorithms. The ten different buffer replacement algorithms investigated include: random (RAND); First In First Out (FIFO-N); CLOCK (CL-N); traditional Least Recently Used (LRU1-N); GCLOCK (GCL-N); Least Frequently Used (LFU-N); Least Recently Used K algorithm with K set to 2 (LRU2-H); GCLOCK algorithm using training data (GCL-T); Least Frequently Used algorithm using training data (LFU-T); Belady's optimum algorithm (OPT-T). Algorithms with a T suffix uses information gathered in the training step of the experiment to help make more accurate replacement decisions during the evaluation step. The N suffix is used for algorithms that do not use training data and also resets statistics for a page when it is first loaded into memory. Algorithms with a H suffix retains history information for a page when it is evicted from memory. However H suffix algorithms do not use training data.

The results from running the above described experiment on two different buffer sizes are depicted on figure 2. The first general observation is that GPC3 outperforms GGP for all buffer replacement algorithms when the buffer size is 2400KB. However for buffer size of 400KB, GPC3 and GGP performed approximately the same, for nine of the ten buffer replacement algorithms tested. We now explain the degradation in relative performance of GPC3 when buffer size is decreased. At smaller buffer sizes the various buffer replacement algorithms find it more difficult to retain in memory pages, belonging to the hot region of GPC3. This failing means clustering hot objects together is less profitable since even when many hot objects are clustered into the same page, the page still has a high probability of being evicted due to the small buffer size.

The only result in which GPC3 performs substantially worse than GGP is when buffer size is 400 KB and the buffer replacement algorithm used is LFU-N (depicted on figure 2 (b)). The reason for GPC3's bad performance in this situation lies in the way LFU-N works. LFU-N does not favor retaining recently loaded pages in memory. All other algorithms with the exception of RAND favor retaining recently loaded pages in memory.

7.2 Variation of Buffer Size Experiment

This experiment examined in more detail the effect of buffer size on the performance of GGP and GPC3. The buffer replacement algorithm used for this experiment is the popular LRU1-N algorithm.

The results of this experiment are shown on figure 3, the abbreviation GPC3-x is used to denote the GPC3 algorithm with a hot region size of x fraction of buffer size. These results show GPC3 outperforming GGP for a large region of buffer sizes (500 KB to 4200 KB). The reason for GPC3 to perform worse than or equal to GGP when the buffer size is smaller than 500 KB is again the fact at smaller buffer sizes the buffer replacement algorithm can not keep many hot pages in memory. The inability to keep hot pages in memory degrades the performance of GPC3, as explained in section 7.1.

When comparing GPC3 with various settings, on figure 3 (b), a hot region size of 0.9 fraction of buffer size performed best, once the buffer size was larger than 1800 KB. This result can be explained by the fact, once the buffer is large enough (thus giving the buffer replacement algorithm a good chance to keep hot pages memory resident), then it is advantageous to be able to fill almost all of the cache with hot pages (as is the case when hot region size is set to 0.9). When hot region is set to 1.2, the hot region is too large to fit entirely into memory and thus performance degrades.

When the buffer size is greater than 4200 KB all clustering algorithms perform the same, since at these buffer sizes the entire working set can fit in memory.

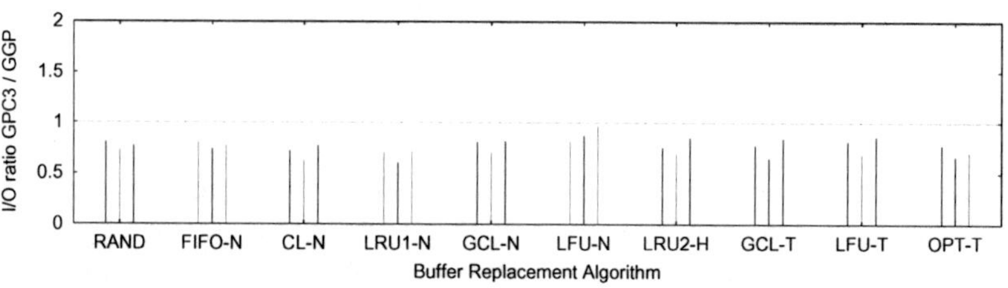

(a) Buffer size of 2400 KB

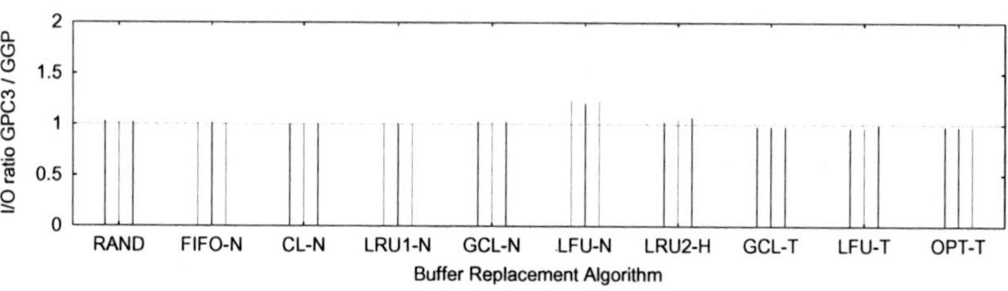

(b) Buffer size of 400 KB

Fig. 2. A performance comparison between GGP and GPC3 for various buffer replacement algorithms. The results depict the I/O ratio of GPC3 over GGP. A result of less than one indicate GPC3 produces less I/O than GGP. A result of 0.5 indicates GPC3 only producing half as many I/Os as GGP. Three results are reported for each buffer replacement algorithm. These results differ in the hot region size of GPC3, 60%, 90%, and 120% size of buffer respectively. The geometric mean across all the buffer replacement algorithms for buffer size of 400KB, are 1.028, 1.024 and 1.034 respectively. Geometric mean for buffer size of 2400KB, are 0.778, 0.731 and 0.806 respectively.

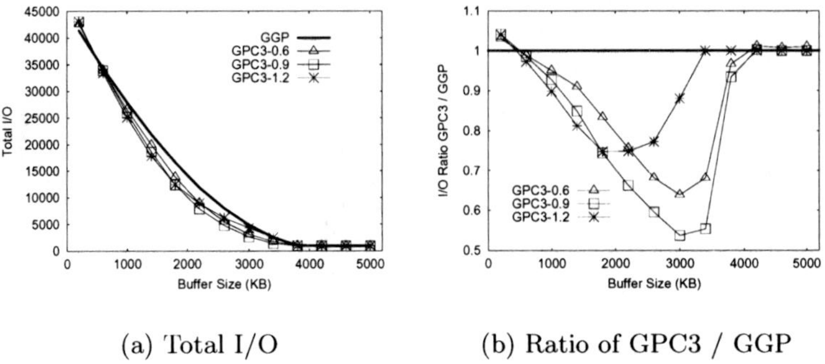

(a) Total I/O (b) Ratio of GPC3 / GGP

Fig. 3. The effects of variation of buffer size on the performance of clustering algorithms.

8 Conclusion

This paper has highlighted the importance of cache consciousness for clustering algorithms. The clustering problem has been restated for the first time to incorporate caching. As a result a new family of clustering algorithms (C3) have been developed. In order to test the performance of C3, GPC3 a concrete example of C3 was proposed.

A performance evaluation of GPC3 was conduct against GGP. GGP is a member of the graph partitioning family of clustering algorithms, which has been shown to provide the best quality of clustering. Results indicate GPC3 outperforms GGP when the buffer size is large compared to the database size and about the same performance for smaller buffer sizes. This implies systems with a large memory size compared to the working set size will benefit more from GPC3.

9 Further Work

An obvious area for further work is to introduce more algorithms that use the C3 approach of clustering. Intelligent ways of finding points at which to cut the sorted sequence of objects in phase one of C3 is an interesting area of further research.

The cache conscious approach to clustering should be introduced into dynamic clustering [15]. A possible way of doing this is to apply OPCF [8] on C3. OPCF is a generic framework by which static clustering algorithms can be transformed into dynamic algorithms.

[15] In dynamic clustering, clustering occurs concurrently with database operation.

Acknowledgement. We would like to thank Jerome Darmont for making the sources of VOODB and OCB freely available. These tools have helped tremendously for our experimental work. In addition we would like to thank John Zigman and Stephen Blackburn for their helpful comments and suggestions.

References

1. Ailamaki, A., Dewitt, D. J., Hill, M. D., and Wood, D. A. DBMSs on a modern processor: Where does time go? In *The 25th VLDB conference, Edinburgh, Scotland* (September 1999), pp. 266–277.
2. Belady, L. A. A study of replacement algorithms for a virtual-storage computer. *IBM Systems Journal 5*, 2 (1966).
3. Benzaken, V., and Delobel, C. Enhaning performance in a persistent object store: Clustering strategies in o_2. Tech. Rep. 50-90, Altair, August 1990.
4. Darmont, J., Petit, B., and Schneider, M. Ocb: A generic benchmark to evaluate the performances of object-oriented database systems. In *International Conference on Extending Database Technology (EDBT)* (Valencia Spain, March 1998), LNCS Vol. 1377 (Springer), pp. 326–340.
5. Darmont, J., and Schneider, M. VOODB: A generic discrete-event random simulation model to evaluate the performances of oodbs. In *The 25th VLDB conference, Edinburgh, Scotland* (September 1999), pp. 254–265.
6. Denning, P. J. The working set model of program behavior. *Commincations of ACM 11*, 5 (May 1968), 323–333.
7. Gerlhof, C., Kemper, A., Kilger, C., and Moerkotte, G. Partition-based clustering in object bases: From theory to practice. *In Proceedings of the International Conference on Foundations of Data Organisation and Algorithms (FODO)* (1993).
8. He, Z., Marquez, A., and Blackburn, S. Opportunistic prioritised clustering framework (OPCF). In *Symposium on Objects and Databases* (June 2000).
9. Knafla, N. *Prefetching Techniques for Client/Server, Object-Oriented Database Systems.* PhD thesis, University of Edinburgh, 1999.
10. Nicola, V. F., Dan, A., and Dias, D. M. Analysis of the generalized clock buffer replacement scheme for database transaction processing. In *Proc. of the 1992 ACM SIGMETRICS Conference* (1992), pp. 35–46.
11. O'Neil, E. J., O'Neil, P. E., and Weikum, G. The lru-k page replacement algorithm for database disk buffering. In *Proc. of the 1993 ACM SIGMOD Conference.* 1993, pp. 297–306.
12. Stamos, J. Static grouping of small objects to enhance performance of a paged virtual memory. In *ACM Transactions on Computer Systems* (May 1984), vol. 2, pp. 155–180.
13. Tsangaris, E.-M. M. *Principles of Static Clustering For Object Oriented Databases.* PhD thesis, University of Wisconsin-Madison, 1992.
14. Tsangaris, M. M., and Naughton, J. F. A stochastic approach for clustering in object bases. In *Proceedings of the ACM SIGMOD conference on Management of Data* (1991), pp. 12–21.

Closed External Schemas in Object-Oriented Databases

Manuel Torres[1] and José Samos[2]

[1] Departamento de Lenguajes y Computación. Universidad de Almería.
Carretera Sacramento S/N. 04120. Almería. Spain
mtorres@ual.es
[2] Departamento de Lenguajes y Sistemas Informáticos. Universidad de Granada
Avenida Andalucía, 38. 18071. Granada. Spain
jsamos@ugr.es

Abstract. Schema closure is a property to guarantee that classes in a schema have not references to classes that are not included into it (*external references*). The existing methodologies solve this point including referenced classes into the schema. In this paper, a new kind of schema closure (*reduction closure*) is put forward. Reduction closure is based on the transformation of classes with external references, removing these references to fulfil the schema closure property. The main benefit of reduction closure is that it can be used as a method to simplify the external schema definition process, because explicit definition of derived classes for hiding external references is avoided. In addition, the explicit definition of derived classes to update the references to modified classes is also avoided. This closure algorithm is part of an external schema generation system for ODMG databases that we are developing, which is also briefly described in this paper.

1 Introduction

Definition of *external schemas* in object-oriented databases can be divided into the following tasks: definition of *derived classes*, selection of classes that make up external schemas and, generation of external schemas.

Definition of derived classes allows us to customize existing classes from which they are defined (*base classes*). Once all the necessary derived classes are defined, the external schema definition process goes on with the selection of a set of classes (base and/or derived) to be included into the external schema. This selection can be carried out by means of a declarative language [Rund92b, Torr00] and takes place in the database repository.

Finally, the generation of external schemas builds closed, valid, and complete external schemas from the set of classes selected. In a *closed* schema, every class referenced by a class included into it, must be also included into it (a class *A* is a class referenced by a class *B*, if *A* is used in the specification of *B*, either as aggregation or as relationship). A *valid* schema contains only consistent (valid) relationships between its classes. A *complete* schema contains all the non-redundant relationships existing between any two classes of it.

In this paper, a new kind of closure, named *reduction closure*, is proposed. Unlike the one used in most existing works [Abit91, Scho91, Rund92a, Bert96, Guer97],

H.C. Mayr et al. (Eds.): DEXA 2001, LNCS 2113, pp. 826–835, 2001.

reduction closure generates closed external schemas without adding classes to the set of classes selected to compose the external schema. Instead, classes with external references are replaced with classes that hide those references. Reduction closure can be used as a method to define external schemas, which avoids the explicit definition of derived classes that hide the external references. If a user wants to include a class without including its external references, he or she has to define explicitly a derived class in order to hide them, and replace the original class with the new derived class. However, classes with external references that have been replaced could be referenced by other classes of the schema, and then, additional derived classes have to be defined in order to update the references to the new classes, and so on. With reduction closure, these definitions are carried out automatically; therefore, the external schema definition process becomes easier. Reduction closure has to be considered as an additional method with respect to the existing ones; the schema definer can select which kind of closure to use, or even, to use different closure policies in the same schema definition process. The proposed reduction closure is part of an external schema definition mechanism that we are developing in the ODMG framework [Samo95, Torr00, Torr01a], since the ODMG 3.0 specifications [Cate00] do not address the definition of external schemas.

The remainder of this paper is organized as follows. Section 2 describes our external schema definition mechanism. In Section 3, the schema closure concept is explained and existing proposals are described. Section 4 puts forward the reduction closure. In Section 5, a hybrid approach is proposed. Finally, Section 6 summarizes the conclusions of this paper and discusses the future work.

2 An External Schema Definition Mechanism for ODMG

In the current specifications of the ODMG 3.0 standard, external schema definition for ODMG databases is not addressed. Only, a very basic *view* mechanism is proposed, *named queries*, which defines a function by means of a query expressed in OQL; the OQL query is evaluated when the function is called. Named queries cannot be considered as a mechanism for defining derived classes, because they cannot be used as input of other named queries and, only selection and projection operations can be used.

Therefore, given that there is a lack in the ODMG standard to define external schemas, we are developing an external schema definition mechanism based on its object model. This means the extension of the ODMG architecture according to the three levels ANSI/SPARC architecture. This mechanism [Torr01a], based on [Samo95], is characterized by the use of the *derivation* relationship [Bert92] into the repository to integrate the derived classes. The use of the derivation relationship in the repository is not an extension of the object-oriented paradigm, because it is not used in end-user schemas (conceptual and external schemas), and the repository schema (metaschema) is still an object-oriented schema [Torr01b].

In our mechanism, unlike in [Sant95, Guer97], classes of the external schemas are related only using inheritance, aggregation and associations (i.e. ODMG relationships). In addition, unlike in [Scho91, Rund92a], external schemas are defined without generating intermediate and possibly meaningless classes. Nevertheless, some intermediate interfaces may be generated when two classes that are not related by means of inheritance have common behaviour.

Figure 1 illustrates the class hierarchy corresponding to an example of a database. The database stores data of people. People may be clients or employees. People have vehicles, which are manufactured by a firm, and a vehicle has only an owner. In addition, the addresses of the people are stored as objects. For sake of simplicity, attributes are not shown in the figure but we assume the existence of some attributes in the following example (i.e., salary and category for employees).

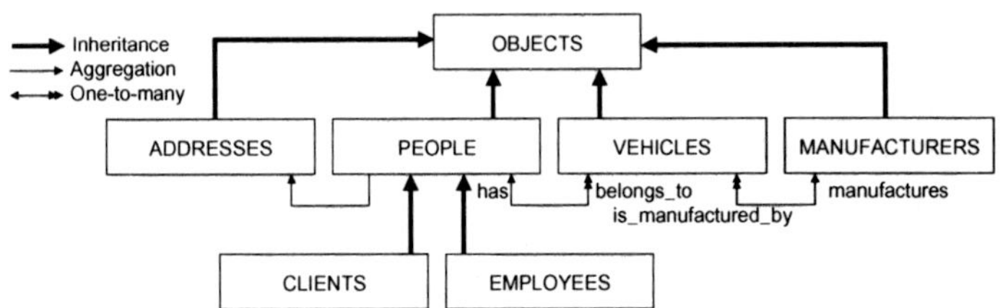

Fig. 1. Class hierarchy representation.

In order to explain how our mechanism works, Figure 2 illustrates the class hierarchies of the repository and of an external schema (the surrounded area). The external schema is defined from the conceptual schema of the previous example, replacing the class `EMPLOYEES` with a derived class `EMPLOYEES'`, which hides the salary and selects only employees that are not managers.

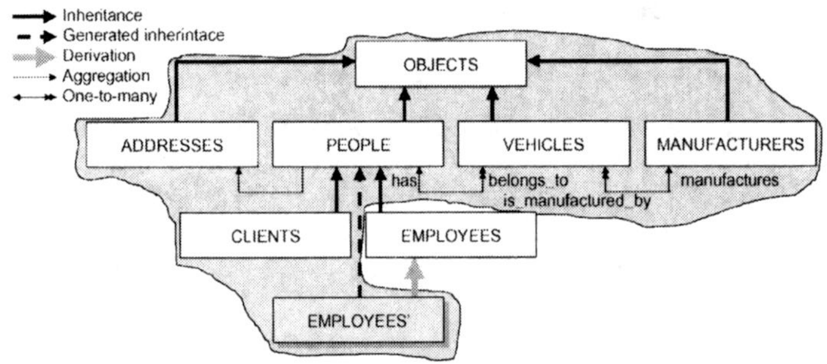

Fig. 2. Repository and external schema (the surrounded area) class hierarchies.

If the approach proposed in [Scho91, Rund92a] had been used, an intermediate class `EMPLOYEES''` would have been defined in order to integrate the `EMPLOYEES'` by means of inheritance. On the other hand, if the approach proposed in [Sant95, Guer97] had been used, `EMPLOYEES'` would be related in the external schema with its base class with a relationship that is not allowed in the ODMG object model. Therefore, our mechanism integrates easily the derived class in the repository, but the object-oriented paradigm is preserved because end-user schemas only use relationships allowed in the ODMG object model. The existence of a mechanism to define derived classes for ODMG is supposed, and therefore its definition is beyond of the scope of this paper.

In Section 4, where reduction closure is explained, derived classes will be integrated by means of derivation. However, the reduction closure concept proposed in this paper is independent of the approach used to integrate derived classes.

3 The Closure Problem: Enlargement Closure

In our proposal, like in [Rund92a], external schema definition specifies the classes to be included into the external schema returning a set of isolated classes. Schema closure is a property to guarantee that no class of a schema includes references to other classes that are not included into it.

A closed schema can be defined in this way [Rund92a]: Let C be the set of classes of a schema and R the set of inheritance relationships defined in it. $Uses(C_i)$ can be defined as the set of classes that use the properties and operations of C_i.

Definition [Closed schema] *A schema $S = (C, R)$ is closed if, and only if, $C = Uses(C_i) \cup C, \forall C_i \in C$*

Rundensteiner's methodology studies the schema closure problem deeply using an enlargement approach. This kind of closure is based on the idea that the user wants an external schema with the specified classes and, if it is necessary, other classes can be also included into it in order to achieve the schema closure.

Figure 3 illustrates the class hierarchy in the repository and an external schema (the surrounded area). The external schema is initially defined selecting only the class PEOPLE. Given that PEOPLE has two references to classes that are not included into the external schema, ADDRESSES and VEHICLES, the enlargement closure adds these classes to the schema. In addition, since the added class VEHICLES has also a reference to MANUFACTURERS, and the latter is not included into the schema either, it has also to be included. Therefore, referenced classes are included recursively. The repository is updated with the definition of the external schema.

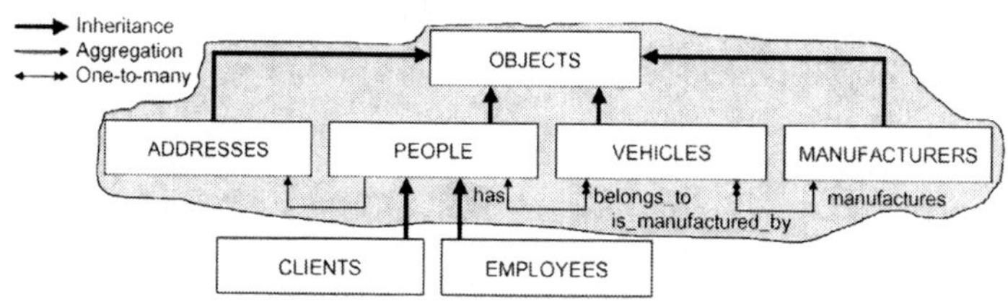

Fig. 3. Resulting schema using enlargement closure.

In [Abit91, Scho91], the closure problem is quoted, but without explaining how to solve it. In [Bert96, Guer97], the inclusion of the necessary classes is mentioned without proposing a solution. In addition, since their external schemas can include only derived classes, a "virtualization" process is used to generate a derived class with the same type and extent of its base class to include it in the external schema.

4 Reduction Closure

Enlargement closure may add some classes to external schemas so that, all the referenced classes are also included into the schema, as well as all the classes referenced by them, and so on. However, in some situations the schema definer may not want to include into the external schema all the referenced classes, or some of them. For example, this would mean that the schema definer selects only the classes `PEOPLE` and `ADDRESSES`, as shown in Figure 4.a, and does not want to include the class `VEHICLES`, which is referenced by the class `PEOPLE`. However, since schema closure must be fulfilled, but no additional classes are wanted, classes with external references must be replaced with another classes, which do no not include external references. This is the premise which reduction closure is based on, that is, to replace classes that have external references in order to remove such references. Thus, schema closure is fulfilled and no classes are added to the schema.

Figure 4.b illustrates the repository as well as the external schema resulting of applying reduction closure (the surrounded area). Given that the defined external schema is not closed because `PEOPLE` has a reference to `VEHICLES`, and `VEHICLES` is not included into the original definition of the external schema (Figure 4.a), reduction closure proposes the replacement of `PEOPLE` with a derived class `PEOPLE'`, which hides the external references of its base class.

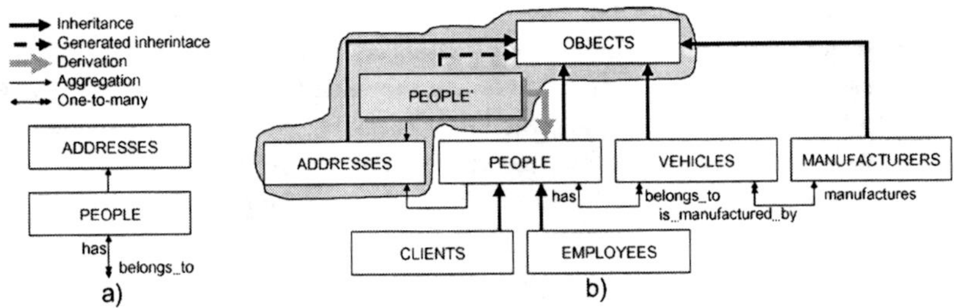

Fig. 4. a) Initial class selection. b) Resulting schema using reduction closure.

Reduction closure assumes that the user only wants to include the classes that have been selected by means of the external schema definition language, and no one else. In order to remove the references to non-included classes, new classes have to be defined to replace them. Classes with external references cannot be directly modified because, if we modify them instead of defining new ones, we would produce collateral effects in other schemas where those classes were also included (the conceptual schema or another external schemas).

4.1 Reduction Closure as a Mechanism to Define External Schemas

Reduction closure can be used as a mechanism to define external schemas because it simplifies the external schema definition process. Derived classes that hide external references are defined automatically, and existing relationships are updated automatically. In the previous example (Figure 4), given that the schema definer wanted to define an external schema only with people and their addresses, but without including their vehicles, a new class derived from class PEOPLE has to be defined in order to replace the class with external references.

However, if other classes of the schema were referencing to the class with external references, new derived classes would have to be defined to update the references, and so on. With reduction closure, explicit definition of this chain of derived classes definitions and reference updates is avoided. We can see it with an example. Let us suppose that the user wants to define an external schema from the conceptual schema of the example we are following along this paper, including all the classes except MANUFACTURERS. The schema is not closed, because VEHICLES references to MANUFACTURERS, and the latter has not been included into it. Therefore, a derived class VEHICLES' projecting out the references to MANUFACTURERS has to be defined. Now, given that VEHICLES has been replaced with VEHICLES' and, PEOPLE was referencing to the former, the definition of PEOPLE in the external schema is not correct yet. Then, a new derived class PEOPLE' has to be defined in order to reference to the derived class instead of to the original class.

Nevertheless, the process does not stop here, since CLIENTS and EMPLOYEES are subclasses of PEOPLE and consequently, they had also a reference (inherited) to VEHICLES. Therefore, a new derived class for CLIENTS and another for EMPLOYEES have to be defined. The result of this process is illustrated in Figure 5, where all the derived classes have been defined and the references have been updated. Note, that all of these changes have to be carried out due to the user did not want to include a referenced class, and this situation is very usual.

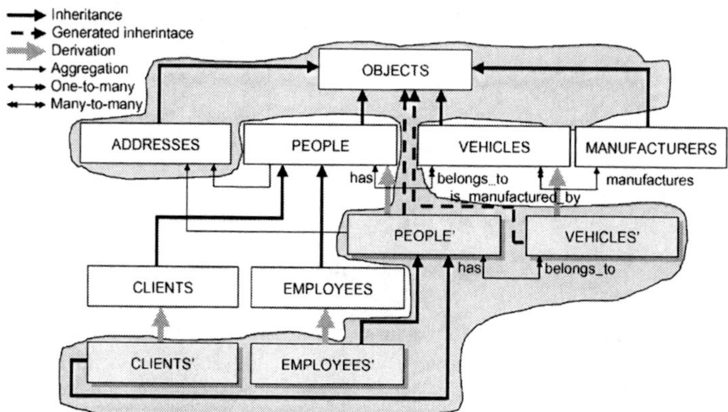

Fig. 5. Reduction closure. Derived classes and new relationships are defined automatically.

As can be seen in Figure 5, changes must be propagated to classes that use or are subclasses of modified classes. Therefore, if a user wants to define an external schema without a class, which is referenced by one of the classes selected to compose it, the external schema definition process becomes hard, since modifications must be propagated. However, if reduction closure is used, the external schema definition process becomes easier because all of these definitions and modifications are carried out automatically.

4.2 Propagating the Modifications

In reduction closure, derived classes have to be defined to project out the external references and to update the references. However, this definition has to be scheduled carefully in order to avoid multiple modifications of derived classes.

Let us suppose a schema like the one in Figure 6, where classes `E` and `G` have external references. If the closure algorithm generates a derived class `E'` in order to hide the external references of `E`, and a derived class `D'` that references to `E'` instead of `E`, then, a derived class `A'` should be generated in order to update the references to `D'`, instead of `D`. Furthermore, since `B` and `C` also have references to `D`, because they inherited it from `A`, a new derived class has to be defined for each one. Therefore, `B` and `C` are replaced with `B'` and `C'`. However, since `G` has also external references, a new derived class `G'` must be defined, which replaces to `G`. `F'` has to be defined to replace to `F` in order to reference to `G'`. Therefore, the derived class `A'` has to reference to `F'` instead of `F`, that is, a new derived class `A''` has to be defined and, as explained above, new classes `B''` and `C''` have also to be defined. The multiple modifications of derived classes would not have happened if the referenced classes had been updated before the classes that were referencing to them.

Therefore, we can use a graph based on the one illustrated in Figure 6, which represents the constraints to be satisfied if we want to define derived classes in only one step. Derived classes that replace `B` and `C` have to be defined after the definition of the derived class `A'` which replaces to `A`. Besides, `A'` should not be defined until `D'` and `F'` are defined, and so on. This is a planning problem, which can be solved with Petri nets or Constraint Satisfaction techniques, between others.

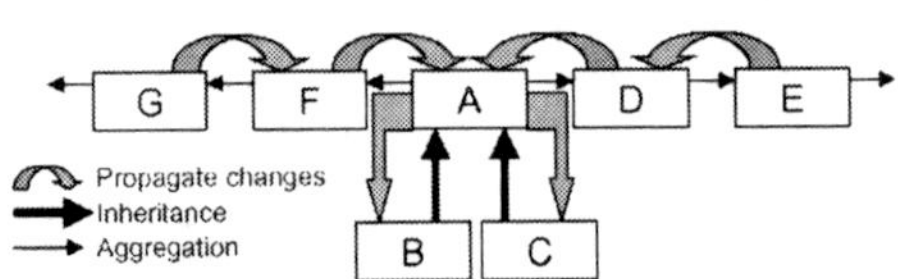

Fig. 6. Propagation of changes.

Then, the problem of generating a closed schema with respect to the reduction closure can be divided into several tasks: a) determine which classes must be transformed, either because they have external references, or because they have references to classes that have to be also transformed; b) determine a sequence of transformations, so that necessary derived classes are defined in one step; and c) define the necessary derived classes using the order obtained in the step above.

Next, a tagging method to indicate whether a class has to be replaced with a derived class is proposed. This method analyses the five cases that may occur, which are illustrated in Figure 7. Aggregated classes of a modified class do not need to be adapted (figure 7.a). If an aggregated class has to be adapted, the classes that reference to it have to be modified after it (figure 7.b). If two classes are related with an association (relationships in ODMG), and at least, one of them has to be modified, both classes have to be adapted (figure 7.c). Subclasses of a modified class must be modified after it (figure 7.d). Superclasses of an adapted class do not need to be modified if they have not to be modified for another reason (figure 7.e).

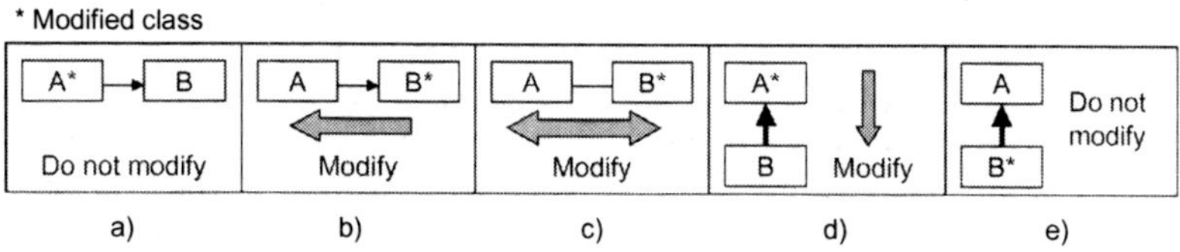

Fig. 7. Cases of propagation of modifications in a schema.

Following these indications, a graph can be built, where nodes represent classes and arcs establish an order to define the derived classes, so that they can be defined in only one step. Figure 8 proposes a draft of the reduction closure algorithm taking as input the set of classes S specified in the external schema definition process.

```
Procedure ReductionClosure(S)
  1.  Find out classes with external references
  2.  Determine affected classes
  3.  Define constraints
  4.  Establish a derived class definition order
  5.  Define derived classes according to the order
End Procedure
```

Fig. 8. Reduction closure algorithm

Therefore, users may define external schemas that are not closed and, the reduction closure is achieved by the system. Generated derived classes are integrated into the repository. In our mechanism, derived classes and their base classes are related by means of derivation relationships; naturally, this fact is also applied to the generated derived classes. However, given that the derived classes that are needed to hide external references can be already defined in other schemas, their existence must be checked in the repository in order to reuse previous definitions.

5 A Hybrid Approach

Given that both enlargement and reduction closure have their own advantages, the schema definer may be interested in using both approaches together in the same schema definition. That is, to apply enlargement closure to some classes, and to apply reduction closure to others. Classes which enlargement closure is applied are those that the schema definer wants to include together with all their details. However, classes which reduction closure is applied, correspond to classes where the concepts they represent are interesting to the users, but not all their details.

This hybrid approach may be solved tagging the classes selected to compose the external schema as *transformable* or *non-transformable* [Samo96]. Transformable classes may be modified applying reduction closure in order to fulfil the schema closure. On the other hand, non-transformable classes must appear in the external schemas without modifying their definition. By default, the classes referenced by a non-transformable class may be also non-transformable and they would be included recursively. However, added classes can be tagged when they are included into the set in an interactive definition process.

Nevertheless, like in the reduction closure, a processing order for the set of classes must be defined. First, the non-transformable classes must be analysed (before the transformable ones) in order to include the classes referenced by them. If transformable classes were processed before non-transformable ones, some transformable classes would have to be modified in order to hide external references; however, classes corresponding to the removed references may be included later, while processing non-transformable classes.

The concept of non-transformable class can be understood as a class whose properties and operations must be preserved, that is, they cannot be projected. However, a non-transformable class may have relationships (inheritance, aggregation or exactly relationships) with another classes of the schema, and some of these classes may have been modified because they were transformable classes. Then, the non-transformable class must be replaced with a derived class, which only has its references updated. This is not a violation of the "non-transformability principle"; new non-transformable classes still have their references, but their links are updated. These changes must be also propagated.

Therefore, the main tasks to be carried out by the external schema definition process under the hybrid approach are the following: When classes are selected, they are tagged as transformable or non-transformable. Then, non-transformable classes are processed in order to include their referenced classes. Finally, a reduction closure is applied to the rest of the classes of the schema (transformable classes).

6 Conclusions and Future Work

In this paper, the concept of schema closure has been studied. Schema closure states that all the referenced classes of a schema must be included into it. The existing approach adds all the referenced classes to the schema in order to fulfil this property, and we name it *enlargement closure*. In this work, an additional schema closure method, named *reduction closure*, has been proposed. Unlike the enlargement closure, it replaces the classes that have external references with derived classes that hide those references. In addition, this replacement must be propagated and may entail the definition of other derived classes. Reduction closure carries out this propagation automatically, simplifying the definition of external schemas

Enlargement and reduction closure have their advantages and drawbacks. A hybrid approach is defined tagging the classes of external schemas as *transformable* or *non-transformable*. A reduction approach is used for transformable classes and an enlargement approach is used for non-transformable classes.

Both enlargement and reduction closure approaches can be used in the external schema definition mechanism we are developing in the ODMG framework. This mechanism is characterized by the integration of derived classes into the repository using the *derivation* relationship. External schemas are generated without extending the object-oriented paradigm (schemas only use relationships allowed in ODMG) and without generating intermediate classes, possibly meaningless to end-users.

Given that both the external schema definition mechanism system and the reduction closure proposed need a derived class definition mechanism, we are currently working on such mechanism, one more elaborated than the ODMG named queries, that takes advantage of the richness of the object-oriented model.

Acknowledgements. This work has been supported by the Spanish CICYT (project TIC 2000-1723-C02-02).

References

[Abit91] Abiteboul, S., Bonner, A. 'Object and Views'. In Proc. ACM SIGMOD International Conference on Management of Data. pp. 238-247. 1991

[Bert92] Bertino, E. 'A View Mechanism for Object-Oriented Databases'. In Proc. of the 3rd International Conference on Extending Database Technology. pp. 136-151. 1992

[Bert96] Bertino, E., Guerrini, G. 'Viewpoints in Object Database Systems'. In Proc. of the SIGSOFT '96 Workshops. pp. 289-293. 1996

[Cate00] Catell, R.G.G. *The Object Database Standard: ODMG 3.0*. Morgan Kaufmann. 2000
[Cate00] Catell, R.G.G. *The Object Database Standard: ODMG 3.0*. Morgan Kaufmann. 2000
[Guer97] Guerrini, G., Bertino, E., Catania, B., Garcia-Molina, J. 'A Formal View of Object-Oriented Database Systems'. In TAPOS. Vol. 3(3). pp. 157-183. 1997

[Rund92a] Rundensteiner, E. 'Multiview: A Methodology for Supporting Multiple Views in Object-Oriented Databases'. In Proc. Of the 18th VLDB. pp. 187-198. 1992

[Rund92b] Rundensteiner, E. A., Bic, L. 'Automatic View Schema Generation in Object-Oriented Databases'. Technical Report WPI-CS-TR-92-15. 1992

[Samo95] Samos, J. 'Definition of External Schemas in Object Oriented Databases'. In Proc. Of 1995 OOIS. pp. 154-166. 1995

[Samo96] Samos, J., Saltor, F. 'External Schema Generation Algorithms for Object Oriented Databases'. In Proc. of 1996 OOIS. pp. 317-332. 1996

[Sant95] Santos, C.S. 'Design and Implementation of Object-Oriented Views'. In Proc. Of DEXA, 6th International Conference. pp. 91-102. 1995

[Scho91] Scholl, M.H., Laasch, C. Tresch, M. 'Updatable Views in Object-Oriented Databases'. In Proc. Of the 2nd Deductive and Object-Oriented Databases. pp. 189-207. 1991

[Torr00] Torres, M, Samos, J. 'Definition of External Schemas in ODMG Databases'. In Proc. of 2000 OOIS. pp. 3-14. 2000

[Torr01a] Torres, M., Samos, J. 'Generation of external schemas in ODMG databases'. To appear in Proc. of IDEAS01.

[Torr01b] Torres, M., Samos, J. 'Metadata for Defining External Schemas in ODMG Databases. A Proposal'. *Submitted for publication.*

Supporting Cooperative Inter-Organizational Business Transactions

Juha Puustjärvi[1] and Harri Laine[2]

[1] Helsinki University of Technology, Software Business and Engineering Institute, P.O.Box 9600, FIN-02015 HUT, Finland
Juha.Puustjarvi@cs.hut.fi
[2] Department of Computer Science, P.O.Box 26 (Teollisuuskatu 23) FIN-00014 University of Helsinki, Finland
Harri.Laine@cs.helsinki.fi

Abstract. A business transaction is an interaction in the real world, usually between an enterprise and a person, where something is exchanged. Business transactions, where dealing is made by first requesting the bids and then making the deal, are common in practice. However, such cooperative bidding-based processes cannot be carried out by traditional transactions. In this paper we present appropriate concepts and methods to execute bidding-based business transactions in a distributed workflow context. The main ingredients of the proposed extended business transaction (EBT) model are persistent buffers and semantic locks.

1 Introduction

The concept of a *workflow* was introduced to facilitate business process reengineering and automation [4]. A problem with workflow models is that they allow users to cooperate only by successive tasks, i.e., a workflow defines the order of task execution or conditions under which tasks must be executed, but negotiation-like cooperation cannot be automated in a reliable way. However, business processes requiring negotiation are common. For example, negotiations where dealing is made by first requesting the bids and then making the deal are common.

In this paper we present appropriate concepts and methods for executing business transactions that require negotiation-like cooperation in a workflow context. The proposed model, called the *Extended Business Transaction* (EBT) model, does not require any specific protocol. The atomicity of EBTs' execution (failure atomicity) is ensured by persistent buffers which are implemented as tables of a relational database system. The isolation requirements of EBTs (execution atomicity) are enforced by semantic locks which are implemented as constraints supported by an SQL-system [8].

We have implemented a workflow management system prototype, called *WorkMan* [7, 5], which will be used for EBTs implementation. The focus of the *WorkMan* project is on ensuring the reliable executions of workflows.

H.C. Mayr et al. (Eds.): DEXA 2001, LNCS 2113, pp. 836–845, 2001.

The rest of the paper is organized as follows. Next section views the concept of a transactional workflow. Section 3 deals with the architecture of the distributed systems supporting EBTs. The way the failure atomicity of EBTs is enforced is the topic of Section 4. Then, in Section 5, it is shown how semantic locking can be used in ensuring the execution atomicity of EBTs. Section 6 concludes the paper.

2 Transactional workflows

A natural and sufficient criterion for workflow isolation correctness is that the execution of workflows is serializable, i.e., equivalent to a serial execution. However, the serializability requirement of long-lasting activities overly restricts the performance of the system.

By using semantic information it is possible to weaken, or give up altogether, the serializability criterion, and yet ensure workflow execution correctness. However, analogous with traditional semantic concurrency control models [6, 3] the use of semantic information makes the specification as well as the management of the system more complex. The way the semantic information is used in executing EBTs is discussed in Sections 4 and 5.

A transactional workflow involves coordinated execution of tasks which may require access to heterogeneous, autonomous and distributed database systems. The coordination requirements are expressed by control-flow dependencies, which specify a precondition for the execution of each task. The preconditions are based on the execution states of other tasks (i.e., whether they are active, committed or aborted), output parameters of other tasks, or on external variables (e.g., on time). For example, the execution structure of the EBT consists of four kinds of tasks (Figure 1).

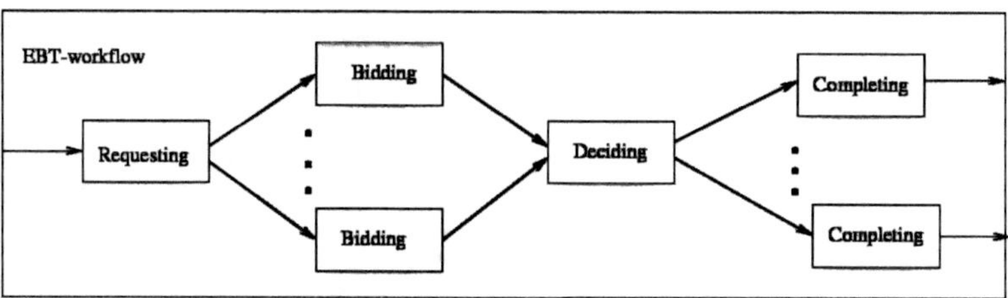

Fig. 1. The execution structure of a transaction based on the EBT.

The functions and the preconditions of the tasks in the EBT-workflow are the followings:

- *Requesting task*: The buyer requests the producers to make a bid of certain products. The prerequisite of the *Requesting task* is the user call including the appropriate parameters.

– *Bidding tasks*: The producers make bids and send them to the buyer. The prerequisite of the *Bidding task* is the output of the *Requesting task*.
– *Decision task*: The buyer makes the decision (which bids are accepted and which are rejected) and sends a message to each producer. The prerequisite of the *Decision task* is the output of one or more *Bidding tasks*.
– *Completing task*: Depending on the decision the producers perform appropriate actions. The prerequisite of the *Completing task* is the output of the *Deciding task*.

By decomposing the execution structure of the EBT to the sites of buyer and producers we get the execution structures presented in Figure 2. At the site of the buyer the function of the workflow system is to coordinate the execution of the tasks *Requesting* and *Deciding*, and at the sites of the producers the workflow system has to coordinate the execution of the tasks *Bidding* and *Completing*. The way the *Bidding task* and the *Completing task* are extended by semantic locking is a topic of Section 5.

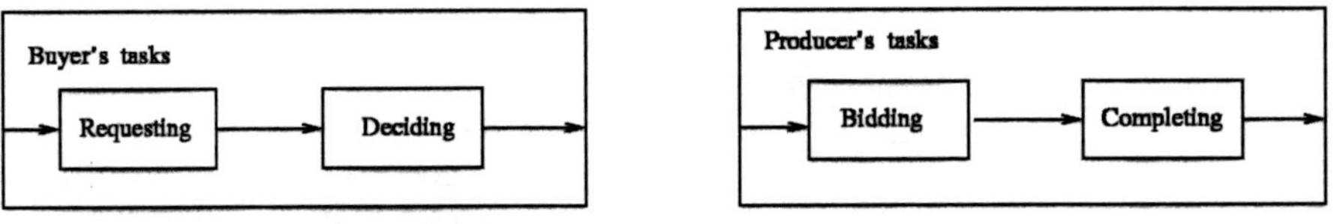

Fig. 2. The tasks of the Buyer and the Procuders.

In order to illustrate the communication requirements between the *buyer* and the *producers* we also model the EBT as a tree-structured transaction (Figure 3). Now the tasks *Requesting* and *Deciding* correspond to the root of the tree and the tasks *Bidding* and *Completing* correspond to the leaves of the tree.

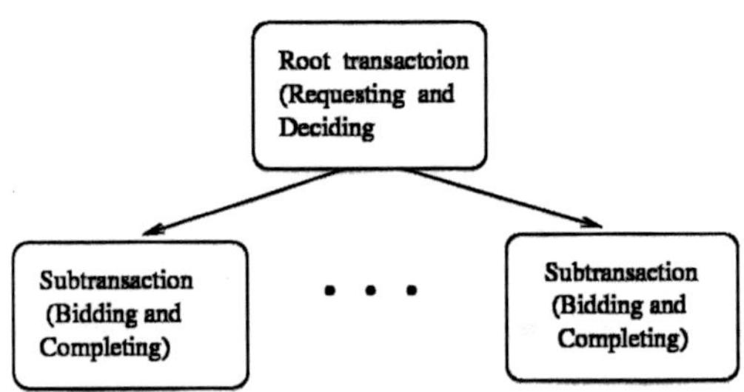

Fig. 3. An EBT as a tree-structured transaction.

The execution of the tree-structured EBT nicely match to the client server paradigm: the buyer corresponds to the client while the producers correspond to the servers. The gains of the client-server architecture based on buffers are discussed in Section 4.

3 EBT-applications

We use the term *EBT-application* to indicate the software where different EBTs can be executed. An *EBT-application* (Figure 4) consists of an *EBT-client*, a *Communication system*, and some *EBT-servers*.

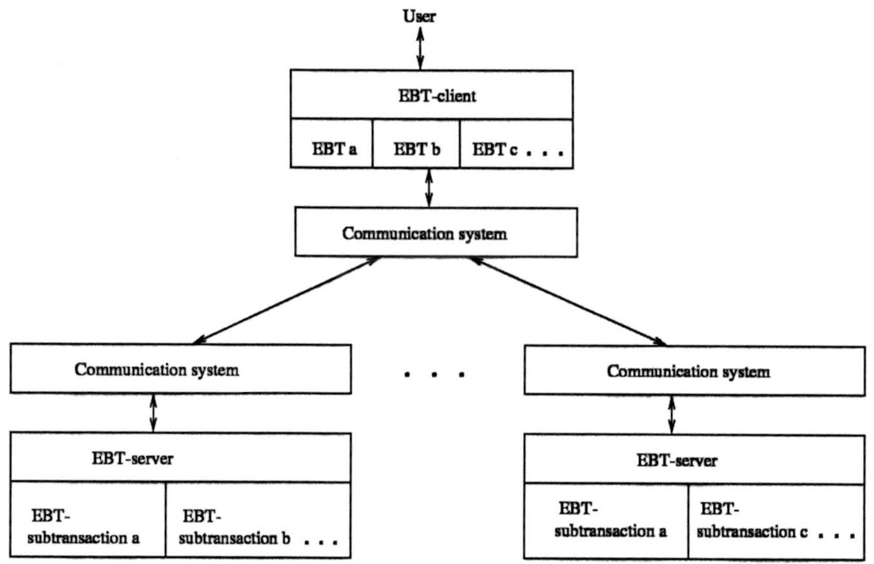

Fig. 4. EBT-applications.

An *EBT-client* gathers the input from the user to execute an EBT. It displays the menus where the user can select the kind of EBT to run and the forms for the user to provide input for the EBTs. For example, in a travel bureau (a buyer) there may be specific forms for requesting a bid for a flight ticket and for requesting a bid for staying in a hotel.

The EBT-client turns the input provided by the user into communication messages and passes them to the *Communication system*. The system moves the messages to the sites where the *EBT-servers* execute the *Bidding tasks* of the EBT. After that the bids are transferred to the EBT-client where they are displayed in an EBT-specific form. Then the user chooses the accepted bid(s), the EBT-client gathers the input from the form and turns it into a communication message and passes it to the *Communication system*. The system transfers them to the appropriate EBT-servers which execute the *Completing tasks* of the EBT.

4 EBT's failure atomicity

The failure atomicity of an EBT means that its execution tolerates system and communication failures. More accurately: if all existing failures are repaired and no new failures occur for a sufficiently long time period, then the EBT will eventually be executed.

The concepts used in ensuring the failure atomicity are presented in Figure 5. In this architecture the client and the servers do not communicate directly but

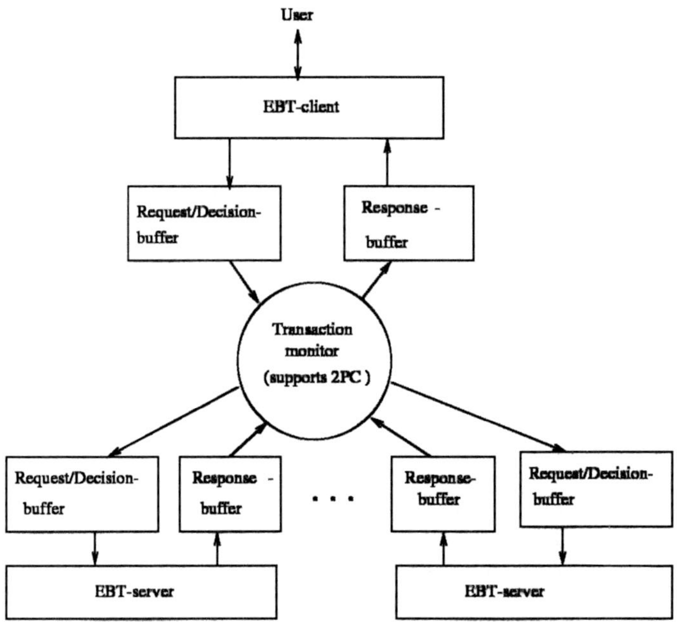

Fig. 5. The buffered execution of EBTs.

rather through the buffers. In addition, the buffers are distributed over the client site and the server sites. An important point is that each buffer is a transactional resource, i.e., operations on a buffer are made permanent or undone depending on whether the transaction that issued the operations commits or aborts. The buffers are implemented as tables of relational database systems.

The execution of an EBT goes as follows:

1. the buyer (client) inserts the bid requests into the buyer's Request/Decision-buffer. The requests may concern one or more producers, i.e., there may be one or more requests in the buffer.
2. The software, which supports the 2PC-protocol (e.g., a transaction monitor), forwards the requests to the Request/Decision-buffers of the producers to be

requested. Specifically, a distributed transaction is executed which takes the message from the buyer's Request/Decision-buffer and inserts it into the producers' Request/Decision-buffers.
3. The producers (clients) take the requests from their Request/Decision-buffers, make their bids and insert them into their Response-buffers.
4. The transaction monitor forwards the bids to the buyer's Response-buffer.
5. The buyer takes the bids from the Response-buffer, makes the decision and inserts appropriate messages (decisions) into its Response/Decision-buffer.
6. The transaction monitor forwards the responses to the Request/Decision-buffers of the producers.
7. The producers take the responses from their Request/Decision-buffers, and take appropriate actions.

If the systems fail or in the case of a communication failure there is no ambiguity about the state of an EBT. To determine what recovery action to take the recovery system has to read the buffers. As a matter of fact the recovery actions to be taken are the same as the recovery actions taken with the queued transaction processing [2].

Note that the reliability is not the only gain of the buffered architecture but the flexibility is another important gain of the architecture. For example, the buyer can send bid requests even if the producers are busy, down or disconnected, as long as its Request/Decision-buffer is available. Respectively, a producer can send its offer even if the buyer is down or disconnected, as long as its Response-buffer is available.

5 EBT's execution atomicity

Execution atomicity ensures that the concurrent transactions do not interleave in a way where they interfere with each other. With EBTs the critical point is in ensuring the execution atomicity of each subtransaction, i.e., the atomicity of *Bidding* and *Completing*. The reason is that each bid is based on the state of a database, and if the bid is accepted the database still has to be in such a state where the bid can be realized.

In order to illustrate the isolation requirements of the EBTs let us assume that a buyer (a retail store) requests bids from producers (wholesalers) concerning 100 sacks of cement. A wholesaler, say wholesaler A, has 120 sacks of cement in its store, and it makes a bid on the requested 100 sacks. Then a customer of A wants to buy 40 sacks of cement and another customer wants to buy 10 sacks of cement. What should the wholesaler A do?

The wholesaler A should make the deal only with the customer requesting 10 sacks of cement, but not with the customer requesting 40 sacks of cement. Otherwise, if the retail store accepts the bid, then A does not have enough cement to deliver for the retail store, i.e., the execution atomicity of the subtransaction including (*Bidding* and *Completing*) would not be preserved.

The actual problem is how the correct actions can be made automatically. If the execution atomicity of a subtransaction (*Bidding* and *Completing*) is ensured in a traditional way (i.e., by using two-phase locking [1]), then the data item indicating the amount of cement in the store is locked before making the bid, and the lock is not released until the decision from the retail store is received, i.e., when the subtransaction is committed. In such a case we face two problems:

- First, the deal concerning 10 sacks of cement cannot be done.
- Second, other transactions cannot update the amount of cement in the store, e.g., even if 500 sacks of cement is brought into the store it cannot be booked in the database until the decision from the retail store is received.

In EBT we avoid these problems by dividing each subtransaction into three transactions called *Locking transaction*, *Accepting transaction* and *Refusing transaction* (Figure 6).

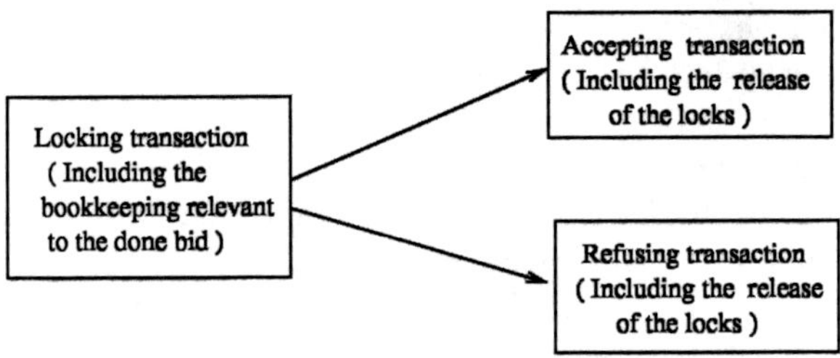

Fig. 6. Semantic locking in a subtransaction of an EBT.

- The Locking transaction sets a semantic lock and makes the bookkeepings (updates) relevant to the bid.
- The Accepting transaction is executed in case the bid was accepted. It makes the bookkeeping relevant to the acceptance, and releases the semantic locks.
- The Refusing transaction is executed in case the bid was refused. It makes the bookkeeping relevant to the refusal and releases the semantic locks.

Ideally the Locking transaction ensures that the Accepting transaction cannot semantically fail as a result of other concurrent transactions. And most important, the locking transaction sets (by using the semantics of the application) as liberal a lock as possible, i.e., a lock which prevents the execution of other transactions only when it is necessary to ensure the execution atomicity of the EBT.

Next we illustrate how the above problems can be solved by semantic locking. Let us assume that the wholesaler has the relation *Bids* for keeping books on the information relevant to the bids done, and the relation *Orders* for keeping books on the information of the accepted bids (Figure 7) and the relation *Inventory* (Figure 8) for indicating the content of the store.

The specification of the relation *Inventory* is presented below. The specification of *Bids* and *Orders* are omitted as they do not include any constraint specifications.

Bids	productNum	amount	clientNum
	111111	40	567-82
	...	...	...

Orders	productNum	amount	clientNum
	212121	120	321-99
	...	...	...

Fig. 7. The relations *Bids* and *Orders*.

Inventory	productNum	productName	unit	amount	reservations
	111111	cement	sack	120	40
	212121	nail	kilogram	12	0
	343434	rope	meter	550	0

Fig. 8. The relation *Inventory*.

```
CREATE TABLE Inventory (
   productNum CHAR(5),
   productName VARCHAR(15),
   unit VARCHAR(15),
   amount INTEGER,
   reservations INTEGER,
   CONSTRAINT Watch CHECK (reservations<= amount));
```

The idea in semantic locking is that the intermediate results of EBT's subtransactions are also modelled, and presented in the database. As a result other concurrent transactions are allowed to see the intermediate results of EBT's subtransactions. This is in contrast with traditional transaction processing (i.e., with ACID-transactions [2]) where the intermediate results of transactions are hidden from other concurrent transactions.

For externalizing the intermediate results of EBTs' subtransactions the attribute *reservations* is included in the relation *Inventory*. So, when wholesaler A makes a bid of 40 sacks of cement it activates the Locking transaction (Figure 6) which tries to increases the attribute *reservations* by 40. As the constraint *Watch* (a semantic lock), which states that the value of the attribute *reservations* is not allowed to exceed the value of the attribute *amount*, this transaction will be committed because the value of the attribute *amount* is 120. Accepting the transaction decreases the value of the attribute *reservations* by 40 and decreases the value of attribute *amount* by 40, as well.

Next we specify the subtransaction, named *Product*, which solves the problems related to wholesaler A. It is defined as follows:

```
EBT-subtransaction <Product>
   Locking transaction:   <ProductBidding>
   Accepting transaction: <ProductAccepting>
   Refusing transaction:  <ProductRefusing>
```

Transactions ProductBidding, ProductAccepting and ProductRefusing are specified as follows:

```
Product Bidding(productNumber, bidAmount, clientNumber)
Begin transaction
  UPDATE Inventory
    SET reservations = reservations + bidAmount
    WHERE productNum = productNumber;
  INSERT INTO Bids
    VALUES (productNumber, bidAmount, clientNumber);
End transaction;

Product Accepting(productNumber, bidAmount, clientNumber)
Begin transaction
  UPDATE Inventory
    SET reservations = reservations - bidAmount,
        amount = amount - bidAmount,
    WHERE productNum = productNumber;
  INSERT INTO Orders
    VALUES (productNumber, bidAmount, clientNumber);
  DELETE FROM  Bids
    WHERE productNum = productNumber and clientNum = clientNumber;
End transaction;

Product Refusing(productNumber, bidAmount, clientNumber)
Begin transaction
  UPDATE Inventory
    SET reservations = reservations - bidAmount,
    WHERE productNum = productNumber;
  DELETE FROM  Bids
    WHERE productNum = productNumber and clientNum = clientNumber;
End transaction;
```

6 Conclusions

We have considered the automation of a business process where dealing is made by first requesting the bids and then making a deal. We have focused on a solution which ensures the reliability of the execution. We believe that such cooperative processes cannot be automated if the reliability of the execution cannot be ensured. However, in general, reliability and high performance are contradicting goals. With traditional (syntactic) transaction models failure atomicity is guaranteed by forcing transactions to hold their data locked until the whole activity either commits or aborts, thereby decreasing the performance of the system. With semantic atomicity models transactions may release their data resources before the whole activity (a workflow or an advanced transaction) is committed or aborted, thus leading to better performance but at the same time exposing dirty data to other concurrent transactions. Within this context, semantic locks used in EBTs represent an intermediate form: transactions (or tasks) hold their data, but only in a liberal way allowing other transactions to access the data as long as it does not jeopardize failure atomicity.

References

1. P. Bernstein, V. Hadzilacos, and N. Goodman. *Concurrency Control and Recovery in Database Systems*. Addison-Wesley, 1987.
2. P. Bernstein and E. Newcomer. *Principles of Transaction Processing*. Morgan Kaufmann, 1997.
3. H. Garcia-Molina. Using semantic knowledge for transaction processing in a distributed database. *ACM Transactions on Database Systems*, 8(2):186–213, June 1983.
4. D. Georgakopoulos, M. Hornick, and A. Sheth. An overview of workflow management: From process modeling to workflow automation infrastructure. *Distributed and Parallel Databases*, 3(2):592–620, 1995.
5. H. Laine and J. Puustjärvi. Modeling business processes as transactional workflows. In *Proc. of the Workshop on Practical Business Process Modeling (in conjuction with CAiSE'00)*, 2000.
6. N.A. Lynch. Multilevel atomicity — a new correctness criterion for database concurrency control. *ACM Transactions on Database Systems*, 8(4):65–76, December 1983.
7. J. Puustjärvi and H. Laine. Workman - a transactional workflow prototype. In *Proceedings of the DEXA'00*, 2000.
8. J. D. Ullman and J. Widom. *A First Course in Database Systems*. Prentice Hall, 1997.

O2PC-MT: A Novel Optimistic Two-Phase Commit Protocol for Mobile Transactions

Zhiming Ding[1], Xiaofeng Meng[2], and Shan Wang[2]

[1] Institute of Computing Technology
Chinese Academy of Sciences, Beijing China,100080
dingzhiming@263.net
[2] Institute of Data and Knowledge Engineering
Renmin University of China, Beijing China,100872
{xfmeng, suang} @public.bta.net.cn

Abstract. Advances in computer and telecommunication technologies have made mobile computing a reality. In mobile computing environment, users can perform on-line transaction processing independent of their physical location. In the last decade, this new kind of computing paradigm has gained great development and posed new challenges to the database community. In mobile database systems, new features such as mobility, disconnection and long-lived transactions make traditional transaction processing schemes no longer suited. To solve this problem, a novel mobile transaction model, O2PC-MT, is proposed in this paper. By combining Optimistic Concurrency Control and Two-Phase Commit, O2PC-MT provides a flexible and effective support for mobile transactions. In order to compare the performance of our model with that of other mobile transaction schemes, we developed a detailed simulation model. The experiment results show that O2PC-MT model outperforms the previously proposed mobile transaction models that utilize the locking mechanism for mobile transaction processing.

1 Introduction

Advances in computer and telecommunication technologies have made mobile computing a reality. In mobile computing environment, users can perform on-line transaction processing independent of their physical location [1]. In the last decade, this new kind of computing paradigm has gained great development and posed new challenges to database researchers. In mobile database systems, new features such as mobility, disconnection, resource restriction and long-lived transactions make traditional transaction processing schemes no longer suited. Therefore, it is necessary to develop new models and algorithms to deal with this new situation.

Research in the area of concurrency control for database systems has led to the development of many concurrency control algorithms. Most of these algorithms are based on one of three basic mechanisms: locking, timestamps, and optimistic concurrency control (OCC) [2]. Although these schemes are well suited for traditional database applications, they can not work very well in mobile database systems. In a mobile database system, both fixed hosts and mobile hosts can submit transactions.

H.C. Mayr et al. (Eds.): DEXA 2001, LNCS 2113, pp. 846–856, 2001.

Transactions originating from mobile hosts are called mobile transactions. Due to limited bandwidth and frequent disconnection, mobile transactions usually become long-lived transactions; Moreover, mobility of computers makes mobile transaction processing a complicated problem; Finally, mobile transactions can visit more heterogeneous data resources and are thus more susceptible to failures [3]. All these factors make mobile transaction processing a challenging research field.

Based on the above analysis, we propose a novel transaction model, Optimistic Two-Phase Commit for Mobile Transactions (O2PC-MT), in this paper. The remaining part of this paper is organized as follows. Section 2 presents a survey of related work; Section 3 describes the mechanism of O2PC-MT model; Section 4 introduces the O2PC-MT Two-Phase Commit algorithm; and Section 5 provides an evaluation to the proposed model and finally concludes the paper.

2 Related Work

Recently, a lot of research has been focused on mobile transaction processing, and many models and algorithms have been proposed. Some models, however, such as the Clustering Transaction model [4], the Kangaroo Transaction model [5], the Adaptable Mobile Transaction Model [6], and the Moflex transaction model [7], relax or redefine the strict ACID properties. Thus they can not completely ensure serializability, which limits their adaptability.

L. H. Yeo and A. Zaslavsky in [8] put forward an efficient mobile transaction model, MDSTPM, based on their work on Multi-Database systems. In MDSTPM model, an entire mobile transaction is submitted to the coordinator in a single request message. Meanwhile, the mobile host also delivers execution control to the coordinator and waits for return of the results of transaction execution. MDSTPM model is typical of a class of mobile transaction models that require a mobile transaction to be submitted in a single request message. Therefore, they do not support interactive mobile transactions.

J. Jing *et. al.* in [9] put forward an effective O2PL-MT mobile transaction model, in which mobile computers can submit a mobile transaction in multiple request messages. A submission unit thus consists of one operation or a group of operations. A subsequent operation can be submitted after the previous operations have been executed and the results have returned from the coordinator. O2PL-MT model is adaptive and provides a flexible support for mobility. However, mobile computers can not leave the current cell until they receive the results of previously submitted operations. Moreover, data items may be locked for a long period of time since it uses the Optimistic Two-Phase Locking mechanism for mobile transaction processing, which may affects the transaction throughput of the whole system.

In order to solve the above problems, a new mobile transaction model, O2PC-MT, is proposed in this paper. Through the combination of OCC and Two-Phase Commit, O2PC-MT model provides an effective support for the long-transaction property. In addition, mobile computers are allowed to submit mobile transactions in multiple request messages and to move arbitrarily during transaction execution. Therefore, O2PC-MT presents a more flexible support for interactivity and mobility.

3 O2PC-MT Mobile Transaction Model

3.1 Mobile Database System Model

Fig. 1 presents a general architecture of the mobile database system similar to that described in [1, 9]. In this architecture, the trusted part is composed of the fixed network and the fixed hosts residing on it. Some of the fixed hosts, called MSS, are augmented with wireless interface to communicate with mobile computers. The current location and state of each mobile computer are managed by the LS.

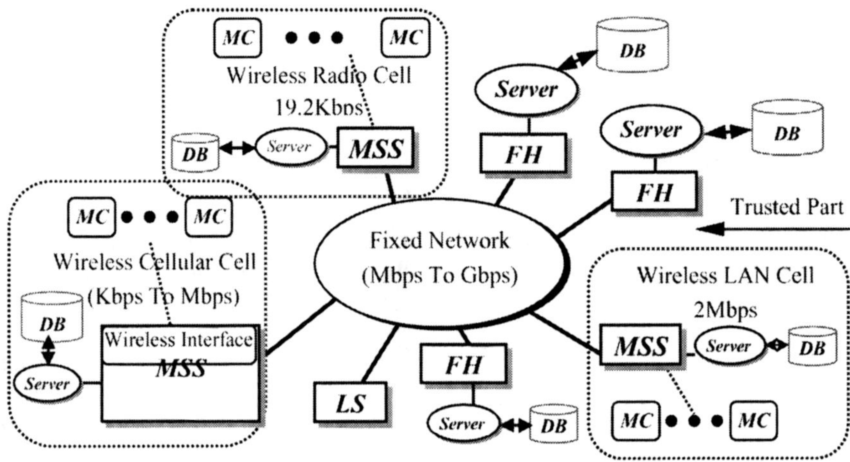

Fig. 1. Architecture of Mobile Database System

In the above architecture, database servers residing on FHs and MSSs compose a distributed database system. Every database server possesses autonomy and supports local transactions through Two-Phase Locking mechanism. Meanwhile it supports global mobile transactions through O2PC-MT scheme.

As a part of the distributed database system, each MSS can also function as a mobile transaction coordinator which receives transaction operations from MCs and coordinates their execution and global commitment.

An MC can move arbitrarily at any moment within a wireless cell or among different cells. When it is connected with the fixed network, it always communicates with the MSS supporting the cell where it is currently located. In addition, it can disconnect from the fixed network at any time. When it reconnects with the fixed network, it fetches back the results of previous operations and sends subsequent operations.

3.2 O2PC-MT Mobile Transaction Model

O2PC-MT model is shown in Fig. 2. In this model, a mobile transaction contains a group of read/write operations which are numbered continuously from 0 through *n*. It begins with Begin-MT(MTID, MODE) and ends with Commit/Abort, where MTID is the unique identifier of the mobile transaction assigned by the MC, and MODE is the transaction submission mode. A mobile transaction can be submitted in one of the following two modes [9] (for simplicity, we suppose that there can be at most one transaction running at an MC at any moment):

1) The entire transaction is submitted in a single request message, and the whole transaction thus becomes one submission unit. This method is only suitable for none-interactive transactions.

2) In contrast, the entire transaction may be submitted in multiple request messages. A submission unit thus consists of one operation or a group of operations, which is called an Operation Series (OPS). This method is suitable for interactive transactions.

No matter which submission mode is used, the receiving of one mobile transaction may concern multiple MSSs. This is because the MC can move to another cell during the submission of the mobile transaction. When handoff happens, one original OPS will be divided into two or more OPSs received by different MSSs.

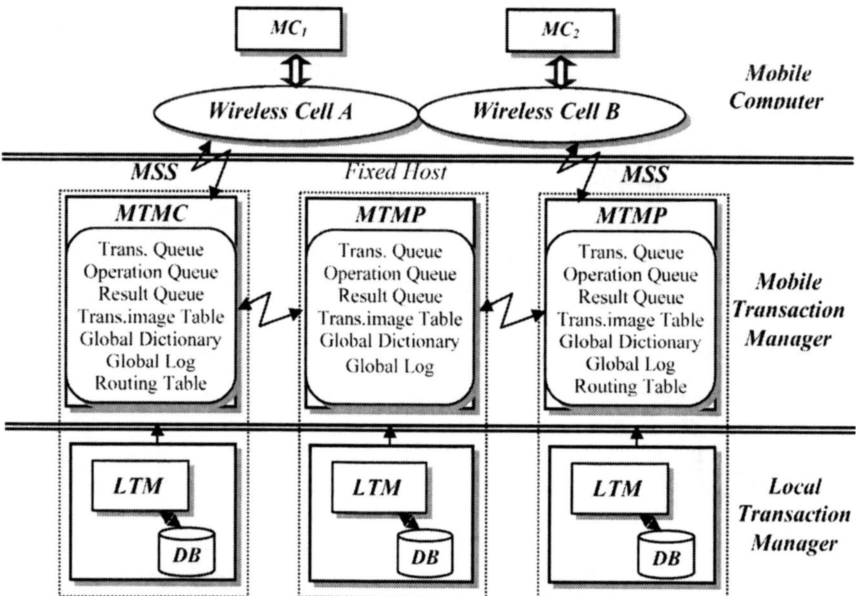

Fig. 2. O2PC-MT Mobile Transaction Model

1) The Receiving and Forwarding of OPSs

After an MSS receives an OPS, the MSS will deal with the OPS according to its type. If the OPS begins with BEGIN-MT(MTID,MODE), then it must be the first OPS of a new mobile transaction. In this case, the MSS becomes the MTMC of the new transaction. The MSS will first generate a global transaction identifier (GTID) for the new transaction by combining MCID and MTID, where MCID is the identifier of the

MC submitting the transaction. Next, it will save the GTID to the transaction queue and save the operations of the OPS to the operation queue. Finally, it will broadcast a message to all MSSs to declare its relationship with the GTID. This message is then saved into the routing table by other MSSs. If the OPS does not begin with BEGIN-MT(MTID,MODE), then the MSS only need to forward the OPS to the right MTMC according to its routing table.

2) The Handling and Coordinating of Mobile Transactions

The MTMC will handle the mobile transaction differently according to different MODE. If the mobile transaction is submitted in the first mode, then the MTMC will initiate the execution of the mobile transaction only after all transaction operations have been received. Mobile transactions of this kind can be dealt with in a way similar to that described in [8]. In the following discussion, we will focus on the mobile transactions submitted in the second mode.

For mobile transactions submitted in the second mode, the MTMC will initiate the transaction execution immediately after the first OPS is received. If any subsequent OPS received by the MTMC contains the Abort statement, then the MTMC will immediately inform all MTMPs to terminate the transaction execution and release all related resources. Otherwise, the new OPS will be saved into the transaction operation queue. Since mobile transaction operations are continuously numbered, the MTMC can restore their original order. According to the global dictionary, transaction operations are sent to relevant MTMPs for single-step execution. If the next operation or the data required by the next operation are not available, the MTMC will suspend the mobile transaction until the condition is satisfied again.

If the MTMC reaches the Commit statement and all previous operations have finished single-step execution, then the mobile transaction will enter into the Two-Phase Commit phase (see Section 4).

3) The Single-Step Execution of Mobile Transaction Operations

Each MTMP serially executes transaction operations sent by the MTMC in a single-step manner. That is, the related locks applied by an operation will be released immediately after the operation has been executed. For read operations, the MTMP will read data items from the write image and the database, and transmit the returning values back to the MTMC. These values will be saved into the transaction result queue and will be transmitted to the MC properly according to the information in LS. Meanwhile, the MTMP will save a copy of the returning values to the read image.

For write operations, the MTMP will save the new values to the write image instead of modifying the database directly. Transaction image table contains 1) the GTID of the mobile transaction, 2) the read images of each operation, and 3) the write image of the mobile transaction.

(Definition 1: Transaction) A transaction (or subtransaction) is defined as **T**= $((T, a_i, e_i))_{i=1}^{n}$, where T is the transaction identifier, a_i is the ith action, and e_i is the data set accessed by a_i.

(Definition 2: Read and Write Sets of Transaction Operation) For any transaction (or subtransaction) **T**= $((T, a_i, e_i))_{i=1}^{n}$, the Read Set and Write Set of the ith action a_i are defined as:

$$ReadSet(a_i) = \begin{cases} e_i & (\text{if } a_i = read) \\ null & (\text{if } a_i = write) \end{cases} \quad WriteSet(a_i) = \begin{cases} null & (\text{if } a_i = read) \\ e_i & (\text{if } a_i = write) \end{cases}$$

(Definition 3: Read and Write Sets of Transaction) For any transaction (or subtransaction) **T**= $((T, a_i, e_i))_{i=1}^{n}$, the Read Set and Write Set of **T** are defined as:

$$RSet(\mathbf{T}) = \bigcup_{i=1}^{n} ReadSet(a_i) \qquad WSet(\mathbf{T}) = \bigcup_{i=1}^{n} WriteSet(a_i)$$

(Definition 4) For any transaction (or subtransaction) **T**= $((T, a_i, e_i))_{i=1}^{n}$, and $\Psi \in$ ReadSet(a_i), define $\xi(\Psi, a_i)$ to be the value of Ψ that a_i reads.

(Definition 5: Read Image of Transaction Operation) For any transaction (or subtransaction) **T**= $((T, a_i, e_i))_{i=1}^{n}$, the Read Image of the ith action a_i is defined as:

$$RImage(a_i) = \{(\Psi, \omega) \mid \Psi \in ReadSet(a_i) \wedge \omega = \xi(\Psi, a_i)\}$$

(Definition 6: Write Image of Transaction) For any transaction (or subtransaction) **T**= $((T, a_i, e_i))_{i=1}^{n}$, assume that η is any data object in $WSet$(**T**) and $\delta(\eta$, **T**) is the new value of η assigned by **T.** The write image of **T** is defined as:

$$WImage(\mathbf{T}) = \{(\eta, \upsilon) \mid \eta \in WSet(\mathbf{T}) \wedge \upsilon = \delta(\eta, \mathbf{T})\}$$

Consider two tables, *Wages* and *Sum*, in MTMP_i's database (see Fig. 3). Assume that $\mathbf{T}_i$ is the subtransaction of mobile transaction **T** executed at MTMP_i, which consists of the following actions: r[a=50], w[a=60], r[P: 'Name=X'], w[X=100]. Then the transaction image table is shown in Table 1 (assume that the GTID of **T** is "MC01•T01").

Wages

No.	Name	Payment
a	X	50
b	X	30
c	X	10
d	Y	60
e	Y	100

Sum

Name	Sum
X	90
Y	160

Fig. 3. Sample Database

Trans. ID	Oper. Read Image	WriteImage
:	:	:
MC01•T01	{(a, 50)} <null> {(a,60),(b,30),(c,10)} <null>	{(a,60),(X,100)}
:	:	:

Table 1. Transaction Image Table

4 O2PC-MT Two-Phase Commit Algorithm

O2PC-MT Two-Phase Commit algorithm is composed of two phases: the Validation phase and the Global-Commitment phase. In the Validation phase, the MTMC sends PREPAER messages in parallel to all MTMPs. After receiving this message, the MTMPs begin to validate the transaction and send the validation results back to the

MTMC. If an MTMP passes the validation, then it will send a READY message to the MTMC; otherwise, it will send an Abort message.

Assume that mobile transaction **T** is jointly accomplished by *m* participants, $MTMP_1$, $MTMP_2$,•••, and $MTMP_m$, and $\mathbf{T_i}$ is the subtransaction of **T** executed at $MTMP_i$. During the Validation phase, $MTMP_i$ will initiate a corresponding base transaction $\mathbf{BT_i}$ which contains exactly the same operations as $\mathbf{T_i}$. When executing $\mathbf{BT_i}$, $MTMP_i$ utilizes the Two-Phase Locking mechanism and needs to detect two kinds of conflicts, Read-Set conflict and During-Execution conflict.

(Definition 7: Read-Set Conflict) For any subtransaction $\mathbf{T_i}= ((T_i, a_j, e_j))^n_{j=1}$, assume that the corresponding base transaction is $\mathbf{BT_i}= ((BT_i, ba_j, be_j))^n_{j=1}$. If one of the following conditions is met, then a Read-Set conflict is detected:

1)$(\exists j \in [1, n]) \wedge (ReadSet(a_j) \neq ReadSet(ba_j))$

2)$(\exists j \in [1, n]) \wedge (\exists \Psi \in (ReadSet(a_j) \cap ReadSet(ba_j))) \wedge (\xi(\Psi,a_j) \neq \xi(\Psi,ba_j))$

(Definition 8: During-Execution Conflict) $MTMP_i$ detects a During-Execution conflict when any operation of $\mathbf{BT_i}$ fails to return a SUCCESS code, which indicates that the operation has not been properly executed.

Many factors may contribute to the During-Execution conflict such as violation of uniqueness constraints or trying to update a data item which has already been deleted.

Theorem 1: For subtransaction $\mathbf{T_i}$ $(1 \leq i \leq m)$, if neither Read-Set conflict nor During-Execution conflict is detected during the execution of $\mathbf{BT_i}$, then $\mathbf{BT_i}$ can be committed at the $MTMP_i$ without violating serializability; Otherwise $\mathbf{BT_i}$ can not be committed.

Proof: If neither Read-Set conflict nor During-Execution conflict is detected, then we can infer the following facts: 1) Since $\mathbf{BT_i}$ and $\mathbf{T_i}$ have the same operations and no Read-Set conflict is detected, according to Definition 7, they see the same data and have the same transaction semantics. Therefore, $\mathbf{BT_i}$ transfers the database from one consistent state to another. 2) Since no During-Execution conflict has been found, every operation of $\mathbf{BT_i}$ has been successfully executed by transaction-commit time. 3) For any other transaction **T** at $MTMP_i$, the serializability of $\mathbf{BT_i}$ and **T** is ensured by the Two-Phase Locking mechanism. Combining 1), 2), and 3), we can conclude that the commitment of $\mathbf{BT_i}$ will not violate serializability.

If any form of conflict exists, then $\mathbf{BT_i}$ can not keep the original transaction semantics and should be aborted. o

In the Global-Commitment phase, if the MTMC receives a READY message from all MTMPs within the time limit, then it will send GLOBAL-COMMIT messages in parallel to all MTMPs; otherwise, it will send GLOBAL-ABORT messages. If receiving a GLOBAL-COMMIT message, $MTMP_i$ $(1 \leq i \leq m)$ will commit $\mathbf{BT_i}$ and send an ACK to the MTMC; if receiving a GLOBAL-ABORT message, $MTMP_i$ will abort $\mathbf{BT_i}$. After the above operations have been finished, $MTMP_i$ will delete relevant information of $\mathbf{T_i}$ from the transaction image table.

When Two-Phase Commit procedure is over, the MTMC will transmit the final results to the MC and broadcast a message to all MSSs, informing them to release related information in their routing table.

5 Performance Analysis and Conclusion

The comparison of O2PC-MT and two representative mobile transaction models, MDSTPM and O2PL-MT, is shown in Table 2. We can see from table 2 that O2PC-MT combines the advantages of MDSTPM and O2PL-MT. First, O2PC-MT maintains transaction ACID properties and serializability through strict validation process. Moreover, O2PC-MT provides a flexible support for interactivity, mobility and disconnection operations. Finally, by utilizing an optimistic method, O2PC-MT reduces the length of lock, and thus improves the performance of the mobile database system (see Section 5.2).

Table 2. Comparison of O2PC-MT with MDSTPM and O2PL-MT

	O2PC-MT	***MDSTPM***	***O2PL-MT***
Support interactive Trans.	√	×	√
Support arbitrary Mobility	√	√	×
Support Disconnection	√	√	×
Maintain ACID Properties	√	√	√
Trans. Submission Mode	1), 2)	1)	1), 2)
Length of Lock	Short	Long	Long

5.1 Simulation Model and Main Parameters

In order to evaluate the performance of O2PC-MT, we developed a detailed simulation model based on KingBase Lite 2.0, a mobile database system developed by Renmin University of China. The simulator is implemented in *Visual* C^{++} *6.0*, which consists of a Fixed Transaction Generator (FTG), a Mobile Transaction Generator (MTG), a Fixed Transaction Processor (FTP), an O2PC-MT Transaction Processor (OMTP), and a G2PL-MT Transaction Processor (GMTP).

FTG and MTG generate transactions that randomly access the data items of the sample database. At each simulation run, at least 5,000 transactions are generated. In order to simulate the features of mobile computing such as low bandwidth, high latency, frequent disconnection, and long-lived transactions, different time delays are introduced by FTG and MTG in generating transaction operations. Fixed transactions generated at FTG are processed by FTP using ordinary Two-Phase Locking mechanism, while mobile transactions generated at MTG are processed by OMTP using O2PC-MT scheme. In order to compare O2PC-MT with the mobile transaction models that utilize the Two-Phase Locking scheme or its variation in mobile transaction processing, we use G2PL-MT, an abstract transaction model which uses the Two-Phase Locking mechanism, as a control in our experiments. A summary of the parameters used in the simulation model is presented in Table 3.

Table 3. Main Simulation Parameters and Their Default Settings

Parameter	*Value*	*Meaning*
DBSize	*5000 tuples*	*Number of tuples in the database*
TupleSize	*256 bytes*	*Size of the tuple in the database*
NumSites	*3*	*Number of sites in the database system*
TransSize	*6*	*Average number of operations per transaction*
Pr	*0.25 – 0.75*	*Proportion of Read-only transactions*
Pu	*0.25 – 0.75*	*Proportion of update operations in an update transaction*
μ	*1*	*Ratio of arrival rates of fixed transactions vs. mobile transactions*
MPL	*1 – 100*	*Multiprogramming level*
$Delay_f$	*1 ms*	*Time delay introduced between operations of fixed transactions*
$Delay_m$	*5 – 300 ms*	*Time delay introduced between operations of mobile transactions*

5.2 Simulation Results and Concluding Remarks

The performance metric used for the evaluation of O2PC-MT model includes Abort Rate and Transaction Throughput. The performance results obtained from the simulation in terms of Abort Rate are shown in Fig. 4. Generally, as illustrated in Fig. 4, Abort Rate increases with multiprogramming level (MPL) increasing. However, before MPL reaches a certain critical point, Abort Rate is very small. In addition, Abort Rate increases with *Pu* increasing or *Pr* decreasing. This is because in O2PC-MT model, the probability of conflicts (including Read-Set conflicts and During-Execution conflicts) increases with the number of concurrently executed update operations increasing. However, before it reaches a certain point, the system is not data-contentious enough for these conflicts to happen frequently.

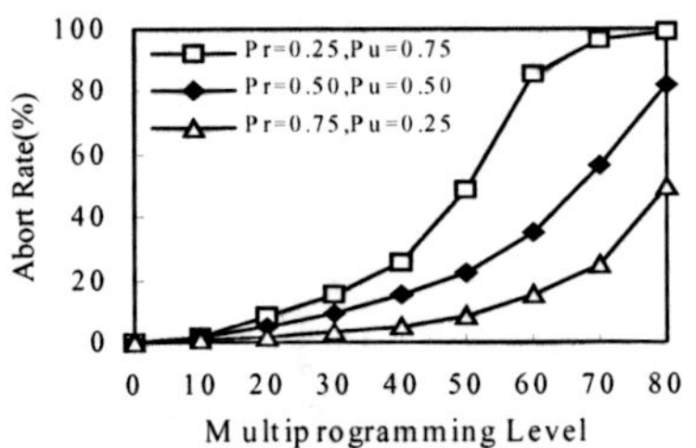

Fig. 4. Transaction Abort Rate of O2PC-MT Model (*$Delay_m$=100ms*)

T_i	T_j	*Conflict Type*
w	*r*	*1*
w	*w*	*2*
r	*w*	*3*

Table 4. Possible Conflict Types between Two Transactions

The performance results obtained from the simulation in terms of Transaction Throughput are shown in Fig. 5.

From the above simulation results we can get the following conclusions. 1) With MPL increasing, the transaction throughput of both O2PC-MT and G2PL-MT first increases and then decreases. 2) On the whole, O2PC-MT, compared with G2PL-MT, provides better performance by increasing transaction throughput. 3) With $Delay_m$ increasing, the performance of G2PL-MT decreases rapidly while the performance of O2PC-MT remains relatively stable. The reason for the above results is as follows.

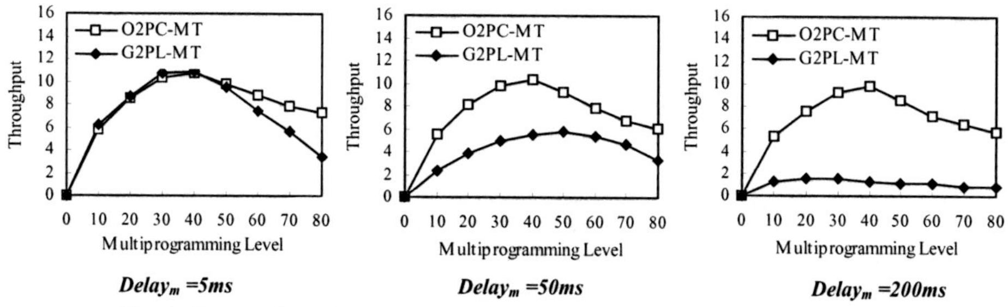

Fig. 5. Transaction Throughput of O2PC-MT and G2PL-MT (*Pr =0.5, Pu =0.5*)

Suppose that $\mathbf{T_i}$ is a mobile transaction, $\mathbf{T_j}$ is any other transaction in the database server, and $\mathbf{T_i}$ has accessed the conflicting data items of $\mathbf{T_i}$ and $\mathbf{T_j}$ before $\mathbf{T_j}$ starts. The possible transaction conflicts between $\mathbf{T_i}$ and $\mathbf{T_j}$ are shown in Table 4.

For the first and second kinds of conflicts, if $\mathbf{T_i}$ is processed with G2PL-MT, then $\mathbf{T_j}$ will have to wait until $\mathbf{T_i}$ is committed/aborted. On the other hand, if $\mathbf{T_i}$ is processed with O2PC-MT, then $\mathbf{T_j}$ will continue to execute and will finally be committed, which will not affect the execution and commitment of $\mathbf{T_i}$. In this case, the transaction schedule is serializable in $\mathbf{T_j} \rightarrow \mathbf{T_i}$ order. Since $\mathbf{T_i}$ is a long-lived transaction, O2PC-MT provides better performance than G2PL-MT which will keep $\mathbf{T_j}$ blocked for long period of time.

For the third kind of conflicts, if $\mathbf{T_i}$ is processed with G2PL-MT, then $\mathbf{T_j}$ will have to wait until the S lock applied by $\mathbf{T_i}$ is released. If $\mathbf{T_i}$ is processed with O2PC-MT, then $\mathbf{T_j}$ will continue to execute and finally commit, but $\mathbf{T_i}$ will be aborted because it has read out-of-date data items. The abortion of $\mathbf{T_i}$ is worthwhile in this case because $\mathbf{T_i}$ is a long-lived transaction, and the transaction flow at the database server is much heavier than that at the MC.

To conclude, by combining the Optimistic Concurrency Control and Two-Phase Commit, O2PC-MT improves the performance of mobile database systems, especially in the environments where update rate (update per second) is not very high.

Acknowledgements. This research was partially supported by the grants from 863 High Technology Foundation of China under grant number 863-306-ZD12-12-1 and from the Natural Science Foundation of China under grant number 60073014. We would like to thank Linwei Li and Rui Ding of Renmin University of China for their valuable help and advice in the experiments and the detailed implementation of the simulation model.

References

1. S. Byun, S. Moon: Resilient data management for replicated mobile database systems, *Data & Knowlwdge Engineering.* Vol.29, 1999, pp. 43-55.
2. R. Agrawal, M. J. Carey, M. Livny: Concurrency Control Performance Modeling: Alternatives and Implications. *ACM Trans. on Database Systems*, 12(4), 1987, pp.609-654.
3. X. He, C. Tan, L. Li, *et. al.*: *Special Database Technologies*, Beijing: Science Press, 2000.

4. E. Pitoura, B. Bhargava: Maintaining Consistency of Data in Mobile Distributed Environments, In: *Proc. of 15th Intl. Conf. on Distributed Computing Systems*, May 1995, pp.404-413.
5. M. H. Dunham, A. Helal: A Mobile Transaction Model that Captures both the Data and Movement Behaviour, *Mobile Networks and Application* (*MONET*), 2 (2),1997.
6. A. Rakotonirainy: Adaptable Transaction Consistency for Mobile Environments. *10th Intl. Workshop on Database and Expert Systems Applications (DEXA'99)*. Florence, Italy. 1999.
7. K. Ku, Y. S. Kim: Moflex Transaction Model for Mobile Heterogeneous Multidatabase Systems. *The 10th Intl. Workshop on Research Issues in Data Engineering*. San Diego, California. Feb. 2000.
8. L. H. Yeo, A. Zaslavsky: Submission of Transactions from Mobile Workstations in a Cooperative Multidatabase Processing Environment, In: *Proc. of the 14th IEEE CS Intl. Conf. on Distributed Computing Systems*, Poland, Jun. 1994, pp372-379.
9. J. Jing, O. Bukhres, A. Elmagarmid: Distributed Lock Management for Mobile Transactions. In: *Proc. of the 15th Intl. Conf. on Distributed Computing Systems*, Vancouver, Canada. 1995.

Quorum-Based Locking Protocol in Nested Invocations of Methods

Katsuya Tanaka and Makoto Takizawa

Dept. of Computers and Systems Engineering
Tokyo Denki University
{katsu, taki}@takilab.k.dendai.ac.jp

Abstract. Objects are replicated in order to increase reliability and availability of an object-based system. We discuss how to invoke methods on replicas of objects in a nested manner. If a method t is invoked on multiple replicas and each instance of t on the replicas invokes a method u on another object y, u may be performed multiple times on some replica of y and then the replica gets inconsistent, i.e. redundant invocations. In addition, if each instance of t issues a request to a quorum, more number of the replicas are manipulated than the quorum number of the method u, i.e. quorum explosion. We discuss an invocation protocol to resolve the redundant invocation and quorum explosion. We evaluate the protocol on how many replicas are manipulated and requests are issued.

1 Introduction

Objects are replicated in order to increase the reliability and availability in object-based applications [13]. The two-phase locking protocol [5] and quorum-based protocol [7] are proposed. *Quorum* numbers N_r and N_w of the replicas are locked for *read* and *write*, respectively, in the quorum-based protocol [7] where $N_r + N_w > a$ for the number a of the replicas. The subset of the replicas is a *quorum*. An object is an encapsulation of data and abstract methods. A pair of methods conflict on an object if the result obtained by performing the methods depends on the computation order. In the papers [14, 15], the quorum concept for read and write is extended to abstract methods. Suppose methods t and u are issued to replicas x_1 and x_2 of an object x. The method t is performed on one replica x_1 and u on x_2 if t and u are compatible. Here, x_1 and x_2 are different but can be the newest ones if u is performed on x_1 and t on x_2. As long as t and u are issued, the methods are performed on replicas in their quorums. If some method v conflicting with t is issued to a replica x_1, every instance of t performed so far is required to be performed on x_1. Even if a replica is updated by t or u, $N_t + N_u \leq a$ only if t and u are compatible.

In the object-based system, methods are invoked in a nested manner. Suppose a method t on an object x invokes a method u on another object y. Let x_1 and x_2 be replicas of the object x. Let y_1 and y_2 be replicas of y. A method t is issued to the replicas x_1 and x_2. We assume that every method is deterministic, i.e. the same computation for t is done on x_1 and x_2. Then, t invokes the other

H.C. Mayr et al. (Eds.): DEXA 2001, LNCS 2113, pp. 857–866, 2001.

method u on y_1 and y_2. Here, u is performed twice on each replica although u should be performed only once on each of the replicas y_1 and y_2. Otherwise, y gets inconsistent. This is a *redundant invocation.* In addition, an instance of the method t on x_1 issues a method u to replicas in its own quorum Q_1, and another instance of t on x_2 issues u to replicas in Q_2 where $|Q_1| = |Q_2| = N_u$ but $Q_1 \neq Q_2$. More number of replicas are manipulated than N_u, i.e. $|Q_1 \cup Q_2| \geq N_u$. If the method u furthermore invokes another method, the number of replicas to be manipulated is more increased and eventually all the replicas are manipulated. This is a *quorum explosion.* In order to increase the reliability and availability, a method issued has to be performed on multiple replicas. On the other hand, the replicas may get inconsistent by the redundant invocations and the overhead is increased by the quorum explosion. We discuss how to resolve the redundant invocation and quorum explosion to occur in nested invocations of methods on multiple replicas.

In section 2, we overview the quorum-based protocol. In sections 3 and 4, we discuss how to resolve the redundant invocation of methods on replicas and the quorum explosion. In section 5, we evaluate the quorum-based protocol.

2 Quorum-Based Replication of Object

An object is an encapsulation of data and abstract methods. Let us consider a *counter* object c which supports three types of methods *increment* (*inc*), *decrement* (*dec*), and *display* (*dsp*). Suppose there are four replicas c_1, c_2, c_3, and c_4 of the object c. *inc* and *dec* are considered to be *write* because the state of the object c is changed by the methods. Hence, $N_{inc} + N_{dec} > 4$, $N_{dsp} + N_{inc} > 4$, and $N_{dsp} + N_{dec} > 4$ according to the traditional quorum-based protocols [7]. For example, $N_{inc} = N_{dec} = 3$ and $N_{dsp} = 2$. The quorum concept for *read* and *write* is extended to methods of objects [14, 15].

[Object-based quorum (OBQ) constraint] If a pair of methods t and u conflict, $N_t + N_u > a$ where a is the total number of the replicas. □

It is noted that $N_t + N_u \leq a$ only if t and u are compatible even if t or u is update. Every pair of conflicting methods t and u of an object x are performed on at least k $(= N_t + N_u - a)$ replicas in the same order. $N_{inc} + N_{dec} \leq 4$, e.g. $N_{inc} = N_{dec} = 2$ because *inc* and *dec* are compatible. Suppose $Q_{inc} = \{c_1, c_2\}$ and $Q_{dec} = \{c_3, c_4\}$. Since either *inc* or *dec* is performed on each replica in the quorums, the states of the replicas in Q_{inc} are different from Q_{dec}. However, if *dec* is performed on c_1 and c_2 and *inc* on c_3 and c_4, all the replicas can be the same. This is an *exchanging procedure* where every method t performed on one replica is sent to other replicas where t is not performed and only methods compatible with t are performed. Suppose *dsp* is issued to three replicas c_1, c_2, and c_3 where $Q_{dsp} = \{c_1, c_2, c_3\}$. *dsp* conflicts with *inc* and *dec*. *dsp* cannot be performed on replicas c_1, c_2, and c_3 because only *inc* is performed on c_1 and c_2 and only *dec* on c_3 as shown at step 1 of Figure 1. Before performing *dsp*, *dec* is performed on c_1 and c_2 and *inc* on c_3. *inc* and *dec* can be performed in any order because they are compatible. Here, c_1, c_2, and c_3 get the same at step 2. *dsp* is performed on c_1, c_2, and c_3 at step 3.

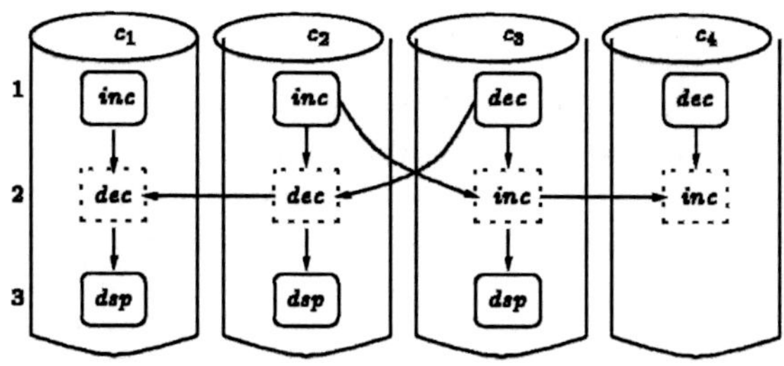

Fig. 1. Exchanging procedure.

3 Redundant Invocation

3.1 Invocation on Replicas

In the object-based system, methods are invoked in a nested manner. Suppose a transaction T invokes a method t on an object x and then t invokes a method u on an object y. Suppose there are multiple replicas $x_1, \ldots, x_a$ of the object x and $y_1, \ldots, y_b$ of the object y. One way to invoke a method t on the replicas is a *primary-secondary* one. First, T issues a request t to a primary replica x_1. Then, a request u is issued to a primary replica y_1 [Figure 2]. After the method commits, the state of the primary replica is eventually transmitted to the secondary ones. Since only one instance of t invokes u, neither redundant invocation nor quorum explosion occur. However, this way implies less availability for the fault of primary replica.

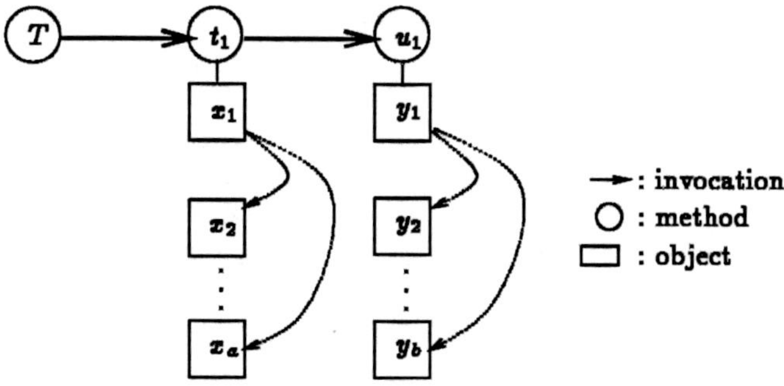

Fig. 2. Primary-secondary replication.

We take another approach where a method is issued to multiple replicas [Figure 3]. Here, a transaction T invokes a method t on multiple replicas of x.

Each instance t_i of t on a replica x_i invokes a method u on multiple replicas of y. Even if some replica is faulty, t is performed on other replicas and u is invoked on replicas of y. Suppose that t invokes a method u on an object y. Let Q_{ui} be a set of replicas of y to which an instance t_i issues u. If $|Q_{u1} \cup \cdots \cup Q_{um}| > N_u$, T manipulates more number of replicas of the object y than N_u, i.e. the quorum of u is *exploded*.

A transaction T issues a method t to replicas in the quorum $Q_t = \{x_1, x_2\}$ and $N_t = 2$. Furthermore, t issues a request u to replicas of the object y in the quorum of the method u, say $N_u = 2$. Let t_i be an instance of the method t performed on a replica x_i ($i = 1, 2$). Each instance t_i issues a request u to replicas in a quorum Q_{ui}. Suppose $Q_{u1} = Q_{u2} = \{y_1, y_2\}$. Here, let u_{i1} and u_{i2} show instances of the method u performed on replicas y_1 and y_2, respectively, which are issued by t_i ($i = 1, 2$) [Figure 4]. Suppose the value of y is multiplied by two through u. However, the replica y_1 is multiplied by four since two instances u_{11} and u_{21} are performed on y_1. Thus, y_1 gets inconsistent. This is a *redundant invocation*, i.e. a method on a replica is invoked multiple times by multiple instances of a method. Since every method is deterministic, the same computation of t is performed on the replicas x_1 and x_2. Here, t_1 and t_2 are referred to as *same crone* instances of a method t. u_{11}, u_{12}, u_{21}, and u_{22} are also same crone instances.

[Definition] A pair of instances t_1 and t_2 of a method t are *same crones* if t_1 and t_2 are invoked on replicas by a same instance or by same crones. □

Each replica has to satisfy the following constraint.

[Invocation constraint] At most one crone instance of a method invoked in a transaction is performed on each replica. □

[Theorem] If every method is invoked on a replica so that the invocation constraint is satisfied, the replica is consistent. □

3.2 Resolution

We discuss how to resolve the redundant invocation in a transaction T so as to satisfy the invocation constraint. In order to resolve the redundant invocation, we have to make clear whether or not every pair of instances issued to a replica are same crones in the transaction. An identifier $id(t_i)$ for each instance t_i invoked on a replica of an object x is composed of a method type t and identifier of the object x, i.e. $id(t_i) = t{:}x$. Each transaction T has a unique identifier $tid(T)$, e.g. thread identifier of T. If T invokes a method t, t is assigned a transaction identifier $tid(t)$ as a concatenation of $tid(T)$ and *invocation sequence number* $iseq(T, t)$ of t in T. $iseq(T, t)$ is incremented by one each time T invokes a method. Suppose an instance t_i on a replica x_i invokes an instance u_k on a replica y_k. $id(t_i) = t{:}x$. The transaction identifier $tid(u_k)$ is $tid(t_i){:}id(t_i){:}iseq(t_i, u_k)$, i.e. $tid(u_k) = tid(t_i){:}t{:}x{:}iseq(t_i, u_k)$. $id(u_k) = u{:}k$. Thus, $tid(u_k)$ shows an invocation sequence of methods from T to u_k.

[Theorem] Let t_1 and t_2 be instances of a method t. $tid(t_1) = tid(t_2)$ iff t_1 and t_2 are same crone instances of the method t invoked in a transaction. □

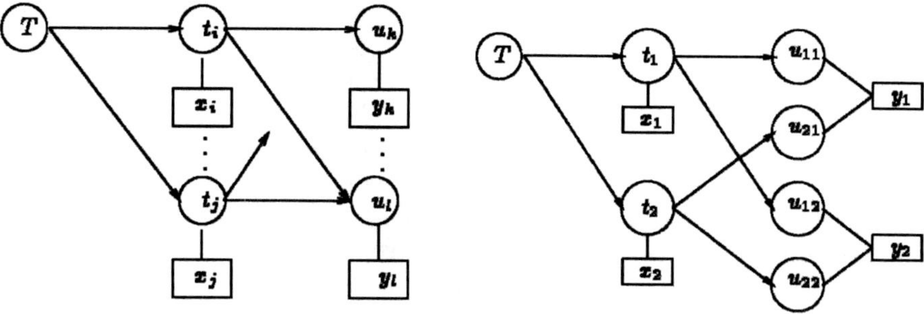

Fig. 3. Invocation on multiple replicas. **Fig. 4.** Redundant invocation.

Suppose $tid(T)$ is assumed to be 6 in Figure 4. Suppose T invokes a method t after invoking three methods, i.e. $iseq(T, t_1) = iseq(T, t_2) = 4$. Since $tid(t_1) = tid(t_2) = tid(T){:}iseq(T, t_1) = tid(T){:}iseq(T, t_2) = 6{:}4$ and $id(t_1) = id(t_2) = t{:}x$, t_1 and t_2 are same crone instances. t invokes another method u after invoking one method. $tid(u_{11}) = tid(u_{12}) = tid(t_1){:}id(t_1){:}2 = 6{:}4{:}t{:}x{:}2$. $tid(u_{21}) = tid(u_{22}) = tid(t_2){:}id(t_2){:}2 = 6{:}4{:}t{:}x{:}2$. Since $tid(u_{11}) = tid(u_{21})$, u_{11} and u_{21} are same crone instances on a replica y_1.

A method t invoked on a replica x_h is performed as follows:

1. If no method is issued to a replica x_h, an instance t_h is performed and a response *res* of t is sent back. $\langle t, res, tid(t_h)\rangle$ is stored in the log L_h.
2. If $\langle t, res, tid(t'_h)\rangle$ such that $tid(t_h) = tid(t'_h)$ is found in L_h, the response *res* of t'_h is sent back as the response of t_h without performing t_h. Otherwise, t is performed on the replica x_h as presented at step 1.

In Figure 4, u_{11} is performed on the replica y_1. $\langle u$, response of u_{11}, $tid(u_{11})\rangle$ is stored in the log L_1. Then, u_{21} is issued. Since $tid(u_{11}) = tid(u_{21})$, u_{11} and u_{21} are same crones. u_{21} is not performed but the response of u_{11} as the response of u_{21} is sent to t_2. By the resolution of the redundant invocation presented here, at most one crone instance is surely performed on each replica. In addition, each method can be performed on some replica even if a replica is faulty.

4 Quorum Explosion

4.1 Basic Protocol

In Figure 4, suppose $Q_{u1} = \{y_1, y_2\}$ and $Q_{u2} = \{y_2, y_3\}$. The method u is performed on each replica in a subset $Q = Q_{u1} \cup Q_{u2} = \{y_1, y_2, y_3\}$. Suppose another transaction manipulates replicas y_3 and y_4 of the object y in the quorum Q_u through the method u. $|Q_{u1} \cup Q_{u2}|$ $(= 3) \geq N_u$ $(= 2)$. This means that more number of replicas are manipulated than the quorum number N_u. Then, the instances of u on the replicas in $Q_{u1} \cup Q_{u2}$ issue further requests to other replicas and more number of replicas are manipulated. This is *quorum explosion*.

[Definition] A quorum of an object x for a method t is *exploded* in a transaction T if same crone instances of t invoked in T are performed on more number of replicas of x than the quorum number N_t of t. □

Suppose a method t on an object x invokes a method u on an object y. Let Q_{uh} be a quorum of u invoked by an instance t_h of t on a replica x_h. In order to resolve the quorum explosion, Q_{uh} and Q_{uk} have to be the same for every pair of replicas x_h and x_k. If $Q_{uh} = Q_{uk} = Q_u$, only the same replicas are manipulated for every instance of u. If some method is frequently invoked, the replicas in the quorum are overloaded. In distributed systems, the quorum information is distributed in networks. If some replica is faulty, the quorum information including the faulty replica has to be updated in the networks. $Q_{ui} = Q_{uj}$ only if t_i and t_j are same crones. $Q_{ui} \neq Q_{uj}$ if t_i and t_j are different crones. We introduce a following function *select* to decide a quorum:

1. A function *select*(i, n, a) gives a set of n numbers out of 1, ..., a for a same initial value i where $n \leq a$. For example, *select*$(i, n, a) = \{h \mid h = (i + \lceil \frac{a}{n} \rceil (j - 1))$ *modulo* a for $j = 1, \ldots, n\} \subseteq \{1, \ldots, a\}$.
2. Suppose an instance t_h on a replica x_h invokes a method u. I = *select*(*numb*(*tid*(t_h)), N_u, b) is obtained, where N_u is quorum number of u and b is a total number of replicas, i.e. $\{y_1, \ldots, y_b\}$. Let *tid*(t_h) be $s_1{:}s_2{:}\cdots{:}s_g$. Here, *numb*(*tid*(t_h)) is $(s_1 + \cdots + s_g)$ *modulo* a. $I \subseteq \{1, \ldots, b\}$ and $|I| = N_h$. Then, $Q_h = \{y_i \mid i \in I\}$.

Every pair of same crone instances have the same transaction identifier *tid* as presented in the preceding subsection. Hence, *select*(*numb*(*tid*(t_h)), N_u, b) = *select*(*numb*(*tid*(t_k)), N_u, b) for every pair of crone instances t_h and t_k. An instance t_h on every replica x_h issues a method u to the same quorum Q_{uh} (= Q_u). Hence, no quorum explosion occurs [Figure 6].

Some replica may be faulty. Suppose a method t invokes a method u on replicas of an object y. Let Y be a set $\{y_1, \ldots, y_b\}$ of replicas of y. Here, suppose some replica y_h is faulty. Here, the quorum number N_u can be decremented by one as far as at most k replicas of y are faulty, i.e. $N_u + N_v - b = k$ for every method v conflicting with u. In one case, an invoker, say t_i, does not know that y_h is faulty. Here, by using *select*, a quorum Q_{ui} including N_u replicas in Y are selected. In another case, t_i knows y_h is faulty. If $y_h \in Q_{ui}$, y_h is removed from Q_{ui}. Here, $|Q_{ui}| = N_u - 1$. Unless $y_h \in Q_{ui}$, $|Q_{ui}| = N_u$. There is no need u is issued to N_u replicas. u is required to be issued to at least $N_u - 1$ replicas. Therefore, one replica y_l is removed from Q_{ui}. For example, a replica y_l where l is the minimum in Q_{ui} is selected and removed from Q_{ui}. If a faulty replica is recovered, *views* on locations and status of the replicas are resynchronized.

4.2 Modified Protocol

Each instance t_h on a replica x_h issues a request u to N_u replicas of the object y. Hence, totally $N_t \cdot N_u$ requests are transmitted. We try to reduce the number of requests transmitted in the network. Let Q_u be a quorum $\{y_1, \ldots, y_b\}$ ($b = N_u$) of the method u obtained by the function *select* for each instance t_h. If each instance t_h issues a request u to only a subset $Q_{uh} \subseteq Q_u$, the number of requests issued to the replicas of the object y can be reduced. Here, $Q_{u1} \cup \ldots \cup Q_{ua} = Q_u$.

In order to tolerate the fault of a replica, each replica y_k in Q_u is required to receive a request u from more than one instance of the method t. Let r (≥ 1) be a *redundancy factor*, i.e. the number of requests of u to be issued to each replica y_k in Q_u. For each instance t_h on a replica x_h in $Q_t = \{x_1, \ldots x_a\}$ where $a = N_t$, Q_{uh} is constructed for the method u as follows ($h = 1, \ldots, a$):

If $a \geq b{\cdot}r$, $Q_{uh} = \{y_k \mid k = \lceil \frac{h_b}{a} \rceil$ if $h \leq r \cdot b\}$, ϕ otherwise.

If $a < b{\cdot}r$,

$Q_{uh} = \{ y_k \mid (1 + \lfloor \frac{(h-1)b}{a} \rfloor) \leq k < [\, 1 + (\, \lfloor \frac{(h+r-1)b}{a} \rfloor - 1)$ *modulo* b $]\}$.

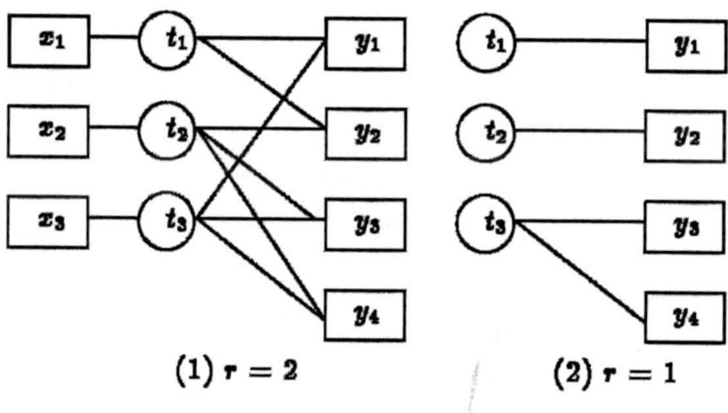

Fig. 5. Invocations.

For example, suppose instances t_1, t_2, and t_3 on replicas x_1, x_2, and x_3 issue a request u to replicas y_1, y_2, y_3, and y_4, i.e. $Q_t = \{x_1, x_2, x_3\}$ and $Q_u = \{y_1, y_2, y_3, y_4\}$. Suppose the redundancy factor r is 2. Hence, $Q_{uh} = \{y_k \mid (1 + (\lfloor \frac{(h-1)4}{3} \rfloor) \leq k \leq (1 + (\lfloor \frac{(h-1)4}{3} \rfloor + \lfloor \frac{8}{3} \rfloor - 1)$ *modulo* $4)\}$. Hence, $Q_{u1} = \{y_1, y_2\}$, $Q_{u2} = \{y_2, y_3, y_4\}$, and $Q_{u3} = \{y_3, y_4, y_1\}$ for $r = 2$ [Figure 5(1)]. Two requests from the instances of the method t are issued to each replica of y. For example, suppose an instance t_1 on x_1 is faulty. t_2 sends u to the replicas y_2, y_3, and y_4 in Q_{u2} and t_3 sends u to the replicas in Q_{u3}. Since $Q_{u2} \cup Q_{u3} = \{y_1, y_2, y_3, y_4\}$, u is sent to every replica in Q_u even if t_1 is faulty. $Q_{u1} = \{y_1\}$, $Q_{u2} = \{y_2\}$, and $Q_{u3} = \{y_3, y_4\}$ for $r = 1$ [Figure 5(2)]. Thus, totally $r \cdot N_u$ requests of the method u are issued to the replicas in Q_u. Even if $(r - 1)$ instances of t are faulty, u is performed on N_u replicas of y.

5 Evaluation

We evaluate the QB protocol to resolve the redundant invocation and quorum explosion in nested invocations of methods on replicas in terms of number of replicas manipulated and number of requests issued. We consider three protocols

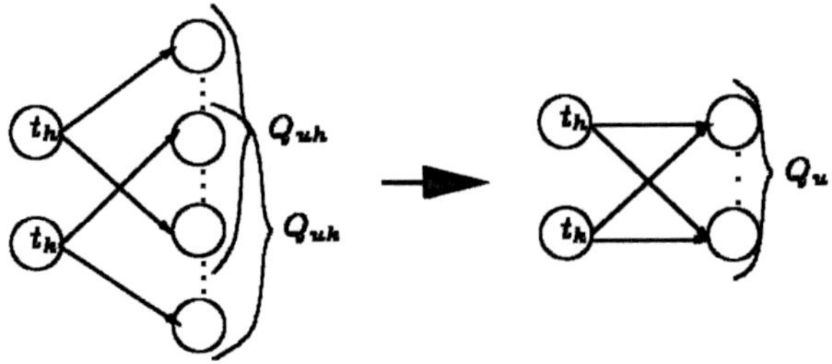

Fig. 6. Resolution of quorum explosion.

R, Q, and N. In the protocol Q, the redundant invocation is prevented but the quorum explosion is not resolved. The protocol R shows the QB protocol where neither redundant invocation nor quorum explosion occurs. In the protocol N, redundant invocation and quorum explosion may occur.

In the evaluation, we take a simple invocation model where a transaction T first invokes a method t_1 on an object x_1, then t_1 invokes t_2 on x_2, $\cdots$ as shown in Figure 7. Here, let a_i be the number of replicas of an object x_i (i = 1, 2, ...). Let N_i be the quorum number of a method t_i ($N_i \leq a_i$), where i shows a level of invocation. A transaction T first issues N_1 requests of t_1 to the replicas of x_1. Then, each instance of t_1 on a replica issues N_2 requests of t_2 to the replicas of x_2. In the protocol N, a method t_2 invoked by each instance of t_1 is performed. Here, totally $N_1 \cdot N_2$ requests are performed on the replicas of x_2. In the protocol Q, at most one instance of t_2 is performed on each replica of x_2 by the resolution procedure of the redundant invocation. Since the quorum explosion is not resolved, the expected number QE_2 of replicas where t_2 is performed is $a_2[1 - (1 - \frac{N_2}{a_2})^{N_1}]$. Then, each instance of t_2 issues requests of t_3 to N_3 replicas of x_3. Here, $a_3[1 - (1 - \frac{N_3}{a_3})^{N_1 N_2}]$ replicas are manipulated in the protocol N and $QE_3 = a_3[1 - (1 - \frac{N_3}{a_3})^{QE_2}]$ replicas in the protocol Q. In the protocol R, t_2 is performed on only N_2 replicas of the object x_2.

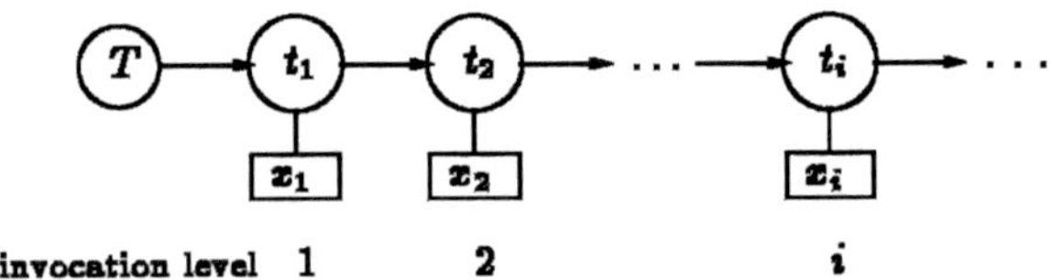

Fig. 7. Invocation model.

We assume that $a_1 = a_2 = \ldots = a = 10$ and $N_1 = N_2 = \ldots = N$ ($\leq a$). Figure 8 shows the ratios of replicas where a method is performed to the quorum number a (= 10) at each invocation level i for $N = 3$. The dotted line with white circles shows the ratio for the protocol R. The straight line indicates the protocol

N and the other dotted line with black circles shows the protocol Q. If methods are invoked at a deeper level than two for $N = 3$, all the replicas are manipulated if neither the redundant invocation nor quorum explosion are prevented. In the protocol R, only the quorum number of replicas, i.e. three replicas, in ten replicas are manipulated at any invocation level.

Figure 9 shows the number of request messages transmitted by crone instances of a method t_i for $N = 3$. The vertical axis shows $log(m)$ for the number m of requests issued. In the protocol N, N^i request messages are issued to replicas of the object x_i because N^{i-1} crone instances are performed on replicas of the object x_{i-1}. In the protocol Q, there are $a[1 - (1 - \frac{N}{a})^{QE_{i-2}}]$ replicas of x_{i-1} where crone instances of a method t_{i-1} are performed. Hence, $a[1 - (1 - \frac{N}{a})^{QE_{i-2}}]N$ request messages are transmitted. In the protocol R, we assume the redundancy factor $r = N$ in this evaluation. N^2 request messages are transmitted.

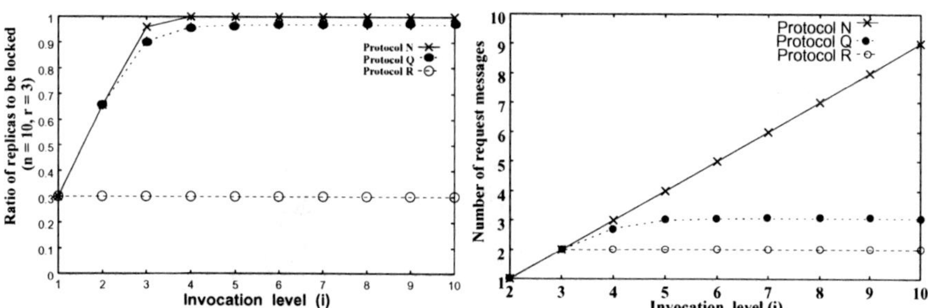

Fig. 8. Ratio of replicas manipulated ($a = 10$ and $N = 3$).

Fig. 9. Number of request messages issued ($a = 10$ and $N = 3$).

Acknowledgment. This research is partially supported by Research Institute for Technology, Tokyo Denki Univ.

6 Concluding Remarks

In this paper, we discussed how transactions invoke methods on multiple replicas of objects. The object supports abstract methods. In addition, methods are invoked in a nested manner. If methods are invoked on multiple replicas, multiple redundant instances of a same method may be performed on a replica and more number of replicas than the quorum number may be manipulated. We discussed the QB (quorum-based) protocol where redundant invocations and quorum explosions to occur are resolved in systems. By using the QB protocol with the resolution of redundant invocations and quorum explosions, an object-based system including replicas of objects can be efficiently realized.

References

1. Ahamad, M., Dasgupta, P., LeBlanc R., and Wilkes, C., "Fault Tolerant Computing in Object Based Distributed Operating Systems," *Proc. 6th IEEE SRDS*, 1987, pp. 115–125.
2. Barrett, P. A., Hilborne, A. M., Bond, P. G., and Seaton, D. T., "The Delta-4 Extra Performance Architecture," *Proc. 20th Int'l Symp. on FTCS*, 1990, pp. 481–488.
3. Birman, K. P. and Joseph, T. A., "Reliable Communication in the Presence of Failures," *ACM TOCS*, Vol. 5, No. 1, pp 1987, pp. 47–76.
4. Borg, A., Baumbach, J., and Glazer, S., "A Message System Supporting Fault Tolerance," *Proc. 9th ACM Symp. on Operating Sys. Principles*, 1983, . 27–39.
5. Carey, J. M. and Livny, M., "Conflict Detection Tradeoffs for Replicated Data," *ACM TODS,* Vol.16, No.4, 1991, pp. 703–746.
6. Chevalier, P. -Y., "A Replicated Object Server for a Distributed Object-Oriented System," *Proc. IEEE SRDS*, 1992, pp.4-11.
7. Garcia-Molina, H. and Barbara, D., "How to Assign Votes in a Distributed System," *JACM*, Vol 32, No.4, 1985, pp. 841-860.
8. Gifford, D. K., "Weighted Voting for Replicated Data," *Proc. 7th ACM Symp. on Operating Systems Principles*, 1979, pp. 150-159.
9. Hasegawa, K., Higaki, H., and Takizawa, M., "Object Replication Using Version Vector," *Proc. of the 6th IEEE Int'l Conf. on Parallel and Distributed Systems* (*ICPADS-98*), 1998, pp. 147–154.
10. Jing, J., Bukhres, O., and Elmagarmid, A., "Distributed Lock Management for Mobile Transactions," *Proc. IEEE ICDCS-15*, 1995, pp. 118-125.
11. Korth, H. F., "Locking Primitives in a Database System," *JACM*, Vol. 30, No. 1, 1983, pp. 55-79.
12. Powell, D., Chereque, M., and Drackley, D., "Fault-Tolerance in Delta-4," *ACM Operating System Review*, Vol. 25, No. 2, 1991, pp. 121–125.
13. Silvano, M. and Douglas, C. S., "Constructing Reliable Distributed Communication Systems with CORBA," *IEEE Comm. Magazine*, Vol.35, No.2, 1997, pp.56–60.
14. Tanaka, K., Hasegawa, K., and Takizawa, M., "Quorum-Based Replication in Object-Based Systems," *Journal of Information Science and Engineering* (*JISE*), Vol. 16, 2000, pp. 317–331.
15. Tanaka, K. and Takizawa, M., "Quorum-Based Replication of Objects," *Proc. 3rd DEXA Int'l Workshop on Network-Based Information Systems* (*NBIS-3*), 2000, pp. 33–37.

Applying Low-Level Query Optimization Techniques by Rewriting

Jacek Płodzień[1] and Kazimierz Subieta[2]

[1]Institute of Computer Science PAS
[2]Polish-Japanese Institute of Information Technology
Warsaw, Poland
{jpl, subieta}@ipipan.waw.pl

Abstract. In the paper we focus on those query optimization techniques that concern low-level mechanisms and data structures used in query processing. In this setting we discuss how such techniques can be applied at a textual level, in other words, how they can be used as rewriting rules. A number of such methods are considered, among others, so-called direct navigation and a widely known technique – indices.
Our rewriting rules are defined in an algorithmic manner, that is, they are associated with code. An important part of such algorithms is a special phase – static analysis – which gathers all the information needed to decide whether a given method can be applied and how.

1 Introduction

The problem of query optimization has been under research for many years. The research has resulted in a great number of optimization methods. A widely used category of such methods is techniques concerning low-level mechanisms and special data structures of query execution. Practice has proved that physical level mechanisms determine to a large degree the effectiveness of a query optimizer, because they can not only significantly support query optimization, but sometimes are indispensable so that the query optimizer could generate an acceptable (for users) evaluation plan. Examples of the most important methods of the physical level in relational *database management systems* (DBMSs) are: *pipelining*, *implementation of joins*, *buffering*, *function caching*, and *clustering*.

Low-level optimization mechanisms applied in relational DBMSs are often also used in object DBMSs; some of them are more or less modified. Examples are *method caching*, *clustering* and *double data buffering*. There are also new ones that have been invented especially for the object approach, for instance: *pointer swizzling* and *path indices* [1]. Another example is *access support relations* (ASRs; [4, 5]). They improve performance of path expression traversal by maintaining redundantly frequently traversed reference chains. More detailed information about these and other concepts can be also found e.g. in [6, 11].

In the paper we deal with those low-level optimization methods that in our approach to query optimization can be applied at a textual level, that is, by rewriting; they include indices, access support relations, and a technique called *direct navigation*. (In our work we have also devised other query optimization techniques,

H.C. Mayr et al. (Eds.): DEXA 2001, LNCS 2113, pp. 867–876, 2001.

for instance, factoring out independent subqueries and removing dead parts of queries. They are discussed e.g. in [8, 10, 13].)

An advantage of our solution is that we define our rules in an algorithmic way, that is, we associate them with code. This enables us to construct complex optimization methods, which could not be defined otherwise, or it would be more difficult.

In order to decide whether a given optimization method can be applied, a special phase of processing is performed: it gathers all the information that is needed to make such a decision. One of its most important tasks is to determine the meaning of each name occurring in a query, which is essential for the precise (and correct) evaluation of it. This operation is called *static analysis*, because it is performed for *static* (i.e., compile-time) optimization. Due to space limit, we are unable to present in this paper the details of our approach to query optimization (including static analysis); the reader is referred to [8, 9, 14].

In our research we use a special object-oriented data model: the *Stack-Based Approach* (SBA) along with its query language (SBQL). SBA is a general object model, which includes, for instance, complex objects, collection-valued attributes, classes, methods, and inheritance. Its description can be found e.g. in [8, 12, 13].

All queries in this paper are defined in SBQL against an example database whose schema (in a little modified UML) is shown in Fig. 1.

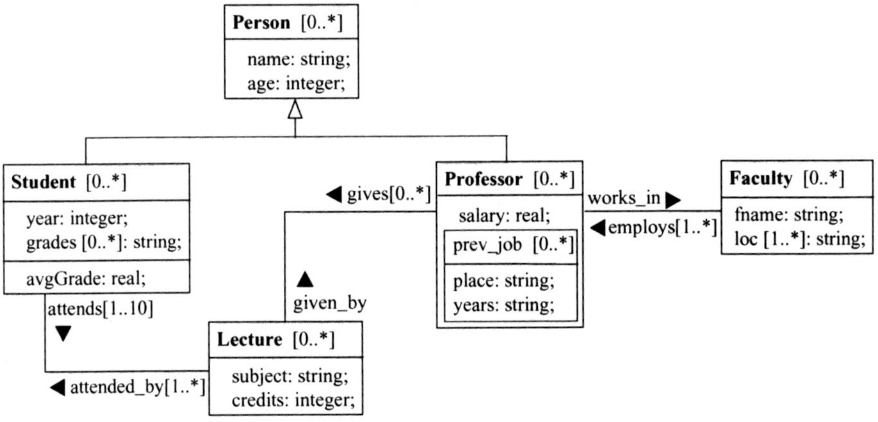

Fig. 1. The class diagram of the example database

The schema defines five classes (i.e., five collections of objects): *Lecture*, *Student*, *Professor*, *Person*, and *Faculty*. The classes *Lecture*, *Student*, *Professor* and *Faculty* model lectures attended by students and given by professors working in faculties, respectively. *Person* is the superclass of the classes *Student* and *Professor*. *Professor* objects can contain multiple complex *prev_job* subobjects (modeling previous jobs). The name of a class (attribute, etc) is followed by its cardinality, unless the cardinality is 1. All of the object attributes and class properties are public.

The rest of the paper is structured as follows. Section 2 presents a general architecture of query processing in our solution. In Section 3 we discuss a general framework of our approach to rewriting, in particular, what we mean by a rewriting rule and how we determine whether it is correct or not. Sections 4 through 6 cover our optimization methods, namely: Section 4 covers indices, Section 5 covers direct navigation, and Section 6 covers access support relations. Section 7 concludes.

2 Architecture of Query Processing

The general query processing architecture is presented in Fig. 2. First, the text of a query is parsed and its syntax tree is constructed. Then, the query is optimized by rewriting. Static analysis, performed by a *query optimizer*, involves a *metabase* (a data structure obtained from a database schema), a structure simulating the *Environment Stack* (static ES denoted by S_ES), and a structure simulating the *Query RESult stack* (static QRES denoted by S_QRES). After optimization the query is evaluated; evaluation involves a run-time object store, ES and QRES.

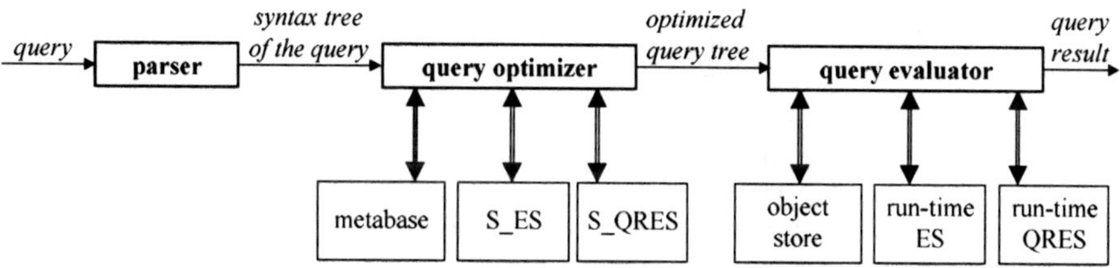

Fig. 2. Architecture of query processing

A metabase stores the definitions of objects from a database schema. It is constructed, because during static optimization we have no access to run-time objects. Instead, we have access to those definitions. Nodes in a metabase may also store additional data that concern given entities, for instance, statistics and the definitions of indices. If an optimization method makes use of such data, we discuss it in the section covering that method.

3 Rewriting Rules

Rewriting rules are a widely used concept in the literature on query optimization ([3, 5, 7] and many others). They are used to describe a query transformation and the queries subject to it. Many rewriting rules are *declarative*, that is, they specify transformations and the queries to which they apply without committing to any code.

Typically, declarative rules have a left-hand side, which is used to match a pattern in the query, and a right hand side, which defines a replacement for the matching pattern [5]:

$l \rightarrow r$

This rule specifies that expression l is replaced by expression r. A disadvantage of such rewriting rules is that they are not universal enough and do not have the expressive power to model some cases or it is very complex [2].

An alternative approach is applied for instance in Starburst [7], where a special procedural language is used to express transformations. An example of a rule is

if (in a SELECT box a quantifier has type = E or A)
{quantifier.distinct = PERMIT;}

It says that existential and universal quantifiers are blind to duplicates.

Our approach to rewriting rules is similar to that in Starburst, but we go farther. We do not use declarative rules, either, but define optimization transformations in a pure algorithmic way. Our algorithms statically analyze queries (i.e., perform static analysis) and gather all the necessary information to rewrite them appropriately (if it is possible). This approach enables us to design sophisticated rewriting rules.

3.1 Semantic Equivalence and Cost Model

A very important aspect of query rewriting is *semantic equivalence*. We apply the following approach: because the text of an SBQL query determines its operational semantics, while discussing its correctness we need to consider only the SBA and SBQL mechanisms referred to by that semantics. Moreover, in the discussion on a given rewriting rule we consider two queries: q_1 and q_2, where q_2 is textually different from q_1, but, as the result of applying some of our rewriting rules to q_1, is usually (very) similar to it; we can say that it is some form of q_1. In consequence, it is enough to consider only the textual differences between such two forms of the query, because only they can potentially invalidate the equivalence.

Another aspect is a *cost model*. The techniques discussed in this paper always improve performance (at least, do not deteriorate it). Therefore, we usually do not have to use a cost model to check whether it is worth applying a given technique (as long as we do not construct a full optimization algorithm). There is, however, one important case when we make use of a cost model: indices. Nevertheless, in order to construct a full cost-based optimization algorithm, one has to devise a general cost model that can be applied to any transformation.

Due to space limit the paper does not cover these issues; see [9] for the discussion.

4 Indices

While using indices we abstract from data structures, access methods and other solutions concerning the implementation level. For us, an index on attribute *Attr* of *Object* objects is implemented as a special procedure of the signature

index_Object_Attr(par) (i)

which can be invoked as a regular (sub)query. The formal parameter *par* is a query returning a single atomic value being of the type compatible with the type of *Attr*. (We assume that every time the administrator creates an index for attribute *Attr* of *Object* objects, he/she also registers an appropriate procedure of the form (i).)

Procedure (i) works in the following manner: it reads from the appropriate index the identifiers of all *Object* objects, for which the value of attribute *Attr* is equal to the result of *par*, and then pushes those identifiers as a one-column table onto QRES. Due to using indices, the evaluation of such a procedure is much faster (sometimes by orders of magnitude) than the evaluation of the corresponding (sub)query

Object **where** *Attr* = *par* (ii)

Note that the procedure can be used only if we want to select objects from the entire extension of *Object* objects.

4.1 How to Apply the Rewriting Rule

Our method of applying indices is as follows. During a static analysis of a (sub)query of the form (we assume that it is semantically correct)

$$Object\ \textbf{where}\ (Attr_1\ op_1\ Val_1\ \textbf{and}\ \ldots\ \textbf{and}\ Attr_{k-1}\ op_{k-1}\ Val_{k-1}\ \textbf{and}\ Attr_k\ op_k\ Val_k\ \textbf{and}\ Attr_{k+1}\ op_{k+1}\ Val_{k+1}\ \textbf{and}\ \ldots\ \textbf{and}\ Attr_n\ op_n\ Val_n\ \textbf{and}\ p) \quad \text{(iii)}$$

where, for $i \in \{1, 2, \ldots, n\}$, $Attr_i$ is an attribute of *Object* objects, op_i is an operator of a binary relation (e.g., =, <, >, **in**; the form of a predicate depends on the operator), Val_i is a query returning a single atomic value, p is a predicate, we rewrite it to

$$index\_Object\_Attr_k(Val_k)\ \textbf{where}\ (Attr_1\ op_1\ Val_1\ \textbf{and}\ \ldots\ \textbf{and}\ Attr_{k-1}\ op_{k-1}\ Val_{k-1}\ \textbf{and}\ Attr_{k+1}\ op_{k+1}\ Val_{k+1}\ \textbf{and}\ \ldots\ \textbf{and}\ Attr_n\ op_n\ Val_n\ \textbf{and}\ p) \quad \text{(iv)}$$

provided that:

- the name *Object* is bound in the base sections of ES, so that the whole extension of *Object* objects will be taken into consideration; to determine where such a name is bound we have to perform a static analysis;
- there is an index on attribute $Attr_k$ of *Object* objects; the information on indices for a given attribute is stored in the metabase node modeling that attribute;
- op_k is the operator of equation.

Note that if *Object* objects have indices on a few (at least two) different attributes $Attr_i$, then we should not choose just any of them. It is the most advantageous to use that index, which is (according to the statistics) the most selective [11]; a cost model is used.

The static analysis applying indices is a little modified version of the standard *static_eval* procedure discussed in [14]. Its modified part is presented below. (Due to space limit the paper presents an algorithm only for the method of indices.)

```
case query is q1 θ q2: (*θ is a non-algebraic operator*)
begin
  n: integer; (*the number of indices that can be
               applied*)

  analyze statically query in the modified way to
  determine binding levels;
  if (query is of the form (iii)) then
    if (the name Object is bound in the base
        sections) then
```

```
      (*the entire extension is searched*)
      begin
        determine the number of indices that can be
        applied - say, it is n;
        if (n >= 1) then
        begin
          if (n > 1) then
            choose the most selective index;
          rewrite query to the form (iv) using the index;
        end;
      end;
  end; (*case*)
```

Procedure (i) works for the operator of equation. However, other operators of binary relations can be considered as well. For instance, for the > operator we could define a procedure

index_Object_Attr_greater_than(*par*)

that selects the identifiers of those *Object* objects for which the value of attribute *Attr* is greater than the value returned by *par*.

4.2 Examples

Below we discuss a few examples of applying indices to query rewriting (we assume that the names being the left operands of the **where** operators are bound in the base sections of ES):

(1) The query returning lectures on biology:

Lecture **where** *subject* = „biology"

can be rewritten to the form

index_Lecture_subject(„biology")

provided that *Lecture* objects have an index on attribute *subject*.

(2) The query getting the Faculty of Engineering along with the names of its professors:

(*Faculty* **where** *fname* = „engineering") | *employs.Professor.name*

can be transformed as follows:

index_Faculty_fname(„engineering") | *employs.Professor.name*

provided that *Faculty* objects have an index on attribute *fname*.

(3) The query retrieving the names of professors who earn more than Professor White:

(*Professor* **where** *salary* > ((*Professor* **where** *name* = „White").*salary*)).*name*

can be rewritten to the form

index_Professor_salary_greater_than((*Professor* **where** *name* = „White").*salary*).
name

provided that *Professor* objects have an index on attribute *salary*. Note that this transformation is even more advantageous than factoring the independent subquery (*Professor* **where** *name* = „White").*salary* out of the **where** operator (the method of factoring out so-called independent subqueries is discussed in detail in [8]):

(((*Professor* **where** *name* = „White").*salary* **as** *s*).(*Professor* **where** *salary* > *s*)).*name*

The first form is evaluated much faster than the latter one, since the index procedure retrieves the appropriate object identifiers directly from the index, while in the other case all *Professor* objects have to be checked.
(4) The query returning professors named Smith who are older than 50 and earn more than 3000:

Professor **where** (*name* = „Smith" **and** *age* > 50 **and** *salary* > 3000)

can be rewritten to the form

index_Professor_name(„Smith") **where** (*age* > 50 **and** *salary* > 3000)

provided that *Professor* objects have an index on attribute *name*. If they have an index on attribute *age*, then we can rewrite the query as follows:

index_Professor_age_greater_than(50) **where** (*name* = „Smith" **and** *salary* > 3000)

If both of those indices exist, then the decision which one of them should be chosen depends on which of them is more selective (see [9] for an example).

5 Direct Navigation

The technique of *direct navigation* concerns a situation when navigation is performed onto attribute *n* of *Object* objects, whose identifiers are returned by some subquery *q*:

q.*n* (i)

Though it is optimization of low level (because it deals with internal data structures like in the case of indices), it can be applied by means of rewriting.

According to the semantics of SBA, query (i) is evaluated as follows: subquery *q* is calculated to retrieve the identifiers of *Object* objects, scopes with sections containing (among others) attributes of those objects are pushed onto ES, and finally those sections are accessed to get the identifier(s) of attribute *n*. However, the cost of such a naive evaluation, that includes manipulating ES and possibly fetching objects from storage, can be significant, because it may involve a large set of objects.

Therefore, we propose a method in which for queries of the form (i) we do not have to either modify ES or fetch any object to get the identifier(s) of *n*. The technique assumes that the identifier of an object attribute can be determined by combining the identifier of the object and the offset of the attribute in that object. (The values of such offsets can be stored in the metabase of a given DBMS; to be precise, in the nodes modeling the corresponding attributes.) To be able to express such a direct navigation at a textual level, we propose to introduce a procedure

dnav(*offset*)

(short for *d*irect *nav*igation), which does the following: for each object identifier from the top one-column table on QRES, it gets the identifier of its attribute whose offset in this object is equal to the value *offset*, then pops that top table, and finally pushes onto QRES a one-column table containing the identifier(s) of the attribute. (This method works well for attributes of cardinality one; for multiple attributes it has to be modified a little.)

We propose to use *dnav* as a unary suffix operator. By means of that operator we can rewrite (sub)query (i) to the form

q dnav(*offset_of_n*)

where *offset_of_n* is the offset of attribute *n* in *Object* objects. For example, the query

Student.name

can be rewritten to the form

Student dnav(*offset_of_name*)

and the query

(*Lecture* **where** *credits* >= 5).*given_by.Professor.works_in.Faculty.fname*

to the form

((((*Lecture* **where** *credits* >= 5) *dnav*(*offset_of_given_by*)).*Professor*
dnav(*offset_of_works_in*)).*Faculty dnav*(*offset_of_fname*))

where the offsets *offset_of_name*, *offset_of_given_by*, *offset_of_works_in* and *offset_of_fname* are the offsets of the appropriate attributes in objects *Student*, *Lecture*, *Professor* and *Faculty*, respectively.

6 Access Support Relations

One of the basic features of the object model is the existence of path expressions, that is, (sub)queries of the form

$n_1.n_2.n_3. \ldots .n_{k-1}.n_k$ (i)

where n_i ($i \in \{1, 2, \ldots, k\}$) is the external name of an object or its attribute. For instance, the path expression below:

Faculty.employs.Professor.gives.Lecture (ii)

navigates from faculties to lectures given by professors employed in those faculties.

In Section 1 we referred to a special data structure used to support efficient evaluation of path expressions: *access support relations*. We propose to use ASRs in order to optimize path expressions in a way similar to the way we optimize queries by means of procedures encapsulating indices: if a given query contains path expression (i) and there exists an ASR modeling navigation from entity n_1 (object, subobject, etc) to entity n_k (object, subobject, etc), then in our approach expression (i) can be replaced with the invocation of a procedure

ASR_n1_nk (iii)

Just like in the case of indices discussed in Section 4, we assume that the administrator registers procedures for ASRs. In our solution, the definition of each ASR is stored in the metabase node modeling the entity whose name begins a given path expression; for instance, for (i) it is n_1. By the definition of an ASR we mean a list of the names of the consecutive entities comprising the corresponding path.

Procedure (iii) does the following: by making use of the appropriate ASR, it gets the identifiers of entities n_k navigated onto from all entities n_1 existing in a database and pushes them onto QRES as a one-column table (in accordance with the semantics of SBA). For instance, the query getting the subjects of those lectures from query (ii) whose credits are greater than five:

(*Faculty.employs.Professor.gives.Lecture* **where** *credits* > 5).*subject* (iv)

can be rewritten to the form

(*ASR_Faculty_Lecture* **where** *credits* > 5).*subject*

provided that there is an ASR navigating from *Faculty* objects onto *Lecture* objects.

We could also consider another version of such procedures:

ASR_QRES_n1_nk (v)

The difference in comparison with procedure (iii) is that (v) does not get the identifiers of entities n_k navigated onto from all entities n_1 existing in a database, but navigated onto only from those of n_1 whose identifiers are on the top of QRES (as a one-column table). Additionally, before pushing the identifiers of n_k onto QRES, (v) pops the top table off the stack.

We propose to use (v) as if it were a unary suffix operator:

q ASR_QRES_n1_nk

where *q* is a subquery pushing onto QRES a one-column table of the identifiers of entities n_1. For example, if query (iv) were of the form

(((*Faculty* **where** *fname* = „physics“).*employs.Professor.gives.Lecture*)
where *credits* > 5).*subject*

then we could not use an *ASR_Faculty_Lecture* procedure, because the first selection excludes faculties other than the Faculty of Physics. However, we can apply a procedure of the form (v) and rewrite the query as follows:

(((*Faculty* **where** *fname* = „physics“) *ASR_QRES_Faculty_Lecture*)
where *credits* > 5).*subject*

7 Conclusions and Future Work

The main goal of this paper was to analyze traditional and new low-level methods for improving performance of query processing in object-oriented DBMSs. As we have discussed, to a big degree this goal can be achieved by applying special rewriting rules. In our approach we make use of a universal object data model (i.e., SBA) and our rules are expressed in an algorithmic fashion. We have discussed three such optimization methods: indices, direct navigation, and access support relations.

Before applying a given method, we analyze a query to decide whether the method can be used or not. Such an analysis (called static analysis) enables us to gather all the necessary information. One of the structures used by static analysis is a metabase – a compile-time model of a run-time database. One of the tasks of a metabase is to store data concerning low-level mechanisms that are used by our optimization techniques.

In our solution a cost model plays a minor role since we focus on transformations that always (with a few minor exceptions) improve query performance. However, such a model is necessary when designing a full cost-based optimization algorithm. We see constructing a cost model as an extension of our research.

References

1. Bertino, E., Guglielmina, C.: Path-Index: An Approach to the Efficient Execution of Object-Oriented Queries. Data & Knowledge Engineering, Vol. 10 (1993) 1-27
2. Chaudhuri, S., Shim, K.: Query Optimization in the Presence of Foreign Functions. Proc. of VLDB (1993) 529-542
3. Freytag, J.Ch.: A Rule-Based View of Query Optimization. Proc. of SIGMOD (1987) 173-180
4. Kemper, A., Moerkotte, G.: Access Support in Object Bases. Proc. of SIGMOD (1990) 364-376
5. Kemper, A., Moerkotte, G.: Advanced Query Processing in Object Bases Using Access Support Relations. Proc. of VLDB (1990) 290-301
6. Kim, W., Reiner, D.S., Batory, D.S. (eds.): Query Processing in Database Systems. Springer-Verlag, Berlin (1985)
7. Pirahesh, H., Hellerstein, J.M., Hasan, W.: Extensible/Rule Based Query Rewrite Optimization in Starburst. Proc. of SIGMOD (1992) 39-48
8. Płodzień, J., Kraken, A.: Object Query Optimization through Detecting Independent Subqueries. Information Systems, Vol. 25, No. 8 (2000) 467-490
9. Płodzień, J.: Optimization Methods in Object Query Languages. Ph.D. Thesis. Institute of Computer Science, Polish Academy of Sciences (2000)
10. Płodzień, J., Subieta, K.: Query Optimization through Removing Dead Subqueries. Proc. of ADBIS, to appear (2001)
11. Ramakrishnan, R.: Database Management Systems. WCB/McGraw-Hill (1998)
12. Subieta, K., Kambayashi, Y., Leszczyłowski, J.: Procedures in Object-Oriented Query Languages. Proc. of VLDB (1995) 182-193
13. Subieta, K., Płodzień, J.: Object Views and Query Modification. Proc. of 4th IEEE International Baltic Workshop on DB and IS (2000) 13-24
14. Płodzień, J., Subieta, K.: Static Analysis of Queries as a Tool for Static Optimization. Proc. of IDEAS, to appear (2001)

A Popularity-Driven Caching Scheme for Meta-search Engines: An Empirical Study+

Sang Ho Lee[1], Jin Seon Hong[1], and Larry Kerschberg[2]

[1] School of Computing, Soongsil University, Korea
{shlee, jshong}@computing.soongsil.ac.kr
http://orion.soongsil.ac.kr/

[2] E-Center for E-Business, Department of Information and Software Engineering
George Mason University, U.S.A.
kersch@gmu.edu
http://eceb.gmu.edu/

Abstract. Caching issues in meta-search engines are considered. We propose a popularity-driven cache algorithm that utilizes both popularities and reference counters of queries to determine cache data to be purged. We show how to calculate query popularity. Empirical evaluations and performance comparisons of popularity-driven caching with the least recently used (LRU) and least frequently used (LFU) schemes have been carried out on collections of real data. In almost all cases, the proposed replacement policy outperforms LRU and LFU.

1 Introduction

Web search engines enable Internet users to search the web. Yet, no single search engine indexes all the information available on the Internet, and the coverage of a single search engine is surprisingly low [5]. A number of meta-search engines have been developed to augment the low coverage of a single search engine [9]. A meta-search engine accesses external search engines to get search results when the user issues a query.

Accessing external search engines in response to user queries is likely to lead to long response times for end-users, as network traffic and slow remote servers can lead to long delays in results delivery. One approach to overcome the slow response time is to cache previously retrieved results, called results cache [1], for possible future reference. In this case, meta-search engines maintain results of search engines (i.e., a collection of HTML pages) for possible use to answer future queries.

Caching is a quite well known technique in various fields of Computer Science and has been studied extensively. Among others, page caching, tuple caching and semantic caching schemes [2, 3, 6] are used in practice. An essential part of caching

+ This work was supported by grant No. (2000-2-51200-002-3) from the Basic Research Program of the Korea Science and Engineering Foundation, and by the E-Center for E-Business, the Virginia Center for Innovative Technology.

H.C. Mayr et al. (Eds.): DEXA 2001, LNCS 2113, pp. 877–886, 2001.

techniques are the cache replacement policies [4, 7, 8], which decide which part of data in the cache will be deleted to accommodate new data. The most popular policy is the least recently used (LRU), which replaces a block that has been in the cache longest with no references to it. The least frequently used (LFU) policy replaces a block that has experienced the fewest references in the cache.

All the above block (page) replacement policies have been studied in the context of operating systems or database systems. They cannot continue to work well in meta-search engines, since circumstances of meta-search engines are quite different. First, query results of search engines do not need to be written back to a search engine's memory. Data consistency issues, which are very important in operating systems and database systems, do not apply in the meta-search context. Second, results of search engines are apt to be stale after a certain period of time has passed since the data was collected. Search engines are not informative or even friendly enough to let users know the staleness of search results. Lastly, results caching is important for meta-search engines, because the underlying search engines may not be accessible to process a query.

A caching scheme in a meta-search engine is considered in this paper. We describe the cache scheme of our meta-search engine, which is being developed as a research vehicle, in terms of its architecture, algorithms, and operational flow. In particular, we propose a popularity-driven cache algorithm that utilizes both popularities and reference counters of queries to determine cached data to be replaced. We show how to calculate query popularity. Empirical evaluations and performance comparisons of popularity-driven caching with commonly used LRU and LFU have been carried out on collections of real data. In almost all cases, the proposed replacement policy outperforms LRU and LFU.

The rest of this paper is organized as follows. Section 2 describes the cache organization of our experimental meta-search engine. The design philosophy is also described. In section 3, we present the notions of popularity, popularity collection and calculation, and a replacement policy based on the popularity of queries. Empirical evaluations are found in section 4, along with our analysis. Section 5 contains closing remarks and future work.

2 Preliminaries

This section briefly describes a meta-search engine, named EzFinder, which is being developed as a research vehicle (Figure 1). EzFinder implements a wrapper-level cache scheme in which each wrapper has its own cache to hold data. The cache in each wrapper stores query results (here, HTML pages) along with queries. Caching in the wrapper could be done in two places: in main memory and in disk. This paper considers caching data in main memory only.

The EzFinder query manager accepts user queries and transforms them into queries in the internal format of each search engine. The transformed queries are transferred to the wrapper manager, which in turn dispatches sub-queries to each wrapper. Each wrapper connects to external search engines, and receives search results from them. All collected query results are transferred to the output manager for post-processing. The output manager processes (such as collating, ranking, etc.) all returned results and presents them to users.

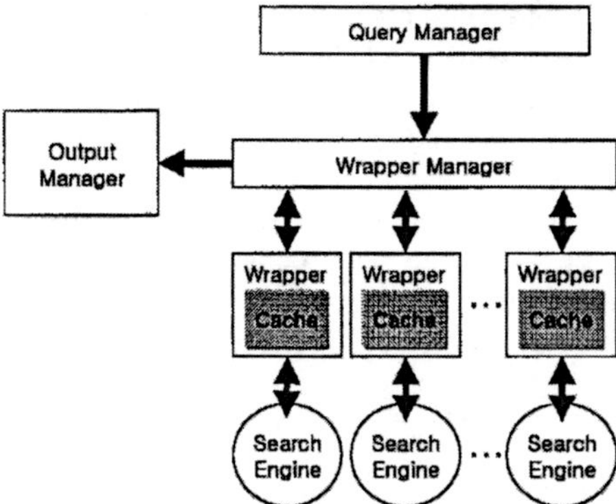

Fig. 1. Cache in EzFinder

We analyzed user queries, which were over 781,550 queries, collected at a popular search engine in Korea in which virtually all queries were issued in Korean. More than 86% of all queries consist of a single word. We have decided that EzFinder shall store query results of only single word queries in the cache. Query results of user queries with more than one word are not stored in the cache, so in these cases wrappers always connect to search engines to get answers.

At this point, we alert readers to language differences between Korean and English. From a syntactic view, words in both languages are delimited by blanks, but the semantic expressiveness of one word is quite different. A single word in Korean often denotes multiple-word expressions in English. For example, "information retrieval" and "computer science" use two words in English, but the corresponding Korean expressions could have only one word. Therefore, the one-keyword query assumption is not exceedingly restrictive.

3 Popularity-Driven Caching Scheme in Meta-search Engines

Popular queries are ones that are presented repeatedly to web search engines by users, and they represent a significant portion of all submitted queries. Popular queries tend to reflect the public interests or trends in Internet searching at a given time. For example, searching expressions about North Korea were heavily posed to search engines in Korea when the historical summit meeting between two Korea's was taking place in June 2000. Generally speaking, popular queries depend on significant events, such as political, social, cultural events; these are sensitive to time and changes over time.

For a query consisting of a single word, we define the notion of popularity, which represents popularity of a query among all queries. The popularity should be normalized on the basis of posting cycles, the number of lists of popular queries, and the predefined maximum number of popular queries in the lists. The values that the popularity can take range from zero to one; the higher value means more popular. Words with zero popularity are ones that never occur in the popular query lists under consideration. Three different popularities are defined, namely *unit popularity* (UP), *accumulated popularity* (AP), and *fused popularity* (FP).

Before we present how to calculate popularities, we need to define one variable W. W is to be set in advance, and it will be used to normalize popularities. The only restriction on W is that it be greater than the expected maximum number of popular queries at all times. W is independent of particular search engines. Once W is set in the beginning, W remains unchanged permanently.

UP is calculated on a single list of popular words. UP is calculated on every posting of popular queries for each search engine. Let $R_i^j(X)$ be the rank of popular query X in the ith search engine's j^{th} posting, $UP_i^j(X)$ denote UP of popular query X in the ith search engine's j^{th} posting. Here is the formula of UP:

$$UP_i^j(X) = \frac{W - R_i^j(X) + 1}{W}$$

$R_i^j(X)$ is always equal to or greater than one. UP is essentially a normalized value of rank of a query in a single list of popular queries. Note that $0 < UP_i^j(X) \leq 1$. If a query is listed at the same rank in the two different lists of popular queries, then the UPs of the query are the same regardless of the number of popular queries in the lists.

AP is obtained by accumulating UP's of the same search engine over a predetermined period of time. The number of accumulations within a time period is called the order. We use AP's to deal with different search engines that post popular query lists in different posting cycles (for example, daily and weekly). AP gives popularities of queries that shall be collected over the same period of time. Let n_i denote the order of AP of the ith search engine, $AP_i(X)$ denote the AP of popular query X in the ith search engine. Then, $AP_i(X)$ is calculated as below:

$$AP_i(X) = \frac{1}{n_i} \sum_{j=1}^{n_i} UP_i^j(X)$$

Since AP is a summation of UP divided by the number of the order, we have $0 < AP_i(X) \leq 1$. A query gets a high value of $AP_i(X)$ if the query X appears often in popular query lists of the ith search engine. If a query appears only once in popular lists, then AP of the query becomes low (precisely speaking, UP is the same as the division of AP by the order).

FP presents integrated popularity collected by different search engines that post popular query lists periodically. The number of search engines in consideration normalizes FP, which is used in our cache scheme. Let N be the number of search engines in consideration. FP is defined as below:

$$FP(X) = \max\left(0, \frac{1}{N} \sum_{i=1}^{N} AP_i(X)\right)$$

All queries, whether they are popular or not, have FP's. A query has a zero value of FP if it does not appear in any of popular query lists.

In our computation, a query gets higher popularity if: (1) it has higher ranking in a popular query list, (2) it appears often in many query lists collected by different search engines over the same period of time or, (3) it appears often in many query lists collected over different time periods by the same search engine. It should be noted that our computation is flexible enough to accommodate any number of query lists that are posted over any period of time by any number of different search engines.

Example 1. Consider two web search engines. Let W be 200. The first engine posts 100 popular queries weekly, and the second posts 50 popular queries daily. The order of AP (n_1) of the first is assigned to be 1, and the order (n_2) of the second is 7.

Now assume that a query "Napster" is listed as follows. In the first search engine, "Napster" has the 2nd rank. In the second search engine, the word is listed in the 15th, 10th, 5th, 1st, 8th, 9th, and 12th rank, respectively in the daily popular query lists. In the first search engine, the accumulated popularity of "Napster" equals the unit popularity, since the order of accumulation is one.

$$AP_1(Napster) = UP_1^1(Napster) = \frac{200-2+1}{200} = 0.995$$

In the second search engine, the accumulated popularity of "Napster" is computed as:

$$AP_2(Napster) = \frac{1}{7}\sum_{j=1}^{7} UP_2^j(Napster)$$

$$= \frac{1}{7}\left(\frac{(200-15+1)+(200-10+1)+(200-5+1)+(200-1+1)+(200-8+1)+(200-9+1)+(200-12+1)}{200}\right) = 0.962$$

Then, FP(Napster), the fused popularity of "Napster", is computed as:

$$FP(Napster) = \frac{1}{2}\sum_{i=1}^{2} AP\ (Napster) = \frac{1}{2}\left(AP_1(Napster) + AP_2(Napster)\right) = 0.9785$$

The fused popularity of "Napster" is then 0.9785. ■

Now we present a popularity-driven replacement (PDR) algorithm. PDR utilizes both FP and reference counters of a query in the cache replacement process. The reference counter of a query holds the number of references (accesses) of the query stored in the cache.

The cache in consideration consists of a number of slots. Each slot has five components (X, FP, C, T, R), where X denotes a query presented by the user, FP denotes the fused popularity of the query X, C denotes the current reference counter of the query X, T denotes the time in which a search result is constructed, and R denotes a search result (here, a collection of HTML pages).

Search engines are known to update their data from time-to-time, perhaps monthly, quarterly, etc. Since we do not want to return stale data to users, we keep track of the time at which search results are collected. For each search engine, we maintain a variable for this purpose. This variable indicates how often a search engine updates its data, and it is used to determine staleness of cached data. If data is stale, we discard cached data and connect to the search engines to receive fresh data. The newly received data will be stored in the slot, and the reference counter of the slot is incremented by one.

Popularity, which is the primary criterion for cache replacement, changes over time. Fused popularities should be updated if necessary. We introduce the notion of *popularity update cycle*. During popularity update cycle, we re-calculate FP's of all queries using new lists of popular queries, and FP's of all queries stored in the cache are updated accordingly. A non-popular query (i.e., a query with zero popularity) in the cache could become a popular query and vice versa on popularity update cycle. However, the reference counter in the slots remains unchanged on popularity update cycle.

Figure 2 shows the pseudo code of PDR. The input of the algorithm is a query X, and the output is a search result (R). When requested data is already cached, we then increment the reference counter by one and return the search result.

```
Function Popularity-base replacement()
  Let EVICT be the slot number such that FP is minimum and not zero;
  If (FP of slot EVICT ≥ FP(X)) then
      Return R and exit;
  End if
  Flush slot EVICT into disk;
  Store (X, FP, 1, T, R) into slot EVICT and return R and exit;
End Function
Function Reference-base replacement()
  Let EVICT be the slot number such that C is minimum and FP is
zero;
  Flush slot EVICT into disk;
  Store (X, FP, 1, T, R) into slot EVICT and return R and exit;
End function

If X is already in the cache (say slot i) then
  Fetch slot i in the cache;
  If slot i is not stale then
      Increment C by one;
      Return R of slot i and exit;
  End if
  Construct the search result (R) of X by accessing search engines;
  Increment C by one;
  Store (X, FP, C, T, R) into slot i and return R and exit;
End if
Construct the search result (R) of X by accessing search engines;
If cache is not full then
  If FP(X) is not zero then
      If ((1 - NP/NS) > ONP)
        /* The ratio of non-popular queries is greater than threshold */
        Get the next available slot (let the slot number be FREE);
        Store (X, FP, 1, T, R) into slot FREE and return R and exit;
      End if
      /* The ratio of non-popular queries is no greater than threshold */
      Popularity-base replacement();
  End if
  /* When X is a non-popular query */
  Get the next available slot (let slot number be FREE);
  Store (X, FP, 1, T, R) into slot FREE and return R and exit;
End if
/* When the cache is full */
If FP(X) is not zero then
  If ((1 - NP/NS) > ONP) then
      /* The ratio of non-popular queries is greater than threshold */
      Reference-base replacement();
  End if
  /* The ratio of non-popular queries is no greater than threshold */
  Popularity-base replacement();
End if
/* When X is a non-popular query */
Reference-base replacement()
```

Fig. 2. The PDR Algorithm

PDR reserves a portion of slots for non-popular queries at all times. Let N_S denote the number of cache slots, N_P denote the current number of popular queries in the cache. Then N_P/N_S denotes the ratio of popular queries over all the queries stored in cache and $1 - N_P/N_S$ denotes the ratio of non-popular queries over all the stored queries. PDR guarantees $(1 - N_P/N_S)$ to be greater than a threshold at all times, i.e., $(1 - N_P/N_S) > O_{NP}$, where O_{NP} is the minimum ratio of non-popular queries over all the loaded queries. O_{NP} is to be set in advance.

Even though there are free slots in the cache, PDR applies the popularity-based replacement if a newcomer is a popular query and the ratio of non-popular queries is less than the threshold. Such replacement is necessary in order to reserve slots for non-popular queries coming later.

In order to achieve this, PDR makes use of two different criteria (i.e., popularities and reference counters) for cache replacement. There are two cases in which the first criterion (popularities) is applied; first, when cache is full, a newcomer has non-zero popularity (a popular query) and the ratio of non-popular queries is no greater than the threshold (O_{NP}), second, when there are free slots in the cache, a newcomer has non-zero popularity (a popular query) and the ratio of non-popular queries is no greater than the threshold. In those cases, a newcomer replaces the slot having the minimum value of popularities, as long as the popularity of the newcomer is bigger than the minimum value of popularities.

The second criterion (reference counters) is applied only when the cache is full. The first case is when a newcomer has zero popularity (a non-popular query), the second case is when a newcomer has non-zero popularity and the ratio of non-popular queries is greater than the threshold. In both cases, a newcomer replaces the slot that has zero popularity and the minimum value of reference counters.

4 Experimental Evaluation

Experimental evaluation of our caching scheme has been carried out. We implemented and evaluated LRU, LFU, and PDR algorithms with Java development kit version 1.3 (JDK1.3). The experiments were performed on a Pentium III-650 machine with 256 Mbytes main memory.

For the experiments, we used real data. We selected three search engines that are posting a reasonable number of popular queries periodically. Two of them are posting popular queries weekly, and one search engine is posting daily. As for users' input queries, we used a log file that was generated by a commercial search engine in Korea. It contained 781,550 queries totally.

In order to see the effect of accumulation of popular queries, we made three different lists of popular queries, each of which was collected over one week (144 popular queries), two weeks (178 popular queries), and four weeks (194 popular queries), respectively. We denote them as PDR-1, PDR-2, and PDR-4, where the suffixes 1, 2, 4 denote the number of weeks. Duplicate terms are always purged in the lists. There is much commonality in the lists posted by search engines, as expected.

The metric we use is a cache hit ratio, which is a ratio of the number of hitting queries over the number of total single queries submitted. The second metric is the performance gain ratio of LFU and PDR over LRU. LRU is the most widely used one in practice, so it can serve as a reference point of performance. The gain ratio of LFU or PDR is calculated by dividing the hit ratios of LFU or PDR over the hit ratio of LRU, and it is presented by percentage.

Our evaluation has been focused on three aspects of the PDR algorithm: performance effect of cache size, the changing of the minimum ratio of non-popular queries in cache, and accumulation of popular queries. For the first evaluation, we have varied the number of slots in the cache. We tested seven cases, with the number of slots 50, 75, 100, 125, 150, 180, and 200, respectively. Figure 3 shows the hit ratios of LRU, LFU and PDR-1. As the number of slots increases, the hit ratio also increases. PDR performed the best in all cases except in the 50-slot case, where LFU was the best. PDR exhibits 6-8% of improvement to LRU in terms of the hit ratio in all cases. W was assigned to be 300 and O_{NP} was 0%.

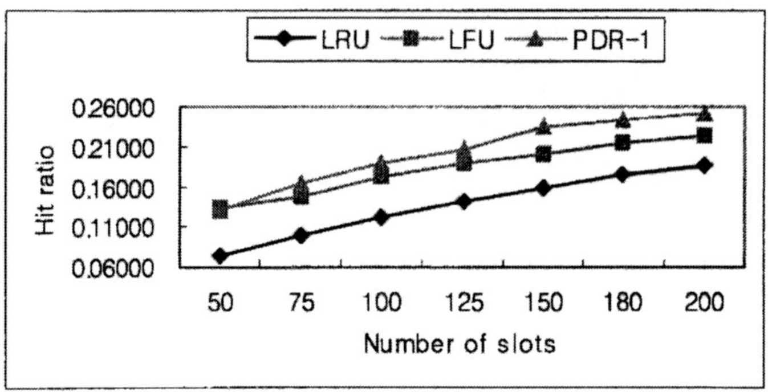

Fig. 3. The Hit Ratios of LRU, LFU, and PDR-1

Figure 4 shows the gain ratios of LFU and PDR-1 over LRU. It is interesting to note that the gain ratios of LFU and PDR decrease as the number of slots increases. But LFU decreases more rapidly than PDR does. In case of the large cache, the performance gain of LFU over LRU becomes marginal, which implies that LRU becomes to work well. One lesson we learned is that the cache size is a critical performance factor in cache replacement schemes.

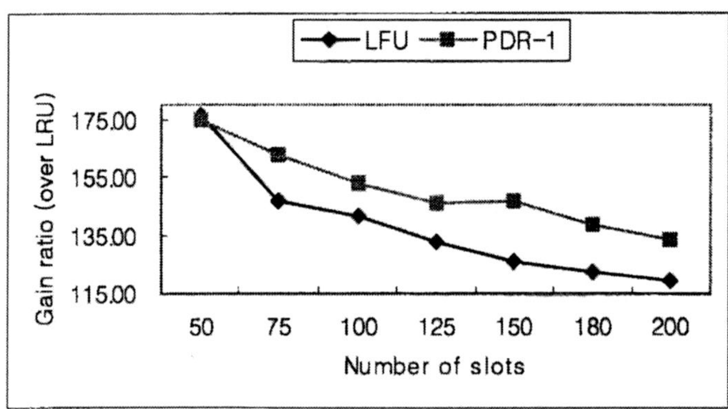

Fig. 4. The Gain Ratios of LFU and PDR-1

Second, we have varied the minimum ratio of non-popular queries in cache. We tested six cases, with 0%, 5%, 10%, 15%, 20%, and 25%, respectively. Figure 5 shows the gain ratios of PDR-1.

Except in the 50-slot case, PDR performs the best in all cases when O_{NP} uses 5%. In almost every case, the gain ratio decreases as O_{NP} increases over 5%. This result implies that loading the cache with too many non-popular queries does not help to increase performance. Note that the gain ratios of 200 slots are the same regardless of O_{NP}. This is because the number of slots is greater than the number of popular queries. Specifically, all 144 popular queries are eventually loaded in the cache, and non-popular queries compete to be loaded in the 56 remaining slots. This phenomenon happened partially when the numbers of slots were 150 and 180.

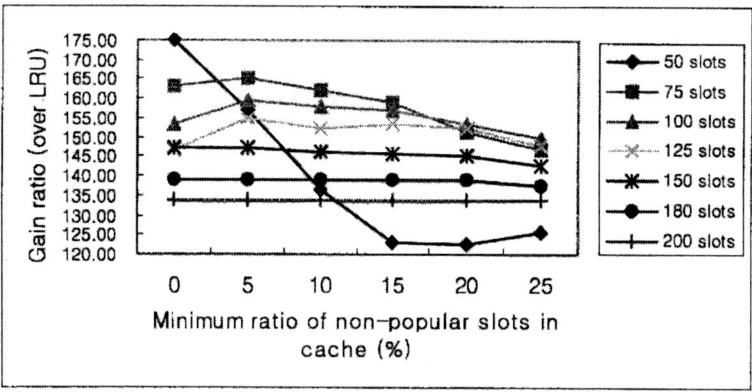

Fig. 5. The Gain Ratio of PDR-1 over LRU

Third, we evaluated the effect of the accumulation of popular queries by running the three fused popularities. Figure 6 shows the hit ratios of PDR-1, PDR-2 and PDR-4. Each accumulation shows similar behavior. When there are some cases (say 50-slot and 200-slot), PDR-2 and PDR-4 beat PDR-1 consistently. This result implies that accumulation of popular queries over a long period of time (say over one month) does not help increase the hit ratio. The accumulation of popular queries over two weeks or one week would be a reasonable choice in terms of caching performance.

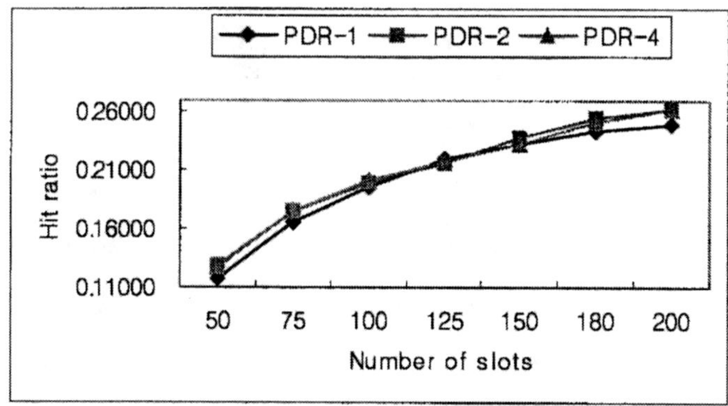

Fig. 6. The Hit Ratios of PDR-1, PDR-2, and PDR-4

With three aspects of performance evaluation, we come to a conclusion as follows: (1) the page replacement policy utilizing both popularities and reference counters of queries works out well, (2) the cache size is a critical performance factor in cache replacement schemes, (3) reserving a portion of slots for non-popular queries help increase performance (in our experiments, it was 5%), (4) accumulation of popular queries does not help.

5 Closing Remarks

We have presented a popularity-driven caching scheme for meta-search engines. Computation of query popularity is given, and the PDR algorithm for cache replacement is described. Empirical evaluations and performance comparisons with LRU and LFU have been carried out on real data. PDR exhibits satisfactory behavior in almost all cases.

On posting popular queries, some search engines have an internal policy that censors indecent queries from their lists of popular queries. A commonly exercised policy in the lists is to exclude pornographic words, which otherwise would appear in the lists as very popular words. The experimental results shown in this paper are therefore conservative, considering that search engines self-censor their lists of popular queries. If we had used unfiltered lists of popular queries for experiments, then PDR would show even better performance than is described here.

Our future work includes expansion of the popularity calculation to consider popular queries that could be collected internally. When EzFinder is operational, we can collect user queries. Such internal popularities can be merged with external ones. If we had accumulated the "indecent" queries on our own list, then we could actually measure the true improvement. This is a topic of future research.

References

1. J. Cheong, and S. Lee: A Boolean Query Processing with a Result Cache in Mediator Systems, Proceedings of Advances in Digital Libraries, IEEE (2000), 218-227
2. B. Chidlovskii, C. Roncancio, and M. Schneider: Semantic Cache Mechanism for Heterogeneous Web Querying, WWW8 (1999), 1347-1360
3. S. Dar, M. Franklin, B. Jonsson, D. Srivastava, and M. Tan: Semantic Data Caching and Replacement, Proceedings of the 22nd VLDB Conference (1996), 330-341
4. T. Johnson, and D. Shasha: 2Q: A Low Overhead High Performance Buffer Management Replacement Algorithm, Proceedings of the 20th International Conference on VLDB (1994), 439-450
5. S. Lawrence, and C. Giles: Accessibility of Information on the Web, Nature, 400 (1999), 107-109
6. D. Lee, and W. Chu: Semantic Caching via Query Matching for Web Sources, Proceedings of the 8th International Conference on Information Knowledge Management (1999), 77-85
7. E. O'Neil, P. O'Neil, and G. Weikum: The LRU-K Page Replacement Algorithm for Database Disk Buffering, Proceedings of the ACM SIGMOD (1993), 297-306
8. J. Robinson, and M. Devarakonda: Data Cache Management Using Frequency-Based Replacement, Proceedings of the ACM SIGMETRICS Conference on Measurement and Modeling of Computer Systems (1990), 134-142
9. Scime, and L. Kerschberg: WebSifter: An Ontology-based Personalizable Search Agent for the Web, Proceedings of the International Conference on Digital Libraries, Research and Practice (2000), 439-446

Towards the Development of Heuristics for Automatic Query Expansion

Jesús Vilares, Manuel Vilares, and Miguel A. Alonso

Departamento de Computación
Facultad de Informática, Universidad de La Coruña
Campus de Elviña s/n, 15071 La Coruña, Spain
jvilares@mail2.udc.es, {vilares,alonso}@dc.fi.udc.es,
http://coleweb.dc.fi.udc.es/

Abstract. In this paper we study the performance of linguistically-motivated conflation techniques for Information Retrieval in Spanish. In particular, we have studied the application of productive derivational morphology for single word term conflation and the extraction of syntactic dependency pairs for multi-word term conflation. These techniques have been tested on several search engines implementing different indexing models. The aim of this study is to find the strong and weak points of each technique in order to develop heuristics for automatic query expansion.

1 Introduction

In Information Retrieval (IR) systems, documents are represented through a set of index terms or keywords. For such a purpose, documents are conflated by means of *text operations* [1,6], which reduce their linguistic variety by grouping together textual occurrences referring to similar or identical concepts. However, most classical IR techniques for such tasks (such as the elimination of *stopwords*, too frequent words or words without seeming significance, or the use of *stemming*, which reduces distinct words to their supposed grammatical root) lack solid linguistic grounding. Even text operations with an apparent linguistic basis (e.g. stemming) which obtain very good results for English, perform badly when applied to languages with a very rich lexis and morphology, as in the case of Spanish. For these languages, we must face such tasks by employing Natural Language Processing (NLP) techniques, which redounds in a greater complexity and a higher computational cost.

2 NLP Techniques for Term Indexing

One of the main problems of natural language processing in Spanish is the lack of available resources: large tagged corpora, treebanks and advanced lexicons are not freely available. In this context, we propose to extend classical IR techniques in two ways: firstly, at word level, using morphological families; and secondly, at phrase level, using groups of related words with regard to their syntactic structure.

H.C. Mayr et al. (Eds.): DEXA 2001, LNCS 2113, pp. 887–896, 2001.

2.1 Morphological Families

Single word term conflation is usually accomplished in English through a *stemmer* [8], a simple tool from a linguistic point of view, with a low computational cost. The results obtained are satisfactory enough since the inflectional morphology of English is very simple. The situation for Spanish is completely different, because inflectional modifications exist at multiple levels with many irregularities [10]. The case of generative morphology is similarly very rich and complex in Spanish [7].

Using a lemmatizer we can solve the problems derived from inflection in Spanish. As a second step, we have developed a new approach based on morphological families [9]. We define a *morphological family* as a set of words obtained from the same morphological root through derivation mechanisms. It is expected that a basic semantic relationship will remain between the words of a given family.

For single word term conflation via morphological families, we first obtain the part of speech and the lemmas of the text to be indexed. Next, we replace each of the lemmas obtained by the representative of its morphological family. In this way, we are covering relations between terms of the type process-result, e.g. *producción* (production) / *producto* (product), process-agent, e.g. *manipulación* (manipulation) / *manipulador* (manipulator), and similar ones. These relations remain in the index because related terms are conflated to the same index term.

2.2 Syntactic and Morpho-Syntactic Variants

A *multi-word term* is a term containing two or more content words (nouns, adjectives and verbs). There exist several techniques to obtain them. The first one is *text simplification*: in a first step, we make a single word stemming, after which stopwords are deleted; in the final step, terms are extracted and conflated employing pattern matching [2] or statistical criteria [3]. As we can see, most operations lack solid linguistic grounding, which often results in incorrect conflations. Nevertheless, this is the easiest and least costly method.

At the other extreme, we find the *morpho-syntactic analysis* of the text by using a parser that produces syntactic trees which denote dependency relations between involved words. This way, structures with similar dependency relations are conflated in the same way.

At the mid point, we have *syntactic pattern matching*, which is based on the hypothesis that the most informative parts of the texts correspond to specific syntactic patterns [5].

We take an approach which conjugates these two last solutions, based on indexing noun syntagmas and their *syntactic and morpho-syntactic variants* [4]. A syntactic or morpho-syntactic variant of a multi-word term is a textual utterance that can be substituted for the original term in a task of information access:

Syntactic variants result from the inflection of individual words and from modifying the syntactic structure of the original term, e.g. *chico gordo* (fat boy) → *chicos gordos y altos* (fat and tall boys).

Morpho-syntactic variants differ from syntactic variants in that at least one of the content words of the original term is transformed into another word derived from the same morphological stem, e.g. *medición del contenido* (measurement of the content) → *medir el contenido* (to measure the content).

From a morphological point of view, syntactic variants refer to inflectional morphology, whereas morpho-syntactic variants also refer to derivational morphology. In the case of syntax, syntactic variants have a very restricted scope, a noun syntagma, whereas morpho-syntactic variants can span a whole sentence, including a verb and its complements, e.g. *comida de perros* (dog food) → *los perros comen carne* (dogs feed on meat). However, both variants can be obtained through transformations from noun syntagmas.

To extract such index terms we will use syntactic matching patterns obtained from the syntactic structure of the noun syntagmas and their variants. For such a task we take as our basis an approximate grammar for Spanish.

2.3 Syntactic and Morpho-Syntactic Variants as a Text Operation

The first task to be performed when indexing a text is to identify the index terms. Taking as our basis the syntactic trees corresponding to noun syntagmas and according to an approximate grammar for Spanish, we apply the mechanisms associated with syntactic and morpho-syntactic variants, obtaining their syntactic trees. Then, these trees are flattened into regular expressions formed by the part of speech labels of the words involved. Such matching patterns will be applied over the tagged text to be indexed, to identify the index terms. In this way, we are dealing with the problem from a surface processing approach at lexical level, leading to a considerable reduction of the running cost.

Once index terms have been identified, they must be conflated. This process consists of two phases. Firstly, we identify relations between pairs of content words inside the multi-word term, to conflate it into syntactic dependency-pairs. Secondly, single word term conflation mechanisms (lemmatization or morphological families) are applied to the words which form such pairs.

The relations we can find in a multi-word term correspond to three types:

1. *Modified-Modifier*, found in noun syntagmas. A dependency-pair is obtained for each combination of the head of the modifiers with the head of the modified terms. For example, *coches y motos rojas* is conflated into *(coche,rojo),(moto,rojo)* [1].
2. *Subject-Verb*, relating the head of the subject and the verb.
3. *Verb-Complement*, relating the verb and the head of the complement.

In the case of syntactic variants, the dependencies of the original term always remain in the variant. In the case of morpho-syntactic variants we cannot guarantee the presence of the original term dependencies unless morphological families are applied. For example, given the term *recorte de gastos* (spending

[1] *red cars and bikes* and *(car, red), (bike, red)*, respectively

cutback) and its morpho-syntactic variant *recortar gastos* (to cut back spending), using lemmatization we obtain the following two different dependency pairs *(recorte, gasto)* and *(recortar, gasto)*, respectively. Whereas, using morphological families and supposing that the representatives are *recorte* (cutback) and *gastar* (to spend), we obtain the same dependency pair *(recorte, gastar)* for both the original term and its variant. Therefore, the degree of conflation obtained when using morphological families is higher than when using lemmatization.

3 Evaluation

The techniques proposed in this paper are independent of the indexing engine we choose to use because documents are preprocessed before being treated. We have performed experiments using the following engines: Altavista SDK[2], SMART[3] (based on a vector model) and SWISH-E[4] (based on a boolean model). For all engines, we have tested five different conflation techniques:

1. Elimination of stopwords using the list provided by SMART (*pln*).
2. Lemmatization of content words (*lem*).
3. Morphological families of content words (*fam*).
4. Syntactic dependency-pairs with lemmatization (*FNL*).
5. Syntactic dependency-pairs with morphological families (*FNF*).

We have tested the five proposed approaches on a corpus of 21,899 documents of a journalistic nature (national, international, economy, culture, ...) covering the year 2000. The average length of the documents is 447 words. We have considered a set of 14 natural language queries with an average length of 7.85 words per query, 4.36 of which were content words.

3.1 Altavista SDK

Average precision and recall are shown at the bottom-right of Fig. 1. Single word term conflation techniques, *fam* and *lem*, has led to a remarkable increase in precision and recall with respect to *pln*. The increase in precision is even higher for multi-word term conflation techniques *FNL* and *FNF*. Moreover, the technique *FNF* attains good recall, which implies that it can significantly increase the precision without seriously affecting the recall.

With respect to the evolution of precision vs. recall, Fig.1 confirms the technique *pln* as being the worst one. The best behaviour corresponds to the technique *FNF*, except for the segment of recall between 0.5 to 0.7, where single word term conflation techniques, *lem* and *fam*, are slightly better. For low recall rates (≤ 0.3) *FNF* is clearly the best one, whilst the other conflation techniques show a similar behaviour. For the segment of recall between 0.3 to 0.5, single

[2] `http://solutions.altavista.com/`
[3] `ftp://ftp.cs.cornell.edu/pub/smart/`
[4] `http://sunsite.berkeley.edu/SWISH-E/`

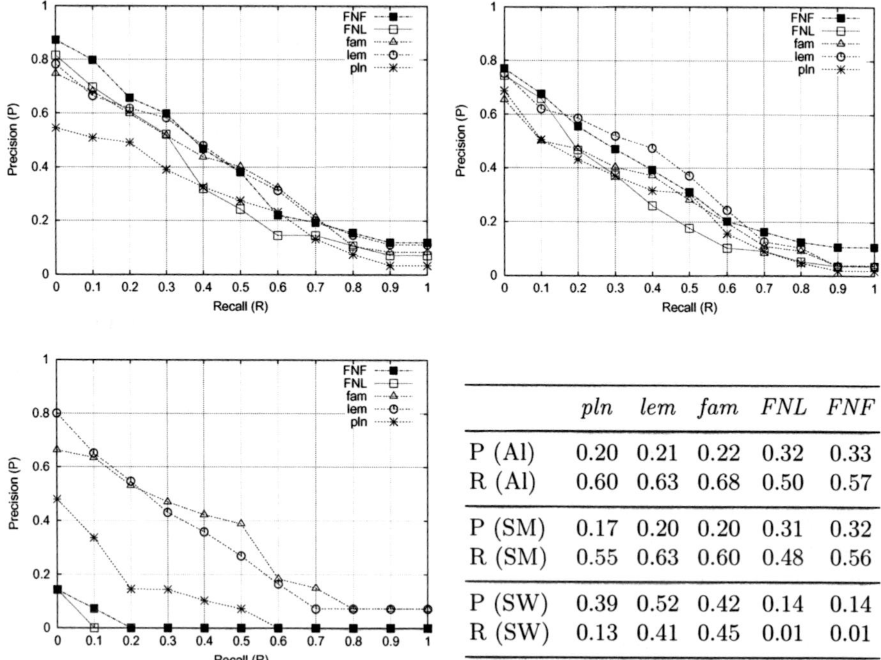

	pln	*lem*	*fam*	*FNL*	*FNF*
P (Al)	0.20	0.21	0.22	0.32	0.33
R (Al)	0.60	0.63	0.68	0.50	0.57
P (SM)	0.17	0.20	0.20	0.31	0.32
R (SM)	0.55	0.63	0.60	0.48	0.56
P (SW)	0.39	0.52	0.42	0.14	0.14
R (SW)	0.13	0.41	0.45	0.01	0.01

Fig. 1. *Global results: Altavista (top-left), SMART (top-right), SWISH-E (bottom-left) and average precision and recall (bottom-right)*

word term conflation techniques are closer to *FNF*, whereas *FNL* is closer to *pln*. For recall rates greater than 0.7, conflation techniques using lemmatization tend to converge, as do the techniques using morphological families.

3.2 SMART

The average recall and precision are similar to those obtained with Altavista SDK, except for the case of single word term conflation via morphological families, *fam*, which does not appear to improve the global behaviour of the system in relation to lemmatization. On the contrary, its efficiency is somewhat reduced, in contrast with the results for Altavista. Nevertheless, the use of such families together with the use of multi-word terms gives a remarkable increase of recall, as in the case of Altavista, with regard to the use of lemmatization with complex terms. In fact, *FNF* improves the recall of *pln*. We can also notice that there is a greater homogeneity in the behaviour of all methods in the case of recall.

With respect to the evolution of precision vs. recall, we can observe in Fig. 1 that the greater complexity of the vectorial model tends to reduce the differences between all techniques. We can observe some noticeable differences between the behaviour of conflating techniques in SMART and Altavista. Firstly, in SMART the behaviour of *fam* technique is clearly worse than the behaviour of *lem* technique. This supports the results obtained for average precision and recall. Another difference we can observe is that in SMART the *FNF* technique only obtains better results than the rest of methods for low and high recalls ($\leq$ 20, 50 $\geq$), while for the rest of the interval the best method is clearly *lem*. On the other hand, we also find some similarities, such as the fact that *pln* and *FNL* have the worst behaviour in comparison with the other methods.

3.3 SWISH-E

The first conclusion we can reach is that the use of multi-word term methods in combination with the boolean model is completely inadequate due to boolean engines require all terms involved in a query to match index terms in a given document, a rare situation when dealing with syntactic dependencies. The use of plain text with a boolean model is also completely inadequate because this model is more sensitive to inflectional variations than the previous engines. When using lemmatization to conflate the text we reach a noticeably higher level of recall, with very high precision. The employment of morphological families for single word term conflation obtains a higher level of recall, but the level of precision is lower than the level of precision attained with *lem*. This is due to the noise introduced by inaccurate families. However, it is also interesting to remark that the precision reached by *pln*, *lem* and *fam* is the highest reached for all the test suite, but at the cost of reducing recall.

3.4 Behaviour for Particular Queries

The behaviour of the different techniques varies according to the characteristics of each particular query. We will try to illustrate this fact with some practical examples obtained during the test process. This study is a first step towards the development of heuristics for automatic query expansion.

The first example we will work with is the query *"experimentos sobre la clonación de monos"* (experiments on the cloning of monkeys), trying to illustrate how multi-word terms can discriminate very specific information. For this query only two relevant documents were found in the corpus. Nevertheless, since cloning is a very popular topic nowadays, there are a lot of related but non-relevant documents which introduce a lot of noise.

We center this discussion on the results obtained by multi-word term conflation techniques. As we can see in the graph of precision vs. recall for Altavista and SMART of Fig. 2 the evolution for techniques based on families (*fam* and *FNF*) is similar, and the same occurs with techniques using lemmatization (*lem* and *FNL*). Nevertheless these last two techniques obtain a lesser degree of recall and precision. However, it is in the table of average precision and recall where we can find very important differences. We can see that the average precision reached by using multi-word term conflation techniques is significatively higher than the average precision obtained by using single word term techniques. Morover, the levels of recall are maintained. This means that the set of documents

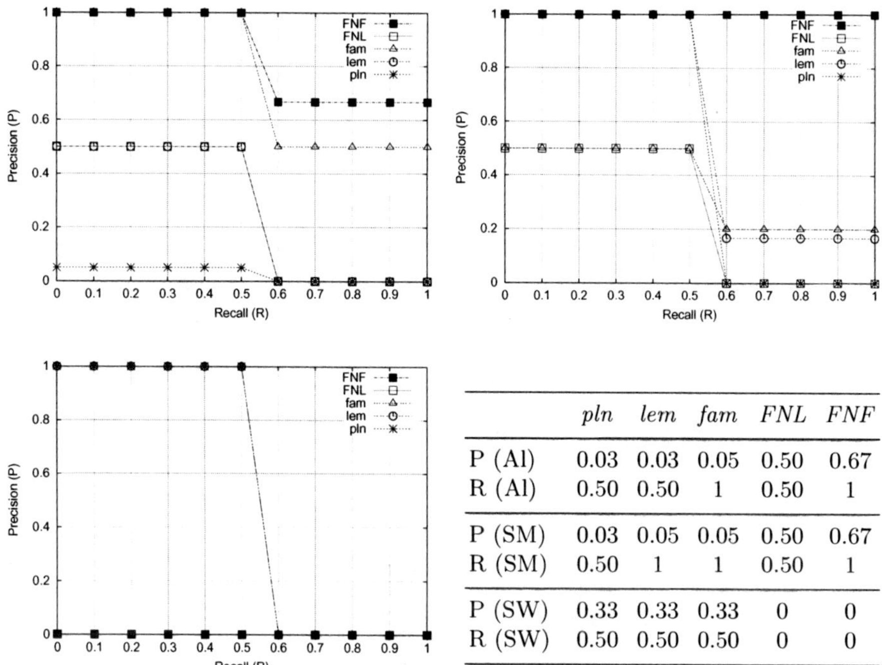

	pln	lem	fam	FNL	FNF
P (Al)	0.03	0.03	0.05	0.50	0.67
R (Al)	0.50	0.50	1	0.50	1
P (SM)	0.03	0.05	0.05	0.50	0.67
R (SM)	0.50	1	1	0.50	1
P (SW)	0.33	0.33	0.33	0	0
R (SW)	0.50	0.50	0.50	0	0

Fig. 2. *"experimentos sobre la clonación de monos"*: results for Altavista (top-left), SMART (top-right), SWISH-E (bottom-left) and average precision and recall

returned is small but precise, because multi-word term techniques have been able to discriminate the relevant documents adequately without losing recall.

As a second example, we consider the query *"negociaciones del PP con el PSOE sobre el pacto antiterrorista"* (negotiations between PP and PSOE about the pact against terrorism) to illustrate a case where single word term conflation techniques achieve a better performance than multi-word techniques. As we can observe in figure 3, there are some similarities in the precision vs. recall graphs for the three indexing engines. In particular, the *fam* technique shows the best behaviour, even better than multi-word techniques. The *lem* technique performs worse than *fam* but better than *pln* for all search engines. These results are due to the fact that lemmatization solves variations caused by inflectional morphology. In addition, morphological families solve variations caused by derivational morphology, retrieving more documents, most of which are relevant because this query involves words with derivatives which frequently appear in the texts referring to the topic of the query, such as *negociación* (negotiation), *negociar* (to negotiate) and *negociador* (negotiator) or *pacto* (pact) and *pactar* (to agree on).

The third example we consider corresponds to the query *"el PSOE reclama un debate entre Aznar y Almunia"* (PSOE demands a debate between Aznar and Almunia). This query refers to the constant demand by the PSOE party for

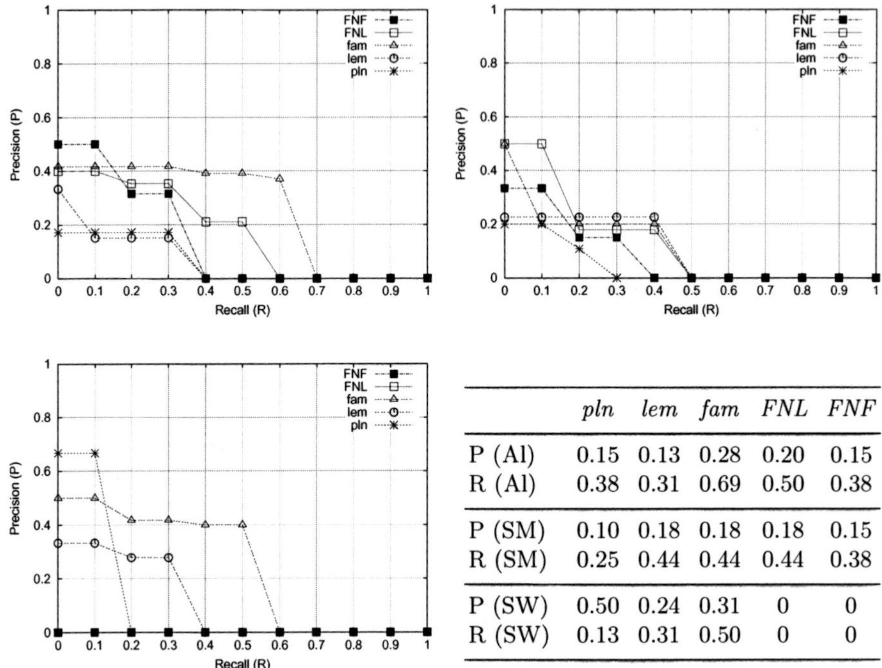

	pln	*lem*	*fam*	*FNL*	*FNF*
P (Al)	0.15	0.13	0.28	0.20	0.15
R (Al)	0.38	0.31	0.69	0.50	0.38
P (SM)	0.10	0.18	0.18	0.18	0.15
R (SM)	0.25	0.44	0.44	0.44	0.38
P (SW)	0.50	0.24	0.31	0	0
R (SW)	0.13	0.31	0.50	0	0

Fig. 3. *"negociaciones del PP con el PSOE sobre el pacto antiterrorista"*: Altavista (top-left), SMART (top-right), SWISH-E (bottom-left) and average precision and recall

a TV debate between the two main candidates in the general elections in the year 2000. We must take into account that words like *PSOE*, *Almunia*, *Aznar* and *debate* appear in several hundreds of non-relevant documents about political issues, introducing a lot of noise. Finally, we have found that only 11 documents were relevant to this query. With this example we try to illustrate the situations where a boolean model beats other indexing models, as is shown in Fig. 4.

Comparing the precision vs. recall graph for SWISH-E with respect to the graphs for Altavista and SMART, we observe that precision in these two last models is lower or similar to precision in SWISH-E for all levels of recall, except for the interval ≤ 0.1. However, the main difference arises in the measures of average precision and recall. Recall in SWISH-E reaches 55%, in contrast to 64% and 73% reached by Altavista and SMART, respectively. Nevertheless, precision in SWISH-E reaches 40%, in contrast to a maximum of 29% reached by multi-word term conflation techniques in the other engines. This increase in precision is due to the high level of discrimination achieved by the boolean model between relevant and non-relevant documents when the query is very similar to the way the information is expressed in the documents, i.e. there exists little variation in the way the concepts involved in the query are expressed.

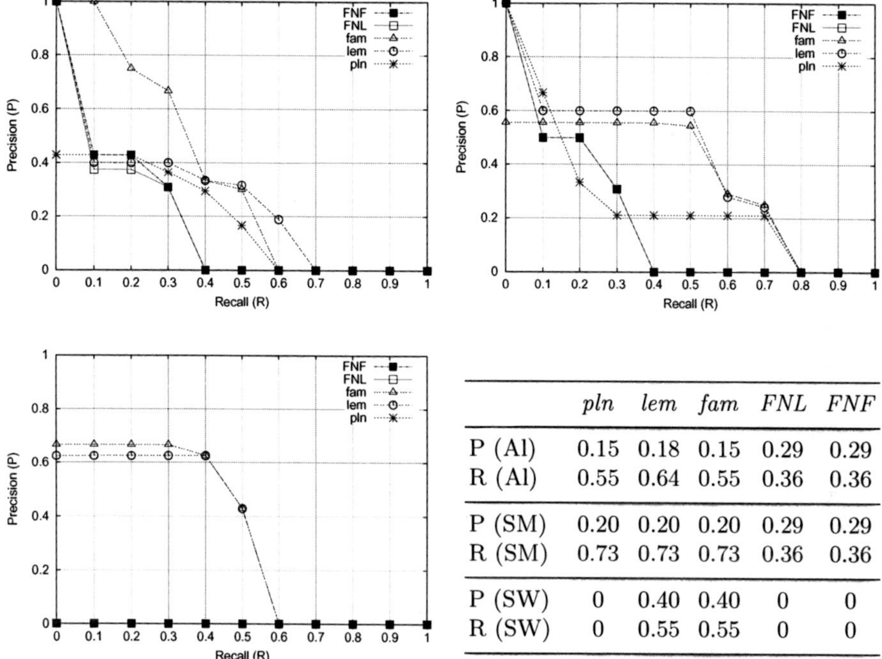

	pln	*lem*	*fam*	*FNL*	*FNF*
P (Al)	0.15	0.18	0.15	0.29	0.29
R (Al)	0.55	0.64	0.55	0.36	0.36
P (SM)	0.20	0.20	0.20	0.29	0.29
R (SM)	0.73	0.73	0.73	0.36	0.36
P (SW)	0	0.40	0.40	0	0
R (SW)	0	0.55	0.55	0	0

Fig. 4. *"el PSOE reclama un debate entre Aznar y Almunia"*: results for Altavista (top-left), SMART (top-right), SWISH-E (bottom-left) and average precision and recall

4 Conclusions

We have shown how linguistically-motivated indexing can improve the performance of information retrieval systems working on languages with a rich lexis and morphology, such as Spanish. In particular, two text operations have been applied to effectively reduce the linguistic variety of documents: productive derivational morphology for single word term conflation and extraction of syntactic dependency-pairs for multi-word term conflation. These techniques require a minimum of linguistic resources, which make them adequate for processing European minority languages. The increase of computational cost is also minimal due to the fact that they are based on finite state technology, which makes them useful for practical systems.

These techniques have been tested on a testsuite of journalistic documents using different search engines. We have found that:

- Indexing of plain text (*pln*) is the worst option, independently of the indexing model used.
- Morphological families show good recall and precision when they do not introduce noise.
- Multi-word term conflation techniques (*FNL*,*FNF*) do not work properly in combination with the boolean model.

- Multi-word term conflation significantly increases the precision in non-boolean models, and when combined with morphological families (*FNF*) it also shows a good level of recall.
- Lemmatization (*lem*) is not the best technique but it is a good balance between all the techniques considered.

In consequence, we can propose an automatic heuristic consisting in the use of morphological families (*fam*) with a boolean model when the words involved in the query have variants with a high frequency of appearance in the corpus of documents. Depending on user need, we can also propose the following heuristics for interaction between the information retrieval system and the user:

- When the user is searching nearly literal utterances, the best option is to employ lemmatized text (*lem*) with a boolean search engine.
- If the user requires high precision, even at the expense of reducing recall, dependency-pairs with families (*FNF*) is the most accurate approach.
- When the user wishes to increase recall, for example if the other techniques return few documents, he may use morphological families (*fam*).

References

1. R. Baeza-Yates and B. Ribeiro-Neto. 1999. *Modern information retrieval.* Addison-Wesley, Harlow, England.
2. M. Dillon and A.S. Gray. 1983. FASIT: A fully automatic syntactically based indexing system. *Journal of the American Society for Information Science*, 34(2):99–108.
3. J.L. Fagan. 1987. Automatic phrase indexing for document retrieval: An examination of syntactic and non-syntactic methods. In *Proceedings of ACM SIGIR'87*, pages 91–101.
4. C. Jacquemin and E. Tzoukerman. 1999. NLP for term variant extraction: A synergy of morphology, lexicon and syntax. In T. Strzalkowski, editor, *Natural Language Information Retrieval*, pages 25–74. Kluwer Academic, Boston.
5. J.S. Justeson and S.M. Katz. 1995. Technical terminology: some linguistic properties and an algorithm for identification in text. *Natural Language Engineering*, 1:9–27.
6. G. Kowalski. 1997. *Information retrieval systems: theory and implementation.* Kluwer Academic, Boston.
7. M. F. Lang. 1990. *Spanish Word Formation: Productive Derivational Morphology in the Modern Lexis.* Croom Helm. Routledge, London and New York.
8. M. Lennon, D.S. Pierce, and P. Willett. 1981. An evaluation of some conflation algorithms. *Journal of Information Science*, 3:177–183.
9. J. Vilares, D. Cabrero, and M. A. Alonso. 2001. Applying Productive Derivational Morphology to Term Indexing of Spanish Texts. In Proc. 2nd International Conference on Intelligent Text Processing and Computational Linguistics, CICLing-2001, Mexico City, Mexico; February 18–24. To be published in *Lecture Notes in Artificial Intelligence.*
10. M. Vilares, J. Graña, and P. Alvariño. 1997. Finite-state morphology and formal verification. In A. Kornai, editor, *Extended Finite State Models of Language*, pages 37–47. Cambridge University Press.

Utilising Multiple Computers in Database Query Processing and Descriptor Rule Management

Jerome Robinson, Barry G.T. Lowden, and Mohammed Al Haddad

Department of Computer Science, University of Essex
Colchester, Essex, CO4 3SQ, U.K.
robij@essex.ac.uk

Abstract. A fundamental problem to be solved in systems that derive rules from database tables to use in query optimisation is the workload involved. If the data server has to do the work it can interfere with query processing and cause slower query answering, which is the opposite of the required effect. This paper reports our investigation of the use of multiple workstations in the same local network as the data server to derive and maintain sets of rules describing data subsets. These rules are used in query optimisation. In a local area network of workstations, one computer accepts SQL queries and data manipulation commands from networked clients. This computer provides an interface to one or more database management systems located on computers in the network. It uses a collection of subset-descriptor rules for query reformulation before forwarding the semantically optimised query. It manages a set of workstations in the network, to derive and maintain the rules. The workstations are ordinary networked computers whose spare computing capacity is utilised by spawning background programs on them.

1 Introduction

Several kinds of rules have been used for Semantic Query Optimisation, including Integrity Constraints [3,5,6], rules generated by Induction triggered by each query [7], and others [17,19,20]. But the type of rule with greatest potential for query optimisation is

(i) generated specifically for that purpose from the data (rather than using rules such as integrity constraints, created for some other purpose), and

(ii) derived in *sets* whose information provides coverage of a whole database table rather than a few data items.

However, the task of examining tables of data to derive sets of rules can be a significant workload. Further work is also needed to maintain those rules when changes occur in the data they describe. Such work is undesirable, if the data server must do the work, since the execution of these additional tasks can *delay* query processing. The purpose of deriving the rules is to *speed up* query processing.

Therefore we seek an additional computational resource to do the work without loading the data server. Workstations in the same local network as the data server provide such a resource. We use them by means of the PVM software system [25].

H.C. Mayr et al. (Eds.): DEXA 2001, LNCS 2113, pp. 897–908, 2001.

This paper reports our investigation of the use of multiple workstations to derive and maintain sets of rules describing data subsets. The structure of the paper is as follows. Section 2 provides background information and explains what is meant by subset descriptor rules, attribute pair rules and histogram rule sets. Rule-set derivation algorithms are discussed in sections 3 and 4. The effect of increasing table size on performance is examined in section 5. Rule Utility is considered in section 6, since there is no benefit in fast derivation and maintenance of rules that are not potentially useful. Conclusions are drawn in section 7.

2 Background

A subset descriptor rule is a < selector, descriptor > pair. The selector is a data-value constraint (a selection condition) which identifies a subset of data items in the database. The descriptor provides information about data items in that subset. Attribute Pairs (AP) rules [13] have been identified as a particularly useful form of subset descriptors for query processing operations such as remote cache management [21,22,23] and semantic query optimisation (SQO) [15,18,19]. A significant part of their value lies in their simple structure which allows fast access, essential in the time-constrained environment of query optimisation.

An AP rule has the form $A \Rightarrow B$, where A and B both have the structure of query selection conditions, but consequent B also *describes* tuples selected by condition A. *For example*, $(10 \leq c \leq 20) \Rightarrow (27 \leq d \leq 36)$ means IF attribute c in a tuple has a value in the range $(10 \leq c \leq 20)$ THEN the value of attribute d is in the range $(27 \leq d \leq 36)$.

AP rules can be extended to rules with multiple consequent assertions. *For example:*

$$(10 \leq c \leq 20) \Rightarrow (27 \leq d \leq 36) \wedge (f \in \{\text{'OMG'}, \text{'TPC'}\}) \wedge (93 \leq h \leq 141)$$

represents three AP rules, all with the same antecedent condition, $(10 \leq c \leq 20)$. A single antecedent look-up in the rule set thus provides multiple assertions about the selected subset. Reducing look-up time for descriptors is important. The consequent is a *vector* of assertions, so that descriptors for different subsets are easily compared or combined by specific vector element. *For example*, a database query selects items with $(75 \leq a \leq 90)$ AND $(10 \leq c \leq 15)$. Two relevant rules describe subsets *containing* the required data items:

$$(70 \leq a \leq 95) \Rightarrow (18 \leq d \leq 43) \wedge (f \in \{\text{'ODMG'}, \text{'OMG'}\}) \wedge (13 \leq h \leq 71)$$
$$(10 \leq c \leq 20) \Rightarrow (27 \leq d \leq 36) \wedge (f \in \{\text{'OMG'}, \text{'TPC'}\}) \wedge (93 \leq h \leq 141)$$

These rules also describe tuples selected by the *subrange* constraints in the query, because those constraints identify *subsets* of the described sets. Pairwise comparison of vector elements in the two rule consequents show *incompatible* values for attribute h. This indicates that the two query conditions select *disjoint subsets* of data items. No tuples can satisfy *both* query conditions so the result set will be empty, and the empty answer can be returned without consulting the database.

Another use of descriptors is to reduce the number of string constants specified in a query, before forwarding the query to the data server. This reduces the comparison time per tuple and so accelerates query processing by the server. Further uses for subset descriptors of this kind are identified in [24,13].

Histogram Rule Sets are a solution to the problem of choosing suitable data subsets to describe. The interval between MIN(a) and MAX(a), for antecedent attribute a, is divided into a number of equal width intervals like those used for the bars in an equi-width histogram. Descriptions of larger data sets can then be produced to match query conditions by combining descriptors from this set of rules. For numeric antecedent attributes, the number of rules in the rule-set decides the *resolution* of subset description, e.g. 1% of attribute a's range if 100 subsets are used to provide a set of 100 rules.

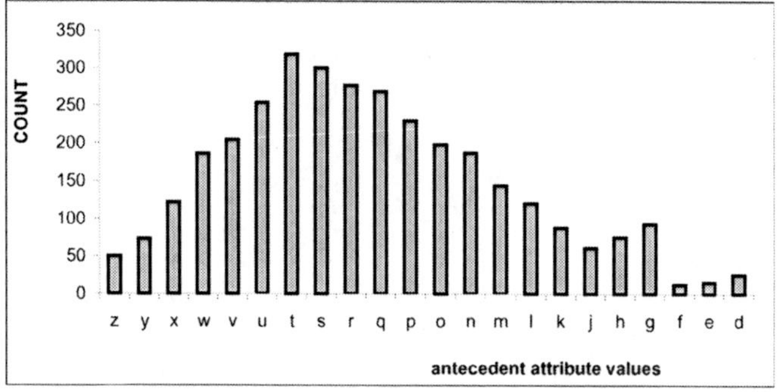

Fig. 1. Each subset bar has a rule associated with it, describing the subset

Histogram rule set derivation is a data reduction process [1], in which very large data sets can be reduced to a few hundred descriptors, using a single scan through the raw data set. A different histogram set is generated for each antecedent attribute.

3 Sorting Data Subsets for Rule-Set Derivation and Maintenance

The data in a Database table or view is partitioned by the Master workstation to whatever number of workstations is available. For an N-row table and H workstations, each Slave workstation receives N/H rows. Partitioning is done by counting rows rather than examining data values, so it is fast. The Master workstation also tells the Slaves which attribute to use as antecedent for the current rule-set. Each slave then sorts its sub-table on that attribute, extracts a rule set from the sorted data, and sends the rule set to the master workstation. The master merges the sets of rules, one from each slave, into a single set for that antecedent attribute.

Receiving and merging rule sets is much faster than merging data sets, because rule sets are small (e.g. 100 rules per set). It takes less than one second to receive and merge rule-sets derived from a 400000-row table, for example, for up to ten slaves. When the antecedent attribute is *numeric* the master tells the slaves how many rules to derive. The master also broadcasts the MIN and MAX values for the attribute so that all slaves use the same set of sub-ranges as rule antecedents. The number of rules produced per slave is therefore constant for numeric antecedents. Sorting the data makes it easy to extract a histogram rule set since the antecedent attribute values are all arranged in order. It also makes *rule maintenance* easy. The master broadcasts to the slaves all data changes. The slaves then revise their rules and notify the master of any changes. The master obtains an updated rule-set describing the changed database table in less than 2 seconds by this method.

Sorting data is usually a slow operation. This would be a disadvantage for the current application, because rules are needed for query optimisation as soon as possible after a query reveals user interest in certain columns of some virtual or base relation. If rules are not produced until the data is sorted then sorting must be done as fast as possible. Our experiments show sorting is significantly accelerated by the parallelism in distributing data to multiple workstations.

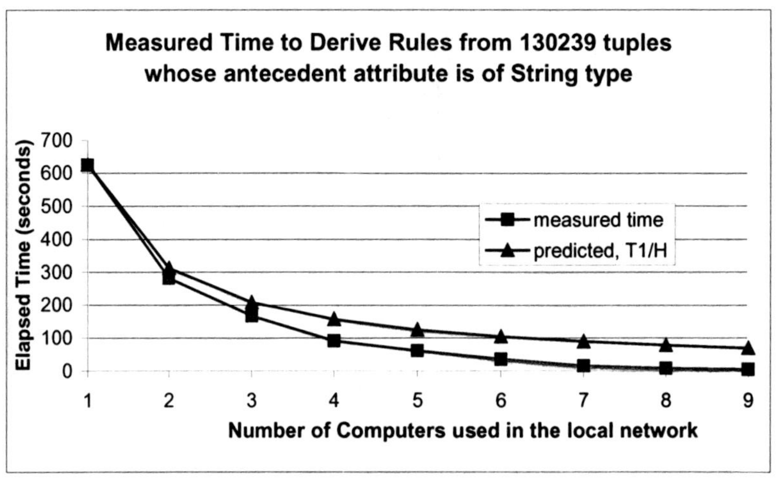

Fig. 2. Measured time for rule set derivation shows better than linear speedup

No. of Hosts, H	1	2	3	4	5	6	7	8	9
Measured time (sec)	625	282	167	91	61	36	16	8	5
Expected 625/H (sec)	625	313	208	156	125	104	89	78	70

Measured time means the observed time taken to create a set of rules (a histogram rule-set) from the 130239-row database table. The roughly hyperbolic curve for measured time suggests xy = constant. In this case we might expect the constant to be 625 seconds, the measured time for one workstation; time to complete a task being inversely proportional to the number of workers involved. Expected Time in the graph is therefore calculated as 625/H where H is the number of workstations used in the local network. The experimental results show even better speedup, as indicated in Fig 2. (Two machines are *more than* twice as fast as one, etc).

The explanation for this better than predicted performance is partly the computational complexity of the Quicksort algorithm used. It has a best case complexity of NlogN for N data items, and a worst case of N^2. We divide N by H and sort the smaller subsets, without the need to recombine the sorted subsets (only the relatively small sets of *rules* are merged). A second factor in the speedup is the amount of virtual memory paging involved. Each page swap between disk and main memory is a significant time delay. Large data sets do proportionately more page swapping.

Fig 2 shows that when 9 workstations are used it took only 5 seconds to distribute and sort the data sub-sets, derive 9 separate histogram rule-sets and merge them into a single rule-set in the master workstation. The same operation performed on a single workstation is seen to take over 5 minutes. The practical significance of this acceleration is that rules can now be generated in response to a query and may be available in time to be used to optimise the next query. This *query-triggering* of rule-set derivation is now a feasible alternative to *speculative generation* of sets of rules from database tables before queries arrive.

The experiments were repeated with various database tables. They varied in antecedent type, table size, degree of prior sorting and total number of workstations used. The graph above is representative of the results to some extent, but larger database tables needed correspondingly larger numbers of workstations to provide fast derivation. Furthermore, the minimum time achievable increased with the size of the database table because data is sent to computers before they start work on it. Data subsets must be sent one after another on the local network until the whole table has been distributed. The network bandwidth therefore imposes a time proportional to table size on the whole process. (Some workstations will have finished their tasks before the final data subset is sent). This undesirable time penalty can be removed by distributing database tables to workstations in advance. Then rule-sets can be derived in a few seconds by broadcasting only the *derivation parameters.* These are the identity of the antecedent attribute, and if it is a numeric attribute the number of rules required in the set plus the MIN and MAX values in that column of the whole table.

4 Direct Mapping to Buckets for Fast Rule Set Derivation

The sorted data subsets in each workstation are useful for rule maintenance, but a rule-set can also be derived using a more direct algorithm which scans once through the database table. During the scan each tuple is mapped to a bucket in a set of buckets corresponding to the required set of rules. Buckets correspond to bars in the histogram.

For numeric antecedent attributes the number of bars and their sub-range limits are known in advance. So mapping each tuple to its bucket is achieved by matching its value for the antecedent attribute to the relevant sub-range. For string antecedents a new bucket is added for each new value of the attribute encountered during the scan.

Each bucket has one rule associated with it, which describes all tuples mapped to that bucket so far. The subset descriptor evolves as more tuples are added to the bucket's subset. *For example,* at some point in the scan one subset descriptor has the form:

$$(15 \le a \le 30) \Rightarrow (71 \le c \le 94) \wedge (101 \le g \le 156)$$

This indicates that all tuples encountered so far whose attribute 'a' value was in the range $15 \le a \le 30$ were found to have values of attribute 'c' in the range 71..94 and attribute 'g' values in 101..156. If the next tuple in the table has values $a = 16$, $c = 96$ and $g = 121$ then the value of the antecedent attribute 'a' maps it to the bucket with antecedent range $(15 \le a \le 30)$, *i.e* this rule. The value $c = 96$ requires the range in the assertion describing all 'c' values to increase from (71..94) to (71..96), and the value of 'g' does not change the descriptor because 121 agrees with the assertion that all 'g' values are in the range 101..156.

Storage space for tuples *in buckets* is not required, because each bucket discards mapped tuples after deciding their effect on the bucket's evolving rule, during the incremental rule derivation process. The scanning algorithm for rule set derivation has the advantage that a single pass through the data generates a rule-set. This is much faster than sorting. The disadvantage is that sorted data, to support subsequent rule maintenance, is not produced.

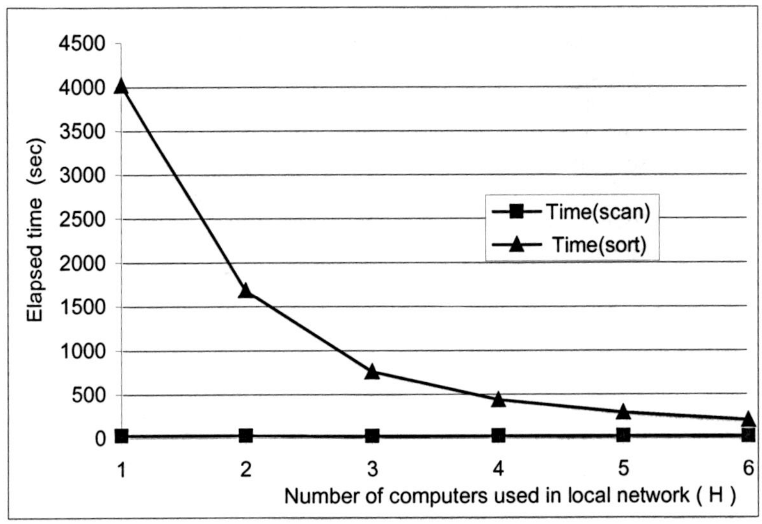

Fig. 3. Comparing rule-set derivation times for sort algorithm and scan algorithm

These measurements are for a 42 Mbyte table with 390731 rows. The scanning algorithm times form a horizontal line on the graph. Elapsed time was 30.5 ± 3.5 sec, independent of H. The time to derive the same set of rules by sorting the data subsets in the workstations varied from 4018 seconds for one workstation down to 205 seconds for six machines.

Since the scan times are fairly constant, independent of number of processors, it is possible to derive *multiple rule sets* simultaneously, one in each host. Each rule set has a different antecedent attribute. The derivation time f*or N sets* of rules is still about 30 seconds for this 42 Mbyte table.

Two or more *sets* of rules can be produced during the scan *in each single computer*. A set of buckets is provided for antecedent attribute 'a' and another set for antecedent 'd', say, in another rule set. Then in each tuple the value of attribute 'a' maps it to a bucket in the first rule set, and the value of attribute 'd' maps it to a bucket in the second evolving rule-set. The observed time to derive two rule-sets in this way is virtually the same as one rule-set, because *data transfer* to slave workstations is the rate-determining step in the process.

5 Scalability

Some database tables are much too large to distribute to ordinary workstations, because the local storage capacity on these general-purpose computers is not large enough to accommodate the data sets. Therefore there is an upper size limit for tables, beyond which the data distribution approach is not applicable.

Performance also declines with increasing table size, before that upper size limit is reached. We examined separately the times for sending data, processing data, and returning results. The third of these components used negligible time, because the result (a set of rules) is tiny in comparison with the data from which it was derived. The time to process the data depends on the rule derivation algorithm used, as discussed above. (Times reported above include all three components). The time taken to send data from the master workstation to a set of slave computers was investigated. Tables of progressively increasing size (from 32560 to 651219 rows, representing database tables up to 70 Mbytes) were sent to sets of 1, 2, 3 .. 8 computers, and the total send time measured. The following graph displays the results. They show that even these relatively small tables suffer from performance degradation related to their size.

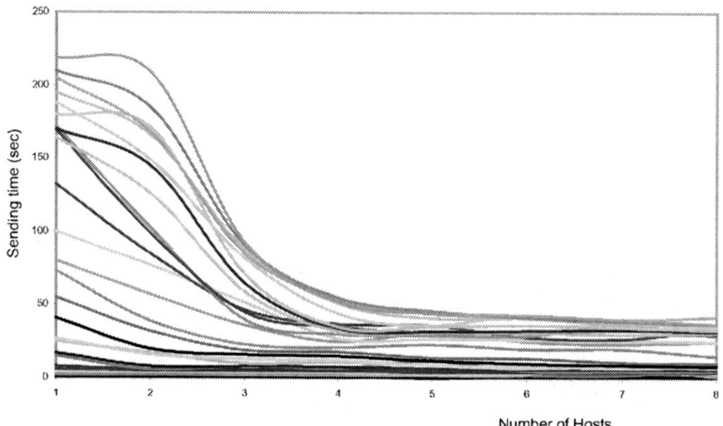

Fig. 4. Time to send data sets of various sizes to varying numbers of workstations

Each table size is shown as a curve on the graph. Small tables appear as horizontal lines near the bottom of the graph. Curves are seen to deviate progressively more from the horizontal as the table size increases, but all become approximately horizontal when the number of hosts becomes 'sufficiently large'. Using more hosts reduces the size of the data set that is sent to each computer, because the number of hosts divides the table. The graph reveals that above a particular data size per computer the time to transfer data between Master and slaves increases dramatically.

All curves become horizontal when the number of table rows per host is 150 000 or less. So 150000 rows for this 112-bytes-per-row table is the maximum size per host (for these particular hosts) to avoid the delay. 150000*112 bytes = 16 Mbytes. This reveals a limitation of the distributed rule derivation system. For FAST operation the maximum table size is 16*H Mbytes, where H is the number of workstations available for use. Larger tables can be processed, but time will increase significantly because of the data transfer time component shown in the graphs. Paging in the Receive Buffer memory space in the slave workstations causes the large increase in data transfer time above 16 Mbytes per workstation. This particular value represents a memory buffer size. Therefore the 16 Mbyte limit, or speed change point, can vary for different systems. But there will always be some such size, above which speed decreases rapidly.

The next physical limitation as table size increases beyond 16*H Mbytes is the size of the swap file used for page swapping. The size of the swap file can be increased, up to the limitation of available disk space accessible to each workstation. The swap file can be placed on any mounted drive, but a computer can slow down dramatically if a remote (shared) disk is used for virtual memory swap space. A large network-accessible disk increases the maximum size of database tables that can be processed, but the resulting slowdown of the workstation (which affects all programs running on it, not just our background processes) is a clear drawback. The workstations used in the experimental network are chosen as typical examples of ordinary PCs in current use, not state of the art machines. Their internal disks are 10 Gbytes capacity. They have Intel PIII 450 MHz processors, 128 Mbytes of main memory, Linux Suse 6.4 operating system, and communicate by Fast Ethernet (100Mbit/sec).

6 Rule Utility

Estimating the potential usefulness of rules derived from data is important, because the number of possible rules that can be derived is extremely large, and only useful ones should be stored. Certain *utility metrics* have been proposed for this purpose [*eg* 8,10,16], but a more fundamental measure of usefulness for a subset descriptor rule is whether its description differs significantly from that for other subsets.

Creating a histogram rule set can be used as a form of data analysis, to decide which antecedent-consequent pairs have potential value in subset descriptor rules. *For example,* if date of birth is used as antecedent attribute then other attributes may show *subrange* dependencies.

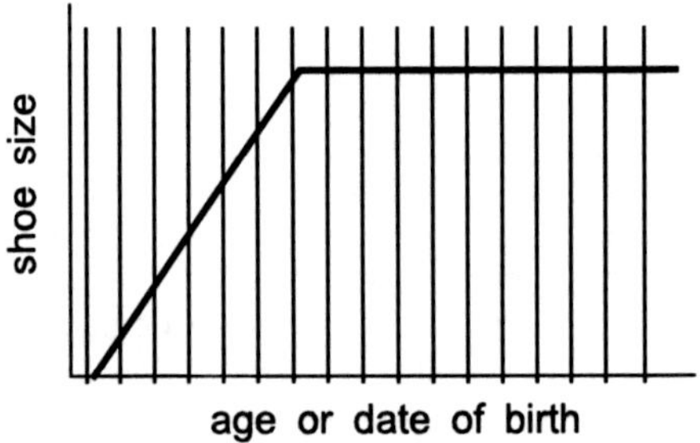

Fig. 5. Subrange dependency

The horizontal axis in this graph is divided into bars for the histogram. So all the bars above a certain age will have a very similar descriptor for attribute shoe_size. All those bars can be automatically merged into a single bar (i.e. a single rule). The single rule *subsumes* the others because its descriptor is the same but it describes a super-set of their data. A rule such as $(35 \le \text{age} \le 40) \Rightarrow (7 \le \text{shoe\_size} \le 10)$ is less useful than $(25 \le \text{age} \le 60) \Rightarrow (7 \le \text{shoe\_size} \le 10)$.

For some consequent attributes, *all bars merge into one* because the description of any subset differs little from the description of the attribute's domain. Such attributes are removed from the set of consequent attributes for this antecedent since they are not useful. They repeat only the domain assertions for their attribute. The histogram rule-set therefore provides a data profile. This information is not available to other rule-generating systems that create individual rules rather than rule sets.

The ability to rapidly derive histogram rule sets from data also allows a *search* for subset dependencies in response to queries. *For example,* a query selects tuples with job_title = "nurse" and $21 \le \text{salary} < 23$ and other attribute conditions. The subset of table rows with job_title = "nurse" can now be taken as the 'database table' for histogram rule-set derivation using *salary* as antecedent attribute. This may reveal useful relationships between nurses salaries and other attributes, which do not exist for salaries of *all* employees.

The usefulness of rules may decrease with time, because queries no longer concern the data described by a particular rule-set. Such rule-sets can be discarded because new sets can now be quickly created if query interest returns to this area of the data. There is no need to maintain the rules as data changes in the mean time.

7 Conclusions

Workstations in the same local network as the data server can provide a dynamically extensible and reconfigurable computing resource for rule derivation and maintenance. This additional resource is provided by utilising existing hardware: workstations that are being used for the intermittent or computationally undemanding tasks which form the usual workload of desktop computers. The work involved in rule derivation and maintenance is thus removed from the data server onto other workstations. The master workstation can measure the workload on each workstation in the network by spawning a short program on the workstation, and measuring the time it takes to finish. Its runtime under various computer workloads is known. So the measured time indicates the workstation's current workload and thus its suitability as a place to run a new rule derivation task.

Deriving a histogram rule set is a way to detect subset dependencies in data. The ability to rapidly derive rule sets from data therefore makes this aspect of data analysis easier. It allows the potential usefulness of rules to be quickly recognised and prevents fruitless attempts to produce rules from data that does not support them.

The scanning algorithm discussed in section 4 is amenable to parallel implementation by either horizontal or vertical partitioning of database tables. The effect, in either case, is the simultaneous derivation of N histogram rule *sets* by partitioning to N workstations. Vertical partitioning, assigning a different pair of columns to each workstation, gives slightly slower rule-set derivation. But it also has the more significant drawback that if the data is subsequently sorted the operation will

be very slow. It requires the one-workstation time rather than the N-workstation time described in section 3.
Experimental results for sorting data on multiple workstations show a useful sub-linear speedup. The effect of sorting by antecedent attribute value is to cluster tuples for each rule antecedent, therefore sorted data allows direct access to the data subset selected by a rule's antecedent condition. Descriptors for that subset can be rapidly revised, following data changes.

A choice must be made about whether to derive rules by the sorting or the scanning algorithm. For 'small' tables the sorting algorithm can be completed rapidly if sufficient workstations are used, so sorted data as well as a rule-set is immediately available. However, the scanning algorithm is faster than the sorting algorithm and the difference becomes increasingly significant as the amount of data per workstation increases. The experimental results suggest that the scanning algorithm should do the initial derivation of each set of subset descriptor rules (unless enough workstations can be used to reduce derivation time, as explained in section 3). This makes rules available for query optimisation as quickly as possible at the time they are needed. Data in the slaves can be sorted *after* rule derivation, to support rule maintenance. The scanning algorithm time being independent of the number of workstations means that one rule-set can be derived *per machine*, so that N workstations can simultaneously create at least N *sets* of rules (each having a different antecedent attribute, for example).

In an ordinary local network bandwidth is limited and data transfer is necessarily sequential. Distributing subsets to workstations therefore takes an amount of time related to the size of the database table. It is not possible to send different subsets simultaneously from the master workstation. Therefore the time to create a rule-set must increase to some extent as table size increases, because of the time needed to copy the table into the workstations.

The sorted raw data in multiple workstations can also provide rapid *data retrieval* for database queries or sub-queries, and this facility can be utilised by the 'master' workstation query interface when deciding the quickest way to answer each query. Some queries will be re-written by semantic query optimisation methods using the information provided in the subset descriptor rules. These re-written queries will then be sent to the DBMS server to answer. Other queries will be decomposed into sub-queries for distributed query processing on some combination of workstations and DBMS data server. The investigation of performance for this distributed query answering system forms part of our continuing research.

The contribution of this paper is to increase the *practicality* of SQO (semantic query optimisation). Databases rarely use SQO at present because (i) the server's workload to derive and maintain the rules tends to cancel the benefits by delaying queries, and (ii) the quality of rules derived without that lengthy data analysis is poor, giving only limited improvement to optimised queries. The current work seeks a solution to these problems by using computers that are separate from the data server. A cost-effective solution is to use existing workstations in the same local network as the data server, and do the work of rule derivation and maintenance on those computers as *background* programs. Rule-sets should be derived *dynamically* (in response to database queries, which indicate the current data area of user interest and also identify attribute connections for Joins and for dependency investigation). Our experimental work in implementing this idea reveals that usefully rapid rule-set derivation and maintenance can be achieved for database tables up to a certain size.

Data transfer time on the LAN between data server and workstations was a limiting factor for *dynamic* rule-set derivation, because of its strict time constraints. Rules must be created from data in time to be used, before query interest moves to other areas of the data. For *static* data (in a data warehouse or data archive, for example) the need for dynamic derivation is removed, so that much larger data sets can be processed (up to the disk space limit of the collection of general-purpose workstations). Data cube creation can be seen as an example of multi-dimensional histogram rule-set production, which generates subset descriptors from static data in preparation for OLAP queries.

References

[1] D. Barbará, W. DuMouchel, et. al., The New Jersey Data Reduction Report. Data Engineering Bulletin 20(4): 3-45 (1997)

[2] Blaszczyk A. and Trinitis C., *Experience with PVM in an industrial environment*, Proc. 3rd European PVM Conference, Munich, Germany, Springer-Verlag, 1996.

[3] Chakravarthy U.S., Grant J. and Minker J., *Logic based approach to semantic query optimisation,* ACM Transactions on Database Systems, Vol. 15, No. 2, 162-207, 1990.

[4] Geist A. and Sunderam V.S., Network based concurrent computing on the PVM system, Journal of Concurrency: Practice and Experience, 4(4), pages 293-311, June 1992.

[5] Godfrey P., Grant J., Gryz J. and Minker J., 'Integrity Constraints: Semantics and applications', Logics for Databases and Information Systems, Kluwer, Ch.9, 1998.

[6] Grant J, Gryz J, Minker J, Raschid, Logic-Based Query Optimization for Object Databases, IEEE Transactions on Knowledge and Data Engineering, 12(1) 2000, pp 529-547.

[7] Hsu C, and Knoblock C.A, Rule Induction for Semantic Query Optimization, Proc 11th International Conference on Machine Learning, 1994, pp112-120.

[8] Hsu C, and Knoblock C.A, Estimating the Robustness of Discovered Knowledge, Proc 1st International Conference on Knowledge Discovery and Data Mining, 1995.

[9] Ioannidis Y.E., Poosala V, Histogram-Based Approximation of Set-Valued Query-Answers. Proc VLDB Conference 1999, pp 174-185.

[10] Lowden B.G.T. and Robinson J., A statistical approach to rule selection in semantic query optimisation, Proc. ISMIS'99, 11th International Symposium on Methodologies for Intelligent Systems, 1999, pp 330-339. (LNCS 1609)

[11] Viswanath Poosala, Yannis E. Ioannidis, Peter J. Haas, Eugene J. Shekita: Improved Histograms for Selectivity Estimation of Range Predicates. SIGMOD Conf. 1996: 294-305.

[12] Poosala V, Ganti V, Ioannidis Y.E., Approximate Query Answering using Histograms. IEEE Data Engineering Bulletin 22(4): 5-14(1999)

[13] Robinson J, Lowden B.G.T., *Attribute-Pair Range Rules*. Proc. DEXA'98, 9th International Conference and Workshop on Database and Expert Systems Applications, 1998, pp 680-691. (LNCS 1460)

[14] Robinson J. and Lowden B.G.T., Data analysis for query processing, Proc. 2nd International Symposium on Intelligent Data Analysis, London, 1997.

[15] Sayli A, Lowden B.G.T., A fast transformation method for semantic query optimisation, Proc. IDEAS'97, IEEE, Montreal, 1997.

[16] Sayli A, Lowden B.G.T., The Use of Statistics in Semantic Query Optimisation, Proc. 13th. European Meeting on Cybernetics and Systems Research, pp 991-996, 1996.

[17] Shekhar S, Hamidzadeh B, Kohli A, Coyle M, Learning Transformation Rules for Semantic Query Optimization: A Data-Driven Approach, IEEE Trans Data and Knowledge Engineering 5(6) 950-964, 1993.

[18] Shenoy S.T, Ozsoyoglu Z. M., Design and implementation of semantic query optimiser. IEEE Transactions on Knowledge and Data Engineering, 1(3) 1989, 344-361.

[19] Siegel, M., Sciore E. and Salveter S., A method for automatic rule derivation to support semantic query optimisation, ACM Transactions on Database Systems, Vol. 17, No. 4, 563-600, 1992.

[20] Yu C. and Sun W., Automatic knowledge acquisition and maintenance for semantic query optimisation, IEEE Transactions on Knowledge and Data Engineering, 1(3) 362-375, 1989.

[21] Robinson J. and Lowden B.G.T., *Extending the Re-use of Query Results at Remote Client Sites*, Proc. 11th Intl. Conf. on Database and Expert Systems Applications, DEXA 2000, pages 536-547. Springer (LNCS 1873).

[22] Dar, S., Franklin, M. J., Jonsson, B. T., Srivastava, D., Tan, M.: Semantic Data Caching and Replacement, Proc. 22nd VLDB Conference (1996) 330-341.

[23] Keller, A. M., Basu, J.: A Predicate-based Caching Scheme for Client-Server Database Architectures. VLDB Journal 5(1) 1996, 35-47.

[24] Robinson J. and Lowden B.G.T., *Semantic Query Optimisation and Rule Graphs*. Proc. KRDB'98, 5th Intl. Workshop on Knowledge Representation meets DataBases, 1998, pp 14.1 - 14.10. http://sunsite.informatik.rwth-aachen.de/Publications/CEUR-WS/Vol-10/

[25] Geist, A, Beguelin A, et. al., PVM: Parallel Virtual Machine, A Users' Guide and Tutorial for Networked Parallel Computing, MIT Press, 1994.

Estimating Object-Relational Database Understandability Using Structural Metrics

Coral Calero[1], Houari A. Sahraoui[2], Mario Piattini[1], Hakim Lounis[3]

[1] Dep. Informática Universidad de Castilla-La Mancha Ronda Calatrava, 5
13071 Ciudad Real Spain
{ccalero, mpiattin}@inf-cr.uclm.es

[2] Dep. d'Informatique et de Recherche Opérationnelle Université de Montréal
CP 6128 succ. Centre Ville
Montréal QC H3C 3J7 Canada
Sahraouh@iro.umontreal.ca

[3] Département d'informatique Université du Québec a Montréal
CP 8888, succ. Centre-ville
Montréal QC H3C 3P8 Canada
hlounis@uqam.ca

Abstract. New Object-Relational Database Management Systems (ORDBMSs) are replacing existing relational ones. In spite of the high expressiveness, application systems built upon ORDBMS are more complex and difficult to maintain due to the mixing of two paradigms, the relational and the object-oriented. This paper describes a suite of metrics for measuring different aspects of an object-relational database. An empirical validation of the usefulness of the proposed metrics in estimating the understandability of an object-relational schema is given. The analysis procedure comprises the use of two techniques: C4.5, a machine learning algorithm, and RoC, a robust Bayesian classifier. The results demonstrate that a subset of the proposed measures is relevant for the estimation of the understandability.

1 Introduction

Software maintenance is the most expensive stage in the software life cycle. It is one of the greatest problems in the software industry, representing between 67% and 90% of total life cycle costs ([3], [11]). Until now, software maintenance efforts have mainly been centered on program maintenance tasks, as data maintenance was relatively easy in simple files or simple relational tables.

Nowadays, we are witnessing important advances in database technology; a new ''generation" of DBMS (Database Management System) is coming out, among which object-relational ones (e.g. Oracle 8, Informix Dynamic Server, DB2) stand out. Object-relational databases will replace relational systems to become the next great wave of databases ([16]). This kind of DBMSs supports a more complex data model having a stronger influence on the overall application maintenance effort.

H.C. Mayr et al. (Eds.): DEXA 2001, LNCS 2113, pp. 909–922, 2001.

Therefore, it is very important to have maintainability metrics for this new kind of databases. Metrics for databases have been neglected in the metric community ([15]). In fact, most of the metrics put forward, as the famous McCabe ([9]) cyclomatic number, have been centered on measuring program complexity, quality, maintenance, etc.

Maintainability is achieved by three factors: understandability, modifiability and testability, which in turn are influenced by complexity ([8]). We must be conscious, however, that a general complexity measure is "the impossible holy grail" ([4]). Henderson-Sellers ([6]) distinguishes three types of complexity: computational, psychological and representational, and for psychological complexity three components are considered: problem complexity, human cognitive factors and product complexity. The last one will be our focus.

In this paper we propose some complexity metrics for measuring object-relational databases and we use them to study their impact on the schema understandability. As understandability is one of the components of maintainability, these metrics may be used as partial indicators of the overall IS maintainability.

However, the goal is not only to propose metrics, because when a new measure is proposed, it is natural to ask whether the measure captures the attribute it claims to describe. We want to be sure that the measures we use reflect the behavior of entities in the real world ([5]). This validation must be made according to two perspectives: theoretical and experimental. The formal verification of the metrics presented can be found in [1]. In this paper we describe two experiments carried out with these metrics.

In the next section we summarize the features of object-relational databases. In Section 3, we describe the proposed metrics. Metrics empirical validation is presented in Section 4. Finally, Section 5 summarizes the paper and draws our conclusions.

2 Object-Relational Databases

Relational databases are widely accepted and used by the database community but they present some problems such as the representativeness limitations (complex elements which are present in several domain like graphics, geography are hard to represent). On the other hand, object-oriented databases propose a more powerful model to represent such elements. However, for multiple reasons, adopting this technology is still difficult. Object Oriented (OO) databases are not as mature as the relational ones. Another more practical reason is the difficulty of converting relational specialists and to convince managers to adopt this new paradigm with all the possible risks involved.

From this point of view, object-relational paradigm proposes a good compromise between both worlds. Object-relational databases combine traditional database characteristics (data model, recovery, security, concurrency, high-level language, etc.) with object-oriented principles (e.g. encapsulation, generalization, aggregation, polymorphism, ...). These products offer the possibility of defining classes or abstract data types, in addition to tables, primary and foreign keys and constraints[1], as do relational databases.

Furthermore, generalization hierarchies can be defined between classes (super and subclasses) and between tables, subtables and supertables. Table attributes can be defined in a simple domain, e.g. CHAR(25), or in a user-defined class as a complex number or image, In Figure 1 an example based on the one presented in [2] is shown.

```
CREATE TABLE house(
idhouse INTEGER,
idagency INTEGER,
price INTEGER,
rooms INTEGER,
size DECIMAL (8,2),
location address,
desc text,
front_view bitmap,
document doc,
seller employee,
PRIMARY KEY (idhouse),
FOREIGN KEY idagency
REFERENCES agency(id));

CREATE TABLE agency(
id INTEGER,
name VARCHAR(20),
location address);
```

```
CREATE TYPE address AS(
street CHAR(30),
city CHAR(20),
state CHAR(2),
zip INTEGER) NOT FINAL;

CREATE TYPE employee
AS(
name CHAR(40),
base_salary DECIMAL(9,2),
bonus DECIMAL(9,2))
INSTANTIABLE NOT FINAL
METHOD salary() RETURNS
DECIMAL(9,2);
CREATE METHOD salary()
FOR employee
BEGIN
...
END;
```

Fig. 1. Example of table definition in SQL:1999

In this example we can notice that part of the data is expressed using relational concepts (tables, primary and foreign keys and references) and the other part using OO concepts (types, and methods). The richness of the resulting model somewhat increases its complexity ([16]). For this reason it is very important to have metrics that allow for the complexity of this kind of databases to be controlled.

3 Working Hypotheses

Our main hypothesis is that the understandability is highly influenced by the complexity of an object-relational database schema.

Moreover, we claim that complexity is itself impacted by the size and the coupling between the elements of the schema (tables and classes). Taking into account this idea and the characteristics of an object-relational schema, we present six metrics which cover these two aspects and which are defined at table level. Three of them have been

---

[1] In this first approximation constraints are not considered for measure purposes.

previously presented and theoretically validated in [1] (TS, DRT and RD). The other three metrics have been defined for the present experiment.

3.1 Description of the Metrics[2]

TS Metric

The table size (TS) measures the size not only in terms of the simple columns (defined using simple domains), but also in terms of complex columns (defined using user-defined classes). Formally it can be defined as the sum of the total size of the simple columns (TSSC) and the total size of the complex columns (TSCC) in the table. TSSC is simply the number of simple columns in the table (considering that each simple domain has a size equal to one). TSCC is defined as the sum of complex columns size (CCS). The size of a complex column is no more than the size of the class hierarchy above the column is defined weighted by the number of complex columns which use the hierarchy. Finally, the size of a class hierarchy is defined as the sum of the size of each class in the hierarchy. For more details about the precise definition of this metric see [1].

RD Metric

Referential Degree (RD) is defined as the number of foreign keys in a table.

DRT Metric

Depth of Relational Tree (DRT) is defined as the longest path among the table concerned and the rest of the tables in the schema database, by considering the later as a graph where nodes are tables and arcs are referential integrity relations 1between tables (Foreign key-Primary key link).

PCC Metric

PCC is defined as the percentage of complex columns.

NIC Metric

NIC is the number of involved classes and it measures the number of all the classes that compose the types of the complex columns of a table using the generalization and the aggregation relationships.

---

[2] On [16] it is possible to find all the basic concepts used for the definition of the metrics presented.

NSC Metric

NSC is the number of shared classes and it measures the number of involved classes for a table that are used by other tables.

Table 1 summarizes the relation between metrics and size and coupling.

Table 1. Relation between our metrics and coupling and size

	SIZE	COUPLING
TS	✓	✓
RD		✓
DRT		✓
PCC	✓	
NIC	✓	✓
NSC		✓

3.2 Example

We present the values for the different metrics for the example presented in Figure 1. For simplifying the calculus, let us assume that all methods have a cyclomatic complexity equal to 1 and that all the large objects (LOBs), such as text or bitmap, also have a size equal to one.

We can calculate the value for the address class (four simple attributes, each one with a size equal to one, divided by two, because there are two tables which use the address class) and the employee class (three simple attributes, size three, plus a method, size equal to one, divided by two, because there are two tables which use the employee class) as

$$CCS_{address} = \frac{4}{2} = 2 \tag{1}$$

$$CCS_{employee} = \frac{3+1}{1} = 4$$

And with these values we can obtain the values shown in Table 2 for each column size of each table:

Table 2. Size for each column

	COLUMN NAME	COLUMN TYPE	COLUMN SIZE
HOUSE	Idhouse	Simple	1
	Idagency	Simple	1
	Price	Simple	1
	rooms	Simple	1
	size	Simple	1
	location	Complex	2
	desc	LOB	1
	front_view	LOB	1
	document	LOB	1
	seller	Complex	4
AGENCY	id	Simple	1
	name	Simple	1
	location	Complex	2

With these data, we obtain the following values for the table size metric:

$$TS_{house} = 5+9 = 14 \qquad (2)$$
$$TS_{agency} = 2+2 = 4$$

The other metrics for the house and agency tables are summarized in Table 3.

Table 3. Metric values for the example of Figure 1

	HOUSE	Comments	AGENCY	Comments
TS	14	See above	4	See above
RD	1	Foreign Key idagency	0	No Foreign Keys
DRT	1	House to Agency	0	No Foreign Keys
PCC	20%	2 complex att. over 10	33%	1 complex att. over 3
NIC	2	address and employee	1	address
NSC	1	Address	1	address

4 Empirical Validation

In this section, we want to evaluate whether or not the proposed measures can be used as indicators for estimating the understandability of an OR database. In the remainder of this section, we present the way we collect the experimental data, the techniques used to assess the usefulness of the measures, and the results of the experiment.

4.1 Data Collection

Five object-relational databases were used in this experiment with an average of 10 relations per database. These databases were originally relational ones. For the purpose of the experiment, they were redesigned as OR databases. The maximum and minimum values for the metrics are given in Table 4.

Table 4. Range of values used in the experiment

	Minimum value	Maximum value
TS	2	17.5
RD	0	5
DRT	0	3
PCC	0%	80%
NIC	0	6
NSC	0	5

Five subjects participated in the experiment (one researcher, two research assistants and two graduate students). All of them are experienced in both relational databases and object-oriented programming. One subject did not complete the experiment, and we had to discard his partial results.

The subjects were given a form, which included three questions for each table. Our idea was that in order to answer these questions, they would need to understand the subschema (objects and relations) defined by the concerned table. A table (and thus the corresponding subschema) is easy to understand if (almost) all the subjects find the right answers in a limited time (2 minutes per table). Formally, a value 1 is assigned to the understandability of a table if at least 10 out of 12 questions are answered correctly in the specified time (4 subjects and 3 questions). A value 0 is assigned otherwise. The tables are given to the subjects in random order and not by database to minimize the effect of familiarity with the schema of a particular table.

After compiling the results, 28 tables were classified as difficult to understand (0) and 22 easy to understand (1).

4.2 Validation Technique

To analyze the usefulness of the metrics proposed in Section 3, we used two machine learning (ML) techniques: C4.5 ([12]), a Top Down Induction of Decision Trees algorithm, and RoC [13], a robust Bayesian classifier.

Most of the work done in ML has focused on supervised machine learning algorithms. Starting from the description of classified examples, these algorithms produce definitions for each class. In general, they use an attribute-value representation language that allows for the learning set statistical properties to be exploited, leading to efficient software quality models. C4.5 is representative of the Top Down Induction of Decision Trees (TDIDT) approach ([12]). C4.5 belongs to the divide and conquer algorithms family. In this family, the induced knowledge is generally represented by a decision tree. It works with a set of examples where each example has the same structure, consisting of a number of attribute/value pairs. One of these attributes represents the class of the example.

Closer to probabilistic approaches, RoC is a Bayesian classifier [7]. It is trained by estimating the conditional probability distributions of each attribute, given the class label. The classification of a case, represented by a set of values for each attribute, is accomplished by computing the post probability of each class label, given the attribute values, by using Bayes' theorem. The case is then assigned to the class with the highest posterior probability. RoC extends the capabilities of the Bayesian classifier to situations in which the database reports some entries as unknown. It can then train a Bayesian classifier from an incomplete database. More information about this process is given in [13].

We uphold the use of these ML algorithms for several reasons. One of them is that real-life software engineering data are incomplete, inexact, and often imprecise; in this context, ML could provide good solutions. ML is also fairly easy to understand and use. However, perhaps the greatest advantage of an ML algorithm –as a modeling technique- over statistical analysis lies in the fact that the interpretation of production rules is more straightforward and intelligible to human beings than principal components and patterns with numbers that represent their meaning. This is very important for us because we want to obtain information about what kind of relationship can exist between our metrics and the understandability.

To evaluate the database schemata understandability characterization model based on our measures, we need criteria for evaluating the overall model accuracy. Evaluating model accuracy tells us how good the model is expected to be as a predictor. If the characterization model based on our suite of measures provides good accuracy it means that our measures are useful in identifying understandable schemes. Two criteria for evaluating the accuracy of predictions are the measures of correctness and completeness.

Correctness is defined as the percentage of database schemes that were deemed as understandable and were actually understandable. We want to maximize correctness because if correctness is low, then the model is identifying more database schemes as being understandable when they really are not understandable. Completeness is defined as the percentage of those schemes that were judged as understandable (response not understandable). We want also to maximize completeness because as completeness decreases, more schemes that were understandable are misidentified as not understandable.

The following table (Table 5) summarizes the formal measures of the learned model classification performance.

Table 5. Formal measures in the learned model

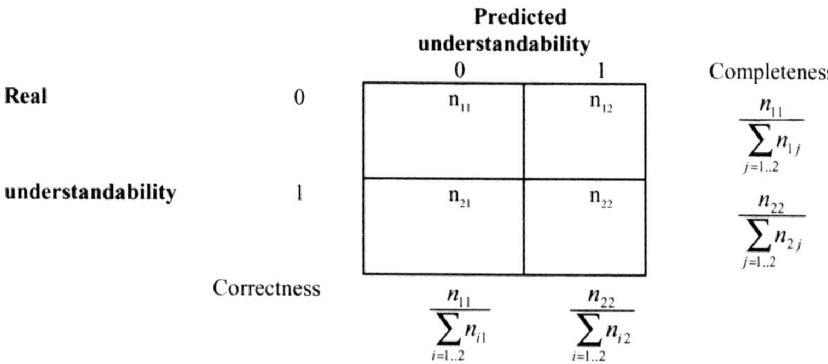

		Predicted understandability 0	**Predicted understandability** 1	Completeness
Real understandability	0	n_{11}	n_{12}	$\frac{n_{11}}{\sum_{j=1..2} n_{1j}}$
	1	n_{21}	n_{22}	$\frac{n_{22}}{\sum_{j=1..2} n_{2j}}$
Correctness		$\frac{n_{11}}{\sum_{i=1..2} n_{i1}}$	$\frac{n_{22}}{\sum_{i=1..2} n_{i2}}$	

Finally the model accuracy measures how correct the model is. It is given by the following formula:

$$Accuracy=\frac{\sum_{i=1..2} n_{ii}}{\sum_{i,j=1..2} n_{ij}} \quad (3)$$

In order to calculate values for correctness and completeness, and thus fill the table given above, we used a cross-validation procedure. In this procedure, the available data is divided into N blocks so as to make each block's number of cases and class distribution as uniform as possible. N different classification models are then built, in each of which one block is omitted from the training data, and the resulting model is tested on the cases in that omitted block. In this way, each case appears in exactly one test set. Provided that N is not too small, the average error rate over the N unseen test sets is a good predictor of the error rate of a model built from all the data.

The next sub-section presents the quantitative and qualitative results obtained following our verification strategy.

4.3 Results

As specified in validation the technique section, we applied RoC and C4.5 to evaluate the usefulness of the OR metrics in estimating the understandability of the tables in an OR schema. After applying these techniques, the results are very promising. The details of the results are given below.

Using the cross-validation technique, the algorithm RoC was applied 500 times. A total of 369 cases were correctly estimated (accuracy 73.8%) and all the other cases were misclassified. Contrary to C4.5, RoC does not propose a default classification rule which guarantees coverage of all the proposed cases. However, in this experiment, it succeeded in covering all 500 cases (100% coverage). These results are summarized in Table 6.

Table 6. RoC quantitative results

Correct:	369
Incorrect:	131
Not classified:	0
Accuracy:	73.8 %
Coverage:	100.0 %

RoC produces the model presented in Figure 2. From this model, it is hard to say which metric is more relevant than another in an absolute manner. However, we can notice that the smaller the TS is the higher the probability that the table is understandable is (for example 54% for TS <= 3). This probability decreases when the table size increases (9.5% for TS >10). Inversely, the same probability increase in estimating the tables that are not understandable (varying from 13.6% for TS <= 3 to 33.6% for TS >10). For the NSC metric, a table that shares classes with other tables is hard to understand and vice versa (the highest probability in the model given by RoC, 80%). For the other metrics, it is hard to draw a conclusion since no uniform variation is shown. This can be explained by the fact that for the sample used in this experiment, the values are defined in a narrow range (for example [0, 3] for DRT metric and [0, 5] for the RD metric).

The model of C4.5 is more accurate in estimating the understandability of a table (94%). As shown in Table 7, the model presents a high level of completeness (up to 100% for not understandable tables) and correctness (up to 100% for understandable tables).

From a qualitative point of view, C4.5 produces a more understandable model (Figure 3). As for Roc, TS seems to be an important indicator for the understandability of the tables. Rules 1, 2 and 7, which determine if a table is understandable, all have as part of the conditions that TS must be small. Inversely, in Rule 5, it is stated that a large size is sufficient to declare the table as not understandable. A small DRT is also required for Rules 1 and 7 as a partial condition to classify the table as understandable. At the same time, a high value of DRT means that the table is hard to understand (Rule 2). The number of shared classes can also be considered as a good indicator since, if there are shared classes, the table is not understandable (Rule 4) and vice versa (Rules 1 and 7). RD, PCC and NIC do not seem to be interesting indicators.

Model

TS

	(1 . 3)	(3 . 5)	(5 . 10)	(10 . 17.5)
0	0.136	0.193	0.336	0.336
1	0.543	0.233	0.129	0.095

DRT

	0	1	2	3
0	0.336	0.221	0.193	0.250
1	0.336	0.371	0.233	0.060

RD

	0	1	2	3	4	5
0	0.319	0.319	0.148	0.09	0.062	0.062
1	0.316	0.247	0.316	0.040	0.040	0.040

PCC

	(0 . 25)	(25 . 80)
0	0.471	0.529
1	0.603	0.397

NIC

	0	1	2	3	4	5	6
0	0.257	0.114	0.229	0.143	0.143	0.057	0.057
1	0.517	0.241	0.069	0.034	0.069	0.034	0.034

NSC

	0	1	2	3	4	5
0	0.462	0.233	0.090	0.090	0.062	0.062
1	0.799	0.040	0.040	0.040	0.040	0.040

Fig. 2. The model generated by RoC

Table 7. C4.5 quantitative results

		Predicted understandability		
		0	1	Completeness
Real understandability	0	28	0	100%
	1	3	19	86.36%
	Correctness	90.32%	100%	

Accuracy = 94%

```
Rule 1:
TS <= 9 ∧ DRT = 0 ∧ NSC = 0 -> class 1         [84.1%]

Rule 2:
TS <= 3 ∧ RD > 1 -> class 1             [82.0%]

Rule 7:
TS <= 9 ∧ DRT <= 2 ∧ NIC > 0 ∧ NSC = 0 -> class 1    [82.0%]

Rule 4:
NSC > 0 -> class 0                 [89.9%]

Rule 5:
TS > 9 -> class 0                  [82.2%]

Rule 6:
DRT > 2 -> class 0                 [82.0%]

Default class: 0
```

Fig. 3. C4.5 estimation model

In conclusion, both techniques indicate that table size and the number of shared classes are good indicators for the understandability of a table. The depth of the referential tree is also presented as an indicator by C4.5, but not clearly by RoC. The rest of the metrics do not seem to have a real impact on the understandability of a table.

A limitation of the presented work is the size and representativeness of the training sample. Object-relational databases are not widely used. The only criterion we used to choose the databases was availability. This kind of sampling, known as convenience sampling (see [10]), does not allow for the results to the whole population of OR databases to be generalized. However, as the 5 databases have small/medium schema size and the distribution of the metrics is uniform, we can consider the results as reasonably accurate for similar databases. For large schema, more experiments are needed to draw a final conclusion.

5 Conclusion

Object-relational database management systems are replacing simpler relational ones. One of the main consequences of this change will be the stronger weight of the ORDBMSs in software systems maintainability.

In this paper, we have presented a first approach for measuring object-relational database maintainability using three different metrics. To validate our measures for the understandability purpose, we have used 5 existing object-relational databases. We have applied two different techniques: C4.5, a machine learning algorithm and RoC, a Bayesian theorem-based algorithm. Two estimation models have been generated according to the two techniques. The results of our experimentation demonstrate that our measures can estimate the understandability of OR tables with a higher level of accuracy. In particular we have found that a sub-set of our measures proved to be quite accurate (table size, depth of referential tree, and number of shared classes). This suggests that these measures can be reasonably used as indicators for the understandability of a table, and to a certain degree of its maintainability.

In spite of the obtained results, this work presents a major limitation related to the threshold values of the two models (C4.5 and RoC). These values are specific to the sample and are hard to generalize for others databases. However, we are convinced that these specific values do not significantly affect the results. The trends shown by the model are more important that the values. To solve the problem of the threshold values, we are working on a machine learning algorithm that derives fuzzy threshold values (a first version is published in [14]).

Acknowledgment. The experience was conducted with the support of CRIM (Computer Science Research Institute of Montreal).

References

1. Calero, C., Piattini, M., Ruiz, F. and Polo, M. Validation of metrics for Object-Relational Databases, International Workshop on Quantitative Approaches in Object-Oriented Software Engineering (ECOOP99), (Lisbon ,Portugal. June 1999), 14-18
2. Cannan, S.J. (1999), The New SQL Standard: Good, Bad or Simply Ugly, Jornadas de Ingeniería del Software y Bases de Datos (JISBD99), Cáceres, Spain, November 1999.
3. Card, D.N. and Glass, R.L. (1990). *Measuring Software Design Quality*. Englewood Cliffs. USA.
4. Fenton, N. Software Measurement: A Necessary Scientific Basis. *IEEE Transactions on Software Engineering,* (1994), 20(3): 199-206.
5. Fenton, N. and Pfleeger, S. L. *Software Metrics: A Rigorous Approach* 2nd edition. London, Chapman & Hall. (1997).
6. Henderson-Sellers, B. *Object-oriented Metrics - Measures of complexity*. (Upper Saddle River, New Jersey, 1996). Prentice-Hall,
7. Langley, P., Iba, W., and Thompson, K. An analysis of Bayesian Classifiers. *In Proc. of the National Conference on Artificial Intelligence*, p. 223-228, (San Mateo, CA, 1992). Morgan Kaufman.
8. Li, H.F. and Chen, W.K. An empirical study of software metrics. *IEEE Trans. on Software Engineering*, (1987), 13 (6): 679-708.
9. McCabe, T.J. A complexity measure. IEEE Trans. Software Engineering, (1976,) 2(5): 308-320.
10. Patton M. Q., Qualitative Evaluation and Research Methods. Sage Publications, 1990.
11. Pigoski, T.M. (1997). Practical Software Maintenance. Wiley Computer Publishing. New York, USA.
12. Quinlan, J.R., C4.5: Programs for Machine Learning, (1993), Morgan Kaufmann Publishers.
13. Ramoni, M. and Sebastiani, P. Bayesian methods for intelligent data analysis. In M. Berthold and D.J. Hand, editors, An Introduction to Intelligent Data Analysis, (New York, 1999). Springer.

14. Sahraoui H. A., Adel Serhani, M. and Boukadoum M. A., Extending Software Quality Predictive Models Domain Knowledge, Proc. of the 5th International ECOOP Workshop on Quantitative Approaches in Object-Oriented Software Engineering, (Budapest, 2001)
15. Sneed, H.M. and Foshag, O. Measuring Legacy Database Structures. *Proc of The European Software Measurement Conference FESMA 98*, (Antwerp, May 6-8, 1998). Coombes, Van Huysduynen and Peeters (eds.), 199-211.
16. Stonebraker, M. and Brown, P. *Object-Relational DBMSs tracking the next great wave*, (California, 1999), Morgan Kauffman Publishers.

CDM – Collaborative Data Model for Databases Supporting Groupware Applications

Waldemar Wieczerzycki

Department of Information Technology
The Poznan University of Economics, Poznan, Poland
wiecz@kti.ae.poznan.pl

Abstract. In the paper the CDM data model for a database that could become a kernel of cooperative applications is presented. The CDM model is oriented for the specificity of multiuser environments, in particular: cooperation scenarios (e.g. sequential, parallel, reciprocal), cooperation techniques and cooperation management.

1 Introduction

A common feature of the majority of cooperative systems is that they require functions and mechanisms naturally available in DBMSs, e.g. data persistency, access authorization, concurrency control, consistency checking and assuring, data recovery after failures, etc. Notice, however, that these functions are generally implemented in collaborative systems from scratch, without any reference to the database technology. Some systems provide gateways to classical databases, however these databases are autonomous and external to them, thus database access is organized in a conventional manner.

Since the theory and technology of classical databases is very mature, commonly accepted and verified over many years, the following question naturally arises: can we apply this technology in collaborative systems, instead of re-implementing database functions from scratch and embedding them in collaborative systems? In other words: can we develop collaborative systems as database applications, thus probably saving time normally spent on re-implementation of selected database functions? As usually we can obviously try, but there is one substantial drawback we have to take into account. The classical database paradigm assumes namely that database users are totally isolated.

In such situation, in order to develop collaborative database applications, we have to extend database technology. The required extensions should be applied simultaneously to both data modeling techniques and transaction management algorithms. Former techniques have to facilitate modeling data structures that are specific to cooperation processes, while the latter techniques have to support human interaction and exchange of non-committed data.

There are many data models proposed in the literature that are addressed to advanced domains of database applications, in particular to computer aided design (CAD) and computer aided software engineering (CASE). Most of them provide

H.C. Mayr et al. (Eds.): DEXA 2001, LNCS 2113, pp. 923–932, 2001.

versioning mechanisms [1, 2, 3, 4, 6, 7]. These models substantially support individual design and development activities of database users. However, they do not sufficiently support group activities. It follows from the common assumption that database users communicate only via committed data. Since the users are totally isolated by the database system, each of them has an impression that the system is dedicated to him. When users collaborate to achieve a common goal, this approach is obviously too restrictive. Collaborators have to communicate directly before they agree on a data value.

Among basic drawbacks of the models mentioned above one can distinguish:

- the lack of data structures used to distinguish information particularly important to groups of collaborating users that could be simultaneously accessed by them without conflicts,
- difficulties with representing collaboration structure and collaboration organization in the data model; the lack of modeling concepts reflecting different levels of collaboration intensity,
- the lack of semantic relationships posed on data that could reflect relationships between the users operating on these data following from different cooperation forms,
- the lack of operations reflecting collaboration techniques and collaboration management.

In this paper we propose a solution of problems mentioned above by the use of a new database model. We propose a new data model CDM (Collaborative Data Model) that is oriented for the specificity of cooperation scenarios, cooperation techniques and cooperation management. In the paper we focus on data manipulation mechanisms of the CDM model and refer to data definition mechanisms already published in [9].

As preciously mentioned, besides new data models for cooperative applications, new transaction models are required. We suggest to apply to databases managed according to the CDM model so called *multiuser transactions* [10]. Contrarily to advanced transaction models proposed in the literature [5, 8], multiuser transactions are flat transactions in which, in comparison to classical ACID transactions, the isolation property is relaxed. The CDM data model and the multiuser transaction model are strictly related to each other. Most of concepts used in the CDM model match the basic concepts of the transaction model, and vice versa.

The paper is structured in the following way. In section 2 the CDM data structures are briefly reminded. In section 3 operations on data structured according to the CDM model are proposed. Section 4 contains concluding remarks.

2 CDM Model

In the CDM model a database is viewed as a set of domains. The *domain* is a set of database objects operated by a group of collaborating users. The users create (modify) domain objects using cooperative database applications associated with the domain.

Every domain is composed of two disjoint subsets of objects: *local objects* and *global objects*. First subset contains objects that are available only in the encompassing database domain. Second subset is composed of objects simultaneously available in all database domains. In other words, the subset of global objects is the intersection of all database domains - it is further called the *database core*.

The database core is a communication mean between database domains. It is composed of non-versionable objects containing basic information concerning the database, that can be potentially useful to all database users, no matter which domain they address.

Local domain objects can be further divided into so called domain content and domain abstract. The *domain content* groups objects created and frequently modified by team members in order to achieve the assumed outputs of cooperative work. Due to multi-stage, multi-thread and multi-variant specificity of the cooperation, the domain content can be versioned. Every version of the domain content is called a *context*.

The *domain abstract* is as subset of non-versionable domain objects playing the role of domain content generalization. It is used to support team members assigned to the respective domain.

The specificity of collaborative work in the database environment imply the necessity of distinguishing different types of contexts. In the CDM model we classify domain contexts in three orthogonal ways, considering respectively: context life-time, context consistency and semantic relationships between contexts.

Taking into account context life-time, we distinguish persistent contexts and temporary contexts. A *persistent context* is stored in the database directly after the commitment of a transaction that has created this context.

Temporary context life-time may not exceed the duration of a transaction related to this context. We mean here a transaction that has explicitly created the context during its execution, or a transaction that has implicitly created the context, as a result of a particular database operation that requires temporary context derivation (c.f. section 3). A temporary context may be addressed only by the transaction related to it. A temporary context may be promoted to a persistent context, thus gaining the features mentioned above.

The second way of context classification, orthogonal to the one considered above, distinguishes consistent and inconsistent contexts. In CDM model a single context extended by a domain abstract and the database core is a unit of consistency. It concerns, however, only consistent contexts, since inconsistent contexts do not contribute in database consistency units. A *consistent context*, augmented by a respective abstract and database core, does not violate integrity constraints defined for the corresponding database domain and it reflects the expectations of users responsible for information stored in this context.

Contrarily, inconsistent context does not fulfill the requirements stated above. It can be created as a result of particular operations automatically performed by the DBMS (c.f. section 3). Furthermore, initially consistent context may also become inconsistent, as result of deliberate operations done by a database user, who is aware of context inconsistency, however, because of some reasons, decides to keep the context in the database.

The third way of context classification refers to semantic relationships between contexts. We distinguish isolated and linked contexts. An *isolated context* is logically independent from all other contexts. Logical independence concerns also isolated contexts from the same domain, in particular a base context and its descendants. Two transactions addressed to two isolated contexts never conflict, even if they operate on the same multiversion object, whose value is physically shared.

Linked contexts have at least one link explicitly defined in the database. A *link* is a semantic relationship of a particular type binding a pair of contexts. A link between two contexts causes in general that an execution of an operation in one context automatically triggers an execution of a derived operation in the second context. Contrarily to isolated contexts, two transactions addressed to two linked contexts may fall into conflicts.

More details concerning the CDM data structures and context types can be found in [9].

3 CDM Operations

In the CDM model we distinguish the following groups of operations: object operations, context operations, domain content operations, domain operations.

Some of operations, e.g. context derivation, have already been intuitively introduced in section 2. In this section we mainly focus on new operations, not mentioned before.

3.1 Object Operations

Before first operation on a database object, a transaction has to address a single context in the scope of a particular domain. Since a domain abstract and the database core are subsets of non-versioned objects, while a single context contains exactly one version of every object belonging to a domain content, a database view perceived by the transaction is monoversion. It simplifies object addressing because there is no need for using object version identifiers. Having the context identifier *cid* and the object identifier *oid*, the database system can automatically identify a respective object version and present it to the transaction.

A transaction can perform classical operations on database objects: read, write, create and delete, as well as operations typical to the CDM data model: generalization, particularization and publishing. Now we focus on the latter set of operations.

Object generalization moves an object from the domain content to the abstract. Since objects in the abstract are non-versioned while objects in the contents are versioned, the object being moved gets the version value from the context addressed by the transaction. If the object has many different versions, then versions from other contexts are irrevocably lost. To avoid losing object versions, the concerned object can be copied in the scope of the domain content, before it is generalized. Object generalization facilitates inter-context communication between cooperating users, since the abstract extends all contexts available in the domain. If contexts are isolated, object generalization is the only way to make the object accessible to users addressing different contexts.

Object particularization is a reverse operation to object generalization. It moves the addressed object from the abstract to the domain content. There are two variants of this operation. In the first one, the object being moved gets its not null value (i.e. value from the abstract) only in the context addressed by the transaction. In the second variant, the object gets the same not null value in all domain contexts, which is physically shared. Object particularization enables further multi-thread object evolution independently in different contexts, by the creation of new object versions.

Object publishing concerns only objects included in a domain abstract. Only sufficiently privileged database users can perform this operation. The object being published moves from the abstract to the database core. As result, the object is still available in its original domain, however its modifications are restricted or even disallowed. Moreover, the object becomes global, i.e. it becomes available in all database domains. Obviously object publishing facilitates inter-domain communication.

3.2 Context Operations

Depending on the scope of visibility, we distinguish two groups of context operations: explicit and implicit. Explicit operations are called by database users. Their results are visible to other users of the same domain. One can distinguish the following four explicit operations: context derivation, context promotion, context linkage and context merge. First two operations require one argument, while the last two operations require two arguments.

Context derivation consists in the creation of a logical copy of the operation argument called base context. Context derivation may be performed by a transaction only once as the first transaction operation. Next the transaction is immediately re-addressed to a newly derived context and operates in its scope. The derived context is visible to other transactions after transaction commitment.

Next three operations due to their specificity are auto-commit operations, i.e. they imply the end of a calling transaction and their result becomes immediately visible to other transactions (database users) working in the scope of the same domain.

Context promotion changes the status of the operation argument from temporary to persistent or from inconsistent to consistent. It is worth to emphasize that the promotion of context to consistent state can be performed only by a verifying transaction.

Context linkage introduces new semantic relationship between two arguments (contexts). Types of possible relationships strictly depend of the domain of database application. If both arguments are isolated contexts then of course the operation changes their type to linked contexts.

Context merge operation derives a new context directly from the context addressed by the calling transaction, being default first argument of the operation. Next, the derived context is combined with the second argument of the operation. The context merge can be performed automatically if a particular merging algorithm available in the system has been selected. Otherwise, context merge is performed manually with the intervention of database users, who point object versions required in the resulting context in case of ambiguity. After automatic context merge the resulting context is in general inconsistent, thus it requires adjustments by a verifying transaction.

Now we present implicit context operations. They are invoked automatically by the database system, as a consequence of special users' requests. The result of an implicit operation is in general not visible to other users. We distinguish three following operations in this group: view definition, save point definition and workspace definition.

The concept of *view* is very useful in collaborative environments. A user who wants to be aware of work progress in different contexts may define views on them and perceive these contexts in a preferred manner, e.g. by selecting particularly interesting subsets of objects, binding with objects conversion mechanisms. Classically a view is a persistent query specified in the database language, automatically invoked by the database system whenever a view is addressed by a transaction. In some cases it can be materialized, i.e. a physical representation of data visible through view can be created. Both cases have some disadvantages. Operations on views stored as queries reduce system efficiency. Materialized views in turn require additional disk space and restrict updates done through views. In CDM data model we propose different approach that solves these problems.

A view is a persistent, linked and consistent context derived by the database system from the context for which a view has been defined. We distinguish two view types: simple and complex. A *simple view* presents objects in original form, while a *complex view* enables to modify object images. A way of modification is defined by particular methods operating on base objects called *conversion methods.* These methods are called automatically by the system whenever base objects are modified.

In a context modeling a simple view all objects visible through a view are physically shared with the base context, while objects out of a view have null values. It means that there is unidirectional weak propagation relationship between the base and derived contexts.

In a context modeling a complex view non-converted objects and objects out of view are treated as in case of a simple view. In case of objects with conversion methods assigned to them, their new versions are created in the derived context that result from applying conversion methods (the conversion methods are stored in the derived context). It means that there is extended unidirectional weak propagation relationship between the base and derived contexts. The extension consists in automatic invocation of conversion methods during the propagation process.

Views are illustrated in Fig. 1. In the simple view *P1* two objects: *A* and *C* are visible in original form (i.e. as in the base context), while object *C* is not visible. Thus, versions of *A* and *C* objects are shared between the base context and the context modeling a view. *P2* is a complex view in which modified objects *B* and *C* are visible. Thus, the context modeling a view stores new, local versions of objects: *B* and *C*, which result from invoking respective conversion methods. Moreover, conversion methods (represented by triangles) are stored together with local object versions. They are automatically used by the database system whenever objects *B* and *C* are modified in the base context.

In case of a complex view, there is additional mechanism available that enables the creation of new objects in a view based on other objects. In this case base objects have null values in the context modeling a view. These null values are bound to mirror conversion methods. In the domain content a new object is created being a result of applying these conversion methods. It has not null value only in the context modeling a view. Whenever one of base objects is modified in the base context, the database system replaces old not null version of this new object by another version resulting from the invocation of conversion methods. In Fig. 1 it is illustrated by the view *P3*. In this view only one object *D* is visible which results from modification of objects *A* and *B* from the base context. Although objects *A* and *B* have null values in the derived context, they are bound to respective conversion methods. Object *D* results from the conversion. It has not null value only in the context modeling the view *P3*.

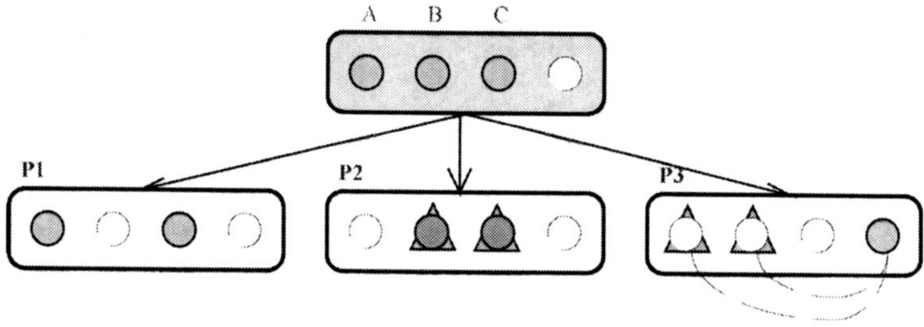

Fig. 1. Views

Defining a save point is the next implicit context operation. A save point represents a particular historical state of the database, perceived by a transaction during its execution. Save points are very useful in case of long-duration transactions that are typical in cooperation processes. They enable a partial roll-back of these transactions. Classically save points are represented in the system by so called database *snap-shots*, taken in a time moment pointed by a transaction, thus supporting partial transaction roll-backs. Another possibility of partial roll-backs comes from the *log file* that stores all operations performed in the system. The first approach has substantial disk space requirements, while the second one introduces substantial time overhead. In the CDM model a different approach is proposed which resolves the above problems.

Defining a save point consists in deriving by the database system a new temporary, isolated and inconsistent context, directly from the context addressed by the transaction which requests save point definition. Since this context is not visible to any transaction (thus, it can not be modified), it stores a frozen image of its base context. A transaction may define many save points during its execution. Every time the same derivation mechanism is applied. If a transaction is committed, save points are useless. Thus, corresponding contexts are simply removed by the database system.

If a transaction requests a roll back, first a respective context is identified by the database system. Next all contexts derived after the identified context are automatically removed. Finally, the historical state of the base context is restored using objects from the context that represents a save point. This operation consists in copying to the base context all values of objects that have been exclusively locked by the transaction (it suggests that they could be modified after the save point definition). Other objects do not change. Earlier save points are potentially still useful, thus corresponding contexts remain unchanged.

Save point definition and partial roll-back is illustrated in Fig. 2. A transaction addresses the context which has one descendant (Fig. 2 a). The transaction modifies two objects from the four available. During its execution, the transaction defines three consecutive save points: *SP1*, *SP2* and *SP3*. (Fig. 2 b). Next, the transaction partially rolls back to the save point *SP2* (Fig. 2 c). In response, the database system first deletes the context representing *SP3*. Next the state of the objects modified by the transaction is restored. Finally, if required, the context representing *SP2* can be removed.

The last implicit context operation is *workspace definition*. A workspace is a subset of database objects on which a user intends to work by the use of transactions. In some approaches [7] workspaces are used to support concurrency control of long-duration transactions. In the CDM model workspaces are primarily used to notify database users working in the same domain context about their mutual activities and scope of activities. Since consecutive transactions of the same user frequently concern the same workspace, in the CDM model workspaces are stored until their explicit removal.

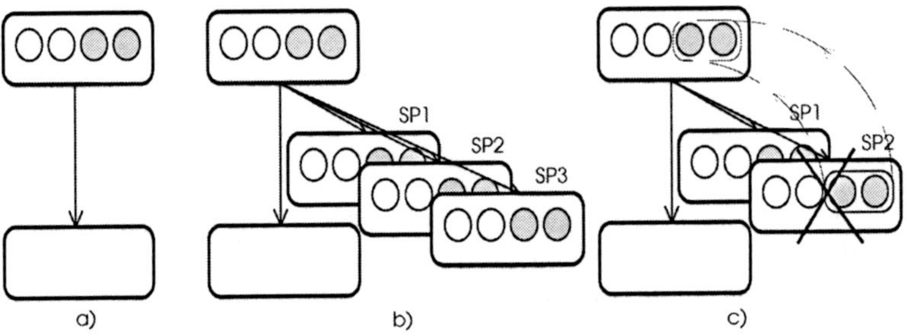

Fig. 2. Partial transaction roll-back

A workspace is a persistent and consistent context, invisible to the user, that is directly derived from the context addressed by the user when a workspace is defined. Workspace definition consists in iterative addition of group of objects with regard to all semantic relationships between objects. Selected objects are shared between derived and base contexts, while others have null values.

After workspace definition, a workspace may be in inactive or active state. *Inactive workspace* is not used by any transaction. In this case, there is a unidirectional propagation relationship of shared objects between base and derived contexts. *Active workspace* is a workspace currently used by a transaction. The transaction addresses the base context, however it is automatically re-addressed by the database system to the derived context (i.e. the context modeling the workspace). Switching from inactive to active states is a result of a particular database event called *workspace activation*. This event implies the change of relationship between base and derived contexts that becomes bi-directional. This means that all updates introduced to the derived context are propagated to the base context.

Workspace activation is sometimes impossible. It happens when another workspace has already been activated for the same context, that has non-empty intersection with a workspace considered. In such situation a users' notification mechanism is triggered by the system and a communication channel is established between respective users. After negotiations they can resolve the problem by shrinking their workspaces.

3.3 Domain Content Operations

The context derivation tree can become very large for some domains. The domain users often are interested only in contexts derived by themselves or by collaborating colleagues. In the CDM model particular views are available which are called prospects.

A *prospect* is a reduced context derivation tree of the domain in which some of nodes and edges are eliminated. There is a possibility to redefine context identifiers in the prospect and adjust them to users' preferences. A prospect can be defined on the basis of a domain content or another prospect. Prospect definition consists in iterative elimination of nodes or subtrees from the base tree.

A user addressing the domain content through a chosen prospect may derive new contexts. In this case, however, there are two restrictions. First, a new context may be derived only from the node visible in the prospect. Second, newly created context appears only in the domain content and the prospect through which it has been created. It means that users using different prospects will not notice a newly created context.

Prospects are illustrated in Fig. 3. In the prospect *P_1* two nodes at the third tree level are eliminated. Prospect *P_2* contains only the left subtree of the context tree (root node is also eliminated). Prospect *P_1_1* is derived (defined) from the prospect *P_1*. In this case, further three nodes have been eliminated: two at the second tree level and one at the fourth level.

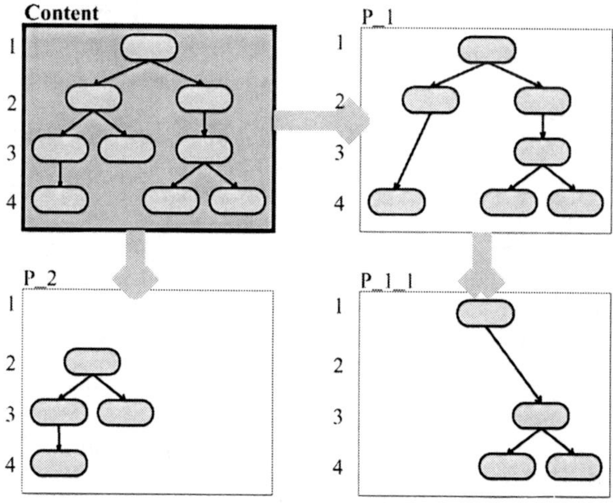

Fig. 3. Prospects

3.4 Domain Operations

Only the database administrator can perform domain operations, due to their scope and specificity. We distinguish the following operations: domain creation, domain removal, and assignment of users to the domain.

Domain operations are natural and straightforward, thus they do not require any further explanation.

4 Conclusions

A particular model of a database supporting collaborative applications has been proposed in this paper that is based on the CDM data model and the multiuser transaction model. The proposed database model is very straightforward and natural, on one hand, and allows practically unrestricted collaboration among members of the same team, on the other hand [10]. During collaborative work, DBMS supports flexible versioning mechanisms and wide information exchange between team members, on one hand, and users' awareness and notification, on the other hand. These functions are extremely important in case of every cooperative system.

The proposed database model supports three typical cooperation strategies: sequential, reciprocal and parallel.

References

1. Agraval R. et al., *Object Versioning in Ode*, IEEE, 1994.
2. Cellary, W., G. Vossen and G. Jomier, *Multiversion object constellations: A new approach to support a designer's database work*, Engineering with Computers, vol. 10, 1995, pp. 230-244
3. Chou H., Kim W., *A Unifying Framework for Version Control in CAD Environment*, Proc. of the 12 Intl. Conf. on Very Large Databases, Kyoto, 1986.
4. Chou H. T., Kim W., *Versions and Change Notification in Object-Oriented Database System*, Proc. of the Design Automation Conf., 1988.
5. Elmagarmid A. (ed.): Database Transaction Models, Morgan Kaufmann, 1992.
6. Katz R. H., Toward a Unified Framework for Version Modeling in Engineering Databases, ACM Computing Surveys, Vol. 22, No 4, 1994.
7. Lamb C., Landis G., Orenstein J., Weinreb D., *The ObjectStore Database System*, Communications of the ACM, Vol. 34, No. 10, 1991.
8. Nodine M., Zdonik S.: Cooperative transaction hierarchies: A transaction model to support design applications, Proc. of VLDB Conf., 1984.
9. W. Wieczerzycki, *Database Model for Web-Based Cooperative Applications*, Eighth International Conference on Information and Knowledge Management, CIKM'99, November 2-6, 1999, Kansas City, MO, USA.
10. Wieczerzycki, *Multiuser Transactions for Collaborative Database Applications*, Proc. of 9th International Conference on Database and Expert Systems Applications - DEXA'98, Vienna, pp. 145-154, 1998.

An Efficient Distributed Concurrency Control Algorithm using Two Phase Priority

Jong Sul Lee, Jae Ryong Shin, Jae Soo Yoo

Department of Computer & Communication Eng., Chungbuk National University, 48 Gaesin-dong, Cheongju Chungbuk, Korea, 361-763
Email: {leejs98, jrshin, yjs}@pretty.chungbuk.ac.kr

Abstract. Many concurrency control algorithms for distributed real-time database systems have been proposed. But there isn't a representative concurrency control algorithm for replication environment. In this paper, we propose an efficient concurrency control algorithm for distributed real-time database systems in replication environment. The main ideas of this paper are promoting priority and trading of data. Promoting priority is that the priority of the transaction that enters into voting phase is elevated. Trading of data is that a holder in the voting phase can lend holding data to other transactions. The proposed algorithm does not cause priority inversion. Therefore it decreases the ratio of restarting transactions and guarantees a transaction to commit at its maximum. Also to reduce blocking times of transactions, it permits data of a transaction in the voting phase to lend to the others. It is shown through the performance evaluation that the proposed algorithm outperforms the existing algorithms such as DO2PL_PA and MIRROR.

1 Introduction

According to the development of computer network, many real-time database applications, especially in the areas of communication systems, military systems and electronic commerce systems, were extended to distribute computing environment. The performance, reliability and availability of such applications can be significantly enhanced through the replication of data on multiple sites of the distributed network[8]. However, it incurs additional complexity of concurrency control and recovery schemes in distributed database systems. The issues of distributed real-time concurrency control and distributed commit protocol to guarantee the serializability and improve the performance have been considered in several researches[1,6,8]. A major issue is the development of an efficient replica concurrency control scheme. Recent researches on replica concurrency control scheme in distributed real-time environments can be classified into two groups in terms of their approaches. One group uses pessimistic concurrency control schemes such as D2PL(Distributed Two Phase Locking), DO2PL(Distributed Optimistic Two Phase Locking) and MIRROR(Managing Isolation in Replicated Real-time Object Repositories). The other group uses optimistic schemes such as OCC-Sacrifice, OCC-Wait and Wait-50[1]. These algorithms, however, cannot avoid priority inversion. Also, blocking

H.C. Mayr et al. (Eds.): DEXA 2001, LNCS 2113, pp. 933–942, 2001.

time of transactions extremely increases as the voting phase is delayed. The OCC wastes resources since transactions need to restart.

Therefore in this paper, we propose an efficient replica distributed concurrency control algorithm, called the PPCC(Promoting Priority Concurrency Control) that minimizes the restart ratio and blocking time of transactions. The PPCC promotes the priority of a transaction in the voting phase to guarantee commit at its maximum. The PPCC eliminates wastes of unnecessary restarting and minimizes the lock holding time of a transaction.

The remainder of this paper is organized in the following fashion: Section 2 reviews related works. In section 3, we describe the PPCC in detail. Then, in section 4, the results of the simulation experiments and discussions are presented. Finally, conclusions of this paper and our future research directions will be given in section 5.

2 Related Works

2.1 D2PL(Distributed Two-Phase Locking)

A transaction that intends to read a data item must get a read lock on any copy of the item but to update an item, write locks are required on all copies. Transactions that request a write lock on a data item are blocked until all copies of the item have been successfully locked by the local cohort and remote updaters. The data locked by the cohort is updated in the data processing phase. Remote copies locked by updaters are updated after those updaters have received copies of the relevant updates with the PREPARE message during the first phase of the commit protocol. Read locks are held until the transaction has entered the voting phase while write locks are held until they are committed or aborted. This algorithm is simple but the processing of transaction is interrupted until locks of all copies are obtained to update replicated data. This extremely decreases the concurrency.

2.2 DO2PL(Distributed Optimistic Two-Phase Locking)

A transaction is processed in the following three phases: execution phase, voting phase and decision phase[2]. The O2PL algorithm can be thought of as a hybrid occupying the middle ground between 2PL and OCC. O2PL handles replicated data optimistically. When a cohort updates a replicated data item, it requests a write lock immediately on the local copy of the item. However, it defers requesting write locks on any of the remote copies until the beginning of the commit phase is reached. As in the OCC algorithm, replica updaters are initiated by cohorts in the commit phase. Thus, communication with the remote copy site is accomplished by simply passing update information in the PREPARE message of the commit protocol. In particular, the PREPARE message sent by a cohort to its remote updaters includes a list of items to be updated, and each remote updater must obtain write locks on these copies before it can act on the PREPARE request. Since O2PL waits until the end of a transaction to obtain write locks on copies, both blocking and abort are possible rather late in the execution of a transaction. In particular, if two transactions at different sites have updated different copies of a common data item, one of the transactions has to be aborted eventually after the conflict is detected. In this case, lower priority transaction is usually chosen for abort in real-time database systems[8]. The DO2PL decreases wastes of resources since it permits write locks on remote copies once transactions reach the voting phase.

2.3 MIRROR(Managing Isolation in Replicated Real-time Object Repositories)

In the MIRROR protocol, a replica concurrency control protocol, the choice of conflict resolution method is a dynamic function of the states of the distributed transactions involved in the conflict. The key idea of the MIRROR protocol is to resolve data conflicts based on distributed transaction states. The state of a cohort/updater is used to determine which data conflict resolution mechanism should be employed. The basic idea is that priority abort(PA) should be used in the early stages of transaction execution, whereas priority blocking(PB) should be used in the later stages since in such cases a blocked higher priority transaction may not wait too long before the blocking transaction completes.

- Priority Abort (PA): This scheme attempts to resolve all data conflicts in favor of high-priority transactions.
- Priority Blocking (PB): This mechanism is similar to the conventional locking protocol in that a transaction is always blocked when it encounters a lock conflict and can only get the lock after the lock is released

To resolve a conflict, the concurrency control manager uses PA if the lock holder has not passed a point called the demarcation point, otherwise it uses PB[8]. In case of the classical priority abort (PA) mechanism, a cohort enters the voting phase after it votes for COMMIT, and a PREPARED cohort cannot be aborted unilaterally. This happens after all the remote updaters of the cohort vote to COMMIT. On the other hand, in the PA_PB mechanism, a cohort reaches its demarcation point before it sends the PREPARE messages to its remote updaters. PA and PA_PB become identical if database are not replicated. Thus, in state-conscious protocols, cohorts or updaters reach demarcation points only after the two phase commit protocol starts. This means that a cohort/updater cannot reach its demarcation point unless it has acquired all the locks. Note also that a cohort/updater that reaches its demarcation point may still be aborted due to write lock conflict. Since the MIRROR does not require additional communications or synchronizations with other sites to acquire state information it achieves good performance in replica distributed environment. However, after demarcation point priority inversion may occur, and deadlock can occur because it uses PB at the voting phase.

2.4 OPT(OPTimistic commit protocol)

The OPT allows higher priority transactions to borrow data items locked by lower priority transactions that are in the voting phase. That is, prepared cohorts lend uncommitted data to higher priority transactions. The lending cohort receives its global decision before the borrowing cohort has completed its execution. If the global decision is "commit", the lending cohort completes its processing in the normal fashion. If the global decision is "abort", then the lender is aborted in the normal fashion, and the borrower is also aborted since it has utilized inconsistent data. The borrowing cohort completes its execution before the lending cohort has received its global decision. The borrower is now "put on the shelf", that is, it is made to wait and not allowed to send a "yes" vote in response to its master's the PREPARE message. The borrower has to wait until either the lender receives its global decision or its own deadline expires, whichever occurs earlier. In the former case, if the lender commits, then the borrower is "taken off the shelf" and allowed to respond to its master's messages. If the lender is aborted, then the borrower is also aborted immediately since it has read inconsistent data.

3 An Distributed Concurrency Control Algorithm

3.1 Overview

The PPCC uses EDF as a scheduling scheme, 2PL(Two Phase Locking), PA(Priority Abort) and 2PC(Two Phase Commit). It is based on DO2PL and avoids an unnecessary restarting of transactions by the promoting priority scheme. Therefore, we divide priority region into normal region and promoting region. For example, when a transaction starts, a priority of normal region is assigned and it steps into the execution phase. If a holder, i.e. a transaction that is holding a lock on a data item, has promoting priority, the requester borrows the data and continues its execution. However, if the holder that has normal priority conflicts with the requester, the conflict is resolved by PA(Priority Abort). When a transaction completes its execution, it enters the voting phase and its promoting priority is reassigned. The transaction in the voting phase checks all of its sub-transactions if all of them are prepared and enter the decision phase. If all of them are in the voting phase, it is committed. Otherwise, it is aborted. Then finally this decision is sent to all sub-transactions.

3.2 Division of Priority

There are two kinds of priorities as described earlier. We assume that the total priority region has fixed numbers. For example, if we use 1 byte unsigned integer to assign priority, the total interval of priorities is from 0 to 255. The total priority region is divided into promoting region and normal region by the middle value. In this case the middle value is 127. Fig. 1 shows the division of priority region. A transaction starts with a normal priority that is from 128 to 255. When it receives the PREPARE message in the voting phase, the promoting priority is reassigned to it. The reassignment is simply done by subtracting the middle value from the normal priority that is assigned at the start point.

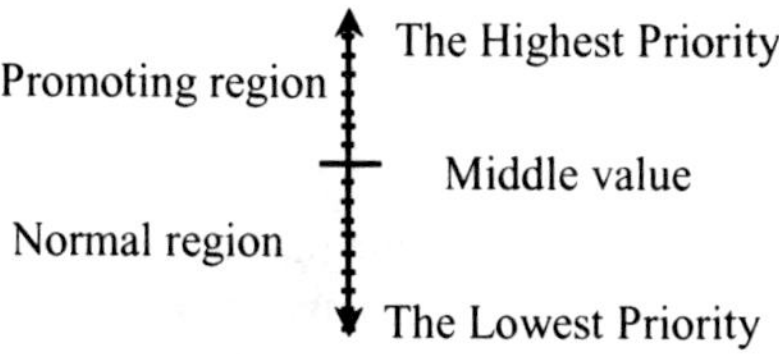

Promoting Priority = Normal Priority - Middle value

Middle value = $\lfloor$ (The Highest Priority + The Lowest Priority) /2 $\rfloor$

Fig. 1. Division of priority region

3.3 Borrowing and Lending of data

In OPT real-time commit protocol, a holder in the voting phase can lend the holding data item to higher priority transactions. We apply the OPT protocol[5] to the PPCC through a little modification. In the PPCC, the cohort transaction can lend its data items to normal priority transactions after receiving the PREPARE message from master. In Fig. 2, we show an example of lending and borrowing process. *Ti* is a normal priority transaction and *Tj* is a promoting priority one. *Ti* requests a lock on the data item that is held by *Tj*. If there is no other borrower of the data item, it borrows the data item from *Tj* and continues its execution. Otherwise, PA resolves the conflict between *Ti* and the borrower. From this example, we can easily know that even though the requester conflicts with the holder it can continue without blocking.

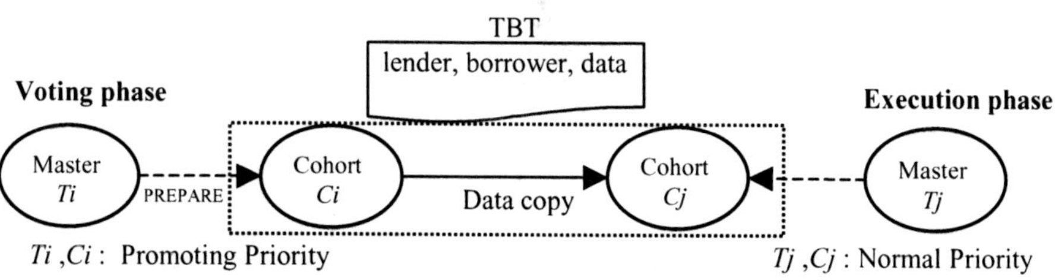

Fig. 2. Borrowing and lending of data

3.4 Execution phase

A transaction *Ti* starts with a normal priority and its sub-transactions also start at associated cohorts. When the *Ti* requests an exclusive lock on a data item that is locked by *Tj* in normal priority region, PA resolves the conflict. However, if the holder(*Tj*) has promoting priority, we check whether there is the borrower of the data item held by *Tj*. When the borrower exists, the conflict between the Ti and the borrower is resolved by PA. Otherwise, the *Ti* borrows the data item and continues its execution. Then *Ti* records the borrowed data item and its lender information to the TBT(Trade Brief Table).

3.5 Voting phase

When a transaction finished its execution, the master sends the PREPARE message to all of its cohorts. The cohorts that received the PREPARE message are reassigned promoting priority. If there is any borrowing cohort among them, the borrower has to wait until the lender is committed or aborted. If the lender is committed, the borrower sends its modified data item list and the PREPARE message to remote updater. Otherwise, the borrower sends abort message to its master. However, if there is no borrower, the cohorts of the transaction send the PREPARE message and modified data list to remote updater without waiting. If the conflict is occurred in the remote updater, it will be resolved by PA. Once the updater obtains locks on all the data item of the list, it sends prepared message to its cohorts. The cohorts that received the prepared message from all updaters send the prepared message to the master.

3.6 Decision phase

The *Ti* sends a commit message to its cohorts after finishing its voting phase successfully and the master writes a commit log record to the log file. Subsequently, all of its cohorts send the commit message to remote updaters. The cohorts that lent a data item update the TBT. All cohorts awake their waiting borrowers and add the commit log record to the log file. Their updaters also add commit log records to the log file and send an acknowledge message to their corresponding cohorts. Then, cohorts that have received acknowledge message send acknowledge messages to the master. Finally the master adds a complete log record to the log file after receiving the acknowledge message from all of its cohorts.

4 Experiments and Results

4.1 Simulation model

We compare proposed concurrency control algorithm with DO2PL using PA and MIRROR. Our simulation model is based on that of MIRROR protocol[8]. The description of the parameters of our simulation model is presented in Table 1. The simulation model is composed of 9 sites. Each site has 1000 pages, each database has 100 pages of replicated data, and each transaction accesses 9 ~ 24 pages. Each transaction is assigned a firm deadline using the Equation (1) where *Deadline*, *ArrivalTime*, and *ResourceTime* are the deadline, arrival time, and resource time, respectively, of a transaction, while *SlackFactor* is a slack factor that provides control of the tightness/slackness of transaction deadlines. The resource time is the total service time at the resources at all sites that the transaction requires for its execution in the absence of data replication.

$$DeadLine = ArrivalTime + SlackFactor * ResourceTime \quad (1)$$

Table 1. Simulation parameters

Parameter	Meaning	Setting
NumSites	Number of sites	9
DBSize	Number of pages in the databases	1000 pages
NumCPUs	Number of CPUs per site	2
NumDataDisks	Number of data disks per site	4
PageDisk	Disk page access time	20 ms
PageCPU	CPU page processing time	10 ms
NumLogDisks	Number of log disks per site	1
BufHitRatio	Buffer hit ratio on a site	0.1
InitWriteCPU	Time to initiate a disk write	2ms
LogDisk	Log force time	5ms
MsgCPU	CPU message send/receive time	1ms
TransSize	Number of pages accessed per trans	16*(0.5 ~ 1.5)
ArrivalRate	Transaction arrival rate	40
ReplDegree	Degree of Replication	10 ~ 100

4.2 Experiment Results

The goal of the first experiment is to investigate the transaction ratio with missed deadline(deadline missing ratio) according as transaction arrival ratio is increased. In the experiment, ReplDegree is 40 %, WriteProbability is 30 % and the values of other parameters are the same Table 1. Fig. 3 shows the result of the first experiment. When the number of transactions arrived per second reaches 30, the transaction ratio with missed deadline of the proposed algorithm is less than that of other protocols. The PPCC significantly decreases the transaction ratio with missed deadline for nearly all rounds from this point. Especially when transaction arrival ratio is 30~70 Trans/Second, the PPCC shows better performance. The write probability of transaction is fixed as 30% in other experiments. However, in the second experiment, we vary write probability. In this experiment, the replicate degree of data is 40 % and the transaction arrival rate is 40 Trans/Second. Fig. 4 shows that the performance of the PPCC outperforms others. The third experiment shows how the size of transaction affects deadline missing ratio in the Fig. 5. The deadline missing ratio of our algorithm is much lower than others. In the distributed database system, the replicate degree of data is closely concerned with the performance of database. Therefore, in the last experiment, we measure missed deadline ratio with varying the replicate degree. Fig. 6, we show the results. Also, in this experiment, our algorithm is affected less by replicate degree.

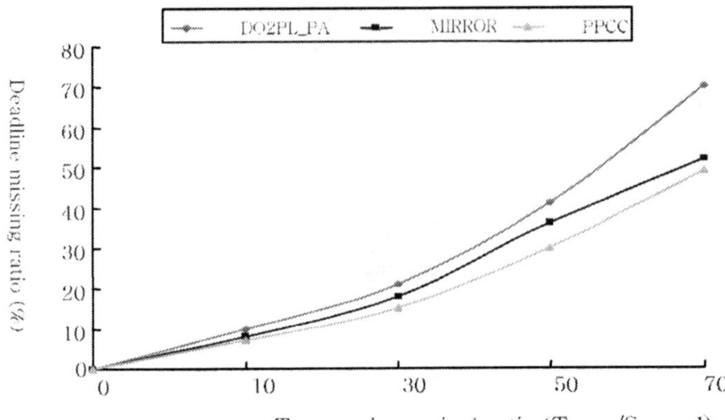

Fig. 3. Deadline missing ratio according to transaction arrival ratio

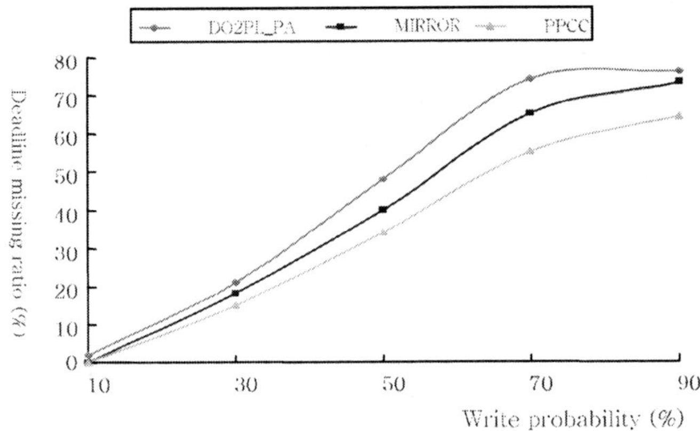

Fig. 4. Deadline missing ratio according to write probability

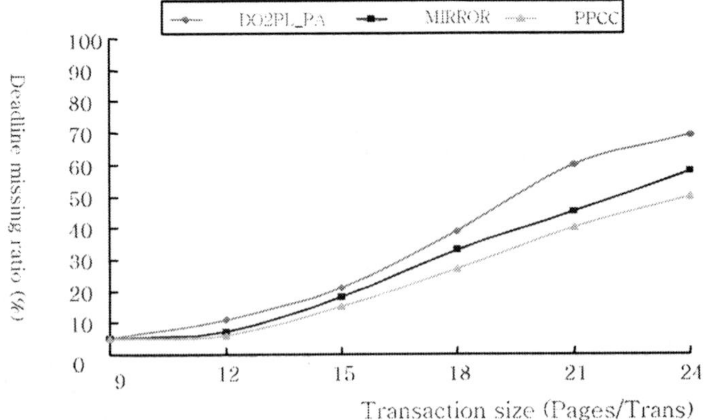

Fig. 5. Deadline missing ratio according to transaction size

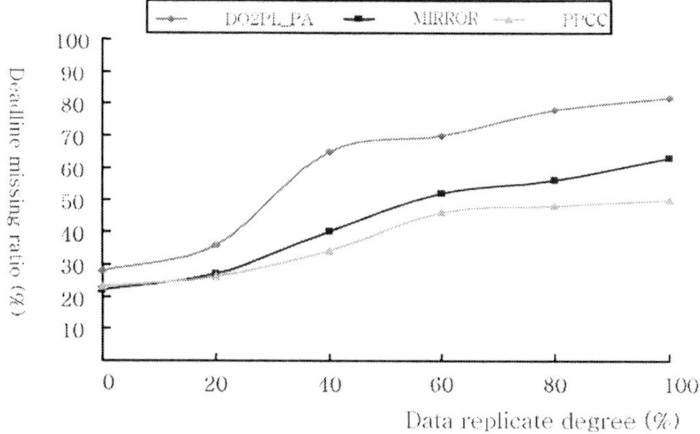

Fig. 6. Data replicate degree and Missed deadline

We could know that the performance of DO2PL using PA is worst. The reason is that transactions in the voting phase can be aborted by higher priority transactions while the PPCC and MIRROR guarantee them to commit. As a result, Figures show that the PPCC is slightly better than the MIRROR because we apply the lending/borrowing scheme to the PPC.

5 Conclusions

In this paper, we have proposed a novel replica distributed concurrency control algorithm, called the PPCC. The features of the PPCC are as followings. First, it promotes priority of transactions that enter the voting phase to guarantee them to commit. Introducing promoting priority scheme, we use just PA as a conflict resolution method while MIRROR uses both PA and PB. Second, we adapted borrowing/lending scheme of the OPT to our algorithm. Finally, the PPCC does not require synchronizations or additional communications with other sites to acquire the state knowledge like the MIRROR. We have also shown through the experiments that our concurrency control scheme achieves better performance than other existing schemes. In the further research, we will adapt the PPCC to the optimistic distributed real-time concurrency control protocol such as OCC-Sacrifice, OCC-Wait, and Wait 50. We will also compare them with the PPCC

Acknowledgement

This work was supported by grant No. (1999-1-303-007-3) from the Basic Research Program of the Korea Science & Engineering Foundation.

References

1. Baothman, F., Sarje, A.K. and Joshi, R.C. "On optimistic concurrency control for RTDBS," TENCON '98. 1998 IEEE Region 10 International Conference on Global Connectivity in Energy, Computer, Communication and Control Volume: 2 , Page(s): 615 -618 vol.2, 1998.
2. Carey, M., and Linvy, M., "Conflict Detection Tradeoffs for Replicated Data," ACM Transactions on Database Systems, Vol. 16, Page(s): 703-746, 1991.
3. C. Mohan, B. Lindsay and R. Obermarck, "Transaction Management in the R* Distributed Database Management System" , ACM TODS, 11(4), 1986.
4. Haritsa, J.. R. and Carey, M.J.; Livny, M. "Dynamic real-time optimistic concurrency control," Real-Time Systems Symposium, Proceedings., 11th , 1990 , Page(s): 94 -103, 1990.
5. Michael J. Carey. and Miron Livny. "Distributed Concurrency Control Performance: A Study of Algorithm, Distribution, and Replication," Proceedings of the 14th VLDB Conference, Los Angels, California Page(s): 13 –25, 1988.
6. Son, S., "Advances In Real-Time Systems," Prentice Hall, 1995.
7. Thomasian, A. "Distributed optimistic concurrency control methods for high-performance transaction processing," Knowledge and Data Engineering, IEEE Transactions on Volume: 10 1, Jan.-Feb. 1998.
8. Xiong, M., Ramamritham, K., Haritsa, J., and Stankovic, J., "MIRROR: A State-Conscious Concurrency Control Protocol in Replicated Real-time Database," Technical Report 98-36, Department of Computer Science, University of Massachusetts at Amherst, 1998.
9. E. Levy, H. Korth and A. Silberschatz, "An optimistic commit protocol for distributed transaction management", Proc. of ACM SIGMOD Conf., May 1991.
10. Anderson, T., Breitbart, Y., Korth, H. and Wool, A., ``Replication, Consistency, and Practicality: Are These Mutually Exclusive" Proceedings of the ACM-SIGMOD 1998 International Conference on Management of Data, Seattle, WA., Page(s) 484-495, 1998.
11. Agrawal, R., Carey, M., and McVoy, L., "The Performance of Alternative Strategies for Dealing With Deadlocks in Database Management Systems", IEEE TOSE, Dec 1987.
12. Ciciani, B., Dias, D. M., Yu, P. S., ``Analysis of Replication in Distributed Database Systems," IEEE Transactions on Knowledge and Data Engineering, Vol. 2, No. 2, June 1990.
13. Gray, J., ``Notes On Database Operating Systems," in Operating Systems: An Advanced Course, R. Bayer, R. Graham, and G. Seegmuller, eds., Springer-verlag, 1979.
14. Ulusoy, O., ``Processing Real-Time Transactions in a Replicated Database System," Distributed and Parallel Databases, 2, Page(s) 405-436, 1994.
15. Wu, K.L., Yu, P.S. and Pu, C., ``Divergence Control for Epsilon-Serializability," In Proceedings of Eighth International Conference on Data Engineering, Phoenix, February 1992.

A New Look at Timestamp Ordering Concurrency Control

Rashmi Srinivasa, Craig Williams, and Paul F. Reynolds Jr.

Department of Computer Science, University of Virginia, Charlottesville, VA 22904
{rashmi, craigw, reynolds}@cs.virginia.edu

Abstract. Popular conception has been that timestamp ordering concurrency control (CC) yields poor transaction processing performance in relation to two-phase locking (2PL). This paper makes two contributions. First, we show the surprising result that Basic Timestamp Ordering (BTO) performs better than 2PL in all cases except when both data contention and message latency are low. When latency or data contention is high, BTO significantly outperforms 2PL. Our second contribution is a new timestamp ordering CC technique (PREDICT) that performs better than 2PL and BTO under low data contention, and continues to perform well under high data contention. We evolve a set of variants of PREDICT, and demonstrate that PREDICT achieves a good balance between lost opportunity cost and restart cost, and outperforms popular CC techniques.

1 Introduction

Concurrency control (CC), an integral part of a database system, is the coordination of concurrent transactions that access shared data and potentially interfere [1]. Two costs are associated with CC: lost opportunity and restart cost. The former cost is significant in conservative methods which involve waiting to ensure that there will be no conflict. Restart cost is significant in aggressive methods which optimistically execute transactions, and restart some transactions if a conflict does arise. A scalable CC technique that has low lost opportunity and restart costs is a desired goal.

Dynamic two-phase locking (2PL) is the CC technique that databases use almost exclusively [2], but it causes thrashing at high data contention. Popular conception has been that timestamp ordering techniques perform poorly as compared to 2PL. In previous studies, Basic Timestamp Ordering (BTO) has been shown to perform poorly because its high restart rate causes it to reach a performance limit imposed by available hardware resources. In light of today's faster processors, it is time to reevaluate BTO. We show the surprising result that BTO outperforms 2PL in all cases except when data contention and message latency are both low. When latency or data contention is high, BTO significantly outperforms 2PL.

The second contribution of this paper is a new timestamp ordering CC technique — PREDICT — that performs well under different levels of data contention. Under low data contention, PREDICT outperforms both 2PL and BTO. Under high data contention, PREDICT outperforms 2PL and its performance is slightly worse than that of BTO. We evolve a set of variants of the PREDICT technique based on reasonable assumptions about network characteristics in a distributed database system. We demonstrate that PREDICT achieves a good balance between lost opportunity cost and restart cost and outperforms popular CC techniques for a wide range of workloads.

H.C. Mayr et al. (Eds.): DEXA 2001, LNCS 2113, pp. 943–952, 2001.

2 Background

We consider a distributed database management system (DDBMS) — a collection of clients and servers interconnected by a network. Each client runs a software module called the transaction manager (TM). Each server runs a data manager (DM) and a concurrency control scheduler (CCS). TMs supervise interactions between users and the DDBMS, CCSs coordinate transactions, and DMs manage data [1]. The database is a collection of data items or *objects*, and each object is managed by a single DM. Users interact with the DDBMS by executing transactions. In order to execute a transaction, a client issues *read*, *predeclare*, *write*, *commit*, *lock-release* and *abort* operations to the servers. A server responds with *read-response*s and *lock-set*s.

CC techniques have been classified as locking, timestamp ordering, optimistic or hybrid [1, 3, 4]. In dynamic 2PL, locks are acquired on demand and in a two-phase manner, and a strategy to prevent or detect deadlocks is required. In BTO, transactions are assigned timestamps when they start execution, and the CCS executes operations in timestamp order, rejecting any operation that arrives too late. A rejected operation results in the transaction being aborted and restarted. 2PL has been shown to outperform BTO in a centralized database system [5]. Another study has reported that 2PL outperforms BTO for a single server connected to clients over a network [6], but the study does not model hardware resource contention. BTO has been reported to perform worse than 2PL in a distributed database for low data contention [7]. The non-replicated case in the study assumes that all of a transaction's accesses are local. The replicated cases assume that the primary copies of all objects accessed by a transaction are located at a single site. There have been no prior studies of the performance of BTO in a truly distributed database environment and a high level of data contention.

3 Qualitative Comparison of BTO to Dynamic 2PL

An important difference between BTO and dynamic 2PL (referred to as simply 2PL in the rest of this paper) is that in 2PL, a lock is acquired as a result of a *read*, whereas in BTO, a *read* does not result in lock acquisition. In both schemes, *write*s have the effect of making the object unavailable until the *write*s are committed. 2PL and BTO also differ with respect to deadlocks. Since deadlock cannot occur in BTO, deadlock detection is unnecessary, while servers in 2PL incur deadlock detection costs. Both techniques have a restart cost, but restarts in 2PL result from deadlock breakage, while restarts in BTO are caused by conflicting operations arriving out of timestamp order. On commit, a client in 2PL must send *lock-releases* to the servers in order to release *read* locks. BTO does not incur this cost since it does not use *read* locks. The overall effect of these differences on performance is explored in §5.

4 A New Timestamp Ordering Technique: PREDICT

We propose a new timestamp ordering technique, PREDICT, that provides a mechanism to control the amount of restart behaviour. PREDICT is based on the *predictability* property, which allows the sender of a message to predict the time by which the message will have arrived at its destinations, where *time* is real-time or logical time in a time frame valid for the system. When a client issues the operations of a transaction, it can predict the time t by which the operations will be delivered to all destinations. The client can schedule the transaction to be executed at a time equal to or later than t. It is possible for the transaction to be executed at the scheduled time at all destinations, since the network guarantees that the transaction's operations will be delivered before the scheduled time.

While perfect predictability in real-time is difficult to achieve, most networks can guarantee imperfect predictability. Studies of network transmission delays have shown that a majority (80-95%) of messages are delivered within a bound of about 1.5-2.5 times the average message latency, while the remaining messages can take an unpredictably long time to reach their destinations [8, 9]. We show that a distributed database can make use of even this imperfect predictability to achieve low restart cost.

Other systems have made the assumption of predictable message delivery for other purposes. An optimistic CC technique that prunes validation information based on loosely synchronized clocks has been proposed [10]. The technique assumes that some synchronization mechanism like Network Time Protocol [11] guarantees bounded clock skews and message transmission delays. Some work on atomic broadcast uses the assumption of bounded transmission delays [12].

We first explain the PREDICT CC technique assuming that the network provides perfect predictability, and then describe why the algorithm works even under imperfect predictability. PREDICT requires transactions to predeclare their accesses. A TM starts the execution of a transaction by issuing all the *read*s and *predeclare*s of the transaction as an atomic action. The network assigns timestamp t to this atomic action, where t is the time by which all the operations will have reached their destinations. On receipt of operation o, the network receiver has two options in delivering o:

1. The conservative option is to wait until time t to deliver o. If all servers execute a transaction's operations at time t, then a total order of transactions is achieved.
2. The aggressive option is to deliver o before time t. The server then rejects conflicting operations that arrive out of timestamp order. Rejected operations cause transaction restarts. The amount of restart behaviour can be estimated and controlled by the difference between t and the delivery time. The control over restart behaviour might be adaptive, based on past behaviour of the system.

The *aggressive limit* is the maximum time interval a receiver allows between the timestamp and delivery time of an operation. On receipt of an operation timestamped t at time t_r, the receiver delivers the operation immediately if $(t-t_r) <=$ aggressive limit. Otherwise, the receiver waits until the time (t-aggressive limit) to deliver the operation. The aggressive limit can vary from zero to no_limit. If the aggressive limit is zero, the receiver always delivers an operation at its timestamp, and the network is delivering transaction operations in a total order. If the aggressive limit is no_limit, the receiver always delivers operations immediately on receipt. The more the aggressive limit, the higher the probability of abort. In addition, a high variance in network latency implies a high probability of messages arriving out of order and hence a high probability of abort. PREDICT can perform well if the number of aborts is sufficiently low.

A server can accept or reject a delivered operation, and buffers accepted *read*s and *predeclare*s in queues corresponding to the object accessed. The server maintains two values — maxRTS and maxWTS — for every object that it stores. These values are the maximum timestamps of *read* and *predeclare* operations that the server has accepted. When the network receiver delivers a *read* with timestamp t to the server, the server rejects the *read* if $t <$ maxWTS for that object. When the network receiver delivers a *predeclare* with timestamp t to the server, the server rejects the *predeclare* if $t <$ maxRTS or $t <$ maxWTS for that object. If the server accepts an operation, it appends the operation to the tail of the appropriate queue, sending an explicit *lock-set* to the client if the operation is a *predeclare*. (Read-responses double as accept notifications for the *read*s.) The server immediately executes a *read* by sending it to the DM, if the *read* is at the head of its queue. As a transaction receives *read* responses, it issues *write*s corresponding to the previously-issued *predeclare*s. The TM does not send these *write*s across the network, but stores them locally. When a transaction has received responses to all of its *read*s and *predeclare*s and has issued all of its *write*s, the transaction issues *commit*s for every *predeclare* that it issued. On the other hand, if the client receives a *reject*, or if it decides to perform a unilateral abort, the client sends out *abort*s for every *predeclare* that it issued. The TM sends *commit*s (carrying the values of the corresponding *write*s) and *abort*s as regular messages rather than timestamped messages. The network does not have to guarantee predictable message delivery for these *commit*s or *abort*s. On receipt of a *commit*, the destination finds the corresponding *predeclare* on its queue, replaces the *predeclare* with a committed *write*, and executes any committed *write*s and *read*s that are ready to be executed. On receipt of an *abort*, a destination finds the corresponding *predeclare*, deletes the *predeclare*, and executes any committed *write*s and *read*s that are ready to be executed. A transaction is complete when all its operations have been committed or aborted.

The network may provide imperfect predictability, in that operations may not always arrive before their timestamp. The algorithm guarantees correct execution even with imperfect predictability. An operation that arrives late simply has a higher probability of rejection. Imperfect predictability does affect performance. The better the network at predicting message delivery time, the lower the restart cost. The predictable delivery guarantee is required only for *read*s and *predeclare*s, and not for other messages. This implies that quality-of-service techniques can be used in order to provide predictable delivery for this limited class of messages.

4.1 Qualitative Comparison of PREDICT to 2PL and BTO

PREDICT differs from 2PL in all the ways in which BTO differs from 2PL (§3), and also in the following ways. PREDICT assumes that the network provides a measure of predictability in message delivery, while 2PL and BTO make no such assumption. A transaction in PREDICT is forced to predeclare all of its accesses, while in 2PL and BTO, access requests are made on demand. Predeclaration allows access requests to be made early, but may result in a longer object-holding time. (The object-holding time is the time for which a *read*, *write* or *predeclare* holds an object, making it unavailable to other transactions.) A difference between PREDICT and BTO is that a network receiver in PREDICT can delay the delivery of a message in order to decrease the probability of abort. Finally, a CCS in PREDICT immediately rejects operations that were delivered out of order. A BTO scheduler accepts operations that were delivered out of order but that can still be executed in timestamp order. A variant of PREDICT is possible in which the CCS behaves like the one in BTO. We propose to study this variant in future work. Note that rejecting operations increases restart cost, but may improve object availability by keeping queues short. Wait-depth locking (WDL) is a variant of 2PL that restricts queue lengths at the expense of restarts [13]. A comparative study of WDL with timestamp ordering methods is left to future work.

5 Performance Evaluation

In addition to BTO, 2PL and PREDICT, we simulated a best-case algorithm that we call Zero-Cost (ZC). ZC assumes no data conflicts and no concurrency control overhead, and *read*s and *write*s are executed immediately without being queued. ZC allows us to isolate the effects of hardware contention from data contention and ordering costs. Note that ZC guarantees a correct execution only in the absence of data contention. Servers in our 2PL simulation do local as well as global deadlock detection using waits-for graphs, but the cost of deadlock detection is set to zero. Locks can be shared or exclusive, with no upgrade from shared to exclusive. When a transaction is aborted in any scheme, a new transaction is started in order to simulate a restart. PREDICT uses a network that provides imperfect predictability, in that the clients know the 90th percentile of the network's delay distribution and use it as the estimated worst-case message latency. In other words, 90% of all messages arrive within the estimated worst-case time, and 10% arrive later. We model message latency as an exponential distribution; therefore, the estimated worst-case message latency (90th percentile of the distribution) is approximately 2.303 times the average

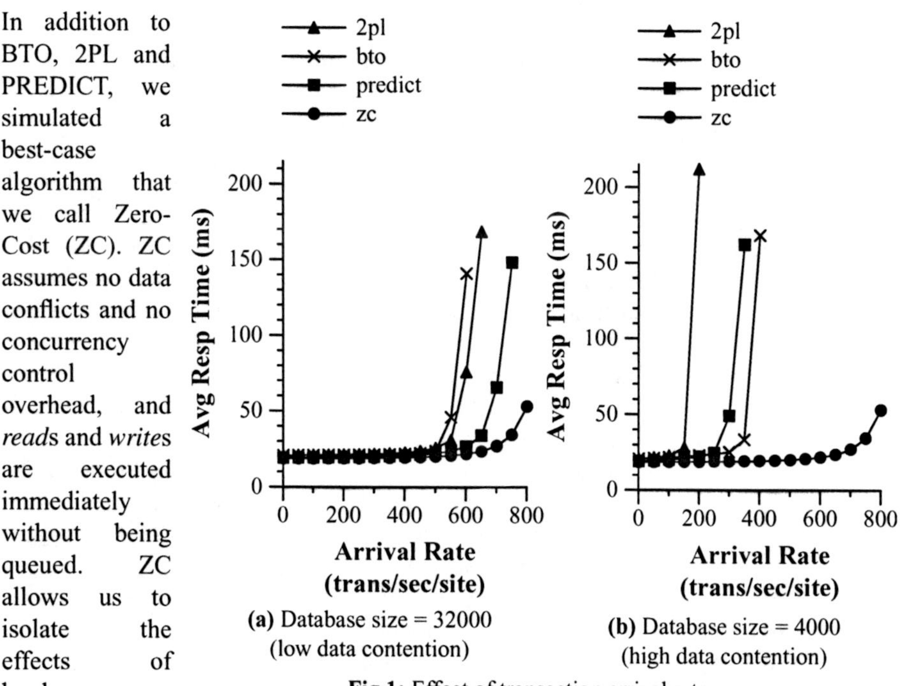

(a) Database size = 32000 (low data contention)

(b) Database size = 4000 (high data contention)

Fig 1: Effect of transaction arrival rate

latency. We assume the network is not a bottleneck at the load levels we are modelling. We model the degree of aggressiveness of the network by the *aggressiveness* parameter, measured as a percentage of the worst-case message latency. The aggressive limit is the maximum interval a receiver will allow between the timestamp and the delivery time of an operation, and is calculated as (aggressiveness * estimated worst-case message latency). Therefore, the aggressive limit can vary from zero to the estimated worst-case message latency. Our baseline parameters [14] are standard ones culled from recent performance studies of CC techniques. Our default average latency is 1.5ms, and default aggressiveness is 50%. We use a b-c pattern of hot spot access, where a fraction *b* of accesses go to a fraction *c* of the database, and $b > c$ [15]. The method of independent replications was used to obtain an accurate estimate of transaction response time. The values in the graphs are midpoints of a confidence interval which is 1% of the sample mean on each side at a 90% confidence level. Wider confidence intervals (<5%) were tolerated in regions approaching peak performance.

5.1 Transaction Arrival Rate and Database Size

Figure 1 shows the effect of varying arrival rate and database size. As arrival rate increases, response time increases for all schemes, hitting a *knee* and then rising steeply as the system goes into an unstable region. The knee for ZC is due to hardware resource contention. For 2PL, BTO and PREDICT, the knee occurs at a lower arrival rate because of data contention. The larger database (size = 32000) represents the case when hardware resource contention is the dominating factor, and the smaller database (size = 4000) represents the case when data contention is the dominating factor. The former case will be called the *low data contention* scenario, and the latter will be referred to as the *high data contention* scenario.

There are two important factors that affect performance of CC schemes - CCS queue length and restart behaviour. As CCS queue lengths increase, operation wait time increases, which increases transaction response time. The increased response time increases object-holding time, which causes queues to get longer. This iterative build-up of data contention is an important cause of performance degradation in all three schemes. The amount of restart behaviour also affects performance. A large number of restarts puts pressure on the hardware resources available, and degrades performance. As processor speeds increase, performance becomes less sensitive to restarts, and it becomes necessary to reevaluate restart-oriented schemes like BTO, which have been perceived as poor performers until now.

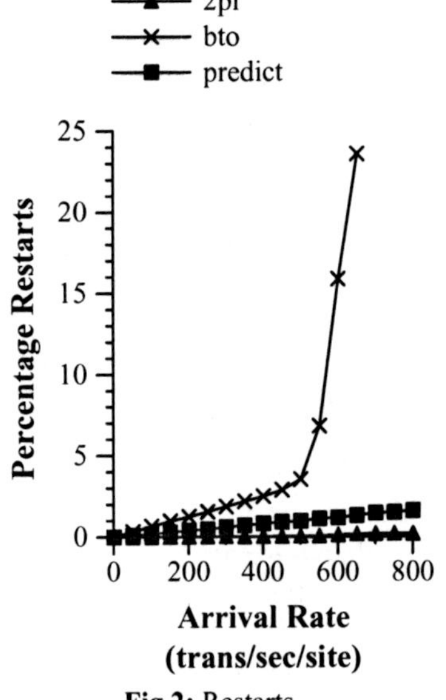

Fig 2: Restarts (low data contention)

Performance of BTO. BTO performs slightly worse than 2PL under low data contention, but significantly outperforms 2PL when data contention is high. The reason for BTO's poor performance under low data contention is apparent in Figure 2 which plots the percentage of restarts. As arrival rate increases, more and more operations arrive out of order in BTO and are rejected. The large number of restarts causes a knee in the performance of BTO due to high hardware resource contention. The percentage of restarts in 2PL is much lower than that in BTO, since deadlocks are not very frequent. BTO succumbs to a large number of restarts and performs worse than 2PL.

BTO significantly outperforms 2PL when data contention is high. The reason for this surprising result is found through an examination of the CCS queue lengths. Figure 3a shows the average queue length for the high data contention scenario. As in the low data contention scenario, restarts increase steadily in BTO, but before BTO can reach a knee due to high hardware resource contention, the steep rise in the number of restarts is reversed (Figure 3b). The reason for this reversal is that the average queue length increases, increasing operation wait time on the CCS queues. The effect of the increased operation wait time is to allow late-arriving operations to be inserted into the queue in timestamp order. This effect reduces the number of rejected operations and, therefore, the number of restarts in BTO. Instead of reaching a knee due to high hardware resource contention, BTO continues until it reaches a knee due to data contention and long queue lengths. The effective queue lengths in BTO are lower than those in 2PL, since *reads* do not lock objects in BTO. This phenomenon allows BTO to significantly outperform 2PL. The reversal of the steep increase in restarts does not occur in the low data contention scenario, because queue lengths are still low when BTO reaches its knee.

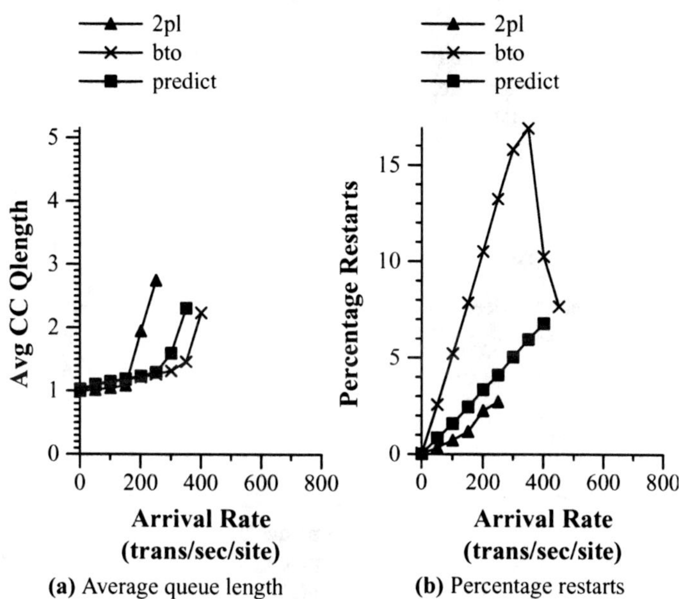

(a) Average queue length **(b)** Percentage restarts

Fig 3: Queue lengths and restarts (high data contention)

Performance of PREDICT. PREDICT outperforms 2PL under low data contention as well as high data contention (Figure 1). Since PREDICT does not require *read* locks, queue lengths in PREDICT stay lower than in 2PL (Figure 3a). Therefore, the performance knee due to data contention occurs at a higher load in PREDICT than in

2PL. At the same time, the number of restarts in PREDICT are not high enough to cause significant deterioration in performance (Figure 2 and Figure 3b).

Since PREDICT predeclares all of its accesses, the probability of operations arriving out of timestamp order is lower in PREDICT than in BTO. Therefore, the number of restarts in PREDICT is lower. This difference in the number of restarts allows PREDICT to outperform BTO in the low data contention scenario. Unlike BTO, PREDICT does not succumb to a knee due to high hardware resource contention. However, BTO outperforms PREDICT under high data contention, because queue lengths in BTO are slightly lower than those in PREDICT (since BTO accesses objects on demand instead of using predeclaration). In summary, while both BTO and PREDICT reduce the lost opportunity cost by keeping operation wait time low, PREDICT also manages to keep the restart cost low. This allows PREDICT to outperform 2PL under both levels of data contention.

5.2 Message Latency and Aggressiveness

We studied the effect of message latency and degree of aggressiveness, in the low data contention scenario. The results are shown in Figure 4. PREDICT is represented by three different curves, depending on the value of the aggressiveness parameter. The *predict-50* curve uses an aggressiveness of 50%, and corresponds to the *PREDICT* curves presented in earlier graphs.

Performance of BTO. As the message latency increases, operations take longer to arrive, and the object-holding times in all three schemes increase, increasing response time. Moreover, at a higher message latency, the object-holding time is higher, which implies that for a given arrival rate, there is a higher probability of data conflict. Therefore, the data contention knee occurs at a lower

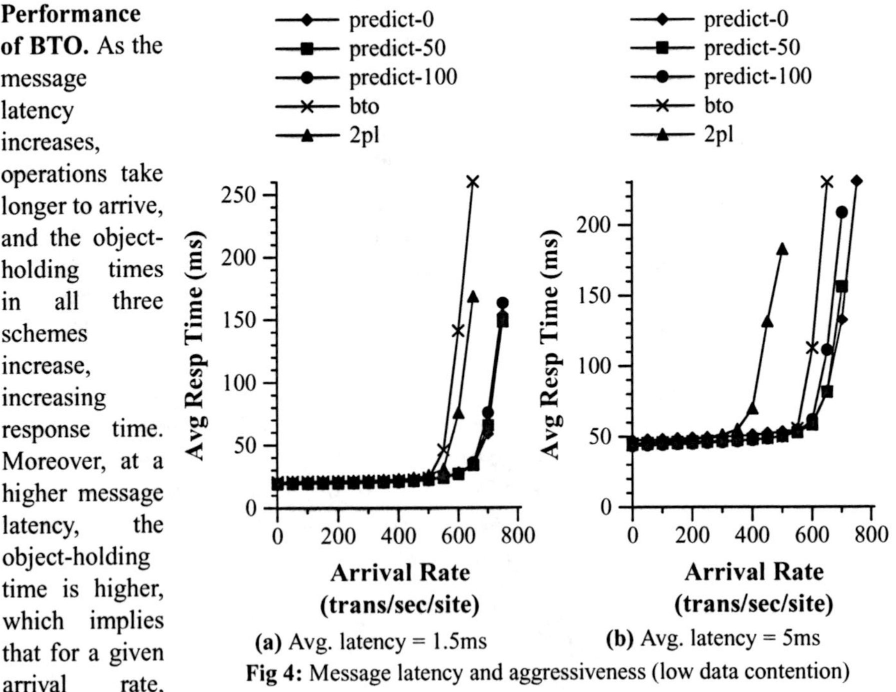

(a) Avg. latency = 1.5ms **(b)** Avg. latency = 5ms

Fig 4: Message latency and aggressiveness (low data contention)

arrival rate when message latency is high. As the message latency increases, the data contention knee of 2PL occurs at lower arrival rates. For high message latency (5ms), the data contention knee of 2PL occurs earlier than the hardware contention knee of BTO. This allows BTO to outperform 2PL at high message latencies (Figure 4b).

Performance of PREDICT. In order to discover how aggressive the network should be in delivering operations, we studied the effect of three different values — 0%, 50% and 100% — for aggressiveness. The higher the aggressiveness, the greater the probability of late-arriving operations, and the higher the probability of abort for PREDICT. On the other hand, the lower the aggressiveness, the longer the network waits before delivering operations, and some of this waiting may be unnecessary if there is little data conflict. Reducing the aggressiveness increases the lost opportunity cost but reduces the restart cost. Increasing the aggressiveness increases the restart cost but reduces the lost opportunity cost. At an average message latency of 1.5ms, all of the PREDICT variants perform better than 2PL, in terms of both the arrival rate at the performance knee, and the average response time at all loads. The number of aborts does increase as the degree of aggressiveness goes up, but the amount of restart behaviour is not high enough to significantly affect overall performance. The effect of varying the degree of aggressiveness is more apparent in the graph for higher message latency. At a latency of 5ms, all of the PREDICT variants still outperform 2PL in terms of knee arrival rate, but the response time of predict-0 is higher than that of 2PL for low arrival rates. This difference in response time at low arrival rates is up to 2ms, and is due to the high lost opportunity cost in predict-0. However, predict-50 and predict-100 have lower response times than 2PL even at low arrival rates. For the cases we studied, it paid to be aggressive (predict-50 and predict-100) when the message latency was high, at the cost of more restarts. In all cases, predict-50 performed slightly better than or as well as the other PREDICT variants.

Increasing the message latency causes a scheme's data contention knee to occur at a lower arrival rate, but does not significantly affect the hardware contention knee. Under low data contention, the hardware contention knee is the dominant factor in the performance of BTO, while the data contention knee is the dominant factor in PREDICT's performance. Therefore, BTO and PREDICT are affected differently by changes in message latency. As the message latency increases, the data contention knee of PREDICT occurs at lower arrival rates, approaching the hardware contention knee of BTO. Therefore, the performance of PREDICT approaches that of BTO as message latency increases.

6 Conclusion

Dynamic 2PL causes system thrashing at high data contention levels, restricting transaction throughput. Popular conception has been that timestamp ordering techniques perform poorly as compared to 2PL. We have shown the surprising result that the performance of BTO is better than that of 2PL in all cases except when both data contention and message latency are low. When message latency or data contention is high, BTO performs significantly better than 2PL.

We have also presented a new timestamp ordering CC technique — PREDICT — that performs well under different levels of data contention. Under low data contention, PREDICT outperforms both 2PL and BTO. Under high data contention, PREDICT outperforms 2PL, but BTO performs somewhat better than PREDICT. We have evolved a set of variants of the PREDICT technique based on reasonable assumptions about network characteristics in a distributed database system. We have demonstrated through simulation that PREDICT achieves a good balance between lost opportunity cost and restart cost, and outperforms popular CC techniques. In future work, we plan to study the effect of high-variance network latencies, queue-length-limiting rules and transaction size and composition on BTO, PREDICT and 2PL.

7 References

1. Bernstein P. A., Hadzilacos V., Goodman N.: Concurrency Control and Recovery in Database Systems, Addison-Wesley, 1987.
2. Gray J. N., Reuter A.: Transaction Processing: Concepts and Facilities, Morgan-Kaufmann, 1992.
3. Thomasian A.: Concurrency Control: Methods, Performance, and Analysis, *ACM Computing Surveys 30/1*, Mar. 1998, pp 70-119.
4. Yu P., Wu K., Lin K., Son S.: On Real-Time Databases: Concurrency Control and Scheduling, *Proc. of the IEEE 82/1*, Jan. 1994.
5. Ryu I. K., Thomasian A.: Performance Analysis of Dynamic Locking with the No-Waiting Policy, *IEEE Trans. on Software Engg. 16/7*, pp 684-698, Jul. 1990.
6. Lin, Nolte: Basic Timestamp, Multiple Version Timestamp and 2-Phase Locking, *Proc. of the 9th VLDB Conf.*, Nov. 1983.
7. Carey M., Livny: Conflict Detection Tradeoffs for Replicated Data, *ACM Transactions on Database Systems 16/4*, pp 703-746, Dec. 1991.
8. Cristian F.: Probabilistic Clock Synchronization, *Distributed Computing 3*, pp 146-158, 1989.
9. Wang J., Keshav S.: Efficient and Accurate Ethernet Simulation, *Proc. of the 24th Conf. on Local Computer Networks (LCN '99)*, Oct. 1999.
10. Adya A., Gruber R., Liskov B., Maheshwari U.: Efficient Optimistic Concurrency Control Using Loosely Synchronized Clocks, *Proc. of the ACM SIGMOD Int. Conf. on the Management of Data*, May 1995.
11. Mills D. L.: Network Time Protocol: Specification and Implementation, *DARPA-Internet Report RFC 1059*, DARPA, Jul. 1988.
12. Cristian F.: Synchronous Atomic Broadcast for Redundant Broadcast Channels, *IBM Research Report RJ 7203*, Dec. 1989.
13. Franaszek, Robinson: Distributed Concurrency Control Based on Limited Wait Depth, *IEEE Trans. on Parallel and Distributed Systems 4/11*, Nov. 1993, pp 1246-1264.
14. Srinivasa R., Williams C., Reynolds P. F.: Distributed Transaction Processing on an Ordering Network, *Technical Report CS-2001-08*, Dept. of Computer Science, Univ. of Virginia, Feb. 2001.
15. Tay Y., Goodman N., Suri R.: Locking Performance in Centralized Databases, *ACM Trans. on Database Systems 10/4*, Dec. 1985, pp 415-462.

On the Evaluation of Path-oriented Queries in Document Databases

Yangjun Chen
Dept. Business Computing
Winnipeg University, Canada
ychen2@uwinnipeg.ca

Gerald Huck
IPSI Institute, GMD GmbH
64293 Darmstadt, Germany
huck@darmstadt.gmd.de

Abstract. In this paper, we propose a new indexing technique: path signature to speed up the path-oriented query evaluation in document databases, by which the paths appearing in a query are fully employed to avoid access to non-related elements. In addition, this technique can be further enhanced by using the so-called signature trees over signature files to expedite scanning of path signatures. Experiments were performed to show that this technique brings really substantial advantages.

1. Introduction

As XML (Extensible Markup Language) is emerging as the data format of the internet era, more needs to efficiently store and query XML data arise. Recently, a lot of efforts have been directed to the integration of database technology into this area to manage documents efficiently.

In this paper, we propose an indexing technique to speed up the evaluation of queries against documents stored structurally. In our system, a document is decomposed into a set of elements and distributed over several relations (tables). In this way, index structures provided in database management system can be used. Especially, we introduce two new indexing techniques: *path signatures* and *signature trees*. The path signatures are used to avoid traversal along useless paths to expedite path-oriented queries. The signature trees are constructed over signature files to speed up the scanning of path signatures. The combination of these two techniques can raise the efficiency by an order of magnitude or more. In summary, the following two benefits can be obtained using our method:

(1) The space overhead for path encoding is low.

(2) Indexing structure can be established over signatures themselves to speed up retrieval of the relevant elements.

The rest of this paper is organized as follows. In Section 2, we give our system architecture to provide a background for the subsequent discussion. Section 3 is devoted to storage of documents in databases. In Section 4, we discuss the technique of path signatures and its combination with signature trees. Section 5 reports the experiment results. Finally, Section 6 is a short conclusion.

2. Logical architecture of the system

In this section, we briefly outline the logical architecture of our system which consists mainly of three parts:

(1) (*parser and base relations*) In the database of the system, documents are stored in several tables. Any document to be stored in the database will be syntactically analyzed and then decomposed into a set of elements, attributes and texts.

The first author is supported by NSERC 239074-01 (242523) (Natural Sciences and Engineering Council of Canada).

H.C. Mayr et al. (Eds.): DEXA 2001, LNCS 2113, pp. 953–962, 2001.

(2) (*query transformation*) A path-oriented query issued by users or from an application will be translated into several SQL queries executable in the corresponding platform database system.

(3) (*output format*) The results of a query will be reorganized into a new XML document by "output format" processor.

Fig. 1 is a pictorial description of the system architecture.

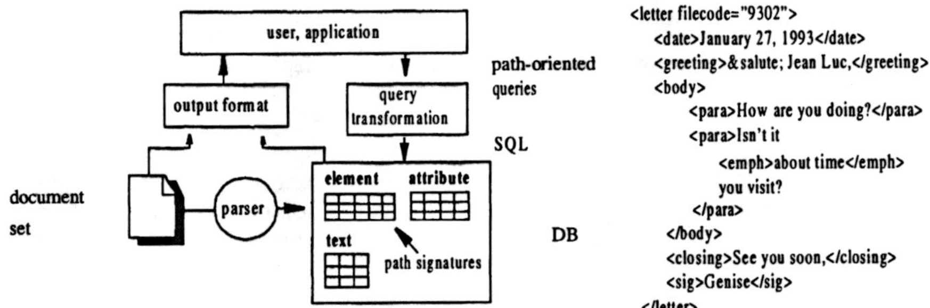


```
<letter filecode="9302">
   <date>January 27, 1993</date>
   <greeting>&salute; Jean Luc,</greeting>
   <body>
      <para>How are you doing?</para>
      <para>Isn't it
         <emph>about time</emph>
         you visit?
      </para>
   </body>
   <closing>See you soon,</closing>
   <sig>Genise</sig>
</letter>
```

Fig. 1. Logical architecture of the system

Fig. 2. A simple XML document

In this system, the path signatures are used to support efficient query evaluation, which are implemented as the values of a hidden attribute of the relation for elements or organized into a tree structure to optimize the signature scanning.

3. Storage of documents in DB

An XML document is defined as having elements and attributes [DD94]. Elements are always marked up with tags; and an element may be associated with several attributes to identify domain-specific information. XML processors (or parsers) guarantee that XML documents stored in databases follow tagging rules prescribed in XML or conform to a DTD (Document Type Descriptor, which specifies what elements may occur and how the elements may nest in an XML document).

3.1 Tree structure representation of an XML document

An XML document can be represented as a tree, and node types in the tree are of three kinds: Element, Attribute and Text. These node types are equivalent to the node types in XSL [W3C98b] data model. There are some other less important node types such as comments, processing instructions, etc. The treatment of those node types is trivial and thus will not be discussed here.

- Nodes of type Element have an element name as the label. Each Element node has zero or more child nodes. The type of each child node is of one of the three types (Element, Attribute and Text).
- Nodes of type Attribute have an attribute name and an attribute value as a label. Attribute nodes have no child nodes. If there are multiple appearances of attributes, the order of the attributes will be ignored since the attribute order is normally not important for the document treatment.
- Nodes of type Text have strings as labels. Text nodes have no child nodes.

In Fig. 3, we show the tree structure representing the XML document shown in Fig. 2.

In Fig. 3, "#PCDATA" represents a data type which is more or less comparable to strings, used to accommodate text data.

3.2 Storing documents

To store documents in databases efficiently, the policies shown below should be followed:

- (*DTD independent*) Database schemas to store XML documents should not depend on DTDs or element types. Any XML document can be manipulated, based on the predefined relations.
- (*no loss of structural information*) The structure of a document stored in a database should be implemented in such a way that it can be operated.
- (*easy maintenance*) The cost of the maintenance of the document structure should be kept minimum. Any update to a document will not cause the storage changes of other documents.

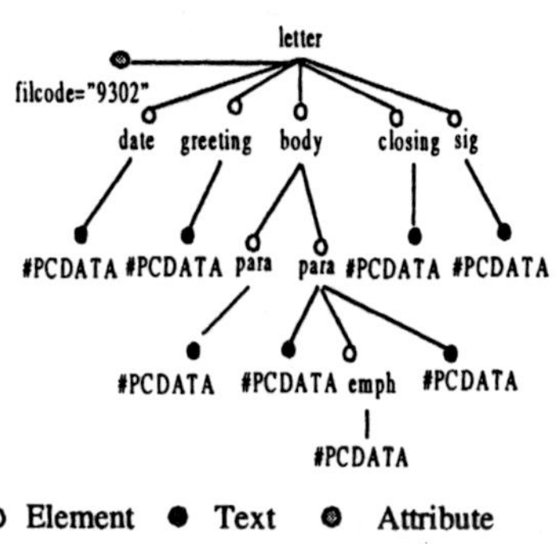

Fig. 3. Tree structure for a Document

Table 1: Element

docID	ID	Ename	parentID
1	1	letter	*
1	2	date	1
1	3	greeting	1
1	4	body	1
1	5	para	4
1	6	para	4
1	7	emph	6
1	8	closing	1
1	9	sig	1

Table 2: Text

docID	parentID	value
1	2	January 27, 1993
1	3	&salut, ...
1	5	How are you ...
1	6	Isn't it
1	7	about time
1	6	you visit?
1	8	See you soon
1	9	Genise

Table 3: Attribute

docID	parentID	att-name	att-value
1	1	filecode	9302

To reach above goals, we decompose a document into a set of elements and distribute them over three relations named: Element, Text and Attribute, respectively.

The relation Element has the following structure:
{DocID: <integer>, ID: <integer>, Ename: <string>, parentID: <integer>}.

where DocID represents the document identifier,
ID represents the element identifier,
Ename is the element name (or tag name) and
parentID is the pointer to the element's parent.

For example, the document given in Fig. 2 may be stored in such a table as shown in Table 1.

The relation Text has a more simple structure:

{DocID: <integer>, parentID: <integer>, value: <string>},

where "parentID" is for the identifiers of elements (stored in relation "Element") which have the corresponding text values in the original document. One should notice that a text takes always an element as the parent node. SeeTable 2 for illustration.

The relation Attribute has the following structure:

{DocID: <integer>, parentID: <integer>, att-name: <string>, att-value: <string>}.

As with the relation "Text", "parentID" is for the identifiers of elements (stored in relation "Element"), in which the corresponding attribute appears. Table 3 helps for a better understanding.

From the above discussion, we can see that the tree structure is implemented through the "parentID" in the relation "Element", which contains pointers from child nodes to their parents. Together with the technique of path signatures to be discussed in the next section, it is especially effective for the evaluation of path-oriented queries since it is quite often to check a path bottom-up after a signature matching succeeds. But it suffers from a serious performance problem when a top-down search is desired. This can be solved by assigning each element e a pair of integers (l_e, h_e) such that if element a is an ancestor of element b, then $(l_a, h_a) \supseteq (l_b, h_b)$. This property makes it easy to find all descendants of an element in terms of our storage strategy discussed above. However, how to determine such pairs is beyond the scope of this paper. We shift the corresponding discussion in another paper in preparation.

4. Path-oriented language and path signatures

Now we discuss our indexing technique. To this end, we first outline the path-oriented language in 4.1. Then, the concept of path signatures will be described in 4.2. In 4.3, we will discuss the combination of path signatures and signature trees, and the corresponding algorithm in great detail.

4.1 Path-oriented language

Several path-oriented language such as XQL [RLS98] and XML-QL [DFF98] have been proposed to manipulate tree-like structures as well as attributes and cross-references of XML documents. XQL is a natural extension to the XSL pattern syntax, providing a concise, understandable notation for pointing to specific elements and for searching nodes with particular characteristics. On the other hand, XML-QL has operations specific to data manipulation such as joins and supports transformations of XML data. XML-QL offers tree-browsing and tree-transformation operators to extract parts of documents and to build new documents. XQL separates transformation operation from the query language. To make a transformation, an XQL query is performed first, then the results of the XQL query are fed into XSL [W3C98b] to conduct transformation.

An XQL query is represented by a line command which connects element types using path operators ('/' or '//'). '/' is the child operator which selects from immediate child nodes. '//' is the descendant operator which selects from arbitrary descendant nodes. In addition, symbol '@' precedes attribute names. By using these notations, all paths of tree representation can be expressed by element types, attributes, '/' and '@'. Exactly, a simple path can be described by the following Backus-Naur Form:

```
<simple path>::= <PathOP> <SimplePathUnit> |
                 <PathOp> <SimplePathUnit> '@' <AttName>
<PathOp> ::= '/' | '//'
<SimplePathUnit> ::= <ElementType> |
                     <ElementType> <PathOp> <SimplePathUnit>
```

The following is a simple path-oriented query:

/letter//body [para $contains$ 'visit'],

where /letter//body is a path and [para $contains$ 'visited'] is a predicate, enquiring whether element "para" contains a word 'visited'.

4.2 Signature and path signature

Signature files are based on the inexact filter. They provide a quick test, which discards many of the nonqualifying values. But the qualifying values definitely pass the test although some values which actually do not satisfy the search requirement may also pass it accidentally. Such values are called "false hits" or "false drops". The signature of a value is a hash-coded bit string of length k with m bit set to 1, stored in the "signature file" (see [Fa85, Fa92]). The signature of an element containing some values is formed by superimposing the signatures of these values. The following figure depicts the signature generation and comparison process of an element containing three values, say "SGML", "database", and "information".

When a query arrives, the element signatures (stored in a signature file) are scanned and many nonqualifying elements are discarded. The rest are either checked (so that the "false drops" are discarded) or they are returned to the user as they are. Concretely, a query specifying certain values to be searched for will be transformed into a query signature s_q in the same way as for the elements stored in the database. The query signature is then compared to every element signature in the signature file. Three possible outcomes of the comparison are exemplified in Fig. 4: (1) the element matches the query; that is, for every bit set to 1 in s_q, the corresponding bit in the element signature s is also set (i.e., $s \wedge s_q = s_q$) and the element contains really the query word; (2) the element doesn't match the query (i.e., $s \wedge s_q \neq s_q$); and (3) the signature comparison indicates a match but the element in fact doesn't match the search criteria (false drop). In order to eliminate false drops, the elements must be examined after the element signature signifies a successful match.

text: ... SGML ... databases ... information ...

representative word signature:		queries:	query signatures:	matchin results:
SGML	010 000 100 110	SGML	010 000 100 110	match with OS
database	100 010 010 100	XML	011 000 100 100	no match with OS
information ∨	010 100 011 000	informatik	110 100 100 000	false drop
object signature (OS)	110 110 111 110			

Fig. 4. Signature generation and comparison

The purpose of using a signature file is to screen out most of the nonqualifying elements. A signature failing to match the query signature guarantees that the corresponding element can be ignored. Therefore, unnecessary element accesses are prevented. Signature files have a much lower storage overhead and a simple file structure than inverted indexes.

The above filtering idea can be used to support the path-oriented queries by establishing path signatures in a similar way. First, we define the concept of tag trees.

Definition 4.1 (*tag trees*) Let d denote a document. A tag tree for d, denoted T_d, is a tree, where there is a node for each tag appearing in d and an edge ($node_a$, $node_b$) if $node_b$ represents a direct sub-element of $node_a$.

Based on the concept of tag trees, we can define path signatures as follows.

Definition 4.2 (*path signature*) Let $root \rightarrow n_1 \rightarrow \ldots \rightarrow n_m$ be a path in a tag tree. Let s_{root} and s_i ($i = 1, \ldots, m$) be the signatures for $root$ and n_i ($i = 1, \ldots, m$), respectively. The path signature of n_m is defined to be $Ps_m = s_{root} \vee s_1 \vee \ldots \vee s_m$.

Example 1 Consider the tree shown in Fig. 3. Removing all the leave nodes from it, we will obtain the tag tree for the document shown in Fig. 2. If the signatures assigned to 'letter', 'body' and 'pare' are s_{letter} = 011 001 000 101, s_{body} = 001 000 101 110 and s_{para} = 010 001 011 100, respectively, then the path signature for 'para' is $Ps_{para} = s_{letter} \vee s_{body} \vee s_{para}$ = 011001111111.

In the following, we show how to use the path signatures to optimize the query evaluation. As an example, consider the sample path-oriented query given in 4.1 once again.

Example 2 Assume that an additional (hidden) attribute is attached to the relation Element, named *PS* to store path signatures for elements. For the path appearing in the query, we first compute its signature:

$$s = s_{letter} \vee s_{body} \vee s_{para} = 011001111111.$$

Then, we transform the sample query into the following form:

select *
from Element *x*, Text *y*
where *x*.Ename = 'para' and *x*.*PS matches s*

and x.docID = y.docID
and x.ID = y.parentID and y.value ⊇ 'visit';

where "*matches*" is a function to do the signature checking as described above. From this example, we can see that the path signature can be used to reduce the amount of tuples to be searched in relation Text. It works like a filter to eliminate non-related elements as many as possible. However, due to the "false drops", it is possible that although the path signature of an element matches a query path signature, the corresponding path is not the path appearing in the query. Therefore, an extra step is needed to check those paths whose path signature survives the signature checking, which may delay the response time.

Another problem is that some elements may share the same path (e.g., the multiple appearance of "para" element in the tree shown in Fig. 3) and thus the same path signature, which will be redundantly stored as the values of "*PS*" attribute. This problem can be removed by storing all the distinct path signatures in a separate file F_{ps} and establish a hidden attribute (named "pointer") in the relation Element to store the pointers to the positions of the path signatures in F_{ps}. In this setting, the above query can be changed into the following form:

Search the path signature file F_{ps} to find positions whose signature matches s;
Let S_{ps} be the set of the resulting positions;
Execute the following statement:
select *
from Element x, Text y
where x.Ename = 'para' and x.*pointer* in S_{ps}
and x.docID = y.docID
and x.ID = y.parentID and y.value ⊇ 'visit';

To mitigate the first problem mentioned above to some extend, we do not store the path signatures simply in a file, but organize them into a tree structure, the so-called *signature tree* to find the matching path signatures quickly. We discuss this issue below.

4.3 Building signature trees over path signatures

In this subsection, we show how to speed-up the path signature scanning.

As in traditional databases, we want to establish index over path signatures just as a B-tree over a primary key attribute. Unfortunately, due to the fact that signatures work only for an inexact filter, the comparison-and-branching mechanism used in a B-tree can not be utilized to build an index tree structure for signatures. As an counter example, consider the following simple binary tree, which is constructed for an Element relation containing only three tuples:

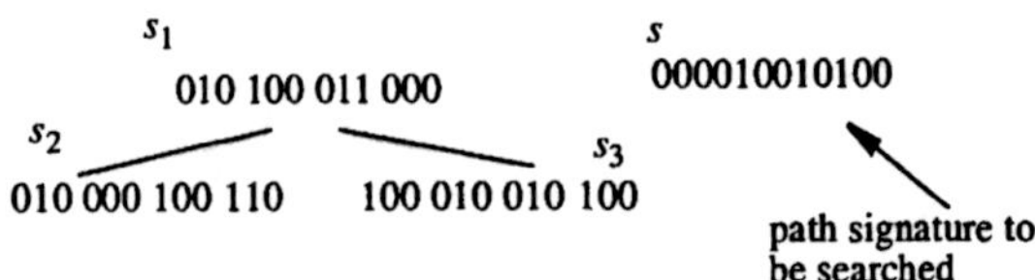

Fig. 5. An counter example

Assume that s = 000010010100 is a signature to be searched. Since $s_1 > s$, the search will go left to s_2. But s_2 does not match s. Then, the binary search will return a 'nil' to indicate that s can not be found. However, in terms of the definition of the inexact matching, s_3 matches s. For this reason, we try another tree structure, the so-called *signature tree* as a index structure over path signatures, and change its search strategy in such a way that the behavior of signatures can be modeled. In the following, we discuss the signature tree in some detail.

Consider a (path) signature s_i of length F. We denote it as $s_i = s_i[1]s_i[2] \ldots s_i[F]$, where each $s_i[j] \in \{0, 1\}$ ($j = 1, ..., F$). We also use $s_i(j_1, ..., j_h)$ to denote a sequence of pairs w.r.t. s_i: $(j_1, s_i[j_1])(j_2, s_i[j_2]) ... (j_h, s_i[j_h])$, where $1 \leq j_k \leq F$ for $k \in \{1, ..., h\}$.

Definition 4.3 (*signature identifier*) Let $S = s_1.s_2 ... .s_n$ denote a signature file. Consider s_i ($1 \leq i \leq n$). If there exists a sequence: $j_1, ..., j_h$ such that for any $k \neq i$ ($1 \leq k \leq n$) we have $s_i(j_1, ..., j_h) \neq s_k(j_1, ..., j_h)$, then we say $s_i(j_1, ..., j_h)$ identifies the signature s_i or say $s_i(j_1, ..., j_h)$ is an identifier of s_i.

Definition 4.4 (*signature tree*) A signature tree for a signature file $S = s_1.s_2 ... .s_n$, where $s_i \neq s_j$ for $i \neq j$ and $|s_k| = F$ for $k = 1, ..., n$, is a binary tree T such that

1. For each internal node of T, the left edge leaving it is always labeled with 0 and the right edge is always labeled with 1.
2. T has n leaves labeled 1, 2, ..., n, used as pointers to n different positions of s_1, s_2 ... and s_n in S (signature file). For a leaf node u, $p(u)$ represents the pointer to the corresponding signature in S.
3. Each internal node v is associated with a number, denoted $sk(v)$ that is the bit offset of a given bit position in the block signature pattern. That bit position will be checked when v is encountered.
4. Let $j_1, ..., j_h$ be the numbers associated with the nodes on a path from the root to a leaf node labeled i (then, this leaf node is a pointer to the ith signature in S). Let $p_1, ..., p_h$ be the sequence of labels of edges on this path. Then, $(j_1, p_1) ... (j_h, p_h)$ makes up a signature identifier for s_i, $s_i(j_1, ..., j_h)$.

Example 3. In Fig. 6(b), we show a signature tree for the (path) signature file shown in Fig. 6(a). In this signature tree, each edge is labeled with 0 or 1 and each leaf node is a pointer to a signature in the signature file. In addition, each internal node is associated with a positive integer (which is used to tell how many bits to skip when searching). Consider the path going through the nodes marked 1, 7 and 4. If this path is searched for locating some signature s, then three bits of s: $s[1]$, $s[7]$ and $s[4]$ will have been checked at that moment. If $s[4] = 1$, the search will go to the right child of the node marked "4". This child node is marked with 5 and then the 5th bit of s: $s[5]$ will be checked.

See the path consisting of the dashed edges in Fig. 6(b), which corresponds to the identifier of s_6: $s_6(1, 7, 4, 5) = (1, 0)(7, 1)(4, 1)(5, 1)$. Similarly, the identifier of s_3 is $s_3(1, 4) = (1, 1)(4, 1)$ (see the path consisting of the thick edges in Fig. 2(b)).

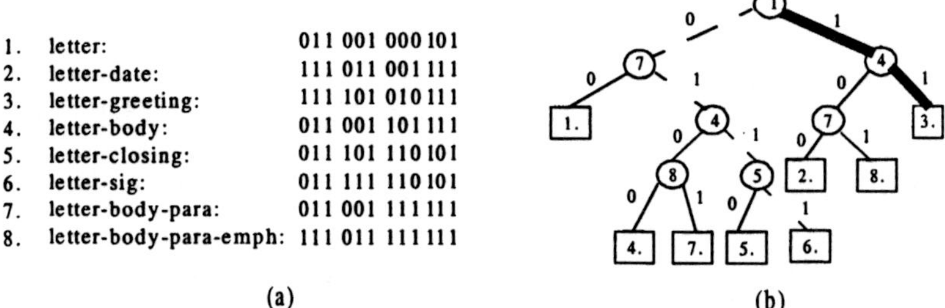

Fig. 6. A set of path signatures and the corresponding signature tree

Below we give only an algorithm to construct a signature tree for a signature file which contains different signatures. It can be easily extended so that it can be applied to the general case that a signature file contains signature duplicates. The algorithm needs only O(N) time, where N represents the number of signatures in the signature file.

At the very beginning, the tree contains an initial node: a node containing a pointer to the first signature.

Then, we take the next signature to be inserted into the tree. Let s be the next signature we wish to enter. We traverse the tree from the root. Let v be the node encountered and assume that v is an internal node with $sk(v) = i$. Then, $s[i]$ will be checked. If $s[i] = 0$, we go left. Otherwise, we go right. If v is a leaf node, we compare s with the signature s_0 pointed by v. s can not be the same as v since in S there is no signature which is identical to anyone else. But several bits of s can be determined, which agree with s_0. Assume that the first k bits of s agree with s_0; but s differs from s_0 in the $(k + 1)$th position, where s has the digit b and s_0 has $1 - b$. We construct a new node u with $sk(u) = k + 1$ and replace v with u. (Note that v will not be removed. By "replace", we mean that the position of v in the tree is occupied by u. v will become one of u's children.) If $b = 1$, we make v and the pointer to s be the left and right children of u, respectively. If $b = 0$, we make v and the pointer to s be respectively the right and left children of u.

The following is the formal description of the algorithm.

```
Algorithm sig-tree-generation(file)
begin
      construct a root node r with sk(r) = 1; (*where r corresponds to the first signature s1 in the signature file*)
      for j = 2 to n do
         call insert(sj);
end

Procedure insert(s)
begin
      stack ← root;
      while stack not empty do
         {v ← pop(stack);
          if v is not a leaf then
             {i ← sk(v);
              if s[i] = 1 then {let a be the right child of v; push(stack, a);}
              else {let a be the left child of v; push(stack, a);}
             }
          else          (*v is a leaf.*)
             {compare s with the signature s0 pointed by p(v);
              assume that the first k bit of s agree with s0;
              but s differs from s0 in the (k + 1)th position;
              w ← v; replace v with a new node u with sk(u) = k + 1;
              if s[k + 1] = 1 then make s and w be respectively the right and left children of u
              else make s and w be the right and left children of u, respectively;}
         }
end
```

In the procedure *insert*, *stack* is a stack structure used to control the tree traversal.

The search of a signature tree is relatively easy. It can be described as follows. Let s_q be a query signature. The i-th position of s_q is denoted as $s_q(i)$. During the traversal of a signature tree, the inexact matching is defined as follows:

(i) Let v be the node encountered and $s_q(i)$ be the position to be checked.

(ii) If $s_q(i) = 1$, we move to the right child of v.

(iii) If $s_q(i) = 0$, both the right and left child of v will be visited.

In fact, this definition just corresponds to the signature matching criterion. To locate a path signature, the corresponding signature tree will be searched. For any "1" in the path signature, we move to the right child node of the current node. Therefore, each time only part of the signature tree will be traversed, which is efficient compared to the scanning of all path signatures.

5. Experiment

In this Section, we present some benchmark numbers for typical queries against a large XML document. We have compared an OODBMS based XML store (OODB) with XQL query processor, and 'Infonyte', the commercial version of our PDOM and XQL processor, by which the technique described in the previous sections are employed. The tests against Infonyte were performed with enabled cache (IE) and disabled cache (ID). All systems run on a machine with the following configuration:

- Dell Poweredge 6300.
- 4 × Intel Xeon Pentium III (500 MHZ).
- 1 GB RAM.
- 4 × 9GB Harddisk.

The OODBMS was configured with 64MB internal in-memory cache, and the Java virtual machine used to run Infonyte is the HotSpot engine that comes with JDK 1.3 from SUN.

The XML document used for the experiments are the 37 plays of Shakespeare marked up by Jon Bosak. The document uses 7.65 Mbyte file space in textual format. It consists of 180,000 elements and a total number of 327.000 DOM nodes.

The following XQL queries are used for the test:

Q1. /WILLIAM/PLAY/TITLE

Q2. //PLAY/TITLE

Q3. //TITLE

Q4. //LINE

Q5. //PLAY[TITLE="The Tempest"]//SPEECH[SPEAKER="Lord"]

Q6. //PLAY//INDUCT//SPEECH[//SPEAKER="Lord"]

Q7. //PLAY[//PROLOGUE//SPEAKER="Chorus"]/TITLE

Q8. //PLAY[//INDUCT//SPEECH[//SPEAKER="Lord"]]/TITLE

The test results are summarized in the following table.

Table 4: Query execution time (*ms.*)

Query	OODB	ID	IE
Q1	40	110	<1
Q2	50	280	1
Q3	640	2200	50
Q4	28800	3500	810
Q5	340	310	28
Q6	60	73	3
Q7	1700	230	2
Q8	1800	200	3

Queries Q1-Q4 are simple path queries which return <TITLE> elements in <PLAY> elements (Q1, Q2); all <TITLE> elements including <ACT> titles and <SCENE> titles (Q3); and all <Line> elements. Q5 returns all <SPEECH> elements where the speaker is "Lord" within the play whose title is "The Tempest", which is in fact an abbreviated form of the following search condition:

//PLAY[TITLE="The Tempest"] and
//PLAY/TITLE//SPEECH[SPEAKER="Lord"]

Queries Q6-Q8 are more complicated path queries which refer to elements <INDUCT> and <PROLOGUE> that occur infrequently.

Generally, our Infonyte system can compete with the OODB, even with caching disabled. Especially Q4 shows the impact of the cache used by the OODB. The large amount of <LINE> elements (170.000) which are the result of this query do not fit into its cache and lead to an enormous performance decrease. With caching enabled, Infonyte outperforms the OODB system at least by a factor of 10.

The execution time for queries Q1-Q4 shows that OODB and Infonyte optimization strategies behave similarly for simple path queries. For the complex path queries Q5-Q8, however, execution time differs significantly. For these queries, our query processor can avoid processing of large, irrelevant subtrees by performing path signature tests, which can seen from Infonyte's uncached evaluation time of queries Q2 (280ms) and Q7 (230ms). Q7 can be thought of as a refinement of Q2 where the filter '[//PROLOGUE// SPEAKER="Chorus"]' needs to be evaluated for each <PLAY> element's subtree. But before the query processor traverses these trees, it can perform a signature test. This test fails often, as only 5 of 37 <PLAY> elements contain a <PROLOGUE> element. For these remaining 5 elements, the subtree needs to be loaded to evaluate the filter expression. Only 2 <PLAY> elements match this filter expression and are processed further, which finally returns their <TITLE> element.

6. Conclusion

In this paper, a new indexing technique: *path signature* has been proposed to speed up the evaluation of the path-oriented queries in document databases. On the one hand, path signatures can be used as a filter to get away non-relevant elements. On the other hand, the technique of pat-trees can be utilized to establish index over them, which make us find relevant signatures more quickly.

References

Bos97 Jon Bosak, XML, Java, and the future of the web, March 1997, http://sunsite.unc.edu/pub/sun-info/standards/xml/why/xmlapps.html.

DD94 S.J. DeRose and D.D. Durand, "*Making Hypermedia Work: A User's Guide to HyTime*," Kluwer Academic Publishers, London, 1994.

DFF98 A. Deutsch, M. Fernandez, D. Forescu, A. Levy and D. Suciu, "XML-QL: A Query Language for XML," Aug. 1988, http://www.w3.org/TR/NOTE-xml-ql/.

Fa85 C. Faloutsos, "Access Methods for Text," *ACM Computing Surveys*, 17(1), 1985, pp. 49-74.

Fa92 C. Faloutsos, "Signature Files," in: *Information Retrieval: Data Structures & Algorithms*, edited by W.B. Frakes and R. Baeza-Yates, Prentice Hall, New Jersey, 1992, pp. 44-65.

ISO86 ISO 8879: 1986, *Information Processing - Text and Office System - Standard Generalized Markup Language (SGML)*, Oct. 1986.

Kn73 D.E. Knuth, *The Art of Computer Programming: Sorting and Searching*, Addison-Wesley Pub. London, 1973.

Mo68 Morrison, D.R., PATRICIA - Practical Algorithm To Retrieve Information Coded in Alphanumeric. *Journal of Association for Computing Machinary*, Vol. 15, No. 4, Oct. 1968, pp. 514-534.

RLS98 J. Robie, J. Lapp and D. Schach : "XML Query Language (XQL)," *W3C QL'98 - The Query Languages Workshop*, December 1998.

W3C98a World Wide Web Consortium, Extensible Markup Language (XML) 1.0. http//www.w3.org/TR/1998/REC-xml/19980210, Febuary 1998.

W3C98b World Wide Web Consortium, Extensible Style Language (XML) Working Draft, Dec. 1998. http//www.w3.org/TR/1998/WD-xsl-19981216.

W3C98c World Wide Web Consortium, "Document Object Model (DOM) Level 1", http://www.w3.org/TR/REC-DOM-Level-1/, Oct. 1998.

Reasoning with Disjunctive Constrained Tuple-Generating Dependencies*

Junhu Wang[1], Rodney Topor[1], and Michael Maher[1,2]

[1] CIT, Griffith University, Brisbane, Australia 4111
jwang, rwt, mjm@cit.gu.edu.au
[2] DMCS, Loyola University, Chicago, USA
mjm@math.luc.edu

Abstract. In extended relational databases, queries and integrity constraints often contain interpreted variables and built-in relations. We extend previous work on semantic query containment for extended relational databases to handle disjunctive constrained tuple-generating dependencies (DCTGDs) which include almost all well-known classes of integrity constraints. After defining this extended class of integrity constraints, we present a method for expanding a query Q, using DCTGDs, to a semantically equivalent set of queries. Our theorems on this method unify and generalize several previous results on semantic query containment. We apply the method to the DCTGD implication problem and prove that, when restricted to regular CTGDs, our method is strictly more powerful than previously published chase algorithms.

1 Introduction

Modern relational database systems storing complex data such as spatial, audio, image, video or temporal data need the ability to store and manipulate built-in relations in addition to database relations. In conventional databases, examples of such built-in relations include arithmetic relations such as $X < Y$ or $Z = X + Y$. In spatial or image databases, examples include topological and directional relations between spatial objects, such as X *contains* Y or X *is north of* Y. In temporal and video databases, examples include temporal relations and kinetic properties. In many cases, evaluation of queries involving built-in relations is highly expensive, computationally, but built-in relations are necessary to achieve a required level of expressiveness. We will adopt the terminology of constraint databases, and refer to built-in relations as *constraints*.

The data in such database systems is also subject to varied application-specific semantic restrictions which, in traditional database systems, are represented as integrity constraints. One of the widest class of integrity constraints is the *constrained tuple-generating dependencies* (CTGDs)[1], which generalize traditional dependencies such as FDs, MVDs, EGDs, TGDs[2] and CGDs[3]. Here, we further extend this class to allow disjunctions. We call the resulting

* This work was partly supported by the Australian Research Council.

H.C. Mayr et al. (Eds.): DEXA 2001, LNCS 2113, pp. 963–973, 2001.

class of integrity constraints ***disjunctive constrained tuple-generating dependencies*** (DCTGDs). Such dependencies are needed to represent a wide array of common semantic relationships. For example, an integrity constraint might state that any student is either male or female:

$$student(x) \rightarrow male(x) \vee female(x)$$

More generally, whenever a class is partitioned into subclassess there is an implicit disjunctive integrity constraint. Disjunctive restrictions may also arise directly from the semantics of the data. For example, an integrity constraint might state that a road crosses a river either over a bridge or through a tunnel:

$$\begin{aligned} &road(rd\ id, rd\ geo), river(rv\ id, rv\ geo), rd\ geo \cap rv\ geo \neq \emptyset \rightarrow \\ &\qquad (\exists b\ id, b\ geo\ bridge(b\ id, b\ geo), b\ geo \cap rd\ geo \cap rv\ geo \neq \emptyset) \vee \\ &\qquad (\exists t\ id, t\ geo\ tunnel(t\ id, t\ geo), t\ geo \cap rd\ geo \cap rv\ geo \neq \emptyset). \end{aligned}$$

As argued in [4], sophisticated query optimization which incorporates understanding of the built-in relations and exploitation of highly expressive integrity constraints will be cost-effective for modern applications where the potential for improvement is much greater than in traditional databases. Two key problems are testing query containment and testing integrity constraint implication. Previous researchers have developed and studied techniques for proving implication of integrity constraints [1, 3, 5, 6], and have proposed techniques for query optimization [4, 7].

We extend this previous work to handle DCTGDs as follows. In Section 2, we define our generalized classes of integrity constraints and queries. In Section 3, we present a procedure for expanding a query Q in the presence of a set of DCTGDs Δ into a semantically equivalent set S of queries. We show that, when this procedure terminates, Q is contained in another query Q' under Δ iff every query in S is contained in Q' ***independently*** of Δ. This effectively reduces a semantic containment problem to a set of standard query containment problems, which can be tested using standard methods such as the above generalization of the containment mapping theorem. We also note the simple conditions under which the query expansion procedure is guaranteed to terminate and other useful properties. When the second query Q' is known in advance, we show that a more efficient query expansion procedure can be used to prove Q is semantically contained in Q' under Δ. This is done in Section 4. In Section 5, we apply our query expansion procedure to the the implication problem for DCTGDs. We show our procedure is strictly more powerful than the chase algorithms of [1]. Section 6 concludes the paper with a comparison with related work. We show that our theorems unify and generalize several results in [6] and [4]. Furthermore, the technique of expansion is substantially simpler than the techniques used in those previous works, so that we achieve a conceptual simplification in addition to unifying results.

2 Preliminaries

In this section, we review the terminology in extended relational databases and introduce definitions and notations which will be used throughout the paper. In particular, we introduce DCTGDs which extend CTGDs[1].

A term is a variable, or constant, or function over terms. An *atom* is a formula of the form $r(t_1, ..., t_n)$ where r is an uninterpreted predicate (i.e, a database relation name) and $t_1, ..., t_n$ are terms[1]. In this paper, a conjunction of atoms $r_1 \wedge \cdots \wedge r_n$ is also written as $r_1, ..., r_n$ for short, and is often treated as a set $\{r_1, ..., r_n\}$. A finite conjunction of atoms is said to be *normalized* if the terms in each atom are distinct variables, and the variables in different atoms are disjoint. For instance, the conjunction $r_1(x, y), r_2(u, v)$ is normalized while $r_1(x, y), r_2(y, z)$ and $r_1(x, 1)$ are not.

A *primitive constraint* over domain $\mathcal{D}$ is a formula of the form $c(x_1, ..., x_n)$ where c is a system built-in, interpreted predicate, $x_1, ..., x_n$ are variables over $\mathcal{D}$, i.e, c defines a n-ary built-in relation which, given an assignment of elements from $\mathcal{D}$ to the variables, can be evaluated to *TRUE* or *FALSE* by the system. A *constraint* is a formula obtained by a combination of the following operations on primitive constraints: renaming, quantification, logical negation, conjunction and disjunction.

If R is a set of atoms, then $Var(R)$ and $Term(R)$ will denote the set of variables and the set of terms, respectively, in R. If C is a constraint, then $Var(C)$ will denote the set of *free* variables in C, and C will denote the logical negation of C.

2.1 Disjunctive Constrained Tuple-Generating Dependencies

Definition 1. *A* disjunctive constrained-tuple generating dependency (DCTGD) *is a formula of the form*

$$P, C \rightarrow \bigvee_{i=1}^{k} (\exists Y_i \; P'_i, C'_i)$$

where P and P'_i are conjunctions of atoms, C and C'_i are constraints, Y_i is a set of variables disjoint from $Var(P)$, $Var(P'_i) \subseteq Var(P) \cup Var(C) \cup Y_i$ and $Var(C'_i) \subseteq Var(P) \cup Var(C) \cup Y_i$ for $i = 1, ..., k$. If P contains at least one atom and $Var(C) \subseteq Var(P)$, we say the DCTGD is regular[2].

In a DCTGD, the left-hand side of the arrow is referred to as the *antecedent* and the right-hand side is referred to as the *consequent*. For convenience, we will assume that the set of atoms in the antecedent is normalized (although we will use more compact forms in some examples). When there is only one disjunct in

[1] In this paper, the functions are assumed to have fixed interpretations which the system understands.

[2] Note that most practical DCTGDs are regular.

the consequent (i.e, $k = 1$ in the above definition) and the constraints in either side of the arrow is a conjunction of primitive constraints, the DCTGD becomes a *constrained tuple-generating dependency (CTGD)*[1].

2.2 General Conjunctive Queries

Definition 2. *A* general conjunctive query (GCQ) *is a formula of the form*

$$\{V : R, D\}$$

where $V = (v_1, ..., v_k)$ *is a* sequence *of variables, R is a conjunction of atoms, D is a constraint, and* $Var(D) \subseteq V \cup Var(R)$. *We call V and R, D the* **output** *and the* **body** *of the query, respectively.*

Note that the conventional conjunctive query [5] is a GCQ in which the constraint in the body is a conjunction of equalities (=), disequalities ($\neq$), and (if the domains are ordered) comparisons such as $<$ and $\leq$. Note also that V is a sequence. But for convenience we sometimes treat it as a *set*.

For any query Q, the *answer set* $Q(\mathcal{I})$ of Q with respect to a database instance $\mathcal{I}$ is the set of all answers to Q with respect to $\mathcal{I}$. A query Q is said to be *contained* in another Q', denoted $Q \sqsubseteq Q'$, if $Q(\mathcal{I}) \subseteq Q'(\mathcal{I})$ for every instance $\mathcal{I}$. Q and Q' are said to be *equivalent*, denoted $Q = Q'$, if $Q \sqsubseteq Q'$ and $Q' \sqsubseteq Q$. Q is said to be *empty*, if $Q(\mathcal{I}) = \emptyset$ for every instance $\mathcal{I}$. Clearly, if Q is a GCQ, then Q is empty if and only if the constraint in its body is unsatisfiable.

The above concepts of query containment and equivalence extend to *semantic* containment and equivalence if we are interested only in instances that satisfy a set of DCTGDs.

Definition 3. *Let Δ be a set of DCTGDs, and Q_1 and Q_2 be queries. If for any instance $\mathcal{I}$ satisfying Δ, we have $Q_1(\mathcal{I}) \subseteq Q_2(\mathcal{I})$, then we say that Q_1 is* (semantically) contained in Q_2 under Δ, *denoted as $Q_1 \sqsubseteq_\Delta Q_2$. If $Q_1 \sqsubseteq_\Delta Q_2$ and $Q_1 \sqsubseteq_\Delta Q_2$, then we say that Q_1 and Q_2 are* equivalent under Δ, *denoted as $Q_1 =_\Delta Q_2$.*

In the sequel, we will assume all of the GCQs are *safe* as defined below.

Definition 4. *A GCQ $\{V : R, D\}$ is said to be* safe *if*
(1) R contains at least one atom, and
(2) Every output variable either appears in $Var(R)$, or is equated to a (interpreted) function of $Var(R)$ or to a constant by D.

For convenience, we sometimes require the GCQs be in normal form.

Definition 5. *A GCQ $\{V : R, D\}$ is said to be* in normal form (NF) *if R is normalized, the variables in the sequence V are distinct, and V and $Var(R)$ are disjoint.*

Clearly every GCQ has an equivalent GCQ which is in NF.

2.3 Containment Mappings

We need two types of containment mappings. The first type is from a regular DCTGD to a GCQ, and is used mainly in expanding GCQs; the second type is from one GCQ to another, and is used in testing containment.

Definition 6. *Let* $f \equiv P, C \rightarrow \bigvee_{i=1}^{k}(\exists Y_i\ P'_i, C'_i)$ *be a regular DCTGD, and* $Q \equiv \{V : R, D\}$ *be a GCQ. A* containment mapping (CM) from f to Q *is a mapping from* $Var(P)$ *to* $Term(R)$ *such that it maps every atom in* P *to an atom in* R.

Definition 7. *Let* $Q_i \equiv \{V_i : R_i, D_i\}$ $(i = 1, 2)$ *be two GCQs. A* containment mapping (CM) from Q_2 to Q_1 *is a mapping from* $V_2 \cup Var(R_2)$ *to* $V_1 \cup Term(R_1)$ *such that it maps the* sequence V_2 *to the* sequence V_1, *and maps every atom in* R_2 *to some atom in* R_1.

Let δ be a CM defined on variables $x_1, ..., x_n$. Given any set of atoms and/or constraints $\mathcal{H}$, $\delta(\mathcal{H})$ denotes the set of atoms and/or constraints that is obtained by simultaneously replacing each occurrence of the variables x_i in $\mathcal{H}$ by $\delta(x_i)$. In addition, two CMs from the *same* DCTGD (to possibly different GCQs) are considered to be the same if they map every variable to the same term.

The following lemma is straightforward.

Lemma 1. *Let* $Q \equiv \{V : R, D\}$ *be a GCQ, and* $f \equiv P, C \rightarrow \bigvee_{i=1}^{k}(\exists Y_i\ P'_i, C'_i)$ *be a regular DCTGD. If* δ *is an CM from* f *to* Q, *then* Q *is equivalent under* f *to the union of*

$Q_0 = \{V : R, D \wedge \delta(C)\}$ *and*

$Q_i = \{V : R, \delta(P'_i), D \wedge \delta(C \wedge C'_i)\}$ $(i = 1, ..., k)$,

where the variables Y_i *are renamed to distinct variables not in* $V \cup Var(R)$.

The next lemma is slightly generalized from [8]. It can be used as a basic tool for detecting GCQ containment and equivalence.

Lemma 2. *Let* $Q_i \equiv \{V_i : R_i, D_i\}$ $(i = 0, 1, 2, ..., n)$ *be GCQs. Suppose* $Q_0 \neq \emptyset$, *and* $Q_1, ..., Q_n$ *are in NF. Then* $Q_0 \sqsubseteq \bigcup_{i=1}^{n} Q_i$ *iff there are CMs* $\delta_{i,1}, ..., \delta_{i,k_i}$ *from* Q_i *to* Q_0 *such that* $D_0 \rightarrow \vee_{i=1}^{n} \vee_{j=1}^{k_i} \delta_{i,j}(D_i)$.

3 Semantic Expansion

3.1 The Procedure *Expand*

Before formally defining the procedure, let us look at the intuition first.

Let Δ be a set of regular DCTGDs and $Q \equiv \{V : R, D\}$ be a GCQ. As shown in Lemma 1, if there is a DCTGD $f_1 \equiv P, C \rightarrow \bigvee_{i=1}^{k}(\exists Y_i\ P'_i, C'_i)$ in Δ and an CM δ from f_1 to Q, then Q is equivalent under f_1 to the union of

$Q_0 \equiv \{V : R, D \wedge \delta(C)\}$ and

$Q_i \equiv \{V : R, \delta(P'_i), D \wedge \delta(C \wedge C'_i)\}$ $(i = 1, ..., k)$,

where the variables in Y_i are renamed to distinct new variables not in $Var(R) \cup V$.

To each of $Q_0, Q_1, \ldots, Q_k$, if there is a CM from $f_2 \in \Delta$, then it can be split into the union of some other GCQs in a similar way, and thus Q will be equivalent under f_1 and f_2 to the union of more GCQs. Continuing this process, we can split Q into the union of more and more GCQs under Δ. In general, regarding the GCQs in the union as a set S, and continuing as above, we hope to be able to reach a point where no matter what DCTGD in Δ and what mapping we use, we can not split any GCQ in S into more GCQs which are not subsumed by other GCQs in S.

Clearly the splitting of a GCQ Q' into $Q'_0, \ldots, Q'_k$ in the above process depends on the application of a (DCTGD, CM) pair. Let us call $Q'_0, \ldots, Q'_k$ the ***child*** queries of Q', and use the name ***descendant*** (query) for a GCQ's child query or its descendant's child query. For efficiency, any (DCTGD, CM) pairs, if already applied in splitting Q', should not be used again to split Q''s descendants. Also, any newly generated GCQs in S which are empty can be removed immediately.

We now formalize the above idea into the procedure ***Expand*** as listed in Fig 1.

Procedure $Expand(Q, \Delta)$
Input: a GCQ Q and a set Δ of regular DCTGDs.
Output: a set of GCQs S.
Local variables: a set $pairs(Q')$ for each GCQ Q' in S.

let $S = \emptyset$; let $pairs(Q) = \emptyset$;
if (Q is empty)
then return S;
else add Q to S;
while (there is $Q' \equiv \{V : R, D\}$ in S and $f \equiv P, C \rightarrow \bigvee_{i=1}^{k} (\exists Y_i\ P'_i, C'_i)$ in Δ,
  and an CM δ from f to Q' such that $(f, \delta) \notin pairs(Q')$) **do**
 let $Q_0 = \{V : R, D \wedge \delta(C)\}$;
  $Q_i = \{V : R, \delta(P'_i), D \wedge \delta(C \wedge C'_i)\}$ $(i = 1, \ldots, k)$;
  where the variables in Y_i are renamed to distinct variables not in $Var(R) \cup V$.
 if (no Q_i $(i = 0, \ldots, k)$ is equivalent to Q')
 then remove Q' from S;
   for $(i = 0, \ldots, k)$ **do**
    if (Q_i is not empty)
    then add Q_i to S; let $pairs(Q_i) = pairs(Q') \cup \{(f, \delta)\}$;
 else let $pairs(Q') = pairs(Q') \cup \{(f, \delta)\}$;
return S;

Fig. 1. The semantic expansion procedure

Procedure $Expand(Q, \Delta)$ may or may not terminate. If it does, we will have a finite set S of GCQs . Let Q^{Δ} be the union of these GCQs if $S \neq \emptyset$, and let Q^{Δ} be an empty query if $S = \emptyset$. It is easy to see that $Q^{\Delta} =_{\Delta} Q$.

Let us call the process defined by the procedure $Expand(Q, \Delta)$ the ***semantic expansion*** of query Q with Δ. Using semantic expansion, query containment under DCTGDs can be reduced to query containment without DCTGDs.

Theorem 1. *Given a set of regular DCTGDs Δ and a GCQ Q, if the procedure Expand(Q, Δ) terminates with result S, then for any query Q', $Q \sqsubseteq_\Delta Q'$ if and only if every GCQ in S is contained in Q' (without the DCTGDs).*

Note that Q' can be any query, including unions and differences of GCQs. In particular, when Q' is the empty query, we get the following corollary.

Corollary 1. *Let Q be a GCQ and Δ be a set of regular DCTGDs. If the procedure Expand(Q, Δ) terminates with result S, then Q is empty under Δ iff $S = \emptyset$.*

Note also that we have assumed the conjunctions of atoms in the antecendents of the DCTGDs are normalized; if not, the above theorem will not hold.

Example 1. Let Δ contain the integrity constraint $f \equiv p(x, y), q(y, z) \rightarrow FALSE$. Let $Q = \{x : p(x, y), q(z, u), y = z\}$. Since there are no CMs from f to Q, *Expand* terminates with $S = \{Q\}$, which is not empty, but Q is empty under f.

When the DCTGDs are limited to disjunctive TGDs, i.e, DCTGDs that do not have constraints in the consequent, we get the next corollary.

Corollary 2. *Let Δ be a set of regular disjunctive TGDs, and Q be a non-empty GCQ. If the procedure Expand(Q, Δ) terminates, then Q is not empty under Δ.*

3.2 Termination and Other Properties

Given that Theorem 1 holds on the condition that *Expand* terminates, it is natural to ask when *Expand* will terminate. In general, the termination problem is undecidable. However, for some special classes of DCTGDs, termination of *Expand* is guaranteed. In this section, we identify some of these special classes.

First, it is trivial to see that when Δ is a set of (disjunctive) CGDs, the expansion terminates for any GCQ Q. The only possible non-terminating case is when there are DCTGDs that contain atoms in the consequent.

Definition 8. *A set of DCTGDs Δ is said to be* recursive, *if it contains a sequence of DCTGDs $f_1, ..., f_n$ ($n \geq 1$) such that some relation names in the antecedent of f_{i+1} appear in the consequent of f_i (for $i = 1, ..., n-1$), and some relation names in the antecedent of f_1 appear in the consequent of f_n.*

Proposition 1. *If the regular DCTGDs in Δ are not recursive, then Expand(Q, Δ) terminates for any GCQ Q.*

Even for recursive DCTGDs, there are simple conditions under which *Expand* terminates on any GCQ Q.

Definition 9. *A regular DCTGD $P, C \rightarrow \bigvee_{i=1}^{k} \exists Y_i\ P'_i, C'_i$ is said to be a* full dependency *if $Var(P'_i) \subseteq Var(P)$ for $i = 1, ..., k$.*

Proposition 2. *If Δ is a set of full dependencies, and the atoms in the consequents of these dependencies do not contain functions, then the procedure* $Expand(Q, \Delta)$ *terminates for any GCQ* Q.

The condition that there are no functions is necessary.

Example 2. If Δ contains $p(x, y) \rightarrow p(x, y+1)$ only [3], and $Q = \{x : p(x, y)\}$, where x, y are from the reals, then the body of Q can be expanded to $p(x, y), p(x, y+1), p(x, y+2), \ldots$, so the procedure $Expand(Q, \Delta)$ will not terminate.

Note that in Proposition 1 and Proposition 2, we have implicitly assumed there are terminating algorithms for solving implication problems of the underlying constraints.

There are many other cases where the semantic expansion procedure terminates. In general, the termination also depends on the query Q. A trivial case of termination, for example, is when there are no CMs from any DCTGDs to Q. The order of choosing a DCTGD from Δ may also affect termination. For example, if Δ contains $p(x, y), x > y \rightarrow FALSE$ and $p(x, y) \rightarrow \exists z\, p(x, z), z > y$, and $Q = \{x : p(x, y), x > y\}$, then *Expand* will terminate immediately if we choose the first DCTGD, but it will not terminate if we always give priority to the second DCTGD.

In practical applications of Theorem 1 (e.g, when testing semantic query containment), we can add extra conditions in the procedure so that it may terminate earlier, as will be seen in Section 4.

In addition, we note the following properties of *Expand*:

1. Although, in general, the number of GCQs in S grows exponentially, there are useful special cases where there will be at most one GCQ in the final S. For example, when there are only CTGDs in Δ and there is no constraint in the antecedent of any CTGD, or when there are only dependencies of the form $P, C \rightarrow FALSE$.
2. In *Expand*, if a (DCTGD, CM) pair is applicable to a GCQ Q' in S but not applied, then it will remain applicable to Q''s descendants (if the descendants are added to S) until it is applied. Thus different orders of choosing a DCTGD or CM will not affect the final result if they all lead to termination of the procedure.
3. There are several variations of *Expand* for which Theorem 1 remains valid. For instance, we can replace "$Q_i = \{V : R, \delta(P_i'), D \wedge \delta(C \wedge C_i')\}$" with "$Q_i = \{V : R, \delta(P_i'), D \wedge \delta(C_i')\}$". We can also relax the condition "**if** (Q_i is not empty)" or replace it with "**if** (Q_i is not contained in the union of the GCQs in S)". The condition "**if** (no Q_i ($i = 0, ..., k$) is equivalent to Q')" can also be relaxed. The differences lie in the efficiency of the procedure.
4. Procedure *Expand* and Theorem 1 extend naturally to the case where Q is a union of GCQs. We only need to modify *Expand* so that every GCQ in the union is added to S before applying the DCTGDs.

[3] Our assumption that the DCTGD is regular and normalized disallows rewriting this integrity constraint to $p(x, z), z = y - 1 \rightarrow p(x, y)$ or $p(x, y-1) \rightarrow p(x, y)$.

4 Application to Testing Semantic Query Containment

Obviously, Theorem 1 can be used to test whether $Q \sqsubseteq_\Delta Q''$ for GCQ Q and an arbitrary query Q'' (provided there are methods to test whether a GCQ is contained in Q''). In fact, if Q'' is given in advance, it is possible that $Q \sqsubseteq_\Delta Q''$ or $Q \not\sqsubseteq_\Delta Q''$ be detected before *Expand* terminates. The procedure *Ctest* listed in Fig. 2 is modified from *Expand* to accommodate Q''.

Procedure *Ctest*(Q, Δ, Q'')
Input: a GCQ Q, a set Δ of regular DCTGDs, and an arbitrary query Q'' .
Output: *TRUE* or *FALSE*.
Local variables: a set $pairs(Q')$ for each GCQ Q' in S.

```
let S = ∅; let pairs(Q) = ∅;
if (Q ⊑ Q'')
then return TRUE;
else add Q to S;
while (there is Q' ≡ {V : R, D} in S and f ≡ P, C → ⋁_{i=1}^k (∃Y_i P'_i, C'_i) in Δ,
      and an CM δ from f to Q' such that (f, δ) ∉ pairs(Q') ) do
   let Q_0 = {V : R, D ∧ δ(C)};
      Q_i = {V : R, δ(P'_i), D ∧ δ(C ∧ C'_i)} (i = 1, ..., k);
      where the variables Y_i are renamed to distinct variables not in Var(R) ∪ V.
   if (no Q_i (i = 0, ..., k) is equivalent to Q')
   then remove Q' from S;
        for (i = 0, ..., k) do
            if (Q_i ⋢ Q'' )
              then if (there is g in Δ and an CM θ from g to Q_i
                          such that (g, θ) ∉ pairs(Q') ∪ {(f, δ)})
                   then add Q_i to S; let pairs(Q_i) = pairs(Q') ∪ {(f, δ)};
                   else return FALSE;
   else let pairs(Q') = pairs(Q') ∪ {(f, δ)};
if (S = ∅)
then return TRUE;
else return FALSE;
```

Fig. 2. The procedure for semantic query containment

Theorem 2. *Let Q be a GCQ and Δ be a set of regular DCTGDs. Let Q'' be any query. If Ctest(Q, Δ, Q'') returns TRUE, then $Q \sqsubseteq_\Delta Q''$. If Ctest(Q, Δ, Q'') returns FALSE, then $Q \not\sqsubseteq_\Delta Q''$.*

The next two examples demonstrate the application of *Ctest*. In Example 3, *Ctest* detects $Q \not\sqsubseteq_\Delta Q''$, but *Expand* does not terminate. In Example 4, *Ctest* detects $Q \sqsubseteq_\Delta Q''$, but, again, *Expand*(Q, Δ) does not terminate.

Example 3. Let $Q = \{x : p(x)\}$, $Q'' = \{x : p(x), q(x, y)\}$. Let $\Delta = \{f_1, f_2\}$, where f_1, f_2 are $p(x), x > 0 \rightarrow \exists y\ q(x, y)$ and $q(x, y), y > 0 \rightarrow p(y)$ repectively. Applying f_1 to Q, we get a GCQ $Q_1 \equiv \{x : p(x), x \leq 0\}$ which is not contained in Q''. Since the only CM from f_1 to Q_1 has been used, and there is no CM from f_2 to Q_1, *Ctest* returns *FALSE*. So we know $Q \not\sqsubseteq_\Delta Q''$.

Example 4. Let $Q = \{y : p(x,y), q(y), y < 0\}$ and $Q'' = \{y : p(x,y), q(y), y < 0, x \leq 0\}$. Let $\Delta = \{f_1, f_2, f_3\}$ where $f_1, f_2,$ *and* f_3 are $p(x,y), x > 0 \rightarrow r(x,y)$; $r(x,y), q(y), z = y, \rightarrow x < -10$; and $q(y), y < 0 \rightarrow \exists z\ p(y,z)$ respectively. Applying (f_1, I) (I is the identity mapping) to Q, we split Q to

$Q_1 \equiv \{y : p(x,y), q(y), y < 0, x \leq 0\}$ and

$Q_2 \equiv \{y : p(x,y), q(y), r(x,y), y < 0, x > 0\}$

Now $Q_1 \sqsubseteq Q''$, so we only add Q_2 to S. Applying (f_2, I) to Q_2, we change Q_2 to

$Q_{2,2} \equiv \{y : p(x,y), q(y), r(x,y), y < 0, x < -10\}$ which is contained in Q''.

Thus *Ctest* stops with an empty S and returns *TRUE*. Therefore, $Q \sqsubseteq_\Delta Q''$.

5 Application to the DCTGD Implication Problem

In this section, we implicitly assume all the DCTGDs are regular.

The DCTGD implication problem is as follows: Given a set Δ of DCTGDs and a single DCTGD g, decide whether $\Delta \models g$, i.e, whether any database instance that satisfies Δ must also satisfy g.

The DCTGD implication problem can be reduced to the semantic containment problem.

Proposition 3. *Let Δ be a set of DCTGDs, and g be $P, C \rightarrow \bigvee_{i=1}^{k}(\exists Y_i\ P_i', C_i')$. Then $\Delta \models g$ iff $Q \sqsubseteq_\Delta Q''$, where $Q = \{X : P, C\}$ and $Q'' = \bigcup_{i=1}^{k}\{X : P, P_i', C \wedge C_i'\}$ (X is a* sequence *of all of the variables in $Var(P)$).*

Thus the procedure *Ctest* provides a method for the DCTGD implication problem.

[1] gives two chase procedures, Chase1 and Chase2 for the CTGD implication problem using the concept of *constrained-tuples*. We claim that, when restricted to regular CTGDs, *Ctest* is more powerful than Chase1 and Chase2 in the sense that any implication or non-implication that can be detected by Chase1 or Chase2 can also be detected by *Ctest*, and that *Ctest* can detect more cases where Δ does not imply g. In addition, *Ctest* is conceptually simpler.

Theorem 3. *Let Δ be a set of CTGDs, and g be a single CTGD. If $\Delta \not\models g$ or $\Delta \models g$ can be detected by Chase1 or Chase2, then it can also be detected by Ctest.*

Example 5 below demonstrates *Ctest* is strictly more powerful than the chase procedures in detecting non-implication.

Example 5. Let Δ be the same set as in Example 3. Let g be $p(x) \rightarrow \exists y\ q(x,y)$. As shown in Example 3, *Ctest* can detect that $\{x : p(x)\} \not\sqsubseteq_\Delta \{x : p(x), q(x,y)\}$, thus we know $\Delta \not\models g$. But Chase2 will not terminate and thus can not detect this. Chase1 can not detect this either, because the constraints do not have the INC property[8].

6 Comparison with Related Work

We have shown in the previous section that *Ctest* is strictly more powerful than the chase algorithms in [1]. Two other most closely related papers are [6] and [4]. The former studies conjunctive query containment under implication constraints and referential constraints, which are both special CTGDs. A main section of [4] is devoted to query containment under CTGDs and gives a necessary condition in the general case and some necessary and sufficient conditions for several special cases. We claim that Theorem 1 unifies and generalizes all the related results in [6] and [4]. In particular, the theorems 2,3,4 in [4] and the theorems 3.1, 4.1 in [6] are all immediate corollaries of Theorem 1 and Lemma 2. Take the main result of [6] as an example. It says

Corollary 3 (Theorem 3.1 of [6]). *Given a set of* implication constraints $N = \{ic_i \equiv P_i, C_i \to FALSE \mid i = 1, \cdots, n\}$, *and a non-recursive set of* referential constraints *(TGDs with one atom on each side of the arrow and no built-in constraints)* M, *a (non-empty) conjunctive query* $Q = \{V : R, D\}$ *is empty under* $N \cup M$ *if and only if there are CMs* $\rho_{i,1}, \cdots, \rho_{i,n_i}$ *from* ic_i *to* Q^M *such that* $D \to \bigvee_{i=1}^{n} \bigvee_{j=1}^{n_i} \rho_{i,j}(C_i)$.

To derive this corollary, we first note that *Expand*(Q, M) generates a single conjunctive query $Q^M = \{V : R, R', D\}$ where R' is the set of the newly added atoms. If there are no CMs from any of the integrity constraints in N to Q^M, then $Q^{M \cup N} = Q^M$, by Corollary 2, Q will not be empty under $M \cup N$. Now suppose $\rho_{i,1}, \cdots, \rho_{i,n_i}$ are all the CMs from ic_i to Q^M, then $Q^{M \cup N} = (Q^M)^N$ will consist of a single CQ (suppose we use a variation of *Expand* where there is no emptiness test) $\{V : R, R', V, D \wedge \bigwedge_{i=1}^{n} \bigvee_{j=1}^{n_i} \delta_{i,j}(C_i)\}$. Thus, by Corollary 1, Q is empty under $M \cup N$ if and only if $D \wedge \bigwedge_{i=1}^{n} \bigwedge_{j=1}^{n_i} \delta_{i,j}(C_i)$ is unsatisfiable, that is, $D \to \bigvee_{i=1}^{n} \bigvee_{j=1}^{n_i} \delta_{i,j}(C_i)$.

References

1. M. J. Maher and D. Srivastava. Chasing constrained tuple-generating dependencies. In *Proc. ACM Symp. PODS, New York, 1996.*
2. R. Fagin and M. Y. Vardi. The theory of data dependencies—an overview. In *LNCS v172,1-22, Springer-Verlag, 1984.*
3. M. Baudinet, J. Chomicki, and P. Wolper. Constraint-generating dependencies. *Journal of Computer and System Sciences 59, 94-115*, 1999.
4. M. J. Maher and J. Wang. Optimizing queries in extended relational databases. In *DEXA2000, Lodon, LNCS1873, p386-396.*
5. J. D. Ullman. *Principles of Database and Knowledge-Base Systems*, volume 1 & 2. Computer Science Press, 1st edition, 1988.
6. X. Zhang and Z. M. Özsoyoglu. Implication and referential constraints: A new formal reasoning. *IEEE TKDE, 9(6):894-910, Nov/Dec 1997.*
7. S. Chaudhuri and K. Shim. Query optimization in the presence of foreign functions. In *Proc. of the 19th international conference on VLDB*, Dublin, Ireland, 1993.
8. M. J. Maher. A logic programming view of CLP. In *Proc. 10th International Conference on Logic Programming*, pages 737–753, Budapest, Hungary, 1993.

A Method for Processing Boolean Queries Using a Result Cache

Jae-heon Cheong[1], Sang-goo Lee[1], and Jonghoon Chun[2]

[1] School of Computer Science and Engineering
Seoul National University, Korea
{cjh,sglee}@cygnus.snu.ac.kr
[2] Division of Computer Science and Engineering
Myongji University, Korea
jchun@mju.ac.kr

Abstract. We propose a new method for processing Boolean queries with a collection of previously answered query results which we called a result cache. We present algorithms to effectively recognize the portions of a given query that can be answered from the result cache and from those should be retrieved from the sources distributed over the network. We allow a semantic decomposition of a representation for an efficient manipulation of it.

1 Introduction

The result cache is a collection of documents that are answers to previously processed queries. It is based on a semantic caching mechanism and is managed as a collection of semantic regions. Each semantic region is represented by a Boolean formula and contains the answer documents that satisfy the formula. When a query is issued, it is decomposed into two sub-queries: a hit query that retrieves cached results from the result cache, and a miss query that fetches non-cached results. The final result is obtained by integrating the results of both the hit query and the miss query.

In this paper, we propose a new representation method for the result cache and utilize that representation to newly propose an efficient processing algorithm for general Boolean queries. Query processing in a mediator makes use of the semantic representation of the result cache to determine which results are locally available in the result cache and which results are needed from information sources. As user queries are submitted, the more complex the representation of the result cache gets. Thus we present a mechanism to reduce the complexity of the representation by allowing multiple representations for the result cache.

The rest of the paper is organized as follows. Section 2 introduces related work; sections 3 and 4 present a new method of processing Boolean queries with a result cache; we present an accommodated replacement strategy in section 5; section 6 describes our experimental results; and finally, section 7 concludes the paper.

H.C. Mayr et al. (Eds.): DEXA 2001, LNCS 2113, pp. 974–983, 2001.

2 Related Work

There are a number of articles on semantic data caching [3][4][5][6]. However, most of them do not consider general Boolean queries but conjunctive ones.

[3] proposes a query optimization method that uses cached queries in a mediator system named HERMES. This system deals with only simple conditions but not with general Boolean expressions. [4] deals with only conjunctive queries also. [5] focuses on the cache replacement strategies based on recency and semantic distance of cached queries.

[6] employs a signature file to represent a result cache. Since a signature file is based on a conjunctive query model, it cannot be directly used for a general Boolean query model. In addition, a signature file cannot completely recognize which portion of the cached results can be used for the given query due to the false drop problem.

In [2], a query-based virtual index (QVI) is proposed. It is based on the fact that most user queries are redundant. However, it does not consider general Boolean queries with multiple query terms and can utilize previous query results only when the current query is exactly matched with at most one among the previous queries. Our method proposed in this paper can process multiple-query-term queries and outperforms the exact matching method as described in section 6.

3 Result Cache Management

We assume that a query is defined as a Boolean formula with atoms connected via three Boolean operators such as AND, OR, and NOT. For notational convenience, we use the symbol '$\wedge$' to denote the Boolean operator 'AND', '$\vee$' to denote the Boolean operator 'OR', and '$\neg$' to denote the Boolean operator 'NOT'.

Definition 1 (Query Result). *For a given query Q, $[Q]$ is the resulting documents for Q.*

Definition 2 (Sub Query). *For two gueries Q_1 and Q_2, Q_1 is a sub query of Q_2 if $[Q_1] \subseteq [Q_2]$.*

3.1 Representation of a Result Cache

For queries Q_1, Q_2,..., and Q_n, the result cache denoted by C is defined as $[Q_1] \cup [Q_2] \cup ... \cup [Q_n]$. The result cache is described by a disjunction of Boolean formulas of previously processed queries. In order to formally represent a result cache, we make use of semantic regions. A *semantic region* groups together semantically related documents. It is represented by a Boolean formula that is qualified for by result documents within the region. The Boolean formula that describes a semantic region is called its *region descriptor*[6][5].

Definition 3 (Representation of a Result Cache). *A result cache consists of one or more semantic regions. A disjunction of their region descriptors is called a representation of the result cache.*

Given a user-submitted query Q, the mediator decomposes it into two sub queries, a hit query and a miss query. The *hit query*, denoted by $H(Q, C)$, is a sub query of Q that describes sub results available from the result cache C. This can be represented by $(Q \wedge C)$. The *miss query*, denoted by $M(Q, C)$, is another sub query of Q that describes the sub results that should be retrieved from information sources other than the result cache C. This can be represented by $(Q \wedge \neg C)$.

Lemma 1. *Suppose R is a representation of the current result cache. Then, the following equalities are always true.*

$$H(a \wedge b, R) = H(a, R) \wedge H(b, R)$$
$$M(a \wedge b, R) = M(a, R) \wedge M(b, R)$$
$$H(a \vee b, R) = H(a, R) \vee H(b, R)$$
$$M(a \vee b, R) = M(a, R) \vee M(b, R)$$

Proof (of the first equality). By the definition of a hit query, $H(a \wedge b, R) = (a \wedge b) \wedge R$ Subsequently, $(a \wedge b) \wedge R = (a \wedge R) \wedge (b \wedge R) = H(a, R) \wedge H(b, R)$ **Q.E.D.**

3.2 Atomic Representation

An atomic representation represents a result cache C as a union of atomic regions. An atomic region is expressed as a minterm [7] that is defined as a conjunction of literals in which every atomic term occurs exactly once, either in its positive or negative form. Accordingly, every two atomic regions are pair-wise disjoint with each other.

Definition 4 (Atomic Representation[1]). *Let a representation denoted by R of the current result cache C is $S_1 \vee S_2 \vee ... \vee S_n$ where S_i is a region descriptor of a semantic region $[S_i]$. If every two semantic regions $[S_i]$ and $[S_j]$ ($i \neq j$ and $i \leq i, j \leq n$) are pair wise disjoint with each other, R is an atomic representation of C.*

Any Boolean expression can be equivalently transformed to a disjunction of minterms. For example, a Boolean formula $a \vee b$ is equivalent to $(a \wedge \neg b) \vee (a \wedge b) \vee (\neg a \wedge b)$ where a is replaced with a disjunction of two minterms $(a \wedge \neg b)$ and $(a \wedge b)$ and b with $(\neg a \wedge b)$ and $(a \wedge b)$. Accordingly, a result cache can be represented by a disjunction of minterms. In this case, each minterm plays the

[1] Throughout, the term 'representation' refers to an atomic representation

role of a region descriptor. In other words, $[m_i]$ is a semantic region described by a region descriptor m_i where m_i is a minterm.

Semantic regions of the result cache are described by corresponding minterms defined by query terms. When one or more new query terms that do not already occur in the representation of the current result cache are introduced by a given query Q, all semantic regions in the representation should be reorganized by splitting. For example, suppose $[S] = [a \wedge b]$ is a semantic region of the current representation of the result cache C, and a query term c is now introduced by a user query. Since c does not occur in S, $[S]$ is split into two new regions $[S_1] = [a \wedge b \wedge c]$ and $[S_2] = [a \wedge b \wedge \neg c]$, where every document that contains a query term c goes to $[S_1]$ and others to $[S_2]$. Consequently, the original semantic region $[S]$ is replaced with $[S_1] \cup [S_2]$. The region descriptor S now becomes as $S_1 \vee S_2$.

3.3 Query Processing

In order to process a given query Q with a result cache C, the query should be rewritten using minterms defined by the set of query terms in Q and C. Once Q and C are represented by minterms, we can get $Q \wedge C$ and $Q \wedge \neg C$ simply by comparing minterms in them [8].

Let R be the representation of the current result cache C. When a new query Q is submitted, it is processed as follows:

Step 1 : If all of the query terms in Q are already in R, go to step 2. If Q contains at least one query term that is not in R, every semantic region of R is split by the new query terms introduced by Q.

Step 2 : Q is rewritten into a disjunction of the minterms defined by the set of query terms in C and Q. and C.

Step 3 : Decompose Q into $H(Q,C)$ and $M(Q,C)$. Since Q and C are represented as disjunctions of minterms, $H(Q,C)$ and $M(Q,C)$ can be obtained by simply comparing the minterms of Q and C. $H(Q,C)$ is equivalent to a disjunction of common minterms of Q and C while $M(Q,C)$ is equivalent to the set of minterms that occurs in Q, but not in C.

Step 4 : Retrieve the results of $H(Q,C)$ and $M(Q,C)$ from the cache and information sources. New semantic regions described by $M(Q,C)$ are added to the result cache.

4 Decomposed Representation

Since every occurrence of a new query term causes the current semantic regions to be doubled, the number of the semantic regions increases exponentially compared to the growth of new query terms. To address this issue, we make it possible for a result cache to have multiple sub-representations by semantically decomposing the original representation.

4.1 Semantic Decomposition

Definition 5 (Semantic Decomposption). *Let R be a representation of the result cache. $R^d = \{R_1, R_2, ..., R_m\}$ is a semantic decomposition of R if the following three conditions are satisfied.*

$[R] \supseteq [R_i]$,
$[R] = [R_1] \cup [R_2] \cup ... \cup [R_m]$, *and*
$|R| > |R_i|$

where $i \leq i \leq m$ and $|R|$ is the number of unit terms in R.

When $R^d = \{R_1, R_2, ..., R_m\}$ is a semantic decomposition of R, R_i is called a sub-representation of R.

Lemma 2. *Suppose $R^d = \{R_1, R_2, ..., R_m\}$ is a semantic decomposition of a representation R. The following equalities are always true.*

$$H(Q, R) = H(Q, R_1) \vee H(Q, R_2) \vee ... \vee H(Q, R_m)$$
$$M(Q, R) = M(Q, R_1) \wedge M(Q, R_2) \wedge ... \wedge M(Q, R_m)$$

Proof. By definition of semantic decomposition,

$$R = R_1 \vee R_2 \vee ... \vee R_m$$

Then,

$$H(Q, R) = H(Q, R_1 \vee R_2 \vee ... \vee R_m)$$

According to the definition of a hit query,

$$\begin{aligned} H(Q, R_1 \vee R_2 \vee ... \vee R_m) &= Q \wedge (R_1 \vee R_2 \vee ... \vee R_m) \\ &= (Q \wedge R_1) \vee (Q \wedge R_2) \vee ... \vee (Q \wedge R_m) \\ &= H(Q, R_1) \vee H(Q, R_2) \vee ... \vee H(Q, R_m) \end{aligned}$$

Similarly,

$$\begin{aligned} M(Q, R_1 \vee R_2 \vee ... \vee R_m) &= Q \wedge \neg(R_1 \vee R_2 \vee ... \vee R_m) \\ &= Q \wedge (\neg R_1 \wedge \neg R_2 \wedge ... \wedge \neg R_m) \\ &= (Q \wedge \neg R_1) \wedge (Q \wedge \neg R_2) \wedge ... \wedge (Q \wedge \neg R_m) \\ &= M(Q, R_1) \wedge M(Q, R_2) \wedge ... \wedge M(Q, R_m) \end{aligned}$$

Q.E.D.

If we employ a semantic decomposition, we can bound the number of semantic regions for one sub-representation to a certain value by limiting its number of query terms. Formally, the maximum number of minterms of a semantic decomposition $R^d = \{R_1, R_2, ..., R_m\}$ is $\sum_{i=1}^{m} 2^{|R_i|}$. Since the same query term can occur in one or more sub representations, $\sum_{i=1}^{m} 2^{|R_i|} \leq 2^{|R|}$. For example, suppose the number of keywords is 20. If the result cache is described with one representation, $2^{20} = 1,048,576$ is the maximal number of minterms to be used. However, Suppose there exist two sub-representations R_1, R_2 and $|R_1| = 10$ and $|R_2| = 11$, then $2^{10} + 2^{11} = 3072$ is the maximal number of minterms.

4.2 Closed Decomposition

According to lemma 2, in order to get a hit query or a miss query, every decomposed sub-representation must be examined. The number of sub-representations to be examined in computing a hit query and a miss query can be reduced by utilizing the notion of closed decomposition.

Definition 6 (Closed Decoposition). *Let Q be a given query whose query terms are $q_1, q_2, ..., q_n$ and $R^d = \{R_1, R_2, ..., R_m\}$ be a semantic decomposition for the representation R. R^d is a closed decomposition for Q if there exists at least one sub representation $R_i (1 \leq i \leq m)$ for every $q_j (1 \leq j \leq n)$ such that*
(1) $[H(q_j, R)] = [H(q_j, R_i)]$ and
(2) $[M(q_j, R)] = [M(q_j, R_i)]$
where $[H(q_j, R_i)] \neq \emptyset$ and $[M(q_j, R_i)] \neq \emptyset$. When R_i does not contain q_j, R_i should be split by means of q_j to get $[H(q_j, R_i)]$ and $[M(q_j, R_i)]$.

If R^d is a closed decomposition of R, a hit query and a miss query for a given query Q can be obtained by considering sub-representation as many as query terms in Q.

Definition 7 (Cascading Decomposition). $R^d = \{R_1, R_2, R_3\}$ *is a cascading decomposition of R if it is a semantic decomposition of R and $[R_1] \subset [R_2] \subset ... \subset [R_m] = [R]$*

In a cascading decomposition, every two representations R_i and R_{i+1} should satisfy $[R_i] \subset [R_{i+1}]$. A simple way to make this possible is to add every semantic regions of R_i to R_{i+1}. Unfortunately, the resulting decomposition cannot be a semantic one, because of the third condition of definition 3.

In order to solve this problem, we extend the notion of atomic term in constructing a minterm. Without loss of generality, we can treat an arbitrary Boolean expression E as a unit term as long as the atoms occurring in E does not occur any where else in the expression. For example, $(a \wedge b)$ can be treated as a unit term in constructing minterms such as $(a \wedge b) \wedge c$, $(a \wedge b) \wedge \neg c$, $\neg(a \wedge b) \wedge c$, and $\neg(a \wedge b) \wedge \neg c$. So, in constructing R_{i+1}, we can treat R_i as a unit term and not allow query terms in R_i to appear anywhere else in R_{i+1}. Then, the resulting decomposition becomes a semantic decomposition of R. Although we do not include the proof here, we can always obtain such a cascading decomposition for R and we can get results from R_{i+1} for query terms in R_i since $[R_i] \subset [R_{i+1}]$.

Theorem 1. *If R^d is a cascading decomposition of R, then it is a closed decomposition for general Boolean queries with arbitrary number of query terms.*

Proof. Let R^d be a semantic decomposition of R and $\{R_1, R_2, ..., R_m\}$

i: Q contains only single query term.
Since R^d is a cascading decomposition of R, $[R_m] = [R]$. Then, the following two equalities are satisfied.

$$[H(Q,R)] = [H(Q,R_m)]$$
$$[M(Q,R)] = [M(Q,R_m)]$$

As a result, R^d is a closed decomposition for Q.

ii: Q contains multiple query terms with AND/OR operators.
We prove this by showing the case with queries with two terms connected by AND/OR operators. Suppose Q contains two query terms a and b connected by AND. According to the lemma 1, the following two equalities are true.

$$H(a \wedge b, R) = H(a,R) \wedge H(a,R)$$
$$M(a \wedge b, R) = M(a,R) \wedge M(b,R)$$

Since R^d is a cascading decomposition, $[H(a,R) = [H(a,R_m)]$ and $[H(a,R) = [H(a,R_m)]$. At the same time, $[H(b,R)] = [H(b,R_m)]$ and $[M(b,R)] = [M(b,R_m)]$. Therefore, R^d is a closed decomposition for $a \wedge b$. Similarly for $Q = a \wedge b$, R^d is a closed decomposition.

Thus for an arbitrary Boolean query Q, R^d id a closed decomposition. **Q.E.D.**

5 Replacement Strategy

In this section, we propose a new replacement strategy that is based on the standard LRU strategy. For the sake of simplicity, we only consider a single representation but not a semantic decomposition. We employ two factors in calculating the replacement value of a semantic region. One is *recency of usage* value and the other is *semantic significance* value. Recency of usage value indicates how recently a semantic region *was* used while semantic significance value describes the potential usefulness of a semantic region.

5.1 Recency of Usage

Firstly, the most recent value denoted by U_{most} is initialized to 1. Each time a query is submitted, U_{most} is incremented by 1 and assigned to all semantic regions induced by the given query as their recency of usage values. If U_i is greater than U_j, it means that a semantic region S_i was more recently used than S_j was.

5.2 Semantic Significance

We assume that every query term has the same probability to occur in user's queries and most users might submit queries only with non-negated query terms. Then, we can reasonably claim that one semantic region denoted by S_1 might have more possibility to be used in answering user's queries than the other region denoted by S_2 does when the number of non-negated query terms in S_1 is larger than that in S_2. The number of non-negated terms in a semantic region S_i is defined as its semantic significance. It is denoted by M_i.

5.3 Replacement Value

The result cache replaces a semantic region whose replacement value is the least among others. The replacement value of a region is calculated by a pre-defined weighted function. If the current replacement value of region S_i is REP_i, we calculate a new replacement function as

$$REP_i' = REP_i + m \cdot M_i + u \cdot U_i \tag{1}$$

where $0 \leq m, u \leq 1$. If m is set to 0 and u to 1, REP_i equivalently simulates the standard LRU strategy.

Since every semantic region varies in its size, we have to consider it in order to determine the replacement value. We employ a size-adjusted LRU startegy, SLRU, mentioned in [9] and choose Larger semantic regions as victims to make room for multiple small regions. If a semantic region has replacement value v and size s, the ratio v/s gives the semantic region's size-adjusted replacement value. Therefore, modified replacement function is as follows:

$$REP_i' = \frac{1}{N_i} \cdot (REP_i + m \cdot M_i + u \cdot U_i) \tag{2}$$

where N_i is the number of documents in a semantic region S_i.

6 Experiment

6.1 Workload

In our experiments, we used the log of real user queries submitted to the Web search engine at Korea, *Naver* (http://www.naver.com). Although this search engine is purposed to search and retrieve general Web pages and most queries have a wide variety, query terms used in this workload are characterized by a high duplication and frequency weight: 30.2% of total query terms are repeatedly used in user's queries and 0.05% of the most frequent query terms occur in 50.4% of the queries. As a whole, 41,000 query terms are used in 1,000 queries.

6.2 Hit Ratio

The size of the result cache varies in range $[20 \cdot S_Q : 200 \cdot S_Q]$ where S_Q is the average size of query answers. The hit ratio is the average size of a query result available from the result cache. For a given query, the hit ratio is calculated as follows:

$$\frac{N_C}{N_T} \tag{3}$$

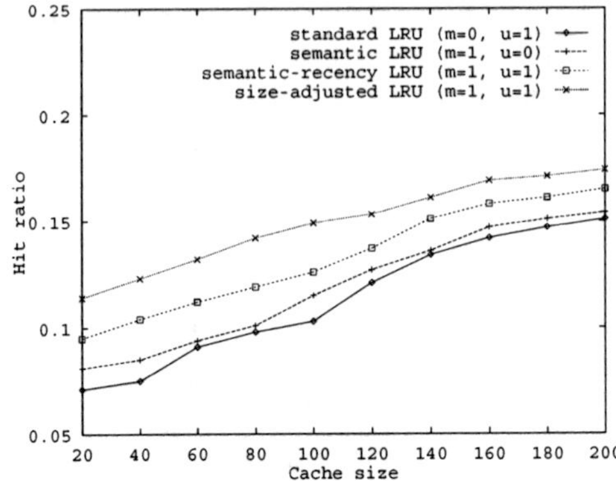

Fig. 1. Hit Ratio

where N_C is the number of results available from the result cache and N_T is total number of results. We examined four replacement strategies such as standard LRU ($m = 0, u = 1$), semantic LRU ($m = 1, u = 0$) that considers semantic significance only, semantic-recency LRU ($m = 1, u = 1$) that considers both semantic significance and recency of usage, and size-adjusted LRU (SLRU $m = 1, u = 1$). Fig. 1 unveils that semantic significance contributes sufficiently more to the hit ratio than recency of usage factor does.

6.3 Performance Comparison

We examine the efficiency of the proposed caching method comparing with two different methods. One is a naive query processing method that does not utilize any cached results (we call it 'NC') and the other uses cached results only when the given query is exactly matched with one among the previously submitted (we call it 'EM'). Every query set consists of 50 distinct queries. On the average, the proposed method (we call it 'DR') improved the retrieval performance by almost 50% as much in the case with no cache as depicted in Fig. 2. Furthermore, DR outperforms EM. The reason is that the EM uses the cached results only when $H(Q, C)$ is equivalent to Q, while DR can utilize them only if $[H(Q, C)]$ is not empty although $H(Q, C)$ is not equivalent to Q. In other words, DR always guarantees higher hit ratio than EM does.

7 Conclusion

In order to improve the query processing performance of mediator systems, it is essential to efficiently recognize the part of a query that can be directly retrieved from the cache. The caching methodology that has been proposed proved to be efficient for this purpose. In addition, the proposed approach is able to be applied to process general Boolean queries while previous methods were somewhat restricted in this aspect. The proposed approach employs an atomic representation

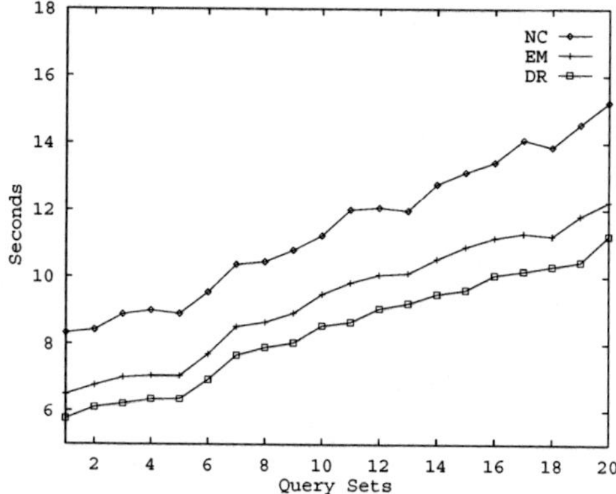

Fig. 2. Average Retrieval Time

in describing the result cache, which can be effectively managed and utilized in processing general Boolean queries. Furthermore, its representation is managed in semantically decomposed form so that the total number of semantic regions can be reduced only with a negligible slight performance degradation.

References

1. G. Wiederhold, Mediators in the Architecture of Future Information Systems, IEEE Computer, Mar. (1992) 38–49.
2. D-G Kim and S-G Lee, QVI: Query-based Virtual Index for Distributed Information Retrieval System, proceedings of ISCA 13th International Conference CATA, (1998) 152–155.
3. S. Adali, K. S. Candan, Y. Papakonstantinou, and V. S. Shubrahmannian, Query Caching and Optimization in Distributed Mediator Systems, proceedings of ACM SIGMOD International Conference on Management of Data, Montreal, Canada, June (1996) 137–148.
4. D. Miranker, M. Taylor, and A. Padmanaban, A Tractable Query Cache By Approximation, Technical Report, MCC, (1998).
5. S. Dar, M. J. Franklin, B. T. Jonsson, D. Srivastava, and M. Tan, Semantic Data Caching and Replacement, proceedings of the 22nd VLDB conference, (1996) 330–341.
6. B. Chidlovskii and U. Borghoff, Semantic Caching of Web Queries, The VLDB Journal, Vol. 9, No. 2, (2000)
7. M. M. Mano, Digital Logic and Computer Design, Prentice-Hall, Englewook Cliffs, NJ, (1979).
8. Jae-heon Cheong and Sang-goo Lee, A Boolean Query Processing with a Result Cache in Mediator Systems, proceedings of the IEEE Intl. Conference on Advances in Digital Libraries, (2000) 218–227.
9. C. Aggarwal, J. L. Wolf, and P. S. Yu, Caching on the World Wide Web, IEEE Trans. Knowledge and Data Engineering, Vol. 11, No. 1, (1999) 94–107

Trends in Database Research

Mukesh Mohania[1], Yahiko Kambayashi[2], A. Min Tjoa[3], Roland Wagner[4], and Ladjel Bellatreche[5]

[1] Dept of Computer Science, Western Michigan University, Kalamazoo, MI 49008, U.S.A. Email: mohania@cs.wmich.edu

[2] Dept of Social informatics, Kyoto University, Kyoto, Japan yahiko@kuis.kyoto-u.ac.jp

[3] IFS, Technical University of Vienna, Vienna A-1040, Austria, tjoa@ifs,tuwin.ac.at

[4] FAW, University of Linz, Linz, Austria, rwagner@faw.uni-linz.ac.at

[5] TIMC - IMAG Laboratory, Faculty of Medicine La Tronche 38706, France, ladjel@imag.fr

Extended Abstract

Research in databases has played a vital role in developing information system technology and also the outcome of this research has been very successful resulting in great potential for industry. The database industry is generating billions of dollars of business annually. It has estimated that the database industry itself has generated $42 billion revenue in 2000 and this market is growing at 11% annually. In the software industry, it is second only to operating system software.

The evolution of database systems started in late 60's when hierarchical and network data models were developed, but these models did not get much momentum because they were not suited for complex applications [9]. In early 70's, Ted Codd proposed a relational data model (for which he was awarded a Turing award) which became the backbone of developing database applications. Although this model was criticized by COBOL/CODASYL group people, it became very popular because of its simplicity. In late 70's and early 80's most of the research work was focused on developing fundamentals of relational database theory, query languages, transaction management and query optimization. In late 80's and early 90's, the database research community grew exponentially and made several breakthrough in many areas like object-oriented, active, deductive, and parallel and distributed databases. The research ideas in these areas have been implemented successfully in different database vendors' products. In early 90's, most of the businesses realize that their business is becoming very competitive and they need some sophisticated tools that can analyze their business data, customers profiles and product information so that they can improve their marketing strategy and management of organization. Data mining and data warehousing technology was developed for satisfying such needs [1].

Data Warehousing is a recent technology [4] that allows information to be easily and efficiently accessed for decision making activities. Knowledge discovery in data warehouses focuses upon the extraction of interesting and previously

H.C. Mayr et al. (Eds.): DEXA 2001, LNCS 2113, pp. 984–988, 2001.

unknown knowledge [3]. Researchers and application developers have designed knowledge discovery systems for number of application domains including finance, health, telecommunications and marketing. The data warehouse stores information of interest to the enterprise from multiple data sources and presents it in an integrated manner to the end user. This *eager* or *in-advance* approach to data integration and query processing from distributed data sources pays rich dividends when it translates into calculated decisions backed by sound analysis [12]. The information stored in the data warehouse facilitates *decision making* activities. On-Line Analytical Processing (OLAP) tools provide an environment for decision making and business modeling activities by supporting ad-hoc queries. The multidimensional data model has been proved to be the most suitable for OLAP applications. One of the issue that is not yet fully addressed is how to define a set of constraints on this model so that we can exploit them in every area of warehouse implementation.

There are many other areas of active research in data warehousing and knowledge discovery, such as integrating active rules in warehouse data [10], view selection and maintenance, multiple query optimization using views, update filtering, on-line view maintenance, fragmentation of multidimensional database, parallel processing, summarizability problem, data expiry, data indexing, instance based data mining, finding emerging patterns in data cubes, and security based on data mining [7]. Some of these issues have been addressed adequately in the literature.

The growth of the internet has dramatically changed the way in which information is managed and accessed. The WWW is a distributed global information resource and it contains large amount of uncontrolled data (HTML or XML documents) relevant to essentially all domains of human activity. To manage and access data available on the web, there is a diagnostic need for effective and efficient tools for information consumers. Users must be able to easily locate required information in the web ranging from unstructured documents and pictures to structured record oriented data. If the information is found, it is generally scattered in a piecemeal fashion. An initial effort of building a virtual warehouse of book data to provide information consumers one point of contact was done by Amazon (www.amazon.com) which now has multi-million dollar revenue from sale of books on Internet. They have a warehouse of data about the books available on Internet and give users one integrated source to find books of their interest.

Several web database system architectures have been proposed LORE [8] WHOWEDA [11], FLORID [6], and W3QS [2]. These systems retrieve and manipulate semistructured data by supporting web query languages. For instance, in W3QS a user can specify content and structure queries on the web and can maintain the results of queries as database *views* of the web. These systems allow users to access any part of web data and manipulate it.

The enormous flexibility provided by this ubiquitous data reservoir, however, has created a number of problems related to information modeling, efficient search of information, indexing, supporting query languages, document clustering, information sharing, web mining (content, structure and log/usage file), and security. Some of these problems, especially information organization, security, and credibility of data in WWW become more complicated because information are continuously added to the web with varied processing requirements. With the increased usage of WWW, several criteria such as accuracy, objectivity, coverage, authority, ownership, are becoming useful for evaluating a web page depending on the purpose.

Another important problem that has not yet been addressed is how to exploit the relationship among web pages. The web pages retrieved by the search engine on a given topic have some relationships among themselves. A few examples of the relationships are Next-to, Previous-to, Similar-to, Example-of, Derived-from, Same-as, Part-of etc. Determining these relationships among static web pages is very important so that user can find the information in more organized way and follow the links depending on the type of relationships.

Agent technology is very useful to solve many web related problems. Several web agents have been designed for specific purpose, such as link validation and repair agent, negotiation and bargaining agent, web page quality control agent, unauthorized access agent, aggregate result formulator agent. Recently, web researchers have started their focus on developing web caching schemes. Caching is important in the World Wide Web since data and the number of users on the web are increasing exponentially, far out pacing the increase of network bandwidth. Caching schemes developed so far are primarily based on data usage in the past (e.g. how often the data has been accessed) to predict the access patterns for the future. Some caching schemes support content-awareness to improve cache efficiency as well as information sharing among users [5].

One of the greatest obstacles to widespread adoption of e-commerce is concern about the security of the system. With the growing use of the Web, security of the web-based system is now an important business decision. Many projects are developing techniques (web materialized views, mobile agents, data mining techniques) to deal with this problem.

We have studied the trends of database research by analyzing the track of accepted papers in DEXA conference in last 10 years. DEXA (Database and Expert Systems Applications) conference started in 1990 with the aim to bring researchers and practitioners together from database and expert system areas to discuss research issues and experience in developing and deploying advanced database systems. Since then, it has become a forum for exchanging ideas and publishing research papers from these areas. As time goes, new technologies emerge and DEXA recognizes, for example, few prime areas of research in databases, such as Data Warehousing, Data Mining, E-Commerce, Web Databases and two different conferences got started in these areas (DaWaK: Data Warehousing and Knowledge Discovery; EC-Web: E-Commerce and Web Technologies) with their roots in databases and knowledge bases.

From the graph, we observe that papers in the fields of OODB, Spatial, Parallel and Temporal DB have remained steady, where as papers in distributed, heterogeneous, Multimedia and Video DB have increased steadily.

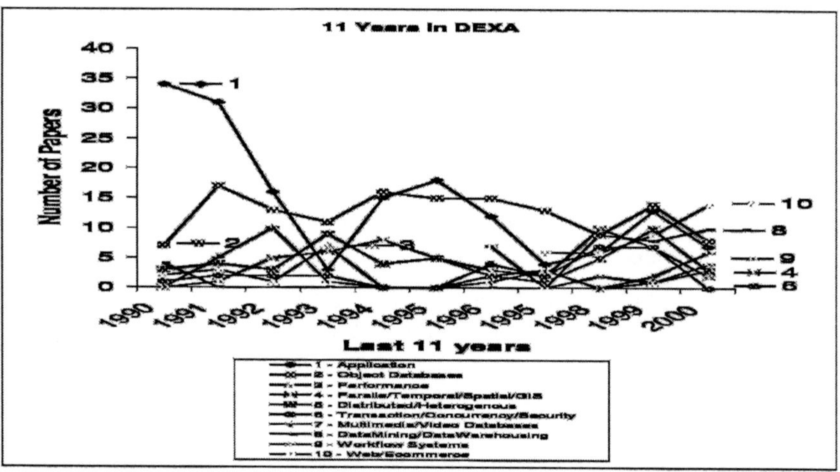

References

1. *Microsoft Data Mining and Knowledge Discovery.* http://www.research.microsoft.com/datamine/.
2. Konopnicki D. and Shmueli O. W3qs: A query system for the world wide web. In *Proc. of International conference on Very Large Databases,* pages 54–65, 1995.
3. U. M. Fayyad, G. Piatetsky-Shapiro, and P. Smyth. From data mining to knowledge discovery: An overview. In U. M. Fayyad, G. Piatetsky-Shapiro, and P. Smyth, editors, *Advances in Knowledge Discovery and Data Mining,* pages 1–34. AAAI Press, Menlo Park, California, 1996.
4. W. H. Inmon. *Building the Data Warehouse.* QED Publishing Group, Boston, Massachussetts, 1992.
5. Cheng Kai, Kambayashi Yahiko, and Mohania Mukesh. Using database technology to improve performance of web proxy servers. In *Proceedings of the Fourth International Workshop on the Web and Databases (WebDB),* pages 73–78, 2001.
6. Bertram L., Rainer H., Georg L., Wolfgang M., and Christian S. Managing semistructured data with orid: A deductive object-oriented perspective. *Information Systems,* 23(8), 1998.
7. Mohania Mukesh, Samtani S., Roddick J. F., and Y. Kambayashi. Advances and research directions in data warehousing technology. *Australian Journal of Information Systems,* 1999.
8. McHugh J.and Abiteboul S., Goldman R.and Dallan Q., and Widom J. *Lore: A Database Management System for Semistructured Data.* http://www-db.stanford.edu/lore, 1994.
9. Michael Stonebraker and Joseph M. Hellerstein, editors. *Readings in Database Systems.* Morgan Kaufmann Publishers, 1998.
10. Thalhammer Thomas, Schre Michael, and Mohania Mukesh. Active datawarehouses: Complementing olap with active rules. *Journal of Data and Knowledge Engineering,* to appear.

11. Ng Wee-Keong, Lim Ee-Peng, Bhowmick S., and Madria S. Web warehousing: Design and issues. In *Proc. of International Workshop on Data Warehousing and Data Mining,* LNCS 1552, 1998.
12. Jennifer Widom. Research problems in data warehousing. In *Proc. Fourth Intl. Conference on Information and Knowledge Management,* 1995.

Author Index

Lecture Notes in Computer Science

For information about Vols. 1–2098
please contact your bookseller or Springer-Verlag

Vol. 2099: P. de Groote, G. Morrill, C. Retoré (Eds.), Logical Aspects of Computational Linguistics. Proceedings, 2001. VIII, 311 pages. 2001. (Subseries LNAI).

Vol. 2100: R. Küsters, Non-Standard Inferences in Description Logocs. X, 250 pages. 2001. (Subseries LNAI).

Vol. 2101: S. Quaglini, P. Barahona, S. Andreassen (Eds.), Artificial Intelligence in Medicine. Proceedings, 2001. XIV, 469 pages. 2001. (Subseries LNAI).

Vol. 2102: G. Berry, H. Comon, A. Finkel (Eds.), Computer-Aided Verification. Proceedings, 2001. XIII, 520 pages. 2001.

Vol. 2103: M. Hannebauer, J. Wendler, E. Pagello (Eds.), Balancing Reactivity and Social Deliberation in Multi-Agent Systems. VIII, 237 pages. 2001. (Subseries LNAI).

Vol. 2104: R. Eigenmann, M.J. Voss (Eds.), OpenMP Shared Memory Parallel Programming. Proceedings, 2001. X, 185 pages. 2001.

Vol. 2105: W. Kim, T.-W. Ling, Y-J. Lee, S.-S. Park (Eds.), The Human Society and the Internet. Proceedings, 2001. XVI, 470 pages. 2001.

Vol. 2106: M. Kerckhove (Ed.), Scale-Space and Morphology in Computer Vision. Proceedings, 2001. XI, 435 pages. 2001.

Vol. 2107: F.T. Chong, C. Kozyrakis, M. Oskin (Eds.), Intelligent Memory Systems. Proceedings, 2000. VIII, 193 pages. 2001.

Vol. 2108: J. Wang (Ed.), Computing and Combinatorics. Proceedings, 2001. XIII, 602 pages. 2001.

Vol. 2109: M. Bauer, P.J. Gymtrasiewicz, J. Vassileva (Eds.), User Modelind 2001. Proceedings, 2001. XIII, 318 pages. 2001. (Subseries LNAI).

Vol. 2110: B. Hertzberger, A. Hoekstra, R. Williams (Eds.), High-Performance Computing and Networking. Proceedings, 2001. XVII, 733 pages. 2001.

Vol. 2111: D. Helmbold, B. Williamson (Eds.), Computational Learning Theory. Proceedings, 2001. IX, 631 pages. 2001. (Subseries LNAI).

Vol. 2113: H.C. Mayr, J. Lazansky, G. Quirchmayr, P. Vogel (Eds.), Database and Expert Systems Applications. Proceedings, 2001. XIX, 991 pages. 2001.

Vol. 2114: Y. Kambayashi, W. Winiwarter, M. Arikawa (Eds.), Data Warehousing and Knowledge Discovery. Proceedings, 2001. XIV, 361pages. 2001.

Vol. 2115: K. Bauknecht, S.K. Madria, G. Pernul (Eds.), Electronic Commerce and Web Technologies. Proceedings, 2001. XI, 347 pages. 2001.

Vol. 2116: V. Akman, P. Bouquet, R. Thomason, R.A. Young (Eds.), Modeling and Using Context. Proceedings, 2001. XII, 472 pages. 2001. (Subseries LNAI).

Vol. 2117: M. Beynon, C.L. Nehaniv, K. Dautenhahn (Eds.), Cognitive Technology: Instruments of Mind. Proceedings, 2001. XV, 522 pages. 2001. (Subseries LNAI).

Vol. 2118: X.S. Wang, G. Yu, H. Lu (Eds.), Advances in Web-Age Information Management. Proceedings, 2001. XV, 418 pages. 2001.

Vol. 2119: V. Varadharajan, Y. Mu (Eds.), Information Security and Privacy. Proceedings, 2001. XI, 522 pages. 2001.

Vol. 2120: H.S. Delugach, G. Stumme (Eds.), Conceptual Structures: Broadening the Base. Proceedings, 2001. X, 377 pages. 2001. (Subseries LNAI).

Vol. 2121: C.S. Jensen, M. Schneider, B. Seeger, V.J. Tsotras (Eds.), Advances in Spatial and Temporal Databases. Proceedings, 2001. XI, 543 pages. 2001.

Vol. 2123: P. Perner (Ed.), Machine Learning and Data Mining in Pattern Recognition. Proceedings, 2001. XI, 363 pages. 2001. (Subseries LNAI).

Vol. 2124: W. Skarbek (Ed.), Computer Analysis of Images and Patterns. Proceedings, 2001. XV, 743 pages. 2001.

Vol. 2125: F. Dehne, J.-R. Sack, R. Tamassia (Eds.), Algorithms and Data Structures. Proceedings, 2001. XII, 484 pages. 2001.

Vol. 2126: P. Cousot (Ed.), Static Analysis. Proceedings, 2001. XI, 439 pages. 2001.

Vol. 2127: V. Malyshkin (Ed.), Parallel Computing Technologies. Proceedings, 2001. XII, 516 pages. 2001.

Vol. 2129: M. Goemans, K. Jansen, J.D.P. Rolim, L. Trevisan (Eds.), Approximation, Randomization, and Combinatorial Optimization. Proceedings, 2001. IX, 297 pages. 2001.

Vol. 2130: G. Dorffner, H. Bischof, K. Hornik (Eds.), Artificial Neural Networks – ICANN 2001. Proceedings, 2001. XXII, 1259 pages. 2001.

Vol. 2132: S.-T. Yuan, M. Yokoo (Eds.), Intelligent Agents. Specification. Modeling, and Application. Proceedings, 2001. X, 237 pages. 2001. (Subseries LNAI).

Vol. 2133: B. Christianson, B. Crispo, J.A. Malcolm, M. Roe (Eds.), Security Protocols. Proceedings, 2001. VIII, 257 pages. 2001.

Vol. 2134: M. Figueiredo, J. Zerubia, A.K. Jain (Eds.), Energy Minimization Methods in Computer Vision and Pattern Recognition. Proceedings, 2001. X, 652 pages. 2001.

Vol. 2136: J. Sgall, A. Pultr, P. Kolman (Eds.), Mathematical Foundations of Computer Science 2001. Proceedings, 2001. XII, 716 pages. 2001.

Vol. 2138: R. Freivalds (Ed.), Fundamentals of Computation Theory. Proceedings, 2001. XIII, 542 pages. 2001.

Vol. 2139: J. Kilian (Ed.), Advances in Cryptology – CRYPTO 2001. Proceedings, 2001. XI, 599 pages. 2001.

Vol. 2141: G.S. Brodal, D. Frigioni, A. Marchetti-Spaccamela (Eds.), Algorithm Engineering. Proceedings, 2001. X, 199 pages. 2001.

Vol. 2142: L. Fribourg (Ed.), Computer Science Logic. Proceedings, 2001. XII, 615 pages. 2001.

Vol. 2143: S. Benferhat, P. Besnard (Eds.), Symbolic and Quantitative Approaches to Reasoning with Uncertainty. Proceedings, 2001. XIV, 818 pages. 2001. (Subseries LNAI).

Vol. 2144: T. Margaria, T. Melham (Eds.), Correct Hardware Design and Verification Methods. Proceedings, 2001. XII, 482 pages. 2001.

Vol. 2146: J.H. Silverman (Eds.), Cryptography and Lattices. Proceedings, 2001. VII, 219 pages. 2001.

Vol. 2147: G. Brebner, R. Woods (Eds.), Field-Programmable Logic and Applications. Proceedings, 2001. XV, 665 pages. 2001.

Vol. 2149: O. Gascuel, B.M.E. Moret (Eds.), Algorithms in Bioinformatics. Proceedings, 2001. X, 307 pages. 2001.

Vol. 2150: R. Sakellariou, J. Keane, J. Gurd, L. Freeman (Eds.), Euro-Par 2001 Parallel Processing. Proceedings, 2001. XXX, 943 pages. 2001.

Vol. 2151: A. Caplinskas, J. Eder (Eds.), Advances in Databases and Information Systems. Proceedings, 2001. XIII, 381 pages. 2001.

Vol. 2152: R.J. Boulton, P.B. Jackson (Eds.), Theorem Proving in Higher Order Logics. Proceedings, 2001. X, 395 pages. 2001.

Vol. 2153: A.L. Buchsbaum, J. Snoeyink (Eds.), Algorithm Engineering and Experimentation. Proceedings, 2001. VIII, 231 pages. 2001.

Vol. 2154: K.G. Larsen, M. Nielsen (Eds.), CONCUR 2001 – Concurrency Theory. Proceedings, 2001. XI, 583 pages. 2001.

Vol. 2157: C. Rouveirol, M. Sebag (Eds.), Inductive Logic Programming. Proceedings, 2001. X, 261 pages. 2001. (Subseries LNAI).

Vol. 2158: D. Shepherd, J. Finney, L. Mathy, N. Race (Eds.), Interactive Distributed Multimedia Systems. Proceedings, 2001. XIII, 258 pages. 2001.

Vol. 2159: J. Kelemen, P. Sosík (Eds.), Advances in Artificial Life. Proceedings, 2001. XIX, 724 pages. 2001. (Subseries LNAI).

Vol. 2161: F. Meyer auf der Heide (Ed.), Algorithms – ESA 2001. Proceedings, 2001. XII, 538 pages. 2001.

Vol. 2162: Ç. K. Koç, D. Naccache, C. Paar (Eds.), Cryptographic Hardware and Embedded Systems – CHES 2001. Proceedings, 2001. XIV, 411 pages. 2001.

Vol. 2163: P. Constantopoulos, I.T. Sølvberg (Eds.), Research and Advanced Technology for Digital Libraries. Proceedings, 2001. XII, 462 pages. 2001.

Vol. 2164: S. Pierre, R. Glitho (Eds.), Mobile Agents for Telecommunication Applications. Proceedings, 2001. XI, 292 pages. 2001.

Vol. 2165: L. de Alfaro, S. Gilmore (Eds.), Process Algebra and Probabilistic Methods. Proceedings, 2001. XII, 217 pages. 2001.

Vol. 2166: V. Matoušek, P. Mautner, R. Mouček, K. Taušer (Eds.), Text, Speech and Dialogue. Proceedings, 2001. XIII, 452 pages, 2001. (Subseries LNAI).

Vol. 2167: L. De Raedt, P. Flach (Eds.), Machine Learning: ECML 2001. Proceedings, 2001. XVII, 618 pages. 2001. (Subseries LNAI).

Vol. 2168: L. De Raedt, A. Siebes (Eds.), Principles of Data Mining and Knowledge Discovery. Proceedings, 2001. XVII, 510 pages. 2001. (Subseries LNAI).

Vol. 2170: S. Palazzo (Ed.), Evolutionary Trends of the Internet. Proceedings, 2001. XIII, 722 pages. 2001.

Vol. 2172: C. Batini, F. Giunchiglia, P. Giorgini, M. Mecella (Eds.), Cooperative Information Systems. Proceedings, 2001. XI, 450 pages. 2001.

Vol. 2174: F. Baader, G. Brewka, T. Eiter (Eds.), KI 2001: Advances in Artificial Intelligence. Proceedings, 2001. XIII, 471 pages. 2001. (Subseries LNAI).

Vol. 2175: F. Esposito (Ed.), AI*IA 2001: Advances in Artificial Intelligence. Proceedings, 2001. XII, 396 pages. 2001. (Subseries LNAI).

Vol. 2176: K.-D. Althoff, R.L. Feldmann, W. Müller (Eds.), Advances in Learning Software Organizations. Proceedings, 2001. XI, 241 pages. 2001.

Vol. 2177: G. Butler, S. Jarzabek (Eds.), Generative and Component-Based Software Engineering. Proceedings, 2001. X, 203 pages. 2001.

Vol. 2180: J. Welch (Ed.), Distributed Computing. Proceedings, 2001. X, 343 pages. 2001.

Vol. 2181: C. Y. Westort (Ed.), Digital Earth Moving. Proceedings, 2001. XII, 117 pages. 2001.

Vol. 2182: M. Klusch, F. Zambonelli (Eds.), Cooperative Information Agents V. Proceedings, 2001. XII, 288 pages. 2001. (Subseries LNAI).

Vol. 2184: M. Tucci (Ed.), Multimedia Databases and Image Communication. Proceedings, 2001. X, 225 pages. 2001.

Vol. 2186: J. Bosch (Ed.), Generative and Component-Based Software Engineering. Proceedings, 2001. VIII, 177 pages. 2001.

Vol. 2187: U. Voges (Ed.), Computer Safety, Reliability and Security. Proceedings, 2001. XVI, 261 pages. 2001.

Vol. 2188: F. Bomarius, S. Komi-Sirviö (Eds.), Product Focused Software Process Improvement. Proceedings, 2001. XI, 382 pages. 2001.

Vol. 2189: F. Hoffmann, D.J. Hand, N. Adams, D. Fisher, G. Guimaraes (Eds.), Advances in Intelligent Data Analysis. Proceedings, 2001. XII, 384 pages. 2001.

Vol. 2190: A. de Antonio, R. Aylett, D. Ballin (Eds.), Intelligent Virtual Agents. Proceedings, 2001. VIII, 245 pages. 2001. (Subseries LNAI).

Vol. 2191: B. Radig, S. Florczyk (Eds.), Pattern Recognition. Proceedings, 2001. XVI, 452 pages. 2001.

Vol. 2193: F. Casati, D. Georgakopoulos, M.-C. Shan (Eds.), Technologies for E-Services. Proceedings, 2001. X, 213 pages. 2001.

Vol. 2196: W. Taha (Ed.), Semantics, Applications, and Implementation of Program Generation. Proceedings, 2001. X, 219 pages. 2001.

CPSIA information can be obtained at www.ICGtesting.com
Printed in the USA
LVOW09s0746120616

492225LV00002B/4/P

9 783540 425274